Strategic Management of Health Care Organizations

Peter M. Ginter
University of Alabama at Birmingham

Linda M. Swayne
University of North Carolina at Charlotte

W. Jack Duncan
University of Alabama at Birmingham

THIRD EDITION

Strategic Management of Health Care Organizations

Copyright © Peter M. Ginter, Linda E. Swayne, W. Jack Duncan, 1998

Second edition published in 1995 by Blackwell Publishers
Third edition published 1998 by Blackwell Publishers
Reprinted 1998

Blackwell Publishers Inc
350 Main Street
Malden, Massachusetts 02148, USA

Blackwell Publishers Ltd
108 Cowley Road
Oxford OX4 1JF, UK

Library of Congress Cataloging in Publication Data
Duncan, W. Jack (Walter Jack)
Strategic management of health care organizations / W. Jack Duncan, Peter M. Ginter,
Linda E. Swayne—3rd ed.
p.   cm.
Includes bibliographical references and index.
ISBN 1–55786–968–5 (hardback)
1. Health facilities—Administration. 2. Strategic planning. I. Ginter, Peter M.
II. Swayne, Linda E.   III. Title.
[DNLM: 1. Health Services—organization & administration. 3. Organizational
Innovation. 4. Marketing of Health Services—methods. W 84.1 D912s 1997]
RA971.D78   1997
362.1'1'068—dc21
DNLM/DLC   97–12153
for Library of Congress   CIP

British Library Cataloguing in Publication Data
A CIP catalogue record for this book is available from the British Library

Manufactured in the United States of America

Contents

PART VI • Cases in the Health Care Sector

Preface

In January 1996, the publishers of *Planning Review* announced that its name would be changed to *Strategy & Leadership,* stating that they had learned from months of research and discussion that "planning is now an integral part of the senior management function and, in many organizations, is no longer viewed as a separate discipline." Similarly, the editor of *Future Survey Annual* noted that strategic management in the past few years, "has taken on a new and promising form that is more holistic, qualitative, visionary, and action-oriented toward shaping the future." These events are not very significant in themselves, however they indicate subtle changes that are taking place in the strategic management field.

Strategic management is a philosophy of managing that is inseparable from leadership. It concerns setting direction for an organization—charting a course for success—but additionally it concerns creating an organizational culture for coping with change. It is no wonder that strategic management is becoming an integral part of leadership.

At the same time that strategic management is evolving, the health care field is changing. A recent article in *Modern Healthcare* entitled, "Health Care Is a Business, Even for Not-for-Profits" indicates that "major transformation of our industry is inevitable" and that the industry is "being driven by consumer demand and market dynamics." Further, it suggests that health care managers are "challenged not only to bring costs in line, but also to rethink how health care should be organized and delivered." Health care organizations, both for-profits and not-for-profits, similar to other businesses, have to be concerned with the implications of their changing environment, setting a viable direction for the future, creating a culture for innovation and change, and emphasizing the bottom line. The success criteria that applies to business organizations now applies equally well to health care organizations.

Strategic leadership is essential to the success of health care organizations. Yet, study after study cites the lack of strategic thinking and poor management as the most important problems facing the health care industry. Clearly, the health care field has had difficulty in dealing with a dynamic environment, holding down costs, providing universal access, diversifying wisely, defining quality, and balancing capacity and demand. Not coincidentally, the health care sector has been slow to adopt modern management methods, particularly strategic management.

Compounding the problems associated with rapid growth, the health care industry has experienced significant environmental change. Political and regulatory "health care reform" measures have initiated a complete restructuring of the industry. Technological advances have continually and rapidly evolved the "state of the art." The economy and competition have forever altered the vision and mission of many of the industry's institutions. In some areas, health care professionals are in short supply; and many of those who remain in the industry have become disenchanted.

Today, no decision-making environment is more difficult or complex than that of health care. The industry presents a truly unfamiliar, unexpected, ambiguous, and uncertain environment. Dramatic change will continue to take place within the technological, social, political, regulatory, competitive, and economic contexts of health care delivery. For this reason, strategic management is gaining a prominent role in the administration of health care. Today, health care organizations that do not have a clear strategy are doomed to mediocrity at best—and failure at worst—resulting in a poor quality of life for the community.

Health care managers will have to understand the changing environment; develop clear, feasible strategies that position their organizations for long-term success; and consistently and logically implement the adopted strategies. Managers have to make strategic decisions today that will influence their organizations for many years.

For these reasons, students of health care administration need to develop a strategic management perspective—a clear understanding of the dynamics of the health care environment and the methods and constructs required to position their organizations for success. At the same time, today's professional health care managers need further experience in assessing strategic health care situations, proposing strategies, and discussing the advantages of their proposals.

This text acknowledges the evolution that is taking place in both strategic management and health care. The objective of this text is to provide readers with a strategic perspective and an understanding of its logic and structure. Therefore, the text provides analytical, rational models of the processes of strategic management. These models may be used to initiate, guide, and track the processes. At the same time, the text encourages strategic thinking, innovation, and leadership. There are no universal models or templates in strategic management that will always work. Thus, the text fosters an understanding of the importance of emergent thinking, intuition, leadership, and learning.

We have used the metaphor of the "map and compass" to explain the need for both rational, sequential models as well as emergent thinking in strategic management. We often need maps to begin our journey and they are extremely useful as we proceed through charted territory. Without some type of map, little progress can be made. However, inevitably we find that the landscape has changed, was poorly charted, or we are entering entirely new territory. Here, the compass is more valuable as it can point our direction, though the route or even the destination may be unclear. Often strategic management is a rational, logical process; sometimes it is an intuitive, entrepreneurial, political, cultural, or learning process.

This book draws upon the literature and experience of the business and health care communities as well as research and practice in both the public and private sectors. This approach provides thought processes and analysis methods from business and health care that have proven effective in dealing with complex tasks in dynamic environments. In combining business and health care methods, we have not lost sight of the fact that health care management has its own unique setting, managerial parameters, and strategic considerations.

Text Organization

The text provides a strategic management perspective through fourteen chapters as well as eighteen cases that deal with strategic issues. Cases allow students to have vicarious experiences in developing pragmatic strategies. In addition, the book contains five appendices that aid in the analysis, research, and presentation of health care strategy. The book is divided into six parts including Part 1, "Initiating the Strategic Management Process;" Part 2, "Strategy Formulation;" Part 3, "Strategic Implementation: Operational Strategies;" Part 4, "Controlling and Creating the Strategy;" Part 5, "Appendices," and Part 6, "Cases in the Health Care Sector." The first four parts introduce the theory and practice of strategic management for health care organizations. The appendices provide important information and help students develop the skills necessary for effective strategic analysis and presentation. The cases provide further insight into the complexity of issues that organizations face, practice in discerning critical issues, application of theory, understanding of the interrelatedness of administrative functions, and a format for the discussion of issues facing the industry.

Retained Features

The text contains features that have been integral to all editions of the book and are designed to help the reader understand the nature and application of strategic management. Some of the most important are these:

- An *integrative model of the strategic management process* guides the reader through the book and provides a framework for unifying all the chapters.
- *Learning Objectives* direct attention to the important points or skills introduced in the chapter.
- A chapter *Introductory Incident* is placed near the beginning of the text material to provide a practical example of the concepts to be introduced and discussed within the chapter.
- A generous number of *examples* and *exhibits* are included for each chapter.
- A minimum of six *Perspectives* drawn from actual health care organizations' experiences or derived from accepted management wisdom provide further insight. These sidebars allow students to relate to particular concepts presented in the text.
- Chapter *Summary and Conclusions* highlight the most important issues covered in each chapter.
- *Key Terms and Concepts in Strategic Management* present the essential vocabulary and terminology relative to the topics discussed in each chapter.
- *Questions for Class Discussion* aid the reader in reviewing the important material and thinking about the implications of the ideas presented.

- *Notes* containing the sources used as support in developing the material in each chapter can be used by those who wish to go to the original sources or who want to read more on a particular topic.
- *Additional Readings* offer the reader additional, up-to-date or classic sources on topics related to the material discussed in each chapter.
- A series of *Appendices* devoted to more detailed discussions of topics assist in expanding the material discussed in the text. Appendices assist readers by presenting ways to analyze health care cases, engage in financial analysis, make oral presentations, and research health care topics.
- A comprehensive *Instructor's Manual* is available for adopters to assist them in preparing for and conducting class sessions. The manual provides chapter outlines, lecture notes, possible responses to discussion questions, and teaching notes for the cases in the text.

Feedback from users of previous editions has reinforced our belief that these features aid in providing an informative, interesting, and pedagogically sound survey of the strategic management of health care organizations.

New Features

Beyond updating text material and changing the Introductory Incidents and Perspectives, the third edition contains some new features and changes from the second edition. The major revisions occur in the first six chapters. Chapters 1 and 2 of the second edition have been merged to present the comprehensive model of strategic management earlier. Most of the subject matter was retained but it was made more concise and readable. Strategic change (formerly in Chapter 2) was moved to Chapter 6 to better connect the strategy evaluation process with strategic change (evolutionary and revolutionary change) and the forces of change.

Chapter 2, "Understanding and Analyzing the External Environment" (formerly Chapter 3), provides methodologies to identify and analyze issues in the general environment. Chapter 3, "Service Area Competitor Analysis," is a completely new chapter to this edition and has been included because of the changing nature of the health care industry. In the past, health care managers did not have to engage in competitor analysis; however, in today's health care environment, this type of analysis is considered essential for both for-profit and not-for-profit segments of the industry.

Chapter 4, "Internal Environmental Analysis," has been completely rewritten to provide a process to assess resources, capabilities, and competencies. Although the traditional strengths and weaknesses orientation is included, it is recognized as being only a part of a more comprehensive and useful approach to analyzing a health care organization's ability to build and sustain competitive advantage from within. The structure of Chapter 5, "Mission, Vision, Values, and Objectives," remains essentially the same but more examples of mission and vision statements from a wider variety of organizations are included. Significantly more attention is given to vision and vision statements.

Chapters 6 through 13 have the same content but have been shortened and made more readable. Chapter 14 has been updated to 1996 and describes the strategic planning activities of the Indiana State Department of Health since completing its initial strategic plan. In addition, there is an expanded bibliography and a more comprehensive index. Of the eighteen cases, five are revised and updated, and four are favorites that reviewers indicated should be retained. Thus over 75 percent of the cases are new.

The book has applications for both students and professional health care managers. Students will find that the text provides an integrative experience that helps pull together their knowledge, skills, and experiences into a unified understanding of the strategic management of health care organizations. Many highly skilled professionals in health care are seeking to expand their expertise in strategic management. Hospital administrators, long-term-care facility managers, medical practice managers, home health care managers, and state and federal public health administrators will find the text a useful guide for developing and implementing strategy.

Acknowledgments

We are indebted to many individuals for their assistance and encouragement in the preparation of this book. First, we would like to thank the Appendix contributors: Mahmud Hassan (Appendix B), Gary F. Kohut and Carol M. Baxter (Appendix C). Their work provides additional fundamental skills important in strategic management. Also Kay Webb, Jackie Frugoli, and Marian S. Lambert made an invaluable contribution typing manuscripts, proofing, aiding in research, and generally supporting all of our activities.

A special note of thanks is due to Dean M. Gene Newport of the Graduate School of Management/School of Business at the University of Alabama at Birmingham, who is returning to the faculty after two decades as dean. Dean Edward M. Mazze of the Belk College of Business Administration at the University of North Carolina at Charlotte, Dean Eli I. Capilouto of the School of Public Health at the University of Alabama at Birmingham, and Dean Charles L. Joiner of the School of Health Related Professions at the University of Alabama at Birmingham have all continued to be supportive of all our projects. We appreciate the support and encouragement of Stuart A. Capper, interim chairperson of the Department of Health Care Organization and Policy, and Robert S. Hernandez, chairperson of the Department of Health Services Administration at the University of Alabama at Birmingham.

In addition, we have benefited greatly from the stimulation and encouragement of other faculty, especially Janet M. Bronstein, Myron D. Fottler, Cynthia C. Haddock, Tee H. Hiett, Howard W. Houser, Merida L. Johns, R. L. Jordan, Stephen T. Mennemeyer, Gail W. McGee, Robert A. McLean, Robert L. Ohsfeldt, John E. Sheridan, Richard M. Shewchuk, and Donna J. Slovensky. Rarely are individuals fortunate enough to have such a large number of supportive colleagues who are so willing to give of their time to facilitate the work of others. Michael A. Morrisey, Director of the Lister Hill Center for Health Policy has generously provided use of office space, logistical support, and unfailing encouragement.

We also thank Barbara A. Mark of the Medical College of Virginia, Arnold Kaluzny of the University of North Carolina at Chapel Hill, Judith W. Alexander of the University of South Carolina, Stephen M. Shortell of Northwestern University, and Howard L. Smith of the University of New Mexico for their initial insights and contribution to the first edition and their encouragement to write it. An additional thanks to all the fine people at Blackwell Publishers for their constant help and guidance, especially Rolf A. Janke, who always believed in us and in this book and whose enthusiasm motivated us all the more, and to Dana Siliman and Mary Beckwith, who have skillfully helped us through every stage of this project and others. We would also like to thank the original reviewers: John A. Baker, University of Arkansas at Little Rock; John D. Blair, Texas Tech University; Roice D. Luke, Medical College of Virginia; and Woodrow D. Richardson, University of Alabama at Birmingham as well as current reviewers: Richard M. Burton, Duke University; Laurel Files, University of North Carolina; Joel Lee, University of Kentucky; E. Jose Proenca, Widener University; and William B. Werther, University of Miami. These colleagues provided valuable guidance in blending concepts from the business and health care fields. They have given a great deal of time and effort to contribute to the education of tomorrow's health care leaders.

A very special note of thanks is extended to a number of people in health care organizations who have opened their organizations to us and allowed us to use them as laboratories to test and refine our ideas and approaches. Chapter 14, "Creating the Strategic Plan: An Example," could not have been developed without the support and encouragement of several people at the Indiana State Department of Health (ISDH). John C. Bailey, M.D., State Health Commissioner, provided us the opportunity to interrelate theory and practice and use the ISDH as the integrative example in this text. Joe D. Hunt, Director of Information Systems, kept the project alive and served as the catalyst at every stage. Nancy Blough, Deputy Commissioner, supported the process, insisted that it stay on schedule, and stepped in to make things happen when the process slowed. Keith Main, now retired but formerly Director of Public Health Research, believed in the process and in us and made the experience enjoyable and a genuine learning experience. Finally, we express our appreciation to all of the employees of the ISDH who participated in the project.

A special thanks to Carole W. Samuelson, M.D., Health Officer of the Jefferson County Department of Health, who has allowed us invaluable access to the health department. Dr. Samuelson's enthusiasm for medicine and her commitment to leadership keeps us motivated and encouraged. Michael E. Fleenor, M.D., M.P.H., Deputy Health Officer, has also provided support and has "run interference" for us in a series of management development and strategic planning projects at Jefferson County.

Other health care professionals who have been instrumental in helping us formulate and refine ideas and concepts are Donald E. Williamson, M.D., State Health Officer, Alabama Department of Public Health; Clyde Bargainer, Director at the Alabama Department of Public Health, Eric T. Baumgartner, M.D., Bureau Chief of Managed Care, State of Texas; Jimmy Guidry, M.D., Assistant Secretary of Health for the State of Louisiana; Pat Cleavland, Director of the New Mexico Division of Public Health; Sandra B. Nichols, M.D., Director of Arkansas Department of Health; and Melinda Rowe, M.D., Director of Jefferson County Health Department, Louisville, Kentucky.

The book would not have been possible without the case writers. Case writing is a difficult art, requiring many hours of library research, personal interviews, and detailed analysis. The case contributors listed in this text represent some of the finest case researchers anywhere. We think you will appreciate and enjoy their craft.

Finally, but most important, we thank our families who have supported and encouraged us through yet another writing project. Support and encouragement are what families are all about and, as usual, we have received full measure of both.

Strategic management is about organizational survival. We live in a competitive world, and health care organizations are no longer protected from the challenges of competition. Health care institutions must compete for patients, markets, revenues, appropriations, employees, and more. Only through a sound, logical process of strategic management can a health care organization understand the changing health care environment and meet the competition now emerging from all sectors. As Avinash Dixit and Barry Nalebuff suggest, "Good strategic thinking . . . remains an art. But its foundations consist of some simple basic principles—an emerging science of strategy."

Peter M. Ginter   Linda E. Swayne   W. Jack Duncan

PART 1

Initiating the Strategic Management Process

Part 1 provides an introduction to strategic management and situational analysis of health care organizations. Chapter 1 discusses the need and rationale for strategic management in today's turbulent health care environment, provides a definition for *strategic management*, traces its foundations, and presents a broad conceptual paradigm for thinking strategically. In addition, the chapter introduces a structured process for conducting strategic management in a health care organization. The process is presented as a model; it represents a map to initiate strategic management. Key elements of the model include the external environment and processes for conducting situational analysis, strategy formulation, strategic implementation, and strategic control.

The starting point in the process of strategic management is to determine precisely where the organization is today and where it wants to be in the future. Situational analysis, covered in Chapters 2 through 5, is the process that determines precisely where the organization is today.

Chapters 2 and 3 focus on identifying issues in the external environment. Chapter 2 contains a comprehensive investigation of the general external environment, and Chapter 3 provides an approach for conducting service area competitor analysis. Because the external environment provides strategic managers with clues as to what they *should* be doing, this is a critically important aspect of situational analysis.

Assessment of the internal environment is accomplished through an analysis of the organization's resources, capabilities, and competencies, as examined in Chapter 4. Once these organizational assets are understood, strategic managers have a better appreciation for what the organization *can* do.

Finally, the concepts of organizational mission, vision, values, and objectives are examined in Chapter 5. The process of developing a mission forces members of an organization to think about their distinctiveness today; developing a vision forces them to think about their hopes for the future; and awareness of organizational values makes members cognizant of the things that should be cherished and not compromised as the mission and vision are pursued. Objectives establish clear targets and help focus organizational activities. Mission, vision, values, and objectives provide the framework for what the organization *wants* to do.

The Nature of Strategic Management

Learning Objectives

After completing this chapter you should be able to:

1. Explain why strategic management has become crucial in today's dynamic environment.

2. Define and differentiate between *strategy, strategic planning,* and *strategic management.*

3. Trace the evolution of strategic management and discuss its conceptual foundations.

4. Understand the necessity for both the analytic and emergent models of strategic management.

5. Describe and explain the strategic management processes used in the analytic model.

6. Understand how an organization may realize a strategy that it never intended.

7. Explain the links between the different levels of strategy within an organization.

8. Describe the various leadership roles within strategic management.

9. Understand the benefits of strategic management for health care organizations.

Managing in a Dynamic Environment

The dramatic changes currently occurring in the health care industry will continue. At no previous time have both public and private health care institutions faced a more turbulent, confusing, and threatening environment. Impetus for significant change will come from many sources, including federal, state, and local health care reform efforts; international as well as domestic economic and market forces; demographic shifts and lifestyle changes; and technological advances within the health care industry. Certainly, the hospitals in Boston and Nashville, described in the Introductory Incident, as well as health care institutions across the nation will look very different in the future. Which health care institutions will survive these changes and prosper? As suggested in the introductory quote, in this environment health care organizations will have to effectively manage change and become "masters of renewal."

A Tale of Two Cities

It was the best of times because the United States had created the most advanced health care system in the world. In the early 1990s, hospitals in America's largest cities spent enormous sums on sprawling megaplexes and high-tech medical equipment. It was the age of wisdom because one breakthrough after another characterized medicine in the United States. People who could afford it traveled from all parts of the world to America to receive the finest medical treatment available.

It was the worst of times because double-digit increases in health care costs were bankrupting the system. Insurers and the public alike were in a furor over the escalating costs. In addition, approximately 41 million Americans were without health insurance. It was the age of foolishness because none of the experts had a way to deal with the problems. By the mid-1990s, despite slower health care cost increases, the industry faced a period of turbulence and "white water change."

Stark, but not unusual, examples of the problems in health care across the nation can be found in a tale of two cities.

Boston

In an environment of increasing costs, calls for reform, an aging population, an overabundance of duplicated services, declining birth rates, declining admissions and lengths of stay, and insurers cutting payments, Boston's largest and most prestigious hospitals were expanding and vying for dominance in a costly market niche. Beth Israel Hospital, a leading medical facility and the site of many major medical advances, is one of the teaching hospitals affiliated with Harvard Medical School. In 1993, it proudly opened a $5 million facility devoted to saving the lives of critically ill babies. With twenty new neonatal beds of its own, Beth Israel no longer had to transport its babies who needed intensive care across the street to the world-famous Children's Hospital or three blocks away to Brigham and Women's Hospital, both Harvard teaching hospitals with international reputations. Tufts University's New England Medical Center opened a multimillion-dollar maternity unit in downtown Boston and St. Elizabeth's Medical Center, another Tufts affiliate in nearby Brighton, opened a new wing dedicated to women's and infants' care. At the same time, Massachusetts General Hospital, perhaps the best known of the Boston hospitals, opened a new obstetrics facility.

By 1995, most of these hospitals no longer stood alone. Brigham and Women's had teamed with Massachusettes General to form Partners HealthCare System; and by the summer of 1996, New England Medical Center joined Partners as well. Pathway Health Network includes New England Deaconess Hospital, Beth Israel, and four other Boston-area facilities. Even the Tufts University School affiliate hospital, New England Medical, the only major Boston teaching hospital without a partner in the spring of 1996, initiated preliminary talks with Pathway.

Nashville

Although buffeted by market forces for years, many of the nineteen hospitals in the Nashville area were not fully aware of the magnitude of the looming environmental changes in their health care market in the early 1990s. The city of Nashville, with a population of about 500,000, had ten general hospitals, and in the seven counties surrounding the city were nine additional hospitals, each with about 100 beds. In the past, these county hospitals sent 40 to 60 percent of their patients to Nashville for treatment—a situation that would likely change.

Nashville's ten hospitals—three for-profit and seven not-for-profit—had an average occupancy rate of approximately 66 percent. Here, the for-profits may not ultimately squeeze out the not-for-profits as in some other of the nation's cities. The strongest hospitals are Nashville Baptist and St. Thomas, not-for-profit hospitals competing to take a larger share of the market by offering a full continuum of care and building statewide networks. Vanderbilt Teaching Hospital may survive under the wing of the university. Nashville Memorial Hospital and Tennessee Christian are insulated by politics and religion, respectively, but are in remote parts of the city and struggling financially. Meharry-Hubbard, a not-for-profit teaching hospital in a predominately black area, has allied with the city's public hospital, Metro-General. Metro-General, where about half the doctors who run the 500 community health centers in the poor rural and inner-city areas in the United States were trained, needs more paying patients. Moreover, its management fears that poor people, given a choice of hospitals, will choose to go elsewhere.

By the mid-1990s, according to a health care executive from Nashville, the hospitals in the area have consolidated into two large networks. One is composed of Baptist, St. Thomas, and Vanderbilt, and the other is the for-profit Nashville-based Columbia/HCA Healthcare Corp. that has been buying up hospitals around the country. Columbia and Baptist have been in a neck-to-neck competitive battle around Nashville during the past year; both are opening women's centers in shopping malls, both are bidding on and buying up hospitals around the state. But only Columbia has bridged the tale of two cities. In May, Columbia completed a joint venture that gives it 80 percent ownership of MetroWest Medical Center, a Boston-area hospital with ties to the Harvard-affiliated teaching hospitals in Boston.

A New Paradigm of Health Care?

The individual hospital of the early 1990s has given way to the network of hospitals of the mid-1990s. What will the picture look like in the year 2000? Will a new health care delivery system be created in the United States? How do organizations know where to compete and where not to compete? How can individual health care organizations chart their way through the changes occurring in the industry? What strategies will help health care organizations cope with all the changes and position them to survive?

Source: Terrie Reeves, Assistant Professor, Texas Woman's University, Institute of Health Sciences, Houston, Texas. Adapted from Laura Walbert, "Reality Is at the Bedside," *CFO,* December 1993, pp. 22–25 and from numerous notices in *Modern Healthcare* (July 31, 1995–July 22, 1996).

One of the greatest challenges for health care organizations is identifying and planning for the changes that are most likely to occur. Interviews with health care professionals and a review of the health care literature suggest that health care organizations will have to cope with some or all of the following:

- Additional legislative health care reform efforts to provide health care access to the 41 million Americans who are without health insurance.
- An increasingly restrictive reimbursement environment as the federal government, business, and the health care industry attempt to curb burgeoning medical costs.
- Demographic shifts, including an aging population, that will place capacity burdens on some health care organizations as a lessening of demand threatens the survival of others.

- Forced mobility of patients from one health care provider to another because of changes in the health plan selected by the employer.
- Critical shortages of nonphysician health care professionals and primary-care physicians, yet a surplus of physicians within some specialties and in some geographic regions.
- The high costs of purchasing new, sophisticated, largely computer-based technologies to meet the demand for high-quality health care.
- Further consolidation within the health care industry because of cost pressures and intensified competition.
- The development of integrated networks of care (the combining of the financing and delivery of care).
- The continuing expansion by health care corporations into segments that have less regulation and into businesses outside of the traditional health care industry.
- The increasing importance of market niche strategies and services marketing.
- Growth in outpatient care and the development of innovative alternative health care delivery systems.
- The rapid growth of home health care influenced by limitations in reimbursement (prospective payment) and the high costs of hospital care.
- The decreasing viability of many of the nation's small, rural, and public hospitals and a reconfiguration of the rural health care delivery system.
- An increase in the acceptance of health maintenance organizations (HMOs) and preferred provider organizations (PPOs) to the point where managed-care plans will cover nearly one-third of the United States population by the year 2000.
- Increasing number of physician executives in leadership roles in health care organizations.
- More emphasis on preventive care through wellness programs and healthy behavior.
- Increased emphasis on cost containment and measurement of outcomes of care (cost/benefit).
- A changing role for public health moving back to "core" activities (prevention, surveillance, disease control, assurance) and away from the delivery of primary care.
- Increased pressure to reduce the costs of administration of health care.[1]

Even the language of health care has changed over the past several years. Perspective 1–1 examines the growing list of health care acronyms that have marked the changes of the 1990s. How can health care leaders deal with these important, complex, and sometimes conflicting issues? Which ones are most important or most pressing? Furthermore, what new issues will emerge? It is likely that there will be new opportunities and threats to health care organizations that have yet to be identified or fully assessed. Even more sobering, it seems certain that there will be more change in the health care industry in the next ten years than there was in the past ten.

Recent Changes

We need only look at some of the changes that took place during the past several years to anticipate the number and magnitude of the changes that may occur in the future. For instance, because of health care cost escalation during the 1970s and 1980s, Medicare's

Perspective 1-1

The Changing Language of Health Care

- **ASO (Administrative Services Only):** a contract between an insurance company and a self-funded plan (usually a large business or government entity) where the insurance company only performs administrative services such as claims processing.
- **CCO (Complete Care Organization):** hospitals and providers working cooperatively to provide care within a community.
- **DRG (Diagnostic Related Group):** a classification system using 383 major diagnostic categories that assign patients into case types. It is used to facilitate utilization review, analyze patient case mix, and determine hospital reimbursement. For example, the classification DRG 320 is for kidney and urinary tract infection.
- **EPO (Exclusive Provider Organization):** structurally similar to a PPO in that an EPO can simply be a network of health care providers; however, the beneficiary cannot go out of network or must pay the entire cost of services. EPO physicians are reimbursed only for services actually provided to plan beneficiaries (rather than a capitated rate).
- **FFS (Fee for Service):** refers to a provider that charges the patient according to a fee schedule set for each service or procedure performed; the patient's total bill will vary by the number of services or procedures actually performed.
- **HCFA (Health Care Financing Administration):** part of the U.S. Department of Health and Human Services, the contracting agency for HMOs that seek direct contractor/provider status for provision of Medicare benefits.
- **HMO (Health Maintenance Organization):** an organization interposed between providers and payors that attempts to "manage the care" on behalf of the health service consumer and payor. HMOs are responsible for both the financing and delivery of comprehensive health services to an enrolled group of patients.
- **IPA (Independent Practices Association):** a legal entity composed of physicians who have organized for the purpose of negotiating contracts to provide medical services. Typically, physicians keep their independent businesses but negotiate as a group with payors. A super IPA has many IPAs rolled into one to contract with payors.
- **IPN (Integrated Provider Network):** a network comprised of primary and secondary hospitals and providers within a city or other geographic unit that have agreed to work together.
- **ISN (Integrated Service Network):** a network of hospitals, physicians, and other health care professionals that provides health services to members or enrollees for a capitated fee. Although ISNs are similar to HMOs, they are intended to be more flexible in terms of their relationships with health care providers and more sophisticated in their management of patient care.
- **MCO (Managed-Care Organization):** any organization whose goal is to eliminate excessive and unnecessary service, thereby keeping health care costs manageable.
- **MSO (Management Service Organization):** a legal corporation formed to provide practice management services to physicians. At one extreme, an MSO could own one practice or several hundred practices. On the other extreme, an MSO may not own any physician practices or provide management services. In that case, the MSO would be strictly an entity that signs managed-care contracts for an affiliated provider group. Typically, an MSO will require a commitment of ten to forty years from the physician or group practice contracting for its services.

- **NP (Nurse Practitioner):** a nurse who serves as the initial contact into the health care system and coordinates community-based services necessary for health promotion, health maintenance, rehabilitation, or prevention of disease and disability. Nurse practitioners work interdependently with other health professionals to provide primary health care in many communities.

- **PA (Physician Assistant):** an allied health professional who, by virtue of having completed an educational program in the medical sciences and a structured clinical experience in surgical services, is qualified to assist the physician in patient-care activities. Physician assistants may be involved with patients in any medical setting for which the physician is responsible, including the operating room, recovery room, intensive care unit, emergency department, hospital outpatient clinic, and the physician's office.

- **PCP (Primary-Care Physician):** a physician responsible for coordinating and managing the health care needs of members. PCPs may be trained in primary care, pediatrics, obstetrics/gynecology, internal medicine, or family medicine. They determine hospitalization and referral to specialists for their patients.

- **PHO (Physician-Hospital Organization):** an organization designed to integrate a hospital and its medical staff so they can contract with payors as a single entity. Physicians retain their independence. A super PHO has many PHOs rolled into one to contract with payors.

- **PMC, PMO, PPM (Physician Management Company, Physician Management Organization, Physician Practice Management):** organizations that provide management expertise to medical practices. They might provide capital for building and expanding physician practices, contracted management, financial and information system services, recruitment of physicians, and so on, usually on a contractual basis.

- **POS (Point of Service):** combines an HMO insurance plan with traditional insurance. "Point of service" refers to members deciding whether to go in or out of the network. The employee belongs to a managed-care plan but can opt for the traditional plan anytime. POS members usually pay less when they stay within the HMO network but can avoid restrictions. When they choose the traditional insurance plan, coverage is typically for that type insurance—meet a deductible and 70 to 80 percent of health care costs are paid. Sometimes POS is called an "HMO with an escape hatch." POS plans grew at a faster rate than HMOs in 1995.

- **PPO (Preferred Provider Organization):** an entity through which various health plans or carriers contract to purchase health care services for patients from a selected group of providers, typically at a better per-patient cost.

- **PPS (Prospective Payment System):** a system designed to control costs for Medicare and Medicaid patients. Rather than reimbursing on a retrospective cost-plus system, PPS legislation in 1983 reimbursed hospitals on a prospective (predetermined) basis. For example, a hospital would know that it would receive a set amount to treat a broken hip. If the patient could be treated at a cost lower than the reimbursed amount, the hospital could keep the "profit." On the other had, if the hospital spent more than the reimbursable amount, for whatever reason, it had to absorb the loss.

- **PPWW (Physician Practice Without Walls):** physicians effectively integrate their practices and become employees of the new entity, yet maintain their separate, existing practice locations.

- **PRO (Peer Review Organization):** a professionally sponsored and operated system for the review of professional judgment about quality or appropriateness of treatment and related matters. The duties of PROs include arbitrating disagreements between or among physicians, dentists, patients, and third parties.

- **PSO (Provider-Sponsored Organization):** integrated groups of doctors and hospitals that assume managed-care (often Medicare) risk contracts.
- **OON (Out of Network):** describes health care services received from providers who do not participate in a managed-care program's contracted network of providers. Typically, patients pay all costs out of pocket (no reimbursement).

- **RBRVS (Resource-Based Relative Value Scale):** a national fee system for Medicare payments to physicians. The fee schedule is designed to shift payment patterns from a number of more costly specialties (such as those in surgery) to primary care.
- **TPA (Third-Party Administrator):** a firm that performs administrative functions such as claims processing and membership for a self-funded plan or a start-up managed-care plan.

prospective payment system (PPS) was implemented in 1983. As a result of PPS, health care delivery today is quite different than it was in the mid-1980s. PPS shifted national priorities from insisting on high-quality care regardless of cost to holding health care delivery costs in check. PPS fundamentally reformed the nation's health care delivery system in a very short period of time, and yet because of the extensive reform efforts of the 1990s, its tenth anniversary passed virtually unnoticed.[2]

The dramatic increase in managed-care systems, including PPOs and HMOs, is another significant change that gained impetus during the 1980s and continued throughout the 1990s. Although often referred to as health care providers, these organizations are actually interposed between providers and payors and attempt to "manage the care" on behalf of the health service consumer and payor. Growth of these organizations was primarily fueled by the prospect of legislated health care reform.

Managed care fostered the growth of integrated health systems. Employers embraced these organizations as a way to control their health care costs. Now more than 60 percent of major employers offer managed-care plans and over 70 percent of inpatient care is covered by some fixed-price, managed-care payment system. In an effort to control rising health care costs and improve quality, managed-care organizations and integrated networks became major forces shaping the health care industry.

Further significant restructuring of the industry began in the 1990s and continues today. The large number of failures of health care organizations, on the one hand, and the large numbers of mergers, acquisitions, alliances, and cooperatives, on the other, indicate the magnitude of the restructuring taking place. For example, in 1995 and then again in 1996, more mergers took place than in any previous time. Furthermore, consolidation is taking place in every segment of the health care industry including hospitals, physician medical groups, long-term care, home health, HMOs, rehabilitation, psychiatric, and so on. As illustrated in Perspective 1–2, even academic medical centers have not escaped restructuring. Such dramatic changes have created a chaotic health care environment. In describing the situation, the chief executive officer (CEO) of Mount Sinai Hospital, which recently reopened as a psychiatric and rehabilitation facility, indicated that "the whole [health care] system is in a state of crisis." The system may have allowed too many hospitals, too many beds, duplication of high-tech services, heavy concentration of hospitals in certain areas, and low concentration in others. In addition, inadequate Medicaid and

Perspective 1–2

The Changing Face of Academic Medical Centers

The academic medical center, an independent, not-for-profit institution of higher learning, research, and patient care may be a thing of the past. Used to having the most difficult cases referred to them, academic medical centers that are not part of a managed-care system find they are being left out. In Oklahoma, the state-owned hospital authority has agreed to enter a partnership with Columbia/HCA. The partnership will merge Columbia's Presbyterian Hospital in Oklahoma City with the university system. Profits will be divided 60 percent to Columbia/HCA, 40 percent to the authority. Tulane University in New Orleans sold an 80 percent interest in its hospital to Columbia/HCA.

Columbia/HCA has entered into a 50/50 management agreement with the Medical University of South Carolina. The deal will include University Hospital, the Children's Hospital, and the Institute of Psychiatry. The Storm Eye Institute has not been addressed at this point.

Two major academic medical centers in the San Francisco Bay area, the University of California San Francisco Medical Center and Stanford University Hospital, are exploring the feasibility and benefits of reducing duplication in investment in new facilities and state-of-the art equipment. Similar to other academic medical centers located in competing markets, the two facilities agree that this proposal would result in more cost-effective patient care. Both schools would remain independent, and both institutions would continue providing patient care at their respective hospital campuses and clinics. The two hospitals have not decided whether it will be a full-asset merger.

In Boston, Dana Farber and Partners Health-Care System, the parent organization of Massachusetts General and Brigham and Women's, will con-solidate cancer facilities and programs of the Harvard Medical School instead of interspersing smaller medical programs to affiliates throughout Boston.

The University of Michigan Medical Center has entered into a joint venture with Principal Health Care, a commercial insurance carrier. Duke University is acquiring primary-care physicians, but is also creating a managed-care company through a joint venture with Sanus Corporation Health Systems.

In Louisville, Kentucky, Jewish and Alliant, two leading private hospitals, created an integrated hospital network by taking control of the management of the University of Louisville Hospital from Columbia/HCA.

As the examples illustrate, the academic medical center of the past is quickly getting a face-lift. Institutions that were either state supported or private university affiliated are seeking alternatives to management and even ownership. One main concern of the facilities seems to be the consolidation of duplicated services. They are reengineering themselves into lean, cost-efficient, less bureaucratic, more market-responsive organizations. They are renegotiating the relationship with the university, state governments, medical schools, and other organizations to which they may be legally or financially tied in order to attain greater flexibility and the ability to innovate. At the present time, these joint ventures may be the "Band-Aid" of choice in the healing process.

Source: Beth Woodard, Ph.D. Student in Health Services Administration, University of Alabama at Birmingham.

Medicare payments have contributed to losses. Henry Nichols of the National Union of Hospital and Health Care Employees added, "There is no strategy, no plan, no leadership at the state level—no strategy, no plan, no leadership at the local level."[3]

Coping with the Environment

Change has become so rapid, so complex, so turbulent, and so unpredictable that it is sometimes called *chaos* or *white water change.*[4] As a result, many health care markets have entered an era of hypercompetition. *Hypercompetition* is a condition of rapidly escalating competitive activity based on price-quality positioning, competition to create new know-how and to gain first-mover advantage, competition to protect or invade established product or geographic markets, and competition based on deep pockets and the creation of even deeper pocketed alliances. In hypercompetition the frequency, boldness, and aggressiveness of dynamic movement by players accelerates to create a condition of constant disequilibrium and change.[5] We truly are moving irrevocably beyond an awareness of "turbulent environments" to a recognition of our participation in a truly chaotic world.[6] Health care leaders will have to cope with white water change and position their organizations to take advantage of emerging opportunities while avoiding external threats. Strategic management can help health care managers sort out and cope with this new era of hypercompetition.

Strategic management has become a major thrust guiding the management of all types of contemporary organizations. Business organizations embraced strategic management as a way to anticipate and cope with a variety of external forces beyond their control. The environmental uncertainties and competitive pressures that have moved business organizations to adopt strategic management now beset health care organizations. Indeed, health care has become a complex business using many of the same processes and much of the same language as the most sophisticated business corporations.

As more and more health care organizations adopt strategic management, it is important that health care managers understand the concept, application, language, and process. Strategic management provides a basic understanding of how and why an organization survives and grows.

Strategy as Organizational Behavior

As illustrated in Exhibit 1–1, *strategy* may be viewed as the "behavior" of the organization. Forces in the external environment influence the strategic behaviors of the organization and suggest "what the organization *should* do." Strategic behavior is additionally influenced by the internal capabilities of the organization and represents "what the organization *can* do." Consistency of the behavior is driven by a set of common organizational values and goals. These values and goals are often the result of considerable thought and analysis by top management and indicate "what the organization *wants* to do."

For example, the strategic behavior of public hospitals across the United States clearly has been shaped by these three forces. Public hospitals are under severe political pressure, reimbursements are being cut, and competitors are vying for their patients. At the same time, resources in these hospitals typically have been limited and even decreasing, facilities are aging, and technology is less than state of the art. Yet, public hospital CEOs and some political leaders see the need for competitive disproportionate-share hospitals (hospitals that treat large numbers of poor people). The stra-

Exhibit 1–1 • Strategy as a Behavior of the Organization

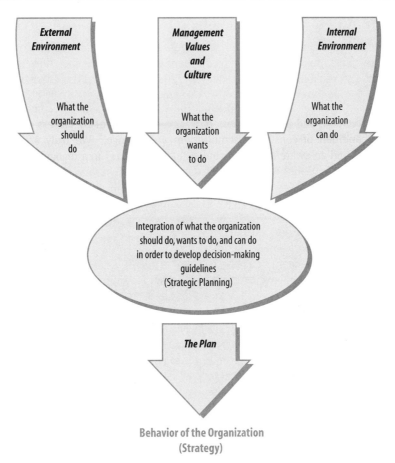

Source: From Fred Luthans, Richard M. Hodgetts, and Kenneth R. Thompson, *Social Issues in Business: Strategic and Public Policy Perspectives,* 6th ed. © 1990, p. 13. Adapted by permission of Prentice-Hall, Inc., Upper Saddle River, NJ.

tegic behavior of these hospitals will be shaped by the external forces, the hospitals' internal capabilities, and the direction provided by the leadership. Perspective 1–3 presents an example of a public hospital that understands what it should do, has strengthened what it can do, and has clear values and goals providing direction for what it wants to do.

Decision consistency is central to strategy; when an organization exhibits a consistent behavior it has a strategy. Therefore, a strategy may be viewed as a behavioral pattern that emerges from a stream of decisions concerning the positioning of the organization within its environment. In other words, when a sequence of decisions relating the organization to its environment exhibits a logical consistency over time, a strategy will have been formed.[7] As a matter of fact, one way to anticipate the next logical strategic move of an organization is to closely examine the logic of past decisions.

Perspective 1–3

Public Hospital Rebuilds to Compete

San Joaquin General Hospital near Stockton, California, understands its external forces, has moved to strengthen its internal capabilities, and has leadership with a vision for the future.

External Forces

San Joaquin County Health Care Services, the hospital's parent organization, serves Medi-Cal (California's Medicaid) and uninsured patients in one of California's poorest regions, nestled in the fruit basket of the vast and arid Central Valley. With a population of approximately 520,000, nearly one-half have no health insurance or are under-insured. Over 20 percent of San Joaquin County's population is foreign born. The county has one of the highest rates of people living in poverty and an unemployment rate that is typically over 10 percent. Medi-Cal covers about 125,000 people in the county.

Yet in today's health care environment, a hospital will not be able to survive by serving only uninsured and Medi-Cal patients. A major threat to San Joaquin General is that the state revised the Medi-Cal program to create more competition for Medi-Cal covered patients. However, there are also opportunities. A state program, passed by the 1989 legislature, pledged state funds to help California's beleaguered disproportionate-share hospitals finance necessary expansions, renovations, replacements, and seismic upgrades.

Internal Capabilities

Founded in 1857, San Joaquin County Health Care Services has a long history of providing good care to its poorest residents and has earned considerable patient loyalty. In order to increase its capabilities, San Joaquin County Health Care Services built a 97-bed partial replacement for the neighboring 212-bed county hospital (built in the 1920s). The hospital has everything a new private hospital would have. A sky-bridge connects it to the old building, which is being renovated for medical-surgical space. Hospital officials are hopeful that the building's handsome design, comfortable accommodations, and state-of-the-art technology will make it a viable alternative in the dawning age of competition for Medi-Cal patients. The challenge is to hold on to their Medi-Cal base (50 percent of their patients are covered under Medi-Cal) and lure privately insured patients.

Values and Goals

Michael N. Smith, director of San Joaquin County Health Care Services, believes that the county needs the public hospital to survive and prosper and therefore mounted the campaign to construct the new hospital. Building a state-of-the-art hospital is important if it is to be competitive in an environment where competition for Medicaid, as well as private patients, is being encouraged. Hospital officials want the public to see San Joaquin General as a quality health care institution—not as a "county hospital."

The strategic behavior of San Joaquin General Hospital is being shaped by changing external forces (what they should do), their capabilities (what they are able to do), and its leadership (what they want to do).

Source: J. Duncan Moore, Jr., "Public Hospital Rebuilds to Compete," *Modern Healthcare* 26, no. 21 (1996), pp. 44–46.

Decision consistency, and therefore a strategy, can be found by examining the behavior of organizations. For example, Premier Medical Group in Denver assessed its situation and developed a consistent strategy to create the medical practice of the future—the "group practice without walls." The organization builds on the group practice concept, except that the group's physicians practice medicine in offices dispersed throughout a particular geographic area rather than physically located in one facility. Premier has approximately 45 primary-care physician employees, and it is expected that the group will eventually include over 100 physicians and their practices. The strategy is aimed at centralizing administration while decentralizing health care delivery. Decision consistency is maintained in the corporation's nine-member board of directors—a group elected by and from the physician owners.[8]

Strategic Planning

The requirements of decision consistency suggest that a strategy is the means an organization chooses to move from where it is today to a desired state some time in the future. Thus, strategy also may be viewed as a set of guidelines or a plan that will help assure consistency in decision making. Strategic plans indicate what types of decisions are appropriate or inappropriate for an organization. As illustrated in Exhibit 1–2 strategy links management's understanding of the organization today with where it wants, can, and should be at some point in the future (say, for example, three to five years from now). The organizational process for identifying the desired future and developing decision guidelines for getting there is called *strategic planning.* The result of the strategic planning process is a plan or strategy.

Strategic Management

Although sometimes used interchangeably with strategic planning, strategic management is much broader. *Strategic management* is an externally oriented *philosophy* of

Exhibit 1–2 • Strategy and Vision

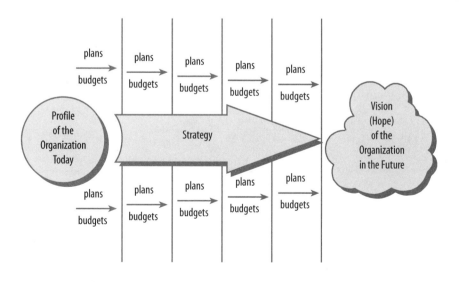

managing an organization that links strategic thinking and analysis to organizational action. Strategic management attempts to orchestrate a fit between the organization's external environment (political, regulatory, economic, technological, social, and competitive forces) and its internal situation (values, culture, finance, organization, human resources, marketing, information systems, and so on). In some cases this may mean responding to external forces (indications of what the organizations should do), whereas in other cases the organization may attempt to actually shape its environment (change the rules for success).

Strategic management goes beyond the traditional focus of strategic planning and incorporates leadership. Strategic management has become an integral part of the senior leadership of organizations and is no longer viewed as a separate discipline. As Max DePree has suggested, "Leaders are obligated to provide and maintain momentum."[9] Although organizations may accomplish superior results for a brief period of time, it takes the orchestration of management as well as leadership to perpetuate these capabilities far into the future.[10] Strategic managers constantly relate the organization to its external environment, not just to ensure compatibility and survival, but also to understand or alter the environmental trends well enough to "create the future."

What Strategic Management Is Not

Strategic management should not be regarded as a technique that will provide a "quick fix" for an organization that has fundamental problems. Quick fixes for organizations are rare; successful strategic management often takes years to become a part of the values and culture of an organization. If strategic management is regarded as a technique or gimmick, it is doomed to failure.

Strategic management is not a process of completing paperwork. If strategic management has reached a point where it has become simply a process of filling in endless forms, meeting deadlines, drawing milestone charts, or changing the dates of last year's objectives and plans, the process is not strategic management. Effective strategic management requires little paperwork. It is an attitude, not a series of documents.

Strategic management is not a process of simply extending the organization's current activities into the future. It is not based solely on a forecast of present trends. Strategic management attempts to identify the issues that will be important in the future. Health care leaders should not simply ask the question *"How* will we provide this service in the future?" Rather, they should be asking questions such as *"Should* we provide this service in the future?" "What *new* services will be needed?" and "What services are we providing now that are no longer needed?"

The Foundations of Strategic Management

In the political and military context, the concept of strategy has a long history. For instance, the underlying principles of strategy were discussed by Sun-tzu, Homer, Euripides, and many other early strategists and writers. The English word *strategy* comes from the Greek *strategos,* meaning "a general," which in turn comes from roots meaning "army" and "lead."[11] The Greek verb *stratego* means "to plan the destruction of one's enemies through effective use of resources."[12] As a result, many of the terms commonly used in relation to strategy—*objectives, mission, strengths, weaknesses*—were developed by the military.

Over the past fifty years, strategic management has been developed primarily in the business sector. The 1960s and 1970s were a time of major growth for strategic planning in business organizations. Leading companies such as General Electric were not only practicing strategic planning but also actively promoting its merits in the business press. Strategic planning provided these firms with a more systematic approach to managing business units and extended the planning and budgeting horizon beyond the traditional twelve-month operating period. In addition, business managers learned that financial planning alone was not an adequate management framework.[13]

In the 1980s, the concept of *strategic planning* was broadened to *strategic management.* This evolution acknowledged the importance of strategy implementation and control as well as strategy formulation and established strategic management as an approach to managing complex enterprises.

Strategic Management in the Health Care Industry

Strategic management concepts have been employed within health care organizations only in the past twenty to twenty-five years. Prior to 1970, individual organizations had few incentives to employ strategic management because most health care organizations were independent, freestanding, not-for-profit institutions, and health services reimbursement was on a cost-plus basis. Efforts at health planning were initiated by either state or local governments and implemented through legislation or private or nongovernmental agencies. For the most part, these planning efforts were disease oriented; that is, they were categorical approaches directed toward specific health problems (for example, the work of the National Tuberculosis Association, which stimulated the development of state and local government tuberculosis prevention and treatment programs).[14]

More recently, a variety of state and federal health planning or policy initiatives have been designed to (1) enhance quality of care—through studies on outcomes measures; (2) provide or control access to care—through the Hospital Survey and Construction Act (better known as the Hill-Burton Act), Medicaid, Medicare, state certificate of need laws; and (3) contain costs—through the National Health Planning and Resource Development Act and implementation of DRGs. Exhibit 1–3 presents the evolution of health planning since 1900.

Strategic Management Versus Health Policy Planning

As suggested in Exhibit 1–3, there has been substantial health planning in the United States; however, strategic management is organization specific. Strategic management helps an individual organization respond to state and federal policy and planning efforts, as well as to a variety of other external forces. The major differences between health planning and strategic planning are that strategic planning:

- is directed toward defining the organization's relationship to its environment;
- considers the whole organization as the unit of analysis;
- is a market-driven and market-based approach;

Exhibit 1–3 • Stages of Health Planning

Stage	Time Period	Major Concern	Control
Private Sector	1900 to late 1950s	Quality of care	Professional
Public Sector, Initial Stage	Late 1950s to early 1970s	Access to care	Administrative, grounded in volunteerism
Public Sector, Advanced Stage	Early 1970s to end of 1970s	Cost containment	Administrative, combined with regulation
Regionalization of Health Planning	1980 to 1994	Managerial efficiency	Market
Health Reform	1994–	Access and cost containment	Market, combined with regulation

Source: From G. Budrys, *Planning for the Nation's Health: A Study of 20th Century Developments in the U.S.,* p. 4a. Copyright © 1986 by Greenwood Press. Reproduced with permission of GREENWOOD PUBLISHING GROUP, INC., Westport, CT.

- places the development of strategic plans under the direct control of the chief executive officer without delegation;
- requires that the strategy must be clearly stated and persuasively communicated throughout the institution;
- creates final planning goals, objectives, and programs that must be vigorously implemented;
- requires that middle management be carefully educated and prepared to engage in strategic planning;
- emphasizes data collection and analysis for the "nuts and bolts" of the health institution's business;
- requires that strategic planning be integrated with other management functions; and
- places a strong focus on gaining and sustaining a competitive advantage.[15]

Strategic management is, in large part, a decision-making activity. The strategy of an organization is the result of a series of managerial decisions. Although these decisions are often supported by a great deal of quantifiable data, strategic decisions are fundamentally judgmental. Because strategic decisions cannot always be quantified, managers must rely on "informed judgment" in making this type of decision. As in our own lives generally, the more important the decision, the less quantifiable it is and the more we will have to rely on the opinions of others and our own best judgment. For example, our most important personal decisions—where to attend college, whether to get married, and so on, are largely judgments. Similarly, the most important organizational decisions, such as entering a market, introducing a new service, or acquiring a competitor, although based on information and analysis, are essentially judgments.

A Systems Perspective

The problems facing organizations are so complex that they defy simple solutions. Understanding the nature of the health care environment, the relationship of the organization to that environment, and the often conflicting interests of internal functional departments requires a broad conceptual paradigm. Yet, it is difficult to comprehend so many complex and important relationships. Strategic managers have found *general systems theory* or "a systems approach" to be a useful framework for organizing and understanding the variables of strategic management. A systems framework provides a basis for understanding and integrating knowledge from a wide variety of highly specialized areas so important to today's health care managers.

A *system* may be defined literally as "an organized or complex whole: an assemblage or combination of things or parts forming a complex or unitary whole."[16] The use of the systems approach requires managers to define the organization in broad terms and to identify the important variables and interrelationships that will affect decisions. A systems approach permits managers to concentrate on those aspects of the problem that most deserve attention and allows a more focused attempt at a resolution. In simple terms, systems thinking enables managers to see the "big picture" in proper perspective and helps them to avoid devoting excessive attention to relatively minor aspects of the total system.[17]

Today, health care organizations are placing increased emphasis on strategic management. A systems approach can provide a logical and consistent conceptual framework for analyzing these decisions. First, rapid environmental change from diverse sources requires leaders to identify and monitor the systems likely to affect the organization. Second, the health care leaders strive to achieve overall organizational effectiveness and avoid allowing the parochial interests of one organizational element to distort overall performance. Third, the strategic leader must do this in an organizational environment that invariably involves conflicting organizational objectives.[18]

Recognizing the importance of systems thinking, health care managers commonly refer to "the health care system" or "the health care delivery system" and strive to develop logical internal organizational systems to deal with the environment. In a similar manner, health care managers must use systems thinking to understand and relate to the external environment. The community and region may be thought of as an integrated system with each part of the system (subsystem) providing a unique contribution. Many contemporary health care strategies are driven by a systems approach as evidenced by the growth of health care systems, networks, cooperatives, and alliances.

As capitation (a set fee for each enrolled member of a managed-care system) increases, it is becoming clear that fully integrated systems are in a better position to control all cost elements in the provision of care. Physicians are best able to control inpatient bed days by carefully managing care, educating patients, and knowing the latest cost-effective treatments. However, these activities are time intensive and benefit the hospital, not the physician. Systems thinking would suggest that physicians should be rewarded for their part in improving the health of a capitated population.

UniHealth Systems of Southern California recognizes the importance of understanding the entire system. UniHealth Systems fully integrated two large medical group practices, hospitals, and a 200,000-member HMO. UniHealth takes responsibility for the entire continuum of care (no carve outs) and uses reinsurance to protect against extreme capitation risks. An income distribution formula for physicians is based on production, utilization, and patient satisfaction.[19]

Strategic Thinking

As suggested earlier, strategic management is an attitude—a way of thinking. Strategic management requires a broad base of leadership throughout the organization and asks everyone to think as leaders. In a strategic context this process is called *strategic thinking.* Vision and a sense of the future are an inherent part of strategic management. Strategic thinkers are constantly reinventing the future—creating windows on the world of tomorrow. All enterprises or projects, big or small, begin in the mind's eye; they begin with imagination and with the belief that what is merely an image can one day be made real.[20] Strategic thinkers draw upon the past, understand the present, and can envision a better future.

Strategic thinkers have built and continue to build health care systems that will serve major metropolitan and rural areas during the next fifty years. Strategic thinkers are visionaries. They know what they want to become and what they want their organizations to be. Strategic thinkers look at assumptions, understand system interrelationships, create scenarios, and calculate the odds. Strategic thinkers forecast external technological and demographic changes, as well as critical changes in the political and regulatory arenas. Planners, on the other hand, figure out how to get where the strategic thinkers want to go. A planner gathers and evaluates data and tells the strategic thinker what it will take to achieve the objective.[21] Perspective 1–4 presents several habits of successful strategic leaders.

Strategic thinking, therefore, is an important foundation of strategic management. However, leadership is not confined to just the CEO or the top level of the organization. Leadership is a performing art—a collection of practices and behaviors—not a position.[22] For strategic management to be successful, everyone should be encouraged to be a leader. Everyone should be encouraged to think strategically. Such thinking is facilitated through a model of the process and an understanding of the possible approaches to strategic management.

Perspective 1–4

Habits of a Successful Strategic Leader

- Develops and communicates an exciting vision for the future.
- Involves people from all levels and backgrounds in meaningful strategic management processes.
- Manages "tomorrow" rather than "today." The CEO's job is assuring a future for the organization rather than current operations.
- Manages by wandering around (MBWA). The CEO understands the employees and their problems because he or she talks to them on a regular basis.
- Allows people to make mistakes. Innovation in products, services, and the management processes requires that people take chances. Sometimes people will fail, but there is little

chance for success without attempts to achieve it.
- Builds leaders throughout the organization. CEOs should encourage others in the organization to take responsibility for setting direction and aligning people, as well as inspiring and motivating others.
- Trusts others in the organization to make the best decisions they can and does not "micromanage."
- Makes heroes out of people who innovate and contribute to the development and accomplishment of the strategic plan.
- Allows time for the process to work.
- Leads by example.
- Empowers employees to solve problems.

Strategic Management Models

Without some type of organizing framework or theory, strategic management becomes overwhelming. If we are to learn from experience, whether from our own or that of others, we must rely on theory. Without theory, it is impossible to guess what is generalizable from a situation and what is specific to it. Without theory, managers run the risk of becoming totally incoherent, confused in perception, and muddled in practice.[23] Therefore, strategic management may be more easily understood, studied, and applied by using a theoretical model.

Models are abstractions that attempt to identify, simplify, and explain processes, patterns, and relationships inherent within a phenomenon. As a result, models are quite useful because they circumvent the need to store masses of data and allow us to recognize the logic underlying a series of interdependent processes. Through a theoretical model, managers can gain an appreciation of the required inputs to strategic management, the processes involved, and the outputs of the process.

Dimensions of Strategic Management

There are many ways to think about strategic management in organizations. In fact, Henry Mintzberg identified ten distinct schools of thought concerning organizational strategy.[24] As described in Exhibit 1–4, three of these approaches were prescriptive or analytical (rational): the design (conceptual) school, the planning (formal) school, and the positioning (analytical) school. Six schools of thought were descriptive (emergent, intuitive) and dealt with approaches to the strategic management process: the entrepreneurial school (a visionary process), the cognitive school (a mental process), the learning school (an emergent process), the political school (a power process), the cultural school (an ideological process), and the environmental school (a passive process). The final school of thought, the configurational school, specifies the stages and sequence of the process and attempts to place the findings of the other schools in context.[25]

Analytical Versus Emergent Models

Given the careful reasoning of the proponents of these various approaches, it is safe to assume that there is no one best way to think or learn about strategy making in complex organizations. Analytical or rational approaches to strategic management rely on the development of a logical sequence of steps or processes (linear thinking). Emergent models, on the other hand, rely on intuitive thinking, leadership, and learning. Both approaches are valid and useful in explaining the process of strategic management. Neither the analytical model nor the emergent assumption, by itself, is enough. David K. Hurst explained that

> the key question is not which of these . . . models of action is right, or even which is better, but *when* and under what circumstances they are useful to understand what managers should do. Modern organizational life is characterized by oscillations between periods of calm, when prospective rationality seems to work, and periods of turmoil, when nothing seems to work. . . . At some times, analysis is possible; at other times, only on-the-ground experiences will do.[26]

Exhibit 1–4 · **Strategy Formation Schools of Thought**

School of Thought	Basic Process	Brief Description
Design School	A conceptual process, simple, judgmental, deliberate (prescriptive)	Strategy formation as a process of informal design, essentially one of conception, process of fitting the organization to its environment
Planning School	A formal process, staged, deliberate (prescriptive)	Formalized the design approach, describing strategy as a more detached, sequential, and systematic process of formal planning
Positioning School	An analytical, systematic process, deliberate (prescriptive)	Focuses on the selection of strategic positions considered generically, emphasizes the content of strategy, selection of the optimal strategy
Entrepreneurial School	A visionary process, intuitive, largely deliberate (descriptive)	Strategy is associated with the vision of a single leader, focuses on personal intuition, judgment, wisdom, experience, insight
Cognitive School	A mental process, overwhelming (descriptive)	Strategy is viewed as a cognitive process of concept attainment, an understanding of the strategist's mind, how individuals handle information to develop strategies
Learning School	An emergent process, informal, messy (descriptive)	The world is too complex to develop clear plans or visions, hence strategies must emerge in small steps or stages, strategy is a process of doing and learning
Political School	A power process, conflictive, aggressive, messy, emergent (descriptive)	Strategy is a process of exploiting power within organizations and by organizations with regard to their external environment
Cultural School	An ideological process, constrained, collective, deliberate (descriptive)	Strategy is rooted in the culture of the organization and thereby depicts it as collective, cooperative, and based on the beliefs shared by the members of the organization
Environmental School	A passive process, emergent (descriptive)	Strategy formation is a passive process and power over it rests not in the organization but the force in the environment
Configurational School	An episodic process, integrative, sequenced (descriptive)	Strategy is composed of behavioral typologies, stages, episodes, or cycles

Source: From Henry Mintzberg, "Strategy Formation Schools of Thought" in James W. Frederickson (Ed.), *Perspectives on Strategic Management,* pp. 105-197. Copyright © 1990 by HarperBusiness. Reprinted by permission of HarperCollins Publishers, Inc.

As a result, both approaches are required. It is difficult to initiate and sustain organizational action without some logical plan. Yet in a dynamic environment, such as health care, we must expect to learn and establish new directions as we progress. In reality the methods are both complementary and contradictory—the analytical model is similar to a map whereas the emergent model is similar to a compass. Both may be used to plot a course to a defined destination but in some cases they may indicate different directions. Maps are better in known worlds—worlds that have been charted before. Compasses are helpful when you are not sure where you are and can get only a general sense of direction.[27] Managers use the analytical model to develop a map as best they can from their understanding of the external environment and by interpreting the capabilities of the organization. Once the journey begins, new understandings and strategies may emerge and old maps must be modified. However, the direction must not be random or haphazard. It must be guided by some form of strategic sense—an intuitive, entrepreneurial sensing of the "shape of the future" that transcends ordinary logic. The compass is a unique blend of thinking, analysis, and intuition.[28]

An Analytical Model of Strategic Management—The Map

A model of the strategic management process that illustrates and organizes the major components for health care organizations is presented in Exhibit 1–5. This comprehensive analytical model serves as a map for health care managers and forms the basis for much of the discussion in this book. In the practice of strategic management, as portrayed in the model, managers engage in several strategic management processes: situational analysis, strategy formulation, strategic implementation, and strategic control.

The strategic management process occurs within the organization's context, referred to as the organizational setting. The setting may be viewed as being made up of the broader general environment and the more specific health care environment (health care industry). As indicated in the model, these environments affect each other as well as directly affecting the organization.

Situational Analysis

Analyzing and understanding the situation is accomplished by three separate processes: (1) external environmental analysis; (2) internal environmental analysis; and (3) the development of the organization's mission, vision, values, and objectives. The interaction and results of these processes form the basis for the development of strategy. These three interrelated processes drive the strategy.

Issues in the external environment directly and simultaneously affect all three situational analysis processes. Issues in the external environment will affect the process of environmental analysis, provide the context for internal analysis, and influence the mission, vision, values, and objectives of the organization. For example, a regulatory change may very well affect independently the analysis of the external environment, the determination of factors to be considered strengths or weaknesses of the organization, and the way managers view the mission, vision, values, and objectives. Moreover, the three situational analysis processes affect one another. They are not completely distinct and separate; they overlap, interact with, and influence one another.

External environmental analysis In order to operate in today's changing environment, health care managers need a method for scanning external information that will affect the organization. This process is referred to as external environmental analysis. As information is accumulated and classified, managers must determine the environmental issues that are significant to the organization. In addition, they must monitor these issues, collect additional information, evaluate their impact, and incorporate them into a strategy.

External environmental analysis is the process by which an organization crosses the boundary between itself and the external environment in order to identify and understand changes (issues) that are taking place outside the organization. These changes will represent both opportunities and threats to the organization and may emanate from either the general environment or the health care environment. It is important that health care managers understand the nature of these opportunities and threats significantly before they affect the organization. Managers must understand and respond to external opportunities and threats because they represent the fundamental issues that

Exhibit 1–5 • The Strategic Management Process in Health Care Organizations

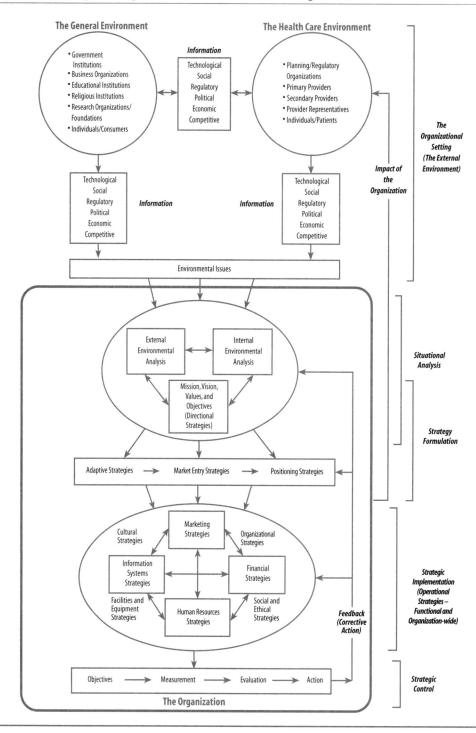

Perspective 1–5

Ambulance Companies Adapt to the Market

The same forces that are driving consolidation among providers are also affecting other segments of the health care industry. Consolidation of the highly fragmented ambulance industry is rapidly taking place led by such companies as American Medical Response, Rural/Metro Corporation, and Laidlaw. As of 1996, private companies have gained nearly 30 percent of the market compared with only 17 percent in 1988. For example, American Medical bought forty-one ambulance companies during 1993 through 1995. Consolidation is creating economies of scale. In addition, paramedic salaries are typically lower than city and county firefighters who have traditionally performed emergency transportation services in many communities. Thus far, consolidation has been on a local or regional basis; however, if emergency medical services follow the trends in health care consolidation, several large companies may emerge. In addition, these companies will team up with other providers in a fully integrated system.

Source: Sandy Lutz, "Ambulance Companies Adapt to Market," *Modern Healthcare* 26, no. 22 (1996), pp. 40–41.

will spell success or failure for the organization. Opportunities and threats should influence the strategy adopted by the organization, that is, what the organization *should* do. Perspective 1–5 illustrates how the emergency medical services segment is responding to external changes. Chapters 2 and 3 examine the processes of general and health care external environmental analysis and service area competitor analysis.

Internal environmental analysis The organization itself has an internal environment that represents the resources, competencies, and capabilities of the organization (what the organization *can* do). An understanding of these factors requires an extensive, in-depth analysis of the internal functions, operations, structure, resources, and skills.

An internal environmental analysis should reveal the strengths and weaknesses of the organization. An understanding of the strengths and weaknesses provides a foundation for strategy formulation and is essential if a strategy is to be developed that optimizes strengths and de-emphasizes and overcomes weaknesses. Chapter 4 examines the processes of internal environmental analysis.

Mission, vision, values, and objectives The mission, vision, values, and objectives of an organization greatly affect the strategy it ultimately adopts. The organization's *mission* represents the consensus and articulation of its understanding of the external opportunities and threats and the internal strengths and weaknesses. Mission is a general statement of what distinguishes the organization from all others of its type and answers the questions "Who are we?" and "What do we do?" *Vision,* on the other hand, is that view of the future that management believes is optimum for the organization (ideally, based on an understanding of the external opportunities and threats and internal strengths and weaknesses) and is communicated throughout the organization. Vision profiles the future and constitutes what the organization *wants* to do.

The *values* of an organization are the fundamental beliefs or "truths" that the organization holds dear. Values are the best indicator of the philosophy of the organization and specify what is important (honesty, integrity, customers, and so on) in the organization. Values are sometimes referred to as guiding principles. The *objectives* of the organization broadly specify the major direction of the organization and link the mission to organizational action. Unlike the mission statement, objectives are specific and measurable.

Mission, vision, values, and objectives are considered part of the situational analysis because they rely on and influence external environmental analysis and internal environmental analysis. Taken together, an organization's mission, vision, values, and objectives express an understanding of the situation, what the organization is now, and what it wants to be. However, mission, vision, values, and objectives are also a part of strategy formulation, because they provide the broadest direction for the organization and are referred to as directional strategies. The development of mission, vision, values, and organizational objectives are explored in more detail in Chapter 5.

Strategy Formulation

Whereas situational analysis involves a great deal of gathering, classifying, and understanding information, *strategy formulation* involves making decisions using that information. These decisions will result in a strategy for the organization. As previously discussed, the first set of decisions concerns the mission, vision, values, and organizational objectives. These decisions provide the general direction for the organization and are therefore called *directional strategies.* Next, more specific strategic decisions must be made. These decisions include determination of the adaptive strategies, market entry strategies, and the positioning strategies.

The *adaptive strategies* are more specific than the directional strategies and indicate the method for carrying out the directional strategies. The adaptive strategies specify how the organization will expand (diversification, vertical integration, market development, product development, or penetration), contract (divestiture, liquidation, harvesting, or retrenchment), or stabilize (enhancement or status quo) operations.

The *market entry strategies* indicate whether the adaptive strategy will be accomplished by buying into the market (through acquisitions, licensing, or venture capital investments), cooperating with other organizations in the market (through mergers, alliances, or joint ventures), or internal development. *Positioning strategies* delineate how the organization's products and services will be positioned vis-à-vis other organizations' products and services in a given market and might include strategies such as cost leadership or product differentiation.

Decisions concerning these strategies are sequential. That is, directional strategies are developed first, then adaptive strategies are formulated. Next, market entry strategies are selected. Finally, positioning strategies are formulated. These strategic decisions explicitly answer the questions: "What business(es) are we in?" "What business(es) should we be in?" "How are we going to compete?" At this point, the broad organizational strategies have been selected. The strategy formulation process is further explored in Chapters 6 and 7.

Strategic Implementation

Once the strategy for the organization has been formulated (including directional, adaptive, market entry, and positioning strategies), operational strategies that support (accomplish) the organizational strategy are developed. *Operational strategies* are made up of strategies developed within the functional areas of the organization and strategies that link the functional areas and develop the capabilities of the organization. *Functional strategies* and supporting programs and budgets must be developed for the key areas in the organization, such as marketing, information systems, finance, and human resources. These functional areas are directly and independently affected by the strategy formulation process, yet functional strategies must be integrated to move the organization toward realizing its mission. In addition to the functional strategies, organizations often develop *organization-wide strategies* that enhance the general capabilities and link organizational processes. These operational strategies include initiatives such as changing the organization's culture, reorganization, upgrading facilities and equipment, and social and ethical policies. These strategies generally affect the entire organization and cut across all functional areas. Implementation strategies are discussed further in Chapters 8 through 12.

Strategic Control

The final stage of strategic management is *strategic control.* This process includes (1) establishment of standards (objectives), (2) measurement of performance, (3) evaluation of organizational performance against the standards, and (4) taking corrective action, if necessary. However, strategic control is much broader and will, in turn, affect the operational strategies, the organization's general strategy, and situational analysis processes. As managers monitor these various organizational processes, they learn what is effective and take corrective action as necessary. The strategic control processes are discussed in Chapter 13.

Using the Model

The model of strategic management provides a useful framework or map for conceptualizing and developing strategies for an organization. The model may be applied to a variety of types of health care organizations operating in dramatically different environments. The model is useful for both large and small organizations and facilitates strategic thinking at all levels of the organization. Chapter 14 provides a comprehensive example of the strategic management model applied in an actual organization.

Emergent and Intuitive Strategic Management—The Compass

Sometimes it is difficult for managers to plan or envision the long-term future of an organization in a dynamic environment. Managers often need to react to unanticipated developments and very new competitive pressures. Different environmental characteristics and different organizational forms require new and different ways of defining strategy.[29] Strategy becomes an intuitive, entrepreneurial, political, culture-based, or learning process. In these cases, maps are of limited value. Managers must create and discover an unfolding future, using their ability to learn together in groups and interact politically in a spontaneous, self-organizing manner. When there are provocative atmospheres conducive to complex learning, organizations may change and develop new strategic direction. In such an environment, the destination as well as the route may turn out to be unexpected and unintended. As a result, strategy emerges spontaneously from the chaos of challenge and contradiction, through a process of real-time learning and politics.[30] For these situations a compass indicating a general direction, steadied by leadership, may be more appropriate.

Intended Versus Realized Strategies

Clearly, rational strategies do not always work out as planned (an unrealized strategy). In other cases, an organization may end up with a strategy that was quite unexpected as a result of having been "swept away by events" (an emergent strategy). Leadership, vision, and "feeling our way along" (learning) often provide a general direction without a real sense of specific objectives or long-term outcomes.

Exhibit 1–6 presents three outcomes for an organization. These outcomes may be summarized as follows:

1. Intended strategies that are realized (*deliberate strategies*);
2. Intended strategies that are not realized, perhaps because of unrealistic expectations, misjudgments about the environment, or changes during implementation (*unrealized strategies*); or
3. Realized strategies that were never intended, perhaps because no strategy was developed at the outset or perhaps because the strategies somehow were displaced along the way (*emergent strategies*).[31]

Obviously, health care organizations formulate strategies and realize them to varying degrees. For instance, as a part of a deliberate strategy to broaden their market, improve service to the community, and retain referral patients, many community hospitals began offering cardiac services such as catheterization and open-heart surgery.[32] As a result, some of these hospitals have built market share and increased profitability. Other community hospitals have not fared so well. Their managers had unrealistic expectations concerning the profitability of cardiac services and the number of procedures required. A large volume is crucial to cardiac services because it allows the hospital to order supplies

Exhibit 1–6 · Intended Versus Realized Strategy

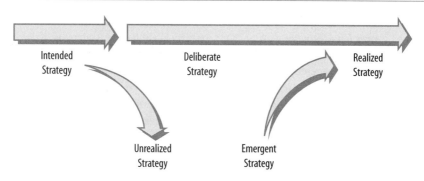

Intended Strategy

Deliberate Strategy

Realized Strategy

Unrealized Strategy

Emergent Strategy

Source: Henry Mintzberg, "Patterns in Strategy Formation," *Management Science* 24, no. 9 (1978), p. 934.

in bulk and provides physician experience that produces better outcomes and shorter lengths of stay. In addition, some community hospital managers misjudged the level of reimbursement from Medicare, thereby further squeezing profitability margins. The strategies of those community hospitals that left the market were not realized.

Still other community hospitals seemed to move into a full range of cardiac services without an explicit strategy to do so. In an effort to retain patients and enhance their images, these hospitals began by offering limited cardiac services but shortly found that they were not performing enough procedures to be "world class." They added services, equipment, and facilities to help create the required volume and, without really intending to at the outset, ended up with emergent strategies to build significant market share in cardiac services.

Mintzberg added several possible outcomes to those presented in Exhibit 1–6. For example, he discussed strategies that, as they were realized, changed form and became, in part at least, emergent; emergent strategies that were formalized as deliberate ones; and intended strategies that were over-realized.[33] It is quite possible that a strategy may be developed and subsequently realized. However, we must be realistic enough to understand that when we engage in strategic management the theoretical ideal (strategy developed, then realized) may not and in all probability will not be the case. A great deal may go wrong. The possibilities include the following:

1. There is a reformulation of the strategy during implementation as the organization gains new information and feeds that information back to the formulation process, thus modifying intentions en route (a function of strategic control).
2. The external environment is in a period of flux and strategists are unable to accurately predict conditions; the organization may therefore find itself unable to respond appropriately to a powerful external momentum.[34]
3. Organizations in the external environment, implementing their own strategies, may block a strategic initiative forcing the activation of a contingency strategy or a period of "groping."

Lessons for Health Care Managers

Strategic management is a complex and difficult task. The 1990s will place a higher premium on effective management and leadership than ever before. Yet, no single approach may be adequate to understand social and organizational processes. Indeed, different organizational situations may call for dramatically different leadership styles.[35] The model presented in this text is designed to provide the essential logic of the process involved in strategic management and therefore is based *first* on the analytical model as a framework for understanding strategy making in organizations. The analytical model provides an excellent starting point for understanding the *concept* of strategy and a foundation for comparing and contrasting strategies. However, the model does not perfectly represent reality and must not be applied blindly or with the belief that "life always works that way."

Strategic management is not always a structured, well-thought-out exercise. In reality, thought does not always precede action, perfect information concerning the environment and organization never exists, and rationality and logic are not always superior to intuition and luck. Sometimes organizations "do" before they "know." For instance, intended strategies are often not the realized strategies. Sometimes managers are able to just "muddle through." Or, managers may have a broad master plan or logic underlying strategic decisions, but because of the complexity of the external and internal environments, incremental adjustments are the best they can do. Managers must realize that, once introduced, strategies are subject to a variety of forces both within and outside the organization. Sometimes we learn by doing.

Levels of Strategy

The strategic management process may be applied at different levels in the organization. The resulting strategies will differ in scope as well as in purpose as we move from one organizational level to another. As illustrated in Exhibit 1–7, strategic management uti-

Exhibit 1–7 • The Link Between Levels of Strategic Management

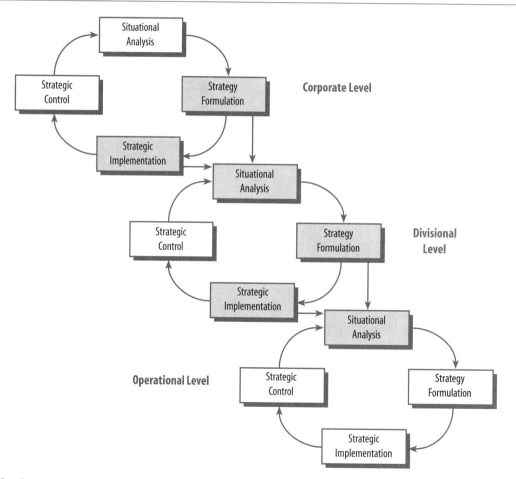

Source: From Peter Lorange, *Corporate Planning: An Executive Viewpoint,* p. 61. © 1980. Adapted by permission of Prentice-Hall, Inc., Upper Saddle River, NJ.

Exhibit 1–8 · Characteristics of Corporate, Divisional, and Operational Strategies

| | | | Operational | |
Attribute of Strategy	Corporate	Divisional SBU/SSU*	Functional	Organization wide
Scope	The entire organization	A single SBU/SSU	A single functional area	Across all functional areas
Type of Decision	Industries	Products/markets	Market approach	Internal/organization wide
Market	Multiple	Single	Segment	Internal
Performance Criteria	Return on investment/market share	Market share	Contribution to strategy	Contribution to strategy

* SBU—strategic business unit; SSU—strategic service unit

lizes a hierarchy of strategies. Each level provides the "means" for accomplishing the "ends" of the next higher level. Thus, the operational level provides the means for accomplishing the ends of the divisional level. The divisional level, in turn, is the means for the ends established at the corporate level.

Corporate-Level Strategy

Exhibit 1–8 summarizes some of the important characteristics of corporate, divisional, and operational strategies and demonstrates the scale of each. Corporate strategies are concerned with the entire organization and its relationship to the entire industry. Corporate strategies address the question, "What business(es) should we be in?" Such strategies consider multiple, sometimes unrelated, markets and typically are based on return on investment and market share or potential market share.

The organizational structure of InterMountain Health Care, Inc. (IHC), a regional system serving the intermountain area of Utah, Idaho, and Wyoming, is illustrated in Exhibit 1–9. The corporate level is the parent holding company, InterMountain Health Care, Inc., which owns various semi-autonomous "businesses" operating in several different markets, each headed by a central board member.

Division-Level Strategy

Divisional strategies are much more focused and provide direction for a single division within a specific product area or market. Divisional strategies are most often concerned with maintaining or increasing market share. Division-level strategic management is concerned with competition in a single market, with a single product line, using technology appropriate for that market. These semi-autonomous units are often referred to as SBUs (strategic business units) or SSUs (strategic service units). Therefore, strategic managers for these units are most concerned with a specified set of competitors within a well-defined market (service area). Strategies at this level are usually limited to the organization's current area of operations (market development, product development, and so on).

In Exhibit 1–9, InterMountain has several subsidiaries carrying the IHC brand name, including IHC Hospitals, Inc., which manages the system's twenty-three hospitals; a foundation, which executes fund development; an insurance company; IHC Affiliated

Exhibit 1–9 • InterMountain Health Care, Inc. Organization

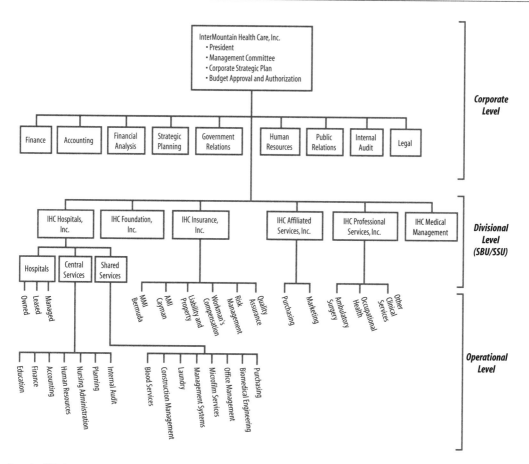

Source: From Gerald E. Sussman, "CEO Perspectives on Mission, Healthcare Systems, and the Environment," *Hospital & Health Services Administration*, Vol. 33, No. 3, (March/April 1985), p. 31. Adapted with permission by Health Administration Press, Chicago.

Services, which provides shared services; IHC Professional Services, which develops and supports alternative modes of health care delivery including ambulatory surgery centers; and a medical management company, which provides professional services to other companies. These SSUs are allowed a great deal of operating independence, yet there is strong central management and control of finances.

Operational-Level Strategy

Operational strategies support divisional strategies in addressing market segments. Operational strategies may be developed within the functional departments of an organization such as marketing, finance, information systems, human resources, and so on. Similarly, linkage strategies that affect all of the functional departments may be developed by SSU managers. Functional strategies address two issues. First, they are intended to integrate the various subfunctional activities. Second, they are designed to relate the various functional area policies with any changes in the functional area environment.[36] Linkage strategies are directed toward integrating the functions themselves and creating internal capabilities across functions (for example, quality programs or changing the organization's culture). As shown in Exhibit 1–9, at InterMountain Health Care, each division has the appropriate supporting functional units to carry out the mission of the division.

The Importance of Leadership

Ultimately, strategic decision making for health care organizations is the responsibility of top management. The CEO is a strategic manager with the preeminent responsibility for positioning the organization for the future. If the CEO does not fully understand or support strategic management, it will not happen.

Leadership Roles Throughout the Organization

In the past, strategy formulation was primarily a staff activity. The planning staff would formulate the strategy and submit it for approval to top management. This process resulted in plans that were often unrealistic, did not fully consider the realities and resources of the divisions or functional departments, and separated planning from leadership.

Over the past decade, many large formal planning staffs have been dissolved as organizations learned that strategy development cannot take place in relative isolation. Today, the *coordination and facilitation* of strategic planning typically is designated as the responsibility of a key manager (often the CEO), and *development of the strategy* has become a line job with each manager responsible for the strategic implications of his or her decisions. The rationale underlying this approach is that no one is more in touch with the external environment (regulations, technology, competition, social change, and so on) than the line manager who must deal with it every day and lead change. However, someone must coordinate the organization's overall strategy and facilitate strategic thinking throughout the organization. As a result, the strategic planner acts as an extension of the chief executive officer to ensure that an organized and used planning process ensues.[37] Perspective 1–6 illustrates the changing role of the strategic planner over the past three decades.

Leadership plays an important role in strategy development. Strategies cannot be created entirely by analysis, but their development can be enhanced by a logical approach. Therefore, planners have critical roles to play.[38] Planners can:

- pose the right questions rather than find the right answers;
- provide alternative conceptual interpretations of situations;
- act as catalysts encouraging managers to think about the future in creative ways;
- help identify and provide information concerning important issues and emerging strategies;
- clarify and express the strategies in terms sufficiently clear to render them operational;

Perspective 1–6

Position Advertisements for Strategic Planners

1970s

An expert at strategic planning, knowledgeable in all strategic planning functions. Will be required to develop a strategic planning process for corporate and divisional units. An ability to build and manage a staff of planning specialists as they perform strategic analysis and complete the strategy formulation and selection process.

1980s

A strategic planning specialist who can guide the CEO and direct reports to explore and identify the strategic alternatives available and evaluate and select the most beneficial for the organization. Will be responsible for conducting strategic analysis and providing input to the CEO and the direct reports.

1990s

Knowledge of strategic planning models and responsible for establishing and monitoring the strategic planning schedule, handling the logistics of planning group meetings, providing strategic analysis and assessments to the strategic planning group, and documenting and distributing strategic planning group meeting results. To function as an extension of the CEO to make strategic management effective in fulfilling the vision for the organization. Assist the CEO to establish, articulate, communicate, and educate those responsible for putting into practice strategies that pay off. Major efforts will be in establishing the criteria for effective strategy and ensuring that they are applied.

Source: From Donald L. Bates and John E. Dillard, Jr., "Wanted: A Strategic Planner for the 1990s," *Journal of General Management* Vol. 18, No. 1 (1992), pp. 51–62. Reprinted by permission of The Coach House.

- break down strategies into substrategies, ad hoc programs, and action plans specifying what must be done to realize each strategy;
- consider the effects of the strategic changes on the organization's operations; and
- communicate and control the strategy.[39]

In organizations that have seriously adopted strategic management, all managers are strategic managers. As part of the job, every manager must be concerned with change and innovation. Each must ask the critical questions: "Should we be doing this in the future?" "How should we be doing this?" "What new things should we be doing?"

Long-Range and Short-Range Perspectives

In the general management and health care literature, you will see references from time to time to "long-range" planning and "short-range" planning. These time references are purposely missing from our discussion. The terms *long range* and *short range* lack the richness implied in the terms *strategic management* and *strategy.* Long-range and short-range planning have the connotation of simply extending present operations to some point in the future. Strategic management, on the other hand, constantly questions the relationship between the environment and organization and the organization's basis for competition.

Although strategies typically take considerable time to implement, and thus are generally long range in nature, the time span is not the principal focus of strategic management. In fact, strategic management compresses time. Competitive shifts that might take generations to evolve instead occur in a few short years.[40] Therefore, it is better to use "long range" and "short range" to describe the time it will take to accomplish a strategy rather than to indicate a type of planning.

The Benefits of Strategic Management

Regardless of the approach, the adoption and further development of strategic management will provide many benefits to health care organizations. Because strategic management is a philosophy or way of managing an organization, its benefits are not always quantifiable. Strategic management:

- ties the organization together with a common sense of purpose and shared values;
- improves financial performance in many cases;[41]
- provides the organization with a clear self-concept, specific goals, and guidance as well as consistency in decision making;
- helps managers understand the present, think about the future, and recognize the signals that suggest change;
- requires managers to communicate both vertically and horizontally;
- improves overall coordination within the organization; and
- encourages innovation and change within the organization to meet the needs of dynamic situations.

Strategic management is a unique perspective that requires managers to cease thinking solely in terms of internal operations and adopt what may be a fundamentally new attitude, an *external* orientation. It is basically optimistic in that it integrates "what is" with "what can be." Strategic management is the exciting future of effective health care management.

Organization of the Book

In our view, managers require a comprehensive strategic management approach for guiding organizations through the general environment and health care industry changes that will occur in the future. We believe that the strategic management concepts, processes, and methods presented in this text will prove to be valuable in coping with these changes. In addition, the internal, nonquantifiable benefits of strategic management will aid health care organizations in better integrating functional areas to strategically utilize limited resources and to satisfy the various publics served.

The processes of strategic management for health care organizations are described in fourteen chapters organized around a comprehensive analytical model. This first chapter provided an overview of the nature of strategic management in health care organizations as well as a specific model of health care strategic management. The remaining chapters examine the strategic processes included within the model.

Following the chapters are five appendices designed to aid in the analysis, discussion, and presentation of health care case studies. Appendix A presents a suggested method for case analysis, and Appendix B provides additional information concerning the specifics of financial analysis for health care organizations. Appendix C provides insights into making presentations to health care professionals (or future health care professionals), including some of the newer electronic presentation tools. Appendix D presents sources for obtaining additional health care and business information. Finally, Appendix E is an extensive bibliography of strategic management references helpful to the health care researcher or strategist. In addition to the chapters and appendices, eighteen comprehensive health care case studies are included to provide actual and timely strategic management situations for analysis by the student.

Summary and Conclusions

This chapter discussed the nature and process of strategic management. Many changes are taking place in the environment that will profoundly affect the success of health care organizations. Strategic management provides a philosophy of health care management that considers these changes in relation to the capabilities of the organization and provides a framework for positioning the organization within the environment.

In exploring the nature of strategic management, it is important to note that strategic management decisions are largely judgmental, yet are crucial to the success of the organization. When an organization makes consistent decisions and exhibits a consistent behavior, it has a strategy. A strategy may also be viewed as a guideline or plan to help assure decision consistency in the future. Strategic management attempts to achieve a fit between the external environment and its internal capabilities.

The concept of strategic management has been successfully used in politics, by the military, and by business organizations. Health care managers are finding it essential for their organizations. Strategic management is organization specific and very different from the health policy planning of the past. Strategic management involves systems concepts, allowing managers to consider and integrate the many important external and internal variables that health care organizations face. In addition, strategic management is a process for thinking about the future. Everyone in the organization should be encouraged to think strategically.

The process of strategic management may be either formal or informal; however, models or theories of complex phenomena are useful in understanding the various processes involved and their interrelationships. Models provide an abstract overview and conceptual anchors for managers to consider as they struggle to deal with complexity. Without some conceptual framework, it would be difficult to begin the process of strategic management. However, strategic management may be both analytical and emergent.

The analytical model of strategic management may be thought of as having two major segments: the setting and the organization itself. The setting consists of the broad general environment and the more specific health care environment. These environments affect one another as well as the organization itself. The overall environment and the health care environment are composed of organizations and individuals that, in pursuit of their own missions and objectives, create information. The strategic manager must consider this information and determine if there are any emerging issues to which the organization could, should, or must respond.

The analytical model was investigated by describing the internal processes (situational analysis, strategy formulation, strategic implementation, and strategic control) that are designed to help managers understand and respond to the external environment. The subprocesses within each (as well as the processes themselves) are not inherently discrete but rather overlap and affect one another. The processes within situational analysis combine to influence the process of strategy formulation. The strategy formulation process in turn affects strategic implementation at the operational level. Finally, the strategic management process must be evaluated and controlled. Strategic control may establish new understandings of the situation, change the fundamental strategy, or modify strategic implementation. Strategic control essentially reinitiates the strategic management process.

The analytical or rational model of strategic management is not itself reality but rather a framework for dealing with reality. The behavior of an organization probably cannot be accurately modeled. In reality, the stages of strategic management may be blended together as the strategy is formed and reformed through leadership, intuition, and organizational learning. The process of implementing the strategy may actually create an entirely new, unintended strategy.

Strategic management may be applied at various levels within the organization. Thus, the strategic management process often involves developing strategies at the operational level to achieve strategies at the divisional level. Division-level strategies, in turn, are the means to achieving corporate-level ends. At any level, however, strategic management must not be separated from leadership.

Health care managers must understand that, although the analytical model provides a framework for thinking about the organization and its future, they must deal with powerful internal and external forces that in many cases are beyond their control. As Mintzberg has said, "practice is always more complicated—and more interesting—than theory. . . ."

Key Terms and Concepts in Strategic Management

adaptive strategies
corporate-level strategy
deliberate strategies
directional strategies
divisional-level strategy
emergent strategies
environmental issues
external environmental analysis
functional strategies
general environment
goals and objectives
health care environment

hypercompetition
intended strategies
internal organizational analysis
linkage strategies
market entry strategies
mission
objectives
operational-level strategy
organizational setting
positioning strategies
realized strategies
situational analysis

strategic business unit (SBU)
strategic control
strategic implementation
strategic management
strategic planning
strategic service unit (SSU)
strategy
strategy formulation
system
unrealized strategies
values
vision

Questions for Class Discussion

1. What types of changes are likely to occur in the health care environment in the next several years?
2. What is the rationale for health care organizations' adoption of strategic management?
3. Explain *white water change* and *hypercompetition*. Why are these occurring? What effect will they have on the management of health care organizations?
4. What is a strategy?
5. Trace the evolution of strategic management. Have the objectives of strategic management changed dramatically over its development?
6. What are the characteristics of strategic management? How is strategic management different from traditional health policy planning?
7. Why is a "systems approach" helpful to strategic managers?
8. What is strategic thinking? How is it different from leadership?
9. What is meant by the statement, "Strategic leaders should try to create the future"?
10. Why are conceptual models of management processes useful for practicing managers?
11. Compare and contrast the analytical model of strategic management with the emergent, learning model. Which is most appropriate for health care managers?
12. Describe the "setting" for health care management. Is the setting too complex or changing too rapidly to accurately predict future conditions?
13. In the analytical model, what are the major processes of strategic management? What types of subprocesses occur within each process? How are they linked together?
14. What is meant by *realized strategies*? How can strategies be realized if they were never intended?
15. What can go wrong with well-thought-out strategies that were developed using all the steps of the analytical model of strategic management?
16. At what organizational level(s) may a strategy be developed? If at more than one level, how are these levels linked by the planning process?
17. How has the role of the strategic planner changed over the past several decades? What new skills will be essential for the strategic planner in the next millennium?
18. Explain and illustrate the possible benefits of strategic management. What types of health care institutions may benefit most from strategic management?
19. Select a health care organization you are familiar with and discuss the demands of strategic management for the organization.

Notes

1. This partial list of issues in the health care industry results from tracking the strategic issues in health care in the professional and trade literature as well as numerous interviews with both public and private health care professionals by the authors.
2. David Burda, "What We've Learned from DRGs," *Modern Healthcare* 23, no. 40 (October 4, 1993), pp. 42–44.
3. Dean Mayer, "The Philadelphia Story: Hospitals in State of Crisis," *HealthWeek* 4, no. 5 (March 12, 1991), pp. 1, 56.
4. H. B. Gelatt, "Future Sense: Creating the Future," *The Futurist* 27, no. 5 (September–October 1993), pp. 9–13.
5. Richard A. D'Aveni, "Coping with Hypercompetition: Utilizing the New 7S's Framework," *The Academy of Management Executive* 9, no. 3 (1995), pp. 45–60.
6. Ruben F. W. Nelson, "Four-Quadrant Leadership," *Planning Review* 24, no. 1 (1996), pp. 20–25, 37.
7. Henry Mintzberg, "Patterns in Strategy Formulation," *Management Science* 24, no. 9 (1978), p. 935.
8. Darrell L. Schryver, Gerald A. Niederman, and Bruce A. Johnson, "Establishing a Group Practice 'Without Walls,'" *Health Care Strategic Management* 11, no. 1 (1993), pp. 18–21.
9. Max DePree, *Leadership Is an Art* (New York: Doubleday, 1989), p. 14.
10. Craig R. Hickman, *Mind of a Manager, Soul of a Leader* (New York: John Wiley and Sons, Inc., 1992), p. 261.
11. Jeffrey Bracker, "The Historical Development of the Strategic Management Concept," *Academy of Management Review* 5, no. 2 (1980), pp. 219–224.
12. Ibid.
13. Ibid.

14. Ernest L. Stebbins and Kathleen N. Williams, "History and Background of Health Planning in the United States," in William A. Reinke, *Health Planning: Qualitative Aspects and Quantitative Techniques* (Baltimore: Johns Hopkins University, School of Hygiene and Public Health, Department of International Health, 1972), p. 3.

15. C. Clemenhagen and F. Champagne, "Medical Staff Involvement in Strategic Planning," *Hospital and Health Services Administration* 29, no. 4 (1984), pp. 79–94.

16. David I. Cleland and William R. King, *Systems Analysis and Project Management* (New York: McGraw-Hill Book Company, 1983), pp. 19–20.

17. Ibid.

18. Ibid., p. 17.

19. Jerry F. Pogue, "Capitation Strategies," *Integrated Healthcare Report* (December 1994), pp. 1–10.

20. James M. Kouzes and Barry Z. Posner, *The Leadership Challenge: How to Keep Getting Extraordinary Things Done in Organizations* (San Francisco: Jossey-Bass Publishers, 1995), p. 93.

21. Donald E. L. Johnson, "Strategic Thinking About Collaboration and Integration," *Health Care Strategic Management* 11, no. 3 (1993), pp. 2–3.

22. Kouzes and Posner, *The Leadership Challenge: How to Keep Getting Extraordinary Things Done in Organizations,* p. 30.

23. David K. Hurst, *Crisis and Renewal: Meeting the Challenge of Organizational Change* (Boston: Harvard Business School Press, 1995), p. 7.

24. Henry Mintzberg, "The Design School: Reconsidering the Basic Premises of Strategic Management," *Strategic Management Journal* 11, no. 3 (1990), pp. 171–195.

25. Ibid.

26. Hurst, *Crisis and Renewal: Meeting the Challenge of Organizational Change,* pp. 167–168.

27. Ibid.

28. Ian H. Wilson, "The 5 Compasses of Strategic Leadership," *Strategy and Leadership* 24, no. 4 (1996), pp. 26–31.

29. John C. Camillus, "Reinventing Strategic Planning," *Strategy and Leadership* 24, no. 3 (1996), pp. 6–12.

30. Ralph Stacey, "Strategy as Order Emerging from Chaos," *Long Range Planning* 26, no. 1 (1993), pp. 10–17.

31. Mintzberg, "Patterns in Strategy Formulation," p. 945.

32. Mary Wagner, "Cardiac Services Find a New Home in Community Hospitals," *Modern Healthcare* (October 29, 1990), pp. 23–31.

33. Mintzberg, "Patterns in Strategy Formulation," p. 946.

34. Ibid.

35. William E. Rothschild, "A Portfolio of Strategic Leaders," *Planning Review* 24, no. 1 (1996), pp. 16–19.

36. Dan E. Schendel and Charles W. Hofer, "Introduction," in *Strategic Management: A New View of Business Policy and Planning,* ed. D. E. Schendel and C. W. Hofer (Boston: Little, Brown, and Company, 1979), p. 12.

37. Donald L. Bates and John E. Dillard, Jr., "Wanted: A Strategic Planner for the 1990s," *Journal of General Management* 18, no. 1 (1992), pp. 51–62.

38. Henry Mintzberg, "The Fall and Rise of Strategic Planning," *Harvard Business Review* 72, no. 1 (January–February 1994), pp. 107–114.

39. Ibid.

40. Bruce D. Henderson, "The Origin of Strategy," *Harvard Business Review* 67, no. 6 (November–December 1989), p. 142.

41. After almost three decades of research, the effects of strategic planning on an organization's performance is still unclear. Some studies have found significant benefits from planning, although others have found no relationship, or even small negative effects. For an extensive survey of the strategic planning/financial performance literature, see Lawrence C. Rhyne, "The Relationship of Strategic Planning to Financial Performance," *Strategic Management Journal* 7, no. 5 (September–October 1986), pp. 423–436 and Brian K. Boyd, "Strategic Planning and Financial Performance: A Meta-analytic Review," *Journal of Management Studies* 28, no. 4 (July 1991), pp. 353–374.

Additional Readings

Champy, James, *Reengineering Management: The Mandate for Leadership* (New York: HarperBusiness, 1996). This book follows Michael Hammer and James Champy's well-received work *Reengineering the Corporation: A Manifesto for Business Revolution* (HarperBusiness, 1993). Hammer and Champy made a convincing argument that because of a rapidly changing environment, organizations must fundamentally rethink what they do and dramatically and radically redesign their operational processes. They suggested that the old ways of managing no long work and demonstrated that reengineering is a process for reinventing the organization and helping it cope with change. In his latest book, Champy goes beyond the redesigning of work and posits that managers should constantly deal with four key questions: "What is the organization for? What kind of culture do we want? How do we do our work? What kind of people do we want to work with?"

Duncan, W. Jack, Peter M. Ginter, and Linda E. Swayne, eds., *Handbook of Health Care Management* (Cambridge: Blackwell Publishers, 1997). The Handbook contains fifteen chapters on highly relevant topics written by as many different experts in health care management and leadership. The book is organized into three major sections: the management of relationships (stakeholders, customers, alliances, and strategic management), key organizational processes (teams, leadership, change and innovation, organizational design, and motivation), and tools for managers to develop and maintain efficient and effective organizations (finance, economics, information systems, marketing, and quality). The contributing writers make important and significant contributions to our understanding of effective health care management.

Mintzberg, Henry, *The Rise and Fall of Strategic Planning* (New York: Free Press, 1994). Mintzberg makes a convincing argument that strategic planning has failed. Strategy cannot be planned because planning is about analysis and strategy is about synthesis. He argues that managers must reconceive the process by which strategies are created. Mintzberg suggests that informal learning and personal vision are the important elements of strategy formation. He exposes three fallacies of traditional strategic planning—discontinuities can be predicted; strategists can be detached from the operation; and the process can be formalized.

Pettigrew, Andrew, *The Management of Strategic Change* (Oxford: Basil Blackwell, 1987). This book is a collection of thoughts by leading strategic thinkers concerning the understanding and management of dynamic environmental and organizational change. The book covers a wide range of strategic issues associated with managing change, including the process of change, the impact of technology, organizational methods to deal with change, and errors in managing strategic change.

Spender, J. C., *Industry Recipes: An Enquiry into the Nature and Sources of Managerial Judgment* (Oxford: Basil Blackwell, 1989). J. C. Spender indicates that new management models are necessary to deal with uncertainty and change. In his book, organizations are considered bodies of knowledge, and management is the process of creating, manipulating, and communicating this knowledge. The key to successful management is creativity and judgment in thinking about and dealing with the organization and its relationship with the external environment.

Understanding and Analyzing the External Environment

Chapter 2

Learning Objectives

After completing this chapter you should be able to:

1. Appreciate the significance of the general external environment's impact on health care organizations.

2. Understand and discuss the specific goals of environmental analysis.

3. Point out some limitations of the environmental analysis process.

4. Describe the various types of organizations in the external environment and how they produce information flows that are of importance to other organizations.

5. Identify major environmental trends affecting health care organizations.

6. Identify key sources of environmental information.

7. Discuss important techniques used in environmental analysis.

8. Conduct an external environmental analysis for a health care organization.

The Importance of Environmental Influences

Fifty years ago the delivery of health care was usually an uncomplicated relationship of facilities, physicians, and patients working together. Government and business stood weakly on the fringes, having little significant influence. Today, a multitude of interests are directly or indirectly involved in the delivery of health care. For instance, private-sector businesses are largely responsible for the development and delivery of drugs and medical supplies; and government agencies regulate much of the actual delivery of health care services. The external environment increasingly has become a factor in the success of health care organizations.

To be successful, health care organizations must have an understanding of the external environment in which they operate; and they must anticipate and respond to the significant shifts taking place within that environment. Futurist Joel Barker has suggested that "in times of turbulence the ability to anticipate dramatically enhances

> "American health care is in a state of hyper-turbulence characterized by accumulated waves of change in payment systems, delivery systems, technology, professional relations, and societal expectation. It can be likened to an earthquake in its relative unpredictability, lack of a sense of control, and resulting anxiety."
>
> • *S. A. Shortell, R. R. Gilies, and K. J. Devers*

Introductory Incident
The Hospital of the Twenty-First Century

The design, services, name, and location of hospitals will undergo a major transformation by the first decade of the twenty-first century. Most health care procedures will be dispersed to alternative sites and, therefore, the hospital will not be a place. The health care system of the twenty-first century will be spread over a wide geographic area and into sites such as homes, churches, and workplaces rather than being bundled together in a very congested and intimidating hospital environment. *Hospital* will no longer mean one monolithic building but a distributed campus. The health care system will be linked together, not by bricks and mortar, but by a common management structure and a uniform computer system.

Hospitals will take on a totally new role and become data centers. Patients will be treated at home through interactive television, while specialists and "super specialists" back at the hospital work with and manipulate the systems to treat them. The hospital will not be a place you go, but something that comes to you.

Something resembling a hospital will continue to be needed for emergency services, inten-

sive care, and some diagnostic work. Other services can be mobile or housed in satellite locations, such as traveling MRIs and radiology clinics located in shopping malls. There will be a blurring between the definition of hospital and ambulatoy care centers. Horizontal development may be more important than vertical development for the hospital of the future.

Hospital designers will abandon the institutional features of today's hospitals and create environments more conducive to healing and comfort. Architecture will have more fluid organic shapes becoming more therapeutic and breaking the institutional grid of 90 degree angles that has become so characteristic of hospitals. Hospital rooms of the twenty-first century will be larger and resemble a comfortable bedroom. Additional space will accommodate family visits, because hospitalized patients in the future will be there principally for critical care.

Source: Rhonda L. Bergman, "2013: The Hospital Is Not a Place," *Hospitals and Health Networks* 67, no. 19 (1993), p. 29.

your chances of success. Good anticipation is the result of good strategic exploration."[1] As indicated in the Introductory Incident, the nature of health care institutions will change dramatically in the next two decades as a result of external technological, social, regulatory, political, economic, and competitive forces. Because of this change, it is unlikely that today's hospital would be successful in the twenty-first century. Institutions that anticipate and recognize the significant external forces and modify their strategies and operations accordingly will prosper. Organizations that fail to anticipate change, ignore the external forces, or resist change will find themselves out of touch with the needs of the market, especially because of antiquated technologies, ineffective delivery systems, and outmoded management.

The introduction of an early recognition system to identify external opportunities and threats is a major task for health care managers. This task has evolved because of the growing impact of economic factors, new technologies, increasing government influence, new centers of power, demographic shifts, changes in motivation for work, and changes in values and lifestyles, as well as changes in the kind and extent of competition.

Examples of organizations "reading" shifts in the external environment and being open to change include the development and growth of outpatient clinics specializing in alternative medicine such as chiropractic therapy, alternative wound care, nonsurgical cardiac care, and mind/body medicine. Changes in the health care delivery system, institutional support, and the public's attitudes are environmental shifts that have provided opportunities in nontraditional medicine.[2]

Efficiency Versus Effectiveness

Because the success or failure of a health care organization depends in large part on influences from outside of the organization, the key to strategic management and, indeed, to the organization's success is to "do the right thing" (effectiveness) and not just "do things right" (efficiency). Organizational effectiveness has an external orientation and suggests that the organization is well positioned to accomplish its mission. Efficiency, on the other hand, has an internal orientation and suggests that economies will be realized in the use of capital, personnel, or physical plant. However, if an organization is doing the wrong thing, no amount of efficiency or good management will save it from decline. Health care organizations, of course, should strive to be both effective and efficient. As illustrated in Perspective 2–1, with increased pressure on health care organizations to reduce costs, a great deal of emphasis has been placed on efficiency throughout the 1990s; in fact, it may be critical to success.

Efficiency and effectiveness must be balanced. Efficiency is established through the institution of routines directed toward achieving a high level of performance. However, routines are aimed at maintaining the status quo and preventing change. As Kouzes and Posner explain, "routines get us into ruts, dull our senses, stifle our creativity, constrict our thinking, remove us from stimulation, and destroy our ability to compete. Yet some routines are essential to a definable, consistent, measurable, and efficient operation."[3] Effectiveness in a dynamic environment, on the other hand, requires learning and change. One of the costs of a learning organization is lowered performance. The dynamics of the learning process hamper performance by discouraging the establishment of routine, whereas the demands of performance inhibit learning by institutionalizing routine.[4] Therefore, managers must carefully balance efficiency, routines, and the requirements for performance with effectiveness, disorder, learning, and lowered short-term performance. Health care managers must be careful not to let routines and efforts directed toward efficiency smother creativity, the organization's external orientation, or its ability to respond to change.

The External Role of Strategic Management

Strategic management should be directed toward positioning the organization most effectively within its changing environment. Environmental analysis is an integral part of the situational analysis section of the analytical strategic management model presented in Exhibit 1–5. This part of the model illustrates the role of the environmental analysis process and its relationship with mission, vision, values, objectives (the directional strategies), and internal analysis. *Environmental analysis* is the process of understanding the issues in the external environment, including the general environment,

Perspective 2–1

Health Care Organizations Purchase Efficiency

In the mid-1990s, many health care organizations were acquiring more administrative equipment to help decrease costs than medical equipment. Rather than expanding medical capabilities through purchases of such items as radiation-therapy equipment and MRIs, many health care organizations were seeking information and operating systems that would help cut overhead costs. In a hospital survey of actual 1995 expenditures and expected purchases for 1996, respondents listed data processing equipment, telecommunications, and energy-saving equipment as the top choices for acquisition. The following bar chart shows the equipment purchases for 443 American Hospital Association (AHA) hospitals in 1995 and their projected 1996 purchases.

Source: Jon Asplund, "Hospital Buying Shifts to Computer Equipment," *AHA News* 32, no. 17 (April 29, 1996), p. 4.

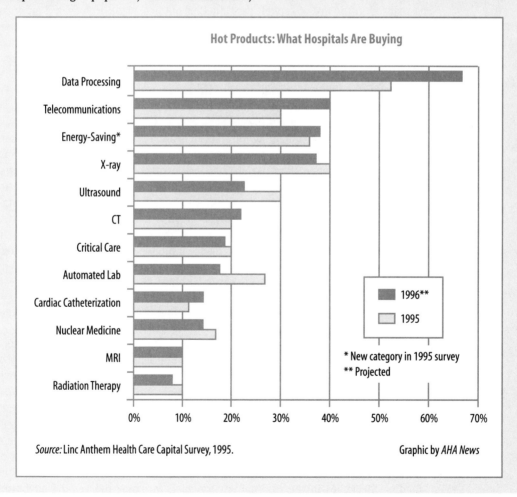

Hot Products: What Hospitals Are Buying

Legend: 1996** ; 1995

* New category in 1995 survey
** Projected

Source: Linc Anthem Health Care Capital Survey, 1995.

Graphic by *AHA News*

the health care industry, and specific competitor strategies to determine their implications for the organization. The results of the environmental analysis process directly influence the development of the organization's mission, vision, values, objectives, and internal analysis. In combination, external environmental analysis, internal environmental analysis, and the formulation of mission, vision, values, and objectives affect the strategy of the organization.

Environmental analysis requires externally oriented leadership. Leaders search for opportunities—ways to radically alter the status quo, create something totally new, or revolutionize processes—opportunities to do what has never been done previously or to do known things in a new way. The fundamental nature of strategic management and the basis of strategic leadership requires the awareness and understanding of outside forces. Leaders encourage passage of new ideas into the system, maintain receptivity to new ways, and expose themselves to broad views. Leaders, through environmental analysis, can remove the protective covering in which organizations often seal themselves.[5] Effective environmental analysis occurs through leadership.

Determining the Need for Environmental Analysis

Based on extensive experience in business, A. H. Mesch developed a series of questions to determine if an organization needs environmental analysis. The questions include:

1. Does the external environment influence the capital allocation and decision-making processes?
2. Have previous strategic plans been scrapped because of unexpected changes in the environment?
3. Has there been an unpleasant surprise in the external environment?
4. Is competition growing in the industry?
5. Is the organization or industry becoming more marketing oriented?
6. Do more and different kinds of external forces seem to be influencing decisions, and does there seem to be more interplay between them?
7. Is management unhappy with past forecasting and planning efforts?[6]

Answering "yes" to any of the questions suggests that management should consider some form of environmental analysis. Answering "yes" to five or more indicates that environmental analysis is imperative. In today's dynamic environment, most health care managers would probably answer "yes" to more than one of these questions and should therefore be performing environmental analysis.

The external environmental analysis process attempts to identify, aggregate, and interpret environmental issues as well as provide information for the formulation of organizational mission, vision, values, objectives, and the analysis of the internal environment. Therefore, environmental analysis seeks to eliminate many of the surprises in the external environment. Organizations cannot afford to be surprised. As one writer has pointed out, "to the blind all things are sudden." However, while certain repetitive patterns, such as seasons, may be predictable, the forecasting of discontinuities, such as technological innovation or price increases, is virtually impossible.[7] Yet, managers who practice environmental analysis are so "close" to the environment that by the time change becomes apparent to others, they have already detected the signals of change and have explored the significance of the changes. These managers are often called visionaries; however, vision is often the result of their striving to detect subtle signals of change.

The lack of forecasting and planning success sometimes is the result of directing processes internally toward efficiency rather than externally toward effectiveness. Such planning systems have not considered the growing number and diversity of environmental influences. Early identification of external changes through environmental analysis will greatly enhance the planning efforts in health care organizations. For example, as it became clear that health care reform was moving toward some form of managed care or managed competition, many physician group practices and solo practitioners joined together to create large physician-driven health care organizations that could compete for prepaid health care contracts. These physicians viewed such organizations as a way to evolve competitively to ensure their survival.[8]

The Goals of Environmental Analysis

Although the overall intent of environmental analysis is to position the organization within its environment, more specific goals may be identified. The specific goals of environmental analysis are:

1. to classify and order information flows generated by outside organizations;
2. to identify and analyze *current* important issues that will affect the organization;
3. to detect and analyze the weak signals of *emerging* issues that will affect the organization;
4. to speculate on the *likely* future issues that will have significant impact on the organization;
5. to provide organized information for the development of the organization's mission, vision, values, objectives, internal analysis, and strategy; and
6. to foster strategic thinking throughout the organization.

There is an abundance of information in the external environment. For it to be meaningful, managers must identify the sources as well as aggregate and classify the information. Once classified, important issues that will affect the organization may be identified and evaluated. This process encourages managers to view environmental changes as external issues that may affect the organization.

In addition to the identification of current issues, environmental analysis attempts to detect weak signals within the external environment that may portend a future issue. Sometimes based on little hard data, managers attempt to identify patterns that suggest emerging issues that will be significant for the organization. Such issues, if they continue or actually do occur, may represent significant challenges. Early identification aids in developing strategy.

Strategic managers must go beyond what is known and speculate on the nature of the industry, as well as the organization, in the future. This process often stimulates creative thinking concerning the organization's present and future products and services. Such speculation is valuable in the formulation of a guiding vision and the development of mission and strategy. For example, the Introductory Incident, which describes the nature of a twenty-first century hospital, was developed through a process of extending and analyzing emerging external issues and speculating on likely future issues and their impact upon the hospital. Perspective 2–2 provides some of the emerging and speculative trends and issues that led to the conclusions reached in the Introductory Incident.

When top managers, middle managers, and front-line supervisors throughout the organization are considering the relationship of the organization to its environment, innovation and a high level of service are likely. Strategic thinking within an organization fosters adaptability, and those organizations that "adapt best will ultimately displace the rest."

The Limitations of Environmental Analysis

Environmental analysis is an important process for understanding the external environment, but it provides no guarantees for success. The process has some practical limitations that the organization must recognize. These limitations include the following:

1. Environmental analysis cannot foretell the future.
2. Managers cannot see everything.

Perspective 2–2

Trends and Issues Influencing Health Care Delivery Systems of the Twenty-First Century

Looking beyond the basic structural changes of health care reform can be helpful in planning for the future. These are some of the forces influencing the vision of the hospital of the twenty-first century described in the Introductory Incident of this chapter. Although some of the following changes are twenty years or more in the future, early signs are apparent now:

- Health care moves from its current "diagnose-and-treat" to "predict-and-manage" approach allowing for intervention well before problems become acute.
- Many acute-care services become broadly decentralized.
- A decline in surgical rates.
- Surges in ambulatory and home care.
- Greater focus on trauma and serious infection in hospitals.
- Cures for diseases such as cancer, AIDS, and Alzheimer's disease.
- Extension of life and a need for more geriatric-health professionals.

- Widespread use of alternative therapies and providers.
- More use of advanced practice nurses.
- Advances in telemedicine and information management bring specialized services and expertise to remote locations.
- "Wearable" personal computers.
- "Biosensor" self-care devices.
- Health risks analyzed using a database of a patient's genetic information.
- Reversal of genetic damage by replacing damaged or defective genes.
- Artificial intelligence or expert systems used routinely in clinical diagnoses.
- Increase in endoscopic techniques and the movement from inpatient to outpatient surgery.

Source: Rhonda L. Bergman, "Quantum Leaps," *Hospitals and Health Networks* 67, no. 19 (1993), pp. 28–35.

3. Sometimes pertinent and timely information is difficult or impossible to obtain.
4. There may be delays between the occurrence of external events and management's ability to interpret them.
5. Sometimes there is a general inability on the part of the organization to respond quickly enough to take advantage of the issue detected.
6. Managers' strongly held beliefs sometimes inhibit them from detecting issues or interpreting them rationally.[9]

Even the most comprehensive and well-organized environmental analysis process will not detect all of the changes taking place. Sometimes events occur that are significant to the organization but were preceded by few, if any, signals.

Perhaps the greatest limiting factor in external environmental analysis is the preconceived beliefs of management. In many cases, what managers already believe about the industry, important competitive factors, or social issues inhibits their ability to perceive or accept signals for change. Because of each manager's beliefs, signals are ignored that do not conform with what he or she believes. What we actually perceive is dramatically determined by our paradigms (ways of thinking, beliefs); and any data that exists in the real world that does not fit our paradigm will have a difficult time getting through our filters. We will see little if any of it.[10] As creativity expert Edward De Bono explains, "We are unable to make full use of the information and experience that is already available to us and is locked up in old structures, old patterns, old concepts, and old perceptions."[11] Despite long and loud signals for change, in some cases organizations do not change until "the gun is at their heads," and then it is often too late.

A Description of the External Environment

Organizations and individuals create change. Therefore, if health care managers are to develop awareness of changes taking place outside of their own organization, they must have a good understanding of the types of organizations that are creating change and the nature of the change. Exhibit 2–1 illustrates the concept of the external environment for health care organizations.

Components of the General Environment

All types of organizations and independent individuals generate important information within the general environment. For example, a research firm that is developing imaging technology may provide "information" that could be used by a variety of other organizations in very diverse industries such as hospitals (magnetic resonance imaging) and manufacturing (robotics). The members of the general environment may be broadly classified in a variety of ways depending on the strategic management needs of the organization analyzing the environment. These groups of organizations and individuals make up the broad context for the health care industry:

1. government institutions,
2. business organizations,
3. educational institutions,
4. religious institutions,

Exhibit 2–1 • The External Environment of a Health Care Organization

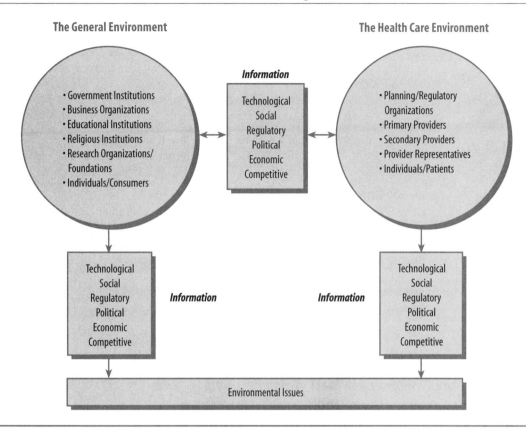

5. research organizations and foundations, and
6. individuals and consumers.

Organizations and individuals in the general environment, acting alone or in concert with others, initiate and foster the macroenvironmental changes within society. These organizations and individuals generate technological, social, regulatory, political, economic, and competitive *information* that will, in the long run, affect many different industries (including health care). Therefore, external organizations, engaged in their own processes and pursuing their own missions, are developing new information that will affect other industries, organizations, and individuals.

In the general environment, information flows usually affect a number of different sectors of the economy (industry environments). For example, during the Reagan and Bush administrations, the shift toward less government oversight and more deregulation affected not only the health care industry but also many others, including transportation, banking, and telecommunications. Similarly, the health care reform initiatives of the Clinton administration affected virtually all institutions in the general environment, not just health care organizations.

A business that develops a breakthrough in computer technology (new information) or a government organization that fosters changes in the general regulatory climate (new information) contributes to macroenvironmental changes that, although perhaps not specifically related to health care, may have a significant and long-lasting impact on the delivery of health care. Although initially developed in the business sector, innovations in computer systems and information processing technologies have significantly affected the delivery of health care.

As illustrated in Exhibit 2–1, the organization itself may be affected *directly* by the technological, social, regulatory, political, economic, and competitive information initiated and fostered by organizations in the general environment. In the aggregate, these information flows represent the general direction of societal change, which may affect the success or failure of any organization. Therefore, an organization engaging in strategic management must try to sort out the general information being generated in the external environment and detect the major shifts taking place. This process is often referred to as *macroenvironmental analysis.* A shift in consumer attitudes and expectations about health care is an example of a societal change that may affect the success or failure of health care organizations. Perspective 2–3 illustrates baby boomer health care attitudes that have directly impacted health care organizations in the 1990s.

Typically, as information is accumulated and evaluated by the organization, information flows will be summarized as *environmental issues* affecting the industry or organization. The identification and evaluation of the issues in the general environment are

---

Perspective 2–3

Baby Boomer Consumers Will Have a Major Influence in the 1990s and Beyond

Broad changes are in store when a generation of health care consumers as large as the baby boomers increasingly gain access to the health care system. Seventy-six million strong, the baby boom generation and its buying habits have helped drive the cost-and-quality revolution in industries ranging from automobile manufacturing to retailing. Health care has had to follow the trend, leading to widespread release of outcomes data through quality report cards and similar mechanisms.

The baby boom generation has different expectations and a far different background for those expectations than older generations. This group generally does not see their doctors as gods and will routinely:

- ask questions about treatment options and costs, then take charge of the decision;

- demand more products and services that promote youthful and healthy aging, because they are uncomfortable with physical decline;
- pore over self-help books, videos, and databases and use hot lines, workshops, survivor groups, and more;
- refuse to accept advice—and advice givers—at face value;
- demand convenience and excellent service;
- ask for evidence of quality and expertise;
- expect continuity of care; and
- explore alternative therapies.

Source: Kevin Lumsdon, "Baby Boomers Grow Up," *Hospitals and Health Networks* 67, no. 18 (1993), pp. 24–34.

important because the issues will accelerate or retard changes taking place within the industry and may affect the organization directly as well.

Components of the Health Care Environment

Organizations and individuals within the health care environment develop and employ new technologies, deal with changing social issues, address political change, develop and comply with regulations, compete with other health care organizations, and participate in the health care economy. Therefore, strategic managers should view the health care environment with the intent of understanding the nature of the issues and changes taking place in technology, social issues, regulation, political attitudes, economic realities, and competition. Focusing attention on these major change areas (information flows) facilitates the early identification and analysis of industry-specific environmental issues and trends that will affect the organization. This process is often referred to as *industry analysis.* The environmental analysis techniques and methods presented in this chapter help surface important general and industry issues. However, in today's environment a more focused *service area competitor* analysis is typically required. Chapter 3 presents a process for accomplishing service area competitor analysis.

The variety of health care organizations make categorization difficult. However, the health care system may be generally grouped into five segments:

1. organizations that plan and regulate primary and secondary providers;
2. organizations that provide health services (primary providers);
3. organizations that provide resources for the health care system (secondary providers);
4. organizations that represent the primary and secondary providers; and
5. individuals involved in health care and patients (consumers of health care services).[12]

Exhibit 2–2 lists the types of organizations and individuals within each segment and provides examples. The categories of health care organizations listed under each of the health care segments is not meant to be all-inclusive, but rather to provide a starting point for understanding the wide diversity and complexity of the industry.

Organizations That Plan and Regulate   A number of organizations plan for or regulate primary and secondary health care providers. These organizations may be generally categorized into four groups: federal regulating agencies, state regulating agencies, voluntary regulating groups, and accrediting groups.

Federal involvement in the regulation of the health care industry has increased in the past thirty years. The passage of the Medicare and Medicaid programs in the mid-1960s and the 1974 enactment of the National Health Planning and Resource Development Act dramatically increased the federal government's participation in the regulation of health care.[13] Important federal health care–regulating organizations include the Department of Health and Human Services (DHHS) and the Health Care Financing Administration (HCFA). In a similar manner, state governments have become concerned about the provision of health care and have created a variety of organizations and agencies to regulate health care within the states. For example, many states enacted certificate of need (CON) legislation in order to regulate provider growth and viability. Similarly, state Medicaid agencies have attempted to ensure health care access to the poor.

Exhibit 2–2 · Organizations in the Health Care Environment

Organizations That Plan for or Regulate Primary and Secondary Providers

- Federal Regulating Agencies
  Department of Health and Human Services (DHHS)
  Health Care Financing Administration (HCFA)

- State Regulating Agencies
  Public Health Department
  State Health Planning Agency (e.g., Certificate of Need [CON])

- Voluntary Regulating Groups
  Joint Commission on Accreditation of Healthcare Organizations (JCAHO)
- Other Accrediting Agencies

Primary Providers (Organizations That Provide Health Services)

- Hospitals
  Voluntary (e.g., Barnes/Jewish/Christian Health System)
  Governmental (e.g., Veteran's Administration Hospitals)
  Investor-Owned (e.g., Columbia/HCA, Tenet)

- State Public Health Departments
- Long-Term-Care Facilities
  Skilled Nursing Facilities (e.g., Beverly Enterprises, Upjohn Healthcare Services, Mediplex)

- Intermediate-Care Facilities
- HMOs and IPAs (e.g., Care America, Complete Health, PruCare)
- Ambulatory-Care Institutions (e.g., Wellesley Medical Management, National Rehabilitation Centers)
- Hospices (e.g., Hospice Care, Inc., Melinda House, Connecticut Hospice, Inc.)
- Physicians' Offices
- Home Health Care Institutions (e.g., Care Givers Home Health, Olsen Healthcare, Visiting Nurses Association [VNA], Kimberly Quality)

Secondary Providers (Organizations that Provide Resources)

- Educational Institutions
  Medical Schools (e.g., Johns Hopkins, University of Alabama at Birmingham [UAB])
  Schools of Public Health
  Schools of Nursing
  Health Administration Programs

- Organizations That Pay for Care (Third-Party Payors)
  Government (e.g., Medicaid, Medicare)
  Insurance Companies (e.g., Prudential, Metropolitan)
  Businesses (e.g., AT&T, IBM)
  Social Organizations (e.g., Shriners, Rotary Clubs)

- Pharmaceutical and Medical Supply Companies
  Drug Distributors (e.g., Bergen Brunswig, Walgreen, McKesson)
  Drug and Research Companies (e.g., Bristol Myers Squibb, Merck, Pfizer, Hoffman-LaRoche, Eli Lilly, Upjohn, Warner Lambert)
  Medical Products Companies (e.g., Johnson & Johnson, Baxter International, Abbott Labs, Bausch & Lomb)

Exhibit 2–2 · **Continued**

Organizations That Represent Primary and Secondary Providers

- American Medical Association (AMA)
- American Hospital Association (AHA)
- State Medical Associations (e.g., Illinois Hospital Association, Kentucky Medical Association)
- Professional Associations (e.g., Pharmaceutical Manufacturers Association [PMA], American College of Healthcare Executives)

Individuals and Patients (Consumers)

- Independent Physicians
- Nurses
- Nonphysician Professionals
- Nonprofessionals
- Patients and Consumer Groups

Source: From Beaufort B. Longest, Jr., *Management Practices for the Health Professional*, 4th ed., © 1990. Adapted with permission of Appleton & Lange.

In addition to federal and state government regulating agencies, there are a number of voluntary regulatory groups and accrediting agencies. These groups include the Joint Commission on Accreditation of Healthcare Organizations (JCAHO) as well as a number of separate discipline accrediting agencies such as the American Dietetic Association, the National League of Nursing, and the Commission on Accreditation of the American Dental Association. With a growing emphasis on quality, it is likely that these types of organizations will expand their role within the industry.

Primary Providers　There are a number of ways to classify the wide and diverse range of primary providers, the most visible component of the health care system. (Note: Primary and secondary providers should not be confused with primary, secondary, and tertiary levels of hospital care.) Exhibit 2–2 suggests one approach that has eight, sometimes overlapping, groups: hospitals; state public health departments; long-term-care facilities; HMOs, PPOs, and IPAs; ambulatory-care institutions; hospices; physicians' offices; and home health care institutions.

These types of organizations make up the delivery portion of the health care industry. In the past, hospitals have been the dominant segment; but as the industry becomes more specialized and fragments further, other primary providers will grow in importance. Institutions that are likely to be more dominant in the future are long-term-care facilities, ambulatory care hospices, home-care institutions, and managed-care organizations. Managed-care organizations have already had a significant influence in the 1990s. The evolution of managed care and its impact on the industry is examined in Perspective 2–4.

Secondary Providers　Essentially composed of support organizations for primary providers, the secondary provider component includes educational institutions, organizations

Perspective 2–4

The Evolution of Managed Care

National health care expenditures totaled $27 billion in the 1960s; however by 1995, spending had exceeded $1.1 trillion. The concept of managing care emerged as a viable method to contain health care costs and has had a profound and lasting influence on the nature and delivery of U.S. health care. Over the past twenty-five years, managed health care systems have evolved in an attempt to manage the cost as well as the quality of health care.

Initially managed care was directed toward limiting benefits and providing utilization reviews, including second opinions for surgery. These first-generation managed-care efforts were typically employer-based health insurance plans. Second-generation managed care provided benefit differentials, provider networks, and utilization management. These second-generation systems were managed by health maintenance organizations (HMOs) and preferred provider organizations.

Third-generation managed-care systems include quantitative quality measures, patient-care management teams, and advanced physician selection and monitoring. Third-generation managed care increasingly involves integrated networks of care. Integrated networks are beyond HMOs in both structure and function. Consumers receive vertically integrated health services from family-oriented medical care to tertiary hospital care, long-term care, and home and mental health services. One umbrella institution organizes and manages this continuum of care. In some cases, the institution owns all or most of the diverse components of the system although in other cases webs of contractual relationships form the continuum of care.

Today the managed health care label describes a variety of complex organizational structures and reimbursement arrangements (see Perspective 1–1). However, regardless of the specific form, managed-care organizations employ a structure that manages a comprehensive set of operations that assume pre-authorization functions and all or partial legal, financial, and organizational risks. Whether it is a pre-authorization structure or an organization that assumes all the risks, the purpose of managed health care is to restrict fee for service, introduce binding contracts, and modify the behavior of both the provider and the consumer in the utilization of health care services.

Source: Steven Findlay, "Networks of Care May Serve as a Model for Health Reform," *Business and Health* 11, no. 2 (1993), pp. 27–31; and Colodia Owens, *Managed Care Organizations: Practical Implications for Medical Practices and Other Providers* (New York: McGraw-Hill, 1996).

that pay for health care, and pharmaceutical and medical supply companies. Educational institutions, through their medical schools, nursing schools, schools of public health, and allied health care programs, educate health care personnel. Organizations that pay for care (third-party payors) include the government (principally through Medicare and Medicaid), commercial insurance companies, and employers.

Another segment of the secondary provider category includes pharmaceutical and medical supply organizations. This is a particularly important segment supporting the research and material needs of primary providers. Major pharmaceutical and medical supply organizations include drug distributors, drug and research companies, and medical products companies.

Representation of the Primary and Secondary Providers The various providers of health care are typically represented by associations whose main purpose is to foster the disciplines and represent the interests of their constituencies. Examples include national associations such as the American Medical Association, the American Hospital Association, the Pharmaceutical Manufacturers Association, and so on. In addition, there are a variety of state and local health care associations.

Individuals and Patients The final segment of the health care industry includes individuals working within the industry (either independently or in health care organizations), patients, and consumer groups. Individuals working within the industry create the culture of the industry and are the source of many issues. Patients are the reason that health care organizations exist. In the past, this group was treated as a mere component of the health care system; but in today's competitive environment the needs and wants of the users of health services are driving the system. Patients create important issues for health care managers. In addition, groups of consumers such as the American Association of Retired Persons (AARP) and the American Cancer Society make their voices heard about health care issues.

The Process of Environmental Analysis

There are a variety of approaches to conducting an environmental analysis. Regardless of the approach, four fundamental processes are common to all environmental analysis efforts (see Exhibit 2–3): (1) scanning to identify signals of environmental change, (2) monitoring identified issues, (3) forecasting the future direction of the issues, and (4) assessing the organizational implications of the issues.[14]

Scanning the External Environment

As suggested earlier in this chapter, the external environment is composed of a number of organizations and individuals in the general and health care environments. Some of the organizations and individuals in the external environment have little direct involvement with the health care industry while others are directly involved. The distinction is not always clear. These organizations and individuals, through their normal operations and activities, are generating information that may be important to the future of other organizations. Information in the general environment is always "breaking through" to the health care environment, as when laser technology was developed outside of the health care industry and was quickly adopted within the industry. This phenomenon sometimes is referred to as "environmental slip."

The environmental *scanning* process acts as a "window" to these organizations. Thus, these general environment information flows may have a direct impact on any one health care organization if it is the member of the health care industry that most immediately sees an application for the information. Through this window, managers engaged in environmental scanning carry out three functions. They:

1. view external environmental information;
2. organize external information into several desired categories; and
3. identify issues within each category.

Exhibit 2–3 · The Environmental Analysis Process

Scanning

- View external environmental information
- Organize information into desired categories
- Identify issues within each category

↓

Monitoring

- Specify the sources of data (organizations, individuals, or publications)
- Add to the environmental database
- Confirm or disprove issues (trends, developments, dilemmas, and possibility of events)
- Determine the rate of change within issues

↓

Forecasting

- Extend the trends, developments, dilemmas, or occurrence of an event
- Identify the interrelationships between issues and between environmental categories
- Develop alternative projections

↓

Assessing

- Evaluate the significance of the extended (forecasted) issues to the organization
- Identify the forces that must be considered in the formulation of the vision, mission, internal analysis, and strategic plan

Strategic issues are trends, developments, dilemmas, and possible events that affect an organization as a whole and its position within its environment. Strategic issues are often ill-structured and ambiguous and require an interpretation effort (forecasting and assessment).[15]

The scanning function, conceptualized in Exhibit 2–4, serves as the organization's "window" or "lens" on the external world. The scanning function is a process of moving the lens across the array of external organizations in search of current and emerging patterns of information. Using the lens, the viewer can focus on diverse and unorganized information generated by external organizations and individuals, and compile and organize it into meaningful categories. Thus, information generated in the external envi-

Exhibit 2–4 • The Concept of Scanning the External Environment

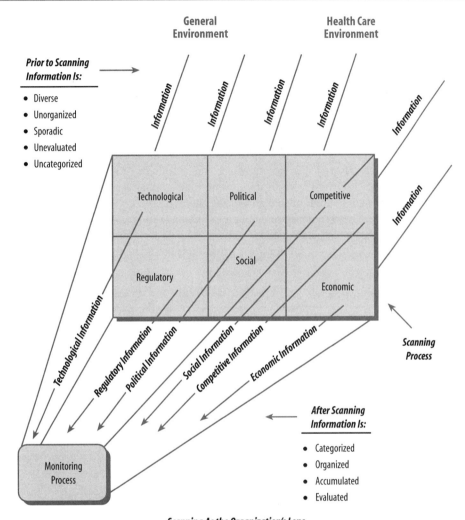

Scanning As the Organization's Lens

The scanning process allows the organization to focus on technological, political, competitive, regulatory, social and economic issues, trends, dilemmas, and events important to the organization. The "viewing process" must sort diverse, unorganized information. This process also filters out information not relevant to the mission of the organization.

ronment is organized through the scanning process. Prior to this interpretation process, information is diverse, unorganized, sporadic, mixed, and undefined. The scanning process categorizes, organizes, accumulates, and, to some extent, evaluates this information. This organized information is then used in the monitoring function.

Information Categories To monitor and further analyze the information, it must be organized into logical categories. Categories not only aid in tracking but also facilitate the later assessment of the information's impact on the organization. The categories most used to classify information are technological, social, political, regulatory, economic, and competitive. These streams of information are assessed and their impact incorporated into the strategy of the organization. Information, of course, is not inherently technological, social, and so on. However, using this approach helps managers to understand the nature of the information and to evaluate its impact. In addition, such classification helps aggregate information and organize it for the identification of important issues that may affect the organization. Through the aggregation and organization process, patterns may be identified and evidence accumulated to support an issue.

Information Sources There are a variety of sources for environmental information. Although organizations create change, they themselves are often difficult to monitor directly. However, a variety of secondary sources (published information) are readily available to most investigators to monitor other organizations. Essentially, people and publications both outside and inside the organization serve as the lens to the external world. These sources are outlined in Exhibit 2–5.

For most organizations, direct sources are far more important than indirect sources. Typically, within the organization, there are a variety of experts who are famil-

Exhibit 2–5 • Information Sources

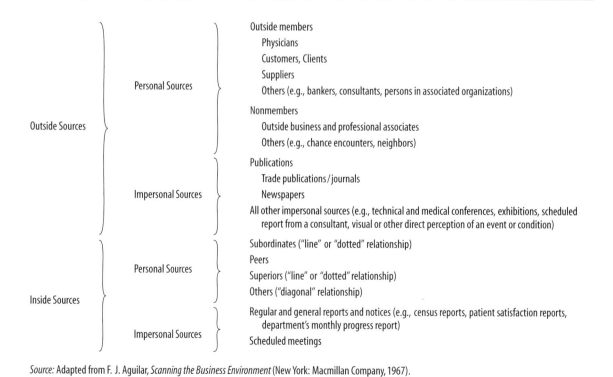

Source: Adapted from F. J. Aguilar, Scanning the Business Environment (New York: Macmillan Company, 1967).

iar with information created outside the organization and who may be the best sources of such information. Outside the health care organization, nonmembers and patients may be considered important direct sources. Indirect sources are mostly newspapers and journals, television, libraries, and public and private databases. (Appendix D of this text provides a comprehensive list of indirect sources of health care and business information.)

Environmental scanning is perhaps the most important part of environmental analysis because it forms the basis for the other processes. In the scanning activity, information flows are specified and sources identified. It is from this beginning that a database for decision making will be built. It is crucial that managers understand the thinking that led to the development and selection of strategic and tactical issues from among those identified in the scanning process. It is therefore advantageous if as many managers as possible take part in the scanning process. An important aspect of environmental scanning is that it focuses managers' attention on what lies outside the organization and allows them to create an organization that can adapt to and learn from that environment.[16]

Monitoring the External Environment

The monitoring function is the tracking of trends, issues, and possible events identified in the scanning process. Monitoring accomplishes four important functions:

1. It researches and identifies additional sources of information for specific issues delineated in the scanning process.
2. It adds to the environmental database.
3. It attempts to confirm or disprove issues (trends, developments, dilemmas, and the possibility of events).
4. It attempts to determine the rate of change within issues.

The monitoring process investigates the sources of the information obtained in the scanning process and attempts to identify the organization or organizations creating change and the sources reporting change. Once the organizations creating change and the publications or other information sources reporting change have been identified for a given health care organization, special attention should be given to these sources.

The monitoring function has a much narrower focus than scanning; the objective is to accumulate a database around the identified issue. The database will be used to confirm or disconfirm the trend, development, dilemma, or possibility of an event and to determine the rate of change taking place within the environment.

The intensity of monitoring is reflected in management's understanding of the issue. When managers believe they understand the issue well, less monitoring will be done. However, when environmental issues appear ill-structured, vague, or complex, issues will require a large amount of data to arrive at an interpretation.[17]

Forecasting Environmental Change

Forecasting environmental change is a process of extending the trends, developments, dilemmas, and events that the organization is monitoring. The forecasting function attempts to answer the question: "If these trends continue, or if issues accelerate beyond their present rate, or if this event occurs, what will the issues and trends 'look like' in the future?"

Three processes are involved in the forecasting function:

1. extending the trends, developments, dilemmas, or occurrences of an event;
2. identifying the interrelationships between the issues and environmental categories; and
3. developing alternative projections.

Assessing Environmental Change

Assessing environmental change is a process that is largely nonquantifiable and therefore judgmental. The assessment process includes evaluation of the significance of the extended (forecasted) issue upon the organization and identification of the issues that must be considered in the formulation of the vision, mission, internal analysis, and strategic plan.

The complexity of what we find and the grossness of most of the data that we collect are not consistent with traditional decision-making methods.[18] There are few procedures for incorporating "fuzzy" issues into the planning process.[19] In addition, even when exposed to identical issues, different managers may interpret their meaning quite differently. Different interpretations are a result of a variety of factors such as perceptions, values, and past experiences.

An excellent example of organizations attempting to assess the significance of an issue upon the organization occurred in late 1993 and throughout 1994, as many organizations tried to anticipate health care reform that might occur as a result of the Clinton administration's efforts. One of the lessons learned from the experience with DRGs was that organizations should not wait for the first set of reform implementation regulations to position themselves but that they must adapt *before* the change.[20]

The assessment or interpretation of a strategic issue is often represented by general labels such as *opportunity* or *threat.* These labels capture management's belief about the potential effects of environmental events and trends. Other dimensions may be used, such as positive/negative, gain/loss, and controllable/noncontrollable.[21]

Unfortunately no comprehensive conceptual scheme or computer model can be developed to provide a complete assessment of environmental issues. The assessment process is not an exact science, and sound human judgment and creativity may be bottom-line techniques for a process without much structure. Fahey and Narayanan conclude that the fundamental challenge

> is to make sense out of vague, ambiguous, and unconnected data. Analysts have to infuse meaning into data; they have to make the connections among discordant data such that signals of future events are created. This involves acts of perception and intuition on the analysts' part. It requires the capacity to suspend beliefs, preconceptions, and judgments that may inhibit connections being made among ambiguous and disconnected data.[22]

Environmental Analysis Tools and Techniques

Several different analysis tools and techniques may be used in environmental analysis. These techniques, which are informal and generally not overly sophisticated, have been variously described as "judgmental," "speculative," or "conjectural."[23] Indeed, environmental analysis is largely an individual effort and is directed to person-specific interests. Environmental analysis techniques usually are not limited to just one of the environmental analysis processes, but rather encompass scanning, monitoring, forecasting, and assessing. The remainder of this chapter will discuss environmental analysis techniques that identify trends and issues in the external environment. Techniques for more specific market segmentation and competitive analysis will be discussed in Chapter 3.

Simple Trend Identification and Extrapolation

Trend identification and extrapolation is a matter of plotting environmental data and then, from the existing data, anticipating the next occurrence. Perhaps because of its relative simplicity, trend extrapolation is a widely practiced analysis method. Obviously, such a method works best with financial or statistical data. However, environmental issues are rarely presented as a neat set of quantifiable data. Rather, environmental issues are ill-structured and conjectural. Thus, in many cases, trend identification and extrapolation in environmental analysis is a matter of reaching consensus on the existence of an issue and speculating on its likelihood of continuance.

Trend identification and extrapolation was applied by the Children's Memorial Hospital (CMH) in Chicago to open a satellite clinic and surgical center in a Chicago suburb. Decision makers at Children's noted that many pediatric hospitals such as La Bonheur Hospital in Memphis, Children's Hospital and Medical Center in Seattle, and Cincinnati Children's Hospital succeeded in establishing similar clinics. In addition, the decision to build the clinic was influenced by careful analysis of CMH's patient population, a substantial portion of which came from the suburban regions where the clinic was to be located. Projected population growth in the service area indicated sufficient demand for the satellite clinic.[24]

In the case of Lake Villa Nursing Home, demographic trends as well as others are of interest. As illustrated in Exhibit 2–6, the trend identification and extrapolation process includes the identification of issues by environmental category, the designation of an issue as an opportunity or threat, and the determination of its probable impact on the organization. Additionally, managers may assess the likelihood that the trend, development, or dilemma will continue or that the event will occur and then identify the sources for additional information.

These issues may then be plotted on the chart shown in Exhibit 2–7. The assumption is that the issues to the right of the curved line in the exhibit have a significant impact (high impact) on the organization and are likely to continue or occur (high probability) and should be addressed in the strategic plan.

The formats illustrated in Exhibits 2–6 and 2–7 are useful for organizing environmental data and providing a starting point for speculating on the direction and rate of

Exhibit 2–6 · Trend/Issue Identification and Evaluation of Lake Villa Nursing Home

Trend/Issue	Opportunity/ Threat	Evidence	Impact on Our Organization (1–10)	Probability of Trend Continuing (1–10)
Aging Population	*Opportunity*	*1 in 5 Americans will*	*9*	*9*
		be at least 65 by 2030		
Wealthier Elderly	*Opportunity*	*Income of those 60 +*	*7*	*6*
		has increased 10%		
		faster than any other		
		group		
Local Competition	*Threat*	*Over past 5 years,*	*7*	*9*
		number of nursing		
		homes in the service area		
		has increased from 5 to 7		

10 = High probability of occurring
1 = Low probability of occurring

change for identified trends. However, as with Children's Memorial Hospital, trend extrapolation of environmental issues requires extensive familiarity with the external environment (the issues) and a great deal of sound judgment.

Solicitation of Expert Opinion

Expert opinion is often used to identify, monitor, forecast, and assess environmental trends. Experts play a key role in shaping and extending the thinking of managers. For example, health care experts have concluded that these managerial skills will be essential throughout the remainder of the decade: the ability to deliver quality care at reasonable cost, the ability to enhance the health status of the community, the ability to gain the respect of the business and medical communities, and the ability to improve outcomes and satisfaction. Health care managers can use these opinions to stimulate their strategic thinking and begin developing human resources strategies.

To further focus managers' thinking and generate additional perspectives concerning the issues in the external environment, there are a number of more formal expert-

Exhibit 2–7 • **Environmental Trends/Issues Plot**

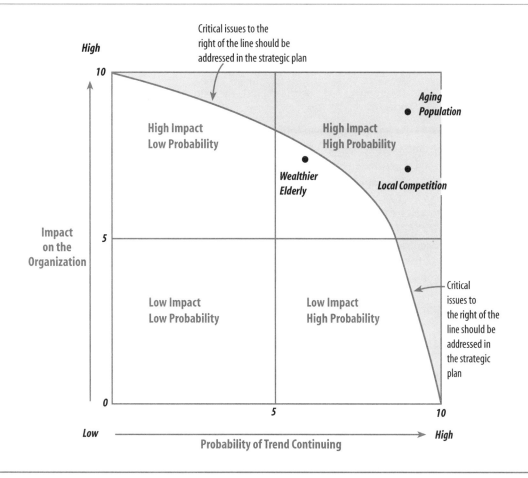

based environmental analysis techniques. These techniques help solicit and synthesize the opinions and best judgments of experts within various fields.

The Delphi Technique   The delphi technique is a popular, practical, and useful analysis technique for considering environmental data. The delphi method may be used to identify and study current and emerging trends within each environmental category (technological, social, economic, and so on). More specifically, the delphi technique is the development, evaluation, and synthesis of individual points of view through the systematic solicitation and collation of individual judgments on a particular topic. In the first round, individuals are asked their opinions on the selected topic. Opinions are summarized and then sent back to the participating individuals for the development of new judgments concerning the topic. After several rounds of solicitation and summary, a synthesis of opinion is formulated.[25]

S. C. Jain found that the traditional delphi method has undergone a great deal of change in the context of environmental analysis. Jain suggests that the salient features of the revised delphi method are to:

1. identify recognized experts in the field of interest;
2. seek their cooperation and send them a summary paper (based on a literature search); and
3. conduct personal interviews with each expert based on a structured questionnaire.[26]

In contrast to traditional delphi methods, there is no further feedback or repeated rounds of questioning. The major advantage is that it is easier to recruit recognized experts because they do not need to commit as much of their time.

The delphi technique is particularly helpful when health care managers want to understand the opportunities and threats of a specific environmental issue. For instance, there are indications that, because of the aging population, home health care is becoming more popular. However, the home-care industry has seen profits decline due to Medicare reimbursement changes and cuts in home medical equipment funding. In addition, HCFA regulations requiring a physician to demonstrate the medical necessity for home health care has, along with increased competition, dampened enthusiasm. A delphi panel can help health care managers better understand the opportunities and threats in the home health care market.[27]

Nominal Group Technique, Brainstorming, and Focus Groups The nominal group technique (NGT), brainstorming, and focus groups are interactive group problem identification and solving techniques. In the NGT, a group is convened to address an issue, such as the impact of consolidation within the health care industry or the impact of an aging population on hospital facilities. Each individual independently generates a written list of ideas surrounding the issue. Following the idea-generation period, group members take turns reporting one idea at a time to the group. Typically, each new idea is recorded on a large flip chart for everyone to consider. Members are encouraged to build on the ideas of others in the group. After all the ideas have been listed, the group discusses the ideas. After the discussion, members privately vote or rank the ideas. After voting, discussion and the group generation of ideas continue. Typically, additional voting continues until a reasonable consensus is reached.[28]

A brainstorming group is convened for the purpose of understanding an issue, assessing the impact of an issue on the organization, or generating strategic alternatives. In this process, members present ideas and are allowed to clarify them with brief explanations. Each idea is recorded, but evaluation is generally not allowed. The intent of brainstorming is to generate fresh ideas or new ways of thinking. Members are encouraged to present any ideas that occur to them, even apparently risky or impossible ideas. Such a process often stimulates creativity and sparks new approaches that are not as risky, crazy, or impossible as first thought.[29] As illustrated in Perspective 2–5, computer technology can enhance and facilitate brainstorming sessions.

NGT and brainstorming could be used to understand and respond to the trend of women's increasing preference for midwives rather than OB/GYN physicians. Women are increasingly fed up with high-tech, highly impersonal prenatal care and delivery.

Perspective 2–5

GDSS Facilitates Brainstorming

Group decision support systems (GDSS) are configurations (local area networks) of computer hardware and software that enhance the decision-making process by merging computer and communi-cation technologies. Accordingly, GDSS are interactive, electronic meeting support systems with the goal of enriching meetings, thereby improving the quality and quantity of alternatives and decisions. One powerful use of GDSS is for electronic brainstorming.

A typical brainstorming session occurs in a conference room where members have their own private microcomputers. Arranged at this central "room of the future," group members generate messages that display on a central "public" projection screen. A skilled facilitator provides guidance throughout each session. Increased creativity occurs by providing group members the ability to generate and share comments simultaneously while remaining anonymous. Possible gains include increased information, synergy, objectivity, stimulation, and learning. Anonymity can prove

useful when there are differences in power and status within the group and help prevent domination and intimidation. Further, simultaneous or parallel communication helps prevent rationing or blocking of speaking time.

Most GDSS field research suggests that larger groups obtain greater benefits. Second, improved meeting outcomes result in improved performance, efficiency, and satisfaction. Third, GDSS are most appropriate for complex tasks. Finally, repeated use increases performance and reactions. Other GDSS tools include a meeting manager, idea organizer, vote compiler, alternatives evaluator, and a policy formulation application.

Source: Written by John Frank Patton, Ph.D. Candidate, Health Services Administration, University of Alabama at Birmingham. Adapted from L. M. Jessup and J. S. Valacich, *Group Support Systems* (New York: Macmillan Publishing Company, 1993).

This trend is partly due to the high risks and high insurance costs for obstetricians. For example, one in eight OB/GYN doctors has stopped delivering babies, one in four will not handle a high-risk pregnancy, and more than one-third do not accept Medicaid patients. In addition, nearly 26 percent of all counties nationwide lack prenatal care clinics. European countries, where infant mortality rates are significantly lower than those in the United States, use midwives for approximately 70 percent of all births. NGT and brainstorming can provide a forum to explore the strength of the midwife trend and clarify the forces underlying the trend.[30]

Similar to brainstorming, focus groups bring together ten to fifteen key individuals to develop, evaluate, and reach conclusions regarding environmental issues. Focus groups provide an opportunity for management to discuss particularly important organizational issues with qualified individuals. For example, a hospital considering the establishment of a satellite clinic might develop a focus group of physicians. On the other hand, if a hospital wanted to understand the patient's viewpoint on the use of a midwife, different perspectives could be explored by convening a focus group of women who used a midwife and another group composed of women who would not use a midwife. The individuals involved can provide new insights for understanding the issues and suggest fresh alternatives for their resolution. Hospitals and large group practices have used focus groups of patients to better understand the perceived strengths and weaknesses of the organization from the patient's view.

Dialectic Inquiry

Dialectic inquiry is a "point and counterpoint" process of argumentation. The nineteenth-century German philosopher Hegel suggested that the surest path to truth was the use of dialectic, an intellectual exchange in which a thesis is pitted against an antithesis. According to this principle, truth emerges from the search for synthesis of apparently contradictory views.[31]

More specifically, in environmental analysis dialectic inquiry is the development, evaluation, and synthesis of conflicting points of view (environmental issues) through separate formulation and refinement of each point of view.[32] For instance, one group may argue that health care costs will be declining after the year 2000 (thesis) because of the prospective payment system, pressure by businesses and labor, health care reform, physician reimbursement reform, and so on. Another group may present a case that the trend toward rising health care costs will continue (antithesis) because of hospital failures, the high cost of new technology, failure of health care reform initiatives, and so on. Debating this issue will unearth the major factors influencing health care costs and implications for the future.

Any health care provider can utilize this technique by assigning groups to debate specific external issues. The groups make presentations and debate conflicting points of view concerning the environment. After the debate, the groups attempt to form a synthesis of ideas concerning the likely future.[33]

Stakeholder Analysis

Stakeholder analysis is based on the belief that there is a reciprocal relationship between an organization and certain other organizations, groups, and individuals. They are referred to as *stakeholders,* that is, organizations, groups, and individuals that have an interest or "stake" in the success of the organization. Examples of possible health care stakeholders, shown as a "stakeholder map," are presented in Exhibit 2–8.

Stakeholders may be categorized as internal, interface, and external. Internal stakeholders are those who operate primarily within the bounds of the organization, such as managers and other employees. Interface stakeholders are those who function both internally and externally, such as the medical staff and the corporate officers of the parent company. External stakeholders operate outside the organization and include such entities as suppliers, third-party payors, competitors, regulatory agencies, the media, the local community, and so on.[34]

Some of these stakeholders are almost always powerful or influential, others are influential regarding only certain issues, still others have little influence and power. If the stakeholders can be identified and evaluated, then the "forces" affecting the organization may be specified. The needs and wants of these constituencies may dramatically affect the strategy of an organization.[35]

Scenario Writing and Future Studies

Scenario writing and future studies have been used extensively in environmental analysis. One study showed that over 50 percent of the *Fortune* 1,000 companies were using

Exhibit 2–8 • A Stakeholder Map for a Large Multispecialty Group Practice

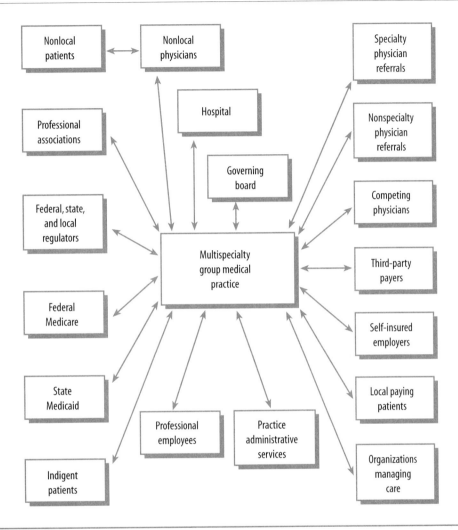

scenario analysis.[36] The popularity of scenario analysis is due in large part to the inability of other, more quantitative forecasting methods to predict and incorporate major shifts in the environment and provide a context for strategic thinking. Scenarios avoid the need for single-point forecasts by allowing users to explore several alternative futures.[37] Scenario analysis is an alternative to conventional forecasting that is better suited to an environment with numerous uncertainties or imponderables.

A scenario is a coherent story about the future using the world of today as a starting point.[38] Based on data accumulated in the scanning and monitoring processes, a scenario or narrative that describes an assumed future is developed. The objective of scenarios and future studies is to describe a point of time in the future as a sequence of time frames or periods of time.[39] Scenario writing often requires generous assumptions, and there are few guidelines as to what to include in the scenario.

In most cases several plausible scenarios should be written. It is an all-too-common mistake to envision only one scenario as the "true picture of the future."[40] Most authorities advocate the development of multiple scenarios. However, to avoid decision makers focusing only on the "most likely" or "most probable" scenario, each scenario should be given a distinctive theme name, such that they appear equally likely.

Multiple scenarios allow the future to be represented by different cause/effect relationships, different key events and their consequences, different variables, and different assumptions. The key question is: "If this environmental event happens (or does not happen), what will be the effect on the organization?" The use of multiple scenarios was particularly helpful as organizations considered the probable impact of health care reform legislation on their organizations. Exhibit 2–9 presents a brief summary of four scenarios or alternative futures for health care in the twenty-first century developed by Clement Bezold, Executive Director of the Institute for Alternative Futures. The scenarios were developed to examine the differences between leadership practices today and the organizational demands that health care leaders will face in the next century. Bezold indicates, "The scenarios were designed to provoke the imagination, raise fundamental questions, and stretch world views."[41]

Selecting the Technique

The intent of environmental analysis is to identify and understand the issues in the external environment. Exhibit 2–10 summarizes the primary focus, advantages, and disadvantages of each technique.

The technique selected for environmental analysis will depend on such factors as the size of the organization, the diversity of the products and services, and the complexity and size of the markets (service areas). Organizations that are relatively small, do not have a great deal of diversity, and have well-defined service areas may opt for simple techniques that may be carried out in-house, such as trend identification and extension, in-house nominal group technique or brainstorming, or stakeholder analysis. Such organizations may include independent hospitals, HMOs, rural and community hospitals, large group practices, long-term-care facilities, hospices, and county public health departments.

Health care organizations that are large, have diverse products and services, and have ill-defined or extensive service areas may want to use techniques that draw upon the knowledge of a wide range of experts. As a result, these organizations are more likely to set up delphi panels and outside nominal and brainstorming groups. In addition, these organizations may have the resources to conduct dialectics concerning environmental issues and engage in scenario writing. Such techniques are usually more time consuming, fairly expensive, and require extensive coordination. Organizations using these techniques may include national and regional for-profit health care chains, regional health systems, large federations and alliances, and state public health departments.

Ultimately, the technique selected for environmental analysis may depend primarily on the style and preferences of management. If used properly, any of the techniques can provide a powerful tool for identifying, monitoring, forecasting, and assessing environmental issues.

Exhibit 2–9 • Alternative Scenarios for Health Care in the Twenty-First Century

Scenario 1: Business as "Usual"

National health care reform was sent back to the states, resulting in substantial diversity as most of the states left reform to the marketplace. Outcome measures and the growing consolidation within the health care industry brought some consistency at the level of therapeutics, but access and specific coverage varied widely. Advances in biomedical knowledge and technology made it possible to forecast and increasingly manage an individual's health and illness over his or her life course, profoundly altering health care delivery to the insured. Health care providers shifted to forecasting and then managing illness far earlier and more successfully.

Expensive advances in technology and therapeutics, including function-enhancing bionics, helped health care's share of GNP grow to 17 percent by 2005. Hospital beds were reduced from more than 900,000 in 1989 to about 450,000 in 2001 and 300,000 by 2010. Hopsitals became smaller and their number declined proportionally as the number of beds decreased. Poverty and lack of access to health care persist.

Scenario 2: Hard Times/Government Leadership

Recurrent hard times and a political revolt against health care led the federal government to take back health care and create universal access to a very frugal capitated or severely restricted fee-for-service care (a Canadian-like health care system). The federal government as the single payer set prices and kept them low, but it gave states discretion over what types of care would be eligible for payment and over the priorities among these. The "Oregon Approach"—involving the public in consciously setting priorities for the services available—was taken not only for the poor but now for the vast bulk of the population.

Innovation slowed dramatically. The system favored expenditures with the greatest return on limited funds. The formerly uninsured were better off because of the greater emphasis on services for all. Heroic measures for terminal patients declined and more frugal—yet successful—approaches to innovation were adopted. Health care's percentage of the GNP was reduced to 11 percent by 2001. Thirty percent of Americans "buy up" to affluent, higher-tech care, and two systems of health care emerge.

Scenario 3: Buyer's Market

Health care's role as a "player" in the marketplace did not induce a more competitive environment that led to better, less expensive service during the 1980s. However, over the next two decades, health care markets did a much better job of giving consumers a range of high-quality services, delivered in convenient ways, at relatively low cost over the long term, while maintaining a high degree of innovation.

When the cost of health care reached $1 trillion and 14 percent of GNP in 1995, a powerful coalition emerged. Policy makers, employers, and consumer groups became convinced that modest changes would not work. National health policy was formulated to make all individuals and families who were not poor or "near poor" responsible for their health expenditures up to the equivalent of 8 percent to 10 percent of their income. Individuals could buy insurance (either indemnity or managed care) though the insurance had to meet certain criteria. Medicare and Medicaid coverage was adjusted to ensure that all poor and near-poor individuals had basic health care.

Local consumers, insurers, and managed-care providers reinforced effective care deliverers and shunned poorly performing providers; buyers and markets became smarter. Since many buyers paid out-of-pocket and the outcomes of all providers could be compared, a diverse and active market for various types of providers and treatments emerged. Even managed-care plans began providing both conventional and alternative therapies. Cost-effective innovation was rapid because the resulting outcomes were quickly known.

Scenario 4: Health Gains and Healing

The fifteen years before 2010 were a time of vision and design for health care. Health care organizations, their customers, and the communities they served joined to develop and pursue powerful shared visions. Healing the body, mind, and spirit of individuals and communities became the focus.

By 2010 health systems had integrated, disintegrated, and "virtualized." Some large players remained, although they only had a fraction of the inpatient beds they had in the 1990s and more ongoing life-enhancing relationships (rather then covered lives). By 2000, the ability to monitor the track record of all health care providers and make this information accessible in consumers' homes allowed successful new entrants to build a reputation quickly. Simultaneously, decreases in health providers' contributions to health gains, or a decrease in cost competitiveness, became visible within six months in most communities.

In the late 1990s, health care systems and the communities they served realized that they could jointly "design out" pathologies, such as drug problems, teenage pregnancy, and the effects of poverty. These generally lead to health gains, through a variety of paths. This noble activity was reinforced by "smarter markets," which allowed consumers and large purchasers to understand the outcomes of health care providers both for individuals and for the communities they served.

Source: Clement Bezold, "Four Futures: Alternative Scenarios for Health Care in the 21st Century," *Medicine and Health PERSPECTIVES* (Washington, DC: Faulkner & Gray, January 15, 1996).

Exhibit 2–10　•　**Primary Focus, Advantages, and Disadvantages of Environmental Techniques**

Technique	Primary Focus	Advantage	Disadvantage
Simple Trend Identification and Extension	Scanning Monitoring Forecasting Assessing	• Simple • Logical • Easy to communicate	• Need a good deal of data in order to extend trend • Limited to existing trends • May not foster creative thinking
Delphi Technique	Scanning Monitoring Forecasting Assessing	• Use of field experts • Avoids intimidation problems • Eliminates management's biases	• Members are physically dispersed • No direct interaction of participants • May take a long time to complete
Nominal Group Technique	Scanning Monitoring Forecasting Assessing	• Everyone has equal status and power • Wide participation • Ensures representation • Eliminates management's biases	• Structure may limit creativity • Time consuming
Brainstorming	Forecasting Assessing	• Fosters creativity • Develops many ideas, alternatives • Encourages communication	• No process for making decisions • Sometimes gets off track
Focus Groups	Forecasting Assessing	• Uses experts • Management/expert interaction • New view points	• Finding experts • No specific structure for reaching conclusions
Dialectic Inquiry	Forecasting Assessing	• Surfaces many subissues and factors • Conclusions are reached on issues • Based on analysis	• Does not provide a set of procedures for deciding what is important • Considers only a single issue at a time • Time consuming
Stakeholder Analysis	Scanning Monitoring	• Considers major independent groups and individuals • Ensures major needs and wants of outside organizations are taken into account	• Emerging issues generated by other organizations may not be considered • Does not consider the broader issues of the general environment
Scenario Writing	Forecasting Assessing	• Portrays alternative futures • Considers interrelated external variables • Gives a complete picture of the future	• Requires generous assumptions • Always a question as to what to include • Difficult to write

Issues in the Health Care Environment

The health care industry is faced with many dynamic issues, and it will have to face a host of new developments in the rapidly changing external environment. Managers of health care organizations should assess these issues and others unique to their organizations in order to provide a foundation for understanding the complexity of health care delivery and to furnish a backdrop for developing strategy. An excellent example of identifying environmental issues, recognizing opportunity, and building a strategy around that opportunity has been implemented by Vencor, a for-profit, publicly owned health care organization specializing in long-term catastrophic care.

Michael R. Barr, the founder of Vencor, discovered a market niche outside the prospective payment system. He observed that Medicare reimbursed long-term-care hospitals based on cost rather than DRGs. Additionally, cash flow for this type of hospital was enhanced by the Medicare practice of reimbursement while care is being given. A large pool of potential patients existed because traditional hospitals emphasized rapid resolution of the patient's disease and discharge. Also, Barr noted the near absence of competition in the long-term catastrophic-care market. Extending the implications of these developments, identifying the interrelationships between the developments and other factors in the external environment, and developing alternative outcome projections led Barr to form Vencor. Barr understood the significance of these issues and formulated a vision and plan for the future of Vencor.

For the foreseeable future, the health care environment will continue to generate numerous complex issues. Using a format similar to that shown in Exhibit 2–6, some of the major health care issues commonly identified by environmental analysis are listed in Exhibit 2–11. This list of issues, although not exhaustive, provides some insight into the dynamics of the health care environment. In addition, this format provides a usable summary of environmental issues and encourages managers to cite specific evidence supporting their beliefs concerning the issues. For instance, the high cost of technology

Exhibit 2–11 • Health Care Environmental Issues for the Year 2000

Issue	Evidence
Technology	
High Cost of Technology	• Hospitals spend billions of dollars on capital equipment each year.
	• Spending on equipment is expected to increase 15 percent per year throughout the 1990s.
	• MRI technology costs $2 million, a lithotripter costs $1.5 million.
DNA Mapping	• Research is being conducted that links diseases to faulty DNA.
	• There are 2,400 genes already mapped.
	• Five thousand scientists are doing research in genetics.
	• NIH and other agencies are set to spend billions of dollars in the next 10 years.
	• Cloning is revolutionizing the manufacture of protein-based drugs and other protein products.
High-Tech Treatments	• Sixteen biotech drugs have been approved by the U.S. Food and Drug Administration, and 132 are in the clinical trial pipeline.
High-Tech Equipment	• MRI imaging is widespread.
	• Computers have increasing applications in health care.
	• The electronic patient record and bedside data entry are possible.
Social	
Demand for Access and Quality	• There are 41 million people without health care insurance.
	• Federal and state governments are initiating health care reform.

continued

Exhibit 2–11 · **Continued**

Issue	Evidence
Social *(cont.)*	
Demand for Access and Quality *(cont.)*	• "Outcomes" research is called for by many within and outside health care.
	• At least seven states have considered universal access legislation and more are expected to investigate it.
	• There are 58.2 million people enrolled in HMOs in 1995, up from 51.1 million from 1994.
	• Health cost increases are slowing; some HMOs hold increases to less than 5 percent.
Disease Trends	• The number of AIDS cases is growing.
	• The cost of individualized care is high.
	• AIDS moves into diverse segments of the population.
	• At least 30,000 cases of multidrug-resistant tuberculosis are reported in the United States (72 to 89 percent mortality rates).
	• A number of epidemics (Washington State *E. coli*, Milwaukee *cryptosporidium*, Four-corners *hantavirus*) have been identified.
Aging Population	• The baby boom generation will need increased access to health care.
	• There is a shortage of affordable long-term-care facilities.
	• Those over 65 account for over 50 percent of inpatient days.
	• 80 percent of older adults have at least one chronic condition.
Focus on Women's Health	• A total of twenty legislative bills have been introduced relating to women's health care issues.
	• Cancer death rates for women are increasing dramatically.
	• The cost of osteoporosis could be as much as $62 billion by the year 2020.
	• Women are the fastest growing group with AIDS.
Death with Dignity	• Laws and "living wills" are reformed.
	• Suicide machines are being built.
	• Right-to-die legislation is being enacted.
Political/Regulatory	
Third-Party Payor's Share of Health Care Costs Is Increasing	• Medicare's catastrophic illness total coverage that called for an individual surtax charge was repealed.
	• Consumers and governments are calling for universal health insurance.
Health Care Reform	• Passage of limited health care insurance reform in 1996 made it easier for people who change jobs to keep their coverage.
	• Medicare Part B payment reforms limiting fees to be phased in over five years began in 1992.
	• Some states passed legislation to publish physician profiles.
IRS Regulations	• Tax-exempt status and issuance of tax-exempt bonds are increasingly restrained.
COBRA	• Antidumping rules and regulations are expanding.
National Budget Deficit	• Funds for research are decreasing.
	• Federal and state governments are increasingly looking toward privatization to solve budget problems.
Medicare/Medicaid Reimbursement	• Medicare reimbursements to hospitals are predicted to decrease over the next several years.
	• Outpatient services will increase.
	• Overhaul of the welfare system cut Medicaid coverage for legal/illegal immigrants.

Exhibit 2–11 · Continued

Issue	Evidence
Economic	
Increased Pressures to Reduce Health Care Costs	• HCFA estimates health care expenditures will exceed 14 percent of GNP.
	• The United States leads all other industrial nations in health care costs.
	• Length of hospital stay is decreasing.
	• Outpatient visits are increasing (18 percent in some states).
	• Drinking and smoking are declining in some states.
	• Exercise and a healthy diet are on the rise.
	• Health care purchasers have called for reforms.
	• Business and labor unions are increasingly concerned with high health care costs.
Personnel Problems	• Nurses and nonphysician personnel are in short supply.
	• There is an oversupply of physicians in urban and suburban areas, an undersupply in rural areas.
	• One-half of the fastest growing occupations are in the health care field.
General Competitive	
Managed Care Will Continue to Grow	• 70 percent of employed people are in some form of managed care.
	• HMO penetration rates continue to grow in urban markets but lag in rural areas.
Continued Health Care Industry Restructuring	• AHA reported hospitals had a 5.1 percent total profit margin in 1995 down from 5.4 percent in 1994.
	• 1995 and 1996 were record years for health care mergers and acquisitions (an average of 2.4 per day among all types of providers in 1996).
	• New forms of delivery are emerging (integrated health network, group practice without walls, physician/hospital organizations, mobile and telemedicine).
	• Integrated delivery is the most significant trend of the mid-1990s.
	• Many academic centers are seeking alliances or mergers.
	• Community care networks are emerging.
	• Alliances and networks are growing phenomenally.
	• Average length of hospital stay decreased in 1995.
	• Average number of hospital outpatient visits rose in 1996.
	• Growth of capitated plans has continued.
	• JCAHO is taking steps toward accreditation based on outcomes.
	• PPS has been extended to some post-acute care providers, e.g., home care.
	• Continued horizontal integration has occurred in major segments, rehabilitation, and group practice management.
Failures/Closures Will Continue	• Record numbers of hospital closings each year—between 1980 and 1990, 761 hospitals closed—some experts predict that there will be 50 percent fewer hospitals by 1998.
	• Many rural hospitals continue to lose money.
	• National Association for Hospital Development estimates 40 percent of the nation's 2,200 acute-care hospitals will be closed or converted to other uses.
	• Emergency rooms close in record numbers.
	• Average hospital occupancy continues to decrease.
	• Nearly one in ten hospitals is in financial difficulty.

is commonly cited as a health care issue, but what is the specific evidence indicating that it is still an issue or is continuing as an issue? As suggested in Exhibit 2–11, the evidence indicates that high technology costs will continue to be a key issue driving health care strategy. Individual health care managers will have to assess the likelihood that these issues will continue and what their impact will be for individual organizations. More specific competitive and service area issues will be examined in Chapter 3.

Summary and Conclusions

This chapter is concerned with understanding and analyzing the general external environment of health care organizations. To be successful, organizations must be effectively positioned within their environment. Organizations involved in making capital allocations, experiencing unexpected environmental changes and surprises from different kinds of external forces, facing increasing competition, becoming more marketing oriented, or experiencing dissatisfaction with their present planning results should engage in environmental analysis.

The goal of environmental analysis is to classify and organize the general and industry information flows generated outside the organization. In the process, the organization attempts to detect and analyze current, emerging, and likely future issues. This information is used to develop the vision, mission, internal analysis, and strategy of the organization. In addition, the process should foster strategic thinking throughout the organization.

Although the benefits of environmental analysis are clear, there are several limitations. Environmental analysis cannot foretell the future nor can managers hope to detect every change. Moreover, needed information may be impossible to obtain or difficult to interpret, or the organization may not be able to respond quickly enough. The most significant limitation may be managers' preconceived beliefs about the environment.

This chapter provides a comprehensive description of the external environment for health care organizations. The environment includes organizations and individuals in the general environment (government institutions and agencies, business firms, educational institutions, research organizations and foundations, and individuals and consumers) and organizations and individuals in the health care industry (organizations that plan and regulate, primary providers, secondary providers, organizations that represent providers, and individuals and patients).

Organizations and individuals in the general and health care environments generate information that may be important to health care organizations. Typically, such information is classified as technological, social, political, regulatory, economic, or competitive. Such a classification system aids in aggregating information concerning the issues and in determining their impact. Sources for environmental information are found both inside and outside the organization and are direct as well as indirect.

The steps in environmental analysis include scanning to identify signals of environmental change, monitoring identified issues, forecasting the future direction of issues, and assessing organizational implications. Scanning is the process of viewing and organizing external information in an attempt to detect relevant issues that will affect the organization. Monitoring is the process of searching for additional information to confirm or disprove the trend, development, dilemma, or likelihood of the occurrence of an event. Forecasting is the process of extending issues, identifying their interrelationships, and developing alternative projections. Finally, assessing is the process of evaluating the significance of the issues. The information influences the formulation of the vision, mission, internal analysis, and strategy of the organization.

Several methods were discussed to conduct the scanning, monitoring, forecasting, and assessing processes. These methods include simple trend identification and extension, solicitation of expert opinion, dialectic inquiry, stakeholder analysis, and scenario writing.

Finally, several relevant issues in the health care environment were explored. The next chapter will examine market segmentation and competitive analysis.

Key Terms and Concepts in Strategic Management

assessing	forecasting	scanning
brainstorming	general environment	scenarios
delphi technique	health care environment	stakeholder
dialectic inquiry	industry analysis	strategic issues
external environmental analysis	monitoring	trends
focus groups	nominal group technique (NGT)	

Questions for Class Discussion

1. Why is environmental analysis important for an organization?
2. Most health care managers would answer "Yes" to many of A. H. Mesch's questions to determine if an organization needs environmental analysis. Are there other questions that seem to indicate that health care organizations should be performing environmental analysis?
3. What are the specific goals of environmental analysis?
4. What are the limitations of environmental analysis? Given these limitations, is environmental analysis worth the effort required? Why?
5. Why is it important to be able to identify influential organizations in the external environment? How may these organizations be categorized?
6. What four processes are involved in environmental analysis? What are their subprocesses?
7. How does the scanning process create a "window" to the external environment? How does the window concept help in understanding organizations and the types of information they produce?

8. Why is the *process* of environmental analysis as important as the *product?*
9. What are some important technological, social, political, regulatory, economic, and competitive issues that are affecting health care today?
10. Which of the environmental analysis tools and techniques are most useful?
11. Using Exhibit 2–8 as an example, develop a "stakeholder map" for a health care organization in your metropolitan area or state. On this map show the important health care organizations and indicate what impact they may have on the industry.
12. Go beyond your immediate data and speculate on the major forces that will affect the delivery of health care after the year 2000.
13. Which of the scenarios in Exhibit 2–9 do you think is most likely? Why? Based on today's available information (trends, issues, dilemma, and so on), develop your own scenario of health care in the twenty-first century.

Notes

1. Joel A. Barker, *Future Edge: Discovering the New Paradigms of Success* (New York: William Morrow and Company, 1992), p. 28.
2. John Burns, "Market Opening Up to the Non-Traditional," *Modern Healthcare* 23, no. 32 (August 9, 1993), pp. 96–98.
3. James M. Kouzes and Barry Z. Posner, *The Leadership Challenge: How to Keep Getting Extraordinary Things Done in Organizations* (San Francisco: Jossey-Bass Publishers, 1995), p. 44.
4. David K. Hurst, *Crisis and Renewal: Meeting the Challenge of Organizational Change* (Boston: Harvard Business School Press, 1995), p. 49.
5. Kouzes and Posner, *The Leadership Challenge: How to Keep Getting Extraordinary Things Done in Organizations*, pp. 47–48.
6. A. H. Mesch, "Developing an Effective Environmental Assessment Function," *Managerial Planning* 32 (1984), pp. 17–22.
7. Henry Mintzberg, "The Fall and Rise of Strategic Planning," *Harvard Business Review* 72, no. 1 (1994), pp. 107–114.
8. Della de Lafuente, "California Groups Join for Survival," *Modern Healthcare* 23, no. 25 (1993), p. 24.
9. J. O'Connell and J. W. Zimmerman, "Scanning the International Environment," *California Management Review* 22 (1979), pp. 15–22.
10. Barker, *Future Edge: Discovering the New Paradigms of Success*, p. 86.
11. Edward De Bono, *Serious Creativity: Using the Power of Lateral Thinking to Create New Ideas* (New York: HarperBusiness, 1992), p. 17.
12. Beaufort B. Longest, Jr., *Management Practices for the Health Professional*, 4th ed. (Norwalk, Connecticut: Appleton & Lange, 1990), pp. 12–28.
13. Ibid., p. 23.
14. Liam Fahey and V. K. Narayanan, *Macroenvironmental Analysis for Strategic Management* (St. Paul: West Publishing Company, 1986).
15. James B. Thomas and Reuben R. McDaniel, Jr., "Interpreting Strategic Issues: Effects of Strategy and the Information-Processing Structure of Top Management Teams," *Academy of Management Journal* 33, no. 2 (1990), p. 288.
16. P. T. Terry, "Mechanisms for Environmental Scanning," *Long Range Planning* 10 (1977), p. 9.
17. Thomas and McDaniel, "Interpreting Strategic Issues," pp. 289–290.
18. W. R. Dill, "The Impact of Environment on Organizational Development," in *Concepts and Issues in Administrative Behavior*, S. Mailick and E. H. VanNess, eds. (Englewood Cliffs, New Jersey: Prentice Hall, 1962).
19. Harold Klein and W. Newman, "How to Use SPIRE: A Systematic Procedure for Identifying Relevant Environments for Strategic Planning," *The Journal of Business Strategy* 5 (1980), pp. 32–45.
20. David Burda, "What We've Learned from DRGs," *Modern Healthcare* 23, no. 40 (October 4, 1993), pp. 42–44.
21. Thomas and McDaniel, "Interpreting Strategic Issues," pp. 288–289.
22. Fahey and Narayanan, *Macroenvironmental Analysis for Strategic Management,* p. 39.
23. H. E. Klein and R. E. Linneman, "Environmental Assessment: An International Study of Corporate Practice," *The Journal of Business Strategy* 5 (1984), pp. 66–75.
24. "Pediatric Clinics and Surgicenters Widen Market Reach," *Health Care Strategic Management* 8, no. 3 (1990), pp. 4–5.
25. James L. Webster, William E. Reif, and Jeffery S. Bracker, "The Manager's Guide to Strategic Planning Tools and Techniques," *Planning Review* 17, no. 6 (1989), pp. 4–13.
26. S. C. Jain, "Environmental Scanning in U.S. Corporations," *Long Range Planning* 17 (1984), p. 125.
27. S. Lutz, "Hospitals Reassess Home-Care Ventures," *Modern Healthcare* 20, no. 37 (September 17, 1990), pp. 22–30.
28. Ricky W. Griffin and Gregory Moorhead, *Organizational Behavior* (Boston: Houghton Mifflin Company, 1986), pp. 496–497.
29. Ibid., pp. 495–496.
30. "Does Doctor Know Best?" *Newsweek* (September 24, 1990), p. 85.
31. Barbara Karmel, *Point and Counterpoint in Organizational Behavior* (Hinsdale, Illinois: Dryden Press, 1980), p. 11.
32. Webster, Reif, and Bracker, "The Manager's Guide," p. 13.
33. Ibid.
34. Myron D. Fottler, John D. Blair, Carlton J. Whitehead, Michael D. Laus, and G. T. Savage, "Assessing Key Stakeholders: Who Matters to Hospitals and Why?" *Hospital and Health Services Administration* 34, no. 4 (1989), p. 527.
35. Ibid., p. 532.
36. R. E. Linneman and H. E. Klein, "The Use of Multiple Scenarios by U.S. Industrial Companies: A Comparison Study, 1977–1981," *Long Range Planning* 16, (1983) pp. 94–101.
37. Audrey Schriefer, "Getting the Most Out of Scenarios: Advice from the Experts," *Planning Review* 23, no. 5 (1995), pp. 33–35.

38. P. Leemhuis, "Using Scenarios to Develop Strategies," *Long Range Planning* 18 (1985), pp. 30–37.

39. Webster, Reif, and Bracker, "The Manager's Guide," p. 13.

40. Fahey and Narayanan, *Macroenvironmental Analysis for Strategic Management,* p. 39.

41. Clement Bezold, "Five Futures," *Healthcare Forum Journal* 35, no. 3 (1992), p. 29.

Additional Readings

Drucker, Peter F., *Managing in Turbulent Times* (New York: HarperBusiness, 1980). This classic book is still relevant today. Drucker comments on how managers will have to deal with the new economic era, new trends, new technologies, new markets, and new institutions. Drucker explains that in turbulent times, the first task of management is to assure the institution's capacity for survival; its structural strength and soundness; and its capacity to survive a blow, adapt to sudden change, and avail itself of new opportunities. He suggests that predicting the future only causes trouble. Management's task is to manage "what is" and to work to create what could and should be.

The Futurist, published by the World Future Society since 1966 (bimonthly). An association for the study of alternative futures, the World Future Society is a not-for-profit educational and scientific organization founded in 1966. This publication is a very readable journal of forecasts, trends, and ideas about the future.

Kotter, John P., *The New Rules: How to Succeed in Today's Post-Corporate World* (New York: Free Press, 1995). Based on a study of 115 members of the Harvard Business School's Class of 1974, Kotter explores the "new rules" to succeed in the "post-corporate world." The book examines the new realities and requirements for success, the new responses and strategies that will pay off, and the new underpinnings or assumptions associated with success. Kotter argues that the greatest opportunities have shifted away from large bureaucratic companies to smaller, more entrepreneurial ones; away from professional management in manufacturing to consulting and other service industries; toward leadership and financial deal making; toward high personal standards and a strong desire to win; and toward a willingness to continue to learn over an entire lifetime.

Mercer, David, ed., *Managing the External Environment* (London: Sage Publications, 1992). The collection of readings in this book is concerned with managing an organization's relationship with its external environment. The readings focus on the need to identify and understand the major forces that may shape that environment in the future as well as the role of strategic planning in both anticipating change and actively creating a desired future. Articles explore the likely nature of the future; developments in the economic, political, social, and technological environments; and methods for developing strategies to ensure success.

Vance, Mike, and Diane Deacon, *Think Out of the Box* (Franklin Lakes, New Jersey: Career Press, 1995). Vance and Deacon use a nine-dot matrix to plot the nine necessary points of a creative culture — people, place, product, involving, informing, inspiring, caring, cooperation, and creativity. The authors indicate that these nine factors are key in creating an organization culture that is open to change. Vance and Deacon illustrate the change in the organization's culture that enables managers to be more innovative and creative in their responses to the external environment.

Service Area Competitor Analysis

► **Learning Objectives**

After completing this chapter you should be able to:

1. Understand the importance of service area competitor analysis as well as its purpose.

2. Understand the relationship between general environmental trend identification and analysis and service area competitor analysis.

3. Be able to define and analyze the service area for a health care organization or specific health services.

4. Be able to conduct a service area structure analysis for a health care organization.

5. Understand strategic groups and be able to map competitors' strategies along important service and market dimensions.

6. Understand the elements of competitor analysis, be able to conduct a comprehensive competitor analysis, and be able to assess likely competitor strategic responses.

7. Be able to aggregate and synthesize general environmental trends and issues and service area competitor issues into specific strategy implications.

The Importance of Competitor Analysis

The process of environmental analysis is one of focusing on increasingly more specific issues. Chapter 2, "Understanding and Analyzing the External Environment," provided the fundamental approach and specific techniques for environmental trend and issues identification, monitoring, forecasting, and assessment. Once the general and industry trends and issues in the external environment have been identified and assessed, a more specific analysis is required. *Competitor analysis* is the process by which an organization attempts to further define and understand its service area through identifying its competitors, determining the strengths and weaknesses of these rivals, and anticipating their strategic moves. It involves collecting data on rivals and analyzing and interpreting the data for strategic decision making.[1]

Introductory Incident — Competitive Pressures Mount in the St. Louis Market

There are thirty-eight inpatient facilities with nearly 11,000 beds in the St. Louis area—40 to 50 percent too many, experts estimate. In recent years, providers have reacted to this intense competition by creating large integrated health care systems. BJC Health System, Unity Health Network, St. Louis Health Care Network, and Deaconess Incarnate Word Health System have emerged from a flurry of consolidations and integrations.

BJC Health System

BJC has thirteen member hospitals including Barnes-Jewish and St. Louis Children's, Christian Northeast and Northwest, and Missouri Baptist. With 30 percent of the ten-county market, BJC has become the largest area health care network. In creating its system, BJC has pursued a strategy of merger instead of affiliation. Physician integration developed slowly. BJC employs 100 primary care physicians and participates with 300 others through IPAs (independent practices associations).

Unity Health Network

With 28.5 percent market share in the ten-county area, Unity, part of the Sisters of Mercy Health System–St. Louis, is right on BJC's heels. This seven-hospital system, located in the affluent west and south St. Louis counties as well as Illinois, has pulled ahead in terms of net income. Through strong PHOs (physician-hospital organizations), Unity is affiliated with nearly 2,000 physicians.

St. Louis Health Care Network

The St. Louis Health Care Network (SLHCN), which includes 1,200 affiliated physicians, seven member health centers, and six affiliates, holds almost 18 percent of the ten-county market. Its parent, the SSM Health Care System, is one of the nation's largest Catholic health care systems. SLHCN has integrated its functional and clinical services to improve quality and reduce costs. With 150 fully aligned physicians, SLHCN has one of the largest physician organizations.

Deaconess Incarnate Word Health System

Formed in late 1995, Deaconess Incarnate Word is a three-hospital system with 1,030 licensed beds and an 8 percent share of the market. Its strength lies in having ninety primary-care physicians financially tied to it.

The future of health care in St. Louis is uncertain. Clearly the market is very competitive. Each of the four systems has its own particular strengths and weaknesses, each is pursuing a strategy that includes system integration, as well as market and services development. Is there a need for four health care systems in St. Louis? Survival in this market will require understanding market segments, rivals' strengths and weaknesses, and competitors' likely future strategies as well as strategic responses. Today, long-term success for health care organizations depends on positioning vis-à-vis the other "players" in the market.

Source: Meg Matheny, "BJC Health System: The Perils of a Proactive Strategy," *Health System Leader* 3, no. 2 (March 1996), pp. 12–19.

Business organizations have long engaged in competitor analysis, viewing it as an essential part of environmental analysis. These companies have learned that the process of competitor analysis aids in the identification of new business opportunities, the clarification of emerging ideas, improved ability to anticipate surprises, and the development of market penetration and market share growth strategies.[2] As a matter of fact, one well-documented reason Japanese automobile firms were able to penetrate the U.S. market successfully, especially during the 1970s, was that they were much better at doing competitor analysis than U.S. firms.[3] For business organizations the task of understanding the industry and specific competitors is a challenge; but it is even more difficult for health care organizations.

In the past, general environmental analysis was sufficient for most health care organizations. General and industry technological, social, political, regulatory, economic, and competitive issues provided enough information to make most strategic decisions. Service area competitor moves and countermoves were not that important. However, during the past decade, because of fundamental changes within the industry brought about by the influences of managed care, efforts to reduce costs and increase efficiency, and the increasing presence of for-profit health care organizations, every segment of the industry has become highly competitive. Certainly, as suggested in the Introductory Incident, aggressive competition has entered the health care market in St. Louis.

Challenges for the Health Care Market

Analyzing this new competitive environment is difficult for health care organizations for a variety of reasons. Perhaps most obvious is that in the recent past, very few health care organizations were concerned with competition. In fact, those in the "helping professions" believed there was no need to compete. Hospitals, long-term-care facilities, and physicians were more concerned with trying to meet the demand for their services. This history of noncompetition changed when legislation led to an increased number of hospital beds and an increased number of physicians (particularly within certain specialties). Eventually, the oversupply led to a more competitive environment. Because they are reluctant to even acknowledge competing with others for patients, it is no surprise that few health care managers have developed expertise in competitor analysis.

Another reason that competitor analysis has received little attention by health care managers is that generally competition has been restricted to a regional area with few competitors. Most people do not travel very far for health care. Those people who live in small towns tend to be treated there or go to the nearest larger town for health care. Only the very wealthy or very well insured travel great distances to well-known medical centers such as the Mayo Clinic or Johns Hopkins. This focus on regional delivery allowed health care managers to know competitors' past behaviors quite well. However, now they need to be able to predict future behavior with less information than was available in the past and with new alliances bringing outside organizations into the region. In addition, as competition has escalated, some formerly friendly competitors have become far more aggressive in attracting and keeping consumers as they sense survival is at stake.

Another major reason for the lack of competitor analysis is that the separation of consumers of health services (patients) from payors (insurance companies and employers) provided few checks on the system. When all the health care providers in a service area were well paid by insured patients, increasingly higher costs for more and more services provided to insured as well as uninsured patients were passed on to the insured patients. This "cost shifting" became a major concern in the tight economy of the early 1990s because employers paid for most insurance coverage for their employees. When U.S. companies felt they could no longer be competitive in world markets because of high health care costs, they began searching for ways to decrease the burden. They brought pressure on health care providers to reduce costs and began focusing on price competition. They began requiring their employees to pay an increasing portion of the costs and they became increasingly interested in "managing health care."

Managed care controls consumer choice to a limited number of providers to achieve greater buying power through economies of scale. When patients' choices of hospitals or physicians are limited, competition emerges among health care providers for the managed-care organization's insured group. Physicians, notably primary-care physicians, become "gatekeepers" into the system and direct patients to only one hospital in order to obtain the best possible rates. Hospitals "compete" for these desirable contracts. Nowhere is this more true than in the Minneapolis/St. Paul area, one of the most advanced managed-care markets in the country. Perspective 3–1 highlights the competitive nature of this market.

Despite the lack of experience in performing competitor analysis and the difficulty in identifying specific competitors for the many services offered, health care organizations need to understand their immediate competitive environment in order to develop successful strategies. Evidence of intense competition has manifested itself in a number of markets, where previously independent hospitals have combined along ownership lines to form competing systems. As illustrated in Perspective 3–2, the New Orleans market is representative of the trend of consolidation and increased competition between for-profit and not-for-profit institutions.

This chapter is directed toward a more focused understanding of the external forces that may affect the organization—the relevant market (service area) and analysis of specific competitors within that service area. Today's competitive health care environment requires that managers provide services for specific segments of the market. In addition, managers must understand the competitive advantages and potential strategic responses of competitors. Strategic response can entail a competitor's reactions to emerging issues in the environment or reactions to another organization's strategies. To undertake service area competitor analysis, it is important that health care managers examine relevant market segments, engage in industry analysis, profile competitors, and predict competitor responses. To create a clear competitive advantage within a service area, these important factors should be investigated.

Strategic Significance of Competitor Analysis

Within the health care community there is a growing understanding that health care organizations must be positioned vis-à-vis their competitors. Competitor information is essential for selecting viable strategies that position the organization strongly within the market. Many health care managers agree that an organized competitor intelligence system is necessary for survival. The system acts like an interlinked radar grid constantly monitoring competitor activity, filtering the raw information picked up by external and internal sources, processing it for strategic significance, and efficiently communicating actionable intelligence to those who need it.[4]

The Purpose of Competitive Analysis

Organizations engage in competitor analysis to gain a general understanding of the competitors in the service area, identify any vulnerabilities of the competitors, assess the

Perspective 3–1

The Dynamics of the Twin Cities Health Care Market

The Minneapolis/St. Paul region covers seven counties in the Twin Cities metropolitan area with a population of about 2.6 million people, a little more than half the state's 4.5 million people. The Minneapolis/St. Paul health care market is one of the most advanced managed-care markets in the United States. Approximately 80 percent of the Twin Cities' population is enrolled in HMOs, PPOs, or self-funded employer plans; 10 percent remain in fee-for-service arrangements; and about 10 percent are uninsured. In addition, there has been a high level of consolidation in the insurance, hospital, and physician sectors. Minnesota has a long history of promoting managed-care and marketplace competition within a structured regulatory framework. Moreover, Minnesota has been in the forefront of state health care reform and has relatively large state-sponsored programs that subsidize coverage for the uninsured.

As a result of horizontal and vertical integration in the insurance, hospital, and purchasing sectors, the market is dominated by three health plans—HealthPartners, Allina, and Blue Cross/Blue Shield. Combined, the three health plans account for 80 percent of the insured market. These plans are pursuing different strategies. Allina, an alliance of an HMO and a large hospital system, is trying to merge its two lines of business into a more integrated system. HealthPartners, the product of several HMO mergers, emphasizes close working relationships with its owned and affiliated physician group practices. Blue Cross/Blue Shield does not own any hospitals or physician groups, but it has sought contractual arrangements with providers.

Aggressive competition among these three health plans as well as pressure exerted by large, organized purchasers have led to increased price competition.

Recent trends indicate that the market consolidation pendulum may have swung too far. Purchasers are increasingly uncomfortable with the high level of consolidation in the health plan market, believing that it reduces their ability to hold health plans accountable and that any further increase in leverage for health plans could lead to higher prices. For instance, several of the major hospital-based systems are beginning to position themselves to compete with health plans by contracting directly with large employers.

The Twin Cities market is expected to become less consolidated, more quality conscious, and more consumer oriented. Although managed-care enrollment will likely increase as more low-income and under-served individuals enroll in managed-care organizations, large health plans will lose some of their former dominance. Purchasers, working together, will become even more value conscious as they seek direct contracts with high-quality, efficient providers and reduce the power of the health plans. Provider groups that are able to deliver what purchasers want will likely gain great advantage.

Source: Adapted from Debra J. Lipson and Jeanne De Sa, "Minneapolis/St. Paul, Minnesota, Site Visit Report," in Paul B. Ginsburg and Nancy J. Fasciano, eds. *The Community Snapshots Project: Capturing Health System Change* (Center for Studying Health System Change, a Robert Wood Johnson Foundation project monitoring health system change), Alpha Center, Washington, DC, 1996.

---

impact of its own strategic actions against specific competitors, and identify potential moves that a competitor might make that would endanger the organization's position in the market.[5] Through this process of analyzing competitors, organizations must identify, create, and sustain a clear competitive advantage—some basis upon which they are willing to compete with anyone. *Competitive advantage* is the means by which the organization seeks to differentiate itself from other organizations. Organizations con-

Perspective 3–2

New Orleans Market Consolidates into Three Strong Competitive Systems

New Orleans-Area Hospitals:	Number of Staffed Beds	New Orleans-Area Hospitals:	Number of Staffed Beds
Tenet		**Not-for-Profit Alliance**	
Mercy Baptist Medical Center:	634	Children's Hospital:	175
St. Charles General Hospital:	173	Ochsner Foundation Hospital:	377
Jo Ellen Smith Medical Center:	186	Pendleton Memorial Methodist	
Doctors Hospital of Jefferson:	114	Hospital:	211
Northshore Regional Medical		East Jefferson General Hospital:	437
Center:	147	Touro Infirmary:	332
Kenner Regional Medical Center:	124	West Jefferson Medical Center:	382
Meadowcrest Hospital:	161	Slidell Memorial Hospital and	
Columbia		Medical Center:	173
Tulane University Hospital:	259	St. Tammany Parish Hospital:	135
Elmwood Medical Center:	108	**Others**	
Lakeland Medical Center:	150	Medical Center of Louisiana:	611
Lakeside Hospital:	122	Medical Center of Louisiana—	
Lakeview Regional Medical		University Hospital Campus:	272
Center:	163	United Medical Center New Orleans:	136

stantly take offensive and defensive actions in their quests for competitive advantage vis-à-vis competitors.[6] Competitive advantage might be centered on image, high-quality services, an excellent and widely recognized staff, or efficiency and low cost, among others.

It is useful to classify competitor information as general, offensive, and defensive. This classification system will aid in strategy development in later stages (strategy formulation) of the strategic management process.

General competitor information is important for an organization in:

- avoiding surprises in the marketplace;
- providing a forum for executives to discuss and evaluate their assumptions about the organization's capabilities, market position, and the competition;
- making everyone aware of significant and formidable competitors to whom the organization must respond;
- helping the organization learn from rivals through benchmarking (specific measures comparing the organization with its competitors on a set of key variables);
- building consensus among executives on the organization's goals and capabilities, thus increasing their commitment to the chosen strategy; and
- fostering strategic thinking throughout the organization.

Offensive competitor information is helpful in:

- identifying market niches and discontinuities;
- selecting a viable strategy; and
- contributing to the successful implementation of the strategy.

Defensive competitor information will aid in:

- anticipating competitor's moves; and
- shortening the time required to respond to competitor's moves.

Depending on the intent of the competitor analysis, an organization might use all of these categories or just one or two. For example, in the early stages of competitor analysis, the organization may seek only general information. As an organization plans to enter new markets, offensive information may be the primary focus of the competitor analysis. In the face of strategic moves by a powerful competitor, defensive information may take precedence. In large complex markets, all of these information categories are appropriate and essential for positioning the organization. For example, Houston, the fourth largest U.S. city, is beginning to feel an acceleration of health care system changes. Horizontal and vertical integration and restructuring in response to growing pressure from payors for efficiency have been slower to develop in Houston; however, the pace of health system change is likely to accelerate sharply in the next few years. Such a market will likely require general, offensive, and defensive competitor information.

Impediments to Effective Competitor Analysis

Monitoring the actions and understanding the intentions of competitors is often difficult. Yet, health care executives agree that it is necessary and growing in importance. Zahra and Chaples have identified six common impediments or "blind spots" that slow an organization's response to its competitors' moves or even cause the selection of the wrong competitive approach. Flawed competitor analysis, resulting from these blind spots, weaken an organization's capacity to seize opportunities or interact effectively with its rivals, ultimately leading to an erosion in the organization's market position and profitability.[7] The six impediments to effective competitor analysis include:

- misjudging industry and service area boundaries;
- poor identification of the competition;
- overemphasis on competitors' visible competence;
- overemphasis on where, rather than how, to compete;
- faulty assumptions about the competition; and
- paralysis by analysis.[8]

A major contribution of competitor analysis is the development of a clear definition of the industry, industry segment, or service area. To avoid a focus that is too narrow, the industry, industry segment, and service area must be defined in the broadest terms that are useful. In today's health care environment, competition may come from very nontraditional competitors (outside the health care industry). For instance, based on their experience in the hotel business, the Marriott Corporation and the Hyatt Corporation have entered the long-term-care and retirement center markets. In the past, multihospital systems and nursing home chains dominated this industry segment. As competition increases from these nontraditional competitors, social activities, meals, and housekeeping may become more important competitive factors.

Typically, health care managers have focused their analysis on locally served markets. They were insulated from other health care organizations outside their geographic service area; however, that is no longer the case. Market entry by competitors from outside the metropolitan area, the region, or the state is now quite common. For example, expansion by multihospital systems such as Columbia/HCA and Tenet represent serious new competitive challenges in many markets. A local or regional focus may lead to delays in recognizing changes in the service area boundaries.

Often, only cursory attention was given to other segments of the health care industry. Hospitals traditionally focused on acute care. They did not envision intermediate care or home care as a competing segment. Yet, because of length-of-stay issues, patients are now being sent to an intermediate-care or home-care situation outside the hospital's purview, which increases revenues to those organizations and decreases the hospital's revenues. Clearly, misjudging how the industry, industry segments, or service area is defined will lead to poor competitor analysis.

Another possible flaw of competitor analysis is the improper or poor identification of precisely which organizations are the competitors. In many cases, health care executives focus on a single established major competitor and ignore emerging or lesser known potential competitors. This is especially true when the perceived strengths of competitor organizations do not fit traditional measures or there is an inflexible commitment to historical critical success factors (traditional inpatient services instead of outpatient approaches). For example, traditional physicians may only regard other traditional medical practices as competitors and ignore emerging alternative health care practitioners.

Another problem in performing competitor analysis is the tendency to be concerned only with the visible activities of competitors. Less visible attributes and capabilities such as organizational structure, culture, human resources, service features, intellectual capital, management acumen, and strategy may cause misinterpretation of a competitor's strengths or strategic intent. Certainly the Mayo Clinic's strong culture of excellence has played an important role in shaping their strategic decisions. Similarly, in an environment of rapid change, intellectual capital represents a primary value-creation asset of the organization.[9] In addition, effective competitor analysis requires predicting how competitors plan to position themselves. Although often difficult, determining competitors' strategic intent is at the heart of competitor analysis. An effective competitor analysis should focus on what rivals *can* do with their resources, capabilities, and competencies—an extension of what competitors are currently doing—to include possible radical departures from existing strategies.[10]

Accurate and timely information concerning competitors is an extremely important first step in competitor analysis. Misjudging or underestimating competitors' resources, capabilities, or competencies is a serious misstep. Faulty assumptions can suggest inappropriate strategies for an organization. Poor environmental scanning perpetuates faulty assumptions.

Because of the quantity of data that can be collected concerning the external environment and competition, paralysis by analysis can occur. In environments undergoing profound change, volumes of data are generated and access to it becomes easier. Under such conditions, information overload is possible and separating the essential from the nonessential is often difficult. As a result, it should be emphasized that the intent of competitor analysis is to support strategic decision making; and over-analysis or "endless" analysis should be avoided. Competitor information must be focused and contribute to strategy formulation.

Service Area Competitor Analysis

Service area competitor analysis is a process of understanding the market and identifying and evaluating competitors. Together with the general trends and issues, service area competitor analysis must be synthesized into the strategic issues facing the organization. The synthesis will be an explicit input into the formulation of the organization's strategy.

As illustrated in Exhibit 3–1, the process of service area competitor analysis begins with an understanding and specification of *services* or *service categories* the organization provides to its customers. Next, the service area must be identified. Then the service area structure or competitive dynamics should be assessed. Competitors providing services in the same category in and around the service area must be analyzed. Each of the organizations can be positioned against the important dimensions of the market and assessed as to their likely strategic moves. Finally, the results of the analysis must be synthesized and implications drawn. These conclusions will provide important information for strategy formulation.

Defining the Service Categories

The first step in service area competitor analysis is to specify the service categories to be analyzed. Many health care organizations have several service categories or products,

Exhibit 3–1 · Service Area Competitor Analysis

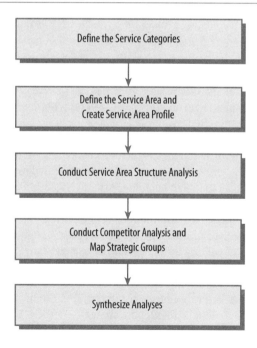

and each may have different geographic and demographic service areas. This is seldom an easy task, and the level of specificity will vary with the intent of the analysis. For a multihospital chain deciding to enter a new market, the service category may be defined as acute hospital care but for a rehabilitation hospital, the service category might be defined as physical therapy or orthopedic surgery. In addition, because many health care services can be broken down into more specific subservices, the level of service category specificity should be agreed on before analysis begins. For example, pediatric care may be broken down into well-baby care, infectious diseases, developmental pediatrics, pediatric hematology-oncology, and so on. Certainly pediatric hematology-oncology would have a far larger service area than well-baby care.

Another example of a service that requires a clear definition is the sub-acute care segment. Sub-acute care, sometimes termed the *middle ground* of health care, provides services for those patients who no longer require inpatient acute care, but need a higher level of care than can be provided in a skilled nursing facility or at home. There are multiple ways to segment this market that includes diverse post-acute care and rehabilitation services. An organization could select one or a combination of services to offer. For example, Community Psychiatric Centers has created a new sub-acute subsidiary, Transitional Hospitals, that will focus on ventilator-dependent patients. Transitional Hospital in Atlanta has selected complex medical cases—those discharged from intensive care—and treats them at a lower cost. Several of the largest nursing home chains, such as Beverly Enterprises and Hillhaven Corporation, have added chronically ill sub-acute care to their services. Living Centers of America, another long-term-care organization, decided to offer infusion therapy, wound care, and rehabilitation services. Thus, to have a clear idea of what is to be accomplished by the service area and competitor analysis, it is important to first understand and define the service category. From this delineation, the next phase of competitor analysis is better focused on direct and indirect (but potentially important) competitors.

Defining the Service Area

Health care organizations generally focus their environmental analyses on their service areas or community. The *service area* is considered to be the geographic area surrounding the health care provider. It is usually limited by fairly well defined geographic borders. Beyond these borders, services may be difficult to render due to distance, cost, time, and so on. Therefore, a health care organization must not only define its service area but also analyze in detail all relevant and important aspects of the service area including economic, demographic, psychographic (lifestyle), and disease pattern characteristics.[11] Contracts with managed-care companies will also influence consumer's access decisions. This information will help in positioning the service category and tailoring the service to the needs of the service area.

Although service area is defined by customers, it is based on the health care providers that are available. For example, in many rural areas there is no doctor, no hospital, no long-term-care facility. People who live there have to travel to the nearest town that has a doctor. The service area for that doctor may be very large in terms of geography (although have few residents). In other more densely populated areas, consumers will drive past some providers to seek health care from the doctor, hospital, long-term-care, or urgent-care facility that they prefer.

Customer preferences dictate one component of service area definition. A number of interacting variables determine customer preference. For instance, the distance that consumers are willing to travel for health care depends on a variety of factors including the kind of care, location of the provider, and the number of competitors that they pass on the way to receive care. Consumers are "shopping" for health care today because of the higher costs of care including insurance premiums, out-of-pocket costs (co-pays and percentages), and wait-time costs.

Exhibit 3–2 models the determinants of a service area including the consumer variables and the market (provider) variables. For the consumer, the services need could include health care that is preventive, alternative, routine, episodic, acute, or chronic. Usage rate would be related to a variety of economic, demographic, psychographic, and

Exhibit 3–2 • Service Area Determinants

Consumer Determinants

Services Type	Personal Values
Usage Rates	Social Values
Brand Predisposition	Epistemic Values
Preferred Image	Past Experiences
Personal State of Health	

Service Area

Location	Services Available
• Drive Time	Service
• Transportation	• Friendliness
• Parking Ease/Access	• Caring
Convenience	• Wait Time
• Hours of Operation	Quality of Information
• Safety	• Phone Consults
• Wayfinding	• Brochures
Price Level	• Instructions
Image	

Market/Organization Determinants

disease pattern variables. Brand predisposition indicates the consumer has a preference for some health care providers over others. For example, if there is only one hospital in town, and the consumer does not like its "looks," location, or perceived quality of care, he or she may prefer to drive to the nearest larger city. For routine medical care, some consumers prefer to go to specialists only, primary-care doctors only, or clinics that have primary-care physicians and specialists, although others prefer physician assistants or nurse practitioners. These different consumer preferences will be determinants in defining the service area.

Another group of consumer determinants will be related to personal factors such as personal and social values, epistemic (knowledge) values, past experiences, and the individual's personal state of health. In concert, these variables develop the individual's preferences for health care providers. However, if providers are not available (there are limited or no options in the immediate area), the consumer will travel greater distances to gain the desired care.

Shopping options are controlled by the health care structure. The market and organizations within it determine what will be offered or made available to the consumer. The "market" contains health care providers in a variety of locations that bear on convenience and image. Location includes drive time from home (or increasingly work), availability of transportation, as well as parking ease and access. Convenience may be hours of operation, safety, availability of food, signs to assist in finding the way, and so on. Image for the market entails positioning among the various providers. The health care provider might have the image of being more caring, friendlier, or more high tech; or it may be perceived as attracting desirable or undesirable demographic, socioeconomic, or ethnic groups. The organization itself has an image of the services (health care provided) as well as the service and the quality of information provided. Location, convenience, and image are all in relationship to the other providers in the area, including those within driving distance and those that are remote but perceived as providing better quality, more services, or some other desirable characteristic.

Managed care interrupts the normal decision making by consumers. An employed individual today usually has some choice in health care insurance. The employer may offer one or more different "plans." Once the consumer has selected a managed-care plan, the ability to choose becomes more restrictive. And, in fact, the more the HMO attempts to control health care costs (structures health care delivery more), the more restricted the choice becomes for consumers.

Determining Geographic Boundaries Understanding the geographic boundaries is important in defining the service area, but is often difficult because of the variety of services offered. For instance, in an acute-care hospital, the service area for cardiac services may be the entire state or region, whereas the service area for the emergency room might be only a few blocks. Thus, for a health care organization that offers several service categories, it may be necessary to conduct several service area analyses. For example the Des Moines, Iowa, market has two geographic components: the metropolitan area of the city and the suburbs of Polk County (population approximately 350,000), as well as the forty-three primarily rural counties of central Iowa that surround the capital (population about 1,000,000). The opportunities and threats for each of these multiple service areas may be quite different; therefore, considerable effort is directed toward understanding and analyzing the nature of the health care organization's various service areas. At the same time, for some organizations, defining only one service category may suffice (such as in the case of a long-term-care facility).

Service areas will be different for different organizations. For instance, a national for-profit chain may define its service area quite generally, whereas an individual hospital, home health care organization, or HMO may define its service area much more specifically. Most health services are provided and received within a well-defined service area, where the competition is clearly identified and critical forces for the survival of the organization originate. For instance, hospitals in rural areas have well-defined service areas for their particular services. These hospitals must be familiar with the needs of the population and with other organizations providing competing services. Similarly, the service areas for public health departments vary within a state, depending on whether they are metropolitan or rural, and may suggest quite different opportunities and threats.[12]

Determining the geographic boundaries of the service area may be highly subjective and is usually based on patient histories, the reputation of the organization, available technology, physician recognition, and so on. In addition, geographic impediments such as a river, mountains, and limited access highways can influence the service area definition. The definition of communities used in community health assessments (see Perspective 3–3) is often helpful in determining a service area.

Service Area Profile Once the geographic boundaries of the service area have been defined, a general service area profile should be developed. Capturing the dimensions of a service area requires tapping and synthesizing information and data from various sources:

- both quantitative and qualitative data for framing and understanding a service area (see Perspective 3–4);
- population-based health status data (specifics of the various health dimensions of an entire population and its subgroups); and
- health services utilization data (specifics on the patterns and frequency of health service use for various health conditions by different groups of individuals in the population).[13]

The service area profile includes key economic, demographic, psychographic (lifestyle), and community health status indicators. Relevant economic information may include income distribution, major industries and employers, types of businesses and institutions, economic growth rate, seasonality of businesses, unemployment statistics, and so on. Demographic variables most commonly used in describing the service area include age, sex, race, marital status, education level, mobility, religious affiliation, and occupation.

Psychographic or lifestyle variables are often better predictors of consumer behavior than demographic variables and include values, attitudes, lifestyle, social class, or personality (referred to as *mind-set/belief* in Perspective 3–3). For example, consumers in the service area might be classified as medically conservative or medically innovative. Medical conservatives are only interested in traditional health care—drugs, therapies, and diagnostics they are familiar with—whereas medically innovative individuals are

Perspective 3–3

Defining a Community to Assess Community Health Status

A community is a group of organizations or people who share a common characteristic, interest, commitment, or living condition within a larger group. Communities may be defined in terms of the following criteria:

1. *Geographic Placement.* The community is defined by proximity or physical boundaries (e.g., neighborhood, health district, areas within clear geographic confines such as rivers or mountains).

2. *Enrolled Population.* The community is defined by the individuals enrolled within a given program or project—by the clients or individuals (not families) who have given consent for records to be kept (including demographic and clinical information) and who receive ongoing services from the program (e.g., Medicaid, HMO).

3. *Social Interaction.* The community is defined by people who congregate in a particular setting (e.g., school, work, place of worship).

4. *Mind-Set or Belief.* The community is defined by people who share specific and similar attitudes, lifestyles, or sets of beliefs (e.g., cultural groups, political parties, religious sects, people with a particular philosophy of health such as those who use alternative therapies).

5. *Political District.* The community is defined according to the political boundaries determined or approved by legislative or government entities (e.g., a political district, city council district, congressional district, school board district).

6. *Shared Experience.* The community is defined by the common problems or shared experiences of individuals (e.g., those with AIDS, those in poverty, war veterans).

For a health care organization, community might be thought of as a "sphere of accountability" (those for whom the organization assumes accountability) or "sphere of influence" (those whose health the organization is able to positively influence). For example, the sphere of accountability and sphere of influence for any health care network will be the same. However, if community is defined as the enrolled population of any one health "network," that network will be limited in its ability to impact many community health status indicators unless it interacts with the communities of other networks' enrolled populations.

Changing structures to support community health ultimately requires that a community be defined geographically, such that all health providers work together to affect those community factors that influence the enrolled populations of all health systems in the area. In short, even if the community health care system is reconfigured to incorporate various health networks, collaborations among these networks and their geographic community will still be necessary.

Source: Voluntary Hospitals of America, Inc., *Community Health Assessment: A Process for Positive Change* (Irving, Texas: VHA, 1993), p. 60.

willing (often eager) to try new alternative drugs, therapies, or diagnostics. Although medically independent individuals are high in self-esteem and assertiveness, often questioning one physician's diagnosis and seeking a second opinion, medically dependent individuals follow what the doctor prescribes exactly and would never think of questioning "doctors orders."

Perspective 3–4

Marketing Research for Health Care Organizations Needs to Look Beyond Statistics

It is important for health care organizations to go beyond traditional databases and health status indicators to understand their patients and markets. Census data and morbidity and mortality data lack the richness of research that asks consumers how they feel about health care. Focus groups, household interviews, questionnaires, town meetings, and informal gatherings provide qualitative data lacking in traditional assessments of community needs.

"The kind of information you collect in a more informal consumer survey is truly more useful," according to Jeffrey C. Bauer, Ph.D., of the Bauer Group in Hill Rose, Colorado. "It includes people's perceptions, their gut-level feelings about health care—things that don't show up in databases. You can analyze data all day and all night and never really know what people's preferences would be."

Stanford University Hospital used psychographic profiling to illustrate that different health care personality "types" rate the same services dif-ferently. Two personality types that dominate Stanford University Hospital's service area tend to rate room accommodations, nursing, and physician care lower than other health care personality types, regardless of the hospital used. An attitude and behavior shared by these two groups is their propensity to gather health care information in order to choose from health care alternatives. According to Frederick Navarro, marketing research manager at Stanford, "This information has shown the hospital the importance of understanding its customers' needs and wants, and that simply trying to provide more services is not the whole answer."

Source: Jill L. Sherer, "Assessment Data Evaluated," *Hospitals and Health Networks* 67, no. 14 (July 20, 1993), p. 38; and Frederick Navarro, "Psychographic Research Enhances Community Profile," *The AHSM Academy Bulletin* (January 1993), p. 7.

Health status of the service area is also important in considering its viability, as disease may be related to age, occupation, environment, or economics. Health status includes all types of data normally considered to represent the physical and mental well-being of a population. The important variables in developing a service area profile are summarized in Exhibit 3–3.[14]

Service Area Structure Analysis

Harvard's Michael E. Porter developed a framework for analyzing the external environment through an examination of the competitive nature of the industry. Such an analysis provides considerable insight into the attractiveness of the service category within the service area and provides a framework for understanding the competitive dynamics.

Porter suggested that the level of competitive intensity within the industry is the most critical factor in an organization's environment. In Porter's model, intensity is a function of the threat of new entrants to the market, the level of rivalry among existing organizations, the threat of substitute products and services, the bargaining power of

Exhibit 3–3 · **Service Area Profile Variables**

Economic	Demographic	Psychographic	Health Status Indicators[†]
Income Distribution	Age Profile	Medical Conservatives	**Mortality**
Foundation of Economy	Sex	Medical Innovators	Deaths from all causes per 100,000 population
Major Employers	Average Income	Medical Dependent	Motor vehicle crash deaths per 100,000 population
Types of Businesses	Race Distribution	Personal Health	Suicides per 100,000 population
Growth Rate	Marital Status	Controllers	Female breast cancer deaths per 100,000 population
Seasonality	Education Level		Stroke deaths per 100,000 population
Unemployment	Religious Affiliation		Cardiovascular deaths per 100,000 population
	Population Mobility		Work-related injury deaths per 100,000 population
	Stage in Family Life Cycle		Lung cancer deaths per 100,000 population
	Occupational Mix		Heart disease deaths per 100,000 population
	Residence Locations		Homicides per 100,000 population
			Infant deaths per 1,000 live births

Notifiable Disease Incidence
AIDS incidence per 100,000 population
Tuberculosis incidence per 100,000 population
Measles incidence per 100,000 population
Primary and secondary syphilis incidence per 100,000 population

Risk Indicators
Percentage of live born infants weighing under 2,500 grams at birth
Births to adolescents as a percentage of live births
Percentage of mothers delivering infants who received no prenatal care
    in first trimester of pregnancy
Percentage of children under 15 years of age living in families at or
    below the poverty level
Percentage of persons living in areas exceeding the U.S. EPA air quality
    standards

[†] From *A Guide for Assessing and Improving Health Status: Community . . . Planting the Seeds for Good Health*, (1993), p. 8. Reprinted by permission of Hospital & Health-system Association of Pennsylvania.

---

buyers (customers), and the bargaining power of suppliers.[15] The strength and impact of these five forces must be carefully monitored and assessed. As illustrated in Exhibit 3–4, Porter's industry structural analysis may be adapted to service areas to understand the competitive forces for health care organizations.

Threat of New Entrants New entrants into a market are typically a threat to existing organizations because they increase the intensity of competition. New entrants may have substantial resources and often attempt to rapidly gain market share. Such actions may force prices and profits down. The threat of a new competitor entering into a market depends on the industry or service area barriers. If the barriers are substantial, the threat of entry is low. Porter identified several barriers to entry that may protect organizations already serving a market:

1. existing organization's economies of scale;
2. existing product or service differentiation;

Exhibit 3–4 • **Service Area Structural Analysis**

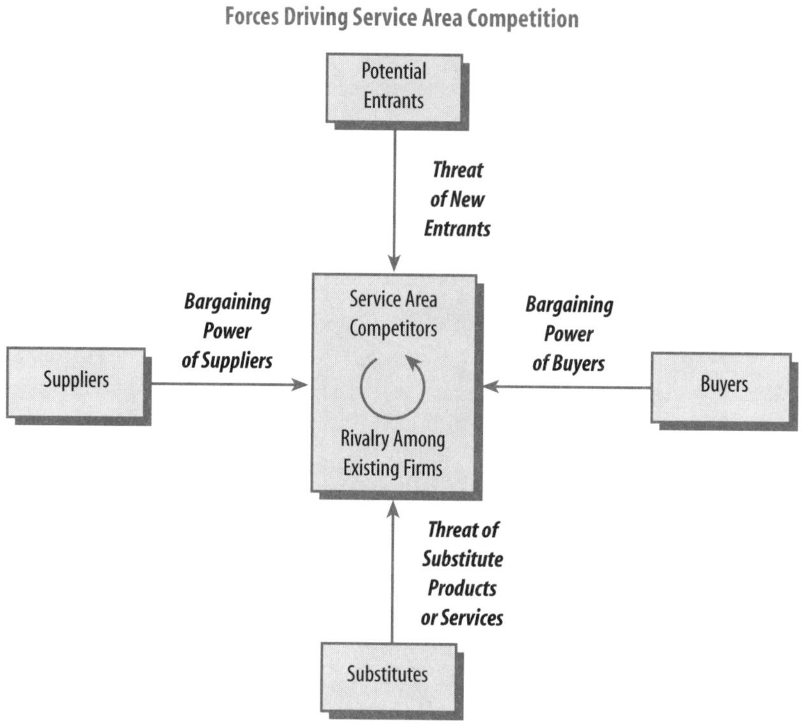

Forces Driving Service Area Competition

Source: From Michael E. Porter, *Competitive Strategy: Techniques for Analyzing Industries and Competitors.* Copyright © 1980. Adapted with the permission of The Free Press, a division of Simon & Schuster.

3. capital requirements needed to compete;
4. switching costs—the one-time costs for buyers to switch from one provider to another;
5. access to distribution channels;
6. cost advantages (independent of scale) of established competitors; and
7. government and legal constraints.

These seven barriers may be assessed to determine the current or expected level of competition within an industry or service area. In health care markets, the barriers to entry for new "players" may be substantial. Consolidation (creation of large health care systems) and system integration (control of physicians and insurers) may make entry into a particular service area difficult because of economies and cost advantages. In an effort to create cost efficiencies, managed care has had the effect of limiting the ease of entry into markets. Where managed-care penetration is high, market entry by new competitors will be more difficult because switching costs for some populations are high. However, the difficulty of adding new service categories for existing organizations in a managed-care market may be lessened. Service categories may be added to better serve a captured (managed-care) market.

Intensity of Rivalry Among Existing Organizations Organizations within an industry are mutually dependent because the strategy of one organization affects the others. Rivalry occurs because competitors attempt to improve their position. Typically, actions by one competitor foster reactions by others. Intense rivalry is the result of:

- numerous or equally balanced competitors;
- slow industry (service area) growth;
- high fixed or storage costs;
- a lack of differentiation or switching costs;
- capacity augmented in large increments;
- diverse competitors—diverse objectives, personalities, strategies, and so on;
- high strategic stakes—competitors place great importance on achieving success within the industry; and
- high exit barriers.

Often consolidation has created several balanced large health care systems in a service area. For example, in the St. Louis market described in the Introductory Incident, consolidation has resulted in three large balanced integrated systems (plus an additional smaller system) with high fixed costs and extremely high strategic stakes. For some markets, consolidation has resulted in competition between large for-profit and not-for-profit systems (see Perspective 3–5). Additionally, because of managed care, switching costs for consumers are high. Because many markets have supported too many providers in the past, the strategic stakes are extremely high. Most experts agree that further consolidations are likely and rivalry will intensify.

Threat of Substitute Products and Services For many products and services there are a variety of substitutes. These products and services perform the same function as established products. Substitute products limit returns to an industry because at some price point consumers will switch to alternative products and services. Usually, the more diverse the industry, the more likely there will be substitute products and services. A major substitution taking place in health care has been the switch from inpatient care to outpatient alternatives. In addition, alternative therapies such as massage therapy, acupuncture, biofeedback, and so on are increasingly substituted for traditional health care (see Perspective 3–6).

Bargaining Power of Customers Buyers of products and services attempt to obtain the lowest price possible while demanding high quality and better service. If buyers are powerful, then the competitive rivalry will be high. A buyer group is powerful if it:

- purchases large volumes;
- concentrates purchases in an industry (service area);
- purchases products that are standard or undifferentiated;
- has low switching costs;
- earns low profits (low profits force lower purchasing costs);
- poses a threat of backward integration;
- has low quality requirements (the quality of the products purchased by the buyer is unimportant to the final product's quality); and
- has enough information to gain bargaining leverage.

Perhaps the greatest change in the nature of the health care industry in the past decade has been the growing power of the buyers. Managed-care organizations purchase services in large volume and control provider choices. The increasing power of the buyers has fueled system integration as well as blurring of providers and insurers.

Bargaining Power of Suppliers Much like the power of buyers, suppliers can affect the intensity of competition through their ability to control prices and the quality of materials they supply. Through these mechanisms, suppliers can exert considerable pressure on an industry. Factors that make suppliers powerful tend to mirror those making buyers powerful. Suppliers tend to be powerful if:

- there are few suppliers;
- there are few substitutes;
- the suppliers' products are differentiated;
- the product or service supplied is important to the buyer's business;
- the buyer's industry is not considered an important customer; and
- the suppliers pose a threat of forward integration (entering the industry).

Traditionally suppliers to the health care industry have tended not to exercise a great deal of control over the industry. However, physicians and other health care professionals have always been important and powerful "suppliers" to the industry because of their importance to health care institutions. Because of the nature of managed care, the physician remains the "gatekeeper" to the system and plays a crucial role in controlling consumer choice. This supplier power has added pressure to include physicians in system integration through the purchase of primary-care individual and group practices by hospital systems.

Porter's approach is a powerful tool for assessing the level of competitive intensity within the health care service area. Porter's framework for analyzing the external environment is applied to a nursing home in Exhibit 3–5.

| Perspective 3–5

For-Profits and Not-for-Profits
Compete in Charleston and Richmond Markets

Both Charleston and Richmond are good examples of markets where consolidation is creating several balanced, highly competitive health care systems polarized along ownership lines (for-profit versus not-for-profit). Large balanced systems will increase the competitive rivalry with extremely high strategic stakes. These markets have been cited as examples of many hospital markets of the future, where systems with competing ideologies will do battle. The key events changing the Charleston and Richmond markets are profiled using time lines.

Source: From David Burda, "No Prisoners: For-Profit vs. Not-for-profit Hospital Skirmishes Intensify," *Modern Healthcare* Vol. 26, No. 17 (1996), pp. 35–41. Copyright Crain Communications, Inc., 740 N. Rush Street, Chicago, IL 60611. Reprinted with permission.

Key events in changing landscape of Charleston, S.C., hospital market

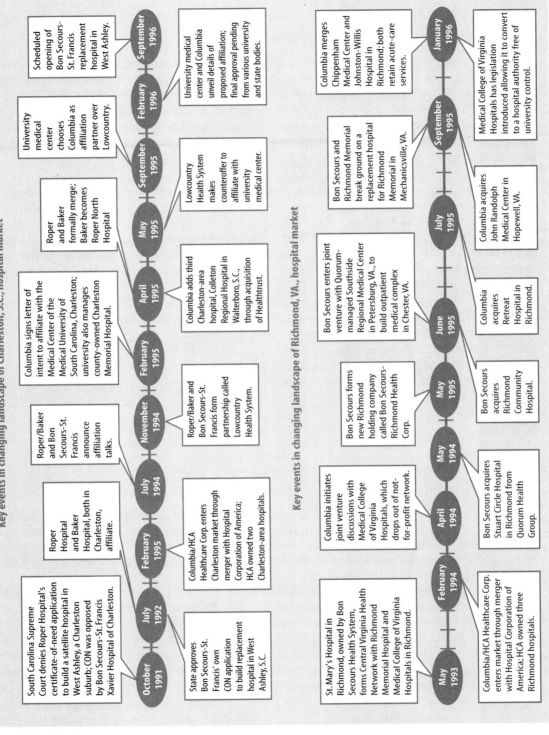

October 1991
South Carolina Supreme Court denies Roper Hospital's certificate-of-need application to build a satellite hospital in West Ashley, a Charleston suburb; CON was opposed by Bon Secours–St. Francis Xavier Hospital of Charleston.

July 1992
State approves Bon Secours–St. Francis' own CON application to build replacement hospital in West Ashley, S.C.

February 1995
Roper Hospital and Baker Hospital, both in Charleston, affiliate.

July 1994
Columbia/HCA Healthcare Corp. enters Charleston market through merger with Hospital Corporation of America; HCA owned two Charleston-area hospitals.

November 1994
Roper/Baker and Bon Secours–St. Francis announce affiliation talks.

Roper/Baker and Bon Secours–St. Francis form partnership called Lowcountry Health System.

February 1995
Columbia signs letter of intent to affiliate with the Medical Center of the Medical University of South Carolina, Charleston; university also manages county-owned Charleston Memorial Hospital.

April 1995
Columbia adds third Charleston-area hospital, Colleton Regional Hospital in Walterboro, S.C., through acquisition of Healthtrust.

May 1995
Roper and Baker formally merge; Baker becomes Roper North Hospital

September 1995
Lowcountry Health System makes counteroffer to affiliate with university medical center.

February 1996
University medical center chooses Columbia as affiliation partner over Lowcountry.

September 1996
Scheduled opening of Bon Secours–St. Francis replacement hospital in West Ashley.

University medical center and Columbia unveil details of proposed affiliation; final approval pending from various university and state bodies.

Key events in changing landscape of Richmond, VA., hospital market

May 1993
Columbia/HCA Healthcare Corp. enters market through merger with Hospital Corporation of America; HCA owned three Richmond hospitals.

February 1994
St. Mary's Hospital in Richmond, owned by Bon Secours Health System, forms Central Virginia Health Network with Richmond Memorial Hospital and Medical College of Virginia Hospitals in Richmond.

April 1994
Bon Secours acquires Stuart Circle Hospital in Richmond from Quorum Health Group.

May 1994
Columbia initiates joint venture discussions with Medical College of Virginia Hospitals, which drops out of not-for-profit network.

Bon Secours forms new Richmond holding company called Bon Secours–Richmond Health Corp.

May 1995
Bon Secours acquires Richmond Community Hospital.

June 1995
Bon Secours enters joint venture with Quorum-managed Southside Regional Medical Center in Petersburg, VA., to build outpatient medical complex in Chester, VA.

Columbia acquires Retreat Hospital in Richmond.

July 1995
Columbia acquires John Randolph Medical Center in Hopewell, VA.

September 1995
Bon Secours and Richmond Memorial break ground on a replacement hospital for Richmond Memorial in Mechanicsville, VA.

Medical College of Virginia Hospitals has legislation introduced allowing it to convert to a hospital authority free of university control.

January 1996
Columbia merges Chippenham Medical Center and Johnston-Willis Hospital in Richmond; both retain acute-care services.

Perspective 3–6

Market Opening to the Nontraditional

Several shifts in the external environment have created opportunities in alternative or nontraditional medicine. These opportunities are the result of a growing acceptance of some unconventional forms of medicine, such as chiropractic therapy, massage therapy, alternative wound care, nonsurgical cardiac care, and mind/body medicine (mind/body medicine utilizes nutrition, massage therapy, meditation, and other natural stimuli to treat an array of illnesses, from arthritis to cancer).

Environmental shifts that have opened up this growing market include changes in the health care delivery system, institutional support, and changes in the public's attitudes. The phenomenal growth of outpatient clinics away from the influence of traditional medicine practiced in a hospital has provided a setting conducive to the growth of unconventional forms of medicine. The serious consideration of including alternative medicine and technologies in overall health care reform has fostered the growth of nontraditional approaches. The National Institutes of Health's Office of Alternative Medicine has been given a $2 million bud-

get to explore previously unaccepted and unconventional medical treatments. In addition, consumers appear to be giving wider support to alternative medicine. A *New England Journal of Medicine* survey indicated that one-third of 1,500 respondents to a survey were treated with unconventional therapy. Americans spend over $15 billion a year on alternative medicine.

Despite the controversy surrounding alternative medicine, it appears that there will be many opportunities (and threats) for organizations in this growing market. No doubt, traditional health care organizations will carefully monitor these trends. In addition, it may be an opportune time for providers of alternative health care to form new relationships with hopsitals, nursing facilities, insurers, and managed-care groups.

Source: John Burns, "Market Opening up to the Non-Traditional," *Modern Healthcare* 23, no. 32 (August 9, 1993), pp. 96–98.

Conducting Competitor Analysis and Mapping Strategic Groups

The next step in the service area competitor analysis process (see Exhibit 3–1) is to evaluate the strengths and weakness of competitors, characterize their strategies, group competitors by the types of strategies they have exhibited, and predict competitive future moves or likely responses to strategic issues and initiatives by other organizations.

Competitor Strengths, Weaknesses, and Strategy In assessing the rivalry of the service area, the competitors were identified. Next, the strengths and weaknesses of each competitor should be specified and evaluated. Organizations have a unique resource endowment and a comparison with a given competitor will help to illuminate the relationship between them and to predict how they compete with (or respond to) each other in the market.[16] Clearly, the Massachusetts General–Brigham and Women's alliance (Partners HealthCare Systems), with $1.7 billion net operating revenue, $1.1 billion cash and investments, and 1,800 inpatient beds serving fully one-third of the population of eastern Massachusetts, has unique capabilities and resources when compared to either

Exhibit 3–5 · Using Porter's Industry Structure Analysis

The Hanover House Nursing Home, a skilled nursing facility, used differentiation as its major competitive advantage. In its early years, in a less regulated environment, the home was very profitable. As the facility began to age, and with increasingly stricter regulations for long-term care, profit margins began to deteriorate. The administrators of Hanover House used Porter's Industry Structure Analysis to better understand the forces in their external environment. The following is a summary of their analysis.

Threat of New Entrants

The supply of nursing homes and other long-term-care facilities is currently limited because there is a moratorium on additional beds within the geographic area. Competition is based on process or quality. If the moratorium is lifted, it will remain costly to enter the market because it is highly regulated. The greatest threat as a new entrant (when the moratorium is lifted) will be hospitals attempting to compensate for decreasing occupancy rates. Switching costs are low for hospitals (the same bed can be used for acute care or long-term care). Access to the distribution channel is high as hospitals have many of the required resources, including access to nurses, familiarity with the regulations, and capability to enter quickly (by converting acute-care beds to long-term care).

Intensity of Rivalry Among Existing Organizations

Although there is competition, the long-term-care industry is not fiercely competitive. Hanover House has six competitors—Mary Lewis Convalescence Center, Hillhaven, Altamont Retirement Community, St. Martins in the Pines, Lake Villa, and Kirkwood—that have relatively stable market shares. Because the service has both quality and dollar value, there is the opportunity to differentiate, and switching costs are high for the consumer. It is a highly regulated area and, therefore, not a great deal of diversity among competitors is apparent. The long-term-care industry is maturing but remains a rapid-growth industry driven by demographic and social trends (the graying of America and the deterioration of the extended family). The most significant factor creating rivalry is the high fixed assets, which make exit difficult and success important.

Threat of Substitute Products and Services

There are few substitute products for nursing home care. Home care is a substitute but an increasingly less available alternative because of the mobility and dissolution of the family unit. Other alternatives include nonskilled homes, retirement housing, and domiciliaries. Increased costs and DRGs have virtually eliminated hospitals as an alternative. On balance, substitutes do not appear to be a strong force in the nursing home industry.

Bargaining Power of Customers

The power of the customer in the industry is generally high. The major consumer, the government, purchases over 45 percent of nursing home care and regulates reimbursement procedures as well as the industry. Therefore, significant levels of information are available. In addition, for private-pay customers, the purchase represents a significant investment and comparison shopping is prevalent. Product differentiation tends to reduce buying power but relatively low switching costs and government involvement make nursing home care a buyers' market.

Bargaining Power of Suppliers

Because the product is simultaneously produced and consumed in service industries, labor is the major supplier in the nursing home industry. Although Hanover House is unionized, it has maintained good labor relations, and the union is not particularly powerful. Most who work in long-term care have selected the field to satisfy their need to care for others or make a contribution rather than to earn large salaries. Suppliers are not a dominant force in the nursing home industry.

Source: Elaine Asper, "Hanover House Nursing Home," an unpublished case study.

New England Medical Center, which is without substantial cash resources, or Cambridge Hospital, a major public facility. Therefore, evaluation of competitors' strengths and weaknesses provide clues as to their future strategies and to areas where competitive advantage may be gained.

Both quantitative and qualitative information may be used. Competitor information is not always easy to obtain, and it is often necessary to draw conclusions from sketchy information. A list of possible competitor strengths and weaknesses is presented in

Exhibit 3–6. Such information may be obtained through local newspapers, trade journals, focus groups with customers and stakeholders, consultants who specialize in the industry, securities analysts, outside health care professionals, and so on.

Identification of competitor strengths and weaknesses will aid in speculating on competitor strategic moves. The range of possible competitive actions available to organizations varies from tactical moves, such as price cuts, promotions, and service improvements that require few resources, to strategic moves, such as service category/area changes, facilities expansions, strategic alliances, and new product or service introductions that require more substantial commitments of resources and are more difficult to reverse. Such competitive actions represent clear, offensive challenges that invite competitor responses.[17]

Critical Success Factor Analysis   Critical success factor analysis involves the identification and analysis of a limited number of areas within an industry in which the organization must achieve at a high level if it is to be successful. The rationale behind critical success factor analysis is that there are five or six areas in which the organization must perform well and that it is possible to identify them through careful analysis of the environment. In addition, critical success factor analysis may be used to examine new market opportunities.

Typically, once the critical success factors have been identified, several objectives are developed for each success factor. At that point, a strategy may be developed around the objectives. Important in critical success factor analysis is the establishment of linkages among the environment, the critical success factors, the objectives, and the strategy. In addition, it is also important to evaluate competitors on these critical success factors.

Exhibit 3–6 • **Potential Competitor Strengths and Weaknesses**

Potential Strengths	Potential Weaknesses
• Distinctive competence	• Lack of clear strategic direction
• Financial resources	• Deteriorating competitive position
• Good competitive skills	• Obsolete facilities
• Positive image	• Subpar profitability
• Acknowledged market leader	• Lack of managerial depth and talent
• Well-conceived functional area strategies	• Missing key skills or competencies
• Achievement of economies of scale	• Poor track record in implementing strategies
• Insulated from strong competitive pressures	• Plagued with internal operating problems
• Proprietary technology	• Vulnerable to competitive pressures
• Cost advantages	• Falling behind in R&D
• Competitive advantages	• Too narrow a product/service line
• Product/service innovation abilities	• Weak market image
• Proven management	• Below-average marketing skills
• Ahead on experience curve	• Unable to finance needed changes in strategy
	• Higher overall costs relative to key competitors

Indeed, excellence in any (or several) of these factors may be the basis of competitive advantage. Further, these factors form the fundamental dimensions of strategy.

Organizational strategies can differ in a wide variety of ways. Michael Porter identified several strategic dimensions that capture the possible differences among an organization's strategic options in a given service area:

- *specialization:* the degree to which the organization focuses its efforts in terms of the number of product categories, the target market, and size of its service area;
- *reputation:* the degree to which it seeks name recognition rather than competition based on other variables;
- *service/product quality:* the level of emphasis on the quality of its offering to the marketplace;
- *technological leadership:* the degree to which it seeks superiority in diagnostic and therapeutic equipment and procedures;
- *vertical integration:* the extent of value added as reflected in the level of forward and backward integration;
- *cost position:* the extent to which it seeks the low-cost position through efficiency programs and cost-minimizing facilities and equipment;
- *service:* the degree to which it provides ancillary services in addition to its main services;
- *price policy:* its relative price position in the market (although price positioning will usually be related to other variables such as cost position and product quality, price is a distinct strategic variable that must be treated separately); and
- *relationship with the parent company:* requirements concerning the behavior of the unit based on the relationship between a unit and its parent company. (The nature of the relationship with the parent will influence the objectives by which the organization is managed, the resources available to it, and perhaps determine some operations or functions that it shares with other units.)[18]

Strategic Groups Service area analysis concentrates on the characteristics of the specific geographic market, whereas strategic group analysis concentrates on the characteristics of the strategies of the organizations competing within a given service area. Strategic groups have been studied in many different industries.[19] A *strategic group* is a number of organizations within the same industry making similar decisions in key areas. The grouping of organizations according to strategic similarities and differences among competitors can aid in understanding the nature of competition and facilitate strategic decision making. There are four implications of the strategic group concept.

1. Organizations pursue different strategies within service categories and service areas. Creating competitive advantage is often a matter of selecting an appropriate basis on which to compete.
2. Organizations within a strategic group are each other's primary or direct competitors. As Bruce Henderson has noted, "Organizations most like yours are the most dangerous."
3. Strategic group analysis can indicate other formulas for success for a service category. Such insight may broaden a manager's view of important market needs.

4. Strategic group analysis may indicate important market dimensions or niches that are not being capitalized on by the existing competitors. Lack of attention to critical success factors by other competitive organizations offering the same or a similar service may provide an opportunity for management to differentiate its services.

Organizations within a group follow the same or similar strategy along the strategic dimensions. Group membership defines the essential characteristics of an organization's strategy. Within a service category or service area, there may be only one strategic group (if all the organizations follow the same strategy) or there may be many different groups. Usually, however, there are a small number of strategic groups that capture the essential strategic differences among organizations in the service area.[20]

The analysis of competitors along key strategic dimensions can provide considerable insight into the nature of competition within the service area. Such an analysis complements Porter's structural analysis but provides some additional insights. As a means of gaining a broad picture of the types of organizations within a service area and the kinds of strategies that have proven viable, strategic group analysis can contribute to understanding the structure, competitive dynamics, and evolution of a service area as well as the issues of strategic management within it.[21] More specifically, the usefulness of strategic group analysis is that it:

- can be used to preserve information characterizing individual competitors that may be lost in studies using averaged and aggregated data;
- allows for the investigation of multiple competitors concurrently;
- allows assessment of the effectiveness of competitors' strategies over a wider range of variation than a single organization's experience affords;
- provides a means of summarizing information to bring key dimensions of strategy in high relief;[22] and
- captures the intuitive notion that "within-group" rivalry and "between-group" rivalry differ.[23]

When analyzing strategic groups, care must be taken to ensure that they are engaging in market-based competition. Many organizations may not be direct or primary competitors because of a different market focus. Organizations will have little motivation to engage each other competitively if they have limited markets in common. It is not unusual for organizations that serve completely different markets yet have similar strategic postures to be grouped together and assumed by analysts to be direct competitors when in fact they are not.[24] For example, a pediatric group practice affiliated with a children's hospital and a community health clinic emphasizing preventive and well care may serve the same population but not be direct competitors because of a different market focus.

Mapping Competitors   For any service category (broadly or narrowly defined) competitors within a service area may be *mapped* based on the critical success factors or important strategy dimensions. Exhibit 3–7 shows strategic groups of assisted-living organizations within a service area. Several strategic maps may be constructed demonstrating different strategic views of the service area. In addition, a single dimension may be so important as a critical factor for success that it may appear on several maps.

Exhibit 3–7 • **Service Area Assisted Living Competitors**

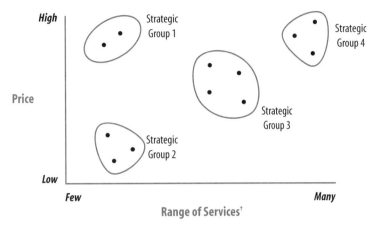

For this service area, assisted living organizations are pursuing four basic strategies—high price with highly specialized services (strategic group 1), low price with few ancillary services (strategic group 2), medium price with some (selected) services (strategic group 3), and high price with many services (strategic group 4). The primary (direct) competitors for these organizations are other organizations within their own strategic group. Customers who seek the attributes of one strategic group, such as highly specialized rehabilitation services, are unlikely to be attracted to another strategic group. These assisted-living organizations should change strategy cautiously as a decision to add services may move an organization to a new strategic group and therefore a new set of competitors. Note that in this example there may be an opportunity to enter or move toward a medium-cost, many services niche and become a strategic group of one

† Range of services includes skilled nursing, organized social activities, outings, physical therapy, education, rehabilitation, speech therapy, Alzheimer's care, nutritional services, infusion, pharmacy, homemaker services, live-ins, companions, and so on.

Source: From Raj-Shekhar G. Javalgi, Thomas W. Whipple, Mary K. McManamon, and Vicki L. Edick, "Hospital Image: A Correspondence Analysis Approach," *Journal of Health Care Marketing,* Vol. 12, No. 4 (December 1992), pp. 34–39. Reprinted with permission by American Marketing Association.

Likely Competitor Actions or Responses

Strategy formulation is future oriented, requiring that management anticipate the next strategic moves of competitors. These moves may be projected through an evaluation of competitor strengths and weaknesses, membership in strategic groups, and the characterization of past strategies. In many cases competitor strategic objectives are not difficult to project given past behaviors. Strategic thinking is a matter of anticipating what is next in a stream of consistent decisions.

As indicated in Chapter 1, a strategy may be viewed as the "behavior" of an organization. This behavior is the result of consistency in decision making, and decision consistency is central to strategy. Therefore, in determining competitors' future strategies, managers must look for the behavioral patterns that emerge from a stream of consistent decisions concerning the positioning of the organization in the past. A thorough analysis of the key strategic decisions of competitors will reveal their strategic intent. A *strategic decision time line* can be helpful in showing "the stream of decisions." A strategic decision time line for MedPartners, a physician-management company is illustrated in Exhibit 3–8. The likely strategic objectives and next strategic moves of MedPartners are

Exhibit 3–8 • Likely Objectives and Strategies of MedPartners

Strengths:
Aggressive management
Clear strategic focus
First-mover advantage
Favorable environmental forces
Largest physician-management company
HMO affiliations
Purchasing economies of scale
Market power
HEALTHSOUTH as stakeholder

Weaknesses:
Very rapid growth
Physicians' resistance to control
Bottom-line orientation
Financial difficulties of Caremark

Strategic Group: MedPartners has created a new strategic group with itself as the only member based on size and national scope. Other firms such as Coastal Physician Group, Pacific Physicians, PhyCor, and OccuSystems are substantially smaller with a focus on regional areas.

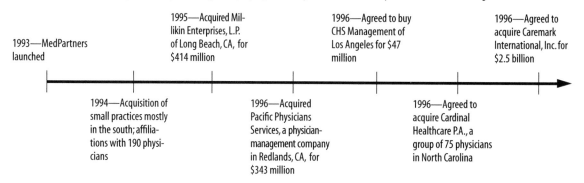

1993—MedPartners launched

1995—Acquired Millikin Enterprises, L.P. of Long Beach, CA, for $414 million

1996—Agreed to buy CHS Management of Los Angeles for $47 million

1996—Agreed to acquire Caremark International, Inc. for $2.5 billion

1994—Acquisition of small practices mostly in the south; affiliations with 190 physicians

1996—Acquired Pacific Physicians Services, a physician-management company in Redlands, CA, for $343 million

1996—Agreed to acquire Cardinal Healthcare P.A., a group of 75 physicians in North Carolina

General Conclusions: MedPartners is engaging in a market development growth strategy through acquisition (horizontal integration). Through this strategy, MedPartners has created the largest physician-management company in the United States with revenues of $4.4 billion and 7,250 employed or affiliated physicians.

Strategic Objectives: MedPartners is attempting to consolidate the physician practice management segment of the health care industry. Likely strategic objectives are to become the largest physician-management company, continue national development, create further purchasing economies of scale, develop further HMO affiliations, and acquire other physician-management companies as well as smaller single and group practices.

Strategic Moves: Likely next strategic moves will be to further increase market share through additional acquisition of physician practices. After a period of integrating recent purchases, MedPartners will probably engage in another round of aggressive acquisitions. Acquisitions will likely be targeted in geographic areas where managed-care penetration is significant and where MedPartners has little or no presence.

anticipated based on its perceived strengths and weaknesses, past strategies, and strategic group membership.

If an organization is planning an offensive move within a service area, an evaluation of competitor strengths and weaknesses, past strategies, strategic group membership, and assumed strategic objectives can anticipate the likely strategic response. For example, Columbia/HCA's analysis of the strategic response of competitors for a new market they are considering is an important variable in their expansion strategy.

Synthesizing the Analyses

In order to be useful for strategy formulation, general external environmental analysis (Chapter 2) and service area competitor analysis (as covered in this chapter) must be synthesized and then conclusions drawn. It is easy for strategic decision makers to be overwhelmed by information. To avoid paralysis by analysis, external environmental analysis should be summarized into key issues and trends including their likely impact.

Example of a Service Area Competitor Analysis

Service area competitor analysis is increasingly important for health care organizations. For-profit as well as not-for-profit health care organizations will have to understand the competitive dynamics of service categories and service areas. Exhibit 3–9 provides a comprehensive example of a service area competitor analysis beginning with service category definition and ending with a synthesis of the analyses. In this example, a large, national acute-care hospital chain is considering expanding into the northwest United States (the Portland, Oregon/Vancouver, Washington metropolitan area). Therefore, the hospital chain primarily has offensive objectives. A service area competitor analysis will help answer key questions such as market viability, opportunities for a new competitor, methods of market entry, and so on.

The Use of General Environmental and Competitor Analysis

In health care organizations today, there is a real understanding that not every organization will survive, that no one health care organization can be "everything to everybody." Understanding the external environment—including the general, health care, and competitor environments—is fundamental to strategic management and survival. A comprehensive general environmental analysis and service area competitor analysis combined with an assessment of the internal strengths and weaknesses (Chapter 4) and establishment of the directional strategies (Chapter 5) provide the basis for strategy formulation.

Summary and Conclusions

Service area competitor analysis is the second phase of environmental analysis. Service area competitor analysis is an increasingly important aspect of environmental analysis because of the changes that have taken place in the health care industry throughout the past decade. Specifically, service area competitor analysis is the process of identifying competitors, determining the strengths and weaknesses of rivals, and anticipating their moves. It provides a foundation for determining competitive advantage and subsequent strategy formulation.

Health care organizations engage in service area competitor analysis in order to obtain competitor information and for offensive and defensive reasons. However, analysts must be careful not to misjudge the service area boundaries, do a poor job of competitor identification, overemphasize visible competence, overemphasize where rather than how to compete, create faulty assumptions, or be paralyzed by analysis.

The process of service area competitor analysis includes an identification of the service category for analysis, service area structure analysis, competitor analysis, and a synthesis of the information collected and analyzed. Identification of the service category provides the basis for the analysis. Service categories may be defined very broadly or quite specifically and will vary with the intent of the analysis. An identification of the service area will

Exhibit 3–9 · Analysis of the Portland, Oregon/Vancouver, Washington Acute-Care Hospital Market

Service Area Competitive Analysis	Portland, Oregon/Vancouver, Washington
Service Category	**Comprehensive Acute Hospital Care**

Service Area—*General*[†]

- Market is changing rapidly.
- Market consists of Washington (OR), Multnomah (OR), Clackamas (OR), and Clark (WA) Counties.
- Providers have been consolidating for the past ten years and will continue to do so.
- Health plans are competing for market share.
- Long history and experience with managed care; penetration rate over 50 percent.
- More heavily dominated by managed care than most U.S. markets.
- Business has been a willing participant in managed care but has not driven the market; providers and health plans have initiated change.
- There is a buyers' market for specialty care.
- Twelve-year drop in the use of inpatient care.
- Outlook for various "players" is positive.

Service Area—*Economic*[†]

- Portland/Vancouver has a generally healthy economy.
- Primary growth in nonmanufacturing sector.
- Clark County growth in biotechnology, electronics, and computer industries.
- Economy characterized by small and medium-sized firms.
- Unemployment rate of less than 5 percent.
- Largest employers are in the public sector—federal and state government, public schools, and Oregon Health Sciences University.
- Large private employers—U.S. Bancorp, US West, Hewlett-Packard, and Intel.

Service Area—*Demographic*[†]

- Approximately 1.6 million people live in the four-county area.
- Population growth rate is approximately 3.5 percent.
- Proportion of elderly parallels the national average but is higher than other western states.
- Poverty rate is slightly below the national average: 40.4 percent under $25,000/year, 56.3 percent $25,000 to $100,000/year, and 3.4 percent over $100,000.
- Ethnic mix is 91.6 percent white, 3.2 percent Asian/Pacific Islander, 2.5 percent African American, 1 percent American Indian/Eskimo/Aleut, and 1.8 percent other.
- There is a mix of blue- and white-collar workers; growth is expected mainly in white-collar jobs.

Service Area—*Psychographic*

- Collaboration among health care providers is common.
- Outdoor lifestyle is preferred.
- Independence is valued.
- Innovative public policy solutions are frequent.

Service Area—*Health Status*[†]

- Survey data (1995) indicates 63 percent of the consumers report their health status as excellent or very good, 22 percent good, and 16 percent fair or poor.
- The Oregon Health Plan (provides universal coverage establishing a basic benefit package by ranking and limiting covered Medicaid services) has contributed to increased access to care for many low-income people.
- No unusual disease patterns exist.

[†] Sections adapted from Paul B. Ginsburg and Nancy J. Fasciano, eds. *The Community Snapshots Project: Capturing Health System Change* (Center for Studying Health System Change, a Robert Wood Johnson Foundation project monitoring health system change); Jill Marsden, "Portland, Oregon/Vancouver, Washington Site Visit Report," Health Policy Analysis Program, Department of Health Services, School of Public Health and Community Medicine, University of Washington, Seattle, Washington, 1996.

Exhibit 3–9 • **Continued**

Service Area Competitive Analysis	Portland, Oregon/Vancouver, Washington
Service Area Structure Analysis—*Threat of New Entrants*	• Trend of hospital downsizing and closures is likely to continue. • Few observers predict that there will be new entrants to the market in the near future. • Barriers to market entry are very high because of established systems.
Service Area Structure Analysis—*Intensity of Rivalry*[†]	• Providers are consolidating and integrating management and service delivery structures among entities that were once separate (e.g., hospitals and physician clinics). • Market has seen rapid development of provider alliances, as well as the horizontal and vertical integration of health systems. • Most of the seventeen facilities are linked in some way to three large delivery systems. • Legacy, Providence, and Kaiser each have 25 to 27 percent of the market. • Legacy owns four hospitals and has a strategic partnership with a fifth; Providence owns three hospitals; Kaiser owns two. • Clark United Providers (CUP) in Vancouver is positioning itself to become a fourth major system in the market. • All but two of the hospitals are not-for-profit organizations. • Tuality Community Hospital formed a physician-community-hospital organization (PCHO). • Each system has a relationship with a health maintenance organization (HMO) though ownership or contract. • Given the development of large systems, competition is keen and intensity of rivalry is high.
Service Area Structure Analysis—*Threat of Substitutes*	• Systems have engaged in vertical integration, and therefore traditional substitutes to the system are few. • Successful nontraditional health care substitutes (massage, acupuncture, etc.) will be subsumed by the large systems.
Service Area Structure Analysis—*Power of Customers*[†]	• The insurance market continues its push toward managed care. • Four competitive health plans dominate—Providence's Good Health Plan, Kaiser, BC/BS of Oregon, and PacifiCare. • Insurers are seeking greater financial security through closer relationships, involving cost- and risk-sharing contracts, with provider networks. • The insurance market is becoming consolidated—five HMOs comprise at least 100,000 enrollees statewide and three PPOs have an enrollment that is greater than 150,000. • Product lines of the managed-care companies are full range and similar. • Some businesses have negotiated aggressively with health plans, taking advantage of competition to obtain favorable rates and negotiate multiyear contracts. • Larger locally based employers tend to self-fund health care. • Some insurers are developing HMOs designed for self-fund employers. • Medicaid enrollees have eleven HMOs from which to choose. • Health care consumers are generally satisfied but not knowledgeable about their health care choices. • Choice remains an important factor for consumers. • Power of the customer is quite strong and will continue.

continued

[†] Sections adapted from Paul B. Ginsburg and Nancy J. Fasciano, eds. *The Community Snapshots Project: Capturing Health System Change* (Center for Studying Health System Change, a Robert Wood Johnson Foundation project monitoring health system change); Jill Marsden, "Portland, Oregon/Vancouver, Washington Site Visit Report," Health Policy Analysis Program, Department of Health Services, School of Public Health and Community Medicine, University of Washington, Seattle, Washington, 1996.

Exhibit 3–9 • **Continued**

Service Area Competitive Analysis	Portland, Oregon/Vancouver, Washington
Service Area Structure Analysis—*Power of Supplier*	• Purchasing consortia have developed. • Acquisition of group practices is occurring. • Because of the development of large systems, the power of suppliers remains relatively weak.
Competitor Analysis—*Competitor Strengths and Weaknesses**	• All the major players have similar strengths and weaknesses. • Strengths are the high degree of integration including physician groups, multiple hospital locations, managed-care affiliations, emphasis on quality and cost cutting, heavy investment in information technology. • All the health care providers have experience with managed-care. • Weaknesses include a fairly rigid structure for managed-care delivery (although that is changing); Providence, as a Catholic system, limits some procedures and emphasizes care for the medically poor, which may lead to financial problems; although there has been an emphasis on quality it is not driving the buying or selling of institutions; and the investment in technology is not yet producing the desired results.
Competitor Analysis—*Critical Success Factors*	• Vertical integration and the development of a large fully integrated system (primary-care feeders) is one success factor. • Ownership or affiliation with managed care is a second factor. • Information technology that provides critical paths, outcomes data, and so on is another.
Competitor Analysis—*Strategic Groups*	• There appear to be three strategic groups with movement toward two groups (CUP is duplicating the strategies of the three large systems). • The market is mature. • The primary strategy has been to build vertically integrated health care systems.
Competitor Analysis—*Mapping Competitors*	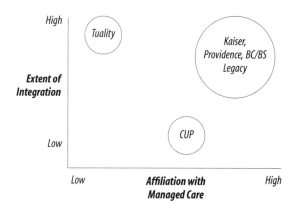

Portland/Vancouver Hospital Provider Market

Competitor Analysis—*Likely Responses*	• The market is fairly evenly divided. • Competition is already aggressive and the entrance of a new player will likely be met with considerable resistance.

*Executives more familiar with the local market would identify strengths and weaknesses for *each* competitor.

Exhibit 3–9 · **Continued**

Service Area Competitive Analysis	Portland, Oregon/Vancouver, Washington
Competitor Analysis—*Likely Responses (cont.)*	• As prices and products grow more alike, competition will hinge on the issue of customer service and other value-added factors, such as breadth of provider panels and quality of care. • Kaiser has already contracted with community physicians and PacifiCare to enlarge its focus beyond large clinics.
Synthesis	• This is a changing and highly competitive market. • Risk sharing is accelerating as the distinction between insurer and provider functions blur. • The health system is characterized by widespread optimism. • Care is generally of high quality. • Managed care and capitation will continue to grow. • The provider community will become further consolidated. • Further vertical and horizontal integration within health systems is expected. • Consolidation is expected to strengthen physicians' bargaining power with health plans. • Continued development of direct contracting by physician groups and vertically integrated provider networks will bring them head-to-head with the health plans. • The acute-care hospital market appears to have few uncovered niches or discontinuities. • Entry into this market should only be initiated through a purchase or cooperation strategy. • Competition within the market will require continued integration (physician groups), an emphasis on quality, and the further development of managed-care options.

include establishing geographic boundaries and developing a service area profile that might include economic, demographic, psychographic, and disease pattern information.

Service area structure analysis may be accomplished through a Porter-type analysis: evaluating the threat of new entrants into the market, the service area rivalry, the power of the buyers, the power of the suppliers, and the threat of substitute products or services. Next, competitor analysis should be undertaken. Comprehensive competitor analysis would include an identification and evaluation of competitor strengths and weaknesses, competitor strategy, strategic groups, critical success factors, and likely competitor actions and responses. Finally, service area and competitor information should be synthesized and strategic conclusions and recommendations drawn.

Chapter 4 will explore how an organization examines its own strengths and weaknesses as a basis for strategy formulation.

Key Terms and Concepts in Strategic Management

competitive advantage	service area competitor analysis	strategic group
competitor analysis	service area profile	strategic mapping
critical success factors	service category	strategic response
service area	strategic decision time line	

Questions for Class Discussion

1. What is competitor analysis? Why should health care organizations engage in competitor analysis? Should not-for-profit organizations perform competitor analysis?
2. What is the relationship between general environmental analysis and service area competitor analysis?
3. What competitor information categories are useful in competitor analysis? Are these categories appropriate for health care organizations? How can these information categories provide a focus for information gathering and strategic decision making?
4. What are some impediments to effective competitor analysis? How may these impediments be overcome?
5. Explain the steps or logic of competitor analysis.
6. Why must the service categories be defined first in competitor analysis for health care organizations?
7. Why is it important to clearly define the service area in competitor analysis? How does managed-care penetration affect service area definition?
8. How does the use of Porter's analysis help identify the major competitive forces in the service area?
9. Why is an identification and evaluation of competitor strengths and weaknesses and the determination of strategy essential in competitor analysis?
10. What are the benefits of strategic group analysis and strategic mapping?
11. Why should a health care organization attempt to determine competitors' strategies and likely strategic responses?
12. What is the purpose of the synthesis stage of service area competitor analysis?
13. Conduct a service area competitor analysis for a health care market with which you are familiar.

Notes

1. Shaker A. Zahra and Sherry S. Chaples, "Blind Spots in Competitive Analysis," *Academy of Management Executive* 7, no. 2 (1993), pp. 7–28.
2. John E. Prescott and Daniel C. Smith, "The Largest Survey of 'Leading-Edge' Competitor Intelligence Managers," *Planning Review* 17, no. 3 (1989), p. 12.
3. David Halberstam, *The Reckoning* (New York: William Morrow, 1986), p. 310.
4. Sumantra Ghoshal and D. Eleanor Westney, "Organizing Competitor Analysis Systems," *Strategic Management Journal* 12, no. 1 (1991), pp. 17–31.
5. Prescott and Smith, "The Largest Survey of 'Leading-Edge' Competitor Intelligence Managers," pp. 6–13.
6. Joel A. C. Baum and Helaine J. Korn, "Competitive Dynamics of Interfirm Rivalry," *Academy of Management Journal* 39, no. 2 (1996), p. 256.
7. Zahra and Chaples, "Blind Spots in Competitive Analysis," p. 9.
8. Ibid.
9. Hubert Saint-Onge, "Tacit Knowledge: The Key to the Strategic Alignment of Intellectual Capital," *Strategy and Leadership* 24, no. 2 (1996), pp. 10–14.
10. Zahra and Chaples, "Blind Spots in Competitive Analysis," pp. 19–20.
11. Carl Pegels and Kenneth A. Rogers, *Strategic Management of Hospitals and Health Care Facilities* (Rockville, Maryland: Aspen Publishers, 1988), pp. 35–36.
12. Joseph P. Peters, *A Strategic Planning Process for Hospitals* (Chicago: American Hospital Publishing, 1985), pp. 71–73.
13. Voluntary Hospitals of America, Inc., *Community Health Assessment: A Process for Positive Change* (Irving, Texas: Voluntary Hospitals of America, Inc., 1993), p. 49.
14. There are several community assessment approaches available such as Voluntary Hospitals of America, Inc., *Community Health Assessment: A Process for Positive Change* (Irving, Texas: Voluntary Hospitals of America, Inc., 1993); The Hospital Association of Pennsylvania, *A Guide for Assessing and Improving Health Status: Community . . . Planting the Seeds for Good Health* (The Hospital Association of Pennsylvania, 1993); and James A. Rice, *Community Health Assessment: The First Step in Community Health Planning* (Chicago: American Hospital Association Technology Series, 1993). Perhaps the best known is *Assessment Protocol for Excellence in Public Health (APEX PH)*, a

collaborative project of the American Public Health Association, the Association of Schools of Public Health, the Association of State and Territorial Health Officials, the Centers for Disease Control, the National Association of County Health Officials, and the United States Conference of Local Health Officers funded through a cooperative agreement between the Centers for Disease Control and the National Association of County Health Officials, 1991.

15. Michael E. Porter, *Competitive Strategy: Techniques for Analyzing Industries and Competitors* (New York: Free Press, 1980), pp. 3–33.

16. Ming-Jer Chen, "Competitor Analysis and Interfirm Rivalry: Toward a Theoretical Integration," *Academy of Management Review* 21, no. 1 (1996), p. 101.

17. Baum and Korn, "Competitive Dynamics of Interfirm Rivalry," p. 257.

18. Adapted from Michael E. Porter, *Competitive Strategy: Techniques for Analyzing Industries and Competitors,* pp. 127–128.

19. For a review of strategic group studies, see Rhonda K. Reger and Anne Sigismund Huff, "Strategic Groups: A Cognitive Perspective," *Strategic Management Journal* 14, no. 2 (1993), p. 104.

20. Michael E. Porter, *Competitive Strategy: Techniques for Analyzing Industries and Competitors*, p. 129.

21. Robert M. Grant, *Contemporary Strategic Analysis: Concepts, Techniques, Applications* (Cambridge, Massachusetts: Blackwell Business, 1995), p. 98–99.

22. K. J. Hatten and M. L. Hatten, "Strategic Groups, Asymmetrical Mobility Barriers and Contestability," *Strategic Management Journal* 8, no. 4 (1987), pp. 329–342.

23. Karel Cool and Ingemar Dierickx, "Rivalry, Strategic Groups and Firm Profitability," *Strategic Management Journal* 14, no. 1 (1993), pp. 47–59.

24. Chen, "Competitor Analysis and Interfirm Rivalry: Toward a Theoretical Integration," p. 102.

Additional Readings

Aaker, David A., *Developing Business Strategies,* 4th ed. (New York: John Wiley & Sons, Inc., 1995). Noted business scholar David Aaker's book on development, evaluation, and implementation of business strategy contains a concise and timely chapter concerning competitor analysis. Aaker suggests a broad process for first identifying and then evaluating competitors. In identifying competitors, customer-based approaches and the use of strategic groups are examined. Competitor analysis includes evaluating competitor size, growth, and profitability; image and positioning; objectives and commitment; current and past strategies; organization and culture; cost structure; exit barriers; and strengths and weaknesses.

Montgomery, Cynthia A., and Michael E. Porter, eds. *Strategy: Seeking and Securing Competitive Advantage* (Boston: Harvard Business School Publishing, 1991). A collection of excellent *Harvard Business Review* articles of the past decade are included in this book. Of particular interest for understanding service area competitor analysis are "How Competitive Forces Shape Strategy" by Michael Porter, "Sustainable Advantage" by Pankaj Ghemawat, "Time—The Next Source of Competitive Advantage" by George Stalk, Jr., and "From Competitive Advantage to Corporate Strategy" by Michael Porter.

Oster, Sharon M., *Modern Competitive Analysis*, 2d ed. (New York: Oxford University Press, 1994). The author believes that fundamental ideas in microeconomics are very important in strategic planning. Accordingly, the book presents three main themes: how interactive forces inside and outside the market affect strategic choices and the outcomes of these choices; strategic management as a way of managing the changing nature of the marketplace; and decision making in the context of limited information and market friction. Oster posits that strategic planning is a way of informing and improving the choices made in organizations; but such planning must recognize that uncertainties will inevitably remain.

Rouse, William B., *Start Where You Are: Matching Your Strategy to Your Marketplace* (San Francisco: Jossey-Bass Publishers, 1996). Rouse demonstrates how to proactively build and shape an organization's future by starting with its current position and understanding the market. Although not focused on health care, Rouse details the ten most common situations that companies experience and discusses how to determine which situation best identifies an organization's current and likely future circumstances. Most important, Rouse illustrates a method to assess an organization's position in the marketplace, a step-by-step plan for determining the strategic situation, and a process for evaluating how strategic actions affect an organization's future.

Zelman, Walter A., *The Changing Health Care Marketplace: Private Ventures, Public Interests, Uneasy Partnerships Among Doctors, Hospitals, and Health Plans* (San Francisco: Jossey-Bass Publishers, 1996). Zelman reviews and evaluates the significance of the environmental trends affecting today's health care marketplace including the rise of managed care, risk sharing, and integration in health care to reduce costs. He examines consolidation and describes how partnerships among physicians, hospitals, and insurers are emerging and will exercise greater control in the future. In addition, Zelman assesses the strengths and weaknesses of the major players forming and leading organized delivery systems and analyzes the impact of increasing competition, regulation, and consumer protection.

Internal Environmental Analysis

Learning Objectives

After completing this chapter you should be able to:

1. Understand the critical role of internal environmental analysis in achieving sustained competitive advantage.

2. Discuss and integrate traditional perspectives of the relationship between the internal organizational environment and sustained competitive advantage.

3. Understand the nature of competitive advantage as visualized by traditional views of strengths and weaknesses, the resource-based approach, value-chain analysis, and stretch and resource leveraging.

4. Understand the importance of organizational resources, competencies, and capabilities in creating and maintaining competitive advantage.

5. Discuss how resources, competencies, and capabilities interact within the value chain.

6. Assess a health care organization's strengths and weaknesses in terms of resources, competencies, and capabilities.

7. Understand how to use the ASSIST model in analyzing the competitive advantage of a health care organization.

8. Discuss different ways health care organizations can leverage their resources in pursuit of sustained competitive advantage.

"To date, the development of tools for analyzing environmental opportunities and threats has proceeded much more rapidly than the development of tools for analyzing a firm's internal strengths and weaknesses."

- *Jay B. Barney*

From External to Internal Considerations

As discussed in the previous chapters, understanding and adapting to the external environment is crucially important to successful strategic management. Focusing on the essentially uncontrollable external environment, including actions and reactions of competitors, highlights the importance of adapting to change, "fitting" organizations to the larger environment, and understanding the "rules of success" that are written outside hospitals, physician practices, or managed-care organizations. Adaptability, fit, and understanding externally imposed rules of success, however, are only part of the strategic management process.

Pricing, Cost, and Competitive Advantage: The Discount Doc

It may seem strange—and to some, it may even seem unprofessional—but to Harold H. Allen, M.D., it spells competitive advantage. The practice of medicine has always been an area where competitive advantage was thought to be built on differentiation. "My doctor is a world-famous surgeon, and people travel from all over the world to acquire her services." "My doctor *delivered* the hospital administrator's *baby*, so he must be good." Price competition has rarely been a part of the marketing plan.

Dr. Allen believes there is another way to compete. According to him, "Health care in the United States is too costly." That is why his professional association, Physicians Surgical Alliance, says it will "beat any price." In his home state, the average cost of removing cartilage from the knee is $3,392. Dr. Allen performs the procedure for $2,529. His price for surgery to alleviate carpal tunnel syndrome is $1,706; the average cost in a hospital is $1,940. Dr. Allen is able to charge lower prices because he reduces his costs wherever appropriate. He secures cheaper leases and shops for bargain-priced new and refurbished equipment. In addition, Dr. Allen's outpatient surgical facility saves money on medications and supplies by monitoring costs on an ongoing basis.

As one might guess, insurance companies appreciate Dr. Allen. Some of his fellow physicians, however, are not so sure about his cost-effectiveness. Critics argue that the competition is unfair because hospitals must absorb expensive overhead such as emergency room operations and other services that lose money. Dr. Allen, however, believes that he is not antihospital and that "if hospitals and doctors would communicate and cooperate instead of having a grab-it-all mentality, we could really help health care." His facility, according to Dr. Allen, "does its share of charity cases" and still achieves a cost and price advantage.

Source: Anne M. Nordhaus-Bike, "Surgery at Discount Prices," *Hospital and Health Networks* 70, no. 9 (May 5, 1996), pp. 56–58.

Effective strategic management also requires an understanding of organizational competencies, capacities, and resources, as well as how each contributes to the formation of organizational strengths to develop competitive advantage. In short, creating and maintaining a competitive advantage demands that health care strategists achieve a delicate mixture of effectiveness and efficiency, focus attention on the short term while keeping an eye on the long term, and skillfully manipulate controllable factors while adapting to things beyond their control.

Strategic Effectiveness Requires Adaptability

The strategic effectiveness of a health care organization rests on its ability to accomplish two equally important tasks: to operate efficiently in the short run and to adapt to change over the long run. In the present, the goal of management is to efficiently use the organizational resources allocated to them through the budgeting process. This requires that costs be carefully controlled and efforts be made to do things as efficiently as possible.

From outside the health care organization, external forces such as technology, the economy, regulations, and so on emerge, requiring that the strategic manager change and adapt to different conditions. Sometimes the ability to adapt requires that managers sacrifice a degree of short-term efficiency, such as when research and development expenditures are made in an attempt to ensure that the latest technologies are available when needed. Or payments might be made to professional lobbyists to influence legislation in ways the hospital's board of directors believes is desirable. In either case, the money must be spent from the present budget and benefits are not realized until sometime in the future. In the short run, the result is that the operation appears less efficient. This is the type of strategic decision that health care managers must make. The demands for long-term adaptability and flexibility must be carefully weighed against costs in terms of short-term efficiency.

Efficiency and Health Care

Efficiency has become increasingly important to health care organizations after the passage of legislation in 1983 placing limits on what Medicare will pay for hospital services. The continued movement of the health care industry toward managed care and capitated rates makes efficiency an increasingly important concern for providers of health services. It is customary under a managed-care system for the employer or insurance company to pay a health care provider a capitated or fixed rate to care for the health needs of members of the covered group. If one employee or family member has difficult and expensive-to-treat problems, the provider will lose money because the cost will be greater than the amount paid to the provider per year. However, for many enrollees, no health services will be required; therefore the provider will make a profit on these employees and use the excess to cover the costs of the more expensive-to-treat employees. There is a strong financial incentive to be as efficient as possible in order to keep individual health service costs below the amount paid per employee per year.

In Exhibit 4–1 the hospital consumer price index (indicator of hospital costs) and the producer price index (indicator of prices charged by hospitals) are illustrated for the period March 1995 to March 1996. The data demonstrate that medical care costs increased 3.7 percent compared to 2.9 percent for the hospital consumer price index. Physician services (5.3 percent) and hospital costs–other services (4.6 percent) were well above the hospital consumer price index. The increasingly competitive nature of the health care market, however, is confirmed by the fact that producer prices increased, in most cases, by less than the cost increases. Prices charged by psychiatric hospitals actually decreased by less than 1 percent. These figures underscore the need for efficiency in health care.

Efficiency versus adaptability represents a delicate balance between managing for the present and managing for the future. The balance achieved between these two, often competing, demands will be influenced by a number of factors. The changing nature of the health care industry will certainly influence the balance sought and achieved but internal factors will influence choices as well. Some of these internal factors will relate to specific operational and logistical expertise whereas others will relate to the "character" or culture of the organization itself.

Internal Environmental Assessment: An Integrated Approach

Understanding competitive advantage is an ongoing challenge for strategic decision makers especially in dynamic industries such as health care. The challenge becomes ever more demanding because competitive advantage laboriously achieved can be quickly lost. Historically, competitive advantage was primarily a matter of "position" where health care organizations occupied certain competitive space and built and defended market share—although in a nonaggressive and highly refined manner. It had a great deal to do with where the hospital, physician practice, or long-term-care facility was located and, therefore, where they chose to provide services. A stable environment allowed static strategies to be successful for years, particularly for large and dominant organizations.

In today's environment, the ability to develop a sustained competitive advantage is increasingly rare. A health care organization enjoys a sustained competitive advantage only so long as the services it delivers have attributes that correspond to the key "buying criteria" of a substantial number of customers in the target market. *Sustained competitive advantage* is the direct result of an enduring value differential between the services of one organization and that of competitors in the minds of patients, physicians, and so on.[1] This reality makes internal environmental factors extremely important. Health care organizations must consider more than the fit between the external environment and the present internal characteristics. They must anticipate what the rapidly changing environment will be like and change their structures, cultures, and other relevant factors so as to reap the benefits of changing times. Sustained competitive advantage has become more of a matter of "movement" than of position. As demonstrated in Perspective 4–1, other technological factors make success depend less on where an organization is physically located than its ability to anticipate the future and respond to changing conditions.[2]

The question of an enduring value differential, therefore, raises the issue of why one or only a few organizations in a particular health care market are able to achieve a

Exhibit 4–1 · Selected Hospital Costs and Prices (March 1995 and March 1996)

Hospital Consumer Price Index (CPI) Component	Yearly Change (%)	Producer Price Index Component	Yearly Change (%)
CPI	2.9	Hospitals (Overall)	2.6
Medical Care (Overall)	3.7	General Medical and Surgical Hospitals	2.7
Medical Care Commodities	2.9	Primary Services	2.7
Medical Care Services	3.9	Inpatient Treatments	2.7
Hospitals–Other Services	4.6	Outpatient Treatments	3.0
Hospital Rooms	3.7	Psychiatric Hospitals	−0.9
Physician Services	5.3	Specialty Hospitals (Except Psychiatric)	2.9
Outpatient Services	3.9		

Source: *AHA News* (May 20, 1996), p. 4, from U.S. Department of Labor data.

Perspective 4–1

Changing the Way Things Are Done at the Wilmer Eye Institute

Not long ago the Wilmer Eye Institute in Baltimore had 120 inpatient beds, a staff to support them, and an average length of stay of almost two weeks. Today, because of the new laser technology used for surgery, most patients do not require an overnight stay. Morton Goldberg, M.D., the institute director, stated, "We were sitting with a lot of empty beds and with nurses who had nothing to do. That couldn't continue."

Things had to change and decision makers had to move fast. The institute could not continue with business as usual. It added two new operating rooms, recruited more surgeons, drastically cut the number of beds to twelve, consolidated four nursing units, and formed the Wilmer Nursing and Trauma Center, complete with "virtual rooms" that could be transformed as needed to suit outpatients, inpatients, and families. In 1995, surgeries were at an all-time high, cross-training among nurses was the order of the day, costs decreased by more than 20 percent, and the Institute was ranked first in the ophthalmology category in *U.S. News and World Report*'s annual listing of America's best hospitals.

Source: Tibbett L. Speer, "With an Eye to the Future," *Hospitals and Health Networks* 70, no. 1 (January 5, 1996), p. 43.

competitive advantage. To understand this, it is necessary to understand why and how organizations differ in a strategic sense.[3] Traditionally, the focus has been on organizational strengths and weaknesses. However, what constitutes a strength and a weakness is a complex question that requires introspection and self-examination.

Internal environmental analysis is much like external environmental analysis except the focus is on the organization rather than environmental forces. In Chapter 2 external environmental analysis was accomplished through the successively more detailed stages of scanning, monitoring, forecasting, and assessing. Internal environmental analysis takes place through the successively detailed stages of surveying, inspecting, investigating, and evaluating. Exhibit 4–2 provides an overview of these four phases.

Phase 1: Surveying Potential Strengths and Weaknesses

Identifying an organization's internal strengths and internal weaknesses is an essential task of health care strategists. The task is difficult because organizational characteristics may initially appear as a strength or weakness, but on closer examination they may offer no competitive advantage or disadvantage. In addition, strengths and weaknesses may be *objective* or *subjective* as well as *absolute* or *relative.*

Some strengths possessed by a health care organization are clear by objective standards. For example, the mere presence of one organization in a particular location may be a strategic strength because it prohibits other organizations from occupying that specific location. An objective weakness occurs when an organization assumes excessive debt financing for its facilities thereby limiting its ability to borrow additional money.

Exhibit 4–2 • Internal Environmental Analysis Process

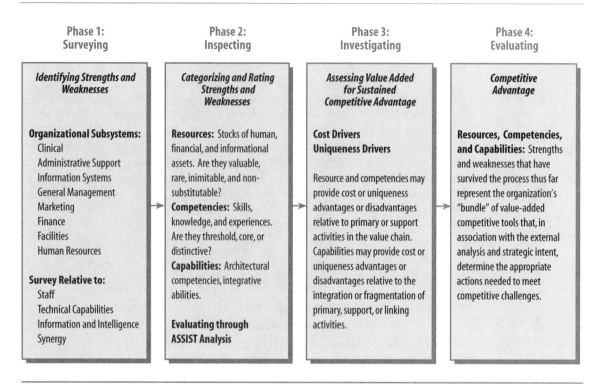

Phase 1: Surveying	Phase 2: Inspecting	Phase 3: Investigating	Phase 4: Evaluating
Identifying Strengths and Weaknesses	*Categorizing and Rating Strengths and Weaknesses*	*Assessing Value Added for Sustained Competitive Advantage*	*Competitive Advantage*
Organizational Subsystems: Clinical, Administrative Support, Information Systems, General Management, Marketing, Finance, Facilities, Human Resources	**Resources:** Stocks of human, financial, and informational assets. Are they valuable, rare, inimitable, and non-substitutable?	**Cost Drivers** **Uniqueness Drivers**	**Resources, Competencies, and Capabilities:** Strengths and weaknesses that have survived the process thus far represent the organization's "bundle" of value-added competitive tools that, in association with the external analysis and strategic intent, determine the appropriate actions needed to meet competitive challenges.
Survey Relative to: Staff, Technical Capabilities, Information and Intelligence, Synergy	**Competencies:** Skills, knowledge, and experiences. Are they threshold, core, or distinctive? **Capabilities:** Architectural competencies, integrative abilities. **Evaluating through ASSIST Analysis**	Resource and competencies may provide cost or uniqueness advantages or disadvantages relative to primary or support activities in the value chain. Capabilities may provide cost or uniqueness advantages or disadvantages relative to the integration or fragmentation of primary, support, or linking activities.	

At times, a strength or weakness may be subjective. Perhaps the administrator of a large physician practice believes her medical staff is superior to all others in the area, even though a review of the qualifications, specialties represented, and services provided does not indicate any substantial differences among the training and qualifications of the medical staffs in competing practices. Weaknesses can also be subjective. The management team may think that the "philosophy" of the board of directors is more conservative than that of other organizations even though there are no concrete data to support the assertion. As a result, the organization's leadership acts in a "timid" manner when it comes to taking risks.

Sometimes organizational strengths and weaknesses are absolute. The Mayo Clinic is known for its excellence in patient care and is frequently used as a standard by which other health care organizations are judged. The Johns Hopkins University School of Medicine is recognized worldwide as a leader in medical education. Because these organizations have been historical "standards" against which others are measured, their images represent an absolute strength.

To illustrate absolute weakness one need only look at the circumstances facing publicly supported indigent care hospitals in view of continuing changes in the health care system. Most observers agree that the future of health care in the United States will involve managed-care systems, and for those individuals who are not employed or for a variety of other reasons are not affiliated with a private managed-care plan, there will probably be some type of government-sponsored safety net. The goal is to "insure" everyone, either through a private or public program, to provide access to health care, and to give each person as much choice as possible in selecting the provider. The public's perception of these hospitals, whether accurate or not, has been that of lower quality services, less patient orientation, outdated technology, and deteriorating facilities. Image becomes an absolute weakness that these facilities will be forced to overcome if they are to survive.

Finally, strengths and weaknesses may be relative. That is, one long-term-care facility may have certain strengths, not in an absolute sense, but relative to its competitors. One facility may have limited financial resources in comparison to national averages but considerably more money than any of its service area competitors. At the same time, a world-renowned academic health center may lose a famous surgeon to a local hospital that is attempting to build a clinical area such as heart transplants. The health center may remain very strong in terms of the services it provides but have a relative weakness with regard to the facility where the surgeon is now located. Perspective 4–2 illustrates Tenet Healthcare Corporation's decision to outsource its information systems. The decision was based on the realization that information systems was not its primary business and that it would always possess a relative disadvantage compared to organizations that were in the information systems business.

Perspective 4–2

Outsourcing Information Systems at Tenet Healthcare Corporation

Tenet Healthcare Corporation is betting that Perot Systems Corporation is better than its own staff at designing and implementing an information system. It has agreed to pay Perot $275 million over seven years to take charge of all its computerized operations including those in its hospitals. Tenet believes the deal will save $100 million. If Tenet's experience is positive, it may encourage other health care organizations to do what they do best—take care of patients. This is the core business of health care organizations, not data processing and information system design.

If the health care organization is relatively inexperienced and ineffective in accomplishing a certain task, one way to overcome that weakness is to outsource the task to companies that have the expertise. According to CEO Jeffrey C. Barbakow, by freeing itself from investing in-house resources into its information system infrastructure, Tenet should "dramatically cut the overhead costs associated with updating the ever-evolving technology while increasing the company's access to sophisticated systems management and development." The decision to outsource is not without risks—for example, there are potential problems with giving up control of software applications that are central to day-to-day operations. However, Tenet management believes that outsourcing will allow it to focus on the core business of health care and is willing to take the chance.

Source: Chuck Appleby, "Tenet's Computer Compact," *Hospital and Health Networks* 69, no. 22 (October 20, 1995), p. 52.

The Concept of the Organization The systems view discussed in Chapter 1 has been traditionally used to survey or suggest potential strengths and weaknesses of the organization. An initial, if superficial, list of possible strengths and weaknesses can be generated by auditing each of the subsystems and linking processes. Exhibit 4–3 provides an illustration of how a health care organization can be viewed as a complex system.

At the heart of the health care organization are clinical personnel—individuals who are the foundation of health care organizations. The term "clinical personnel" is used to include physicians, nurses, and others who are involved in direct patient care as well as groups that provide support to the clinical staff, such as pharmacy, pathology, medical laboratories, rehabilitation services, and others. Assessing the strengths and weaknesses of the clinical subsystem is especially complicated because of accreditation standards for different clinician specialists.

The effectiveness of clinical services is also influenced by the administrative support available to the people who provide direct patient care. Determination of the support available requires a survey of the administrative services subsystem including the clerical support staff and system. With regard to the information and intelligence issues, the surveying of potential strengths and weaknesses must evaluate the present developmental stage of the information systems supporting medical, administrative, and overall decision-making systems.

The technical capabilities of administrative services are important and must be surveyed as well. As part of this, the pressing question of technology must again be addressed. Few question the importance of technology as it relates to patient diagnosis and treatment. The effectiveness of administratively oriented technologies, for example payroll and patient billing, are also important.

The first step in an audit of the potential strengths and weaknesses of the marketing subsystem is an articulation of the organization's marketing philosophy. A survey of the experiences of the marketing staff is particularly important for health care organizations.

Exhibit 4–3 • Framework for Discussion of the Internal Environment

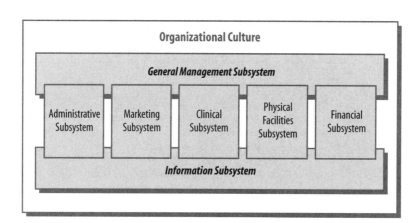

Because marketing has not been a high priority, marketing activities have been assumed by individuals with little knowledge of the most effective concepts and tools. Marketing information and intelligence systems have not been as highly developed as in other industries, and marketing research has been lacking.

A survey of the organization's financial subsystem's potential strengths and weaknesses is an integral part of the overall administrative audit. After determining if the basic skills are available, it is important to evaluate the responsiveness of the finance personnel to their internal customers. Next, the quality of the financial information system should be surveyed. It is important to ensure that the financial information system is integrated into the larger management information system. The financial information system needs to be able to store historical data so that managers may track financial trends. The technical capabilities of the finance function are important. The finance function should regularly track, report on, and make recommendations regarding liquidity, earnings, leverage, and other related indicators. Appendix B discusses financial measures of this nature and ways they can be developed and used.

Identifying the potential strengths and weaknesses of the general management subsystem of a health care organization is a difficult yet essential aspect of internal assessment. When surveying general management capabilities, the fundamental concern is accomplishing the basic management functions of planning, organizing, coordinating, and controlling. Perhaps the most important function of the general management subsystem is to ensure that all the various subsystems are coordinated in a way that builds and maintains organizational synergy.

Finally, the physical facilities of an organization must be surveyed and the organization's potential strengths and weaknesses relative to them examined. Although it is tempting to overlook, it must be recognized that the effectiveness and efficiency of human and nonhuman resources are influenced by the physical facilities within which they must operate.

Identifying Strengths and Weaknesses Exhibit 4–4 provides an initial list of some potential strengths and weaknesses resulting from a survey of the internal environment of a regional acute-care hospital. This list was generated by surveying the six major functional subsystems: clinical, administrative services, marketing, financial, general management, and facilities. An evaluation of the adequacy of the organization's information system was an integral part and a primary means of connecting all the subsystems and was therefore included across every element in the audit.

There are many possible issues that could, and should, be discussed with regard to each of these subsystems. Therefore, in each of these areas, the exhibit provides only an outline of important questions that would normally be asked using the traditional audit approach. The "audit checklist" of possible strengths and weaknesses includes a review of four similar factors in each functional subsystem. These are:

1. *Staff.* Do we have an adequate staff in terms of both numbers and qualifications for our present activities? Can the staffing base support our expected future development? Do we have the managerial expertise needed to coordinate all the functional areas? Indicators include number of employees, estimates of adequate career paths, leadership depth and succession plans, ratio of managers to nonmanagerial employees, and so on.

Exhibit 4–4 • A Summary Checklist for Selected Organizational Subsystems in a Regional Acute-Care Hospital

Criteria	Clinical Subsystem	Administrative Services Subsystem	Marketing Subsystem	Financial Subsystem	General Management Subsystem	Physical Facilities
1. Staff	The medical staff (physicians, nurses, technicians) have the credentials and training appropriate for the services they deliver. (S) Professional clinical staff have appropriate types and numbers of support personnel and services. (S) Nurse practitioner and patient assistance programs in many specialties. (S) Staffing levels are inappropriate on all shifts for the services provided requiring use of excessive overtime. (W)	The administrative staff have the training and experience needed to support clinical personnel. (S) Staffing levels are appropriate to support clinical personnel. (S) Human Resources recruits and hires qualified personnel. (S) There is no understood management succession plan. (W)	Marketing staff is appropriately trained and creative. (S) Marketing staff have too little and untimely input into the introduction of new services. (W) Marketing staff does not interact effectively with clinicians and other personnel in the organization. (W)	Finance and accounting staff have the training and experience needed to effectively manage an organization of our size and complexity. (S) Finance staff respond to special requests in a timely manner. (S) Finance staff provide decision makers with information that is not timely and is suspect in terms of reliability. (W)	Executives are committed to long-run success and are not easily distracted by short-term considerations. (S) Executives are comfortable allowing decisions to be made at the appropriate level. (S) Executives are acquainted with the "big picture" and effectively coordinate diverse functions. (S)	Craft and maintenance staff have the training and experience needed to effectively do their jobs. (S) Physical facilities are state of the art and appropriately support mission accomplishment. (S) All shifts are not adequately staffed with support and maintenance personnel. (W)
2. Information and Intelligence	The management information system provides useful and timely decision-making support. (S) The telemedicine link connects the hospital with referring physician database. (S)	The necessary systems are in place to support our business-related activities. (S) Effective and efficient purchasing and inventory control systems have been implemented. (S)	The marketing information system provides valuable information about our customer base. (S) The marketing information system includes patient satisfaction surveys. (S)	The organization possesses databases needed to keep informed about performance over time and the performance of our competitors. (S) Financial information is effectively integrated into decision making. (S)	Managers insist on two-way communication in the organization. (S) Managers are interested in and informed about what is going on, in general, in and throughout the health care industry. (S)	The information system provides support staff with the information they need to do their work in an efficient and timely manner. (S) Facilities are sufficient to allow effective responses to changes in information technology. (S)

Exhibit 4–4 · **Continued**

Criteria	Clinical Subsystem	Administrative Services Subsystem	Marketing Subsystem	Financial Subsystem	General Management Subsystem	Physical Facilities
2. Information and Intelligence *(cont.)*	Information systems do not support the diagnostic and support needs of the clinical staff. (W) There are no established systems and procedures for keeping up-to-date on clinical areas and relevant medical knowledge. (W)	Human Resources information system is not integrated into the general information system. (W) Clinical information system provides little support for decision making. (W)	The marketing information system has insufficient information about competitors' actions. (W) The marketing information system does not support high-quality market research. (W)	The financial information system does not integrate well with the management information system. (W) More archival capacity is needed to provide baseline information on organization. (W)	Managers are effective listeners and keep their finger "on the pulse" of the organization. (S) Managers do not effectively communicate the importance of cross-functional interaction. (W)	Maintenance and other support services are not automated enough to ensure effective and efficient services. (W) Facilities planning technology is not appropriate for the future of the organization. (W)
3. Technical Capabilities	Medical diagnosis, treatment, and laboratory technologies are appropriate to provide state-of-the-art services. (S) Technical personnel are trained and experienced in the use of the latest technologies. (S) Facilities are appropriate for the latest diagnostic and treatment technologies. (S) Heart transplant and level-one trauma units are the only ones in the region. (S)	Business technologies and equipment are sufficient to support our administrative staff. (S) Business systems are appropriate for the support of our medical mission. (S) Business systems are not well integrated into clinical systems. (W)	Managers have a good sense of the market share goals we are pursuing relative to various services. (S) Marketing resources are allocated in a way that supports our marketing strategy. (S) Tracking patient satisfaction and integrating data into decision making are not effective. (W) There is no systematic review of the service mix. (W)	The financial condition is monitored to ensure resources are available to take advantage of strategic opportunities. (S) The financial structure is appropriate for the business strategy. (S) Decision makers are aware of financial performance relative to that of competitors. (S) Fund-raising expertise has provided large endowment. (S)	Employees understand the decision making process and are involved whenever possible in making the decisions that affect them. (S) Management has developed a proprietary patient flow engineering model. (S) Mission, vision, values, and objectives are not well formulated or communicated to all staff. (W) The organizational structure is not appropriate for our plans and strategies. (W)	The patient care facilities support the mission and strategies. (S) The location of facilities does not support the patient care mission and ensure competitiveness with other providers. (W) Facilities are not very attractive and reflect a negative image for the organization. (W)

continued

Exhibit 4–4 · **Continued**

Criteria	Clinical Subsystem	Administrative Services Subsystem	Marketing Subsystem	Financial Subsystem	General Management Subsystem	Physical Facilities
4. Synergy	Clinical staff share the common goal of high-quality patient care. (S) Efforts are made to encourage clinical staff to respond to the needs of all stakeholders. (S) The clinical staff is the center (hub) of the integrated health care system. (S) Real-time medical laboratory testing and reporting system improves clinical capabilities. (S)	There is a minimum amount of conflict among staff and clinical personnel. (S) Administrative staff understand the needs of clinical staff. (S) The integrated patient admission and discharge system is effective. (S) Service follow-up with home health integration keeps patients in the system. (S) Line and staff personnel do not interact effectively. (W)	Marketing staff relate effectively and listen to the ideas of staff in other functional areas. (S) Marketing research personnel are responsive to the needs of other units. (S) The patient advocacy system links medical specialties and business operations. (S) Marketing data are not always integrated into decision making. (W)	Financial personnel protect rather than share information. (W) Financial personnel do not have an attitude of service in their dealings with internal customers. (W) Financial systems are not user friendly and do not respond to the needs of those who use them. (W)	Executive managers move around the organization and attempt to understand what is happening in all aspects of operations. (S) The business process system assures low costs. (S) General management and information systems are not useful in linking organization-wide decision making. (W)	The physical facilities and maintenance staff understand their role in accomplishing organizational mission. (S) Physical facilities planning is carefully integrated into strategic planning. (S)

2. *Information and Intelligence.* Is the internal information flow relative to clinical operations, administrative services, finance, marketing, and general management sufficient to support day-to-day activities, and do we have a system for obtaining strategic information (intelligence) outside the organization? Indicators include incidents of recurring needs to outsource programming services, overtime trends among key personnel needed to overcome information systems bottlenecks, and delays in getting planned applications operational.

3. *Technical Capabilities.* Do we have the equipment, facilities, and knowledge necessary to accomplish the tasks required in each functional area? Indicators include complaints of space limitations, inability to decentralize computing because of limited local area networks, and so on.

4. *Synergy.* Are the objectives of the functional areas appropriate to accomplish organizational goals given the organization's competitive position, resources, and opportunities? Indictors include communication of organizational strategies and goals to functional areas, ability of diverse information systems to interact with one another, and so on.

Perspective 4–3

Public Systems and the Future of Health Care

Analyzing internal strengths and weaknesses focuses attention on an organization's capability to compete in the health care environment. This involves an objective assessment of human and nonhuman resources, facilities, and even policies and procedures. Some public hospital systems are concluding reluctantly that they simply do not have the ability to compete with private enterprise. The result is to seek outside management.

An official of the Alameda (California) County health care system stated it plainly: "County supervisors don't understand all of the health care issues affecting the market and can't respond quickly enough to them. . . . [T]he competition is fierce . . . change is so fast in the industry they [the county supervisors] are overwhelmed." In Washington, D.C., consideration is being given to the formation of a District of Columbia Health and Hospital Corporation, which would combine eleven community health clinics. This separate financial entity would increase competitiveness by allowing the corporation to operate more as a business without cumbersome budget approval processes, bureaucratic personnel systems, and nonresponsive procurement policies.

Source: Jeffrey Green, "Public Hospital Systems Lean Toward Outside Management," *AHA News* (March 11, 1996), p. 5.

Although this traditional approach is useful in developing a list of possible organizational strengths and weaknesses and is essential in providing initial indicators, some precautions are needed. First, checklists and audits are useful tools to guide the thinking process, but they are never exhaustive; important issues for individual organizations and specific circumstances are omitted in even the most comprehensive audit. Therefore, it is important to remain alert to items and issues that may not be stated explicitly in the checklist of questions. Second, strengths and weaknesses (even potential ones) cannot be assessed within the framework of a single function or subsystem.

Some of the organization's most important strengths and weaknesses are not its financial or marketing expertise but how it "links" or coordinates the various subsystems as illustrated in Perspective 4–3. The initial survey is based on general, and sometimes impressionistic, indicators. The goal of the survey is accomplished when a list is generated of potential strengths and weaknesses that can be investigated in greater detail and with more demanding measures.

Phase 2: Inspecting Organizational Differences

Understanding the internal environment's relationship to competitive advantage cannot end with an initial survey. In his classic book, *Functions of the Executive,* Chester Barnard emphasized the need for a deeper understanding by noting that unless strategic managers possess a commitment to the organization's purpose and understand the capabilities of the organization, the environment has no meaning. Environments are, in fact, so complex that they are simply "mere messes of things" until an understanding of our purpose and capabilities converts the environment into something meaningful, significant, and interesting.[4]

After health care strategists have completed the initial survey (phase one in Exhibit 4–2), the second phase of internal environmental analysis involves more detailed inspection of the potential strengths and weaknesses highlighted by the survey. An effective way to begin this phase is to think of the potential strengths and weaknesses in terms of organizational resources, competencies, and capabilities and to develop more specific measures of each. This is an important phase because ultimately resources, competencies, capabilities, along with the purpose that makes the organization different, suggest the paths to competitive advantage.

Resources   A *resource-based view* of strategy argues that valuable, expensive-to-copy resources provide the key to sustainable competitive advantage.[5] The basic assumption of this view is that "resource bundles" used to create and distribute services by health care organizations are unevenly developed, which explains to some extent the ability of each to effectively compete.[6] Organizations with marginal resources break even, those with inferior resources disappear, and those with superior resources make profits.

"Basing strategy on the [resource] differences between firms should be automatic rather than noteworthy."[7] However, the argument is far from evident, especially in light of the overwhelming attention given to the external environment in strategy formulation. In order to delve deeper into the resource-based view, it is necessary to understand several concepts. Often used in a variety of ways and sometimes interchangeably, the concepts defined are particularly important because according to a resource-based view any or all of them can be sources of sustained competitive advantage.

Resources are the stocks of human and nonhuman factors that are available for use in producing goods and services. Resources may be tangible as in the case of land, labor, or capital; or they may be intangible as in the case of intellectual property, reputation, and goodwill.[8] Resources create worth because of one or more interrelated reasons. First, they may be valuable or not valuable, in and of themselves. The "good name" of a health care organization is a valuable, intangible resource. Second, resources that are rare are worth more than resources that are abundant. Capital is worth a great deal because of the relative scarcity of financial resources, whereas unskilled labor demands less compensation because it is widely available. Third, resources that are difficult to imitate are worth more than those that are easily copied. The location of a hospital's physical plant can be worth a great deal simply because there is no easy way to duplicate a location that will provide equal or better patient convenience. Finally, resources that have no available substitute take on a particular worth. A gamma knife is a valuable resource for a hospital competing for patients who can uniquely benefit from surgeries employing this technology.[9]

Health care organizations with considerable resources are, at least temporarily, able to define the field upon which competition will occur. A survey by Linc Anthem, a Chicago-based management and financial services company, reported that health care decision makers plan to shift their purchases of capital equipment away from radiation-therapy equipment such as MRIs to information and operating systems that are designed specifically to cut costs.[10] This reinforces the earlier discussion that the focus in health care is increasingly toward cost control and efficiency and suggests that the competitive energy in the near future will be focused on cost leadership.

Competency   *Competency* is defined as knowledge and skills that may be a source of sustained competitive advantage.[11] In the pharmaceutical industry, for example, strategically important competency is acquired by developing disciplinary expertise (i.e., medicinal chemistry, crystallography) or expertise in a particular disease category (i.e., cancer, heart disease). Competency in the pharmaceutical industry, however, often comes at a high price. For example, in 1996 American drug companies were expected to spend almost $16 billion on research and development for new drugs. In 1980 these companies spent only $2 billion on research and development and less than $9 billion as recently as 1990. The companies are developing 215 medicines for more than twenty types of cancer, 107 new medicines for heart attacks and strokes, 110 for AIDS and related conditions, and 132 medicines to treat more than fifteen major diseases related to aging.[12]

Some writers prefer to include competencies within the general category of intangible resources and thus make them inclusive of things such as technology, management information systems, and so on. Although there is no inherent problem with this classification, competency is knowledge and skill based and, therefore, inherently human. Competency, in many cases, is socially complex and requires large numbers of people engaged in coordinated activities.[13] Note, however, that the "purposeful coordination of resources and competencies" is yet another potential source of sustained competitive advantage.[14]

Capabilities   *Capabilities* are a health care organization's ability to deploy resources and competencies, usually in combination, to produce desired services. Unfortunately, "there are almost as many definitions of organizational capabilities as there are authors on the subject."[15] However, capabilities, variously defined, usually fall into one of the following categories. The organization either has:

- the ability to perform the basic activities of the organization (surgeries, outpatient services, and so on) better than competitors;
- the ability to make dynamic improvements to the organization's activities through learning, renewal, and change over time; or
- the ability to develop strategic insights and recognize and arrange resources and competencies or to develop novel strategies before or better than competitors.

In a sense, capabilities are architectural[16] or bonding mechanisms[17] whereby leaders make use of resources and competencies and integrate them in new and flexible ways so as to develop new resources and competencies as they learn, change, and continually renew themselves and their organizations. The point is that capabilities represent integrative and coordinating abilities that bring together resources and competencies in ways that are superior to those of competitors. Perspective 4–4 illustrates how integrated health systems attempt to achieve competitively relevant capabilities.

Sustained competitive advantage is based on resources and competencies, both of which possess important relationships to the external environment. As noted, resources

| Perspective 4–4

Integrated Health Systems and Capabilities

Fully integrated health systems can be effective means of building organizational capabilities. Vertically integrated systems attempt to develop sustained competitive advantage by possessing threshold or core competencies in a number of services. However, the real competitive advantage results from the combination of competencies into a system (capability) that is more difficult for competitors to imitate than a single competency.

The Henry Ford Health System in Detroit has attempted to build a competitive advantage by developing capabilities that transcend any single competency. For example, the system includes six hospitals, a 1,000 multispecialty physician group practice, and an HMO with 500,000 members. In addition, it offers home health and nursing services as well as operating a chemical dependency center. A large system of this nature creates the innovative possibilities of providing unique patient services (one-stop shopping), economies of scale, and numerous other advantages. Integrated health systems provide interesting attempts to capitalize on combinations of competence and convenience as sources of competitive advantage.

Source: Gary Luggiero, "Gail L. Warden: President and CEO of Henry Ford Health System," *AHA News* (January 15, 1996), p. 4.

must be rare, have value, be inimitable, and lack substitutability.[18] In order to enter a particular market or offer specific services, the organization must possess, at a minimum, *threshold competencies.* These competencies are the minimally required knowledge and skills necessary to compete in a particular area. In order to offer cardiac services, an acute-care hospital must have a minimum number of clinical personnel with specific knowledge and skill. Although all organizations offering cardiac services presumably possess threshold competencies, only one or two will develop the knowledge and skills to the point where it becomes a distinctive competency. This type of competency is a highly developed strength that can be critical in developing a sustained competitive advantage.[19]

Resources and capabilities that are merely present rarely represent competitive advantages. In order to be competitively significant, the specialized resources and competencies must be marshaled in a way that allows them to become genuine strategic assets resulting in the accumulation of economic returns greater than could be achieved in any alternative use.[20] Accomplishing this important task requires highly developed and maintained strategic capabilities.

The stock of resources and the knowledge and skills contained in a health care organization may not be sufficient to ensure a sustained competitive advantage. It is likely that two or more organizations competing in the same health care market may have essentially the same resources and similar competencies. Yet, one of the organizations may consistently "win" in a competitive sense. When this is the case, the competitive advantage may be the result of different capabilities or a "set of business processes strategically understood."[21] In other words, capabilities are best thought of as processes or ways of bringing together and organizing competencies and resources so as to obtain competitive advantage. Capability, as used here, is what Prahalad and Hamel refer to as the core competency of the organization; and although the usage is somewhat different, the ability to muster resources, skills, and knowledge in unique ways is, indeed, an important competency. Capabilities, in this sense, become the "collective learning in organizations, especially how to coordinate diverse operational skills and integrate multiple streams of technologies."[22]

Therefore, health care organizations that do not have superior resources or unique competencies may still derive sustainable competitive advantages if they are extraordinarily good at "architectural competencies"; that is, if they can convert the ordinary resources and threshold skills they possess into genuine strategic assets.[23] This results in services that respond uniquely to customer needs and, thereby, provide a competitive advantage. The development of this type of capability is based on four interrelated principles. These principles are as follows:

1. The building blocks of strategy are not products, services, and markets but processes.
2. Competitive success depends on transforming an organization's key processes into strategic capabilities that consistently provide superior value to customers.
3. Organizations create these capabilities by making strategic investments in a support infrastructure that link together and transcend traditional functions.
4. Because capabilities necessarily cross functions, the champion of capabilities-based strategy must be the chief executive.[24]

This recognition of the importance of "transfunctional" capabilities underscores the importance of general management in the traditional complex systems view of internal environmental assessment. However, the strategic importance of transfunctional capabilities can be better illustrated with ASSIST analysis, which enables a management team to view the organization in terms of its potential for creating a position of cost leadership or for differentiating its services.

ASSIST Analysis (ASSessment Internally for STrategy) To develop an ASSIST analysis, first identify the most important strategic resources, strategic competencies, and strategic capabilities from the initial survey of potential strengths and weaknesses. These should be reframed and restated in terms more directly related to the suspected competitive potential (potential for creating lower cost or service uniqueness). In accomplishing this, each of the following questions should be answered about each resource, competency, and capability:

1. *Question of Value.* Does the resource, competency, or capability add value by allowing us to take advantage of an opportunity or avoid a threat?
2. *Question of Rareness.* How many of our competitors possess the resource, competency, or capability?
3. *Question of Imitability.* Do our competitors face a cost disadvantage in obtaining the resource, competency, or capability relative to us?
4. *Question of Organization.* Are we able to obtain the full competitive potential of the resource, competency, or capability?
5. *Question of Sustainability.* Are we able to maintain the value, rareness, inimitability, or organizational advantage of the resource, competency, or capability?[25]

The third step is to assign a value between one (1) and five (5) for each of the questions. Each value should be assigned according to the following definitions.

Adequate = 1. Assign this value to a particular question if you believe the resource, competency, or capability identified is the minimum required to "be in this business" or to minimally compete.

Attractive = 2. Assign this value if you believe the resource, competency, or capability identified is greater than the minimum required to compete but does not represent a strong advantage. It would, in other words, "get the attention of appropriate individuals" but does not represent an impressive advantage.

Potential = 3. Assign this value if you believe the resource, competency, or capability identified is sufficient to attract attention and represents an important strategic consideration.

Competitive = 4. Assign this value if you believe the resource, competency, or capability identified represents a clear competitive advantage over others in your strategic group.

Distinctive = 5. Assign this value if you believe the resource, competency, or capability identified is something that none of your competitors can duplicate.

Exhibit 4–5 provides the results of how decision makers in the regional acute-care hospital introduced earlier converted the initial survey of strengths and weaknesses into ASSIST analysis by determining the resources, competencies, and capabilities and estimated the impact of each on the hospital's competitive advantage relative to its strategic group. Note that the final column in Exhibit 4–5 labeled "Summary Judgment" represents the management team's best evaluation of an overall ranking but should not be a simple average of the other rankings. For example, being at the center of an integrated system may have great value; but it is unlikely that such an advantage is sustainable as more and more organizations affiliate with health networks. Therefore, the lack of sustainability over the long run may greatly overcome the temporary advantage of today and result in a significantly lower summary judgment.

The process of more detailed inspection reduced the number of potential strengths and weaknesses to five strategic resources, competencies, and capabilities. In the judgment of the management team, only four in each category proved to be relevant to competitive advantage. Competitive advantage ultimately is built and maintained by adding value to health care services. Value is added in one of two ways: (1) by providing equal quality services at a lower cost than competitors; or (2) by providing higher quality services at the same cost. The first results in cost leadership and the second in differentiation. As Exhibit 4–2 illustrates, understanding precisely how each strategic resource, competency, and capability affects cost and uniqueness is an important aspect of understanding how, or if, each adds value to the services provided.

Investigating Competitive Advantage: The Value Chain

Few strategists have the ability to look at the organization as a whole and recognize opportunities for creating competitive advantage. That is why the traditional method of surveying strengths and weaknesses divides the organization into smaller, more manageable subsystems. It is also why the resource-based view looks for competitive opportunities in

Exhibit 4–5 · ASSIST Analysis

Dimension	Value Rating	Rareness Rating	Imitability Rating	Organization Rating	Sustainability Rating	Summary Judgment
Strategic Resources:						
State-of-the-art physical facilities including convenient and safe parking areas	4	3	4	4	5	4
Large discretionary endowment	5	5	5	4	5	5
Telemedicine link with 150 referring regional health care facilities	4	4	1	4	4	4
Proprietary physician referral database	5	5	2	4	3	4
Regional leader of employees with graduate degrees in field	2	2	2	1	2	2
Strategic Competencies:						
Only heart transplant team in region	3	5	5	2	2	2
Only level-one trauma unit in region	5	5	5	4	4	5
Proprietary patient flow engineering model dedicated to reducing waiting time	3	3	3	3	4	3
Nurse practitioner and patient assistance program in numerous specialties	4	3	1	3	3	3
Business process system dedicated to ensuring low-cost services in all areas	5	4	3	4	3	4
Strategic Capabilities:						
Center of totally integrated health care system	4	4	3	4	3	4
Integrated patient admission and discharge system	4	3	3	4	4	4
Real-time medical laboratory testing and reporting system	4	3	3	5	3	3
Patient advocacy system linking medicine specialties and business operations	4	3	2	4	4	4
Service follow-up system with home health integration	4	4	3	3	3	4

Source: From Jay B. Barney, "Looking Inside for Competitive Advantage," *Academy of Management Executive* Vol. 9, No. 4 (1995), pp. 49–61. Adapted with permission.

light of the organization's unique competencies, capabilities, and resources. Once potential strengths and weaknesses have been translated in terms of resources, competencies, and capabilities, it is important to investigate deeper relationships and determine how and where these factors actually add value to health care services. Michael E. Porter's value chain, illustrated in Exhibit 4–6 is a useful tool for disaggregating an organization "into its strategically relevant activities in order to understand the behavior of costs and the existing and potential sources of differentiation."[26]

Basic Concepts of Value-Chain Analysis The regional hospital's value chain is part of a larger value system. Suppliers of human and nonhuman resources (supplier value

Exhibit 4–6 · **Example of Organizational Value Chain with the Value System**

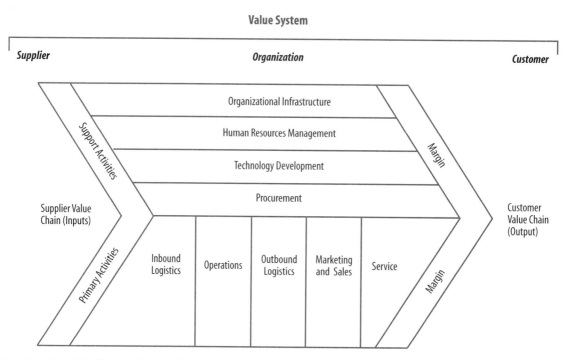

chain) influence the hospital's value chain by determining the quality of the inputs into the system. The quality of the physicians, nurses, and allied health personnel produced by professional schools significantly impact on the value of the hospital's services. Pharmaceutical firms influence the cost and quality of services through the drugs they supply, and so on. At the other end of the organization's value chain is the customer value chain. It is important for hospital decision makers to understand the way they "fit" into the value chain of the physicians, patients, and insurers who buy hospital services. An interesting illustration is reported in Perspective 4–5 relating to the value of academic medical centers as engines for economic development within the community.

Value is indirectly measured by the amount customers are willing to pay for the hospital's services. As illustrated in Exhibit 4–6, an organization's value chain consists of value activities (primary and support activities) and margin. Value activities are the distinct actions it performs in providing services and are the "building blocks" by which the organization creates valuable services for its customers. Understanding the value chain enables decision makers to better understand and control the primary cost drivers that differentiate their services by capitalizing on their uniqueness drivers.[27] Margin is the difference between the total value generated (revenues) and the collective costs of accomplishing all the value activities.

Perspective 4–5

Value Added, Economic Development, and Academic Medical Centers

Why should a state support academic medical centers? Because of their unique research and teaching mission and the patient mix, costs are almost always higher than at other hospitals. The quality of their services may or may not be better than that of competitors.

In addition to patient care, academic medical centers can be valuable aids for economic development. Three academic medical centers in Virginia, for example, have reported that they spend $2.7 billion each year on goods and services, employ 26,520 people, and create an additional 31,591 jobs among private sector firms that sell goods and services to the centers. The resulting impact is significant:

1. One dollar in every $84 in the state can be traced to academic medical centers.
2. State government receives more than $116 million in tax revenue as a direct result of the centers' operations.

3. Visiting clinicians, patients, and students inject another $103.8 million into the state's economy.
4. Patients from outside Virginia who came to the state for specialized care spend $30.6 million on nonhealth-related goods and services.
5. In 1995, biomedical research conducted at the medical centers brought in more than $160 million in research funds.

The report, based on a study by Tripp, Umback, and Associates of Pittsburgh, indicated that academic medical centers are good investments and add considerable value to the state's economic development activities.

_____

Source: "Academic Medicine," *Hospitals and Health Networks* 70, no. 6 (March 20, 1996), p. 14.

Value Activities Value activities may be either primary or support activities. *Primary value activities* are listed along the bottom of Exhibit 4–6 and are directly involved in the creation, sale, transfer, and follow-up of health care services provided by the organization. *Support activities* facilitate the primary activities and each other by providing purchased inputs, technology, and human resources. Organizational infrastructure is associated with the entire value chain.

There are five generic classifications for primary value activities. These activities are critical to creating and maintaining sustainable competitive advantage because each can be a source of cost efficiency or service differentiation. Each value activity is related to the strategic resources, competencies, and capabilities in Exhibit 4–5.

1. *Inbound Logistics.* These are activities relating to the receiving, storing, and disseminating of inputs into the services created by the organization. (Example: Proprietary patient referral database.)
2. *Operations.* This is synonymous with the clinical subsystem and involves activities associated with the transformation of inputs into health care services. (Examples: Heart transplant, level-one trauma unit, real-time laboratory testing and reporting system, nurse practitioner and patient assistance programs.)

3. *Outbound Logistics.* These are activities relating to distributing services to customers involving discharge planning and, in the case of integrated systems, scheduling into downstream elements in the overall value system. (Examples: Services follow-up and home health integration.)

4. *Marketing and Sales.* These activities relate to providing a means for customers to purchase services and encouraging them to do so through promotion, channel selection and relations, and pricing. (Example: Media campaign to develop preference for the hospital's maternity programs.)

5. *Service.* These activities relate to maintaining value by enhancing services through patient follow-ups, consultations on treatment effects, and so on. (Example: Patient contact by nurse or pharmacist at specific time to inquire about effects of treatments and ongoing patient satisfaction surveys.)

The support activities associated with providing health care services are divided into four generic categories for purposes of discussion.

1. *Procurement.* This relates to all the activities involved in purchasing inputs used in the value chain rather than the actual purchased items. Procurement takes place throughout the value chain and restricting the concern to the purchasing department greatly underestimates the magnitude of these activities. (Example: Business process system—careful design of all functions related to business activities—encourages decentralized procurement.)

2. *Technology Development.* This occurs in many parts of the organization from clinical support technology to telecommunications to office automation to research and development. (Examples: Telemedicine link with regional referral facilities, patient flow engineering model, and business process system.)

3. *Human Resources Management.* This involves the recruiting, hiring, training, development, and compensation of all types of personnel and, again, is much broader than the activities performed in personnel departments. (Example: Regional leader in employees who have graduate degrees because of the priority placed on continuing education and development.)

4. *Organizational Infrastructure.* This supports the entire value chain and the accounting, finance, quality, and general management activities of the organization. (Examples: Business process system, large endowment, and state-of-the-art facilities.)

Linking Value Activities   Value activities are the building blocks of competitive advantage because resources and competencies may reside in any or all components of the value chain. At the same time, the way that parts of a system of interrelated activities are linked to one another is sometimes as important as how the activities are performed. These linking activities are similar to the capabilities discussed previously. Effective linkage of value activities can lead to competitive advantage either by optimizing activities or by coordinating them in unusually effective ways. Value activities often involve trade-offs to obtain cost advantages. For example, service costs might be reduced in a hospital's laboratory operations by increasing the quality demands for laboratory supplies as well as operational incentives for zero rework with regard to tests performed (optimizing the trade-off among inbound logistics, operations, and service).[28]

In another case, the department of pharmacy in an acute-care hospital noted that patients were consistently discharged with an average of three unfilled prescriptions in their possession. In most cases the patient's family held the prescriptions and had them filled in neighborhood pharmacies with a corresponding loss of revenue to the hospital. Careful coordination among operations (clinical personnel), outbound logistics (discharge scheduling), and marketing and sales made it possible for the outpatient pharmacy to differentiate their services and gain a competitive advantage by offering to have the prescriptions filled and waiting for patients when they left the hospital. In other words, it is important to recognize that effectively linking activities can itself be an important aspect of value creation, and such opportunities should not be overlooked either horizontally or vertically in the value chain.

In the case of the regional acute-care hospital discussed in this chapter, the fact that it has a telemedicine link with referring facilities, a physician referral database, patient flow engineering models, and business process systems allows it to provide high value to patients, physicians, and insurers. It can "put things together" in ways that result in reasonably priced, high-quality, and conveniently delivered health care services; and in doing so, it delivers genuine value.

Evaluating Competitive Advantage and Overcoming Limitations

The basic endowment of resources in a health care organization and the way these resources are allocated are critical determinants of the organization's ability to effectively compete. Although the regional hospital is fortunate to have a large endowment, state-of-the-art facilities, and well-trained employees, resources should not be looked on as absolute determinants of competitive abilities. In fact, it has been argued that the essential character of new directions in strategic thinking is the acceptance of "an aspiration that creates, by design, a chasm between ambitions and resources." It is further argued that spanning the chasm and encouraging *stretch* "is the single most important task senior management faces."[29]

Stretch is accomplished through resource leveraging or systematically getting the most possible from the available resources. That is why CNN has been able to compete with major news networks, why Apple was able to compete effectively with IBM in selected markets, and why Kmart and Wal-Mart were able to compete with Sears. And, if they are to survive, that is how smaller, less resource-rich health care organizations must compete against large and powerful national and regional health networks and managed-care organizations. Leveraging can be accomplished by concentrating, accumulating, complementing, conserving, and recovering resources.[30]

Resources are more effectively directed toward strategic goals when they are concentrated. Prioritizing goals and focusing on a relatively few things at one time aids the concentration of limited resources. Finally, successful concentration of resources requires not only focusing on relatively few things but focusing on the right things—those activities that make the greatest impact on patients' perceived value. Nurses, receptionists, maintenance employees, and others come into contact with patients and observe organizational realities in ways that are different from physicians, CEOs, and management personnel. The stockpiles of experience accumulated by these individuals can be valuable competitive resources if properly mined and extracted.

Resources can be combined to create synergy or "higher order value." In the previous value-chain discussion, linking activities provide unique opportunities to integrate functions such as operations, service, and technological development. In other words, there is a "creative interweaving of different types of skills" to create competitive advantage.

The more often a particular competence is used, the greater the potential for resource leveraging. Being able to quickly switch hard-won knowledge from delivering one service to another conserves service development resources and reduces cycle time in introducing and perfecting service delivery. Restricting exposure of resources to unnecessary risks is essential to the conservation of limited resources. An aspiring competitor in a health care market should think carefully before attacking the dominant player "head on" at the point of the competitor's greatest strength. To do so would be to subject limited resources to excessive risks and would likely be unsuccessful. Competing with a stronger competitor requires creativity and innovation.

Expediting success—increasing the resource multiplier by reducing the time between expenditure of resources and their recovery through revenue generation—is an important means of resource leveraging. Reducing the payback period of technological improvements in health care organizations is a substantial resource recovery challenge. On one hand, high-quality service delivery depends on state-of-the-art technology. On the other hand, this type of technology is expensive and usually has a relatively short economic life. Careful planning is required to ensure that paybacks are evaluated and accelerated in every possible way. Exhibit 4–7 provides a summary of the key methods of resource leveraging.

Interestingly, a great deal of resource leveraging is a matter of attitude and willingness to take reasonable risks, do things in new and innovative ways, learn from the experiences of others, and generally pursue excellence in all aspects of organizational performance. In fact, Hamel and Prahalad note that traditional strategic as well as

Exhibit 4–7 • **Summary of Resource-Leveraging Techniques**

Technique	Description
Converging	Preventing diversion of resources over time by building consensus on strategic goals. Strategic intent is important.
Focusing	Preventing dilution of resources at a given time by specifying precise improvement goals. Coordination is a critical element in this short-run equivalent to converging.
Targeting	Directing resources toward high-impact activities. It is impossible to give equal attention to all activities.
Learning	Making maximum use of existing knowledge by fully using the intelligence of every employee.
Borrowing	Accessing resources and expertise of partners. A critical aspect of strategic alliances and joint ventures.
Blending	Combining skills in new ways in order to multiply the value for each. Always look for potential synergies.
Balancing	Securing and ensuring complementary strategic assets. A key consideration in all cooperative strategies.
Recycling	Reusing skills and resources. Not only using skills but improving them is important.
Co-opting	Finding common causes and interests with others.
Protecting	Shielding resources from competitors and unreasonable risks.
Expediting	Minimizing time from investment to payback.

Source: From Gary Hamel and C.K. Prahalad, *Competing for the Future: Breakthrough Strategies For Seizing Control of Your Industry and Creating the Markets of Tomorrow*, p. 175. Copyright © 1994. Reprinted by permission of Harvard Business School Press, Boston, MA. All rights reserved.

behavioral factors lead to competitive advantage by stating that "cross-functioning teams, focusing on a few core competencies, strategic alliances, programs of employee involvement, and consensus are all parts of stretch."[31] In the end, the evaluating phase of internal environmental analysis (see Exhibit 4–2) requires an integration of what health care strategists know about the external environment with an understanding of organizational resources, competencies, capabilities, and aspirations. The issue of organizational aspirations and intent—mission, vision, values, and strategic objectives—will be discussed in Chapter 5. Finally, the process of internal environmental analysis, as Perspective 4–6 illustrates, requires diverse skills on the part of health care leaders.

Summary and Conclusions

A variety of topics relating to analyzing the internal environment of health care organizations have been introduced. With the information presented here and that covered in previous chapters, it is possible to relate the internal environment to the critical external forces that affect an organization. The objective is to relate both the external and internal environmental analyses to the organizational aspirations and goals to be discussed in Chapter 5.

Perspective 4–6

Some Essentials for Successfully Competing from Within

Health care leaders who engage in internal environmental analysis will recognize that organizations that compete successfully from within must be outstanding at a variety of dissimilar tasks. Three of the most important abilities are the following:

1. *Acquisition of Resources and Competencies.* Sustained competitive advantage is built on organizational differences. In order to be different, leaders of successful health care organizations need resource acquisition skills. This means the ability to attract nonhuman resources as well as the ability to identify, recruit, and maintain individuals with skills and experiences with which distinctive competency can be achieved.

2. *Synergistic Skills.* Merely being different is not enough to ensure that a health care organization develops a sustainable competitive advantage. Competitive advantage demands that the differences be integrated in a way that provides added value when compared to other members of the strategic group. Strategic leaders, in other words, must configure resources and competencies in ways that add value.

3. *Competitive Insight.* Ultimately, sustained competitive advantage is built on incremental value; and value is a function of cost leadership or uniqueness. Health care organizations that achieve sustained competitive advantage must be highly creative. This requires not only achieving cost leadership or uniqueness but an ability to articulate and communicate the value-added potential for the organization.

Rarely are resources and competencies alone enough to obtain sustained competitive advantage. Stretch and leverage are essential. Many successful organizations effectively overcome limitations in resources, competencies, and capabilities by leveraging what they have and "outstretching" competitors.

It is important to understand the differences between the traditional approach to surveying internal strengths and weaknesses and the resource-based view of competitive advantage. Careful distinctions must be drawn between resources, competencies, and capabilities and the role of each in achieving and sustaining competitive advantage. Resources are assets that are used in creating and delivering services. Resources assume strategic significance to the extent that they are valuable, rare, inimitable, and nonsubstitutable. Competencies are skill based and inherently human in nature. They are the skills, knowledge, and experiences individuals bring to and develop in organizations. Competencies may be threshold, core, or distinctive in nature. Capabilities represent the ability to coordinate and utilize resources and competencies in unique and innovative ways. Understanding resources, competencies, and capabilities represents a more detailed investigation of the items identified in the survey of potential strengths and weaknesses. The value chain was used in the third phase of internal environmental assessment as a means of analyzing strategic resources, competencies, and capabilities in terms of cost and uniqueness drivers.

As important as resources, competencies, and capabilities are, however, an organization's vision or strategic intent should never be limited by its present stocks of resources, competencies, or capabilities. Often the most important role of the strategic leader is to create a gap or chasm between the aspirations of employees and the organization and the resources, competencies, and capabilities it has available to realize the aspirations. This introduces the dual concepts of stretch and resource leveraging. In concluding, competitive advantage ultimately requires three things on the part of health care strategists: an understanding of the external environment, an understanding of the internal environment, and an understanding of the organization's aspirations and strategic intent. Organizational aspiration is the subject of Chapter 5.

Key Terms and Concepts in Strategic Management

administrative services subsystem
ASSIST analysis
capabilities
clinical subsystem
competency
financial subsystem
general management subsystem

human resources subsystem
internal strength
internal weakness
marketing subsystem
physical facilities subsystem
resource-based view
resource leveraging

resources
stretch
sustained competitive advantage
threshold competency
value-chain analysis

Questions for Class Discussion

1. Discuss the statement: "Internal strengths and weaknesses only have meaning when related to external opportunities and threats."

2. Discuss an efficiency-adaptability dilemma for a health care organization in your region of the nation.

3. What does it mean when it is said that a health care organization has a sustained competitive advantage?

4. What is the difference between objective and subjective strengths and weaknesses? What is the difference between absolute and relative strengths and weaknesses?

5. What are the subsystems an organization should monitor to assess its relative strengths and weaknesses? Are any of these subsystems more or less important than any others?

6. What is the difference between organizational information and an organizational intelligence system? Which is more important?

7. Why is the ability to coordinate all the organizational subsystems so important in an evaluation of the strengths or weaknesses of the general management of an organization?

8. Describe the resource-based view for internal environmental analysis. Why is it so important to determine health care organizational differences to effectively use this approach?

9. What is meant by competency as used in strategic management? How do threshold competencies, core competencies, and distinctive competencies differ? How are they similar?

10. What is the difference between a competency and a capability? How can these concepts be accurately related to value-chain analysis?

11. Why is the ASSIST model useful to health care managers in determining competitive advantage?

12. What is a value-chain analysis? What is the importance of this chain to strategic management? What is the difference between primary and support activities?

13. What is meant by the term *resource leveraging?* How is leveraging related to stretch?

14. How would you define *stretch?* Is this really a meaningful strategic term? Why or why not?

Notes

1. This argument is presented in George Stalk, Philip Evans, and Lawrence Shulman, "Competing on Capabilities: The New Rules of Corporate Strategy," *Harvard Business Review* 70, no. 2 (March/April 1992), pp. 57–69.

2. Richard Hall, "A Framework for Linking Intangible Resources and Capabilities to Sustainable Competitive Advantage," *Strategic Management Journal* 14, no. 6 (1993), pp. 607–618.

3. Glen R. Carroll, "A Sociological View on Why Firms Differ," *Strategic Management Journal* 14, no. 4 (1993), pp. 237–249; and Giovanni Azzone and Umberto Bertele, "Measuring Resources for Supporting Resource-Based Competencies," *Management Decision* 33, no. 9 (1995), pp. 57–58.

4. Chester I. Barnard, *The Functions of the Executive* (Cambridge, Massachusetts: Harvard University Press, 1938), pp. 195–196.

5. Stuart L. Hart, "A Natural-Resource-Based View of the Firm," *Academy of Management Review* 20, no. 4 (1995), pp. 986–1014.

6. Margaret A. Peteraf, "The Cornerstones of Competitive Advantage: A Resource-Based View," *Strategic Management Journal* 14, no. 3 (1993), pp. 179–191.

7. Birger Wernerfelt, "The Resource-Based View of the Firm: Ten Years After," *Strategic Management Journal* 16, no. 3 (1995), p. 173.

8. Jay B. Barney and Mark H. Hansen, "Trustworthiness As a Source of Competitive Advantage," *Strategic Management Journal* 15, no. 3 (1994), pp. 175–190; and Jay Barney, "Firm Resources and Sustained Competitive Advantage," *Journal of Management* 17, no. 1 (1991), pp. 99–120.

9. Alan L. Brumagim, "A Hierarchy of Corporate Resources," in *Advances in Strategic Management: Resource-Based View of the Firm*, vol. 10, part A. eds. Paul Shrivastava, Anne S. Huff, and Jane E. Dutton (Greenwich, Connecticut: JAI Press, 1994), pp. 81–112.

10. Jon Asplund, "Hospital Buying Shifts to Computer Equipment," *AHA News* (April 29, 1996), p. 4.

11. Rebecca Henderson and Ian Cockburn, "Measuring Competence? Exploring Firm Effects in Pharmaceutical Research," *Strategic Management Journal* 15, no. 1 (1994), pp. 63–84.

12. Jim Montague and Hilarie Pitman, "Pharmaceuticals: Record Spending on R&D," *Hospitals and Health Networks* (March 20, 1996), p. 12.

13. Raphael Amit and Paul J. H. Schoemaker, "Strategic Assets and Organizational Rent," *Strategic Management Journal* 14, no. 1 (1993), pp. 33–46.

14. Hart, "A Natural-Resource-Based View of the Firm," p. 986.

15. Dave Ulrich and Dale Lake, "Organizational Capability: Creating Competitive Advantage," *Academy of Management Executive* 5, no. 1 (1991), pp. 77–85.

16. David J. Collis, "Research Note: How Valuable Are Organizational Capabilities?" *Strategic Management Journal* 15, no. 2 (1994), pp. 143–152.

17. Henderson and Cockburn, "Measuring Competence," p. 66.

18. Amit and Schoemaker, "Strategic Assets and Organizational Rent," p. 35.

19. Janice A. Black and Kimberly B. Boal, "Strategic Resources: Traits, Configurations, and Paths to Sustainable Competitive Advantage," *Strategic Management Journal* 15, no. 2 (1994), pp. 131–148.

20. Amit and Schoemaker, "Strategic Assets and Organizational Rent," p. 37.

21. Stalk, Evans, and Shulman, " Competing on Capabilities," p. 62.

22. C. K. Prahalad and Gary Hamel, "The Core Competency of the Corporation," *Harvard Business Review* 68, no. 3 (May/June 1990), p. 82.

23. Constantinos C. Markides and Peter J. Williamson, "Related Diversification, Core Competencies, and Corporate Performance," *Strategic Management Journal* 15, no. 3 (1994), pp. 149–165.

24. Stalk, Evans, and Shulman, "Competing on Capabilities," p. 62.

25. Jay B. Barney, "Looking Inside for Competitive Advantage," *Academy of Management Executive* 9, no. 4 (1995), pp. 49–61.

26. Michael E. Porter, *Competitive Advantage: Creating and Sustaining Superior Performance* (New York: Free Press, 1985), Chapter 2. See also Michael E. Porter, "Toward a Dynamic Theory of Strategy," *Strategic Management Journal* 12, no. 1 (1991), pp. 95–117.

27. Daniel R. Gilbert, Jr., Edwin Hartman, John J. Mauriel, and R. Edward Freeman. *A Logic for Strategy* (Cambridge, Massachusetts: Ballinger Publishing, 1988), p. 92.

28. Stalk, Evans, and Shulman, "Competing on Competencies," p. 69.

29. Gary Hamel and C. K. Prahalad, "Strategy As Stretch and Leverage," *Harvard Business Review* 71, no. 3 (March/April 1993), pp. 75–84.

30. This discussion has been adapted from Gary Hamel and C. K. Prahalad, *Competing for the Future* (Boston: Harvard Business School Press, 1994), Chapter 7.

31. Gary Hamel and C. K. Prahalad, "Competing in the New Economy: Managing Out of Bounds," *Strategic Management Journal* 17, no. 1 (1996), pp. 237–242.

Additional Readings

Estes, Ralph, *Tyranny of the Bottom Line* (San Francisco: Berrett-Koehler Publishers, 1996). Most responsible health care managers have asked themselves, "As managers, can we maintain our responsibilities for financial survival without injuring people and communities by the hard decisions that must be made?" This book illustrates how the corporate system that was originally created to serve the public interest has actually acquired great power over the public. Estes provides an insightful view of how management must consider the interests of all stakeholders even when it means less domination or tyranny by the bottom line.

Halé, Jacques, *From Concepts to Capabilities* (New York: John Wiley & Sons, 1996). Rapid change and uncertainty are two important constraints in health care organizations. This book discusses an approach to process redesign and offers techniques for converting change from a threat to a powerful strategic weapon. Case studies are used to provide examples of improvements in productivity and profits through use of this approach.

Hayes, Robert H., Gary P. Pisano, and David M. Upton, *Strategic Operations* (New York: Free Press, 1996). This combination text and case book emphasizes the manufacturing process itself as a means for achieving competitive advantage. The authors propose new explanations for ways that organizations can achieve competitive advantage through the development of operational capabilities.

Trotter, Jeffrey P., *The Quest for Cost-Effectiveness in Health Care: Achieving Clinical Excellence while Controlling Costs* (Chicago: AHA Press, 1996). This book offers instructions to health care executives for introducing new drug therapies, equipment, and other health care technologies in a cost-effective manner. The author describes innovative tools to assist in achieving better clinical outcomes while controlling costs.

Stacey, Ralph, *Complexity and Creativity in Organizations* (San Francisco: Berrett-Koehler Publishers, 1996). Health care organizations today are characterized by faster technological development and information flow, increasing inter-connectedness between organizations, and much greater diversity among employees that result from these developments. This book describes how the "science of complexity" provides managers with useful frameworks for making sense out of life in organizations and, thereby, rethinking our actions to creatively solve problems.

Mission, Vision, Values, and Strategic Objectives

Chapter 5

Learning Objectives

After completing this chapter you should be able to:

1. Understand the relationships among organizational mission, vision, values, key performance areas, and strategic objectives.

2. Identify the characteristics and components of organizational mission statements.

3. Write a mission statement.

4. Recognize the important characteristics of a well-conceived organizational vision and statement of values.

5. Appreciate the importance of the manager's role as the "keeper of the organization's vision."

6. Suggest a set of key performance areas for a health care organization.

7. Develop strategic objectives related to key performance areas.

8. Understand the motivational potential of clearly established and communicated directional strategies.

> "What distinguishes leaders from laggards, and greatness from mediocrity, is the ability to uniquely imagine what could be."
> • *Gary Hamel and C. K. Prahalad*

Directional Strategies

Mission, vision, values, and strategic objectives are types of organizational goals or desired end results. The mission attempts to capture the organization's distinctive purpose or reason for being. The vision is what the managers, employees, physicians, patients, and other interested groups want the organization to be when it is accomplishing its purpose or mission—the hope for the future. Values are the principles (innovation, integrity, teamwork, and so on) that guide decision making and are held dear by members of the organization. These are principles the managers and employees will not compromise while they achieve the mission and pursue the vision.

Once the mission statement is properly conceived it is possible to identify a relatively few key performance areas for the organization. These areas identify the activities that absolutely must be accomplished if the organization is to achieve its purpose and realize its mission.

Daughters of Charity National Health System–East Central (DCNHS–East Central): Our Mission in Action

Ask any sample of health care executives what they think about mission statements and at least a small number will answer with skepticism. Some believe a mission statement is a necessary, but not particularly useful, part of a strategic plan. Some believe it is a good thing to have because the public relations department needs it for press releases and annual reports. A few really believe in mission statements, but think of them as ends in themselves.

To be effective, the mission must be at the heart of operations and drive all aspects of planning. At the DCNHS–East Central the mission serves a unique function relative to planning and business activities. The mission is at the center of a circular flow process connecting planning and operations. It is the basis for planning; and when it is accomplished, the mission generates the resources needed to continue operations.

The diagram highlights the fact that maintaining operational and financial strength is a fundamental stewardship responsibility. It calls for ongoing evaluation and continuous improvement because changes are needed to enable local health ministries to perform well and meet community needs effectively in a dynamic environment. This mission integration cycle illustrates that ongoing evaluation, high performance standards, and continuous improvement are the hallmarks of the DCNHS–East Central.

Source: From Daughters of Charity National Health System–East Central, *Our Heritage, Our Vision* (1995). Reprinted with permission.

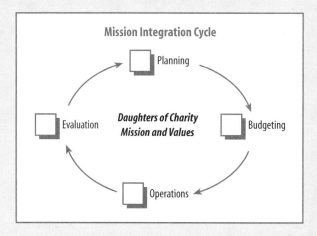

Finally, relative to each key performance area, several strategic objectives are needed to provide tangible performance targets for the organization. The mission is a statement of distinctiveness, the vision is a hope, the values are guiding principles, key performance areas must be accomplished for success, and objectives are specific quantitative desired end results. The conceptual framework for this analysis is summarized in Exhibit 5–1.

Exhibit 5–1 • **From Organizational Mission to Strategic Objectives**

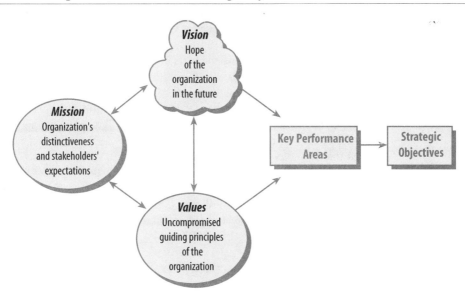

Organizational Purpose and Mission

Chester Barnard, in *The Functions of the Executive,* stated that only three things are needed to have an organization: (1) communication, (2) a willingness to serve, and (3) a common purpose. The inculcation of the "belief in the real existence of a common purpose" is, according to Barnard, "the essential executive function."[1] This purpose, among other things, helps managers make sense of the environment. When the purpose of an organization is clearly understood, the complexity of the environment can be reduced and organized in a way that can be analyzed in light of the goals the organization wishes to achieve.[2]

For example, if the CEO of a large managed-care plan considers all the changes taking place in the organization's environment, they may appear confusing and overpowering. Can anyone effectively track the changes taking place in the biotechnology, cultural values, and political arenas? However, if the CEO were to focus on only those aspects relating to the elderly (such as the aging trend of the population, the increased financial condition of this group of aging people, and selected social values) from the perspective of the mission of the managed-care plan, the task becomes more manageable.

The common purpose (mission) to which Barnard referred is the reason that organizations exist. Some organizations exist to make money for the owners, some are founded to provide health care to indigent patients, others are started to deliver health services in as convenient a way as possible or to provide the care needed by groups of individuals who belong to the same managed-care plan.

Mission: A Statement of Distinctiveness

In the hierarchy of goals (end results and organizational plans to accomplish them), the mission is the most general. Although a well-conceived mission is general, it is more concrete than vision. Organizational missions are not expressions of hope. On the contrary, they are attempts to capture the essence of the organizational purpose and commit it to writing.

Unfortunately, mission statements are rarely the true "living documents" that are capable of inspiring high performance. One leading authority on strategic planning stated that most mission statements are "worthless."[3] The evidence, however, does not support this view. For example, the well-known consulting firm of Bain and Company indicated that in a survey of executives asking which of twenty-five management tools were used most often, mission statements were ranked first. The list of tools included things such as activity-based costing, value-chain analysis, and so on. Interestingly, the mission statement has been ranked first every year since the study began in 1989, whereas other tools such as total quality management (TQM) have lost ground. TQM, for example, was ranked third from 1989 to 1993 but seventh in 1995.[4]

One study of hospital mission statements found that almost 85 percent of the respondents had mission statements. Unfortunately, most of the executives who completed the survey did not perceive a high level of commitment to the statement by employees or that specific actions were very much influenced by the mission.[5] A more recent study of state-level departments of public health indicated that more than 90 percent had formal, written mission statements.[6]

Despite the frequency with which formal mission statements are encountered, a great deal of disagreement remains regarding their value and the influence these statements actually have on behavior within organizations. This is unfortunate, because the mission statement is a crucially important part of strategic goal setting. It is the "super-ordinate goal" that stands the test of time and assists top management in navigating through periods of turbulence and change.[7] It is, in other words, the "stake in the ground" that provides the anchor for strategic planning and management. It must be emphasized, however, that mission statements, even at their best, can never be substitutes for well-conceived and strongly formulated strategies.[8]

An organizational *mission* is a broadly defined but enduring statement of purpose that distinguishes a health care organization from other organizations of its type and identifies the scope of its operations in product, service, and market (competitive) terms.[9] Although mission statements are relatively enduring, they must be flexible in light of changing conditions. As Perspective 5–1 illustrates, missions sometimes must be accomplished in different ways than originally intended.

When formulated correctly and used properly, mission statements force managers in health care organizations to ask a series of questions.[10] The answers radically affect how the organization performs. These questions include:

1. *Are we not doing anything new that we should be doing?* Perhaps an academic medical center, after analyzing the environment and studying its own strengths and weaknesses, determines that it should purchase a long-term-care facility. Historically, the medical center has not been involved in long-term care, but the aging

Perspective 5–1

Holding Fast to the Mission Even in Changing Times

In New York, as in other areas of the nation, managed care seems to be the order of the day. In 1996, New York City had about 25 percent managed care in all its forms, and the percentage was increasing. Some of the city's hospitals hoped to cushion the impact of lost referrals for inpatient care by buying primary-care physicians' practices. Some observers believe that for many of the hospitals the action was "too little, too late."

Mount Sinai Medical Center, however, started planning for the changes two years earlier by forming a strategic network called the Mount Sinai Health System. This alliance of twenty-one hospitals and twelve long-term-care facilities in several counties in New York as well as New Jersey and southwest Connecticut has actually increased inpatient volume. Mount Sinai is now adding beds

when most hospitals are planning for lower occupancy rates. John Rowe, M.D., president of the medical center and the Mount Sinai School of Medicine, believes that his main advantage was that moving early allowed him more time to plan. According to Dr. Rowe, "We're not going to change our mission of providing excellent care, research, and training for physicians, but we need to create a system that gives us enough money to train the next generation of physicians to work in ambulatory-care settings, community-based facilities, and other primary-care sites."

Source: "How One New York Hospital Is Moving to Head Managed Care off at the Pass," *Hospital and Health Networks* 70, no. 2 (January 20, 1996), pp. 22–23.

population and the need to train personnel to work with the elderly suggest that the time is right to alter the mission to include long-term-care facilities.

2. *Are we doing some things now that we should not be doing?* The same academic medical center, after proper analysis, may conclude that its burn unit no longer serves the purpose for which it was created and decides that the resources dedicated to the unit could be better used in other ways.

3. *Are we doing some things now that we should continue to do, but in a different way?* Perhaps the academic medical center concludes that it should continue to provide certain kinds of technician programs to train needed personnel but that it should no longer try to do it in the traditional manner. Perhaps a joint venture with a local junior college, where most of the classroom training could be conducted, would be better for everyone. Perspective 5–2 illustrates how one Medicaid HMO contracted with a city health department to provide immunizations rather than attempting to offer them directly.

Characteristics of Mission Statements

The mission statement definition presented previously highlights several important characteristics.

1. *Missions are broadly defined statements of purpose.* Well-formulated mission statements are written and communicated to those involved in doing the work of the organization. They are broad but also, in a sense, specific. That is, mission

| Perspective 5-2

Different Ways to Accomplish a Mission

Mercy Health Plan, a Medicaid HMO in Philadelphia, is a subsidiary of Mercy Health Corporation of Southeast Pennsylvania and run by the Sisters of Mercy. A major part of its mission is to care for the poor. However, with regard to providing immunizations, it has found a better way to accomplish its mission without its providers tooling up to do things they are not prepared to do.

The HMO gave $1.3 million to the city health department to create "express-lane immunizations" at four public health clinics. The goal was to have children immunized in 30 minutes or less even without appointments. Half the grant was devoted to hardware and software purchases for the city's immunization data system. Doctors had to have immunization records to ensure shots were up to date and to avoid duplication. The data

system could assist in providing the needed information.

One observer, looking at the Philadelphia experience, noted that Medicaid HMOs should bring into their networks the community health clinics that already have expertise in caring for the needy population and are located in strategic areas. This way, patients will continue to get care from providers who specialize in addressing their needs, and the HMO "won't have to reinvent the wheel."

Source: "Happily Ever After: Managed Care and Public Health," _Hospital and Health Networks_ 69, no. 20 (October 20, 1995), p. 31.

statements should be vague enough to allow for innovation and expansion into new activities when advisable, yet narrow enough to provide direction.
2. _Mission statements are enduring._ The purpose, and consequently the mission, of an organization does not change often and should be enduring. People are committed to ideas and causes that remain relatively stable over time.
3. _Mission statements should underscore the uniqueness of the organization._ Good missions distinguish the organization from all others of its type.
4. _Mission statements should identify the scope of operations in terms of service and market._ It is important that the mission statement specify what business the organization is in (health care) and who it believes are the primary stakeholders.

Lovelace Medical Center's mission statement "to provide high quality, cost effective health care that is consumer oriented and physician directed" makes it clear that the medical center is committed to providing quality care as determined by physicians. At the same time, the mission precludes the center from entering industries such as textiles or heavy manufacturing but allows the center to maintain its options to actively participate in other areas such as home health care, health maintenance organizations, and so on.

Although missions are enduring, this should not imply that the mission will never or should never change. New technologies, demographic trends, and so on might be very good reasons to rethink the mission of an organization. For example, a number of hospitals have incorporated the desire to be an "independent provider of health care" in their statements of mission. In today's managed-care-oriented health care environment, that aspect of mission may need to be revisited.

These characteristics of mission statements illustrate the essential properties of well-conceived and communicated mission statements. They outline worthy ideals that are not often achieved by strategic managers in business firms or health care institutions. Nevertheless, the mission provides direction. Good mission statements are not easy to write, but fortunately there is general agreement on what they should include.

Components of Mission Statements

There is no single way to develop and write mission statements. Mission, in order to define the uniqueness of an organization, must highlight those things that constitute uniqueness. Some of the more important components of a mission are listed below and illustrated with the use of mission statements from a variety of health care institutions.[11]

1. *Mission statements target customers and markets.* Frequently the mission statement provides evidence of the kind of customers or patients the organization seeks to serve and the markets where it intends to compete. The mission statement of a long-term-care facility, for example, might make explicit the organization's intent to serve patients with special needs, such as those suffering from Alzheimer's disease, as well as general geriatric patients.

   The mission statement of the Children's Hospital of Wisconsin emphasizes, as does the name of the institution, that children are the patients the hospital is dedicated to serving (see Exhibit 5–2). As the only children's hospital in the state, it is clear that patient care, research, and teaching activities all revolve around the unique needs of children. Other health care organizations such as Chronimed, Inc. in Minnetonka, Minnesota, are dedicated to the care of patients with specific diseases. Chronimed's mission statement is: "To manage costs, improve outcomes, and enhance the quality of life of individuals with chronic health conditions." Consistent with its mission, Chronimed specializes in the treatment of patients with diabetes, HIV/AIDS, and other chronic conditions.

2. *Mission statements indicate the principal services delivered by the organization.* A specialized health care organization such as Hospice Care, Inc. would highlight the special services it provides in its mission statement. Similarly, Living Centers of

---

Exhibit 5–2 • Mission Statement of Children's Hospital of Wisconsin

Children's Hospital of Wisconsin is a private, independent, not-for-profit, pediatric medical center whose mission is to be one of the nation's premier pediatric hospitals.

- Children's Hospital of Wisconsin provides high-quality, comprehensive health care services to children appropriate for their needs.
- Children's Hospital of Wisconsin is a center for the education of health professionals in the care of children.
- Children's Hospital of Wisconsin supports research and training activities that increase the knowledge and understanding of the health care needs of children.
- Children's Hospital of Wisconsin provides leadership and expertise as a community, state, and regional resource to advocate the health and well-being of children.

Source: From *1994 Annual Report: 100 Years of Caring: 1894–1994*, p. 19. Copyright © 1994. Reprinted by permission of Children's Hospital of Wisconsin.

America, the nation's third-largest operator of long-term-care centers offers more diverse but still relatively well-defined services as illustrated in Exhibit 5–3.

3. *Mission statements specify the geographical area within which the organization intends to concentrate.* This element is most frequently included when there is a regional aspect to the organization's service delivery. The mission statement of the Parkland Memorial Hospital, for example, states that "our mission is to give Dallas County residents access to the highest standards of health care, regardless of ability to pay, while providing patient-centered services that acknowledge each patient's value system." As indicated in the name, the Rapid City Regional Hospital's mission statement (see Exhibit 5–4) specifies its geographical domain as the region.

4. *Mission statements identify the organization's philosophy.* Frequently the mission of an organization will include statements about unique beliefs, values, aspirations, and priorities. This is particularly true for health facilities operated by religious groups.

    The mission statement for Wesley Homes is included as Exhibit 5–5. The mission statement reflects the organization's philosophy of establishing a caring community that values independence, integrity, and personal dignity. It reflects the overall commitment to enhance the lives of residents by providing support for physical, spiritual, and social needs.

5. *Mission statements include confirmation of the organization's preferred self-image.* The manner in which a health care organization views itself may constitute a uniqueness that should be included in the mission. The mission statement of American Medical Response (see Exhibit 5–6) illustrates how this organization views itself as a "partnership of entrepreneurs" that has successfully brought together the "best" service providers and the "finest" systems and expertise for the benefit of the patients it serves.

Exhibit 5–3 • **Mission Statement of Living Centers of America**

Living Centers of America's Mission is to be the preferred provider for health, rehabilitation, and support services in the communities we serve. Our customers will choose us because we provide high-quality, cost-effective, customer-responsive care and services.

Source: From "LCA Committed to New Mission Statement and Values," *Quality Quarterly* (January 1995), p. 6. Reprinted with permission of the Living Centers of America.

Exhibit 5–4 • **Rapid City Regional Hospital Mission Statement**

Rapid City Regional Hospital's mission is to provide leadership in maintaining and improving the health care of all the people in the region. The hospital demonstrates its commitment to this endeavor by providing quality services through innovative programs, comfortable and convenient facilities, and a staff of caring physicians, employees, and volunteers.

Source: Circle of Life: Report to the Community (Rapid City, South Dakota: Rapid City Regional Hospital, 1994), back cover.

6. *Mission statements specify the organization's desired public image.* This customarily manifests itself in statements such as the organization's desire to be a "good citizen" in the communities where its operations are located or a similar concern. However, organizations may have a unique approach or focus that they want to communicate to the public. Sierra Health Services, Inc., for example, has followed a strategy of marketing managed-care products to employer groups and individuals. Therefore, Sierra's mission statement (see Exhibit 5–7) highlights the importance of managed care and its employees' commitment to ensuring high-quality, cost-effective services.

Not every one of the characteristics discussed can or necessarily should be included in a single mission statement. Any particular statement will likely include one or several of these aspects but almost never will all of the components be included. Interestingly, in the study of mission statements previously noted, it was suggested that higher performing organizations generally have more comprehensive mission statements. Moreover, it

Exhibit 5–5 • **Mission Statement of Wesley Homes**

Wesley Homes strives to enhance quality of life by providing the residents a variety of living choices and supportive services to meet their physical, social, and spiritual needs. We are a caring community that values independence, integrity, and the personal dignity and uniqueness of those who are served as well as those who provide service.

Source: From promotional brochure for Wesley Homes. Reprinted by permission.

Exhibit 5–6 • **Mission Statement of American Medical Response**

Our mission is straightforward: to provide the most effective and highest quality care for our patients in the most efficient manner possible. To accomplish this, American was initially formed as a "partnership of entrepreneurs" where the best ambulance service providers could bring together the finest systems and know-how and then deploy them throughout the country.

Source: From "When Every Second Counts," *1993 Annual Report*, p. 3. Reprinted by permission of American Medical Response.

Exhibit 5–7 • **Mission Statement of Sierra Health Services, Inc.**

The company mission is to develop people who provide high-quality services and products in the managed health care and insurance environments in order to maximize value to its patients, customers, and shareholders. The company defines managed health care as quality care delivered in an organized and cost-effective manner. Managed care requires that providers, insurers, and patients work together. It necessitates that all providers are accountable for both the treatments dispensed to the patient and the charges billed to the payors for this treatment. The system further requires that the care delivered be necessary, appropriate, and fairly priced.

Source: From "All the Benefits of Good Health," *1994 Annual Report*, p. 4. Reprinted by permission of Sierra Health Services, Inc.

seemed that components such as organizational philosophy, self-concept, and desired public image were particularly associated with higher performing organizations in the sample studied.[12]

Building a Mission Statement

First, there has to be a leader who begins the discussion concerning the need to examine or reexamine the organization's mission and attempt to clearly state its purpose. This statement helps all employees focus their efforts on the most important priorities. A group of interested personnel (administrative and nonadministrative) should be assembled to begin the task of developing a mission statement. Prior to actually writing the mission statement, a series of meetings should be held to ensure that there is desire for a well-understood and widely communicated statement of organizational distinctiveness. Once commitment has been determined, assessments should be made of what makes the organization successful from the perspectives of employees as well as other key stakeholders. Further, consideration should be given to what these perceptions of success would likely be in the future.

To stimulate some initial thinking on the part of the group, each person could be asked to think about the points noted in Exhibit 5–8. Recognizing that few members of the health care community have been previously involved in writing a mission statement, this exhibit was developed to encourage some initial thought without introducing too much structure into the process.

After the management staff has been given time to think about the organization, its distinctiveness in its environment, and the likely future it would face, the group can meet in a planning retreat format. There is a great deal to recommend being away from the office, phones, and beepers to focus on the organization's mission. At the retreat, the components of the mission can be developed with the aid of Exhibit 5–9. This exhibit simply provides a listing of mission statement factors previously discussed with space provided for participants to elaborate on their concept of the different components. After discussion and fine-tuning the language, a draft of the mission statement can be developed. The draft should be circulated among key individuals to gain their input and eventually their support for the mission.

Exhibit 5–8 · **Writing the Components of the Mission Statement**

Mission Statement Components	Descriptions [Key Words] of Our Mission
1. Target Customers/Clients and Markets	
2. Principal Services Delivered	
3. Geographical Domain of Operations	
4. Commitment to Specific Values	
5. Explicit Philosophy	
6. Other Important Component(s)	

Exhibit 5–9 • **An Aid for Thinking About Our Mission**

1. *The mission of the* _____ *is to…*

How would you broadly define our purpose? Be sure what you say will be meaningful to the people who work here. Be specific yet broad enough to allow innovation in how things are done, the development of new activities when advisable, and so on. Our purpose should be independent of time —it should be enduring.

2. *We accomplish our unique purpose by …*

What is the scope of our services? This should be meaningful to external stakeholders, who are unaware of the details of our operations, as well as employees.

3. *We provide our services to …*

Who are our customers or clients and where are their locations? Do not be limited by the obvious.

4. *The principles we intend to observe in our relationships with customers/clients and stakeholders are …*

What are the standards of conduct to which we are committed? These standards should provide philosophical guides to employee and management behavior in dealing with others and among ourselves.

5. *Our philosophy includes …*

Although our statement of values will list specific guiding principles, the mission statement should underscore or reinforce any particularly important over-arching commitments of the organization.

Top-Level Leadership a Must for Mission Development

If a mission statement is to be a "living document," employees must develop a sense of ownership and commitment to the mission of the organization. For this reason, employees should be involved in the development and communication of the mission. However, top-level leadership must be committed if the process is to actually begin. Developing a mission statement is a challenging task. Frequently, attempts are made to formulate "blue sky" statements of constraints and little more. For example, it is of little real value to state that our health maintenance organization is devoted to being a good citizen of the local community and to paying wages and benefits comparable to those of other organizations in the area. Realistically, the HMO must be a good citizen and, if it wants employees, its wages and benefits must be competitive.

The role of the chief executive officer in formulating the mission can never be underestimated. Mission statement development is not a task that should be delegated to the planning staff. The CEO, selected line officers, and other key individuals who will be instrumental in accomplishing the mission should have input into the document.

Of necessity, this process of developing a sense of mission is built with top management leadership. Although the process appears to be simple, the actual work of writing a mission statement is time consuming and complex, with many "drafts" before the final document is produced. The forms (Exhibits 5–8 and 5–9) can help and be useful aids to strategic thinking about clients, services, and domain; but the development and communication of a well-conceived mission statement is challenging. Although developing a mission statement is not an easy task, it is a necessary one.

Vision: Hope for the Future

The mission is developed from the needs of all the stakeholders or groups who have a vested interest in the success and survival of the organization. Vision, on the other hand, is an expression of hope. It is a description of what the organization will be like and look like when it is fulfilling its purpose.[13] The Fallon Healthcare System of Worcester, Massachusetts, created the vision statement included as Exhibit 5–10. This statement illustrates the importance attached to a variety of stakeholders—the community, patients, and employees.

Effective visions possess four important attributes including: idealism, uniqueness, future orientation, and imagery.[14] Visions are about ideals, standards, and desired future states. The focus on ideals encourages everyone in the organization to think about possibilities. Visions communicate what makes our organization unequaled and sets us apart from everyone else. The focus, as with missions, is on distinctiveness. Organizational members need leaders who are forward-looking. Effective visions are "statements of destination" that map where we collectively want to go. Finally, visions are built on images of the future. If you ask someone to describe a desirable place or thing, they almost always do so in terms of images. Rarely do we focus on tangible characteristics. Images motivate people to pursue the seemingly impossible. Perspective 5–3 suggests some different ways employees may react to a vision.

Exhibit 5–10 • Fallon Healthcare System Vision Statement

The Fallon Healthcare System, committed to creating healthier lives in our communities:

- will relentlessly pursue unparalleled quality, value, and patient, customer, and staff satisfaction;
- will create the national model for integrated health care delivery and financing;
- will continuously rethink, reshape, and refine solutions to health care challenges;
- will create healthier communities by creatively challenging individuals to be more responsible for their personal health status; and
- will be cherished as the best place to come for care and the best place to work.

Source: From Fallon Healthcare System vision statement. Reprinted by permission.

Perspective 5–3

Reactions to a Vision

People react in different ways to visions. Some of the possible reactions are listed below:

- *Commitment.* Employees want a vision, a sense of direction into an uncertain future and will "create the rules" to make it happen.
- *Enrollment.* Employees want the vision and, although they are less passionate than those who are committed, they will do what can be done within the rules of the organization to make it happen.
- *Genuine Compliance.* Employees see the benefits of the vision and will do everything expected of them—and sometimes even more—to make it happen. They are "good soldiers" in pursuit of the vision.
- *Formal Compliance.* Employees on the whole see the benefits of the vision and will do what is expected of them to make it happen.

- *Grudging Compliance.* Employees do not see the benefit of the vision but are afraid they will lose their jobs if they do not "play." They do what is expected because they have to; but they let it be known they are not on board.
- *Noncompliance.* Employees do not see the benefit of the vision and will not do what is expected.
- *Apathy.* Employees are neither for nor against the vision. They have no interest and no energy to pursue it.

Source: From Peter M. Senge, *The Fifth Discipline*, pp. 219–220. Copyright © 1990. Adapted with permission of Doubleday, a division of Bantam Doubleday Dell Publishing Group, Inc.

Origins of Vision

Health care managers acquire vision from an appreciation of the history of the organization, a perception of the opportunities present in the environment, and an understanding of the strategic capacity of the organization to take advantage of these opportunities. All of these factors work together to form an organization's hope for the future.

History and Vision   An organization's history is made up of a variety of things that affect the development of vision. The founder's philosophy is important if the organization's inception is sufficiently recent to recall who actually started the hospital, clinic, long-term-care facility, or home-care agency.

Consider, for example, the Mayo Clinic in Rochester, Minnesota, an organization that is rich in history and tradition. Children's books tell successive generations how a destructive tornado in Rochester one night caused the Sisters of Saint Francis to aid the elder Dr. Mayo in caring for storm victims and encouraged his two sons, Will and Charlie, to follow in their father's footsteps.

The result is a world-famous research, teaching, and patient care facility that continues to thrive and expand far beyond the boundaries of Minnesota. Anyone who hopes to succeed at the Mayo Clinic and understand its unique vision must be aware of the founders and the past. The history of an organization is instrumental in the formation of its image and its vision or hope for what it is capable of becoming.[15]

Vision and the Environment   Another important determinant of a manager's vision for an organization is his or her environmental view. Some organizations have "bad" experiences with environmental forces such as the government. Many private physicians and health care managers look at attempts by the government to get involved in setting rates, regulating quality, and so on as unnecessary and unwarranted interventions in private enterprise. When this view is adopted, enemies are seen "out there" in the environment and the vision becomes altered accordingly.[16] The vision is compromised, and lack of accomplishment is blamed on these external forces. Sometimes the past experiences of organizations and the uncontrollable nature of environmental forces cause managers to engage in strategies that either over- or under-react to crises.

Vision and Internal Capacity   A manager's vision is also related to the perceived strengths and weaknesses of the organization. The challenge to reconcile vision and internal capacity is illustrated by Senge's integrative principle of creative tension.[17] *Creative tension* comes into play when management develops a view of where they want to be in the future (vision) and tells the truth about where they are now or "current reality." The current reality is greatly determined by the organization's present internal capacity and how this capacity relates to aspirations. Organizations deal with this creative tension in different ways. If the organization has been successful in the past, it may be aggressive about the future and raise its current reality in pursuit of the vision. If it has experienced failure, limited success, or merely has a cautious philosophy, management may choose instead to revise and reduce the vision to bring it more in line with current reality.

Managers have visions, and organizations gain and lose competitive advantage based on how the vision "fits" the environment and the strategic capability of the organization to capitalize on opportunities. However, developing a vision is "messy work," and for this reason we will examine more closely what organizational vision actually means.[18]

Health Care Strategists as Pathfinders

The job of building a vision for an organization is frequently referred to as *pathfinding.*[19] When the manager of a health care organization functions as a pathfinder, the focus is on the long run. The goal of the pathfinder is to provide a vision, find the paths the organization should pursue, and provide a clearly marked trail for those who will follow. As Senge notes, pathfinders have an ability to create a natural energy for changing reality by "holding a picture of what might be that is more important to people than what is."[20]

Strategic managers are the key to establishing a vision for an organization. A "vision-led" organization is guided by a philosophy to which managers are committed but that has not yet become obvious in the daily life of the organization. The vision-led approach hopes for higher levels of performance that are inspiring although they cannot yet be achieved.[21] A primary role of management under this approach is to clarify goals and priorities and to ensure that they are understood and accepted by employees.[22] Perspective 5–4 lists some guidelines for building a vision that makes a difference.

The role of the strategic manager, however, is more than pathfinding. As Barnard noted, because executives are responsible for inculcating the purpose into every employee, the manager must also be the "keeper of the vision." This means being a

Perspective 5–4

Building a Vision That Matters

- *Put the customer at the center.* Identify the customer and what makes him or her unique.
- *Connect the customer's key needs and desires with how you intend to fulfill those needs and desires.* Identify the characteristics that are important to the customer and plan to deliver services that respond uniquely to the desired characteristics.
- *Talk about the vision.* How will our services "feel" to the customers?
- *Use metaphors.* There is nothing wrong with aspiring to be the Mayo Clinic of the Southwest!
- *Use powerful language.* The language of leadership is critical to effective visioning.
- *Squeeze everything you want to say into a paragraph.* Make complexity as simple as possible. Some suggest that if the vision cannot be written in a paragraph, it is not clear to the writer and, therefore, will certainly not be clear to the reader (audience).

- *Communicate the vision.* Put it in speeches, plaster it on the wall, repeat it at every opportunity.
- *Live the vision.* If you do not live the vision, your sermons about it will not be effective.
- *Stick to it.* Timing is everything. Do not hold to an irrelevant vision but do not abandon one that simply has not had time to work.
- *Change it.* No vision lasts forever. Know when you need a new one. Thinking constantly about the vision will suggest when changes are needed.

Source: From J. Daniel Beckham, "How to Construct a Vision that Matters," *The Healthcare Forum Journal*, Vol. 33, No. 3 (March/April 1994), p. 64. Reprinted with permission.

cheerleader and holding on to the vision even when others lose hope. Employees want to believe that what they are doing is important, and nothing convinces employees of the importance of their jobs more than the manager who keeps the inspirational vision before them (especially when things are not going well).

Characteristics of Effective Vision

If vision is really based on hope, it is a snapshot of the future that the health care manager wants to create. For example, the president of the Regional Medical Center in Tennessee stated in the organization's annual report: "Our vision of becoming not just the most respected health care organization in this region but the best public hospital in the United States is a possible dream." Although this vision is short and to the point, it highlights some of the important characteristics of effective visions. It has been said that for an organizational vision to be successful it must be clear, coherent, consistent, have communicative power, and be flexible.[23]

A clear vision is simple. Basic directions and commitments should be the driving forces of a vision, not complex analysis beyond the understanding of most employees. A vision is coherent when it "fits" with other statements including the mission and values. It is consistent when it is reflected in decision-making behavior throughout the organization. A vision "communicates" when it is shared and people believe in the importance of cooperation in creating the future that managers, employers, and other stakeholders desire.[24] Finally, to be meaningful, a vision must be flexible. The future, by definition, is uncertain. Therefore, the effective vision must remain open to change as the picture of the future changes and as the strategic capabilities of the organization evolve over time.

According to Tom Peters, to effectively outline the future and facilitate the pursuit of organizational and individual excellence, visions should possess certain characteristics:[25]

1. *Visions should be inspiring, not merely quantitative goals to be achieved in the next performance evaluation period.* In fact, visions are rarely stated in quantitative terms. They are, however, nothing less than revolutionary in character and in terms of their potential impact on behavior. The vision of OrNda HealthCorp involves excellence through the provision of value-added hospital and related services (see Exhibit 5–11).

2. *Visions should be clear, challenging, and about excellence.* There must be no doubt in the manager's mind about the importance of the vision. If the "keeper of the vision" has doubts, those who follow will have even more. There is no doubt that the Nalle Clinic, a 120-physician multispecialty clinic, emphasizes the characteristics of prestige, national reputation, and excellence in its vision statement (see Exhibit 5–12).

3. *Visions must make sense in the relevant community, be flexible, and stand the test of time.* If the vision is pragmatically irrelevant, it will not inspire high performance.

4. *Visions must be stable, but constantly challenged and changed when necessary.* Mercy Health Services of Phoenix, Arizona, for example, acknowledges the sponsorship of the Sisters of Mercy Regional Community of Detroit and the vision of its foundress, Sister Catherine McAuley of Dublin, Ireland. The centuries-old tradition of the Roman Catholic Church of assisting the economically poor continues to be the challenge. However, the methods for accomplishing this ministry have changed over time and involve, among other things, advocacy for the health care needs of

Exhibit 5–11 • The OrNda HealthCorp Vision Statement

OrNda HealthCorp will be recognized for creativity and excellence in delivering value-added hospital and related services that meet or exceed patient, physician, and payor expectations.

Source: "A New Force in Health Care," OrNda HealthCorp, *1992 Annual Report* (Nashville: 1992), p. 2.

Exhibit 5–12 • Nalle Clinic Vision Statement

To become the most prestigious multispecialty group practice in our region, with a national reputation for excellence.
Source: The Nalle Clinic.

the poor and building partnerships and alliances with other faiths and lay organizations that share similar goals. This is illustrated in Mercy Health Services' vision statement in Exhibit 5–13.

5. *Visions are beacons and controls when everything else seems up for grabs.* A vision is important to provide interested people with a sense of direction.

6. *Visions empower our own people first and then the clients, patients, or others we propose to serve.* The vision must first call forth the best efforts of our own people. Because visions are about inspiration and excellence, it is critical to recognize that employees are the ones who must be inspired first. Employees must ultimately be inspired to achieve excellence.

7. *Visions prepare for the future while honoring the past.* Effective visions always maintain a sense of where the organization has been and how its past influences where it can go. In the previous discussion about the vision statement of the Mercy Health Services, the reference to the "centuries-old tradition of the Roman Catholic Church" illustrates the importance of history to that organization.

8. *Visions come alive in details, not in broad generalities.* Although inspirational visions are generally unconcerned with details, the accomplishment of the vision eventually has to lead to tangible results, whether in health care, business, government, or education. In Exhibit 5–14, the WellCare HMO's Vision 2000 statement lists seven principles upon which its vision is based to ensure that the "details" of the vision are understood.

Unfortunately, although many organizations have given substantial attention to writing mission statements, relatively few have written and published vision statements. However, there are some useful aids that can assist managers in thinking about their vision and the direction they desire for the future. Exhibit 5–15 provides some initial considerations as the vision formulation process develops. This exhibit provides a series of questions that are useful to think about in the process of formulating a vision statement. Exhibit 5–16 describes specific components that can direct construction of an effective vision statement. Strategically, visionary leaders are the most important element in the difference between the merely well-managed and the excellent organization.

Exhibit 5–13 • Mercy Health Services Vision Statement

Mercy Health Services will work toward creating the future envisioned in the following statements:

1. Mercy Health Services will apply the values and spirit of the Sisters of Mercy throughout its health care ministry.

2. Mercy Health Services will demonstrate a preferential option for the economically poor.

3. Mercy Health Services will work with others in providing comprehensive health services to improve the health status of the communities we serve.

4. Mercy Health Services will work with other health care providers to facilitate inter-congregational and lay-sponsored health care in order to strengthen Catholic health care in the United States.

5. Mercy Health Services will participate in shaping public policy to improve health status at local, state, national, and international levels, emphasizing in these efforts the needs of the economically poor.

6. Mercy Health Services will assist people in taking responsibility for their own health by actively promoting wellness and facilitating healing.

Source: From public documents of the Mercy Health Services. Reprinted by permission.

Exhibit 5–14 · The WellCare HMO's Vision 2000

Vision 2000 has seven principles:

1. Primary-care is the entry point into the entire health care delivery system.
2. Primary-care access and availability must meet the needs of WellCare HMO members.
3. Primary-care contracting is used to provide economic incentives for physicians to provide both high-quality and cost-effective medicine.
4. There must be reasonable accessibility and availability to all specialty and supplemental health care referral services.
5. Special relationships with high-quality specialists and other health care providers are necessary. (These relationships should employ state-of-the-art methods for reimbursement and risk sharing, electronic data sharing, and paperwork-reducing strategies.)
6. Providers must have a commitment to quality service, cost management, and the ideals of managed care.
7. We need a strong quality assurance component built around a state-of-the-art management information system.

Source: The WellCare Management Group, Inc., *1993 Annual Report* (Kingston, New York: 1993), p. 8.

Exhibit 5–15 · Thinking About Our Vision

When thinking about the vision for our organization, consider the following points:

1. *As we look toward the future, we believe our organization will/should become . . .*

   If we are successful at everything we are trying to accomplish today, what will our organization look like five years from now?

2. *We want our organization to be "thought of" as . . .*

   What attributes do we most want our organization to achieve? What characteristics should be considered as the essence of excellence in our field of endeavor?

3. *In the future, our employees will have and be seen as . . .*

   What characteristics reflect significant professional achievements in health care and are recognized as reflections of competence by all relevant stakeholders?

4. *The realization of this vision will bring _____ to all of us . . .*

   What fundamental, positive changes will occur to us and our stakeholders if we achieve the vision we have set for ourselves?

A Cautionary Note: The Problem of Newness

Visionary managers provide their greatest service by making the organization flexible and able to enter new markets, disengage from old ones, and experiment with new

Exhibit 5–16 • **Components of a Vision Statement**

Vision Statement Components	Descriptions [Key Words] of Our Vision
1. A Clear Hope (Profile) for the Future	
2. Challenging and About Excellence	
3. Inspirational and Emotional	
4. Empowers Employees First and Clients/Customers Second	
5. Prepares for the Future	
6. Memorable and Provides Guidance	

Source: From Fallon Healthcare System vision statement. Reprinted by permission.

ideas. By getting into a new market first, organizations can obtain certain *first-mover* advantages.[26] A reputation for pioneering can be generated and market position can be more easily established when there are no or only a few competitors. Sometimes it is expensive (monetarily and emotionally) for clients and patients to "switch" to other providers once loyalty and mutual trust have been developed.

However, visionary change when directed toward early entry into markets has its disadvantages. This has been referred to as the *liability of newness.* Unfortunately, the innovators often experience pioneering costs. Pioneers make the mistakes that others learn from and eventually correct. First movers face greater uncertainty because the demand for the service has not been verified. Patient and client needs may change and, particularly when large technological investments are required, the first mover can be left with expensive equipment and little demand.

Therefore, it is important that the demand for visionary management be tempered with realistic knowledge of the market, consumers, and other factors that will affect the organization. The rewards often go to the first mover, but the risks are greater.

Values as Guiding Principles

Values are the things organizations and people stand for—the fundamental principles that, along with the mission, make an organization unique. Most often, discussions of organizational values relate to ethical behavior and socially responsible decision making. To be sure, these values are extremely important, not just to a single hospital, HMO, or long-term-care facility, but to society in general.

There are, however, other values that are very specific to particular organizations and the type of behavior that has either characterized its members' behavior in the past or behavior to which members collectively aspire in the future. Total quality management or continuous improvement is in this sense a value, as is entrepreneurial spirit, teamwork, innovation, and so on.[27] It is important that managers, employees, and key stakeholders understand the values that are expected to drive an organization. The statement of values of the Cleveland Clinic Foundation (Exhibit 5–17) illustrates the five fundamental values upon which the foundation's culture is built.

Exhibit 5–17 · Cleveland Clinic Foundation's Statement of Values

The Cleveland Clinic Foundation was established by visionary leaders who believed in simple, guiding principles. Five fundamental values form the foundation of the Cleveland Clinic culture.

Collaboration   The phrase "to act as a unit" forms the basis of the Cleveland Clinic's group practice. This value, established as a guiding principle when the Cleveland Clinic was founded, ensures that all patients will benefit from the collective wisdom of a team of health care professionals.

Quality   A commitment to quality has created the Cleveland Clinic's legacy of achievement and innovation resulting in excellent and cost-effective patient care. Nationally, the Cleveland Clinic has taken a leadership role in establishing standards for measuring and reporting guidelines for health care.

Integrity   An adherence to scientific and professional integrity are the ethical cornerstones that underlie our delivery of patient care, basic and clinical research investigations, education of residents and allied health professionals, as well as the fiscal and administrative management of the Cleveland Clinic.

Compassion   A commitment to compassionate care includes a respect for our patients' and their families' needs for emotional support during their illness. The Clinic believes in providing the highest level of services to its patients and families.

Commitment   As an institution, the Cleveland Clinic recognizes its responsibilities to the community in which it resides, and to the trustees who oversee the management of its resources.

Source: The Cleveland Clinic Foundation, Division of Health Affairs, Cleveland, Ohio, 1994.

Core values, beliefs, and philosophy seem to be clear during the early stages of an organization's development and become less clear as the organization matures.[28] The distinctive values of the Mayo Clinic were no doubt clearest while the founding brothers were active in its operations. As with mission and vision statements, although values may certainly change over time, it is important that organizations reexamine their values, reaffirm them, change them, communicate them, and perhaps commit them to writing for all to see.

Exhibit 5–18 illustrates a particularly well-developed and articulated set of organizational values. Note that this "credo" focuses on what the organization believes are its key responsibilities—to patients, employees, the future, and so on. Throughout the credo are references to ideals such as compassion, excellence, and respect. Anyone reading this credo or set of guiding principles can understand the motivational force it might have on employees and the comfort it might give patients. The credo ends in a particularly effective manner with the statement of the motto: "Skill, tenderly applied, works wonders."

Not all statements of values or guiding principles are as elaborate as that of the Jewish Hospital of St. Louis. However, they need to be as well conceived. In the case of the credo outlined in Exhibit 5–18, much of the focus is on responsibilities to various stakeholders—physicians, patients, employees, community, and so on. In addition, value statements can be useful in clarifying to employees the specific behaviors that are expected of them as a member of the organization.

Mission, vision, and value statements are tools for "getting better at what we do." The usefulness of any of these statements is the ownership developed on the part of employees and the commitments observed by stakeholders. Framed mission, visions, values, and credos are merely exercises—and futile ones at that—if they are not made real by commitments and actions.[29] The point, of course, is not to write fancy statements. The point is to motivate and guide all employees, managerial and nonmanagerial,

Exhibit 5–18 • Credo of the Jewish Hospital of St. Louis, a Member of BJC Health Systems

"We believe our first responsibility is to our patients. In meeting their needs, we will deliver our services with skill, compassion, and respect for the patient's dignity and privacy, regardless of race, creed, or religious affiliation.

"We will provide superior care across a broad spectrum of medical disciplines, emphasizing the clinical areas in which we have distinctive strengths. We will support that emphasis through the recruitment of outstanding physicians and employees and the provision of state-of-the-art equipment and facilities. We will deliver treatment in the most appropriate setting, whether inpatient, outpatient, or homebound.

"We are responsible to our employees, the men and women who enable us to care for our patients. We respect our employees' dignity, recognize their merit, and value their contributions to Jewish Hospital. We will provide the resources needed to uphold their dedication to excellence.

"We recognize that superior patient care depends on outstanding physicians. We will recruit and support a medical staff that ranks among the best in the nation. Through our affiliation with the Washington University School of Medicine, we will foster the crucial link between medical science and patient care. We believe teaching and research programs enhance the quality of our treatment, and we are committed to their advancement.

"Our responsibility to deliver excellent patient care extends beyond our walls to the community. We strive not only to serve the ill but also the healthy. We will serve—to the best of our financial ability—those unable to afford care.

"Our final responsibility is to the future. We will manage our resources in a manner that sustains our ability to serve the community.

"Our future will be built on our Judaic foundation, stressing a dedication to learning and compassion. We best express those values in our motto: Skill, tenderly applied, works wonders."

Source: From promotional material for The Barnes-Jewish Hospital of St. Louis, a member of BJC Health System. Reprinted by permission.

provide high-quality care, and respond to external as well as internal customers; to distinguish the organization from others in the perceptions of key stakeholders; and to let everyone know the organization stands for something important.

These statements and beliefs, as mentioned in Chapter 2, are directional strategies that provide the focus and parameters for the more operational strategic objectives. In addition, they provide a means of determining the essential things that must be accomplished if the organization is to be effective.

Key Performance Areas and Strategic Objectives

Once management is confident that the mission, vision, and values are well formulated, understood, communicated, and expressed in writing, it has to develop a means of focusing on the things that will make the most progress toward accomplishing the vision. The identification of key performance areas or mission-critical activities is an extremely important step in this process. It is tempting when setting strategic goals to develop as many as possible. Unfortunately, when a large number of goals are established, the task appears to be so great that little progress is made with regard to the really important issues.

Key Performance Areas

Key performance areas or critical success factors, as was noted in Chapter 3, highlight those "few key areas of activity necessary for a particular organization to achieve its purpose."[30] Perspective 5–5 illustrates Oxford Health Plan's identification of a single factor—speed—that its management believes accounts for the company's continued success. It helps to note that these key performance areas represent major commitments for

Perspective 5–5

The Oxford Health Plan—Built for Speed

When it comes to administering health care, performance is measured in seconds. Oxford Health Plan believes the key reason for its continued success is speed—speed in bringing unique products to the marketplace and speed in responding to the needs of its members, providers, and employees. Every investment Oxford has made focuses on improving the speed and accuracy of operations. These are some of its significant achievements:

- Faster claims processing is now possible through an electronic data interchange (EDI) initiative. EDI allows providers to file claims electronically and makes possible a reduction in claims processing and payment from fourteen to four days.
- Increased recording accuracy is achieved through digital document imaging that makes

an electronic replica of any paper claim or letter for cataloging and instant retrieval.
- Members have easier access to computer records through Touch-Tone telephones.
- More responsive customer service is made possible by an on-line reference system that gives service representatives instant access to complete, up-to-the-minute information on benefits and policies pertaining to each member. To date, response time has been reduced 20 percent with increased accuracy.
- Rapid employee training programs allow new recruits to perform at 95 percent after six weeks of training.

Source: The Oxford Health Plan, *1993 Annual Report* (Darien, Connecticut: Oxford Health Plan, 1993), p. 9.

the organization and are not limited to those things that are easy to measure. If difficult-to-measure areas are believed to be genuinely critical to success, they should be included as well.

The things that make the difference can, and often do, vary with the nature of the industry, the stage of a particular organization in its life cycle, and so on. For example, Alex. Brown, and Sons, Inc., an investment research service, indicated that there are five keys to success for providers of specialty health care services: (1) ability to serve an entire market; (2) strong information systems; (3) lowest cost structure; (4) ability to replicate its services in other geographical markets; and (5) ability to accept near-term risks. Quorum Health Group, Inc. indicated that "while there are many ingredients which blend together to result in excellent performance," six receive primary attention. These are: (1) taking actions to ensure service quality; (2) retaining customers; (3) providing value to those we serve; (4) achieving carefully considered, strategic growth; (5) managing profitability dynamics aggressively; and (6) operating with integrity in all that we undertake. Regardless of the industry or life cycle stage, successful leaders recognize that they cannot manage everything. They must focus on a few things and these critical factors must be the factors that make a real difference in success or failure.

To illustrate the importance of this challenge, consider the key performance areas identified by the management of a large local health department. After careful consideration and analysis, the management determined that the success or failure of the organization depended on six key performance areas or critical success factors. These were

(1) accurate assessment of community needs; (2) adequate human and nonhuman resources—facilities, staff, financial; (3) clear legal authority; (4) high credibility and favorable image with key stakeholders; (5) state-of-the-art technology for service delivery; and (6) high-quality services. Exhibit 5–19 illustrates how the key performance areas were logically related to the department's mission, vision, and values. Note that various service centers such as disease control, vital records, nutrition, dental health, and so on set strategic objectives deliberately designed to contribute to the accomplishment of the department's critical success factors.

Setting Strategic Objectives

Whereas well-developed missions are abstract and provide general direction, strategic objectives are specific and to the point. Strategic objectives should possess the following characteristics:

1. Objectives should be as *explicit* and *measurable* as possible. Objectives should reflect organizational priorities to assist managers in making decisions with regard to the distribution of resources. When formulated in this manner, they provide a basis for control and performance evaluation.[31] HEALTHSOUTH Corporation's strategic objective, for example, is to implement its integrated service model of diagnostic centers, acute rehabilitation services, outpatient surgery, and outpatient physical therapy in the top 300 health care markets in the United States with populations of more than 100,000 people. This objective is both explicit and measurable.

2. Objectives should be *attainable*—challenging yet achievable. Objectives are motivational only if they are feasible. Although a statement of hope (vision) does not

Exhibit 5–19 • Structure of Strategic Objectives in a Local Health Department

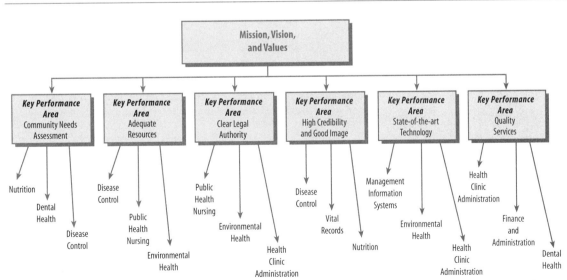

have to be achievable to be motivational, an objective that is used eventually for performance appraisal must be feasible or it will lose its motivational impact.

3. Objectives should *relate to the key performance areas* identified by management. Because managers are often tempted to set more objectives than they can properly attend to, it is a good idea to restrict the number of strategic objectives to two or three for each key performance area. Thus, if five key performance areas are identified, managers should focus on a maximum of fifteen objectives for the year rather than be consumed by the "trivial many." In addition, this is important for purposes of evaluation. If a single objective identifies more than one output, confusion will result if only part of the objective is accomplished.

4. Objectives should be *written.* There should be no confusion about what is to be accomplished, by what date, by whom, and what resources are available to finance the accomplishment. Good objectives include a time deadline for accomplishment and a budget constraint to make clear the maximum amount of organizational resources to be devoted to the accomplishment. For example, FHP Southeast Medical Center in Albuquerque, New Mexico, indicated that continued success required, among other things, attracting, developing, and retaining the best employees in the managed health care industry as well as managing and controlling costs. Management set strategic goals to: (1) train and generate 75 percent of FHP's managers internally; (2) achieve health care costs of 80 percent of revenue or better company-wide within five years; and (3) achieve non–health care expenses of 11 percent of revenue company-wide within five years. These objectives were written and distributed widely within the company and in the annual report.

As a practical matter, few things are more essential for effective management than carefully established and communicated objectives. Objectives are no less important for the three-physician practice than for the 900-bed research and teaching hospital. In addition to all the other benefits, precise and understood objectives are effective motivators of performance. They focus the attention of employees on important factors, regulate how hard a person actually works, and increase an individual's resolve and persistence.[32] Perspective 5–6 presents the strategic objectives for the American Hospital Association. It is clear from these objectives that the AHA intends to be recognized as the national leader in representing provider-based integrated health care delivery systems and to be the "single most influential national organization" for hospital systems.

To illustrate the importance of a well-established set of strategic objectives and how they can be important elements for focusing attention on a relatively few critical activities, review Exhibit 5–20. Premier Health Systems, Inc. was formed in 1993 as a managed-care organization by a joint venture of Providence Hospital and Baptist Healthcare System of South Carolina. By the end of 1994, a network of over 500 physicians and three hospitals had been developed. To be successful, Premier Health Systems, Inc. must develop a statewide network of physicians and hospitals as well as market its services to large and small businesses. The importance of these key performance areas are clearly illustrated in its strategic objectives. The objectives provide focus to individual units and ensure that each unit contributes to the overall vision of the company.

Perspective 5–6

Strategic Objectives of the American Hospital Association

The American Hospital Association hopes to achieve the following major outcomes for 1999:

- Remain the recognized national leader in representing and promoting provider-based integrated delivery systems and the single most influential national organization for hospitals, hospital systems, and integrated delivery systems.
- Make progress in returning coverage and access to the national agenda.
- Remain a recognized national leader for learning, research, resources, and networking for the building and improving of provider-based integrated delivery systems.
- Have members learning from one another to implement a systems-based approach to quality.

- Lead the establishment of community efforts to improve health status.
- Demonstrate leadership to improve community health status and patient care through collaborative activities with other national organizations.
- Have a highly satisfied and strong membership base, financial stability, and a highly motivated and productive workforce.

Source: From "AHA Sets Lofty Goals," *Modern Healthcare* Vol. 26, No. 30 (July 22, 1996), p. 2. Copyright Crain Communications, Inc., 740 N. Rush Street, Chicago, IL 60611. Reprinted by permission.

Exhibit 5–20 • **Strategic Objectives of Premier Health Systems, Inc., 1996–1997**

1. To complete our efforts to become a comprehensive statewide PPO network with at least thirty-six hospitals and three thousand physicians and complementary ancillary providers by the end of 1996. This allows us to be competitive in statewide and regional markets.
2. Complete agreement with at least three more insurance companies to "lease" our network. This allows small businesses as well as large businesses to take advantage of the lower insurance premiums the Premier Health System network discount brings.
3. To have an enrollment of more than 40,000 lives by January 1997.
4. Analyze needs for other products such as a "gatekeeper" PPO.
5. Select (or have designed) an information system that will allow administration to be streamlined and more efficient by September 1997.
6. To reach a "break-even" financial status by having 60,000 lives enrolled at the end of 1997.

Source: Public documents of Premier Health Systems, Inc. Reprinted by permission.

In January 1996, Premier had a membership of over 23,000 covered lives and a network of more than 2,000 physicians and thirty hospitals. In view of this, the goal of thirty-six hospitals and 3,000 physicians by the end of 1996 is challenging yet attainable. Further, Premier Health Systems' objectives are measurable. Often it is tempting to substitute trivial yet measurable goals to ensure that some outcomes are successfully achieved. Quantification is an important aspect of strategic objectives and should be insisted on when practical and reasonable.

Finally, as a concluding note, it should be mentioned that in addition to financial and productivity objectives, organizations sometimes establish targets for contributions to society, communities where they operate, or other specific localities. These "public-oriented" objectives are often less easily measured than the objectives just discussed, but they are no less important. Counter to what one might expect intuitively, research has shown that public welfare goals are as important to investor-owned health care organizations as they are to not-for-profit organizations.[33]

Summary and Conclusions

The topics in this chapter relate to the superordinate goals or outcomes that health care organizations plan to achieve. Managers should recognize that strategic planning is a logical process. The goal progression discussed in this chapter illustrates the importance of strategic logic. The mission of the organization drives decision making because it is the organization's reason for existing. The vision provides the hope for the future, and the values tell everyone—employees, stakeholders, patients, and so on—how the organization will operate.

A mission alone is not enough. The mission is a systematic statement of purpose that distinguishes the organization from all others of its type, such as the care given to patients, physical location of the health care facility, the unusual commitment of physicians to research as well as to healing, or any other factor that is important in the minds of those served. However, it is only the first step. The mission may motivate a few physicians and department managers, but real motivation comes from visionary leadership. The vision is a hope that says what key stakeholders think the organization should look and be like when the purpose is being achieved. Values, as guiding principles, can be powerful motivating forces, as well.

Even a well-developed and communicated mission is likely to leave the health care strategist with far too many areas of responsibility, resulting in an impossible task. For this reason, key performance areas must be identified and strategic objectives must be set with regard to each of the performance areas. This helps make the strategist's job feasible. It is likely that most managers in all types of organizations attempt to manage far too many aspects of the job. The logic of this chapter should help managers focus more effectively on those tasks that really make a difference with respect to organizational success.

Management research shows that the existence of specific objectives with deadlines and resource constraints can be extremely motivating. Clearly stated and communicated objectives provide a sense of direction—they specify what managers are expected to accomplish and remove anxiety from those who want to succeed. If managers provide the opportunity to do so, employees generally accept the chance to provide some input into the goals that will ultimately influence, for better or worse, their occupational success or failure.

Well-developed and communicated objectives provide a framework for evaluating how the organization is doing and what might be needed to improve performance. Formulating mission, vision, values, key performance areas, and strategic objectives is often "messy" and unappreciated work. In the end, however, it is an important responsibility of all strategic managers.

Key Terms and Concepts in Strategic Management

creative tension
first mover
goals
guiding principles

keeper of the vision
key performance areas
organizational mission

organizational vision
pathfinding
strategic objectives

Questions for Class Discussion

1. Is it necessary for all organizational mission statements to include the multiple components discussed in this chapter? How do we decide what components to include?

2. Think of an organization that you know relatively well and attempt to construct a mission statement in light of the components of missions discussed in this chapter.

3. Where do organizational missions originate? How do you explain the evolution of organizational missions as the organization grows and matures? What types of changes are likely to take place in the mission statement?

4. Should leaders encourage or resist changes in the mission statement? Explain your response.

5. Indicate two ways in which an organizational vision is different from other types of organizational goals.

6. It has been said that vision is necessarily a responsibility of leaders. Do you agree or disagree with this statement? Why or why not?

7. Why is the pathfinder's role so important in health care strategic management? Who in the organization is best equipped to fulfill this role and why?

8. Why are values referred to as an organization's guiding principles? In what sense do values constitute a directional strategy for the organization?

9. Who determines the guiding principles of a health care organization? Who should determine these values? What are some guiding principles that you think should be common to all health care organizations? What types of values might, in your opinion, be organization specific?

10. What is a key performance area? How do key performance areas keep us from becoming preoccupied with the "trivial many" factors that can consume a strategic manager's time?

11. What is the relationship among an organization's mission, vision, values, key performance areas, and strategic objectives?

12. Why is it appropriate for an organizational mission to be broad and enduring and strategic objectives to be specific and dynamic?

13. How can health care managers more effectively use goals to stimulate higher levels of performance among all personnel?

14. For the same organization identified in Question 2, attempt to write three strategic objectives that possess the characteristics discussed in this chapter.

15. From the standpoint of the individual employee, is the mission, vision, values, or strategic objectives more important? Explain your answer.

Notes

1. Chester I. Barnard, *The Functions of the Executive* (Cambridge, Massachusetts: Harvard University Press, 1938), p. 87.

2. W. Jack Duncan, *Great Ideas in Management: Lessons from the Founders and Foundations of Managerial Practice* (San Francisco: Jossey-Bass, 1989), pp. 117–118.

3. Russell L. Ackoff, "Mission Statements," *Planning Review* 15, no. 4 (July/August 1987), pp. 30–31.

4. Dennis Mosner, "Mission Improbable," *Across the Board* (January 1995), p. 1.

5. C. Kendrick Gibson, David J. Newton, and Daniel S. Cochran, "An Empirical Investigation of the Nature of Hospital Mission Statements," *Health Care Management Review* 15, no. 3 (Summer 1990), pp. 35–46.

6. W. Jack Duncan, Peter M. Ginter, and W. Keith Kreidel, "A Sense of Direction in Public Organizations: An Analysis of Mission Statements in State Health Departments," *Administration and Society* 26, no. 1 (May 1994), pp. 11–27.

7. Romuald A. Stone, "Mission Statements Revisited," *SAM Advanced Management Journal* 61, no. 1 (Winter 1996), pp. 31–43.

8. John A. Pearce II, "The Company Mission as a Strategic Tool," *Sloan Management Review* 23, no. 2 (Spring 1982), p. 15.

9. Perry Pascarella and Mark A. Frohman, *The Purpose Driven Organization* (San Francisco: Jossey-Bass, 1989), p. 23.

10. R. D. Ireland and M. A. Hitt, "Mission Statements: Importance, Challenge, and Recommendations for Development," *Business Horizons* 35, no. 3 (1992), pp. 34–42.

11. These components adapted from John A. Pearce II and Fred David, "Corporate Mission Statements and the Bottom Line," *Academy of Management Executive* 1, no. 2 (1987), pp. 109–116.

12. Ibid.

13. Cecilia Falbe, Mark Kriger, Lauri Larwood, and Paul Miesing, "Structure and Meaning of Organizational Vision," *Academy of Management Journal* 38, no. 3 (1995), pp. 740–767.

14. James M. Kouzes and Barry Z. Posner, "Envisioning Your Future: Imagining Ideal Scenarios," *The Futurist* 30, no. 3 (1996), pp. 14–19.

15. Stanley Harris, Kevin W. Mossholder, and Sharon Oswald, "Vision Salience and Strategic Involvement: Implications for Psychological Attachment to Organization and Job," *Strategic Management Journal* 15, no. 3 (1994), pp. 477–489.

16. Manfred F. R. Kets de Vries, "The Leadership Mystique," *Academy of Management Executive* 8, no. 3 (1994), pp. 73–83.

17. Peter M. Senge, "The Leader's New Work: Building Learning Organizations," *Sloan Management Review* 31 (Fall 1990), pp. 13–14.

18. Montgomery Van Wart, "The First Step in the Reinvention Process: Assessment," *Public Administration Review* 55, no. 5 (1995), pp. 429–438.

19. G. B. Morris, "The Executive: A Pathfinder," *Organizational Dynamics* 16 (1988), pp. 62–77.

20. Senge, "The Leader's New Work," p. 8.

21. James C. Collins and Jerry I. Porras, "Organizational Vision and Visionary Organizations," *California Management Review* 34, no. 1 (1991), pp. 30–52.

22. Timothy W. Coombs and Sherry J. Holladay, "Speaking of Visions and Visions Being Spoken," *Management Communication Quarterly* 8, no. 2 (1994), pp. 165–189.

23. Ian Wilson, "Realizing the Power of Strategic Vision," *Long Range Planning* 25, no. 5 (1992), pp. 18–28.

24. David Silvers, "Vision—Not Just for CEOs," *Management Quarterly* 35, no. 2 (1994), pp. 10–15.

25. Tom Peters, *Thriving on Chaos* (New York: Alfred A. Knopf, 1988), pp. 401–404.

26. The term *liability of newness* was suggested by James March. However, the most extensive treatment of "first-mover" advantages and disadvantages is presented in Michael E. Porter, *Competitive Advantage* (New York: Free Press, 1986), pp. 186–191.

27. L. D. DeSimone, "How Can Big Companies Keep the Entrepreneurial Spirit Alive?" *Harvard Business Review* 73, no. 5 (1995), pp. 183–186.

28. Gerald E. Ledford, James T. Strahley, and Jon R. Wendenhof, "Realizing a Corporate Philosophy," *Organizational Dynamics* 23, no. 3 (1995), pp. 4–19.

29. For some criticisms of these tools see Colin Coulson-Thomas, "Strategic Vision or Strategic Con: Rhetoric or Reality?" *Long Range Planning* 25, no. 1 (1992), pp. 81–89.

30. Jeffrey K. Pinto and John E. Prescott, "Variations in Critical Success Factors over the Stages in the Product Life Cycle," *Journal of Management* 14, no. 1 (1988), pp. 5–18.

31. For a discussion of organizational goals and objectives, see Max D. Richards, *Setting Strategic Goals and Objectives,* 2d ed. (St. Paul, Minnesota: West Publishing, 1986).

32. E. A. Locke and G. P. Latham, *Goal Setting for Individuals, Groups, and Organizations* (Chicago: Science Research Associates, 1984).

33. John Kralewski, "Profit Versus Public Welfare Goals in Investor-Owned and Not-for-Profit Hospitals," *Hospital and Health Services Administration* 33, no. 3 (Fall 1988), pp. 312–329.

Additional Readings

Abrahams, Jeffrey, *The Mission Statement Book: 301 Mission Statements from America's Top Companies* (New York: Ten Speed Press, 1995). The mission statements of some of the leading companies in the United States such as Baxter Healthcare Corporation, Bausch and Lomb, Columbia/HCA are included. It is a useful guide to different organizations' perceptions of their own distinctiveness.

Graham, J. W., and W. C. Havlick, *Mission Statements: A Guide to the Corporate and Nonprofit Sectors* (New York: Garland Publishing, 1994). A collection of mission statements from both the for-profit and not-for-profit sectors, this book is useful for those who wish to compare and contrast some of the differences in mission statements in different industrial sectors.

Jones, P., and L. Kahaner, *Say It and Live It: The 50 Corporate Mission Statements That Hit the Mark* (New York: Doubleday, 1995). The focus in this book is on corporations that take their mission statements seriously and attempt to make them genuine living documents.

Schmeling, Winnie, *Facing Change in Health Care: Learning Faster in Tough Times* (Chicago: American Hospital Association Press, 1995). This book goes beyond managing or dealing with change and proposes ways of building a visionary future for health care. The experiences of twenty hospitals in the United States are recounted and the lessons learned are highlighted. The hospitals include rural and urban facilities as well as those with primarily teaching and community service missions. Each of these hospitals was able to improve patient care as well as the bottom line through large-scale organizational change.

Schwartz, Hillel, *Century's End: An Orientation Manual Toward the Year 2000* (New York: Doubleday, 1996). According to the author, all centuries end in a similar way and the twentieth century is no exception. There have been massive changes in technology, literature, and even human values. These changes call forth predictions of decay and disaster. We now face alarming forecasts of terrorism, depleted natural resources, bankrupt industries, and outdated careers. However, as the author notes, change also creates opportunities. Schwartz argues for a new spirit of renewal as the new century begins.

PART 2

Strategy Formulation

Strategy formulation is concerned with making strategic decisions using the information gathered during the situational analysis. Part 2 has two chapters: Chapter 6 presents the basic strategic alternatives available to health care organizations and Chapter 7 presents and discusses methods to analyze and evaluate the alternatives.

Chapter 6 provides a decision logic for strategy formulation and demonstrates that strategic decisions should be made sequentially with each decision more explicitly defining the strategy. Each of the strategy types— directional, adaptive, market entry, and positioning—has several strategic alternatives that may be adopted by health care organizations. In addition, the chapter discusses strategic change and the benefits of strategic management models.

Chapter 7 discusses how to evaluate the strategic alternatives under each type of strategy. These evaluation methods do not make the strategy decision but rather are constructs or maps for helping managers think about the organization and its relative situation, thus enabling them to understand the risks and benefits of their decisions.

Developing
Strategic Alternatives

Learning Objectives

After completing this chapter you should be able to:

1. Understand the decision logic of the strategy formulation process and be able to discuss its steps.

2. Identify the hierarchy of strategies and strategic decisions.

3. Understand the nature of directional strategies, adaptive strategies, market entry strategies, positioning strategies, and operational strategies.

4. Identify strategic alternatives available to health care organizations.

5. Provide the rationale as well as advantages and disadvantages for each of the strategic alternatives.

6. Understand that strategies may have to be used in combination to accomplish the organization's goal.

Strategy Formulation

Strategic management and the development of a strategy are essentially parts of a decision-making process—making a choice from among many possibilities. Therefore, strategy formulation is not a single decision but rather a series of increasingly more specific decisions. As indicated in the Introductory Incident, Eastern Health System is pursuing several different types of strategies. In addition, there is a decision logic for strategy formulation. For instance, the development of the cancer and diabetes clinics and the creation of Eastside Ventures and Health Services East are part of a well-considered strategy. Similarly the acquisition of one health care organization by another generally is part of a series of decisions rather than a single decision or an end in itself. In other words, there is a broader strategy that precipitated the acquisition decision; and there will be subsequent strategic decisions that will have to be made to support the acquisition and make it successful.

Eastern Health System: Anatomy of Growth

As Somerset Maugham said, "For the complete life, the perfect pattern includes old age as well as youth and maturing." Eastern Health System, Inc. (EHS), a not-for-profit health care organization, has taken Maugham's dictum to heart as it strives to ensure its own long-term success. EHS, pursuing an expansion adaptive strategy, has vertically integrated its operations to offer patient services literally from cradle to grave. Although centered around vertical integration, the EHS expansion strategy has included diversification, product development, market development, and penetration strategies.

EHS's acute-care full-service hospital, Medical Center East, built in the early 1990s, includes labor/delivery/recovery rooms as well as several intensive care units. Contiguous to the hospital are the Cancer and Diabetes Clinics and office buildings for the physicians on staff. Eastside Ventures, Inc., a unit of EHS, serves a multitude of health care business needs from medical consulting and media management to construction, workers' compensation programs, and grounds maintenance. During late 1995 and early 1996, EHS expanded the geographic region in which it operates. EHS entered into agreements to manage two regional hospitals, St. Clair Regional and Blount County Memorial, both located to the east and north of Medical Center East. Patients from these two regional hospitals are sent to Medical Center East for tertiary care or for consultation with specialists.

One of the company's ongoing goals is to meet all the health care needs of older adults. To this end, in addition to its hospitals and a Physician Information Line that provides the names of area specialists, EHS through its Health Services East, Inc. (HSE) subsidiary, turned one of its older hospitals into Lake Villa, an independent and assisted-living facility. HSE Home Care Services will send the health care workers to the home of a patient if care in the home is preferred. If the patient requires a private nurse, Private Duty Nursing provides one-on-one nursing twenty-four hours a day, seven days a week. The Hospice, another HSE Home Care Service, provides care in the home for the terminally ill. Respite Care is available at Lake Villa in case a primary caregiver in the home must be out of town or needs a break. In addition, Lakeview Nursing Home, Inc., a skilled nursing facility, is available for older adults requiring a more intense level of care.

If an older adult already has living accommodations, the Friendship Center Adult Day Care Program provides assistance for adults during the day only. Active older people can join HSE Goldenagers, which provides members with fellowship, field trips, volunteer services, and discounts at local retail establishments. The HSE Goldenagers also market the Emergency Response Program that provides a device attached to a necklace to be used to signal for emergency personnel if the need arises.

Through its Eastside Ventures, Inc. subsidiary, EHS provides durable medical equipment delivered to the patient at the hospital or at home. A patient needing help with home repairs can call Eastside Ventures Construction Services, which provides home renovations and builds physicians' offices. The Apothecary, with a location at Medical Center East as well as a central freestanding location, is a full-service pharmacy. The Diabetes Clinic offers all patients the convenience of complete facilities and evaluation processes, from dental care, eye evaluations, and podiatry service, to pulmonary, vascular, and cardiovascular studies, and includes the most technologically advanced radiology tests. For any patients unable to drive, transportation is provided to doctor and dentist appointments or to the Friendship Center by the MCE Shuttle Care.

EHS provides community education programs. It has opened the Wellness Place in a local shopping mall to provide blood screenings, blood sugar tests, and blood pressure checks for free or at low cost. The Liz Moore Low Vision Center caters to the older adult by providing educational materials and referrals for people with poor vision and training on the use of low-vision equipment. The Woman's Resource Center at Medical Center East provides informational brochures or videotapes and has registered nurses and other health care professionals available to speak to civic groups on a wide variety of topics. Recently, to supply information booklets, brochures, and even prescription forms, EHS went into the printing business with its Print Shop.

Thus, instead of diversifying into other "sectors," EHS's strategy appears to be one of vertical integration, both upstream and downstream from its expanded hospital core. Given the changing demographics of the United States, EHS's decision to integrate all services, especially those for the older adult, seems to be a good strategy for future success.

Source: Terrie Reeves, Assistant Professor, Texas Woman's University, Institute of Health Sciences, Houston, Texas. Adapted from Eastern Health System, Inc. publications.

The strategy formulation process includes developing strategic alternatives, evaluation of alternatives, and strategic choice. This chapter classifies the types of strategies and develops a hierarchy of strategic alternatives available to health care organizations. Chapter 7 discusses methods for analyzing these alternatives to make a strategic choice.

The relationship of strategy formulation to situational analysis and strategic implementation can be reviewed in Chapter 1, Exhibit 1–5. Situational analysis provides information concerning the external and internal environments that is used in strategy formulation to develop strategic alternatives and select the strategy for the organization. Operational strategies then may be developed to implement the broader organizational strategy.

The Decision Logic of Strategy Formulation

Decisions concerning the five types of strategies making up the strategy formulation process—directional strategies, adaptive strategies, market entry strategies, positioning strategies, and operational strategies—should be made sequentially with each subsequent decision more specifically defining the activities of the organization. The strategy types form an "ends-means chain." Therefore, directional strategies must be made first, followed by adaptive strategies as the adaptive strategies are the means to accomplish the directional strategies or the desired end result. Further, market entry strategies are the means to accomplish the adaptive strategies. Next, the products or services are introduced or reintroduced to the market in a way to be different (or similar to) competitive products (positioning strategies); and finally, specific functional and organization-wide action plans are developed (operational strategies). Operational strategies are the means to accomplish positioning strategies. The decision logic for strategy formulation is illustrated in Exhibit 6–1.

Exhibit 6–1 · **The Decision Logic of Strategy Formulation**

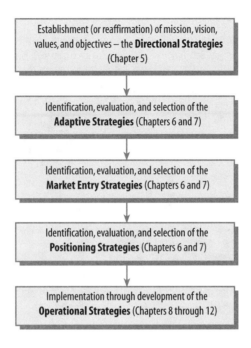

The organization must first reaffirm or establish and reach consensus on its mission, vision, values, and broad objectives. These decisions set the direction for the organization and, as noted in Chapter 5, are referred to as directional strategies. Next, the adaptive strategies must be identified. *Adaptive strategies* are concerned with the variety of methods available to expand, contract, or stabilize (maintain) operations. The potential adaptive strategic alternatives must be evaluated and a specific strategy or combination of strategies adopted. The adaptive strategies outline the major strategic emphasis for the organization to accomplish its vision and objectives (the directional strategies). Third, market entry strategies must be identified, evaluated, and specified. *Market entry strategies* indicate how expansion or stabilization strategies will be carried out. Fourth, a positioning strategy must be identified, evaluated, and selected. *Positioning strategies* indicate the place in the market (or buyers' perceptions) of the products and services in relation to other market "players." Finally, *operational strategies* (both functional and organization-wide) to carry out the adaptive, market entry, and positioning strategies, must be identified, evaluated, and selected. The scope and role of the five strategy types are summarized in Exhibit 6–2.

Recall that all decisions are made following a comprehensive situational analysis and should be based on as much information as possible. Before the plan is formalized, it is important to remember that organization-wide understanding of and commitment

Exhibit 6–2 • Scope and Role of Strategy Types in Strategic Formulation

Strategy	Scope and Role
Directional Strategies	The broadest strategies set the fundamental direction of the organization by establishing a mission for the organization (Who are we?) and providing a vision for the future (What should we be?). These strategies create an understanding of the philosophy or values and set benchmarks for success — objectives.
Adaptive Strategies	These strategies are more specific than directional strategies and provide the primary methods for achieving the vision of the organization. These strategies delineate how the organization will expand, contract, or stabilize operations.
Market Entry Strategies	These strategies carry out the expansion and stabilization strategies through purchase, cooperation, or internal development. These strategies provide methods for access or entry to the market. Market entry strategies normally are not necessary for contraction strategies.
Positioning Strategies	These strategies position the organization vis-à-vis other organizations within the market. These strategies are market oriented and best articulate the competitive advantage within the market. These strategies may be marketwide or directed to particular market segments.
Operational Strategies	The most specific strategies are developed for the functional areas (marketing, finance, information systems, human resources, and so on) and for the entire organization. Organization-wide strategies include culture, organization, facilities and equipment, ethics and social responsibility, and so on. In combination, these actions must accomplish the positioning, market entry, adaptive, and directional strategies.

to the strategies must be developed if they are to be successful. The choice of a strategic alternative creates momentum or direction for an organization and subsequently shapes its internal systems (organization, technology, information systems, culture, policies, skills, and so on). This momentum is reinforced as managers understand, commit, and make decisions according to the strategy.

Exhibit 6–3 presents a comprehensive schematic or map of the hierarchy of strategic alternatives. The hierarchy represents a multitude of strategic alternatives available to health care organizations. In this context, strategy development should be viewed as a sequential decision-making process—a process of evaluating and selecting from various alternatives. This map not only identifies the alternatives but also the sequential relationships among the strategies. Using Exhibit 6–3, each strategy type and the available alternatives will be discussed in the remainder of this chapter.

Using an organizing framework or decision logic (analytical model) in strategy formulation keeps the process from becoming overwhelming. Therefore, the decision logic is the map to initiate the strategy formulation process and encourage managers to start thinking strategically. However, as pointed out in Chapter 1, managers may also have to use a compass and rely on intuitive thinking, leadership, and learning. As managers work through the strategic decisions, new understandings, insights, and strategies may (and in fact, should) emerge. Thinking can never be replaced by how-to formulas and techniques. Many of our greatest achievements in science, law, government, medicine, or other intellectual pursuits are dependent on our development of rational, logical thinkers; however, linear thinking can limit the potential.[1] That is why leadership is essential to foster creativity and innovation and allow for the reinvention of the process. Strategy formulation often is the

Exhibit 6–3 • Hierarchy of Strategic Decisions and Alternatives

Directional Strategies	→ Adaptive Strategies	→ Market Entry Strategies	→ Positioning Strategies	→ Operational Strategies
	Expansion	**Purchase**		
• Mission	• Diversification → Related / Unrelated	• Acquisition	**Marketwide**	**Functional**
• Vision	• Vertical Integration → Forward / Backward	• Licensing	• Cost Leadership	• Marketing
• Values	• Market Development → Geographic / Segmentation	• Venture Capital Investment	• Differentiation	• Information Systems
• Objectives	• Product Development → Product Line / Product Enhancement		**Market Segment**	• Finance
	• Penetration → Promotion / Distribution / Pricing	**Cooperation**	• Focus/Cost Leadership	• Human Resources
	Contraction	• Merger	• Focus/ Differentiation	**Organization-wide**
	• Divestiture → Total / Partial	• Alliance		• Culture
	• Liquidation → Operations / Assets	• Joint Venture		• Organizational Structure
	• Harvesting → Fast / Slow	**Development**		• Facilities and Equipment
	• Retrenchment → Personnel / Markets / Products / Assets	• Internal Development		• Ethics and Social Responsibility
	Stabilization			
	• Enhancement → Quality / Efficiency / Innovation / Speed / Flexibility	• Internal Venture		
	• Status Quo			

management of dilemmas, tolerance for ambiguity, and coping with contradictions. Finally, the strategy process cannot ignore the entrepreneurial spirit, politics, and culture. Despite the need for flexibility in the process, the decision logic at least provides a starting point.

Directional Strategies: Mission, Vision, Values, and Objectives

Chapter 5 explored mission, vision, values, and objectives and indicated that these elements are part of both situational analysis and strategy formulation. They are a part of situational analysis because they describe the current state of the organization and codify its basic beliefs and philosophy. However, mission, vision, values, and objectives are also a part of strategy formulation because they set the boundaries and indicate the broadest direction for the organization.

The mission, vision, values, and objectives should provide a sensible and realistic planning framework for the organization. Within this planning framework, more specific strategic alternatives are selected. Therefore, it is important that environmental analysis has been used to identify the current and emerging issues (opportunities and threats) that will affect the success of the organization. Concurrently, management should have carefully analyzed the organization and be attuned to its resources, competencies, and capabilities (strengths and weaknesses). Having assimilated and evaluated all this information, management then decides what strategic alternatives are appropriate for the organization.

Because formulation of the mission, vision, values, and objectives provides the broad direction for the organization, directional strategic decisions must be made first. Then the adaptive strategies provide further strategic momentum by specifying product/market expansion, contraction, or stabilization. The adaptive strategies form the core of the strategy formulation process and are most visible to those outside the organization.

Adaptive Strategies

From a practical standpoint, whether the organization should expand, contract, or remain stable is the first decision that must be made once the direction of the organization has been set (or reaffirmed). As shown in Exhibit 6–3, several specific alternatives are available to expand operations, contract operations, or stabilize operations. These alternatives provide the major strategic choices for the organization.

Expansion Strategies

If expansion is selected as the best way to perform the mission and realize the vision of the organization, several alternatives are available. Two of the alternatives are corporate-level strategies and three are division-level strategies. The *expansion strategies* include:

- diversification (corporate level),
- vertical integration (corporate level),
- market development (divisional/strategic service unit [SSU] level),
- product development (divisional/SSU level), and
- penetration (divisional/SSU level).

Corporate-level strategies consider the best mix of semi-autonomous divisions operating in separate markets with distinct products or services. Therefore, corporate-level strategies generally address the current viability and potential of a portfolio of separate businesses (divisions). Corporate strategies are not concerned with one market or product/service, but rather with several "businesses" assembled to fulfill the mission of the organization given the demands of the external environment. Corporate-level strategies address the question, "What business(es) should we be in?" Thus, an integrated health system must consider what portfolio of businesses—acute-care hospital, long-term care, home health, and so on (or businesses outside the health care industry)—best serves the mission of the system. Corporate expansion strategies increase the scope of the organization.

In contrast to corporate strategies, divisional strategies are concerned with a single well-defined market and with a product/service line that serves a specific market or service area. Division-level strategies deal with the question, "How should an organization compete in a given market?" Therefore, division-level strategic alternatives are concerned with an organization's current area of operations and are used by organizations such as SSUs, single-unit hospitals, and small group practices to compete within a service area.

Diversification   *Diversification* strategies, in many cases, are selected because markets have been identified outside of the organization's core business that offer potential for substantial growth. Often, an organization that selects a diversification strategy is not achieving its growth or revenue objectives within its current market, and these new markets provide an opportunity to achieve them. There are, of course, other reasons organizations decide to diversify. For instance, health care organizations may identify opportunities for growth in less-regulated markets such as specialty hospitals, long-term-care facilities, or managed care. An interesting diversification strategy is that of the Healthcare Financial Management Association (HFMA). Membership in the association was formerly restricted to acute-care sites; however, in an acknowledgment of a decreasing market, the association decided to diversify into broader markets (outside their core market). Association chairman Warren Hern indicated, "My primary goal is to maintain the relevance of the association as the industry transforms. To accomplish that goal, the HFMA first must broaden its membership to include other nonacute-care delivery sites. Health care professionals used to think hospitals were the center of health care delivery. In fact, half of the hospitals will likely be closed in ten years." The diversification initiative targets finance professionals at physician practices and managed-care organizations.[2]

Diversification is generally seen as a risky alternative because the organization is entering a relatively unfamiliar market or offering a product/service that is different from its current products or services. Organizations have found that the risk of diversification can be reduced if markets and products are selected that complement one another. Therefore, managers engaging in diversification seek synergy between corporate divisions (SSUs).

There are two types of diversification: related, or concentric, diversification and unrelated or conglomerate diversification. Exhibit 6–4 illustrates possible related and unrelated diversification strategies for one type of primary health care organization.

In *related diversification,* an organization chooses to enter a market that is similar or related to its present operations. This form of diversification is sometimes called *concentric diversification* because the organization develops a "circle" of related products/services. Exhibit 6–5 illustrates the circle of related products for a hospital that is interested in diversifying into another segment of the health care market, the long-term-care market.

The general assumption underlying related diversification is that the organization will be able to obtain some level of synergy (a complementary relationship where the total effect is greater than the sum of its parts) between the production/delivery, marketing, or technology of the core business and the new related product or service. For hospitals, the two primary reasons for diversifying in the 1990s are to introduce nonacute- or

Exhibit 6–4 • Related and Unrelated Diversification by a Primary Provider

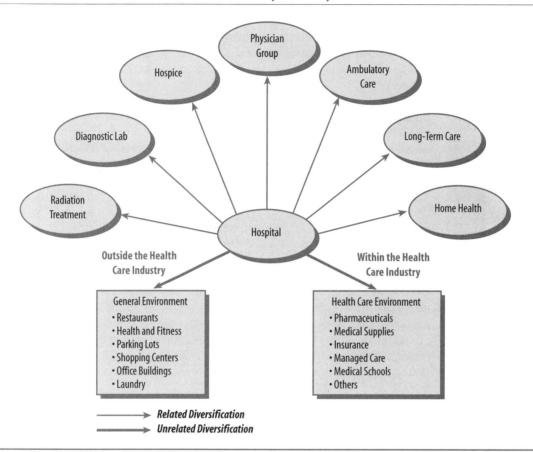

subacute-care services that reduce hospital costs and to offer a wider range of services to large employers and purchasing coalitions through capitated contracts.[3] The movement of acute-care hospitals into skilled-nursing care is an example of related diversification.

On the other hand, in *unrelated diversification,* an organization enters a market that is unlike its present operations. This action creates a "portfolio" of separate products/services. Unrelated diversification, or *conglomerate diversification,* generally involves semi-autonomous divisions or strategic service units. An example of unrelated diversification would be a hospital diversifying into the operation of a restaurant, parking lot, or medical office building. In such a case, the new business is unrelated to health care although it may be complementary (synergistic) to the provision of health services. Unrelated diversification, however, has been generally unsuccessful in generating revenue for acute-care hospitals, as illustrated in Perspective 6–1.

Vertical Integration A *vertical integration* strategy is a decision to grow along the channel of distribution of the core operations. Thus, a health care organization may

Exhibit 6–5 • Long-Term-Care Options for Hospital Diversification

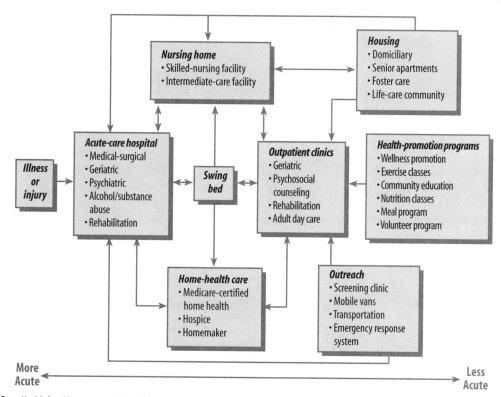

Source: From *Health Care Management Review,* Vol. 15, No. 1, p. 73. Copyright © 1990. Reprinted by permission of Aspen Publishers, Inc.

grow toward suppliers or toward patients. When an organization grows along the channel of distribution toward its suppliers (upstream) it is called *backward vertical integration.* When an organization grows toward the consumer or patient (downstream) it is called *forward vertical integration.*

Vertical integration can reduce costs and enhance an organization's competitive position. Reductions may occur through lower supply costs and better integration of the "elements of production." With vertical integration, management can better ensure that supplies are of the appropriate quality and delivered at the right time. For instance, some hospitals have instituted technical educational programs because many health professionals (the major element of production in health care) are in critically short supply.

A decision to vertically integrate further commits an organization to a particular product or market and therefore management must believe in the long-term viability of the product/service and market. As a result, the opportunity costs of vertical integration must be weighed against the benefits of other strategic alternatives such as diversification. Examples of vertical integration would be a hospital chain acquiring one of its major medical products suppliers (backward integration) or a drug manufacturer moving into drug distribution (forward integration). An interesting form of forward vertical

---

Perspective 6–1

Unrelated Diversification Difficult for Hospitals

In the 1980s hospitals were buying dude ranches in Montana and bottling companies in Ohio. They were expanding into janitorial services, catering firms, condominiums, travel agencies, and health clubs. Unrelated diversification was intended to spread risks or develop new sources of revenues to support acute-care operations; however, many of the diversified businesses have been divested or liquidated as losing money or not in the best interests of a health care organization. Some unrelated diversifications broke even or were marginally profitable, but they did not justify the diversion of executive time. Many hospital administrators lacked the skills to manage these nonacute-care businesses. In addition, boards of trustees questioned the additional capital needed and wondered

when these diversified businesses would become profitable.

In the 1990s, health care organizations are more apt to employ related diversification to create or move into a new market or vertical integration to manage the health of a population. Simply owning an asset to increase revenue has not been an effective strategy. Often related diversification and vertical integration are achieved through collaboration or joint ventures with similar providers.

Source: Jay Greene, "Trying a New Line? Diversifier Beware" and "Diversification, Take Two," *Modern Healthcare* 23, no. 39 (1993), pp. 28–32.

---

integration in the 1990s has been hospitals opening retail operations in malls. For example, in Louisville, Kentucky, Jewish Hospital HealthCare Services runs health and information centers staffed by registered nurses in four malls within twenty miles of its campus. Visitors can watch videos, check out books, attend health screenings, and get free or low-cost lessons on diabetes management, yoga, smoking cessation, and numerous other health topics. Retail business has proven to be a good partner for some urban hospitals trying to tap the suburban market.[4] Additional reasons for vertical integration in the 1990s are presented in Perspective 6–2.

Whether a strategic alternative is viewed as vertical integration or related diversification may depend on the objective or intent of the alternative. For instance, when the primary intent is to enter a new market in order to grow, the decision is to diversify. However, if the intent is to control the flow of patients to various units, the decision is to vertically integrate. Thus, a decision by an acute-care hospital to acquire a skilled-nursing unit may be viewed as related diversification (entering a new growth market) or vertical integration (controlling downstream patient flow). For example, Jane Phillips Episcopal Medical Center in Bartlesville, Oklahoma, developed a home health unit that delivers care to patients recently discharged from the hospital and to those with chronic medical problems that do not require hospitalization. Because Jane Phillips' actions are clearly motivated to control the flow of patients in order to manage inpatient stays and provide continuity of care, it is vertical integration.

In the area of supplying patients to various health care units, several patterns of vertical integration may be identified.[5] In Exhibit 6–6, an inpatient acute-care facility is the strategic service unit or core technology that decides to vertically integrate. Example 1 is

Perspective 6–2

Reasons for Vertical Integration in the 1990s

The health care industry is rushing toward vertical integration just when some other industries are moving away from vertical integration. Integrated health care systems are being formed and consolidated to:

- Compete with other integrated systems and managed-care organizations in the delivery of high-quality care to enrollees and other patients;
- Give providers enough market clout to force managed-care organizations to renegotiate

contracts that are more favorable to them; and

- Dominate markets so that providers and their managed-care components will be virtually free of meaningful competition.

Source: Donald E. L. Johnson, "Integrated Systems Face Major Hurdles, Regulations," *Health Care Strategic Management* 11, no. 10 (1993), pp. 2–3.

a hospital that is not vertically integrated. The hospital admits and discharges patients from and to other units outside the organization. Example 2 is a totally integrated system in which integration occurs both upstream and downstream. In this case, patients flow through the system from one unit to the next, and upstream units are viewed as "feeder" units to downstream units.

Example 3 represents a hospital that has vertically integrated upstream. In addition, more than one unit is involved at several stages of the integration. For instance, there are two wellness/health promotion units, three primary-care units, and three urgent-care units. The dashed line represents the receipt of patients via external or market transfers. Example 4 illustrates a multihospital system engaged in vertical integration. Three hospitals form the core of the system, which also contains three nursing homes, two rehab units, a home health unit, three urgent-care facilities, three primary-care facilities, and a wellness center.

Finally, a quirk of the health care system is illustrated in Example 5. Some health care systems are closed systems with fixed patient populations entirely covered through prepayment. Thus, whereas in the second example, the health care organization is vertically integrated, in the fifth example, patients are a part of the system. This insurance function is shown as an additional unit and identified by the letter *i* in the example.

It is important to note that simply adding members to create an integrated health system is not enough. Institutions must be truly integrated and create a "seamless" system of care. Perspective 6–3 provides some insight into the requirements for system integration.

Market Development *Market development* is a divisional strategy used to enter new markets with present products or services. Specifically, market development is a strategy designed to achieve greater volume, through geographic (service area) expansion or by targeting new market segments within the present geographic area. Typically, market development is selected when the organization is fairly strong in the market (often with

Exhibit 6–6 • **Patterns of Vertical Integration Among Health Care Organizations**

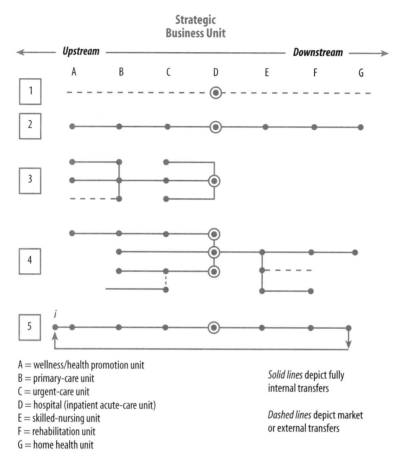

A = wellness/health promotion unit
B = primary-care unit
C = urgent-care unit
D = hospital (inpatient acute-care unit)
E = skilled-nursing unit
F = rehabilitation unit
G = home health unit

Solid lines depict fully
internal transfers

Dashed lines depict market
or external transfers

Source: Adapted in part from K.R. Harrigan, "Formulating Vertical Integration Strategies," *Academy of Management Review,* Vol. 9, No. 4 (1984), pp. 638–652. Reprinted by permission of Academy of Management. And adapted in part from Stephen S. Mick and Douglas A. Conrad, "The Decision to Integrate Vertically in Health Care Organizations," *Hospital and Health Services Administration,* Vol. 33, No. 3 (Fall 1988), p. 351. Reprinted by permission from Health Administration Press, Chicago.

a differentiated product), the market is growing, and the prospects are good for long-term growth. A market development strategy is strongly supported by the marketing, financial, information systems, organizational, and human resources functions. An example of a market development strategy would be a chain of outpatient clinics opening a new clinic in a new geographic area (present products and services in a new market). Of course new markets may be entered via acquisition as is a common strategy for HEALTHSOUTH Corporation. For instance, HEALTHSOUTH pursued a market development strategy by acquiring Professional Sports Care Management that operates thirty-six outpatient rehabilitation facilities in Connecticut, New Jersey, and New York in order to create a significant presence in the Northeast.

Perspective 6–3

To Play the Systems Game, You Need More than the Pieces

Health care organizations attempting to create systems do not do well by simply making deals—it is the integration that determines success. Certainly, the concept of providing a seamless continuum of patient care is admirable. To achieve it, services beyond acute care must be added to a health care system's product lines. However, making the pieces work together is the challenge. A collection of institutions is not a system.

Just because a management team can successfully run a hospital does not mean that they can successfully run a home-care agency or outpatient clinics. The challenge over the next five years will be for boards and executives to knit the pieces of their network or alliance together to work as one.

Key in making a network function is a philosophy of interdependence. Interdependence will have to be part of the system's vision, mission, values, and objectives. The CEO and the entire senior management team must feel a deep sense of responsibility for reinforcing the value of interdependence and making integration a priority. Employees will have to think in terms of the system—not the individual components of that system. This philosophy will require a strong sense of trust among the parts of the system. Trust is the foundation of true interdependence within any organization or team.

In creating an effective system of care, each acquisition, merger, alliance, or joint venture should add strategic value (competitive advantage). It might be geographic coverage, excellent information systems, clinical expertise, or a successful track record of managing outpatient sites. Bigger is not better unless it adds strategic value.

Amassing the pieces of an integrated delivery system is revolutionary, but creating a culture of interdependence and integration is evolutionary. The process of integration must be managed with great care.

Source: Edward A. Kazemek and Nancie Noie, "To Play the Systems Game, You Need More than the Pieces," *Modern Healthcare* 26, no. 26 (June 24, 1996), pp. 142–144.

Product Development *Product development* is the introduction of new products/services to present markets (geographic and segments). Typically, product development takes the form of product enhancements and product line extension. Product development should not be confused with related diversification. Related diversification introduces a new product category (though related to present operations), whereas product development may be viewed as refinements, complements, or natural extensions of present products. Product development strategies are common in large metropolitan areas where hospitals vie for increased market share within particular segments of the market, such as cancer treatment and open-heart surgery. Another good example of product development is in the area of women's health. Many hospitals have opened clinics designed to serve the special needs of women in the present market area.

Penetration An attempt to better serve current markets with current products or services is referred to as a market penetration strategy. Similar to market and product development, *penetration* strategies are used to increase volume and market share. A market penetration strategy is supported by aggressive functional strategies, particularly within marketing. Market penetration is centered on promotional, distribution, and pricing strategies and often includes increasing advertising, offering sales promotions, increasing publicity efforts, or increasing the number of salespersons.

An example of a penetration strategy is Baptist Medical Center's (BMC) response to the expansion of the prestigious Mayo Clinic into the Jacksonville, Florida, area. BMC believed that it was unlikely that the Mayo Clinic would compete in pediatric care. Therefore, BMC capitalized on its major strength and initiated an aggressive adaptive/penetration strategy in pediatric care. To enhance availability to the market, BMC formed alliances (a market entry strategy) to develop a regional children's health center. BMC allied with the 450-bed University Medical Center, the University of Florida Health Science Center in Gainesville, and the Nemours Foundation of Wilmington, Delaware (a source of competition in the past). In addition, BMC opened a new $45 million children's hospital. BMC has supported this strategy with extensive promotion to inform the public of its strategic emphasis.[6]

The various expansion strategies, their relative risks, and their rationales are summarized in Exhibit 6–7.

Contraction Strategies

Contraction strategies decrease the size and scope of operations either at the corporate level or divisional level. Contraction strategies include:

- divestiture (corporate level),
- liquidation (corporate level),
- harvesting (divisional level), and
- retrenchment (divisional level).

Divestiture *Divestiture* is a contraction strategy in which an operating strategic service unit is sold off as a result of a decision to permanently and completely leave the market despite its current viability. Generally, the business to be divested has value and will continue to be operated by the purchasing organization. For example, Tenet Healthcare Corporation divested its 42 percent stake in Westminster Health Care Holdings, a London-based nursing home chain, for $120 million. The sale completed the hospital chain's plan to sell non-core assets and refocus on its domestic hospitals.[7]

Within the past decade, the strategy of "unbundling" (divesting by a hospital of one or more of its services) has become common. Thus, hospitals are carving out non-core services previously performed internally and divesting them. Typical services and products produced in a hospital that are not necessarily part of the core bundle of activities include laboratory, pharmacy, X-ray, physical therapy, occupational therapy, and dietary services.[8] In addition, "hotel" services (laundry, housekeeping, and so on) formerly performed by hospitals are contracted to outsiders. Even medical services in such specialty areas as ophthalmology are increasingly being performed outside the hospital in "surgi-centers" and may be candidates for divestiture.

Divestiture decisions are made for a number of reasons. An organization may need cash to fund more important operations for long-term growth or the division/SSU may be not achieving management's objectives. Some multihospital systems have divested

Exhibit 6–7 • **Rationales and Relative Risks of Expansion Strategic Alternatives**

Strategy	Relative Risk	Rationale
Related Diversification	Moderate	• Pursuit of high-growth markets • Entering less-regulated segments • Cannot achieve current objectives • Synergy is possible from new business • Offset seasonal or cyclical influences
Unrelated Diversification	High	• Pursuit of high-growth markets • Entering less-regulated segments • Cannot achieve current objectives • Current markets are saturated or in decline • Organization has excess cash • Antitrust regulations prohibit expansion in current industry • Tax loss may by acquired
Backward Vertical Integration	High	• Control the flow of patients through the system • Scarcity of raw materials or essential inventory/supplies • Deliveries are unreliable • Lack of materials or supplies will shut down operations • Price or quality of materials or supplies variable • Industry/market seen as profitable for long period
Forward Vertical Integration	High	• Control the flow of patients through the system • Faster delivery required • High level of coordination required between one stage and another • Industry/market seen as profitable for long period
Market Development *(geographic and segmentation)*	Moderate	• New markets are available for present products • New markets may be served efficiently • Expected high revenues • Organization has cost leadership advantage • Organization has differentiation advantage • Current market is growing
Product Development *(product line and product enhancement)*	Moderate	• Currently in strong market but product is weak or product line incomplete • Market tastes are changing • Product technology is changing • Maintenance or creation of differentiation advantage
Penetration *(promotion, distribution, and pricing)*	Moderate	• Present market is growing • Product/service innovation will extend market of product life cycle • Expected revenues are high • Organization has cost leadership advantage • Organization has differentiation advantage

their HMOs so that they could concentrate on care delivery. One such system was Advocate Health Care of Oak Brook, Illinois, which sold Health Direct, its 122,000-enrollee managed-care organization to Healthsource, a New Hampshire HMO company. The CEO indicated that Advocate would focus on its core strategy of building a competitive provider network.[9]

Some practical guidelines for the divestiture of services are presented in Exhibit 6–8. If eight or more responses support reinvesting, the organization should continue with the activity; however, if eight or more support divestiture, consideration should be given to selling the service. If the responses are relatively even, significant modifications in the service should be considered.

Liquidation   *Liquidation* involves selling the assets of an organization. The assumption underlying a liquidation strategy is that the unit cannot be sold as a viable and ongoing operation. However, the assets of the organization (facilities, equipment, and so on) still have value and may be sold for other uses. Organizations, of course, may be partially or completely liquidated. Common reasons for pursuing a liquidation strategy include bankruptcy, the desire to dispose of nonproductive assets, and the emergence of a new technology that results in a rapid decline in the use of the old technology.

Upon leaving a market, an aging hospital building may be sold for its property value or an alternative use. In a declining market, a liquidation strategy may be a long-term strategy to be carried out in an orderly manner over a period of years. Recently many hospitals have been liquidating their emergency helicopter operations. Historically,

Exhibit 6–8 · Guidelines for Divestiture of Services

	Reinvest	Divest
1. Were the actual financial results equal to or better than those anticipated in the strategic plan?	Yes	No
2. Has the organization been in operation less than eighteen months?	Yes	No
3. Is there at least an example of a known profitable operation of approximately the same size as your operation?	Yes	No
4. If utilization targets have not been achieved, what is the reason?	Not achieved, but still reasonable	Overestimated
5. Is your payor mix the same as or better than you expected?	Yes	No
6. Is this a high fixed-cost operation with excess capacity?	Yes, could increase utilization without adding much expense	No, expanding services means adding expenses
7. Can you quantify spin-off benefits to the system?	Yes	No
8. Can you identify any real competitive advantages this service has in the marketplace?	Yes	No
9. Can you identify specific management actions that can reverse the losses?	Yes	No
10. Is this a mature product or market?	No	Yes
11. Would you use your own money to invest in this venture?	Yes	No

Source: Adapted from Jay Greene, "A Strategy for Cutting Back," *Modern Healthcare,* August 18, 1989, p. 29, developed by the Society for Healthcare Planning and Marketing, American Hospital Association.

these programs have been allowed to operate as loss leaders because they brought prestige and positive public relations to the hospital. However, because of increasing costs and limited reimbursements, many hospitals have shut down and liquidated helicopter operations.

Harvesting A *harvesting* strategy is selected when the market has entered long-term decline. The reason underlying such a strategy is that the organization has a relatively strong market position but industry-wide revenues are expected to decline over the next several years. Therefore, the organization will "ride the decline," allowing the business to generate as much cash as possible but at the same time investing no new resources.

In a harvesting strategy, the organization attempts to reap maximum short-term benefits before the product or service is eliminated. Such a strategy allows the organization an orderly exit from a declining segment of the market by planned downsizing. Harvesting has not been widely used in health care but will be more frequently encountered in the future as markets mature and organizations exit various segments. For instance, some regional hospitals that have developed rural hospital networks have experienced difficulty in maintaining their commitment to health care in small communities. The twenty-bed hospitals frequently found in rural networks tend to struggle financially because of a lack of support from both specialists and primary-care physicians, an aging population, and flight of the young to urban areas. Twenty-bed rural hospitals are probably in a long-term decline with little hope for survival. On the other hand, fifty-bed hospitals have managed to maintain or improve their financial position because of effective physician recruitment, good community image, and the continued viability of the communities themselves. Therefore, regional hospitals with rural networks may have to employ a harvesting strategy for the twenty-bed hospitals while using one of the development or stabilization strategies for the fifty-bed and larger hospitals.

Retrenchment A *retrenchment* strategy is a response to declining profitability usually brought about by increasing costs. The market is still viewed as viable, and the organization's products/services continue to have wide acceptance. However, costs are rising as a percentage of revenue, putting pressure on profitability. Retrenchment typically involves a redefinition of the target market, selective cost elimination, and asset reduction. Retrenchment is directed toward reduction in personnel, the range of products/services, or the geographic market served and represents an effort to reduce the scope of operations.

Over time, organizations may find that they are overstaffed given the level of demand. As a result, their costs are higher than those of competitors. When market growth is anticipated, personnel are added to accommodate the growth, but during periods of decline, personnel positions are seldom eliminated. A reduction in the staff members who have become superfluous or redundant is often central to a retrenchment strategy.

Similarly, in an attempt to "round out" the product or service line, products and services are added. Over time, these additional products/services may tend to add more costs than revenues. In many organizations, less than 20 percent of the products account for more than 80 percent of the revenue. Under these circumstances, retrenchment may be in order.

Finally, there are times when geographic growth is undertaken without regard for costs. Eventually, managers realize they are "spread too thin" to adequately serve the market. In addition, well-positioned competitors are able to provide quality products/ services at lower costs because of their proximity. In this situation, geographic retrenchment (reducing the service area) is appropriate.

In many cases, a retrenchment strategy is implemented after periods of aggressive market development or acquisition of competitors. For example, Columbia/HCA Healthcare Corporation closed Columbia HEB Hospital, a 200-bed facility in Bedford, Texas, and transferred patients to another nearby Columbia/HCA facility, Columbia North Hills Hospital in North Richland Hills, Texas. Columbia HEB was the third hospital that Nashville, Tennessee-based Columbia/HCA had closed in the Dallas/Fort Worth area, although it dominated the region with sixteen hospitals and eight surgery centers.[10]

The various contraction strategies, their relative risks, and their rationales are summarized in Exhibit 6–9.

Stabilization Strategies

Often organizations pursue *stabilization strategies* when management believes the past strategy has been appropriate and few changes are required in the target markets or the organization's products/services. Stabilization does not necessarily mean that the organization will do nothing; it means that management believes the organization is progressing appropriately. There are two stabilization strategies: enhancement and status quo.

Exhibit 6–9 · **Rationales and Relative Risks of Contraction Strategic Alternatives**

Strategy	Relative Risk	Rationale
Divestiture	Low	• Industry in long-term decline • Cash needed to enter new, higher-growth area • Lack of expected synergy with core operation • Required investment in new technology seen as too high • Too much regulation
Liquidation	Low	• Organization can no longer operate • Bankruptcy • Trim/reduce assets • Superseded by new technology
Harvesting	Low	• Late maturity/decline of the product life cycle • Consider divestiture or downsizing • Short-term cash needed
Retrenchment *(personnel, markets, products, assets)*	Moderate	• Market has become too diverse • Market is too geographically spread out • Personnel costs are too high • Too many products or services • Marginal or nonproductive facilities

Enhancement When management believes that the organization is progressing toward its vision and objectives but needs to "do things better," an *enhancement strategy* may be used; neither expansion nor contraction of operations is appropriate but "something needs to be done." Typically, enhancement strategies take the form of quality programs (CQI, TQM) directed toward improving organizational processes or cost-reduction programs designed to render the organization more efficient. In addition to quality and efficiency, enhancement strategies may be directed toward innovative management processes, speeding up the delivery of the products/services to the customer, and adding flexibility to the design of the products or services (marketwide customization).

Many times after an expansion strategy, an organization engages in stabilization/ enhancement strategies. Typically after an acquisition, organizations initiate enhancement strategies directed toward upgrading facilities, reducing purchasing costs, installing new computer systems, enhancing information systems, improving the ability to evaluate clinical results, reducing overhead costs, and improving quality.

Status Quo A *status quo strategy* is based on the assumption that the market has matured and periods of high growth are over. Often, the organization has secured an acceptable market share and managers believe the position can be defended against competitors. This strategy is sometimes referred to as a maintenance strategy.

In a status quo strategy, the goal is to maintain market share. Although the organization attempts to keep services at current levels, additional resources may be required. Management attempts to prolong the life of the product/service for as long as possible. Environmental influences affecting the decline of the products or services should be carefully analyzed to determine when decline is imminent. An example of this strategy would be a full-service hospital investing heavily in marketing to prevent market share erosion for inpatient services.[11] Typically, organizations attempt a status quo strategy in some areas while engaging in market development, product development, or penetration in others to better utilize limited resources. For instance, a hospital may attempt to hold its market share (status quo) in slow-growth markets such as cardiac and pediatric services and attempt market development in higher growth services such as intense, short-term rehabilitation care (renal dialysis, ophthalmology, or intravenous therapy, for example).

In mature markets, industry consolidation occurs as firms attempt to add volume and reduce costs. Therefore, managers must be wary of the emergence of a single dominant competitor that has achieved a significant cost differential. A status quo strategy is appropriate when there are two or three dominant providers in a stable market segment because, in this situation, market development or product development may be quite difficult and extremely expensive. The various stabilization strategies, their relative risks, and their rationales are summarized in Exhibit 6–10.

Market Entry Strategies

The selection of the expansion or stabilization strategies from among the adaptive strategic alternatives dictates that the next decision to be made is which of the *market entry strategies* should be used. If a contraction adaptive strategy is selected, normally there is no market entry decision and market entry strategies are not used. The expansion strategies specify entering or gaining access to a new market, and the stabilization strategies

Exhibit 6–10 · Rationales and Relative Risks of Stabilization Strategic Alternatives

Strategy	Relative Risk	Rationale
Enhancement *(quality, efficiency, innovation, speed, and flexibility)*	Low	• Organization has operational inefficiencies • Need to lower costs • Need to improve quality • Improve internal processes
Status quo	Low	• Maintain market share position • Maturity/late maturity stage of the product life cycle • Product/market generating cash but has little potential for future growth • Extremely competitive market

call for obtaining new resources. Therefore, the next important decision that must be made for these strategies concerns how the organization will enter or develop the market.

There are three ways to enter a market. As illustrated in Exhibit 6–3, an organization can use its financial resources and purchase into the market, team with other organizations and use cooperation to enter a market, or use its own resources and develop its own products and services. It is important to understand that market entry strategies are not ends in themselves but serve a broader aim—the adaptive strategies. Any of the adaptive strategies may be carried out using any of the market entry strategies but each one places different demands on the organization.

Purchase Strategies

Purchase market entry strategies allow an organization to use its financial resources to enter a market quickly, thereby initiating the adaptive strategy. There are three purchase market entry strategies: acquisition, licensing, and venture capital investment.

Acquisition *Acquisitions* are entry strategies to grow through the purchase of an existing organization, a unit of an organization, or a product/service. Thus, acquisition strategies may be used to carry out both corporate and divisional strategies. The acquiring organization may integrate the operations of the newly acquired organization into its present operations or may operate it as a separate business/service unit. Acquisitions offer a method for quickly entering a market or securing a needed channel member to improve or secure distribution. It is usually possible to assess the performance of an organization before purchase and thereby minimize the risks through careful analysis and selection. However, even a small acquired organization can be difficult to integrate into the existing culture and operations. Often it takes several years to "digest" an acquisition or to combine two organizational cultures. For example in medical-surgical distribution, the combination of Owens and Minor and Stuart Medical was followed by service declines and a price increase. Many of the troubles were because of the difficulty in blending operations and cultures.[12]

Acquisition of a direct competitor is called horizontal integration. *Horizontal integration* is a method of obtaining growth within a market by purchasing direct competitors rather than using internal operational/functional strategies to take market share from competitors. Typically, organizations select horizontal integration for rapid geographical expansion or acquisition of a new technology.

Much of the growth of the for-profit hospital chains has been via a market development/acquisition/horizontal integration strategy. For example, before and since the merger of Columbia and HCA, an aggressive market development strategy through acquisition strategies of independent hospitals has been used to build the nation's largest private for-profit hospital chain. In the past two decades, horizontal integration and vertical integration through acquisition and alliances have been key entry strategies for initiating rapid market growth by health care organizations as well as by non–health care businesses.

Licensing Acquiring a technology or product through *licensing* avoids the financial, time, or market risks of technology or product development and may be viewed as an alternative to acquiring a complete company. License agreements provide rapid access to proven technologies and generally reduce the financial and marketing risk to the organization. However, the licensee usually does not receive proprietary technology and is dependent on the licensor for support and upgrade. In addition, the up-front dollar costs may be high. Typical of licensing is CareMap Corporation, which licenses operations software to hospitals for developing critical-care paths.

Venture Capital Investment *Venture capital investments* offer an opportunity to enter or "try out" a market while keeping risks low. Typically, venture capital investments are used to become involved in the growth and development of a small organization that has the potential to develop a new or innovative technology. By making minority investments in young and growing enterprises, organizations have an opportunity to become close to and possibly later enter into new technologies.[13]

In other cases, venture capitalists invest in growing industries and often profit from their acquisition. For instance, Dynamic Health, a small rural hospital company based in Tampa, Florida, operates five hospitals in three states and was founded by two former American Medical International executives through venture capital from Continental Equity Capital Corporation, a unity of Continental Bank Corporation and Shamrock Investments, a Los Angeles–based investment banking firm. In 1996, Dynamic was acquired by Community Health Systems in a horizontal integration strategy.[14]

Cooperation Strategies

Probably the most used and certainly the most talked about strategies of the 1990s are cooperation strategies. Many organizations have carried out adaptive strategies—particularly diversification, vertical integration, product and market development strategies—through cooperation strategies. Cooperation strategies include mergers, alliances, and joint ventures.

Merger *Mergers* are similar to acquisitions; however, in mergers two organizations combine through mutual agreement to form a single new organization, often with a new name. Increasing market share and eliminating competitors to improve patient volume and profitability are the primary reasons for many recent hospital mergers. For example, when the Penrose Health System and St. Francis Health System, both in Colorado Springs, Colorado, were consolidated through a national merger of the health care operations of Sisters of Charity Health Care Systems, Inc. of Cincinnati, Ohio, and Franciscan Healthcare Corporation of Colorado Springs, the new Penrose–St. Francis Healthcare System set as its objectives:

- greater efficiency in the delivery of health care services;
- reduction in duplication of services;
- improved geographic dispersion;
- increased service scope;
- restraint in pricing increases; and
- improved financial performance.[15]

Reflecting the recent trend in mergers and acquisitions of academic medical centers, New York Hospital–Cornell Medical Center and Columbia Presbyterian Medical Center agreed to merge creating one of the largest not-for-profit hospital corporations. The renamed New York and Presbyterian Hospitals, Inc. is expected to attain 17 percent share of the New York market. This merger typifies the quandary academic health centers are facing. They are being forced to consider consolidation strategies simply to survive in the changing market place. Similar steps have been taken by other academic health centers such as Mount Sinai (New York) and NYU Medical Centers, University of California San Francisco Medical Center and Stanford University Hospital as well as Boston's Brigham and Women's Hospital and Massachusetts General Hospital.[16]

As in acquisitions, a major difficulty in a merger is the integration of two separate organizational cultures. Mergers offer a more difficult problem than acquisitions because a totally new organization must be forged. In an acquisition, the dominant culture remains and subsumes the other. In a merger, a totally new organizational culture (the way we do things) must be developed. In the Penrose–St. Francis consolidation, because of significant changes in the organizational structure, governance, senior and middle management, service mix, product mix, and outside relationships, management realized that merging two distinctly different corporate cultures would be a challenge. Therefore, at Penrose–St. Francis a great deal of time was spent in communications at all levels in the organization. Medical staff and employees were engaged in a reformulation of the vision, mission, and statement of the shared values of the new organization. Work groups met and planned how to effectively and efficiently meet the needs of patients. Internal and external communications were given top priority.[17] Despite such efforts, truly merging the two organizational cultures into one will take years to complete.

Mergers and acquisitions continue to be important market entry strategies for health care organizations. An environment conducive to large health care combinations, institutional coordination, demands for efficiency, and the continuum of care (seamless care) has fostered many of these mergers and acquisitions. As a result, 1995 and 1996 were record years for large mergers and acquisitions (see Perspective 6–4).[18]

Alliance *Strategic alliances* are loosely coupled arrangements among existing organizations that are designed to achieve some long-term strategic purpose not possible by any single organization.[19] They are an attempt to strengthen competitive position while

Perspective 6–4

Record Years for Mergers and Acquisitions

- Of the nation's hospitals, 735 were involved in mergers and acquisitions in 1995.
- In 1995, 230 mergers or acquisitions were either completed or pending (184 in 1994).
- One in five U.S. community hospitals changed hands in the past two years.
- Columbia was clearly the biggest single deal-maker—in addition to the Healthtrust merger, it was involved in fifty-one mergers and acquisitions and closed twelve hospitals,

merging them with other Columbia/HCA-owned facilities.
- Record pace of mergers and acquisitions continues in 1996.

Source: Sandy Lutz, "1995: A Record Year for Hospital Deals," *Modern Healthcare* 25, no. 51 (December 18, 1995), pp. 43–50 and Sandy Lutz, "Merger, Acquisition Activity Hits Records in 1st Quarter, Report Says," *Modern Healthcare* 26, no. 22 (May 27, 1996), pp. 2–3.

maintaining the independence of the organizations involved. Strategic alliances are cooperative agreements that go beyond normal company-to-company dealings but fall short of merger or full partnership.[20]

In health care, the term alliance often has been used to refer to the voluntary organization that hospitals joined primarily to achieve economies of scale in purchasing. For some, this type of alliance provided the benefit of being part of a large system, yet allowed them to exist as freestanding, self-governing institutions. Examples of some major hospital alliances include Premier, Voluntary Hospitals of America (VHA), and University Hospital Consortium. This is a different type of alliance than that based on an expansion/cooperation strategy.

Strategic alliances, although not mergers, have many of the same problems—previously unrelated cultures have to learn to cooperate rather than compete; numerous "sessions" are required to determine what will be shared, what is proprietary, and how to balance the two; and efforts must be made to maintain cooperation over time within such a "loose" cooperative effort. On the other hand, strategic alliances offer several opportunities such as shared learning, access to expertise not currently "owned" by the organization, strengthened market position, and direction of competitive efforts toward others instead of each other. In some cases, an alliance can lead to a merger. For example, Breech Medical Center in Lebanon, Missouri, moved its affiliation agreement with St. John's Health System of Springfield, Missouri, to a full-asset merger over a several-year period.

More recently, as the environment becomes more unpredictable and reform efforts appear to be directed toward increased integration, a number of health care providers have been seeking strategic alliances. Many primary providers have turned to alliances as vehicles for providing services, soliciting physician loyalty, and reducing investments in operations.[21] Strategic alliances between physicians and hospitals must be anchored in their common purpose—improving patient care. The physicians involved may not concur with the hospital in its management of facilities, staffing, and so forth. In addition, conflict may emerge as hospitals diversify into areas that compete more directly with the physicians' own clinics, ambulatory-care centers, and diagnostic centers. Finally, although the hospital would prefer to have many qualified physicians admitted to the staff (who could refer more patients), allied physicians would prefer to limit credentialing of outside physicians (controlling competition).

Health care reform and the pressures of a rapidly changing environment have initiated some unique alliances. In Columbia, South Carolina, four hospitals—one Baptist, one Catholic, and two public hospitals—have agreed to participate in the Midlands Partnership for Community Health. It has undertaken three major joint projects: helping fund the relocation of the Columbia Free Clinic to a larger site, adding staff to the local AIDS consortium, and conducting a community health assessment. Although the hospitals are collaborating on some projects and hoping to do more, they are still competitive.[22] As this example illustrates, cooperative strategies are becoming more complex. As illustrated in Perspective 6–5, multiple-partner mergers and alliances are a trend of the 1990s.

Joint Venture   When projects get too large, technology too expensive, or the costs of failure too high for a single organization, joint ventures are often used.[23] A *joint venture* is the combination of the resources of two or more separate organizations to accomplish a designated task. A joint venture may involve a pooling of assets or a combination of

---

Perspective 6–5

Multiple-Partner Cooperation Strategies

Hospital mergers are becoming more complicated and typically include multiple partners, shared equity (purchase of minority interest), and joint operating agreements. Similarly, joint ventures used to be a simple transaction between two partners. Now some include three or more partners or two partners joining together to buy a third. It is no longer uncommon that a for-profit and a not-for-profit hospital team together to buy a third hospital. Some not-for-profit hospitals have engaged in multiple-partner deals as a defensive measure because of for-profit hospitals that are aggressively vying for market share. In some cases partners in joint ventures are buying multiple hospitals as well as entering into other joint ventures. In addition, many alliances include both vertical and horizontal arrangements and may be a prelude to full merger agreements.

A major reason for multiple-partner deals is that they diffuse risk. If operations turn sour, there are more institutions involved to solve the problems. Another advantage is that typically one partner represents local board control and franchise (recognition and preference) and the other brings capital to the deal. That is especially important in agreements in which an investor-owned chain and a regional system pair up. For example, Columbia/HCA Healthcare Corporation has twenty hospitals operating as joint ventures with other partners. Joining an existing network automatically means multiple-partner associations.

On the other hand, multiple partnerships can be more time consuming and problematic. In addition, although the financial risks will not be as great, neither will the rewards.

Source: Sandy Lutz, "Multiple-Partner Deals Let Players Hedge Their Bets," *Modern Healthcare* 26, no. 26 (June 24, 1996), pp. 146–150.

the specialized talents or skills of each organization. The most common organizational forms used in health care joint ventures are:

1. *Contractual Agreements.* Two or more organizations sign a contract agreeing to work together toward a specific objective.
2. *Subsidiary Corporations.* A new corporation is formed, usually to operate nonhospital activities.
3. *Partnerships.* A formal or informal arrangement in which two or more parties engage in activities of mutual benefit.
4. *Not-for-Profit Title-Holding Corporations.* Tax legislation enacted in 1986 allowed not-for-profit organizations to form tax-exempt title-holding corporations (providing significant benefits to health care organizations engaged in real estate ventures).[24]

With the dynamic health care environment, hospitals engage in joint ventures to lower costs and improve and expand services. Joint ventures can be an innovative way to generate revenues, supplement operations, and remain competitive.[25] Through the mid-1990s, the most common use has been hospital/physician joint ventures. Hospital/physician joint ventures were popular in the 1990s because they allowed the hospital to preempt physicians as competitors and, at the same time, stabilize their referral base. Often joint ventures with hospitals increased physicians' profitability. In the early 1990s, physicians entered joint ventures with hospitals to protect their incomes and autonomy whereas hospitals were motivated to form joint ventures as a means of controlling medical care costs and gaining influence over physician utilization of hospital services. Changes in third-party payor methods have created competition based on price, and joint ventures have been created to enable hospitals to have the capability of reducing costs and competing more effectively.[26]

Development Strategies

Organizations may enter new markets by using internal resources. This entry strategy takes the form of internal development or internal ventures. Diversification and vertical integration through internal development or internal ventures usually take considerably longer to establish than through acquisition.

Internal Development *Internal development* uses the existing organizational structure, personnel, and capital to generate new products/services or distribution strategies. Internal development may be most appropriate for products or services that are closely related to existing products or services. Internal development is common for growing organizations particularly when they can use existing resources, competencies, and capabilities.

Internal Ventures *Internal ventures* typically set up separate, relatively independent entities within the organization. Internal ventures may be most appropriate for products or services that are unrelated to the current products or services. For instance, internal ventures may be appropriate for developing vertically integrated systems. Thus, initial efforts for a hospital developing home health care may be accomplished through an internal venture. Similarly, in 1996, Columbia/HCA was expanding into the physician liability insurance business through an internal venture "pilot" program in several markets in order to evaluate whether it would be a long-term business for Columbia.

The major advantages and disadvantages of the market entry strategies are summarized in Exhibit 6–11. The adaptive and market entry strategies work in combination. The market entry strategies are the means for accomplishing the adaptive strategies. This relationship is demonstrated as organizations struggle with cost containment and their managed-care strategies. Perspective 6–6 illustrates how different organizations have opted for a variety of adaptive and market entry strategies to deal with HMOs. Although ownership of HMOs has a certain appeal in developing fully integrated systems, they do represent risk.

Positioning Strategies

Having selected the adaptive strategies and market entry strategies, managers must decide how the products and services will be positioned vis-à-vis competitors' products

Exhibit 6–11 • Advantages and Disadvantages of Market Entry Strategies

Market Entry Strategy	Major Advantages	Major Disadvantages
Acquisition	• Rapid market entry • Image already established • Performance known before purchase	• New business may be unfamiliar to parent • Takes a long time to assimilate organization's culture • New management team may be required • High initial cost
Licensing	• Rapid access to proven technology • Reduced financial exposure	• Not a substitute for internal technical competence • Not proprietary technology • Dependent on licensor
Venture Capital Investment	• Can provide window on new technology or market • Low risk	• Alone, unlikely to be a major stimulus of growth • Extended time to profitability
Merger	• Uses existing resources • Retains existing markets and products • Reduces competition	• Takes a long time to merge cultures • Merger match often difficult to find
Alliance	• Fills in gaps in product line • Creates efficiencies (e.g., purchasing power) • Reduces competition in weak markets • Focuses growth in critical areas	• Potential for conflict between members • Limits potential markets/products
Joint Venture	• Technological/marketing joint ventures can exploit small/large organizational synergies • Spreads distribution risks	• Potential for conflict between partners • Objectives of partners may not be compatible
Internal Development	• Uses existing resources • Organization maintains a high level of control • Presents image of developing (growth) organization	• Time lag to break even tends to be long • Unfamiliarity with new markets • Obtaining significant gains in market shares against strong competitors may be difficult
Internal Venture	• Uses existing resources • May enable organization to hold a talented entrepreneur • Isolates development from organization's bureaucracy	• Mixed record of success • Organization's internal climate often unsuitable

Perspective 6–6

HMOs Generate a Variety of Strategic Alternatives

Because the share of the heath care dollar spent on inpatient care is declining (and expected to continue to decline), hospital managers have searched for alternatives to maintain their position of dominance in the health care system. HMOs seemed to offer what hospitals needed in their efforts to develop fully integrated systems. However, many hospitals are rethinking the benefits and risks of HMO ownership.

Most multihospital systems are launching or expanding their HMOs. Others are bucking the trend and divesting their HMOs to focus solely on care delivery through market development, service development, or penetration rather than attempting to manage insurer risk. These multihospital systems have abandoned their vertical integration through internal development strategy by eliminating the HMO or insurer "middleman." To effectively manage risk, health plans had to grow to a sufficient size to support sophisticated information and management systems. The increasing consolidation resulting in larger HMOs has made it harder for small hospitals to develop a competitive HMO. Selling is attractive because hospitals are able to maintain their patient base as they sell assets and gain a partner. They manage to realize value while still retaining the market share initially sought in starting a health plan.

Large HMO companies and other provider-owned HMOs are interested in purchasing these smaller hospital-owned plans as part of their expansion strategy—market development through acquisition (horizontal integration). In the process, the HMO companies are creating payor-provider partnerships that appear to benefit both parties.

Rapidly growing hospital-owned plans are looking for stronger partners to support further market development (primarily geographic expansion). Systems that are selling their provider-owned plans want to solidify and expand their provider network and achieve the security that comes from affiliation with the leading provider network and managed-care organizations in the area.

Despite the sell-offs by smaller organizations, market activity has not been dominated by hospitals selling all or part of their health plans. Provider systems continue their strategies of vertical integration by forming or buying HMOs. Hospitals have been trying to regain a form of control over the delivery and business of health care by organizing networks and their own health plans. Many of these are joint venture arrangements with insurers. In addition, in a related diversification move, medical associations in several states, including California, New York, and Washington, have formed or are planning to form HMOs.

Source: Louise Kertesz, "Systems Begin Pruning HMOs from Holdings," *Modern Healthcare* 26, no. 25 (June 17, 1996), pp. 77–88.

and services. An organization must consciously position its products and services within a market through one of the marketwide or market segment positioning strategies. Michael Porter proposes three *generic positioning strategies*—cost leadership, differentiation, and focus.[27] Exhibit 6–12 presents Porter's concept of the three generic strategies.

Marketwide Strategies

Marketwide strategies position the products/services of the organization to appeal to a broad audience. These products and services, therefore, are not specifically tailored to the

Exhibit 6–12 • **Porter's Matrix**

Strategic Advantage

	Uniqueness Perceived by the Customer	Low Cost Position
Marketwide (broad)	Differentiation	Overall Cost Leadership
Particular Segment Only (narrow)	Differentiation/Focus	Cost/Focus

Strategic Target

Source: From Michael E. Porter, *Competitive Strategy: Techniques for Analyzing Industries and Competitors.* Copyright © 1980. Reprinted with permission of The Free Press, a division of Simon & Schuster.

particular needs of any special segment of the population. As shown in Exhibit 6–12, differentiation and cost leadership are marketwide positioning strategies.

Cost Leadership *Cost leadership* is a positioning strategy designed to gain an advantage over competitors by producing a product or providing a service at a lower cost than competitors' offerings. The product or service is often highly standardized to keep costs low. Cost leadership allows for more flexibility in pricing and relatively greater profit margins.

Cost leadership is based on economies of scale in operations, marketing, administration, and the use of the latest technology. Cost leadership may be used effectively as the generic strategy for any of the adaptive strategies and seems particularly applicable to the primary providers segment of the health care industry. As Porter suggests, "Cost leadership requires aggressive construction of efficient-scale facilities, vigorous pursuit of cost reduction from experience, tight cost and overhead control, avoidance of marginal customer accounts, and cost minimization in areas such as R&D, service, sales force, advertising, and so on."[28] Therefore, in order to use cost leadership, an organization must be able to develop a significant cost advantage and have a reasonably large market share. This strategy must be used cautiously within health care as consumers often perceive low price to mean low quality. However, cost leadership allows the organization the greatest flexibility in pricing.

An industry segment where cost leadership is being used successfully is in the area of long-term care. Long-term-care facilities are a "thin-margin business" in which profit margins range from approximately 1.2 percent to 1.7 percent. In this industry, older facilities are at a competitive disadvantage relative to new facilities. However, long-term-care facilities that have been able to drive costs down while maintaining quality have enjoyed higher margins. In addition, many of these facilities have been upgraded to be more efficient and have instituted tight cost controls. Advertising has been used to keep occupancy above 95 percent, which is often required in the industry to be profitable.

Differentiation *Differentiation* is a strategy to make the product or service different (or appear so in the mind of the buyer) from competitors' products or services. Thus, consumers see the service as unique among a group of similar competing services.

The product or service may be differentiated by emphasizing quality, a high level of service, ease of access, convenience, reputation, and so on. There are a number of ways to differentiate a product or service, but the attributes that are to be viewed as different or unique must be valued by the consumer. Therefore, organizations using differentiation strategies rely on brand loyalty (reputation or image), distinctive products or services, and the lack of good substitutes.

The most common forms of differentiation in the health care industry have been based on quality and image. Many acute-care hospitals emphasize and promote quality care as the difference between them and other hospitals in their service area. Similarly, a "high-tech" image is often the basis for differentiation among health care organizations. Affiliation with a medical school, performing the most sophisticated procedures or using the latest (often expensive) technology, may promote the image of "the best possible care."

Market Segment Strategies

As shown in Exhibit 6–12, market segment strategies are directed toward the particular needs of a well-defined market segment and often are called focus strategies. A *focus strategy* identifies a specific, well-defined "niche" in the total market that the company will concentrate on or pursue. Because of its attributes, the product or service or the organization itself may appeal to a particular niche within the market. A focus strategy may involve tailoring the product or service to meet the special needs of the segment the organization is trying to serve. Focus strategies may be based on cost leadership (cost/focus) or differentiation (differentiation/focus).

Because of the complexity of medicine and the entire health care industry, focus strategies are quite common. Just as physicians have specialized, the institutions within the field have tended to focus on specialized segments. Examples of focus strategies are rehabilitation hospitals, psychiatric hospitals, ambulatory-care centers, Alzheimer's centers, and so on. These specialty organizations may be further positioned based on cost leadership or differentiation.

Each of the generic strategies results from an organization making consistent choices for product/services, markets (service areas), and distinctive competencies—choices that reinforce each other. Exhibit 6–13 summarizes the choices appropriate for each generic strategy. Exhibit 6–14 presents the advantages and disadvantages of each of the positioning strategies.

Operational Strategies

As was shown in Exhibit 6–3, both functional and organization-wide operational strategies are developed to support the higher-level strategies. Functional-level strategies are developed within departments (marketing, information systems, finance, human resources, and

Exhibit 6–13 • **Product/Market/Distinctive Competency Choices and Generic Competitive Strategies**

	Cost Leadership	*Differentiation*	*Focus*
Product Differentiation	Low (by price)	High (by uniqueness)	Low to High (price or uniqueness)
Market Segmentation	Low (mass market)	High (many market segments)	High (only one or a very few segments)
Distinctive Competency	Operations and Materials Management	Research and Development/Marketing	Any Kind of Distinctive Competency

Exhibit 6–14 • **Advantages and Disadvantages of Positioning Strategies**

Positioning Strategy	Major Advantages	Major Disadvantages
Cost Leadership	• Provides clear competitive advantage • Provides clear market position • Provides opportunities to spend more than competition	• Must obtain large volume • Product/service must be standardized • Product/service may be viewed as low quality
Differentiation	• Product/service viewed as unique • Often viewed as high quality • Greater control over pricing	• Often difficult to adequately differentiate product or service • Product/service may be higher priced
Focus	• Appeals to specialized market • May develop good relations with market	• Market may be small • Expansion of market may be difficult

so on), and organization-wide strategies are developed across all functions (culture, organization, facilities, social responsibility). Both functional and organization-wide operational strategies are the means for implementing directional, adaptive, market entry, and positioning strategies. Each major function within the organization develops an "implementation" strategy, and for major strategic shifts there will be changes in organization-wide strategies as well.

The major areas for which functional strategies must be developed include marketing, finance, information systems, and human resources. The functional strategies must be linked to the higher-level strategies. Chapters 8 through 11 examine the functional strategies appropriate for each of the higher-level strategies. Typical organization-wide operational strategies may include changing the organizational culture, reorganization, upgrading facilities and equipment, and social responsibility initiatives. These strategies are addressed in Chapter 12.

Combination Strategies

Combination strategies are often used, especially in larger complex organizations, because no single strategy alone may be sufficient. For example, an organization may concurrently divest itself of one of its divisions and engage in market development in another. Perhaps the most frequent combination strategy of the 1990s for hospital-based systems has been vertical integration through acquisition and alliances combined with market development through acquisition (horizontal integration). As conceptualized in Exhibit 6–15, the intent of these strategies has been to create regional fully-integrated systems with wide market coverage and a full range of services (often referred to as providing the continuum of care).

As illustrated in Perspective 6–7, Carolinas Health Care System, previously known as Charlotte/Mecklenburg Hospital Authority, demonstrates the successful use of combination strategies. Beginning with a single county hospital as the base, Carolinas Health Care System used practically every type of adaptive and market entry strategy to achieve its vision of a fully integrated regional health system with Carolinas Medical Center as its foundation.

Exhibit 6–15 • Vertical and Horizontal Integration Combination Strategy

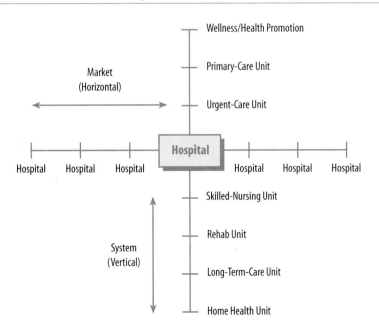

Integration at Carolinas Health Care System

Carolinas Health Care System (formerly Charlotte/Mecklenburg Hospital Authority) (4,386 beds)

Owns

Carolinas Medical Center (843 beds)
  Two helicopters, one jet
  Home Health Care
University Hospital (130 beds)
Mercy Hospital (336 beds)
Mercy-South (97 beds)
Sardis Nursing Home (125 beds)
Huntersville Nursing Home (377 beds)
Center for Mental Health
Institute for Rehabilitation (114 beds)
Carolinas Physician Network
  (300 Primary-Care Physicians)

Manages

Kings Mountain Hospital
Cleveland Memorial Hospital
Union Regional Medical Center
Valdese General Hospital
Mecklenburg County Department of Health

Affiliates

Carolinas Network of nine County Hospitals
  (1,700 beds)

In addition to an organization using several different strategies at once, a strategy may have several phases. It may be necessary to "string together" several strategic alternatives as phases or elements to implement a broader strategic shift. In a two-phase strategy, an organization may employ a retrenchment strategy in phase one and an enhancement strategy in phase two.

The strategic alternative or set of alternatives should be selected that best meets the requirements of the external environment, the resources, competencies, and capabilities of the organization, and the mission, vision, values, and objectives of management. As illustrated in Exhibit 6–16, top management's vision often extends through several strategic alternatives or phases. Such vision helps provide long-term continuity for the entire management team. However, management must be aware that, in a dynamic environment, circumstances may change and later phases may have to be modified or revised to meet the needs of the unique and changing situation. Strategic management is a continuous process of assessment and decision making.

The decision logic for the formulation of the strategic plan was illustrated in Exhibit 6–1. At this point, it would be useful to return to Exhibits 6–1 and 6–3 to review the complete strategy formulation process. In addition, as a review, Exhibit 6–17 provides summary definitions and examples of all of the strategic alternatives.

Summary and Conclusions

This chapter introduces a hierarchy of strategic alternatives. There are several types of strategies, and within each type, several strategic alternatives are available to health care organizations. In addition, there is a sequential decision logic in the strategy formulation process. First, directional strategies must be articulated through the organization's

Exhibit 6–16 • Vision of Strategy Combinations and Phases

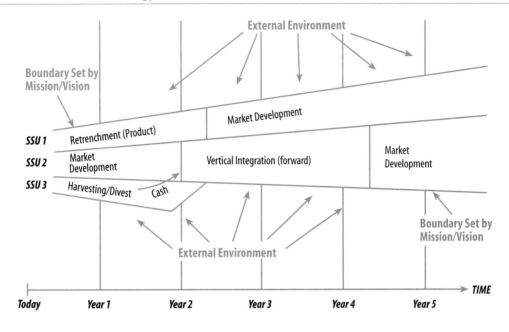

mission, vision, values, and objectives. Second, adaptive strategies must be identified, evaluated, and selected. The adaptive strategies are central to strategy formulation and delineate how the organization will expand, contract, or stabilize operations. Expansion strategies include diversification, vertical integration, market development, product development, and penetration. Contraction strategies include divestiture, liquidation, harvesting, and retrenchment. Finally, stabilization strategies include enhancement and status quo.

The third type of strategic decision concerns the market entry strategies. The expansion and stabilization strategies call for a method to carry out the strategy in the marketplace. Therefore, some method for entering or gaining access to that market is required. Market entry strategies include acquisitions and mergers, internal development and internal ventures, alliances and joint ventures, licensing, and venture capital investments. Any of the market entry strategies may be used to carry out an adaptive strategy.

The fourth type of strategy is the positioning strategy. Positioning strategies relate consumers' perceptions of products and services vis-à-vis competitors. These positioning strategies, often called generic strategies, include cost leadership and differentiation, which are marketwide strategies, and focus, which is a market segment strategy. Each of the generic strategies places different demands on the organization and requires unique resources, competencies, and capabilities.

Finally, operational strategies are discussed. Operational strategies are developed within the organization's functional departments (marketing, finance, human resources,

Exhibit 6–17 · Definition and Examples of the Strategic Alternatives

Strategy	Definition	Example
Adaptive Strategies		
Related Diversification	Adding new related product or service categories. Often requires the establishment of a new division.	Sun Healthcare, a long-term-care chain, purchases Mediplex Group, specializing in subacute care. The principal reason for the purchase was to enter a growth market.
Unrelated Diversification	Adding new unrelated product or service categories. Typically requires the establishment of a new division.	The University of Alabama Medical School owns a motel.
Forward Vertical Integration	Adding new members along the distribution channel (toward a later stage) for present products and services or controlling the flow of patients from one institution to another.	Merck & Company (pharmaceuticals) purchases Medco Containment Services (mail-order drug distributor).
Backward Vertical Integration	Adding new members along the distribution channel (toward an earlier stage) for present products and services or controlling the flow of patients from one institution to another.	San Angelo Texas Community Hospital moved into the wellness market by developing a fitness center open to those aged fifty and over in the community.
Market Development	Introducing present products or services into new geographic markets or to new segments within a present geographic market.	Brentwood, Tennessee-based Community Health Systems purchases Marion (Illinois) Memorial Hospital in order to move into the Midwest.
Product Development	Improving present products or services or extending the present product line.	San Pedro (California) Peninsula Hospital expanded its psychiatric program by establishing a therapy program for elderly patients who require little or no hospitalization.
Penetration	Seeking to increase market share for present products or services in present markets through marketing efforts (promotion, channels, price).	Integrated Medical Systems is trying to increase its market share of automated communications between physicians' offices and health care delivery organizations through industry advertising.
Divestiture	Selling an operating business unit or division to another organization. Typically, the business unit will continue in operation.	Baxter International divests its $675 million diagnostics manufacturing business.
Liquidation	Selling all or part of the organization's assets (facilities, inventory, equipment, and so on) in order to obtain cash. The assets may be used by the purchaser in a variety of ways and businesses.	MedCare HMO was liquidated by the state of Illinois.
Harvesting	Taking cash out while providing few new resources for a business in a declining market. Sometimes referred to as "milking" the organization.	Many state health departments are planning harvest strategies for primary-care services if comprehensive health care reform is passed. Health departments will slowly harvest these services as private providers assume patient loads.
Retrenchment	Reducing the scope of operations, redefining the target market, and selectively cutting personnel, products and services, or service area (geographic coverage).	Because of low utilization, Columbia/HCA Healthcare Corporation closed two of three hospitals it acquired in the Tampa Bay area.
Enhancement	Seeking to improve operations within present product or service categories through quality programs.	After acquisition, St. Luke's Regional Medical Center of Boise, Idaho, replaced aging facilities of Wood River Medical Center, the parent of Blaine County Medical Center and Moritz Community Hospital.
Status Quo	Seeking to maintain relative market share within a market.	Many public health departments offering personal health services (primary care) call for steady state until the impact of managed-care, system integration, and other reforms are clearer.

Exhibit 6–17 · **Continued**

Strategy	Definition	Example
Market Entry Strategies		
Acquisition	Strategy to grow through the purchase of an existing organization, a unit of an organization, or a product/service.	Horizon Mental Health Management, one of the largest contract managers of mental health programs acquired American Day Treatment Centers, which owns 22 partial-hospitalization centers in a deal valued at $17.5 million.
Licensing	Acquiring an asset (technology, market, equipment, etc.) through contract.	GE Medical Systems licenses diagnostic software used to maintain imaging equipment.
Venture Capital Investment	Financial investment in an organization in order to participate in its growth.	Continental Equity Capital Corporation and Shamrock Investments provide venture capital to start Dynamic Health Systems, a rural hospital company.
Merger	Combining two (or more) organizations through mutual agreement to form a single new organization.	Holston Valley Hospital and Medical Center (383 beds) in Kingsport, Tennessee, and 336-bed Bristol (Tennessee) Regional Medical Center merged to form Wellmont Health System.
Alliance	Formation of a formal partnership.	Rural Huntington (Indiana) Memorial Hospital signed a clinical affiliation agreement with urban Lutheran Hospital of Indiana (Fort Wayne) to share clinical services.
Joint Venture	Combination of the resources of two or more organizations to accomplish a designated task.	Marion (Ohio) General Hospital and Smith Clinic, a 53-physician multispecialty group formed a joint venture to consolidate physician and hospital services in Marion County.
Internal Development	Products or services developed internally using the organization's own resources.	Swedish Covenant Hospital of Chicago developed a 37,000-square-foot health and fitness center out of their cardiac rehabilitation program.
Internal Venture	Establishment of an independent entity within an organization to develop products or services.	Columbia University's College of Physicians and Surgeons established a center for alternative and complementary medicine.
Positioning Strategies		
Cost Leadership	Low cost/price strategy directed toward entire market.	Many outpatient clinics attempt to be cost and price leaders for a wide range of primary-care services.
Differentiation	Development of unique product/service features directed toward entire market.	Holy Cross Medical Center of Mission Hills, California, opened a regional cancer center where patients will receive treatments in private or semiprivate cabana-type rooms equipped with televisions, videocassette recorders, and other audio equipment. Other support therapies include acupressure, art, yoga, and pain management.
Focus—Cost Leadership	Low cost/price strategy directed toward particular market segment.	HEALTHSOUTH Rehabilitation Corporation is a cost and price leader in rehabilitation.
Focus—Differentiation	Development of unique product/service features directed toward particular market segment.	Hanger Orthopedic Group, Bethesda, Maryland, focusing on being the largest U.S. distributor of prosthetic and orthotic supplies and components.

and so on). Often there are organization-wide strategies (changing the organization's culture, reorganization, and so on) as well. Functional and organization-wide strategies are developed to implement the higher-level strategic alternatives. These strategies and their linkages with the higher-level strategies are discussed in Chapters 8 through 12.

It is unlikely that a single strategy will suffice for an organization. Several strategic alternatives may have to be adopted and used in combination. For instance, one product may require market development whereas a different product may require harvesting. Similarly, one division may be positioned as a cost leader and another may be pursuing differentiation. In addition, several strategic alternatives may be seen as phases or sequences in a broader strategic shift.

Chapter 7 will discuss methods for evaluating the strategic alternatives presented in this chapter.

Key Terms and Concepts in Strategic Management

acquisition
adaptive strategy
alliance
backward vertical integration
combination strategy
concentric diversification
conglomerate diversification
contraction strategy
cost leadership
differentiation
directional strategy
diversification
divestiture
enhancement strategy

expansion strategy
focus
forward vertical integration
functional strategy
generic strategies
harvesting
horizontal integration
internal development
internal venture
joint venture
licensing
liquidation
market development
market entry strategy

market penetration
merger
operational strategy
organization-wide strategy
penetration
positioning strategy
product development
related diversification
retrenchment
stabilization strategy
status quo
unrelated diversification
venture capital investment
vertical integration

Questions for Class Discussion

1. What five types of strategies make up the strategy formulation process? Describe the role each plays in developing a strategic plan.

2. Why are the directional strategies both a part of situational analysis and strategy formulation?

3. Name and describe the expansion strategies, the contraction strategies, and the stabilization strategies. Which of the adaptive strategies are corporate and which are division level? Under what conditions may each be appropriate?

4. Why does the selection of the strategic alternative(s) create "direction" or "momentum" for the organization?

5. Which of the strategic adaptive alternatives is selected most frequently by for-profit chains? Provide some examples of such strategies.

6. What is the difference between related diversification and product development? Provide examples of each.

7. Describe vertical integration in terms of patient flow.

8. Explain the difference between an enhancement strategy and a status quo strategy.

9. How is market development different from product development? Penetration? Provide examples of each.

10. Compare and contrast a divestiture strategy with a liquidation strategy.

11. How might a retrenchment strategy and a penetration strategy be linked together? What are some other logical combinations of strategies?

12. Which of the market entry strategies provides for the quickest entry into the market? Slowest?

13. Explain Porter's generic strategies. How do they position the organization's products and services in the market?

14. How do functional strategies support higher-level strategies?

15. What are combination strategies? How may a combination of strategies be related to vision?

16. Work through Exhibit 6–3, "Hierarchy of Strategic Decisions and Alternatives," for several organizations with which you are familiar. Practice selecting different alternatives under each strategy type.

Notes

1. Richard Farson, *Management of the Absurd* (New York: Simon and Schuster, 1996), p. 21.

2. Karen Pallarito, "At 50 HFMA Looks to Broaden Its Membership," *Modern Healthcare* 26, no. 27 (July 1, 1996), pp. 2–3.

3. Jay Greene, "Diversification, Take Two," *Modern Healthcare* 23, no. 28 (1993), pp. 28–32.

4. Mary Chris Jaklevic, "Hospitals Expand via Mall Centers," *Modern Healthcare* 26, no. 23 (June 3, 1996), pp. 50–51.

5. Stephen S. Mick and Douglas A. Conrad, "The Decision to Integrate Vertically in Health Care Organizations," *Hospital and Health Services Administration* 33, no. 3 (Fall 1988), p. 352.

6. E. Gardner, "Baptist Uses Expansion Alliances to Bypass Mayo Jacksonville Beachhead," *Modern Healthcare* 20, no. 32 (August 13, 1990), pp. 34–39.

7. "For the Record," *Modern Healthcare* 26, no. 21 (May 20, 1996), p. 16.

8. Mick and Conrad, "The Decision to Integrate Vertically," p. 348.

9. Louise Kertesz, "Systems Begin Pruning HMOs from Holdings," *Modern Healthcare* 26, no. 25 (June 17, 1996), pp. 77–88.

10. "For the Record," *Modern Healthcare* 26, no. 21 (May 20, 1996), p. 16.

11. Charles L. Breindel, "Nongrowth Strategies and Options in Health Care," *Hospital and Health Services Administration* 33, no. 1 (Spring 1988), p. 42.

12. Lisa Scott, "Will We Like Tomorrow's Giants?" *Modern Healthcare* 26, no. 32, (August 5, 1996), p. 86.

13. Edward B. Roberts and Charles A. Berry, "Entering New Businesses: Selecting Strategies for Success," *Sloan Management Review* 25 (Spring 1985), p. 7.

14. Jonathan Gardner, "Community to Buy Dynamic Health," *Modern Healthcare* 26, no. 32 (August 5, 1996), p. 32.

15. Sharon Roggy and Ron Gority, "Bridging the Visions of Competing Catholic Health Care Systems," *Health Care Strategic Management* 11, no. 7 (1993), pp. 16–19.

16. L. Lagnado, "Top New York Medical Centers to Merge," *Wall Street Journal* (July 5, 1996), p. A1.

17. Roggy and Gority, "Bridging the Visions of Competing Catholic Health Care Systems," pp. 16–19.

18. Sandy Lutz, "1995: A Record Year for Deals," *Modern Healthcare* 25, no. 51 (December 18, 1995), pp. 43–52; and Sandy Lutz, "Merger, Acquisition Activity Hits Records in 1st Quarter, Report Says," *Modern Healthcare* 26, no. 22 (May 27, 1996), pp. 2–3.

19. Howard S. Zuckerman and Arnold D. Kaluzny, "Strategic Alliances in Health Care: The Challenges of Cooperation," *Frontiers of Health Services Management* 7, no. 3 (1991), p. 4.

20. Michael E. Porter, *The Competitive Advantage of Nations* (New York: Free Press, 1990), p. 65.

21. Sandra Pelfrey and Barbara A. Theisen, "Joint Ventures in Health Care," *Journal of Nursing Administration* 19, no. 4 (April 1989), p. 39.

22. Kathryn S. Taylor, "Columbia, SC," *Hospitals and Health Networks* 67, no. 21 (November 5, 1993), p. 45.

23. Roberts and Berry, "Entering New Businesses," p. 6.

24. Pelfrey and Theisen, "Joint Ventures in Health Care," pp. 39–41.

25. Ibid., p. 42.

26. Donna Malvey, "Hospital-Physician Joint Ventures: Unstable Strategies for a Rapidly Changing Environment," Unpublished Working Paper, School of Health Related Professions, University of Alabama at Birmingham (1994).

27. Michael E. Porter, *Competitive Strategy* (New York: Free Press, 1980), p. 35.

28. Ibid.

Additional Readings

Andersen, Ronald M., Thomas H. Rice, and Gerald F. Kominski, eds., *Changing the U.S. Health Care System: Key Issues in Health Services, Policy, and Management* (San Francisco: Jossey-Bass Publishers, 1996). This book offers insights into the composition and workings of the full spectrum of health care services in the United States, outlining key trends and future policy options. Important topics include access to health care, the costs of health care, quality of care, special populations, and directions for change.

Nutt, Paul C., and Robert W. Backoff, *Strategic Management of Public and Third Sector Organizations: A Handbook for Leaders* (San Francisco: Jossey-Bass Publishers, 1992). The authors consider the unique needs of public and third-sector organizations and provide strategic approaches designed especially for these institutions. The book offers a framework for understanding strategic issues, explains strategic management concepts and describes their step-by-step process, examines planning techniques, discusses specific examples, and includes forms and work sheets for carrying out the process.

Spiegel, Allen D., and Herbert H. Hyman, *Strategic Health Planning: Methods and Techniques Applied to Marketing and Management* (Norwood, New Jersey: Ablex Publishing Corporation, 1991). Using a six-step strategic planning process framework, the authors provide an extensive and comprehensive compilation of methods and techniques for each aspect of health care planning. They provide insight into identifying and resolving problems existing in the delivery of health care services. The book is particularly helpful in pinpointing needs in geographic service areas; garnering material, financial, and staff resources; creating, selecting, and ranking strategic options; implementation; and evaluating outcomes.

Yuan, Gao, *Lure the Tiger out of the Mountains: The Thirty-Six Stratagems of Ancient China* (New York: Simon and Schuster, 1991). The book provides a summary of thirty-six general strategies developed by ancient Chinese military leaders and tacticians, politicians, merchants, philosophers, and writers, as well as ordinary people. The thirty-six stratagems are of practical use to anyone and were developed over five millennia of wars, coups d'état, court intrigues, economic innovations, and competition. The thirty-six stratagems teach a way of thinking and means of understanding other people's behavior and for analyzing all types of situations. The stratagems' historical and legendary origins are traced through ancient tales and anecdotes illustrating their use.

Evaluation of Alternatives and Strategic Choice

Learning Objectives

After completing this chapter you should be able to:

1. Understand the rationale underlying the various decision tools used to evaluate strategic alternatives.

2. Discuss, evaluate, and select appropriate adaptive strategic alternatives for a health care organization.

3. Discuss, evaluate, and select appropriate market entry strategic alternatives.

4. Discuss, evaluate, and select appropriate positioning strategic alternatives.

5. Understand the role of the functional and organization-wide operational strategies.

> "If the grand strategy is correct, any number of tactical errors can be made and yet the enterprise proves successful."
> - General Robert E. Woods (1879–1969), President, Sears, Roebuck & Company

Evaluation of the Alternatives

There are several methods that may be used to aid in the determination of the appropriate strategic alternatives for each type of strategy (adaptive, market entry, and positioning). All of these methods incorporate the results of external and internal analyses, which in turn have been conducted within the context of the directional strategies—mission, vision, values, and objectives. In using these selection methods, all of the strategic alternatives discussed previously should be available for consideration. As suggested in the Introductory Incident there are many possible strategies, and careful analysis (understanding the internal requirements and external conditions) of the strategic alternatives is essential to assure a coherent and integrated strategy.

The methods for evaluating and selecting strategic alternatives are actually constructs or frameworks for helping managers think about the organization and its situation relative to the general environment, competitors, and consumers. In other words, they are maps to help managers work through the variables in their strategic decisions. These constructs or maps allow health care managers to consciously balance organizational motives with community health needs. Thus, market share and revenue issues may be seen in a context of

Introductory Incident

Evaluation of Strategy Is Important

The following announcements were taken from a single issue of *Modern Healthcare:*[1]

Columbia/HCA announces its intent to acquire Roger Williams Medical Center in Providence, Rhode Island. The 150-bed hospital would provide a base for Columbia/HCA to compete with two developing health networks as well as the adjacent area of southern Massachusetts.

Alexandria Health Services Corporation, the parent company of 321-bed Alexandria Hospital, unveiled a proposed merger with Springfield, Virginia-based Inova Health System that operates Alexandria's only other acute-care hospital, 229-bed Mount Vernon Hospital. The merger would give the combined systems acute-care monopolies in Alexandria, Fairfax, and Falls Church, Virginia.

The parent corporations of *Yale–New Haven Hospital and Bridgeport Hospital* completed an affiliation agreement announced last year. Yale–New Haven Health System will oversee the annual budget and capital spending decisions of Southern Connecticut Health System, the parent of Bridgeport Hospital.

Three Oregon medical groups, *Corvallis Clinic, HealthFirst Medical Group*, and *Medford Clinic,* have agreed to merge their assets and form a physician practice management company called Physician Partners. Physician Partners, 98 percent physician owned, includes 288 physicians at twenty-eight locations.

Allina Health System and several Wisconsin hospitals and clinics are considering the formation of a joint venture in the eastern suburbs of the Twin Cities. The intent is to develop health care services such as information systems or specialty physician services that emerge as the area becomes more urban. In addition, the joint venture will make it easier for Allina to market its managed-care products in the St. Paul suburbs.

Long Island Jewish Medical Center and *Beth Israel Medical Center* announced a memorandum of understanding to create a single parent corporation. The partnership is structured to strengthen the two institutions by creating one broad geographic network that is attractive to managed-care companies.

Announcements of changes in strategy such as these are common in health care publications. However, preceding these announcements a great deal of analysis and evaluation has typically taken place. Given all the strategic alternatives (adaptive, market entry, and positioning) available to health care organizations, how do these organizations decide which strategy is best? Is diversification more appropriate than vertical integration? What conditions would call for market development or a penetration strategy? When should harvesting begin and when is the right time for retrenchment? Is acquisition better than a full-asset merger? When is an alliance more appropriate than acquisition or internal development? How should a health care organization differentiate itself? What services should be cost leaders?

Certainly, there are new market realities for all health care organizations. Integration and linking with managed-care systems are behind much of the consolidation and positioning taking place within the industry. The "right" strategy seems more important than ever before. Although there is no tried and true answer to the question of which strategy is best, there are frameworks for categorizing external and internal variables and relationships. As the engineer and inventor Charles F. Kettering said, "A problem well stated is a problem half solved." Further, there are clear external conditions and internal requirements that are appropriate for each of the strategies. There are advantages and disadvantages associated with each strategic alternative.

---

[1] From *Modern Healthcare*, Vol. 26, No. 28 (July 8, 1996). Copyright © Crain Communications, Inc., 740 N. Rush Street, Chicago, IL 60611. Reprinted with permission.

providing health and well-being to "real people." However, none of the methods provides a definitive answer to the question of appropriate strategy. None of the methods *makes* the strategic choice. Rather, the methods categorize and demonstrate the relationships inherent in the situation. The various methods help to structure the thought processes of decision makers.

Although the evaluation methods fine-tune the manager's perspective and organize thinking, ultimately, the manager must make the decision. Managers need to understand the risks, make judgments, and commit the organization to some course of action. Therefore, the evaluation methods cannot be used to obtain "answers," but rather to gain perspective and insight into a complex relationship between organization and environment. There is no right answer. As Peter Drucker has pointed out: "It is a choice between alternatives. It is rarely a choice between right and wrong. It is at best a choice between 'almost right' and 'probably wrong'—but much more often a choice between two courses of action neither of which is probably more nearly right than the other."[1] As suggested in Perspective 7–1, in order to have the proper perspective, it is important that managers be involved with customers, vendors, and the organization and talk to people to get a real feel for the culture, competitive advantage, and organizational opportunities and threats.

Perspective 7–1

Managing by Wandering Around

Tom Peters and Robert Waterman popularized the term "managing by wandering around" (MBWA) in their book *In Search of Excellence.* They found that excellent companies are a vast network of informal, open communications. Getting managers out of their offices to see things for themselves was cited as a major contributor to informal exchanges.

Later, Tom Peters and Nancy Austin devoted an entire chapter to the concept in *A Passion for Excellence.* They believe MBWA is about common sense, leadership, customers, innovation, and people. Simple wandering—listening, empathizing, staying in touch—leads to better communication and "hands-on" problem solving. "To 'wander' with customers (at least 25 percent of the time) and vendors and our own people, is to be in touch with the first vibrations of the new. It turns out that hard-data-driven information is usually a day late and always sterile."

Peters and Austin posit that a major managerial problem is leaders who are out of touch with their people, customers, and vendors. Being in touch cannot be achieved without being there. "Being in touch means tangible, visceral ways of being informed." It facilitates innovation, and makes possible the teaching of values to every member of the organization. "Listening, facilitating, and teaching and reinforcing values." Peters and Austin conclude, "MBWA is the technology of leadership."

Source: Thomas J. Peters and Robert H. Waterman, Jr., *In Search of Excellence* (New York: Harper and Row, Publishers, 1982); and Tom Peters and Nancy Austin, *A Passion for Excellence: The Leadership Difference* (New York: Warner Books, 1985).

Evaluation of the Adaptive Strategies

As discussed throughout Chapter 6, once the directional strategies have been developed, consideration is given to the adaptive strategies. The adaptive strategies are central to the strategy formulation process and are the broadest interpretation of the directional strategies. This level of strategic decision making specifies whether the organization wants to grow (expansion), become smaller (contraction), or remain about the same (stabilization). In addition, the method to accomplish expansion, contraction, or stabilization (diversification, divestiture, enhancement, and so on) must be formulated.

Several constructs help managers think about adaptive strategic decisions. However, as expressed previously, these constructs help show relationships of the organization to its markets and competitors; they do not make the decision. Methods to evaluate the adaptive strategies include:

- a threats, opportunities, weaknesses, and strengths (TOWS) matrix,
- product life cycle (PLC) analysis,
- Boston Consulting Group (BCG) portfolio analysis,
- extended portfolio matrix analysis,
- strategic position and action evaluation (SPACE), and
- program evaluation.

For the most part, any of these methods may be used to evaluate the adaptive strategic alternatives for all types of health care organizations—for-profit as well as not-for-profit. As illustrated in Perspective 7–2, the strategic thinking requirements and resultant strategies are often quite similar for both for-profit and not-for-profit institutions.

Perspective 7–2

For-Profits and Not-for-Profits Pursue Similar Strategies

Of particular significance in the development of hospital systems is the blurring of differences between investor-owned systems and not-for-profit systems. With the exception of large public hospital systems (and even here the distinctions are fading), the not-for-profit systems are behaving more like investor-owned systems in terms of increasing attention given to balance sheets, the external environment, and competitive strategies. Not-for-profit systems have adopted corporate models, established for-profit subsidiaries, and narrowed the profitability gap when compared to investor-owned systems. Meanwhile, the role of the large investor-owned system has been diminishing. Recognizing that health care is a local business and that survival depends on dominance in local and regional markets, investor-owned systems are no longer focusing on national competition. Instead, they are pursuing growth strategies similar to not-for-profit systems. Investor-owned systems are concentrating on smaller local and regional markets and are abandoning markets where they are poor competitors. These systems have streamlined, reorganized, and refinanced, plus divested themselves of unprofitable acquisitions.

Source: Donna Malvey, Ph.D., Department of Health Administration, University of Arkansas at Little Rock.

Because strategy formulation is a process of "fitting" the organization to its environment, each of these evaluation methods uses the organization's external opportunities and threats and factors as inputs to the process. The threats, opportunities, weaknesses, and strengths constitute the *strategic assumptions* on which strategic decision making will be grounded. Although the strategic assumptions are based on extensive information gathering and analysis, managers cannot always be certain that the assumptions are correct. Therefore, it is often useful to have more than one set of likely strategic assumptions, particularly regarding the external environment. This provides several "backdrops" or contexts for the formulation process and facilitates strategic thinking. Depending on the environmental analysis method used, several sets of simple trend, expert opinion, stakeholder, scenario, or competitor analysis (see Chapters 2 and 3) assumptions may be generated to evaluate strategy. For example, in evaluating the adaptive strategic alternatives several possible scenarios about the external environment (see Exhibit 2–9) or service area structure analyses (see Exhibit 3–4) may be used as a basis for evaluating alternatives. Different strategic assumptions can provide the basis for contingency plans should the assumptions prove to be wrong or change over time.

TOWS Matrix

Within a framework provided by the mission, vision, values, and objectives, the internal and external factors may be combined to develop and evaluate specific adaptive strategic alternatives using a *TOWS* (threats, opportunities, weaknesses, strengths) *matrix.*[2] As illustrated in Exhibit 7–1, the internal strengths and weaknesses of the organization are summarized on the horizontal axis and the external environmental opportunities and threats are summarized on the vertical axis. The TOWS matrix indicates four strategic conditions that the organization may encounter. Adaptive strategic alternatives may be developed by matching the organization's strengths with external opportunities, strengths with threats, weaknesses with opportunities, and weaknesses with threats.

Adaptive strategic alternatives are suggested by the interactions of the four sets of variables. In this example, the primary concern is the adaptive strategic alternatives, but this analysis could also be applied to the development of any type of strategy.[3] In practice, particularly in open discussion sessions, some of the alternatives developed through the TOWS matrix may be adaptive, market entry, positioning, or operational.

The Survival Quadrant An organization faced with significant internal weaknesses and external threats is in a difficult position. Because the organization must attempt to minimize both weaknesses and threats, this quadrant is often referred to as the *survival quadrant.* Obviously, the organization must respond to this situation with an explicit strategy. Adaptive alternatives that may be pursued by an organization in this situation include unrelated diversification (if financial resources are available), divestiture, liquidation, harvesting, and retrenchment. For instance, a PPO may have the internal weaknesses of declining enrollments and an image of declining quality in the face of growing external threats from HMOs, AHPs (accountable health plans), and industry-wide consolidation. Such conditions may suggest retrenchment.

Exhibit 7–1 · **TOWS Matrix**

	List Internal Strengths 1. 2. 3. 4.	List Internal Weaknesses 1. 2. 3. 4.
List External Opportunities 1. 2. 3. 4.	**4** ***Future Quadrant*** • Related diversification • Vertical integration • Market development • Product development • Penetration	**2** ***Internal Fix-It Quadrant*** • Retrenchment • Enhancement • Market development • Product development • Vertical integration • Related diversification
List External Threats 1. 2. 3. 4.	**3** ***External Fix-It Quadrant*** • Related diversification • Unrelated diversification • Market development • Product development • Enhancement • Status quo	**1** ***Survival Quadrant*** • Unrelated diversification • Divestiture • Liquidation • Harvesting • Retrenchment

Source: From Heinz Weihrich, "The TOWS Matrix: A Tool for Situational Analysis," *Long Range Planning* Vol. 15, No. 2 (1982), p. 60. Reprinted by permission of Elsevier Science Ltd., The Boulevard, Langford Lane, Kidlington OS5 1GB, UK.

The Internal Fix-It Quadrant The second quadrant indicates that managers should attempt to minimize internal weaknesses and maximize external opportunities. Typically, an organization will recognize an external opportunity but have internal weaknesses that prevent it from taking advantage of the opportunity. Therefore, this quadrant is referred to as the *internal fix-it quadrant.*

If actions are taken to strengthen the organization (often an operational-level strategy), it may be able to pursue the opportunity. Strategies in this quadrant may require two phases (a combination strategy): first, fixing the internal weakness, and second, pursuing the opportunity. Strategic alternatives that are frequently selected in this quadrant include retrenchment, enhancement, market development, product development, vertical integration, and related diversification. For example, a for-profit hospital may have an external opportunity to enter an attractive new market but presently lacks the financial resources to do so. After addressing this weakness (perhaps by selling additional stock), the opportunity may be pursued (market development).

The External Fix-It Quadrant   In this quadrant, the organization recognizes that it has significant strengths but that it must deal with external environmental threats. Therefore, managers must attempt to maximize the organization's strengths and minimize the external threats. This quadrant may be referred to as the *external fix-it quadrant.* As in the internal fix-it quadrant, strategies in this quadrant may require two phases. Strategies that are often employed in this quadrant include related and unrelated diversification, market development, product development, enhancement, and status quo. For instance, an investor-owned skilled-nursing home with internal strengths of strong management, financial resources, and customer loyalty may encounter the external threat of a powerful new competitor planning to enter the service area. The nursing home may use a preemptive strategic response by engaging in status quo in the skilled-nursing home segment while using related diversification into domiciliaries and retirement communities to expand its presence in the total market.

The Future Quadrant   This quadrant represents the best situation for an organization. The organization tries to maximize its strengths and take advantage of external opportunities. Therefore, this quadrant may be referred to as the *future quadrant* because it represents the strategies that the organization will adopt for future growth. Strategies in this quadrant lead from the strength of the organization and use its internal resources to capitalize on the market for its products and services.[4] Typical strategic alternatives that might be selected in this quadrant include related diversification, vertical integration, market development, product development, and penetration. For example, a metropolitan hospital with the internal strengths of access to technology, economies of scale in purchasing, and capable management may be presented with an external opportunity to initiate affiliations with several rural or specialty hospitals and thus create a more extensive referral system for the hospital (vertical integration). The major reasons that the health care industry has engaged in vertical integration in the 1990s include:

- competing with other integrated systems and managed-care organizations in the delivery of high-quality care to enrollees and other patients;
- giving providers enough market clout to force managed-care organizations to renegotiate contracts that are more favorable to them; and
- dominating markets so that providers and their managed-care components will be virtually free of meaningful competition.[5]

Product Life Cycle Analysis

Product life cycle (PLC) analysis can be useful in selecting strategic alternatives based on the principle that all products and services go through several distinct phases or stages. These stages relate primarily to the changing nature of the marketplace, the product-development process, and the types of demands made on management. In evaluating product life cycles, the evolution of industry sales and profits (or a surrogate for sales such as the number of subscribers, hospital visits, or competitors) is tracked over time. This evolution will have strategic implications for the organization. A typical product life cycle and the attributes of each stage are presented in Exhibit 7–2.

Products and services have an introductory stage during which sales are increasing yet profits are negative. In this stage, there are few competitors, prices are usually high,

Exhibit 7–2 · The Product Life Cycle

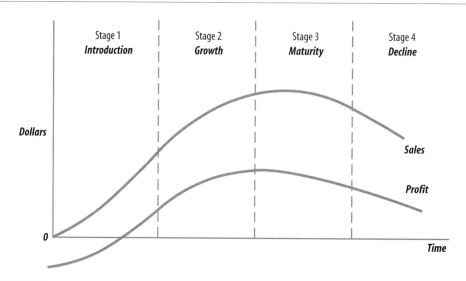

	PLC Stage Characteristics			
	Introduction	**Growth**	**Maturity**	**Decline**
Sales/Revenue	Low	Rapid growth	Slow growth	Declining
Profits	Negative	Peak levels	Declining	Low
Competitors	Few	Growing	Many	Declining
Cash Flow	Negative	Moderate	High	Low
Capital Access	Venture	Equity/debt	Debt/internal	Minimal

Source: From Philip Kotler, *Marketing Management: Analysis, Planning, Implementation, and Control,* 7th ed., (1991), p. 365. Reprinted by permission of Simon & Schuster.

promotion is informative about the product category, and there are limited distribution outlets. In the growth stage, sales and profits are both increasing, and, as a result, competing organizations enter the market to participate in the growth. During this stage, prices are still high but may begin to decline, promotion is directed toward specific brands, and there is rapid growth in the number of outlets.

The maturity stage of the PLC marks the end of rapid growth and the beginning of consolidation. In addition, market segmentation (defining narrower and narrower segments of the market) occurs. In this stage, prices have stabilized or declined, price promotion becomes common, and distribution is widespread. In the decline stage, total revenues and profits for the product or service are declining and will likely continue to decline over the long term. Perspective 7–3 describes the PLC for health maintenance organizations.

There are two important questions for strategy formulation when using product life cycles: "In what stage of the life cycle are the organization's products and services?" "How long are the stages (and the life cycle itself) likely to last?"

The Product Life Cycle Concept Applied to Health Maintenance Organizations

The health maintenance organization (HMO) industry is an excellent example of product life cycle (PLC) phases. HMOs had an extremely long introductory period. The first HMO prototype, the Ross-Loos Clinic in Los Angeles, became operational in 1929. Forty years later, in 1970, there were only thirty-three, generally not-for-profit, HMOs in the United States, serving approximately 3 million enrollees.[1]

The boost that pushed HMOs from introduction into growth included the passage of the Health Maintenance Organization and Resources Act of 1974, which provided development funding of over $350 million for ten years.[2] Additionally, the market for HMOs was expanded with the passage of the HMO Act Amendments, which resulted in acceptance of federal qualifications.

In addition to the federal funding for development and growth, HMOs sought additional capital in the early 1980s. One method to accomplish this was to convert from a not-for-profit to a for-profit HMO. U.S. Health Care Systems, Inc. (then known as HMO of Pennsylvania) converted to for-profit status in 1981 and obtained a venture capital investment of $3 million from Warburg, Pincus and Co., Inc. Two years later, U.S. Health Care Systems, Inc. became the first HMO to offer stock to the public and raised $25 million in two public offerings. Others followed suit, and for several years HMOs were the darlings of Wall Street as record growth and earnings were reported. Not-for-profit HMOs also sought additional capital to fund growth. Kaiser-Permanente Medical Care Program, the country's largest HMO, offered $75 million in tax-exempt bonds. By 1983, there were 280 HMOs serving some 12 million enrollees.

Signs of the shift to maturity were typified by the acquisition of Health-America Corporation by Maxicare Health Plans, Inc. in late 1986. In many parts of the country HMOs were changing hands as the returns began to decrease and the growth phase entrepreneurs and investors pulled out.[3]

Some hospital providers sought to enter the industry. Recognizing that development would require too much time and investment, organizations such as the Voluntary Hospitals of America (VHA) entered into joint ventures with insurance companies seeking to merge insurance and health provider skills. Insurance companies also invested in HMOs. Prudential continued with its own internal development, whereas others such as Travelers Corporation purchased HMOs. Insurance companies have the available capital from other sources to fund a long-term commitment. From a business perspective, there is also a health insurance product decision involved.

By the mid-1990s, many urban markets experienced high managed-care penetration signifying maturity. In many cases, HMOs led the way as the most cost-effective alternative. Overall HMO enrollment grew 14 percent to 58.2 million in 1995 from 51.1 million in 1994, and enrollment was expected to increase to nearly 70 million in 1996. Nearly 80 percent of HMOs offered point-of-service (POS) plans and virtually all conducted consumer satisfaction surveys and relied on them for feedback, evaluation, and quality improvement. Approximately 44 percent of HMOs served Medicare beneficiaries with another 34 percent planning to offer Medicare benefits.[4]

HMO consolidation in major markets continued, and company strategies were typical of market maturity—price competition, extensive channel development, aggressive promotion, and product differentiation. Although, confusing the picture, rural and non-urban markets continued to develop very slowly because of a lack of economies of scale and a sufficient number of providers. In addition, few new players were entering the market in these areas.

The maturity shakeout among HMOs will continue. In the long term, as with other sectors of the insurance business, the margins generated by HMOs will be small. It will be those organizations with well-managed, cost-effective operations that will be able to succeed.

Despite its limitations, the product life cycle is a useful tool for business planning. It provides a framework for assessing existing activities as well as new lines of business. The decomposition and critical review of market characteristics in conjunction with the PLC can serve as a guideline for strategy development. A PLC framework is particularly useful for product, marketing, and management strategies. In addition, it can clarify access and types of capital available as well as the intrinsic PLC risk.

In the consideration of new lines of business, a PLC analysis can help to answer not only whether an activity is attractive for the organization, but also which way is best to enter the market. Historically, hospitals have developed the businesses or services that they offer. However, development makes sense only if the business is in introductory or growth stages of the life cycle. If the hospital chooses to enter a mature business, it is usually better to joint venture the business with an experienced party or acquire an existing provider. Introducing new products during late maturity or decline carries great risk.

[1] Susanna E. Krentz and Suzanne M. Pilskaln, "Product Life Cycle: Still a Valid Framework for Business Planning," *Topics in Health Care Financing* 15, no. 1 (Fall 1988), pp. 47–48.

[2] 42 U.S. Code sec. 300e.

[3] J. Graham, "Initial Public Offerings Slow as HMOs Fail to Extract Substantial Profits," *Modern Healthcare* 16, no. 13 (1985), p. 62.

[4] Louise Kertesz, "HMO, PPO Enrollment Growth Solid," *Modern Healthcare* 26, no. 26 (1996), p. 52.

Stage of the Product Life Cycle By determining the stage in the product life cycle for a product or service, management may formulate a strategic response and determine the level of resources to be committed to a particular product or service. Exhibit 7–3 shows logical strategic alternatives for each stage of the product life cycle.

Length of the Product Life Cycle The relevance of the strategies shown in Exhibit 7–3 depends on management's perception of the timing of the cycle. Products and services that management determines have lengthy stages (or a long PLC) will require dramatically different strategies than those management concludes have short stages or a short PLC. For instance, extensive vertical integration may be justified in the growth stage and even in the mature stage of the PLC if the cycle is judged to be a long one. However, the investment in and commitment to the product required in vertical integration may not be justified when the PLC is viewed as being relatively short.

Determining the PLC Stage and Its Length To determine the stage of the PLC, management must use a great deal of judgment. Total industry revenues and profits may be monitored as an initial indicator. In addition, information obtained in external environmental analysis concerning technological, social, political, regulatory, economic, and competitive change is valuable in assessing both the current stage and the expected length of the cycle.

The usefulness of product life cycles can be seen in tracking hospital outpatient and inpatient revenue trends. As shown in Exhibit 7–4, there has been a significant reduction in hospital inpatient revenues since 1985. This decline can be attributed largely to

Exhibit 7–3 • **Strategic Choices for Stages of the Product Life Cycle**

Stage 1
Introduction

- Market development
- Product development

Stage 2
Growth

- Market development
- Product development
- Penetration
- Vertical integration
- Related diversification

Stage 3
Maturity

- Market development
- Product development
- Penetration
- Enhancement
- Status quo
- Retrenchment
- Divestiture
- Unrelated diversification

Stage 4
Decline

- Divestiture
- Liquidation
- Harvesting
- Unrelated diversification

Exhibit 7–4 • **Percent of Revenues from Outpatient and Inpatient Services**

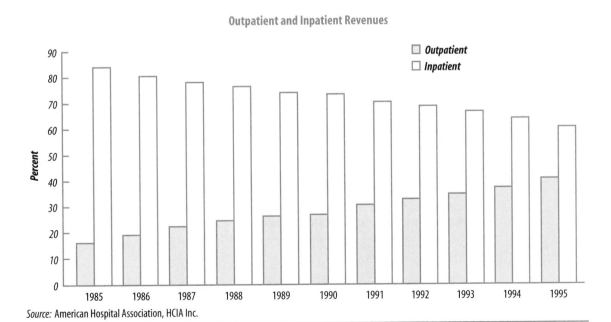

Outpatient and Inpatient Revenues

Source: American Hospital Association, HCIA Inc.

a shift to less costly services, efforts by public and private payers to contain their outlays for health care, and hospital efforts to contain or reduce staff and beds. As a result, outpatient visits and revenues have been on the increase. Therefore, for hospitals, it appears that inpatient services have reached the mature or even decline stage of the PLC, whereas outpatient services appear to still be in a growth stage. Administrators of a hospital who are considering product/service mix decisions may initiate a status quo or harvesting strategy for inpatient services and engage in a market development strategy for outpatient services (or related diversification into outpatient services). In addition, hospital administrators should continue to monitor, forecast, and assess these trends because new forces in the environment could change the life cycles or create entirely new life cycles.

The product life cycle may be represented by tracking the number of competitors. For example, the growth in the number of preferred provider organizations (PPOs) progressed through the introduction and growth stages and is entering the mature stage of the PLC. As predicted by PLC theory, as of 1996 there are fewer competitors entering the market, further market segmentation, greater consolidation among plans, and an emphasis on price. Organizations in this market have adopted aggressive market development and penetration strategies or enhancement strategies (quality and efficiency). Some experts suggest that if PPOs persist as discounted fee-for-service arrangements with less utilization review than HMOs, they might quickly enter the decline stage of the product life cycle. The principal reason for the decline will be that PPOs have been less effective than HMOs in containing costs and the quality of care often varies widely from provider to provider. However, the product life cycle may be extended (or a new PLC created), as happened in the early 1990s, if PPOs begin to incorporate more complex utilization management techniques, assume risks, ensure quality and patient satisfaction, create specialty products such as centers of excellence or exclusive provider organizations (EPOs) to segment risks, and deliver specific patient services at specific prices (diversification and product development).[6]

The PLC may also be represented by tracking enrollment, but caution is necessary. By the mid-1990s, many urban markets had experienced high managed-care penetration signifying early stages of maturity.[7]

HMO consolidation in major markets continued and company strategies were typical of market maturity—price competition, extensive channel development, aggressive promotion, and product differentiation. However, as suggested in Exhibit 7–5, overall HMO enrollment appears to be in the growth stage or in a completely new PLC after a period of relative maturity. Confusing the picture are the rural and non-urban markets that continue to develop very slowly because of a lack of economies of scale and a sufficient number of providers. In addition, few new players are entering the market in these areas. Overall enrollment shows growth, but hides two separate HMO PLCs—urban maturity and rural/nonurban growth.

Portfolio Analysis

Portfolio analysis, popularized by the Boston Consulting Group (BCG), has become a fundamental tool for strategic analysis. The market position of the health care organization as a whole or its separate programs can be examined in terms of its share of the

Exhibit 7–5 • **Growth of HMO Enrollment**

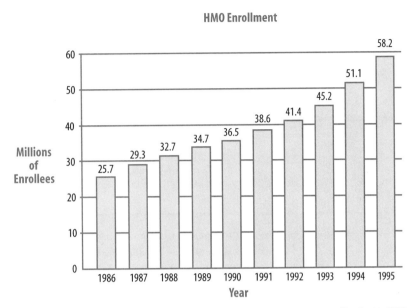

HMO Enrollment

Source: Data for 1987-1992 from Frank Cerne, "Dinosaur or Chameleon?" *Hospitals and Health Networks,* Vol. 67, No. 20 (October 20, 1993), p. 41. Copyright 1993, American Hospital Publishing, Inc. Reprinted with permission
From Louise Kertesz, "HMO, PPO Enrollment Growth Solid," *Modern Healthcare,* Vol. 26, No. 26 (1996), p. 52. Copyright Crain Communications, Inc., 740 N. Rush Street, Chicago, IL 60611. Reprinted with permission.

market and the rate of industry growth.[8] As illustrated in Exhibit 7–6, the traditional BCG portfolio analysis matrix graphically portrays differences among the various products/services (stars, cash cows, problem children, and dogs) in terms of relative market share and market growth rate.

Relative market share is defined as the ratio of a SSU (strategic service unit) to the market share held by the largest rival organization. The midpoint of the horizontal axis is usually set at .50, which corresponds to a SSU whose market share is half that of the leading provider. Thus, all SSUs that are smaller than the largest competitor would have values of less than 1; only the largest SSU would have a value of 1.

Growth rate is usually measured by the changes in level of gross patient service revenues or by population or service utilization growth (e.g., admissions or inpatient days).[9] Classification as high, medium, or low may be determined through comparison with national or regional health care growth figures, the prime rate, return on alternative investments, or the stage in the product life cycle.[10]

An example of portfolio analysis for one institution is illustrated in Exhibit 7–7. Service lines in the upper left quadrant such as women's services, geriatrics, cardiology, and so on, have high market growth and a relatively high market share (and most likely high profitability). These services are the most attractive for the institution and should be provided additional resources and encouraged to grow (and become cash cows). Services in

Exhibit 7–6 • BCG Portfolio Analysis

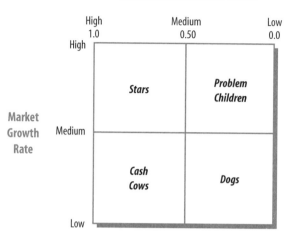

Relative Market Share Position

Stars

Products and services that fall in this quadrant (high market growth and high market share) represent the organization's best long-run opportunity for growth and profitability. These products and services should be provided resources. Market development, product development, penetration, vertical integration, and related diversification are appropriate strategies for this quadrant.

Cash Cows

Products and services in this quadrant have low market growth (probably in maturity and decline stages of the PLC) but the organization has a high relative market share. These products and services should be maintained but should consume few new resources. For strong cash cows, appropriate strategies are status quo, enhancement, penetration, and related diversification. For weak cash cows, strategies may include retrenchment, harvesting, divestiture, and perhaps liquidation.

Problem Children

Problem children have a low relative market share position, yet compete in a high-growth market. Managers must decide whether to strengthen the products in this quadrant with increased investment through market development or product development or get out of the product/service area through harvesting, divestiture, or liquidation. A case may also be made for retrenchment into specialty niches.

Dogs

These products and services have a low relative market share position and compete in a slow- or no-growth market. These products and services should consume fewer and fewer of the organization's resources. Because of their weak position, the products or services in this quadrant are often liquidated or divested or the organization engages in dramatic retrenchment.

the upper right-hand quadrant (neurology/neurosurgery, G.I./urology, emergency services, and so on) over time will move into the stars quadrant or the dogs quadrant. It is important to nurture the services that will most likely move to the stars quadrant. Services such as psychiatry, vascular surgery, pediatrics, and so on have low growth rates as well as a low relative market share (and most likely low profitability) and may be targets for contraction strategies. However, in health care some "dogs" quadrant services may be slated for stabilization or even expansion because of community needs. Cash cow services (plastic surgery and substance abuse) have achieved high market share but the

Exhibit 7–7 · BCG Portfolio Analysis for a Health Care Institution

Relative Market Share Position

	High	Medium	Low
High	Women's Services Geriatrics Cardiology/Cardiovascular Oncology Pulmonary Orthopedics		Neurology/Neurosurgery G.I./Urology Emergency Services Ambulatory Surgery, Adult Ambulatory Surgery, Pediatrics
Market Growth Rate — Medium			
	Plastic Surgery Substance Abuse		Psychiatry Vascular Surgery Pediatrics E.N.T. Ophthalmology General Medicine
Low			

Source: From Doris C. Van Doren, Jane R. Durney, and Colleen M. Darby, "Key Decisions in Marketing Plan Formulation for Geriatric Services," *Health Care Management Review*, Vol. 18, No. 3, pp. 7-20. Copyright © 1993, Aspen Publishers, Inc. Adapted by permission.

growth rate has slowed. These services should generate excess cash that may be used to develop stars and problem children services.

Extended Portfolio Matrix Analysis

Although the BCG matrix may be used by health care organizations, portfolio analysis must be applied with care. For example, health care organizations typically have interdependent programs, such as orthopedics and pediatrics, that make SSU definition difficult. Additionally, underlying the BCG matrix is an assumption that high market share means high profitability and that profits may be "milked" to benefit other programs with growth potential. In health care organizations, however, it is quite possible to have a high market share and no profit. For example, because of reimbursement restrictions, a high number of Medicare patients may cause a physician practice to be unprofitable. Similarly, programs such as obstetrics, pediatrics, neonatal intensive care, and psychiatry may have high market share but be unprofitable.[11]

The profitability issues suggest that portfolio analysis for health care organizations might better utilize an *extended portfolio matrix analysis* that includes a profitability dimension. The profitability dimension is measured by high or low profitability according to positive or negative cash flow or return on invested capital. The expanded matrix is presented in Exhibit 7–8.

Exhibit 7–8 • **Expanded Product Portfolio Matrix**

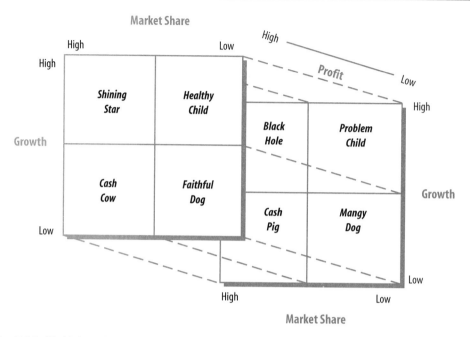

Source: From Gary McCain, "Black Holes, Cash Pigs, and Other Hospital Portfolio Analysis Problems," *Journal of Health Care Marketing,* Vol. 7, No. 2 (June 1987), p. 58. Reprinted by permission of American Marketing Association.

Shining Stars Shining stars have high market growth (typically in the early stages of the PLC), a high market share, and high profitability. This quadrant represents the best situation for a health care organization; however, it is likely that high profitability will attract competitors. Therefore, aggressive enhancement or product development will be required; market development may be difficult because of the already high market share. In addition, the organization will want to consider vertical integration and related diversification.

Cash Cows Cash cow products and services have low market growth but a high market share and high profitability. In this situation, the organization has a dominant position in the market (perhaps 100 percent) and further growth is unlikely. Again, the high profitability may attract competition, and the organization may have to defend its market share. Thus, strategies should be directed toward maintaining market dominance through enhancement. If the PLC is viewed to be long, the organization may want to engage in vertical integration or related diversification.

Healthy Children In this quadrant, products and services have high market growth, a low market share, and high profitability. This quadrant demonstrates that there are situations in which it is possible to have a low share of the market and be profitable (at least in the short term or through segmentation). This situation is potentially attractive to the organization, which may be able to move the product or service into the shining star and, ultimately, cash cow quadrant. These products and services will require investment to nurture them and gain relative market share. Strategies may include market development, product development, penetration, and vertical integration coupled with strong functional support.

Faithful Dogs In this situation, the products and services have low market growth and a low market share, but have been profitable. For example, many hospital services involve less-dominant units showing slow growth. But if they are profitable, such units make a positive contribution to the overall health of the hospital.[12]

For faithful dogs, managers must assess if increased market share will add to profitability. For instance, if profitable segments can be identified, it may be more advantageous to withdraw from broader markets, concentrate on a smaller segment, and maintain profitability. In such situations, a status quo or retrenchment strategy may be appropriate. If profitability is likely to decline over time, a harvesting or divestiture strategy may be employed.

Black Holes Black hole products and services have high growth and a high market share but low profitability. Not all high-growth, high-share programs are profitable in health care. For instance, costly technological equipment may make an organization the sole provider of a service whose high cost cannot be recovered from individual patients. However, such services may contribute to the overall image of the organization and increase the profitability of other services.

Nevertheless, having a high share for a service that is low or negative in profitability is quite disturbing. There must be a concentrated effort to reduce costs (enhancement strategy) or to add revenue without adding costs to such a program (a functional-level strategy). "When circumstances prevent a service from generating most of its own cash inflow, it becomes a 'black hole'—a collapsed star sucking in light (profit or cash)—rather than shining and generating cash or profits."[13]

If a black hole product or service cannot be made into a shining star, it is likely to become a cash pig. Therefore, enhancement and retrenchment strategies may be most appropriate. In addition, functional strategies should be employed to reduce costs and increase revenue.

Problem Children Low-share, high-growth, and low-profitability products and services present both challenges and problems. Some of the products and services represent future shining stars and cash cows although others represent future black holes and mangy dogs. Management must decide which products and services to support and which to eliminate. For supported products, market development with strong functional commitment is appropriate. For products that management does not feel can become shining stars, divestiture and liquidation are most appropriate.

Cash Pigs In this quadrant, products and services have a high or dominant share, are experiencing low growth, and have low profitability. Health care cash pigs are likely to be those well-established SSUs with dominant shares that once were considered to be cash cows. Typically, they have well-entrenched advocates in the organizational hierarchy who support their continuance.[14]

A possible solution to the cash pig problem is to cut costs and raise prices. Therefore, aggressive retrenchment may be required. This strategy may allow the organization to give up the market share to find smaller, more profitable segments and thus create a smaller cash cow.

Mangy Dogs   Products and services with low growth, a low share, and poor profit have a debilitating effect on the organization and should be eliminated as soon as possible. In this situation, it appears that other providers are better serving the market. Probably the best strategy at this point is liquidation, as it will be difficult to find a buyer for products and services in this quadrant.

Strategic Position and Action Evaluation

Strategic position and action evaluation (SPACE), an extension of two-dimensional portfolio analysis (BCG), is used to determine the appropriate strategic posture of the organization. By using SPACE, the manager can incorporate a number of factors into the analysis and examine a particular strategic alternative from several perspectives.[15]

SPACE analysis suggests the appropriateness of strategic alternatives based on factors relating to four dimensions: industry strength, environmental stability, the organization's competitive advantage, and the organization's financial strength. The SPACE chart and definitions of the four quadrants are shown in Exhibit 7–9. Listed under each of the four dimensions are factors to which individual numerical values ranging from 0 to 6 can be assigned. The numbers are then added together and divided by the number of factors to yield an average. The averages for environmental stability and competitive advantage each have the number six subtracted from them to produce a negative number. The average for each dimension is then plotted on the appropriate axis of the SPACE chart and connected to create a four-sided polygon. Factor scales for each dimension are presented in Exhibit 7–10, which has been filled in for a regional hospital. The resulting shape of the polygon can be used to identify four strategic postures—aggressive, competitive, conservative, and defensive. The quadrant with the largest area is the most appropriate general strategic position.

The factor scales shown in Exhibit 7–10 are for a California-based regional hospital system specializing in health services for the elderly and chemically dependent. As illustrated in Exhibit 7–10, this hospital system is operating in a fairly turbulent environment with many competitive pressures and many technological changes (environmental stability axis). However, the hospital's industry segments (industry strength axis) show good growth potential, which attracts strong competition. Increasing competition requires increased investment in new facilities and technology. The hospital still has a competitive advantage (competitive advantage axis) derived from early entry into the market, and it has been able to retain customer loyalty because of high-quality service. However, the hospital's financial position (financial strength axis) is weak because it financed new facilities through a substantial amount of debt. Its liquidity position has eroded and cash flow continues to be a problem.

Exhibit 7–9 • Strategic Position and Action Evaluation (SPACE) Matrix

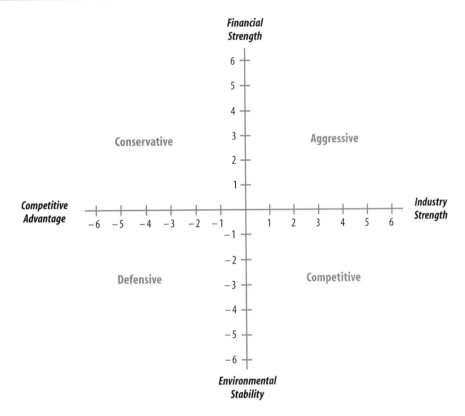

Aggressive Posture

This posture is typical in an attractive industry with little environmental turbulence. The organization enjoys a definite competitive advantage, which it can protect with financial strength. The critical factor is the entry of new competitors. Organizations in this situation should take full advantage of opportunities, look for acquisition candidates in their own or related areas, increase market share, and concentrate resources on products having a definite competitive edge.

Competitive Posture

This posture is typical in an attractive industry. The organization enjoys a competitive advantage in a relatively unstable environment. The critical factor is financial strength. Organizations in this situation should acquire financial resources to increase marketing thrust, add to the sales force, extend or improve the product line, invest in productivity, reduce costs, protect competitive advantage in a declining market, and attempt to merge with a cash-rich organization.

Conservative Posture

This posture is typical in a stable market with low growth. Here, the organization focuses on financial stability. The critical factor is product competitiveness. Organizations in this situation should prune the product line, reduce costs, focus on improving cash flow, protect competitive products, develop new products, and gain entry into more attractive markets.

Defensive Posture

This posture is typical of an unattractive industry in which the organization lacks a competitive product and financial strength. The critical factor is competitiveness. Firms in this situation should prepare to retreat from the market, discontinue marginally profitable products, aggressively reduce costs, cut capacity, and defer or minimize investments.

Source: From Alan J. Rowe, Richard O. Mason, Karl E. Dickel, and Neil H. Snyder, *Strategic Management: A Methodological Approach,* 3rd ed. (1989), pp. 145–150. Reprinted by permission.

Exhibit 7–10 · Strategic Position and Action Evaluation Factors

Factors Determining Environmental Stability

		0	1	2	3	4	5	6	
Technological changes	Many	0	(1)	2	3	4	5	6	Few
Rate of inflation	High	0	(1)	2	3	4	5	6	Low
Demand variability	Large	0	1	2	3	(4)	5	6	Small
Price range of competing products/services	Wide	0	(1)	2	3	4	5	6	Narrow
Barriers to entry into market	Few	0	1	2	(3)	4	5	6	Many
Competitive pressure	High	0	1	(2)	3	4	5	6	Low
Price elasticity of demand	Elastic	0	1	2	3	(4)	5	6	Inelastic
Other: _____		0	1	2	3	4	5	6	_____

Average $-6 = \underline{-3.3}$

Critical factors

Fairly turbulent environment; strong competition; many technological changes.

Comments

Necessary to maintain financial stability because of turbulence in the environment; demand in market segments relatively stable; protect market niche against competition.

Factors Determining Industry Strength

		0	1	2	3	4	5	6	
Growth potential	Low	0	1	2	3	(4)	5	6	High
Profit potential	Low	0	1	2	3	4	(5)	6	High
Financial stability	Low	0	1	(2)	3	4	5	6	High
Technological know-how	Simple	0	1	2	3	4	(5)	6	Complex
Resource utilization	Inefficient	0	1	2	3	(4)	5	6	Efficient
Capital intensity	High	0	1	(2)	3	4	5	6	Low
Ease of entry into market	Easy	0	(1)	2	3	4	5	6	Difficult
Productivity, capacity utilization	Low	0	1	2	3	4	(5)	6	High
Other: Flexibility, adaptability	Low	0	1	2	3	4	(5)	6	High

Average $\underline{3.7}$

Critical factors

Good growth and profit potential; strong competition.

Comments

Very attractive industry segment, but strong competition; degree of capital intensity increasing.

Factors Determining Competitive Advantage

		0	1	2	3	4	5	6	
Market share	Small	0	1	(2)	3	4	5	6	Large
Product quality	Inferior	0	1	2	3	4	5	(6)	Superior
Product life cycle	Late	0	1	2	(3)	4	5	6	Early
Product replacement cycle	Variable	0	1	2	3	(4)	5	6	Fixed
Customer/patient loyalty	Low	0	1	2	3	(4)	5	6	High
Competition's capacity utilization	Low	0	1	2	3	(4)	5	6	High
Technological know-how	Low	0	1	2	3	(4)	5	6	High

Exhibit 7–10 · **Continued**

		0	1	2	3	4	5	6	
Vertical integration	Low	0	1	②	3	4	5	6	High
Other: _____	_____	0	1	2	3	4	5	6	_____

Average − 6 = −2.4

Critical factors

Market share low; product/service quality very good.

Comments

The organization still enjoys slight competitive advantage because of quality and customer loyalty; can be expected to diminish, however, because of improving performance of competitive organizations.

Factors Determining Financial Strength

		0	1	2	3	4	5	6	
Return on investment	Low	0	1	2	3	④	5	6	High
Leverage	Imbalanced	0	①	2	3	4	5	6	Balanced
Liquidity	Imbalanced	⓪	1	2	3	4	5	6	Balanced
Capital required/capital available	High	0	①	2	3	4	5	6	Low
Cash flow	Low	0	①	2	3	4	5	6	High
Ease of exit from market	Difficult	0	1	2	3	④	5	6	Easy
Risk involved in business	Much	0	①	2	3	4	5	6	Little
Other: Inventory turnover	Slow	0	①	2	3	4	5	6	Fast

Average 1.6

Critical factors

Very little liquidity; too much debt.

Comments

Financial position very weak; cash inflow has to be increased in order to improve liquidity; outside financing difficult because of high leverage.

Source: From Alan J. Rowe, Richard O. Mason, Karl E. Dickel, and Neil H. Snyder, *Strategic Management: A Methodological Approach*, pp. 148–149. Reprinted by permission.

Which of the adaptive strategic alternatives is most appropriate for this regional system? The dimensions for this organization are plotted on the SPACE matrix shown in Exhibit 7–11, which demonstrates that the hospital is competing fairly well in an unstable but attractive industry segment. This organization cannot be too aggressive because it has few financial resources and the environment is a bit unstable. Therefore, it should adopt a competitive posture.

It is important to remember that the SPACE chart is a summary display; each factor should be analyzed individually as well. In particular, factors with very high or very low scores should receive special attention.[16] Exhibit 7–12 examines various possible strategic profiles that may be obtained in a SPACE analysis, and Exhibit 7–13 shows the adaptive alternatives for each strategic posture.

The regional hospital system examined previously was plotted into a competitive profile. Accordingly, the most appropriate strategic alternatives are penetration, market

Exhibit 7–11 • SPACE Profile for a Regional Hospital System

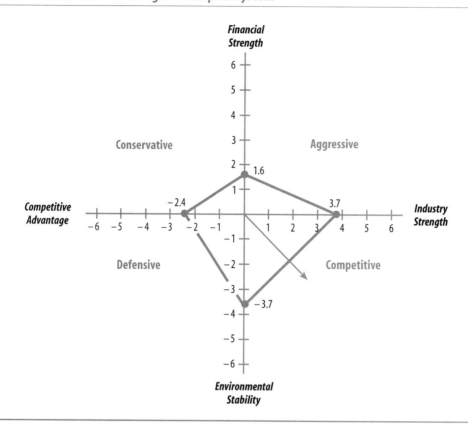

development, product development, status quo, or enhancement, with the most likely being enhancement. The hospital should continue to differentiate itself but must rectify its financial position because an unstable environment may place unanticipated demands on the organization that will require an additional infusion of capital. In light of its financial problems, the hospital may have to pursue its objectives (for example, market development) through a cooperation market entry strategy. As pointed out in Perspective 7–4, cooperation strategy—joining a network—may be important in an environment where health care systems, continuums, and referral networks are the key to market development and penetration. In the end, the adaptive and market entry strategic decisions are inextricably linked.

Program Evaluation

Program evaluation is especially useful in organizations where market share, industry strength, and competitive advantage are not particularly important or not relevant. Such organizations are typically not-for-profit, state and federally funded institutions such as

Exhibit 7–12 • Space Strategy Profiles

Aggressive Profiles

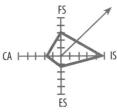

A financially strong organization that has achieved major competitive advantages in a growing and stable industry segment

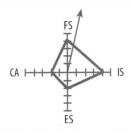

An organization whose financial strength is a dominating factor in the industry segment

Conservative Profiles

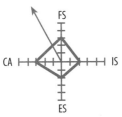

An organization that has achieved financial strength in a stable industry segment that is not growing; the organization has no major competitive advantages

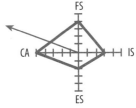

An organization that suffers from major competitive disadvantages in an industry segment that is technologically stable but declining in revenue

Competitive Profiles

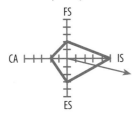

An organization with major competitive advantages but limited financial strength in a high-growth industry segment

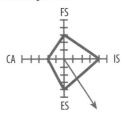

An organization that is competing fairly well in an industry segment where there is substantial environmental uncertainty

Defensive Profiles

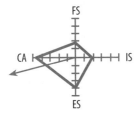

An organization that has a very weak competitive position in a negative-growth, stable but weak industry segment

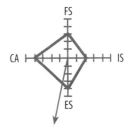

A financially troubled organization in a very unstable and weak industry

Source: From Alan J. Rowe, Richard O. Mason, Karl E. Dickel, and Neil H. Snyder, *Strategic Management: A Methodological Approach* (1982), p. 155. Reprinted by permission.

Exhibit 7–13 · Strategic Alternatives for SPACE Quadrants

Conservative	Aggressive
• Status Quo • Unrelated Diversification • Harvesting	• Related Diversification • Market Development • Product Development • Vertical Integration
Defensive	Competitive
• Divestiture • Liquidation • Retrenchment	• Penetration • Enhancement • Product Development • Market Development • Status Quo

state and county public health departments, state mental health departments, Medicaid agencies, community health centers, and public community hospitals. Despite the fact that these organizations are public and not-for-profit, they should develop explicit strategies and evaluate the adaptive strategic alternatives open to them. Although TOWS and a form of portfolio analysis may be used to evaluate public health programs,[17] evaluation methods that consider increasing revenue and market share may be inappropriate or difficult to use.

Public and not-for-profit institutions typically maintain any number of programs funded through such sources as state appropriations, federal grants, private donations, fee for service, and so on. In a public health department, such programs might include HIV/AIDS education, disease surveillance, disease control, immunizations, food sanitation inspection, on-site sewage inspection, and many more. Usually, these programs have been initiated to fill a health care need within the community that has not been addressed through the private sector. These "health care gaps" have occurred because of federal or state requirements for coordination and control of community health and because of the large number of individuals without adequate health care insurance or means to pay for services.

Within the context provided by an understanding of the external environment, internal environment, and the directional strategies, these not-for-profit institutions must chart a future through a set of externally and internally funded programs. The set of programs maintained and emphasized by the organization constitutes the adaptive

Perspective 7–4

Joining a Health Network Is a High-Stakes Decision for a Specialty Hospital

Regardless of their area of expertise, specialty hospitals—rehabilitation, pediatrics, psychiatry, or others—face questions over network involvement as they consider their futures in the changing delivery system. However, the stakes are high for specialty providers because patients are more seriously ill and often require a greater concentration and coordination of health care services. What factors should specialty hospitals consider in deciding whether to become a part of an integrated health care network?

• Specialty providers generally draw patients from large, regional referral bases. Restricting themselves to a single network may not allow for an adequate number of referrals. If faced with a choice, would referring physicians keep their patients locally or send them to the specialty hospital?

• The more unique the services in their markets or regions, the more specialty hospitals may want to leave the door open to provide some services to several networks. Could other providers easily replicate some or all of our services in competing networks or health care plans, thus increasing the competition?

• Good location, high quality, and efficiency increase options for the specialty hospital and increase the desirability of the services provided by the specialty hospital.

• Networks desiring to close down their own specialty unit to eliminate duplication of services may pressure the specialty hospital for exclusive association. Do emerging networks already have the capacity or capability for the specialty?

• Are the traditions, mission, and values of the specialty hospital compatible with the network?

• Will capitation (as part of a managed-care network) put the specialty hospital at a disadvantage?

• Will there be a loss of organizational identity and autonomy by joining the network?

• Will referrals decline if the hospital is not part of a health care network? What is the relationship to referring physicians? How strong are those links?

• Are links to other parts of the health care continuum important and provided as a part of the network?

Source: Information taken from Kevin Lumsdon, "Specialty Gamble," *Hospitals and Health Networks*, Vol. 67, No. 21 (November 5, 1993), pp. 32–36. Copyright 1993, of American Hospital Publishing, Inc. Reprinted by permission.

strategy. The degree to which they are changed (expansion, contraction, stabilization) represents a modification of the adaptive strategy. Therefore, the fundamental question is, "Does our current set of programs effectively and efficiently fulfill our mission and our vision for the future?" This question may be addressed through a process of program evaluation. Two program evaluation methods that have been used successfully are needs/capacity assessment and program priority setting.

Needs/Capacity Assessment   The set of programs in not-for-profit organizations such as public health departments essentially are determined by (1) community need and (2) the organization's capacity to deliver the program to that community. Of course, some programs may be mandated by law, such as disease control, disease surveillance, and the maintenance of vital records (birth and death records). However, the assumption is that the legislation is a result of an important need and, typically, the mandate is supported by nondiscretionary or categorical funding (funding that may be used for only one purpose). Therefore, in developing a strategy for a public health organization or not-for-profit organization serving the community, community needs must be assessed, as well as the organization's ability (capacity) to address the needs.

Community need is a function of (1) clear community requirements (environmental, sanitation, disease control, and so on) and personal health care (primary care) gaps, (2) the degree to which other institutions (private and public) fill the identified health care gaps, and (3) public/community health objectives. Most not-for-profit institutions enter the health care market to provide services to those who otherwise would be left out of the system. Despite efforts to reform health care, these gaps are likely to remain for some time. Health care gaps are identified through community involvement, political pressure, and community assessments such as those carried out by the Centers for Disease Control (CDC). These gaps exist because there are few private or public institutions positioned to fill the need. Where existing institutions are willing and able to fill these gaps, public and not-for-profit organizations should probably resist entering the market. In addition, public and community health objectives must be considered when developing strategy. National, state, and community objectives such as the *Year 2000 Objectives* should be included as a part of a community needs assessment.[18]

Organization capacity is the organization's ability to initiate, maintain, and enhance its set of adaptive strategy programs. Organization capacity is composed of (1) funding to support programs, (2) other organizational resources and skills, and (3) the program's fit with the mission and vision of the organization. Availability of funding is an important part of organization capacity. Many programs are supported with categorical funding and accompanying mandates (program requirements dictated by a higher authority, usually federal or state government). Often, however, local moneys supplement federal- and state-funded programs. For other programs, only community funding is available. Thus, funding availability is a major consideration in developing strategy for public and not-for-profit organizations. In addition, the organization must have the skills, resources, facilities, management, and so on to initiate and effectively administer the program. Finally, program strategy will be dependent upon the program's fit with the organization's mission and vision for the future. Programs outside the mission and vision will be viewed as luxuries, superfluous, or wasteful.

Exhibit 7–14 presents the adaptive strategic alternatives indicated for public organizations as they assess community needs and the organization's capacity to fill the identified needs. Where the community need is assessed as high (significant health care gaps, few or no other institutions addressing the need, and the program is a part of the community's objectives) and the organization's capacity is assessed as high (adequate funding, appropriate skills and resources, and fit with mission/vision), then the organization should adopt one of the expansion adaptive strategies (upper left-hand quadrant). Appropriate strategies might include vertical integration, related diversification, product development, market development, and penetration. When the community need assessment is low (no real need, the need has abated, need is now being addressed by another institution, or the need does not fit with community objectives), but organization capac-

Exhibit 7–14 • **Public Health and Not-for-profit Adaptive Strategic Decisions**

Organizational Capacity

	High	*Low*
High	**Expansion Strategies** • Vertical Integration • Related Diversification • Product Development • Market Development • Penetration	**Stabilization / Contraction** • Enhancement • Status Quo • Retrenchment • Harvesting
Low	**Contraction / Stabilization** • Related Diversification • Retrenchment • Harvesting • Status Quo	**Contraction** • Liquidation • Harvesting • Divestiture • Retrenchment

Community Need (row axis: High / Low)

ity is high (adequate funding, appropriate skills and resources, and fit with mission/ vision), there should be an orderly redistribution of resources, suggesting contraction and stabilization adaptive strategies (lower left-hand quadrant). Contraction strategies should be given priority as the community need diminishes; however, phasing out a program may take some time or the uncertainty concerning the changing community needs may dictate stabilization in the short term. Appropriate adaptive strategies include related diversification, retrenchment, harvesting, and status quo.

Where community needs have been assessed as low (no real need, the need has abated, need is now being addressed by another institution, or the need does not fit with community objectives) and the organization has few financial or other resources to commit to programs (low organization capacity), one of the contraction adaptive strategies should be adopted (lower right-hand quadrant). These strategies include liquidation, harvesting, divestiture, and retrenchment. When community needs have been assessed as high but organizational capacity is low, stability and contraction strategies are appropriate (upper right-hand quadrant). Stabilization strategies should be given priority because of the high community need but, if resources dwindle or funding is reduced, contraction may be required. Appropriate adaptive strategic alternatives include enhancement, status quo, retrenchment, and harvesting. As resources become available, organization capacity increases and programs in this quadrant will move to the upper left-hand quadrant and more aggressive (expansion) strategies may be selected.

Program Priority Setting   The second method of developing adaptive strategies for public programs involves ranking programs and setting priorities. This process is significant because community needs (both the need itself and the severity of the need) are constantly changing and organizational resources, in terms of funding and organization capacity, are almost always limited. Invariably more programs have high community need than resources are available. Therefore, the most important programs (and perhaps those with categorical funding) may be expanded or stabilized. The organization must have an understanding of which programs are the most important, which should be provided incremental funding, and which should be the first to be scaled back if funding is reduced or eliminated.

The nature and emphasis on programs is the central part of strategy formulation in many public and not-for-profit organizations. However, a problem in ranking these programs is that typically all of them are viewed as "very important" or "essential." This is particularly true when using Likert or semantic differential scales to evaluate the programs. Therefore, it is necessary to develop evaluation methods that further differentiate the programs. One method that can be used is to list all the programs of the agency or clinic, each on a separate paper posted in different areas of the room. Provide three different colors or types of stickers, one for each of the adaptive strategies—expansion, contraction, and stabilization. Each member of the management team is asked to sort the organization's programs into categories—those that should be expanded, reduced, or remain the same—based on their perceived importance to the organization's mission and vision. The group may agree upon several programs. Discussions can then be focused on those programs where there is disagreement. After points have been raised and discussed, the programs can be ranked again, hopefully leading to greater consensus from the group.

The Q-sort method provides a more formal method of differentiating the importance of programs and setting priority. Q-sort is a ranking procedure that forces choices along a continuum in situations where the difference between the choices may be quite small. The *program Q-sort evaluation* is particularly useful when experts may differ on what makes one choice preferable over another. By ranking the choices using a Q-sort procedure, participants see where there is wide consensus (for whatever reasons used by the experts) and have an opportunity to discuss the choices for which there is disagreement (and, hopefully, reach greater consensus).

The Q-sort is a part of *Q-methodology,* a set of philosophical, psychological, statistical, and psychometric ideas oriented to research on the individual. Q-sort evaluation helps overcome the problem of ranking all programs as very important by forcing a ranking based on some set of assumptions. Therefore, the Q-sort is a way of rank-ordering objects (programs) and then assigning numerals to subsets of the objects for statistical purposes. Fred N. Kerlinger, in *Foundations of Behavioral Research,* characterized the Q-sort as "a sophisticated way of rank-ordering objects."[19]

Q-sort focuses particularly in sorting decks of cards (in this case each card representing a program) and in the correlations among the responses of different individuals to the Q-sorts. Kerlinger reports good results with as few as forty items (programs) that have been culled from a larger list, but usually greater statistical stability and reliability results from at least sixty items and not more than one hundred.[20]

For ranking an organization's programs, only the first step in using Q-methodology is used—the Q-sort. In the Q-sort procedure, each member of the management team is asked to sort the organization's programs into categories based on their perceived importance to the organization's mission and vision. To facilitate the task, the programs are printed on small cards that may be arranged (sorted) on a table. To force ranking of programs, managers are asked to arrange the programs in piles from most important to least important. The best approach is that the number of categories be limited to nine and that the number of programs to be assigned to each category be determined in such a manner as to ensure a normal distribution.[21] Therefore, if a public health department had forty-nine separate programs that management wished to rank (culled from a larger list of programs), they may be sorted as shown in Exhibit 7–15. Notice that to create a normal distribution (or quasi-normal), 5 percent of the programs are placed in the first pile or group, 7.5 percent in the second group, 12.5 percent in the third, and so on. In this case, there are two programs in the first group, four programs in the second group, six in the third, and so on.

Depending on in which group it is placed, each program is assigned a score ranging from 1 to 9 where 1 is for the lowest and 9 is for the highest ranked programs. The score indicates an individual's perception of that program's importance to the mission and vision of the organization. A program profile is developed by averaging individual member's scores for each program.

Based on the results of the Q-sort, programs may be designated for expansion, contraction, or stabilization. For the public health programs in Exhibit 7–15, food sanitation and epidemiology, sewage planning and operation, sexually transmitted disease (STD) control, and so on might be earmarked for expansion. Cancer prevention, lodging/jail inspection, injury prevention, and so on might be slated for stabilization, whereas plumbing inspection, hearing aid dealer board regulation, and animal control may be marked for contraction.

The Q-sort procedure works well using several different sets of strategic assumptions. For example, the programs may be sorted based on different scenarios or sets of assumptions. For example, the programs may be sorted several times, each based on a different scenario. Then the group can determine which of the scenarios is most likely and make decisions accordingly.

Evaluation of the Market Entry Strategies

Once expansion or enhancement stabilization adaptive strategies are selected, one or more of the market entry strategies must be used to break into or capture more of the market. All of the expansion adaptive strategies require some activity to reach more consumers with the products and services. Similarly, enhancement stabilization strategies indicate that the organization must undertake to "do better" what it is already doing, which requires market entry analysis. Contraction strategies are methods to either rapidly or slowly leave markets and therefore do not require a market entry strategic decision.

The market entry strategies include acquisition, licensing, venture capital investment, merger, alliance, joint venture, internal development, and internal venture. Any

Exhibit 7–15 • Department of Public Health Q-Sort Results[*]

Most Important	Next Most Important	Next Most Important	Next Most Important	Next Most Important	Next Most Important	Next Most Important	Next Most Important	Next Most Important
				Cancer Prevention 4.88				
			Seafood Sanitation 6.11	Lodging/Jails Inspection 4.88	Microbiology 4.44			
			Infection Control 5.77	Injury Prevention 4.77	Home Health 4.22			
		Immunization 6.99	Health Education 5.66	Disaster Preparedness 4.77	Quality Assurance 4.11	Administrative Support 3.99		
		Tuberculosis Control 6.88	Family Planning 5.66	Public Health Nursing 4.75	Primary-Care Support 4.11	Vector Control 3.99		
	Sewage Regulation 7.22	Licensure and Certification 6.77	Child Health 5.55	Lead Assessment 4.62	School Health Education 4.0	Dental Health 3.87	Medicaid Waiver 3.33	
	STD Control 7.22	Newborn Screening 6.62	Emergency Medicine 5.50	HMO Regulation 4.55	WIC 4.0	Diabetes 3.77	Swimming Pools 3.11	
Food Sanitation 8.0	Milk Sanitation 7.0	Health Statistics 6.44	Radiation Control 5.44	Hypertension 4.55	Vital Records 4.0	Indoor Air Quality 3.66	Adolescent Health 2.66	Hearing Aid Regulation 1.88
Epidemiology 8.0	HIV/AIDS Planning and Control 7.0	Solid Waste 6.33	Maternity 5.22	Myco-bacteriology 4.55	Serology 4.0	Public Health Social Work 3.44	Plumbing Inspection 2.55	Animal Control 1.44
5%	7.5%	12.5%	15%	20%	15%	12.5%	7.5%	5%

* Program name and mean score in each box.

one (or several) of these strategies may be used to enter the market; however, mergers and alliances have received most of the media attention in the 1990s. Mergers and alliances are the principal cooperation strategies.

The specific market entry strategy considered to be appropriate depends on (1) the internal resources, competencies, and capabilities, (2) the external conditions, and (3) the objectives of the organization. Each of these three areas should be scrupulously evaluated in the selection of the appropriate market entry strategy.

Internal Requirements

Each market entry strategy requires different resources, competencies, and capabilities (see Exhibit 7–16). Before selecting the appropriate market entry strategy, a review of the internal strengths and weaknesses should be undertaken (see Chapter 4). If the required skills and resources, competencies, and capabilities are available, the appropriate

Exhibit 7–16 • Internal Requirements for the Market Entry Strategies

Market Entry Strategy	Required Resources, Competencies, and Capabilities
Acquisition	• Financial resources • Ability to manage new products and markets • Ability to merge organizational cultures and organizational structures • Rightsizing capability for combined organization
Licensing	• Financial resources (licensing fees) • Support organization to carry out license • Ability to integrate new product/market into present organization
Venture Capital Investment	• Capital to invest in speculative projects • Ability to evaluate and select opportunities with a high degree of success
Merger	• Management willing to relinquish or share control • Rightsizing capacity • Agreement to merge management • Ability to merge organizational cultures and organizational structures
Alliance	• Lack of competitive skills/facilities/expertise • Desire to create vertically integrated system • Need to control patient flow • Coordinate board/skills • Willing to relinquish share control
Joint Venture	• Lack of a distinctive competency • Additional resources/capabilities are required
Internal Development	• Technical expertise • Marketing capability • Operational capacity • Research and development capability • Strong functional organization • Product/service management expertise
Internal Venture	• Entrepreneur • Entrepreneurial organization • Ability to isolate venture from the rest of the organization • Technical expertise • Marketing capability • Operational capacity

market entry strategy may be selected. On the other hand, if they are not present, another alternative should be selected or a combination strategy of two or more phases should be adopted. The first phase would be directed at correcting the weakness prohibiting selection of the desired strategy, and the second phase would be the initiation of the desired market entry strategy. In some cases a total redesign or *reengineering* of a process may be required before a strategy may be implemented. Perspective 7–5 provides some insight into the requirements of reengineering.

External Conditions

The next consideration in the selection of the market entry strategy is the evaluation of the environment. A review of the external environmental opportunities and threats and supporting documentation (see Chapters 2 and 3) should provide information to determine which of the market entry strategies is most appropriate. Exhibit 7–17 provides a list of representative external conditions appropriate for each of the market entry strategies.

Organizational Objectives

Along with the internal and external factors, organizational objectives play an important role in evaluating the appropriate market entry strategies (see Perspective 7–6). As shown in Exhibit 7–18, internal development and internal ventures offer the greatest degree of control over the design, production, operations, marketing, and so on of the

Exhibit 7–17 · External Conditions Appropriate to Market Entry Strategies

Market Entry Strategy	Appropriate External Conditions
Acquisition	• Growing market • Early stage of the product life cycle or long maturity stage • Attractive acquisition candidate • High volume economies of scale (horizontal integration) • Distribution economies of scale (vertical integration)
Licensing	• High capital investment to enter market • High immediate demand for product/service • Early stages of the product life cycle
Venture Capital Investment	• Rapidly changing technology • Product/service in the early development stage
Merger	• Attractive merger candidate (synergistic effect) • High level of resources required to compete
Alliance	• Market demands complete line of products/services • Market is weak and continuum of services is desirable • Mature stage of product life cycle
Joint Venture	• High capital requirements to obtain necessary skills/expertise • Long learning curve in obtaining necessary expertise
Internal Development	• High level of product control (quality) required • Early stages of the product life cycle
Internal Venture	• Product/service development stage • Rapid development/market entry required • New technical, marketing, production approach required

Perspective 7–5

Reengineering—Rethinking Health Care Delivery

Reengineering has been used as part of strategic planning to help organizations rethink the way processes are managed in organizations. Many health care organizations are using reengineering to cut across departmental lines to completely redesign a process. Its founders and leading proponents, Michael Hammer and James Champy, define reengineering as "the fundamental rethinking and radical redesign of process to achieve dramatic improvements in critical, contemporary measures of performance, such as cost, quality, service, and speed." Key words in this definition are *radical* and *process.*

Reengineering goes beyond quality improvement programs that seek marginal improvements and asks a team to "start over" and completely and *radically* redesign a process. It does not mean tinkering with what already exists or making incremental changes that leave basic structures intact. It ignores what *is* and concentrates on what *should be.* The clean sheet of paper, the breaking of assumptions, the throw-it-all-out-and-start-again flavor of reengineering has captured and excited the imagination of managers from all industries. Radical redesign requires creativity and a willingness to try new things, questions the legitimacy of all tasks and procedures, questions all assumptions, breaks all the rules possible, and draws upon customer desires and needs.

A *process* is a complete end-to-end set of activities that together create value for a customer. Many organizations have become so specialized that few people understand the complete process of creating value for the customer. In the past, organizations have focused on improving the performance of individual tasks in separate functional units rather than on complete processes that usually cut across many functions. Everyone was watching out for task performance, but no one was watching to see if all the tasks together produced the results they were supposed to for the customer. Dramatic improvement can be achieved only by improving the performance of the entire process.

In order to be successful, management must be willing to destroy old ways of doing things and start anew. Many changes take place in an organization or unit when reengineering is initiated.

- Work units change—from functional departments to process teams;
- Jobs change—from simple tasks to multidimensional work;
- People's roles change—from controlled to empowered;
- Job preparation changes—from training to education;
- The focus of performance measures and compensation change—from activity to results;
- Advancement criteria change—from performance to ability;
- Values change—from protective to productive;
- Managers change—from supervisors to coaches;
- Organizational structure changes—from hierarchical to flat; and
- Executives change—from scorekeepers to leaders.

Sources: Michael Hammer and James Champy, *Reengineering the Corporation: A Manifesto for Business Revolution* (New York: HarperBusiness, 1994); and Michael Hammer, *Beyond Reengineering: How the Process-Centered Organization Is Changing Our Work and Lives* (New York: HarperBusiness, 1996).

product or service. On the other hand, licensing, acquisition, mergers, and venture capital investment offer the quickest market entry. Alliances and joint ventures offer relatively quick entry with some degree of control. The trade-off between speed of entering

| Perspective 7–6

The Strategic Logic Behind an HMO

William L. Dowling, vice president of planning and development at Sisters of Providence Health Systems, Seattle, discusses the reasons the system started HMOs in Oregon and Washington.

We wanted to rationalize the flow of payment into the delivery system and be able to turn around and rationally allocate resources internally. With the aggregate dollars, we can decide to allocate more beds to long-term care or pay a nurse to provide well-baby care. If the hospital and physicians are being paid independently, this is difficult to do. For instance, you could have both DRGs and fee-for-service payments, which create different incentives.

As a Catholic-sponsored system, we are committed to serving all segments of the community. We use the HMOs to that end. For instance, the health plans that contract with us may decide they don't want Medicaid enrollees. With our own health plan, we can reach out to poor and rural areas. We've invited federally qualified clinics that service needy populations to be providers in our HMOs. Many of these clinics are too small to be at risk by themselves.

The HMO is an important tool for bringing market perspective into an organization. We can learn how to be more cost-effective in the delivery of patient care. We are directly dealing with those footing the bill for health care and must listen to them. The HMO collects intelligence and brings it into the organization.

The HMO helps providers gear up to deliver managed care. Providers see the need for clinical treatment protocols and work out clinical interfaces between primary care physicians and specialists. It allows comprehensive data to be gathered, not just data from one provider. Then we can look at entire episodes of treatment for given conditions and profile cost-effective treatment regimens. The HMO is a tool for both assessing and evaluating care. For instance, it enables us to look at immunization levels and flagship services that need to be delivered. It's a powerful educational tool.

Source: From William L. Dowling, quoted in interview by Terese Hudson, "Learning by Doing," *Hospitals and Health Networks*, Vol. 67, No. 22 (November 20, 1993). Reprinted by permission of American Hospital Publishing, Inc.

the market and organizational control over the product or service must be assessed by management in light of organizational objectives.

Evaluation of the Positioning Strategies

After the market entry strategies have been selected, the products/services must be positioned within the market using the generic strategies of cost leadership, differentiation, or focus. All of the expansion, contraction, and stabilization strategies require explicit positioning strategies and operational strategies. As discussed in Chapter 6, products/services may be positioned marketwide or for a particular market segment.

Exhibit 7–18 • **Market Entry Strategies and Organizational Objectives**

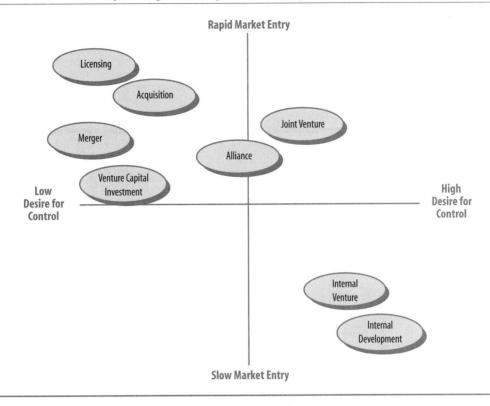

Cost leadership and differentiation are used as marketwide strategies or they are used to focus on a specific segment of the market.

Presence in a market requires that the products and services be positioned vis-à-vis competing products and services. Similar to the other strategy types, positioning depends upon the strengths and weaknesses of the organization and the opportunities and threats in the external environment. In other words, how a product or service is positioned depends on the organization's competitive situation. Therefore, the positioning strategies must be selected based on their required, resources, competencies, and capabilities, as well as environmental risks. For example, it would be difficult for an urban public community hospital dependent on limited county funding to be positioned as the high-technology hospital in the region (differentiation strategy). Conversely, a well-funded hospital using the latest technology most likely would not be positioned as the cost leader.

Internal Requirements

Exhibit 7–19 presents the internal requirements for each of the positioning strategies. In order for an organization to use a cost leadership strategy, it must have or develop the ability to achieve a real *cost* advantage (not price) through state-of-the-art equipment and facilities and low-cost operations. This competitive advantage must be maintained

Exhibit 7–19 · Internal Requirements for the Positioning Strategies

Generic Strategy	Resources and Competencies	Organizational Capabilities
Cost Leadership	• Sustained capital investment and access to capital • Process engineering skills • Intense supervision of labor • Products and services that are simple to produce in volume • Low-cost delivery system	• Tight cost control • Frequent, detailed control reports • Structured organization and responsibilities • Incentives based on meeting strict quantitative targets
Differentiation	• Strong marketing abilities • Product/service engineering • Creative flair • Strong capability in basic research • Reputation for quality or technological leadership • Long tradition in the industry or unique combination of skills • Strong cooperation from channels	• Strong coordination among functions in R&D, product/service development, and marketing • Subjective measurement and incentives instead of quantitative measures • Amenities to attract highly skilled labor, scientists, or creative people
Focus	• Combination of the preceding skills and resources directed at a particular strategic target	• Combination of the preceding organizational requirements directed at a particular strategic target

Source: From Michael E. Porter, *Competitive Strategy: Techniques for Analyzing Industries and Competitors* (1980), pp. 40–41. Copyright © 1980 by The Free Press. Adapted by permission of Simon & Schuster.

through tight controls and emphasis on economies of scale. Differentiation requires the ability to distinguish the product or service from other competitors. Typically, this requires technical expertise, strong marketing, a high level of skill, and an emphasis on product development. A focus strategy is directed toward a particular segment of the market; however, either cost leadership or differentiation may be used. Therefore, the required competencies are the same for a market segment and for marketwide strategies. It is important that organizations adopting a focus strategy closely monitor their market so that specialized needs may be fully addressed and changes in the segment carefully monitored. Otherwise, changes in the market may negate the differentiation or cost leadership. Often *benchmarking* (see Perspective 7–7) can be used to assess current internal requirements for successfully implementing strategies.

External Conditions

Each of the generic positioning strategies has its own external risks that must be evaluated by the organization (see Exhibit 7–20). Perhaps the biggest risk for cost leadership is technological change. Technological change in processes may allow competitors to achieve cost advantages. Technological change in the product/service may result in differentiation, making the cost leader's product less desirable. The most significant risks for the organization that chooses a differentiation strategy are that emphasis on differentiation pushes costs too high for the market or that the market fails to see, understand, or appreciate the differentiation. In addition, there are risks for the organization adopting a focus strategy. Often, the focusing organization is dependent on a small segment that may diminish in size, or purchasers may turn to the broader market for products or services. Movement toward marketwide products and services will occur if the differences in cost or differentiation become blurred.

Benchmarking: A Valuable Tool for Health Care Managers

Benchmarking is a management process of comparing one organization with a set of its peers. Benchmarking is generally considered to be part of an organization's "learning" or continuous-improvement efforts. As a concept, benchmarking is akin to "taking a picture" of one's organization and comparing this picture to pictures of other organizations. Some organizations simply identify a peer organization and try to emulate it. However, this perspective deals with benchmarking in the context of an ongoing, long-lived process for senior management that is designed to gather and disseminate both process and performance information throughout an organization.

The benchmarking process begins with the identification of a set of peers. The peers should be organizations that are similar, but not necessarily identical, to the organization and should operate on a scale that will not distort the understandings. The peers should not be direct competitors because of the collaborative nature of the process that will ensue. For example, a steel fabricator with sales of $200 million may seek a paper converter with $50 million in sales as a benchmarking peer or a large health care system might use a telecommunications company as a benchmarking peer.

Senior management of the peer organizations should be contacted to initiate a dialog. The initiator of the benchmarking process is seeking a group of senior managers with whom every intimate detail concerning the strategies of the organizations may be shared. In other words, the initiator should describe the desire to share strategies, financial data, personnel data, and so on, as though the benchmarking participants are part of the senior management team of each organization. The number of participants in a benchmarking group probably should be limited to seven or fewer in order to allow all participants equal opportunities to participate and gain from the experience.

Once a set of willing participants has been recruited, an initial meeting should be scheduled for the purpose of establishing protocol—a set of ground rules for the operation of the benchmarking group. Although there is no well-established standard for such a protocol, it focuses on creating an atmosphere in which full disclosure and frank discussion is facilitated. The meeting can be held at the location of one of the participants or it can be at a neutral site. Ground rules should deal with frequency of meetings, confidentiality, format of the meetings, processes for establishing agenda for subsequent meetings, and the process of choosing the locations of meetings.

It may be useful to hire a professional facilitator for the first meeting and to determine whether such a person would be helpful in further meetings of the group. Each participant should leave the first meeting with the agenda for the second meeting and a set of work assignments to be completed by the next meeting. Work assignments might include detailed descriptions of the handling of customer complaints, how orders are processed and filled in a minimum of time, or whatever activities were identified as worthy of discussion by the group. At each meeting, detailed minutes (perhaps a transcript) of the meeting should be taken, produced, and distributed to the participants in a timely manner. The purpose of the minutes is to formalize the process and to minimize misunderstandings that may arise from failed memories.

Subsequent meetings should have a formal agenda, with reports from each of the participants. The frequency of meetings should be such that they can have an impact on the practices and procedures of the participants. For the most positive impact, meetings should occur on a quarterly basis.

The benchmarking process is not completed when the meetings end. The lessons learned and the insight gained must be shared with subordinates. Participants in benchmarking processes should schedule regular meetings with subordinates for dissemination of information. In other words the lessons should be shared widely within the organization in order to gain the greatest impact.

Source: "Andrew C. Rucks, Ph.D., Executive Assistant to the Chief Executive Officer, Jemison Industries, LLC, Birmingham, Alabama.

Exhibit 7–20 • **External Risks Associated with Positioning Strategies**

Generic Strategy	External Risks
Cost Leadership	• Technological change that nullifies past investments or learning • Low-cost learning by industry newcomers or followers, through imitation or through their ability to invest in state-of-the-art facilities • Inability to see required product or marketing change because of the attention placed on cost • Inflation in costs that narrow the organization's ability to maintain sufficient price differential to offset competitors' brand images or other approaches to differentiation
Differentiation	• The cost differential between low-cost competitors and the differentiated firm too great for differentiation to hold brand loyalty; buyers therefore sacrifice some of the features, services, or image possessed by the differentiated organization for large cost savings • Buyers' need for the differentiating factor diminishes, which can occur as buyers become more sophisticated • Imitation narrows perceived differentiation, a common occurrence as the industry matures
Focus	• Cost differential between broad-range competitors and the focused organization widens to eliminate the cost advantages of serving a narrow target or to offset the differentiation achieved by focus • Differences in desired products or services between the strategic target and the market as a whole narrows • Competitors find submarkets within the strategic target and outfocus the focuser • Focuser grows the market to a sufficient size that it becomes attractive to competitors that previously ignored it

Source: From Michael E. Porter, *Competitive Strategy: Techniques for Analyzing Industries and Competitors* (1980), pp. 40–41. Copyright © 1980 by The Free Press. Adapted by permission of Simon & Schuster.

Summary and Conclusions

Several strategic alternatives are available to health care organizations. It is important that the organization has a process in place for understanding the internal and external environments and methods for evaluating strategic alternatives. This chapter provides the methods for evaluating strategic alternatives—adaptive strategies, market entry strategies, and positioning strategies.

There are a number of methods for deciding which of the adaptive strategic alternatives is most appropriate for an organization. The TOWS (threats, opportunities, weaknesses, and strengths) matrix, product life cycle analysis, portfolio analysis, SPACE (strategic position and action evaluation) analysis, and program evaluation were examined in considerable depth. Using these methods, managers can classify internal and external factors to gain perspective on which adaptive strategic alternative or combination of alternatives is most appropriate.

Once the most appropriate adaptive strategy (or combination of adaptive strategies) has been selected, a market entry strategy must be selected. Expansion and stabilization strategies are initiated through one or more of the market entry strategies. Entry strategies include acquisition, licensing, venture capital investment, merger, alliance, joint venture, internal development, and internal venture. The organization's internal resources, competencies, and capabilities, the external conditions, and the organization's objectives will determine which of these strategies is most appropriate.

After the market entry strategy has been selected, positioning strategies should be evaluated and selected. Positioning strategies include cost leadership, differentiation, and focus. The most appropriate positioning strategy may be selected through an evaluation of the internal skills and resources of the organization and the external conditions.

Chapters 8 through 12 discuss various operational strategies. Chapter 8 will address strategic implementation through marketing strategies.

Key Terms and Concepts in Strategic Management

BCG portfolio analysis

benchmarking

extended portfolio matrix analysis

management by wandering around

needs/capacity assessment

product life cycle analysis

program evaluation

program priority setting

program Q-sort evaluation

reengineering

SPACE analysis

strategic assumptions

TOWS matrix

Questions for Class Discussion

1. Explain how external opportunities and threats are combined with internal strengths and weaknesses to develop strategic alternatives.

2. Using the TOWS matrix, what adaptive strategic alternatives might be appropriate for each quadrant?

3. Describe the product life cycle. How is it useful for thinking about the adaptive strategy of a health care organization?

4. Why is the length of the product life cycle important for strategy formulation?

5. What adaptive strategic alternatives are indicated for each stage of the product life cycle?

6. Is portfolio analysis useful for developing adaptive strategic alternatives for health care organizations?

7. Explain the rationale for expanding the traditional BCG portfolio matrix.

8. Identify appropriate adaptive strategic alternatives for each quadrant in the expanded portfolio matrix.

9. Explain the strategic position and action evaluation (SPACE) matrix. How may adaptive strategic alternatives be developed using SPACE?

10. Why should program evaluation be used for public health and not-for-profit institutions in the development of adaptive strategies?

11. What are the critical factors for determining the importance of programs within a not-for-profit organization?

12. Why should public health and not-for-profit organizations set priorities for programs?

13. Describe program Q-sort. Why would an organization use program Q-sort?

14. How are market entry strategies evaluated? What role do speed of market entry and control over the product or service play in the market entry decision?

15. How may the positioning strategic alternatives be evaluated?

Notes

1. Peter F. Drucker, *Management: Tasks, Responsibilities, Practices* (New York: Harper and Row Publishers, 1974), p. 470.
2. Heinz Weihrich, "The TOWS Matrix: A Tool for Situational Analysis," *Long Range Planning* 15, no. 2 (1982), pp. 54–66.
3. Ibid., p. 61.
4. Ibid.
5. Donald E. L. Johnson, "Integrated Systems Face Major Hurdles, Regulation," *Health Care Strategic Management* 11, no. 1 (1993), pp. 2–3.
6. Frank Cerne, "Dinosaur or Chameleon?" *Hospitals and Health Networks* 67, no. 20 (1993), pp. 41–43.
7. Louise Kertesz "HMO, PPO Enrollment Growth Solid," *Modern Healthcare* 26, no. 26, (1996), p. 52.
8. Robin E. Scott MacStravic, Edward Mahn, and Deborah C. Reedal, "Portfolio Analysis for Hospitals," *Health Care Management Review* (Fall 1983), p. 69.
9. Gary McCain, "Black Holes, Cash Pigs, and Other Hospital Portfolio Analysis Problems," *Journal of Health Care Management* 7, no. 2 (June 1987), p. 56.
10. Ibid., pp. 56–57.
11. MacStravic, Mahn, and Reedal, "Portfolio Analysis for Hospitals," p. 70.
12. McCain, "Black Holes, Cash Pigs," p. 60.
13. Ibid., p. 61.
14. Ibid., p. 62.
15. Alan J. Rowe, Richard O. Mason, Karl E. Dickel, and Neil H. Snyder, *Strategic Management: A Methodological Approach,* 3d ed. (Reading, Massachusetts: Addison-Wesley Publishing Company, 1989), p. 143.
16. Ibid., p. 145.
17. Peter M. Ginter, W. Jack Duncan, Stuart A. Capper, and Melinda G. Rowe, "Evaluating Public Health Programs Using Portfolio Analysis," *Proceedings of the Southern Management Association,* Atlanta (November 1993), pp. 492–496.
18. *Healthy Communities 2000 Model Standards: Guidelines for Community Attainment of the Year 2000 National Health Objectives,* 3d ed. (Washington D.C.: American Public Health Association, 1991); and *Healthy People: National Health Promotion and Disease Prevention Objectives* (Washington, D.C.: U.S. Department of Health and Human Services, Public Health Service, 1991).
19. Fred N. Kerlinger, *Foundations of Behavioral Research* (New York: Holt, Rinehart and Winston, Inc., 1973), p. 582.
20. Ibid., p. 584.
21. J. Block, *The Q-Sort Method in Personality Assessment and Psychiatric Research* (Palo Alto, California: Consulting Psychologist Press, 1978), p. 137.

Additional Readings

Dixit, Avinash K., and Barry J. Nalebuff, *Thinking Strategically: The Competitive Edge in Business, Politics, and Everyday Life* (New York: W. W. Norton & Company, 1991). The authors indicate that strategic thinking is the art of outdoing an adversary, knowing that the adversary is trying to do the same. All of us are involved in some form. Dixit and Nalebuff suggest that strategic thinking has as its foundation some simple principles derived from game theory. The book is not confined to any particular context but rather illustrates strategic thinking in a variety of circumstances including literature, movies, and sports. Through strategic thinking, the goal of the authors is to make readers more effective managers, negotiators, athletes, politicians, or parents.

Hofer, Charles W., and Dan Schendel, *Strategy Formulation: Analytical Concepts* (St. Paul, Minnesota: West Publishing Company, 1978). This classic book defines the concept of strategy and explains the reasons for its central role in the management of organizations. Distinctions of strategy formulation and content are drawn at the corporate, divisional, and functional levels of the organization. Many of the concepts, models, and techniques useful for the formulation of strategy are discussed.

Savage, Charles M., *5th Generation Management: Co-creating Through Virtual Enterprising, Dynamic Teaming, and Knowledge Networking* (Boston: Butterworth-Heinemann, 1996). This revised edition of a book that first appeared in 1990 challenges managers to form new types of organizations to meet the changing demands of the environment. Savage argues that instead of just selling to customers, organizations will have to co-create new products and services with them. Virtual enterprising is the process of combining the talents, capabilities, knowledge, and experience of many organizations to produce a product or service. Dynamic teaming is the process of teaming and reteaming resources both within an organization and between organizations to take advantage of market opportunities. Knowledge networking is the process of combining and recombining one another's knowledge, experiences, talents, skills, capabilities, and aspirations. With the movement in health care toward cooperative strategies, this book will help managers think about possible future organizational configurations and strategies.

Shortell, Stephen M., Robin R. Gillies, David A. Anderson, Karen Morgan Erickson, and John B. Mitchell, *Remaking Health Care in America* (San Francisco: Jossey-Bass Publishers, 1996). The authors present the results of a comprehensive study of eleven health care systems' responses to managed care and cost containment pressures. The book examines the successes and failures of the current system and provides extensive examples and recommendations for developing and implementing integrated delivery systems. The authors promote a community-wide approach that includes alliances, linkages, and partnerships with public health and community social services agencies.

PART 3

Strategic Implementation: Operational Strategies

Strategic implementation deals with putting strategies to work. Implementation requires that the coordinated efforts of clinical, marketing, information systems, finance, and human resources be directed toward the accomplishment of the organization's mission and its vision for the future. Clinical operations are left to health care professionals and are not covered in this book. Strategic marketing (Chapter 8), strategic information systems (Chapter 9), strategic financial planning (Chapter 10), and strategic human resources (Chapter 11) are examined in greater detail.

Chapter 12 discusses the organization-wide operational strategies that undergird the implementation strategies. Organizational culture, organization structure, facilities and equipment, and ethics and social responsibility are a backdrop for the entire organization's decision making, regardless of the direction charted by different strategies.

In the final analysis, implementation is critical. Situational analysis may be sophisticated and impressive. Strategy formulation may be creative and even brilliant. However, if strategies are poorly implemented, little is likely to change, and the process of strategic management will contribute nothing to the success of the organization.

Strategic Marketing

Learning Objectives

After completing this chapter you should be able to:

1. Define marketing and its role in health care organizations.

2. Understand the movement from a services-oriented to a selling-oriented to a marketing-oriented organization.

3. Understand the interrelationships among the various customers for health care and be able to identify an appropriate target market for a health care provider.

4. Understand the role of strategic marketing within the strategic management process.

5. Understand the role marketing plays in situational analysis.

6. Link the various marketing strategies to the health care organization's directional, adaptive, market entry, and positioning strategies.

7. Suggest some market development, product development, and penetration strategies for health care strategists.

8. Appreciate the unique challenges involved in marketing health care services.

Because of its customer focus, marketing is the first type of operational strategy to be discussed. However, the planning and coordinating of the operational strategies in marketing, information systems, finance, and human resources actually have to be done concurrently to achieve synergy in accomplishing organizational objectives.

What Is Health Care Marketing?

Marketing is often defined as an exchange process whereby customers buy goods and services from the selling company, and the selling company accomplishes its objectives at a profit. Therefore, marketing has been viewed by some health care providers as unprofessional, inappropriate, or even as "crass commercialism."

| Introductory Incident | Focusing on Global Markets for HMOs |

According to the American Association of Health Plans (AAHP), selected cities such as Albuquerque, New Mexico; Rochester, New York; Tucson, Arizona; and San Diego, California, have over 60 percent of their population enrolled in managed-care plans. Although many regions of the country do have high percentages enrolled in HMOs, U.S. HMOs have less than 5 percent of the market share of the combined population of 470 million people in Canada, the European Union, and Mexico. At the same time, the Academy for International Health Studies indicates that total health care spending in countries such as France, Germany, and the Netherlands has almost doubled as a percentage of gross domestic product over the past two decades. Mickey Herbert, incoming president of the AAHP noted the international marketing opportunities for U.S. HMOs by stating: "Other countries are crying out for help from our health plans. American companies have to skate to where the puck is going to be." He believes the international marketing opportunities are significant.

Expansion into the international health care arena probably requires pursuing overseas partners who can share financial risks and help navigate the uncertain regulatory channels of other nations. However, there is some urgency to form these partnerships or be left with only the less-desirable partners. Last year, for example, a three-way partnership was formed in South Africa called Southern Healthcare Joint Venture. This for-profit venture was formed by United Healthcare Corporation of Minneapolis; Anglo-American, one of South Africa's largest employers; and Southern Life, a South African life and property insurance company. The venture is to be an American-style managed-care organization that contracts with health care providers to offer services to customers. United Healthcare has a 20 percent stake in the new company and is responsible for providing managed-care expertise, top management personnel, and information technology. Many observers visualize this type of venture as one of the great health care marketing opportunities of the future.

Source: Charlotte Snow, "U.S. HMOs Aim to Go Global via Overseas Deals," *Modern Healthcare* 26, no. 26 (June 24, 1996), pp. 130–132ff.

Broadened Definition for Health Care

Philip Kotler and Sidney J. Levy, in their classic article in the *Journal of Marketing,* advocated that the concept of marketing should be broadened beyond the traditional definition.[1] In its broadest sense, marketing is a process of providing want-satisfying goods and services in exchange for value. Rather than the traditional business definition of profit, value for health care providers might be dollars that are exchanged for the health services provided. This "value" might be used to provide an emergency room, staff a hospital, or buy the latest equipment. For health care, value might be the "psychic" value of "doing something for someone else" as perceived by a volunteer or donor. There are two parties to the health care exchange, and both the user or consumer (buyer) and the provider (seller) must receive benefits.

The Uniqueness of Marketing Services

The marketing of services, such as health care services, is not the same as marketing products such as automobiles, beer, or computers. It is important to differentiate between *services* and *service.* "Competitors commonly offer the same services and different service."[2] In the early 1980s, when marketers began differentiating between physical goods and services, Len Berry defined a *good* as an object, a device, or a thing; a *service* was defined as a deed, a performance, or an effort.[3] Because physical goods do contain some elements of service and services contain some physical components, marketers think of products (the inclusive term used to mean goods, services, or ideas) as ranging along a goods/services continuum. As indicated in Exhibit 8–1, most primary health care providers (hospitals, physicians, hospices, and so on) would be located further to the right on the continuum. Secondary providers, such as pharmaceutical manufacturers, would be further to the left on the continuum.

The differences between goods and services are based on intangibility, inseparability, perishability, and variability. A good can be picked up, inspected, put in a bag to be taken home, and stored until it is needed. Services, in contrast, are intangible. There are no samples to feel, try out, or return if the purchase is unsatisfactory. Services are generally inseparable as production and consumption occur simultaneously. An appointment is made, and then a physician is physically present to ask questions, examine, and make a diagnosis for the patient who participates in the process. Because services are inseparable, they cannot be inventoried and are therefore perishable. Even when a clinic has no appointments scheduled during some hours, the facility, staff, and so on are still available. Therefore, an important task of health care providers is to match services availability with services demand. Finally, services are, in many regards, more heterogeneous than physical goods, resulting in greater variability. Quality of care varies from physician to physician, nurse to nurse, and so on in the same practice or hospital. Moreover, the quality of care from the same physician or nurse will vary from day to day. People-based services (as opposed to machine-based services) are very difficult to standardize.

France and Grover have suggested that several other differences translate into unique marketing problems for health care services:

1. Health care is probably the most intangible service because the consumer cannot sample it before the purchase and usually cannot evaluate it after "consumption."

Exhibit 8–1 • **Health Care Goods/Services Continuum**

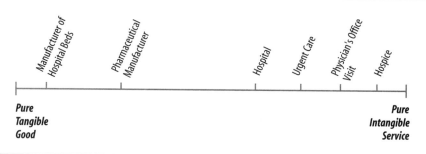

2. The mismatch between consumer expectations and actual delivery may be greater for the health care product because of the uniqueness of individual diagnosis, response to medications, and treatment. In addition, the multiplicity of health care professionals with whom the patient interacts results in greater variation in the quality of care.

3. The demand for a health care product is less predictable, although some possibilities exist to better control usage. For example, incentives can be offered to induce physicians to perform elective surgery in the afternoons and over weekends when the operating room is virtually unused.

4. Distinguishing the decision maker from the consumer may be more involved for the health care product because the physician often recommends specific hospitals, long-term-care facilities, home-care agencies, therapists, and others to the patient who customarily—but not always—follows that advice.

5. Frequently, the patient does not pay directly for the health care service.[4]

Although services, and health care services in particular, have a number of differences when compared to physical products, they have many more similarities. The basic approach to marketing does not change. Health care organizations, as services providers, need to understand and adopt marketing practices if they are to survive in today's competitive environment. Perspective 8–1 illustrates the close relationship between

---

Perspective 8–1

Making Room for Families

Although Juneau is the capital of Alaska, it is difficult to imagine its isolation. The city is 900 miles from Seattle by air and 600 miles from Anchorage. No roads connect Juneau and its 30,000 residents to the mainland of North America. For residents of this area, Bartlett Memorial Hospital is their lifeline. The hospital provides care for southeastern Alaska and serves over 70,000 people. As the only hospital, you might expect Bartlett executives to think and act as monopolists with little attention given to patients or the families of injured fishermen, loggers, and other people who are brought to the level III trauma center for stabilization. However, this is not the case.

Juneau's seclusion and its beauty make it attractive to nature lovers who force the price of scarce hotel rooms beyond the limit of many patients and patient's families who are required to remain in the city for an extended time. An average hotel room during tourist season costs about $185 per day if you are lucky enough to find one. "Spouses are left to fend for themselves," says hospital administrator Robert Valliant. In many cases staff members have shared their homes.

To deal with this problem, the municipally owned hospital is planning to build eight apartments on land adjacent to the facility. The units would house the families of the 400 out-of-town patients who use the 56-bed hospital. Some argue that hospitals should not be in the housing business. But Bartlett's efforts are the result of a concern for their customer. It may be the only way to ensure that families are not greeted with a "no vacancy" sign just at the time they have many other and more pressing concerns.

Source: Peter MacPherson, "Making Room for Families," *Hospitals and Health Networks* 70, no. 5 (March 5, 1996), p. 39.

marketing and thinking of the needs of the patient and the needs of his or her family members.

Developing a Marketing-Oriented Philosophy

Competition, consumerism, and cost containment are mandates for health care professionals to think about marketing. Competition has increased across the range of health care providers. The rising costs of health care in the 1990s have led to demands for reform, health care that is more responsive to patient needs, and cost containment. The influence of government legislation, insurance, business, and others in the environment have propelled health care providers to develop a marketing-oriented philosophy. Typically, an organization moves through two stages before adopting a marketing orientation.

The Services (Production) Orientation

In the early days, health care professionals and health care administrators focused on delivery of health care or a *services (production) orientation.*[5] If a new piece of equipment meant better care for a patient or was requested by a physician, it was purchased. If a community was without a hospital, money was raised, taxes were assessed, and a hospital was built. Because health care organizations were dominated by professionals whose primary commitment was to their own professional practice, managers tended to be services (production) oriented. They were concerned with filling a preconceived number of beds or with the number of patients seen or with the number of procedures or tests that had been administered. Emphasis was on quality of delivery, as perceived by the professional. Needs, as perceived by the patients, received little consideration. After all, "What did the patient know about health care?"

Interestingly, the overbuilding of hospitals and medical schools and the increasing costs associated with this orientation led to more intense competition. Many beds remained empty causing communities to contribute more and more resources to maintain the local hospital. Physicians attempted to draw new patients by opening satellite offices.

The Selling Orientation

Because of empty beds, health care professionals began to try to "sell" the community on using the local hospital—a *selling orientation.* Since the inception of hospital marketing in the 1970s, the focus has been on the promotional component of marketing rather than the entire strategy. Marketing was equated with advertising. The focus was on short-term results: "What can be done to fill more beds?"

Marketing is not merely advertising in various media. It entails determining the appropriate customer (target market), designing services that will satisfy that customer, pricing the service at a level that is acceptable to the customer while allowing the organization to survive, and developing a plan to make the service available where the customer wants or is able to obtain it. Once these activities have been completed, the information about the service has to be made available to potential customers. Only then does advertising become involved.

The Marketing Orientation

The *marketing orientation* focuses on the premise that customer wants and needs have to be met for the health care organization to survive. If hospitals or extended-care facilities treat patients merely as bodies on which a certain number of procedures are to be performed in a given day without regard for patient preferences, or if doctors feel that bedside manner makes no difference because of medical training and skill, patients can and will find alternatives. Patients feel they have a right to be treated with respect and have their questions answered.

Today, outside forces are focusing greater attention on patient satisfaction—the net result of a successful marketing effort. Total quality management or continuous quality improvement uses patient satisfaction as a key indicator of success at the same time that satisfying patients is becoming more difficult because of reduced lengths of stay, heavier workloads for hospital personnel, and more critical and demanding patients.[6] The marketing orientation focuses on customer needs as determined by the customer. As Peter Drucker so aptly stated, "The aim of marketing is to know and understand the customer so well that the product or service fits him and sells itself."[7]

Marketing is in part a "state of mind." It is a willingness to always think of the client or patient first, recognizing that when the patient is satisfied, other organizational goals can be realized as well. Patient-centered care, a relatively new approach by hospitals, clinics, and physician practices, reorients the entire organization around the patient rather than functions or departments. In a survey by *Hospitals* and ServiceMaster Company, nearly half of the hospitals that responded indicated that they were either planning to or already implementing patient-centered care programs. More than 90 percent of the existing programs are three years old or less.[8] Perspective 8–2 illustrates the patient-centered program at Omaha's Bergan Mercy Medical Center.

It makes little sense to spend thousands of dollars developing a marketing strategy to increase the patient load of a private physician's practice or long-term facility while ignoring basic "antimarketing" behavior among employees. For example, the same physicians who are often willing to pay for marketing studies fail to see that patients are being lost every day because of the way they have been treated by the receptionist, nurse, or doctor, or because of excessive waiting time. Other health care organizations have similar non-patient-oriented activities that need to be investigated and changed.

Few organizations, whether for-profit or not-for-profit, health care or manufacturing, have managed to truly adopt the philosophy of a customer orientation. In a 1991 study published in the *Journal of Health Care Marketing,* Naidu and Narayana concluded that only about 20 percent of hospitals are marketing oriented.[9] Most organizations pay lip service to the concept and then cannot understand why marketing does not work. A major underlying factor of a marketing orientation is that money will be spent to determine what customers actually want. Often time-consuming and expensive marketing research is needed to identify the customer and his or her needs and wants. If marketing takes its rightful place at the center of provider decision making and focuses on the customer, it can have a significant impact on many of the important factors affecting cost[10] and profitability.[11]

In the McDermott, Franzak, and Little study of medium- and large-size hospitals that related marketing activities and profitability, they found that market intelligence

Perspective 8–2

A Kinder, Gentler Emergency Room

Emergency rooms are rarely thought of as customer friendly. Instead, they are characterized by high drama where health care professionals are in charge, making decisions, and cannot be concerned with the kinder and gentler things of life. At Bergan Mercy Medical Center in Omaha, Nebraska, there is an attempt to lower the anxiety level of the emergency room and, hopefully, lower blood pressure and heart rates at a time when these numbers matter most.

Bergan has attempted to humanize and demystify its emergency department for the approximately 100,000 people who enter the medical center via the emergency room each year. Bergan has adopted the patient-centered model developed by the Planetree organization in San Francisco. "At first, people on the staff get offended, wondering how we could even question that what we do isn't patient-centered," says Kevin Schwedhelm, Director of Emergency Services. However, he notes that, at some point, "light bulbs started going on. It's amazing what comes out once you start making decisions from the patient's point of view."

Many of the changes were relatively simple—hiding wheelchairs, crash carts, and equipment in storage bays to remove clutter and reduce anxiety, replacing overhead lights with wall fixtures and green plants, and providing erasable display boards in examination rooms where nurses could jot down their names and list the tests patients were scheduled to receive. In children's rooms, televisions and VCRs were added with plenty of Disney cartoons. However, the changes were more than merely cosmetic. Nurses now telephone all patients who visit the ER to check on their progress, answer nagging questions, and ensure that prescriptions are filled. Perhaps the proof is really in the results. In 1994, before introduction of the Planetree model, patients lodged thirty-seven formal complaints against the emergency department. In 1995, the number was down to only two. According to one nurse executive, "The funny thing is, once you start thinking differently, the environment changes. A table and chairs in the right place can make a big difference to patients."

Source: Kevin Lumsdon, "Inside Track: A Kinder, Gentler ER," *Hospitals and Health Networks* 70, no. 3 (February 5, 1996), pp. 44–46.

activities, such as surveying the general public, evaluating performance against marketing objectives, evaluating effectiveness of marketing expenditures, and analyzing competitors' strengths and weaknesses, were positively related to profitability. In addition, an integrated, team-oriented approach (reorganizing to speed the flow of resources across departments, involving other department heads in the marketing planning process, sharing competitor information with other departments, and organizing interdepartmental teams to call on potential customers) was positively related to profitability.[12]

Identifying the Health Care Customer

One of the difficulties with health care marketing is that there are many, very diverse customers to satisfy in the market. Health care organizations by nature have some inherent specializations—long-term care, emergency medicine, oncology, dermatology, and so on—that determine who the customer will be. Yet within these specializations are customers with varying needs, wants, and desires.

Segmentation is the process of identifying recognizable groups that make up the market and then selecting a group as the target market. Several groups may be targeted, but each one requires different marketing activities to achieve customer satisfaction. Exhibit 8–2 illustrates the many customers for a hospital and the segments a physician (one of the hospital's customers) may consider. The process of segmentation for a general practice would be more challenging than for an oncology practice, which is more specialized, but many segments can be identified among cancer patients—those with leukemia, skin cancer, lung cancer, and so on. Specialization of the hospital, nursing home, or physician's practice would be a first step in the segmentation process, but other demographic, psychographic, geographic, and benefits factors must be considered as well.

Physicians

Physicians are a major target for marketing efforts because they recommend other health care providers for their patients. Estimates are that physicians control 80 percent of health care costs as they prescribe pharmaceuticals and medical equipment and determine hospitalization and diagnostic and surgical procedures. Doctors are an important customer base for hospitals because almost all patients are admitted by physicians who have staff privileges at the hospital. If physicians choose not to admit patients to a given hospital, the hospital will have no patients. Thus, major efforts have been undertaken by

Exhibit 8–2 • **Determining the Health Care Customer**

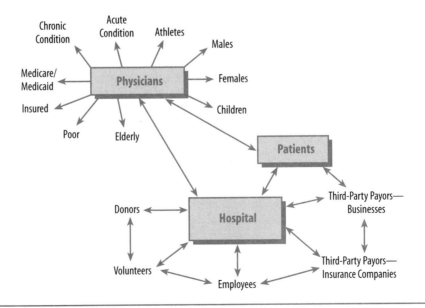

hospitals to "market" to physicians through personal selling, provision of new products (facilities, equipment, programs, and so on) that the physicians want, improved locations, advertising, and referral services.

Physicians use a referral system when patients need care outside their expertise. With the abundance of specialists, physicians are learning that marketing to other physicians is also important. Because a long-term-care facility is often recommended by a physician, nursing homes, rehabilitation centers, home health care organizations, and others have targeted physicians with their marketing efforts. Typically the patient or responsible caregiver chooses a facility from the group recommended by the physician. If a health care provider is not in the suggested group, there is little chance a patient will consider it.

Patients

The patients themselves are customers. However the buyer/seller relationship of traditional exchange processes has to be modified in much of health care because the patient has a professional dependency on the doctor. Most people have no knowledge of medical terminology nor the complexity of medical diagnosis or care and cannot accurately evaluate the medical care provided. Hence patients are dependent on the professional.

At one time, patients would never have questioned their doctor's choice of a hospital. Today, a patient whose physician does not have privileges at the hospital of the patient's choice may change physicians. In a national study by Professional Research Consultants and American Hospital Publishing, Inc., more than 42 percent of the participants said they would change physicians to be admitted to the hospital they preferred.[13] When considering maternity care, 58 percent of pregnant women select a hospital before choosing a physician.[14] In addition, as third-party payors and the popular press have encouraged consumers to seek "second opinions" before having surgery, patients' preferences for a particular hospital have become part of the decision-making process. Moreover, the physician who provided the original diagnosis may not be the physician who continues the patient's care.

A variety of marketing efforts have been directed to patients. Advertising has been used to communicate with patients concerning the benefits (satisfaction) available from the health care provider. However, the services offered must be carefully developed to satisfy consumers before advertising will be effective. Public relations activities, such as heart transplant recipient reunions, health fairs, baby fairs, and others, provide additional opportunities to make information available to the public.

Third-Party Payors

Third-party payors (insurance companies and employers) are customers as well and must be satisfied that the health care provider is efficiently treating patients, or their considerable financial influence will dictate that patients go elsewhere. For example, because of their dissatisfaction with escalating health care costs, Hershey Foods Corporation and Xerox Corporation have developed their own systems to contain health care costs. Through price incentives employees are encouraged to participate in the HMOs determined by the corporations to be the most efficient and provide the best quality of care.

Xerox's HealthLink monitors the satisfaction of its enrollees on a constant basis. Employees can select from a variety of HMOs, but those that Xerox has determined provide the highest quality care and customer satisfaction at the lowest cost are designated as "HealthLink" HMOs and are offered at no cost to the employee. To participate in other programs, the employee has to pay higher premiums and co-payments. Xerox holds the HMO to specific stated standards. If the specific target (designated satisfactory percentage) for childhood immunizations or mammograms or blood pressure checks is not achieved in a given year by an HMO in HealthLink, it may not be a participant in the future.

As payors, insurance companies (and managed-care organizations) are a major customer of nursing homes, hospitals, and others. If they are not satisfied with the quality of care or the charges for procedures, they can use their considerable clout to make changes. If the insurance company's customers (the patients) are not happy with the health care provided, the company will react as well. Perspective 8–3 notes that patient satisfaction surveys are becoming increasingly important, not only to individual providers but also to policy makers.

Others

State health departments actively compete with other agencies for public funding. It is important that the community (the health department's customer) and the legislators (elected representatives for the general public) are aware of and understand the services provided by the health department. If the general public is not aware of the needs being met (benefits provided), government funding will be very difficult to obtain. Similarly, hospitals and other health care providers have community, state, and federal regulatory groups and funding agencies to satisfy.

Perspective 8–3

The Largest Health Care Consumer Survey Ever Attempted

At the end of 1996, HCFA planned to launch the largest health care consumer survey ever undertaken. The plan was to survey four million beneficiaries of Medicare in an effort to determine their satisfaction with the services they receive. It was likely that the survey would be completed by telephone and would ask for information that will be used to compile comparisons between HMOs and between managed-care and fee-for-service systems.

"We're looking for ways to ask beneficiaries of competing plans and delivery systems about issues that go to satisfaction and quality," said Bruce Fried, Director of HCFA's Office of Managed Care. As the purchaser of health care for its benefi-

ciaries, HCFA is extremely interested in consumer satisfaction. However, since there is no one universally accepted measure of quality, HCFA will use the consumer satisfaction results, along with the National Committee for Quality Assurance's "report cards" and outcome measures developed by the Foundation for Accountability, to make its evaluation of the current state of health services financed by Medicare.

Source: Louise Kertesz, "HCFA Plans Huge Medicare Patient Survey," *Modern Healthcare* 26, no. 12 (March 18, 1996), p. 21.

Not-for-profit health care organizations have contributors and volunteers whose needs must also be satisfied. Contributors want to feel that their donations are being given to a worthwhile organization and that they can make a difference. As seen in Exhibit 8–3, a Red Cross blood donation advertising campaign has successfully appealed to the need to make a difference.

Exhibit 8–3 • Red Cross Advertisement

When you give blood
you give another birthday,
another anniversary,
another day at the beach,
another night under the stars,
another talk with a friend,
another laugh,
another hug,
another chance.

American Red Cross

Please give blood.

Volunteerism is an important part of the not-for-profit health care organization's ability to appear less "institutional" and more caring and friendly. Patients appreciate the volunteers who are common in many not-for-profit hospitals and extended-care facilities. Because of the increased number of women in the workforce, the ranks of volunteers have thinned, and many organizations compete for their time. Volunteers' needs must be satisfied if they are to continue to contribute.

Another group that has to be considered are current and potential employees of the organization. Because of the shortages in health care professions (current and projected), recruiting becomes a marketing activity aimed at satisfying the needs of potential employees, not just at the time of hiring, but over their careers as well. Retention of the best and brightest has the potential to ease the marketing effort, especially in people-based services.

The impact of a change in marketing strategy to one group must be assessed in terms of the potential impact on other groups. Critical-care mapping, although viewed favorably by hospital administration and nurses, is often less enthusiastically supported by physicians. It has to be demonstrated to them that it brings better efficiency and outcomes for the patient and may actually free them up to spend more time on the more difficult cases.[15]

Because there are many diverse customers to serve, a coordinated effort must be directed toward the various customers of health care institutions. When a specific group of customers is identified, it is called the *target market.* Each target market requires different marketing efforts and activities to successfully satisfy the group. As illustrated in the discussion of customers, health care organizations by their very nature have a number of target markets to satisfy. Therefore, strategic marketing has an important role to play in the organization.

Marketing in the Strategic Management Process

Specific marketing inputs to the situational analysis are presented in Exhibit 8–4. Although marketers are involved in scanning all the components of the external environment, they focus on market analysis, competitor analysis, and customer analysis. Internally marketers attempt to maintain a customer-oriented focus when assessing the strengths and weaknesses of the various facets of the organization. Specific internal marketing activities are reviewed under Internal Environment in Exhibit 8–4. Finally, marketing people should be involved in development of mission, vision, values, and strategic objectives as illustrated in Exhibit 8–5. The senior marketing executive for the health care organization should be involved in all levels of strategic management; however, the greatest contribution from strategic marketing usually occurs in carrying out the positioning and operational strategies.

The *strategic marketing process* starts by conducting a thorough situational analysis (covered in Chapters 2, 3, and 4), contributing to and understanding the organization's mission, vision, and objectives (covered in Chapter 5), and contributing to and understanding marketing's role in the organization's adaptive, market entry, and positioning strategies (covered in Chapters 6 and 7). The next phase is to develop marketing objectives that will contribute to accomplishing the corporate objectives. Finally, marketing strategies are developed as part of the strategic implementation process. Marketing

Exhibit 8–4 · Marketing Input to Situational Analysis

Situational Analysis	Marketing Input to Situational Analysis
External Environment	
Market Analysis	Determine actual size, forecast potential, estimate rate of growth, market profitability, cost structure, distribution patterns, critical success factors.
Customer Analysis	Forecast demand from current and new customers, analyze lost customers; study diffusion of innovation, customer buying behavior and motivation; uncover unmet needs, benefits sought, brand loyalty of segments, price sensitivity, purchasing patterns, intensity of distribution required, information needs of customers; identify sources of information and media usage patterns, demographic and socioeconomic trends.
Competitive Analysis	Identify generic, specific, service, brand competition; estimate strength of each competitor in terms of finances, profitability, management; determine market share, competitor size, growth rate; identify number of substitutes; compare product quality, customer service, comparative advantage, brand loyalty, length/breadth/depth of product line, distribution, pricing levels and flexibility, advertising and promotion, public relations activity, amount of positive and negative publicity; segmentation for each direct competitor and selected indirect competitors.
Internal Environment	
Marketing	Develop/evaluate the marketing strategy—segmentation and target market(s) identified; product positioning strategy; image development; usage rates; pricing strategy; advertising, personal selling, sales promotion, publicity; distribution strategy. Measure against objectives—sales growth, market share increase, profitability by product, share of mind, sales efficiency, customer complaints and compliments, accuracy of forecasts.
Mission, Vision, Values, and Objectives	Ensure an understanding of customer, services, competitor; focus on customer orientation; include personal ethic, customer and employee expectations; participate in development of corporate objectives; develop marketing objectives to accomplish corporate objectives.

strategies occur at the operational level as functional strategies to be implemented by marketing management.

Prior to developing marketing strategies, the health care organization has to undertake a situational analysis that includes its market definition, the important environmental factors, and the competition that exists in the defined market. Understanding these factors are instrumental in determining the best strategic marketing alternatives.

Situational Analysis

In developing a marketing strategy, health care providers must understand their current situation in the market. "How well are they satisfying the various customers they currently serve? Are competitors better meeting customer needs? What new needs will occur in the near future that should be in the planning stages today?" Frequently, the necessary information is not available, and marketing research must be conducted to understand patient satisfaction, medical staff satisfaction, competitive offerings, and so on. Often it is important to collect data from patients and staff who do not use (or occasionally use) the facility as well as current users.

Market Definition From a marketing perspective, the key to developing a situational analysis that will assist in providing the organization with strategic direction lies in

Exhibit 8–5 · Strategic Marketing Input to Strategic Management

Hierarchy of Strategic Decisions	Strategic Marketing Input
Directional Strategies	
Mission	Ensure understanding of the customer, services, and competition.
Vision	Focus on customer orientation.
Values	Include personal ethic, customer and employee (internal customer) expectations.
Objectives	Participate in developing corporate objectives; development of marketing objectives to accomplish corporate objectives.
Adaptive Strategies	
Expansion	
Diversification—Related	Assist in identifying products, services needed to fill in the line of current offerings.
Vertical Integration—Forward	Identify customers that, if acquired, would enable the health care organization to satisfy consumers even more.
Market Development	Identify unserved segments and geographic areas; analysis of size; predict level of achievable penetration; analysis of extent of competition.
Product Development	Identify new products/services to add to the line; analysis of profit potential; extent of competition.
Penetration	Enhance current products/services—greater differentiation; increase promotion—advertising, personal selling, public relations, sales promotion; reduce price; increase distribution.
Contraction	
Divestiture	Recommend products/services no longer satisfying current customers for divestiture; identify buyers, suggest ways to enhance the offering to make it more salable; assist in determining a fair market value.
Liquidation	Recommend products/services no longer satisfying current customers.
Harvesting	Recommend products/services no longer meeting organization objectives but still satisfying some current customers; recommend appropriate phase-out time.
Retrenchment	Recommend areas where limiting the geographic scope or product line will turn around the organization's ability to profitably satisfy customers.
Stabilization	
Enhancement	Identify product/service features to improve customer acceptance, provide greater differentiation; improve comparative advantage.
Status Quo	Recommend product enhancement activities; increase promotion, reduce price, or increase distribution to maintain position, market share, or revenues.
Market Entry Strategies	
Purchase	
Acquisition	Recommend organizations/products/services to acquire based on ability to integrate and then market the acquired entity; analyze market share, position, comparative advantage, profitability of potential acquiree.
Licensing	Recommend attractive licenses to purchase based on fit with current products/services; analyze benefits of licensing versus internal development to enhance the product line; analyze profitability, comparative advantage, market share with and without licensed product/service.
Cooperation	
Merger	Analyze fit with current products/services; assess whether increased size will lead to a dominant or more significant position in the market; if the merger is with a cash-rich entity detail how the added capital can enhance current products/services.
Alliance	Analyze fit with current products/services; assess whether alliance will lead to a dominant or more significant position in the market.

continued

Exhibit 8–5 · **Continued**

Hierarchy of Strategic Decisions	Strategic Marketing Input
Cooperation *(cont.)*	
Joint Venture	Analyze anticipated market share, position, dominance, and profitability of new products/services developed in cooperation with another organization; is it worth the cost in lost control?
Development	
Internal Development	Direct traditional marketing activities—select the appropriate target market and develop the product, price, promotion, and distribution to satisfy it.
Internal Venture	Contribute intrapreneurial marketing person to the team.
Positioning Strategies	
Marketwide	
Cost Leadership	Design or redesign product to be cost efficient but meet quality standards of customers; lower price or increase value; promote position selected; match distribution with selected position.
Differentiation	Study market to determine relative positioning perceived by customers; analyze competitors' image and positioning; understand our image and positioning; identify positioning we want; develop marketing strategy to develop the image and positioning desired to achieve comparative advantage.
Market Segment	
Focus—Cost Leadership	Determine segment for concentration, design or redesign product to be cost efficient but meet quality standards of customers; lower price or increase value; promote position selected; match distribution with selected position.
Focus—Differentiation	Determine segment for concentration; determine if it is large enough to be profitable; study market to determine relative positioning perceived by customers; analyze competitors' image and positioning; understand our image and positioning; identify positioning we want; develop marketing strategy to achieve the image and positioning desired to achieve comparative advantage.
Operational strategies	
Functional—Marketing	Direct traditional marketing—select the appropriate target market and develop the product, price, promotion, and distribution to satisfy it.

determining the service category and service area definition. The question "What business are we in?" needs to be answered in customers' terms. The customer's needs and wants must be identified and understood in the first stage of the situational analysis. The health care provider's market definition can be deduced from the mission statement and is central to identifying the market to be served. A market consists of those prospective buyers who are willing and able to purchase the organization's offering. The market can be defined on the basis of geography, demographics, or benefits sought.

Perhaps one of the more interesting developments in health care marketing is the prospect of the globalization of health care. The Introductory Incident illustrates this emerging trend. However, it should be noted that historically health care has been a rather localized phenomenon with service areas clearly defined. The need to grow by large integrated systems is changing the entire concept of service area in health care. Significant market potential is represented by other nations that are interested in the expertise of American health care organizations (see Perspective 8–4).

Perspective 8–4

Exporting U.S. Health Care?

Globalizaton of American business is no longer an issue. It is a reality and has been for a decade or more. Globalization of health care? That is a different matter. It is hard to imagine health care in a global context. However, all signs point to international markets and their growth potential. But, why would American health care providers be interested in international markets? There are at least four reasons:

- Costs are increasing. In Europe, the rate of health care inflation has outpaced gross domestic product growth since 1990.
- Some nations are looking to privatize health care and shift the risk from the government to employers, insurers, and providers.
- There is a developing middle class in many nations that can afford to spend more on health care.
- A large percentage of the population is aging. In the United States, 12.2 percent of the population is 65 and older. In the United Kingdom, the percentage is 15.5, and in Sweden, it is 17.6 percent.

These figures, of course, provide an answer to why U.S. health care organizations are interested in going global. But, why would other countries be interested in having U.S. firms as competitors? There are five important reasons.

- Managed care has shown it can help slow the growth in U.S. health care spending.
- Managed-care techniques are untried in most European and Asian nations.
- Many nations are facing the same challenges of spiraling health care costs that plagued the United States in the 1980s.
- Providers in other nations believe they can learn from our mistakes, tap into our experiences, and shorten the managed-care learning curve.
- Patients are demanding higher quality and improved access to health care services.

The stage is set and the opportunities are present. The question is how well U.S. health care leaders can adjust their thinking to the uniqueness of the global context. How well can they adjust to even more environmental changes as they attempt to compete in completely new markets?

Source: Clark W. Bell, "U.S. Healthcare Piques Interest Abroad," *Modern Healthcare* 26, no. 13 (March 25, 1996), p. 78.

Customer Analysis Segmentation, or the process of investigating the defined market to identify specific subgroups, has in fact been done by hospitals and physicians. When a hospital determines how many private, semiprivate, and ward rooms should be constructed, the number should be based on the expected demand for each type of room in the given community. Information such as major employers, general income levels, previous history, and so on should be investigated and then a number of each type of room determined.

Physicians segment the market, in part, by their choice of office location. Unfortunately, this is not often a planned process as most doctors do not study the demographics of the area where they plan to locate. However, as health systems become larger and more complex, segmentation based on location is more feasible as illustrated in Perspective 8–5. Segmentation, and the subsequent selection of specific segments to satisfy, leads to more effective and efficient marketing.

| Perspective 8–5

Marketing Convenient Health Care

OccuSystems in Dallas/Fort Worth, Texas, has fourteen (soon to be sixteen) clinics clustered near industrial parks. This is no coincidence because it is easier for employers to send workers to Occu-Systems for drug screenings, physical examinations, and treatment of on-the-job injuries. The CFO says that most people using the clinics drive no more that 15 minutes.

Convenience has helped OccuSystems capture half the initial reported on-the-job injuries in the Dallas/Fort Worth market. It has been instrumental in the company's growth to the No. 1 provider of integrated occupational health care service in the United States. Although OccuSystems has been careful in planning its locations, it has other selling points, such as its aggressive efforts to get injured workers back on the job sooner than competitors. Also, by coordinating care, it can cut 30 to 60 percent of a company's workers' compensation costs.

OccuSystems coordinates specialty and ancillary services and operates proprietary software to help physicians identify the best treatments. It even assists in identifying alternative duties for employees who are not able to return to their former jobs.

These are significant marketing advantages. It is estimated that work-related injuries cost American employers $60 to $70 billion a year. Only about half the costs are medical. The rest are in lost productivity, retraining, and other costs that accrue while the employee is out of work. With its specialized focus, OccuSystems is putting pressure on hospital-based occupational health programs to reduce costs and improve services.

Source: "Marketing Convenience Is Key to Firm's Success," *Modern Healthcare* 26, no. 13 (July 4, 1996), p. 39.

Competitive Analysis To develop an effective marketing strategy, it is important to identify which health care institutions are direct competitors and which are indirect competitors. Because competition is identified in customers' terms, it is often necessary to conduct marketing research to identify the competition from the customer's point of view rather than the provider's point of view. A few questions to recent maternity patients could determine the competition for the OB/GYN service of a hospital: "Which hospitals did your physician recommend? If the hospital you selected had been full, where would you have gone for delivery? Which hospitals did you consider? Which hospitals did you visit? Why did you choose this hospital for your baby's delivery? How satisfied were you with the experience? Would you choose the same hospital for the birth of your next child?"

Understanding consumers' perceptions and their evaluation of a health care organization's image is essential for the institution's long-term survival and prosperity. *Image* can be defined as the aggregate of beliefs, attitudes, impressions, and ideas that people have for something. A consumer's image of a health care organization is based on his or her perception of that organization in relationship to other competitors in the environment. It is a function of the health care organization's strategies, how they are implemented, and how the consumer perceives the organization.

Images are formed from past experiences, word of mouth, and marketing communications. Image is important for health care organizations to ensure strong public support, favorable legislation, tax breaks, outside funding, and a supply of volunteers. Whether management is concerned with relating to prospective or current patients, physicians, employees, volunteers, boards of trustees, government agencies, or special interest groups, image management is crucial to the strategic management process.

Javalgi, Whipple, McManamon, and Edick used a correspondence analysis approach to understand the image of Lake Hospital System's (LHS) two hospitals (Lake-East and LakeWest) in relation to the fourteen other hospitals in the Northeast Ohio area.[16] The study asked consumers (through telephone interviews) to identify the hospitals that had certain features. Thirteen features were studied including expert emergency treatment, heart disease prevention and treatment, rehabilitation services, cancer treatment, call-in health information services, women's health services, laser surgery, outpatient services, doctors keeping up with medical advances, staff giving personal attention, special programs for seniors, offering community programs, and advanced technological equipment. The image map (See Exhibit 8–6) created through the analysis of responses was used to develop strategy.

The results of the image study enabled the LHS strategic planners to assess the hospitals' competitive positions by comparing consumer perceptions with the results of an internal analysis of clinical strengths and weaknesses. For the strong programs that did have an external image associated with LHS (special programs for seniors), new markets were created and communications activities were increased. To reduce the likelihood of losing customers to competitors in areas of perceived clinical weaknesses, LHS undertook defensive measures (cancer treatment, women's health services, outpatient services) by first strengthening the products and then increasing communications about the services at LHS. Although LHS was perceived favorably as a hospital system known for offering community programs, more internal resources had been expended to implement strategies to increase technological capabilities. It was clear from the study that management had not successfully communicated about the technologically advanced equipment available at the hospital. Armed with the information concerning consumers' views of the hospitals, management developed strategies to live up to its image in the community and develop clearer positioning strategies.[17]

Marketing Objectives

Once the marketing manager is satisfied that the situation has been thoroughly analyzed, the marketing objectives must be determined. Marketing objectives are not set in a vacuum. A hierarchy of objectives exists, as indicated in Chapter 5. Therefore, after the situational analysis, a review of the organization's mission and objectives are the starting point for determining the marketing objectives. If the marketing objectives are achieved, they should help the organization accomplish its overall objectives. Marketing objectives typically include revenues, market share, growth, innovation, and public responsibility.

Revenues   Merely setting an objective for the dollar amount of money that should come into the health care organization can be shortsighted, because the outflow of money is a major consideration. Moreover, the revenue objective should be tied to a growth (or status quo) objective. An example of a marketing revenue objective would be to generate revenues of $12,500,000 by year end while holding expenses to budgeted amounts.

Exhibit 8–6 · Image Map for Lake Hospital System

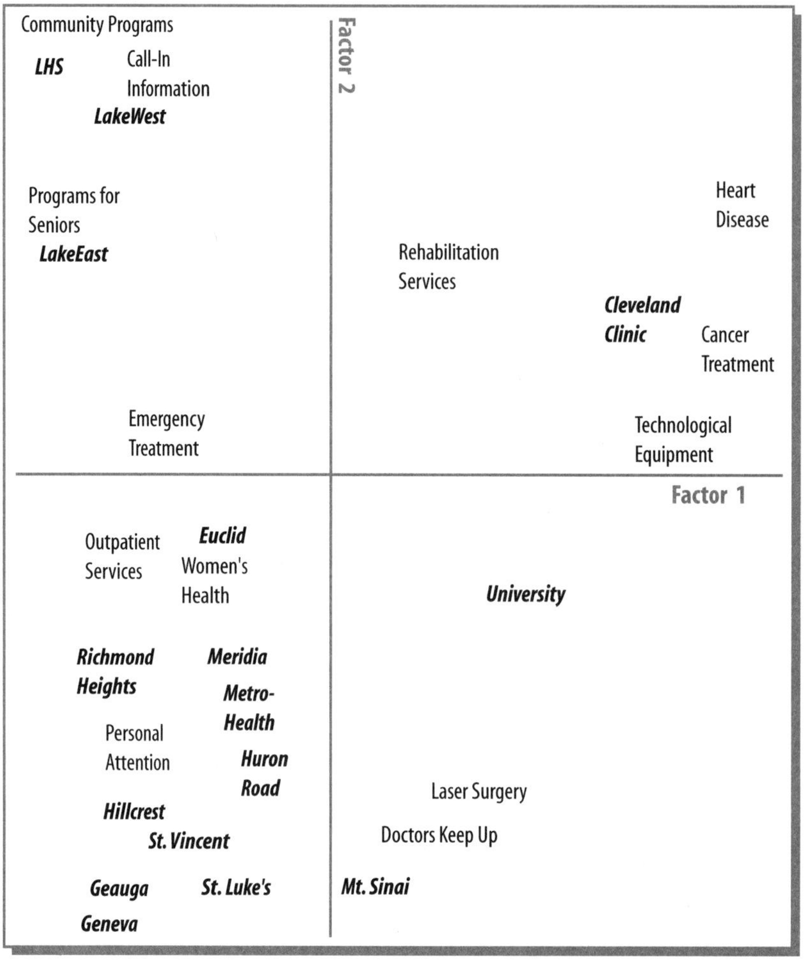

How to Read the Image Map

Cleveland Clinic is most closely associated with cancer treatment, heart disease prevention and treatment, and having advanced technological equipment.

Meridia Health System hospitals (Euclid, Huron Road, and Hillcrest) are closely associated but their image as a system is not distinguishable from the images of Metro-Health, Richmond Heights, and St. Vincent. Euclid has the most distinct image in the quadrant for outpatient services and women's health.

LakeEast and LakeWest are perceived as a cohesive hospital system with a distinct image but not for high technological equipment.

Source: Rajshekhar G. Javalgi, Thomas W. Whipple, Mary K. McManamon, and Vicki L. Edick, "Hospital Image: A Correspondence Analysis Approach," *Journal of Health Care Marketing* 12, no. 4 (December 1992), pp. 34–39.

Market Share   Market share objectives are tricky because the percentages are based on the quantity and quality of competitors in the selected "market." In the hospital software market, the top five vendors account for over 44 percent of the market. The leader, at 12.3 percent market share, has 1,454 applications. For any one application, the market share figures would be much different.[18]

A local community hospital could say that it has 100 percent share of the market (town) where it is located. But the important question is, "How many people leave town for their medical care?" Therefore, hospitals use a variation of market share based on occupancy rates or bed census data.

Growth   Growth is usually set as a percentage over the previous year in terms of revenue, market share, or census rates. Growth for growth's sake is not always desirable. Almost any organization can reach growth objectives, but what will the cost be? Often, remaining the same size and increasing profitability is a more important objective.

Innovation   Innovation objectives could include new services to be offered or speeding service delivery. Or, the organization could strive to become the leader in developing or offering new technology.

Public Responsibility   Most not-for-profit hospitals, nursing homes, hospices, and so on have publicly mandated social responsibility objectives, but many for-profit providers have also included public or social responsibility in their objectives. For example, some hospitals aim to serve a certain percentage of indigent patients or to return a certain amount of money to the community in the form of health benefits.

Strategic Implementation Through Marketing

No position of leadership lasts forever. Every health care organization that succeeds at differentiation serves as a model for new competitors.[19] The dynamic health care market and ever-changing technology mean that no competitive advantage can be sustained in the long run without a great deal of thought and effort. To further complicate the strategic process, the long run itself is becoming shorter as the rate of change becomes increasingly rapid.

There is no single established way in which a health care organization can assure success; rather, a number of possibilities exist. As discussed in previous chapters, the organization determines its directional strategies through mission, vision, and objectives; adaptive strategies determine whether the organization strives for growth or stabilization or for managing contraction. Positioning strategies are based on cost leadership, differentiation, and focus. As illustrated in Exhibit 8–7, marketing is involved with accomplishing each of these strategies in a number of different ways.

Adaptive/Expansion Strategies

Markets are often defined for expansion opportunities, as discussed in Chapter 6. Market penetration, market development, and product development are implemented through marketing strategies.

Expansion/Market Penetration   Market penetration attempts to improve revenues or market share by better satisfying current customers with current products. *Product enhancement* (modifying the product to make it more appealing to the target market) is

Exhibit 8–7 • Summary of Marketing Implementation Strategies

Strategic Alternatives	Marketing Strategies and Tactics
Adaptive Strategies	

Expansion/Market Penetration	• Product enhancement
	   Improve quality of service
	   Faster service delivery
	   Technological innovation
	   Reliability
	• Reduce price
	• Increase promotion
	• Make services more available in current market area

Expansion/Market Development	• New service areas near current area • New service areas beyond current area • Innovative delivery sites
Expansion/Product Development	• New products/services lines • Expansion within product lines • Increase product variations
Contraction/Decrease Scope	• Reduce product lines • Reduce number of offerings within the lines • Reduce the number of product variations
Contraction/Decrease Service Area	• Close entire facilities • Close units/wings • Limit promotional efforts to smaller geographic area • Only offer some services in a limited geographic area
Contraction/Demarketing of Services	• Educate to reduce demand • Promote alternatives as superior • Be less customer oriented

Stabilization/Enhancement	• Less aggressive use of:
	   Increased differentiation
	   Improved quality
	   Reduced price
	   Increased promotion

Stabilization/Status Quo	• Maintain product quality, service, and reliability • Monitor competitive prices and maintain current position • Monitor competitive promotional activities, maintain "share of mind"
Positioning Strategies	
Marketwide/Cost Leadership	• Lowest cost • Best value
Marketwide/Differentiation	• Be first • Be best • Be unique • Be most prestigious • Position against the leader • Position against competitors • Promote your position

Market Segment/Cost Leadership	• For a specific segment be:
	   Lowest cost
	   Best value

Exhibit 8–7 · **Continued**

Strategic Alternatives	Marketing Strategies and Tactics
Market Segment /Differentiation	• For a specific segment: Be first Be best Be unique Be most prestigious Position against the leader Position against competitors Promote your position

a fundamental component of market penetration strategies, although pricing, promotion, and distribution are used as well.

Improved quality of service is one way to increase market penetration. Most health care providers like to think they can enhance their institution on the basis of the service they offer to their various customers. "Quality" is frequently used in discussions by health care providers, but they do not determine what quality is. The consumer's perception of what constitutes quality must be used to judge it. To the consumer, quality is achieved only when the service meets or exceeds expectations.[20]

Realistically, quality can be perceived by the consumer only from other environmental cues, because few people have the expertise to actually judge competent medical care. Thus, friendly nurses, clean and pleasant surroundings, prompt response to patient call buzzers/lights and questions, convenient hours of operation, and so on are used to judge quality for many hospitals, long-term-care providers, and private practices.

Individual consumers are not the only health care customers to judge quality, however. Physicians and other health care professionals are more likely to judge the quality of an institution by assessing equipment, physicians who are currently on staff (or who have staff privileges), the competence of the nursing staff, and the organization and leadership provided by the nonmedical staff.

Strategies can be formulated to improve (expansion strategy) or maintain (stabilization strategy) quality over time. When quality is allowed to deteriorate, whether planned (contraction) or unplanned, use of the facility will eventually decline. A hospital's emergency room is generally a cash user but can increase admissions by 25 percent or more. If a community hospital's emergency room is using cash and does not lead to at least some increase in admissions, it might be neglected and allowed to deteriorate over time; it is therefore likely that this perception of deterioration would carry over to the rest of the institution. To avoid this unplanned side effect, it might be better to face the issue squarely. Many CEOs overlook the role that the public relations staff can play in relating the appropriate message to the community.[21] In the case of a community hospital, public meetings could be held to demonstrate to the citizens that the hospital cannot afford to provide quality emergency care and, with group consensus, decide to close the unit (contraction).

Faster service delivery can be used to increase penetration. Consumers are increasingly impatient. They value their time and will not wait for service.[22] Horror stories about such things as long waits in the emergency room and sick patients being left in wheelchairs outside the X-ray room are shared with family and friends. To avoid negative word-of-mouth communication, hospitals need to think about service delivery. To "speed service delivery" does not mean to do things faster, but to rethink why the delays occur and correct the underlying reasons. Faster responsiveness can develop into a sustainable competitive advantage.

Waiting time in physicians' offices represents another opportunity. One busy professional calls the doctor on the morning of his appointment and politely informs the receptionist that it is his policy to wait no longer than fifteen minutes for the doctor. He then inquires as to the doctor's current schedule. If the doctor is behind for whatever reason and the caller would have to wait longer than fifteen minutes, he reschedules the appointment. If it happens more than once, he changes doctors. Most people understand emergencies, but when a doctor's staff consistently overschedules so that patients have long waiting times, many will find a new physician.

Another way a health care organization may improve patients' or potential patients' perception that it provides quality care is to educate them about some of the special diagnostic capabilities and treatment expertise the hospital or clinic offers. To pursue expansion through technological innovation, large sums of money must be available because breakthroughs in medical equipment are costly. The price for new technology generally decreases over time, but to maintain technological innovation as a competitive strategy, financial resources must continue to be accessible to purchase new equipment as soon as it becomes available. This represents an example of the importance of the marketing/finance interface. Communicating information about the new technology to patients is another necessary and expensive part of maintaining technological innovation as a competitive advantage.

Reliability, or standardization to achieve consistent quality, is another differentiating strategy. Service reliability is a goal for most health care organizations. Services are difficult to standardize because the consumer participates in the simultaneous production and consumption of services; and as previously indicated, the human beings involved in health care delivery (patient, doctor, nurse, and so on) are not capable of performing in the same way every time they might encounter the same situation. However, a prescribed routine known to all can achieve some level of consistency in admitting or new patient procedures, pre-op preparation, and so on.

Many freestanding urgent-care facilities have attempted to standardize procedures, thereby providing the additional benefit of avoiding long emergency room waiting time. However, the procedures that are more unusual and do not fit the standards are often sent on to the more sophisticated hospital emergency rooms.

When demand is elastic, reducing the price generally increases the demand. In the competitive environment of the 1990s, the health care organization may be able to grow by reducing the price. Certainly this is true if the customer is a third-party payor. For Xerox, price is one of the important factors; however, quality must be maintained at acceptable levels. As deductibles and co-payments have become more common, consumers are asking more frequently about price.

Demand for health care services may be expanded by advertising, personal selling, sales promotion, and publicity (promotion). There is limited demand for some health care services. For example, an individual needs only one appendectomy. However, that individual may tell several others about his or her experiences with the lab technician, physician, hospital, nurse, and so on. Therefore, health care organizations wanting to expand through market penetration might develop a newsletter for previous patients to encourage them to return when the need arises for some other type of procedure. A hospital's image, in part, is developed by the communications it develops and makes available in its community. By increasing the number of times potential patients receive that message, the more likely they are to remember it when the need for health care arises.

Greater availability of services in the current market area can increase penetration. A health care provider might relocate within the current service area to improve convenience for consumers, or increase parking, or furnish another examining room. A pharmaceutical company that increased the intensity of distribution (sold the products to more retail locations in the service area) would increase availability. A long-term-care facility that added beds in another nearby facility would be expanding distribution as well. The health care organization is trying to grow *within* the service area.

Expansion/Market Development   When expansion is outside the "normal" service area to new markets, the organization has selected a market development strategy. This may be accomplished by using purchase or cooperation market entry strategies. However, if an internal development strategy has been selected, marketing will be involved to implement expansion. Specific areas for a new location have to be identified through market research. Competitive activity in the area has to be monitored and an exact site located. Some health care organizations have reached an optimum size in the current location and to grow they will need another facility. Decisions have to be made concerning whether to locate near the current facility or further away. More distant facilities can bring in entirely new customers, but sometimes the interaction of clinical staff, managers, and so on becomes far more difficult.

A location that is attractive because of its proximity to patients' homes and work is a valuable asset, especially if other health care providers cannot duplicate the location. Because people do not want to travel great distances for most health care, demographic studies of population are an important part of choosing a location for a facility. Satellite offices and hospital branches have become increasingly important in order to be available where patients want to receive care. Although satellite offices/hospitals do not typically cut costs for the organization, they do cut costs for the patient, which can lead to an increased market share and improved efficiency for the health care provider.

Some hospitals are finding it worthwhile to establish education centers in shopping malls. These centers can enhance a hospital's reputation by demonstrating its commitment to providing easily accessible outpatient care and can increase the hospital's visibility, which can then lead to increased bed census rates and economies of scale.[23] Perspective 8–6 illustrates an interesting use of educational technology by Blue Cross and Blue Shield of Massachusetts.

Mobile units are another method of achieving the optimum in health care delivery. Long practiced by the Red Cross to gain more blood donations, other institutions are

Perspective 8–6

Shopping for Doctors

It was, no doubt, just a matter of time before two of today's trendiest terms—multimedia and managed care—came together for the practical benefit of health care consumers. Targeting customers accustomed to using technology is the goal of Blue Cross and Blue Shield of Massachusetts, with its ATM-like interactive, multimedia information on wellness, prescription drugs, and other health-related topics.

The Health Navigator is designed to get information to consumers wherever and whenever it is needed. By selecting the "members only" option and swiping their ID card, members can obtain a printout of their membership profile and even change primary-care doctors. "What's critical is that the consumer can pick a primary care physi-

cian, know the hospital he or she is associated with, and then see them soon using real-time information," says Russell J. Ricci, M.D., President of New Health Ventures, a Division of Blue Cross and Blue Shield of Massachusetts.

Ultimately, the plan is to incorporate videos of primary-care physicians talking about their practices to aid customers in selecting doctors. Also in the pipeline is a plan to install Health Navigator next to ATMs in the stores of major grocery chains that also happen to be Blue Cross and Blue Shield clients.

Source: Chuck Appleby, "Doc Shopping," _Hospitals and Health Networks_ 69, no. 14 (July 20, 1995), pp. 49–50.

using movable diagnostic equipment to be closer to patients. Approximately 200 mobile mammography units are in operation in the United States to increase women's use of this excellent but expensive tool.[24]

Once the decision has been made to expand the service area, promotion becomes important to build awareness for the new facility. If the organization has a definite image, it can be transferred to the new site, as was the case when the Mayo Clinic opened another office in Jacksonville, Florida. If the organization has a less well-developed image, it will need to invest in promotional activities. Advertising can inform consumers of the opening and services offered. Personal selling will be important to inform third-party payors in the area. Publicity may be garnered with the proper planning.

Expansion/Product Development Offering new services that satisfy customer needs can be an opportunity. The first hospitals that offered a physician referral service met the needs of two of their customers—patients and physicians. The hospital that developed the referral service first could use it as a differentiating strategy. When others copy the new service with a similar "me too" offering, there is less opportunity to differentiate. Although it is good to have a quality offering, it is better still to have a quality offering, be the first to offer it, and tell everyone about it.[25]

Product development can occur through expansion of the width, length, or depth of the health care organization's offerings. _Product line width_ refers to the number of product lines offered. For a hospital, programs such as oncology, pediatrics, cardiology, orthopedics, and obstetrics represent product lines. If obstetrics were to expand into infertility treatment and childbirth classes in addition to its usual labor and delivery services, the _product line length_ has been extended. The _product line depth_ is increased if natural childbirth were added to regular and C-section childbirth services.[26]

Adaptive/Contraction Strategies

The scope of the market often has to be narrowed when there are limited resources, whether financial, natural, or human. The shortage of health professionals in some areas has caused hospitals to have to close wings until the necessary number of nurses, physical therapists, and so on could be recruited. Generally, the scope is broadened (multisystem hospitals) with successes over time as additional resources become available and economies of scale can be achieved.

Contraction/Decrease Scope Because of decreasing revenues, personnel, or available space, a health care organization may decide to serve fewer customers. When the Chicago hospitals eliminated emergency room service they were decreasing the scope. When Dade County, Florida, OB/GYN doctors refused to deliver babies because of the high cost of malpractice insurance, they decreased the scope of their practices to gynecology patients only.

Contraction/Decrease the Service Area A health organization can withdraw from the market by closing, selling, or merging. Entire facilities can be closed or selected units or wings can be closed. Careful analysis of the contribution margin of the facility, unit, or wing should be undertaken before the decision is announced. In the long run, all hospital costs have to be covered and provide a satisfactory return for the organization to survive. However, in the short run, incremental costs are important.[27]

Promotional efforts should be limited to a smaller geographic area or indicate the current services mix. If the services mix has been reduced, a positive, proactive campaign should be initiated. For example, few consumers object to having more attention from the physician or easier accessibility to him or her, when the physician decides to accept no new patients. If the long-term-care facility decides to accept only Alzheimer's patients, many families would be pleased with this contraction in services.

Contraction/Demarketing of Services One hospital administrator conferred with a consultant about the hemorrhaging costs of the emergency department (ED). The consultant's advice was demarketing the ED by maintaining insufficient staff, closing the parking lot next to the ED, and reducing housekeeping activities so that it became dirty. This is demarketing at its worst. In actuality, *demarketing* attempts to educate customers in order to reduce demand (when toddlers have a temperature over 102° for longer than 24 hours bring them to the ED), shift demand by pointing out the benefits of alternatives (no long waits at the medical center next door to the hospital), or place less emphasis on total customer satisfaction (longer waits). The health care organization that engages in demarketing through education and stressing the superiority of alternatives will not infuriate consumers and cause them to develop negative attitudes toward all services offered by the provider.

Adaptive/Stabilization Strategies

There are times when a health care provider is best served by maintaining its current place in the market. A hospital, nursing home, or physician might not be in a financial position to try to grow its service area. Sometimes, aggressive strategies on the part of one health care provider may "raise the stakes" so much that all of the providers in a community would be negatively affected. At other times, because of intense competition, an organization will have to engage in market penetration-type strategies simply to maintain its market share.

Stabilization/Enhancement Strategies In a dynamic health care environment the organization often has to develop new products or enhance current products to maintain its position in the market. Pricing needs to be monitored to make sure that it remains in line with other "like" competitors, and promotional activities have to be maintained in relation to its competition. If the organization strives for evolutionary change or incremental growth it may not upset the "balance" in an otherwise stable industry. If one organization begins to aggressively develop new products, offensively price, and increase promotion, its more aggressive expansion efforts will be noticed by its competition and retaliation may occur.

Stabilization/Status Quo To maintain status quo may be extremely challenging. Typically, health care organizations that select stabilization strategies perceive their own particular environment as "stable." They believe that they need not make significant changes to maintain their market share and revenues or that they have limited capital and cannot aggressively pursue growth strategies. Most of the expansion strategies can be used less aggressively to achieve stabilization.

Implementation Strategies May Occur in Phases or Concurrently

Riverside Health System illustrates concurrent and phases of strategic implementation (Perspective 8–7). Based on its mission, the hospital system engaged in contraction of its inpatient acute care as it focused on prevention. Then expansion strategies were carried out through product development, market development, and market penetration.

Marketwide Positioning Strategies Through Cost Leadership

Being the low-cost producer in the service area can be a significant competitive advantage. It allows the organization to make many more choices in terms of such things as product quality and development, expansion of the service area, increasing awareness of the organization through paid media, pricing, and profitability. In health care, low cost strategies must be selected carefully because few people want to think that they are receiving "cheap" (poor quality) care. Although cost leadership strategies are generally associated with having low costs that can be translated into low prices, a high-price strategy can effectively position an organization as a high-quality health care provider. However, the consumer must perceive that the benefits (aesthetically pleasing surroundings, attentive care, latest technology, and so on) are worth the high price.

Reduced Overhead This strategy is usually selected when an organization is mature. Overhead generally consists of rent, utilities, and other expenses that would occur even if there were no patients. It can also include administrative salaries, insurance, and other costs that are ongoing.

It might be that the health care provider invested too much in overhead during times of growth. Many organizations are quick to add employees and facilities when

Perspective 8–7

From Mission to Marketing Strategy

Riverside Health System made a commitment to a vision of prevention-driven health care more than a decade ago. The organization stated as its mission, "The only reason for our existence is to improve the health status of the community we serve." Management believed that preserving the illness-based model of care no longer was useful.

Riverside's first commitment to prevention was to obtain a failing racquet club and turn it into a fitness center. The racquet club was donated for the tax write-off, and in 1982 Riverside's first wellness and fitness center was opened. Over the next ten years, four more centers were opened, each one in a different geographic location, with the specific groups living in those areas as its targets. Over 20,000 paying members have made the effort profitable, including the finances to improve, replenish, and update the center's personnel, equipment, facilities, programs, and services.

The five wellness and fitness centers have become the core business, the "heart" of Riverside's health care system, linking a variety of components from hospitals to home health care. Riverside embraced the shift from sick care to well care by making its wellness and fitness centers the building blocks for its health care delivery system. Members have annual health risk assessments to turn up indications of new conditions that may require physician intervention. Management expects this information to become a database of wellness information that will eventually link all points of care and enable Riverside to offer proac-

tive rather than reactive care. For example it will indicate which members should be called to remind them that it is time for a blood cholesterol check, mammogram, prostate exam, or other diagnostic.

Riverside has committed to health and wellness so completely that it has formed a joint venture with Blue Cross/Blue Shield of Virginia to form Peninsula Health Plan to provide care on a capitated basis. It is management's hope that those who join and use the centers will be entitled to lower insurance premiums and eventually lower costs for other types of care.

Twenty thousand members did not join Riverside's wellness and fitness centers without a well-conceived marketing strategy. Not only did each fitness center have to have its own specific decor and activities for an identified target market, but each had to become "known" in its community and pricing had to be high enough to cover costs and maintain Riverside's image, yet reasonable enough for people to afford. Although some are recuperating patients covered by third-party payors, most of Riverside's wellness and fitness members pay out of pocket. Riverside's vision of maintaining wellness rather than sick care is being implemented though an effective marketing strategy.

Source: M. Caroline Martin, "Working out for the Best," *Healthcare Forum* 36, no. 6 (November/December 1993), pp. 57–63.

times are good but they rarely cut back when times are difficult. The result is excessive overhead. One way for a hospital to reduce overhead is to close off a wing or eliminate an infrequently used department. Sometimes spending *more* money can reduce overhead, such as when a physician moves to a newer building with a more energy-efficient heating and cooling system.

Control Raw Materials Access to factors of production can provide a competitive advantage in terms of price as well as availability. When the Carolinas Medical Center (Charlotte, North Carolina) was having difficulty recruiting nurses, the administration decided to develop a school of nursing. By reducing or eliminating the cost of tuition to those students who would agree to practice nursing at the center after graduation, Carolinas Medical Center gained much more control over the hospital's major factor in services production—its nurses.

Reduced Labor Costs This appears to be a very difficult strategy to implement for today's health care organizations. As with other service industries, health care is labor intensive. In addition, the industry requires skilled labor. With the shortage of trained personnel, wages and salaries are going up rather rapidly. Moreover, certification standards for qualified personnel must be met. Thus, certification standards, shortages of skilled labor, and wage inflation make it very difficult to reduce labor costs. Rather than focus on reducing the costs of labor, greater emphasis must be placed on proper scheduling. By better matching consumer demand and labor availability, costs can be reduced.

Redesign of the Offering Another strategy is to change the product offered so that it becomes less costly, but no less desirable. An extended-care facility that enjoys an excellent reputation in the community for cleanliness, good food, and competent and sympathetic caregivers could probably reduce the square footage in patients' rooms—and thereby reduce the cost of construction, heating/cooling, and maintenance—without harming its image.

Automation Labor-intensive services are difficult to automate, but not impossible. Blood pressure checks have been automated. Additionally, a finger stick for routine blood work could be automated by using a machine; but would the public accept a machine instead of a nurse? In another service industry, many bankers held on to their belief that consumers would want to talk to a real person when cashing checks or depositing money. Those banks that were the first to automate with teller machines have been very profitable. "Can similar results be achieved in health care?"

In addition, monitoring and data entry for patient records are increasingly done through automation in many hospitals. Although not pervasive, individual patient stations instead of a larger nurses' station are the technology of the future.

Increased Government Subsidy Many not-for-profit hospitals, extended-care facilities, hospices, and so on are subsidized by city, county, state, or federal government. Those that have done an excellent job of keeping the public and the lawmakers informed of the benefits they provide often have an easier time obtaining increased subsidies.

No Frills In this strategy, all "extras" are eliminated from the services, through a rather direct approach that tells consumers from the beginning that there will be no frills and that in return they will receive a lower price. Home health care offered by a hospital seems to fit this strategy. On the other hand, for many who are admitted to a large hospital ward, few "frills" are perceived. Caution has to be exercised in positioning "no frills" so that the patient perceives that only the "extras" have been eliminated. Otherwise the perception may be of poor quality care.

Combination of Low Cost and High Quality Most managers believe that high quality always leads to higher costs. More expensive facilities, more staff, more customized (personalized) services, and so on do usually cost more. However, by offering higher cost services only to consumers that prefer it, overall costs can actually be reduced by moving along the experience curve and achieving economies of scale (brought about by increased market share). Accurate assessment of demand, careful planning, and increased expertise (actual movement along the experience curve) are crucial to the successful implementation of a high-quality/low-cost strategy.

Marketwide Positioning Strategies Through Differentiation

Differentiation is typically used in reference to a product offering that is superior to competitive offerings in quality, prestige, features, value, performance, convenience in use, reliability, or service. Brand names are important in differentiating the product. For example, only the Mayo Clinic can use the name. Columbia, it is rumored, is committed to spending $26 million on a national advertising blitz designed to make it a household name.[28] Location (distribution) can be a differentiating feature if the health care organization has a convenient location with easy access to parking in a pleasant, or at least safe, area. Price is usually higher because of the "extra" features, prestige, and so on. Promotion, particularly advertising, is the way health care organizations inform their customers that the facility *is* different from others. Those hospitals, long-term facilities, and physicians that have invested heavily in developing patient-centered care have to inform consumers that it is available.

Several hospitals are differentiating on the basis of "efficient care." This product is offered to customers who "want not only high quality hospital care, but also physicians who can provide the quick route to health."[29] They want a physician who has enough clinical experience and judgment to reduce the amount of unnecessary tests, drugs, and days in the hospital. Not overwhelmingly adopted, efficient care has met some obstacles that may be diminishing in today's health care reform environment.

Using Differentiation Strategies Some caution must be exercised in selecting any of the differentiation strategies. Differentiation will not work when the superior attribute highlighted is meaningless or unimportant to the consumer. Additionally, if the health care provider has a differentiating attribute that provides benefits but consumers do not know about it, there is no advantage. For example, suppose a new technology is used to better diagnose a patient's problem, but the patient is unconscious when the equipment is used. The patient will not perceive the benefit unless he or she is told that the hospital cares enough to purchase the wonderful, new equipment that works so much faster (or is less intrusive, or whatever the benefit may be).

Providing "quality care" has been overused by so many health care organizations as a differentiation strategy that it is virtually meaningless. In addition, how many patients can judge quality of care? When severity-adjusted mortality and morbidity data become available to more consumers, will they use it to judge quality of care?

If the health care organization does not appear to provide quality care, only those who have no choice will use it. It is important for health care managers to realize that there is a cost in not providing quality in the delivery of health care—including lawsuits.

Furthermore, costs are associated with doing things incorrectly. Consider a hospital or nursing home billing statement that contains errors. Not only is there the cost of finding the error and redoing the statement, there is also the cost of losing a positive consumer attitude and perhaps a patient.

Positioning Strategies Through Market Segment Focus

Sometimes called niche strategies, focus strategies are often implemented when an organization has limited resources. The organization does not compete across the board, but in selected areas. The market definition is narrowed to identify a select group to serve. Enough resources can then be devoted to that customer group to achieve some degree of prominence or even dominance. In addition, increased specialization may lead to development of greater understanding and satisfaction on the part of the particular group targeted, which may in turn increase usage and loyalty.

Market scope is easily (and often preferably) narrowed when a large enough set of customers will be satisfied by a specific benefit. For example, some centers of excellence are marketing their expertise nationally, providing significant cost savings and improved outcomes despite the patient having to travel to fairly distant cities. Perhaps the best example of this is the Shouldice Hospital in Toronto. Shouldice treats only one illness—inguinal hernias—and attracts patients from all over Canada, the United States, and Europe. It succeeds with this very narrow scope because its services are highly efficient and of the highest quality. Patients who have had the Shouldice method for hernia repair have reoccurrences at 0.5 percent—the lowest in the world.[30]

A sharply focused strategy has the benefit of being difficult for the competition to attack. Yet at the same time such a strategy often restricts the organization's ability to grow. Take, for example, the case of EMI, which made only CAT scanners. The company was plagued by its inability to field enough service people. To avoid expensive downtime for the machine, quick response by service personnel was necessary. Larger competing firms selling broad product lines that included CAT scanners and other diagnostic equipment could support bigger and better trained service staffs, resulting in faster response times for repair work.[31]

Focused Cost Leadership Strategies All of the previously discussed cost leadership strategies can be focused on a given segment. Being the low-cost producer in a segment rather than the entire market still provides an opportunity for developing a sustainable competitive advantage.

Focused Differentiation Strategies A focused product is one part of a product line. Rather than attempting to offer a complete product line, which usually includes some mangy dogs and underperforming cash cows, the organization offers only a part of a product line. Usually an organization will focus on a product in which it has greater expertise and in which it believes some economies of scale may be achieved. Because there is less of a "one-stop shopping" orientation, the product (service) does need to be differentiated from competition as it may be less convenient to obtain.

A birthing center has selected a focus or niche strategy based on the segment served. Another example is a nursing home that focuses on Alzheimer's patients. Within all nursing homes in a community, it may be differentiated on the basis of the

Alzheimer's care offered; however, if other long-term or home-care organizations offer the service, differentiation is required.

Most community hospitals use geography as part of their strategy. They serve a specific geographic market and are the only hospital in the area. The private practice of an individual physician who attempts to find a convenient location for patients with no other similar type physicians located nearby uses a geographic area differentiation focus strategy as well. As the practice develops and flourishes, a second office may be opened that extends the geography.

Low-share markets are those that are not of sufficient size to interest the larger health care providers. A hospital or physician practice that specializes in less common diseases can satisfy a smaller market extremely well and thereby capture virtually all of the patients with that disease. This strategy can be more profitable than trying to capture a very small part of a larger market that includes many large and knowledgeable competitors. This strategy emphasizes profitability rather than size or growth.

Implementing the Strategy

Once the general implementation strategy has been selected, marketing management's task is to translate the generalities of the strategy into meaningful distinctions for consumers. The selected strategy becomes the marketing strategy when a target market is selected and a *marketing mix* is developed to meet the target market's needs. As shown in Exhibit 8–8, the elements of the marketing mix—product, price, distribution (location of delivery), and promotion—must be designed and coordinated to present the competitive advantage to the targeted consumers. The answers to each of the questions

Exhibit 8–8 • Concurrent Decisions Involved in Developing a Marketing Strategy

Target Market: Of the identified market segments, which one or ones should we satisfy?
Product: Which health care services shall we offer? What position in the market can we capture? Should our service offering be given a brand name?
Price: What shall we charge for our services? Can we cover the cost of indigent care in prices set for others?
Promotion: Shall we advertise? If so, where and in what media? How much shall we spend? Shall we create a special public relations event? Should we hire a salesperson?
Place: Where shall we locate? Should we establish additional facilities? Where?

posed in the exhibit would be different depending on which marketing implementation strategy had been selected—differentiation, cost leadership, or focus.

Once the target market is identified and the marketing mix determined, the marketing strategy should provide the sustainable competitive advantage and serve as the cornerstone for making decisions. In addition, it should be reviewed on a periodic basis to make sure the organization's competitive advantage still exists and is desired by consumers. When competitive pressure is increasing, revenue is decreasing or static in what should be a time of growth, or the excess of revenues over expenses is declining, health care managers must reassess whether the competitive advantage is still meaningful to consumers.

The market naturally works to cut the competitive advantage of a leader by technological and environmental changes that erode protective barriers. Additionally, competitors learn how to imitate the leader and negate or equalize the competitive advantage. The organization itself may not take action to protect its position.[32] This passive reaction may occur because the organization does not perceive a threat from competitors or the threat is dismissed as unimportant. Sometimes an organization does not respond because any action is considered to be detrimental to the organization's overall strategy.

An organization can engage in defensive moves to thwart prospective challengers.[33] One defensive move is to signal intentions to defend a position. If a smaller hospital announces its intention to build specialized labor/delivery rooms, a larger competitor in the region could increase its advertising budget to promote its already-in-place specialized maternity care. It has signaled that it will defend its position.

Others will attempt to foreclose avenues for attack, as when a large group practice adds previously uncovered specialties to provide comprehensive care. "Raising the stakes" is another way to combat competition. A hospital that purchases high-tech diagnostic equipment that no other hospital in the area can afford is raising the stakes.

Finally, a competitor can attempt to reduce the attractiveness of the market by using the mass media, which has covered health care extensively. For example, a number of articles have been written about the financial and personal difficulties faced by home health care organizations. Potential entrants to the industry may find it less attractive if they are exposed to a number of such articles or commentary in the mass media.

The final step in implementing any strategy should be assessment or control. The marketing audit looks at all marketing activities to determine if there are areas where marketing could be improved; if the marketing effort is supporting the organization's mission, goals, and strategic objectives; and if the results of the marketing effort were as planned.[34] The marketing audit is a part of organizational control, which Chapter 13 investigates more thoroughly.

Summary and Conclusions

Marketing is relatively new to most health care organizations. This chapter traces the evolution of acceptance that most organizations follow from a production orientation through a selling orientation to a marketing orientation. The basics of a marketing-oriented health care provider include customer satisfaction, an integrated marketing effort, and the provision of value for both parties in the exchange process.

A variety of health care customers—including physicians, patients, third-party payors, volunteers, employees, and so on—are discussed and their interdependence illustrated. Patients have to be admitted to a hospital by a physician; third-party payors influence physician choice, length of stay, and so on; volunteers and employees may also be patients; government entities interpret the need for additional health care subsidies from the public.

Because of the competition and complexity in the market, health care providers must implement strategic marketing to survive. The strategic marketing process involves determining the market served, analyzing the situation (including customers, competitors, and environmental factors), reviewing the organization's mission and objectives, setting marketing objectives, and determining marketing strategy.

The chapter illustrates how the directional, adaptive, market entry, and positioning strategies are implemented through marketing strategies. Marketers are intricately involved in strategic management of the health care organization. Marketing strategies are implemented through decisions concerning the selected target market and the appropriate marketing mix—product, price, distribution, and promotion—to satisfy that market.

The next chapter discusses strategic information systems.

Key Terms and Concepts in Strategic Management

demarketing	marketing mix	selling orientation
differentiation	marketing orientation	service
health care consumer	positioning	services
market definition	product line depth	services (production) orientation
market share	product line length	strategic marketing process
marketing	product line width	target market

Questions for Class Discussion

1. Why have health care providers been forced to think about marketing?
2. What "clues" can you identify that would indicate whether a health care organization is really applying the marketing concept?
3. How does the marketing of a service differ from the marketing of a physical product (good)?
4. Explain the strategic marketing process. How does it fit within strategic management?
5. Discuss the various ways that health care providers can define the market that they want to serve.
6. Explain how you would select between a differentiating, focus, or cost leadership positioning strategy for a nursing home in New York City and for one in Butte, Montana.
7. What recommendations would you make to the CEO of a local hospital that is attempting to differentiate itself from others in the area?
8. Name several ways that marketing can implement adaptive strategies for growth.
9. Does marketing have a role to play in the market entry strategies? Explain your answer.
10. Explain the role that health care marketing plays in each stage of the strategic planning process. Why do you think it took health care managers so long to appreciate the strategic importance of marketing?

Notes

1. Philip Kotler and Sidney J. Levy, "Broadening the Concept of Marketing," *Journal of Marketing* 33, no. 1 (January 1969), pp. 10–15; and Roger C. Nauert, "The Quest for Value in Health Care," *Journal of Health Care Finance* 22, no. 3 (1996), pp. 52–61.

2. Valarie A. Zeithaml, A. Parasuraman, and Leonard L. Berry, *Delivering Quality Service* (New York: Free Press, 1990), p. 11.

3. Leonard L. Berry, "Services Marketing Is Different," *Business* (May–June 1980), pp. 24–30.

4. Karen Russo France and Rajiv Grover, "What Is the Health Care Product?" *Journal of Health Care Marketing* 12, no. 2 (June 1992), p. 32.

5. For a more in-depth study of health care organizations and their movement toward a marketing orientation, see Robert Stensrud and Barbara Arrington, "Marketing-Oriented Organizations: An Integrated Approach," *Health Progress* (March 1988), pp. 86–89, 95.

6. Les J. Hauser, "Hospitals Must Advance Beyond Advertising to True Marketing," *Modern Healthcare* 23, no. 6 (February 8, 1993), p. 25.

7. Peter F. Drucker, *Management: Tasks, Responsibilities, Practices* (New York: Harper and Row, 1973), p. 64.

8. Jill L. Sherer, "Putting Patients First," *Hospitals* 67, no. 3 (February 5, 1993), p. 14.

9. G. M. Naidu and C. L. Narayana, "How Marketing Oriented Are Hospitals in a Declining Market?" *Journal of Health Care Marketing* 2, no. 1 (1991), p. 30.

10. Dan F. Duda, "Marketing Must Turn Savage," *Modern Healthcare* (April 16, 1990), p. 50.

11. Dennis R. McDermott, Frank J. Franzak, and Michael W. Little, "Does Marketing Relate to Hospital Profitability?" *Journal of Health Care Marketing* 13, no. 2 (Summer 1993), pp. 18–25.

12. Ibid.

13. "Smart Consumers Present a Marketing Challenge," *Hospitals* (August 20, 1990), pp. 42–47.

14. "It's a Woman's Market . . . ," *Hospitals and Health Networks* 67, no. 18 (September 20, 1993), p. 30.

15. Kevin Lumsdon and Mark Hagland, "Mapping Care," *Hospitals and Health Networks* 67, no. 20 (October 20, 1993), p. 39.

16. Rajshekhar G. Javalgi, Thomas W. Whipple, Mary K. McManamon, and Vicki L. Edick, "Hospital Image: A Correspondence Analysis Approach," *Journal of Health Care Marketing* 12, no. 4 (December 1992), pp. 34–39.

17. Ibid.

18. Charles J. Austin, *Information Systems for Health Services Administration* (Ann Arbor, Michigan: AUPHA Press, 1992), p. 108. To calculate market share, an individual organization's revenues are divided by the total revenues for the market. Other alternatives to revenue market share can be calculated such as share of occupied beds (the number of adjusted occupied beds compared to the total number of beds available in a community, state, nation, or world) or "share of mind" interpreted as the percent of the target market that recalls the health care organization's name or what it is known for without prompting.

19. George S. Day, *Market Driven Strategy: Processes for Creating Value* (New York: Free Press, 1990), p. 163.

20. For an excellent discussion of quality in service organizations, see Valarie A. Zeithaml, A. Parasuraman, and Leonard L. Berry, *Delivering Quality Service* (New York: Free Press, 1990).

21. For further information, see Julie Johnsson, "Survey: Many CEOs Overlook PR Staff's Role in Strategic Planning," *Hospitals* 66, no. 17 (September 5, 1992), pp. 34–40.

22. For suggestions on how to speed up health care service delivery, see Dan Beckham, "Making Speed a Priority," *Marketing to Doctors* 5, no. 11 (November 1992), pp. 1–3.

23. "Education Centers Are Subtle Marketing Tools," *Hospitals* (September 20, 1989), p. 76.

24. Mary Wagner, "Mobile Mammography Tries to Enhance Its Image, Revenue Through Strategic Ties," *Modern Healthcare* (January 8, 1990), p. 78.

25. Al Ries and Jack Trout, *Positioning: The Battle for Your Mind* (New York: McGraw-Hill, 1981), p. 22.

26. For a more thorough discussion of expansion of the product line, see France and Grover, "What Is the Health Care Product?" pp. 31–38.

27. For greater understanding of incremental cost analysis, see Shahram Heshmat, "The Role of Cost in Hospital Pricing Decisions," *Journal of Hospital Marketing* 6, no. 1 (1991), pp. 155–161.

28. Mary C. Jaklevic, "Branding Time at Columbia," *Modern Healthcare* 26, no. 34 (August 19, 1996), pp. 26–28.

29. Jon A. Chilingerian, "New Directions for Hospital Strategic Management: The Market for Efficient Care," *Health Care Management Review* 17, no. 4 (Fall 1992), pp. 73–80.

30. Ibid., p. 79.

31. Day, *Market Driven Strategy,* p. 202.

32. Ibid., p. 213.

33. For further discussion of defensive positioning, see Day, *Market Driven Strategy,* Chapter 8.

34. Ellen Pearson, "Marketing Audit Reveals Holes and Opportunities," *Health Care Strategic Management* 8, no. 7 (July 1990), pp. 17–18; and Franklyn A. Manu, Philip D. Cooper, and

Walter Reinhart, "The Status of Marketing in the Health Care Industry: Perspectives of Marketing Practitioners," *Journal of Hospital Marketing* 10, no. 2 (1996), pp. 11–24.

Additional Readings

Barlow, Janelle, and Claus Moller, *A Complaint Is a Gift* (San Francisco: Berrett-Koehler Publishers, Inc., 1996). These authors make the unusual argument that a complaint can actually be the avenue to strategic advantage. Their argument revolves around the point that customer feedback can actually be used as a strategic tool when the concerns of customers, as defined by customers, are taken seriously.

Berkowitz, Eric N., *Essentials of Health Care Marketing* (Gaithersburg, Maryland: Aspen Publishers, 1996). Divided into three main parts—the marketing process, understanding the consumer, and the marketing mix—this book captures the basics of marketing for health care professionals new to the field. Although fundamentally a no-frills approach to marketing, each chapter contains a number of current examples and models to enhance the basic concepts provided. The glossary and index are particularly useful for those being introduced to the discipline.

Cooper, Philip D., *Health Care Marketing: A Foundation for Managed Quality,* 3d ed. (Germantown, Maryland: Aspen Publishers, 1994). A revision of a well-known introduction to health care marketing. This revision pays particular attention to the role of marketing in managed-care settings.

Kessler, Sheila, *Measuring and Managing Customer Satisfaction* (Burr Ridge, Illinois: Irwin Professional Publishing, 1996). Customer satisfaction is ultimately what makes an organization in any industry a success or a failure. Leaders need to hire the right people and train them to recognize and be sensitive to customer needs. This book is useful in designing and developing an effective customer assessment system. The book is a step-by-step approach to planning, implementing, and getting results from a successful customer service strategy.

McCalley, Russell W., *Marketing Channel Management: People, Products, Programs, and Markets* (Westport, Connecticut: Greenwood Publishing, 1996). This book provides concepts and applications of market channels using actual organizational examples. It is designed to be a lively and informative treatment of marketing that should prove useful to managers in a variety of industries.

Moore, James F., *The Death of Competition: Leadership and Strategy in the Age of Business Ecosystems* (New York: HarperBusiness,

1996). This book takes a fundamentally different look at business strategy. The author introduces biological ecology as a way of stimulating strategic thinking about radically new cooperative and competitive marketing relationships.

Rados, David L., *Marketing for Nonprofit Organizations* (Westport, Connecticut: Greenwood Publishing, 1996). A useful book for anyone interested in marketing in the not-for-profit sector. It covers the entire field, from discussing what marketing is to describing the role of marketing in the not-for-profit organization. The book offers suggestions on pricing, distribution, and marketing communications.

Vitberg, Alan K., *Marketing Health Care into the Twenty-First Century* (Binghamton, New York: Haworth Press, 1996). This book explores the competitive health care environment from a strategic marketing perspective. The author believes that participants in the health care "wars" have to be aggressive in competing for patients, enrollees, and physicians. In addition, it includes information about the changes that are being implemented in Medicare and Medicaid programs. Vitberg's focus is on developing competitive advantage through brand identification, product differentiation, and marketing communications to motivate consumers.

Wennberg, John, *Dartmouth Atlas of Health Care* (Chicago: American Hospital Publishing, 1996). This atlas offers an unparalleled tool for making more informed strategic decisions. It contains a tremendous amount of information supplemented by a number of add-on CD-ROM databases. The *Atlas* highlights regional disparities in resources and costs as well as utilization data on the nation's 306 hospital referral regions.

Zimmerman, David, Peggy Zimmerman, and Charles Lund, *The Healthcare Customer Service Revolution* (Burr Ridge, Illinois: Irwin Professional Publishing, 1996). What is the impact on revenue for a health care organization that fails to measure and monitor patient satisfaction? These authors contend the impact is likely to be significant. Providers who understand the importance of patient satisfaction will be the survivors in the increasingly competitive health care market. This book helps managers in health care settings to shift their organization's orientation toward customer-focused services.

Chapter 9

Strategic Information Systems

*"*The organization of the future is rapidly becoming a reality—a structure in which information serves as the axis and as the central support system."

• *Peter Drucker*

Learning Objectives

After completing this chapter you should be able to:

1. Define strategic information and its role in health care organizations.

2. Think of creative ways to use information in strategically managing health care organizations.

3. Understand the importance of strategic information in strategic management.

4. Understand the importance of information in situational analysis.

5. Explain how a strategic information system can be a competitive advantage for a health care organization.

6. Relate change in the way work is done through new ways of thinking and doing to understand the impact of information on this process.

7. Explain how information systems and electronic data interchanges link various internal and external constituencies of health care organizations.

8. Identify the strategic issues facing strategic information systems managers in health care organizations.

Information must be considered a tool of strategic management similar to marketing, human resources, and finance. Used to its fullest capabilities, an information system is a strategic weapon. "Information, intelligently used, and information systems, carefully planned, can be great assets to the health services manager."[1] A *strategic information system* (SIS) has been defined as one that is any combination of computers, workstations, software systems, and communications technology used to gain competitive advantage.[2] In contrast, traditional information support systems focus on improved efficiency. This chapter describes ways that health care organizations can effectively use strategic information systems not only to improve the direct care of patients but also to improve the organization's ability to compete.

Patient Care and the Internet

Home pages, many of which are electronic marketing brochures, were health care organizations' first tentative steps onto the World Wide Web. Now the Internet is actually aiding in patient care. Visiting nurses at Medlantic Healthcare Group use laptop computers to send prescription requests to doctors and eliminate typical telephone delays. Community Hospital and Medical Center in California registers patients on-line and avoids long waits when they arrive at the facility. Group Health Cooperative in Seattle puts a PC on the desk of its 1,000 physicians and uses the Internet to disseminate clinical guidelines instantly. Florida doctors can fulfill continuing medical education requirements and complete exams at home or office using MedONE, a joint on-line service of the Florida Medical Association and Sprint.

These examples are just the tip of the iceberg of the potential uses of the Internet in health care. Two areas seem to hold particular promise. One is private networks or intranets which run on the Internet and move internal data seamlessly at a fraction of the cost of traditional computing systems. Intranets could be used to link all the pieces of the health care systems and managed-care organizations as well as to connect providers, payors, and health plans in regional networks.

The second area is the public Internet which could help patients manage their own health and navigate through the health system. Some have even suggested that the Internet could be used to build community health information networks (CHINs), which are regional networks of payors and providers that share clinical and financial information. Since Oracle Systems unveiled a working model of a $500 network computer with no internal processor, designed specifically to run only off the Internet, computing or information appliances appear, for the first time, to be available to larger segments of the population and the possibilities multiply.

Source: Mary Chris Jaklevic, "Internet Technology Moves to Patient-Care Front Lines," *Modern Healthcare* 26, no. 10 (March 11, 1996), pp. 47–50.

The Importance of Information in Strategic Management

For strategic management to successfully direct the organization to accomplish its mission and vision, information is essential. Information can be gleaned through the information system; by management's reading of newspapers, professional association newsletters, and journals; and by word of mouth, to name a few sources. However, properly planned and implemented, the information system is the most critical source. "In order for health services organizations to effectively use information technology to gain strategic advantage, two conditions (among others) are essential: (1) information systems planning must be guided by the strategic directions of the organization, and (2) information systems managers must think, plan, and act in *strategic* rather than *technical-operational* ways."[3] Operational planning requires specific detailed information that is internal to the organization and is used repeatedly (e.g., day, date, and time of emergency room admissions to the hospital). Strategic planning requires a broad range of data from a variety of diverse sources (both internal and external) and focuses on the development of relationships and analysis of trends.[4] In actuality, a considerable amount of strategic internal information is available in the organization's operational systems; however, without proper planning it may not be accessible. For example, internal billing statements could provide outcomes research data on the efficacy of drugs and medical devices for various surgeries—if the system were planned to allow capturing of all billing information by procedure. Through the use of outcomes data, competitive positioning could be developed or enhanced.

Situational Analysis

Information is vital to the strategic management process of situational analysis. The process of monitoring the external environment for threats and opportunities and the methodologies to do so were covered extensively in Chapter 2, and service area competitor analysis was explained in Chapter 3. Chapter 4 discussed the assessment of the internal environment. All of these analyses require information. Exhibit 9–1 summarizes the areas of greatest contribution to situational analysis by strategic information systems.

The application of information technology to situational analysis to collect, analyze, and manipulate data is well documented. According to Peter Drucker, "Information is data endowed with relevance and purpose. Converting data into information thus requires knowledge."[5] Information systems specialists have to know and understand the

---

Exhibit 9–1 • Information Systems Input to Situational Analysis

Situational Analysis	Information Systems Input to Situational Analysis
External Environment	
Economic	Monitor and provide information on the economy and aspects that affect the health care organization.
Regulatory	Access databases that provide the latest information on regulatory changes from national, state, and local governments and regulatory groups; convert it to useful information.
Competitor Analysis	Develop a database of competitive activity to include market share, revenues, costs, profitability, productivity, services offered, number of employees, and so on.
Market Analysis	Develop a database of the market—its size, changes, potential, rate of growth, profitability, cost structure, critical succcess factor measures.
Customer Analysis	Develop a database that profiles current customers and usage patterns, previous customers; match demographics of the area with customer profiles to predict future usage.
Internal Environment	
Information Systems	Assess the information provided to marketing, finance, accounting, human resources, clinical/medical staff, administrative staff, executive staff, and facilities against goals.
Mission, Vision, Values, and Objectives	
	Identify whether SIS can be a competitive advantage; provide information on customers, services, competition; provide information that can empower the vision; include personal ethic, confidentiality of patient information; participate in developing corporate objectives by providing historical and projected future information; develop strategic information systems objectives to accomplish corporate objectives.

technology of data organization, storage, retrieval, and manipulation and use their knowledge to convert the data into information for various organizational purposes, one of which is situational analysis. The general environment as well as the health care environment has to be monitored in terms of social, regulatory, political, economic, competitive, and technology changes. Although information is the basis for decision making in strategic management, there are additional specific and identified roles that it can serve.

Scanning the Information Technology Environment It is important to note that the field of information technology should be incorporated into situational analysis as well as the more traditional areas of the economy, competition, and so on. Although it is only one area of situational analysis, it is important because of the rapid changes occurring in information technology over the past three decades in hardware, software, and telecommunications plus the high costs committed to providing information for the organization. "In addition, each application and technology decision is both enabling and constraining—it opens some doors and closes others."[6] For example, information system decisions made today will affect the organization's ability to respond to changes in video, voice, and document imaging in the near future. Errors in judgment are costly in terms of both time and money.

Environmental scanning should forewarn the organization and allow time to plan for an orderly transition to new software if, for example, a vendor goes out of business or decides to stop marketing (and supporting) the software purchased by the health care organization. If the health care organization has developed proprietary programs (software developed in-house), it still has to know what is available because the competition may choose to purchase it.

Developing Competitive Advantage

In today's fast-paced environment, health care professionals are searching for any competitive advantage that might be available. According to Perspective 9–1, health care managers are using information systems more than any other industrial group, but they have not developed the ability to use the information. An important contribution of strategic information systems in strategic management is developing competitive advantage through decision support systems and improved customer service levels. Examples of information systems that increase market share, raise profitability, add value to products, and change the competitive position of an organization have many CEOs reexamining the role of information technology in their corporate strategy.[7]

Decision Support Systems Decision support systems (DSSs) attempt to take vast quantities of unorganized data and turn them into useful information for managers to make better decisions. Although DSSs have been available in health care for some time, they have been unknown, mistrusted, or ignored.[8] DSSs involve organizing the data, selecting the models that will analyze the data, and interpreting the output. It is not sufficient simply to provide the reports to the decision maker. Sometimes there is a need to interpret and clarify the data relative to the assumptions that were used. Because decision support systems attempt to investigate *future* activities, the assumptions are critical. The organization that can design a DSS that is pertinent, relatively accurate, and timely will

---

| Perspective 9–1

Strategic Information Systems and Health Care

A survey of one hundred large American businesses found that health care organizations are far more likely (89 percent) to have a formalized system to dig up competitive, technological, or business information than firms in other fields (58 percent). However, the real value of information is in how it is used; and so far, it seems that health care is not capitalizing on what it knows. Although health care organizations collect more strategic information, they are less likely to have a formal mechanism for getting the critical information to decision makers (56 percent compared to 68 percent in other business areas).

Interestingly, health care firms are less likely to have information concerning the regulatory climate than other business sectors (78 percent for others and only 32 percent for health care). Also of interest is the fact that health care firms appear to have more data on global economic conditions than the average participant in this survey (32 percent compared to 11 percent). Although health care organizations appear to have a lead, strategic information systems are among the least used throughout all industries.

Source: "Healthy Sleuthing," *Hospitals and Health Networks* 69, no. 33 (September 5, 1995), p. 14.

---

have developed a competitive advantage. "Inappropriate use and interpretation of decision support models can be dangerous, but appropriate use of these models can be a powerful tool in the hands of an informed decision maker."[9]

Improved Customer Service Levels Competitive advantage can be created through improved response times—the time it takes to call up a patient's record, the speed with which the pharmacy can reorder a drug, the accuracy with which drugs are prescribed (see Perspective 9–2), or the ability to quickly access a database for incidence of disease. Another competitive advantage could be in the quantity of data handled and stored in a shorter period of time with greater accuracy. These superior "service levels" can become the organization's opportunity to differentiate itself from others in its field.

Service levels have to be developed based on customer expectations. Internally, customers (other organizational users of information technology) negotiate with the information specialists based on costs and benefits to determine the level of service that will be provided. Another customer-oriented measure is the number of transactions completed per hour. Users understand and can compare this measure of performance. They can then compute the time to complete the processing and determine the time to complete their own job. Externally, service levels are determined by customer expectations and competition. Service levels must be expressed in the customers' terms. For example, response time is how long the customer has to wait for information at the terminal, not the processing time of the central processor.

Once a service level has been established as satisfactory it still has to be reviewed periodically, because there are changes in hardware and software as well as competitive activity. Any deterioration of service levels, whether response speed or number of transactions, should be carefully monitored and corrected before it negatively affects users.

Perspective 9–2

Prescription for Accuracy

One reason why information systems should be a top priority of every health care CEO is that they can reduce and hopefully eliminate harmful or deadly drug errors. It has been found that nearly one-third of all serious drug errors are preventable. Brigham and Women's Hospital responded to this figure by installing a computerized drug ordering system that allows doctors to type in prescriptions at any of Brigham's 4,000 PC workstations. The system reduces errors that can develop when pharmacists attempt to decipher handwritten prescriptions.

The drug ordering system was originally intended as part of Brigham's house clinical software; but doctors did not make it a priority until a study reporting the seriousness of the drug error problem was published in the *Journal of the American Medical Association.* The study further noted that 50 percent of the preventable drug errors occurred during the ordering stage: 11 percent occurred during transcription, 14 percent were the result of incorrect dispensing, and 26 percent took place when the drug was actually administered. Obviously, the front-line in reducing preventable drug errors was the ordering stage.

The new system should all but eliminate ordering errors. The system cross-checks each order against the patient's medication profile and searches for other drugs that may cause adverse interactions. Presently, studies are under way to see just how the new system compares with the old system in terms of accuracy.

Source: Chuck Appleby, "Prescriptions for Accuracy," *Hospitals and Health Networks* 69, no. 23 (November 20, 1995), p. 46.

This requires considerable attention to long-range planning to maintain a competitive advantage by forecasting when additional increments of information technology resources will be necessary and to bring them on-line at the appropriate time. Providing customers what they want and need is a dynamic process.

A supplier can develop competitive advantage by the degree and duration of training. Users will need training and support to solve the problems they encounter (or create). In addition, a user-friendly system may encourage use.

Finally, a sophisticated information system has become the competitive advantage in many industries. For example, in the pharmaceutical and hospital supply industries, those organizations with an automated order entry and distribution system are more competitive than those without. Hospitals and other health care organizations have realized the value of just-in-time (JIT) ordering to reduce storage costs and release space for other uses. In many situations, electronic data interchange is mandatory to just "stay in the game" and compete. For expansion strategies, cutting-edge information is required.

To satisfy customers, provide a quality product, and do it with great cost efficiencies, today's health care managers need the most current information to make decisions affecting the long-term viability of their organizations. Many community and urban hospitals have closed because they could not manage costs. A variety of additional reasons may be noted, but accurate information could have assisted the manager—if with nothing else at least in determining when the operation should have been closed to minimize the losses.

Information Technology As a Catalyst for Change

Many top managers have looked upon information systems as a necessary aspect of company operations but did not recognize the impact on the traditional "bottom line." According to Sprague and McNurlin that view is changing, and "information technology can be used strategically as a catalyst for fundamentally revamping ways of doing business—ways that were appropriate for slower, paper-based processes but impede speedier computer-based operations."[10] For example, a survey of 339 chief information officers and information systems managers revealed that less than half were satisfied with the products they received from vendors. Dissatisfaction was greatest on the West Coast where managed-care penetration is highest. For the most part, the systems being installed now were designed more than a decade ago when few hospitals needed to be electronically linked to physicians' offices, home health sites, and other locations in health networks.[11]

Rather than evolutionary thinking, health care organizations need to respond in terms of revolutionary thinking. Organizational processes tend to evolve over time (evolutionary thinking). Mead Corporation has identified the analogy of "cow paths" to clarify the revolutionary thinking that must occur to achieve the best benefits of information systems.[12] In covering the distance from the pasture to the barn, cows follow meandering paths as they avoid obstacles and rough terrain. Even after the obstacles have been removed, the cows continue to follow the old meandering path rather than create a new, more direct route. The organization often does the same by attempting to more efficiently "follow the path" rather than rethinking the processes. Old assumptions must be questioned.

Information technology can be used as a catalyst for change not only to improve automated processes but also to improve the way work is performed. This may lead to restructuring the organization or to support for greater external linkages, including strategic alliances or other partnering activities. The on-line world of the future will allow far greater fluidity in organizational structure. Work teams will come together and disband as needed. Individuals will control what they do while managers think for the future.

Reengineering Forces Strategic Thinking   Reengineering incorporates this same type of revolutionary thinking. Rather than focusing on improving speed and accuracy of information processing and reports, reengineering is oriented to new ways of thinking and performing operations. Michael Hammer identified seven principles for organizational reengineering.[13]

1. *Organize around outcomes, not tasks.* The old ways are task oriented—one person works on one file at a time to generate one bill for one patient. By focusing on the desired outcome, people consider new ways to accomplish the work.
2. *People who use the output should perform the process.* Why should purchasing order IV tubing when the emergency department runs low? With approved vendors, safety stock numbers, and order quantities determined, the information system can order IV tubing when the emergency department reaches a predetermined level.
3. *Include information processing in the "real" work that produces the information.* Those who produce the information should also process it. This eliminates the overspecialization where one group collects the data and another processes it,

reducing errors and time. Patient bedside data entry would be an example. Rather than having a written patient chart with dictated physician input given to another individual in another location to enter and transcribe the data at another time (impeding the timeliness of information), nurses, physicians, and others enter data as they examine, prescribe, and document decisions for the patient's care. The reality of the electronic medical record is slowly emerging as discussed in Perspective 9–3.

4. *Treat geographically dispersed resources as if they were centralized.* By using networks and systems, organizations can achieve economies of scale and at the same time offer flexibility and responsiveness. Pharmacy and nurses stations are geographically separated; but by centralizing the information, various physicians can better prescribe, monitor, and manage drug therapies for administration by the nursing staff.

5. *Link parallel activities rather than integrate them.* By coordinating similar kinds of work while it is in process rather than after completion, better cooperation can be fostered and the process accelerated. Information on the availability of organs for transplantation and the patient's readiness to receive the donated organ have to be linked for the best results.

6. *Let "doers" be self-managing.* By putting decisions where the work is performed and building in controls, organizations can eliminate layers of managers. Expert systems can aid the "doers" in decision making.

| Perspective 9–3

Improving Information Transfer

Not long ago, M. D. Anderson Cancer Center in Houston issued wheelchairs to patients who returned frequently. However, the wheelchairs were not issued to assist the patients in moving from appointment to appointment. Instead, the cancer center resorted to using this fleet of special carts to haul the patient's medical records, which were often several feet thick and included doctors' notes, radiation therapy reports, and lab results.

Pinpointing the location of paper records can, and usually does, pose problems at all health care organizations. At M. D. Anderson, lab results and transcribed reports were the only things that could be tapped via computer. In all, the center had more than 150 software systems running on a hodgepodge of personal computers. Executives knew that managed care would demand ready access to both clinical and financial data, so they formed a committee to look into the costs and benefits of developing an electronic record that would serve all purposes. The result is a plan that would take ten years to complete but would ensure that information would be easy to call up and save, aid doctors in patient-care decisions, and improve appointment scheduling as well as other routine tasks.

Among the major challenges are to ensure that any plan developed makes business sense and builds in the possible information technology scenarios that may develop over the next decade. It is a task that will require genuine strategic thinking.

Source: Kevin Lumsdon, "On the Record," *Hospitals and Health Networks* 69, no. 23 (November 20, 1995), p. 45.

7. *Capture information once and at its source.* Because of on-line capabilities, the information can be shared everywhere it is needed after it has been entered. Patients are particularly vocal about having to tell their name, address, telephone number, insurance, and so on to various nurses, physicians, technicians, and administrative personnel in a hospital. Most of the data does not change during one admission.

Reorganizing Based on New Ways of Thinking Once the work has been redesigned because of revolutionary thinking, the old organization structure may need to be reassessed. In the centralized form of organization, the decisions are made at the top and directed down the hierarchy. Middle-level managers are expected to apply the policies determined by top managers to the work they and their subordinates perform. In decentralized organizations, middle-level managers have relative autonomy to do what they consider appropriate "to get the work done."

Although few organizations operate at these extremes, centralized control operates most effectively when the environment is relatively stable and the work is homogeneous. Decentralized control is most effective when the environment is dynamic and the work is very different, requiring creativity on the part of lower-level managers. Information systems can blend these extremes and modify the organization on an as-needed basis. In other words, the organization becomes more fluid, responding to change as it occurs.

In his information-systems-oriented book *Shaping the Future,* Peter Keen predicted eight events. Several of the events are the results of information technology impacting the organizational structure.

1. Every large firm in every industry will have from 25 to 80 percent of its cash flow processed on-line.
2. Electronic data interchange will be the norm.
3. Point-of-sale and electronic payments will be core services.
4. Image technology will be an operational necessity.
5. Work will be distributed, and reorganization will be commonplace.
6. Work will increasingly be location independent.
7. Electronic business partnerships will be standard.
8. Reorganizations will be frequent, not exceptional.[14]

Information Linkages Through Electronic Data Interchange

Several trends are occurring that will bring about greater information linkages or electronic communication both internally and externally. In the internal context, the linkages can improve efficiency and lower costs. For example, inventory control and billing can be linked through an automated updating process. Any time a drug, special diet, medical device, or other item is prescribed or ordered for a patient, the inventory can be automatically adjusted and the cost of the item added to the patient's bill and reimbursement filing forms. Internal linkages between departments, including the management of information systems, must be planned for in the strategic management process.

This same system can be expanded externally through interorganizational linkages to automatically reorder from specified suppliers to keep sufficient safety stock on hand.

Thus, advanced order entry systems in the health care industry can reduce ordering costs for both the customer and the supplier. Suppliers are linking with their customers to electronically process ordering. Third-party payors are linked with health care providers for billing and reimbursement procedures. Providers can connect, by various methods, with medical centers as shown in Perspective 9–4. Government regulators are linking for documentation and research purposes. Finally, as health care organizations form strategic alliances, they will need to be linked and information technology will be heavily involved. There is some discussion that the Joint Commission on Accreditation of Healthcare Organizations is readying requirements for a minimum level of information sharing that can be accomplished only through a computer.[15]

The success of these interorganizational systems depend on eight characteristics according to Sprague and McNurlin:

1. *Interorganizational systems require partners.* There has to be a willingness for two or more parties to cooperate.
2. *Standards play a key role.* For linkages to be successful in the future, the programs and processes developed today should be easily expandable to other links whether they are community, regional, state, industry, national, or international.
3. *Education is important.* The more advanced information technology partner will pull the others along through education.
4. *Third parties are often involved.* They operate as electronic intermediaries to facilitate the flow of information.
5. *The work must be synchronized.* A change in any one of the cooperating systems has to be coordinated with all the others.

Perspective 9–4

Communicating Without Wires

At the John Muir Medical Center in California, a wireless computer system delivered by a vendor clashed with the hospital's cordless telephone network. Immediately, the staff went to work to create a system that would connect clinicians to Muir's computer network by radio—using laptop computers that look like high-tech clipboards. Doctors and nurses can access point-of-care data, send E-mail, and look up patients' insurance status without wasting time tracking down paper files or even going to a computer terminal.

"The phone system empowered people to communicate," stated one staff member, "but local area network empowers them to get patient data wherever they are—in a hallway or a patient's room." Staff were inspired to explore the limits of LAN technology in light of what they believed would be the next step in information technology. In addition to current uses, clinicians may soon be able to access and communicate case management, utilization review, performance and home health data using the new system, as well as store all that information in a common, centralized data depository. The common depository would allow for more integrated examination of patient records, such as those who have been treated in alternate sites such as home health.

Source: Jim Montague, "Look Ma, No Wires!" *Hospitals and Health Networks* 70, no. 8 (April 20, 1996), pp. 78–79.

6. *Work processes are often reevaluated.* When electronic ordering is implemented, paper invoices can be eliminated and payments made without an invoice.
7. *Technical aspects are not the major issue.* Relationship issues are the key to making interorganizational systems work.
8. *Efforts often cannot be secretive.* By using standards, the cooperating organizations have to be involved in the ongoing development of the standards.[16]

Many organizations are using *electronic data interchange* (EDI) for standard business transactions. Many health care organizations, particularly physicians' practices, are still operating at the lowest level of computer-to-computer linkage; however, some organizations are reaching the second level of applications-to-applications linkage (ordering to billing). Few organizations have achieved the third level of process-to-process linkage. At this point in time, EDI provides the greatest potential when standard transactions require accuracy, making it easier for the customer to buy. In the future, less standardization will be required as processes are used.

Refinement of EDI, however, is becoming critical to the success of community health information networks (CHINs), which are electronic highways "providing seamless connectivity to all components of a health delivery system."[17] The seamless connectivity of providers, employers, payors, pharmacies, and regulatory agencies is a technological challenge, but the potential for cost reduction and improvement in the quality of care is significant. The Wisconsin health information network, which is jointly owned by Ameritech and Aurora Health Care, has been in operation since 1993 and supports the exchange of both clinical and administrative information.[18]

Time Value of Information

A time value is associated with information. The reduction in time required or improved timeliness of delivery of information can be developed into a competitive advantage. Anyone who has had to wait for results of tests until they can be read by the specialist knows the cost of time. Emergency medical services understand the time value of information. They work in a time-based environment. Telecommunications will play an increasing role in time-valued operations.

The major time-related factors for information technology include response time for serving customers; time-based competitive differentiation; efficiency in inventory, ordering, and out-of-stocks; and eliminating distance as a barrier.

Importance of Strategic Information Systems

Organizations of all sizes have come to rely on computers. From small private physician practices to the largest hospital systems, computers have enabled information to be collected, stored, and manipulated for payroll and billing, diagnostics (both clinical and managerial), records management, facilities control, and decision making. Because information transfer is required among all the major functional areas of the health care organization, an integrated information system (one where the various departments/ functional areas can communicate and share information) is superior. In a study by Hewlett-Packard Company and the Healthcare Information and Management Systems Society, more than 50 percent of the 571 hospital information system specialists surveyed indicated that connecting with outside facilities including physicians' offices, clinics, HMOs, and others was one of the driving forces in hospital computerization. Over 60 percent indicated that integrating existing systems was a top priority.[19] However, integration remains primarily a goal rather than a reality. Some providers are even abandoning traditional approaches of seeking systems from vendors and entering joint ventures with them to codevelop systems that specifically meet their needs.[20] An integrated approach requires great effort in a rapidly changing environment such as health care, and much work remains before integrated systems become commonplace.

Rapidly Changing Environment

Because of the potential changes in the regulatory environment, many health care organizations are using market entry strategies such as alliances, mergers, and so on. Multi-institutional health care systems must communicate across institutions as well as within institutions. Communication is particularly important for vertically integrated health care organizations. All of these linkages require increasingly sophisticated information technology and expanded strategic information systems.

Information technology has played a part in many aspects of change in health care delivery. *Medical informatics* is the term used to describe the technology associated with the organization and management of information in support of patient care, medical information, and medical research.[21] For example, collecting the data on the number of C-sections by hospital and by physician nationwide has allowed researchers to determine that it may be practice patterns instead of clinical evidence dictating that a patient give birth by C-section rather than vaginal delivery. That information, in combination with the general public's perception of "excessive costs," has affected the number of C-sections performed. In the past, that data could have been collected but the process would have taken so long that it would have been meaningless by the time it became available. Thus technology allows information to be generated and evaluated faster, causing an increase in the speed with which events occur and the pace with which managers and organizations have to respond.

Federal government reform efforts are causing changes in the health care environment as well, dictating the need for more information to make informed decisions. It appears that health care reform will continue to focus on increased clinical accountability, efficiency of administrative and other operations, and detailed knowledge of costs. Managed care and capitation force health care managers to understand every cost decision and the resulting implications.

Some states have legal requirements that hospitals provide information on admissions, discharges, lengths of stay, and so on to the public. Federal and state regulations determine specific information that must be collected, but there is still some uncertainty over the format for the information when it is submitted electronically. As Perspective 9–5 illustrates, there are a number of efforts under way to better collect and disseminate health care data.

In addition, federal and state governments specify the length of time that records must be maintained and housed. In the recent past, all electronic medical records systems were required to have paper backup. Optical disk manufacturers were required to prove that their storage medium would contain data for at least twenty-five years before

Perspective 9–5

The Ten Best Health Care Web Sites

The ten best health care web sites, according to St. Anthony Publishers are:

- *Go Ask Alice.*
  www.cc.columbia.edu/cu/healthwise
  Columbia University Health Services' no-holds-barred question and answer website (30,000 hits a day).
- *The ABCs of EDI.*
  www.hibcc.org
  Authoritative electronic data interchange information run by the Health Industry Communications Council.
- *General Accounting Office.*
  www.gpo.ucop.edu /
  Database of General Accounting Office reports.
- *Med Help.*
  medhlp.netusa.net/index.html
  Consumer health information run by not-for-profit Med Help International.
- *The Medical Student Lounge.*
  falcon.cc.ukans.edu/~nsween/index.html
  Handbook for anyone interested in medical schools. Run by the University of Kansas Medical Center.
- *Outbreak.*
  ichiban.objarts.com/ebola/ebola.html

Disease tracking and reporting system run by volunteers.
- *PRACTICENET.*
  www.practice-net.com/practicenet.html Slick site by physician recruitment firm Merritt, Hawkins, and Associates of Dallas, Texas (700 hits a day).
- *SeniorSites.*
  www.seniorsites.com
  Tour long-term-care facilities compliments of the California Association of Homes and Services for the Aging.
- *The Body.*
  www.thebody.com/index.html
  HIV and AIDS information run by the Body Health Resources Corporation of New York.
- *Wellness Web.*
  www.wellweb.com/wellness
  Claims to be the first site founded by patients and run by the Wellness Web Company in Pennsylvania.

Source: From "10 Best Health Care Web Sites," *Modern Health*, Vol. 26, No. 10 (March 11, 1996), p. 50. Copyright © Crain Communications, Inc., 740 N. Rush Street, Chicago, IL 60611. Reprinted by permission.

they could be used to store medical records. Fortunately, these requirements are changing almost as rapidly as the environment.

Quantity of Information Generated and Stored

In health care organizations, the sheer quantity of information generated and the requirements that much of it be maintained over time has elevated the importance of strategic information systems. Health care providers must maintain meticulous records that document a patient's ailment (from his or her perspective), the physician's diagnosis, and the recommended course of treatment. This information is used by a variety of reimbursement sources, including insurance companies, the federal government (Medicare patients), state government (Medicaid patients), and an individual's records for reimbursement and taxes. In addition, it may be used in malpractice cases, research studies, outcomes measurement, and so on. Every time the patient is admitted to the hospital or a long-term-care facility, the information is expanded as nurses and a variety of technicians add to the physician's documentation of the patient's care.

Information Systems Affect Health Care Delivery

Several additional factors occurring in the health care environment affect the increasing use of information technology. Examples include an increased focus on quality from the customer's perspective, concern over the environment, consumers' abilities and increasing expectations to use computers, acceleration of the development process for new technology, the ability to provide sophisticated health care away from the hospital, and so on. The focus on quality has caused management to examine and redesign many processes to improve organizational performance. Information systems themselves are used in the redesigning of work.

Children learn to operate computers in their toys and become skilled in programming without noticing. It takes somewhat greater effort for adults; but most people have learned to use an automatic teller machine. There is the opportunity to teach patients how to access and check their health care billing information through the telephone, how to use at-home medical diagnostic equipment such as diabetes and oxygen monitoring, or even how to order prescription drugs through telephone access to the pharmaceutical company's internal information system.

Alteration of the Service Area   Expansion of the traditional delivery area is occurring through information technology by use of video diagnostics, the information highway, and so forth. Shortened product development time and product life cycles underscore the need for timely information. The development of lightweight powerful computers have enabled many health care professionals to work outside the traditional confines of the hospital. Home health care is expanding rapidly because of the ability to access through a modem any patient information and add to the database keeping it current.

Point-of-service (POS) systems are heavily computer dependent. Kaiser Permanente, one of the largest HMOs, provides health care services on a prepaid basis exclusively to enrollees. Competitive pressures are forcing Kaiser to give enrollees the option of receiving services from non-Kaiser physicians.[22] U.S. Healthcare, Inc., based in Pennsylvania, offered point-of-service options to its enrollees and grew 13 percent. According to Sprague and McNurlin, "Information systems can and do influence competitive measures. Systems are competitive tools."[23] Without massive communication capabilities, POS systems could not be offered. Although they have to pay somewhat more, consumers prefer POS options because they have greater choice. Within the industry there is some doubt that point-of-service options will continue because of increasing cost pressures,[24] although others expect accelerated growth for POS options.

Alteration at the Point of Delivery   Information technology is pervasive. Most nursing stations have workstations, and bedside computers are predicted to be the way of the future. These computers will be interconnected via local area networks to large sophisticated mainframes. The technology is expandable to all health care settings including physicians' offices, hospitals, long-term-care facilities, public health departments, and others. In addition, all the patient's health information could be portable after being recorded on a magnetic strip affixed to a plastic card. According to Frenzel, "The penetration of electronic information processing into the fabric of human activity will continue unabated into the foreseeable future."[25] However, the electronic patient record that assists in patient care, billing, and so on, is somewhat more challenging to develop.

Alteration of the Industry An *information highway* is expected to electronically connect all hospitals before the turn of the century. Moynihan and Norman developed a model of the complex myriad of information flows for health care providers (see Exhibit 9–2). Although integration of health facilities is occurring rapidly under the predictions of looming health care reform, health care is an $800 billion cottage industry.[26] When more and more health care organizations can access each other or come under one umbrella through the information highway, those outside the system will be at a distinct competitive disadvantage.

Financial Commitment

Purchasing sophisticated computers and telecommunications equipment is a major financial commitment for most organizations. Developing software and training personnel add to the high cost of information systems. Thus, there are long-term consequences to decision making. Management must incorporate information requirements into its vision of the future and consider future needs in current information technology pur-

Exhibit 9–2 • Health Care Industry Trading Partners

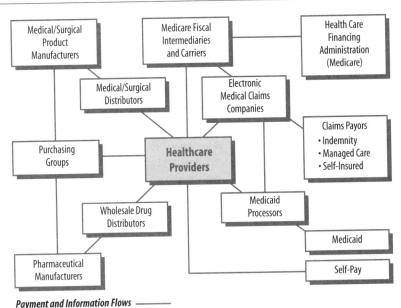

Payment and Information Flows ───────

Source: From James J. Moynihan and Kathryn Norman, "Networking Providers—Data Highways of the '90s," *Journal of American Health Information Management Association,* Vol. 64, No. 11 (November 1993), p. 46. Reprinted by permission.

chasing. To convert an information system is a monumental, time-consuming, and expensive task; it is far better to prepare for the future. However, because of the rapidly changing technology in the field, the future is extremely difficult to predict.

Importance of Planning

The core of strategic management is planning for the future. This long-term plan is articulated through the mission, vision, and objectives of the organization as discussed in previous chapters. The attainment of many of these objectives will be determined by the quality and efficiency of the information system. Therefore, when organizational planning occurs, information systems planning should be incorporated.

Sprague and McNurlin suggest that the goal for information systems should be "to improve the performance of people in organizations through the use of information technology."[27] Information technology managers would need to keep abreast of changes in technology in the areas of processors, storage devices, telecommunications, operating systems, communications software, programming tools, vendor application software, and systems management tools to assess the ways that information technology can improve the performance of people.

Critical success factors (CSFs), a concept developed by John Rockart of the Sloan School of Management at MIT in the late 1970s, define the information needs of top managers. "CSFs identify those areas where things must go right; they are the executive's necessary conditions for success."[28] The CSF method can help organizations identify information systems that need to be developed. Rockart identified four major areas to investigate for critical factors: the industry, the organization itself, the environment, and temporal organizational factors (requiring intense attention for a short period of time). He further divided CSFs into either monitoring or building types. Monitoring CSFs keep track of ongoing operations (patient billing, ordering of pharmaceuticals, and so on). Building CSFs are those operations determined by the manager as important to bring about change within the organization.[29]

Critical success factors can be incorporated into the strategic planning process by listing the corporate objectives and identifying factors that are critical for accomplishing the objectives. Then several measures need to be identified for each objective. Hard, factual data is the easiest to identify; the qualitative information such as opinions, perceptions, and hunches is more challenging and requires greater persistence to identify the underlying sources of information.

Information systems planning and organizational systems planning are becoming increasingly linked. However, in some cases, especially where information has a great deal of time value, information systems may *lead* organizational strategy to develop competitive advantage.

Most information systems are developed in a piecemeal fashion; add-ons abound. The laboratory and radiology departments, for example, are two areas that developed computer-based information systems early. However, in many hospitals one system cannot communicate with (access) the other. The results are problems with inefficiencies, duplication of work, lack of access, and difficulty of use. Because of a focus on crisis-type problem solving, strategic information planning often is pushed aside to attend to the current critical problem of the day. Charles J. Austin advocates a specific planning process for information systems that starts with a review of the organization's mission and major strategic objectives for the next five years. The entire process is outlined in Exhibit 9–3.

Information Technology Strategic Issues

Several strategic issues are driving information technology. First, routine transaction processing is relatively the norm across organizations. Only minimal future gains in cost reduction and speed of processing are possible. "In a sense the playing field has been leveled as far as transaction processing is concerned."[30] Because most of the benefits of routinized transaction processing have been achieved, time and resources will be directed to more innovative uses of information technology. Specifically, there has been greater emphasis on using information technology to accomplish organizational goals and objectives rather than using it to reduce costs.

Information Technology Positions the Organization

Information technology is being used to analyze competition (through such models as that suggested by Michael Porter discussed in Chapter 3) and to develop competitive advantage. The belief that information has time value dictates that speed can provide competitive advantage. On-line systems for patient databases can provide speed of access to many different users plus offer the added benefit of requesting the data from the patient just a single time. Time can be an asset internally as well as externally. Externally, response time to customers, markets, and changing market conditions can be sources of competitive advantage. Internally, time is of value in planning, implementing, and controlling.

Properly conceived information systems can provide enormous advantages to their owners. "Advances in technology shape the products and services of the future and offer opportunity for innovative organizations to increase their value in the stream of economic activity."[31] Information technology is particularly important because of its pervasiveness in the processes leading to advances in most other industries. Advances in information technology have a compounding effect on other technological advances across the spectrum.[32]

Resistance to Information Technology

When increased emphasis is placed on information technology, not all organizational participants are enthusiastic. There is a normal resistance to change, particularly in the art of practicing medicine. Many providers focus on computers detracting from personal relationships in health care delivery rather than the increased speed, accuracy, and convenience that computers can provide in the clinical setting. In addition, many feel that the high costs of increasing information technology may have an impact on the budget in such a way that other areas in the health care organization are denied important allocations. However, as Perspective 9–6 argues, the reality is simple—it will be impossible to compete in the managed-care world of the future without increasingly sophisticated health care information systems.

Exhibit 9–3 • **Strategic Information Systems Planning Process Flowchart**

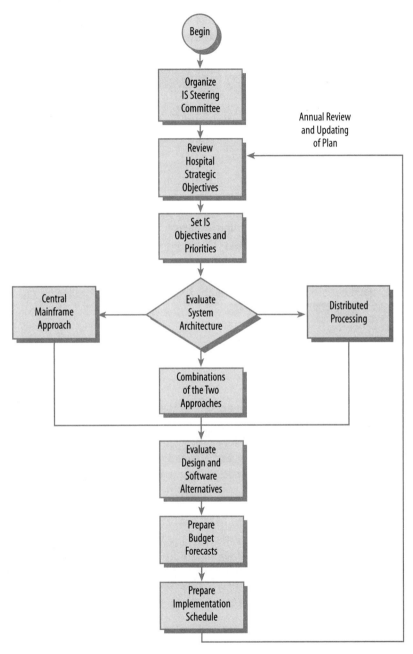

Source: From Charles J. Austin, *Information Systems for Health Services Administration,* 4th ed. (1992) p. 53. Reprinted by permission of Hospital Administration Press, Chicago.

Financial Implications

Financial considerations are an important strategic issue because although the cost of information technology in terms of speed per function is declining, the total dollar costs of these new systems are increasing. The cost of hardware is declining (if the organization does not continually upgrade in terms of capacity and speed), but the cost of software is increasing. Surveys of the health care industry indicate that organizations generally are committed to increasing their capital budgets for information systems by 10.9 percent over the next three years. However, the spending is not evenly distributed throughout the industry. A third of the health care organizations surveyed planned to increase their spending by 15 percent or more, but more than half were projecting increases of 10 percent or less. It was suggested that this diversity may reflect the differences in thinking between hospitals that are forming networks and hospitals that are destined to be absorbed by some other network.[33]

Another cost is associated with recruiting, hiring, training, and retaining skilled personnel for information technology. These professionals extend their knowledge to the data to make information available to others. Their work involves sophisticated equipment that is constantly changing, and as an employment category, they are in demand. The hiring organization needs to understand the needs of this group of people, who are typically working under pressure, to have the opportunity to work on the newest equipment and to be constantly exposed to new technology.

Perspective 9–6

Health Care and Information Technology

Charles Singer, President of Charles J. Singer and Company, a health care information technology consulting firm in Boston, has stated, "The largely mainframe systems that exist today were built mostly as financial transaction systems, not to automate clinical care." He estimates that it will take twenty years for the health care industry to overcome the obstacles to building the information infrastructure required by managed care. Perhaps the primary obstacle is the fragmented nature of the nation's 600,000 physicians who are only loosely aligned and lack incentives to adopt compatible computer systems. A related problem is the lack of standards for sharing digital information, which is comparable to everyone having a telephone that will not connect to all other telephones.

Health care systems reap two primary benefits from upgrading their communication systems, according to Francine Gaillour, M.D., Medical Director of Pharmis. First, there are fewer record-keeping errors, which immediately improves patient care. Second, there is the blending of the best of clinical practices into clinical care. The bottom line is that before managed care, business operations were independent of research and clinical operations. Managed care forces an alignment of all systems.

Source: Chuck Appleby, "The Mouse That Roared," *Hospitals and Health Networks* 70, no. 4 (February 20, 1996), pp. 31–36.

Perhaps one of the most visible changes is the rise of the chief information officer (CIO). CIOs are no longer heads of data processing units but are individuals capable of providing expert advice, vision, and consultation through the high-risk information systems to future-directed health care organizations. This type of expertise demands higher compensation. The average compensation for CIOs in hospitals with revenues over $200 million is approximately $110,000 per year, and this can easily rise to more than $150,000 annually for CIOs in hospitals with revenues between $550 and $950 million.[34]

Preserving Privacy of Patient Records

Data security is a particularly important component of the information system for health care organizations. According to consultant Dale Miller, "A primary application of information technology, the computer-based patient record, will be found at the heart of the next generation of health care information systems."[35] With this forecast of increased emphasis on the computer-based patient record and concerns about security for all electronic information, strategic managers should be planning to protect the patient's right to privacy.

An individual's diagnosis and treatment are confidential, and the data should be protected. The *Manual for Accreditation* published by the Joint Commission on Accreditation of Healthcare Organizations has been revised to include a chapter on information management that specifies security requirements. Court decisions in lawsuits have confirmed the patient's right to privacy and have held health care organizations and their managers liable for preserving that privacy.

Passwords and limited access should be implemented and properly used. Information systems professionals cite poor password management, the sharing of passwords among physician/office staff members, unattended but logged-in terminals, improper disposal of printed reports, and similar problems as the major threats to security. However, information systems professionals often do not monitor their own department's violations.

Information technologists are exposed to legal action if they allow unlimited and unrecorded access to patient information by systems managers, network managers, and programmers as they test or back up the system; allow vender access; or have inadequate controls with network connections. "Ideally, no person should be aware of confidential patient information without the knowledge and authorization of the patient. The publicity about patient confidentiality and privacy affords an excellent opportunity for CIOs to include information security in the strategic plans for systems and networks."[36]

Information Systems' Contribution to Strategic Management

Information systems managers provide a significant amount of information for strategic management as illustrated in Exhibit 9–4. Although the exhibit by no means contains an exhaustive list of information input to strategic management, it is evident that information permeates the strategic management process. In addition, other implementation strategies are affected by having good information. Specifically, operational strategies in

Exhibit 9–4 • Strategic Information Systems Input to Strategic Management

Hierarchy of Strategic Decisions	Strategic Information Systems Input
Directional Strategies	
Mission	Identify whether SIS can be a competitive advantage, provide information on customers, services, competition.
Vision	Provide information that can empower the vision.
Values	Include personal ethic, confidentiality of patient information.
Objectives	Participate in developing corporate objectives by providing historical and projected future information; develop strategic information systems objectives to accomplish corporate objectives.
Adaptive Strategies	
Expansion	
Diversification—Related	Provide information about current products/services gaps; financial information on ability to acquire; analysis of competitive activity.
Diversification—Unrelated	Provide financial information on ability to acquire; analysis of competition and profitability in new area.
Vertical Integration—Forward	Provide financial information on ability to take over customers; analysis of competition and profitability.
Vertical Integration—Backward	Provide financial information on ability to take over suppliers; analysis of competition and profitability.
Market Development	Access to databases of information on developing markets, underserved markets, and unserved markets; provide information for analysis of competition and profitability.
Product Development	Provide information on usage of current products; market share; analyze information on competitive offerings and potential profitability of new services.
Penetration	Provide information about services that are not meeting objectives and require additional marketing effort and those that are exceeding objectives to capitalize on customer demand.
Contraction	
Divestiture	Provide information on services, facilities, equipment, etc. not meeting objectives over time for a divestiture decision; provide information to determine a fair market value.
Liquidation	Provide information on services, facilities, equipment, etc. not meeting objectives over time to liquidate; provide information to determine remaining investment.
Harvesting	Provide information on services, facilities, equipment, etc. not meeting objectives for eventual phaseout.
Retrenchment	Provide information on personnel costs/productivity for determining optimum size of labor force; provide information to assess market profitability for decisions about markets and services to eliminate; provide information for analysis of costs/benefits of facilities, equipment, and other assets.
Stabilization	
Enhancement	Provide information on competitive activity; compare with the organization's own results.
Status Quo	Provide information on competitive activity; compare with the organization's own results.
Market Entry Strategies	
Purchase	Provide information on the organization's ability to purchase; expected future profitability; scan for potential purchases.
Cooperation	Provide information on profitability (risk) of cooperating organization(s); determine if there is information system compatibility.
Development	Provide information systems specialist to better delineate any information systems needs of the new development.

Exhibit 9–4 • **Continued**

Hierarchy of Strategic Decisions	Strategic Information Systems Input
Positioning Strategies	
Marketwide	
Cost Leadership	Provide continuous information on market share, competitor costs and prices, and productivity for the market.
Differentiation	Provide continuous information on market share, patient satisfaction with current services, consumer preferences, competitive offerings, changing demographics, and so on for the entire market.
Market Segment	
Focus—Cost Leadership	Provide continuous information on market share, competitor costs and prices, and productivity for the identified market segment.
Focus—Differentiation	Provide continuous information on market share, patient satisfaction with current services, consumer preferences, competitive offerings, changing demographics, and so on for the the identified market segment.
Operational Strategies	
Functional—Information Systems	Plan, develop, and maintain information systems (hardware, software, telecommunications, EDI) for clinical, administrative, and executive decision support.
Organization-Wide—Structure	Provide flexibility to organizational structure because availability and use of information systems allows the organization to opt for centralized or decentralized operations (or vice versa) depending on the number of individuals and units involved in decision making.
Organization-Wide—Facilities and Equipment	Enhance efficiency and productivity of various subsystems within the facility (such as energy, scheduling of housekeeping, maintenance of equipment) by improving monitoring and control.
Control	Provide the information of "control" that measures performance and compares performance against the objectives; identify areas in need of management attention.

clinical areas, marketing, finance, and human resources benefit from an effective information system. The information specialist has to be able to work with multiple constituencies including the administration, the clinical staff, and the operating departments.

Apart from the input to strategic management, the strategic information system itself is affected by the organization's choice of directional and adaptive strategies. If the future of health care is in integrated networks, and most believe it is, information technology will be a primary determinant of how rapidly organizations can move into expansion strategies. At the same time, the direction of development in health information systems will be greatly influenced by the types of networks implemented. For example, when Washington state adopted a fee-per-patient financial model to control costs in its Medicaid program, providers such as MultiCare Health Systems responded immediately with information-based strategies. MultiCare's Mary Bridge Children's Hospital in Tacoma used a computerized patient record system to reduce the number of costly visits to its emergency department.[37] This illustrates not only a limitation but an opportunity for information-based strategies and shows how they can be used strategically.

Expansion Strategies

In most growth situations, the information system should grow as rapidly as the health care organization. Rather than hiring new employees for the information system department, rapid growth is oftentimes addressed by outsourcing or by using consultants (especially if the need is perceived to be of short-term duration or an extremely specialized situation). By using outsourcing or consultants, capital is not tied up in computer equipment—freeing the health care organization to invest in facilities and equipment more directly related to patient care.

Outsourcing generally means that an outside organization is hired to be "staff" and is paid by the hour. It can refer to buying or adapting hardware and software or codeveloping a system. Purchasing requires an excellent working knowledge of which vendor's products can meet the organization's needs and perform as stated, as well as of vendor pricing strategies. This can be a time-consuming activity.

Outside consultants, familiar with the health care information systems industry, can save the organization time and money. Many health care organizations have purchased systems in the past that did not meet expectations. Consultants can save a health care organization millions of dollars by helping it avoid making a mistake in an information technology purchase.[38] Consultants should be hired when the expertise is not available in-house or the expertise will be needed for a short period of time, or the CEO can afford the expertise for only a short period of time. Consultant services include selection and evaluation of information systems, contract negotiations, implementation support, systems testing, documentation, telecommunication/networking, interface support, cost justification, and so on. To gain the best results with consultants, Elizabeth Ball suggests: check the references of information system consultants, strive to avoid a learning curve (hire consultants that have had experience doing what needs to be done), agree to estimated due dates and checkpoints, and require weekly status reports.[39] Consulting costs can escalate rather rapidly if they are not carefully managed.

Contraction Strategies

Downsizing of the information systems area is expected with mergers, alliances, and so on, as considerable duplication exists. In addition, increasingly limited resources affect information systems as it does other areas of the health care organization. Because health care organizations exist to provide care to patients, developing a sophisticated information system when contraction strategies are being implemented detracts time and money away from organization goals. Rather than maintaining information system specialists, outsourcing could be used in contraction strategies because the health care organization would pay on an as-needed basis. It does not guarantee that the costs will be less, however.

Stabilization Strategies

Rightsizing is a term that could be applied to stabilization strategies for information systems. If a health care organization decides to pursue a steady course in terms of market share, revenues, and so on, it does not necessarily follow that it should maintain the status quo in terms of information systems. Status quo is not possible without having information about what is going on in the general environment as well as in the health care environment.

Summary and Conclusions

Strategic information systems are changing health care delivery by providing information for situational analysis and development of competitive advantage. Decision support systems provide information for better clinical decision making as well as improving timeliness and accuracy of administrative information (billing, inventory control, third-party reimbursements, cost data, and so on).

Information systems are a catalyst for change in a health care organization because they assist in quality improvements and reengineering many aspects of delivery of care. Electronic data interchange will occur through the information highway that enables all health care facilities to communicate electronically. This increase in linkages can accelerate efficiencies as the organization quickly and accurately communicates with internal and external constituencies.

Planning for strategic information systems is important because of the rapid changes in information technology, the quantity of information generated and stored in health facilities, the high cost and time commitment to any change in the SIS, and the change it causes in health care delivery—alteration of the service area, alteration at the point of delivery with bedside data entry, and alteration of the industry through the information highway.

SIS affects and interacts with every department in a health care organization. At the same time, it is an independent department similar to others in the organization and has to determine how its operational strategies support the strategic plan. The next chapter discusses implementation strategies for finance.

Key Terms and Concepts in Strategic Management

community health information networks (CHINs)
decision support system (DSS)
electronic data interchange (EDI)

information highway
information technology
medical informatics

outsourcing
point-of-service (POS) system
strategic information system (SIS)

Questions for Class Discussion

1. Explain the impact of decision support systems on the provision of direct patient care (clinical decision making).
2. How can a strategic information system (SIS) be used to develop competitive advantage?
3. Explain how SIS changes are also a catalyst for change.
4. Why is EDI important for vertically integrated health care organizations?
5. Does an information system differ for internal linkages versus external linkages?

6. Explain your plan for an electronic patient record.
7. Why is the patient record so critical to the further development of information systems in health care?
8. What changes are information systems bringing to health care?
9. Why is planning for SIS important?
10. Discuss the impact of SIS on the directional, adaptive, and operational strategies of a health care organization.

Notes

1. Charles J. Austin, *Information Systems for Health Services Administration,* 4th ed. (Ann Arbor, Michigan: AUPHA Press, 1992), p. 7.
2. Ibid.
3. Ibid., p. 299.
4. Lynda M. Applegate, Richard O. Mason, and Darryl Thorpe, "Design of a Management Support System for Hospital Strategic Planning," *Journal of Medical Systems* 10 (1986), pp. 82–83.
5. Peter F. Drucker, "The Coming of the New Organization," *Harvard Business Review* 66, no. 1(January/February 1988), p. 45.
6. Peter G. Spitzer, "A Comprehensive Framework for I/S Strategic Planning," *Computers in Healthcare* 14, no. 5 (May 1993), p. 28.
7. David D. Moriarty, "Strategic Information Systems Planning for Health Service Providers," *Health Care Management Review* 17, no. 1 (Winter 1992), p. 85.
8. Homer H. Schmitz, "Decision Support: A Strategic Weapon," in *Healthcare Information Management Systems,* ed. Marion J. Ball, Judith V. Douglas, Robert I. O'Desky, and James W. Albright (New York: Springer-Verlag, 1991), pp. 42–48.
9. Ibid., p. 47.
10. Ralph H. Sprague, Jr., and Barbara C. McNurlin, *Information Systems in Practice,* 3d ed. (Englewood Cliffs, New Jersey: Prentice-Hall, 1993), p. 69.
11. Rhonda Bergman, "Stone Age Solutions?" *Hospitals and Health Networks* 69, no. 5 (February 5, 1995), pp. 27–32.
12. Sprague and McNurlin, *Information Systems in Practice,* p. 31.
13. Michael Hammer, "Reengineering Work: Don't Automate, Obliterate," *Harvard Business Review* 68, no. 4 (July/August 1990), pp. 104–112.
14. Peter G. W. Keen, *Shaping the Future: Business Design Through Information Technology* (Boston: Harvard Business School Press, 1991), p. 111.
15. John Morrissey, "Time to Put Info System in Order?" *Modern Healthcare* 23, no. 47 (November 22, 1993), p. 64.
16. Sprague and McNurlin, *Information Systems in Practice,* pp. 94–96.
17. P. Hanlon, "Charting the Evolution of Community Health Information Networks," *Journal of Healthcare Information and Management Systems Society* 9, no. 2 (1995), pp. 10–14.
18. F. Bazzoli, "Health Information Networks: Where Are We Headed?" *Health Data Management* 2, no. 9 (1994), pp. 39–47.
19. Elizabeth Gardner, "Hospitals on the Road to Data 'Highways,'" *Modern Healthcare* 23, no. 24 (June 7, 1993), p. 32
20. Bergman, "Stone Age Solutions?" p. 32.
21. R. A. Greenes and E. H. Shortliffe, "Medical Informatics: An Emerging Academic Discipline and Institutional Priority," *Journal of the American Medical Association* (February 1990), pp. 1114–1120.
22. Paul J. Kenkel, "Kaiser Planning to Boost Point-of-Service Options," *Modern Healthcare* 23, no. 38 (September 20, 1993), p. 38.
23. Sprague and McNurlin, *Information Systems in Practice,* p. 68.
24. "Point-of-Service: Transitional Product or Here to Stay?" *HMO Magazine* (March/April 1993), pp. 49–51.
25. Carroll W. Frenzel, *Management of Information Technology* (Boston: boyd & fraser, 1992), p. 17.
26. James J. Moynihan and Kathryn Norman, "Networking Providers—Data Highways of the '90s," *Journal of AHIMA* 64, no. 11 (November 1993), p. 42.
27. Sprague and McNurlin, *Information Systems in Practice,* p. 14.
28. Frenzel, *Management of Information Technology,* p. 27.
29. Ibid.
30. Ibid., p. 41.
31. Ibid., p. 57.
32. Ibid.
33. John Morrissey, "Full Speed Ahead," *Modern Healthcare* 26, no. 9 (March 4, 1996), pp. 97–108.
34. Linus Diedling and Joseph Welfeld, "The Rise of the CIO," *Hospital and Health Networks* 69, no. 5 (February 5, 1995), pp. 34–38.
35. Dale Miller, "Preserving the Privacy of Computerized Patient Records," *Healthcare Informatics* 10, no. 10 (October 1993), p. 72.
36. Ibid., p. 73.
37. Chuck Appleby, "The Mouse That Roared," *Hospital and Health Networks* 70, no. 4 (February 20, 1996), pp. 31–36.
38. Bill W. Childs, "Consulting: State of the Art," in *Healthcare Information Management Systems,* p. 319.
39. Elizabeth E. Ball, "Maximizing the Benefits of Using Consultants," in ibid., pp. 326–330.

Additional Readings

Abdelhak, Mervat, Sara Grostick, Mary Alice Hanken, and Ellen Jacobs, Editors, *Health Information: A Strategic Resource* (Philadelphia: W. B. Saunders Company, 1996). Nineteen chapters deal with all aspects of health information technology and management. This book is a valuable guide to all health managers and is an essential reference book for the libraries of health care organizations.

Cronin, Mary J., Editor, *The Internet Strategy Book* (Boston: Harvard Business School Press, 1996). The book, from the author of *Doing Business on the Internet* and *Doing More Business on the Internet,* is the first book to combine the advice and experience of ten leading experts on how to use the information superhighway to gain competitive advantage.

Hammer, Michael, *Reengineering Recycled* (New York: HarperBusiness, 1996). Although this book deals specifically with reengineering, it is really a book about organizational change. Hammer changes the emphasis in this book, however, from radical change and focuses more on process. He notes that, in reality, the process, whether in health care or other industries, is the development of end-to-end activities that create value for customers. Reengineering, therefore, has as much to do with information systems as it does with operations.

Hasenyager, Bruce W., *Managing the Information Ecology* (Westport, Connecticut: Quorum Books, 1996). This book describes the new information ecology in many large organizations and suggests ways to build and manage the complexities of information technologies. It is a useful discussion of how information ecologies evolve in organizations and how this valuable resource can be effectively utilized.

Tenner, Edward, *Why Things Bite Back* (New York: Alfred A. Knopf, 1996). This is a book about the benefits and costs of technology. Tenner's book goes beyond simply bashing technology and offers genuine solutions to the technological problems faced by all individuals living in the modern world as well as health care managers who are called on to manage increasingly complex technologies.

Strategic Financial Systems

➤ **Learning Objectives**

After completing this chapter you should be able to:

1. Understand the relationship between overall strategic plans and strategic financial planning.

2. Discuss the strategic financial implications of adaptive strategies relating to expansion and stabilization.

3. Discuss the necessity and means to finance market entry strategies associated with expansion and stabilization.

4. Understand how the efficient management of financial resources can assist in building and sustaining competitive advantage.

5. Discuss alternative ways of obtaining the funds needed to support strategic decisions.

6. Understand the advantages and disadvantages associated with different methods of financing market entry strategies.

7. Evaluate the effectiveness of different methods of implementing financial strategies.

8. Appreciate the importance of integrating financial strategies into the strategic management process.

The Introductory Incident illustrates an important fact. Capital is an essential and, perhaps next to threshold competency, the first requirement to compete in any organizational activity. Physicians have skills, experience, and knowledge but rarely the financial resources to mount large enterprises required to compete effectively in today's managed-care environment. The alternatives are to attempt to compete on a small scale and risk losing all patients or to sell out to a managed-care company and forfeit a great deal of decision-making authority. The American Medical Association's Physicians Capital Source attempts to provide another alternative—matching physicians with funding sources so that they can develop their own health plans and compete on a grander scale.

Introductory Incident
Helping Doctors Find the Capital to Compete

Although managed care continues to grow in importance, physicians remain uneasy about the decision-making authority they lose under this approach to health care. At the same time, they are understanding a fact of economic life: the party that puts up the money for managed-care organizations is in the financial driver's seat. The Physicians Capital Source program of the American Medical Association is an initiative designed to make capital available to doctors to finance their own health plans and consequently retain greater decision-making control.

The AMA does not plan to invest any money in Physicians Capital Source but rather to function as a "catalyst" to bring together "physician-friendly" sources of capital and physicians and physician groups. To earn this distinction, potential sources of capital must demonstrate that they have experience in financing health care deals, a track record in working with physicians, a good reputation in their field, and references from at least three physicians with whom they have worked. Currently, the list includes banks, investment bankers, physician practice management companies, and venture capitalists.

In March 1996, the Physicians Capital Source was instrumental in cementing a deal between Michigan Provider Network and Southern California–based CareAmerica that developed a new multiple-option health plan to serve southeastern Michigan. The Michigan Provider Network is a consortium of 2,200 physicians. Network physicians will occupy half of the seats on the plan's board of directors and will control 60 percent of the quality management committee that oversees patient-care issues. CareAmerica Michigan will target small to medium-sized employers in a four-county area where approximately 95 percent of all employers have fewer than fifty employees.

The Physicians Capital Source is expected to be an important force in providing doctors better access to the capital they need to effectively compete in a managed-care world. The Source currently has more than forty projects under active consideration.

Source: Chuck Appleby, "A Capital Way to Put Doctors in Charge," *Hospitals and Health Networks* 70, no. 11 (June 5, 1996), pp. 63–64.

This chapter is about strategic financial management in health care organizations. More specifically, it is about the strategic financial implications of the overall strategic management process at the organizational level. No attempt has been made to deal with the broader issues of the national or public policy aspects of health care financing. Although it is true that the way health care services are financed greatly influences decision making, this is basically a public policy issue and beyond the scope of this text.

Although only one part of the strategic plan, financial considerations at the level of strategic implementation are important. Overall strategic decisions are influenced by the quality and quantity of financial resources. (Appendix B provides some additional details on specific aspects of financial analysis.) The financial function should be an aid to the overall strategic plan rather than its driving force. Without adequate financial planning, the organization's strategic plan has little practical meaning. At the same time, strategic thinking should not be limited by finances alone. To do so would unnecessarily restrict the vision of creative health care managers.

Integrating Strategic Planning and Financial Planning

Financial planning is important for all health care organizations. Because a large part of what an organization hopes to accomplish with sound strategic management is to "propel the organization from the present to a predetermined desired future," there must be some idea as to whether the financial resources are capable of taking the organization to where it wants to go.[1] Strategic financial planning is a type of reality check, because without it there is no way of knowing if the goals are even feasible.[2]

Links Between Strategic Planning and Financial Planning

The financial strategies of an organization should contribute to the accomplishment of its directional strategies. They should be consistent with the mission and values and support the vision. Financial plans should fit logically into the clearly defined pattern of strategic decisions.

It is important that all aspects of financial planning maintain a consistent and logical relationship with the strategic plan. Exhibit 10–1 illustrates a continuum of refinement that demonstrates this type of relationship. This continuum highlights the proper relationship that should exist between strategic financial planning and budgeting.[3]

Note that the first two stages of the process relate specifically to strategic concerns. This avoids the conflict that frequently develops in financial planning between strategic planners, who correctly see budgets as being driven by the organization's overall strategic plan as well as the strategic financial plan, and budgetary planners, who see strategic plans as being driven by unit and departmental budgets. In this continuum of refinement, it is not until Stage 3 that the budget becomes operational or is converted into the familiar revenue and cost projections that represent the output of the budgetary financial planning process.

This method focuses on the strategic plan and has the advantage of being more efficient, because lower-level managers who are responsible for developing specific budgetary requests gain the benefit of knowing how the budget relates to the total strategic plan. Budgeting then becomes a refining process for the overall plan rather than a compilation of isolated decisions provided by each department. The individuals actually

Exhibit 10–1 • **Strategic Planning and Financial Planning**

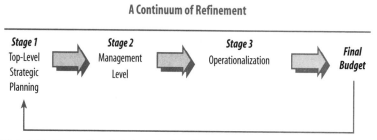

A Continuum of Refinement

Stage 1 Top-Level Strategic Planning → *Stage 2* Management Level → *Stage 3* Operationalization → *Final Budget*

Source: From Donald Cook, "Strategic Plan Creates a Blueprint for Budgeting," *Healthcare Financial Management,* Vol. 44, No. 5, (May 1990) p. 26. Copyright © 1990 by the Healthcare Financial Management Association. Reprinted by permission.

making department-level decisions see how their choices relate to overall financial strategies and the strategic plan. The importance of financial managers to successful strategic management is discussed in Perspective 10–1.

Strategic Financial Planning

There are several important steps in successful strategic financial planning:[4]

1. Establish specific financial performance objectives that are directly linked to the directional strategies of the organization.
2. Compare the return and cost of strategic alternatives to assist in determining overall priorities.
3. Evaluate the costs of different financing options.
4. Assess the financial impact of alternative pricing and marketing strategies.
5. Provide comparative financial data for capital investment alternatives, and present alternatives in a way that is useful for decision-making purposes.

This brief list demonstrates that the role of strategic financial planning is to assist in the accomplishment of directional strategies by providing accurate analyses and evaluations of the financial implications of alternative strategic options.

Although financial considerations can be one of the primary elements of strategic performance, they should not be allowed to reduce the organization's vision.[5] At times,

---

Perspective 10–1

Strategic Financial Planning: Getting the Job Done

William H. Nelson, Chairman of the Healthcare Financial Management Association stated, "To develop successful strategic plans, health care executives must realize that an accurate and realistic financial strategy must be part of the overall plan." Health care financial managers play a critical role in strategic management because they have the skills and the abilities to evaluate the health services marketplace—to assess its challenges, risks, and opportunities and to design plans of action that reflect market and financial realities.

Ultimately, the key to financial success is engaging in an information-based and dispassionate evaluation of the local health services industry, including its various market segments, and understanding what factors influence performance in each segment. Nelson argues: "Ironically, the success the health services industry has achieved over the past 20 years may be its most difficult barrier to

overcome." During the past two decades, health care organizations have often achieved their missions and even exceeded their visions. The challenge is to remain realistic and avoid the temptation of strategic plans that are too optimistic and impossible to implement in today's era of rapid change.

Health care organizations must have solid information systems to aid financial managers in producing the data that will help them create meaningful strategic plans. Projecting future needs is the essence of strategic planning. It cannot be successful unless plans account for financial results and help inject financial discipline into health care organizations.

Source: William H. Nelson, "Vantage Point: Strategic Financial Management: Getting the Job Done," *Healthcare Financial Management* 51, no. 2 (1996), p. 10.

the hostile financial environment facing health care organizations appears overwhelming. Insurance companies set their own reimbursement schedules and refuse to pay full charges, capital markets are in disarray causing interest-rate projections to be virtually impossible, and private donors are reluctant to pledge support for deserving projects. At the same time, a health care organization's unique vision and mission should not imply that it cannot operate in a financially efficient manner, even if its primary purpose is service. This point is convincingly made in Perspective 10–2.

No one would debate that uncertainties exist in health care. However, the vision of a health care organization is, as noted in Chapter 5, a hope of what the organization will and should be at some time in the future. Strategic managers should not allow financial considerations to make them so timid that they fail to strive for the full potential of the organization; nor should they assume that the pursuit of compassionate care, community service, and medical ministries automatically eliminates the possibility of financial fitness.

For example, consider the need to carefully integrate not just strategic, operational, and budgetary financial planning but also the strategic, operational, and budgetary plans of different health care providers in a single health network. The affiliation of Christian Health Services, Barnes Hospital, and Jewish Hospital in St. Louis was initiated to consolidate services and planning while allowing the three involved organizations to maintain separate identities. As with other affiliations, however, the extent to which this structure is successful will depend to a great degree on how the organizations can integrate their strategic and financial planning to most effectively deploy and allocate the resources at their disposal.[6]

Perspective 10–2

Reasons for Transforming Hospitals Go Beyond Financials

Advocates of patient-centered care believe it will be cost effective but at the same time they stress that the reasons for moving hospitals in this direction go beyond financial considerations. They believe it is strategically the right thing to do. The president of Mid-Columbia Medical Center in Oregon stated that they moved to patient-centered care because "it is the correct way to treat patients." The executive director of the Vanderbilt University Hospital and Clinic in Nashville, Tennessee, stated that they were convinced the "traditional hospital structure was not working" so that moving in the direction of patient-centered care was the right direction.

A survey by *Hospitals* found that 42 percent of the hospitals implementing patient-centered care were uncertain about its financial impact. Because start-up costs are significant, it is not sur-

prising that many of the hospitals moving toward patient-centered care are financially healthy institutions. Only 7 percent of the respondents estimated that patient-centered care would cost them less than $50,000, and 26 percent thought it would cost more than $1 million. Almost 60 percent expected savings to be primarily in the area of labor costs, 51 percent thought it would come through combining departments, and 23 percent expected to obtain savings by eliminating departments. All indicated that changes of this nature will be difficult but will ultimately prove to be a sound strategy.

Source: H. J. Anderson, "New Planning Models: Reasons for Transforming Hospitals Go Beyond Financials," *Hospitals* (February 5, 1993), pp. 20–22.

An Integrative View

One way to illustrate the integration of strategic planning and financial planning is with the aid of Exhibit 10–2. Numerous long-term consequences are involved when an organization provides the health services called for in its mission. As hospitals, long-term-care facilities, physicians' practices, and so on provide services for patients, facilities depreciate, technologies evolve and need updating, and fund balances accumulate or become depleted. The result is that organizations need to grow, diversify, vertically integrate, modernize facilities, and expand. Alternatively, some organizations will be faced with contraction, divestiture, and even liquidation.

All of these long-term consequences create the need for long-term, strategic, financial decisions. New financial resources will be required under some circumstances and correction of resource misallocations will be required for others. It is not unusual for strategic decision makers to be faced with the tasks of obtaining new financial resources and reallocating existing resources at the same time. This is particularly true in view of the fact that financing alternatives are greatly influenced by the external environment— especially the economy.

Historically, for example, strategic financial decision makers have made capital budgeting decisions assuming the continuation of the specialty-driven, hospital-based model. Under this assumption, major sources of revenue result from income from operations, depreciation, acquisition of debt, and philanthropy. As an interesting exercise, consider the issues that could emerge when different scenarios of health care delivery are examined from the perspective of their financial impact. For example, what would

Exhibit 10–2 • Integrating Strategic and Financial Planning

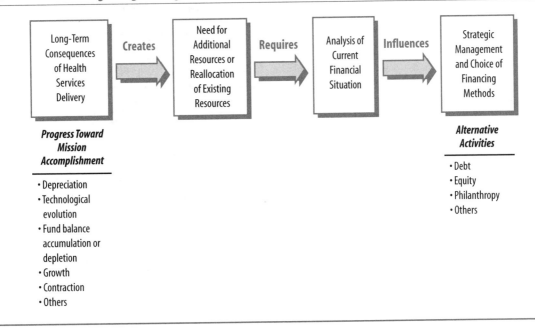

the mix of revenue sources be assuming only three simple financing arrangements such as fee for service, contracting, and capitation rates?[7] There is a definite relationship between adaptive strategies and the financial strategies necessary to accomplish them.

A Framework for Financing Strategic Decisions

To accomplish the adaptive strategies of expansion, contraction, or stabilization, a variety of strategic financial actions are available, as illustrated in Exhibit 10–3. However, conditions in the external economic and competitive environments greatly influence the options available at any particular time. For example, debt funding, along with cash reserves and equipment leasing, has been a preferred means of financing expansion. Unfortunately, for many health care providers this option is becoming less available and more expensive.

Analysts at Moody's Investors' Service argue that health care is increasingly becoming a buyers' market with too many hospitals and systems chasing too few patients. Moreover, the buyers are becoming increasingly powerful through strong HMOs. This is a fundamentally different situation than the one that existed throughout most of the

Exhibit 10–3 · Adaptive Strategies and Strategic Financial Decisions

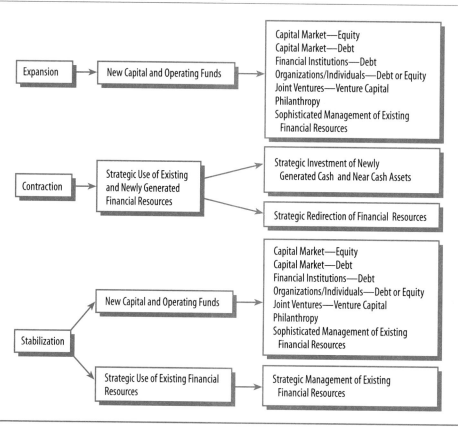

modern history of health care in the United States. The result is overcapacity. Hospitals and physicians are consolidating, but not fast enough. Inpatient admissions are down 15 percent over the past decade and annual inpatient days fell 21 percent during the same period. However, staffed hospital beds dropped by only 10 percent. Financially, the impact has been predictable. In a recent year, there were more downgradings of health care providers' credit worthiness than upgrades.[8]

This presents a particularly dangerous situation for publicly traded, high-growth health care organizations. The companies typically have stock prices that represent high multiples of earnings, and if expectations of their ability to sustain record-breaking growth year after year develops, their stock prices can fall sharply. As Perspective 10–3 illustrates, any such fall in stock prices can be accentuated by short sellers.

Perspective 10–3

Is Wall Street Betting Against Health Care?

It is not a pretty picture. High flying health care stocks that are trading at fifty times earnings fail to make a quarterly earnings projection and investor confidence starts to fall. Sell-off begins and stock prices drop. Not everyone loses, however. Standing in the wings are people on Wall Street "poised to pounce and profit" from the fall. These short sellers, as they are called, borrow stock of the high-growth companies from specialized stock lenders and sell it, betting that they can buy the shares back later at lower prices to return to the lenders. In April 1996, health care stocks helped fuel the largest short-selling binge in the history of the New York Stock Exchange, hitting a record number of 2.2 billion short sells. Columbia/HCA Healthcare was fourth on the list of companies with the largest short position (volume of stock being short sold). SmithKline Beecham, Cardinal Health, and Foundation Health were also in the top twenty.

Strategically, a company with a large short position may be in a serious predicament. In reality, investors are betting against it. They are expecting the stock to drop and that spells trouble, particularly if the company has ongoing capital needs to sustain growth. Some executives such as Victor Campbell, Senior Executive Vice President

at Columbia/HCA, "totally ignore the whole issue." According to him, short position has nothing to do with the fundamental financial strength of a company. "Real investors interested in the long-run and upon which a company must depend for capital pay zero attention to the short interest in a stock," according to Campbell.

Many believe that, in reality, the appearance of four health care companies on the list of the top twenty short-sell candidates has little to do with investors betting against health care. Rather, it is the fact that a number of health care firms have experienced phenomenal growth that investors doubt can be sustained. Eleanor Kerns, a health care analyst at Alex. Brown, and Company, stated that "short sellers are not betting against health care" but against the multiples of earnings many of the companies have achieved relative to their stock prices. Regardless of the motivation, short sellers are a market reality that can dampen the ability of high-growth health care companies to continue spectacular performance.

Source: Chuck Appleby, "Betting Against Health Care," *Hospitals and Health Networks* 70, no. 4 (June 20, 1996), pp. 34–38.

Stabilization strategies directed toward enhancement of facilities, equipment, quality of services, and so on will often require new capital and operating funds. For example, an organization may have to acquire new property and relocate in its efforts to change the image held by physicians who might join its staff and the patients who might use its facilities. New technology may be demanded as well for this change in image or for significant improvement of services. Therefore, expansion and stabilization frequently make it necessary for health care organizations to enter the capital market or make arrangements to borrow money from one or more financial institutions. Joint ventures are often financed by attracting other individuals, such as physicians, to invest in promising ideas or equipment along with the hospital. Organizations with sufficient financial resources may even act as venture capitalists for promising new ideas.

Another avenue of funding available to many health care organizations is private philanthropy. Organizations with long histories of service to a particular area or those that are particularly well known for their good works can, and frequently do, attract gifts from individuals who wish to be a part of the organization's future. Sometimes these gifts are restricted and must be used for specific purposes, although many times the gifts can be used at the discretion of the organization.

Contraction strategies require equally challenging financial decision making. Divestiture, liquidation, and harvesting converts financial resources, at least temporarily, into cash or near cash assets. This forces the decision maker to consider alternative uses of the funds and ensure that the funds are appropriately invested until they are needed for other uses. Contraction requires careful reevaluation and possible redirection of the use of financial resources. For example, a hospital experiencing financial distress, after careful analysis, might decide that its emergency room is too expensive to continue to operate in view of limited demand by the community. The high level of specialized staffing for around-the-clock operations is a financial burden that cannot be justified economically. The decision to close the emergency room would temporarily free financial resources that could be allocated to more profitable areas and relieve some of the pressure on the hospital.

Because it is a moving target, stabilization strategies directed toward maintaining the status quo may require additional capital. Stabilization demands that health care managers effectively and efficiently use existing and newly generated financial resources. In view of all these factors, a series of financial issues will be discussed in terms of their relationship to adaptive and market entry strategies. These factors are:

- capital acquisition—equity and debt,
- other forms of debt acquisition,
- fund-raising and philanthropy, and
- effective investment and management of financial resources.

Capital Acquisition—Equity and Debt

There are two major reasons why capital investments are significant financial challenges. First, they involve large sums of money. Second, they relate to long time periods. The larger sums cause greater exposure to financial risks, and the longer time period commits management to actions that are not easily altered.[9]

Capital investments are extremely important to health care organizations because the industry is very "capital intense." State-of-the-art medical equipment is essential to the delivery of quality medical care, yet this type of equipment is very expensive. The inability or unwillingness of a hospital to obtain the most advanced technology can result in a loss of medical staff, patients, reputation, and ultimately, market share.[10] The ability of a health care organization to effectively manage its capital investments is an important strategic strength. Management of capital investments requires an understanding of such specific techniques as the time value of money and the benefits of collecting income streams as soon as possible to take advantage of reinvestment opportunities. In addition, it requires the ability to use the suitable financial management concepts necessary to evaluate long-term capital projects.

Acquiring Equity Funds In the health care industry, equity funding comes from several sources. Financing mergers, acquisitions, and other market entry strategies may require that private health care organizations issue new stock or pursue increased investment from existing owners. If a health care organization is closely held, it may be built with personal investments from physicians and other interested investors who see an opportunity for a good return on their money. If it is a larger facility, it may have the ability to raise its funds by going public and offering equity (shares of stock) to investors throughout the region or nation. In many cases, joint ventures between a health care organization and physicians or other firms represent equity investments. Equity funding may also be obtained through the reinvestment of profits.

The attractiveness of issuing new stock to finance expansion, however, depends to a great extent on how well health care stocks are performing relative to other stocks and related investments. Perspective 10–4 discusses how health care stocks have performed relative to the stock market as a whole.

As in any industry, not all areas of health care perform to the same degree. Throughout 1995, for example, the Furman Selz/Modern Healthcare composite index increased 36 percent although industry segments varied significantly. (Note in Perspective 10–4 that health care stocks, in general, increased about 40 percent.) Pharmaceuticals and pharmaceutical supply stocks increased 43.4 percent, health care provider stocks increased only 17.2 percent, medical technology stocks increased 57.3 percent, and biotechnology stocks increased 66.3 percent. Clearly, the attractiveness of equity funding for health care organizations, as in other industries, is a matter of the industry segment within which one competes.[11] Health care stocks have become so popular that Morgan Stanley and Company now has three indices that chart the performance of health care stocks. They are quoted on the American Stock Exchange under the symbols RXP for health care products, HMO for health care payors, and RXH for health care providers.

If top management decides to pursue equity funding from the public, it is necessary to weigh some important advantages and disadvantages. Some of the more important pros and cons of going public are presented in Exhibit 10–4.

By going public, it is possible that equity capital can be raised at stock prices that are high multiples of earnings, resulting in large amounts of capital in exchange for relatively few shares of stock. The fewer number of shares translates into less dilution of the original investors' ownership. However, this apparently low cost of equity financing can be deceptive. Underwriting costs are usually high, and the clerical costs of providing

Perspective 10–4

Health Care Stocks Continue to Be Good Investments

Although the Dow Jones industrial average increased almost 34 percent during 1995, health care stocks increased 40 percent. Mutual fund managers have increasingly channeled funds into health care stocks. Health care companies are achieving profits through consolidation and restructuring. Investors recognize the results and willingly purchase health care stocks which, in turn, pushes up the stock price.

Health care, however, is a complicated field—not just from the standpoint of science but from the perspective of the stock market as well. Many small investors simply do not know enough about the industry to pick the real winners. Those who recognize their limitations often pool their money with other less knowledgeable investors and let professional mutual funds managers do their investing. In January 1996, a record $24.5 billion was invested in equity mutual funds alone—a major reason why mutual funds have been so instrumental in the increases in health care stock prices. Invesco Strategic Health Sciences and Global Health Sciences have almost $2 billion invested exclusively in health care companies. The results have been impressive. In 1995, Strategic Health Sciences was up 59 percent and Global Health Sciences was up 68 percent.

Financial managers in health care organizations, however, need to recognize the risks of equity funds and the attraction of mutual funds. Just as institutional investors can amplify market increases, market decreases can also be amplified. This can be particularly significant to companies such as Community Health Services, Health Management Associates, Vencor, Columbia/HCA Healthcare Corporation, and Universal Health Services. Institutional investors own 81.5 percent of Community Health Services, 80.8 percent of Health Management Associates, 66.4 percent of Vencor, and almost 60 percent of Columbia/HCA and Universal Health Services.

Some fund managers see trouble for health care in the near future. Budget cuts in Medicare and Medicaid and forecasted "decelerations in industry fundamentals" have caused some institutional investors to begin reducing their holdings of health care stocks, although they remain bullish on the industry. A particularly favorable sector appears to be physician management companies.

Source: Sandy Lutz, "Healthcare Stocks Stoke Mutual Funds," *Modern Healthcare* 26, no. 9 (March 11, 1996), pp. 61–62.

Exhibit 10–4 • **Advantages and Disadvantages of Going Public**

Advantages

- Raises capital at lower cost.
- Keeps control in hands of insiders if they purchase additional shares.
- Maintains leveraging potential.
- Increases ability to obtain more equity.
- Retains shareholders' liquidity.
- Makes acquisition easy.

Disadvantages

- Makes disclosure of information necessary.
- Dilutes insiders' control.
- Costs to underwrite.
- Reduces original investors' percentage of ownership.
- Lessens ownership control in decision making.
- Increases taxes.

Source: From G. B. Shields and G. C. McKann, "Raising Health Care Capital Through the Public Equity Markets," *Topics in Health Care Financing,* Vol. 12, No. 3 (Spring 1986), pp. 38–40. © 1986, Aspen Publishers, Inc. Adapted by permission.

proper documentation as well as the loss of control by the present owners can be costly. This option is chosen, however, for reasons other than cost. Successfully going public usually makes it easier to raise equity capital in the future. Moreover, the improved equity position enables the organization to obtain additional debt funding based on the increased owners' equity.

Acquiring Debt   When funds are needed for expansion strategies, it is possible to reach the capital market through debt financing. Long-term debt in the form of tax-exempt bonds has been one of the largest single sources of capital funds for hospitals over the past two decades. However, demands to increase public services and the reluctance of elected officials to enact more taxes cause many to question whether or not governments at all levels will continue to allow tax exemptions. Indeed, the volume of hospital tax-exempt bond issues has declined from a high of almost $30 billion in 1993 as the result of capital investment and uncertainties about public attitudes.[12] To qualify for the federal tax exemption, bonds are issued by a state or local authority and the health care facility leases the financed assets from the authority, which holds the title until the indebtedness is repaid.[13]

In 1995, for the first time in a decade, Standard and Poor's Corporation raised more ratings of not-for-profit hospitals and health care organizations than it lowered. The credit-rating agency upgraded sixty-three health care ratings representing $2.4 billion of debt and downgraded fifty-five ratings representing $1.9 billion of debt. This is a significant reversal from 1994 when downgrades outpaced upgrades by a factor of 10 to 1. Obviously, the difference in the number of organizations upgraded and downgraded is relatively small. The difference in the amount of debt affected is accounted for by the fact that the organizations upgraded were generally larger and tended to carry more debt.[14]

Whether considering tax-exempt bonds, FHA-insured or conventional mortgages, or public taxable bonds, it is important to consider several issues before committing to long-term debt financing. The cost of long-term debt is determined by the coupon rate or the amount that must be paid to borrow the necessary money. In addition, costs are involved in issuing the debt. If the debt is privately held by a relatively few investors, the costs can be greatly reduced. However, if the bond issue is made to the public, certificates must be printed, information must be supplied to regulating authorities, the underwriters' spread must be paid, and sometimes reserve funds in the form of an escrow account must be maintained to minimize the public's risk.

Risk is an important consideration. To a great extent, the coupon or interest rate that must be paid reflects the perceived risk by the investors. However, the organization that issues the long-term debt must consider the risks as well. If debt is issued at a time when interest rates are very high, it may be desirable to build in a "call feature" whereby the debt can be refinanced when interest rates are lower. Despite a prepayment fee being charged, it may be beneficial to call in the debt if interest rates drop significantly.

Another aspect of risk is the ability of the organization to service the debt. If revenues are not available to pay the interest in a timely manner and retire the debt, closure is possible. Therefore, margin is an important indicator of a health care organization's ability to effectively service its debt payments (interest and contribution to loan reduction). In recent years, hospitals in particular have recorded lower margins. This results from accelerating expense increases and shorter lengths of stay. At the same time, margins have been reinforced by increases in admissions and outpatient visits.[15]

In deciding whether to use long-term debt, strategic managers are favorably influenced by the fact that control over operations and decision making can be maintained more easily than with equity financing. Although it is true that creditors can require restrictive covenants that reduce flexibility and control, the organization's ability to obtain financing for a promised return, without having to broaden participation in decision making, is attractive.

Other Forms of Debt Acquisition Health care organizations may prefer to deal with a single financial institution rather than numerous individuals and underwriters in the capital market. In such a case, funds can be obtained from banks or other financial institutions. The risks of bank financing, however, are the same as with other forms of debt. For example, OrNda HealthCorp purchased the St. Vincent Healthcare System using a substantial portion of the proceeds of a $168 million stock offering to reduce existing bank indebtedness. Prior to the public offering, OrNda was nearing its debt limit and the reduction of bank loans reopened its access to additional debt.

Other interesting and promising arrangements for financing are being developed in an effort to offset increased competition, pressure on profit margins, and related difficulties faced by companies that supply the goods and services needed by health care organizations. For instance, manufacturers of imaging equipment have abandoned the use of one or a relatively few standard financing packages in an effort to maintain the viability of the market.

Even some relatively nontraditional (at least in health care) financing methods are beginning to appear. One particular method, known as merchant banking, was pioneered in Europe centuries ago. Merchant bankers are people who engage in venture capital services with their own funds rather than pools of funds acquired from the general public. Thus, health care consultants and other industry insiders use their own money to invest directly in small to midsized health care companies that appear particularly promising.[16] Perspective 10-5 provides an illustration of how even strategic alternatives such as alliances and partnerships can be primarily motivated by the need for capital.[17]

These examples, although not exhaustive, illustrate some of the sources health care organizations have used to obtain capital and operating funds. Of course, the attractiveness of debt financing is influenced primarily by interest rates. Because rates have been at all time lows during the 1990s, debt financing has been particularly appealing.

Fund Raising and Philanthropy

During a time when capital markets are uncertain, when there is public resistance to tax increases (some of which might eventually assist health care organizations), and when a host of other problems complicate long-term financing, philanthropy is being "rediscovered" and pursued seriously by many health care organizations. Because of the need for earnings, the cost of public offerings, and the desire of many health care organizations to retain their tax-exempt status, private philanthropy has become more important as a source of funds in health care. In 1995, health-related not-for-profit organizations received over $11 billion in charitable contributions. Not-for-profit hospitals accounted for almost $5 billion—a 29 percent increase over 1994. Exhibit 10-5 illus-

Perspective 10–5

Finding the Capital to Recapture a Community Focus

More than 30 percent of San Diego, California's population is covered by HMOs. There is a considerable oversupply of hospital beds. For Sharp HealthCare, this spells trouble. Sharp began in the mid-1980s when it merged six solo hospitals under one corporate umbrella. In addition, it bought the assets of a large physician practice and attempted to retrofit the operations of the system in a manner that could effectively compete in a managed-care environment. Sharp's CEO was frustrated by the fact that tax-exempt financing was primarily dedicated to bricks and mortar projects, whereas bricks and mortar were not what he needed to deal effectively with current realities. Moreover, for-profit operations such as Columbia/HCA could always get capital cheaper than Sharp, thus providing a significant competitive disadvantage.

Access to capital is one of the major reasons Sharp began investigating an alliance with Columbia/HCA. If approved by California regulators, Sharp could stand to collect as much as $400 million to pay off debt and "boost its charitable mission." Programs relevant to health problems of the community such as wellness, disease prevention, and health education simply could not meet the financial requirements in San Diego's highly competitive health care environment. Some estimate that Sharp may have lost as much as $15 million in 1995. Sharp hopes that Columbia/HCA's ability to provide ready capital will be a logical match with Sharp's prestige and, although it has lost money in recent years, Sharp believes it has considerable "managed-care savvy."

Source: Kevin Lumsdon, "A Sharper Edge?" *Hospitals and Health Networks* 70, no. 5 (March 5, 1996), pp. 37–38.

trates the approximate distribution of charitable contributions for various causes in 1995. Giving to health-related causes ranks high in overall terms with almost 10 percent of total gifts. However, it is tied in relative terms with human services and far behind religious and educational causes.

It is important to note that over the past decade the sources of giving have changed in relative importance. According to the American Association of Fund-Raising Council, Inc., in 1984 corporations provided about 6 percent of total contributions, foundations 5 percent, bequests accounted for another 5 percent, and individuals 82 percent. However, in 1994, the corporate shares dropped to 5 percent, foundations increased to 8 percent, bequests represented about 6 percent of the total, and individuals gave 81 percent.

Private individual, corporate, and foundation gifts will remain an important source of funds for health care organizations. However, as with many other areas of activity, fund-raising is more competitive than ever. Educational, religious, and environmental organizations are actively seeking and acquiring funds. In the future, hospitals and other health care organizations will be pressured to become even more aggressive and innovative just to maintain their historical share of available gifts.

Effective Management of Financial Resources and Investment

Prior to pursuing the acquisition of new capital and operating funds, a careful examination of the utilization of existing financial resources should be conducted. Moreover,

Exhibit 10–5 • Distribution of Charitable Contributions to Not-for-profit Organizations in 1995

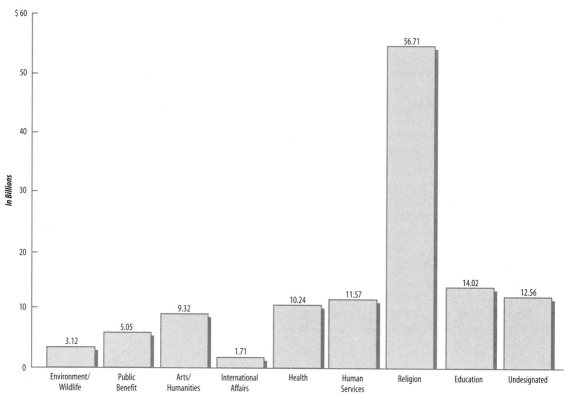

Source: From Giving USA 1996/American Association of Fund–Raising Council, Inc. Trust for Philanthropy. Reprinted by permission.

some strategic alternatives might actually be able to be funded through the better utilization of existing financial resources. For example, if the leadership of a long-term-care facility determines that enhancing quality demands significant increases in training expenditures, the funds for training might be acquired by reducing the amount in the cash account, more carefully managing and reducing inventories, or similar actions.

Some decisions may actually provide organizations with excess cash and near cash assets, at least temporarily. Divesting parts of an organization or liquidating major pieces of equipment will provide financial resources that must be carefully invested to ensure the highest possible returns or reallocated in some systematic manner.

Managing Financial Resources Health care organizations constantly face financial problems and the need to develop innovative ways to increase revenues, control costs, and thus increase profitability. Even in not-for-profit organizations, the extent to which income exceeds costs is an important measure of financial viability. Perspective 10–6 illustrates an ongoing controversy regarding hospital responses to Medicare reimbursement rates.

Perspective 10–6

Financial Realities of Medicare Reimbursement

Medicare inpatient hospital margins are up, and costs are dramatically down. Many health care policy experts say these are signs that cost-containment efforts under Medicare's prospective payment system are paying off; although others argue that the figures are misleading and may be impossible to sustain.

Don Young, Executive Director of the Prospective Payment Assessment Commission, has stated, "In the past two years, Medicare margins have shot up. Hospitals have controlled costs better in the private sector." Carmela Dyer, Vice President for Policy at the American Hospital Association, to some degree agreed and commented: "Medicare margins have improved because hospital care is more efficient. It's good management and we're proud of that."

AHA Health Statistics Group Vice President Joe Martin, however, urges caution. Martin is skeptical about how well PPS matches Medicare patients' needs and questions the success that recent margin figures seem to indicate. According to Martin, "The method for reporting costs is absolutely insensitive to special daily nursing costs of older patients." He continued that "reports overstate margins to the extent that Medicare inpatients need more nursing services." PPS margins, therefore, may be significantly overstated.

Source: Laurie Larson, "Weight of the World," *AHA News,* (June 10, 1996), p. 7.

Although not-for-profit organizations do not make profits as such, they do attempt to generate a surplus of revenues over expenses and thereby develop a fund balance or, at the very least, make enough income to cover costs. Not-for-profit health care organizations may not be as focused on the bottom line as for-profit organizations, but cost containment and revenue generation remain important and often critical issues. Therefore, all types of health care managers must carefully evaluate how effectively revenue-earning assets are used.[18]

In fact, much of strategic financial management relates to what is sometimes called the *financial management paradox.* This dilemma is derived from the fact that, in the management of financial resources, decision makers are forced to choose between two appealing outcomes: liquidity or profitability (excess of income over expenses). The great challenge for financial managers is to balance the organization's need to pay bills when due (liquidity) and the need to keep assets earning additional funds (profitability).

Liquidity relates to the speed and convenience with which noncash assets can be converted into cash. If the hospital's accounts receivable are current (no more than thirty days old), there is a high likelihood that they will be collected. Thus, they are considered to be very liquid because they can be converted quickly into cash. The older the accounts are, the less likely collection will occur, and therefore the less liquid are the assets.

The most liquid asset is cash. However, holding cash in the hospital safe or in a checking account at the local bank further illustrates the financial management dilemma. If the health care organization holds the cash in the safe, it earns no interest and generates no profit. Managers could put the cash into a savings account, use it to build more inventory, or purchase a specialized piece of medical equipment. Although these actions have the potential to generate profits, they also place cash assets into a less-convertible (less-liquid) state.

In not-for-profit organizations, the need for liquidity is as important as it is in any for-profit organization. Salaries must be paid at the end of each week, and vendors demand payment for supplies placed in inventories within thirty days in not-for-profit as well as for-profit settings. Therefore, although the not-for-profit health care organization does not specifically have the bottom-line profit figure to direct decision making, it must get the best return it can on its reserves and resources to accumulate funds to replace equipment, purchase new technologies, and so on. The Sisters of Mercy Health System in St. Louis, as discussed in Perspective 10–7, is an organization that has achieved financial results that are impressive by any standard.

Perspective 10–7

Not-for-Profit System Is a Model of Financial Management

Health care systems with stocks of cash, a strong balance sheet, and high bond ratings are usually thought of as for-profit business operations. However, the Sisters of Mercy Health System of St. Louis, a not-for-profit health care organization, has impressive credentials in this area. Even when its affiliation with Unity Health System is factored in, long-term debt represents less than 25 percent of total capital. The System has almost 225 days cash on hand; the median of other highly rated health care providers is only 177 days. In fact, the Sisters of Mercy Health System is one of only sixty-seven not-for-profit health care providers rated AA by Standard and Poor's Corporation. Moody's Investors' Service maintains an Aa rating for the System based on its "very good profitability, high levels of liquidity, and a modest debt load." In practical terms, what does such a high rating mean to a health care system? It means a great deal.

For one thing, because of its financial strength, the Sisters of Mercy Health System of St. Louis was able to sell $73.3 million worth of a $103.3 million tax-bond issue at variable interest rates. Although variable interest rates are more risky than fixed rates, the financial strength of the System allowed it to engage in this riskier strategy, which it believes will save interest costs over the twenty-year term of the debt. In order to bet on longer term interest savings, a health care organization has to have the financial strength to tolerate interest-rate peaks that may occur before maturity. The ability to assume such risks will allow the System, according to its calculations, to save $12 million dollars in interest cost compared with more traditional fixed-rate alternatives.

In addition, the Sisters of Mercy Health System was able to negotiate some favorable and unusual features into its bond covenants. This bond deal eased or eliminated covenants normally required of tax-exempt issuers of debt. Covenants establishing minimum levels of additional debt, property disposals, mergers, and so on are absent from this transaction. According to one financial expert: "Their [Sisters of Mercy Health System of St. Louis] strength was enough so that their liberal covenants did not impair the rating. Their practice of maintaining strong cash reserves and prudent use of debt provided some comfort."

Source: Karen Pallarito, "Not-for-Profit System a Model of Fiscal Fitness," Modern Healthcare 26, no. 1 (January 8, 1996), pp. 48–49.

In view of this ever-present conflict, paradox, or dilemma, the financial manager is required to constantly weigh the advantages and disadvantages of actions based on the impact each will have on liquidity and profitability. Although no attempt will be made to examine the details of assessing the financial management of a health care organization, the following section attempts to provide more insight into this challenging area.

Measuring Financial Capabilities   Information concerning key indicators of financial strength and weakness must be obtained and used in decision making. In analyzing key indicators, it is important to look at two types of measures. The first relates to how the organization compares with other similar organizations in the same industry. The second relates to how the measures for an organization are changing over time; that is, what trends can be identified for our own hospital, health department, or long-term-care facility?

Health care organizations customarily use a variety of measures to evaluate their financial capabilities. Two of these measures have been introduced. The first was *liquidity,* a measure of an organization's ability to convert its assets to cash and near cash assets. As previously noted, high liquidity implies that the organization is able to take all its assets and convert them into cash in a short time. Certain assets, such as petty cash, are perfectly liquid. Inventories and accounts receivable, depending on their age, are somewhat liquid and can be converted into cash by collecting the receivables or finding a buyer for them. Often this conversion does not result in a dollar-for-dollar exchange but the funds received are usually close to the dollar value. Many not-for-profit facilities have to plan for uncollectibles from indigent and uninsured patients.

The second measure was profitability (or, in the case of not-for-profit organizations, the extent to which income exceeds expenses). A customary measure of profitability is operating income divided by revenues. Further, the net profit margin and rate of return on investments are useful profitability measures. In recent years, as would be expected, for-profit health care organizations have achieved higher operating margins, on the average, than not-for-profit organizations. However, differences in organizational mission and focus account for much of the difference in profitability. Moreover, the higher margins come at a price, as illustrated in Perspective 10–8.

Three additional areas should be investigated: leverage, growth, and activity levels. As a measure of financial strength *leverage* relates to the choices strategic decision makers have made between debt and equity. The leverage of a health care organization indicates how much of its capital is borrowed compared to the amount invested by owners. Leverage is most often measured by the debt-to-equity ratio, or the result obtained when total debt is divided by stockholders' equity. When the health care organization is not owned by private investors, different measures such as fund balances must be substituted for stockholders' equity.

Growth measures are important factors in attempting to assess the financial strengths and weaknesses of a health care organization. Financial indicators of growth document the organization's progression in terms of its development in important areas such as revenues generated, contributions to fund balances, price/earnings ratio of the stock, and so on.

Finally, *activity measures* relate to how the management of the organization "turns over" certain assets such as inventories, receivables, and even beds in some cases.

Perspective 10–8

For-Profit Versus Not-for-Profit: What Do People Really Think?

A survey of public opinion by Louis Harris and Associates uncovered some interesting ideas Americans have regarding the relative merits of for-profit and not-for-profit health care organizations. According to the survey, most people believe that for-profit hospitals, HMOs, and health insurance plans provide better quality services but that not-for-profit health care organizations cost less and are more responsive to community needs.

Americans appeared particularly uneasy about the growth of for-profit hospital chains. Seventy percent of the more than 1,000 adults surveyed thought that local for-profit hospitals are better for the community than national for-profit chains. More than half (59 percent) of the respondents indicated that for-profit hospitals provided higher quality care, whereas only 35 percent thought that the services of not-for-profit hospitals were higher quality. However, 73 percent believed not-for-profit hospital services were less expensive.

When asked whether for-profit or not-for-profit HMOs provided the better services, the results were mixed. Forty-nine percent voted in favor of for-profits and 43 percent thought not-for-profits delivered better services. Fifty-four percent thought the trend toward for-profit health care was a "bad thing," but 46 percent indicated that they "trusted" for-profits as much as not-for-profits.

The survey uncovered several misunderstandings. Over 60 percent of the respondents thought hospitals were being purchased by organizations that specialized in businesses other than health care. Forty-six percent believed that state and local governments owned and operated more hospitals today than they did three years ago.

Source: Karen Pallarito, "Poll: For-Profits, Not-for-Profits Both Have Advantages," *Modern Healthcare* 25, no. 46 (December 18, 1995), p. 3.

Often, tracking the age of accounts receivable to determine an average collection period is used as one important measure of activity.

Decision makers usually look at comparative financial data for the industry as well as measures of liquidity, profitability, leverage, growth, and activity that apply to their own specific organizations to suggest the types of financial goals that might be achieved in a particular planning period. Frequently, it is necessary to use a variety of databases such as the Financial Analysis Service of the Healthcare Financial Management Association or the Strategic Operating Indicators, which provides sixty key indicators of hospital financial performance by city, region, bed size, bond rating, and so on.[19]

The liquidity versus profitability paradox and the assessment of financial strength have obvious implications for day-to-day operations, but the strategic implications are less obvious. However, it is important to remember that strategy and operations are closely linked. For example, the liquidity of a health care organization, in addition to providing some measure of how well current assets and liabilities are managed, will also influence the degree to which additional debt can be acquired from financial institutions. Moreover, the current financial strength of an organization determines to a great extent how aggressive it can be in entering new markets, what entry strategies it might use in introducing new services, and the extent to which it can invest in the latest medical technologies.

Effectively Managing Cash Flow One of the more difficult problems faced by health care organizations is the effective management of cash flow. Increasingly, all organizations have recognized that it is not enough to be profitable or to grow at a rate equal to or better than others in the industry.[20] The inflow of cash must be related to the outflow. That is, certain things such as salaries, rent, and utility bills must be paid by a particular date, and most health care organizations must plan carefully so that sufficient cash is on hand when needed. Although the organization may have large billings to patients, if payment has not been received, it will be forced to borrow to meet obligations at the end of the month. This involves extra expenses and is simply not good financial management. Therefore, cash-flow management is an important measure of the organization's financial capability.[21]

Cash flow is managed through a combination of two actions. The first is to accelerate cash inflows by converting accounts receivable to cash at the earliest possible time (get payments in the bank as fast as possible, impose a service charge on late payments, and provide incentive discounts for early payment). Accounts receivable are often singled out for special attention in improving cash flow because they constitute one of the more complex problems facing health care organizations. Unlike most business firms, health care organizations routinely deal with third-party payors such as Blue Cross, private health insurance companies, and federal and state governments. Often the necessity to file the proper forms (in the format dictated by each of the many third-party payors) and related logistical problems delay payment to health care providers.

Organizations, including hospitals and physicians' practices, sometimes sell their accounts receivable to companies that specialize in collecting the accounts. This provides an earlier inflow of cash for the organization. Customarily, the purchasers buy the accounts for some percentage of their value and make a return on the collections. When the accounts receivable become old and less likely to be collected, a collection agency may be employed to assist.[22]

Some companies, such as Principal Residential Advisors, buy bad debts of hospitals and physician practices. First-party accounts receivable that are four to six months and older may be considered uncollectible and sold for whatever can be obtained in the marketplace. Fraser Memorial Hospital, for example, sold Principal Residential Advisors over $1 million in bad debt for 4.7 cents on the dollar. Principal, in turn, sold the portfolio to United Asset Recovery for $52,000, kept 25 percent of the proceeds and gave Fraser Memorial Hospital the remaining $39,000. Although the recovery from the original amount was small, the hospital believed taking what it could get for these accounts was a better alternative than attempting to collect them or turning them over to a standard collection agency.[23]

The second approach to cash-flow management is to delay cash outflows as long as possible. This can be done by paying bills at the latest date possible to receive discounts, centralizing the payables function to ensure that procedures for avoiding early payments are followed, and keeping payroll funds in interest-bearing accounts as long as possible. Studies show that most employees wait a day or so before cashing their salary checks; therefore, with the proper data, an organization can probably keep payroll funds in interest-bearing accounts a few days longer and still cover salary checks when they are presented for payment.

Budgeting and Financial Planning   Planning is key to effective financial management and a crucial factor in estimating the ability of an organization to take strategic actions. An effective budgeting system is a health care organization's means of identifying the most efficient use of resources and the primary control mechanism to ensure that resources are used effectively.[24]

An effective budgeting system can assist an organization in accomplishing one of the most difficult strategic tasks facing managers: reallocating resources away from the less beneficial to the more beneficial programs. A variety of approaches to budgeting can be used in health care organizations. Which is the most appropriate will depend to a great extent on how the organization generates its support. If the health organization is supported by private investors, available corporate budgetary systems will likely apply. On the other hand, if the organization is publicly supported, techniques used effectively in government, such as zero-base budgeting and planning/programming/budgeting systems, may be more applicable.[25]

Managing Operations   Still another important source of financial resources is the improved management of existing operations. If work could be accomplished with fewer employees, collections made sooner, and the demand for external funding reduced, the health care organization's costs could be reduced.

Fortunately, new management techniques such as reengineering have the potential to greatly reduce billing cycles and collection times. One interesting case illustration is that of Maricopa Medical Center in Phoenix, which completed a year-long redesign of its finance department. In one fiscal year, Maricopa Medical Center had a $20 million loss on net patient revenues of slightly over $116 million. With the aid of Andersen Consulting, the medical center redesigned every major business function in finance, admitting, and patient registration in an effort to streamline the work.[26] One of the Medical Center's reengineering efforts is illustrated in Exhibit 10–6.

The important benefit from this reengineering project was improved use of existing financial resources so that more resources were available for alternative uses. Before reengineering, almost twenty activities were required to bill Medicaid. The process took from one to two months to complete. After reengineering, less than ten activities were required and the process could be completed in twelve to twenty-five days. Reengineering of this type can save considerable sums when the costs of the personnel required for the less-efficient process are included in the savings picture. This issue of saving funds through the more efficient and effective use of human resources highlights another important area that must be considered in any systematic strategic decision making.

Integrating Financial and Strategic Management

Strategic financial management is an important aspect of strategic management in health care organizations. Financial resources must reinforce the overall strategies of the organization or managers will be continuously frustrated in their ability to accomplish planned strategies. Exhibits 10–7 and 10–8 are included to provide a summary of the role finance and strategic financial management play in the overall situational analysis and strategic management of health care organizations.

Exhibit 10–6 • Reengineering the Medicaid Billing Process at Maricopa Medical Center

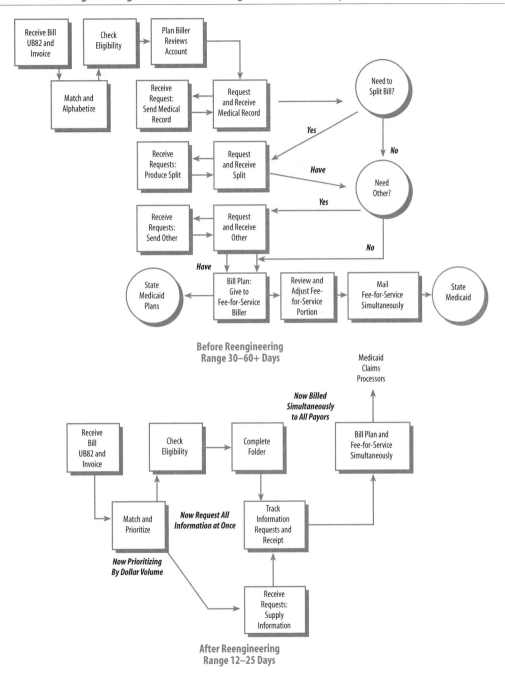

Before Reengineering
Range 30–60+ Days

After Reengineering
Range 12–25 Days

Source: From Judith Nemes, "Reconfiguring the Finance Department," *Modern Healthcare*, Vol. 23, No. 7 (February 15, 1993), p. 60. Copyright © Crain Communications, Inc., 740 N. Rush Street, Chicago, IL 60611. Reprinted by permission.

Exhibit 10–7 · **Financial Input to the Situational Analysis**

Situational Analysis	Financial Input to Situational Analysis
External Environment	
Financial Analysis	Determine the condition of financial markets including financial aspects of the economic environment, interest rate trends and projections, assessment of trends in philanthropic giving, determination of likely sources of funds other than customary financial institutions.
Competitive Financial Analysis	Comparison of financial data on competitors and potential competitors; analysis of financial strength of industry and various market segments; comparative financial ratios and industry standards for financial growth, liquidity, and activity measures.
Financial Market Analysis	Determine the purchasing capabilities of potential customers and the credit status of groups of potential customers in present and potential industries and locations.
Internal Environment	
Finance	Develop indicators of present financial strength; evaluate the strategic financial capacity of the organization; determine the degree to which the organization is capable of financing different strategies from internally generated sources.
Mission, Vision, Values, and Objectives	Ensure management understands the financial requirements for present and future operations; determine financial implications of possible changes in organizational mission; establish financial benchmarks and objectives to accomplish organizational mission and vision.

Exhibit 10–8 · **Strategic Financial Management Input to Strategic Management**

Hierarchy of Strategic Decisions	Financial Input
Directional Strategies	
Mission	Ensure understanding of financial requirements for building and maintaining organizational distinctiveness.
Vision	Determine ways of obtaining financial resources necessary to accomplish the organization's hope for tomorrow.
Values	Include clarification of importance of personal ethics and organizational responsibility in financial decision making.
Objectives	Participate in the formulation of organizational objectives; develop financial objectives to support accomplishment of organizational objectives.
Adaptive Strategies	
Expansion	
Diversification— Related and Unrelated	Assist in obtaining the funds necessary to finance the movement into related and unrelated services; assess the relative advantages of expanding existing operations or moving into related and unrelated areas; determine the relative mix of different sources of capital.
Vertical Integration— Forward and Backward	Assist in obtaining the funds necessary to finance the movement into backward and forward operations; assess the relative financial advantages of diversification and vertical integration; determine the relative mix of different sources of capital.
Market Development	Identify the sources of funds available for expanding the underserved geographical areas and market segments; determine the relative mix of different sources of capital.
Product Development	Evaluate the financial costs and benefits of different services that have been identified as possible additions to the service mix.
Penetration	Assess the availability of funds to support greater service differentiation, fuel promotional activities and other marketing efforts. Evaluate the effect of aggressive pricing strategies.

Exhibit 10–8 • **Continued**

Hierarchy of Strategic Decisions	Financial Input
Contraction	
Divestiture	Ensure the effective financial management of temporary excess funds until additional investment opportunities are located; focus on effective utilization of existing and newly generated financial resources through divestment activities.
Liquidation	Ensure the effective financial management of funds generated through liquidation of assets; evaluate alternative investment opportunities for financial resources generated from liquidation strategy.
Harvesting	Financial management of funds generated; evaluation of alternative uses of financial resources made available by harvesting.
Retrenchment	Evaluate and recommend areas where the greatest use of financial resources can be utilized in view of the more limited scope of operations.
Stabilization	
Enhancement	Identify sources of financial resources to be used in enhancement programs; assess the financial impact of alternative enhancement activities—quality programs, training and development, and so on.
Status Quo	Ensure effective financial management of existing resources.
Market Entry Strategies	
Purchase	
Acquisition	Evaluate the financial viability of target organizations; assess the organization's ability to finance the acquisition; recommend the appropriate sources of capital.
Licensing	Evaluate the financial impact of creating additional competition through the licensing process versus the potential gains from a licensing arrangement; assess the opportunities and financial impact of expanded licensing agreements.
Cooperation	
Merger	Examine and evaluate the financial condition of the merger target; assess the financial impact of the addition of the target organization to the present organization's service line; evaluate the consolidated financial strength of a new and larger organization.
Alliance	Evaluate the financial condition of partner(s); assess the financial synergies likely to result from cooperation.
Joint Venture	Assess the potential financial benefits and costs from entering a joint venture; consider the financial implications of association with a joint partner; evaluate the possibility of financial gains from additional joint venture arrangements.
Development	
Internal Development	Assess the availability of financial resources to support the proposed internal development activities.
Positioning Strategies	
Marketwide	
Cost Leadership	Evaluate the impact of a cost leadership strategy relative to the earnings goal of the organization; suggest ways of increasing efficiency in the use of financial resources without sacrificing quality of financial services.
Differentiation	Evaluate the financial impact of potential increases in costs resulting from differentiation relative to the projected increases in revenues resulting from differentiation efforts.
Market Segment	
Focus— Cost Leadership	Project the potential financial effects of cost leadership activities, expected increases in efficiency, and resulting effects on revenues for a given segment.
Focus— Differentiation	Project the potential financial effects of increasing differentiation—expected cost increases relative to forecasted revenue increases for a given segment.
Operational Strategies	
Functional—Finance	Ensure that financial operations are as efficient and effective as possible; assess the orientation of financial personnel to the internal customers of the organization; develop the strategic financial plan to support the mission and strategies of the organization.

Summary and Conclusions

In this chapter the financial implications of the adaptive strategies of expansion, contraction, and stabilization are discussed. Although financial resources are important reality checks to strategic decision making, the vision of management should not be limited by the financial resources available. Because vision is a hope for the future, it may be necessary to acquire more and different types of financial resources if future aspirations of the organization and its key stakeholders are to be achieved.

The strategic management of financial resources should be carefully integrated into the overall strategic management of health care organizations. Attention should be given to ensure that strategic financial planning is an integral part of overall strategic management.

Expansion strategies such as diversification and vertical integration frequently require additional financial resources. Implementation will require investigation of the different options for obtaining capital. A few of the more important sources of new capital are equity, debt, raising philanthropic funds from individuals or organizations, and more efficient use of existing financial resources.

Contraction strategies place different demands on financial resources. A health care organization that divests itself of existing programs, harvests the benefits of present operations, or liquidates parts of its business will likely find itself, at least temporarily, with excess funds in a liquid state. These overly liquid financial resources will have to be invested until more profitable long-term uses can be implemented. Stabilization strategies such as enhancing existing operations, services, and facilities require a great deal of expertise in the management of the steady state.

Financial resource strategies must be consistent with adaptive strategies and address the realities created by their implementation. Financial resources are one of the important "enablers" that determine to a great extent the success of decision makers in realizing the vision of the organization.

Key Terms and Concepts in Strategic Management

activity measures
budgetary financial planning
cash flow
comparative financial data
continuum of refinement

debt financing
equity funding
financial management paradox
going public
growth measures

leverage
liquidity
philanthropy
profitability
strategic financial planning

Questions for Class Discussion

1. Explain what is meant by the term *continuum of refinement.* Why is this concept important to effective financial planning in health care organizations?

2. What relationship does financial resource planning have to strategic planning? Should financial resource capabilities determine the aspiration levels of a health care organization? Explain your answer.

3. What are the important differences between budgetary and strategic financial planning? Which is more important? Explain your response.

4. What are the primary differences in the financial strategies needed for expansion, contraction, and stabilization? Which type of adaptive strategy is most difficult to implement from a financial perspective? Why?

5. List some of the primary advantages and disadvantages of going public. If you were the chief financial officer of a large health care organization, what advice would you give the CEO about going public to raise operating funds? Under what specific conditions would you advise in favor of a public offering?

6. Health care organizations are sometimes able to attract philanthropic funds from individuals and organizations to finance capital expansion. What are the advantages and disadvantages of using this type of funding to accomplish expansion plans?

7. Why is it important to relate stakeholder relations and the need for philanthropic fund-raising on the part of health care organizations? Do you think philanthropic gifts will become more or less important in the future as a source of funding? Explain your response.

8. Briefly explain the financial management paradox. Provide an illustration of this dilemma in the health care setting.

9. In what ways are financial growth measures different from financial activity measures? Which is more important in assessing the financial strength of a health care organization? Why?

10. How can the profitability needs of health care organizations be balanced with their unique mission to see to the health care needs of all people regardless of ability to pay?

Notes

1. R. D. Stier and C. L. Pugh, "The Strategic Linkage of Marketing and Finance," *Healthcare Forum Journal* 20, no. 2 (April 23, 1989), p. 37.

2. J. C. Folger, "Integration of Strategic, Financial Plans Vital to Success," *Healthcare Financial Management* 43, no. 1 (January 1989), pp. 22–32.

3. Donald Cook, "Strategic Plan Creates a Blueprint for Budgeting," *Healthcare Financial Management* 44, no. 5 (May 1990), pp. 21–25.

4. Adapted from Dale Anderson, "Impact of Strategic Financial Planning in the Health Care Industry," *Topics in Health Care Financing: Strategic Financial Planning* 11, no. 3 (Summer 1985), pp. 1–16.

5. A. E. Glenesk, "Six Myths That Can Cloud Strategic Vision," *Healthcare Financial Management* 44, no. 5 (May 1990), pp. 38–43.

6. Frank Cerne, "Balancing Complex Choices," *Hospitals and Health Networks* 67, no. 10 (June 20, 1993), pp. 28–30.

7. Robert Saunders, J. J. Mayerhofer, and W. J. Jones, "Strategic Capital Planning Scenarios for the Future," *Healthcare Financial Management* 48, no. 4 (April 1993), pp. 50–55.

8. "Buyers' Clout Costs Hospitals Credit," *Hospitals and Health Networks* 70, no. 8 (April 20, 1996), p. 12.

9. J. H. Arnold, "Assessing Capital Risks: You Can't Be Too Conservative," *Harvard Business Review* 64, no. 5 (September/October 1986), pp. 113–121.

10. William O. Cleverley, "Assessing Present and Future Capital Expense Levels Under PPS," *Healthcare Financial Management* 40, no. 9 (September 1986), pp. 62–72.

11. "Furman Selz/Modern Healthcare Composite Stock Index," *Modern Healthcare* 26, no. 1 (January 8, 1996), p. 48.

12. William O. Cleverley, "Capital Formation," in *Handbook of Health Care Accounting and Finance,* 3d ed., vol. 2, ed. William O. Cleverley (Rockville, Maryland: Aspen Publishers, 1989), pp. 803–821.

13. Frank Cerne, "Street Wise," *Hospitals and Health Networks* 69, no. 6 (March 20, 1995), p. 42.

14. Karen Pallarito, "Debt Ratings Rebounded in 1995 at Not-for-Profits," *Modern Healthcare* 26, no. 3 (February 5, 1996), p. 20.

15. David Burda, "AHA Paints Gloomier Portrait of 1995's Hospital Performance," *Modern Healthcare* 26, no. 10 (May 20, 1996), p. 3.

16. Karen Pallarito, "Old Financing Concept Gains New Ground," *Modern Healthcare* 25, no. 31 (July 31, 1995), pp. 34–35.

17. Jay Greene and Sandy Lutz, "A Down Year at Not-for-Profits; For-Profits Soar," *Modern Healthcare* 25, no. 10 (May 22, 1995), pp. 43–52.

18. L. C. Gapenski, W. B. Vogel, and Barbara Langland-Orban, "The Determinants of Hospital Profitability," *Hospital and Health Services Administration* 38, no. 1 (Spring 1993), pp. 63–80; and W. B. Vogel, Barbara Langland-Orban, and L. C. Gapenski, "Factors Influencing High and Low Profitability in Hospitals," *Health Care Management Review* 18, no. 2 (1993), pp. 15–26.

19. William O. Cleverley, "How Boards Can Use Comparative Data in Strategic Planning," *Healthcare Executive* 4, no. 17 (May 6, 1989), pp. 32–33; and James B. Goes and ChunLiu Zhan, "The Effects of Hospital-Physician Integration Strategies on Hospital Financial Performance," *Health Services Research* 30, no. 4 (1995), pp. 508–530.

20. William O. Cleverley and R. K. Harvey, "Profitability: Comparing Hospitals Results with Other Industries," *Hospital Financial Management* 44, no. 3 (March 1990), pp. 42–52.

21. C. E. Chastain and S. T. Cianciolo, "Strategies in Cash-Flow Management," *Business Horizons* 29, no. 5 (May/June 1986), pp. 65–73.

22. T. J. Kincaid, "Selling Accounts Receivable to Fund Working Capital," *Healthcare Financial Management* 47, no. 4 (April 1993), pp. 27–31.

23. Lisa Scott, "Firm Offers to Sell Bad Debts to Highest Bidder," *Modern Healthcare* 23, no. 6 (February 8, 1993), p. 34.

24. F. Hashimoro, A. Bell, and S. Marshment, "A Computer Simulation Program to Facilitate Budgeting and Staffing Decisions in an Intensive Care Unit," *Critical Care Medicine* 15, no. 1 (1987), pp. 256–259.

25. For some useful examples, see S. Duncombe and R. Kinney, "Agency Budget Success: How It Is Defined by Budget Officials in Five Western States," *Public Budgeting and Finance* 7, no. 1 (1987), pp. 24–37; and V. B. Lewis, "Reflections on Budgeting Systems," *Public Budgeting and Finance* 8, no. 1 (1988), pp. 4–19.

26. Judith Nemes, "Reconfiguring the Finance Department," *Modern Healthcare* 23, no. 7 (February 15, 1993), pp. 51–64.

Additional Readings

Bazerman, Max H., *Judgment in Managerial Decision Making* (New York: John Wiley & Sons, Inc., 1994). This book is a comprehensive review of the decision-making process with a focus on the importance of judgment. It provides a convincing argument that the purely quantitative aspects of decision making should not limit the vision of managers and organizations.

DeMuro, Paul R., *The Financial Manager's Guide to Managed Care and Integrated Delivery Systems* (Burr Ridge, Illinois: Irwin Professional Publishing, 1996). An overview of managed care and an applied view of how it fits into integrated delivery systems are the benefits of this book. The author traces financial trends and discusses the methods of provider payment, managed-care contracting, and capitation as preferred payment mechanisms. It is a practical guide to the detailed operations of managed care and integrated delivery systems.

Kolb, Deborah S., and Jennings Ryan, *Assessing Organizational Readiness for Capitation* (Chicago: American Hospital Publishing, 1996). Capitation creates a whole new financial reality for health care organizations. This book provides a self-administered survey that can help health care organizations determine their readiness for capitation. Evaluation takes place with regard to both structural and information readiness. Completion of the survey can assist organizations in actually setting priorities in preparing for managed care and capitation.

McLean, Robert A., *Financial Management of Health Care Organizations* (Albany, New York: Delmar Publishing, 1997). A comprehensive examination of financial management for health care organizations, this book focuses on the unique financial considerations in health care. Attention is given to the long-term as well as working capital needs. It includes information that is readily applicable to all types of heath care organizations.

Pyenson, Bruce S. (Editor), *Calculated Risk: A Provider's Guide to Assessing and Controlling the Financial Risk of Managed Care* (Chicago: American Hospital Publishing, 1995). This book provides tools and techniques to make informed decisions about risk-taking arrangements with managed-care organizations. Underpricing, fluctuation, and business risk are explained as are levels of risk associated with various payment mechanisms. A model is proposed that allows providers to gauge their ability to assume risk and formulate financial strategies relative to managed care.

Strategic Management of Human Resources

Learning Objectives

After completing this chapter you should be able to:

1. Understand the special nature of human resources in health care organizations and the role these resources play in accomplishing the unique mission of health care.

2. Understand the relationship between strategic human resources management and overall strategic management of health care organizations.

3. Discuss the human resources implications of adaptive strategies relating to expansion, contraction, and stabilization.

4. Understand the potential human as well as strategic issues involved in contraction strategies as they relate to human resources.

5. Understand the role of human resources in enhancing performance in stabilization strategies.

6. Discuss the decisions necessary to provide appropriate human resources for market entry strategies associated with expansion and stabilization.

7. Evaluate different methods of implementing human resources strategies.

8. Appreciate the importance of integrating human resources strategies into the strategic management process.

> "The average professional is different from the average worker in other environments: a difference based, I suspect, not on such things as educational levels, but on the psyche of those who choose professional careers."
>
> • *David H. Maister*

The Introductory Incident illustrates that organizations do not have to be mean to be lean. In fact, the Franciscan Health System of Cincinnati has managed to build human resources flexibility as well as preserve employee morale and productivity.

Health care organizations are faced with many conflicting demands. For example, the public continues to encourage health care organizations to be innovative, provide high-quality services, increase access, and contain costs. Often these desires are in conflict, and at times they are mutually exclusive. To illustrate the magnitude of the problem, consider how human resources management strategies relate to the three adaptive strategies of health care organizations.[1] Human resources strategies and implications are outlined in Exhibit 11–1.

Introductory Incident

Franciscan Health System of Cincinnati

Layoffs are a thing of the past at Franciscan Health System of Cincinnati. In 1991, the System began what it calls the employment security list. This program assures employees who lose their jobs because of job redesign and related improvements that they will stay on the payroll with their old salaries and benefits. They are placed in temporary jobs. While in these temporary jobs, a period which can last from a week to a year, displaced employees are offered retraining and educational opportunities designed to prepare them for a new position.

Since the beginning of the program, 356 employees have been placed on the list and 297 (83 percent) have been reassigned. Forty-nine employees resigned and ten are currently on the list. During this period Franciscan reduced its total number of employees by 14 percent—from 2,935 to 2,538 through attrition and elimination of unnecessary positions. Leaders believe the list has been instrumental in reducing the high cost of turnover and maintaining morale in a time of downsizing. The System calculates that it saved almost $10 million in labor costs over the five-year period.

The last layoff at Franciscan Health Systems in Cincinnati was in 1988 when 40 of its 3,000 positions were eliminated to reduce operating losses of $5.5 million between 1989 and 1991. The program, in other words, was started at a time when Franciscan was in the red; however, things turned around quickly and the losses were eliminated the following year.

The Franciscan Health System of Cincinnati has continued its innovative efforts with programs such as its quality improvement program designed to reduce costs. Through more than one hundred action teams, this program has been able to save almost $20 million in five years by streamlining clinical and administrative services.

Source: Jay Greene, "Security List a Win-Win for Workers, Health System," *Modern Healthcare* 26, no. 7 (February 26, 1996), p. 82.

Cost-reduction strategies require a particular type of human resources management system. The emphasis is on carefully designing and defining jobs that contribute to efficiency. Performance appraisal systems emphasize short-term results that directly affect quantified goals. Because jobs are narrowly defined, career paths tend to be equally narrow. Under a cost-reduction strategy, nurses enter the organization as nurses, do their jobs, and retire as nurses or perhaps nurse supervisors. The same is true of engineers and financial administrators. There is relatively little training and development because of the expense required and the uncertainty of a direct payoff.

When the focus is on quality, the human resources management strategy must change. Jobs tend to remain relatively fixed and narrow, but the "experts" or specialists have more input into how their jobs should be done in order to improve quality. Although appraisals tend to be short term and oriented toward specific results, more emphasis is placed on group performance. Because high quality demands the latest information, there is a high commitment to training and development.

Innovative competitive strategies require innovative human resources management strategies. They must focus on job designs that require close interaction and coordination among groups of individuals. Job descriptions in innovative organizations tend

Exhibit 11–1 · Strategic Human Resources Decisions

Cost-Reduction Strategy

1. Stable job descriptions that allow little room for confusion.
2. Narrowly designed jobs and narrow career paths that encourage specialization and efficiency.
3. Short-term, results-oriented performance appraisals.
4. Close monitoring of market pay levels in compensation decisions.
5. Minimal levels of employee training and development.

Quality-Enhancement Strategy

1. Fixed and explicit job descriptions.
2. High levels of employee participation in matters relating to the job itself.
3. Mix of individual and group performance appraisals that emphasize short-term results.
4. Egalitarian treatment of employees with some employment guarantees.
5. Extensive and continuous training and development.

Innovation Strategy

1. Jobs that require interaction and coordination among groups of individuals.
2. Performance appraisals that reflect long-run, group-based achievements.
3. Jobs that allow employees to develop skills that can be used in other parts of the organization.
4. Compensation that emphasizes internal equity rather than external markets.
5. Pay rates that tend to be lower but that allow employees flexible compensation packages.
6. Broad career paths that encourage employees to develop wide arrays of skills.

Source: From R.S. Schuler and S.E. Jackson, "Linking Competitive Strategies with Human Resource Management Practices," *Academy of Management Executive,* Vol. 1 (August 1987), p. 213. Adapted by permission of Academy of Management.

to be less specific to allow employees to develop multiple skills. In addition, these "loose" job descriptions allow for broader career paths and encourage individuals to move to where they are needed most in the organization. Although pay levels are not always high, compensation programs emphasize equity among group members and flexibility so that employees can design their own compensation packages to the extent possible.

Some Special Human Resources Challenges in Health Care

Health care organizations present a number of unique human resources management challenges. One of the most difficult problems facing hospitals, long-term-care facilities, and HMOs relates to the different skill levels required to accomplish the organization's mission. Simultaneously motivating and retaining physicians, plumbers, engineers, nurses, electricians, and the janitorial staff can be a human resources manager's nightmare. Research has shown that human resources management issues such as recruiting, staffing, evaluation, and training and development are directly affected by strategic choices at both the corporate and SSU levels.[2]

Managing Occupational Diversity

The art of effectively managing professionals despite their occupational diversity is essential in health care organizations.[3] Some professionals (nurses, laboratory scientists, and hospital-based physicians) are salaried, and others are independent such as private physicians with hospital staff privileges.

The changes and projected changes taking place in the health care environment make it difficult to predict precisely which health-related human resources will be demanded most in the future. Experts agree that health-related personnel will continue to be in high demand, as discussed in Perspective 11–1, although they may be needed in different types of organizations. For example, as hospitals downsize, many of those displaced will find employment in managed-care organizations, long-term-care facilities, and so on.

One area that has received too little attention is the retention of employees once they are hired. By focusing more on retention, a health care organization can reduce the necessity of competing directly for scarce human resources. A comprehensive study of employee retention in health care organizations suggested the following five-part program for retaining valued employees.[4]

1. *Pay for productivity.* Health care organizations of all types are attempting to reduce personnel costs. Accomplishing this objective will require that the most productive employees be retained and rewarded for exceptional performance that leads to significant productivity improvement.
2. *Encourage employee development.* Employees, especially professionals, view their current jobs from the perspective of career development. Effective staffing strategies demand that employees be given incentives and rewards for continuing their professional development.

| Perspective 11–1

Health Care Hiring Continues to Heat Up

Health care hiring accounted for one of every six new jobs in the United States during the 1980s. This outpaced other sectors of business by 250 percent. Most of the growth occurred in nonacute-care areas such as physician's offices, where employment grew by 74 percent.

A study entitled "Employment Trends in Hospitals 1981–1993" published in *Inquiry* outlined some of the more significant changes. One particularly interesting finding was that managed care has not halted the health care hiring as many predicted. During the years covered by the study, there was no significant difference in the growth of health care employment based on whether a state was saturated with managed-care firms or barely affected by them. Although the numbers are impressive, it is important to note that a great amount of uncertainty exists in health care because of downsizing and rumors of layoffs. It is important to remember that, in the area of human resources, often the human response is not based on statistics so much as it is on emotions.

Source: "Human Resources: Health Care Hiring Heats Up," *Hospitals and Health Networks* 70, no. 14 (July 20, 1996), p. 10.

3. *Match individual and organizational goals.* Beginning with initial recruitment, increased attention is needed to ensure that individual and organizational goals match. One effective motivator, as noted in Chapter 5, is to constantly keep the vision and purpose of the organization before all employees and do everything possible to ensure that the vision and purpose are related to individual aspirations.

4. *Encourage employees to voice dissatisfaction.* To keep valued employees, health care managers should provide opportunities for people to voice dissatisfactions rather than allow an atmosphere of fear and intimidation to develop.

5. *Reward loyalty.* Although longevity is not necessarily related to performance, those employees who remain loyal to the organization over the long term should be recognized and rewarded.

Special Staffing Problems Relating to Physicians

The strategic decisions of health care organizations are always affected to some extent by the staffing strategies designed to ensure an adequate supply of physicians. Because physicians ultimately determine whether a patient will be admitted to a particular hospital, human resources managers must focus a great deal of attention on physician recruitment and retention.[5] Frequently, staff physicians are given minimum income guarantees, relocation expenses, and even initial signing bonuses. Nonhospital-based physicians are sometimes given equally appealing incentives to admit patients to a particular hospital, such as favorable rental fees in professional office buildings and opportunities to spread some of the cost of insurance over a larger base.

One of the more innovative and elaborate strategies used to attract and retain physicians is the hospital/physician joint venture. This represents a type of partnership in which the private physician and the hospital decide to jointly purchase expensive equipment, buildings, or laboratory facilities. The advantage to the hospital is that the physician has a mutual interest in the success of the venture and the organization because of his or her cooperative investment. The physician benefits from the funds made available by the hospital.

As more physicians become high-level health care executives, they will also receive executive pay packages that have the effect of allowing them to participate in the success of high performance and assume the risk of low performing health care organizations. Some recent trends in the use of long-term incentives are presented in Perspective 11–2.

Emphasizing the Unique Mission of Health Care

The public health sector is likely to continue to experience a competitive disadvantage relative to the private sector in terms of money and benefits. Even in the for-profit health care sector, there are dedicated personnel whose attraction to the field goes beyond monetary rewards alone. If the personnel shortages among health professionals are to be properly addressed by strategic decision makers, it will be necessary to focus on some of the "strategic uniquenesses" of health care that were discussed in Chapter 5.

Some of these important unique characteristics of the health care field can be effectively used as "currencies" to attract and retain professional employees.[6] The term

---

| Perspective 11–2

Long-Term Incentives in Health Care Organizations

If health care organizations are serious about positioning themselves for the long term, they have to ensure a continuing supply of experienced executives. If executives are expected to engage in long-term strategic thinking, there must be an incentive for such action. Incentive programs have been used successfully in other industries to encourage this long-range orientation, and they are becoming more widely used in health care organizations.

For example, a survey of 237 health care organizations by the William M. Mercer Company reported some interesting results. About 17 percent of the surveyed organizations had long-term incentive plans and another 41 percent were considering such plans. Further, the researchers examined proxy statements from fifty of the largest publicly held health care companies and found that all of them used long-term incentives.

Of the 237 health care organizations surveyed, 35 percent of the for-profits used long-term incentives, 50 percent offered executive stock options, and 22 percent used pay-for-performance plans. Only 13 percent of the not-for-profits had long-term incentive programs, but 100 percent had pay-for-performance plans. Of the organizations surveyed, only 10 percent had long-term incentives available to direct-care providers but 76 percent involved providers in pay-for-performance plans. Twenty-seven percent of the managed-care organizations in the sample used long-term incentives, 61 percent had pay-for-performance plans, and 28 percent used stock options.

Source: "Rewards over the Long Haul," *Hospitals and Health Networks* 70, no. 4 (February 20, 1996), p. 17.

---

currency is used in this context to describe any type of resource that can be exchanged for something else of value. In this case, the question becomes, what can the health care organization offer in terms of a strategic or long-term nature that might give it an advantage in attempting to attract scarce resources in the labor market? Some examples might be:

1. *Inspiration-related currencies.* Health care professionals can be offered the vision of being involved in a unique type of work that helps other people. Public-sector employees can be offered the vision of offering unique services to people regardless of their ability to pay. Excellence, the opportunity to do important things well, and the moral correctness of providing health services to everyone are important inspiration-related currencies as well.

2. *Task-related currencies.* Health care strategists can offer unique attractions to health professionals by giving them opportunities to learn new and challenging technologies and by offering resources that encourage professionals to obtain the educational and work experiences that will allow them to remain up to date in their professions.

3. *Position-related currencies.* Health care organizations can recognize professionals for high levels of performance and provide opportunities for networking that will give them visibility and recognition beyond a single organization.

4. *Relationship-related currencies.* Being a part of a highly professional environment can offer unique opportunities for interaction with other individuals who share similar interests and vision.

5. *Personal-related currencies.* Perhaps the greatest currency of all is the strategic manager's ability to offer professionals an important return on the time and energy they have invested in preparing for a career of service. The return includes gratitude, a sense of ownership, freedom from bureaucratic hassles, and affirmation of the basic service-oriented values that attracted them to the profession initially.

This "strategic reorientation" away from a salary- and benefits-driven recruitment and motivation philosophy could do much to attract and retain the kinds of health care professionals who are capable of providing the high-quality services desired in both private and public health care organizations. Certainly, compensation rates must be reasonable and equitable. However, we increasingly recognize the truth in the statement: "The difference between employees who perform well and those who do not is not how much they are paid but how they are treated."[7] Specifically, with respect to professional employees it is clear that meaningful products from their labor, freedom to use personal judgment, time to do quality work, and challenge are the primary motivators of high performance.[8] Perspective 11–3 provides an illustration of how one HMO attempts to

---

Perspective 11–3

Get with the Program and Prosper

HMOs are known for driving their doctors and pinching pennies. ConnectiCare, Inc. realized that keeping physician salaries as low as possible was self-defeating. It certainly would not result in organizational loyalty.

Senior Vice President Paul Buestein, M.D., stated that "we wanted doctors to feel good about what they do, instead of feeling an HMO is only interested in money." So ConnectiCare, Inc. devised a bonus system that rewarded physicians for achieving plan goals. Three hundred doctors were surveyed and asked what criteria and behaviors were important enough to warrant a bonus. The resulting Primary Care Recognition Program rewards doctors on the basis of quality of care, member satisfaction, resource management, member access, and participation in the plan. Some criteria were weighted higher than others.

ConnectiCare physicians can earn up to 25 points for the quality of care they give, which is determined by a review of the medical charts. Patient satisfaction is also worth 25 points and is determined by patient surveys. Complaints about doctors are factored into the scores. Resource management and cost-effectiveness are also monitored.

The program is a year old, and the first bonuses will be distributed soon. Although the HMO probably will not save money in the short run, Buestein hopes that encouraging practice efficiencies will cut health care costs in the long run. He said, "We wanted to go beyond money and educate physicians about how we wanted them to practice in a managed-care environment."

Source: Katherine Morrall, "A Payoff to Get with the Program," *Hospitals and Health Networks* 70, no. 2 (January 20, 1996), pp. 50–51.

reward doctors for things the doctors believe are important as well as for financial performance.

Human Resources Decisions in Adaptive Strategies

Adaptive strategies force human resources issues. Expansion, contraction, and stabilization demand an ongoing evaluation of governance and organizational structures. In addition, they demand that specific actions be taken to ensure human resources are employed in an efficient and effective manner, as illustrated in Exhibit 11–2. Expansion requires different human resources actions, depending on the specific positioning strategy employed.

In understanding the various strategic choices and their implications, refer to Exhibit 11–2 for a summary of the more important aspects of human resources implications. Organizations go through a number of stages in their life cycles. Although there are many theories and even more labels for the different stages, most agree that organizations experience growth, maturity, and decline. The magnitude of change required on the part of health care organizations in each stage will depend on how prepared they are

Exhibit 11–2 • **Adaptive Strategies and Human Resources Decisions**

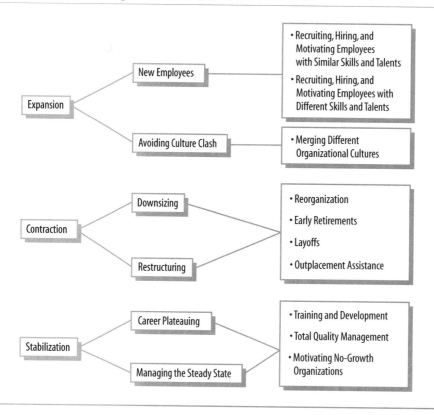

to deal with the different strategic, organizational, and human resources management problems of each phase of the organizational life cycle.

Human Resources Considerations During Expansion

Expansion strategies such as related diversification will make it necessary to recruit new personnel with skills and talents similar to those already in the organization. Unrelated diversification and backward and forward vertical integration will create the need for human resources with skills and talents different from those presently employed. The necessity of recruiting, hiring, and leading individuals with different skills and talents is a major reason that these strategies are "riskier" than related diversification. Any one of these strategies requires the merger of similar or dissimilar organizational cultures, presenting yet another human resources challenge.

Exhibit 11-3 provides an example of the growth-preparedness matrix and illustrates how different changes are needed under different conditions. If the organization is in the mature stage, the primary focus is on efficiency. An organization such as a general hospital with a reasonably long history generally has its services well defined and the human and nonhuman resources to deliver the services efficiently in place. The hospital may not, however, be prepared for rapid growth. If new opportunities develop that present the potential for significant growth (such as expansion into psychiatric hospitals), the organization must be prepared to take advantage of the opportunity for expansion. Organizational changes will be required to accommodate the increased size and diversity of the organization. Staffing and human resources management strategies will require similar changes.

Diversification and Vertical Integration   More attention has probably been devoted to related and unrelated diversification than to any other strategic alternatives.[9] Diversification, as noted in Chapter 6, is selected as a strategic alternative when management believes that markets outside the organization's core operations offer significant growth

Exhibit 11–3 · Growth-Preparedness Matrix

Source: From C.A. Lengnick–Hall and M.L. Lengnick–Hall, "Strategic Human Resources Management: A Review of the Literature and a Proposed Typology," *Academy of Management Review*, Vol. 13 (July 1988), p. 461. Adapted by permission of Academy of Management.

opportunities. Theoretically, diversification is chosen to improve performance by entering new and promising areas or to reduce the risk of having "all our eggs in one basket." Some evidence suggests that there is indeed a trade-off between risk and performance.[10] That is, the more an organization engages in unrelated diversification to avoid financial risk, the less likely it is that it will obtain high levels of performance in overall operations because of potential organizational and human resources management problems. This seems to occur so consistently in health care organizations that strategic managers frequently end up divesting unrelated operations to concentrate more on what they know best—health care.[11]

One study of 570 hospitals that belong to eight hospital systems found four primary practices that distinguished the successful from the unsuccessful organizational diversifications.[12] These *best practices,* as they were called, involved (1) a diversification plan that was closely linked to physicians' interests; (2) plans that were strategically driven and focused on the markets to be served; (3) new services that were different from the acute-care inpatient services already offered but close enough to benefit from present expertise and past experience; and (4) market entry at an opportune time. In other words, the most successful diversification experience has occurred when the strategy was deliberate and planned, when it recognized the reality of dependence on physician acceptance, took advantage of experience and expertise, and was well timed. The necessity of physician acceptance as well as the importance of individual experience and expertise illustrates the importance of human resources for the successful implementation of strategies. Perspective 11–4 illustrates the importance of thinking carefully about engaging in seemingly risk-free strategies such as physician-hospital integration.

Although diversification and integration are two very different strategic choices, they require similar types of organizational and human resources management responses. In these illustrations, one underlying fact is clear: when diversification or integration is selected as a strategic alternative, the potential exists that organizational size and diversity will increase as will the demand for more specialized human resources management services.

Moreover, to ensure that organizations are structured properly and human resources management is coordinated, certain types of transaction costs between and among the different organizations and organizational units must be taken into account. These transaction costs are the costs associated with handling market or interunit transfers within an organization, such as the transfer prices charged by the hospital-owned laundry that provides services for a number of other facilities.[13] The costs associated with this type of operation are not always evident on the financial statements of the organization. For example, the costs of recruiting laundry staff as well as the administrative costs associated with motivating and leading individuals in the laundry must be considered. As noted earlier under occupational diversity, the needs and skills of laundry workers are quite different from the needs and skills of nurses and physicians. This requires sensitive management, and the costs of providing this attention should be carefully monitored so that the true costs of diversification and integration are known.

When a hospital decides to enter the long-term-care market, it ventures outside its area of expertise—short-term acute care. For this reason, organizational and human resources management problems are likely. As size increases, there may be pressure to add another functional unit to specialize in long-term care. In addition, special organi-

Perspective 11–4

Making Deals for Good Reasons Only

Hospital-physician integration has been a popular strategy during the 1990s. Because some experts estimate that physician decision making affects 80 percent of health care costs, tremendous strategic and financial advantages should be achieved through this type of integration. As promising as this type of strategy may be, many, if not most, of the determinants of success relate to human as well as financial resources. The following guidelines have been suggested in evaluating the potential of a hospital-physician integration strategy.

1. Cost management will require innovative solutions to physician relations. Clinical pathways, formulary selections, and related areas offer considerable opportunities for cost savings. Physicians influence all of these important decisions.

2. Trust is the first element of a successful business plan. In light of today's competitive environment and tight margins, trust is as important as profits.

3. Governance is more than ownership. Physicians want more than an equity interest. Board membership and involvement in setting strategic direction is a must.

4. Primary care is essential but not sufficient. Primary care may be the foundation of an integrated system but specialty care remains a major source of profits. Ideally, successful integration fosters a group practice culture.

5. It has to be right. Never get caught up in merger mania. If the human resources side as well as the numbers are not right, walk away from the deal.

Source: Chris Kane and Karen Duke, "Ready. Set. Wait!" *Hospitals and Health Networks* 70, no. 12 (June 20, 1996), p. 51.

zational units may be needed to deal with domiciliary housing, health promotion programs, outreach efforts such as alcohol and substance-abuse programs, and other forms of rehabilitation. Recruitment, performance appraisal, training and development, compensation, and employee relations become more complex. New services and new clients require different specialists. The typical hospital does not have an established network to effectively recruit specialists in the newer fields nor sufficient knowledge of the work to evaluate the performance with confidence. In addition, there is little understanding of the training and development needs of the new professional staff and limited information about compensation customs.

The acquisition of new technologies, different medical services, and additional health care professionals greatly complicates the staffing or human resources management function. Once these new types of resources are identified and employed, it is necessary to review and probably revise the performance-appraisal system to ensure that the new employees are fairly evaluated and compensated. The increasing diversity of the skills required by the organization makes employee relations more difficult to develop and maintain. Professional and occupational jealousies and conflict place tremendous demands on human resources personnel and line managers.

There is increasing need for managed-care specialists within all types of health care organizations, from hospitals to home health care providers. The ultimate goal of managed care is to provide quality medical services at reasonable costs. This requires an entire array of health professionals who have clinical training and experience as well as a "head for business." To be successful, managed-care firms "need to combine business astuteness with medical knowledge and medical understanding."[14]

Whether to centralize or decentralize human resources management is a question that must be addressed. Centralization occurs when a single human resources management unit is established to develop staffing and related policies, recommend evaluation procedures, and ensure that all regulatory requirements are met. If the human resources management activities are delegated more to the individual functional units and the central human resources staff provides only overall management support, decentralization has occurred.

One illustration is the divisional structure put in place when Methodist Medical Center, a 465-bed medical center in St. Joseph, Missouri, merged in the early 1980s with the 205-bed St. Joseph Hospital to form Heartland Health System. Specialized units were added to provide an organizational home for the new services provided and to combine these new services with those already available to clients. In addition to the physician and service changes, Heartland developed a divisionalized structure located in the Heartland Center with services relating to the elderly, rehabilitation, and chronic diseases. The Heartland Samaritan Center for Human Development specialized in addiction recovery and mental health. By establishing these specialized, relatively autonomous units, decision making for specialized care could take place at the level closest to the patient.[15]

In organization structures such as Heartland's, human resources management and staffing activities are usually very decentralized, and the challenge is to ensure that excessive duplication of administrative functions does not take place. Because the divisions are relatively autonomous, it is tempting for each one to have its own human resources, data processing, and accounting units. Thus, the trade-off is important—those activities that are truly unique to the SSU should be focused at that level with only oversight at the corporate level, whereas those activities that do not relate specifically to the SSU should be centralized to achieve economies of scale.

Finally, it is important to remember that whenever a health care organization grows, diversifies, or integrates through acquisitions or mergers, there is potential for *culture clash.* Different organizations, which may have been former competitors, have different histories, missions, and traditions. The combined organizations do not "fit" together without effort. A new mission and vision must be conceived and communicated. The importance of achieving synergy is paramount.[16] Before the Sioux Valley Hospital and New Ulm Medical Clinic in Minnesota merged, the two organizations were going in different directions, and no effort was made to coordinate actions or policies. To build the kind of "oneness" required for future success, great care was taken to foster the development of a single culture to avoid any form of culture clash.[17]

When organizations are combined, there is considerable concern about what happens to the employees in the acquired health care organization. One study found that 75 percent of the executives in acquired industrial firms were gone after five years.[18] Because health care has been growing so rapidly, the outlook appeared to be somewhat better. Despite the fact that jobs might have been eliminated in one organization, there have been opportunities in others. However, in light of economic pressures, health care may become more similar to industrial firms.

Human Resources and Other Expansion Strategies In health care, there are a number of hybrid organizational arrangements that have strategic implications for health care organizations and are used in many cases as means of facilitating expansion. Some of these arrangements, such as pooled purchasing and facility management groups, are not new. Others are not only new but innovative.

Hybrid organizational arrangements involve two or more independent organizations that combine to pursue common interests.[19] These organizations are commonly referred to as *quasi-firms* because they are composed of highly autonomous organizations loosely coupled to achieve long-term strategic purposes. Some of these arrangements are very familiar in the health care sector. Preferred provider organizations (PPOs), independent practice associations (IPAs), and some health maintenance organizations (HMOs) are quasi-firms.[20]

Although quasi-firms have a variety of structures, they all share one important characteristic: they are the result of cooperative expansion strategies. In each case, strategists make a decision to cooperate rather than compete, even if the cooperation is relatively uncoordinated, to take advantage of certain perceived long-term advantages.[21] These arrangements can vary from extremely tight and formal legal arrangements to relatively "loose" group practices "without walls" similar to that implemented by Premier Medical Group, P.C. in Denver, Colorado. This type of practice allows physicians to centralize many support functions such as data processing and human resources, develop a more powerful marketing strategy, and experience a number of other economies of scale while preserving the autonomy and practice style of each physician.[22]

All of these cooperative expansion strategies, including the joint operating company discussed in Perspective 11–5, have important human resources implications. For example, physicians and hospitals sometimes decide to "pool" their resources to pursue an opportunity neither is prepared to pursue alone. These internal corporate joint ventures (ICJVs) are unique in that the parties remain independent and invest their own money, although the activity takes place within the organizational structure and is subject to the governance of the overarching health care organization.

One study examined fifty-three hospitals and their physicians who initiated such arrangements. The goals of the ICJVs were to expand primary-care services to the community, increase referrals within the group, and increase the hospital's market share of admissions.[23] This analysis of ICJVs offered several important insights for organization structure and human resources management. First, hospitals and their boards of directors assumed responsibility for the ICJVs' performance and maintained the right to make policy decisions relative to operations. Each ICJV, however, was established as an organizational entity with its own bylaws, mission statement, and strategic goals. The organizational unit was staffed internally and thereby maintained a great deal of operational autonomy. Finally, the ICJVs annually negotiated with the hospital to determine compensation levels and the range of services to be rendered.

Pragmatically, the ICJV possesses many of the characteristics of a SSU in the divisionalized form of organization. In fact, the study cited previously pointed out one of the often unanticipated problems that can develop when such a "division" is given autonomy not afforded to others. Initially, there was a significant amount of staff resistance to the establishment of the ICJVs. Some insiders feared that the new ventures would compete with the hospital for patients, beds, and services. Others simply had a philosophical disagreement with the hospital over forming such associations.

Perspective 11-5

Overcoming Barriers to Cooperation

It looked like it might never happen. Leaders had a vision of Mid-America Health First, an affiliation among St. Luke's Health System, Shawnee Mission, and five other hospitals in the Kansas City, Missouri, area. Last year the original plan to merge St. Luke's, Shawnee, Carondelet Health System's two hospitals, and two other area hospitals fell apart. Eventually, the idea of a joint operating company emerged and resolved the primary stumbling blocks, at least between St. Luke's and Shawnee Mission. Under this arrangement, there is a single governing body and a single management team to operate both organizations. The assets will not be merged but the cash flows, operating income, and debt will be merged in order to achieve tight financial control.

Although the assets will be owned by the sponsoring boards, management responsibility will rest in a new twenty-member board with ten members from St. Luke's, seven from Shawnee Mission,

and three physicians. The joint operating company makes sense for both partners because it provides economies of scale, sophisticated management, and gives the two organizations a real "sense of presence" in a market where other systems are emerging. Ultimately, it allows the partners to share instead of compete. The challenge, as is often the case, will be avoiding governance and culture clash problems because St. Luke's is almost three times as large as Shawnee. Integrating former competitors can be expected to surface human issues and problems. This is especially true in health care organizations where physical space, personalities, and trust-valued ways are unique to the setting.

Source: J. Duncan Moore, Jr., "Kansas City–Area Hospitals in Link," *Modern Healthcare* 26, no. 8 (April 15, 1996), p. 16.

The primary human resources issues are related to the ICJV's ability to develop its own management team, marketing strategies, and budgetary controls. Some of these, of course, could be centralized and provided by the larger administrative infrastructure already in place in the hospital. However, it is important to provide as much operational autonomy as possible for the ICJV or it becomes nothing more than a SSU of a single organization.

Organizational alliances are more common, loosely coupled arrangements. These cooperative groups consist of three or more hospitals (or other health care organizations) that pool their resources to achieve strategic objectives.[24] Cooperative expansion strategies (joint ventures, quasi-firms, alliances, and so on) avoid some of the more troubling organizational and human resources management problems because the loosely coupled organizations remain autonomous. However, there are issues of organizational governance that must be considered. In the case of a group purchasing alliance, provisions for policy making and representation of the individual member organizations must be addressed. At the same time, because a staff will be required to manage the day-to-day operations, understandings must be reached about the extent of each person's authority.

To this point, we have examined appropriate organizational/human resources management responses to expansion strategies. Although the problems are difficult and demanding, expansion is always more fun to manage than maturity and decline. During maturity, the emphasis is on efficiency. Human resources management practices must be constantly refined and improved to ensure that things are done in the best way at the least cost. However, organizations do not always successfully manage maturity, and markets erode and even disappear. Therefore, it is important for the strategic health care manager to also understand how to manage the organizational and human resources aspects during market contraction.

Contraction and Human Resources

Contraction involves different human resources management skills. Incentives must be devised to encourage employees to find other jobs or to retire earlier than anticipated. For some, layoffs may be necessary, and the organization will be forced to determine its responsibility in assisting displaced employees to find alternative employment opportunities. At times, health care organizations may assist employees by retraining them for different tasks that will be needed as contraction takes place.

In Chapter 6, several contraction strategies such as divestiture and liquidation were discussed. Although terms such as divestiture and liquidation imply financial actions, they have important human resources implications in the form of restructuring and reorganizing, early retirements, layoffs, and so on.

Specifically, in the case of divestiture or liquidation, recruitment for new personnel to fill essential positions is extremely difficult. It is not easy to attract qualified applicants who might assist in turning the organization around when less-essential employees are being terminated. Recruitment is difficult (if not impossible) in times of organizational decline. Employee relations are difficult as well. It is a challenge to maintain morale and productivity in the midst of organizational decline even though compensation, training and development, and appraisal activities may be simplified.

More serious, however, are the human resources decisions that require actual layoffs of personnel. These decisions, sometimes referred to as *downsizing* or *rightsizing,* can come in a variety of forms. Cost-driven downsizing takes place when health care organizations remove a specific number of employees from the payroll to reduce costs by a certain percent or absolute amount. Downsizing may also take place through attrition, hiring freezes, and so on.[25] Targeted restructuring takes place when particular parts of the organization such as the emergency room are eliminated or people in a certain department are laid off. Chicago's Rush-Presbyterian-St. Luke's Medical Center, for example, eliminated 220 positions through a combination of attrition, consolidation of jobs, and a layoff of eighty-five employees to "decelerate the increase in prices."[26]

It is difficult to determine precisely how many hospital employees have been laid off in recent years through downsizing, reengineering, and work improvement methods. It has been estimated that from 1993 to January 1996, 140 hospitals or health systems laid off a total of almost 24,000 employees or an average of a little over 170 per hospital.[27]

The human resources implications of downsizing and layoffs for those who lose their jobs are obvious. However, it is important to note that reorganizations can carry implications for the performance of the organization. A study by E. C. Murphy, Ltd., a New York–based research and consulting firm, found that hospitals that reduce staff for financial reasons are up to four times more likely to experience increases in patient morbidity and mortality. The study examined the staffing structures of 281 general acute-care hospitals and the work practices of more than 72,000 health care workers and concluded that hospitals that make across-the-board staff reductions of 7.6 percent or more for financial reasons were 400 percent more likely to experience increases in patient death or injury.[28] Interestingly, in an American Management Association survey of downsizing companies, including health care organizations, only one-third of the respondents were successful in accomplishing their primary objectives in the layoffs. Unless general work practice changes, such as through reengineering, are combined with staff reductions, organizations simply have fewer people doing inefficient operations.[29] The adverse effects on patient care are worse than before the downsizing.

The real and potential adverse effects of layoffs, no matter what they are called, are simply too serious in health care organizations for many leaders to assume the risks of reductions in the quality of services and patient care. When InterMountain Health Systems in Salt Lake City determined that it needed to eliminate fifty jobs, a program was developed to prevent future layoffs. Under InterMountain's Salary and Benefits Continuation Program, employees displaced because of job and work redesign are placed in temporary positions until new positions are found. Similarly, since the Mayo Clinic's layoff of 400 employees in 1994, much of its quality improvement efforts have been directed toward averting layoffs while maintaining its reputation as a health care leader.[30]

A more dramatic case of contraction (closure after merger into a larger system) is provided by Woodruff Hospital in Cleveland, Ohio.[31] The acquiring organization made provisions to rehire more than 40 percent of the initially displaced personnel; and because of the market area, almost all personnel eventually found comparable employment. Unfortunately, before the final merger was completed, year-long negotiations with another hospital were terminated and employees were not informed about the differences in the proposals under discussion. The result was that the agreements of the final merger were very different (especially in regard to the effect on personnel) than what had been communicated originally to employees.

The direct short-term effects on personnel were quite significant. Almost half of the employees blamed the closing of Woodruff on poor management, and a majority did not believe they had been adequately informed or prepared for the closing. Three-quarters of those who lost jobs indicated that the closing was an extremely stressful experience. The greatest problems were considered to be tangible loss of wages and a sense of not belonging. The long-term effects, however, appeared less dysfunctional, although about one-quarter of the terminated employees reported being unemployed at the time of the follow-up study about four months later. Of those who had been reemployed, 50 percent had obtained similar-level jobs, 30 percent had lower-level jobs, and about 20 percent had actually received promotions.

Strategically, the process of managing organizational degeneration is challenging and difficult. Studies of organizational decline (including bankruptcy and liquidation) show certain patterns. Decision makers tend to become paralyzed by the events and indecisive about what to do to prevent further decline. When they do act, the actions are often wrong. For example, managerial imbalances develop when executive-level decision makers from critical functional areas such as nursing, medicine, marketing, and finance are replaced by individuals with less knowledge concerning these important areas.[32] Additional ill-advised actions include an excessive focus on centralization of control and efficiency measures at a time when innovation is needed.[33] At no other time are decision makers more likely to focus exclusively on short-term solutions to serious and recurring problems.

Effective management of organizational contraction demands clear and courageous decision making. The environment created by decline makes the quest for excellence difficult if not altogether impossible. Uncertainty characterizes the organization and insecurity can increase the likelihood of reductions in the quality of services delivered. The challenges to the effective management of organizational decline are great. If a turnaround is to be achieved, inspiration as well as good decision making is crucially important. Perhaps more than anything, honest and timely communication is needed to reduce as much as possible the uncertainty and insecurity faced by the very people who must perform if the organization is to survive.

Managing Stabilization Strategies

The benefits of systematically managing the human resources dimension under expansion and contraction strategies are somewhat obvious. The need for carefully managing stabilization strategies is equally important, if not as obvious.

Stabilization strategies almost always require training and development activities. Enhancement strategies through total quality management programs involve significant commitments to continuous learning on the part of the individual and the organization. Status quo requires the challenging task of keeping people motivated in the face of career plateaus.

When an organization reaches a point in its life cycle where it is no longer growing, it must work extremely hard to keep from contracting. Strategic decision makers may adopt a conservative strategy, such as managing the steady state or status quo. As was noted in Chapter 6, the assumption underlying this strategy is that the expansion phase of the organization's evolution is over, maturity has been achieved, and that acceptable market shares have been attained. Relative to human resources strategies, the goal is likewise conservative. The organization attempts to replace personnel with employees of similar skills and training and works to keep existing personnel up to date and technologically prepared to perform their jobs at high levels of effectiveness.

Stabilization can present an opportunity to enhance current levels of operation. This stage of organizational development can be looked on as a temporary "breather," and preparation can commence for the next period of growth. Or, decision makers can simply think of stabilization in a dynamic sense and recognize that they must work hard just to maintain their current position. In this case, they may choose to enhance their facilities, improve the quality of their services, increase the speed with which they respond to patients and make decisions, and create new and better ways of doing things.[34] Human resources strategies are important to support any attempt at enhancement because ultimately it is the employees that must improve quality, innovate, and work faster if things are to improve.[35]

Organizational Enhancement Through Human Resources Strategies

Different management methods have human resources implications. However, few have received as much attention and emphasis in recent years as total quality management. Exhibit 11–4 provides an overview of some specific ways in which the total quality

Exhibit 11–4 • Human Resources Issues and TQM

Human Resources Characteristics (corporate culture)	Traditional Paradigm (individualism, profits, autocratic, specialization)	TQM Paradigm (teamwork, autonomous work groups, coaching, customer/patient focus)
Communication	Top Down	Multidimensional
Voice and Involvement	Employment at Will	Due Process, Quality Circles, Attitude Surveys
Job Design	Industrial Engineering Focus	Cross Functional, Empowerment, Innovation
Training	Job Related and Technical	Continuous Learning, Problem-Solving Skills
Performance Measurement and Evaluation	Individually Focused	Team Focused
Rewards	Individual Merit	Team Merit
Health and Safety	Treat Problems	Prevent Problems
Recruitment, Promotion, Career Development	Supervisor Driven	Driven by Contribution to Team Effort

Source: From Richard Blackburn, "Total Quality and Human Resources Management: Lessons from Baldrige Award–Winning Companies," *Academy of Management Executive,* Vol. 7, No. 3 (August 1993), p. 51. Adapted by permission of Academy of Management.

management and continuous improvement philosophies can be implemented relative to human resources considerations.[36] Overall, as the top portion of the exhibit illustrates, the traditional culture paradigm based on individualism, autocratic leadership, profits, and productive efficiency is replaced with collective efforts (teamwork), cross functioning rather than specialized work groups, coaching and enabling, and a focus on customer/patient satisfaction. Human resources management plays an important role in achieving this culture change.

Organizational communication, traditionally viewed as top down, is encouraged to become multidimensional—top down, bottom up, lateral, or some other combination. Employment at the pleasure of management gives way to due process in disciplinary matters, quality circles, and employee attitude surveys. Job design based on industrial engineering concepts moves to autonomous work teams that facilitate innovation and better ways of doing things. Training is oriented more toward continuous development and problem solving and less toward traditional technical skills-oriented learning. Performance measurement and evaluation are based less on individual attainment, financial focus, and supervisory grading and more on team accomplishments, customer satisfaction outcomes, and service delivery. Rewards likewise are less individual in character and more team oriented. In recognition of the contemporary realities facing health care organizations, health and safety issues are more preventive in character and less problem focused. Finally, hiring, promotion, and career development revolve less around the judgment of supervisors and more on group input. Downsizing and maturity cause career development to be horizontal and less hierarchical.

Enhancement through a focus on quality is significantly changing all types of industries, and health care organizations are becoming increasingly involved in this movement. Numerous organizations have attempted to develop approaches that uniquely fit their situation. Regardless of the characteristics, it is important for an organization to develop a benchmark based on the best practices in the industry. Perspective 11–6 illustrates how practice guidelines software has been useful in reducing the cost of medical treatment.

Perspective 11–6

Enhancing Operations with Practice Guidelines

Insurance companies and self-insured employers are in a constant battle to control health care costs. Historically, the costs have won. Insurers and self-insured employers are leveling the playing field somewhat through the use of practice guideline software packages. Health Risk Management, Inc. has offered practice guidelines software since 1978.

In Minneapolis, Minnesota, QualityFIRST uses practice guidelines software to assist doctors and care managers in selecting the best treatment option for each patient. Potential cost savings are based on the belief that front-end diagnosis offers the greatest opportunity for savings. The goal is to select the right therapeutic option in the first place. Accepting the computer-generated guidelines is complicated by the somewhat unique nature of health care services. On one hand, it is personal and knowledge based. On the other hand, it is reduced to protocols that make it particularly suited for simulation and programming. This is a threatening prospect for many caregivers.

QualityFIRST guidelines are based on the published medical literature and consider both the quality and effectiveness of treatment options. When more than one treatment option is available,

the software identifies the most appropriate. Presently, there are guidelines available for over 200 medical/surgical and behavioral health diagnoses. New ones are added every three months.

Health Risk Management practice guidelines have been applied extensively to workers' compensation areas and have claimed impressive results. By using guidelines early, injured employees can be provided the types of care that will aid their recovery and ensure a faster return to work. For example, in one case of an injured railroad worker, it was estimated that the cost of treatment could have gone as high as $13,611 with a loss of twenty-four workdays. According to observers, the practice guidelines made it possible for the railroad's occupational medical clinic to treat the worker for $800 and hold the loss of workdays to seventeen. A thirty-day follow-up found no evidence of problems or complications resulting from the recommended treatment.

Source: Anne Nordhaus-Bike, "How to Save Big Bucks: Insurers," _Hospital and Health Networks_ 70, no. 5 (March 5, 1996), p. 22.

Enhancement Through Redesign Reengineering and redesigning have made an impact on all areas of organizational life. Health care is no exception. The results of reengineering and redesign efforts have been mixed; yet health care executives, in their quest to control costs and improve services, continue to look for all possible options to aid in accomplishing these goals.[37]

Jersey Shore Medical Center in Neptune, New Jersey, initiated a redesign effort that was expected to cut 25 percent of controllable costs. The means of achieving the savings included collapsing whole departments and patient-care units, eliminating job categories, creating a few new ones, and changing completely the way drugs and other supplies traveled from storage rooms to patients. The 25 percent reduction is, of course, a stretch goal but it was established to symbolize the seriousness of the program and also to underscore the importance of becoming increasingly efficient in response to managed care. The Jersey Shore redesign is the sum of sixty subplans affecting many departments and satellite operations. Ultimately, the objective is to cut the budget by more than $19 million. Redesign and reengineering efforts almost always have direct human resources implications because job specialization is reduced as are the number of job descriptions, and work becomes redefined in terms of completing a process rather than merely doing a task or a job.

Although reengineering and redesign efforts are relatively new, there are some emerging guidelines from actual experiences that can assist in avoiding some of the traps and obstacles such efforts involve. Five of the most important are discussed below.

Always Tell the Truth Sinai Hospital of Baltimore had to cut $26 million or 11 percent of its budget. No thank you notes were received by CEO Warren Green when he shared the news with Sinai's 3,000 employees. However, according to him, "That's the price you pay for honesty." In the end it is hoped that the whole truth and concrete actions will build trust. Sinai, for example, has cut its management positions almost in half and has involved employees in identifying where the savings can be achieved with the least impact on patient care.

Plan, Plan, and Plan Some More Reengineering and redesign rarely happen the first time. So much of strategic management is learning by doing, which means that plans must be constantly reevaluated and revised. At Jersey Shore, COO (chief operating officer) Michael Schwartz compares the redesign program to navigating the Amazon. He has a compass and provisions but no one can assure him he will arrive at the planned destination. There are too many surprises and too many traps to focus on a single path. Flexibility and rethinking are essential.

Plan, Yes; But Also Commit At Sinai Hospital, the cost of the reengineering effort has reached $2.5 million. That is why the CEO says this type of strategy is "not for the faint of heart." Remember this investment is taking place while devoted and loyal employees are worrying about their jobs. Even the most conscientious may ask, "Why spend so much on consultants, meetings, and planning? Why not save jobs instead?" These are good questions, and any honest leader has to be prepared to deal with them. Jobs are important, but preparation for the future requires significant and sometimes risky investments in the present.

Expect Resistance Several years ago Jersey Shore experienced a nurses' strike that lasted 98 days. It resulted from the hospital's refusal to drop a plan for giving pay raises based on merit rather than seniority. Less than a year later, management returned with a reengineering proposal that would likely cost two dozen registered nurses their jobs. This is risky business. Even though health care professionals may agree, in theory, that redesigning the nurses' jobs to remove activities that did not require their degree of training stands the tests of business and professional logic, workforce reductions will be resisted. Again, honesty in the beginning and throughout the process is the best policy.

Change Hurts At Jersey Shore 300 employees will have to apply for new jobs and engage in extensive and intensive training in order to assume expanded duties. However, massive layoffs have been avoided by filling only the most critical vacancies and offering early retirement to others. There are a substantial number of vacant positions for which displaced employees may apply if they are properly qualified. That, however, means retraining, adjusting to new conditions, and uncertainty. As has been noted, strategic management is about change. It recognizes that change hurts; but it also illustrates that change is the key—perhaps the only key—to long-term organizational and occupational survival.

Even the best intentions, however, will not ensure success in work reengineering and redesign. Medical City Dallas Hospital decided to drop its Care Redesign program to reduce fear and improve employee morale. The hospital CEO stated that the program had good intentions but there were problems of implementation. One of the goals of the program was to reduce the number of job categories from more than 250 to a dozen or so. These efforts appeared to many as a threat to job security, and predictable morale problems developed.[38]

This concluding section of the chapter has discussed many of the human resources implications of different strategies in health care organizations. Human resources provide important reality checks to strategic decisions in health care organizations. If the human resources necessary to support today's mission and tomorrow's vision are not developed, strategies will not be realized. Exhibits 11–5 and 11–6 assist in summarizing some of the ways in which human resources contribute to situational analysis and to the overall strategic management of health care organizations.

Summary and Conclusions

This chapter discusses the human resources implications of expansion, contraction, and stabilization. It is important that human resources planning be carefully integrated into the overall strategic management process of health care organizations. However, the vision of management should not be limited by the existing quantity or quality of human resources. Human resources, similar to financial resources, are important "enablers" and reality checks but not the sole determinant of what a health care organization should aspire to become as evidenced by the vision of its leaders.

Expansion strategies such as diversification and vertical integration frequently require additional and different types of human resources. If expansion strategies such as related diversification are adopted, the new employees may possess the same skills

Exhibit 11–5 · Human Resources Input to Situational Analysis

Situational Analysis	Human Resources Input
External Environment	
Analysis of Human Resources	Assess elements of macroenvironment that possess human resources implications: availability of adequately trained workforce; socioeconomic status of present and potential employees; cultural diversity.
Competitive Human Resources Analysis	Evaluate available pool of employees relative to competitive organizations; carefully assess critical human resources areas such as nursing and physicians.
Internal Environment	
Human Resources	Assess present strength relative to human resources; inventory existing skills relative to mission and vision for the future; evaluate succession planning activities.
Mission, Vision, Values, and Objectives	Ensure management understands the human resources requirements for present and future operations; determine human resources implications of possible changes in organizational mission; establishment of human resources benchmarks and objectives to accomplish organizational mission and vision.

Exhibit 11–6 • Human Resources Management Input to Strategic Management

Hierarchy of Strategic Decisions	Human Resources Input
Directional Strategies	
Mission	Ensure understanding of human resources requirements for building and maintaining organizational distinctiveness.
Vision	Determine ways of obtaining human resources necessary to accomplish the organization's hope for tomorrow.
Values	Include clarification of importance of personal ethic and organizational responsibility in human resources decision making.
Objectives	Participate in the formulation of organizational objectives; develop human resources objectives to support accomplishment of organizational objectives.
Adaptive Strategies	
Expansion	
Diversification— Related and Unrelated	Assess available human resources pool relative to similar skills needed for related diversification; build network to assist in obtaining the unfamiliar skills needed for unrelated diversification; evaluate advantages of decentralized versus centralized human resources operations.
Vertical Integration— Forward and Backward	Build a network to obtain the unfamiliar skills needed to staff vertically integrated operations; evaluate advantages of decentralized versus centralized human resources operations.
Market Development	Identify the sources of human resources needed for expanding the underserved geographical areas and market segments; determine the incremental human resources needed to support market development.
Product Development	Evaluate present human resources and assess the additions needed to support service development activities.
Penetration	Assess the availability of human resources needed to support greater service differentiation, staff promotional activities, and marketing efforts.
Contraction	
Divestiture	Assess the capacity of the organization to absorb human resources displaced by divestiture; evaluate the organization's commitment to assisting displaced employees with outplacement efforts; evaluate any acquiring organization's commitment to provide opportunities for existing employees.
Liquidation	Evaluate the organization's responsibility to displaced employees; consider the use of outplacement services; assess the organization's capacity to absorb employees from liquidated operations; evaluate acquiring organization's willingness to continue employment of present human resources.
Harvesting	Initiate efforts to retrain employees presently in areas of harvesting; develop a program to offer retraining opportunities to employees desiring such services and outplacement opportunities for those who do not.
Retrenchment	Evaluate and recommend areas where greatest use of human resources can be achieved despite more limited scope of operations; evaluate the capacity of the organization to absorb employees displaced by retrenchment activities.
Stabilization	
Enhancement	Identify specific training and development activities needed to support enhancement efforts.
Status Quo	Ensure effective management of human resources.
Market Entry Strategies	
Purchase	
Acquisition	Assess the human resources of the target organization; evaluate the target organization's culture relative to present organizational culture and plan for any expected culture clash; evaluate the ability of the organization to absorb the human resources of the acquired organization.
Licensing	Negotiate the precise relationship and responsibilities to employees of other organizations as part of a licensing agreement.

Exhibit 11–6 · **Continued**

Hierarchy of Strategic Decisions	Human Resources Input
Cooperation	
Merger	Assess the possibility of culture clash from merging of organizations; evaluate advantages of decentralized versus centralized human resources operations and any possible human resources synergies from the merger.
Alliance	Evaluate the human resources condition of the partner(s); assess human resources synergies likely to result from cooperation; precisely state the reciprocal responsibilities of cooperating organizations to employees of all organizations.
Joint Venture	Consider the combined human resources capabilities of joint venture partners for possible synergies; evaluate the human resources that will be needed to support the venture but are not currently available in either partner to the venture.
Development	
Internal Development	Assess the availability of human resources to support the proposed internal development activities.
Positioning Strategies	
Marketwide	
Cost Leadership	Assess the human resources implications of cost leadership—particularly any temporary or permanent displacement of employees resulting from efficiency measures; assist employees that may be displaced by efficiency measures.
Differentiation	Consider whether different types of human resources will be required for increased differentiation efforts; plan for acquisition of any human resources needed to support the differentiation strategy.
Market Segment	
Focus— Cost Leadership	Project the potential human resources effects of cost leadership activities and expected increases in efficiency.
Focus— Differentiation	Project the potential human resources effects of increasing differentiation; assess the pool of human resources needed for increased differentiation relative to those currently available.
Operational Strategies	
Functional— Human Resources	Ensure that human resources operations are as efficient and effective as possible; assess the orientation of human resources personnel to the internal customers of the organization; develop the strategic human resources plan to support the mission and strategies of the organization.

and training as present employees. Unrelated diversification and vertical integration, on the other hand, will require employees with different skills and training. This is one of the primary risk factors for expansion, as little may be known about how to hire, manage, and lead these new types of employees.

Human resources implications of contraction strategies are particularly threatening because they often mean downsizing, layoffs, early retirements, and alternative career paths for devoted and loyal employees. Although there are no easy solutions to contraction strategies when it comes to human resources, a convincing argument can be made that systematic planning can sometimes eliminate the need to take extremely radical actions and allow time for employees to find alternative careers and employment.

Stabilization strategies such as enhancing existing operations and improving the quality of services have a direct impact on human resources. Reengineering processes demand that traditional ways of doing things be altered and improved. Those who have devoted years to learning how to succeed under existing systems may find reengineering, redesign, and work transformations almost as threatening as layoffs. Total quality management offers an appropriate option for enhancing operations and improving services. However, although total quality management has become an increasingly popular method for enhancing operations, some believe that data remain too limited to assess the success or failure of TQM and related techniques.

Key Terms and Concepts in Strategic Management

benchmarking

best practices

culture clash

growth-preparedness matrix

inspiration-related currencies

occupational diversity

personal-related currencies

position-related currencies

relationship-related currencies

task-related currencies

Questions for Class Discussion

1. What are some useful ways to deal with the diversity of employees in health care organizations? Briefly discuss each factor.

2. What is meant by the term *currency* as used in this chapter? List and briefly define some of the more unique currencies valued by health care organizations.

3. Why is it important to avoid allowing the quantity and quality of present human resources to determine the vision of a health care organization? What is the proper role of human resources when planning for the future?

4. What are the primary differences in the human resources strategies needed for expansion, contraction, and stabilization? Which type of adaptive strategy is most difficult to implement from a human resources perspective? Why?

5. Are work redesign and reengineering really worth the investment it takes in terms of time, money, and energy? What do you see as the primary problem involved in evaluating the effectiveness of reengineering and work redesign projects in terms of their impact on human resources?

6. Why do you think job redesigns and work transformations are so threatening in health care organizations? Do you think

employees in industrial organizations are more or less threatened by these measures? Why or why not?

7. Can human resources strategies be effectively implemented without addressing the issue of organizational culture? How is culture related to job redesign and work transformations?

8. What type of adaptive strategy is most likely to benefit from systematic benchmarking and the consequent development of best practices? Why did you select this strategy?

9. Do you think employees resist enhancement strategies that alter the way they do their jobs? Explain your answer.

10. Is honesty really the best policy when it comes to human resources strategies that adversely affect job security? If you agree that honesty is the best policy, what are some important costs of honesty? What are the likely outcomes if something less than total honesty becomes the organizational policy?

11. What are five specific actions leaders could take to make reengineering efforts more acceptable to health care employees? Explain your response.

Notes

1. Scott A. Snell and Mark A. Youndt, "Human Resource Management and Firm Performance: Testing a Contingency Model of Executive Controls," *Journal of Management* 21, no. 4 (1995), pp. 711–731.

2. R. S. Schuler and S. E. Jackson, "Linking Competitive Strategies with Human Resources Management Practices," *Academy of Management Executive* 1, no. 3 (August 1987), pp. 207–219.

3. J. A. Raelin, "An Anatomy of Autonomy: Managing Professionals," *Academy of Management Executive* 3, no. 3 (August 1989), pp. 216–228.

4. H. L. Smith and Richard Discenza, "Developing a Framework for Retaining Health Care Employees," *Hospital Topics* 67, no. 3 (May/June 1989), pp. 26–32.

5. David Burda, "And What Is Your Bid for This Loyal Admitter? Please, Don't Hold Back," *Modern Healthcare* 20, no. 2 (January 15, 1990), pp. 22–27ff.

6. For an innovative application of the currency metaphor, see A. R. Cohen and D. L. Bradford, *Influence Without Authority* (New York: John Wiley & Sons, 1990), Chapter 4.

7. J. S. Livingston, "Pygmalion in Management," *Harvard Business Review* 65, no. 5 (September/October 1987), p. 118.

8. David H. Maister, *Managing the Professional Service Firm* (New York: Free Press, 1993).

9. For a debate on the pros and cons for diversification in health care, see Jeffrey A. Alexander and Beaufort B. Longest, Jr., "Diversification in Health Care: Point and Counterpoint," *Strategic Issues in Health Care Management,* ed. W. J. Duncan, P. M. Ginter, and L. E. Swayne (Boston: PWS-Kent Publishing Co., 1992), pp. 11–33.

10. Yegmin Chang and Howard Thomas, "The Impact of Diversification Strategy on Risk-Return Performance," *Strategic Management Journal* 10, no. 5 (May/June 1989), pp. 271–284.

11. J. R. Williams, B. L. Paez, and L. Sanders, "Conglomeration Revisited," *Strategic Management Journal* 9, no. 5 (September/October 1988), pp. 403–414.

12. S. M. Shortell, Ellen Morrison, and Susan Hughes, "The Keys to Successful Diversification: Lessons from Leading Hospital Systems," *Hospital and Health Services Administration* 34, no. 4 (Winter 1989), pp. 471–492.

13. S. S. Mick, "Explaining Vertical Integration in Health Care: An Analysis and Synthesis of Transaction-Cost Economics and Strategic Management Theory," in S. S. Mick and Associates, eds., *Innovations in Health Care Delivery* (San Francisco: Jossey-Bass, 1990), pp. 207–240.

14. R. C. Harnett, "Managed Health Care Needs Its Own Kind of Specialists," *HealthWeek* 4, no. 21 (June 11, 1990), p. 73.

15. See L. C. Kruse, "Heartland Health System: Merged Hearts and Minds," *Healthcare Executive Briefings*, (May/June 1989), pp. 3–4.

16. J. W. Hunt, "Changing Pattern of Acquisition Behavior in Takeovers and the Consequences for the Acquisition Process," *Strategic Management Journal* 11, no. 1 (January 1990), pp. 69–78.

17. Bill Siwicki, "Hospital, Clinic Merger Proves Advantageous, Perhaps Prophetic," *Healthcare Financial Management* 48, no. 4 (April 1993), p. 26; and "Developing a Collaborative Culture in a Hospital Setting," *Health Care Strategic Management* 11, no. 1 (January 1993), pp. 7–10.

18. Caren Siehl, Dayle Smith, and Ann Omura, "After the Merger: Should Executives Stay or Go?" *Academy of Management Executive* 4, no. 1 (February 1990), pp. 50–60; and J. E. Gutknecht and J. B. Keys, "Mergers, Acquisitions, and Takeovers: Maintaining Morale of Survivors and Protecting Employees," *Academy of Management Executive* 7, no. 3 (August 1993), pp. 26–36.

19. Bryan Byrys and D. B. Jemison, "Hybrid Arrangements as Strategic Alliances: Theoretical Issues in Organizational Combinations," *Academy of Management Review* 14, no. 2 (April 1989), pp. 234–249.

20. Roice Luke, J. W. Begun, and D. D. Pointer, "Quasi-Firms: Strategic Interorganizational Forms in the Health Care Industry," *Academy of Management Review* 14, no. 1 (January 1989), pp. 9–19.

21. B. B. Longest, Jr., "Interorganizational Linkages in the Health Sector," *Health Care Management Review* 15, no. 1 (1990), pp. 17–28.

22. D. L. Schryver, G. A. Niederman, and B. A. Johnson, "Establishing a Group Practice Without Walls," *Health Care Strategic Management* 11, no. 1 (January 1993), pp. 18–21.

23. S. M. Shortell and E. J. Zajac, "Internal Corporate Joint Ventures: Development Processes and Performance Outcomes," *Strategic Management Journal* 9, no. 6 (November/December 1988), pp. 527–542.

24. H. S. Zuckerman and T. A. D'Aunno, "Hospital Alliances: Cooperative Strategy in a Competitive Environment," *Health Care Management Review* 15, no. 2 (1990), pp. 21–30; and Douglas Gregory, "Strategic Alliances Between Physicians and Hospitals in Multihospital Systems," *Hospital and Health Services Administration* 37, no. 2 (Summer 1992), pp. 247–258.

25. "Hospital-Staff Downsizing Can Have Effect on Patient Mortality and Morbidity," *AHA News* (November 8, 1993), p. 3.

26. Geri Aston, "Employees Bear Brunt of Hospital Push to Streamline Operations," *AHA News* (August 2, 1993), pp. 1, 5.

27. "Retooling Without Layoffs," *Modern Healthcare* (February 26, 1996), p. 76.

28. "Hospital-Staff Downsizing Can Have Effect on Patient Mortality and Morbidity," p. 3.

29. Sharon B. Schweikhart and Vicki Smith-Daniels, "Reengineering the Work of Caregivers: Role, Redefinition, Team Structures, and Organizational Redesign," *Hospital and Health Services Administration* 41, no. 1 (1996), pp. 19–36.

30. This case is based on information from M. K. Petchers, Sandra Swanker, and M. K. Singer, "The Hospital Merger: Its Effect on Employees," *Health Care Management Review* 13, no. 4 (1988), pp. 9–14.

31. "Retooling Without Layoffs," p. 76.

32. R. A. D'Aveni, "The Aftermath of Organizational Decline: A Longitudinal Study of the Strategic and Managerial Characteristics of Declining Firms," *Academy of Management Journal* 32, no. 3 (September 1989), pp. 577–605.

33. M. D. Fottler, H. L. Smith, and H. J. Muller, "Retrenchment in Health Care Organizations: Theory and Practice," *Hospital and Health Services Administration* 31, no. 3 (Fall 1986), pp. 29–43.

34. K. M. Eisenhardt, "Speed and Strategic Choice: Accelerating Decision Making," *Planning Review* 20, no. 5 (September/October 1992), pp. 30–32.

35. Bryan Dieter and Doug Gentile, "Improving Clinical Practices Can Boost the Bottom Line," *Healthcare Financial Management* 47, no. 9 (September 1993), pp. 38–40; and T. H. Davenport, "Need Radical Innovation and Continuous Improvement? Integrate Process Reengineering and TQM," *Planning Review* 22, no. 3 (May/June 1993), pp. 6–12.

36. R. J. Schonberger, "Is Strategy Strategic? Impact of Total Quality Management on Strategy," *Academy of Management Executive* 6, no. 3 (August 1992), pp. 80–87.

37. Much of this section is summarized from Kevin Lumsdon, "Mean Streets: Five Lessons from the Front Lines of Reengineering," *Hospital and Health Networks* 69, no. 19 (October 5, 1995), pp. 44–52.

38. Sandy Lutz, "Healthcare Update," *Modern Healthcare* 26, no. 5 (February 5, 1996), p. 20.

Additional Readings

Flannery, Thomas P., David A. Hofrichter, and Paul Platten, *People, Performance, and Pay* (New York: Free Press, 1996). A valuable resource for executives in health care who are attempting to seriously think about the role of human resources in reengineered organizations. This book attempts to link business strategy, organizational culture, and change. Linking the compensation and reward system with strategy, culture, and change is emphasized.

Halal, William E., *The New Management: Democracy and Enterprise Are Transforming Organizations* (San Francisco: Berrett-Koehler Publishers, Inc., 1996). As one of the pioneers of the "internal markets" view of organization, Halal illustrates that managers today are bewildered by a blur of change. This book attempts to cut through the confusion and integrate emerging practices into a coherent whole. The author shows how enterprise and democracy are moving inside organizations and transforming them into institutions ready to deal with problems presented in the twenty-first century.

Hilmer, Frederick G., and Lex Donaldson, *Management Redeemed* (New York: Free Press, 1996). A provocative "counterintuitive" book that argues how an antimanagement sentiment has led leaders to flatten and reengineer, emphasize vision over analysis, and surrender organizational control to outsiders. They maintain, instead, that there is enormous organizational power in hierarchy, bureaucracy, middle management, rules and policies, and quantitative analysis. Unlike many who predict the demise of management and the domination of leadership, these authors believe managers will grow in number and importance in the near and distant future.

Kaplan, Robert S., and David P. Norton, *The Balanced Scorecard: Translating Strategy into Action* (Boston: Harvard Business School Press, 1996). These authors deal with one of the most elusive elements of strategy—the connection between strategy and performance appraisal. Using what they call a balanced scorecard approach that translates the organization's vision and strategy into a set of coherent performance measures, they demonstrate that the balanced scorecard can be used as a driver of change and corporate strategy.

Ulrich, David, *Human Resource Champions: The Next Agenda for Adding Value and Delivering Results* (Boston: Harvard Business School Press, 1996). The human resources function has been under question for years in organizations of all kinds. Whether or not human resources units really add value remains a matter of faith rather than fact. The author "sets a new agenda" for the human resources function. He argues that the role of human resources professionals must be redefined to meet competitive challenges and add value in times when cost leadership is increasingly critical.

Organization-Wide Strategies

Learning Objectives

After completing this chapter you should be able to:

1. Discuss the differences between organizational cultures that contribute to long-term excellent performance and those that do not.

2. Understand the fundamental characteristics of organizational culture.

3. Understand seven factors that relate to building a culture based on organizational excellence.

4. Appreciate the importance of changing organizational culture as an element in implementing strategic change.

5. Understand the relationship between organization structure, culture change, and the implementation of different strategies.

6. Discuss the primary areas of facilities management and their impact on organizational strategies.

7. Understand the importance of ethical and social responsibility constructs in the strategic management of health care organizations.

8. Appreciate the relationship between ethical decision making and strategic health care management.

"Health care ... can no longer afford the maxim, 'if it ain't broke, don't fix it.' Rather, 'if it isn't perfect, make it better,' is becoming the credo of leading hospitals."

- *Michael Everett and James C. Brent*

Health care for the homeless is a serious problem in most American cities. The only options for millions of homeless people is to present themselves for medical care at the only place they can access—the emergency room. Usually, by the time the homeless arrive at the emergency room, the illness has become serious and often life threatening. Expensive services are the only recourse. The Introductory Incident provides an illustration of a cooperative effort that is both socially responsible and economically sound.

In addition to the functional strategies discussed in the previous chapters, four important *organization-wide strategies* are needed to support strategic implementation. Strategies must be developed, such as initiatives to change the organization's culture, reorganize operations to more effectively support new and emerging strategies,

A Clinic for the Homeless
That Makes Good Business Sense

Columbia Health Care Systems, Florida Hospital, and Orlando Regional Health Care Systems are usually fierce competitors. However, in one area cooperation was more effective and helped the community and the homeless in the process. These three health care organizations donated $500,000 to start the Health Care Center for the Homeless as well as funds to keep it operating. About fifty homeless people file through the clinic's primary-, dental-, and eye-care facilities every day. Last year health care delivered at the clinic would have cost over $1 million on the open market. For example, if a homeless person goes to the emergency room of any of the participating organizations, the average price tag will be $450. A clinic visit costs only $38.

There is an effort to give the homeless an alternative to emergency care. A mobile van, for example, takes nurses to ill people on the street in an effort to avoid emergency treatment. Hospitals provide nonemergency care vouchers valued at $150,000 that can be "cashed in" at the facilities for nonemergency surgeries and similar services.

The Health Care Center for the Homeless is an example of the potential for cooperation among private enterprises, philanthropic organizations, and community volunteer groups. In addition to the three participating organizations, the Robert Wood Johnson Foundation has provided funding; and almost 300 physicians, nurses, and dentists donate their time to make the clinic a success. The Health Care Clinic for the Homeless is an example of social responsibility that has become a good economic investment in Orlando.

Source: Silvia K. Foti, "A Clinic That Heals the Homeless," *Hospitals and Health Networks* 70, no. 6 (March 20, 1996), p. 84.

upgrade equipment and facilities, and develop and implement philosophies that ensure the organization's fit into the prevailing social and culture realities that cross multiple boundaries. Because organization-wide strategies extend beyond any functional strategies, they are usually the responsibility of the CEO or other top officer of the organization.

Organizational Excellence and Culture

Many organizations in health care, business, education, and government are very good at achieving their mission. In a competitive enterprise, an organization has to be good in terms of efficiency and effectiveness or it will not survive. In the public sector, unless an organization does at least a satisfactory job at what taxpayers created it to do, it will not survive. The result is that many organizations do a very good job of accomplishing their purpose. Many hospitals with respectable mortality rates admit and discharge patients. Hundreds of public health clinics see patients without making them wait so long that they become frustrated and leave. Thousands of pharmacies fill the prescriptions of millions of customers every day without making serious mistakes. Although literally millions of organizations around the world do an adequate job, perhaps even a commendable job, at accomplishing their mission, relatively few are truly excellent.

Why is this? What is the difference between very good and truly excellent organizations? The answer, according to Tom Peters and Nancy Austin in *A Passion for Excellence,* is that excellence is at the margin. Many organizations consistently operate at the 80 to 90 percent level. However, excellent organizations consistently operate at 95 percent or better. Excellence is a "game of inches."[1] Excellence is consistently working a few percentage points above the competition with regard to patient services, innovation, teamwork, and other areas of importance.

Culture permeates the organization and, as Perspective 12–1 illustrates, successful leaders understand the critical nature of culture. Therefore, to successfully bring about strategic change and foster excellence something must be known about how to build, change, and maintain organizational culture. That requires understanding the basic nature of organizational culture. Culture may be supportive of efforts to improve organizational performance or it may actually resist changes that alter the accepted ways of doing things. If the latter occurs, the implementation process will require modification of the culture. Although culture change is difficult, it is an important factor in moving the organization toward excellent performance.

Perspective 12–1

Building and Maintaining a Healthy Organizational Culture

If organizational culture is to be used as a tool in strategic management, health care leaders must understand its potential advantages and disadvantages and be willing to change the culture when necessary. To successfully do this, several guidelines may help.

1. *Learn the history of the organization.* When history is recognized as important, managers can use the traditions to motivate and maintain high levels of performance. One health care executive assigned a person to each of the eight decades of the hospital's history to highlight the accomplishments and significant events in each period. Old timers were visibly moved and newcomers reported feeling a part of the hospital for the first time.

2. *Reinforce existing cultural patterns.* Health care managers can be important symbolic leaders. One hospital executive reinforced the organization's commitment to cost containment by moving to a very Spartan office in the basement.

3. *Change and reshape culture.* Health care leaders must be careful to avoid jumping into new directions without assuring some stability for those who find security in a well-established culture. When Vanderbilt University Hospital and Clinic moved to its new facilities, morale and productivity suffered because the old symbols were lost—the sycamore trees outside the windows as well as the interaction that was possible in the old facility. Once the issue surfaced and changes were made to preserve and transfer as much as possible of the old environment, performance and morale improved dramatically.

Source: Terrence E. Deal, "Healthcare Executives as Symbolic Leaders," *Healthcare Executive* 5, no. 2 (March/April 1990), pp. 24–27; and A. L. Wilkins and J. J. Bristow, "For Successful Organizational Culture, Honor Your Past," *Academy of Management Executive* 1, no. 3 (August 1987), pp. 221–229.

Understanding Organizational Culture

Most managers agree that there is something that characterizes a health care organization's customary way of doing things, the values that most members of the organization share, and the things that must be learned and subscribed to by new members if they are to be satisfied and productive in their jobs. This customary way of doing things, referred to collectively as the culture of an organization, is important in assessing strategic strengths and weaknesses, achieving stretch, and ultimately in building sustained competitive advantage because it can either aid or hinder an organization's response to external opportunities and threats.

A Definition of Organizational Culture

Organizational culture is an elusive concept that is the subject of considerable controversy in modern management. Although most agree that it is real and affects the accomplishment of organizational goals, there are no widely accepted techniques for measuring and precisely altering culture.

Organizational culture is defined as the "implicit, invisible, intrinsic, and informal consciousness of the organization which guides the behavior of individuals and which shapes itself out of their behavior."[2] Organizational culture possess three important characteristics.

Organizational Culture Is Learned The culture of a health care organization is made meaningful by experience. Those who work in an organization gradually accept its expectations. Culture influences all aspects of what goes on in the organization, including how we feel about what we do, how we do our job, what we believe is important to accomplish, and why we think different things are important or unimportant.[3]

For example, consider an organization such as the Mayo Clinic that has a strong culture. Mayo is built on three primary values that permeate its culture and can be traced directly to the founders: (1) pursuit of service rather than profit; (2) concern for the care and welfare of individual patients; and (3) interest by every member of the staff in the progress of every other member.[4] Anyone working at the Mayo Clinic will soon be confronted with these three core values and his or her success will depend to a great extent on how well these values are learned and accepted.

Organizational Culture Is Shared Shared understandings and meanings are important because they help employees know how things are to be done. If an employee knows that the culture of the hospital dictates that the patient is all-important, decisions can be made according to this understood value system even when a policy, procedure, or rule is not available in a particular situation.[5]

People who "fit in" at the Mayo Clinic soon find themselves sharing the culture with others. In fact, over the years leaders have asked residents and others to state what they think makes the Mayo Clinic great. The responses are summarized into twelve characteristics, three of which—team orientation, special spirit, and trust in those who have "passed the Mayo test"—illustrate the importance of sharing basic beliefs in order to become part of the culture. When the Mayo Clinic made a strategic decision to geographically expand by aggressively establishing a presence in Florida and Arizona, one of the greatest concerns was whether the "Rochester ethic" (culture) could be transferred to the Sun Belt.[6]

Culture Is Subjective and Objective   Shared assumptions, meanings, and values are subjective. The objective aspect of organizational culture can be heard and witnessed. Health care organizations are often quite rich in objective culture, which includes the heroes of the organization, the stories that are told from one generation of employees to another, the ceremonies and rituals of the organization, and so on.

Culture and the Bottom Line   The jury is still out on the strategic significance of a strong organizational culture. Organizational cultures such as the one at Mayo do have the potential to inspire aggressive and calculated managerial action whereas a weak culture is likely to do little more than encourage managers to be mere caretakers. Strong cultures build group cohesiveness, and when the other members of the group insist on high levels of performance each individual is encouraged to do his or her best.[7] A surgical team performing complex operations is a good example of how the culture of the group demands that each individual perform at the highest possible level if membership is to be maintained.

Unfortunately, strong cultures can also discourage change. When organizations become too committed to "how we do things around here" and "what we believe in," it may be difficult, at least in the short run, to change the culture. Opportunities can be missed and competitive advantages can be lost simply because the culture is so strong that it will not tolerate new ideas and directions. However, organizational cultures, when they encourage key success factors such as patient-centered care, can be positive contributors to the overall success of an organization.

Developing Cultures That Are Adaptive

Kotter and Heskett reviewed much of the literature on organizational culture and studied numerous organizations in an attempt to understand the relationship between an organization's culture and its long-term performance.[8] They found that the strength of an organization's culture and its "fit" with the demands of the external environment only partially explained the culture/performance relationship. Instead, adaptive cultures or those cultures that assisted in anticipating and adapting to environmental changes were associated with superior performance over the long run.[9]

An *adaptive culture* is one that allows for reasonable risk taking, builds on trust and a willingness to allow people to fail, and exhibits leadership at all levels.[10] In organizations with adaptive cultures everyone, regardless of position, is encouraged to initiate changes that are in the best interests of patients, employees, and managers. The fear of failure is reduced by tolerating creative, and sometimes risky, efforts to make the organization a better place to work and more responsive to all stakeholders. In other words, adaptive cultures are necessary for organizational excellence. Perspective 12–1 provides some guidelines for building and maintaining a healthy organizational culture.

A Model of Organizational Excellence

Exhibit 12–1 illustrates factors that are instrumental in developing an organizational culture that fosters excellence. Although none of the factors is more important than any other, it is significant to note that the three factors in the center of the exhibit—mission/vision,

Exhibit 12–1 • Model of Organizational Excellence

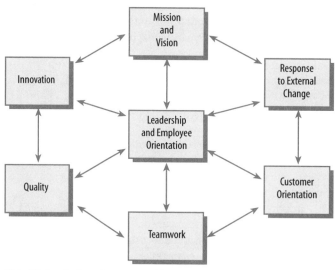

Source: From George A. Steiner and John F. Steiner, *Business, Government, and Society.* Copyright © 1980. Reproduced with the permission of The McGraw-Hill Companies.

leadership, and teamwork—are fundamental to the development and maintenance of the other factors.

A Sense of Mission and Vision   Mission, vision, and values are the building blocks of organizational culture. If people are to be expected to creatively adapt to change, they must understand what the organization is, where it is going, and what it stands for through good times and bad.

Leadership and Employee Orientation   In excellent organizations, leadership is exhibited at all levels, not just in the executive suite. People willingly take responsibility to ensure that jobs are accomplished. Leaders make sure employees and colleagues know that they care about them as people and understand the importance of everyone to accomplish the organizational mission.

The "language of leadership" is very different from management-oriented communication.[11] Conger notes that the language of leadership can be divided into framing and rhetorical crafting. *Framing* involves defining for others in a meaningful way the mission of the organization for today along with the vision for the future and the higher purposes it hopes to fulfill. The focus is on the importance and necessity of the mission, the heroic behavior that makes it happen, and the importance of the organization succeeding at what it was designed to do (its purpose). *Rhetorical crafting*, when done well, is what makes the language of leadership inspirational. Metaphors as well as analogies are used to bring a genuine "alikeness" between the leader and those who are listening. Great orators and some political leaders are highly skilled at inspiring people to do the impossible, think about the unthinkable, and make things happen where others have failed.

In reality, leadership is more than communication. It is role modeling as well. If leaders are to inspire others, they must be prepared to model the valued behaviors. This is what Eire Chapman tried to do as president of Riverside Methodist Hospital in Columbus, Ohio.[12] Every month Chapman puts on the uniform of the housekeeper, nurse aide, parking attendant, or dietary employee and conducts "walkabouts" to find out what it is like to be that kind of employee at Riverside Methodist. Chapman's counterparts in other health care organizations wondered how the busy executive could afford the time to do these jobs. He did not understand how they "could afford not to do them." Chapman says, "The CEO does not take care of patients, the CEO takes care of people who take care of patients." This is an important responsibility and requires dedicated strategic leadership.

Thinking and Working As Teams   It is not uncommon for top leadership in health care organizations to discover after spending time, energy, and resources on strategic planning that the organization simply does not have a culture that is capable of strategic thinking or implementing strategies. Usually the tasks required for implementation demand that people work together as teams. Team building, therefore, is usually a prerequisite to or an integral part of the implementation process.

Researchers have observed that groups pass through four stages in their progression to becoming a team. This evolution is descriptive of the way an organization's culture changes to one that fosters teamwork.[13] In the *forming* stage, members of the organization who are experienced at working and being rewarded as individuals begin to "test the water" of teamwork. Many will not like it and some will resist efforts to become real team players. Inexperienced team players are highly dependent on other things during this stage—leaders, more experienced team members, and the guidelines (rules and regulations) on which team interaction is built.

Storming is the second stage of change as individuals move toward becoming team players and as organizations move toward accepting the group concept. Earlier converts may come to genuinely question the wisdom of moving to a team-oriented culture and become less zealous. Those who were never true believers may take the loss of enthusiasm and natural conflicts as an opportunity to sabotage the process. This is a critical point in the development of a team-oriented culture. At this time it is important to showcase some "small victories" of the power of group performance.

For example, a hospital's pharmacy department had experienced ongoing conflict between registered pharmacists and pharmacy technicians. The pharmacists believed the technicians unnecessarily complained about the condescending way they were treated by the "professionals." The technicians believed the pharmacists, as a group, thought they were "too good" to perform certain routine tasks and, by refusing to do so, reduced the services delivered to the patients. A joint working group of pharmacists and technicians implemented a "put yourself in my shoes" program whereby pharmacists and technicians switched roles for two hours a week. Pharmacy supervisors report that a new understanding has developed between pharmacists and technicians and the two groups are working more as a team.

The third stage in the evolution of a team-oriented culture is *norming.* During this stage the desired cohesion begins to develop. More people become believers in the power of team performance. Fewer people engage in social loafing and teams become the norm.[14] Members become more willing—even enthusiastic—about working in teams. Cooperation becomes the natural way of doing things. The challenge implicit in the small victories taking place during the earlier storming stage is to find ways to make sure the good ideas and improvements are adopted and become the "norm."

The final stage of team development is *performing.* Groups in this stage become mature and develop into high performing teams. There is an established structure, and the purpose and role of the team are well understood by all its members. At the organizational level, the cultural transition is complete. The organization is structured around teams and problems to be resolved rather than the more traditional departmental functions. The emphasis is on results to be achieved and the common good of the team.

Realistically, teams are difficult to form—especially in organizational cultures built on and proud of their commitment to individualism. Perspective 12–2 illustrates that it is easier to form relatively autonomous alliances among physician partners than group practices. However, merely envisioning the potential power of a team can cause a leader to become a believer and an advocate. Teams can achieve tasks that individuals can only dream about, and teams can provide a feeling of satisfaction and accomplishment to equal that of individual achievement when the culture recognizes and rewards the group. It has been stated that: "The opportunity for increased performance [in teams] is too great to let misunderstanding, inexperience, uncertainty, or false assumptions—or even past team failures—stand in the way."[15] Teams are essential to excellence in organizations.

| Perspective 12–2

Teamwork and the Reality of Medical Practice

Alta Bates Medical Center in Berkeley, California, set up an organization to help physicians improve the management of their practices and attract managed-care contracts. Because the doctors who affiliated divided into two camps, two separate organizations were developed to serve the needs of the different cultures. The first organization focused on helping a number of individual practices (one or two physicians) act as one in securing contracts while maintaining their independence and autonomy. The second attempted to merge thirty primary-care doctors into a single group practice.

The first organization has experienced phenomenal success. In five years, it has signed up about 600 doctors and the patient network has grown from 8,000 to more than 100,000. This group has now affiliated with a regional network and has expanded its number of patients to more than 160,000. The second organization, after limping along for over two years, has abandoned

its strategy and retrenched. The goal now is to help subsets of the group settle into practices of seven to twenty physicians. The doctors will own their practices and Alta Bates will assist in billing, contract negotiations, and so on.

In the end, physicians are not used to making group decisions, and attempting to manage their practices in such a manner is very difficult. Often, according to observers of the discontinued effort, "tempers flared, not only over decisions themselves but over the time spent in making them." Perhaps the most fundamental element of success in group settings is trust. Trust, however, rarely exists. It has to be built and constantly nurtured.

Source: Kevin Lumsdon, "Why Doctors Don't Trust You," *Hospital and Health Networks* 70, no. 6 (March 20, 1996), pp. 27–32.

Innovation, Culture, and Excellence Excellent organizations are creative and innovative in the way they do things. Not only do they develop truly new products and services, they adopt creative ways from other organizations to solve problems. Unfortunately, innovativeness is not easy to instill within organizations. "Trying to be more innovative," according to Schein, "will not help if the corporate culture and employees are not open to the process—organizations [if they wish to be innovative] must change the way managers and employees think."[16]

Trying to improve through innovation assumes that many, perhaps most, ideas will not be successful. However, as the CEO of the Allegheny Health Systems noted, "The heroes and heroines of tomorrow will have failed their way to success."[17] The people who make a difference in organizations are willing to try something new when the odds of success seem reasonable or the potential gains are sufficient to justify even extreme risks.

Normal organizational inertia means that very few new and creative things will happen in organizations of any type if a champion does not foster change. People have new ideas and the knowledge to implement them. Therefore, whether innovative thinking is adopted depends on some person or group that champions the idea and overcomes resistance.[18] It is important to identify and nurture these people to ensure a steady flow of new ideas. Exhibit 12–2 provides a summary of selected characteristics possessed by individuals who emerge as champions of change and the characteristics of a nurturing environment for encouraging them to be innovative.

Champions, whether in the executive suite or in the operating room, are natural leaders because of their ability to articulate the vision of what "might be." They are confident, perhaps even overly optimistic, and have little doubt that their ideas better enable the organization to accomplish its mission. And, perhaps most important, they are persistent. Champions persist. They keep the pressure on to rethink ways of doing things and are always available to discuss their own pet projects. The role of strategic managers relative to champions of change is to nurture and protect them.

Quality and Continuous Improvement Excellent organizations always expect more of themselves than they did last year or even last month.[19] This process of "raising the hurdle" is important to ensure that the organization and all its members continuously move toward being the best they can be. The image of quality that is developed in this manner frequently translates into a tangible competitive advantage in the marketplace.[20]

Making sure that quality is ever present in the thoughts and actions of all employees, at all levels, at all times, demands attention from leaders. Peters and Austin summarized it accurately in their statement that quality is "about care, people, passion, consistency, eyeball contact, and gut reaction."[21] Quality does not just happen. It must be reinforced and nurtured if it is to survive. There is no resting with regard to quality. It is, "a race without a finish line."[22]

Response to External Change Excellent organizations appreciate the importance of external factors, develop ways of assessing their importance, and change the way they do things when external factors demand responses. Often they see change as an opportunity and make adjustments before change is required. Excellent organizations are still surprised occasionally by external events but they are consistently better able to deal with change than their "ordinary competitors." Waterman notes that some organizations

Exhibit 12–2 • Champions of Change

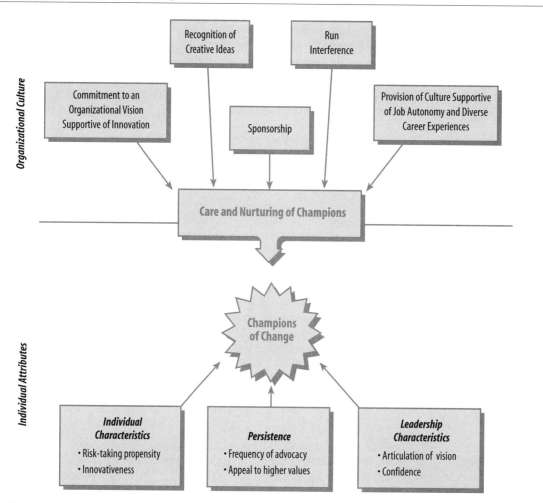

Source: Adapted in part from Jane M. Howell and Christopher A. Higgins, "Champions of Change: Identifying, Understanding, and Supporting Champions of Technological Innovations," *Business Horizons*, Vol. 33, No. 3 (Summer 1990), p. 52. Reprinted by permission of JAI Press Inc. and adapted in part from "Champions of Technological Change," *Administrative Science Quarterly*, Vol. 35, No. 3 (1990), pp. 317–341. Reprinted by permission.

are "continuously adapting . . . to the shocks and prosper from the forces that decimate their competition. They move from strength to strength, adjusting to crises that bedevil others in their industry."[23]

Customer/Patient Orientation   In health care organizations as in business firms, government agencies, or universities, there are two types of customers: the *external customer,* patient, student, or citizen—the person who pays the bills—and the *internal customers*—colleagues within the organization that rely on someone or some other unit to accomplish a task. Nursing, for example, is an internal customer of the medical records department because nurses depend on medical records to properly maintain patient information.

There is an emerging emphasis on the importance of the patient as a customer in health care organizations. Today, almost all health care organizations provide quality care. Therefore, as it is no longer a competitive advantage, health care organizations have to transition beyond merely providing quality care. Excellent organizations seem to understand better than others the true importance of a satisfied customer and focus their energies at all levels to accomplish this goal.

Making the Structure Responsive to the Strategy

Although there has been justified controversy over whether strategic changes cause changes in the organizational structure or vice versa, there is general agreement that changes in one of these important factors almost always requires changes in the other. One of the most important organization-wide implementation strategies, therefore, is the consistent pattern of decisions that leads to a structure that will encourage and facilitate the overall strategic change.

If organizations are to foster innovation and risk taking, the structure must relax control and delegate decision-making authority to the point that employees can activate the rapid responses necessary to take advantage of opportunities detected in the environment. If management hopes to encourage leadership at all levels, the "distance" between managers and employees must be reduced, and the upper levels of leadership must be accessible enough to ensure everyone knows and understands the mission and vision of the hospital, health department, or HMO. Often, when a particular philosophy of organization has been in place for a considerable length of time, changes in the structure will necessitate culture changes similar to those discussed previously.

As environmental issues provide incentives for change in the organization and the culture becomes receptive to accomplishing the organizational mission in new and innovative ways, pressure inevitably increases for change in the structure of the hospital, HMO, or physician practice. Hierarchical organizations with tight operational controls are barriers to team building, innovation, and empowerment. Therefore, one important organization-wide strategy is making the structure more responsive to strategic change.

Components of Organizations

Organizations have many component parts. Three are of particular importance to strategic management: governing boards, management, and operations.

Governing Boards   Boards of directors or boards of trustees in all types of organizations are responsible for making policies—the general guidelines under which the organization will operate. As Perspective 12–3 illustrates, boards can be facilitators of organizational vision and achievement, or they can inhibit progress. The selection and composition of board members is a critical strategic decision.

In health care there are different types of governing boards. *Philanthropic governing boards* are service oriented and concerned primarily with spanning the boundary between the health care organization and the community. These boards are larger and

| Perspective 12–3

Organizational Governance and Boards of Directors

In 1987, Cambridge Hospital was on the brink of disaster. It was $10 million in the red but by 1991 it had eliminated losses as well as the excessive debt service, and it even won the American Hospital Association's Foster G. McGaw Prize for its impressive turnaround. A name change to Cambridge Community Health Hospital completed its transition. CEO John O'Brien gave most of the credit to the board of trustees because they were "truly visionary role models for the rest of us. They're very businesslike, set high standards, and hold themselves accountable." Mr. O'Brien is fortunate. Not all CEOs can say the same about their boards. Gerald McManis, a health care consultant, maintains that one of the most important barriers to change "has been trustees."

Boards of trustees have a difficult job. Often they are appointed because of the diverse interests in the community and must be responsive to community needs. Often this results in boards that are too large to be effective and individual members who are not informed decision makers in light of the realities of health care. Dennis Pointer of San Diego State University states that "the most common indication that trustees are lost is when they cross the line between governing and managing." Some boards spend a huge amount of time approving salary increases and pay levels. He contends the real responsibilities of boards are formulating the organization's vision, mission, and goals; ensuring financial health; promoting efficient management; ensuring quality of care; and monitoring their own effectiveness.

Source: Anne Nordhaus-Bike, "Blessed Be the Board," *Health and Hospital Networks* 70, no. 4 (February 20, 1996), pp. 49–52.

more diverse to gain as much community representation as possible. The inclusion of different types of stakeholders is important and requires that board members be selected from among business leaders, physicians, local politicians, consumers of health care services, and so on.

Corporate governing boards are more involved in strategic planning as well as policy making. This type of board is smaller and composed of individuals who possess expertise that will aid the organization in accomplishing its goals.[24] Membership diversity is important, but less so than the actual skills possessed by the members. The current trend in health care organizations is toward the corporate board. To a great extent, this is the result of the increasingly competitive environment facing health care organizations and the need for expertise in dealing with the complexities of the economic environment.[25]

This experience supports the findings of research on boards of directors, which suggest that when profound or radical organizational change confronts a hospital, the corporate board is more likely to effect a positive response. Philanthropic boards, on the other hand, are more likely to be associated with either no change or negative responses to profound changes.[26] As a specific case in point, it was found that the boards of directors in health care organizations undergoing corporate restructuring (defined as the "segmentation of [the organization's] assets and functions into separate corporations to reflect specific profit, regulatory, or market objectives"), tended to become less philanthropic and more corporate in composition and the way they operated.[27]

Other research has provided additional information about various types of governing boards in health care organizations. When compared to boards of directors of successful high-technology firms, for example, it was found that governing boards in a sample of multihospital health care systems were almost twice as large (eleven to fifteen members).[28] In fact, boards are frequently too large to be effective aids in decision making, and where the goal is stakeholder representation, board members often know so little about health care that CEOs are forced to spend a great deal of their time informing and educating lay members.

One final study examined the issue of outside directors in large investor-owned health care organizations. Four major subsamples were examined, including hospitals, elder-care organizations, HMOs, and alternative-care facilities such as psychiatric clinics and ambulatory-care centers.[29] This study found that, in general, governing boards of health care organizations were composed of more members from outside, rather than inside, the organization. Outside representatives were primarily physicians, financial professionals, attorneys, and academics. The inclusion of physicians was found to be particularly significant in terms of bottom-line performance. It was suggested that this resulted primarily from the fact that the presence of physicians on governing boards enhanced the support of the medical community to improve the market share and quality.

Although it is dangerous to generalize, some inferences can be drawn from the research on governing boards in health care organizations. First, when health care organizations are profit oriented, their boards take on more corporate characteristics. They tend to be smaller, to compensate members for service, to select members for specific expertise, to involve the CEO as a voting member and make him or her formally accountable to the board, and to require the participation of board members in strategic decision making. From the perspective of the board member, the motivation may be to provide a valuable service, but board membership may be an important source of income as well.

In not-for-profit health care organizations, governing boards tend to display characteristics more in line with the philanthropic model. They are generally large (in fact, too large to be effective aids in strategic decision making), do not compensate the members, select members primarily as stakeholder representatives, and do not hold the CEO formally accountable for performance. In this case, the primary motivation for board membership is service and recognition.

Management and Policy Implementation The role of the board of directors or board of trustees is to make policy. The role of professional management personnel such as CEOs, presidents, or administrators is to implement policies. Boards of directors/trustees are representatives of the stakeholders, and as such, they attempt to identify the desires of stakeholders and translate their desires into policy statements.

Managers are responsible to the board for effective policy implementation. The board, for example, may develop a policy relating to the degree of risk a multisystem health care organization may assume in financing expansion into other services. The job of management is to ensure the organization experiences only that degree of risk exposure expressed in the policy. Conforming to that policy may require specific choices such as issuing stock rather than engaging in long-term borrowing. Once strategic choices are made, management's responsibility is to develop appropriate operational strategies to implement the strategic choices.

Strategic management has traditionally focused on top management, particularly the CEO. This individual is considered the person most responsible for scanning and influencing the environment, developing adaptive strategies, and managing key constituencies.[30] Unfortunately, the exclusive focus on the CEO's role in strategic management has implied that middle management has little or no involvement in determining the strategic direction of the organization. Admittedly, the primary responsibility of middle management is strategy implementation. However, certain strategic directions require middle-management leadership. Middle management, for example, is a key resource in the development of employee commitment to the organizational mission and vision. The increasing importance of quality as a strategic objective and middle management's role in keeping this objective before all employees is a good example.[31] Quality has become an important "value" to which employees at all levels can be committed, and middle managers are in the best position to encourage and reinforce this commitment.

Another important area in which middle management ought to be involved is in the redefinition of organizational vision. Grand strategies and futuristic visions are important for health care organizations. If the vision is to become meaningful to nurses, pharmacists, medical laboratory technicians, and others, middle- and first-line managers must take the lead in redefining the organizational vision in terms that are meaningful to departments and work groups. Finally, with regard to building involvement and commitment to service and quality, middle managers are in the best position to appeal to the social and economic motives important to health care employees.

Operations Operational-level personnel are responsible for accomplishing the tasks required by the policies of the board and derived from the strategic choices and action plans of management. It is the organizational level that will be directly and immediately affected by strategic decisions such as selling off a series of specialty hospitals or engaging in a contractual arrangement with an independent laboratory. Operational-level personnel are in many ways the "heart" of the health care organization.

Organizing for Strategic Change

In a classic study of General Motors, Standard Oil of New Jersey, Sears and Roebuck, and duPont, Alfred Chandler documented the way in which an organization's structure must respond to its strategy.[32] Chandler's analysis focused on the developmental stages of an organization (its life cycle) ranging from the initial problems of accumulating and organizing resources to entering new and different markets. Through each change in strategy, organizational changes were required to facilitate the new strategic demands on the firms.

The organizational life cycle is only one way of relating strategy to structure. Another approach is based on the interaction of three important variables—client homogeneity, service diversity, and organizational size. These variables are defined as follows:[33]

1. *Client homogeneity.* How similar are the patients, clients, or customers the organization serves? If different adaptive strategies are being considered (such as moving from related to unrelated diversification or vertical integration) will the differences in the new clients be sufficient to demand a new organizational structure? The

more dissimilar the clients (low homogeneity), the more likely is the need for organizational units specifically designed and staffed to deal with them.

2. *Services diversity.* Again, the more diverse the services offered (high), the more likely the need for units that specialize in particular services with the relevant types of specialists to provide them. If a highly diversified health care organization decides to divest unrelated operations such as parking decks, will the resulting focus back on related health care activities allow a simplification of the organization structure?

3. *Size of the organization.* This may or may not be related to the stage of the organizational life cycle. The important question is whether the organization is large enough (adequate or inadequate) to take advantage of economies of scale if it is divided into departments or autonomous units.

To illustrate the relationship between organization structure and strategic change, consider the case of Sentara Health Systems. Sentara began the decade of the 1990s as a large organization with diverse services and little homogeneity among its clients as illustrated by Exhibit 12–3. In an effort to deal with this diversity and homogeneity, the various business units were operated with distinct boards which, in theory, were pulled together at the top by the Sentara Health System board.

Exhibit 12–3 · Sentara Health System Governance As a Diversified System

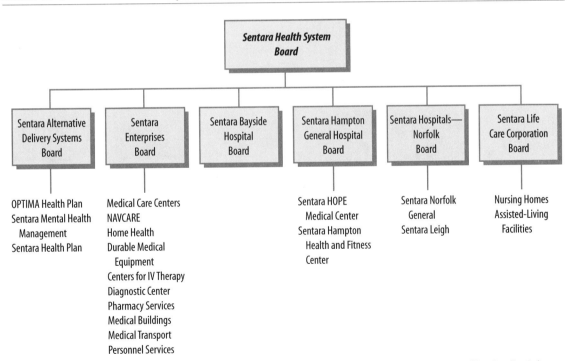

Source: From "Executive Chartbook" *Hospitals and Health Networks*, Vol. 69, No. 11 (June 5, 1995), p. 93. Reprinted by permission of American Hospital Publishing, Inc.

Although Sentara's financial position was stronger than at any other time in its history, leadership recognized certain potential problems. For example, the Norfolk, Virginia, region was experiencing a decrease in the need for hospital beds. The response was a new strategic plan with radical changes in the organizational governance structure. One of the most important changes was the increased representation of physicians in organizational governance. Half of the strategic planning committee, for example, was composed of doctors with the remaining half made up of executives and board members.

Perhaps the most tangible result of the Sentara Health System governance and organizational effort has been the move from a diversified to an integrated model. Exhibit 12–4 demonstrates a more integrated structure where the number of boards has

Exhibit 12–4 · Sentara Health System Governance As an Integrated System

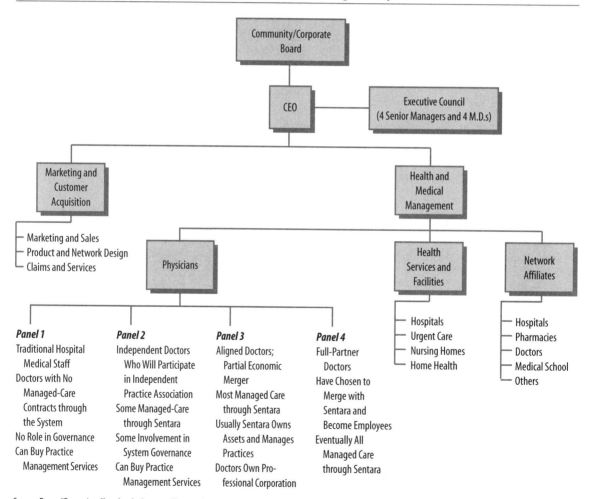

Source: From "Executive Chartbook: Sentara, Then and Now," *Hospitals and Health Networks*, Vol. 69, No. 11 (June 5, 1995), p. 92, 93. Copyright 1995, American Hospital Publishing, Inc. Reprinted by permission.

been reduced from seven to one. With this structure it is possible to ensure a more unified thrust and more consistent systemwide decision making. The policy-making responsibility of the single board of directors makes it possible to formulate and execute strategies that have the potential of obtaining the greatest synergies and thereby accomplish the primary goal of integrated health systems.

Strategic Facilities Management

Facilities management is the broad term used to delineate the management of the physical environment of the health care organization. It is the "shell" in which health care is delivered. Although the departments or areas included in facilities management vary by institution, it generally includes such diverse areas as design and construction of new facilities and renovation of older facilities, technology management, operations and maintenance, clinical engineering, environmental services, safety and security, materials management, and food service. Each component affects the health care organization's ability to implement its strategy.

Facilities management is an area of increasing concern to top management of health care organizations for a variety of reasons. One of the most important is the changing technology that has fostered tremendous growth in the number and kind of alternative delivery systems requiring different strategies for success. Freestanding outpatient clinics, ambulatory (same day) surgery centers, diagnostic and imaging centers, and others are challenging traditional inpatient health care delivery. To survive, hospitals have altered their strategies to expand vertically and horizontally or to diversify into these new delivery systems. However, each type is subject to entirely different design needs for buildings as well as different regulatory guidelines—a challenge for the facilities manager.

These integration and diversification strategies have caused the facilities and related support systems to increase in complexity and cost, another reason why top management has an increased interest in facilities management. With the advent of PPS, controlling costs within areas supervised by facilities management became critically important. Pressure mounts to increase efficiencies and deliver more cost-effective support without impeding the quality of patient care.

Facilities support delivery of quality patient care. Facilities management can identify activities that will lead to continuous improvements in the quality of patient care. "Patient satisfaction can be enhanced by a well-designed and well-maintained facility, the quality of foodservice, and the general courteousness and service orientation of all employees."[34] However, patient-centered care is straining financial resources as significant remodeling must be undertaken to implement the strategy. In addition, with rapidly changing technology, a convenient location and sufficient space are needed to house new diagnostic equipment, for example, a new PET scanner. Will the hospital choose to sell its older scanning equipment (the MRI? the CT scan?) or add on to the facility to house the new equipment?

Another reason for the importance of facilities management within strategic management is that the physical aspects of the health care organization are the first encountered by patients, visitors, and employees. If the health care facility is difficult to find, parking is limited and challenging to navigate, and the outside environment is unmanicured and ill kept, it presents an image of an institution that does not care.

Designing a Health Care Facility

A variety of components are to be considered in the design of a health care facility: medical technology, the full range of medical procedures from routine exams to complicated life-saving activities, medical staff, sanitation, prevention of injury, economics, patients, and visitors. From the patients' perspective, the facility includes "curb appeal," ease of access to the main entrance, ease of parking, ease of *wayfinding* (finding the department, room, diagnostic area, or other area where the patient is expected), comfort, and convenience. Designing the facility with the human experience in mind recognizes that people's perceptions of health care are multidimensional; the facility helps them define the care they receive. Sending a "we care" message cannot stop with the staff but must be designed into the facility itself.[35] Perspective 12–4 illustrates the importance of facility design in the long-term-care industry.

When the health care organization decides on a high-tech, a high-touch, or some other strategy, the facility provides the first impression. The design, layout, color scheme, and so on should reflect the desired image to improve the implementation of the strategy. "Unlike the quality of medical care, health facility design is something that can readily be understood and judged, for better or worse, by the public."[36]

The quality of the health care environment has ramifications beyond its image, however. Research has shown that the design of the facility, its color scheme, arrange-

---

Perspective 12–4

Designing Family Friendly Long-Term-Care Facilities

"We want to break down the barriers that make people uncomfortable with the traditional medical environment and there are many ways to do that using proportion and color," says health care architect Lloyd Landow of Success, New York. Landow and Landow employs three generations of the Landow family whose firm seeks to meet the needs of residents when designing long-term-care facilities, diagnostic and treatment centers, and assisted-living residences.

In order to make facilities more cost effective, the firm typically moves the housekeeping department out of the basement and saves valuable staff time. In addition, it places lounges, supplies, bathing, and soiled utility rooms midway along halls, and not at the ends, saving even more time. Patient rooms are designed to give roommates equal access to the window and heater. To ease the depressing effect of long halls, the Landows design

small, angled alcoves where room entrances are located. This creates little areas similar to front porches where patients and visitors can sit and watch what is happening without being lined up along a sterile corridor. These little "porches" make the halls feel like streets, thus achieving a technique the architect calls "neighborhooding." This allows residents to feel more like they are a part of the ongoing life of the facility. Landow's ninety-six-year-old mother, who lives in a long-term-care facility, sums it up best: "Nursing home residents may not be able to communicate sometimes but they can still think and feel. Creating a good environment that makes them and the staff feel better is really accomplishing something."

Source: Jim Montague, "Family Designs," *Hospital and Health Networks* 69, no. 11 (June 5, 1995), p. 94.

ment of furniture, availability of windows, music, and accommodation for family members contribute to a patient's progress toward recovery.[37] Any way that the facility can relieve stress, not only for patients but also the health care staff, is an organizational strength. Patients and visitors have needs for wayfinding, physical comfort, regulation of social contact (privacy and personal space), and symbolic meaning (the sights, sounds, and smells that blend into the total image of a caring place).[38]

Technology Affects Facilities

Effective technology management is an integral part of strategic management and should be approached in a systematic way. Because health care technology changes rapidly, is costly, and often requires changes in the facility, it must be assessed and carefully planned for in order to operate the facility at its greatest potential. Physicians generally want the latest technology—using the "latest" equipment or newest procedure provides prestige with colleagues and patients and may save more lives or provide less discomfort to patients. However, there may be questions about how many lives will be saved and how much the discomfort will be lessened. In the dynamic environment of the 1990s, costs and benefits are being assessed before decisions are made to purchase new technology and build or remodel the space to house it.

According to Berkowitz and Swan, technology decisions involve technology assessment, planning, acquisition, and management.[39] They advocate that a committee assess requests for new and emerging technology alongside the capital budget requests for new and replacement technology. The committee should report to senior hospital management and should set mission-based, strategic priorities for new, emerging, and replacement technologies. Many hospitals do not incorporate into the budget the costs of redesign and "space" for new technology, nor do they investigate ways to reduce maintenance, insurance, and outside service contract costs. The planning process has to take into account what the competition is planning for the acquisition of new and emerging technology as well as assessing the services offered by competitors.

Clinical engineering (sometimes called *biomedical engineering*) is a relatively new department in most health care organizations. Its responsibilities include applying engineering technology to diagnostic and treatment devices used by health care facilities through testing, maintaining, and repairing equipment; training; consultation with clinical staff concerning the capabilities, efficiencies, and accuracy of the equipment; environmental testing; and incident and recall investigations that involve diagnostic or treatment equipment. The number and sophistication of technologies within health care institutions has increased significantly in the past decade. From 1980 to 1991, the number of diagnostic or treatment devices per occupied bed in an acute-care facility went from 1.5 to nearly 7.[40] Because of the expertise required for such a large variety of equipment, some health care organizations use outside service contracts for some or all of their technological equipment.

Risk management is an important part of diagnostic equipment testing. Testing standards are implemented by a number of governmental and regulatory agencies. Equipment failures and user errors must be documented, and for some equipment they must be reported for further follow-up.

Operations and Maintenance

The goal of the department responsible for the physical plant and its internal machinery (often referred to as the *engineering and maintenance department*) is to operate the physical plant in an efficient, cost-effective manner and to ensure the maximum comfort and safety of the facility's patients, visitors, and employees. Mechanical systems (including heating, ventilating, and air-conditioning systems; plumbing; fire protection; and the medical gas system) and electrical systems make up about 40 percent of the nonequipment construction costs of a new or replacement facility, and it is not unusual that they would account for 50 percent of the costs.[41] In addition, these systems have very high operating costs compared to similar systems in other types of facilities. In part this is because of the many regulations by federal, state, and local governments and codes and guidelines by regulatory agencies such as the Department of Health and Human Services and the Joint Commission on Accreditation of Healthcare Organizations.

Mechanical and electrical systems are rarely noticed by patients, visitors, and employees—unless something is not working properly. Although the engineering and maintenance department does not deal directly with patient care in the facility, virtually every aspect of its operation has some indirect effect on the care of the facility's patients, visitors, and staff. The physical environment supports the efforts of the health care professionals to provide excellent care to patients.[42]

Additional Facilities Management Areas

The value of an *environmental services* department (sometimes called *housekeeping, facilities maintenance, domestic services,* or *janitorial services*) is immediately evident to everyone who enters the health care facility.[43] In addition to keeping the facility clean, this group is typically responsible for laundry, groundskeeping, minor maintenance, pest control, and waste management.

Security of patients, visitors, and staff, as a responsibility of the health care organization, has been verified repeatedly in the court system. The liability as a result of inadequate or negligent security, coupled with the negative impact of theft, pilferage, and waste, represents a serious threat to health care organizations.[44] Safety is another area that is potentially a threat. Exhibit 12–5 illustrates some of the safety issues in a typical health care organization.

Materials management includes the acquisition, warehousing, inventory, distribution and transportation, and processing of supplies and equipment. Materials management has a significant impact on health care organizations both in terms of operations and finances. Studies have consistently shown that ordering, procuring, storing, moving, and using supplies consume up to 45 percent of a hospital's operating budget. This percentage includes the time that clinical and support staff are handling supplies; the supplies themselves are 13 to 23 percent of the operating budget.[45] The goal for most materials managers in health care organizations today is to achieve greater efficiency and cost-effectiveness without sacrificing the quality of patient care. Standardization of items and purchasing procedures, minimum inventory, enhanced purchasing through vendor management or cooperative buying groups, and on-line purchasing are being used to achieve the goal. Technology has become an increasingly important factor in the

Exhibit 12–5 • Safety Threats for a Health Care Organization

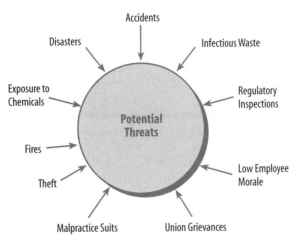

Source: From Linda F. Chaff, "Safety," in V. James McLarney (Ed.) *Effective Health Care Facilities Management,* p. 63. Copyright © 1991. Reprinted by permission of American Hospital Publishing, Inc.

area of materials management; although as Perspective 12–5 illustrates, some technological advances do not immediately realize the cost savings they promise.

Food service is another area of health that has undergone significant change in the past decade. Increased knowledge about diet and health has increased the demand for nutritionists for health care facilities. In addition, patients are not the only consumers of food service. Food-service needs of family and visitors of the patient as well as employees of the facility become important sources of revenue. Thus, cafeterias, vending machines, coffee shops, and others generate additional profit for the health care organization.

Ethical and Social Responsibilities of Health Care Organizations

By their very nature, hospitals, physicians, nurses, and other health professionals seek to help people. Most not-for-profit and public health care organizations that provide service for those who cannot pay for it have long been involved in operating with social responsibility. "Historical attitudes about competition, lack of profit motive, and not-for-profit status have both helped and hindered the health services system."[46] The absence of economic incentives has contributed to public health services organizations feeling good about themselves because they were doing good rather than concentrating on performing effectively and efficiently. Many of the private and for-profit organizations have performed well but have not focused on social responsibilities beyond their particular customers.

As health care has moved more toward the competitive model and more health care organizations are operated as "businesses," the concept of social responsibility must be investigated and given considerable attention by management. For example, not-for-profit status (tax exemption) may be denied if a health care organization does not

Perspective 12–5

Automated Supply Cabinets Do Not Automatically Save Money

The benefits of automated drug and supply cabinets are not always what they are cracked up to be. In the Scott and White Memorial Hospital in Temple, Texas, it was estimated that an automated cabinet would save $1.5 million over four years. The hospital now believes they will be lucky to get $75,000 savings per year, and that will come primarily through staff reduction. Despite the disappointing savings, Scott and White leases more than fifty cabinets in its fifteen nursing units at a cost of almost $80,000 per year, primarily because they make it possible to create and maintain valuable information about inventory utilization.

Automated drug and supply cabinets provide secure storage on nursing units. These units are often compared to automated tellers in a bank because they keep a computer log of the entry of access codes and the withdrawal of supplies. The primary benefits of the cabinets may be the automation of billing and the materials tracking they make practical. Automated cabinets designed for dispensing narcotics have been very popular. In 1995, sales of these cabinets at San Diego–based Pyxis Corporation grew 25 percent to over $175 million and netted almost $36 million to the company.

Source: Lisa Scott, "Materials Management: Automated Supply Cabinets Aren't a Financial Cure All," *Modern Healthcare* 26, no. 8 (February 26, 1996), pp. 84–86.

provide care for the indigent. In addition, governmental bodies established during the 1970s underscore that the national policy officially recognizes the environment, employees, and consumers to be significant and legitimate stakeholders. For executives, the question has become how to balance commitments to owners and their obligations to an ever-broadening group of stakeholders who claim both legal and ethical rights.

Archie Carroll, in a *Business Horizons* article, viewed these social responsibilities in a pyramid, as illustrated in Exhibit 12–6.[47] First and foremost, the organization was created as an economic entity to provide goods and services to societal members at a "profit" (enough revenues to cover costs and survive). Next, organizations are legal entities and are required to fulfill laws and legal obligations established by the lawmakers. The next level, ethical responsibilities, embodies the standards, norms, or expectations that employees, customers, and stakeholders in the community-at-large regard as fair. Ethical responsibilities go beyond what is legally acceptable. They reflect a higher standard of performance than that currently required by law.

Philanthropic responsibilities encompass those activities that respond to society's expectations that the organization be a good community "citizen," including actively engaging in acts or programs to promote human welfare or goodwill. Philanthropy is thus more discretionary or voluntary on the part of organizations, although there is a societal expectation that all organizations provide some. Many health care organizations have made significant commitments to fulfilling philanthropy goals. For example, Bristol-Myers Squibb began a corporate program over twenty years ago to provide life-saving drugs to those who cannot afford to pay for the necessary pharmaceuticals.

Stakeholder management has been defined as the process by which managers reconcile their own organization's objectives for "profit" with the claims and expectations

Exhibit 12–6 • The Pyramid of Social Responsibility

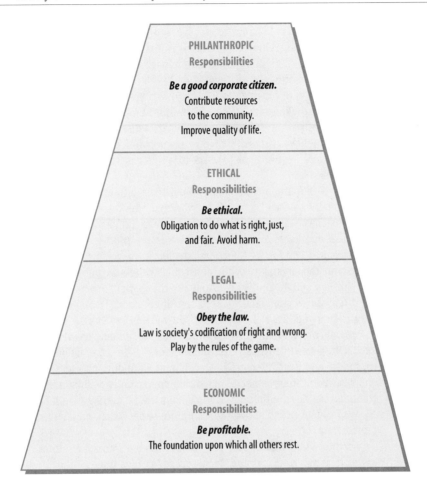

PHILANTHROPIC
Responsibilities

Be a good corporate citizen.
Contribute resources
to the community.
Improve quality of life.

ETHICAL
Responsibilities

Be ethical.
Obligation to do what is right, just,
and fair. Avoid harm.

LEGAL
Responsibilities

Obey the law.
Law is society's codification of right and wrong.
Play by the rules of the game.

ECONOMIC
Responsibilities

Be profitable.
The foundation upon which all others rest.

Source: From Archie B. Carroll, "The Pyramid of Corporate Social Responsibility: Towards a Moral Management of Organizational Stakeholders," *Business Horizons*, Vol. 34, No. 4 (July–August 1991), pp. 39–48. Reprinted by permission of JAI Press Inc.

being made on it by various stakeholder groups.[48] Of course, the challenge of stakeholder management is to ensure that the firm's primary stakeholders achieve their objective while other stakeholders are also satisfied. It is a legitimate and desirable goal for management to pursue protection of the organization's long-term survival.

Social Responsibility Stakeholders

Health care organizations have ethical and social responsibilities to at least five different stakeholders or constituencies: owners/shareholders, employees, customers, suppliers, and the general public.[49] The owners of a health care organization are often the public who, through contribution of their tax dollars and financial and time donations, expect the organization to survive and provide the services that are needed for the community. Thus, there is an inherent social responsibility for the organization to generate more revenues than costs in order to survive and serve the community. Publicly owned, for-profit organizations, whether health care organizations or others, have a legal and social responsibility to their shareholders to manage the investment of those shareholders in a manner that provides return.

In health care organizations, employees are an important constituency group, and strategies must take them into consideration. Employees have a right to be treated fairly and to expect that the strategy choice will not disadvantage them. If hardship cannot be avoided, they have a right to receive proper notice and as much guidance as possible. Employees also have a right to work in a safe environment and be treated with dignity and respect.

Health care organizations have a particular ethical responsibility to their customers to provide the service in the best way that they can. If the health care organization makes mistakes—as it sometimes will because humans deliver health care—the organization that admits its mistakes and makes every effort to correct them will be respected for its ethical conduct. "Anecdotal evidence suggests that patients and families can understand that mistakes occur and things do go wrong. Organizations that acknowledge this fact and do all they can to make things right are much better served than those that circle the wagons and make a last ditch stand."[50] A guiding question perhaps is, "How would you like to be treated if you were in the situation?"

Many complain about the way patients are actually treated in health care organizations. Often the historical environment of health care facilities, professional power structures, and even medical protocols make patients feel less like people at the very time a caring attitude is needed most. Perspective 12–6 illustrates how one hospital has attempted to deal with rape victims in a more caring manner and thereby meet a responsibility over and above the minimum expectation of delivering high-quality health services.

In the 1990s, health care reform is receiving significant attention. Many aspects of reform deal with ethical and social responsibility issues—the "right" to health care, death and dying, and so on. Balancing the needs of stakeholders is a challenging task. There are no easy answers when resources are finite and needs are infinite.

Strategic Management and Ethical and Social Responsibility

"The manager is the organization's conscience."[51] Management is responsible for managing the enterprise. The CEO is responsible for management. Therefore, all ethical considerations start with the CEO. His or her perception of ethics determines whether and how strategy is linked to ethical behavior. "A company that truly cares about ethics and corporate social responsibility is proactive rather than reactive in linking strategy and ethics."[52] The ethical organization does not deal with unethical suppliers or employees. The products and services are safe for customers to use. An ethical organization recruits and hires employees who are ethical as well.

Health care organizations must consider ethical and social responsibilities, and their orientation should be reflected in the organization's mission, vision, values, poli-

Perspective 12–6

Treating Crime Victims Well, While Tightening the Chain of Evidence

What happens to the typical rape victim in America? They are taken to the closest emergency department; sometimes they wait for six to ten hours to be examined; and eventually they are interviewed by the police. Even if they "stick to the rules of evidence" and do not eat, drink, wash, or use the bathroom while they wait, many of the physical signs needed to prosecute the rapist are dissipated, disappear, or are destroyed during the delay. That no longer happens in the Long Beach Community Hospital Medical Center.

Rape victims are whisked to the hospital and admitted to a private waiting area and a private examination room with its own bath, comfortable reclining examination table, and homelike furnishings. They are interviewed by police detectives, and a sexual assault nurse painstakingly gathers tiny particles of evidence. A sexual assault crisis agency volunteer is available to provide support and follow-up counseling.

The Sexual Assault Response Team (SART) at Long Beach Community Hospital "makes a horrible experience as compassionate and efficient and private as possible," says the director of Forensic Nurse Specialist, a private company that provides RN sexual assault examiners. SART is an example of one hospital's attempt to deal responsibly with one of the most demanding health care situations in modern society. Too often the patient—the person—is forgotten or ignored in trying emergency situations. Saving life, collecting evidence, and convicting criminals are all important goals. However, seeing to the emotional and personal needs of victims cannot be ignored or excused by the tension of the emergency room.

Source: Karen M. Sandrick, "Tightening the Chain of Evidence," *Hospitals and Health Networks* 70, no. 11 (June 5, 1996), pp. 64–66.

cies, and procedures. Without proper forethought, the organization may become governed by the events rather than governing the events. The organization's philosophy affects its strategic planning as the organization's views of its social responsibility are incorporated into the mission statement. The development of the mission is the responsibility primarily of the organization's governing body; however, the implementation is the responsibility of senior management. A difficult balance is to be achieved between social responsibility and economic performance.

In addition to mission and vision, some health care organizations have a statement of philosophy. A *statement of philosophy* should include some reference to the organization's relationship with patients, staff, community, and other institutions. By answering questions about the health care organization's relationship to its community, the organization can pose important questions to itself on its role prospectively. Although this is a useful exercise in developing organizational philosophy, it also provides an opportunity for introspection and staff involvement in creating a corporate culture. Major differences in moral philosophies inhibit cooperative efforts. An organization defines its mission based on its vision and philosophy and determines by what means its mission will be achieved. "This exercise *prospectively* resolves conflicts among competing but legitimate ends."[53]

Organizations have philosophies that are value laden, and individuals have a personal ethic. When the personal ethics of the individuals are concurrent with the organization's philosophy, there are few problems. When they differ, the personal ethic is often subsumed to the organizational philosophy because the individual does not wish to lose his or her job, but this dissonance causes considerable discomfort. To be an effective leader, an individual should maintain certain elements of a personal ethic. One way to judge whether an action is ethical is to look at what is being contemplated and ask a series of questions about how others would view this activity. "If you don't get caught, it's okay" is not an ethical position. In addition, ethics should be applicable to everyone in the organization. If the manager at the top says one thing and does another, it will be translated by all employees as an acceptable thing to do. Further, if certain goals are stated but rewards are given for the achievement of different goals, the employees have no ethical dilemma—they will do what is rewarded.

If not identified and handled early, ethical problems can multiply into culture-deteriorating events that can threaten the organization's survival. Many managers are uncomfortable dealing with ethical problems. They do not believe that they are responsible, they are not sure they know how to recognize ethical problems, and they do not believe they have the skills to solve such problems. Sometimes managers consider ethics to be the purview of the clinical staff, yet ethical dilemmas have an administrative aspect in health care organizations.

Managers are problem solvers. Developing problem-solving skills is an important part of management education, and solving ethical problems is really an extension of basic problem-solving skills. Ethical problems are solved in the same manner as other managerial problems. That is, there is an awareness of the problem, gathering of facts, evaluating the various alternatives, selecting the best alternative, and evaluating the results. Implementation of the solution is an important part in ethical dilemmas.

Guidance for Managers

Steiner and Steiner prepared a list of guidelines that are applicable to health care organizations. Although not every topic included in Exhibit 12–7 is appropriate for every health care organization, the list stimulates thinking about social responsibilities.

The major source of guidance for managers within their organizations are the individual's ethics supplemented by the codes of his or her professional group and the organization's philosophy. In addition, specific policies and management committees and task forces help identify and solve administrative ethical problems. Conflict of interest is the most often reported administrative ethical problem confronting health services organizations. Conflict of interest occurs when a person owes duties to two or more persons or organizations and meeting a duty to one of them causes a derogation of duty to another.[54]

For example, conflict of interest occurs when a member of the hospital or long-term-care facility board of trustees is also a major stockholder or CEO of a supplier of goods and services to that organization. Another administrative ethical issue is fiduciary duty, defined as a relationship that exists whenever confidence and trust on one side result in superiority or influence on the other. The health care organization's governing body members (trustees) are fiduciaries. It is their ethical duty to avoid using their position for personal gain, and they must act only in the best interests of the health care

Exhibit 12–7 · Guidelines for Organizational Social Responsibility

1. Think carefully about the organization's social responsibilities.

2. If applicable, make full use of tax deductibility laws through contributions—when profit margins permit.

3. Share the social costs of the community when it is possible to do so without jeopardizing the organization's competitive or financial position.

4. Concentrate action programs on limited objectives. No single organization can remake the entire social system, culture, or government. But an organization can make a difference in a single community or with a single objective or a single activity.

5. Concentrate action programs on areas strategically related to the present and prospective functions of the organization—begin close to home and deal with what appears to be the most urgent areas of concern that in some way can be related to the organization.

6. Facilitate employee actions that can be taken as individuals rather than as representatives of the organization—free them to do good deeds but do not force them.

7. An organization can do many things that are socially responsible as well as profitable, if not in monetary terms at least in improved image in the community.

8. Actions taken in the name of social responsibility should enhance the economic strength of the organization.

9. Take socially responsive actions continuously. Plan for it.

10. Examine carefully before proceeding responsibly. Investigate the community's needs, weighing the contribution the organization can make, the risk involved, and the potential benefits to both the organization and society.

Source: Adapted from George A. Steiner and John F. Steiner, *Business, Government, and Society* (New York: Random House, 1980).

organization. A major conflict of interest occurs when physicians and health care organizations participate in prepaid plans, where the institution benefits by minimizing the cost of caring for the patient although that may not be in the patient's best interest. This dilemma will become increasingly important as health care reform efforts succeed at instituting more managed care.

Another major ethical dilemma for health care organizations is the allocation of health care resources. Some people believe that every individual has a right to health care. At the other end of the continuum are people who believe that access to health care is not a right but a privilege. A middle ground that many people subscribe to is that routine, basic services ought to be available to all people. Where to draw the line is a political decision and depends on society's willingness to provide the resources needed. Our country continues to debate health care reform. What we are really trying to do is to decide where to draw the line, how much we can afford to spend on health care, and what services will be available to all.[55] For the health care manager, allocation of resources is a difficult decision because resources are limited. "Should the health care organization purchase new technology that will significantly help a limited number of people, or should it hire more nurses to staff the emergency room that would incrementally help many people?"

Consider the following example. The CEO of a successful hospital was approached by a physician who had recently attended a seminar on a new outpatient procedure that was stated to be quick and profitable. However, the procedure was still considered experimental, and some authorities considered it to be of questionable value. The physician wanted to offer this new procedure and promote it through a media campaign. The CEO was faced with a dilemma. Should the health care organization promote an experimental, perhaps unnecessary, service that would add profits to the hospital? Ultimately, the CEO decided against the new procedure. The physician then contracted with a freestanding surgical center, and the promotion was extremely successful. Because of this ethical issue, the hospital lost a source of revenue plus the physician's goodwill. The CEO had to decide whether the price was worth it.[56]

The starting point for determining a decision on this issue would be to review the organizational philosophy and mission. If this health care organization's mission included leading-edge technology, it would be expected that not every new technology would be successful. Therefore, the expectation of patients at this hospital would be that some of the procedures might be experimental. However, if the mission was to serve patients in need, then the health care organization would have to use its resources to improve the general health of the population that it serves. Yet the hospital lost the opportunity for additional profits that could have been used to provide additional services to improve the community's health. There are no easy answers. Perspective 12–7 illustrates a novel approach to assisting organizations with ethical dilemmas.

Have a Plan for Ethics

Health care executives can develop and implement a comprehensive, long-term initiative in organizational ethics according to David Perry, a former consultant of the Ethics Resource Center in Washington, D.C. He advocates that organizations first assess the organizational values and vulnerabilities to misconduct. Management should find out what kinds of ethical issues employees really face in their day-to-day jobs. Not only does this highlight what the code of ethics should cover, it also enlightens management as to

---

Perspective 12–7

The Moralsmobile Rolls In

Imagine an ethics SWAT team showing up at the hospital. Although it is hardly a SWAT team, the Park Ridge Center for the Study of Health, Faith, and Ethics does its best to get out into the real world of clinical decision making. The Chicago-area center goes to hospital boardrooms and bedsides providing ethical consulting and educational services. Although the Center often works with facilities in the Advocate Health Care System, the Center's parent organization, it is available to help any health care organization that finds itself facing ethical dilemmas. It helped one hospital create a client ethics program for areas such as respiratory therapy and rehabilitation services. Personnel in these areas are offered educational opportunities using ethical scenarios. One nursing home asked the Center's advice about what to do if they had a brain-damaged patient who could not swallow. The adult children did not want the patient fed through

a tube and she was sent home. Changes in the patient's condition and attitude when she was returned home caused the Center to assist the nursing home in developing new policies to address reconsidering actions in light of a patient's changing decision-making ability.

The ethics service deals with more than patient-centered issues. Sometimes health professionals need ethics training to address their problems. Doctors and other clinicians who are entrusted with life-and-death decisions need help. The Center for the Study of Health, Faith, and Ethics attempts to pick up where technology and human healers leave off.

Source: Terese Hudson, "The Moralsmobile Rolls In," *Hospitals and Health Networks* 70, no. 12 (June 20, 1996), p. 56.

the kinds of problems that employees within the organization face. For example, management, through goal-setting practices, often develops incentives and reward systems that may not encourage ethical conduct because employees perceive that something other than what is stated is rewarded. Although it may be stated that quality and safety are paramount, if employees in practice are rewarded only for cutting costs, employee values will be directed toward cost cutting.[57]

Second, management should create opportunities to discuss organizational values and risks. Management has to reach a consensus on the high-priority issues as well as the action plans that need to be implemented within an ethical construct. Employees need to understand that an ethics program is not merely a temporary fad but a long-term commitment. Therefore, organizational values, risks, and ethics should be discussed freely and frequently. Third, management should develop and communicate clear standards of conduct. A written code of ethics can be created or revised to relate to management systems and practices. It should affirm a basic set of organizational values, establish ground rules, provide illustrations and guidelines in some of the gray areas that are pertinent for a particular organization, and explain how employees can obtain further information and counsel without fear of retaliation.

Finally, management should refine its systems and practices to support the ethics program. In other words, when management develops the mission and strategic goals at the top departmental and individual levels—including incentive and reward systems, performance appraisals, and disciplinary practices—they need to be evaluated according to whether they reinforce the ethics program. Ethics has to be incorporated into the organization's basic culture and operating values. "When the entire organization operates on treating customers, suppliers, and employees fairly and honestly, there is nothing but benefit to be gained for the overall reputation and success of the organization."[58] Having a "plan for ethics" can provide some unanticipated outcomes as Perspective 12–8 illustrates.

Administrative Code of Ethics

The basic goal of a code of ethics is to guide the behavior and decisions of people who want to do the right thing but may need guidance in determining what that is. The American College of Healthcare Executives has had a code of ethics since 1939, just six years after its founding. The current version of the code was adopted in 1993. Its emphasis is on ethical issues in management, including conflict of interest, confidentiality, governing body/medical staff relations, resource allocation, and the manager's personal ethical behavior. A variety of other codes and groups, as summarized in Exhibit 12–8, help managers with ethical dilemmas.

Guiding Principles for Health Care Organizations

Robert Goldman believes that four ethical principles apply to health care organizations: (1) put the patient's welfare first, (2) avoid unnecessary services, (3) maintain high standards of honesty and accuracy, and (4) be accountable to the public. He believes that health care marketing efforts must reflect the highest ethical standards because health care customers lack the knowledge needed to make truly educated choices. "Patients must come before profits if the hospital is to profit."[59]

Perspective 12–8

Ethical Guidelines for Managed-Care Contracting

Robert Stanek, COO of Mercy Health System of Western New York was thrilled when he finally closed the deal with Independent Health Association, the largest HMO in western New York state. The deal was a good one; but what thrilled Stanek most was the HMO's agreement to pay for a $300,000 van that provides primary health care to underserved residents of inner-city Buffalo and poor rural areas.

This "groundbreaking" agreement would not have happened without a prearranged set of ethical guidelines for managed-care contracting. The guidelines, according to Stanek, "helped us challenge the insurance carriers to cover the needs of the underserved in western New York." The creation of ethical guidelines for managed care was the first challenge tackled by the Shared Corporate Ethics Committee formed by Eastern Mercy Health Systems (of which Stanek's organization is a member) and Mercy Health System. The resulting document has been widely circulated among executives and is used to help ensure that the organizational mission of service to the underserved is upheld in all negotiations with managed-care organizations.

Source: Chuck Appleby, "True Values," *Hospitals and Health Networks* 70, no. 13 (July 5, 1996), pp. 20–26.

Other Ethical Considerations

"Strategy ought to be ethical."[60] A phrase often used is "no money, no mission" to justify an organization's termination of care provided for those who cannot afford to pay for it. Hospitals with large amounts of uncompensated care have to manage the organization so that it offers some services that have better reimbursements (such as rehabilitation and cosmetic surgery) as a way to offset losses. More fiscally sound hospitals must ask themselves whether they are meeting a general duty under the principle of justice to offer unprofitable but needed services that benefit the wider community.

Technology is central to the ethical and legal problems about death and dying that have arisen. New technology may solve some problems, but it is likely to create other dilemmas as it solves existing problems. Most death and dying issues for the very old and very young would not even be under consideration were it not for technology.

Several marketing activities have ethical components. True marketing attempts to satisfy customer needs. To know what those needs are, marketers study information about consumers and try to project and predict what their needs will be. Need is subjective. For example, with all the clinical evidence that is available, why would a woman request a radical mastectomy when her physician indicates that it is not necessary? More than likely, for her, the worry and concern about reoccurring cancer would change her life. With the radical mastectomy, she may feel better in control. Are we to tell her she is wrong?

Reasonable people can reach different conclusions as to what patients need and whether the demand that arises from that need should be met by the health care system. Should people be denied elective procedures such as cosmetic surgery simply because other people judge such procedures as trivial or because what they seek to correct is not

Exhibit 12–8 • Resources for Ethical and Social Responsibility

Patient Bills of Rights

A variety of organizations, including the American Hospital Association, American Medical Association, the Joint Commission on Accreditation of Healthcare Organizations, the Department of Veteran's Affairs, and the American Civil Liberties Union have developed patient bills of rights. They have in common the patient's right to confidentiality and consent. There is considerable variation thereafter but the objective is to point out that patients have rights and must be consulted. The information that patients provide must be kept confidential. The bills of rights reflect the law, but a patient bill of rights is not legally binding.

Professional Codes of Ethics

Self-regulation is one of the factors that differentiates the learned professions—law, medicine, and others. They require members to adopt a code of ethics, complete competency requirements, and determine sanctions. The different professional organizations have expressed guidelines for those who violate the organization's "rules." Membership, the rules, and sanctions are all governed by members of the profession. Licensure statutes (enacted in each state) are reviewed by members of the profession that the statutes are designed to regulate. This gives ethical considerations determined by the profession the force of law. Breaching them could lead to license suspension or revocation. It is important to note that this has not been done with great enthusiasm or frequently.

There are codes for physicians written by the American Medical Association, for nurses written by the American Nurses Association, for health care executives written by the American College of Healthcare Executives, for nursing home administrators written by the American College of Health Care Administrators, for hospitals by the American Hospital Association, and for nursing facilities covered by the American Healthcare Association. In addition to ethical codes developed by the various professional associations, nearly all clinical groups are regulated by state laws.

Institutional Review Boards

Institutional review boards (IRBs) are required by the Department of Health and Human Services and the Food and Drug Administration as well as the Environmental Protection Agency, the National Science Foundation, and the Consumer Product Safety Commission when human subjects participate in experimentation. Health care organizations that receive grant funds for research and use human subjects must use an institutional review board. Acceptable IRBs have a minimum of five members, who are expected to have varying backgrounds (at least one member must have professional interests that are nonscientific) and who are capable of reviewing research proposals and activities of the type commonly performed by the organization.

Institutional Ethics Committees

Institutional ethics committees (IECs) have no specific guidelines. Sometimes these groups are responsible to the organization's administration, sometimes they report to the governing board, and sometimes to the clinical staff.[1] Generally they are used for administrative issues as well as biomedical ethical issues. Because there is such a variety in the activities that this group might undertake, each IEC should develop a statement of its ethics, derived from the organizational philosophy and mission. In some institutions, the IECs have a very limited scope—they answer questions about the terminally ill, specifically whether to continue life support. These so-called god squads help determine when life support should be withdrawn and the patient declared dead. Typically, most IECs have a broader role and have undertaken activities such as developing do-not-resuscitate (DNR) orders and patient consent policies as well as educational programs.

Infant Care Review Committees

Infant care review committees (ICRCs) have become more common since the enactment in 1984 of federal legislation that directs the Department of Health and Human Services to encourage their establishment within health care facilities, especially those with tertiary-level neonatal care units. ICRCs specialize in the biomedical ethical problems of infants with life-threatening conditions. Recommended membership includes a practicing physician who specializes in infants including pediatricians, neonatologists, pediatric surgeons or others; a practicing nurse; a hospital administrator; a social worker; a representative of a disability group; a lay community member; and a member of the facility's medical staff, who should serve as chair. DHHS recommends that these committees have adequate staff support including legal counsel; procedures to ensure that hospital personnel and patient families are fully informed of its existence, functions, and 24-hour availability; that it inform itself of pertinent legal requirements and procedures, including state laws; and that it maintain records of its deliberations and summary descriptions of the cases considered and their disposition.[2]

continued

[1] For further discussion of institutional ethics committees, see Judith Wilson Ross, et al., *Health Care Ethics Committees: The Next Generation* (Chicago: American Hospital Publishing, 1993).

[2] Department of Health and Human Services, "Services and Treatment for Disabled Infants: Model Guidelines for Health Care Providers to Establish Infant Care Review Committees," *Federal Register* 50, no. 72 (April 15, 1985), p. 14893.

Exhibit 12–8 · Continued

Advanced Directives

Individuals have requested a variety of advanced directives.

Living wills, based on state statutes, are acceptable in forty-two states.[3] Patients must rely on the willingness of caregivers to accept such documents. In general, the laws recognize a patient's right to instruct physicians to withhold or withdraw life-sustaining procedures. The problem arises in that the patient must have completed all documentation at a time when he or she was mentally competent, and in some states patients must reaffirm the living will at the time of their terminal illness (which may not be possible). Problems continue to surface concerning living wills: how to determine the patient's mental status, establishing the presence of a terminal illness, and determining whether the patient comprehends the effect of what is being done.

Durable power of attorney provides for someone else, typically a family member or the individual's attorney, to act in their behalf concerning withdrawing or withholding life support.

Do-not-resuscitate orders should be applied based on policies determined by the health care organization that affirm the right of patients to provide direction to their caregivers regarding the aggressiveness of life-saving efforts.

[3] Kurt Darr, *Ethics in Health Services Management,* 2d ed. (Baltimore: Health Professions Press, 1991), p. 187.

life threatening? This level of infringement on individual autonomy is greater than the public is likely to accept at this point in history.[61]

Managers have an ethical duty to ensure the confidentiality of all patients' medical records. This means a health care organization that uses its patients for a mailing list is violating confidentiality if they select heart patients (or AIDS patients), for example. To be ethically safe, all past patients would have to be sent the same mailing.

Managers who are responsible for health care teaching institutions have a major ethical concern with consent. When a patient requests a specific physician to do surgery, signs a consent form for that physician to do the surgery, and then a resident actually performs the surgery, the patient may be justifiably angry. Patients have a right to know. They need to be thoroughly informed of any experimental procedures and give permission for the physician to perform these procedures or to have someone else perform the procedures under the physician's guidance.

Managers often think that they have no responsibility in decisions concerning death and dying because these are "clinical matters." Doubtlessly, physicians are prime decision makers in this area but health care organization managers must be knowledgeable and participate in policy development and implementation to guide physicians within the context of their health care organizations. A major problem is how we define death and when we are willing to terminate life. This includes beginning-of-life issues with infants born with severe disabilities and end-of-life issues for the elderly, as well as individuals who have been irrevocably harmed and cannot be expected to ever come out of a persistent vegetative state.

Functional and Organization-Wide Strategies As the Means

As suggested in Chapter 1, organizations are managed through a hierarchy of strategies that leads to a decision logic for strategy formulation. Strategic decisions should be made sequentially with each decision more explicitly defining the strategy. The directional strategies provide a picture of the general direction of the organization. The adaptive strategies, market entry strategies, and positioning strategies provide further focus for the organization. In a sense, these strategies clarify the *ends* the organization would like to achieve, and the functional and organization-wide strategies provide the *means* for accomplishing those ends. The functional and organization-wide strategies must *do,* or carry out, the broader organization's strategy. Therefore, it is important to ensure that all activities associated with the functional and organization-wide strategies make a specific and clear contribution to the organization's directional, adaptive, market entry, and positioning strategies. The only justification for functional and organization-wide strategies is to achieve the broader ends of the organization. Functional managers must remember that their functional areas are not the ends but rather the means. Similarly, the only reason to change the organization's culture, structure, facilities, or ethical and social policies is so they make a greater contribution to the overall goals of the organization. In addition, the functional and organization-wide strategies must be coordinated and complement each other. Exhibit 12–9 summarizes the organization-wide input to strategic management. Strategic control, examined in Chapter 13, can help ensure functional strategies are coordinated and contribute to the broader organizational strategy.

Exhibit 12–9 • Organization-Wide Input to Strategic Management

Hierarchy of Strategic Decisions	Organization-Wide Input
Directional Strategies	
Mission	*Culture:* Ensure culture is consistent with the stated mission.
	Structure: Determine that present structure complements the mission.
	Facilities: Determine the facilities needed to accomplish the organization's mission.
	Ethics: Ensure that the mission is morally and socially acceptable.
Vision	*Culture:* Communicate necessary changes in the culture to achieve the organization's hope for the future.
	Structure: Initiate structural alterations needed to support the vision.
	Facilities: Determine appropriate facilities to realize the vision.
	Ethics: Ensure that the vision incorporates morality and social responsibility.
Values	*Culture:* Ensure that the culture is supportive of the stated values.
	Structure: Ensure that the structure facilitates stated values.
	Facilities: Physical environment should facilitate values.
	Ethics: Ensure that values are consistent with prevailing views of community and social responsibility.
Objectives	*Culture:* Assess the ease with which objectives can be accomplished within present cultural constraints.
	Structure: Determine if the present structure inhibits accomplishment of the objectives.
	Facilities: Determine if the organization's objectives require new or remodeling of facilities.
	Ethics: Ensure that objectives complement ethical and social responsibility values.
Adaptive Strategies	
Expansion Strategies	
Diversification—Related and Unrelated	*Culture:* Suggest cultural changes needed for expansion into related areas and the suitability of culture for entering unfamiliar areas of operation.
	Structure: Determine the most appropriate way to organize the expanded related or unrelated operations.

continued

Exhibit 12–9 • Continued

Hierarchy of Strategic Decisions	Organization-Wide Input
Diversification—Related and Unrelated *(cont.)*	*Facilities:* Evaluate the adequacy of existing facilities for expansion into related areas and new and different kinds of facilities for unrelated operations. *Ethics:* Determine if there are any ethical traps in present areas or unknown ethical minefields in unrelated areas.
Vertical Integration—Forward and Backward	*Culture:* Determine the cultural changes needed for entering unfamiliar areas of operation. *Structure:* Assess the changes that will be required for managing vertically integrated operations. *Facilities:* Recommend changes to the facility for expansion into vertically integrated operations. *Ethics:* Determine if unique ethical risks are associated with expansion into vertically integrated operations.
Market Development	*Culture:* Facilitate cultural changes needed to expand into new market segments and geographic areas. *Structure:* Define and implement structural changes needed to effectively manage new market segments and areas. *Facilities:* Construct and equip new facilities for new markets and areas. *Ethics:* Analyze potential ethical dangers of market development.
Product Development	*Culture:* Evaluate the organizational culture's capacity to develop and deliver new services. *Structure:* Determine and implement changes in the organization structure needed to manage new services. *Facilities:* Assess the adequacy of existing facilities to develop and deliver new services. *Ethics:* Analyze possible ethical dangers of developing and delivering new services.
Penetration	*Culture:* Assess the organizational culture's receptivity to measures necessary to expand through penetration activities (i.e., advertising). *Structure:* Analyze the capacity of the present structure to absorb the functions needed to reinforce the penetration strategy. *Facilities:* Determine any new facilities needed to support penetration efforts. *Ethics:* Evaluate contemporary ethical and social responsibility attitudes relative to promotion and other efforts required for penetration.
Contraction Strategies	
Divestiture	*Culture:* Assess the impact of divestiture on the current or desired organizational culture. *Structure:* Recommend structural changes to implement after divestiture. *Facilities:* Analyze alternative uses and markets for any facilities and equipment no longer needed after divestiture. *Ethics:* Evaluate the ethical and social implications of divestiture on individuals and the community. Will the divested services still be available in the community?
Liquidation	*Culture:* What effect will liquidation of all or parts of the organization have on the culture of the surviving parts? *Structure:* Determine the changes in structure that will occur after liquidation. *Facilities:* Analyze the market potential for the assets that will be liquidated. *Ethics:* Determine the effect of the liquidation on the health of the community.
Harvesting	*Culture:* Assess the effects of harvesting (short range) on the organization's culture. *Structure:* Assess possible ways in which structural streamlining can facilitate the goals of harvesting. *Facilities:* Project the effect of harvesting on the need for and the value of facilities and equipment. *Ethics:* What will be the effect of a harvesting strategy on the health of individuals in the community?
Retrenchment	*Culture:* Assess the impact of retrenchment on current and desired organizational culture. *Structure:* Evaluate streamlining of the organization's structure as a reinforcement to retrenchment. *Facilities:* If facilities are "cut back" during retrenchment, can the organization catch up in the future? *Ethics:* Analyze possible ethical and social implications of retrenchment.

Exhibit 12–9 · **Continued**

Hierarchy of Strategic Decisions	Organization-Wide Input
Stabilization Strategies	
Enhancement	*Culture:* Communicate the necessity of an organizational culture that values and rewards enhancement efforts.
	Structure: Evaluate the contribution that changes in structure can make to efficiency of operations and improvement in services delivery.
	Facilities: Determine contributions that will enhance efficiency and quality.
	Ethics: Highlight the ethical and social desirability of enhancement efforts.
Status Quo	*Culture:* Evaluate the actions needed to maintain a positive culture in a no-growth environment.
	Structure: What organizational changes should be deferred in light of the commitment to the status quo?
	Facilities: Emphasize maintenance and repair of current facilities and equipment.
	Ethics: Ensure that no ethical or social issues arise from the conscious decision to commit to the status quo.
Market Entry Strategies	
Purchase	
Acquisition	*Culture:* Assess the cultural compatibility of the target organization and the willingness of the existing culture to absorb the acquired operations.
	Structure: Evaluate the relative advantages of centralized versus decentralized operations of the newly formed organization.
	Facilities: Determine the contribution acquired facilities and equipment can make to the new organization.
	Ethics: Assess the ethical and social implications of the acquisition.
Licensing	*Culture:* Evaluate licensing in light of historical modes of operating and project needed changes in organizational culture.
	Structure: Develop a structure to incorporate a new way of doing business.
	Facilities: Determine how and when the organization can use the facilities of others.
	Ethics: Evaluate the ethical and social perceptions of licensing agreements.
Cooperation	
Merger	*Culture:* Determine how to avoid culture clash among individuals of the merging organizations.
	Structure: Evaluate the structural changes needed to ensure maximum synergies from the merger.
	Facilities: Analyze synergies of facilities and equipment of the merging organizations.
	Ethics: Consider the ethical and social implications of the merger.
Alliance	*Culture:* Assess the receptivity of aligning parties to a cooperative culture.
	Structure: Evaluate any structural changes needed to facilitate an alliance.
	Facilities: Determine any facilities and equipment not currently available that are needed to ensure success of the alliance.
	Ethics: Analyze any possible adverse ethical and social implications of cooperation.
Joint Venture	*Culture:* Assess the cultural receptivity of both parties to a joint venture.
	Structure: Determine the organizational changes needed to ensure success of the joint venture.
	Facilities: Analyze the facility needs versus those needed for the success of the joint venture.
	Ethics: Analyze any possible adverse ethical and social implications of the joint venture.
Development	
Internal Development	*Culture:* Determine the capacity of the organizational culture to encourage, reinforce, and tolerate internal development.

continued

Exhibit 12–9 · **Continued**

Hierarchy of Strategic Decisions	Organization-Wide Input
Internal Development *(cont.)*	*Structure:* Determine organizational components that should be added or deleted to facilitate the success of internal development.
	Facilities: Ensure that facilities are available that will be necessary to support internal development.
	Ethics: Assess ethical and social implications of an internal development strategy.
Positioning Strategies	
Marketwide	
Cost Leadership	*Culture:* Assess the present culture's interpretation of a cost leadership strategy and the efficiency measures needed to achieve it.
	Structure: Assess structural changes that could contribute to cost efficiencies.
	Facilities: What can facilities management contribute to increase cost efficiencies?
	Ethics: Evaluate ethical and social implications of actions taken to attain cost leadership.
Differentiation	*Culture:* Analyze the tolerance of the present culture to actions designed to differentiate services.
	Structure: Evaluate the structural changes that may be necessary to effectively manage more differentiated services.
	Facilities: How much differentiation of facilities will be required to differentiate services?
	Ethics: Evaluate ethical and social implications of a differentiation strategy.
Market Segment	
Focus—Cost Leadership	*Culture:* Assess the present culture's interpretation of a focused cost leadership strategy and the efficiency measures needed to achieve it.
	Structure: Assess structural changes that would be necessary to support this strategy.
	Facilities: What can facilities management contribute to increase cost efficiencies?
	Ethics: Evaluate ethical and social implications of actions taken to attain cost leadership.
Focus—Differentiation	*Culture:* Analyze the tolerance of the present culture to actions designed to further differentiate services for a specific segment.
	Structure: Evaluate the structural changes that may be necessary to effectively manage differentiated services for one segment.
	Facilities: How will differentiation of services impact facilities?
	Ethics: Evaluate ethical and social implications of a differentiation strategy focused on one segment.
Operational Strategies	
Functional—Organization-Wide	*Culture:* Ensure that an organizational culture exists that will facilitate the strategy of choice.
	Structure: Ensure that the appropriate organization structure is in place to facilitate the selected strategy.
	Facilities: Determine the facilities that are necessary to accomplish the organization's mission.
	Ethics: Incorporate ethical and social concerns in all strategic decision making.

Summary and Conclusions

In this chapter four important organization-wide strategies are examined—organizational culture, organization structure, physical facilities, and ethical and social responsibilities. These strategies have two things in common—they are directed at the entire organization, and they are critically important in the implementation of the directional, adaptive, and market entry strategies. In other words, the organization-wide strategies discussed in this chapter are designed to support strategic management.

If excellence is to be achieved, the culture of the organization must support and reinforce an understanding of the mission and vision, the emergence of leadership at all levels, teamwork, responsiveness to external change, innovation, quality, and a passion for patient service. Adaptive cultures allow for reasonable risk-taking behavior. Although adaptive cultures are not easy to build and maintain, successful organizations seem to be especially good at sensing those things in their history that should be preserved while readily modifying others in light of changing conditions.

One of the most important yet difficult changes to make is in an organization's structure. Organization structures often become a symbol of what makes an organization successful. People become comfortable with "where they fit" and established reporting arrangements. As a result, efforts to change the organization chart is often seen as a threat to be resisted. In reality, however, organization structures must be changed if any significant improvements are to be made in the organization's culture. An organization chart is one of the most cherished "artifacts" of culture because it defines communication and authority patterns. If employees are expected to exercise leadership, assume responsibility for things not normally in their job descriptions, and assume reasonable risks, the organization will have to be less hierarchical and authority driven.

Another important element of an organization's culture is its physical facilities. These facilities are more accurately thought of as the "shell" within which health care is delivered. It includes the total physical environment. The way in which facilities are designed and maintained says much about the culture and values of an organization. Physical facility strategies need to consider more than the design and construction of general- and special-purpose buildings. A comprehensive physical facilities strategy includes operations and maintenance, security, materials management, and others that can enhance or detract from the health care organization's strategy.

The final organization-wide strategy discussed in this chapter is the ethical and social responsibilities of health care organizations. Ethical and socially responsible decision making is an important element in strategic management. In Chapter 1, strategic management was referred to as a "philosophy" or system of thinking that values adjusting the organization in whatever ways are necessary to fit the external environment. Fitting the organization to the ethical and social values of the larger society is essential to success in the health care environment.

Although it is recognized that ethical and social commitments of strategic leaders in organizations are, to a large extent, based on personal background, religious convictions, and experiences, there are useful aids to encourage ethical and socially responsible strategic decision making. For example, it is important to have a plan for ethical behavior. These plans are often greatly facilitated by the existence of recognized codes of ethical behavior for health care managers.

Key Terms and Concepts in Strategic Management

adaptive cultures	code of ethics	environmental services
champions of change	conflict of interest	ethics
clinical engineering	corporate boards of directors	facilities management

fiduciary duty	organization-wide strategies	social responsibility
forming (stage of group development)	performing (stage of group development)	statement of philosophy
framing (stage of group development)	philanthropic boards of directors	storming (stage of group development)
materials management	rhetorical crafting	wayfinding
norming (stage of group development)	role modeling	

Questions for Class Discussion

1. Why are there so few excellent organizations? What are some of the excellent organizations you can identify? What is it that makes an organization excellent?

2. Why is culture change so difficult in health care organizations? What are some ways leaders could make culture change easier?

3. What are some of the actions that can be taken to make work groups function more as teams? Why is teamwork so hard to build in organizations? What role do mission, vision, and values play in building teamwork?

4. Which do you think changes first, strategy or structure? After formulating your answer and making your case, argue the opposite position.

5. What are the primary differences between corporate and philanthropic boards of directors? Why do you think corporate boards are becoming increasingly popular in health care organizations?

6. Why is facilities management an increasing concern for strategic management?

7. How do facilities affect a health care organization's strategy?

8. Do you think the "environment" has an impact on a patient's recovery time?

9. Who is responsible for ethical acts and practices within the health care organization?

10. What stakeholders have ethical and social responsibility claims on the organization?

11. How are ethical problems similar to other managerial problems? How are they different?

12. Explain how a statement of philosophy instills a sense of ethics into an organization's culture.

13. Explain how a conflict of interest might arise in a health care organization. How would you prevent conflicts of interest?

14. Discuss the process you would initiate to introduce a greater emphasis on ethics in a health care organization.

15. What are the four ethical principles that apply to health care organizations?

Notes

1. Tom Peters and Nancy Austin, *A Passion for Excellence: The Leadership Difference* (New York: Random House, 1985), p. 46.

2. Ralph Stacey, "Strategy as Order Emerging from Chaos," *Long Range Planning* 26, no. 1 (1993), pp. 10–17; and Malcom J. Morgan, "How Corporate Culture Drives Strategy," *Long Range Planning* 26, no. 2 (1993), pp. 110–118.

3. R. H. Kilmann, M. J. Saxton, and R. Serpa, "Issues in Understanding and Changing Culture," *California Management Review* 28, no. 2 (1986), pp. 87–94.

4. Robert W. Fleming, "Understanding the Mayo Culture," *Medical Group Management* (May/June 1989), pp. 46–49.

5. B. Z. Posner, J. M. Kouzes, and W. H. Schmidt, "Shared Values Make a Difference: An Empirical Test of Corporate Culture," *Human Resource Management* 24, no. 3 (1985), pp. 293–309.

6. J. E. Sheridan, "Organizational Culture and Employee Retention," *Academy of Management Journal* 35, no. 4 (December 1992), pp. 1036–1056.

7. D. R. Denison, "Bringing Corporate Culture to the Bottom Line," *Organizational Dynamics* 12, no. 12 (Autumn 1984), pp. 5–22.

8. John P. Kotter and James L. Heskett, *Corporate Culture and Performance* (New York: Free Press, 1992).

9. Ibid., p. 44.

10. For a more detailed discussion of adaptive cultures see P. J. Frost, L. F. Moore, M. L. Louis, C. C. Lundberg, and Joanne Martin, eds., *Reframing Organizational Culture* (Newbury Park, California: Sage Publications, 1991).

11. This discussion of the "language of leadership" is from Jay A. Conger, "Inspiring Others: The Language of Leadership," *Academy of Management Executive* 5, no. 1 (1991), pp. 31–45.

12. Paula Eubanks, "CEO Walkabouts Get Firsthand Look at Employee Problems," *Hospitals* (May 5, 1990), pp. 50–51.

13. G. M. Parker, *Team Players and Team Work: The New Competitive Business Strategy* (San Francisco: Jossey-Bass, 1990), Chapter 6.

14. W. Jack Duncan, "Translations: Why Some People Loaf in Groups and Some People Loaf Alone," *Academy of Management Executive* 8, no. 3 (1994), pp. 79–80.

15. J. R. Katzenbach and D. K. Smith, *The Wisdom of Teams: Creating the High-Performance Organization* (Boston: Harvard Business School Press, 1993), p. 263.

16. Edgar H. Schein, "Corporate Culture Is the Real Key to Creativity," *Business Month* (May 1989), p. 73.

17. Michael Bice, "Corporate Culture Must Foster Innovation," *Hospitals* (November 1990), p. 58.

18. Ari Ginsberg and Eric Abrahamson, "Champions of Change and Strategic Shifts: The Role of Internal and External Change Advocates," *Journal of Management Studies* 28, no. 3 (March 1991), pp. 173–190.

19. D. J. Daniel and W. D. Reitsperger, "Linking Quality Strategy with Management Control Systems: Empirical Evidence from Japanese Industry," *Accounting, Organizations, and Society* 16, no. 1 (1991), pp. 601–618.

20. G. L. Clark, P. F. Kaminski, and D. R. Rink, "Consumer Complaints: Advice on How Companies Should Respond Based on an Empirical Study," *Journal of Services Marketing* 10, no. 6 (1992), pp. 41–50; and Cynthia A. Lengnick-Hall, "Customer Contribution to Quality: A Different View of the Customer-Oriented Firm," *Academy of Management Review* 21, no. 3 (1996), pp. 791–824.

21. Peters and Austin, *A Passion for Excellence,* p. 98.

22. Richard Reed, David J. Lemak, and Joseph C. Montgomery, "Beyond Process: TQM Content and Firm Performance," *Academy of Management Journal* 21, no. 1 (1996), pp. 173–202.

23. R. H. Waterman, Jr., *The Renewal Factor* (New York: Bantam Books, 1987), p. xii.

24. J. A. Alexander, L. L. Morlock, and B. D. Gifford, "The Effects of Corporate Restructuring on Hospital Policymaking," *Health Services Research* 23, no. 2 (1988), pp. 311–338; and A. R. Kovner, "Improving Hospital Board Effectiveness: An Update," *Frontiers in Health Services Management* 6 (Spring 1990), pp. 3–27.

25. S. M. Shortell, "New Directions in Hospital Governance," *Hospital and Health Services Administration* 34, no. 1 (Spring 1989), pp. 7–23.

26. M. L. Fennell and J. A. Alexander, "Governing Boards and Profound Organizational Change," *Medical Care Review* 46 (Summer 1989), pp. 157–187.

27. J. A. Alexander and L. L. Morlock, "CEO-Board Relations Under Hospital Corporate Restructuring," *Hospital and Health Services Administration* 33, no. 3 (Winter 1988), p. 436.

28. A. L. Delbecq and S. L. Gill, "Developing Strategic Direction for Governing Boards," *Hospital and Health Services Administration* 33, no. 1 (Spring 1988), pp. 25–35.

29. R. A. McLean, "Outside Directors: Stakeholder Representation in Investor-Owned Health Care Organizations," *Hospital and Health Services Administration* 34, no. 1 (Spring 1989), pp. 25–38.

30. H. S. Zuckerman, "Redefining the Role of the CEO: Challenges and Conflicts," *Hospital and Health Services Administration* 34, no. 1 (Spring 1989), pp. 25–38.

31. A. D. Kaluzny, "Revitalizing Decision Making at the Middle Management Level," *Hospital and Health Services Administration* 34, no. 1 (Spring 1989), pp. 39–51.

32. A. D. Chandler, Jr., *Strategy and Structure* (Cambridge, Massachusetts: MIT Press, 1962).

33. Adapted from J. R. Montanari, C. P. Morgan, and J. S. Bracker, *Strategic Management: A Choice Approach* (Chicago: Dryden Press, 1990), Chapter 6.

34. V. James McLarney, Preface, *Effective Health Care Facilities Management* (Chicago: American Hospital Association Publishing, 1991), p. xiv.

35. Janet R. Carpman and Myron A. Grant, *Design That Cares: Planning Health Facilities for Patients and Visitors,* 2d ed. (Chicago: American Hospital Publishing, 1993).

36. Ibid., p. 19.

37. R. S. Ulrich, "Effects of Interior Design on Wellness: Theory and Recent Scientific Research," *Health Care Interior Design* 3 (1991), pp. 97–109.

38. Carpman and Grant, *Design That Cares,* pp. 9–10.

39. David A. Berkowitz and Melanie M. Swan, "Technology Decision Making," *Health Progress* 74, no. 1 (January/February 1993), pp. 42–47.

40. Gary D. Slack, "Clinical Engineering," in *Effective Health Care Facilities Management,* ed. V. James McLarney et al. (Chicago: American Hospital Publishing, 1991), p. 16.

41. Hugh O. Nash, Jr., James Robin Barrick, Edward Spivey Lipsey, Jr., and Branton B. Blount, "Engineering and Maintenance," in ibid., p. 1.

42. Augustine O. Agho and Stacey T. Cyphert, "Problem Areas Faced by Hospital Administrators," *Hospital and Health Services Administration* 37, no. 1 (Spring 1992), p. 78.

43. Aralee Scardina, "Environmental Services," in *Effective Health Care Management Facilities,* p. 29.

44. Sherman G. McGill, Jr., "Security," in ibid., p. 58.

45. Patrick E. Carroll, Clarence W. Daly, and Jamie C. Kowalski, "Materials Management," in ibid., p. 97.

46. Kurt Darr, *Ethics in Health Services Management,* 2d ed. (Baltimore: Health Professions Press, 1991), p. 231.

47. Archie B. Carroll, "The Pyramid of Corporate Social Responsibility: Towards a Moral Management of Organizational Stakeholders," *Business Horizons* 34, no. 4 (July–August 1991), pp. 39–48.

48. Ibid.

49. A. E. Singer, "Strategy as Moral Philosophy," *Strategic Management Journal* 15, no. 3 (1994), pp. 191–213.

50. Darr, *Ethics in Health Services Management,* p. 144.

51. Ibid., p. 2.

52. Arthur A. Thompson, Jr., and A. J. Strickland III, *Strategic Management: Concepts and Cases,* 8th ed. (Homewood, Illinois: Richard D. Irwin Company, 1995) , p. 52.

53. Darr, *Ethics in Health Services Management,* p. 44.

54. Ibid., p. 95.

55. The state of Oregon has pioneered this effort in the United States. Current literature on the Oregon Plan abounds. Oregon identifies the specific medical procedures that will be paid for by the state based on outcomes and budget available. The people of Oregon have been heavily involved in "drawing the line" for their state.

56. Robert L. Goldman, "Practical Applications of Health Care Marketing Ethics," *Healthcare Financial Management* 47, no. 3 (March 1993), p. 47.

57. David L. Perry, "Keys to Creating an Effective Ethics Program," *Healthcare Executive* 8, no. 2 (March/April 1993), p. 26; and Larue Tone Hosmer, "Strategic Planning As If Ethics Mattered," *Strategic Management Journal* 15, no. 1 (Special Issue 1994), pp. 17–34.

58. Ibid.

59. Goldman, "Practical Applications of Health Care Marketing Ethics," p. 46.

60. Thompson and Strickland, *Strategic Management,* p. 51.

61. Darr, *Ethics in Health Services Management,* p. 223.

Additional Readings

Champy, James, and Nitin Nohria, *Fast Forward: The Best Ideas on Managing Business Change* (Boston: Harvard Business Review Press, 1996). A collection of outstanding articles, two by the editors, that urge executives to seize the opportunities presented by change and to set goals for their organizations to accomplish. These essays should prove useful to executives in industries such as health care where the environment is always changing in fast forward time.

Ghoshal, Sumantra, and Christopher A. Bartlett, *The Individualized Corporation* (New York: HarperBusiness, 1996). This book is based on a three-part series of articles in the *Harvard Business Review* arguing that the key to success is leading rich organizational cultures rather than attempting to control and retool corporate machines. The book is a thought-provoking treatment representing a radically changing management paradigm.

Gift, Robert G., and Catherine F. Kinney, Editors, *Today's Management Methods: A Guide for the Health Care Executive* (Chicago: American Hospital Publishing, 1996). A practical guide that provides brief overviews of the latest management techniques and places them within a systems context. The book employs a framework that allows even busy executives to see how individual management methods fit into the organization-wide framework for effectiveness.

Gomes, Hélio, *Quality Quotes* (Milwaukee: Quality Press, 1996). More than 1,500 quotes on every aspect of quality by 550 authors, business leaders, scientists, and Nobel Prize winners. A valuable reference book to help in making oral and written presentations by adding credibility and inspiration.

Hood, John M., *The Heroic Enterprise* (New York: Free Press, 1996). An interesting argument that goes against conventional wisdom but underscores a great deal of classical economic thinking. It states that corporations do the most good when they do what they were created to do—make profits. Profit seeking is seen as more than a mere economic incentive. It is a dynamic element in our social order and may be the best measure of ultimate social responsibility.

Controlling and Creating the Strategy

Part 4 completes the strategic management process with chapters that discuss strategic control and a comprehensive strategic plan. Chapter 13, "Control of the Strategy," illustrates that the strategic management process must be monitored, evaluated, and adjusted when necessary. A framework for controlling the strategy is presented with questions for validating the strategic assumptions, as well as the directional, adaptive, market entry, positioning, and operational strategies.

The last chapter pulls the entire strategic management process together through a complete and comprehensive example. Chapter 14 chronicles three years of strategic management experience of the Indiana State Department of Health. Each of the strategic management processes is described in detail along with the actual methods used and the results achieved. This chapter demonstrates the actual use of the concepts presented in this text and the practicality of their application.

Control of the Strategy

➤ **Learning Objectives**

After completing this chapter you should be able to:

1. Understand the nature of control and discuss why health care organizations need strategic control.

2. Discuss the relationship between planning and control.

3. Understand the characteristics of effective control in health care organizations.

4. Describe and discuss a practical framework for controlling organizational strategies.

5. Understand that the type of strategic change is determined by management's assessment of the urgency of strategic issues and the capability of the organization to deal with these issues.

6. Determine the need for evolutionary change or revolutionary change.

7. Identify and discuss organizational mechanisms for implementing strategic control.

8. Understand the role of contingency planning in strategic control.

9. Understand strategic change, the frequency of such change, and the forces that put pressure on organizations to engage in strategic change.

The Nature of Strategic Control

As suggested in the Introductory Incident, the control process may be applied at any level in an organization. For instance, *operational control* focuses on controlling individual performance, work groups, or specific processes such as operations, inventory, scheduling, and so on. These types of controls are necessary and a part of the overall control of an organization. Generally, control involves agreeing upon objectives, measuring performance, evaluating performance against the objectives, and taking corrective action, if necessary. More specifically, *control* is defined as a combination of components that act together to ensure that the level of actual performance comes as close as possible to a set of desired performance specifications.

Health Management Associates Controls Its Strategy

Health Management Associates (HMA) has prospered by understanding its market niche and controlling its strategy at several different levels. HMA has become one of the most successful hospital chains by concentrating on the rural and non-urban hospital markets (there are approximately 2,400 acute-care facilities outside metropolitan statistical areas). Typically, managed-care pressures in these markets are less intense and physicians perceive opportunities to establish practices that have fewer competitors. HMA has been the most successful company at acquiring these hospitals and operating them in the black despite intense cost pressures.

HMA pays close attention to margins, revenue growth, and return on investment. It has far better financial ratios than any of the competition. In 1995, HMA had record income of $63.3 million on net patient service revenues of $531.1 million. Over the first half of the decade, HMA's revenues have grown an average of 21 percent a year while its earnings have jumped to an annual average of 29 percent. HMA's controls, however, are not limited to financial measures.

HMA controls its strategy by only acquiring undervalued rural and non-urban hospitals where it can become the sole or dominant provider in the market. In turn, the rural hospitals gain access to millions of dollars in capital that helps them add tertiary services and improve their patient base. In controlling the strategy, HMA does not want to own the greatest number of rural and non-urban hospitals; rather the company wants its hospitals to own its markets. William Schoen, HMA's president, chief executive officer, and chairman of the board stated, "Within three years, we become the sole provider or dominant provider in the areas we

go into. We try to provide all of the health care in that community." Having a well-focused strategy keeps HMA out of unfamiliar territory and away from larger competitors that have concentrated primarily on urban markets.

In addition, HMA controls its operations and culture. As the company grows larger, management has persisted in acting and governing itself as a small company. HMA employs forty-four people at its headquarters in Naples, Florida—a number that has changed very little over the years. More than 8,000 other employees work at HMA's twenty-five hospitals. HMA has created innovative information systems and effective marketing. Moreover, the company has a strong relationship with physicians who constitute one-third of the directors in HMA hospitals. HMA has over 600 managed-care contracts.

Upon acquisition, the value of an HMA hospital rises rapidly because it can take advantage of other HMA-developed controls. For example, the company's Quality Service Management Program compiles surveys of patients' experiences while in the hospital. Patient approval scores must be maintained above 90 percent. In addition, HMA has instituted its Nurse First program, ensuring that a nurse is the first person a patient sees on entering the hospital. These various control systems appear to be effective. HMA has never had a malpractice claim settled for more than $1 million at any of its hospitals, a claim that few others can make.

Source: Bruce Japsen, "Investor-Owned Chains Seek Rich Rural Harvest," *Modern Healthcare* 26, no. 27 (July 1, 1996), pp. 32–37.

Strategic control is much broader and is an important part of the strategic management process. *Strategic control* provides top management a means of determining whether the organization is performing satisfactorily; it is an explicit process for refining or completely altering the strategy. Strategic control is an inherent part of situational analysis and strategy formulation and difficult to separate from them.

A *strategic control system* is a system to support managers in assessing how well the organization's strategy compares to its progress in the accomplishment of its objectives and, when discrepancies are detected, to support areas that need attention.[1] Therefore, the strategic control system monitors, evaluates, and adjusts the strategic implementation (the operational strategies), the strategy itself (directional, adaptive, market entry, and positioning strategies), and the situational analysis processes (validates the strategic assumptions).

The Need for Control

The need for strategic control is a logical extension of the need for strategy. There is a compelling case for the establishment of an explicit strategic control system within organizations. Specifically, strategic control systems:

- provide a means to coordinate the efforts of everyone in the organization;
- motivate managers to achieve objectives;
- provide an early detection system that indicates when strategic assumptions are wrong or when environmental conditions have changed; and
- provide a method for management to intervene to correct an ineffective or inefficient strategy.[2]

Agreement by management on the objectives and how those objectives will be measured helps to coordinate the efforts of everyone in the organization. As discussed in Chapter 5, although objectives are a part of the planning process, they are part of the control process as well. Objectives not only provide standards of performance but also suggest a means for the evaluation of performance. Therefore, objectives should be clear, precise, and measurable. These attributes provide direction for a coordinated effort, establish explicit measures of progress, and point out where corrective action may be required.

Objectives and the subsequent evaluation of progress toward those objectives motivate employees. The control system assigns individual responsibility for the accomplishment of objectives and bases individual reward on the achievement of organizational goals. Thus, the control system provides the personal incentives that align individual and organizational objectives and motivates managers to devote their best efforts to achieving the organization's objectives.[3]

Management may have formulated a strategy based on an erroneous assumption, or it may have correctly matched the strategy with environmental conditions, but those conditions may have changed. The strategic control system, as it monitors the progress of the organization, should provide early warning signals that something may be wrong. If the organization is not making progress toward achieving its objectives, the strategic control process will call for additional investigation. This process may reveal the faulty reasoning of the past or the new environmental conditions that may impair the strategy in the future.

Even the best-laid plans will sometimes fail or need major adjustments. The control system provides a method for managers to evaluate the strategy and initiate required changes. Such changes may be directed toward the operational, market entry, or positioning strategies in the form of strategic adjustments (evolutionary change) or at the directional or adaptive strategies in the form of strategic change (revolutionary change). By monitoring performance and identifying deviations from agreed-upon objectives, the strategic control system provides the signals that trigger management intervention in the selection, adjustment, or implementation of the strategy. As suggested in Perspective 13–1, management is a controlling activity.

Many hospitals in the nation are carefully reevaluating their missions to be sure they have not "abandoned the values" that have been traditional in health care. One particular area is the importance of recognizing the community as a key stakeholder. Some observers fear that as health care organizations become more cost conscious and technologically intense, the needs of the community will be lost. The Greater Southeast Community Hospital in Washington, D.C., was awarded the Foster G. McGaw Prize for Community Service for its intentional efforts to reassess its mission and involvement in community activities.[4]

The Concept of Control

Organizational control systems, whether operational or strategic, have several fundamental elements. As illustrated in Exhibit 13–1, the control system forms a feedback or self-correcting loop to assure a steady state. Such feedback provides information to ensure that progress is being made toward achieving objectives. All control systems have standards, periodically measure progress, make comparisons to the objectives, determine the problems, and take corrective action, if necessary.

Perspective 13–1

To Manage Is to Control—To Control Is to Manage

To *control* means to regulate, guide, or direct. To *manage* means to control, handle, or direct. Therefore, management *is* control and control *is* management. The very act of managing suggests controlling the behavior or outcome of some process, program, or plan. Vision, mission, values, and strategies are types of controls. Similarly, policies, procedures, rules, and performance evaluations are clearly organizational controls. All of these are attempts to focus organizational efforts toward a defined end. Yet, if these tools are improperly used, employees may perceive control to be dominating, overpowering, dictatorial, or manipulative.

When processes are poorly managed, control runs afoul as well. It is interpreted as domination when management enforces too much control and manages too closely by controlling subprocesses or too many details. Management requires the right touch. If control is too great, we create hopeless bureaucracy. If control is too weak, we have a lack of direction causing difficulty in accomplishing organizational goals. When there is too much management (control), then innovation, creativity, and individual initiative will be stifled; when there is too little, chaos ensues. Management should focus efforts but not be dictatorial or manipulative.

Given how easy it is to overdo management (control), a general rule of thumb is that "less is best." Setting direction and empowering people to make their own decisions on how best to achieve the vision seems to work. Effective management (control) is essential if organizations are to renew themselves; however, overmanaging (overcontrolling) can destroy initiative and be viewed as meddling, often reducing motivation as well.

Exhibit 13–1 • The Concept of Control

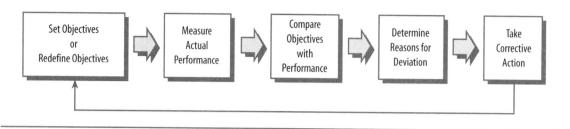

The Characteristics of Control

It is impossible, as well as undesirable, to control everything in an organization. In addition, too much emphasis on control can discourage the exploration of new opportunities and dampen innovation. Therefore, in order to be effective, it is important that organizational controls have certain characteristics. For controls to be effective, they should:

- be based on accurate, relevant, and timely information;
- be directed at controlling only the critical elements;
- be flexible;
- be cost effective;
- be simple and easy to understand;
- be timely; and
- emphasize the exceptions.

All types of control require information; control will be only as good as the information on which it is based. Care should be taken that the information used by managers to assess performance is accurate, relevant to the element being controlled, and current (the latest information available). Strategic control relies primarily on information obtained through external and internal environmental analyses. This information is used to test management's assumptions and assess the organization's performance.

Control should be directed at only a few critical elements. Typically, for most any process only three or four results must occur for the process to be effective. Management must identify and control these essential results. Broadly, the central factor for strategic control is the overall performance of the organization through the appropriateness of the strategy.

Control systems should be both flexible and cost effective. An overzealous application of controls can lead to excessive dogmatism, which may inhibit the real objective of control. Hence, controls should not determine decisions; rather, managers should be allowed to make decisions within acceptable boundaries. Control can be time consuming and costly. Therefore, the fewer and more economical the controls, the better the control system. In strategic management, planning processes and control processes are closely aligned or identical, so flexibility must be an inherent characteristic.

Controls need to be simple and easy to understand. Controls that are overly complex or difficult to apply are often ignored or applied incorrectly. Therefore, management should work to keep controls simple. In addition, control systems need to alert management to possible deviations early in the process. Signals of danger after significant damage has occurred are not effective. Generally, strategic control processes are simply a review of the planning process. Furthermore, this review is accomplished periodically so that deviations may be identified and discussed as early as possible.

Finally, control systems should emphasize the exceptions. Managers can never monitor all the activities within their areas of responsibility at all times. For this reason, controls are effective when they highlight exceptional or out-of-control activities. Strategic controls should alert managers that the organization's mission, vision, values, objectives, strategy, or strategic implementation are not appropriate, effective, or efficient.

A Framework for Controlling Strategy

The logic underlying strategic control is to evaluate the organization's strategy and make changes if necessary. This is the same fundamental logic underpinning the general concept of control that was shown in Exhibit 13–1. The steps of the strategic control model are compared with the general concept of control in Exhibit 13–2. Strategic control provides a more explicit framework for controlling the strategy and determining whether revolutionary or evolutionary change is needed.

Establish Performance Standards

Significantly, the strategic management internal processes (situational analysis, strategy formulation, and strategic implementation) generate the objectives and standards of the organization. Thus, planning and control are inherently intertwined. The development of the directional strategies (mission, vision, values, and objectives) establish the broadest standard for comparison with organizational performance. Similarly, the adaptive, market entry, and positioning strategies, developed through an analysis of the external and internal environments of the organization, must be supported by explicit operational objectives. These planning elements provide the starting point for strategic control.

The standards of performance (evaluation criteria) for control will vary with the strategy of an organization. For example, an organization pursuing a retrenchment adaptive strategy would have different standards of performance than an organization pursuing market development. Managers must decide which objectives are most appropriate for their particular circumstances.

Frequently, the way in which outcomes are measured and monitored can actually change the character of the service. Blue Choice of Rochester, New York, developed procedures for measuring the quality of medical services provided by HMOs. Employers such as Eastman Kodak could then use the data when entering into HMO agreements. The knowledge that such monitoring takes place can significantly affect the care provided by an individual HMO by requiring HMO managers to include objective quality considerations in their strategic decision making.[5]

Measure and Compare Organizational Performance

As discussed in Chapter 1, internal factors, external factors, and performance factors exert pressure for change on organizations. Organizational performance factors are the

Exhibit 13–2 • The Concept of Control and a Framework for Strategic Control

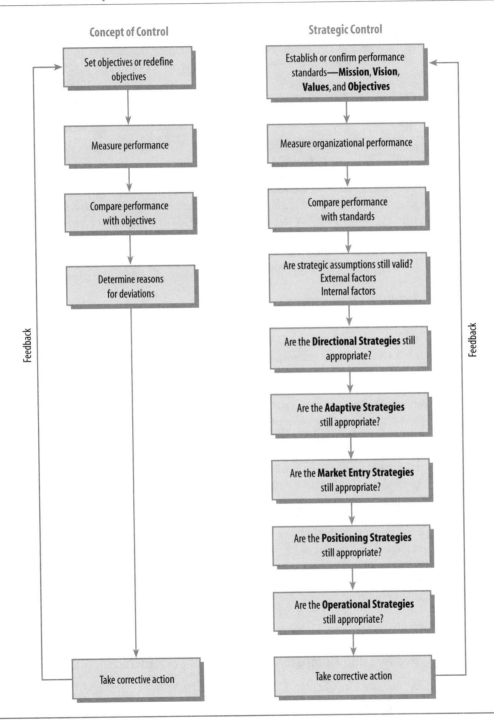

clearest indicators that the strategy is performing well or poorly. As a result, negative organizational performance provides significant insight and incentive to take corrective action if the strategy is not meeting expectations.

Qualitative and quantitative measures are commonly used to gauge the performance of an organization. For mission, vision, and values, the measures of performance are largely qualitative. Managers must match the actions of the organization to the standards provided by the statements of mission, vision, and values, which is another reason why it is important that they be clearly stated and communicated throughout the organization.

The most commonly used quantitative measures of performance are financial ratios and market standing. Typically, these performance measures are related directly to the objectives of the organization. Although perhaps not the best measures, they are relatively easy to obtain and widely used to evaluate and compare organizations.

Commonly used financial ratios include:

- return on investment (ROI),
- return on equity (ROE),
- profit margin,
- debt to equity,
- earnings per share,
- revenue growth, and
- asset growth.

Commonly used market standing measures include:

- overall market share,
- share of the target market, and
- market share as a percentage of the market leader.

These ratios and measures may be used to assess the performance of an organization by comparing the present period with previous periods, comparing the organization with similar competing organizations, and comparing organizational measures with industry averages. In addition to financial and market standing measures, patient satisfaction measures influence strategic decisions.

Peter Drucker has suggested using a mix of quantitative and qualitative measures of performance. Drucker indicates that five measures can provide a clear picture of performance for most organizations. The five measures are:

1. *Market Standing.* Is the share increasing? Is it increasing, decreasing, or remaining the same in particular submarkets and niches?
2. *Innovative Performance.* Are there new products in growth areas?
3. *Productivity.* How much value has been added per resource input?
4. *Liquidity and Cash Flow.* Can the organization generate adequate cash to sustain operations?
5. *Profitability (Revenue over Expenses).* Is there adequate return to the organization, investors, owners, and so on?[6]

Health Management Associates (HMA), discussed in the Introductory Incident, is a good example of an organization that has a balanced set of strategic controls. HMA stresses financial, marketing, and operational measures to control the strategy. Revenue,

revenue growth, and earnings are important but market standing is a key control as well. Recall that one of HMA's criteria for growth is to be the sole or dominant provider in small rural and non-urban markets. In addition, at the operational level, the company places strong emphasis on controlling personnel growth, information systems, and service quality.

Determine the Reasons for Deviations

The fundamental question in strategic control is, "Why has the organization's performance not met the previously established standards?" In the model for strategic control presented in Exhibit 13–2, efforts to determine the reasons for deviations from performance expectations are directed toward three areas. Strategic managers must determine if there have been or should be changes in the strategic assumptions (external and internal factors), in the organizational strategy (directional, adaptive, market entry, or positioning strategies), or in strategic implementation (operational strategies).

Evaluation of the strategic assumptions begins with the key question, "Are the assumptions that underlie the strategy still valid?" The selection of the organization's strategies is based on conclusions concerning the opportunities and threats in the external environment and the internal strengths and weaknesses of the organization. If these factors have changed, operational strategies may be inappropriate, the organizational strategy may need altering, or the mission may no longer be appropriate (although this is rare). Therefore, strategic evaluation and control is concerned with validating the *basis* for the strategy, as well as the strategy itself. Strategic control provides a means of validating and adjusting the organization's strategy.

In addition to validating the strategic assumptions, the strategic control process must be concerned with:

1. *Validity of the organization's directional strategies.* Is the mission still valid as well as the assumptions underlying the vision, values, and objectives?
2. *Appropriateness of the organization's adaptive, market entry, and positioning strategies.* Is the current strategy correct and moving the organization toward its objectives and mission?
3. *Effectiveness and efficiency of the operational strategies.* Are the functional and organization-wide strategies (strategic implementation) making the appropriate contribution?

Take Corrective Action

The purpose of strategic control is to ensure that the organization has the appropriate strategies and is performing as expected. The strategic control process should identify any deviations in these areas so that management may take the necessary corrective action. In strategic control, revision is directed toward:

- directional strategies—mission, vision, values, and objectives;
- adaptive strategies—expansion, contraction, or stabilization;
- market entry strategies—purchase, cooperation, or development;
- positioning strategies—marketwide or market segment; or
- operational strategies—functional and organization-wide (implementation) strategies.

The scope of corrective action in strategic control is conceptually illustrated in Exhibit 13–3. The controlled elements in strategic management should be few enough in number to allow management to focus specifically on them. These elements form a hierarchy, with change occurring relatively rarely at the top and more frequently farther down the hierarchy. Additionally, a change in one element will likely call for a change in every element below it. For example, a change in directional strategies will probably necessitate a change in the adaptive, market entry, and positioning strategies, as well as the operational strategies. Similarly, if the directional strategies are seen as appropriate but the adaptive strategy must be changed, then all subsequent strategies will require modification. A careful assessment of each element is required to determine any need for change.

Strategic Change

The adoption of a new directional or adaptive strategy suggests a major strategic change for an organization. Such change, although relatively infrequent, is often very difficult for an organization and is implemented over an extended period of time. For example, a decision by a multihospital corporation to expand by diversifying into nursing homes would be relatively dramatic and change the nature of the corporation. Such major shifts in strategic direction are not made frequently or arbitrarily.

Strategic evaluation and control decisions are perhaps the most important decisions managers will have to make. Strategic control decisions *change* the organization—its rules, procedures, policies, strategies, philosophy, and direction. Major organizational change is often frustrating and always disruptive. Therefore, decisions to make changes in these fundamental elements of the organization must not be taken lightly. Such changes may take years to implement and may affect the success or failure of the organization.

As illustrated in Exhibit 13–4, changes in directional or adaptive strategies essentially are a reorientation of the organization and have been called "revolutionary" or "frame breaking."[7] Thus, in *revolutionary change* the pattern of decision making is dramatically altered. Changes in the market entry, positioning, or operational strategies, on the other hand, may be viewed as refinements (strategic adjustments or "frame bending") and represent periods of incremental or *evolutionary change;* that is, change that takes place within the confines (guidelines) of the established and accepted broader strategies. Changes in market entry, positioning, and operational strategies typically do not represent a major strategic reorientation but may require internal (operational, structural, human resource, and so on) alterations. These changes, though sometimes dramatic, are still viewed as evolutionary in nature.

Frequency of Change

For most organizations, changes in strategy occur only at *strategic pressure points.* Thus, there are relatively short periods of strategic change between longer periods of relative stability during which few changes occur. These periods have been described as "waves of change and continuity" and "spurts and pauses"—bold, risky leaps into the future followed by a time of catching up or consolidation.[8] Spurts may be viewed as a

Exhibit 13–3 · The Scope of Strategic Control

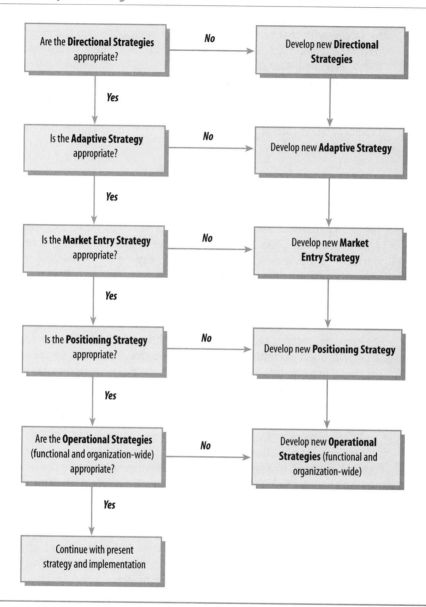

way of focusing resources and energy to take advantage of strategic windows of opportunity, while pauses provide time for maintenance and stability.[9] The concept of strategic change is illustrated in Exhibit 13–5.

Change occurs at strategic pressure points. Pressure for change builds to the point where management feels change is more important than the "costs" associated with the

Exhibit 13–4 • The Strategies and Revolutionary and Evolutionary Change

	Type of Change					
	Revolutionary Change		**Evolutionary Change**			**No Change**
Strategies	Changes in directional strategies	Changes in adaptive strategies	Changes in market entry strategies	Changes in positioning strategies	Changes in operational strategies	No change, same strategies
Nature of Change	Reorientation (frame breaking)	Reorientation (frame breaking)	Adjustment (frame bending)	Adjustment (frame bending)	Adjustment (frame bending)	Same frame
Example	Change the mission	Diversify into new business	Move from merger strategy to alliances	Move from one market segment to another	Change marketing strategy	Continuity

Exhibit 13–5 • The Concept of Revolutionary and Evolutionary Change

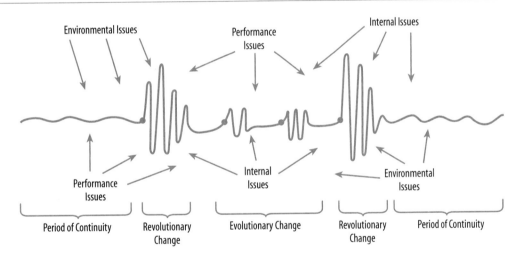

Revolutionary change requires changes in directional and adaptive strategies.

Evolutionary change requires changes in market entry, positioning, and operational strategies.

● = *Strategic pressure point*

change. Generally, pressure for revolutionary change (shifts in directional and adaptive strategies) do not occur frequently; changes in market entry, positioning, and operational strategies occur more often and are followed by periods of continuity.

Forces for Change

There are a vast number of forces pressing for changes in the strategies of health care organizations. These forces may be categorized as external issues, internal issues, and performance issues.[10] External issues that may influence strategies could be technological, regulatory, political, social, economic, or competitive, as discussed in Chapters 2 and 3. As a result of analysis of the external environment, management may conclude that a revolutionary or frame-breaking change is required. Or management may conclude that the basic strategy is sound and only a change in the operational-level strategy is needed. Perhaps the most significant change facing health care in the 1990s is the growth of managed care. Its phenomenal growth has forced many hospitals, physicians, and physician groups to adopt frame-breaking (backward vertical integration) and frame-bending (entering into alliances) strategies. Managed care involves an entirely new way of "doing business" for many health care providers.

In addition to external issues, internal issues may suggest a need for a strategic change. For example, the internal assessment process by a pharmaceutical company may indicate strengths or weaknesses that call for a change in strategies. One pharmaceutical company determined that its two- to ten-year developmental process in R&D was too long for the organization to be competitive. Through reengineering it cut R&D time by 50 percent, increasing its competitive position.

Organizational performance, especially financial performance, may alert management that strategic change is required. Typically, low financial performance mounts pressure on management to engage in evolutionary (market entry, positioning, or operational) strategies in the short term and revolutionary strategies (directional or adaptive) in the long term.

External, internal, and performance issues may, of course, work together to create pressure for strategic change. As management becomes aware of these issues (separately or in concert), pressure builds until the "strategic pressure point" is reached and management makes a decision and takes action. Introducing change in an organization is difficult whether it is a change in strategy or the introduction of a new program or way of performing a process. Indeed, the introduction of strategic management as the basic management philosophy can be very difficult. As illustrated in Perspective 13–2, with the introduction of any major change in an organization, managers should expect various stages of resistance.

Determining the Need for Change

As suggested in the model of strategic control presented in Exhibit 13–2, the key to controlling the strategy is the process of identifying and evaluating deviations to determine if strategic change is required. Thus, it is necessary to validate the existing strategic assumptions, the strategic alternatives, and strategic implementation. This process is referred to as *strategic issue diagnosis (SID)*. Strategic issues are those trends, events, or developments that have the potential to influence the organization's strategy. Through the SID process, strategic issues are detected and interpreted. The understanding formed in SID creates the momentum for strategic change. Much of the control process

Stages of Resistance to Change

Often people do not like change, and their first reaction may be to resist any changes management may wish to make. When instituting changes in an organization, whether it is changing the strategy, initiating the strategic planning process, or attempting to change the culture, managers find people in various stages of resistance. It is often necessary to "pull" people through these stages if the change is to be successful.

Stage One: RESISTANCE

Often the first reaction to something new is to resist the change. Because organizations have frequent changes and in many cases management has tried several techniques before, employees may see a new program or management effort as another fad that will soon go away (as have the others). Therefore they openly resist (or even sabotage) the proposed change. In this stage managers often hear such comments as, "Here we go again, new manager, new program, new technique" or "This will never work" and "We tried this ten years ago."

Stage Two: PASSIVENESS

In stage two, employees are not resistant, they simply do not want to get involved. These people do not like change and believe that if they "bury their head in the sand" (go about their usual work) the change will just go away. In many cases these people do not understand the vision for the future, or they have never been told about it or how they fit in it. In this stage managers often hear such comments as, "This is just a job" or "I put in my eight hours" or "I'll be here when they're gone."

Stage Three: CONVINCE ME

Some people in organizations are ready to change and will work hard if they believe it will really improve the organization. However, they have been "let down" by the organization before. In some cases, programs were started or promises were made but management neither completed the programs nor fulfilled the promises. These people will give it their best if management can show them that the result will be worth their effort. In this stage, managers often hear such comments as, "Show me that we can improve the way we work and I'll be your biggest supporter" or "Give me some indication that this can be an interesting and challenging place to work, and I'll give it a shot."

Stage Four: HOPE

Many people, especially when they start their careers, want to be a part of something important—to make a difference. They have hope that they can make the organization better and be a part of something significant. These people are usually willing to try anything and want to be a part of meaningful change. However, management should follow through because if previously proposed changes have not occurred, these people will be difficult to convince the next time management wants to change something. In this stage, managers often hear such comments as, "I don't know if we can succeed but look at the possibilities if we do" or "Wouldn't it be great if we actually pulled it off?"

Stage Five: INVOLVEMENT

In this stage, people typically understand that the organization must change and continually renew itself if it is to succeed. They are willing to get involved and be a part of any change that will keep the organization viable. They understand that some new things do not work very well and therefore other change agents must be tried. In this stage, managers often hear such comments as, "I don't know if this will work, but we have to try something" or "The world is changing and we have to change with it."

Stage Six: ADVOCACY

People in this stage believe not only that change is important in a changing world but that this program can really make an important difference. They are ready for a long-term commitment to the program or process and will lead and be responsible for its implementation and progress. These people will convince others to be a part of the change and will keep the process on track. In this stage, managers often hear such comments as, "This is our chance for real long-term success" or "I'm a believer; this can work if we stay committed over the long term."

outlined in Exhibit 13–2 is actually a process for identifying and diagnosing issues that are relevant to strategic change.

Jane Dutton and Robert Duncan depict strategic issue diagnosis as an iterative, cyclical process (see Exhibit 13–6). The SID process has two major parts: strategic issues recognition and strategic issues assessment. Recognition of issues may be a part of the normal activities of the organization, or it may occur as a part of the formal strategic planning and control process. Issues assessment involves determining the urgency of taking action on the issue and the feasibility of dealing with the issue.[11] On the basis of these assessments, momentum for change is created and the forces for organizational responses are set into place. These responses may be radical (revolutionary) change or incremental (evolutionary) change.[12]

An example of the strategic issue diagnosis process may be seen in the actions of many urban hospitals in response to the alarming trends in medical emergencies. Nationwide, there has been a fivefold increase in medical emergencies over the past several years, many due to violence and drugs. Because trauma patients consume vast amounts of resources and the majority of them have no health insurance, these patients are causing a severe financial strain on hospitals. As management monitors the rise in trauma cases and the rising costs (losses) for the hospitals, a serious strategic issue is identified and evaluated.

For many Chicago hospitals, this issue has been assessed as extremely urgent, because continued losses were threatening the very survival of several of the institutions—seven trauma centers together were losing $10 million to $12 million annually. Several of these hospitals believed that the only way to deal with the issue was to leave the trauma network. As a result, there has been momentum for change in Chicago's health care system. Four hospitals have left the trauma network: the 543-bed University of Chicago Hospital, the 272-bed Louis A. Weiss Memorial Hospital, the 567-bed Foster G. McGaw Hospital (the teaching facility of Loyola University of Chicago), and the 649-bed Michael Reese Hospital and Medical Center.[13] These institutions are engaging in both revolutionary and evolutionary change.

Issue Recognition—Triggering Mechanisms

The strategic control process encourages decision makers to actively engage in methods to recognize, isolate, and understand emerging strategic issues. As in the other strategic management processes, issue identification and evaluation are decision-making pro-

Exhibit 13–6 • Strategic Issue Diagnosis

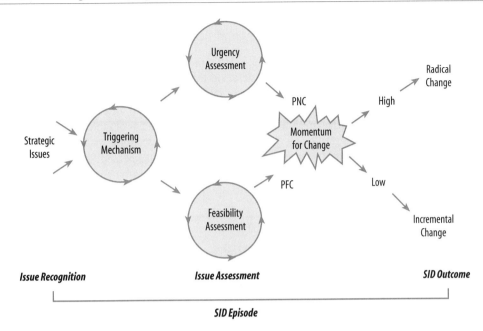

PNC—Perceived need to change
PFC—Perceived feasibility for change

cesses. These decisions are difficult and require the weighing of a mix of quantitative data, qualitative information, opinions, weak signals, and so on. For instance, in one hospital a patient-complaint feedback system was used to detect the need for changing the existing philosophies and the means to improve the delivery of health care services.[14] In addition, health care strategic information systems are becoming more sophisticated and are aiding management in detecting weak signals of change. In many cases, health care executives can access the mainframe computer through personal computers at their desks to evaluate financial and competitive trends.

Although it may be supported with a great deal of data, determining whether the organization has deviated or should deviate from the current strategy will, in the end, require management's best judgment. Clearly, there can be no hard-and-fast rules for deciding whether evolutionary change, revolutionary change, or a change in the fundamental values of the organization is required.

A series of questions for each element of the strategic control model will be useful in detecting and evaluating emerging strategic issues. In addition, these questions are useful in generating discussion among concerned managers. These questions often call for judgments and opinions regarding the appropriateness of strategic change. This approach is used in the following sections based on the major elements in the strategic control model.

Issue Assessment—Urgency and Feasibility

As illustrated in Exhibit 13–6, once strategic issues have been identified (triggered), decision makers attempt to understand the degree of issue urgency and feasibility. *Issue urgency* is the perceived cost of not taking action or the importance of taking action on an issue. Management's greater perception of the need for change arises from pressures from the external and internal environments as well as organizational performance.

Issue feasibility, on the other hand, is the perception that the means for resolving the issue are available and accessible. Management's perception of feasibility arises primarily from the assessment of the capabilities and resources of the organization. Both urgency and feasibility assessments are largely subjective or judgmental in nature.

Impetus for Strategic Change

Management's assessment of the urgency and feasibility of change creates a momentum for change in the strategy. The momentum for change is the level of effort and commitment managers are willing to devote to action designed to resolve an issue. Where effort and commitment are high, strategic managers are willing and motivated to consider radical responses to emergent issues. Where momentum is low, more conservative changes will likely be made.[15]

The matrix in Exhibit 13–7 shows the link between urgency and feasibility assessments in strategic issue diagnosis and likely organizational responses. For the most part, when managers assess urgency and feasibility to be low, decision makers are unconcerned with resolution. For low urgency/low feasibility issues, the impetus to take action is lacking. Where urgency is assessed as low but the feasibility is viewed as high, change will likely be initiated but only at an opportune time for the organization. Management is in no hurry but will move to address the issue in time. Such movements are likely to be evolutionary changes. Low urgency/high feasibility assessments may lead to further modification in implementing a strategy already in place.

An assessment that results in a belief that the issue has high urgency and low feasibility may result in a number of responses, including:

- ignoring or minimizing the issue,
- adjusting current scanning/monitoring or control mechanisms,
- more intensive research,
- preparing to defend against the change, or
- ousting the decision makers.[16]

Often management is frustrated with the organization's inability to respond to the issue in this situation. Thus, management may choose to ignore the issue (and hope it will go away), adjust the scanning or control to obtain new types of information, attempt to obtain more information, or simply remove the decision makers because of their inability to deal with the situation. (This is the fate of many a baseball manager who faces high urgency—the need to win, especially late in the season—and low feasibil-

Exhibit 13–7 • Issue Urgency, Feasibility, and Organizational Response

Assessments of Feasibility

	Low	High
Low	*No Responses*	*Opportunistic Responses*
High	*Coping, Ousting Responses*	*Reorienting Responses*

Assessments of Urgency

From Jane E. Dutton and Robert B. Duncan, "The Creation of Momentum for Change Through the Process of Strategic Issue Diagnosis," *Strategic Management Journal*, Vol. 8, No. 3 (1987), p. 281. Copyright © John Wiley and Sons, Limited. Reproduced with permission.

ity—a poor team.) If the issue is viewed as extremely urgent, management may prepare to defend itself against the change to minimize the impact.

Where the assessment of urgency is high and the assessment of feasibility is high, the greatest momentum for change is generated. Urgency and feasibility combine to produce more radical change involving reorientation of the organization. In this case a change in strategy (revolutionary change) is most likely (and probably most appropriate). As discussed in the earlier example, the Chicago hospitals participating in the trauma network viewed the urgency of the issue as extremely high because their financial viability was threatened. In addition, the hospitals' managers believed their ability to deal with the situation was high. Therefore, the hospitals formulated and implemented exit strategies rather quickly. Issues of urgency and feasibility suggest the sometimes paradoxical nature of strategic management. Further examples of the paradoxical nature of strategic management are included in Perspective 13–3.

Validating the Strategic Assumptions

The strategic plan is based on an analysis of the external and internal environments. These analyses provide the basic beliefs or assumptions that management holds concerning external opportunities and threats and internal strengths and weaknesses. Therefore, validating the strategic assumptions involves determining whether issues in the external or internal environments have changed and to what extent.

Exhibit 13–8 provides a series of questions designed to surface signals of new perspectives regarding these assumptions. The first section examines management's understanding of the external environment and the effectiveness of the strategy. The second

Perspective 13-3

Strategic Management Paradoxes

- **The more chaotic (unpredictable) the external environment, the more strategic planning is needed.** Placid environments do not require a great deal of planning. However, where there is a great deal of change, anticipating, recognizing the signals of change, and repositioning the organization are important.
- **Strategic management is a top-down bottom-up process.** Top management must initiate and support strategic management; however there must be wide participation. Strategic planning staffs generally are less effective because they do not involve the line managers who must implement the strategy. When managers are involved in the planning process, they are more likely to support strategic management.
- **Strategic management is a democratic process where the boss (CEO) is in control.** Although everyone has something to offer and should be involved in the process, final responsibility for the viability of the organization rests with the CEO.
- **Strategic management is an organized/ messy process.** There are clear steps in the process of strategic management; however, each step raises many questions, controversies, and disagreements. Often, it is an inefficient process of consensus building and decision making.
- **Strategic management is about defining the "big picture" and emphasizing the details.** The strategic management process defines the organization's relationship with its environment and sets direction. However, implementation involves coordinating numerous details.
- **Strategic management concerns destruction and renewal.** Sometimes in the process of reinventing an organization, parts of the old organization must first be dismantled in order to put new processes in place.

- **Major changes are often easier to make than small changes.** A major shift in strategy (revolutionary change) is often easier to communicate to employees and implement than subtle adjustments (evolutionary change).
- **The rules for success are written outside the organization (in the environment), but competitive advantage is created inside the organization.** Opportunities and threats are external to the organization. However, management must find the appropriate internal resources, capabilities, and competencies to build sustainable competitive advantage.
- **People cannot perform strategic management until they "get it" (understand the process and its implications); and people cannot "get it" until they perform strategic management.** Sometimes the full implications of strategic management as a way (philosophy) of managing cannot be fully appreciated until people have experienced it. (You cannot really learn to swim until you have been in the pool.)
- **Everybody wants a strategic *plan* but it is the *process* that is important.** Often managers think the plan (the document) is the objective of strategic management. However, the real objective is to set direction through the processes of communicating, reaching consensus, and decision making.
- **Strategic management is easy but difficult.** The processes are not complicated but it is often difficult to get people to overcome their fear of change.
- **Strategic management is a philosophy composed of techniques.** It is management by the compass, but there are many maps to get you started.
- **Strategic management concerns effectiveness and efficiency.** Strategic management concerns doing the right thing as well as doing things right.

- **Managers seek quantifiable data but strategic management is basically a qualitative art.** Strategic management uses quantifiable data but basically involves judgment. There are no such things as cold, hard, objective facts, only opinions about those facts. Strategic management is a matter of interpretation and opinion.
- **Strategic management controls and empowers.** Strategic management focuses organizational efforts toward a vision and well-defined objectives; however, the process allows for individual decision making, innovation, and self-expression. If organizations are to successfully renew themselves, there must be enough freedom for employees to question assumptions, strategic decisions, and the way things are done.

part explores the internal demands of the strategy and the relationship of the organization to its environment. These questions may be used by the board of directors, planning staff, or management itself as a beginning point to validate the assumptions underlying the strategy. Such an "audit" may indicate the emergence of new external or internal factors that will affect the organization and may suggest areas where additional information will be required in future planning efforts. Current, accurate information may mean survival for many health care organizations. Questions concerning the external environment may reveal that a group practice knows far too little about the views of its major constituents (stakeholders), or the existence of new competitors and their strategies, or how well the current strategy is understood and implemented by members of the practice. A validation (or invalidation) of the strategic assumptions provides a basis for controlling the strategy.

Changes in Strategy

Changes in strategic assumptions will cause changes in an organization's strategy. Some changes require a revolutionary response whereas others will be merely evolutionary in scope.

Controlling Revolutionary Change—Directional and Adaptive Strategies Strategic control at this level is not a matter of keeping the organization on track, but rather one of deciding if a completely new track or approach is warranted. Managers must decide if conditions require a change in the organization's fundamental strategies. Lorange, Morton, and Ghoshal have called this decision *controlling the strategic leap.* They suggest:

> Here the challenge is to reset the trajectory of the strategy as well as to decide on the relative levels of thrust and momentum for the new strategic direction. The critical underlying assumptions that underpin the strategy are no longer viable, and the rules that govern the strategy must be redefined. This situation involves a mental leap to define the new rules and to cope with any emerging new environmental factors. Such a recalibrating of strategy requires a personal liberation from traditional thinking, an ability to change one's mindset, and confront the challenge of creating advantage out of discontinuity. The question now is how to achieve a quantum leap in one's strategy to capitalize on emerging environmental turbulence. One must proceed by redefining the rules rather than by clinging to the unrealistic hope that the old rules are still valid.[17]

Exhibit 13–8 • Questions for Validation of the Strategic Assumptions

	Yes/No	Evaluation

External Environment

1. Is the strategy acceptable to the major constituents?
2. Is the strategy consonant with the competitive environment?
3. Do we have an honest and accurate appraisal of the competition? Have we underestimated the competition?
4. Does the strategy leave us vulnerable to the power of a few major customers?
5. Does the strategy give us a dominant competitive edge?
6. Is the strategy vulnerable to a successful strategic counterattack by competitors?
7. Are the forecasts on which the strategy is based really credible?
8. Does the strategy follow that of a strong competitor?
9. Does the strategy pit us against a powerful competitor?
10. Is our market share sufficient to be competitive and generate an acceptable amount of profit?
11. Is the strategy subject to government response?
12. Is the strategy in conformance with the society's moral and ethical codes of conduct?

Internal Environment

13. Does the strategy really fit management's values, philosophy, know-how, personality, and sense of social responsibility?
14. Is the strategy identifiable and understood by all those in the organization?
15. Is the strategy consistent with the internal strengths, objectives, and policies?
16. Is the strategy divided into appropriate substrategies that interrelate properly?
17. Are the operational strategies in conflict?
18. Does the strategy exploit the strengths and avoid the major weaknesses of the organization?
19. Is the organizational structure consistent with the strategy?
20. Is there sufficient capital to support the strategy?
21. What are the financial consequences associated with the allocation of capital to the strategy?
22. Is the strategy appropriate with respect to the physical plant?
23. Are there identifiable and committed managers to implement the strategy?
24. Do we have the necessary skills among both managers and employees to successfully carry out the strategy?

From George A. Steiner, John B. Minor, and Edmund R. Gray, *Management Policy and Strategy*, 3rd ed., pp.150–154. Copyright © 1986. Adapted by permission of Prentice–Hall, Inc., Upper Saddle River, NJ.

After the organization's performance has been compared with its objectives and standards and the strategic assumptions have been evaluated, the directional strategies should be reevaluated. The objective of this process is to determine whether the mission, vision, values, and objectives are still appropriate. Exhibit 13–9 provides several questions that will aid managers in their thinking concerning the appropriateness of the organization's directional strategies. Decisions to change an organization's mission, vision, values, and objectives are complex and involve many variables. This control process calls into question the fundamental activities and direction of the organization: "Are we not doing anything new that we should be doing? Are we doing some things now we should not be doing?"

Exhibit 13–9 • Questions for Evaluation of the Directional Strategies

	Yes/No	Evaluation
1. Are we not doing anything now that we should be doing?		
2. Are we doing some things now that we should not be doing?		
3. Are we doing some things now we should continue to do but do in a different way?		
4. Do our mission and vision allow for innovation?		
5. Do our mission and vision allow for expansion?		
6. Is our mission relatively enduring?		
7. Are our organization's mission and vision unique in some way?		
8. Is our scope of operations clear (market, products/services, customers, geographic coverage)?		
9. Do our mission, vision, and objectives fit the needs of our stakeholders?		
10. Do our fundamental values and philosophy still make sense?		
11. Is the image of the organization what it should be?		

A number of major tertiary-care hospitals are faced with the problem of whether to continue as highly specialized centers of excellence or to diversify and expand into new markets more akin to general trends in the industry.[18] For example, the growth of the outpatient sector of the health care industry may alter the traditional mission of some health care organizations. Further, a decision to alter the basic mission or vision of the future of the institution could mean becoming a multihospital system with all the opportunities as well as the demands and risks. Generally, there is competition from other institutions offering similar specialized services. Technological changes are allowing procedures that formerly were performed in a hospital to take place in nonhospital settings. As other hospital systems diversify in an attempt to develop new and successful markets, the board of directors will ask, "Why aren't we doing the same?"

Concurrently and counter to the impetus for diversification are the strong financial and administrative requirements for maintaining state-of-the-art technology and specialization in a single institution rather than draining off resources for other hospitals in a system. In addition, specialization may suggest strengthening areas of excellence by developing strong feeder institutions and expanding the organization's proven markets.[19]

Perhaps the best approach for controlling the directional strategies is to place the CEO's vision for the future, the existing mission statement, statement of values, and the organization's general objectives next to the questions in Exhibit 13–9 and ask the board of directors or trustees and the executive management team to freely discuss and reach a consensus on each question. This process will either validate the existing mission, vision, values, and objectives or generate momentum for a change. This process invites clarification, understanding, and reinforcement of exactly "what this organization is all about."

Changes in the adaptive strategy also create revolutionary change. Such revolutionary change is relatively rare in stable environments but somewhat more frequent in dynamic environments. Signals that the basic strategy for the organization needs to be changed must be carefully monitored because the change will have serious long-term consequences. The questions presented in Exhibit 13–10 are helpful in surfacing such signals and they provide a starting point for discussion of the appropriateness of the organization's adaptive strategy. The assumption underlying Exhibit 13–10 is that the mission, vision, values, and general objectives are still appropriate but that the organization's adaptive strategy should be questioned.

A recalibration of the strategy and the challenge of creating advantage out of discontinuity were faced by Comprehensive Care Corporation (CompCare), the largest provider of chemical-dependency programs to hospitals. CompCare's board approved a major retrenchment strategy as a result of increased competitive pressures, hospital cost cutting, and a failed merger attempt. The CEO of CompCare indicated, "We determined that we didn't have time to consider further alternatives. We needed to reassert full control and start doing things ourselves."[20] CompCare was indeed, engaging in revolutionary change.

Controlling Evolutionary Change—Market Entry, Positioning, and Operational Strategies If the directional and adaptive strategies of the organization appear to be appropriate, then the market entry, positioning, and supporting operational strategies must be examined to determine if they are still appropriate. This type of change represents an evolutionary alteration or a strategic adjustment. Thus, strategic control at this level focuses on maintaining a particular strategic direction while coping with environmental turbulence and change. Lorange, Morton, and Ghoshal referred to this type of

---

Exhibit 13–10 · Questions for Evaluation of the Adaptive Strategies

	Yes/No	Evaluation

1. Has the adaptive strategy been tested with appropriate analysis, such as return on investment and the organization's ability and willingness to bear the risks?
2. Does the adaptive strategy balance the acceptance of minimum risk with the maximum revenue potential?
3. Is the payback period acceptable in light of potential environmental change?
4. Does the strategy take the organization too far from its current products and markets?
5. Is the adaptive strategy appropriate for the organization's present and prospective position in the market?
6. Is the strategy consonant with product life cycle as it exists or as the organization has the power to make it?
7. Is the organization rushing a revolutionary product or service to market?
8. If the adaptive strategy is to fill a currently unfilled niche in the market, has the organization investigated whether the niche will remain open long enough to return the capital investment?
9. Have the major forces inside and outside the organization that will be most influential in ensuring the success of the strategy been identified and evaluated?
10. Are all the important assumptions on which the strategy is based realistic?
11. Has the strategy been tested with appropriate analytical tools?
12. Has the adaptive strategy been tested with appropriate criteria, such as past, present, and prospective economic, political, and social trends?

control as *controlling the strategic momentum* and explained: "The basic continuity of the business is still credible, and one can hence speak of an extrapolation of the given strategy, even though a lot of operational changes may be taking place. The challenge here is to manage the buffeting of the given strategy and to maintain the strategy on course."[21]

Evaluation of the effectiveness of the market entry strategies provides insight into how well the adaptive strategies are being carried out in the marketplace (see Exhibit 13–11). The adaptive strategies and market entry strategies may be appropriate, but if the product or service is not positioned effectively the organization may not achieve its objectives (see Exhibit 13–12).

Each of the functional strategies and organization-wide strategies should be examined separately to determine whether management has correctly defined the role of these strategies in supporting the organization's overall strategy. In addition, management must determine whether the functional and organization-wide strategies are well integrated and support one another.

For instance, a diversification strategy may be appropriate but refinements are called for in marketing, financing, or clinical operations. Scott and White Corporation of Temple, Texas, which owns the 415-bed Scott and White Memorial Hospital, has found unrelated diversification into a hotel and restaurant across the street from its campus to be successful, but the complex has required some operational and positioning modifications.

The questions listed in Exhibit 13–13 provide a format for examining and controlling the operational strategies. These questions should be applied to each of the functional areas supporting the strategy (marketing, finance, human resources, information systems,

Exhibit 13–11 • Questions for Evaluation of the Market Entry Strategies

	Yes/No	Evaluation
1. Have the adequate financial resources been allocated to enter the market?		
2. Does management understand the important market forces?		
3. Does management understand the unique requirements of the market entry strategy (purchase, cooperation, development)?		
4. Is the market entry strategy the best way to accomplish the adaptive strategy?		
5. Is the market entry strategy compatible with the adaptive strategy?		
6. Does the selection of the market entry strategy affect the ability of the organization to effectively position its products/ services in the market?		
7. Is the market entry strategy compatible with the positioning strategy?		
8. Is the market entry strategy the most appropriate way to achieve the mission, vision, and objectives of the organization?		
9. Is the market entry strategy consonant with the values of the organization?		
10. Does the market entry strategy place unusual strains on any of the functional areas?		
11. Have new stakeholder relationships developed as a result of the market entry strategy (customers, vendors, channel institutions, and so on)?		
12. Has the relationship between the desire and need for rapid market entry been properly analyzed?		
13. Has the desired and appropriate level of control over the products and services been achieved?		
14. Have the trade-offs between costs and control been properly analyzed?		

Exhibit 13–12 • Questions for Evaluation of the Positioning Strategies

	Yes/No	Evaluation

1. Is the product or service positioned appropriately in the market?
2. Can the organization use one of the other generic positioning strategies?
3. Is the positioning strategy appropriate considering the external opportunities and threats?
4. Will market forces allow for the selected positioning?
5. Is the positioning strategy best suited to capitalize on the organization's strengths and minimize the weaknesses?
6. Is the positioning of the organization's products and services unique in the marketplace?
7. Is the positioning strategy defensible against new players trying to position in a similar fashion?
8. Is the positioning strategy compatible with the market entry strategy?
9. Does the positioning strategy provide the appropriate image for the organization?
10. Is the positioning strategy sustainable?
11. Is the appropriate distribution channel being used?
12. Is the current promotional strategy appropriate?
13. Is the pricing strategy appropriate?

Exhibit 13–13 • Questions for Evaluation of Strategic Implementation

	Yes/No	Evaluation

1. Overall, can the strategy be implemented in an efficient and effective manner?
2. Has the organization's overall strategy been well communicated to all members of the functional areas of the organization?
3. Is there a high level of commitment to the strategy within the functional unit?
4. Has the functional area developed a realistic strategic plan to implement the overall strategy?
5. Is the functional strategy appropriate for the position in the market?
6. Has the functional strategy been well communicated to all of the members of the functional areas of the organization?
7. Is there a system of communication and control that best supports the organization's strategy?
8. Does the functional area have the managerial and employee capabilities required to successfully implement the organization's strategy?
9. Does the functional area have the resources required for successful implementation of the strategy?
10. Is the organization's culture appropriate for the overall strategy?
11. Are the facilities and equipment up to date and appropriate to carry out the overall strategy?
12. Does the organization structure help facilitate the overall strategy?
13. Does the organization have the appropriate social and ethical relationships with its communities?
14. Is there a better way to implement the organization's overall strategy?
15. Is the timing of implementation appropriate in light of what is known about market conditions, competition, and so on?
16. Has the strategy been tested with appropriate criteria, such as performance indicators?

Source: Adapted from George A. Steiner, John B. Minor, and Edmund R. Gray, *Management Policy and Strategy,* 3d ed. Copyright © 1996. Adapted by permission of Prentice-Hall, Inc., Upper Saddle River, NJ.

and so on) as well as the organization-wide initiatives. The logic underlying these questions is that the organization's strategy is fundamentally sound but the organization's performance in carrying out the strategy may not be as effective or efficient as possible.

McKinsey's 7-S Framework

McKinsey and Company has developed a model, known as the *7-S framework*, to evaluate the implementation of the strategy.[22] The McKinsey model may be used to assess all of the elements in the "determining the reasons for deviation" stage of the strategic control model. Additionally, the 7-S framework provides a model for testing the "strategic fit" or the match between the strategy and the organization. As illustrated in Exhibit 13–14, the elements of this model are strategy, structure, systems, style, staff, shared values, and skills.

The basic premise underlying the model is that all seven of these variables must fit with one another if the strategy is to be successfully implemented. Thus, all of the elements must be "pulling in the same direction" if the organization is going to reach its full potential. Examination of the strategic fit of these elements provides a workable checklist for evaluating the implementation capabilities and efforts of the organization. A health care organization in which the seven variables are pulling together is Allegheny General Hospital (AGH) of Pittsburgh. Exhibit 13–15 demonstrates the high level of excellence that can be achieved when strategy, structure, systems, style, staff, shared values, and skills are complementary.

Organizational Mechanisms for Strategic Control

The mechanisms for strategic control are integrated into the managerial processes, procedures, style, and technologies of the organization. Strategic control is not a separate process imposed on an organization; rather, strategic control is an inherent part of the organization and the way it operates. Strategic control should be regarded as a normal and necessary part of what the organization and its managers do. Moreover, control is not an end in itself, but is incorporated into managerial processes to make the processes themselves more effective and efficient. A good example of the integration of control is found in the model of strategic management that serves as a framework for this text. Control is part of the process, not separate from it. Strategic management without an inherent control element is a meaningless activity unrelated to the real world.

Types of Organizational Controls

It is easier to identify and discuss strategic control systems if they are classified by type or category. Doz and Prahalad identified three types of strategic control mechanisms: data management mechanisms, management mechanisms, and conflict resolution mechanisms.[23]

Data Management Mechanisms   Data management mechanisms include the information system, strategic management processes (situational analysis, strategy formulation, and strategic implementation), performance measurement, resource allocation procedures, and budgeting procedures. These processes exercise strategic control by providing

Exhibit 13–14 · McKinsey 7-S Framework

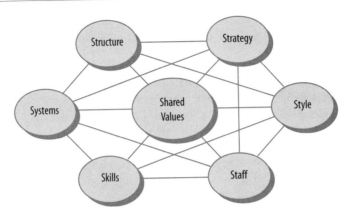

Strategy
A coherent set of actions aimed at gaining a sustainable advantage over competition, improving position vis-à-vis competitors, or allocating resources.

Structure
The organization chart and accompanying documentation that show who reports to whom and how tasks are both divided up and integrated.

Systems
The processes and flows that show how an organization gets things done from day to day (information systems, capital budgeting systems, service delivery systems, quality control systems, and performance measurement systems all would be good examples).

Style
Tangible evidence of what management considers important by the way it collectively spends time and attention and uses symbolic behavior. It is not what management says that is important; it is the way management behaves.

Staff
The people in an organization. Here it is very useful to think not about individual personalities but about corporate demographics.

Shared Values
The values that go beyond, but might well include, simple goal statements in determining corporate destiny. To fit the concept, these values must be shared by most people in the organization.

Skills
A derivative of the rest. Skills are those competencies that are possessed by an organization as a whole as opposed to the people in it. (The concept of corporate skill as something different from the aggregate of the skills of the people in it seems difficult for many to grasp; however, some organizations that hire only the best and the brightest cannot get seemingly simple things done while others perform extraordinary feats with ordinary people.)

Source: Reprinted from Robert H. Waterman, Jr., "The Seven Elements of Strategic Fit," *Journal of Business Strategy* 2, no. 3 (Winter 1982), pp. 69–73. © 1982 Warren, Gorham & Lamont, Inc. Used with permission.

management with information concerning competitive conditions and organizational performance. Thus, information received by management forms the basis for the organization's strategy and objectives as well as control.

It is apparent that the organization's information systems are extremely important in controlling the strategy. Great effort should be made to ensure that the appropriate information is obtained concerning the external environment and that the information reaches decision makers in a useful form and timely manner. Similarly, the internal

Exhibit 13–15 • McKinsey 7-S Model Applied to Allegheny General Hospital

Allegheny General Hospital (AGH) is a 714-bed tertiary-care hospital in Pittsburgh, Pennsylvania. AGH has been cited as the top hospital in an extremely competitive market that includes such formidable tertiary-care competitors as 500-bed Mercy Hospital of Pittsburgh, 583-bed Presbyterian-University Hospital, 729–bed St. Francis Medical Center, and 452-bed Western Pennsylvania Hospital. How can AGH excel in one of the nation's most sophisticated health care markets? Allegheny seems to have found the correct strategic fit.

Strategy
Through strategic planning, AGH has identified its strategy: Establish Allegheny General Hospital as *the* regional referral center in Pennsylvania for tertiary-care services. AGH offers specialized patient care, teaching, and research.

Structure
AGH has medical school affiliation with Medical College of Pennsylvania, located in Philadelphia, and maintains Allegheny Singer Research Institute, which has a $30 million annual research budget to conduct research in eighteen clinical areas.

Systems
AGH has a system of objectives and strategies to guide the hospital's progress. The organization maintains advanced systems for matching specialists with referring physicians, medical staff development plans, and clinical services development plans to guide decisions about new services and technology. AGH engages in financial planning and has supportive budgeting systems as well as plant and equipment replacement plans. In addition, AGH has created a system of hospital-wide productivity measures and quality targets.

Style
Management at Allegheny is direct and aggressive. Management has clear objectives and pursues them vigorously. Management is externally oriented, attempting to understand and respond to the region's health care needs. Management also has an internal orientation and emphasizes efficiency. Management is highly committed to being the best hospital in the region.

Staff
AGH has 4,000 employees, including 565 medical staff members, 1,221 registered nurses, and 132 practical nurses. AGH conducts a residency program for third- and fourth-year students of the Medical College of Pennsylvania. The medical school affiliation helps AGH attract highly sought-after specialists who want to teach as well as practice medicine. AGH has a medical staff development plan that weighs the medical needs in the community with the ability of the hospital's current staff to meet those needs.

Shared Values
The medical staff and employees value excellence, the highest level of technology, and community involvement. The emphasis at AGH is on supporting employees through development programs and gain-sharing programs.

Skills
AGH has many specialists, specialty services, and high-tech procedures. AGH has been highly successful in its ability to entice primary-care physicians to refer patients to specialists on the hospital staff. AGH is highly skilled at marketing its services to both the public and referring physicians. Thirty-five people work in the corporate communications department, whose objective is to make primary-care physicians aware of the specialty services and to help its specialists make contact with referring physicians. Allegheny performs a variety of highly specialized procedures, including heart, liver, kidney, pancreas, and single-lung transplants. AGH offers specialized training to its nurses.

Source: David Burda, "Allegheny: A Tertiary Titan with All the Right Moves,"*Modern Healthcare* (February 12, 1990), pp. 50–58.

information systems need to be designed to provide management with decision-making information, not just data. Ultimately, the quality of management's decisions rests on the quality of the information it receives and understands.

Management Mechanisms Strategic control is exercised by managing the managers. Through the setting of objectives, the performance appraisal process, the compensation program, and so on, managers' actions are coordinated toward agreed-upon organizational objectives. Such controls become part of the operating procedures and culture (shared values) of the organization. Perspective 13–4 illustrates how performance appraisal and compensation may be tied directly to the strategy of the organization.

As health care executives manage their organizations, one of the most powerful strategic controls has been the emphasis on quality. In health care, quality has proven to be a winning strategy. As Heskett, Sasser, and Hart expressed in their book on services breakthroughs, "The mark of an outstanding service organization is the continued effort it devotes to widening the gap between itself and its major competitors on both service quality and productivity (efficiency). The effort is both diligent and persistent, almost crusade-like in nature."[24]

Other writers have observed that a strong management commitment to service quality energizes and stimulates an organization to improved service performance.[25] In these types of organizations, quality becomes the central value. Peter Drucker has called this type of control "the strategy of doing better what we already do well."[26] The

---

Perspective 13–4

Performance Appraisal and Compensation

People in organizations do what they get rewarded for doing and ignore most other organizational dictates. As Steve Kerr reminded us in a classic management article, often management expects "A," but rewards "B" and then cannot understand why "A" never occurs.

If strategic management is to become a philosophy or way of managing an organization, people must see a connection between what they do and strategic management. Therefore, unless strategic management is translated into individual efforts and acknowledged through the performance appraisal and reward systems, it is unlikely that everyone will work for the strategic plan. Just as organizational divisions and units must be linked to the strategic plan, so should the work of the individuals involved.

After initiating a strategic planning effort, it is necessary to rewrite job descriptions and performance appraisal standards. Every position, from secretary to CEO, should be linked back to the strategic plan. An effective way to accomplish this linkage is to create duties within the job description related specifically to strategic management processes. Thus, each job description should have

sections entitled "Contribution to Vision," "Contribution to Mission," "Contribution to Values," "Contribution to Strategic Objectives," "Contribution to Strategy," and "Contribution to Strategy Implementation." Each job should be structured to show explicitly how it contributes to one or more of these processes. There is no justification for any activity that does not specifically contribute to the organization's strategy.

An effective way to redesign job descriptions is to ask three strategic questions for each position:

1. In order to make the maximum contribution, what is this person not doing now that he or she should be doing?

2. In order to make the maximum contribution, what is this person doing now that he or she should not be doing?

3. In order to make the maximum contribution, what is this person doing now that he or she should continue to do but in a different way?

Similarly, performance appraisal forms may be structured around the strategic management processes. Then compensation may be tied directly to the employee's contribution to the strategy.

emphasis on quality is apparent in all strategic decisions because the underlying consideration for the mission, objectives, strategy, and so on is, "How will it affect the quality of the services we offer?" Thus, outcomes management and quality programs can work well together. Managers assess qualitative objectives, strategies, and implementation by asking, "What have we contributed in the past three years that made a difference?" and "What do we plan to contribute?"[27] In health care, merely good service may not be good enough to differentiate the organization from other organizations (or good enough for the patient). Quality-oriented organizations value doing the right thing, even when it is inconvenient or costly.

Conflict Resolution Mechanisms   Conflict resolution creates strategic and administrative integration between diverse organizational groups (division- and corporate-level units). Thus, formal and informal task forces, boards of directors or trustees, committees, ad hoc groups, and group retreats facilitate a shared understanding of environmental conditions, organizational capabilities, vision and mission, objectives, and strategies.

University Hospital in London, Ontario, demonstrates the use of all three categories of strategic control. Strategic control was introduced into the organization by modifying the strategic planning process to include the establishment and integration of objectives, performance measurement, resource allocation, and budgeting. Individual departments and managers themselves were evaluated using a performance appraisal system tied to the strategy and objectives of the organization. Through formal and informal meetings, committee gatherings, and group retreats, the members evaluated strategy and reached consensus on planning assumptions and effectiveness. Strategic control has become an inherent part of University Hospital's managerial processes.

Levels of Strategic Control

Boards of directors or trustees are being used increasingly for strategic control, particularly in multihospital systems. This reliance on boards of directors of system-owned hospitals has been effective for strategic control when member hospitals have high degrees of autonomy over the organization of their services, services are diverse, member hospitals are geographically dispersed, and systems are large or newly formed.[28]

Peter Lorange has suggested a more explicit approach to strategic control. He proposes establishing strategic controls at the corporate, divisional, and operational levels of the organization. In addition to tracking the key assumptions on which the strategy is based, for each level he suggests establishing:

- strategic objectives (objectives of the corporate and division strategy);
- strategic programs and milestones (the tasks and timetable by which the strategic objectives will be accomplished);
- strategic budgets (resources for strategic programs); and
- operating budgets (resources for support programs).[29]

Performance for each of the control areas must be evaluated and action taken as appropriate. Such a strategic control effort will help ensure coordinated organizational effort both vertically and horizontally throughout the organization.

Contingency Planning as Strategic Control

Contingency planning may be incorporated into the normal strategic management process and provide for strategic control. *Contingency plans* are alternative plans that are put into effect if the strategic assumptions change quickly or dramatically or if organizational performance is lagging. Thus, if the organization unexpectedly reaches a strategic pressure point, plans are already in place that provide management with a course of action until further analysis can be undertaken. The more turbulent, discontinuous, and unpredictable the external environment, the more likely it is that unexpected or dramatic shifts will occur and the greater the need for contingency planning.

Strategic plans are based on the events and trends that management views as most likely (the strategic assumptions). However, these events may not occur, or trends may weaken or accelerate far faster than management anticipated. Therefore, contingency plans are normally tied to key issues or events occurring or not occurring. For instance, if management has based the strategy on an expanding economy but is presented with clear evidence that the economy is slipping into a recession, contingency plans may be activated. Similarly, the announcement that a major competitor is leaving the market may present an opportunity that initiates contingency plans for market development. Such contingency planning forces managers to think in terms of possible outcomes of the strategy.

An example where contingency plans may be developed is in the area of home health care. Many hospitals have viewed home health care as a fertile area for diversification. However, the home medical-equipment segment of the business is quite volatile because of major changes in Medicare reimbursement policies (home medical-equipment businesses traditionally have relied on Medicare reimbursements for at least half of their revenues). As a result, hospitals have seen profit margins from medical equipment units decline, and some have incurred substantial losses.[30]

A hospital may formulate a strategic plan for its home medical-equipment business based on the knowledge that federal government proposals call for dramatic cuts in spending. Therefore, a hospital that has diversified into this segment of the market may also formulate a contingency strategy to divest its home medical-equipment operations if new restrictive legislation is enacted or if profit margins continue to erode. On the other hand, home health infusion therapy is growing despite its restricted reimbursement from Medicare. Many hospitals perceive that home care in general will be a necessary part of their strategy to develop a continuum of care. In addition, health care reform may significantly improve reimbursement for all aspects of home care.

In providing strategic control for organizations, Linneman and Chandran suggest that effective contingency planning involves a seven-step process. The seven steps are:

1. Identify both favorable and unfavorable events that could possibly derail the strategy or strategies.
2. Specify trigger points. Calculate a likely timetable for contingent events to occur.
3. Assess the impact of each contingent event. Estimate the potential benefit or harm for each contingent event.
4. Develop contingency plans. Be sure that contingency plans are compatible with current strategy and are economically feasible.

5. Assess the counterimpact of each contingency plan. That is, estimate how much each contingency plan will capitalize on or cancel out its associated contingent event. Doing this will quantify the potential value of each contingency plan.
6. Determine early warning signals for key contingent events. Monitor the early warning signals.
7. For contingent events with reliable early warning signals, develop advance-action plans to take advantage of the available lead time.[31]

Strategic Control—A New Beginning

The model of strategic management introduced in Chapter 1 presented strategic control as the last stage of the model. However, control is an inherent part of all the strategic management processes; strategic management itself is an attempt to control the future of the organization. Managers exercise the explicit process of control as they consider the reasons for strategic change.

There is a valid argument that strategic control is the first stage of strategic management. Strategic control addresses making changes in what the organization is currently doing. Perhaps the best explanation is that strategic management is logically a circular process, and all of its processes are continuous. For instance, situational analysis is not halted so that strategy formulation may begin. Both are continuous and affect one another.

Nevertheless, strategic control provides the momentum for change, and change is a fundamental part of survival. Because managers understand the relationship between change and survival, there have been many management approaches to changing organizations (see Perspective 13–5). As health care managers control and change their organizations, they chart new courses into the future. In effect, they create new beginnings, new chances for success, new challenges for employees, and new hopes for patients. Therefore, it is imperative that health care managers understand the changes taking place in their environment; they should not simply be responsive to them, but strive to create the future. Health care managers must see into the future and create new visions for success.

The Map and Compass

Chapter 1 introduced the concept of the map and the compass. Recall that maps provide explicit directions and start the organization on its journey. Sometimes as we progress, however, the landscape or landmarks have changed or in other cases the organization is not really sure exactly where it should be headed. In these instances the compass is more valuable to chart the course. Organizations create plans (maps) for the future but must be willing to abandon the plan as the situation changes, new opportunities become visible, or managers find out what really works. This takes leadership—leaders recognize discontinuities and the need for change.

Each chapter in this text has presented a map (rational model) for accomplishing the strategic management processes. These maps provide step-by-step guidelines for strategic management including general environmental analysis, service area competitor

Perspective 13–5

What Are These?

1950s	1960s	1970s
• Theory "Y" • Management by Objectives • Quantitative Management • Diversification	• Managerial Grid • T-Groups • Matrix Management • Conglomeration • Centralization/Decentralization	• Zero-Based Budgets • Participative Management • Portfolio Management • MBAs
1980s	**1990s**	**2000s?**
• Theory Z • One-Minute Managing • Organization Culture • Intrapreneuring • Downsizing • MBWA (Management by Wandering Around) • TQM/CQI	• Strategic Thinking • Customer Focus • Quality Improvement • Reengineering • Benchmarking	

Management fads? Management techniques? Management fads is usually the flippant answer. However, each of these management approaches was a genuine attempt to change and improve the organization—to focus efforts, improve the quality of the products and services, to improve employee morale, to do more with less, to put meaning into work, and so on. Some of the approaches worked better than others; some stood the test of time and others did not. Yet, it would be too harsh to simply dismiss them as fads or techniques. The goals for all of these management approaches were to control and shape the organization—to make it better, to make it an excellent organization. One of the things that has distinguished all of these "fads" is the enthusiasm and commitment they have engendered among managers and workers. For many, these approaches have significantly increased the meaning of work—no small accomplishment in an era in which people are increasingly hungry for meaning. And certainly organizations need to create meaning.[1]

When management approaches such as these fail, it is usually because they become an end in themselves. Managers lose sight of the real purpose of the approach and the process becomes more important than the product. Managers start working for the approach rather than letting the approach work for them.

Important Thoughts for the Future

What will be the "management fads" of the next decade? Will you be a part of these attempts to make the organization better or will you simply dismiss them as fads? Perhaps benchmarking, quality improvement, or strategic thinking will turn your organization around. One of these approaches may help make your organization truly excellent or save it from decline.

Is strategic management just another fad? Will it stand the test of time? If strategic management becomes an end in itself, if the process does not foster and facilitate thinking, it will not be useful. However, if the structured process helps managers think about the future and guide their organizations through this turbulent decade, strategic management will have succeeded.

———————

[1] J. Daniel Beckham, "The Longest Wave," *Healthcare Forum Journal* 36, no. 6 (November/December 1993), pp. 78, 80–82.

analysis, internal analysis, and so on through strategic control. The maps keep us from being overwhelmed and provide some perspective to chart where we are going and what we want to accomplish. In addition, the maps initiate action—get us going—on the move toward renewing the organization. However, similar to an organization's plans, these rational models cannot anticipate everything nor can they be universally applied. They will not be a perfect fit for every organization, yet they can provide the initial logical direction for exploring and learning. Therefore, the organization must reinvent the processes and learn as it goes. True creativity, the kind that is responsible for breakthrough innovations in our society, always changes the rules. Do not work for the model, allow it to work for you. When the model no longer provides direction and insight, dare to innovate and re-create the process—use your compass. Use your vision for the organization and its future to determine what to do today to make it happen. To summarize, Perspective 13–6 presents some general do's and don'ts for successful strategic management.

Finally, strategic management is hard work and takes practice. Lasting change will be made only through a lifelong commitment to a continuing discipline. Lasting organizational change (renewal) comes from thinking strategically and adopting sound management principles that are practiced on a continuing basis. There are no quick fixes.

Summary and Conclusions

Strategic control is an integral part of the strategic management process. Strategic control helps managers determine the relevance of the organization's strategy and assess its progress toward achieving objectives. Where progress is not satisfactory, managers must take corrective action.

Strategic control is a major part of coordination within an organization and can help motivate employees to achieve organizational objectives. In addition, strategic control provides managers a means to make major changes in the direction and strategy of the organization.

Generally, the control process has five elements: (1) setting objectives or standards, (2) measuring performance, (3) comparing objectives with performance, (4) determining the reasons for deviation, and (5) taking corrective action. To be effective, this process should be based on accurate information, focused on controlling only the critical elements, flexible, cost effective, simple, and timely, as well as emphasize the exceptions.

Perspective 13–6

The Do's and Don'ts of Strategic Management

Do:

- Understand that strategic management is a philosophy or way of managing, not simply a technique. Strategic management transcends techniques.
- Remember that in strategic management, the process (strategic thinking) is more important than the product (a plan).
- Involve everyone possible in the process. Those who participate will better understand the benefits and will be more willing to buy into the process.
- Ensure that people within the organization take ownership of the process and its results.
- Realize that because the "rules for success" are written outside the organization, understanding the external environment is an essential task of strategic management.
- Expect that strategic management is *really* hard work and that it may take years before people really manage (and think) strategically.
- Remember that strategic management is about organizational renewal. Be ready to learn and reinvent the process (and the organization).
- Expect things to get worse before they get better (people are typically confused at first and resistant to change).
- Remember that you will never get it quite right. Strategic management is about constant organizational rethinking, reinvention, re-creation—renewal.
- Expect the process to be exciting and challenging.

Don't:

- Expect strategic management to be the "magic bullet" that will fix everything.
- Start strategic management without full commitment from top management—their support, time, and resources.
- Expect perfection. Strategic management is a "messy" and sometimes inefficient process.
- Rely too much on consultants, outsiders, or a small staff group. It should not be *their* plan but rather *our* plan.
- Follow the process (map) of strategic management blindly. A compass is necessary to go where the organization has not gone before.
- Expect someone to provide a strategic management "template" that will overlay perfectly with your organization.
- Expect strategic management to be easy or take only a few months or a year.
- Expect that everyone will understand the full implications of strategic management *("get it")* at first. People learn by doing.
- Expect immediate results. Strategic management may be a fundamental change in doing business.
- Expect the future to be an extension of the past. The only thing we know for certain is that the future will be different.
- Expect that your organization will survive without change. Organizations that fail to change, fail.

Strategic control is broader than operational control but it has the same underlying logic. Specifically, strategic control is directed toward controlling the strategic assumptions (perceived threats, opportunities, weaknesses, strengths); directional and adaptive strategies (revolutionary change); and the market entry, positioning, and operational strategies (evolutionary change).

Both qualitative and quantitative performance measures are used to evaluate an organization's performance. Typically, qualitative measures are used in controlling the strategy. However, a number of quantitative measures provide management with signals or indicators of organizational performance. These indicators are primarily financial and marketing oriented. When there are deviations from the planned objectives, management's responsibility is to determine why and take corrective action.

The development and adoption of a new strategy for an organization represents a major change. However, major changes in the organization's strategy (directional or adaptive strategies) are relatively infrequent and represent revolutionary change for the organization. Changes in marketing entry, positioning, and operational strategies occur more frequently and may be viewed as evolutionary change or strategic adjustments. Typically, change occurs when pressure from external issues, internal issues, and performance issues reaches the point that managers believe that they must act. The point at which a change is made is referred to as a strategic pressure point.

To determine a need for strategic change, managers engage in strategic issue diagnosis. Strategic issue diagnosis involves the recognition of issues that will influence the strategy. Once strategic issues have been identified, management must assess their urgency and the feasibility of the organization's dealing with them. The combination of urgency and feasibility will indicate management's willingness and commitment to initiate strategic change (momentum for change). This momentum may result in radical (revolutionary) or incremental (evolutionary) change.

Judgment and opinion must be used to determine the relevance of the strategy and progress toward organizational goals. To aid in the identification and evaluation of strategic issues, a series of questions designed to trigger analysis and discussion may be used.

Mechanisms for strategic control are integrated into the policies, procedures, and practices of management. These mechanisms are typically found within data management, management of managers, and the conflict resolution methods of the organization. Therefore, strategic planning, the information systems, resource-allocation procedures, performance-appraisal procedures, boards of directors or trustees, retreats, and so on are inherently strategic evaluation and control mechanisms of the organization. In addition, contingency planning (developing alternative strategic plans) is an effective strategic control. Typically, contingency plans are initiated when change occurs more rapidly than expected or when unexpected events render the current strategy inappropriate.

Key Terms and Concepts in Strategic Management

contingency planning	issue urgency	strategic change
control	operational control	strategic control
controlling strategic leap	organizational performance	strategic control systems
controlling strategic momentum	revolutionary change	strategic issue diagnosis (SID)
evolutionary change	standards of performance	strategic pressure point
issue feasibility	strategic assumptions	7-S framework

Questions for Class Discussion

1. Define strategic control. Why is it important that managers establish strategic control within their organizations?
2. How are strategic planning and strategic control related? Can you distinguish control from planning?
3. What are the fundamental elements of control? Do all organizational control systems have these elements?
4. What are the characteristics of effective control?
5. Strategic control is concerned most with what three areas?
6. What are the steps involved in strategic control of a health care organization?
7. What part do judgment, opinion, beliefs, and values play in strategic control?
8. How is organizational performance measured? Are the measures of performance for health care organizations different from the measures for business organizations?
9. Do health care organizations change directional and adaptive strategies often? Why are these changes called *revolutionary?*
10. What is *evolutionary* strategic change?
11. What events can create pressure on an organization and lead to a strategic *pressure point?*
12. What is strategic issue diagnosis? What are its elements? Is it a part of strategic control?
13. How does management's assessment of issue urgency and the feasibility of the organization's to deal with the issue combine to influence strategic change?
14. What are an organization's strategic assumptions? How may the strategic assumptions be evaluated?
15. Is it possible to determine if the mission, vision, and values of an organization are valid? How can we approach this determination?
16. How can revolutionary and evolutionary change be strategically controlled? What organizational mechanisms facilitate controlling the strategy?
17. What is the McKinsey 7-S framework? What is the purpose of the framework? Is it a practical strategic control tool?
18. What is contingency planning? How may contingency planning be viewed as strategic control?

Notes

1. Peter Lorange, Michael F. Scott Morton, and Sumantra Ghoshal, *Strategic Control* (St. Paul: West Publishing Company, 1986), p. 10.
2. Michael Goold and John J. Quinn, "The Paradox of Strategic Controls," *Strategic Management Journal* 11, no. 1 (January 1990), p. 44.
3. Ibid.
4. Thomas W. Chapman, "Rediscovering Abandoned Values," *Health Management Quarterly* 12, no. 2 (1990), pp. 20–23.
5. Carolyne K. Davis and Frederick B. Abbey, "Keeping Score Alters the Game," *Health Management Quarterly* 11, no. 2 (1989), pp. 6–9.
6. Peter F. Drucker, "If Earnings Aren't the Dial to Read," *The Wall Street Journal* (October 30, 1986), p. 15.
7. L. Tushman, W. H. Newman, and E. Romanelli, "Convergence and Upheaval: Managing the Unsteady Pace of Organizational Evolution," *California Management Review* 29, no. 1 (1986), pp. 29–44.
8. Sharon Topping, "Strategic Change in Multi-Hospital Systems: A Longitudinal Study of the Nature of Change," dissertation, The University of Alabama at Birmingham, 1991.
9. Ibid.
10. Ibid.
11. Jane E. Dutton and Robert B. Duncan, "The Creation of Momentum for Change Through the Process of Strategic Issue Diagnosis," *Strategic Management Journal* 8, no. 3 (1987), pp. 279–295.
12. Ibid.
13. Lynn Wagner, "Hospitals Feeling Trauma of Violence," *Modern Healthcare* (February 5, 1990), pp. 23–32.
14. Sara Carmel, "Patient Complaint Strategies in a General Hospital," *Hospital and Health Services Administration* 35, no. 2 (Summer 1990), pp. 277–288.
15. Dutton and Duncan, "Creation of Momentum for Change," p. 287.
16. Ibid., pp. 287–288.
17. Lorange, Morton, and Ghoshal, *Strategic Control,* p. 11.
18. Gerald E. Sussman, "CEO Perspectives on Mission, Healthcare Systems, and the Environment," *Hospital and Health Services Administration* 30, no. 1 (Spring 1985), pp. 27–29.
19. Ibid.
20. Karen Southwick, "Ailing CompCare Retrenches," *HealthWeek* 3, no. 22 (November 6, 1989), pp. 1, 64.
21. Lorange, Morton, and Ghoshal, *Strategic Control,* p. 11.
22. Robert H. Waterman, Jr., "The Seven Elements of Strategic Fit," *Journal of Business Strategy* 2, no. 3 (Winter 1982), pp. 69–73.
23. Y. Doz and C. K. Prahalad, "Headquarter Influence and Strategic Control in MNCs," *Sloan Management Review* 22, no. 4 (Fall 1981), pp. 15–29.
24. James L. Heskett, W. Earl Sasser, Jr., and Christopher W. L. Hart, *Service Breakthroughs: Changing the Rules of the Game* (New York: Free Press, 1990), p. 112.

25. Valarie A. Zeithaml, A. Parasuraman, and Leonard L. Berry, *Delivering Quality Service: Balancing Customer Perceptions and Expectations* (New York: Free Press, 1990), p. 3.

26. Peter F. Drucker, *Managing the Non-Profit Organization* (New York: HarperCollins Publishers, 1990), p. 60.

27. Ibid., p. 62.

28. R. D. Kosnik, "Coordination and Control in Multi-Hospital Systems: The Role of Boards of Directors," *Academy of Management Proceedings* (1987), pp. 91–95.

29. Peter Lorange, ed., *Implementation of Strategic Planning* (Englewood Cliffs, New Jersey: Prentice-Hall, 1982); and Peter Lorange, "Monitoring Strategic Progress and Ad Hoc Strategic Modification," in *Strategic Management Horizons,* ed. J. Grant (Greenwich, Connecticut: JAI Press, 1988).

30. Sandy Lutz, "Hospitals Reassess Home-Care Ventures," *Modern Healthcare* (September 17, 1990), pp. 23–30.

31. Robert Linneman and Rajan Chandran, "Contingency Planning: A Key to Swift Managerial Action in the Uncertain Tomorrow," *Managerial Planning* 29, no. 4 (January/February 1981), pp. 23–27.

Additional Readings

Adams, Scott, *The Dilbert Principle: A Cubicle's Eye View of Bosses, Meetings, Management Fads and Other Workplace Afflictions* (New York: HarperBusiness, 1996). There is a great deal of truth in most humor, and Scott Adams takes a humorous look at the management of modern organizations. The book is particularly relevant to control, because it takes the point of view of employees and suggests the inconsistencies in many management control techniques. Topics include TQM, reengineering, empowerment, downsizing, flattening the organization, communication, business plans, budgeting, change, performance reviews, team-building, leadership, and much more. The book provides some interesting insights into managing modern organizations.

Bennis, Warren, and Robert Townsend, *Reinventing Leadership: Strategies to Empower the Organization* (New York: William Morrow and Company, 1995). Bennis and Townsend discuss how organizations can make changes and move away from conventional standards and practices. Chapters such as "The Guiding Vision," "Creating a Trusting Organization," "Empowerment," and "Strategies for the New Work Paradigm" are particularly important in selecting the right controls for organizations. Bennis and Townsend illustrate how to embrace change, turn mistakes into valuable opportunities, transform vision into reality, and lead an organization into the future.

Biehl, Bobb, *Stop Setting Goals If You Would Rather Solve Problems* (Nashville: Moorings, 1995). Bobb Biehl suggests that there are people that are comfortable with goal setting and others that are frustrated by the goal-setting process and are more comfortable with problem solving. Biehl indicates that both types of people are essential to organizational success. However, many organizations require everyone to be goal setters. Goal setters are future oriented and set future agendas whereas problem solvers are better at identifying, solving strategic problems, maintenance, prevention, and making adjustments (control). The author posits that a good team will contain both goal setters and problem solvers and both should be allowed to do what comes naturally.

Pettigrew, Andrew, Ewan Ferlie, and Lorna McKee, *Shaping Strategic Change* (London: Sage Publications, 1992). This book examines the processes of the management of strategic service change within a specific health care setting—the National Health Service (NHS) of England. In exploring the nature of change, the book reviews the literature that has been used to study organizational change processes and explains why an approach based on the study of organizational transitions and adaptations is preferred. In studying strategic change, the authors examine the introduction of general management within the NHS, explore the influences of and barriers to strategic change, and examine the skills associated with change management. In addition, the book provides a generic model for understanding strategic service change.

Weiss, Alan, *Our Emperors Have No Clothes: Incredibly Stupid Things Corporate Executives Have Done While Reengineering, Restructuring, Downsizing, TQM'ing, Team-building, and Empowering . . . in Order to Cover Their Ifs and "Buts."* (Franklin Lakes, New Jersey: Career Press, 1995). In this book, Alan Weiss asks the question, "Do our corporate leaders really know what they are doing?" The book is about incompetence and gross ineptitude at the top levels of corporations and the devastating impact it has had on the workforce and the economy. Weiss explores the shortcomings of recent management "fads" and "magic bullet" management solutions that organizations have initiated and usually bungled. He suggests that we can no longer afford, nor tolerate, stupid management and offers solutions that may be used to implement effective leadership.

Creating the Strategic Plan: An Example

Learning Objectives

After completing this chapter you should be able to:

1. Understand how the steps in the strategic planning process logically fit together.

2. Apply the appropriate analysis methods to develop an actual strategic plan.

3. Use the methods and approaches discussed in the preceding chapters creatively—adapting them to facilitate your understanding of situational analysis, strategy formulation, implementation, and control.

4. Understand the complete model of strategic management.

5. Develop a comprehensive strategic plan for an actual organization or an organization presented in a case study.

6. Think strategically.

Developing a Strategic Plan

Some health care organizations have extensive experience in strategic management and developing strategic plans. However, as suggested in the Introductory Incident, other organizations may have had little experience with strategic management, or when they have developed a strategic plan, it was little used and ended up gathering dust on a shelf. Regardless of the level of expertise, strategic management requires a thorough understanding of the situation; developing, analyzing, and selecting strategic alternatives (formulation); implementing the strategy; and controlling the strategy.

Using the strategic management model presented in Chapter 1 (refer to Exhibit 1–5) plus the methods and approaches discussed throughout the book, this chapter illustrates development of a comprehensive strategic plan for the Indiana State Department of Health (ISDH). Each stage of the strategic management process as well as the various methods and approaches used are examined in detail.

In some instances it will be apparent that the methods presented in previous chapters may have been modified to meet the particular

Introductory Incident   Initiating the Strategic Planning Process

After being appointed state heath commissioner of the Indiana State Department of Health (ISDH), John C. Bailey, M.D., reviewed the plans and organization of the Department of Health and decided that a major strategic planning effort was required to better establish the role of the public health department in Indiana and to set the future direction for the department. In addition, it was Bailey's belief that the changing health care environment—and changing role of public health—would require a new direction for public health and a new way of operating. He believed that the organization had not dealt with change very well and over the years had grown far too bureaucratic to be effective in a rapidly changing environment.

Bailey believed that strategic management would provide an understanding of the trends and issues that the Department of Health would have to address in the next several years and that the

process would be instrumental in developing a course of action for the department. Therefore, Dr. Bailey committed to engage in a year-long strategic planning effort that would provide a foundation for determining the future direction of the department. It was Bailey's belief that everyone should be a part of strategic management, and therefore, he invited participation by employees from throughout the department and all organizational levels. He envisioned that the year-long process would provide the basis for ongoing strategic management of the organization.

Although poised to begin, several questions remained. "What was the best way to initiate the process? How should it be organized? What was the best approach? Who should facilitate the planning effort? Would this be a worthwhile endeavor or merely a long exercise? Did people have the time to participate?"

needs of the ISDH. It is important to realize that each organization is unique and the methods and approaches presented in this book cannot be applied blindly; rather, they must be understood in terms of the objectives of the organization and the logic of the situation. Managers must always make a method or approach *work* for them; they should not work for the method. When working through a process, if a method or approach is not contributing to greater understanding, then it should be modified to better serve the organization's needs or abandoned in favor of an approach that does contribute to improved effectiveness in reaching a decision. A manager's job is to *think*. After studying the previous chapters, you should be familiar with the theories and concepts of strategic management. Now it is time to *apply* the theories and concepts to think strategically.

Organization of the Process

Because the ISDH had not engaged in agencywide strategic management for a number of years, facilitators were used to provide guidance in the process and work directly with Joe Hunt, the director of the Office for Policy Coordination. The director was responsible for coordination of the strategic management activities throughout the agency, development of the written strategic plan, and development of future strategic management activities. A brief profile of the director of the Office for Policy Coordination is presented in Perspective 14–1.

It is often difficult for "outsiders" to independently develop the strategy of an organization. It takes a significant amount of time to understand any organization—its mission, values, tasks, culture, and so on. In addition, if people from all levels of the organization are involved in the development, the strategy will ultimately be better as well as more likely to be accepted. On the other hand, outsiders can be excellent facilitators, examine sensitive issues, and provide more objective opinions.

Wide participation by personnel throughout the agency was believed to be essential to the strategic management effort. Therefore, employees from all levels and all functional specialties within the organization were to be included in the process. A task force structure with five working groups was adopted to carry out the strategic management process. Each group had about twenty members. Thus, at the outset, approximately one hundred employees were involved. In addition, the executive staff, composed of the deputy commissioner and the assistant commissioners, supported and guided the process. Nancy C. Blough, deputy state health commissioner, was committed to the process and ensured that the project remained on schedule. The work groups and their general responsibilities are presented in Exhibit 14–1 and a profile of Blough is provided in Perspective 14–2.

As an additional aid in organizing the strategic management process, a milestone chart was developed (see Exhibit 14–2). The milestone chart helped everyone visualize the entire process and the interrelationships of the individual elements. In addition, the milestone chart highlighted specific priorities and the appropriate sequence for accomplishing the required tasks.

| Perspective 14–1

Profile of Joe D. Hunt, Director of the Office for Policy Coordination

Joe D. Hunt is director of the Office for Policy Coordination of the Indiana State Department of Health. In this capacity, Hunt manages and directs activities of the office, which is responsible for:

- developing policy for the ISDH on issues of public health significance;
- coordinating the ISDH role in health care reform;
- encouraging and supporting strategic thinking within the ISDH;
- monitoring emerging health issues for possible impact on public health in Indiana; and
- assisting programs in assessing policy options.

In his tenure with the ISDH, Hunt has served as assistant commissioner of the Public Health Policy Commission, assistant commissioner of the Health Marketing Commission, director of the Bureau of Policy Development, director of the Planning Program, as well as other positions within the ISDH.

Hunt received the B.S. degree in environmental science from Rutgers University and M.P.H. degree with a major in public health administration from the University of Michigan. He serves on numerous public service groups and as adjunct faculty, Indiana University–Purdue University, Indianapolis School of Public and Environmental Affairs.

Exhibit 14–1 · ISDH Strategic Management Organization

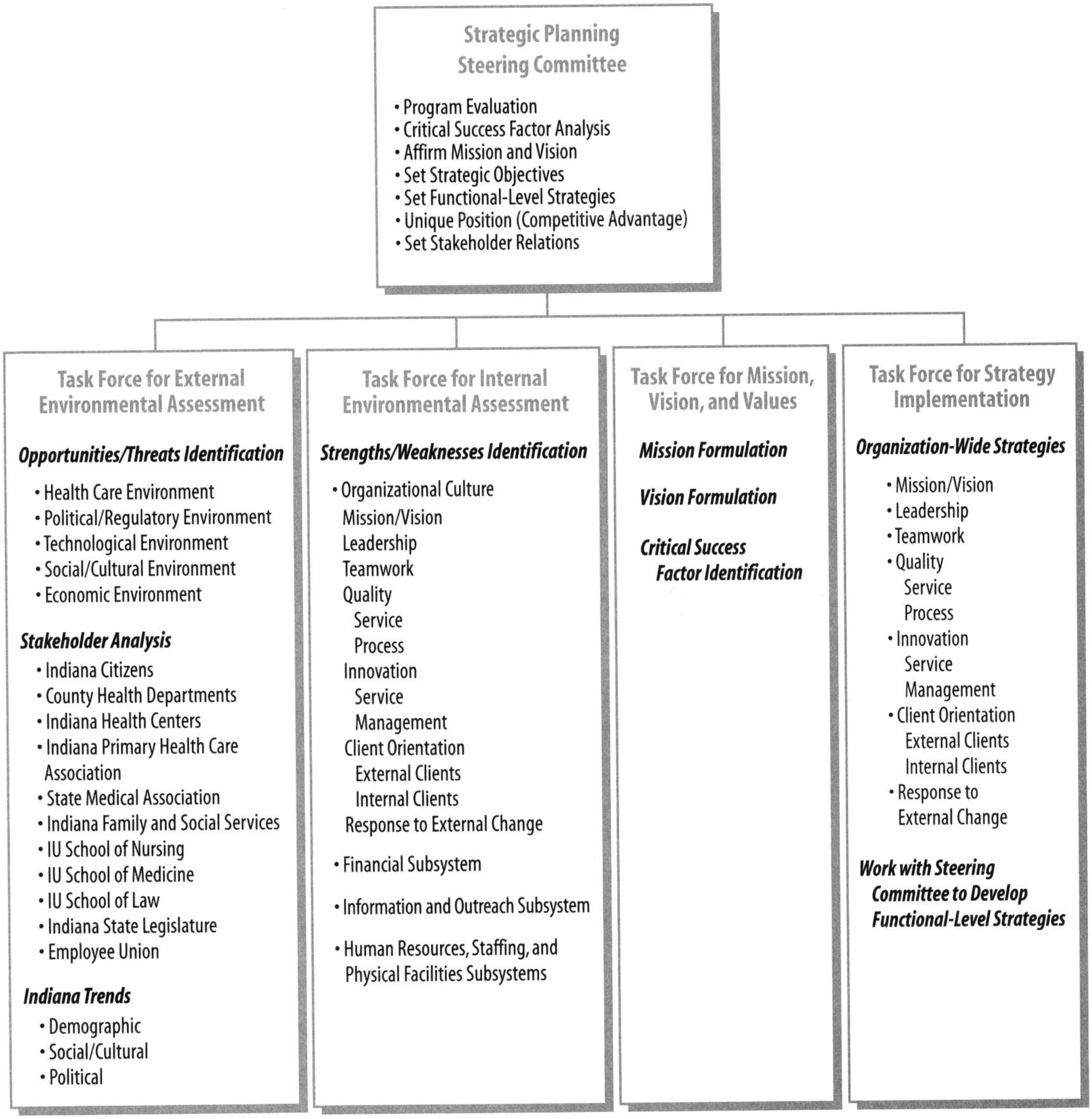

Strategic Planning
Steering Committee

• Program Evaluation
• Critical Success Factor Analysis
• Affirm Mission and Vision
• Set Strategic Objectives
• Set Functional-Level Strategies
• Unique Position (Competitive Advantage)
• Set Stakeholder Relations

Task Force for External Environmental Assessment

Opportunities/Threats Identification

• Health Care Environment
• Political/Regulatory Environment
• Technological Environment
• Social/Cultural Environment
• Economic Environment

Stakeholder Analysis
• Indiana Citizens
• County Health Departments
• Indiana Health Centers
• Indiana Primary Health Care Association
• State Medical Association
• Indiana Family and Social Services
• IU School of Nursing
• IU School of Medicine
• IU School of Law
• Indiana State Legislature
• Employee Union

Indiana Trends
• Demographic
• Social/Cultural
• Political

Task Force for Internal Environmental Assessment

Strengths/Weaknesses Identification

• Organizational Culture
  Mission/Vision
  Leadership
  Teamwork
  Quality
    Service
    Process
  Innovation
    Service
    Management
  Client Orientation
    External Clients
    Internal Clients
  Response to External Change

• Financial Subsystem

• Information and Outreach Subsystem

• Human Resources, Staffing, and Physical Facilities Subsystems

Task Force for Mission, Vision, and Values

Mission Formulation

Vision Formulation

Critical Success Factor Identification

Task Force for Strategy Implementation

Organization-Wide Strategies

• Mission/Vision
• Leadership
• Teamwork
• Quality
    Service
    Process
• Innovation
    Service
    Management
• Client Orientation
    External Clients
    Internal Clients
• Response to External Change

Work with Steering Committee to Develop Functional-Level Strategies

Situational Analysis

As shown on the milestone chart, the first five months of the strategic management process were spent developing the situational analysis. By thoroughly examining the external environment, internal environment, and the mission, vision, values, and critical

Perspective 14–2

Profile of Nancy C. Blough, J.D., Deputy State Health Commissioner

Nancy C. Blough is an attorney and was appointed deputy state health commissioner at the Indiana State Department of Health in 1992. Her responsibilities include overseeing the day-to-day operations of the Public Health Quality Assurance, Prevention and Community Health, and Planning and Information Commissions. Prior to her appointment as deputy state health commissioner, Blough served as assistant commissioner of public health services. In addition, she was an executive assistant to the state health commissioner, providing both legal and policy advice. Prior to working at the State Department of Health, she held the title of equal employment opportunity manager for the Indiana Department of Highways.

Blough received her undergraduate degree in public administration, masters of business administration, and doctorate of jurisprudence from Indiana University. She is a certified mediator in the state of Indiana and is a member of the local bar association, the American Bar Association, and the National Association of Health Lawyers. In addition, she serves as an advisor to the Law, Medical, and Health Institute associated with Indiana University School of Law and is a member of the Indiana Environmental FORUM.

success factors, the ISDH's unique situation was brought into perspective. The information gathered during the situational analysis phase was then used to provide the basis for strategy formulation.

General Situation and Background

The citizens of Indiana are very independent and generally do not favor government "interference." The population's "home rule" attitude has limited the influence of state and federal government and created an unusual operating environment. To understand the setting of the ISDH and its unique set of circumstances, it is helpful to review Perspective 14–3, which contains general information concerning the state of Indiana.

County Governance   Most county governments have two governing bodies, a board of commissioners and a county council. Generally, the board of commissioners performs the executive and legislative functions of county government and the county council serves as the fiscal body. Counties in Indiana follow this home rule authority as granted in Title 36 of the Indiana code, which specifies that counties have the powers granted by law and other powers necessary or desirable to conduct county affairs.[1]

The Indiana State Department of Health   The Indiana State Department of Health is a freestanding, independent state agency. The state health commissioner, John C. Bailey, M.D., serves as the chief executive officer of the department and as the secretary of the eleven-member executive board of the state board of health. Perspective 14–4 provides a profile of Bailey. The commissioner is appointed by and serves at the pleasure of the governor. As chief executive officer, the commissioner is responsible for overall management of the ISDH. The eleven individuals who serve on the executive board of the state board of health are also appointed by the governor. The executive board is responsible

Exhibit 14–2 • ISDH Strategic Management Milestone Chart

Months	May	June	July	August	September	October	November	December	January	February	March	April
Weeks	1 2 3 4	1 2 3 4	1 2 3 4	1 2 3 4	1 2 3 4	1 2 3 4	1 2 3 4	1 2 3 4	1 2 3 4	1 2 3 4	1 2 3 4	1 2 3 4

TASKS

- Organization of the Process
- External Environmental Assessment
  Opportunities and Threats Identification
  Stakeholder Analysis
  Indiana Trends Identification
- Internal Environmental Assessment
  Strengths and Weaknesses Identification
  Financial Subsystem
  Information and Outreach Subsystem
  Human Resources, Staffing, and
    Physical Facilities Subsystem
- Mission, Vision, and Values
  Mission Formulation
  Vision Formulation
  Critical Success Factor Identification
- Steering Committee
  Critical Success Factor Analysis
  Affirm Mission and Vision
  Set Strategic Objectives
  Program Evaluation
  Formulate Statement of Strategy
  Set Functional-Level Strategies
  Set Organization-Wide Strategies
- Implementation
  Organization-Wide Strategies
  Coordinate Functional Strategies

Weeks	1 2 3 4	1 2 3 4	1 2 3 4	1 2 3 4	1 2 3 4	1 2 3 4	1 2 3 4	1 2 3 4	1 2 3 4	1 2 3 4	1 2 3 4	1 2 3 4
Months	May	June	July	August	September	October	November	December	January	February	March	April

for providing policy advice and guidance for the ISDH.[2] An organization chart for the ISDH is presented in Exhibit 14–3.

An important role of the ISDH staff members is to function as consultants to staff members of local (county) health departments within the state. In addition, there is a division of local support services whose staff are assigned on a geographical basis to work directly with local health departments. These staff members provide both technical and management consulting services. Interaction between state and local public health agencies in Indiana is highly decentralized. Under this arrangement, local governments somewhat independently operate and finance their own local health departments.[3]

| Perspective 14–3

The Organization Setting—General Information Concerning Indiana History

The Midwestern territory known as Indiana entered the Union on December 11, 1816, as the nineteenth state. The citizens of Indiana consider themselves to be "typically American." The capital of the state, Indianapolis, lies at the geographic center of Indiana and at the "crossroads of America." The state itself is rectangular, with a maximum length of 280 miles and a breadth of 160 miles. In land area, Indiana is the thirty-eighth largest state.

Economic Base

Of the land in Indiana, 70 percent is devoted to agriculture. Corn and soybeans are the state's primary cash crops. In addition, wheat, oats, tobacco, hay, rye, apples, and peaches contribute meaningfully to the economy. However, service industries account for 60 percent of the gross state product. The northwest portion of the state is a major industrial area fostered by the close proximity to industrial centers in Chicago, Detroit, and Toledo. Iron, steel, and petroleum products are major manufacturing outputs. Other manufactured products include aluminum, chemicals, clay products, furniture, and automotive parts. On a national basis, Indiana is a major producer of pharmaceuticals, manufactured housing, and musical instruments.

Population

In 1990 the population of Indiana was approximately 5.5 million. However, the population growth is slowing. From 1980 to 1990 the growth rate was 1 percent. In addition, the population of Indiana is getting older. In 1990, about 13 percent of the population was 65 years or older as compared to 12 percent in 1986. About 9 percent of the population is nonwhite.

Education

Indiana has thirty-four colleges and universities. In 1990, about 76 percent of the population age 25 years and older had an educational attainment of high school graduate or higher. About 16 percent attained a level of bachelor's degree or higher.

State Spending

Marion County, including the capital city of Indianapolis, is governed by a mayor/council form of government. All other counties are governed by a board of county commissioners. In 1988, the state had total general expenditures of $8.4 billion. On a per capita basis, it ranked thirty-seventh among the states. The major categories of state expenditure included $3.66 billion for education, $1.48 billion for public welfare, $903 million for highways, $604 million for health and hospitals, and $117 million for the management of natural resources.*

Health

High-priority statewide health needs that have been identified and are being actively addressed include high-risk pregnancies, child/abuse neglect, unintentional injuries, older adults, environmental health, and the medically underserved. The ten leading causes of death in 1990 were diseases of the heart, cancer, cerebrovascular diseases, pneumonia, other chronic obstructive pulmonary diseases, diseases of the arteries, diabetes mellitus, motor vehicle accidents, accidents excluding motor vehicle accidents, and suicide.

Selected Sociodemographic Indicators

Indicator	Indiana	United States
Population	5,556,000	245,803,000
Population Density (per square mile)	154.6	69.4

Indicator	Indiana	United States
Number of Counties	92	3,139
Median Age	31.3	31.7
Percent Below Poverty Level	12%	14%
Percent Rural Population	36%	26%
Percent White Population	91.2%	83.1%
Percent Nonwhite Population	8.8%	16.9%
Median Years of Education	12.4	12.5

Source: Public Health Practice Program Office, Division of Public Health Systems, Centers for Disease Control, *Profile of State and Territorial Public Health Systems: United States, 1990,* U.S. Department of Health and Human Services, Public Health Service, Centers for Disease Control, Atlanta, Georgia (December 1991), p. 121.

*Abstracted from *The Travel Guide,* Mobil Oil Corporation, Prodigy Interactive Personal Service, 1993; *Academic American Encyclopedia,* Grolier Electronic Publishing, Inc., Prodigy Interactive Personal Service, 1993; and *Statistical Abstracts of the United States,* 111th ed. (Washington, D.C.: U.S. Bureau of the Census), p. 289.

Perspective 14–4

Profile of John C. Bailey, M.D., Indiana State Health Commissioner

John C. Bailey, M.D., was appointed by Governor Bayh to the Executive Board of the Indiana State Department of Health in 1989, and he became state health commissioner in November 1990. As state health commissioner, he oversees the agency operations and serves as secretary of the eleven-member executive board.

Bailey graduated from the Indiana University School of Medicine and did his residency in internal medicine at St. Vincent Hospital and the Indiana University Medical Center in Indianapolis. After serving as a U.S. Army Medical Corps artil- lery surgeon in Vietnam, Bailey returned to the Indiana University School of Medicine in 1970 for a United States Public Health Service Trainee Fellowship in cardiology. Subsequently he was appointed as research associate and the senior research associate at the Krannert Institute of Cardiology in Indianapolis and promoted to professor at the Indiana University School of Medicine. Bailey's twenty-year career encompasses widely published scientific research, professional consultantships, academic appointments, private practice, and public service.

Indiana has ninety-six local health departments: ninety county, one multicounty, and five city health departments (see Exhibit 14–4). According to state law, the ISDH is the "superior agency" to each of the local health departments. In this capacity the ISDH is charged with the responsibility for recording the appointments of local health officers and overseeing the programs and activities of the local health departments; however, staff members of local health departments are employed and supervised by

Exhibit 14–3 · Indiana State Department of Health Organizational Chart

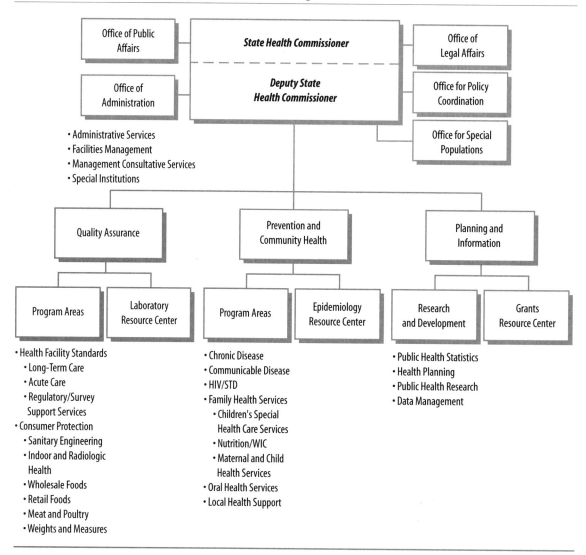

the local jurisdiction. The number of staff members for a local health department ranges from 1 to 550.[4]

Because of the quasi-autonomy of the local health departments, public health services vary widely from county to county depending upon local funding and the decisions of the commission and county council. Therefore, services provided in one county may not be provided in a contiguous county, or these services may be carried out in a different manner or with varying levels of enthusiasm. In general, the services offered by the local health departments may be classified as (1) assessment, (2) policy development,

Exhibit 14–4 • Types of Local Health Departments by Jurisdiction, State of Indiana

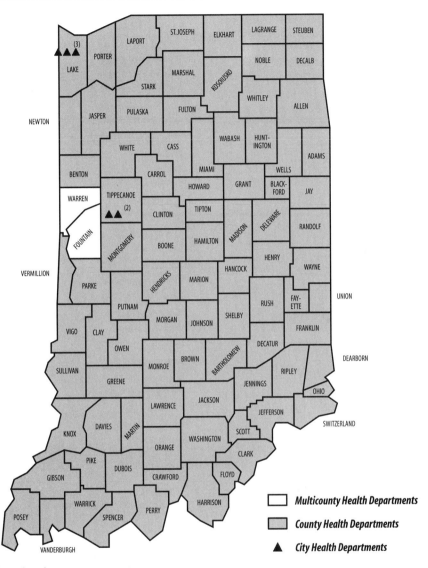

Source: Centers for Disease Control

and (3) assurance activities. Exhibit 14–5 provides a list of these services and identifies the number of local health departments that provide each service in Indiana.

Within this setting and without a great deal of strategic management experience, the Indiana State Department of Health began its determined effort to incorporate strategic management into the administrative philosophy of the organization. The first

Exhibit 14–5 • Services Provided by Local Health Departments

Services	Number of Departments Providing Each Service	Services	Number of Departments Providing Each Service
Assessment Activities		**Assurance Activities** (cont.)	
Data Collection/Analysis		Public Water Safety	51
Behavioral Risk Assessment	13	Radiation Control	17
Morbidity Data	38	Sewage Disposal Systems	87
Reportable Diseases	71	Solid Waste Management	61
Vital Records and Statistics	89	Vector and Animal Control	76
Epidemiology/Surveillance		Water Pollution	65
Chronic Diseases	38	Personal Health Services	
Communicable Diseases	85	AIDS Testing and Counseling	22
Policy Development		Alcohol Abuse	3
Health Code Development and Enforcement	51	Child Health	61
Health Planning	49	Chronic Diseases	50
Priority Setting	21	Dental Health	9
Assurance Activities		Drug Abuse	6
Inspection		Emergency Medical Service	4
Food and Milk Control	67	Family Planning	16
Health Facility Safety/Quality	21	Handicapped Children	53
Recreation Facility Safety/Quality	30	Home Health Care	45
Other Facility Safety/Quality	8	Hospitals	2
Licensing		Immunizations	89
Health Facilities	6	Laboratory Services	17
Other Facilities	63	Long-Term-Care Facilities	1
Health Education	56	Mental Health	4
Environmental		Obstetrical Care	11
Air Quality	41	Prenatal Care	29
Hazardous Waste Management	50	Primary Care	5
Individual Water Supply Safety	76	Sexually Transmitted Diseases	26
Noise Pollution	9	Tuberculosis	75
Occupational Health and Safety	12	WIC (women, infant, children) Program	30

Note: Ninety-four of ninety-six local health departments reported.
Source: Public Health Practice Program Office, Division of Public Health Systems, Centers for Disease Control, *Profile of State and Territorial Public Health Systems: United States, 1990* (Atlanta: U.S. Department of Health and Human Services, Public Health Service, Centers for Disease Control, 1991), pp. 121–122.

phase of the process involved situational analysis—environmental analysis, internal analysis, and the development of mission, vision, and values.

External Environmental Analysis

The department had to understand and respond to external opportunities and threats because they represent the fundamental issues that would spell success or failure. The specific objectives that guided the Task Force for External Environmental Assessment were to:

- classify and order information generated outside of the department;
- identify and analyze current important issues that will affect the department;
- detect and analyze the weak signals of emerging issues that will affect the department;
- speculate on the likely future issues that will have significant impact on the department;
- provide organized information for the development of the department's vision, mission, objectives, and strategy; and
- foster strategic thinking throughout the department.

External analysis for the ISDH was carried out in two phases. First, stakeholder analysis was used to identify the relationships of the ISDH with other organizations. Second, the department used trend/issue identification and analysis to focus on the issues considered to be most important.

Stakeholder Analysis An enthusiastic task force identified over 250 stakeholder groups and organizations, twelve of which were considered to be central to the department's mission. These key stakeholders are identified in the stakeholder map shown in Exhibit 14–6. Stakeholder analysis was selected because of the belief that these outside organizations would be in a good position to suggest areas of excellence within the ISDH and areas for improvements. Further, the stakeholders had important perspectives on the changing economic, social, and political environment of Indiana and the future role that the ISDH should play.

Interviews with the twelve stakeholder groups were conducted to determine the general purpose or mission of the stakeholder and the nature of the relationship between the stakeholder and the ISDH. Results of the interview process are presented in Exhibit 14–7.

The conclusions of the stakeholder analysis were that relations with stakeholders were generally positive, although relations were sometimes strained between the ISDH and the local health departments. There was a high level of cooperation with other agencies, and the members generally understood the reciprocal relationship between their agency and the ISDH. Most of the agencies wanted an even closer working relationship with the ISDH.

The major deficiency in stakeholder relations was with the county health departments. As indicated in the background section, the quasi-autonomous county health departments delivered most public health services. That is, the county health departments actually provided the services such as food inspections, immunizations, health code enforcement, and so on. The ISDH created policy and supported the activities of the counties. However, the relationship between the counties and state was not always viewed positively. Often counties saw the ISDH as bureaucratic, unresponsive, and inappropriately staffed to serve the needs of the counties.

Trend/Issue Analysis In an effort to identify the major trends and issues, the External Environmental Assessment Task Force was divided into five subcommittees, corresponding

Exhibit 14–6 · Indiana State Department of Health Stakeholder Map

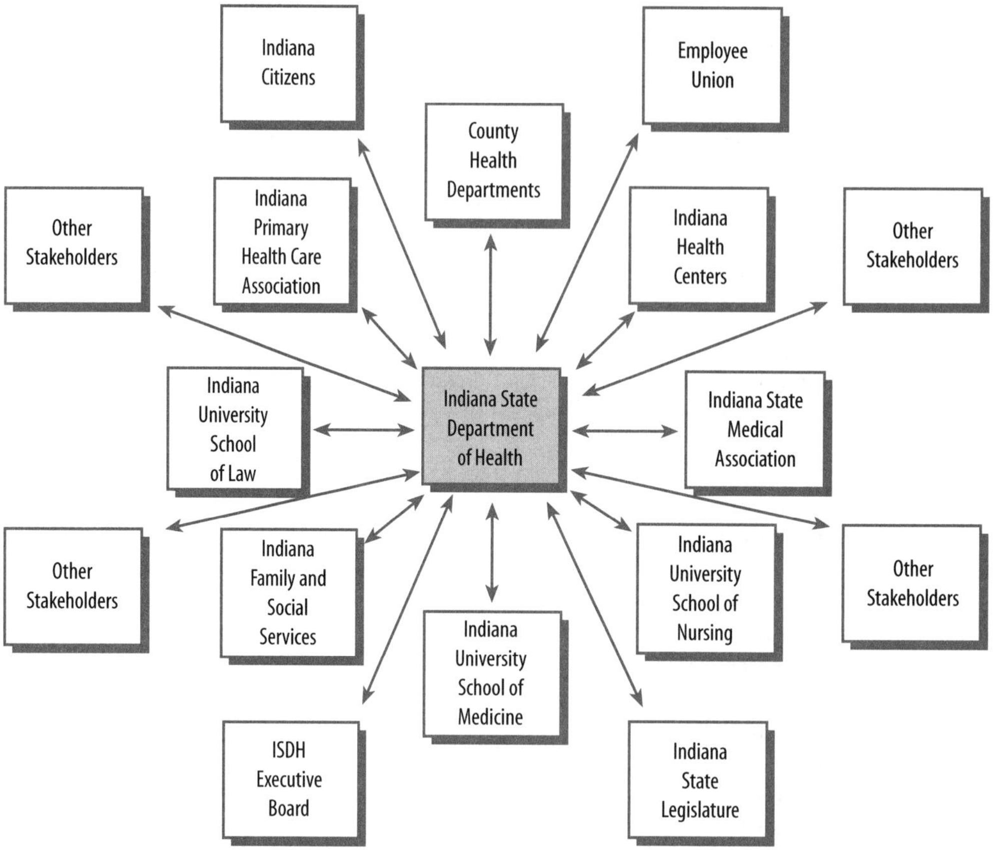

to the five "environments" that the ISDH believed represented the major classifications of the public health environment in Indiana:

- health care,
- political/regulatory,
- technological,
- social/cultural, and
- economic.

Each subcommittee was given the responsibility of gathering information, using internal/external and personal/nonpersonal sources of data to identify key trends and issues within its category. The data-gathering strategy used in trend and issue identification is conceptualized in Exhibit 14–8.

After the initial data-gathering activity, the External Environmental Assessment Task Force decided that the trends and issues identified by the various subcommittees should

Exhibit 14–7 • Indiana State Department of Health Stakeholder Relationships

Stakeholder	General Purpose/Mission	Nature of the Relationship
Indiana Citizens	To achieve health and happiness.	The medically underserved depend on ISDH for clinical services; entire community depends on department for prevention and protection.
County Health Departments	To deliver public health services such as clinical services, permits, inspections, birth and death certificates, and so on, at the county level.	Provide for the direct delivery of public health in Indiana; policy guidance from the state-level organization; rely on state expertise and advice; little financial dependence; semi-autonomous, county departments prefer to stay independent (home rule) but also need the expertise of the state.
Indiana Health Centers	To provide health services to those, who because of poverty or location in rural areas, do not have access to affordable health care; emphasis is on farmworkers.	ISDH provides many important regulatory functions and contracting opportunities for Indiana Health Centers.
Indiana Primary Health Care Association	To provide family care to the underserved through health centers/clinics, advocacy, data analysis, and so on.	Cooperative agreement with ISDH; have a similar mission, want to maintain a close relationship.
Indiana Medical Association	Professional association to represent state physicians; provides licensure services as well as lobbying activities.	ISDH has important regulatory functions and collects useful epidemiology and vital statistical data; both organizations tend to be on the same side of the lobbying issues; Indiana Medical Association would like to see more mutual efforts to communicate with ISDH.
Indiana Family and Social Services	To protect and serve families in need of human services resources or support, including family and children, mental health, Medicaid, aging, and rehabilitative services.	Similar mission to serve the public; clients overlap; would prefer more communication with ISDH.
ISDH Executive Board	To provide advice from different perspectives to facilitate the highest quality of strategic decision making in ISDH.	Board composed of a panel of relevant experts willing to volunteer time and assistance to ISDH.
Indiana University School of Nursing	To provide undergraduate and graduate education, the largest nursing school in the United States.	ISDH is seen as a key player in the debates concerning nursing practice and licensure; School of Nursing wants statutes changed to allow independent nursing practices.
Indiana University School of Medicine	To ensure the highest quality of medical education, contribute to medical research, and provide health services.	Participation in joint research ventures; reciprocal assistance to ISDH when mutually beneficial.
Indiana University School of Law	To provide high levels of teaching, research, and service to the legal community and citizens of Indiana.	Some limited participation in mutually beneficial joint activities.
Indiana State Legislature	To provide informed governance to citizens of Indiana through enlightened and responsive legislation.	Primary funding agency of ISDH; ISDH directly assists through contribution to the legislature's health care agenda.
Employee Union	To represent department employees.	Membership of approximately 20 percent of department employees.

be classified by (1) *scope* (national, state, or county issues) and (2) *strength* (current, emerging, or speculative issues). To illustrate the classifications, the economic environment is shown in Exhibit 14–9. A conceptualization of the process for the entire external environment is presented in Exhibit 14–10. Overall, the external environment for the

Exhibit 14–8 • External Environmental Task Force Data Gathering Strategy

	Personal Sources		Nonpersonal Sources	
Subcommittee	**Internal Experts**	**External Stakeholders**	**Internal Department Studies**	**External databases, Libraries**
Economic Environment				
Social/Cultural Environment				
Political/Regulatory Environment				
Competitive Environment				
Technological Environment				
Health Care Environment				

Exhibit 14–9 • Classifications of the Economic Environment

		Scope of the Issue		
		National	**State**	**County**
Issue Strength	**Current**	• No growth in total economy results in less tax revenue • Increasing hospital and nursing home closures	• No growth in total economy results in less tax revenue • Twelve percent of households earn less than $10,000	• Continued shortage of health care workers in rural areas
	Emerging	• Less health insurance benefits offered by employers • Limited funding for public health	• Less discretionary money for the average Indiana citizen • Limited funding for public health	• Limited funding for public health
	Speculative		• Increasing hospital and nursing home closures	

ISDH was viewed as having five major categories or environments, each with national/state/county and current/emerging/speculative issues. This organization of the process helped members of the task force to better focus data gathering and evaluation.

Exhibit 14–10 • Concept of the External Environment

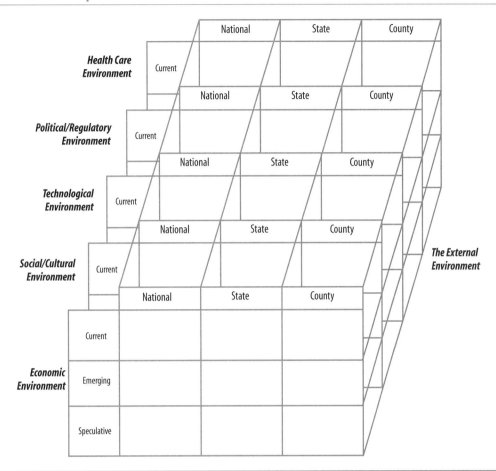

Using this approach, each subcommittee identified numerous (over fifty) national, state, and county; current, emerging, and speculative issues. However, the subcommittees concluded that many of the issues were trivial or would have little direct impact upon the department. Furthermore, only the most important issues ultimately could be addressed by the strategic plan. Therefore, each subcommittee reduced the list to ten or fewer trends/issues by assessing the importance of the impact of the trends and issues on the ISDH. Subsequent discussions and the combination of some issues resulted in a total of thirty-four environmental issues (see Exhibit 14–11).

To verify the validity of the trends and issues identified by the subcommittees of the External Environmental Assessment Task Force, 317 external stakeholders (including the administrators of the ninety-six local health departments) were surveyed. The stakeholders were asked to evaluate each of the thirty-four trends and issues as being very important, important, less important, or not important. Using the same instrument, the External Environmental Assessment Task Force also evaluated the trends and issues.

Exhibit 14–11 · Trends/Issues by Environmental Classification

Economic Environment	Code	Social/Cultural Environment	Code	Health Care Environment	Code	Technological Environment	Code	Political/Regulatory Environment	Code
No growth in total economy with less tax revenue	E-1	Increasing ethnic/racial diversity	S-1	Increasing long-term-care needs for those with chronic disease	HC-1	Inadequate support by ISDH in some technical areas	T-1	Impact of health care reform	PR-1
12 percent of households earn less than $10,000	E-2	Increasing number of single heads of households	S-2	Increasing need for collaboration between public and private providers	HC-2	Testing for environmental health problems (lead, water, food safety, PCBs, etc.)	T-2	Increasing emphasis on the measurement of health care outcomes	PR-2
Fewer health insurance benefits offered by employers	E-3	Increasing emphasis on women's health	S-3	Inadequate access to health care within the state	HC-3	State bureaucracy which does not facilitate procurement of latest technology	T-3	Increasing number of federal and state mandates	PR-3
Less discretionary money for the average Indiana citizen	E-4	Increasing concern for gender/racial/sexual discrimination	S-4	Increasing need for emphasis on prevention (communicable diseases, smoking, substance abuse, etc.)	HC-4	Low budget allocations for the procurement of technology	T-4	Increasing influence of special interest groups on health policy	PR-4
Continued shortage of health care workers in rural areas	E-5	Increasing amount of violence (child abuse, rape, etc.)	S-5	Medicaid reform	HC-5	Low image of ISDH as a technology leader	T-5	Increasing demand for cooperation between state and local health departments	PR-5
Increasing hospital and nursing home closures	E-6	Increasing number of homeless	S-6	Increasing number of senior citizens	HC-6	Increasing number of new required lab tests and procedures	T-6	Increasing demand for community-based services	PR-6
Limited funding for public health	E-7	Increasing amount of substance abuse	S-7	Increasing need for primary care in rural settings	HC-7			Increasing need for cooperation among community, state, and federal agencies	PR-7

Mean scores for each trend were calculated, and stakeholder and task force results were compared. The trends and issues rated as very important (mean scores above 3.38) for both groups are presented in Exhibit 14–12.

Exhibit 14–12 • Trends/Issues Rated As Important by Stakeholders and Task Force Members

Trends with Means Greater than 3.38 for Stakeholders but Not External Task Force	Code	Trends with Means Greater than 3.38 for Both Stakeholders and External Task Force	Code	Trends with Means Greater than 3.38 for External Task Force but Not Stakeholders	Code
No growth in total economy with less tax revenue	E-1	Limited funding for public health	E-7	Inadequate access to health care within the state	HC-3
Fewer health insurance benefits offered by employers	E-3	Increasing amount of violence (child abuse, rape, etc.)	S-5	Inadequate support by ISDH in some technical areas	T-1
Increasing amount of substance abuse	S-7	Increasing need for emphasis on prevention (communicable diseases, smoking, substance abuse, etc.)	HC-4	Low budget allocations for the procurement of technology	T-4
Increasing number of federal and state mandates	PR-3	Medicaid reform	HC-5		
Increasing need for collaboration between public and private providers	HC-2	Impact of health care reform	PR-1		
		Increasing demand for community-based services	PR-6		
		Increasing need for cooperation among community, state, and federal agencies	PR-7		

After considerable discussion concerning the survey results, the task force decided that the views of the stakeholders *and* the task force should be considered by combining several of the important individual trends and issues under broader headings. The total number of trends and issues could be reduced yet still retain the subtlety of the individual factors considered important by both groups. By collapsing the trends and issues under broader headings, eight significant areas were identified (see Exhibit 14–13). Note that twenty-five of the original thirty-four issues were subsumed under the eight broad headings. It was felt that this approach provided general areas of focus for the ISDH, but retained the necessary detail to guide the strategy.

It was the belief of the task force that each of the eight trends and issues represented both opportunities and threats for the ISDH. To highlight this belief, the task force began identifying the implications of the opportunities and threats for each of the eight issues. The points identified were the initial thoughts of the task force and designed to stimulate strategic thinking of the steering committee as well as the entire department. The implications of the trends and issues for the ISDH are conceptualized in Exhibit 14–14.

Internal Environmental Analysis

The general objective of the internal environmental analysis at the ISDH was to provide the steering committee with an assessment of the strengths and weaknesses of the major operating systems as discussed in Chapter 4. These included the culture of the organization as well as the financial, human resources, information, and physical facilities subsystems (marketing was determined not to be a major system of the

Exhibit 14–13 • External Environment Significant Trends/Issues

Trend/Issue	Codes
• Impact of Health Care Reform	
Health care reform	PR-1
Medicaid reform	HC-5
Increasing need for primary care in rural settings	HC-7
Continued shortage of health care workers in rural areas	E-5
• Need for Cooperation-Based Strategies	
Increasing need for cooperation among community, state, and federal agencies	PR-7
Increasing need for collaboration between public and private providers	HC-2
Increasing demand for cooperation between state and local health departments	PR-5
Increasing demand for community-based services	PR-6
• Limited Funding for Public Health	E-7
Increasing number of federal and state mandates	PR-3
No growth in total economy with less tax revenue	E-1
Fewer health insurance benefits offered by employers	E-3
• Increasing Amount of Violence (child abuse, rape, etc.)	S-5
• Increasing Need for Emphasis on Prevention (communicable diseases, smoking, substance abuse, etc.)	HC-4
• Access/Care for Special Populations	
Inadequate access to health care within the state	HC-3
Increasing ethnic/racial diversity	S-1
Increasing emphasis on women's health	S-3
Increasing concern for gender/racial/sexual discrimination	S-4
Increasing numbers of homeless	S-6
Increasing numbers of senior citizens	HC-6
• External Technological Advancements	
Inadequate support by ISDH in some technical areas	T-1
Low budget allocations for the procurement of technology	T-4
Testing for environmental health problems (lead, water, food, safety, PCBs, etc.)	T-2
Low image of ISDH as a technology leader	T-5
• Increasing Amount of Substance Abuse	S-7

department). The specific objectives of the Internal Environmental Assessment Task Force were to:

- identify the key organizational subsystems that collectively determine the strategic capability of the department (i.e., culture, finances, information, human resources, physical facilities);
- isolate the organizational systems and analyze the strengths and weaknesses associated with each;

Exhibit 14–14 • **Significant Trends/Issues as Opportunities and Threats**

Trend/Issue	Opportunities for Action	Threats from No Action
Impact of Health Care Reform	More emphasis placed on core public health—assurance, policy development, and assessment.	Major populations remain without access to health care; no meaningful provisions for rural populations.
Need for Cooperation-Based Strategies	Integrated health care initiatives; public and private partnerships; state and counties share common goals; higher level of community-based services.	Health care remains fragmented and inconsistent throughout the state.
Limited Funding for Public Health	Emphasis on efficiency and essential services.	Decline in community health; provision of fewer services; lag in technology; lower level of cooperation between state and counties.
Increasing Amount of Violence	New programs directed toward vulnerable populations; education; counseling safety; etc.	Continued increase in violence; fewer intervention services.
Increasing Need for Emphasis on Prevention	More emphasis on core public health; improved community health.	Breakdown in disease control, epidemiology.
Access/Care for Special Populations	Special population programs designed to meet specialized needs.	Increasing large segments of the population without access; inadequate health care.
External Technological Advancements	Upgrade of technology—lab, computers, etc.	Low image of ISDH remains; inefficiency; public turns to other organizations for technology-based services.
Increasing Amount of Substance Abuse	New programs for substance abuse—education, etc.	Continued rise in substance abuse among more populations.

- analyze the results of the organizational excellence questionnaire administered to all members of the department;
- identify specific strengths and weaknesses of the department relative to each key organizational subsystem;
- recommend, based on the findings of the analysis, actions for maintaining strengths and eliminating weaknesses; and
- foster strategic thinking throughout the department.

Operationally, the Internal Environmental Assessment Task Force decided to form four groups to cover these areas—organizational culture, finance, information systems, and human resources. At the first meeting, the information systems group was redefined as the information and outreach group to highlight the importance and uniqueness of the department's communication with external organizations and the public. The human resources group became the human resources, staffing, and physical facilities group.

Assessing the Organizational Culture The organizational culture group assessed the culture of the ISDH with the aid of a self-administered questionnaire. The questionnaire had sixty-one items designed to obtain the opinions of the department's 900 employees regarding seven different areas: mission/vision, service and managerial innovation, leadership and employee orientation, responsiveness to external change, teamwork, external and internal customer/client orientation, and quality.[5] All items on the organizational excellence questionnaire were stated in positive terms, with response scales ranging from strongly disagree to strongly agree. In addition to the sixty-one questions, respondents were provided an opportunity to elaborate on any responses through open-ended comments. More than 500 usable questionnaires were returned.

The open-ended comments were used, in conjunction with the objective responses, to discover problems or potential problems. For example, although most of the employees were familiar with the mandated purpose or mission of the ISDH, they were not sure about the department's vision or its direction over the next five years. (It should be noted that these responses were obtained during the health care reform debate, and there was a great deal of uncertainty about the future direction of health care, in general, and public health, in particular.) In addition, most employees believed that changes in the purpose and vision by the leadership in the department were not effectively communicated.

Relative to innovation, the respondents did not believe that the department was a highly creative organization. Comments from respondents indicated that they perceived innovation to be severely limited due to regulatory mandates and excessive policies and procedures imposed on all state agencies. However, respondents believed that department leadership valued new ways of doing things and that individuals were allowed to experiment with new procedures without excessive fear of punishment for failure.

Leadership and employee orientation was a particularly troublesome area as reported on the questionnaire. It received the second lowest evaluation of all factors and indicated a need for substantial attention by top management. There was a widespread belief that top leadership was excessively distant from the operational level of the department, that leaders were not as concerned as they should be about the welfare of employees, and that management was too concerned with political pressures to the detriment of key public health priorities. Much of the discontent, no doubt, resulted because the employees had not had a wage increase in three years and the recently enacted state budget virtually assured no raises for two more years.

The highest ranked factor was the department's ability to deal with external changes. Although this area was perceived as needing improvement, open-ended comments indicated that most employees believed that the ISDH was aware of changing forces in the external environment, had some means of monitoring and forecasting trends, and generally responded to environmental changes.

Teamwork was not ranked very high by employees. There was a belief that most employees were more concerned with their individual jobs and the welfare of their work units than with the overall success of the department. As a result, people sometimes protected rather than shared information, made decisions based on the welfare of their unit rather than the ISDH, and did not work effectively as teams. Competition among work groups was perceived to be more common than cooperation.

The items on the customer/client orientation section of the questionnaire were designed to assess employee responses to both external and internal customers. Relatively few of the ISDH employees, except for those in vital records and similar units, interacted regularly with external customers. Each employee, however, had a number of internal customers—ISDH employees who relied on other ISDH employees to successfully accomplish their jobs.

Considerable agreement existed that employees respected and responded to external and internal customer needs. On the other hand, there was the belief that rules and regulations were more important to many than a true devotion to serving customers. Additionally, it was thought that many people attempted to make their own jobs easier by hiding behind rules and regulations rather than trying in every practical way to facilitate responsiveness to all customers. Consensus was clear that everyone could do more to improve customer orientation.

Finally, concern for quality was widespread in the department. It was generally agreed that employees were professional, well trained for what they did, and committed to public service. However, respondents often indicated that high levels of service quality were not adequately emphasized or rewarded; that the hiring, retention, and promotion policies were not based on the quality of services provided; and that the general work environment made high levels of quality difficult to ensure.

In summary, the results of the questionnaire indicated a perceived need for improvement in all seven areas. There was a need to more clearly state and communicate the future direction of the department to all employees and reduce as much as possible the excessive policies that frustrated many managers and nonmanagerial employees in performing their jobs in the most effective manner. In addition, more managers needed to exercise leadership and encourage teamwork.

Financial Subsystem As previously noted, finance was a particularly serious problem for the ISDH (as well as other state agencies). State employees had not been able to maintain their incomes, and programs and facilities reflected the deteriorating financial situation. In an attempt to isolate the most important strategic considerations, the financial assessment group examined the present, past, and projected future financial resources, interviewed financial personnel at other Midwestern state health departments, and conducted internal interviews and surveys.

Before beginning with the specific analysis, the financial situation of the ISDH was put in perspective based on what was happening in other states in the region. In the year immediately prior to the beginning of the strategic planning process, Illinois and Michigan reduced their public health workforce and Ohio endured about an 11 percent decrease in public health funding.

During the five years prior to the initiation of the strategic planning process, the ISDH's proportion of annual state appropriations was relatively fixed at less than 1 percent of the state general fund. According to the Public Health Foundation, this level of funding placed Indiana as forty-ninth out of the fifty states in per capita funding for public health. As illustrated by Exhibit 14–15, state general funds for all purposes increased about 9 percent in 1990 and gradually declined to an increase of a little over 3 percent by 1993. By comparison, the ISDH appropriations from the general fund in 1990 were about 3 percent over 1989. However, 1993 funding was about the same as 1992 funding. It is clear that increases in state general funds have declined significantly over the past five years and that, of the smaller increases, public health has received increasingly smaller shares.

The one bright spot in the ISDH funding picture can be inferred from Exhibit 14–16. During the past five years when actual budget receipts (not appropriations) from the

Exhibit 14–15 • **Percentage Increase in State General Funds Versus ISDH Appropriations**

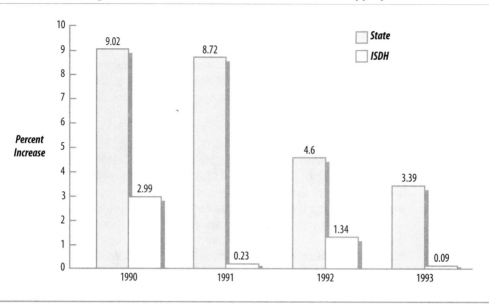

Exhibit 14–16 • **State and Federal Budget Receipts**

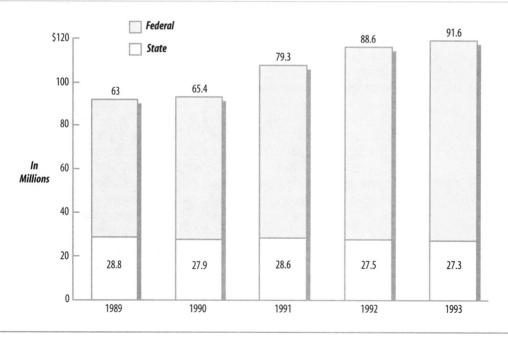

state general fund were virtually level, the department's federal funding increased significantly. In 1989, for example, the ISDH received approximately $63 million in federal funds. This amount increased to more than $90 million in 1993.

With this general background, the group proceeded with its assessment of financial strengths and weaknesses (see Exhibit 14–17). Relative to financial strengths, the group identified three important aspects of the financial operations that were favorable. The first was the ISDH's ability to attract federal funds. Over the five-year period immediately preceding the initiation of the strategic planning process and during a period when state funding was almost level, federal funds increased by 45 percent. Second, although not a strength in an absolute sense, it was certainly a relative strength that the ISDH had not been forced to reduce its public health work force as had its sister states of Illinois and Michigan. Finally, the Finance Division had apparently developed a strong internal customer orientation. A survey of internal users conducted by the division indicated that virtually everyone who responded was satisfied with the manner in which the payroll, travel reimbursements, and similar services were accomplished. There were a number of suggestions concerning how purchasing, contract development, and budget support activities could be improved.

The group identified four important financial weaknesses. First, although industry, state governments, and health care were moving toward increased automation and computerization, the Finance Division had not "kept up" technologically. Personal computers were available only to do the work of the division. Moreover, the capability for on-

Exhibit 14–17 • **Financial Strengths and Weaknesses**

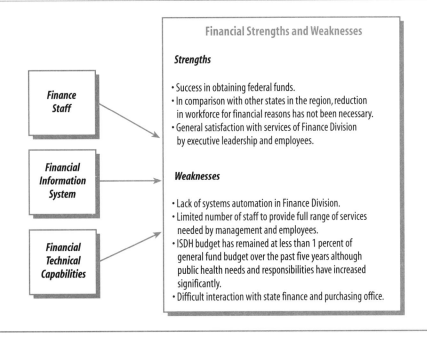

line assistance with financial services was extremely limited, representing a significant restriction on the staff's ability to provide needed services, particularly in the area of budget development and administration.

In real terms, the decline in funding for the department over the past five years had not reduced public expectations and demands for public health services. As a result, despite a period of extremely limited funding, services had increased, making the financial plight of the ISDH even more critical. Finally, much of the criticism regarding the delays in purchasing resulted from an inability to "get things through" the centralized state purchasing system. Although this was to a great extent beyond the control of the division, it caused frustration for everyone and the Finance Division often had to take the blame.

Information and Outreach Subsystems The information systems analysis was divided into two major components. The first related to internal information systems and information resources, and the second related to external or outreach information. Information concerning these key subsystems was obtained by a survey of internal users of information resources as well as through interviews with several of the department's external stakeholders. The analysis of this information resulted in the significant strengths and weaknesses listed in Exhibit 14–18.

The analysis of the information and outreach subsystems indicated that the department had several important strengths when compared to other state agencies and other organizations. The individuals in Management Information Systems (MIS) and the Office of Communications were resourceful and able to accomplish a great deal despite limited resources. The department was fortunate to have found the resources that enabled it to interface with a large number of useful electronic databases. In addition, a "satellite feed" made it possible to communicate electronically with locations throughout the nation and the world.

Internally, it was perceived that the MIS staff understood the problems of the overall system and that the Office of Communications used the power of the "public health message." That is, external communications focused on those issues that captured the interest of the citizens relative to public health issues in Indiana. The department was considered to be well prepared to assure the security of confidential information.

The group identified some generally agreed-on weaknesses in the information and outreach areas that needed attention. First, there was a lack of consistently effective communication up and down the organization as well as with external groups. There was substantial confusion about the protocol for contact and communication with the media. Some of this was attributable to the lack of external and internal customer/client orientation on the part of both MIS and the Office of Communications. It was agreed that the human resources information system was nonfunctioning and did little, if anything, to help managers and employees with personnel matters. There was no parity in the internal distribution of information processing resources and the internal telecommunications infrastructure—telephone system, E-mail, and fax—was inadequate and unreliable. The central MIS could not afford to employ the human resources necessary to keep all the hardware and software operating on a timely basis, and computer expertise to temporarily "fix" things until help arrived was inadequate. There was inadequate physical space for effective hardware operations not only for centralized MIS but also for the individual work units.

Exhibit 14–18 · **Information and Outreach Systems Strengths and Weaknesses**

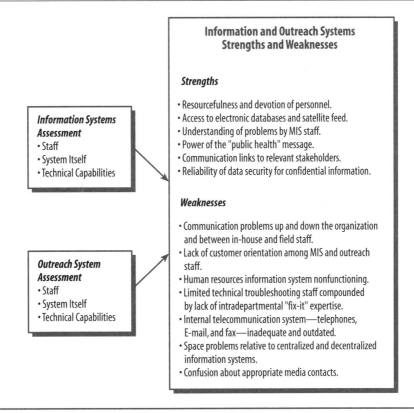

Information Systems Assessment
• Staff
• System Itself
• Technical Capabilities

Outreach System Assessment
• Staff
• System Itself
• Technical Capabilities

Information and Outreach Systems Strengths and Weaknesses

Strengths

• Resourcefulness and devotion of personnel.
• Access to electronic databases and satellite feed.
• Understanding of problems by MIS staff.
• Power of the "public health" message.
• Communication links to relevant stakeholders.
• Reliability of data security for confidential information.

Weaknesses

• Communication problems up and down the organization and between in-house and field staff.
• Lack of customer orientation among MIS and outreach staff.
• Human resources information system nonfunctioning.
• Limited technical troubleshooting staff compounded by lack of intradepartmental "fix-it" expertise.
• Internal telecommunication system—telephones, E-mail, and fax—inadequate and outdated.
• Space problems relative to centralized and decentralized information systems.
• Confusion about appropriate media contacts.

Overall, the picture relative to the information and outreach systems was consistent. The devotion and hard work of the individuals at all levels had made the systems work adequately despite severely limited resources. In the process, however, the staff of both the Management Information Systems and the Office of Communications processing units had become internally oriented and lost sight of the importance of identifying and serving all their relevant customers/clients.

Human Resources, Staffing, and Physical Facilities Assessment In attempting to gauge the quality, quantity, and distribution of these resources, the group assigned to assess these factors employed several data-gathering methods, including employee surveys and interviews with management and nonmanagement staff members. This information was used to formulate the departmental strengths and weaknesses as listed in Exhibit 14–19.

The basic human resources, staffing, and physical facilities infrastructure were primary concerns of the employees of the department. Again, it was perceived that colleagues—managerial and nonmanagerial—were committed to the success of the department and to public health in Indiana. Because of this devotion, loyalty, and hard work, the department was able to accomplish a great deal with relatively little in terms of

Exhibit 14–19 · Human Resources, Staffing, and Physical Facilities Strengths and Weaknesses

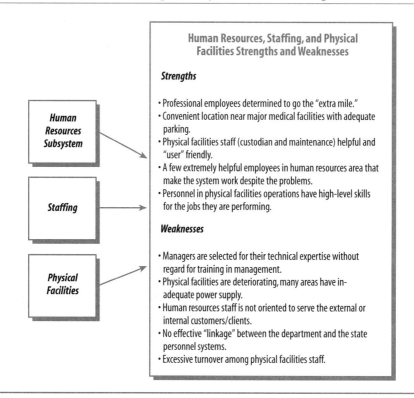

There were, however, a number of weaknesses. As is the case with many high-technology organizations, people were promoted to management positions based on their technical expertise rather than their existing or potential management skills and little management training was provided. As a result, there were many good public health technicians and scientists who became frustrated and unremarkable managers.

There was widespread concern over the inadequacy of the physical facilities. Air quality, ventilation, storage space, and power supply were not adequate for the quality of work expected of employees. More than a few employees suggested that the department would probably "fail" its own health inspections. Finally, as with MIS and the Office of Communications, it was believed that the human resources staff was not properly oriented to serve either external or internal customers/clients.

Mission, Vision, and Values

The ISDH determined early in its strategic planning process that the formulation of directional strategies, similar to assessment of the external and internal environments, had to come from consensus building among as many employees (managerial and non-managerial) as possible. Therefore, it was decided to form a task force to address the formulation of the departmental mission and vision, to suggest the values that would become the basis for decision making, and to develop an initial list of critical success factors for the department. The general objectives of the task force were to:

- generate and develop consensus for a clear, concise statement of the department's primary clients, principal services, geographical domain, philosophy, and desired public image;
- incorporate these items in a clear, concise statement of the mission of the Indiana State Department of Health;
- reach a consensus on a challenging, exciting, and inspiring statement of vision (hope) of the ISDH;
- review the results of the external environment, organizational culture, and internal environmental assessments and suggest a series of critical success factors for the department; and
- foster strategic thinking throughout the department.

Drafting the Mission and Vision Statements   To assist in developing a draft of the ISDH mission statement, the group decided to use the general template presented in Exhibit 5–8. This template is reproduced and adapted to the ISDH in Exhibit 14–20. The components of a mission statement are listed in the first column and the descriptions and key words, obtained through interviews with personnel from all functions and levels throughout the agency, are presented in the second column. From this information, the draft mission statement was developed.

The same process was used to develop the vision statement, except that only senior managers were interviewed (see Exhibit 14–21). The group decided not to develop a separate value statement for the department because values such as respect

Exhibit 14–20 • Components of the ISDH Mission Statement

Mission Statement Components	Descriptions (Key Words) about ISDH's Mission
1. Target Customer/Clients and Markets	People in Indiana—especially those in need, as identified by measures of health and economic status.
2. Principal Services Delivered	Training and technical assistance, prevention and health education programs, surveillance and analysis of health data, policy development, and planning and evaluation.
3. Geographical Domain of Operations	Borders of Indiana.
4. Commitment of Specific Values	Respect for the individual, quality services, innovation, personal integrity, trust, concern, and high ethical standards.
5. Explicit Philosophy	Proactive leadership through the application of public health sciences and epidemiology and the quest for efficiency of operations.
6. Other Important Component(s)	Recognition of interdependence with the larger world.

Exhibit 14–21 • Components of the ISDH Vision Statement

Vision Statement Components	Descriptions (Key Words) in ISDH's Vision
1. A Clear Hope for the Future	A future where communities, local health agencies, and the private sector cooperate to increase the span of healthy life for all Hoosiers, reduce the disparities among segments of the population, and assure access to preventive services for all people.
2. Challenging and Excellence Concerns	Strive for excellence, display initiative, and demonstrate achievement.
3. Inspirational and Emotional	Forging alliances with public and private sectors to ensure timely, cost-effective, public health interventions with primary commitment to local health departments.
4. Empowers Employees First and Clients/Customers Second	Value employees.
5. Prepares for the Future	Catalyst for progress that will result in healthier people and a healthful environment.
6. Memorable and Provides Guidance	Memorable terms—catalyst for progress, public health leader in the Hoosier state, core values integral to public health, innovation, and so on.

for all individuals, quality, trust, concern, ethical standards, and so on were integral parts of both the mission and vision statements. The mission provided a sense of "what is," and the vision statement created a clear picture of the possibilities of what "might be" or "could be" when the mission was being accomplished to the mutual benefit of all citizens of Indiana. These draft statements were forwarded to the steering committee for discussion, revision, and adoption.

From Mission and Vision to Critical Success Factors Having achieved some consensus concerning what the department is today (mission) and its vision for the future, the task force proceeded to formulate critical success factors. A careful review of the mission and vision, the external environmental analysis, the organizational excellence questionnaire, and the internal environmental assessment resulted in the formulation of a draft of six critical success factors that the task force members believed *absolutely must* happen if the department were to be successful:

1. *Public health workforce.* Become the employer of choice for public health professionals and support staff rather than employer of last resort.
2. *Communications.* Improve expertise with internal communication as well as with external stakeholders.
3. *Funding.* Secure adequate and stable funding.
4. *Collaboration.* Expand and improve the network of collaborative relationships with local health departments and other relevant public and private agencies.
5. *Service quality.* Improve quality of services from the viewpoint of external clients and internal clients.
6. *Organizational focus.* Concentrate on professionalism and scientifically identified causes of disease, prevention, disability, and premature death.

Similar to the mission and vision statements, the draft of critical success factors was regarded as a starting point for organization-wide discussion and forwarded to the steering committee for revision and finalizing.

Strategy Formulation

Based on the results of the situational analysis, the ISDH began the process of finalizing the directional strategies and developing adaptive, market entry, and positioning strategies. These decisions (strategies) would set the future course of the ISDH.

Results of the internal analysis suggested that regardless of strategy, the agency needed to create a more participative decision-making environment and foster teamwork. Therefore, it was decided that the steering committee, responsible for coordinating strategy formulation, and the implementation task force could begin their work concurrently. As illustrated in Exhibit 14–22, the activities of these groups were divided into two phases, which allowed some implementation activities to proceed simultaneously with strategy formulation activities.

In Phase I, the steering committee finalized the directional strategies (mission, vision, and strategic objectives) and developed the adaptive, market entry (if necessary), and positioning strategies. In Phase II, the steering committee coordinated implementation (development and implementation) of the operational or program strategies. The steering committee objectives were to:

- review and confirm the external opportunities and threats and internal strengths and weaknesses;
- finalize the mission, vision, and critical success factors;
- specify the set of programs and services that would achieve the mission and vision;
- operationalize the critical success factors with clear and concise strategic objectives (later called *agency goals*) to provide direction for departmental operations;
- coordinate the development of the adaptive, market entry, and positioning strategies;

Exhibit 14–22 • Strategic Decision-Making Phase

	Steering Task Force	Implementation Task Force
Phase I	• Understand information gathered, analyzed, and summarized by the task forces	• Set objectives for cultural change using the seven factors of excellence plus critical success factors
	• Finalize external issues, internal strengths and weaknesses, and mission, vision, and critical success factors	• Develop organization-wide implementation actions to achieve the objectives
	• Set strategic objectives for the organization (based on external analysis, internal analysis, and mission, vision, and critical success factors)	• Develop milestone charts for implementation
		• Submit objectives and actions to steering task force for review and suggestions
	• Develop the statement of strategy	• Make final recommendations to management concerning cultural change
	• Develop the adaptive, market entry, and positioning strategies	
	• Work with unit managers and develop unit-specific implementation actions for the strategic objectives	
Phase II	• Coordinate implementation of actions developed in Phase I	• Develop organization-wide implementation actions for objectives developed by the steering task force
	• Coordinate activities of implementation committee	• Coordinate organization-wide and unit-specific implementation action plans
	• Aid programs in developing implementation work plans	
	• Ensure implementation is proceeding as planned	

- coordinate the development of program implementation work plans; and
- foster strategic thinking throughout the department.

During Phase I, the implementation task force formulated organization-wide strategies directed toward improving the organizational culture. During Phase II, it developed organization-wide strategies to support the strategic objectives that had been developed by the steering committee. This approach provided adequate time for strategic thinking and yet allowed the strategic management process to proceed at two levels. In addition, this approach kept a large number of people involved, maintained the momentum of the project, and helped ensure an atmosphere of change.

The Directional Strategies

The steering committee reviewed the external environmental issues, internal capabilities, and the draft of the directional strategies that were developed, analyzed, and summarized by the three task forces. After this review, the committee set out to finalize the directional strategies.

Finalizing the Mission and Vision   The first task of the steering committee was to finalize the mission and vision statements initially developed by the mission, vision, and values task force. The mission and vision statements were revised after considerable discussion with employees, interviews with members of all of the task forces, and discussion throughout the agency. The final statements appear in Exhibits 14–23 and 14–24. Because of the crucial nature of these statements, it was essential that the steering committee members and the ISDH executive staff play a part in shaping and approving the statements. However, it was believed that the original spirit of the documents should be maintained because they were developed through wide participation throughout the organization.

Exhibit 14–23 • Indiana State Department of Health Mission Statement

The Indiana State Department of Health (ISDH) is dedicated to promoting health and wellness among people in Indiana through planning, prevention, service, and education. The ISDH serves to help people attain the highest level of health possible. The ISDH is a proactive leader and collaborator in assessment, policy development, and assurance, based on science, innovation, and efficiency.

ISDH affirms that health includes physical, mental, and social well-being, and is dependent on economic and environmental factors, access to health care, and individual responsibility and choice. Although the ISDH primarily serves people within Indiana's geographic boundaries, we recognize our interdependence with the larger world.

To achieve our mission, the ISDH supports:

- Training and technical assistance,
- Disease prevention and health education programs,
- Epidemiology for surveillance and analysis of health data for intervention and program evaluation,
- Development of policies and regulations to optimize health,
- Planning and evaluation,
- Staff recruitment and development to accomplish our mission, and
- Collaboration with the public, local health departments, governmental agencies, the scientific community, and special populations.

The ISDH is dedicated to quality service, innovation, respect for every individual, affirmative action, personal integrity, trust, and high ethical standards.

Exhibit 14–24 • Indiana State Department of Health Vision Statement

The Indiana State Department of Health is committed to act as a catalyst for progress that will result in healthier people in a healthful environment.

As a public health leader in the Hoosier State, the department will incorporate strategic management to implement a core set of values that are integral to public health. We will translate science and technology into action to safeguard the public's health. We will apply innovative, sound, and reasonable solutions to traditional public health challenges and emerging issues. At the same time, we will retain that which is good with public health in the state. We will expand knowledge through epidemiology and applied research on health and environmental issues.

The department recognizes its ties with other health and human service agencies to respond to global, national, state, and local public health concerns. We will forge alliances with public and private sectors to ensure that timely, cost-effective, public health interventions are planned and implemented. We will strengthen our commitment to collaborate with local health departments.

Our employees are our most valuable resource. We will provide an environment in which our employees strive for excellence, display initiative, and demonstrate achievement. Our employees will continue to promote health; work to prevent diseases, disability, and premature death; and help to assure access to health care for all populations.

This vision of the future is one in which the Indiana State Department of Health, communities, local health agencies, special institutions, and the private sector across the state cooperate to develop plans, programs, and resources. It guides our work to increase the span of healthy life, to reduce health disparities among different populations, and to assure access to preventive services for all.

Finalizing the Critical Success Factors The next task of the steering committee was to review and finalize the critical success factors developed by the mission, vision, and values task force. Again, input and discussion concerning the critical success factors were solicited from all divisions and levels of the ISDH. There was a great deal of agreement that the critical success factors generated by the mission, vision, and values task forces were important, but the committee believed that one factor (organizational focus) should be expanded and that further rationale or explanation of each factor would help clarify and provide focus for subsequently setting organizational objectives. The revised critical success factors and rationale are presented in Exhibit 14–25.

Developing Agency Goals (Strategic Objectives) Strategic objectives (called *agency goals* by the ISDH) were developed for each of the critical success factors presented in Exhibit 14–25. The steering committee believed that it was better to have a few well-defined goals rather than a long list of objectives that would be impossible to accomplish in view of resource limitations. Therefore, it was decided that one agency goal relative to each critical success factor would be developed. A great deal of effort was put into making the goals simple and straightforward. For each goal, specific activities were outlined to guide the various programs toward the achievement of the agency goals. Individual programs could then develop their own set of objectives, using the ISDH goals and actions as models. The logic of the process used to develop each of the agency goals for the ISDH is illustrated in Exhibit 14–26.

The exhibit demonstrates how the mission, vision, and external and internal environmental factors, identified during the data-gathering stage of the strategic planning process, relate to the development of the workforce (a critical success factor), which in turn translates into an agency goal (strategic objective) and actions for orientation, training, and development. In the example, the mission underscores "support for staff recruitment and development" and the vision statement emphasizes the value placed on employees. The data from the external environmental analysis indicated that relevant

Exhibit 14–25 • Critical Success Factors and Rationale

Workforce: The ISDH must provide a working environment and resources that will attract and retain qualified staff members and empower them to achieve or exceed agency goals. The working environment will support responsive personnel policies, competitive compensation, adequate training, advancement opportunities, trust, sensitivity to diversity, and efficiency, innovation, and excellence.

Communication: The ISDH must communicate effectively both internally with employees and externally with local, state, and federal public health agencies and other stakeholders. Communication must accurately and consistently reflect the mission, vision, and activities of the agency.

Funding: The ISDH must establish funding priorities, pursue innovative strategies to obtain adequate, stable financial resources for ensuring that fundamental public health services are available, and monitor use of funds to achieve established objectives.

Collaboration: The ISDH must expand and improve internal teamwork and external partnerships with local health departments and other local, state, and federal public and private organizations to promote public health.

Service: The ISDH must maintain a client orientation and assure the quality of all services for internal and external clients.

Leadership: The ISDH must be a visible, active, and persistent advocate on behalf of its employees and public health. This leadership must be based on efficiency, innovation, respect for the individual, and science. Leadership qualities will be recognized and promoted at all levels of the agency.

Management: The ISDH must implement a process that plans and sets priorities within the constraints of available resources and in the context of strategic thinking. Management processes must promote interprogram coordination and cooperation to achieve agency goals.

Data and Information: The ISDH must acquire and use timely and accurate data to assess needs, develop policy, and assure quality services. The data and information acquired must be shared with all people who need it to carry out their responsibilities.

public health technologies would continue to develop and require increasingly qualified and committed personnel. Finally, if the ISDH was to be successful, agency staff would have to understand the directional strategies, the interrelationship of programs, their individual roles, and the expectations of the organization. Only when the department has a reputation for providing ongoing training and development opportunities and employees believe they are more important than policies, rules, and procedures, will the department be able to further develop highly qualified personnel. Exhibit 14–27 presents agency goals and illustrates their relationship to the critical success factors.

The Adaptive Strategies

On completion of the directional strategies (mission, vision, and objectives), the steering committee began to develop a statement of strategy and the adaptive strategies (the fundamental strategies for the organization). After reviewing the methods for analyzing the adaptive strategies (TOWS, portfolio approaches, PLC, SPACE, and so on), the steering committee decided that program evaluation would provide the best results. Because of the not-for-profit nature of the agency, funding from state appropriations and grants, and the program orientation of the ISDH, the steering committee thought that both approaches to program evaluation—program priority setting and needs/capacity assessment—would best facilitate strategic thinking within the agency. Program priority setting was used to initiate the strategic thinking process, and needs/capacity assessment was used to corroborate the results of program priority setting.

Program Priority Setting   Joe Hunt, the director of the Office for Policy Coordination, with the aid of the steering committee and executive staff, developed a complete listing

Exhibit 14–26 • Agency Goals Relative to Critical Success Factor: Workforce

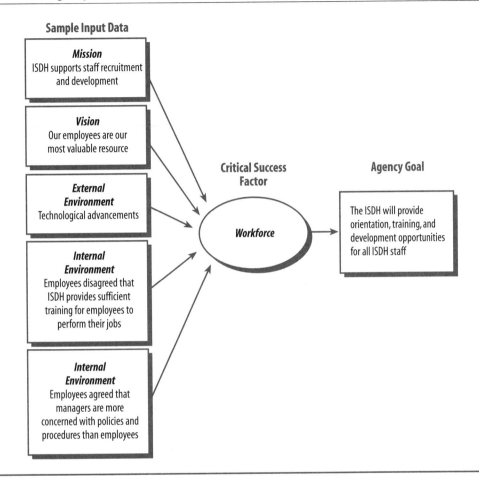

of the programs of the ISDH. Seventy-three separate ISDH programs were identified. The steering committee decided to use the Q-sort method to set priorities for the department's programs. Further, the steering committee believed that several different perspectives of program priorities would enhance strategic thinking. Therefore, two groups—the executive staff and a group of middle-level managers—were asked to "sort" the ISDH's programs.

To provide a context for evaluating the programs, all of the Q-sort participants were provided with and became familiar with the results of the external environmental analysis, internal environmental analysis, and the revised mission, vision, critical success factors, and agency goals. In addition, because the prospects of health care reform (both industry evolution and legislation) was such a dominant environmental theme, three possible scenarios for health care reform were developed as a backdrop for sorting the programs. These scenarios are presented in Exhibit 14–28.

Exhibit 14–27 • Situational Analysis, Critical Success Factors, and Agency Goals

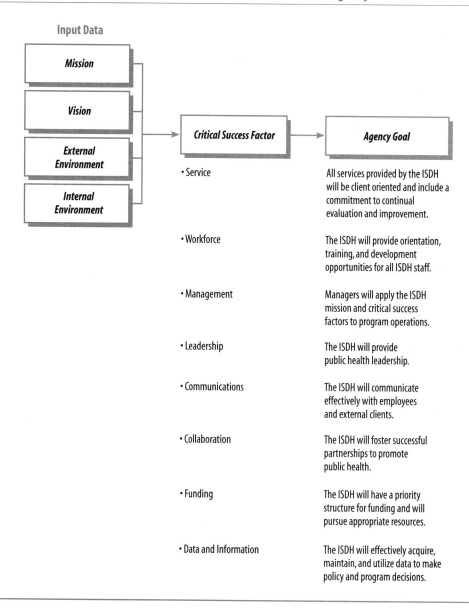

Input Data

Critical Success Factor	Agency Goal
• Service	All services provided by the ISDH will be client oriented and include a commitment to continual evaluation and improvement.
• Workforce	The ISDH will provide orientation, training, and development opportunities for all ISDH staff.
• Management	Managers will apply the ISDH mission and critical success factors to program operations.
• Leadership	The ISDH will provide public health leadership.
• Communications	The ISDH will communicate effectively with employees and external clients.
• Collaboration	The ISDH will foster successful partnerships to promote public health.
• Funding	The ISDH will have a priority structure for funding and will pursue appropriate resources.
• Data and Information	The ISDH will effectively acquire, maintain, and utilize data to make policy and program decisions.

The executive staff believed that given the environmental forces, any of the scenarios was possible for the short term; but in the long term, scenario one—Return to Core Public Health—was most likely. Exhibit 14–29 illustrates the short- and long-term views of the committee. Therefore, Q-sort participants were asked to sort the ISDH's programs

Exhibit 14–28 • Health Care Reform Scenarios

Scenario I: *Return to Core Public Health.* In this scenario comprehensive health care reform legislation is passed that provides some form of health insurance for everyone. Thus, individuals who formerly relied on public health agencies and emergency rooms for primary care, now have access (through their insurance) to private providers. In addition, providers have found it advantageous to serve this population. Under this assumption, the private sector would assume virtually all of the personal primary-care responsibilities. The department would emphasize data collection, monitoring, health promotion, education, regulation, assessment, environmental health, disease control, research, and policy leadership. In this situation, the department's focus would be almost exclusively on community health issues rather than the provision of personal primary care.

Scenario II: *Core Public Health Plus Special Care Needs.* In this scenario health care reform is passed; however, because of high costs, major gaps in coverage remain. Under this assumption, most treatments and special populations would be covered by the private sector; however, significant "gaps" in coverage will continue. The only source of care for these populations or treatments will be in the public sector. In this scenario, the department would emphasize community health (core public health) but would continue to provide primary health care for special populations and treatments not covered under any type of (revolutionary or evolutionary) health care reform.

Scenario III: *Health Care Reform Bogs Down.* In this scenario no significant health care reform legislation is passed. Even the evolutionary restructuring of the health care industry has left major "gaps" for significant populations and treatments. Under this assumption, any type of health care reform fails to significantly change the ratio of people without access to primary care. Primary care may even be expanded under this assumption as the Health Department plays a larger role in ensuring access. In this scenario, the department would emphasize community health and the provision of primary care about equally.

Exhibit 14–29 • Three Possible Views of the Future

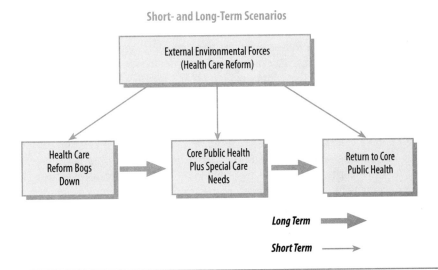

three times, based on the strategic assumptions embodied in the three scenarios. In addition to the executive staff, twelve middle- and upper-level managers sorted the agency's seventy-three programs. The Q-sort results of the twelve managers were quite similar to those of the executive staff. Both sets of Q-sort rankings were used in the subsequent deliberation of strategy. After considerable discussion of the different scenarios, the executive staff chose to use the results of Q-sorts according to the second scenario—health care reform would not be *fully* implemented in the next two to five years but that there would be some type of reform. Q-sort results for the second scenario by the executive staff are presented as Exhibit 14–30.

Needs/Capacity Assessment   To corroborate the results of the program priority setting process by the executive staff and managers throughout the agency, four members of the executive staff, including Joe Hunt and the deputy commissioner Nancy Blough, independently made a needs/capacity assessment. The four members of the executive staff evaluated each of the agency's seventy-three programs based on their perceptions of the community need for the program and the capacity of the agency to meet that need (using the assumptions underlying scenario two). The programs were rated as very high, high, low, or very low for both community need and organizational capacity. Mean scores were calculated and the program number was plotted on a needs/capacity grid. Results of this process are presented in Exhibit 14–31.

The needs/capacity assessment generally corroborated the results of the priority setting Q-sorts and provided an additional perspective on program priority. Based on these evaluative tools, the executive staff began discussions on programs that needed to be expanded, stabilized, or contracted (adaptive strategies). For example, programs with high community need but low organization capacity and a "high" Q-sort ranking might be marked for expansion. Programs with low community need, high capacity, and a "low" Q-sort ranking could be considered for contraction.

Developing the Statement of Strategy   Based on the results of the program priority setting and needs/capacity assessment, an adaptive strategy was developed. The adaptive strategy was viewed as a process of evolving the agency toward a desired profile or portfolio of programs. The makeup of that profile was influenced by the strategic assumptions (external issues, internal issues, and mission, vision, and objectives). Dominant in the strategic assumptions was the belief that, in the *long term,* health care reform would be successful and the agency would move toward more community or core public health (scenario one) activities. However, it was the belief of the steering committee and executive staff that, in the *short term,* special populations and certain medical treatments would be "uncovered" and the health department would have to remain in (or enter) those segments (scenario two). Therefore, the ISDH adaptive strategy was characterized as moving slowly and carefully toward more community health but assuring personal health needs as long as gaps in coverage remained. With this strategy, managers would have to be able to shift resources from personal health care to community health as health care reform progressed.

With this understanding of the changing environment, the following statement of strategy emerged from discussions of the executive staff concerning the agency's adaptive, market entry, and positioning strategies.

> Within the scope of the mission and vision, the ISDH's strategic directions will be expansion in core public health areas with an emphasis on assessment (data collection, epidemiology), policy development, and assurance (health promotion, disease control). The expansion strategies will be primarily market development (expanding the service population), product development

Exhibit 14–30 • Executive Staff Q-Sort Results: Scenario Two—Core Public Health Plus Special Care Needs

Most Important	Next Most Important	Next Most Important	Next Most Important	Next Most Important	Next Most Important	Next Most Important	Next Most Important	Next Most Important
				Oral Health Services 5.13				
				Legal Affairs 5.13				
				OA: Finance 5.13				
				HFS: Regulatory/ Support 5.13				
			CDP: Injury Control 5.88	FHS: Women's Health 5.13	Policy Coordination 4.75			
			Adolescent Health 5.75	Retail Food 5.13	Wholesale Food 4.75			
		PHR: County Assessment 6.63	MCH: Program 5.75	CS: Meat and Poultry 5.13	Environmental Health Lab 4.63	FM: Asset Service 4.25		
		Child Special Services 6.5	Health Planning 5.63	MCH: Lead Poisoning 5.0	Lab Support Services 4.5	Environmental Services 4.13		
		CTS/STD 6.5	OPA: Health Education 5.63	Disability Concerns 5.0	Manufactured Food 4.5	Pregnancy Risk 4.13		
		OSP: Rural Health 6.5	Grants Resource Center 5.5	Birth Problems Registry 4.88	Residential Sewage 4.5	FM: Security 4.0		
	PHS: Vital Records 7.5	Disease Control Lab 6.38	OA: Human Resources 5.5	ACS: Health Inspections 4.88	SE: Vector Control 4.5	MCH: SIDS 4.0	HP: Financial Disclosure 3.25	
Local Health Support 8.0	Chronic Disease 7.38	MCH: Genetic Disease 6.25	Long-Term Care 5.5	HIV/STD Clinical Data 4.88	Environmental Health 4.5	FM: Safety Programs 3.88	CS: Weight and Measures 3.13	HE: Film Library 1.88
Communicable Disease 7.88	Public Health Statistics 7.13	MCH: Healthy Pregnancy 6.25	MCH: Prenatal Substance 5.25	Consumer Health Lab 4.88	OA: Administrative Services 4.38	SE: Plan Review 3.88	Consultive Services 2.5	Correspond Center 1.88
Epidemiology Center 7.75	Nutrition/ WIC 7.0	Public Health Research 5.88	OPA: Media Relations 5.25	MCH: Family Help Line 4.75	OA: Purchasing 4.38	Breastfeed Promotion 3.63	HP: Certificate of Need 2.25	OPA: Photographer 1.63
Management Information 7.63	HIV Prevention 6.75	Minority Health 5.88	WFD: Milk 5.25	MCH: Family Planning 4.75	Physical Plant 4.25	Indoor Radiologic Health 3.5	OPA: Print Shop 2.0	HE: Library 1.5

Note: Mean scores are the result of forced choice and therefore indicate only relative position rather than absolute value of a program (improving or extending current services), and penetration (increasing the ISDH role in the particular service). The ISDH will use contraction strategies in personal health programs where community need is decreasing or where other providers are available and in other programs where there is duplication of effort or where consolidation could offer enhancement in the quality and timeliness of service. Stabilization/enhancement strategies, emphasizing quality improvement and efficiency, will be used for all other programs.

Exhibit 14–31 • Needs/Capacity Assessment Program Plot

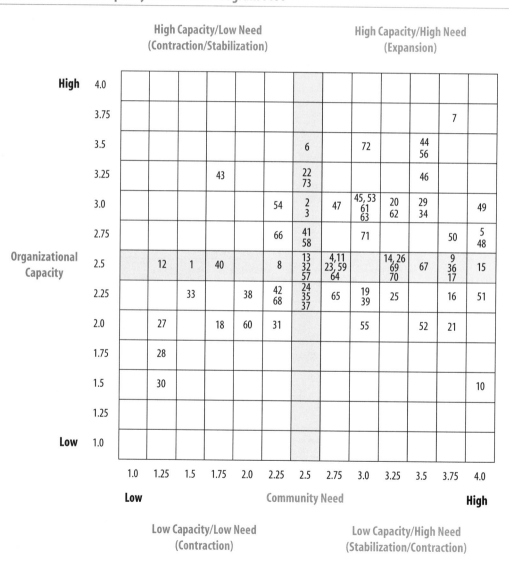

Translating Program Evaluation into Program Adaptive Strategies Given the view of the future and the selected strategy, the executive staff believed that the agency's portfolio of programs might be enhanced through the addition of new programs that addressed anticipated community health needs or health care reform gaps. Therefore, several new programs were proposed and discussed. The importance of the programs was evaluated in relation to the ISDH's existing programs. However, after discussing the results of the program priority setting, the needs/capacity assessment, and the likely nature of health care reform, it was determined that no new programs would be initiated at this time. The discussion of the program evaluation results convinced the executive staff that the ISDH must continue to aggressively manage its programs to meet changing external needs. Within this context, and because of the consistency of the results of the strategic analysis, the agency's programs were grouped under the broad categories of expansion, stabilization, and contraction.

The programs marked for expansion emphasized improving data collection and epidemiology, health promotion, and disease control. Expansion of these programs was consistent with the view that health care reform would begin to substantively affect public health in the next two to three years. The role of public health as a source of information for needs assessment, program evaluation, and epidemiology would therefore increase. In addition, a national emphasis on outcomes of care would require extensive data on the results of all types of health care. This data would have to be of high quality to support the tracking of disease in the population and to link health problems to the health care system.

Health promotion will be essential for improving the health of the population and contributing to long-term cost control. Keeping people healthy longer will save money in earlier years of life and result in a healthier older adult population. Public health agencies are uniquely situated to provide, support, and encourage health promotion through direct service, community-based programs, and through education and encouragement to health providers.

Disease control is a traditional public health program. Effective disease reporting and case follow-up are critical to health care reform. The early identification of disease outbreaks will enable health care services, both individual and community based, to be targeted to early intervention and control.

The majority of the ISDH programs were identified as candidates for stabilization. Stabilization meant that these programs had a departmental commitment to maintain the present level of resources. Stabilization, however, did not mean that these programs were expected to remain unchanged. For instance, these programs could focus on improved quality of services, efficiency, or development of different services with the same resources (enhancement). The specific alternative for each program would be developed by the program director in consultation with the appropriate assistant commissioner or office director. The ISDH was to maintain a strong commitment to these programs as part of assuring quality service to meet identified needs.

Stabilization was to be the adaptive strategy for regulatory and support programs. Health promotion programs that had experienced significant growth in resources in the past few years were identified for stabilization. These programs faced changing needs. Stabilization assured the basic level of resources but allowed programs to select different uses of these resources to meet current and changing needs.

A few programs were identified for contraction. In general, these programs were still important to the ISDH, but their roles may have diminished or may have been completed, in part, by action in other programs. The essential functions would be maintained while activities that were not critical to the ISDH would be eliminated. Resources in these programs would be redirected according to an implementation work plan to areas of higher priority. These programs also had an opportunity to redefine their role within the agency to contribute to high-priority activities or to enhance the way they fulfilled their responsibilities. The programs identified for contraction included the library, film library, Renal Disease Program, video/graphics/photography, the Sudden Infant Death Syndrome (SIDS) Project, and the correspondence center.

In addition to services and service population decisions concerning expansion, stabilization, or contraction, the executive staff believed that program managers should understand the agency's resource commitment to the various programs. For each program, the executive staff labeled funding and staffing needs as "expand," "stable," or "contract." A summary of the results of this process indicating strategies for funds, staff, market development, and product/service development strategies for the ISDH programs are presented in Exhibit 14–32, which shows the portfolio of the ISDH programs and the directions for future growth.

To provide program managers with a clearer idea of how expansion, stabilization, and contraction could be accomplished, specific definitions and examples were developed. These definitions were the ISDH's (public health) adaptations of traditional market development, product development, penetration, and enhancement strategies. The definitions and examples provided program managers a starting point for developing specific program strategies (see Exhibit 14–33).

Market Entry Strategies and Positioning Strategies

Generally, the market entry used by the ISDH programs was internal development. However, the health care reform environment presented the ISDH with opportunities to use cooperation strategies, particularly alliances, for new and future programs. Because of the nature of the ISDH, most of the programs were positioned as market segment (focus) strategies.

Strategic Implementation: Operational Strategies

Although it was understood that there would be some overlap and duplication with the efforts of the steering committee, Phase I of strategic implementation began concurrently with strategy formulation. The objectives of the implementation task force were to:

- review and discuss the internal strengths and weaknesses;
- develop goals and action plans for each of the seven organizational excellence factors;
- develop specific organization-wide action plans to achieve the strategic objectives; and
- foster strategic thinking throughout the department.

Exhibit 14–32 • Program Strategies

Program	Funds	Staff	Market Development	Product/Service Development
Office of Public Affairs				
Health Education	Stable	Stable	Expand	Expand
Health Education: Film Library	Contract	Contract	Expand	Expand
Health Education: Library	Contract	Contract	Contract	Stable/Contrast
Office of Public Affairs: Media Relations	Stable	Stable	Stable	Expand
Office of Public Affairs: Video/Graphics/Photo	Stable/Contract	Contract	Expand	Expand
Office of Public Affairs: Print Shop	Stable	Stable	Stable	Expand
Office of Administration				
Office of Administration: Administrative Services	Stable	Expand	Expand	Expand
Office of Administration: Correspondence Center	Contract	Contract	Contract	Contract
Office of Administration: Finance	Expand	Expand	Expand	Expand
Office of Administration: Purchasing	Expand	Expand	Expand	Expand
Office of Administration: Human Resources	Expand	Expand	Expand	Expand
Office of Administration: Management Consultive Services	Expand	Expand	Expand	Expand
Facilities Management: Safety Programs Coordination	Stable	Stable	Expand	Expand
Facilities Management: Environmental Services	Stable	Stable	Expand	Expand
Facilities Management: Physical Plant	Expand	Stable	Expand	Expand
Facilities Management: Security	Stable	Stable	Stable	Stable
Facilities Management: Asset Service Center	Stable	Stable	Stable	Expand
Office of Legal Affairs				
Office of Legal Affairs	Stable	Stable	Stable	Stable
Office for Policy Coordination				
Office for Policy Coordination	Expand	Expand	Expand	Expand
Office for Special Populations				
Special Populations: Disabilities	Stable	Stable	Expand	Expand
Office for Special Populations: Black and Minority Health	Expand	Expand	Expand	Expand
Rural Health Initiative	Expand	Expand	Expand	Expand
Quality Assurance Commission				
Consumer Protection:				
Retail Food Division	Stable	Stable	Stable	Stable
Meat and Poultry	Stable	Stable	Stable	Stable
Manufactured Food Section	Stable	Stable	Stable	Stable
Consumer Services: Weights and Measures	Stable	Stable	Stable	Stable
Wholesale Food Division	Stable	Stable	Stable	Stable
Milk	Stable	Stable	Stable	Stable
Residential Sewage Disposal	Stable	Stable	Stable	Stable
Vector Control Group	Stable	Stable	Expand	Expand

continued

Exhibit 14–32 · Continued

Program	Funds	Staff	Market Development	Product/Service Development
Consumer Protection: *(cont.)*				
Plan Review Section	Stable	Stable	Stable	Stable
Indoor and Radiologic Health	Stable	Stable	Stable	Stable
Environmental Health Section	Stable	Stable	Stable	Stable
Health Facilities Standards:				
Long-Term-Care Inspections	Stable	Stable	Stable	Stable
Survey Support Services	Stable	Stable	Stable	Stable
Acute-Care Services	Stable	Stable	Stable	Stable
Laboratory Resource Center:				
Laboratory Support Services	Stable	Stable	Stable	Stable
Environmental Health Lab	Stable	Stable	Stable	Stable
Disease Control Lab	Expand	Stable	Stable	Stable
Consumer Health Lab	Stable	Stable	Stable	Stable
Prevention and Community Health Commission				
Chronic Disease:				
Injury Control Program	Stable	Stable	Expand	Expand
Renal Program	Contract	Contract	Contract	Contract
Cancer Registry	Expand	Expand	Expand	Expand
PHBG Supported Activities	Stable	Expand	Expand	Expand
Antitobacco Activities	Stable	Stable	Expand	Expand
Communicable Disease:				
Communicable Disease Program	Expand	Expand	Expand	Expand
HIV/STD:				
CTS/STD Program	Expand	Stable	Expand	Expand
HIV Prevention Activities	Expand	Stable	Expand	Expand
HIV/STD Clinical Data and Research	Stable	Stable	Expand	Expand
Family Health Services:				
Family Health Services: Women's Health	Expand	Stable	Expand	Expand
Maternal and Child Health:				
MCH: Family Help Line	Stable	Stable	Expand	Stable
MCH: Genetic Disease/Newborn Screening	Stable	Stable	Expand	Expand
MCH: Childhood Lead Program	Stable	Expand	Expand	Expand
MCH: Prenatal Substance Abuse Program	Stable	Stable	Expand	Stable
MCH: Adolescent Health	Expand	Expand	Expand	Expand
MCH: Family Planning Program	Stable	Stable	Expand	Stable
MCH: Breast-feeding Promotion Program	Stable	Stable	Expand	Expand
MCH: Pregnancy Risk Assessment Monitoring System (PRAMS)	Stable	Stable	Expand	Expand
MCH: Prenatal Care, Primary Care/Managed Care, School-Based Clinics	Stable/Expand	Stable	Expand	Expand

Exhibit 14–32 • **Continued**

Program	Funds	Staff	Market Development	Product/Service Development
MCH: Healthy Pregnancy/Healthy Baby Campaign	Stable	Stable	Expand	Expand
MCH: Sudden Infant Death Syndrome (SIDS) Project	Contract	Contract	Expand	Stable
Children's Special Health Care Services:				
Children's Special Health Care Services	Stable	Stable	Expand	Expand
Nutrition/WIC Program:				
Nutrition/WIC	Stable	Stable	Expand	Expand
Oral Health Services:				
Oral Health	Stable	Stable	Expand	Stable
Epidemiology Resource Center:				
Epidemiology Resource Center	Expand	Expand	Expand	Expand
Local Health Support:				
Local Health Support	Expand	Expand	Expand	Expand
Planning and Information Services Commission				
Management Information	Expand	Expand	Expand	Expand
Health Planning	Stable	Stable	Expand	Expand
Health Planning: Certificate of Need	Stable	Stable	Stable	Stable
Health Planning: Hospital Financial Disclosure	Stable	Stable	Expand	Expand
Public Health Research	Expand	Expand	Expand	Expand
County Health Needs Assessment	Stable	Stable	Expand	Expand
Public Health Statistics	Expand	Expand	Expand	Expand
Vital Records	Stable	Stable	Expand	Expand
Public Health Statistics: Birth Problems Registry	Expand	Expand	Expand	Expand
Grants Resource Center	Stable	Stable	Expand	Expand

Organization-Wide Strategies

Three related organization-wide implementation strategies were initiated by the ISDH—organization-wide cultural changes (based on the seven factors of excellence), agency goals and implementation priorities, and reorganization of the agency.

Changing the Culture   Phase I of the implementation was directed toward changing the culture of the agency (an organization-wide strategy). The implementation task force formed seven subcommittees to address the seven factors of excellence thought to be important in shaping the culture of the organization. Each subcommittee was asked to identify a few targeted short-term activities or "quick victories" that would make an immediate impact on "the way work is done" in the excellence area assigned to it. The quick victories were considered important in fixing well-defined, short-term problems and in assuring employees that the strategic management process was progressing. In

Exhibit 14–33 • Definitions for Expansion, Stabilization, and Contraction—ISDH Statement of Strategy

The ISDH Statement of Strategy identifies the ISDH commitment of resources to support services and a commitment to the levels and types of the services. The commitments are described as expansion, stabilization, or contraction. The following definitions help explain what the ISDH means by the commitment to expand, stabilize, or contract resources and services.

Expansion of resources is a commitment by the ISDH to identify and allocate additional funding or staff to selected programs. The source of funds can include:

- Grant funds,
- New general fund appropriations,
- Possible fee-supported dedicated funds,
- Redirection of current funding, or
- Funds from collaborative efforts with other agencies.

The sources of personnel could include:

- New staff supported by grant funds,
- Reassignment of current staff,
- Staff available through collaborative efforts with other agencies,
- Federal assignees, or
- Students.

Expansion of programs includes both changes in service population and in the characteristics of the services offered. Expansion of service population can be achieved by:

- Increasing the number of people eligible for a service who actually use the service,
- Serving new population groups not currently targeted either by geographic area or new categories of population,
- Developing collaborative efforts with ISDH/other programs to increase the number of people served, or
- Increasing program efficiency to enable the program to serve more people with the same funding and staffing levels.

Expansion of services can include:

- Developing new service offerings such as screening or data reports,
- Changing the current service or offering the service in different ways to increase the range of services offered, or
- Developing collaborative efforts with ISDH/other programs to develop new services or expand the scope of services offered.

Stabilization of resources means that the current allocation of funding and staff will remain the same for the next fiscal year. Managers will develop work plans to match the resource level to program expectations.

Stabilization of programs means that the level of services offered will remain the same. This does not necessarily mean maintaining the status quo. Each program manager is expected to review programs for possible enhancements such as improved efficiency or quality. Enhancements within stabilization can include:

- Work process streamlining to improve efficiency,
- Quality improvement for services provided,
- Focusing on customer service aspects of care to increase client satisfaction with services,
- Redefining the way services are provided within stable resources, or
- Changing the service mix to meet higher priority needs within stable resources.

Contraction of resources will be accomplished over the next fiscal year. Contraction strategies include:

- Readjusting work flow to reduce resources needed to provide the same service,
- Improving efficiency to reduce resources needed to provide the same service,
- Shifting staff to higher priority activities, with appropriate training for new responsibilities,
- Eliminating or shifting surplus vacant positions to complete work,

Exhibit 14–33 · **Continued**

- Shifting equipment to higher priority activities, or
- Sharing positions between two programs to support activities in both.

Contraction of programs means that a program will stop offering a service or reduce the amount of services offered. Contraction strategies include:

- Eliminating unnecessary services,
- Developing collaborative relationships with ISDH/other programs to assume responsibility for part of the work conducted by your unit,
- Reducing the units of service available through evaluation of requests for service and providing only those services essential to community need, or
- Arranging for another agency to assume responsibilities for a service currently offered by the ISDH.

Managers, working with their assistant commissioners or office directors, will develop specific steps to implement the Statement of Strategy. These steps will become each ISDH program's work plan for the next year.

---

addition to the quick victories, the subcommittees developed strategies that clearly addressed less-well-defined, long-term cultural problems.

Agency Goals and Implementation Priorities Phase II of strategy implementation involved a translation of the agency goals into organization-wide actions incorporating the overall strategy into the operations of the individual programs. Specific organization-wide actions (agency implementation priorities) were developed for each of the eight agency goals. Recall that these goals were tied directly to the critical factors for success and were viewed as essential for development of the entire organization. The implementation actions accomplish the agency goals, which in turn address the critical success factors. The critical success factors, agency goals, actions items, and implementation dates are presented in the agencywide work plan in Exhibit 14–34.

Reorganization In addition to the organization-wide cultural initiatives and agency goals, the ISDH made several changes to the organization structure to better accomplish the strategy. One of the strategic objectives was to further promote public health by working more closely with community health organizations. Therefore, an entirely new commission (Community Health Services) was created to focus on community health needs including local health support services, institutions, and consumer protection.

Because health policy as a core public health function would be critical, given the ISDH's strategy, the Office of Policy was expanded to include research and grant efforts so that grants could be linked to outcomes research. In addition, the name was changed to the Office of Policy and Research to reflect its new emphasis. Finally, the role of the Quality Assurance Commission was expanded. This commission would work with program areas throughout the agency to incorporate quality assurance into the programs. In addition, this commission would be responsible for continuing the strategic planning process and integrating the quality program into the strategic planning process. Joe Hunt assumed the leadership role in this endeavor. The new Indiana State Department of Health organization chart is shown in Exhibit 14–35.

Exhibit 14–34 • **Agencywide Work Plan**

Critical Success Factor	Agency Goals	Action Items	Target Date
Service:			
The ISDH must maintain a client orientation and assure the quality of all services for internal and external clients.	All services provided by the ISDH will be client oriented and include a commitment to continual evaluation and improvement.	All areas will have a customer service plan by October 1994.	October 1994
		All areas will conduct baseline assessments of customer satisfaction by December 31, 1994, driven from customer service plan. (MIS will assist with design and nonduplication.)	December 1994
Workforce:			
The ISDH must provide a working environment and resources that will attract and retain qualified staff members and empower them to achieve or exceed agency goals. The working environment will support responsive personnel policies; competitive compensation; adequate training; advancement opportunities; trust; sensitivity to diversity; and efficiency, innovation, and excellence.	The ISDH will provide orientation, training, and development opportunities for all ISDH staff.	ISDH will have a training options packet for all employees by June 1994 designed by the training task force with input from executive staff and Human Resources.	June 1994
		Managers will evaluate employee training needs and make recommendations to each employee regarding training needs by his or her next annual review.	Annually
		By August 1994, Human Resources will develop and deliver a comprehensive staff orientation to all new employees.	August 1994
Management:			
The ISDH must implement a process that plans and sets priorities within the constraints of available resources, in the context of strategic thinking. Management processes must promote interprogram coordination and cooperation to achieve agency goals.	Managers will apply the ISDH mission and critical success factors to program operations.	Managers will develop work plans based on at least three agency goals by August 1994.	August 1994
		Managers will incorporate mission, vision, and critical success factors into employee job descriptions by December 1994.	December 1994
		Managers will do a personal assessment of their training needs by October 1994.	October 1994
Leadership:			
The ISDH must be a visible, active, and persistent advocate on behalf of its employees and public health. This leadership must be based on efficiency, innovation, respect for the individual, and science. Leadership qualities will be recognized and promoted at all levels of the agency.	The ISDH will provide public health leadership.	Executive staff will establish criteria that define leadership by June 1994.	June 1994
		Executive staff will create an enhanced recognition program including leadership by September 1994.	September 1994
		Health Reform think tank will develop transition plans for ISDH to assist in outlining Indiana's plan by December 1994.	December 1994
Communication:			
The ISDH must communicate effectively both internally with employees and externally with local, state, and federal public health agencies and other stakeholders. Communication must accurately and consistently reflect the mission, vision, and activities of the agency.	The ISDH will communicate effectively with employees and external clients.	By June 1994, the ISDH will implement a communication plan designed by the Office of Public Affairs with input from program areas.	June 1994
		By December 1994, program areas will develop strategies to implement the communication plan in their program.	December 1994

Exhibit 14–34 • **Continued**

Critical Success Factor	Agency Goals	Action Items	Target Date
Funding: The ISDH must establish funding priorities and pursue innovative strategies to obtain adequate, stable financial resources for ensuring that fundamental public health services are available and monitor use of funds to achieve established objectives.	The ISDH will have a priority structure for funding and will pursue appropriate resources.	Executive staff will design a system for priority setting of projects and funding for the agency annually.	End of each March
		Grants Resource Center will identify three funding opportunities for programs listed for expansion annually.	End of each August
		Designated program areas that are listed for expansion will develop at least one new grant application or alternative funding stream based on priorities set by executive staff annually.	End of each December
Collaboration: The ISDH must expand and improve internal teamwork and external partnerships with local health departments and other local, state, and federal public and private organizations to promote public health.	The ISDH will foster successful partnerships to promote public health.	Executive staff, with program input, will identify agencywide collaboration projects that match mission, vision, and critical success factors by the end of each January.	End of each January
		Managers will meet with at least two different program areas and form or improve internal partnerships.	December 1994
		Program areas will identify all existing external collaborative efforts by September 1994.	September 1994
		Grant applications to ISDH must support strategies consistent with mission, vision, and critical success factors for the agency.	Immediately— ongoing
		A strategic plan for strengthening local health departments' relationship with ISDH will be in place by December 1994.	December 1994
Data and Information: The ISDH must acquire and use timely and accurate data to assess needs, develop policy, and assure quality services. The data and information acquired must be shared with all people who need it to carry out their responsibilities.	The ISDH will effectively acquire, maintain, and utilize data to make policy and program decisions.	Management Information Services will have a database architecture plan that describes data sources and relationships by December 1994.	December 1994
		Managers will validate the data and information service needs assessment conducted by Management Information Services by May 1994.	May 1994
		Management Information Services will create a policy-setting work group on data needs by May 1994.	May 1994— ongoing

Functional Strategies

Functional areas in the ISDH are the programs (programmatic areas such as health education, meat and poultry, and vector control, plus support services such as human resources, finance, planning, and so on). Therefore, it was up to the program directors

Exhibit 14–35 • New Indiana State Department of Health Organizational Chart

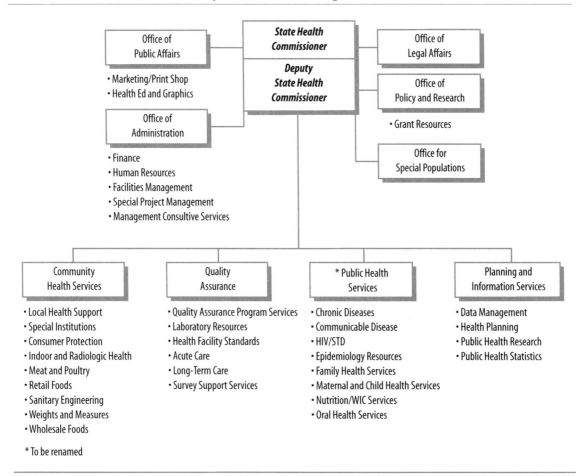

and their staffs to develop the functional implementation strategies. As shown in Exhibit 14–36, situational analysis had produced three organizational change initiatives—a change in strategy (statement of strategy), a change in strategic objectives and implementation priorities, and cultural change initiatives. Although there were organization-wide strategies for implementation of the strategic objectives and cultural change, program directors were expected to address all three organizational change initiatives in their program work plans (see Exhibit 14–36). Therefore, in addition to the organization-wide implementation actions, program directors developed specific work plans to carry out their respective expansion, stabilization, or contraction adaptive strategies. They also had to address the strategic objectives and implementation priorities and cultural change within their respective programs. Development of the work plans generally followed the flowchart of activities shown in Exhibit 14–37. An example of a typical work plan developed for one of the ISDH programs is presented in Exhibit 14–38.

Exhibit 14–36 • Development of Work Plans

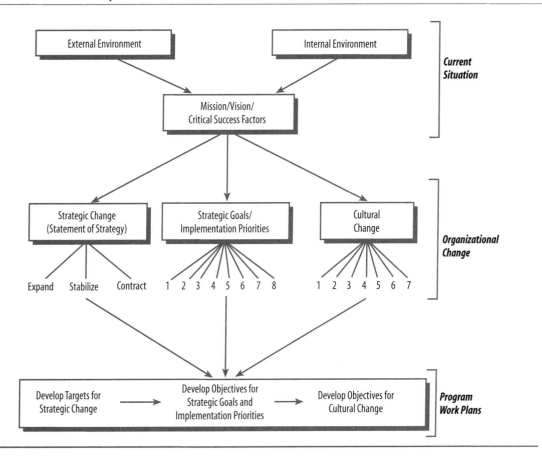

Strategic Control

A strategic control system monitors, evaluates, and adjusts the situational analysis processes, the strategy itself, and strategic implementation as appropriate. Therefore, the ISDH set out to formalize the control process so that progress toward the strategy could be maintained. Realizing that the strategic management process itself was a strategic control, Joe Hunt began to institutionalize the strategic management process. A formal year-long schedule was developed for strategic planning events, including environmental analysis, internal analysis, reassessing the mission, vision, critical success factors, strategy formulation, and so on.

The executive staff played a key role in guiding the agency. Therefore the staff was provided with questions for validation of the strategic assumptions; questions for the evaluation of the directional strategies, adaptive strategies, market entry strategies, and positioning strategies; and questions for the evaluation of strategic implementation. These questions served as an additional strategic control and fostered strategic thinking.

Exhibit 14–37 • Development of Implementation Work Plans

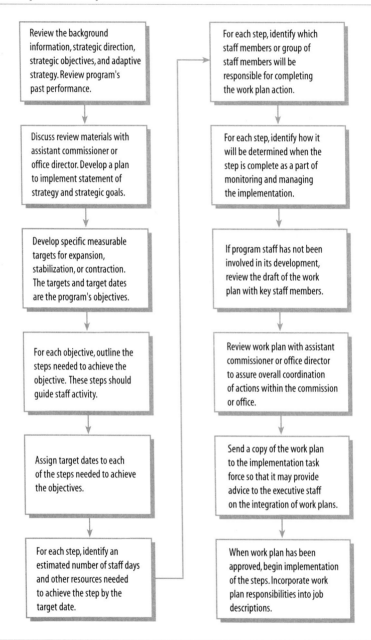

In addition to the strategic management process, the implementation dates specified in the agency work plan (Exhibit 14–34) and the individual program work plans (Exhibit 14–38) were to be monitored and evaluated periodically. As an additional part of the integration of

Exhibit 14–38 • Typical Work Plan for Children's Special Health Care Services (slated for stabilization): Children's Special Health Care Services Program Goals

I. Promote the delivery of high-quality, family-centered services to children with special health care needs.

II. Stress efforts that emphasize early evaluation, prevention of regression in health status, promotion of maximum function, and community-based services.

III. Promote systems development to improve the organization and delivery of services for children with special health care needs.

IV. Develop, promote, and improve the standards of care for children with special health care needs.

V. Provide culturally relevant care coordination and case management for children with special health care needs.

VI. Facilitate accomplishment of program mission statement.

Sample Work Plan and Dates for Completion for Goal I — Promote the delivery of high-quality, family-centered services to children with special health care needs.

A. *Outreach Plan (Communication, Management)*
   1. Develop plan for outreach efforts. — April 30
   2. Present plan to advisory council. — September 30
   3. Begin implementation of outreach plan. — April 30

B. *Health Care Reform (Leadership)*
   1. Keep up to date with the status of health care reform. — Ongoing
   2. Present to director as necessary, the impact of health care reform on: — April 30
       a. Children with special health care needs.
       b. Division of CSHCS.
       c. Impact of FSSA's system.
   3. Present quarterly to staff the changes in health care reform. — April 30

C. *Part H Liaison (Collaboration)*
   1. Work with director of Part H by meeting quarterly to assure all needs of children with special health care needs are met. — April 30
   2. Continue to work on the Interagency Memorandum of Agreement PL99-457 to assure collaboration between agencies. — June 30
   3. Develop plan to pay for diagnostic services and enroll children in CSHCS. — April 30

D. *Interagency Agreements (Collaboration, Leadership)*
   1. Assign staff to assure Medicaid interagency agreement is implemented. — April 30
   2. Assign staff to assure completion and implementation of the interagency agreement between OPIN and CSHCS. — April 30
   3. Assign staff to assure completion and implementation of the interagency agreement between FSSA and CSHCS in regards to MMIS project. — April 30
   4. Assign staff to assure completion and implementation of the interagency agreement between Shriners Hospital and CSHCS. — September 30
   5. Assign staff to assure completion and implementation of the interagency agreement between Part H and CSHCS. — June 30

E. *Credentials (Service)*
   1. Develop policy to assure applications are processed in allowed time frames. — June 30
   2. Develop quality assurance system to assure credentials are processed appropriately. — June 30
       a. Data input.
       b. Medical eligibility.
       c. Financial eligibility.
   3. Cross-train assigned staff. — June 30

continued

Exhibit 14–38 · **Continued**

F. *Provider Relations (Communication, Leadership)*

1. Assure all providers understand the program expectations by mailing a provider update at least quarterly.	April 30
2. Assign staff to respond to provider inquiries.	March 31
3. Develop a plan to work with the multiple providers for outreach.	April 30
4. Implement a plan, reporting status to division director monthly.	June 30
5. Develop plan to assure 90 percent of providers for CSHCS program sign provider agreement in collaboration with EDS.	April 30
6. Work with EDS to develop CSHCS portion of provider manual.	June 30
7. Create a position for provider relations.	April 30

G. *Primary-Care Linkage (Service)*

1. Develop policy to assure all new children enrolled in the program are linked to a primary-care physician within forty-five calendar days of their approval.	April 30
2. Develop policy that allows participants to change primary-care physicians when requested.	June 30
3. Collect and analyze data for those participants declining the primary-care linkage.	June 30
4. Develop list of data needs for tracking primary-care linkage.	April 30

H. *Specialty-Care Linkage (Service)*

1. Develop policy to assure all children who need a specialist are linked to a specialty-care provider.	April 30
2. Assure 90 percent of all children needing linkage are linked to a specialty-care physician by monthly report from tracking system.	May 31

I. *Dental-Care Linkage (Service)*

1. Develop policy to assure all children who are eligible to receive dental care are linked to a dentist.	April 30
2. Assure 90 percent of all children who are eligible to receive dental care are linked to a dentist through monthly report from tracking system.	June 30

J. *Staff Development/Training (Workforce)*

1. Analyze the training needs assessment and develop a plan for staff training.	May 31
2. Develop staff training schedule to include coding training, medical terminology training, and prior authorization training.	May 31
3. Provide claims staff training quarterly.	March 31/ongoing

K. *Case Worker Training/Bill Back (Collaboration/Funding)*

1. Develop relationship with FSSA by meeting quarterly with FSA staff regarding case worker issues.	June 30
2. Negotiate an agreement for bill-back system for CSHCS applications completed by case workers.	June 30
3. Track case worker inquiries, report/respond quarterly.	April 30
4. Develop informational letter quarterly to be sent to the case workers explaining policy changes within the program.	April 30/ongoing

L. *Parent Manual (Communication)*

1. Develop parent manual for all families interested in the program.	June 30
2. Consult OPIN on the development of the manual.	
3. Distribute parent manual to all participants in the program.	September 30

M. *SSDD Outreach (Collaboration)*

1. Meet with SSDD staff to develop outreach plan.	March 31
2. Begin implementation of outreach program.	June 30

N. *Multiagency Review Meeting (Collaboration)*

1. Assign appropriate staff to attend review of applications for alternative or residential services.	March 31
2. Assure all information is transferred.	June 30

operations into the strategic management process, performance evaluations (both personal and program evaluation) were specifically tied to the accomplishment of the strategy.

Summary of the Strategic Management Process

The summary of the strategic plan brings the process together into a single document that provides a quick reference and serves as a guide for decision making. The ISDH strategic plan was summarized into a four-page booklet. Oftentimes these documents are proprietary (confidential) because of the competitive environment. However, this was not a problem for the ISDH. Therefore, the summary was communicated to all personnel and other stakeholders including the public.

Adopting a Strategic Management Philosophy

Dr. Bailey's comment quoted at the beginning of this chapter, "Since we started thinking strategically, we manage in a fundamentally different way," acknowledges the managerial transformation that has taken place at the ISDH in the three years since the strategic management project began. Nancy Blough's statement that "strategic management is not something we have to consciously think about—it's just the way we do things" illustrates that strategic management has been adopted as the managing philosophy of the ISDH and is being inculcated into daily management activities. Joe Hunt, an early and passionate advocate for strategic planning, indicates that everyone in the organization is questioning, "How can my current activities better contribute to the strategic plan?" Everyone is beginning to understand the importance of strategic thinking.

ISDH is rapidly becoming a strategically managed organization. However, it required a great deal of hard work by management to keep the strategic priorities in front of managers and encourage everyone to think strategically. Although it was not easy, ISDH now has a better sense of what public health should be in Indiana, has created clear momentum to achieve that vision, and better "owns" its future.

Managing Strategically

Two years after the strategic plan was completed, the ISDH reviewed their directional strategies. The executive staff decided that although the mission was still accurate, it needed to be shortened. A more succinct statement would better communicate what the ISDH was all about to stakeholders and employees alike. The revised mission statement was posted throughout the building and incorporated into many ISDH documents. The ISDH, revised mission statement, goals for 1995 and 1996, critical success factors, areas to measure, and implementation tools are presented in Exhibit 14–39.

Once the vision for public health in Indiana became clear and programs prioritized according to the vision, mission, and external and internal issues, the ISDH allocated resources based on program priority and mission. The mission of each program was reviewed as to its appropriateness, and it was changed where necessary. During the past two years, the ISDH has systematically shifted personnel and financial resources to the higher priority programs. Exhibit 14–40 presents the Q-sort of the ISDH programs to illustrate the personnel changes. The numbers at the bottom of the Q-sort columns indicate the net change in personnel within the column. Note that, for the most part, programs on the left side of the Q-sort have experienced personnel increases, whereas

Exhibit 14–39 • Revised ISDH Mission Statement

Mission Statement

The Indiana State Department of Health (ISDH) is dedicated to promoting health and wellness among the people in Indiana through planning, prevention, service, and education. The ISDH serves to help people attain the highest level of health possible. The ISDH is a proactive leader and collaborator in assessment, policy development, and assurance, based on science, innovation, and efficiency.

Goals	Critical Success Factors	Health Status Indicators and Priorities	Tools
1995			
• State health data center	• Service	• Cardiovascular disease	• Surveillance
• Regulatory reform	• Workforce	• Cancer	• Education/ health promotion
• Get out of things that are not public health	• Management	• Infant mortality	• Quality assurance
• Determine what we want from labs	• Leadership	• High-risk pregnancies	• Policy setting
• Increase external funding	• Communications	• Vaccine-preventable diseases	
	• Funding	• HIV and other STDs	
1996	• Collaboration	• Foodborne diseases	
• Good management practices	• Data/information	• Emerging infectious diseases	
• Collection, use, and validation of data to make policy and program decisions		• Waterborne diseases	
		• Oral health	
• Focus on community-based health services		• Unintentional injuries	
		• Diseases related to environmental contamination	

those on the right side have undergone decreases. Some programs, such as Management Information, Nutrition/WIC, and OSP Minority Health, although on the left side of the Q-sort, decreased in personnel because of program mission changes and redirection of the program.

Recall that the ISDH's strategic direction (in the statement of strategy) was "an expansion in core public health areas with an emphasis on assessment, policy development, and assurance." Exhibit 14–41 presents budget allocations to core public health functions over the past two years. There has been a 54 percent increase in funds allocated to core public health.

Challenges for the Future

Recent discussions at the ISDH suggest that the organization feels it can become completely strategically managed within another three years. In other words, it will take approximately six years for the whole organization to be managed strategically. The first three years set the direction for the organization, began the process of reshaping public health delivery in Indiana, and created the organizational infrastructure for strategic management. The next three years will be spent tying individual jobs and performance appraisals to the strategic plan and creating individual ownership of the strategic plan. Specifically, each job will be connected to the vision, mission, strategic goals, values, and strategy, resulting in strategic thinking by each member of the ISDH. The strategic plan has been, and continues to be, a worthy achievement for the people of Indiana.

Exhibit 14–40 • Personnel Changes Based on Program Priority

Key

- Increase in Employees
- Decrease in Employees
- No Change in Employees

Most Important	Next Most Important	Next Most Important	Next Most Important	Next Most Important	Next Most Important	Next Most Important	Next Most Important	Next Most Important
				Oral Health Services				
				Legal Affairs				
				OA: Finance				
				HFS: Regulatory/ Support				
			CDP: Injury Control	FHS: Women's Health	Policy Coordination			
			MCH: Adolescent Health	Retail Food	Wholesale Food			
		PHR: County Assessment	MCH: Program	CS: Meat and Poultry	Environmental Health Lab	FM: Asset Service		
		Child Special Services	Health Planning	MCH: Lead Poisoning	Lab Support Services	FM: Environmental Services		
		CTS/STD	OPA: Health Education	OSP: Disability Concerns	Manufactured Food	MCH: Pregnancy Risk		
		OSP: Rural Health	Grants Resource Center	PHS: Birth Problems Registry	SE: Residential Sewage	FM: Security		
	PHS: Vital Records	Disease Control Lab	OA: Human Resources	ACS: Health Inspections	SE: Vector Control	MCH: SIDS	HP: Financial Disclosure	
Local Health Support	Chronic Disease	MCH: Genetic Disease	HFS: Long-Term Care	HIV/STD Clinical Data	SE: Environmental Health	FM: Safety Programs	CS: Weight and Measures	HE: Film Library
Communicable Disease	Public Health Statistics	MCH: Healthy Pregnancy	MCH: Prenatal Substance	Consumer Health Lab	OA: Administrative Services	SE: Plan Review	OA: Consultive Services	OA: Correspondence Center
Epidemiology Resource Center	Nutrition/ WIC	Public Health Research	OPA: Media Relations	MCH: Family Help Line	OA: Purchasing	MCH: Breast-feed Promotion	HP: Certificate of Need	OPA: Photographer
Management Information	HIV Prevention	OSP: Minority Health	WFD: Milk	MCH: Family Planning	FM: Physical Plant	Indoor Radiologic Health	OPA: Print Shop	HE: Library
Most Important	**Next Most Important**	**Next Most Important**	**Next Most Important**	**Next Most Important**	**Next Most Important**	**Next Most Important**	**Next Most Important**	**Next Most Important**
+27	+28	+13	+28	−13	−12	−1	−7	−18

Exhibit 14–41　•　**Funds Shifted to Core Public Health**

	FY 1994	FY 1996
Assessment		
Health Data Center	0	5,893,095
Epidemiology Resource Center	797,288	2,116,646
Policy	124,547	325,760
Assurance		
Consumer Health Services	260,283	400,769
Medicare/Medicaid	6,028,274	7,967,433
Legal	342,067	470,107
Consumer Protection	6,604,644	6,626,170
Labs	3,398,984	3,252,984
Totals	$17,556,087	$27,052,964

Note: The above figures represent a 54 percent increase of funds to the core functions.

Impact of Strategic Management at ISDH

The ISDH developed a brochure that has been distributed to all employees and has become an important part of new employee orientation. "Strategic Planning: What Does It All Mean to Me?" reviews the strategic planning process used by the agency. Its introduction states:

> Strategic planning has helped us sharpen our focus, decide which functions we wish to perform and which ones we do not, and has resulted in some truly positive change in a relatively short time.
>
> Strategic planning is working for ISDH—and for the people it serves. What follows is intended to detail exactly what the ISDH Strategic Plan is so that every employee will understand its importance, and will use the Plan in our everyday work decisions.
>
> ISDH believes that the Plan has improved the organization in the following ways:
>
> 1. The development of program work plans tied to the agency's goals.
> 2. The Strategic Plan has been—and will be—used to make decisions about budgets, grants, and personnel.
> 3. The significant investment of agency resources in improving our data and information systems.
> 4. Internal communications have been improved to ensure that there are no communications gaps from top to bottom, and from the bottom to the top, of the agency.
> 5. The building is cleaner and safer.
> 6. We understand our customers and know better how to serve them.

7. The Strategic Plan has helped guide us in rethinking our philosophy of regulatory functions that we perform.
8. We realized that we needed to invest more in our most important resource—our employees.
9. We now have in place a more formalized, more extensive Employee Recognition Program to recognize employees for the good work that they do.
10. And we're not through trying to improve ourselves—we'll keep monitoring our progress and looking for other opportunities to improve.

The ISDH's Strategic Plan has not been put on the shelf and ignored. All employees recognize that they have a part to play in the ISDH accomplishing its mission and achieving its vision. ISDH's Strategic Plan is a living document that is encouraging the entire organization to create its future.

Questions for Class Discussion

1. In your opinion, what aspects of strategic management did ISDH do well?
2. In your opinion, what aspects of strategic management could ISDH do better?
3. What deviations or modifications in the process did ISDH make from those described in the text?
4. Discuss the success of the strategic management process at ISDH.

Notes

1. Public Health Practice Program Office, Division of Public Health Systems, Centers for Disease Control, *Profile of State and Territorial Public Health Systems: United States, 1990* (Atlanta: U.S. Department of Health and Human Services, Public Health Service, Centers for Disease Control, 1991), p. 121.
2. Ibid., pp. 121–122.
3. Ibid.
4. Ibid.
5. Early development of the underlying factors for the questionnaire can be examined in W. Jack Duncan, Peter M. Ginter, and Stuart A. Capper, "Excellence in Public Administration: Four Transferable Lessons from the Private Sector," *Public Productivity and Management Review* 14 (Spring 1991), pp. 227–236.

PART 5

Appendices

Analyzing Strategic Health Care Cases

How does a manager learn to make strategic decisions in health care organizations? The most obvious way, and maybe the most valuable if the opportunity is available, is to work your way up the organization and observe how senior executives deal with strategic issues. Then, when the opportunity presents itself, combine what you have learned from others and your own management philosophy and do the best you can. Unfortunately, learning by observing others is not practical in most rapidly changing organizations.

Even if this approach were feasible, it would be very risky; and business firms, hospitals, health maintenance organizations, long-term-care facilities, and other organizations trust important strategic decision making only to the most "seasoned managers." As a result, cases have been successfully used as a method to give aspiring managers opportunities to make strategic decisions without "betting the organization" on the outcome. In other words, cases offer an opportunity to deal with real decisions in a low-risk environment.

Cases contain situations actually faced by managers in health care organizations and are documented in a way that makes them useful in training decision makers. The decisions required to solve cases represent a wide range of complexity so that no two are addressed in exactly the same manner. In the following discussion, one method of case analysis is presented. This approach, illustrated in Exhibit A–1, offers a process or way of thinking about cases rather than prescribing one way to approach case analysis. Exhibit A–1 is the model or outline used throughout this book to direct thinking about strategic management in health care organizations. The model can be effective in analyzing cases as well. This approach to case analysis is useful because it is a logical method of decision making.

First, it is important to understand the economic, social, technological, and political environments facing the industry and organization. After developing a knowledge of these aspects of the general environment, it is possible to progress to the specifics of the health care industry. Next, as many facts as possible should be gathered about the environment of the organization under examination. This may be a hospital, health maintenance organization, public health agency, or long-term-care facility. At this point it is important to relate the strategic capabilities of the organization to the external environment. To do this, a thorough and objective analysis of internal strengths and weaknesses is required. There are many ways to look introspectively at a health care organization. One of the most useful ways, however, is to examine it in terms of its resource base, the

Exhibit A–1 • **An Outline for Case Analysis**

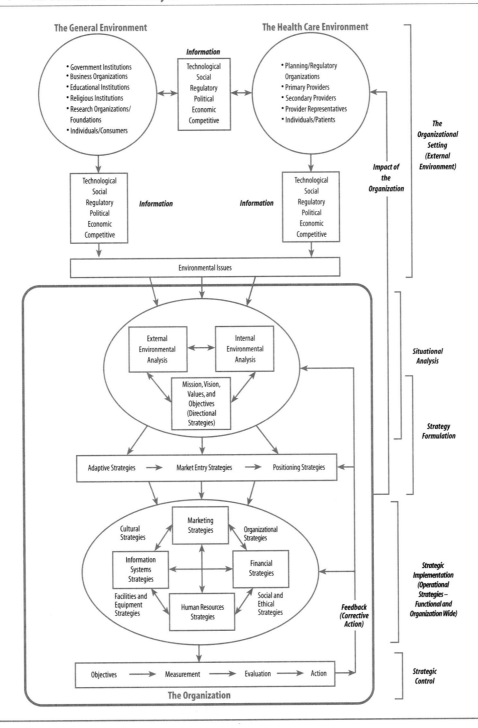

competencies possessed by its professional and nonprofessional employees, and the effectiveness of its leaders in actually "putting" the resources and competencies together (capabilities) and converting them into a competitive advantage. It is also necessary to understand the unique culture of the organization, its mission, and its strategic objectives.

Once the situation analysis is complete, strategic alternatives can be generated as possible solutions to the problems identified in the case. This is the strategy formulation stage, and it is an important part of solving strategic management cases.

When the strategic direction is determined based on the unique "fit" between the organization's internal resources, competencies, and capabilities and the external opportunities and threats, the sufficiency of the various subsystems such as marketing, finance, operations, and so on must be evaluated. These subsystems will determine, to a great extent, the likelihood that a particular strategy will be implemented.

Finally, the effectiveness of the chosen strategic alternative must be evaluated. Because of the nature of case analysis, this aspect of strategic control is not always possible. However, at least some thought must be given to the likely outcomes resulting from different strategic choices.

Although the approach outlined here is logical, it is important to remember that a case should be approached and appreciated as a unique opportunity for problem solving. The organization, environment, and situation make each case different.

Cases: Real and Hypothetical

Many different types of cases are used in strategic management texts. Sometimes cases are invented to illustrate a specific point. Usually these appear as "Ajax Hospital and Medical Center" or some similar name. Other cases are real but disguised. A writer may, for example, have information from an organization such as the Mayo Clinic or Massachusetts General Hospital but for some reason has been asked not to use the name of the institution.

The best cases, like those in this book, are real and undisguised. Cases such as HEALTHSOUTH and the University of Texas at Tyler Medical Center are obviously about real organizations. Of course, less well-known organizations also have been selected because of the important issues they present to prospective managers. Sometimes the issues presented are not even problems. Often the greatest challenge facing an organization is recognizing and acting on an opportunity rather than solving a problem.

Cases that have obvious solutions upon which everyone agrees are not good decision-making aids. Managers in health care organizations rarely face decisions where the solution is obvious to everyone. This does not mean that there are no good and bad answers or solutions in case analysis. However, the evaluation of a case analysis is often based more on the approach and logic employed than the precise recommendation offered.

Cases, Strategic Management, and Health Care

Cases add realism that is impossible to achieve in traditional lecture classes. Realism results from the essential nature of cases, although we may complain that cases fail to provide all the information necessary for decision making. The complaint is valid because cases rarely give us everything we need. However, decision makers in health care organizations never have all the information they want or need when they face strategic decisions. Risks must be taken in case analysis just as in actual decision making.

Risk Taking in Case Analysis

Decisions about the future involve uncertainty. Strategic decision making, because it is futuristic and involves judgment, is particularly risky. Decision making under conditions of uncertainty requires that means be devised for dealing with the risks faced by managers. Cases are valuable aids in this area because they allow us to practice making decisions in low-risk environments. A poor case analysis may be embarrassing, but at least it will not result in the closure of a hospital. At the same time, the lessons learned by solving cases and participating in discussions will begin to build problem-solving skills.

Unfortunately, many future health care decision makers are not familiar with how to analyze cases. Customarily, prospective managers learn how to succeed as students by taking objective examinations, writing occasional term papers, and crunching numbers on a computer, but they seldom solve real case problems. For this reason this appendix has been included—not to prescribe how all cases should be solved but to offer some initial direction on how to "surface" the real issues presented in the cases.

Solving Case Problems

Solving a case is much like solving any problem. First, the issues are defined, information is gathered, alternatives are generated, evaluated, selected, and implemented. Although the person solving the case seldom has the opportunity to implement a decision, he or she should always keep in mind that recommendations must be tempered by the limitations imposed on the organization in terms of its human and nonhuman resources. As the success or failure of the recommendations is analyzed, lessons are learned that can be applied to future decision making.

Alternative Perspectives: Passion or Objectivity

Different hypothetical roles can be assumed when analyzing cases. Some prefer to think of themselves as the chief executive officer or administrator in order to impose a perspective on the problems presented in the case. This provides the case analyst the liberty of becoming a passionate advocate of a particular course of action. Others prefer to observe the case from the detached objectivity of a consultant who has been employed by the organization to solve a problem.

Either perspective can be assumed but the first offers some unique advantages. Because there are no absolutely correct or incorrect answers to complex cases, the most important lesson to learn is why managers behave as they do, why they select one alternative in preference to all others, and why they pursue specific strategies under the conditions presented in the case. Becoming the manager, at least mentally, helps us learn the lessons case histories have to teach.

Consider the situation of the Professional Services Division at UniHealth in Burbank, California. Under the leadership of John H. Austin, M.D., the division has been realigning the overall goals of the organization while pursuing a strategy of developing and affiliating with medical groups throughout California regardless of current or possible affiliation with UniHealth hospitals. This strategy is considered unique in health care.[1]

The strategy was developed because of the uncertainty associated with the hospital and HMO markets. A decision was made to build relationships "where the patients were." That decision suggested the need to forge alliances with physician groups. Another interesting "twist" to the strategy has been that the Professional Services Division is less interested in relationships with a particular specialty group than it is with a group that is successful in its local market. In some areas, alliances are formed with primary-care groups, and in others specialty groups have been developed. There are no guarantees that this approach will be successful. "Will this prove, over the long run, to be a strategy that will be supported by corporate executives? Is success in local markets regardless of specialty the appropriate basis for forging alliances or do affiliations with primary-care groups make better business sense?"

To answer these questions from the administrator's perspective, it is important to "get inside" the decision maker's head. Feel the excitement and fear of doing new and innovative things in dynamic and complex health care markets. The passion and frustration of the administrator suggest why some prefer to assume the objective posture of a consultant. Not being in the trenches can sometimes suggest alternatives that cannot be seen by those directly involved in making the payroll and paying the bills.

The consultant's perspective allows the student to step back, look at decision makers who are engaging in strategies that are radically different from their counterparts in the same service area and objectively assess the likely outcomes of their actions. The consultant can more easily play the devil's advocate and point out how actions are at odds with current theory. Although the fun and excitement of case analysis is enhanced by assuming the decision maker's role, the options can often be expanded through a more objective and detached outlook.

Homework: An Essential Aspect of Case Analysis

Effective case analysis begins with data collection. This means carefully reading the case, rereading it, and sometimes reading it yet again. Rarely can anyone absorb enough information from the first reading of a comprehensive case to adequately solve it. Therefore, collect information and make notes about details as the case unfolds.

Getting Information

The information required to successfully solve a case comes in two forms. The first type of information is given as part of the case and customarily includes things such as the history of the hospital, long-term-care facility, or home health care agency; how it is organized; its management; and its financial condition. This is the easy part because the author of the case has typically done the work.

Occasionally, a case will include information about the industry and maybe even some problems shared by competing firms. If the case involves a chain of long-term-care facilities, a health maintenance organization, or a pharmaceutical company, the industry must be thoroughly understood before looking at specific problems.

A second type of information is "obtainable." This information is not provided in the case or by the instructor but available from secondary sources in the library in familiar magazines and related publications. Obtainable secondary information helps us understand the nature of the industry, the competition, and even some managers, past and present, who have made an impact on the industry. Examples of sources of obtainable information are given in Appendix D.

If the case does not include industry information, the instructor may expect the class to do some detective work before proceeding. This means you should find out what is happening in the industry and learn enough about trends to position the problems discussed in the case in a broader health care context. The culture of the organization or the style of the chief executive officer may also constitute relevant information.

Threats and Opportunities

From the very first reading of the case, start to list the strategic threats and opportunities facing the organization. When a threat is discovered mark it for more detailed examination. "Are the threats financial? Do the primary issues appear to be those of human resources, capital investment, or marketing?" Perhaps there are few, if any, apparent threats. The strategic issue facing the organization may be an opportunity to be exploited or at least investigated.

For example, the trend in the health care industry toward managed care has created some interesting problems, and opportunities, for drug companies. Managed care often means there are larger buyers of pharmaceutical products, and larger buyers will mean that greater discounts must be given to compete effectively. In attempts to maintain profits while offering larger and larger discounts, drug companies began to announce layoffs of personnel. Merck and Company, the world's largest pharmaceutical firm, stated that it would eliminate over 2,000 jobs and at the same time announced it would purchase Medco Containment Company and enter the mail-order drug market. Industry trends can create problems and opportunities almost simultaneously.

Analyzing the Present Situation

After pinpointing the organization's mission and the initial impressions of the major strategic issues in the case, the next step is to understand where the organization, the industry, and the decision makers are at the time a strategic decision is needed. This is called *situational analysis* because we must understand the circumstances and the environment facing the organization if good decisions are to result from our analysis.

Selected Aspects of Situational Analysis

Situational analysis is one of the most important steps in analyzing a case. The list below highlights some of the important areas that should be included in this stage of case analysis.

1. *The environment* of the health care organization.
   A. *Size*. What is the size of the industry? What are the growth trends?
   B. *Nature of the competition*. How many direct competitors are there, and is the competition increasing or decreasing? What are the relative market shares of the different competitors? Which organizations compete in the strategic group?

      C. *Macroenvironmental factors*. What are the prevailing economic conditions, regulatory philosophies, lifestyle and demographic factors, and technological forces that are likely to influence strategic decision making in health care? What is the industry's and the organization's history with respect to labor/management relations?

  2. *The market*.

      A. *Customers*. Who are the organization's primary customers—patients, elderly residents of long-term-care facilities, the home-bound ill? To what extent are the patients or customers loyal to the organization's services? Is price the major determinant in the purchasing decision? Will patients and clients travel and be otherwise inconvenienced to obtain the organization's services?

      B. *Services (Service Categories)*. Does the organization offer a full range of services? Is the present service mix complementary or does the organization compete with itself in some areas? Could the overall level of business be significantly increased if selected new services were added? Exhibit A–2 illustrates some important service trends for acute-care hospitals over a ten-year period that could be extremely helpful to a decision maker in thinking about services provided.

      C. *Geography (Service Area)*. Is the market for the organization's services geographically concentrated?

      D. *Marketing*. How sophisticated are the organization's clients/patients in terms of their buying habits and processes? What does this tell management about advertising and promotion?

      E. *Demographics*. Are market segments easily identified? Are different strategies for each feasible or advisable?

  3. *The organization*.

      A. *Mission*. Does the organization have a clear sense of mission? Is there a mission statement? Is it communicated to those responsible for accomplishing it?

Exhibit A–2 · United States Hospital Trends 1984–1994

Indicator	1984	1994	Percent Change
Hospitals	5,759	5,229	−9.2
Beds (thousands)	1,017	902	−11.3
Average Number of Beds per Hospital	177	173	−2.3
Admissions (thousands)	35,155	30,718	−12.6
Average Daily Census (thousands)	702	568	−19.1
Average Length of Stay (days)	7.3	6.7	−8.2
Inpatient Days (thousands)	256,603	207,180	−19.3
Surgical Operations (thousands)	19,908	22,988	15.5
Bassinets (thousands)	75	66	−13.0
Births (thousands)	3,456	3,809	10.2
Outpatient Visits (thousands)	211,961	382,924	80.7

Source: American Hospital Association "U.S. Hospital Trends," 1996 *AHA News* (March 25, 1996), p. 1.

Are there well-developed and communicated long- and short-range objectives? Does the organization have the human and nonhuman resources necessary to accomplish its mission?

B. *Culture.* What do we know about the culture of the organization? Will the culture allow innovation or are management and employees bound to familiar ways of doing things?

C. *Marketing Strategies.* How sophisticated is the organization in terms of its marketing? Has serious thought been given to a promotion strategy? Has the appropriate channel(s) of distribution been identified and utilized? How flexible are the organization's marketing policies? When was the last time management tried something innovative in the area of marketing? More important perhaps, has the organization ever done any serious marketing of its services?

D. *Finance.* Are the financial resources needed to compete available or is the organization undercapitalized, too highly leveraged, or not leveraged enough? How do the key financial ratios of this organization compare with others in the industry and region?

E. *Information Systems.* Are the information systems providing information that is used by decision makers? Can data on outcomes be generated so that the organization can make informed judgments about rates and contracts?

Note that Chapter 4 provides a discussion of how to think about the internal environment of a health care organization. Make an attempt to identify the competitively relevant resources, competencies, and capabilities of the organization.

Threats, Opportunities, Weaknesses, and Strengths

Once the situation has been reviewed, a better evaluation of the opportunities and threats facing the organization can be made. Moreover, we must be able to look objectively at the hospital or long-term-care facility and ask, "Given the organization's apparent resources, competencies, and capabilities, how can we convert these competitively relevant strengths into actions that allow us to take advantage of our opportunities and avoid the dangers in the environment?" Try to work through the phases of internal environmental analysis—surveying, inspecting, investigating, and evaluating. Attempt an ASSIST analysis. An effective way of summarizing the results is through the use of a simple two-by-two chart listing the threats, opportunities, weaknesses, and strengths. Exhibit A–3 presents an example of how these can be organized.

To illustrate how to relate threats, opportunities, weaknesses, and strengths, suppose that you are presently analyzing a case. In the case, the administrator of a large general hospital is evaluating an opportunity to purchase a regional long-term-care chain and thereby diversify the services offered to existing patients. An environmental analysis confirms the need for long-term-care beds in the future. The population is aging in this country and long-term-care facilities are generally not meeting present or forecasted needs.

The administrator believes that the hospital has a number of internal strengths. It has, for example, a reputation for high-quality and price-competitive services. In addition, it has a medical and administrative staff with proven records of flexibility in responding to new ventures. The hospital has always been able to go into the labor market and get the number and quality of employees needed—even in the highly competitive market for nurses.

The administrator does worry about the hospital's ability to easily enter the nursing home market even with the purchase of the regional chain. Few members of the management team have any experience with long-term care, and only a few are really experienced dealing with elderly patients' unique demands and needs. Moreover, a review of the hospital's financial statements raises serious doubts about its ability to absorb the additional debt financing needed to purchase the long-term-care chain. Financially, the chain does not offer the kind of strength that would overcome an excessive degree of financial leverage.

In addition, the recent trend in interest rates has been upward, so that even if funds could be borrowed, the expense involved would be substantially more than the board of directors would want to pay. Through an examination of the threats, opportunities, strengths, and weaknesses, the administrator can make a more informed decision (see Exhibit A–3).

Purpose or Mission of the Organization

Peter Drucker says that anyone who wants to "know" a business must start with understanding its purpose or mission.[2] If a mission statement is included in the case, does it serve the purpose of communicating to the public why the organization exists? Does it provide employees with a genuine statement of what the organization is all about?

Exhibit A–3 · **Threats, Opportunities, Weaknesses, and Strengths for a General Hospital**

Internal Strengths	Internal Weaknesses
1. Existing expertise 2. Reputation for quality service 3. Adaptive medical and support staff	1. Little experiences with long-term-care facilities 2. Large amount of debt used to finance hospital 3. Proposed acquisition will not overcome adverse financial ratios
External Opportunities	**External Threats**
1. Relaxation of certificate-of-need (CON) regulations 2. Emerging medical technology 3. Favorable demographic indicators	1. Attraction of new competition 2. Rising interest rates 3. Uncertain long-term-care facility market

Mission statements provide valuable information, but they may leave much to be inferred and even imagined. Missions are broad, general statements outlining what makes the organization unique. When the mission is understood, a number of things are known that will help in arriving at a good solution to the case.

As discussed in Chapter 5, a good mission should answer a series of questions. When you read the assigned case, ask if you know enough about the organization's mission to confidently speculate about the following:[3]

1. Who are the customers? The customers may be children, older adults, women, or patients in the hospital. The group or groups must be identified before any serious strategic analysis of the organization can be initiated.
2. What are the organization's principal services? Does the organization have unique experience and expertise in home health care, rehabilitation services, psychological counseling, open-heart surgery, or some other area of specialization?
3. Where does the organization intend to compete? Is the case about a small group medical practice that competes in only one local market, or is it a regional or national force in the delivery of health care services?
4. Who are the competitors? Is the case about an academic research and teaching hospital with a few well-known competitors, or does the hospital operate in a market along with other rural hospitals? In other words, how much competition is actually present in the market(s) where the organization competes or intends to compete?
5. What is the preference of the organization with regard to its public image? If the long-term-care facility wants to be perceived in certain ways, it may have to limit its options when defining and solving strategic issues. Is it, for example, important to the home's leadership that it be regarded as a uniquely caring or affordable "citizen" of the community, or is the mere fact that it creates a large number of jobs sufficient?
6. What does the organization want to be like in the future? Does the information in the case indicate that the organization wants to continue to operate as it does at the present time, or does it wish to expand its markets and the services it offers or even change its own basic operating philosophy?

If a formal mission statement is not presented in a case, it is important to attempt to construct one from the information given.

Objectives: More Specific Directions

Mission statements are broad and provide general direction. Objectives should be specific and explicitly point to where the organization is expected to be at a particular time in the future. Sometimes the case will indicate what the health care organization plans to achieve in the next year, where it hopes to be in three years, or even in five years. As with mission statements, if the objectives are not explicitly stated, there is a need to speculate about them, because they will be the standards against which the success or failure of a particular strategy will be evaluated.

When constructing or modifying hospital or other health care organization objectives, be sure they are as measurable as possible. This is important so that decision makers can use them as a reflection of organizational priorities and as a way of determining how to set their own personal and professional priorities. Make sure that the objectives are motivational and inspirational, yet feasible and attainable. Moreover because strategic management is futuristic and no one can predict the future with complete accuracy, objectives should always be adaptable to the changing conditions taking place in the organization and in the industry. Sometimes an organization will have to face a major strategic problem simply because it was unwilling to alter its objectives in light of changing conditions in the industry.

As a test of your understanding of the case and the health care organization under examination, before attacking problems, reflect on what an initial reading of the case reveals about the mission and objectives of the organization:

1. Identify two or three of the primary values of the organization and speculate about the type of objectives it would like to accomplish. How important, for example, is the quality as well as the quantity of medical services delivered by the organization?

2. Speculate about the indicators that should be used to judge whether or not the values are being realized and objectives are being accomplished. Is there an adequate means of professional review and evaluation to ensure outcomes are really achieved and that the basic values are not simply given lip service?

3. Are the aspirations of the organization's managers realistic in view of the competition and the organization's strengths and weaknesses?

4. Are the objectives being pursued consistent with what you understand to be the mission of the organization?

If the questions raised cannot be easily answered, reread the case yet again.

Finding Problems and Opportunities

Situation analysis is designed to surface present and potential problems. In case analysis, problems include not only the usual idea of a "problem" but also situations where things may be working well but improvements are possible. As noted previously, the "problem" may actually be an opportunity that can be capitalized on by the organization if it acts consciously and decisively.

When we analyze things carefully, patterns can be detected, and discrepancies between what actually is and what ought to be become more apparent. In other words, fundamental issues, not mere symptoms, begin to emerge.

Looking for Causes, Not Symptoms

It is important to realize that the things observed in an organization and reported in a case may not be the "real" or essential problems and opportunities. Often what we observe are the symptoms of more serious core problems. For example, increasing interest rates and cash flow discrepancies appear to be problems in many case analyses. In reality, the problem is the fundamental absence of adequate financial planning. The lack of planning is simply manifested as a cash flow problem, and increasing interest rates certainly complicate cash flow.

Frequently, hospitals conclude that they have operational problems in the area of marketing when bed occupancy rates decline. Someone may suggest that the marketing department is not doing a good job in convincing physicians to use the hospital. Sometimes people will complain that the hospital is not spending enough on promotion. The real problem, however, might be fundamental changes in the demographics of the market area or an outdated services mix that no amount of promotion will overcome. In organizations as complex as health care facilities, problems may have more than a single cause, so do not be overly confident when a single, simple reason is isolated. In fact, the suggestion of a simple solution should increase rather than decrease skepticism.

Getting to core problems requires that information be carefully examined and analyzed. Often, quantitative tools can help. Financial ratio analysis of the exhibits included in the case will sometimes be helpful in the identification of the real problems. Appendix B illustrates how financial analysis and information can be used to identify core problems in an organization.

In arriving at the ultimate determination of core problems, try not to be "paralyzed by analysis" and waste more time than is necessary on identifying problems. At the same time, don't make premature judgments about problem areas because you might risk missing the "real" issues.

Always review the obtainable sources of data before moving to the next step. One general guideline is that when research and analysis cease to generate surprises, the analyst can feel relatively, though not absolutely, sure that adequate research has been conducted and the core problems have been identified.

The threat and opportunity discovery process should not become myopic. There may be a tendency on the part of individuals interested and experienced in accounting and finance to see all problems in terms of accounting and finance. A physician approaching the same case will likely focus on the medical implications. This is too limited a view for effective strategic decision makers. Strategic analysis is the work of "general managers" or those who effectively transcend a single function.

Successful case analysis depends on correctly identifying issues. Insistence on approaching case analysis exclusively from the viewpoint of one's own expertise and training is not likely to produce an accurate overall picture of the situation facing the organization, nor is this approach likely to improve the organization's performance.

Never accept information, either given or obtained, at face value. The ratios on a hospital's financial statements may look strange, but are they? Before jumping to such a conclusion, look at the financial ratios in a historical perspective. Even better, look at the history (as well as similar ratios) of other hospitals of the same nature during the same time period.

Identifying Important Issues

Once the problems are identified, they must be precisely stated and their selection defended. The best defense for the selection of the core problem is the data set used to guide the problem discovery process. The reasons for selection of the problems and issues should be briefly and specifically summarized along with the supportive information on which judgments have been based.

The problem statement stage is not the time for solutions. Focusing on solutions at this point will reduce the impact of the problem statement. If the role of consultant has been assumed, the problem statement must be convincing, precise, and logical to the client organization, or credibility will be reduced. If the role of the strategic decision maker has been selected, you must be equally convincing and precise. The strategic decision maker should be as sure as possible that the correct problems have been identified in order to pursue the appropriate opportunities. After all, the manager will be the one responsible for ensuring that the strategies are implemented.

The statement of the problem should relate only to those areas of strategy and operations where actions have a chance of producing results. The results may be either increasing gains or cutting potential losses. Long- and short-range aspects of problems should be identified and stated. In strategic analysis, the emphasis is on long-range problems rather than merely handling emergencies and holding things together.

It is important to keep in mind that most strategic decision makers can deal with only a limited number of issues at a single time. Therefore, identify key result areas that will have the greatest positive impact on organizational performance.

Analysis

After the problem(s) is satisfactorily defined, the case must be analyzed. This involves (1) developing a theoretical perspective, (2) generating alternative solutions or actions, and (3) evaluating the alternatives.

Developing a Theoretical Perspective

One of the most serious mistakes made in case analysis is to attempt analysis inside a "theoretical vacuum." Although strategic management is not highly theoretical compared to other areas of management, it is important that the problems be defined and opportunities be evaluated according to some consistent theoretical perspective.

Are the problems the kind that cash flow analysis can assist in solving? Are the strategic issues facing the firm problems of leadership, organization, or control? It might be that problems concerning lack of revenue growth are really problems of not responding adequately to patient needs—the lack of a marketing orientation. In the past, health care organizations have tended to disregard the importance of the "strategic decision" to focus on patients.

Many revenue shortfalls could be resolved with the use of the relatively simple marketing philosophy. A proper theoretical perspective, for example, might suggest that patients are less concerned with the location of a clinic than they are with how they are treated when they arrive.

Alternative Actions and Solutions

If the job of obtaining and organizing information has been done well, the generation of alternatives will be a challenging yet attainable task. To investigate options, the given and obtained information must be matched with what is known about financial analysis, statistics, marketing, and management so that actions that are promising, feasible, and consistent with the mission can be generated.

Good alternatives possess specific characteristics. They should be *practical* or no one will seriously consider them. Alternative courses of action that are too theoretical or abstract to be understood by those who have to accomplish them are not useful. Alternatives should be *carefully stated* with a brief justification as to why they could be used to solve at least one of the core problems in the case.

Alternatives should be *specific.* Relate each alternative to the core problem it is intended to address. This is a good check on your work. If the alternatives generated do not directly address core problems, ask how important they are to the case analysis.

Finally, alternatives should be *usable.* A usable alternative is one that can be reasonably accomplished within the constraints of the financial and human resources available to the organization. Alternatives should be ones that can be *placed into action* in a relatively short period of time. If it takes too long to implement a proposed solution, it is likely that the momentum of the recommended action will be lost. Of course, implementation should always take place in light of potential long-range effects of shorter-term decisions.

After the alternatives have been generated and listed, each one must be (1) evaluated in terms of the core problems and key result areas isolated in the prior analysis, (2) evaluated in terms of its relative advantage or disadvantage compared to other possible solutions to core problems, and (3) justified as a potentially valuable way of addressing the strategic issues found in the case.

Evaluating Alternatives

Alternatives should be evaluated according to both quantitative and qualitative criteria. Financial analysis provides one basis for examining the impact of different courses of action. However, a good alternative course of action is more than merely the one with the highest payoff. It may be that the culture of the organization cannot accommodate some of the more financially promising alternative courses of action.

For example, an established policy and practice in the organization may tolerate no more than a certain percentage of debt financing. Although the financial analysis illustrates that additional debt is a low-cost way to finance expansion, top management can be expected to reject the level of debt required, which will make other options necessary. On the more qualitative side, a hospital with a reputation for avoiding layoffs at all costs could be expected to reject any strategic alternative that involves closing part of the facility and reducing staff.

Once the alternatives have been evaluated, one must be selected. At this point it is *essential* to completely understand the criteria upon which the selection is being made and the justification for the criteria. Sometimes the key to identifying the criteria is in the case itself. The chief executive officer may have clearly stated the basis on which decisions are to be made.

At other times it is necessary to look outside to what is going on in the industry. Is competition for services so fierce that capital investment decisions are likely to radically affect our ability to compete with other organizations? If so, should the hospital intentionally postpone short-term actions to ensure sufficient resources are dedicated to the modernization of facilities and the purchase of up-to-date technologies to improve the chances of long-range growth and development?

Action Planning

Once the strategic alternative(s) has been selected, an action plan is required. Action planning moves the decision maker from the realm of strategy to operations. Now the question becomes, "How do we get all this done in the most effective and efficient way possible?"

The task of case analysis does not require that the student implement a decision in a real firm. However, because our alternatives must be "implementable," it is necessary that thought be given to how each alternative would actually be put into action. This is called *action planning* and requires three important steps for each recommended alternative. First, the decision maker must decide what activities are needed to accomplish the alternative action. This involves thinking through the process and outlining all the steps that will be required.

Next, the list of required activities should be carefully reviewed and tasks should be logically grouped. Those that relate to accounting go into one group, medical service delivery activities go into another, and financial activities go into a third. Each itemized activity must be placed into such a group, and any activities that do not fit neatly into the existing organization should be placed in another category of miscellaneous tasks. (Note that if this "other" list is too long, it may suggest that the structure of the organization needs revision.)

Finally, the responsibility for accomplishing the different groups of tasks must be clearly assigned to the appropriate individuals in the organization. Although this is not always possible in case analysis, it is important that consideration be given to how, in a real organization, the recommendations would be accomplished. If, in the process of thinking about getting the different activities completed, it becomes apparent that the organization lacks the resources or the structure to accomplish the recommendations, other approaches should be proposed.

The process of action planning should never be neglected. Organizations sometimes spend large amounts of money and resources developing strategic plans only to discover that they are not prepared to implement them in an effective manner.

Making Recommendations

Making good recommendations is a critical aspect of successful case analysis. If recommendations are theoretically sound and justifiable, people will pay attention to them. If they are not, little is likely to result from all the work done to this point.

One effective method for presenting recommendations is to relate each one to organizational strengths. Or, if necessary, a recommendation can illustrate how it assists in avoiding known weaknesses. If the organization has sufficient financial strength, the recommendations should highlight how each alternative will capitalize on the strong financial condition. If, on the other hand, the resources are limited, it will be important to avoid recommendations that rely on resources that are not available.

It will be particularly useful to ask the following questions when making recommendations:

1. Does the health care organization have the financial resources needed to make the recommendation work?
2. Does the organization have the personnel to accomplish what will be required by each recommendation?
3. Does the organization have the controls needed to monitor whether or not the recommendations are being accomplished?
4. Is the timing right to implement each recommendation? If not, when will the timing be right? Can the organization afford to wait?

Finalizing the Report

The preparation and presentation of the case report is the final part of case analysis. The report can be either written or oral depending on the preference of the instructor. Although the form is slightly different, the goal is the same—to summarize and communicate in an effective manner what the analysis has uncovered. This final section will provide only a brief outline of how to construct and present a case report. Appendix C deals with oral presentations in greater detail.

Decision making is the intended result of the report. The analysis must be complete; but the emphasis should be on making the entire report brief enough to encourage people to read it and comprehensive enough to ensure no major factors are overlooked that might adversely affect the decision. A brief outline of the important sections of a case analysis report follows.

Executive Summary

One of the most important things case analysis can teach prospective managers is how to organize and present ideas in a direct, concise, persuasive manner. Always keep in mind that the reader is a busy person who needs the essential facts about the case quickly. The executive summary (usually one page and rarely more than two pages) functions as an abstract. Its purpose is to force the writer to carefully evaluate what is really important in all the accumulated facts and data and to familiarize the reader with the organization and the industry.

The executive summary should clearly state the major problems and opportunities facing the organization. The outline of strategic issues should be followed by a list of recommendations and a brief justification for each. This summary will allow the reader to quickly see what has been done and understand the logic in the following report. In addition, it forces the analyst to think about the organization's problems and formulate recommendations in a direct manner, rather than hiding them away in the body of the case report.

Body of the Case Report

The body of the case analysis should be broken into several sections. The first section should report what you found in the *situational analysis.* What is the state of the organization today? What type of industry is it in, and what is happening with regard to the competition?

The *strategic problems* should be introduced after the situational analysis. In this section, the three to five most important strategic issues facing the firm should be listed and a justification provided for the inclusion of each. Consideration should also be given to the operational strengths and weaknesses inside the organization and how they relate to the basic strategic problems.

It is a particularly good practice when matching the strategic issues and the organization's strengths and weaknesses to think about the structure and the personnel. When the strategic issues are presented, it will be useful to outline them in terms of the functional areas of the organization most critical for the implementation of the recommendation. Therefore, the body of the report should include careful consideration of the production, financial, marketing, information processing, and human resources implications of the different recommended courses of action.

This final point is particularly important. All strategic actions must ultimately be accomplished by people. Therefore, the action plan for accomplishing recommendations should include an audit of the individual capabilities required to ensure the actions are taken. Who will be responsible for getting each of the recommendations accomplished? Is this individual likely to have the skills required to complete the task? If not, what actions will be necessary before the recommendation can be fully implemented?

In view of the strategic *problems* and the operational condition of the organization, the *alternatives* can now be generated and listed. Each of the alternatives can then be *evaluated.* When the evaluation is complete, the *recommendations* should be presented in considerable detail and particular attention should be given to the problem of *implementation.*

Finally, provide a list of sources that might be useful to decision makers so they can follow up on points made in the body of the report. Do not attempt to impress the professor with the length of the reading list used in compiling the references. To the contrary, find some very good sources that apply to the case analysis and list these valuable sources in a way that any reader who wishes to do so can follow up on them. It is particularly helpful to abstract the most useful sources. This will not do away with the reader's need to review the sources, but it will help him or her decide precisely which sources need to be read in greater detail.

Conclusions

Case analysis is an art. There is no one precise way to accomplish the task. Adapt the analysis to the case problem under review. The thing to keep in mind is that case analysis is a logical process that involves (1) understanding the organization, industry, and environment; (2) clearly defining strategic problems and opportunities; (3) generating alternative courses of action; (4) analyzing, evaluating, and recommending the most promising courses of action; (5) and providing at least some consideration of the operational aspects of how and by whom the recommendations will be accomplished.

The work of case analysis is not over until all these stages are completed. Often a formal written report or oral presentation of the recommendations is required. Case problems provide a unique opportunity to integrate all you have learned about decision making and direct it toward specific problems and opportunities faced by real organizations. It is an exciting way to gain experience and decision-making skills. Take it seriously and develop your own, systematic, and defensible way of solving management problems.

Notes

1. "Interview: Staying Alive," *Hospital and Health Networks* 70, no. 6 (March 20, 1996), pp. 38–39.
2. Peter F. Drucker, *Management: Tasks, Responsibilities, and Practices* (New York: Harper and Row, 1974).
3. John Pearce II and Fred David, "Corporate Mission Statements: The Bottom Line," *Academy of Management Executive* 1, no. 2 (May 1987), pp. 109–116.

Additional Sources of Interest

Barnes, Louis B., C. Roland Christiansen, and Abby J. Hansen, *Teaching and the Case Method*, 3d ed. (Boston: Harvard Business School Press), 1994.

Christiansen, C. Roland, and Abby J. Hansen, *Teaching and the Case Method*, (Boston: Harvard Business School Publishing Division), 1987.

Edge, Alfred G., and Denis R. Coleman, *The Guide to Case Analysis and Reporting*, 3d ed. (Honolulu: System Logic, 1986).

Ronstadt, Robert, *The Art of Case Analysis* (Dover, Massachusetts: Lord Publishing, 1980).

Financial Analysis for Health Care Organizations

by Mahmud Hassan

Appendix B

The purpose of this appendix is to explain some basic concepts of finance as they relate to health care. Finance in health care does not require a different methodology but it does occur in a different context. Unlike most other sectors of the economy, the health industry is composed of both for-profit and not-for-profit organizations. In addition, it is dependent on technology and is heavily regulated by the government. These special characteristics of the industry have prompted the development of innovative ways to survive and grow financially.

To analyze the financial health of a hospital, long-term-care, or other health care organization, you need to understand how to read the financial statements. The income statement and balance sheet are the two most important financial reports of an organization. Not-for-profit organizations do not produce income statements, but they may prepare balance sheets. In this appendix, we will compute financial ratios, net income, and other financial performances for Memorial Hospital, a for-profit hospital company, for the years 1995 and 1996. The detailed financial statements are available in the *Annual Report* of Memorial Hospital. Copies of these statements are shown in Exhibits B–1 and B–2 (the notes that accompany the statements can be found in the *Annual Report* and are an integral part of the financial statements).

As previously mentioned, not-for-profit organizations are not required to prepare balance sheets or income statements. However, some not-for-profit health care organizations do prepare balance sheets to satisfy requirements of the Securities and Exchange Commission (SEC) and the rating agencies (Moody's or Standard and Poor's) when they borrow money by selling bonds. For example, University Hospital (a not-for-profit organization) borrowed money in 1997 from the capital market by selling bonds. It had to prepare a balance sheet for three years, 1994 through 1996, to have its bonds rated. The balance sheet for University Hospital is shown in Exhibit B-3. Publicly traded for-profit hospitals are required by their charters to produce balance sheets and income statements each year. As mentioned earlier, we will analyze the financial statements of Memorial Hospital in this appendix.

The contents of balance sheets vary by company depending on the nature of the business and the type of ownership. Memorial Hospital's balance sheet contains some information regarding investments in subsidiaries, whereas the not-for-profit University Hospital reported a trust fund in its balance sheet. Not-for-profit organizations show their equity share as a fund balance. For University Hospital, the amount of equity

Exhibit B–1 • Memorial Hospital Consolidated Statement of Income (in thousands of dollars except per share amounts)

	1994	1995	1996
Revenues	$2,973,643	$3,435,397	$4,087,994
Operating expenses	2,340,178	2,786,230	3,401,884
Depreciation and amortization	180,197	195,651	209,469
Interest expense	154,156	145,938	138,477
Interest income	(30,923)	(46,064)	(60,570)
	2,643,608	3,081,755	3,689,260
Income before income taxes	330,035	353,642	398,734
Provision for income taxes	147,196	126,602	142,747
Income before extraordinary items and cumulative effect of a change in accounting principle	182,839	227,040	255,987
Extraordinary loss on early extinguishment of debt, net of income tax of $9,597	—	(16,133)	—
Cumulative effect on prior years of a change in accounting principle for retirement plan actuarial gains, net of income tax of $9,645	—	16,214	—
Net income	$182,839	$227,121	$255,987
Earnings per common share:			
Income before extraordinary item and cumulative effect of a change in accounting principle	$1.86	$2.30	$2.56
Extraordinary loss on early extinguishment of debt	—	(.16)	—
Cumulative effect on prior years of a change in accounting principle for retirement plan actuarial gains	—	.16	—
Net income per share	$ 1.86	$ 2.30	$ 2.56

investment in 1996 was over $185 million, as shown in Exhibit B–3 under "fund balance." All other items in Exhibit B–3 are comparable with those in Exhibit B–2.

Financial ratios for University Hospital can be computed using the same formulas as shown for Memorial Hospital, but some financial ratios will require information from income statements. Because not-for-profit hospitals do not prepare income statements, the ratios for days in accounts receivable, average payment period, days' cash on hand, times interest earned, debt service coverage, operating margin, markup, return on assets, and so on cannot be computed for University Hospital.

In addition to the analysis of the income statement and balance sheet, we have provided an analysis of the cost of capital. This is an important topic for the health care industry because of its dependence on technology and because of reimbursement issues involving third-party payors.

The Income Statement

Income statements are prepared by proprietary hospitals for the computation of net profit and incurred tax. (A not-for-profit hospital is not required to prepare an income statement but it may choose to do so to keep its various constituencies informed. The IRS does require "informational reports" to be filed for not-for-profit organizations generating over $25,000 in revenue.)

Exhibit B–2 · Memorial Hospital Consolidated Balance Sheet (in thousands of dollars except per share amounts)

	1995	1996
Assets		
Current assets		
Cash and cash equivalents	$140,202	$105,340
Marketable securities	106,490	79,104
Accounts receivable less allowance for loss of $157,505–1996 and $110,909–1995	507,141	616,210
Inventories	69,786	80,632
Other current assets	104,788	133,615
Total current assets	928,407	1,014,901
Property and equipment, at cost		
Land	168,761	177,275
Buildings	1,678,685	1,759,959
Equipment	1,086,374	1,211,401
Construction in progress (estimated cost to complete and equip after August 31, 1996–$114,000)	41,729	57,719
Gross fixed assets	2,975,549	3,206,354
Less accumulated depreciation	987,790	1,154,868
Net fixed assets	1,987,759	2,051,486
Investments of insurance and health plan subsidiaries	315,875	462,541
Other assets	189,921	167,646
Total assets	$3,421,962	$3,696,574
Liabilities and common stockholders' equity		
Current liabilities		
Trade accounts payable	$107,666	$115,338
Salaries, wages, and other compensation	82,184	95,760
Other accrued expenses	173,956	229,201
Medical claims reserves	141,773	194,925
Income taxes	95,475	106,241
Long-term debt due within one year	32,680	35,045
Total current liabilities	633,734	776,510
Long-term debt	1,210,618	1,140,366
Deferred credits and other liabilities	422,993	452,722
Common stockholders' equity		
Common stock, 16 2/3¢ par; authorized 200 million shares; issued and outstanding 98,438,852 shares–1996 and 97,886,147 shares–1995	16,314	16,406
Capital in excess of par value	233,898	243,398
Other adjustments	(11,047)	(11,029)
Retained earnings	915,452	1,078,201
Stockholders' equity	1,154,617	1,326,976
Total liabilities and stockholders' equity	$3,421,962	$3,696,574

Exhibit B–3 • University Hospital Balance Sheet

	Fiscal Year Ended September 30		
	1994	1995	1996
Assets			
Current assets			
Cash and short-term investments	$ 5,768,785	$ 7,184,131	$ 2,084,610
Accounts receivable	51,415,071	40,085,497	53,338,410
Inventory	1,518,012	2,097,327	2,677,247
Prepaid expenses and other current assets	6,971	0	0
Total current assets	58,708,839	49,366,955	58,100,267
Property, plant, and equipment	171,270,793	197,572,904	212,140,823
Less accumulated depreciation	61,175,801	72,626,040	85,433,535
Net property, plant, and equipment	110,094,992	124,946,864	126,707,288
Capital fund	23,233,852	26,730,346	20,657,000
Trustee funds	6,992,981	6,731,182	7,034,719
Total assets	$199,030,664	$207,775,347	$212,499,274
Liabilities and fund balance			
Current liabilities			
Accounts payable	$2,684,893	$3,911,504	$2,638,836
Accrued salaries	462,326	663,161	1,084,692
Advances from third-party payors	1,051,000	0	0
Deferred revenue	61,561	85,554	85,554
Current portion of long-term debt	2,022,140	2,068,744	1,659,565
Other current liabilities	69,623	17,038	561,853
Accrued interest expense	983,277	805,688	768,511
Total current liabilities	7,334,820	7,551,689	6,799,011
Long-term debt	21,792,410	21,525,786	19,866,221
Fund balance	169,903,434	178,697,872	185,834,042
Total liabilities and fund balance	$199,030,664	$207,775,347	$212,499,274

The income statement shows all revenue receipts and expenditures during a year. Receipts are usually shown as gross revenue and net revenue. Net revenue is equal to gross revenue minus any uncollectibles such as contractual allowances, bad debt, charity care, and business discounts. In the case of Memorial, the net revenue for 1996 was (all figures for Memorial are in thousands of dollars):

Net revenue: $4,087,994

Memorial does not report gross revenue or uncollectibles.

Operating expenses represent selling, general, and administrative expenses.

Operating expense: $3,401,884

Depreciation and amortization are noncash expenses (there is no cash payment for these items, but a company uses them as expense items to compute taxable income) due to wear and tear or decline in the useful life of an asset. Depreciation can be on a straight-line basis or an accelerated basis. For straight-line depreciation, the assumption is that there will be equal wear and tear on the asset each year of its useful life. Accelerated depreciation assumes the wear and tear is high during initial years and declines over time.

Depreciation and amortization:	$209,469

Interest expense is the amount paid to creditors on the total amount of debt the organization holds.

Interest expense:	$138,477

Interest income is computed by subtracting dividends and capital gains from the investment income. In the case of Memorial, this amount is a positive quantity for 1996 and hence entered as a negative quantity in the expense category (see Exhibit B–1).

Interest income:	$60,570

Income before income taxes can be computed by subtracting operating expense, depreciation, amortization, interest expense, and interest income from net revenue.

Income before income taxes:	$398,734

Provision for state and federal taxes is computed at the statutory rate (35.8 percent for Memorial) on the income before income taxes.

Provision for income taxes:	$142,747

Net income is computed by subtracting provision for income taxes and other adjustments from the income before taxes.

Net income:	$255,987

The Balance Sheet

A balance sheet is a statement of the financial status of an organization at a particular point in time (date). It is divided into two sides: assets are shown on the left side and liabilities and owners' equity are shown on the right side. Assets are divided into current assets and fixed assets. Current assets include cash, marketable securities, accounts receivable (less uncollectibles), inventories, and other current assets. Marketable securities are short-term government securities. Other current assets include prepaid expenses such as insurance premiums, advertising charges for the next year, and so on.

In the case of Memorial in 1996:

Cash and cash equivalents:	$105,340
Marketable securities:	79,104
Accounts receivable less uncollectibles:	616,210
Inventories:	80,632
Other current assets:	133,615
Total current assets:	$1,014,901

In this case, cash equivalents include investments in securities with a maturity of three months or less. Fixed assets are land, buildings, equipment, and construction in progress.

Land:	$177,275
Buildings:	1,759,959
Equipment:	1,211,401
Construction in progress:	57,719
Gross fixed assets:	$3,206,354

Accumulated depreciation is the sum of all the depreciation expenses (as found in the income statement) since the inception of the organization.

Accumulated depreciation:	$1,154,868

Net fixed assets are computed by subtracting the accumulated depreciation from the gross fixed assets.

Net fixed assets:	$2,051,486

Memorial shows investments in its subsidiaries in a separate category:

Investments in health plan subsidiaries:	$462,541
Other assets:	167,646
Total assets:	$3,696,574

On the other side of the balance sheet, liabilities include current liabilities, long-term liabilities, and other liabilities. Current liabilities are accounts payable, salaries, wages and other compensation payable, other accrued expenses, medical claim reserve, income taxes payable, and that portion of long-term debt due within one year. Other accrued expenses include any other unpaid amounts. Medical claim reserves include outstanding claims from Memorial's insurance business.

Total current liabilities:	$776,510

All debts not due within one year are listed under long-term debt.

Long-term debt:	$1,140,366

Owners' equity includes the value of common stock outstanding (at par value), the value of the stocks in excess of par value, other adjustments in the value of stocks, and retained earnings. For not-for-profit hospitals, the owners' equity is represented by a fund balance. Retained earnings are the accumulated net income minus the amount of the dividends paid to shareholders.

Owners' equity:	$1,326,976

Financial Ratios

Thus far, different items on Memorial's income statement and balance sheet have been explained. Now we can proceed with the computation of different financial ratios that are used to evaluate the financial health of an organization. The four types of financial ratios usually computed are liquidity ratios, capital structure ratios, activity ratios, and profitability ratios.

Liquidity ratios consist of different measures of liquidity (how rapidly a noncash asset can be converted into cash without losing its value) and the cash position of an organization; capital structure ratios include measures of leverage (the amount borrowed compared to the amount invested by owners) and equity (investment or ownership). Different types of efficiency measures are included in the activity ratios, and a variety of profitability measures (the extent to which income exceeds expenses) are included in the profitability ratios. Each of these four types of ratios are computed and described. The first example is for 1996, and the second example is for 1995.

Liquidity Ratios*

Current Ratio

$$\frac{\text{current assets}}{\text{current liabilities}} = \text{current ratio}$$

$$\frac{1,014,901}{776,510} = 1.31$$

$$\frac{928,407}{633,734} = 1.46$$

Current ratio is one of the most widely used financial ratios. It represents the firm's ability to pay current financial obligations out of current assets. A higher value of current ratio is better than a lower value. A value of 1.31 in 1996 means that for every dollar of current liability, Memorial has $1.31 in current assets. The value declined from 1.46 in 1995. This means that Memorial's liquidity (ability to pay financial claims) deteriorated in 1996. It is possible for a firm with a high current ratio to experience payment problems if its current assets are not available in liquid form (cash or short-term investments) in time to meet the current obligations. A large current ratio may also imply idle cash, too much investment in inventory, or bad collection policies resulting in large accounts receivable. To verify the possibility that a high current ratio may indicate overinvestment in current assets or a high number of days in accounts receivable, the current-asset turnover and inventory ratios should be analyzed. Hospitals with low current ratios can reduce the probability of short-term liquidity problems by carrying larger balances of liquid assets.

Quick Ratio

$$\frac{\text{current assets} - \text{inventory}}{\text{current liabilities}} = \text{quick ratio}$$

$$\frac{1,014,901 - 80,632}{776,510} = 1.20$$

$$\frac{928,407 - 69,786}{633,734} = 1.35$$

*In thousands of dollars except for ratios.

The quick ratio is a more stringent test of liquidity than the current ratio. A higher quick ratio implies a better liquidity position for the organization. However, because it includes accounts receivable, a high value could indicate a bad collection policy, and a low quick ratio is not necessarily indicative of a future liquidity problem. For example, a large accounts payable (due to construction) might result in a lower quick ratio, but the construction accounts payable does not require payment from the current assets. It is paid out of construction-in-progress assets. In the case of Memorial, the quick ratio declined from 1.35 in 1995 to 1.20 in 1996. This says that Memorial can pay off its current liabilities from its current assets without liquidating inventory, even though the quick ratio declined between 1995 and 1996.

Acid Test Ratio

$$\frac{\text{cash plus marketable securities}}{\text{current liabilities}} = \text{acid test ratio}$$

$$\frac{105,340 + 79,104}{776,510} = 0.24$$

$$\frac{140,202 + 106,490}{633,734} = 0.39$$

The acid test ratio is the most stringent test of liquidity. It measures the firm's ability to pay its current liabilities out of cash and marketable securities only. A high value is a good indication of a favorable liquidity position, although a very high value may imply too much idle cash and inefficient investment-portfolio management. The primary source of funds for paying current liabilities is usually collections from accounts receivable. Firms with large variances in collection of accounts receivable should maintain higher levels of cash and short-term investments, which would result in a higher acid test ratio. Memorial's acid test ratio declined from 0.39 in 1995 to 0.24 in 1996. This means that in 1996 Memorial could pay off $0.24 of every dollar of its current liabilities from its cash and marketable securities. An increase in the quick ratio and a decrease in the acid test ratio indicate an increase in the days in the accounts receivable ratio.

Days in Accounts Receivable (A/R) Ratio

$$\frac{\text{net accounts receivable}}{\text{net revenue}} \times 365 = \text{days in A/R ratio}$$

$$\frac{616,210}{4,087,994} \times 365 = 55.02$$

$$\frac{507,141}{3,435,397} \times 365 = 53.88$$

This ratio represents the average collection period. The value for this ratio provides a measure of the average time that receivables are outstanding. A value of 55 in 1996 implies that a patient discharged from Memorial Hospital pays the bill on the 55th day from the date of his or her discharge. High values imply a longer collection period and thus a greater sum in accounts receivable. An increase in the number of days in the collection period may result in a shortage of cash. The short-term solution would be to borrow or to liquidate a part of the investment portfolio. A continuing increase in the collection period would require an increase in operating margin or equity financing. To reduce the A/R collection period, the health care organization might improve management of the business office and improve third-party payor relationships.

Average Payment Period Ratio

$$\frac{\text{current liabilities}}{\text{operating expenses} - \text{depreciation}} \times 365 = \text{average payment period ratio}$$

$$\frac{776,510}{3,401,884 - 209,469} \times 365 = 88.78$$

$$\frac{633,734}{2,786,230 - 195,651} \times 365 = 89.29$$

The average payment period ratio is the counterpart to the days in accounts receivable ratio. The average payment period provides a measure of the average time that elapses before current liabilities are paid. A high value for this ratio indicates a liquidity problem. Low values for this ratio may not always imply a good liquidity position; they might simply be due to a change in policy. For example, changing payroll from biweekly payments to weekly payments will decrease the value for this ratio. A very low value for this ratio might also indicate poor cash management, including poor investment-portfolio management. In both 1995 and 1996, Memorial took about 89 days to pay off its current liabilities.

Days' Cash-on-Hand Ratio

$$\frac{\text{cash} + \text{marketable securities}}{\text{operating expenses} - \text{depreciation}} \times 365 = \text{days' cash-on-hand ratio}$$

$$\frac{105,340 + 79,104}{3,401,884 - 209,469} \times 365 = 21.09$$

$$\frac{140,202 + 106,490}{2,786,230 - 195,651} \times 365 = 34.76$$

Days' cash-on-hand ratio measures the number of days of average cash expenses that a firm maintains in cash and marketable securities. A high value for this ratio implies a greater ability to meet short-term financial obligations. However, high values for the days' cash-on-hand ratio are not always in the best interest of the organization. They may imply overinvestment in liquid assets that have a very low rate of return.

An increase in days in the accounts receivable ratio may be associated with a reduction in the days' cash-on-hand ratio. If the increase in days in the accounts receivable ratio is permanent, some alternative financing may be necessary. In 1996, Memorial had 21 days of operating expenses in cash and marketable securities.

Capital Structure Ratios

Equity Ratio

$$\frac{\text{fund balance or stockholders' equity}}{\text{total assets}} = \text{equity ratio}$$

$$\frac{1,326,976}{3,696,574} = 0.36$$

$$\frac{1,154,617}{3,421,962} = 0.34$$

The equity ratio measures the proportion of total assets that have been financed with equity. High values for this ratio imply that a greater amount of equity relative to debt has been used to finance the total assets. Creditors usually consider this a sign of good financial health because it means less debt and therefore less likelihood of insolvency. A high equity ratio does not always imply solvency. Poor profitability may result in a cash-flow problem that weakens the liquidity position. Equity financing of 100 percent is not desirable because it increases the cost of capital. In practice, some mix of debt and equity is used to finance an organization's total assets. In 1996, Memorial invested $0.36 of its own funds in every dollar of total assets. The remaining $0.64 came from borrowed funds.

Long-Term Debt-to-Equity Ratio

$$\frac{\text{long-term debt}}{\text{fund balance or stockholders' equity}} = \text{long-term debt-to-equity ratio}$$

$$\frac{1,140,366}{1,326,976} = 0.86$$

$$\frac{1,210,618}{1,154,617} = 1.05$$

Long-term debt and equity are permanent capital because they are not repaid within one year. A higher ratio implies a greater amount of external capital in the form of debt relative to equity. This is viewed unfavorably by creditors, although a high long-term debt-to-equity ratio may not prohibit future debt financing (nor does a low ratio guarantee a favorable credit line). The ability to repay debt, rather than the amount of debt, is the important issue. A high long-term debt-to-equity ratio can be risky for an organization if it has high and stable values for debt service coverage (loan payments) and low times-interest-earned ratios. In 1996, Memorial had $0.86 in long-term debt for every dollar of its own fund. The value had declined somewhat in 1996 from $1.05 in 1995. This is an indication of a more favorable financial condition for Memorial in 1996.

Fixed-Asset Financing Ratio

$$\frac{\text{long-term debt}}{\text{net fixed assets}} = \text{fixed-asset financing ratio}$$

$$\frac{1,140,366}{2,051,486} = 0.56$$

$$\frac{1,210,618}{1,987,759} = 0.61$$

The fixed-asset financing ratio measures the extent of long-term debt invested in fixed assets. A high value is considered by creditors to be an indicator of future debt repayment problems. The numerator of the ratio represents a future demand for cash and the denominator is the source to generate that cash in the form of depreciation charges. In 1996, 56 percent of Memorial's net fixed assets were funded by long-term debt.

High values for the fixed-asset financing ratio are associated with low equity financing and high long-term debt-to-equity ratios. The risk of insolvency due to a high value of the fixed-asset ratio can be partially offset by achieving high values for the times-interest-earned and the high debt service coverage ratios.

Times-Interest-Earned Ratio

$$\frac{\text{excess of revenues over expenses} + \text{interest expense}}{\text{interest expense}} = \text{times-interest-earned ratio}$$

$$\frac{686,110 + 138,477}{138,477} = 5.95$$

$$\frac{649,167 + 145,938}{145,938} = 5.45$$

The times-interest-earned ratio measures the ability of a firm to pay its interest expense obligation. The higher the value, the better the financial ability of the firm to pay its interest obligation. Note that this ratio does not measure the ability of the firm to repay the principal. Therefore, it is important to consider both the times-interest-earned and debt service coverage ratios when evaluating a firm's ability to pay its total debt obligation (interest expense plus principal payment).

Debt Service Coverage Ratio

$$\frac{\text{excess of revenues over expenses} + \text{depreciation} + \text{interest}}{\text{principal payment} + \text{interest expense}} = \text{debt service coverage ratio}$$

$$\frac{686,110 + 209,469 + 138,477}{63,980 + 138,477} = 5.11$$

$$\frac{649,167 + 195,651 + 145,938}{256,387 + 145,938} = 2.46$$

(*Note:* Principal payments for 1996 and 1995, respectively, are $63,980 and $256,387. These are not shown in the financial statements here but are provided in the detailed cash-flow statements of Memorial's 1996 *Annual Report.*)

The debt service coverage ratio measures the firm's ability to pay its total debt obligation (both interest and principal). High values are considered favorably by creditors. However, this interpretation could be misleading in some cases, especially in the early years of a capital-expansion program when debt principal is not yet due but the depreciation expense has started. In this situation, the times-interest-earned and the fixed-asset financing ratios are better measures of the debt repayment ability of a firm.

It is important to maintain a high debt service coverage when new debt financing is being considered. The ability to attract debt capital with favorable terms may be related to past debt service coverage ratios.

Activity Ratios

Asset Turnover Ratio

$$\frac{\text{total revenue}}{\text{total assets}} = \text{asset turnover ratio}$$

$$\frac{4,087,994}{3,696,574} = 1.11$$

$$\frac{3,435,397}{3,421,962} = 1.00$$

The asset turnover ratio measures the dollar amount of revenue generated per dollar of investment. This is a measure of efficiency. Higher values for this ratio imply better usage of the available resources. In 1996, Memorial generated $1.11 in revenue for every dollar invested in assets. This ratio should not be the only criterion of efficiency because the age of the plant affects this ratio rather significantly. As the plant gets older, the book value of the asset, net of depreciation, gets smaller, resulting in a higher asset turnover ratio. The point is that the age of the plant needs to be considered when analyzing asset turnover ratios.

Fixed-Asset Turnover Ratio

$$\frac{\text{total revenue}}{\text{net fixed assets}} = \text{fixed-asset turnover ratio}$$

$$\frac{4,087,994}{2,051,486} = 1.99$$

$$\frac{3,435,397}{1,987,759} = 1.73$$

This ratio computes dollars of revenue generated for each dollar of investment in fixed assets. The items included in fixed assets are land, buildings, equipment, and furniture. It represents those assets not intended for sale that are used over and over again to provide the services of the hospital or other health care organization. High values for the fixed-asset turnover ratio are usually regarded as a positive indication of operating efficiency.

The fixed-asset turnover ratio is also likely to be affected by the age of the plant, as in the case of the asset-turnover ratio. The fixed-asset turnover ratio decreases immediately after an expansion or replacement program.

Current-Asset Turnover Ratio

$$\frac{\text{total revenue}}{\text{current assets}} = \text{current-asset turnover ratio}$$

$$\frac{4,087,994}{1,014,901} = 4.03$$

$$\frac{3,435,397}{928,407} = 3.70$$

The current-asset turnover ratio measures the dollars of revenue generated per dollar of investment in current assets. The lower the investment in current assets and the higher the current-asset turnover ratio, the more efficient the organization. This does not imply that the investment in current assets should be cut to a minimum; that would cause delivery of services to be impaired, which would create severe short-term operating problems.

A high value for the current-asset turnover ratio is better than a low value, but a lower value might be the result of an expansion program during which the hospital holds more liquid assets. A low or high value for the current-asset turnover ratio can be further investigated and diagnosed by analyzing the days' cash-on-hand ratio, the days in accounts receivable ratio, and the inventory turnover ratio.

Inventory Turnover Ratio

$$\frac{\text{total revenue}}{\text{inventory}} = \text{inventory turnover ratio}$$

$$\frac{4,087,994}{80,632} = 50.70$$

$$\frac{3,435,397}{69,786} = 49.23$$

An inventory turnover ratio measures the dollars of revenue generated per dollar of investment in inventory. A higher value for this ratio indicates operating efficiency because the organization is not tying up a lot of money in inventory. Customer service (being out-of-stock) is not considered, however.

A hospital using just-in-time (JIT) inventory management would have a high inventory turnover ratio. Other reasons for low investment in inventory (resulting in a high inventory turnover ratio) include geographic location, access to suppliers, unavailability of quantity discounts, and so on.

Profitability Ratios

Deductible Ratio

$$\frac{\text{gross revenue} - \text{net revenue}}{\text{gross revenue}} = \text{deductible ratio}$$

(*Note:* Memorial does not report gross revenue.)

The deductible ratio measures the proportion of gross revenue that is not expected to be realized due to contractual allowances, bad debts, charity care, volume discounts, and so on. In the hospital industry, this ratio is very important because of the widespread presence of contractual allowances for insurers, HMOs, PPOs, and charity care to indigent patients. From a profitability point of view, increasing values of the deductible ratio result in lower profitability. A high deductible ratio may not imply poor profitability if the organization has a high markup or a large amount of nonoperating revenue (philanthropic donations).

The deductible ratio should be closely monitored against changes in the collection process, reimbursement management, or the organization's charity-care policy.

Markup Ratio

$$\frac{\text{gross revenue}}{\text{operating expenses}} = \text{markup ratio}$$

(*Note:* Memorial does not report gross revenue.)

The markup ratio measures the multiples by which prices are set above expenses. Higher numbers for this ratio imply a higher price per dollar of expenses and the likelihood of achieving greater profitability. If a high markup ratio is associated with a high deductible ratio, then the hospital may not be any better off. Hospitals with relatively old plants and a high debt-to-principal payment schedule may need to maintain relatively high markup ratios. However, if markups are too high, the hospital may lose patients and eventually become insolvent. If it is too low, then the hospital may also become insolvent. The markup ratio is directly related to the operating margin ratio, the return on total asset ratio, the return on equity ratio, the debt service coverage ratio, and the times-interest-earned ratio. An increase in prices may improve profitability; but depending on the third-party payor mix, it may also increase the deductible ratio, driving profitability downward.

Operating Margin Ratio

$$\frac{\text{net income}}{\text{total revenue}} = \text{operating margin ratio}$$

$$\frac{255,987}{4,087,994} = 0.06$$

$$\frac{277,040}{3,435,397} = 0.07$$

This ratio is a measure of profitability. Net income is before any extraordinary items. Alternative measures of profitability include return on total assets or return on equity. A low operating margin is not necessarily an indication of poor profitability if the hospital has significant nonoperating revenue from investment income, philanthropic donations, or any other sources. Improvement in the operating margin usually results in higher working capital, which in turn improves liquidity ratios.

Operating Margin Price-Level Adjusted Ratio

$$\frac{\text{net income} + \text{depreciation} - \text{price-level depreciation}}{\text{total revenue}} = \text{operating margin price-level adjusted ratio}$$

$$\frac{255,987 + 209,469 - 242,984}{4,087,994} = 0.05$$

$$\frac{277,040 + 195,651 - 219,129}{3,435,397} = 0.06$$

(*Note:* The age of the plant in 1996, as computed earlier, is six years. This indicates that investments in plant assets were made in 1990. Price-level depreciation is defined as the amount of annual depreciation expressed in the year of the investment. In this case, because the investments were made in 1990, the annual depreciation for 1995 and 1996 should be expressed in 1990 dollars. Assume the purchasing power of the dollar declined to 0.88 and 0.84 in 1995 and 1996, respectively, using 1990 as the reference year. Thus, a dollar in 1990 is worth only $0.88 in 1995 and $0.84 in 1996 due to inflation. The Consumer Price Index (CPI) for 1995 and 1996 was 1.12 and 1.16, respectively, using 1990 as the reference (base) year. The price-level depreciation for 1995 and 1996 is computed as the product of annual depreciation expenses and the CPI of each year.)

This ratio is the same as the operating margin ratio except the depreciation expenses are adjusted for inflation. When equipment is purchased, a depreciation schedule is developed that identifies the future deductions from the operating revenue for the depreciation expense. The dollar values posted are based on the year the equipment was acquired. Because of inflation, those posted dollar values can be worth less than the original estimate. Therefore, the operating margin should be computed to reflect the inflation-adjusted depreciation, not the originally estimated depreciation.

Higher inflation translates into higher inflation-adjusted depreciation, and hence the lower the operating margin in the price-level adjusted ratio. In 1996, Memorial's operating margin ratio was 6 percent; but after the depreciation expense was adjusted for inflation, the operating margin dropped to 5 percent.

Return on Total Assets (ROA)

$$\frac{\text{net income}}{\text{total assets}} = \text{return on total assets}$$

$$\frac{255{,}987}{3{,}696{,}574} = 0.07$$

$$\frac{277{,}040}{3{,}421{,}962} = 0.07$$

The return on total assets measures the amount of net income earned per dollar of investment in total assets. It is a measure of profitability. This ratio is affected by the age of the plant. A hospital with a relatively old and largely depreciated plant may show a higher return on assets ratio. If the hospital is planning a major replacement, this high profit rate may be misleading for creditors.

Return on Equity (ROE)

$$\frac{\text{net income}}{\text{fund balance or shareholders' equity}} = \text{return on equity}$$

$$\frac{255{,}987}{1{,}326{,}976} = 0.19$$

$$\frac{277{,}040}{1{,}154{,}617} = 0.20$$

This ratio, similar to the return on assets ratio, measures the extent of profitability but uses return on equity investment instead of total assets. Many analysts consider the return on equity as the primary test of profitability. Unless a satisfactory return on equity is generated, the hospital may find it very difficult to raise future equity capital by selling new shares. Not-for-profit hospitals may not be very interested in analyzing this ratio.

A high return on equity may not imply sound financial health, because the organization might have huge debt and earned the profit on monthly debt-financed (leased) assets. Further analysis of the return on equity ratio compared to the return on assets ratio would indicate the effect of debt-financed assets. If replacement needs are expected to be financed from operating income, the return on total assets ratio may be a better indicator of profitability than the return on equity ratio.

Other Financial Information

Age of the Facility

$$\frac{\text{accumulated depreciation}}{\text{depreciation expense}} = \text{age of the facility}$$

$$\frac{1,154,868}{209,469} = 5.51$$

$$\frac{987,790}{195,651} = 5.05$$

This is a very crude formula to estimate the age of the plant in years. This measure is more reliable if straight-line rather than accelerated depreciation is used. With the accelerated depreciation method, this formula tends to underestimate the age of newer plants and overestimate the age of older plants. When inflation is occurring, the formula underestimates the age of the plant because the annual depreciation expense increases with inflation.

Working Capital

$$\text{current assets} + \text{current liabilities} = \text{working capital}$$

$$\$1,014,901 + 776,510 = \$1,791,411$$

$$\$928,407 + 663,734 = \$1,592,141$$

The amount of working capital, defined as current assets plus current liabilities, is very important for an organization in its day-to-day operations. An organization's liquidity depends on the amount of working capital.

Net Working Capital

$$\text{current assets} - \text{current liabilities} = \text{net working capital}$$

$$\$1,014,901 - 776,510 = \$238,391$$

$$\$928,407 - 663,734 = \$294,673$$

Many analysts want to find out the net liquidity position (net working capital) of an organization. Net liquidity is computed by subtracting current liabilities from the current assets. If the organization were to pay its current obligations (current liabilities), how much working capital would be left? The answer is the net working capital.

The duPont System

Return on assets can be increased by a higher profit margin or higher asset turnover. To observe the dominant factors in return on assets, some analysts compute return on assets as the product of profit margin and asset turnover. Recall that the profit margin or operating margin ratio was computed as net income divided by total revenue and the asset turnover ratio was defined as total revenue divided by total assets. This can be written:

$$\text{return on assets}_{(\text{duPont})} = \frac{\text{net income}}{\text{total revenue}} \times \frac{\text{total revenue}}{\text{total asset}}$$

The return on assets computed in this manner is called the *duPont System* because it was developed by the duPont Company. This ratio can also be used to compute return on investment (ROI).

In the case of Memorial, the ROI using the duPont System for 1995 and 1996 were:

$$1995_{(\text{duPont})} \frac{227,040}{3,435,397} \times \frac{3,435,397}{3,421,962} = 0.07$$

$$1996_{(\text{duPont})} \frac{255,987}{4,087,994} \times \frac{4,087,994}{3,696,574} = 0.07$$

Limitations of Ratio Analysis

The financial ratios we have discussed provide valuable information concerning the financial health of an organization. We computed different ratios for Memorial for two consecutive years, which indicates changes in financial performance by the organization. However, every ratio can also be compared with national or regional averages that are available annually from the Financial Analysis Service (FAS) of the Healthcare Financial Management Association (HFMA). These national or regional averages are called the *standards* of the industry. An individual hospital's ratios are compared with these standards and financial performances are evaluated. If a hospital is older or newer than the rest of the hospitals in the region, then comparing its financial ratios with the regional averages is not quite as meaningful. Financial ratios reflect the activities of the organization in the past year or years. However, financial ratios do not reflect strategic planning by the hospital. It is possible that a hospital is going through a structural change to achieve future benefits, which would affect many of the ratios. Thus, the long-term planning of the hospital must be considered as well as the financial ratios. Using financial ratios alone may give the wrong signal to analysts.

The presence of severe inflation in the early or later years of a trend analysis makes the analysis less reliable. *Values* for the financial ratios also depend on the accounting practices and policies of the organization. For example, the value of investment in inventory depends on the valuation policies of the organization (first in, first out or last in, first out), the depreciation policies (straight-line or accelerated), which in turn determine the value of net assets, and so on. To the extent these policies vary, financial ratios will also vary.

Cost of Capital

When hospitals borrow money, they have to pay interest on the debt. If a hospital chooses to use its own funds for the acquisition or replacement of an asset, an opportunity cost is associated with that decision, called the *cost of equity*. In many cases, some combination of debt and equity is used to finance a capital investment. The weighted average cost of capital (WACC) is derived as an average cost of debt (k_d) and cost of equity (k_e). (A numerical example follows later in the section.)

$$\text{WACC} = Dk_d + (1-D)k_e$$

where D is the ratio of debt to assets.

Some insurers reimburse hospitals on a cost basis so that a portion of the cost of debt (k_d) is considered a pass-through. Assuming M is the proportion of cost-based reimbursement, the cost of debt is $(1 - M)k_d$. Some insurers pay on a cost-plus basis to for-profit hospitals where the payment above the cost represents some agreed upon (or at least known) return on equity. For-profit hospitals pay taxes on income at the current tax rate (t_c). Interest payments by for-profit hospitals work as a tax shield because tax liability decreases with an increase in interest payments. However, for-profit organizations have to pay taxes on any return they earn on their equity investment. Assuming k_e^m as the return on equity and m' as the proportion from the payor that uses the cost-plus basis, then the WACC for not-for-profit (np) and for-profit (fp) can be written as:

$$\text{WACC}_{\text{np}} = D(1-M)k_d + (1-D)k_e$$
$$\text{WACC}_{\text{fp}} = D(1-M)(1-t_c)k_d + (1-D)(k_e - m'[1-t_c]k_e^m)$$

Cost of Debt

To compute the cost of debt (k_d), data must be collected on the types and amount of debt and the corresponding interest rates for different hospitals over several years. For each year, a weighted average cost of debt can be computed using the individual debt information. Assume that the cost of debt (k_d) for not-for-profit and for-profit hospitals in 1996 is 5.4 percent and 7.5 percent, respectively. Further assume that the proportion of payors who pay cost-based reimbursement (M) are 10 percent and 8 percent for not-for-profit and for-profit hospitals, respectively. The effective corporate tax rate (t_c) for the for-profit hospitals in 1996 is assumed to be 22 percent.

The cost of debt for the not-for-profit and for-profit hospitals can then be computed as:

$$\text{Not-for-profit cost of debt} = (1 - M)k_d$$
$$= (1 - 0.10)5.4$$
$$= 4.86 \text{ percent}$$
$$\text{For-profit cost of debt} = (1 - M)(1 - t_c)k_d$$
$$= (1 - 0.08)(1 - 0.22)7.5$$
$$= 5.38 \text{ percent}$$

The cost of debt is usually available from the for-profit hospital's annual reports. The cost of debt for not-for-profit hospitals is usually lower than for the for-profit hospitals. The reason is that the not-for-profit hospitals use tax-exempt revenue bonds to borrow money from the capital market.

Cost of Equity

Cost of equity can be estimated using the capital asset pricing model (CAPM). The expected rate of return on the share of equity i, $E(R_i)$, depends on the expected return on a market portfolio $E(R_m)$ and a risk-free bond rate R_f. Specifically,

$$E(R_i) = R_f + \beta_i[E(R_m) - R_f]$$
$$\text{where } \beta_i = \text{Cov}(R_i, R_m)/\text{Var}(R_m).$$

The expected rate of return on the share of i is the sum of the risk-free rate of return plus a risk premium. To compute the risk premium, $\beta_i[E(R_m) - R_i]$, we need an estimate of β_i for the hospital industry. Assume the β_i of the for-profit and not-for-profit hospitals is 1.41 and 1.46, respectively. Value Line estimates β of different companies on a periodic basis. The rate of return of the efficient market portfolio $E(R_m)$ and the risk-free rate of return R_f for 1996 are assumed to be 8.5 percent and 5.4 percent, respectively. These rates of return are available in the University of Chicago's Center for Research in Security Prices (CRSP) files.

Now, applying the CAPM equations, we can estimate the cost of equity for 1996 as:

$$\text{For-profit } E(R_i) = 5.4 + 1.41\,(8.5 - 5.4)$$
$$= 9.77 \text{ percent}$$
$$\text{Not-for-profit } E(R_i) = 5.4 + 1.46\,(8.5 - 5.4)$$
$$= 9.93 \text{ percent}$$

Note that cost of equity is greater than cost of debt. This makes sense because equity holders are residual claimants of the property in the case of bankruptcy. They take more risks; hence, the cost of equity is greater than the cost of debt.

Weighted Average Cost of Capital

Assuming the debt-to-asset ratio, D, for for-profit and not-for-profit hospitals is 0.53 and 0.48, respectively, the weighted average cost of capital (WACC) for 1996 can be estimated as:

$$WACC_{np} = (0.48)(4.86) + (1 - 0.48)(9.93)$$
$$= 7.50 \text{ percent}$$
$$WACC_{fp} = (0.53)(5.38) + (1 - 0.53)(9.77)$$
$$= 7.44 \text{ percent}$$

Medicare Reimbursement Under the Prospective Payment System

On October 1, 1983, Medicare started reimbursing hospitals for inpatient nonphysician services under a DRG-based prospective payment system (PPS). Several types of hospitals were exempt from this DRG-based payment system, including psychiatric, rehabilitation, children's, and long-term-care hospitals. About 500 DRGs have been identified from the International Classification of Diseases, 9th Revision, Clinical Modification (ICD-9-CM). Total payments made to a hospital under Medicare include two components: (1) prospective payment and (2) reasonable cost payment. Prospective payment is further divided into operating payment and capital payment. (Effective October 1, 1992, Medicare began using prospective payments for capital payments. Prior to this date, capital payments were paid on a reasonable cost basis.) Reasonable cost payment includes direct medical education costs, kidney acquisition costs, and outpatient costs.

Each of the DRGs has been assigned a weight to indicate the relative resource requirement to provide the service. For example, DRG 103 (heart transplant) has a weight of 14.0323 and DRG 320 (kidney and urinary tract infection) has a weight of 1.0002. This means that DRG 103 is about fourteen times more expensive than DRG 320. When the Health Care Financing Administration (HCFA) announced a nationwide payment for the labor and nonlabor component of the operating payment, every hospital in the country was preassigned a wage index for the labor component. Reimbursement for a particular DRG is computed as follows:

Reimbursement = DRG weight × [(labor amount × wage index) + (nonlabor amount)]

The reimbursement may be further increased by an additional payment to cover the costs of indirect medical education, disproportionate share, and outlier payments. Teaching hospitals incur additional costs because of extra laboratory and other teaching demonstrations. The allowance for indirect medical education covers these additional costs. Hospitals that treat a large percentage of Medicare and Medicaid patients receive an additional payment under PPS. This additional payment is referred to as a disproportionate share payment. The outlier payments are additional payments for patients who use an unusually large amount of resources indicated by either a long length of stay or cost.

The capital component of the prospective payment that began on October 1, 1992, has a ten-year phase-in period, blending federal and hospital components of payments. The hospital component of the capital costs include interest, depreciation, and lease costs. Taxes and insurance are also considered capital costs if they are related to capital assets. There is a federal payment for capital costs that is similar to the national rates for labor and nonlabor costs discussed earlier.

Physician Reimbursement under the Resource-Based Relative Value Scale

Beginning January 1992, Medicare started paying physicians using a resource-based relative value scale (RBRVS). Physician services are categorized into approximately 7,000 different codes using the current procedural terminology (CPT). Resource-based relative value (RBRV) has three components: (1) a work unit that represents physician time, level of stress, and skill; (2) a unit of practice expense representing the costs of support personnel and office expense; and (3) a unit of cost that represents the cost of malpractice insurance.

The level of RBRV for a particular CPT code is obtained by adding the products of each of the three components and multiplying the RBRV by a conversion factor, determined by the Health Care Financing Administration each year. The products of the three factors are generated by multiplying the work unit, practice cost expense, and malpractice insurance cost by the regional cost index for each. The regional cost index is based on the difference in costs geographically as well as the inflation rate.

In Exhibit B–4, Medicare's RBRV reimbursement for an office visit is computed. The physician's level of work depends on the predetermined CPT codes. The example is for a CPT designated "midlevel" office visit (other options would include minimum-level and extensive office visits) for a San Francisco physician in 1996. The $103.11 reimbursement is significantly less than what the physician charged self-pay or insured patients. For this reason, many physicians limit the number of Medicare patients they accept; too many patients paying below practice costs means they close the practice.

Capitation

The health care industry has experienced a tremendous increase in managed-care insurance plans in recent years. These types of plans are expected to have even higher rates of penetration (defined as the percentage of population covered by managed-care plans) in the future. Managed-care plans consisting of health maintenance organizations (HMOs) and preferred provider organizations (PPOs) negotiate with health care providers to arrive at a predetermined price schedule. Many of the negotiations conclude with contracts between the plans and health care providers for a fixed monthly payment per insured individual. Because the providers receive only a fixed amount of revenue from the managed-care plans for a given number of insured individuals (known as enrolled members), financial risk of a shortfall in revenues over expenses is shifted from the insurer to the provider. The providers receive their revenue in the form of capitation—a set sum of money received based on membership rather than services delivered, usually

Exhibit B–4 • Physician Reimbursement for an Office Visit in San Francisco, 1996

1. Relative Value

Physician's work (based on CPT code)	1.71	
× Cost index	× 1.068	
Adjusted value		1.826
Practice expense (based on CPT code)	0.78	
× Cost index	× 1.330	
Adjusted value		1.037
Malpractice insurance (based on CPT code)	0.08	
× Cost index	× 0.596	
Adjusted value		0.048
Total value		2.911

2. Conversion factor (determined by HCFA each year) — × 35.42

3. Medicare's office visit reimbursement — $103.11

---

expressed in amounts per member per month (PMPM). Under capitation, profit accrues by controlling costs as well as utilization of services. Because revenue is fixed, profit is maximized by either cutting unit cost or controlling utilization of services or some combination of both. In this section, we shall discuss several methods of determining the capitation amount in the form of a monthly payment for each enrollee known as PMPM. In negotiating the capitation rate, providers typically use the fee-for-service (FFS) rate as the basis of calculation. Specifically:

$$\text{PMPM} = \frac{\text{Forecasted annual utilization rate} \times \text{FFS rate}}{12 \text{ months}}$$

Suppose an HMO is negotiating the capitation rate with a hospital for the inpatient care of its members. Past utilization of hospital inpatient services by the enrollees of the HMO show that for every 1,000 enrollees, 350 inpatient days were used in a year and the average charge was $1,050. Thus, the corresponding PMPM rate is:

$$\text{PMPM} = \frac{(350 \text{ inpatient days}/1000 \text{ members}) \times \$1,050}{12 \text{ months}} = \$30.63$$

Similarly, the capitation rate can be determined for any specific service (i.e., outpatient, dental, surgical, drug, and others). As an example, assume an HMO randomly selected 1,000 of its members to monitor their utilization of inpatient hospital care for medical and surgical services separately, and they found forty admissions for medical services and twenty admissions for surgical services during a one-year period. Assume the length of stay for medical service equals 3.5 days at an average daily cost of $1,050, and the length of stay for surgical service equals 4.8 days at an average daily cost of $1,800. Now, the capitation rates for medical and surgical services can be computed as follows:

$$\text{Medical: } \frac{(40 \times 3.5/1,000) \times \$1,050}{12} = \$12.25 \text{ PMPM}$$

$$\text{Surgical: } \frac{(20 \times 4.8/1,000) \times \$1,800}{12} = \$14.40 \text{ PMPM}$$

Hence, the capitation rate for the total hospital inpatient care equals $12.25+$14.40 or $26.65 PMPM.

Let us now compute the capitation rate for a primary-care physician (PCP). Assume the physician's fee for an office visit is $50. A random sample of 1,000 members of an HMO show a total of 3,500 visits to physicians during a one-year period. That is, on the average, each member has 3.5 visits in a year. Thus, the capitation rate for PCP is:

$$\frac{3.5 \times \$50}{12} = \$14.58 \text{ PMPM}$$

Obviously, the utilization rates for specialists' services is a much smaller number; therefore the PMPM for such physicians is normally lower than their PCP counterparts. If the fee of a neurosurgeon is $900 per service and the annual average use of such service is 5 per 1,000 members, then the PMPM for such specialist is:

$$\frac{5/1,000 \times \$900}{12} = \$0.38 \text{ PMPM}$$

The per member per month rate can be computed for each service and an aggregate PMPM calculated by adding all the services for a comprehensive capitation rate, unless the parties concerned agree on some carve outs (i.e., to leave some services outside the capitated payments).

The aggregate capitated amount is then adjusted for the cost of reinsurance, cost of administration, and margin. The final amount is risk adjusted for age, gender, and family status.

Medicare is now experimenting with capitated payment by contracting with federally approved HMOs in many states for the health care services of a defined population of Medicare enrollees in a market. Under the contract, HMOs receive a fixed amount of payment from the Health Care Financing Administration for each Medicare enrollee in each month. The HMO is responsible for all the Medicare-approved health care services for the enrolled members. The Medicare PMPM is based on the actual average per capita cost (AAPCC) of the HMO-enrolled Medicare patients. The actual expenses of this population (as paid by HCFA in the previous time period on the DRG-based system) is adjusted for age, gender, welfare status, and geographic location of the enrollees to compute the AAPCC.

Additional References

Asper, Elaine, and Mahmud Hassan, "The Impact of PPS Legislation on the Systematic Risk of Hospitals," *Journal of Economics and Finance* 17, no. 3 (Fall 1993), pp. 121–135.

Cleverley, William O., and Paul C. Nutt, "The Decision Process Used for Hospital Bond Rating—And Its Implications," *Health Services Research* 19, no. 5 (December 1984), pp. 615–637.

Cleverley, William O., and W. H. Rosegay, "Factors Affecting the Cost of Hospital Tax-Exempt Revenue Bonds," *Inquiry* 19 (Winter 1982), pp. 317–326.

Sloan, Frank A., Joseph Valvona, Mahmud Hassan, and Michael A. Morrisey, "Cost of Capital to the Hospital Sector," *Journal of Health Economics* 7, no. 1 (March 1988), pp. 25–45.

Oral Presentations for Health Care Professionals (and Soon-to-Be Professionals)

by Gary F. Kohut and Carol M. Baxter

Appendix C

Presenting information orally requires careful thought. At any time you might be called on to present a proposal to accept a new treatment, give a report to persuade higher management to adopt a new policy, or present a service area status report. Whether you are presenting information to a group of your peers, your supervisor, a group of community leaders, or members of the health care profession, effective oral communication involves three major steps: planning, organizing, and delivering the subject matter.

Planning the Presentation

Several factors must be considered before you can plan a presentation effectively. You must determine the type of presentation you will make, analyze your audience, conduct some research, and consider the logistics of the speaking site.

Determine the Type of Presentation to Make

Generally, oral presentations are divided into two broad categories: informative and persuasive. Informative presentations convey information or ideas, whereas persuasive presentations sell an idea or a product to an audience. Informative presentations include progress reports, instructions, and explanations. For example, you may give a progress report to your supervisor detailing your efforts on an assigned project, or you may give similar information to a small group if it is a team-related task. On the other hand, you may be directing a group of volunteers in a fund-raising effort, and as coordinator you may inform them about their responsibilities.

Many presentations in the health care field are instructional. For example, you might instruct individuals on how to operate a magnetic resonance imaging device, how to administer a new drug, or how to complete a new form required by Blue Cross/Blue Shield.

Explanatory presentations are common in the health care industry as well. For example, you may be asked to explain features of a planned hospital wing to members of the media. Other examples of explanatory presentations include informing family members of a patient's condition and orienting new employees to the policies of the health care facility.

The second category, persuasive presentations, includes proposals and requests. For example, you may have to make a persuasive presentation to get authorization to purchase an expensive piece of equipment. Or, you may present a proposal to your supervisor to conduct market research about outpatients.

In the classroom, when you analyze a case, you are attempting to persuade your audience to understand the logic of your arguments and accept your recommendations.

Analyze the Audience

Because you will give your presentation to a specific audience, you need to analyze that audience carefully. *Audience analysis* is a method of examining the knowledge, interests, and attitudes of the people who will hear your presentation. Your analysis will help you determine how to organize your material, select supporting information, choose the appropriate wording, and select or produce appropriate visual aids.

Audience analysis is critical to ensuring that your information is accepted. Many presentations might be well delivered, but they fail because speakers do not anticipate audience reaction. You need to consider such characteristics as the size of the group, their level of knowledge about your subject, their interest in the material, their attitude and predispositions toward the subject, and their organizational relationship to you. For example, if your audience consists of five people, select a site that is small and personal when you present the information. If your audience is large, make sure all members can both hear and see the information you are presenting.

Although individuals within the health care industry tend to be very well educated, their technical expertise is usually very specific. Therefore, when planning a presentation, you must ask, "What does this audience already know about this subject?" Never assume that your audience is as knowledgeable about the topic as you are. You may want to ask yourself the following questions: "What information will I use to impress my audience? Will I employ technical data, demonstrations, or statistical comparisons?" Whatever information you use, care should be taken to reach your intended audience. This is particularly true when presenting ideas to laypeople, who generally know much less about the material than health care professionals. Choose your vocabulary and your examples to meet the audience's needs. Within the industry, people tend to have high interest in their respective areas but may have less interest in subjects that affect them less directly. Laypeople are often especially interested in their own health but may be easily confused about the technical details.

Every audience is unique. All audience members have different perceptions based upon personal experiences, which influence their attitudes about any subject. Understanding these predispositions will prevent your making bold assumptions that may offend the audience. For example, if your audience consists of people sixty to seventy-five years of age, avoid any current slang lest you appear flippant and uncaring. Similarly, if your audience consists of young adults, avoid examples that they cannot understand because they have not experienced them. Because experience is such an important factor in understanding perceptions, you would not use the same explanations and examples with an audience of parents as you would with a childless audience. Good questions to ask when analyzing an audience are, "What does this group want/need/expect from me?" and "How can I give that to them?"

Types of Appeal: Ethical, Emotional, and Logical

With persuasive presentations, the audience's predisposition will strongly affect the type of appeal in your presentation. Three appeals are used in persuasion: the ethical, the emotional, and the logical. The *ethical appeal* addresses the speaker's or the organization's credibility. It is impossible to separate the speaker's effect on an audience from the content of a message. If listeners regard the speaker highly, they will adopt a more favorable attitude toward the service or idea than if they have a negative impression of the person. Consequently, a speaker must bring to the platform a strong, positive, personal style. Credibility hinges on believability; you may have a high ethical appeal with members of an audience if they perceive that you have acted with integrity in the past. If you have acted rudely, unethically, or unprofessionally toward the audience, your ethical appeal will be very low. Many characteristics such as honesty, dependability, and expertise help to develop credibility. Although it takes some time to establish credibility, it takes only an instant to lose it by saying or doing something unexpected.

The *emotional appeal* uses the audience's motivations to change their thinking or behavior. Because emotion provokes action, speakers often seek to arouse the feelings of their listeners. The emotional appeal is characterized by the use of fear, sympathy, love, jealousy, sex, the desire for attention, the desire for security, or a host of other emotions to persuade the audience. To use the emotional appeal, first analyze the specific emotions to which the audience will respond. Then determine which words, pictures, or actions will best evoke the desired emotion. Once members of the audience are drawn into the persuasion by the emotional "hook," it is easy to ask them to take action to meet the need or to satisfy the emotion that was touched. For example, most people are touched by the vulnerability of children, so when you show them a cute photograph of a child or a sad photograph of a child, you may be able to capitalize on their emotions to get them to do whatever you suggest, such as financially supporting research on childhood diseases. Speakers should be aware, however, that attempts to arouse emotions excessively can lead to a rejection of their arguments by an audience. Thus, the emotional appeal should be used with restraint.

The *logical appeal* draws on an audience's ability to think and reason. This appeal uses good reasons to show members of an audience why they should change their opinions or actions. The reasoning process and the supporting materials used to give credence to an argument comprise the elements of the logical appeal. For example, if you needed to persuade an audience to reengineer a department in the hospital, you might stress making work more meaningful, more customer friendly, and more cost effective.

Gather Information

Your effectiveness as a speaker depends on what you say about the topic you have selected. For case analyses, a thorough understanding of the case is crucial. Knowing *where* to look is a starting point for finding the best possible information on your topic. Sometimes the information will come from your personal knowledge, experience, or research. At other times, you may use information collected by others, such as census data, admissions/discharge records, inventory records, or pricing information. Furthermore, information from electronic databases or from the Internet can provide current data that may enhance the quality of your presentation.

Your credibility as a speaker—your ethical appeal—will be largely determined by the quality of the information you present. For example, if you are talking about recent trends, data from the 1980 census would damage your credibility. Conversely, up-to-date health care reform legislation passed by various states would be beneficial to an audience that needs to plan strategy in an unstable legislative environment.

Consider the Logistics of the Speaking Site

Before you can organize your presentation, you must consider some logistical concerns. First, how much time will you need to give the presentation? Sometimes you have no control over how long you will speak; you are given a specific amount of time. In such cases, it is imperative that you stay within your time limit. When the time is exceeded, the audience becomes less receptive to your ideas. When given some choice over the length of a presentation, most speakers take too much time. Remember that it is difficult to hold people's attention beyond twenty to thirty minutes. To improve effectiveness, speakers need to watch the audience for verbal and nonverbal feedback to evaluate whether their message is being comprehended.

Second, you need to know where you will make the presentation. Will it be made in a conference room, a traditional classroom, a large auditorium, an office, or a dining hall? The location of your presentation will determine the kind of delivery and the types of visual aids that you will use as well as how you set up the room. Some guidelines for setting up the speaking site are:

1. Arrange seating so that every member of the audience can see and hear you. The horseshoe arrangement is preferred if the room and the size of the audience will allow for it.
2. Check the lighting, temperature, and noise level of the site to ensure that your audience will be comfortable. Avoid high-traffic areas, such as a room next to a kitchen, which may distract your audience.
3. Check any equipment you intend to use to be sure that it can be easily viewed or heard by your audience.

Remember, if anything can go wrong, it generally will. Therefore, try to anticipate any problems before they occur. For example, when using any kind of projected visual aids, you should carry an extra bulb or have alternate visual aids in case the equipment breaks down. If you are speaking at a site that you have not visited previously, you may even want to bring an extension cord and an adapter plug, tape, push pins, or other supplies that may not be available at the site.

Organizing the Presentation

In an oral presentation, your audience probably will not have the opportunity to refer to written material; therefore, you must structure the information so that it is very easy to understand the first time it is heard. Every effective presentation has an introduction, body, and conclusion. If these are well planned, the audience will be able to follow your ideas easily. We suggest that you prepare a written outline of the information you want to include in these three parts.

Introduction

Because people tend to remember the beginning and end of presentations, prepare a strong introduction. Good introductions fulfill three purposes: (1) they gain the audience's attention, (2) they establish rapport or goodwill with the audience, and (3) they introduce the audience to the topic.

Getting the audience's attention is one goal of an effective introduction. Attention-grabbers may include the following:

1. *A reference to the event or the occasion.* "On Wednesday, October 12, Health Care Delivery Systems treated our 10,000th patient. Although this is only year two of our operation, we cannot rest on our laurels. We need to build a strategic plan for the next decade. That is what I'd like to talk about today."

2. *A brief story that relates to the topic.* "On May 18 John Miller survived complications from an automobile accident the night before. Medical personnel at Our Lady of Mercy Hospital diagnosed his condition and the potential for complications with an X787 scanner. This presentation will review the life-saving qualities of this miracle of modern science and its sales potential for the coming year."

3. *A quotation by a recognized authority on the subject.* "The Surgeon General of the United States has recommended that we reduce our fat intake by 40 percent. Three out of four Americans have too much fat in their diets. This serious problem is one of many reasons why we need to begin our health awareness program."

4. *A thought-provoking question that requires the audience members to participate by answering the question or to get involved by raising their hands.* "How many of you have been hospitalized in the past year? (Pause for an audience response.) If you have, you know the importance of having a family physician. Today, I'm going to talk about what qualities consumers are looking for in a family physician."

5. *A startling statement; it may or may not be a statistic.* "If our costs continue to increase over the next three years at the rate they have been over the past decade, we will have to increase our initial office consultation charge to $200. Today, I will present five strategies for reducing costs in . . ."

6. *A personal story or reference about the topic.* "Seven years ago I suffered from a serious disease. Locatril was prescribed to treat my illness. I'm happy to say that I am fully recovered and owe much of my recovery to this miracle drug. Locatril was just one of the drugs we developed in the past decade. We continue to add new products. This presentation will preview two of them: Daconaise and Zacarin."

7. *A joke.* This can be particularly tricky in health care as most people feel poor health is not a joking matter. The key is to know your audience and when in doubt . . . don't.

Stating the thesis is the second function of an effective introduction. Once you have successfully chosen an attention-getting statement, tell the audience the purpose of your presentation by stating the thesis. The *thesis* is a statement that tells what you want to accomplish in the presentation. Although the introduction is designed to get the audience members to think about the topic, you must be sure that they understand what you intend to do with the topic. The thesis statement helps focus the entire presentation. Below are examples of thesis statements from two team members making a case analysis presentation to the class:

> Speaker One: Our team believes that New York Hospital should pursue aggressive market development to increase our patient base and become a major player in this increasingly competitive market.

> Speaker Two: Our team proposes an alternative strategy of vertical integration. We believe that the New York Hospital should provide the total continuum of care to compete in a managed-care environment.

Previewing the main points of your presentation keeps your audience attuned to what you are saying. The attention span of an audience varies from one occasion to the next. Below are two examples of previews that come after the thesis statement in a case analysis by team members:

> Speaker One: We need to take immediate action to maintain our number one position in the service area. Because competition is increasing, we have a number of empty beds, and Columbia/HCA just purchased the Sisters' Hospital.

> Speaker Two: Our census has been declining, and competition is increasing. Providing the complete continuum of care means that we must become more than merely a hospital. We need to establish feeder organizations to maintain a stream of patients. Also, because lengths of stay are becoming shorter, our patients need a place where they can still receive the quality care they need.

Later, during the body of the presentation, you will develop in more detail each point mentioned in the preview.

Body

Various methods are available to develop the body of the presentation. Below are some common ones:

1. Use statistics or other facts.
2. Cite quotations or expert testimony.
3. Employ examples, real or hypothetical.
4. Refer to personal experiences.
5. Use comparisons, contrasts, or analogies to the audience's experiences.

Whatever method you choose to employ, smooth transitions are the key aspect of organization. A link must be established between one idea or issue and another so the audience sees the relationship. This link may take the form of a short summary that simply states that a new point will now be discussed or contrasts what has just been presented with that which is to follow. Another technique is the repetition of key words or phrases for emphasis. Some examples include:

- "The first way Daconil differs from our earlier products is . . . "
- "Now for the second difference . . ."
- "Also . . ."

- "To begin . . ."
- "Finally . . ."

Conclusion

The end of your presentation should contain a brief summary of the main points of your presentation. Do not introduce any new information in your conclusion lest you appear unfinished. If some action is expected from the audience, the speaker's expectations should be made clear and easy to follow. Too often, speakers just trail off with a "That's all. Thank you very much" ending. Whatever the specific nature of your conclusion, it should clearly communicate that the speaker is ending.

A presentation can have an excellent introduction and body but still not be effective. Good speakers must leave a favorable impression in the minds of the audience. An effective conclusion can accomplish this objective. Conclusions can be developed in a number of ways:

1. Summarize your main points.
2. Ask the audience to take some action such as buying your product or service or contributing to a particular cause.
3. Recall the story, joke, or anecdote in the introduction and elaborate on it or draw a "lesson" from it.

Now that you have structured your presentation, you must find ways to enhance it further. Visual aids are the tools to accentuate the information you want to share.

Visual Aids

Because we live in a visually oriented society, we expect to see as well as hear information. Therefore, effective speakers show as well as tell their points. Research indicates that audiences remember only 10 to 20 percent of what they hear but 80 percent of what they see. Remember that your audience must understand the material that is being presented to remember it. Visual aids help maintain audience attention and involvement. Two broad categories of visual aids are available to enhance presentations. One category, *direct viewing visuals,* includes such things as real objects, models, flip charts, handouts, and chalkboards or whiteboards. The second category, *projected visuals,* includes slides, videotapes, overhead transparencies, and computer presentations.

Direct Viewing Visuals

Real objects are often the best visuals when the audience is small and when seeing "the real thing" will be more convincing than a drawing, diagram, or photograph. For example, if you are touting the quality of a product, it might be good to show how a particular component is manufactured—what it looks like, feels like, sounds like, and so forth. This can best be done by using real items.

Models are very effective for showing how a dialysis unit, operating room, or visitor waiting room will look. This type of visual can be very persuasive if the audience is small enough that everyone can see the model as it is being discussed.

Flip charts are excellent for use with audiences that are small enough to see the information on the chart. Most speakers "write as they talk" when using flip charts. This flexibility gives an informal, conversational tone to a presentation. However, some information, such as key words, may be put on the chart ahead of time and elaborated on during the speech. If this method is used, the words should be covered by leaving the top page blank and lifting it when ready to show the key words.

Handouts allow you to fit more information on a printed page than with other visuals, but avoid doing so. Keep handouts simple. Summarize major points, but do not provide the audience with your entire presentation. If possible, distribute the handout when it is needed rather than at the beginning of the presentation. Otherwise, the audience may read the handout while you are explaining background information needed to understand the ideas presented in the handout.

Chalkboards or *whiteboards* are useful for presenting informal visuals to small groups. Some major problems presented by chalkboards and whiteboards are the time necessary to write the information, lack of cleanliness of some boards, poor penmanship of the user, and failure of the user to erase items once they have been considered. If you plan to use a board, practice and make certain you have all the necessary equipment (appropriate markers, eraser, and so on). If your visual is complex, you may find it helpful to place it on the board before your presentation. Many portable chalkboards or whiteboards have two sides, thus permitting you to keep your material from view until you need it.

Projected Visuals

Slides can be effective when showing how something looks at particular phases, such as the stages in the progress of a disease. Of course, slides should be organized before they are loaded into the projector. The speaker should practice using them so none are in upside down or backward or out of sequence. Remember to allow enough time to develop the slides if you are producing them yourself.

Videotapes are effective if you need to show a process. Few other types of visuals can capture the drama of a videotape. For example, if you were demonstrating a surgical procedure, a videotape could be excellent. It could show exactly how to perform the surgery and could even be done in slow motion or freeze-frame to allow surgeons to see particularly delicate processes. Or, it could be used to demonstrate the ease of a minor surgical procedure to a patient to dispel anxiety.

Overhead transparencies work best when a large amount of material must be presented and there is little time or money for a more sophisticated type of presentation. Overheads give you a great deal of flexibility. For example, you can circle an important point or change a number or label. In addition, you can place one transparency over another to create a multilayered look. Prepared overheads, such as charts or diagrams can offer a neat appearance and a more polished presentation. The use of overheads allows you to vary the size of the image through adjusting the distance from the projector to the screen. Finally, even if a transparency is created "on the spot," it still has the advantage of giving you the opportunity to face the audience. In this way you can maintain eye contact and observe audience feedback while you talk about your material.

Computer presentations are being prepared by increasing numbers of speakers. When using presentation software such as Microsoft® PowerPoint®, Lotus® Freelance®, and Corel Presentation®, speakers should consider the following points:

1. Input your ideas into a built-in outliner that will help you organize your thoughts. On-screen assistance is generally available to those needing help with various organizational plans.
2. Select features for displaying your text (font, type size, color, texture, border, and so on).
3. Edit each visual, indicating the exact sequence of each visual and special effects (graphics, transitions, sounds, and motion).
4. Generate printed handouts, slides, transparencies, or a slide show for an on-screen presentation.

Many programs provide templates (prepared designs) that suggest features and colors that work well together. You simply select the template, and your information (text or graphics) is formatted automatically. After viewing the results, you can revise the format if you wish. These templates help the novice presenter resist the temptation to create overwhelmingly complex visuals simply because the technology is available.

Running an on-screen presentation takes some practice. Depending on the length of your presentation it may be difficult to remember what information is on each slide. Experience teaches us to rehearse the material to help develop our verbal introduction, develop effective transitions from one slide to another, and conclude effectively. Although they are very effective for large audiences, on-screen presentations may overwhelm a smaller audience. Rather than focusing on the material, the audience may be distracted by the special effects used to move from one idea to another. In addition, on-screen presentations limit audience interaction, which may be an important part of your presentation.

Guidelines for Selecting Visual Aids

Visual aids attract and hold attention, clarify the meaning of your points, emphasize ideas, or prove a point. Several factors must be considered in selecting the appropriate visual aid:

1. *The constraints of the topic.* Some topics will limit your choice of visual aids. For example, if you were explaining to a group of laypeople how microsurgery is performed on a hand, you would not use a flip chart because it would be ineffective. Also, you would probably not show a videotape of the surgery being performed because the sight of blood may upset some individuals. Instead, you might use a model of the hand. However, a videotape might be very effective in teaching surgeons how to perform the procedure.
2. *The availability of the equipment.* If the speaking site does not have an overhead projector, you could not use transparencies. Similarly, if the site does not have an electrical outlet near the podium, you would not be able to use a projected visual. Always check to see what equipment is available or bring your own. Also, verify that your computer presentation will run on the version of software installed on the available equipment.

3. *The cost of the visual.* If your budget is very small, a transparency, flip chart, or a handout may be preferable to the more elaborate types of visual aids such as slides or videotapes.

4. *The difficulty of producing the visual.* If you have only two days to prepare for your presentation, it may be impossible to assemble a scale model of a labor/delivery room interior or process slides of a sequence of cancer growth.

5. *The appropriateness of the visual to the audience.* The type of audience and the nature of the presentation affect the choice of visual aids. Some charts, graphs, and diagrams may be too technical for anyone but specialists to grasp. Detailed and complicated tables and charts that require considerable time to digest should be avoided. When in doubt, keep your visuals short and simple.

6. *The appropriateness of the visual to the speaker.* Visual aids require skill in order to be effectively presented. A speaker must be able to write large and legibly and draw well-proportioned diagrams to use a flip chart. Projected visuals require skill in handling slides, videotape, or film. Unless you feel comfortable with a particular visual medium, avoid using it.

7. *The appropriateness of the visual to the time limit.* The speaker should carefully check the time required to display and explain a visual aid to make sure the main ideas of the presentation will not be neglected. Any visual aid that needs too much explanation should be avoided. An appropriate visual aid should be simple, clear, and brief.

Once you have planned and organized the content of your presentation and prepared your visual aids, you are ready to deliver your presentation.

Delivering the Presentation

The situation, the audience, and the speaker determine the type of delivery a speaker will use. The formality or informality of the situation greatly affects delivery. The more formal it is, the fewer gestures and movements speakers make. They limit themselves more to their position behind the lectern and use a more emphatic speaking style. In very informal situations, speakers are free to move away from the podium and interact with the audience.

The available equipment will also determine delivery. For instance, if the size of the audience necessitates a microphone, speakers should not move away from the microphone. They may also need to adapt themselves to various tables or other unusual speaking platforms that will hold their notes, visuals, or other forms of support.

The larger the audience, the louder speakers must talk unless there is a microphone. Likewise, eye contact is more challenging with large groups. Therefore, delivery to small groups can be more informal and conversational than with large groups.

Types of Delivery

There are several methods for delivering material to an audience and each has its unique advantages. The four methods of delivery are (1) impromptu, (2) manuscript, (3) memorized, and (4) extemporaneous.

Impromptu delivery requires speaking spontaneously on a topic. This type of delivery is generally inappropriate for technical or complex material because you may forget crucial information if the presentation has not been carefully planned. Impromptu delivery is often used at social occasions such as introductions at an after-dinner speaking engagement or at a professional meeting where you are asked to "sit in" for someone who was going to introduce a speaker but was called out because of an emergency.

Manuscript delivery requires that the speaker read from a prepared text. This type of delivery is ineffective in most presentations because audiences generally prefer more eye contact (they also dislike having material read to them). However, manuscript delivery is a must in one particular situation: when a crisis has occurred. For example, if someone receives the wrong medication and dies in a hospital, the media will immediately "look for the story." The spokesperson for the hospital should never deliver the information in an impromptu manner. Rather, the response should be carefully prepared and *read* to the media because any misstatement in such a situation could result in litigation against the organization.

Memorized delivery is self-explanatory. In most cases it should be discouraged because memorized presentations usually sound "canned" rather than natural. However, this type of delivery might be appropriate in situations where the presentation will be only a few minutes long, such as introducing a speaker or "saying a few words" about someone leaving the organization.

Extemporaneous delivery is the preferred approach for most presentations. This type of delivery involves using notes or an outline to deliver your information. The speaker should talk in a conversational tone but refer periodically to notes to be sure that all the information is covered. Some people prefer following a precise outline whereas others prefer using note cards to deliver a presentation. Each person must find what works best for him or her. Although notes can be a valuable resource for a speaker, they can easily become a psychological crutch. To make sure that they do not become a crutch, remember to use notes only when absolutely necessary. Delivery helps build the speaker's credibility in the eyes of an audience. Sometimes the visual aids can also serve as notes to "jog the speaker's memory" in an extemporaneous presentation.

Practicing the Delivery

Preparation influences a speaker's delivery. A speaker who is well prepared and has something valuable to communicate will be more comfortable physically and vocally. If speakers are unsure of themselves and the material, they may be tempted to read word for word from their outline. Being too self-conscious or nervous can create physical and vocal qualities and mannerisms that detract from the message. Too much concern with oneself or the ideas and too little with the audience will also hinder a speaker's delivery. Always practice aloud what you want to say. It will not only give you confidence but will also help you to hear any awkward phrasing or words that are hard to pronounce.

Delivery is not something added to a speech but a part of it. Consider the following when delivering a presentation:

1. *Avoid speaking distractions.* Effective speakers should avoid such distractions as fiddling with a pen or pencil, scratching the nose, playing with the hair, and jingling coins in one's pocket.

2. *Work toward being heard and understood.* A speaker's voice must be loud enough to be heard in the very last row. Pronunciation and articulation must be distinct. Only practice can guarantee this goal.
3. *Convey enthusiasm.* An essential part of delivery is to keep the audience listening. One way of conveying enthusiasm is to vary the characteristics of the voice such as volume, rate, and pitch. The speaker's movements and gestures should also be varied and natural and not choreographed.
4. *Stress the main points.* Some points in a speech are more important than others. If all ideas are spoken in exactly the same way, the significance of your key points will be lost. A slower speaking rate, a pause before or after an idea, a shift in body position, an increase or decrease in volume are only a few of the many ways to emphasize points through delivery.
5. *Involve your audience.* Each member of the audience should feel that the speaker is imparting information to her or him personally. Consequently, eye contact is a critical part of effective delivery. The speaker should look at all audience members, talking to each one from time to time but with no particular person or segment of the audience for a prolonged time.

Establishing Credibility

Credibility is crucial to effective presentations. As mentioned earlier, credibility refers to the confidence an audience has in a speaker. Several factors in the delivery of a presentation work together to determine credibility, including the speaker's enthusiasm, expertise, and trustworthiness.

Enthusiasm is projected through tone of voice, eye contact, and energy. Obviously, the major ways speakers can display these characteristics are by believing in the subject and acting as if they enjoy conveying the information. For example, a sincere smile at the beginning of a presentation sets the tone for both the speaker and the audience.

Expertise is conveyed through the accuracy of your information, the amount of experience you have had with the subject, and the confidence with which you speak. Make sure you check your facts before you communicate them to the audience.

Trustworthiness refers to whether the speaker is perceived as biased. Consistency in conveying information over a period of time is important to establishing trust with an audience.

One factor that detracts from credibility is *speech anxiety.* Most speakers are nervous, but they have learned techniques for handling the condition so that there are few outward signs of anxiety. Several techniques are recommended for managing speech anxiety:

1. Avoid taking medications that will dry your mouth and produce more anxiety. If you have "dry mouth" take a glass of water to the podium.
2. Practice deep breathing exercises just before speaking to reduce your anxiety. Close your eyes, put your hand on your stomach, and breathe deeply enough so that your breath forces your hand to move up and down.
3. Reduce tension by squeezing your hand into a fist and releasing it, tensing your leg muscles and releasing them, or stretching your facial muscles with exaggerated expressions.

4. Avoid alcohol as a means of relaxation because it only exacerbates the problem.
5. Avoid milk products just before speaking because they thicken the saliva and make it difficult to pronounce words.
6. Rehearse your presentation aloud so that you are comfortable and confident with the material.
7. Get a good night's sleep. Just before falling asleep, visualize yourself making an outstanding presentation.

Use of effective visuals can enhance presentations; poor use of them can actually hurt your credibility. Some guidelines for using visual aids are as follows:

1. Avoid turning your back on the audience while you look at a visual aid; talk to the audience, not to the visual aid.
2. Show the visual aid only when you are using it; otherwise, the audience may be distracted from what you are saying. For example, if you are using transparencies, cover everything except the information you are talking about at the moment.
3. Refrain from removing the visual before the audience members have had an opportunity to look at the information for themselves. Also, avoid talking about something on a visual aid after you have put it aside.
4. Organize the visuals in the order in which you will use them so you will appear prepared and confident.

Managing Nonverbal Communication

Nonverbal communication enhances or detracts from the credibility you have worked to establish. Several dimensions of nonverbal communication include (1) *kinesics,* the way people use their bodies to communicate; (2) *proxemics,* the way people use space to communicate; and (3) *paralanguage,* the way people use their voice to enhance the verbal message.

When making presentations, two of the most important types of kinetic behavior are gestures and eye contact. Speakers are rarely credible when they stand rigidly behind a podium, grasp it as if it were a crutch, and seldom glance from their notes to look at the audience. Similarly, poor posture, hands in pockets, and playing with objects, such as chalk or pointers, lessen a speaker's impact.

Speakers who recognize that "space communicates" will use it wisely. For example, if an audience is very small, it may be better to sit at the head of the group rather than to stand to deliver your information. Also, if you are conveying unfavorable information, stand close to the audience to appear sincere and understanding.

Aspects of the voice that affect credibility include volume, rate, pitch, tone, and voice quality. The "sound" of the voice (voice quality) such as raspiness or a nasal whine evokes images in the mind of listeners; however, it is very difficult to change the voice quality you have. On the other hand, tone, pitch, rate, and volume are easily controlled. For example, a person who has a monotone can make the voice seem less monotonous by saying some words softly and others quite loudly. Even though the speaker's tone has not changed, the audience perceives that the tone is varied. Pitch is often associated with nervousness. Speakers should start speaking at the lowest pitch they can achieve, since a lower pitch is generally viewed as more credible in our culture.

Handling Questions from the Audience

Some speaking situations require that the speaker give the audience an opportunity to ask questions. At other times, the speaker may simply want to involve the audience by following a presentation with a question-and-answer session. Whether or not you use this procedure depends on the occasion, the audience, and the amount of time available. You can use this procedure to reinforce key points and gain acceptance of your ideas. Any question-and-answer period should be well organized and brief. To make the most of the available time, follow these guidelines:

1. Ask for questions in a positive way. For instance, you could say, "Who has the first question?" If no one asks a question, you may say, "You may be wondering . . . " or "I am often asked . . . " After supplying an answer to the question you have asked, you may ask, "Are there any other questions?"
2. Look at the entire audience when answering a question. You are addressing everyone, not just the person asking the question.
3. If the question being asked cannot be heard by the entire audience, repeat it for the rest of the group.
4. Keep your answers concise and to the point; do not give another speech. You risk losing the audience's attention as well as discouraging further questions.
5. Cut off a rambling questioner politely. If the person starts to make a speech without getting to the question, wait until he or she takes a breath and then interrupt with, "Thanks for your comment. Next question." Then look to the other side of the room.
6. Remain in control of the situation. Establish a time limit for questions and answers and announce it to the audience before the questions begin. Anticipate the types of questions your audience may ask and think how you will answer. Never lose your temper as you respond to someone who is trying to make you look bad. You may respond with something like, "I respect your opinion even though I don't agree with it." Then restate your response to the issue.
7. Watch your nonverbal communication when answering questions. For example, pointing a finger at the audience, putting your hands on your hips, or raising your voice above the pitch of the presentation may give the appearance of authoritarianism and rudeness.

Because your presentation does not end when you finish your speech, your credibility can be enhanced or lost in the question-and-answer period. Prepare intelligently and establish strategies for handling difficult situations.

Developing the skills needed to present your point of view in a convincing manner is essential to reaching your personal and career goals. Presenting information orally is a challenging task. However, if you follow the guidelines we have suggested, your presentation will be rewarding to both you and your audience.

Information Sources for Health Care Administration

In case analysis it is often useful to perform at least part of the situational analysis by investigating secondary data. Although the cases in this text have about as much information as the decision maker had at the time, further information can be obtained. However, it is wise to check with your professor as to his or her preference for your investigating the organization through library research. Some professors want students to use only the information provided in the case, but others insist that students investigate the organization and the industry using additional materials. Still others want students to research the organization but only up to the time of the decision in the case.

Some students believe that a successful approach to case analysis is to find an article about the organization and the decision that was made and then write up the decision that was implemented as the "correct" solution to the case. However, knowing what the organization did may prejudice your thinking and limit your ability to develop a creative solution. Consider this question: "If the organization had the opportunity to do it over, would management implement the same decision?" If the results were impressive, a student might be tempted to say yes; but would a different decision have yielded even greater benefits?

As an aid to locating information, sources that are typically available in university libraries, along with a brief description of each, are listed. This nonexhaustive list is organized by abstracts, bibliographies, dictionaries, directories, electronic databases, financial data, handbooks and guides, indexes, industry information, journals, loose-leaf services, newspaper and periodical indexes, statistical sources, and guides to sources not described. It suggests sources that might be used by a student or health care professional in a situational analysis.

Abstracts

Abstracts of Health Care Management Studies   Ann Arbor, Michigan: Health Administration Press for the Cooperative Information Center for Health Care Management Studies, School of Public Health, University of Michigan (quarterly).
This publication is focused primarily on the delivery of health care and provides abstracts of materials recently published on management, public policy, and planning.

Excerpta Medica   Amsterdam: Excerpta Medica (ten issues per year, with semiannual accumulations).

An international abstracting service, this publication can be used as a general index as well as a specialized resource because it covers all aspects of health care.

Health Planning and Services Research: An Abstract Newsletter   Springfield, Virginia: National Technical Information Service (weekly).

This newsletter contains information on health services and facilities use; health personnel requirements, use, and education; health-related costs; and methods of funding.

Hospital Abstracts   London: Her Majesty's Stationery Office (monthly).

The organization and management of hospitals are covered in this publication through listings of both books and periodicals. Abstracts are listed according to subject and relate to all aspects of hospital administration as well as specific publications of Great Britain's Ministry of Health.

Medical Care Review   Ann Arbor, Michigan: Bureau of Public Health Economics, School of Public Health, University of Michigan (monthly).

Abstracts from articles as well as entire journal articles are included in this monthly review of the literature. Federal and state legislation is an added feature.

Standard and Poor's Industry Surveys   New York: Standard and Poor's Corporation (quarterly).

This source contains a wealth of data for sixty-nine major domestic industries. Examples include health care, leisure time, computer and data processing equipment, liquor, and photography.

Bibliographies

The Administrator's Bookshelf   Denver: Medical Group Management Association (annually).

Health care administration is the primary focus of this bibliography. Books and periodical articles are included.

Administrator's Collection   Chicago: American Hospital Association (annually).

This is a listing of publications on all aspects of health administration. The materials are arranged by subject categories, and there is an additional listing for periodicals.

A Business Information Guidebook   By Oscar Figueroa and Charles Winkler, New York: AMACOM, 1980.

A reference book that provides direction for business people, consultants, students, or anyone seeking information on available markets, competition, and financing.

Business Information Sources, Rev. Ed.   By Lorna M. Daniells, Berkeley: University of California Press, 1985.

This guide provides a selected, annotated list of books and reference sources for businesses (including the health care industry).

Current Management Resources for Health Care Professionals, 2d ed.   Elaine C. Foster, Editor, Chicago: American Hospital Association, 1985.

This bibliography of health services administration sources is intended for the professional in the health care field. It includes abstracts.

Encyclopedia of Business Information Sources, 7th ed.   By James Woy, Detroit: Gale Research Company, 1988.

This is a bibliographic guide to approximately 20,000 citations, covering about 1,000 subjects. It contains abstracting and indexing services, almanacs and year-books, bibliographies, directories, financial ratios, on-line databases, periodicals and newsletters, price sources, research centers and institutes, statistics sources, trade associations, and professional societies. The health industry is included.

Federal Information Sources in Health and Medicine: A Selected Annotated Bibliography   By Mary G. Chitty, New York: Greenwood Press, 1988.

Annotates approximately 1,200 government publications and 100 databases from 90 federal agencies, institutes, and information centers. An appendix gives addresses of the federal agencies and other departments. The index gives all perti-nent information about each title. The annotated subject bibliography is divided by types of publications.

Health Administration and Organization   By Cortus T. Koehler, Monticello, Illinois: Vance Bibliographies, 1980.

This bibliography includes a comprehensive listing of pertinent sources in the administration and organization of hospitals and other health care institutions.

Health Care Administration: A Guide to Information Sources   By Dwight A. Morris and Lynne D. Morris, Detroit: Gale Research Company, 1978.

This basic annotated guide includes listings of associations, libraries, audiovisual sources, and publishers in health care as well as graduate schools offering majors in health care administration.

Medical Books and Serials in Print: An Index to Literature in the Health Sciences New York: Bowker (annual).

This index includes a listing of books and other materials in the medical and allied health sciences fields currently available from publishers.

Public Health Administration Monographs, 1970–1987   By Mary Vance, Monticello, Illinois: Vance Bibliographies, 1988.

This source combines information in the public administration field as well as the health administration area. It is noteworthy because of the time span covered.

Where to Find Business Information: A Worldwide Guide for Everyone Who Needs the Answers to Business Questions, 2d ed.   By David M. Brownstone and Gorton Carruth, New York: John Wiley and Sons, 1982.

This book contains a descriptive list of over 5,000 sources of current business information, concentrating on periodic publications and services such as maga-zines, newsletters, and computerized databases.

Computerized Information Services

Many of these electronic database services are available to "members" who have paid a membership or subscriber fee and then are charged for access time. Although the electronic databases are expensive to use, they have the advantage of speed and comprehensiveness.

ABI/Inform   Louisville, Kentucky: UMI/Data Courier.

All phases of business management and administration are indexed in this on-line information service. ABI/Inform is the largest and oldest database of bibliographical information. Over 680 business periodicals are indexed as well as the major health care administration journals. A 150-word summary is included for each article. The database covers from 1971 to the present.

Business Periodicals Index   New York: H. W. Wilson Co.

This database, available on CD-ROM, contains the same information as the hardcopy version previously described.

CompuServe   Columbus, Ohio: CompuServe, Inc.

An on-line database, CompuServe offers a variety of services through a time-sharing computer system. Terminal access to the service can be made through the TYMNET system. Two distinct services are offered by CompuServe: Micronet and CompuServe Information Services (CIS). Micronet is designed for those who are familiar with programming and software. CompuServe is menu-driven and provides access to newspapers and specific topics such as health care, finance, entertainment, communications, and so on.

Dow Jones News/Retrieval   New York: Dow Jones and Co., Inc.

Subscribers to this database can obtain the latest price quotations (no delay) for more than 6,000 stocks traded on nine different exchanges. It also allows for text searches for up-to-date news from the Dow Jones News Service Wires, the *Wall Street Journal, Barron's,* and the *Washington Post.*

Health Periodicals Database   Foster City, California: Information Access Company.

This is a full-text database that provides references to journals covering the entire range of health issues.

Health Planning and Administration   Bethesda, Maryland: U.S. National Library of Medicine.

Contains references to nonclinical literature on all aspects of health care planning, management, human resources, and licensing and certification. References are compiled from the *Hospital Literature Index* and *Medline.*

InfoTrac   Forest City, California: Information Access Company.

Available on CD-ROM, *InfoTrac* indexes articles from 1,100 business and general-interest periodicals and newspapers.

Medline   Bethesda, Maryland: U.S. National Library of Medicine.

This database is the major source for information in the biomedical literature. All aspects of medicine are included. Although most of this database is devoted to developments in medical science, many economic, finance, and administrative sources are included.

Nursing and Allied Health   Glendale, California: Cumulative Index to Nursing and Allied Health Literature Corporation.

Over 300 English-language journals are included in this database. All disciplines in nursing and allied health are included and citations are provided from *Index Medicus* as well as other sources.

The Source   Source Telecomputing Corporation.

Also known as "America's information utility," *The Source* is a database service of Source Telecomputing Corporation. By dialing a Source access number and supplying a password, subscribers gain access to hundreds of databases. Some of the files included in *The Source* are United Press International (UPI), *New York Times* News Summary, Aware Financial Services, and Business and Finance.

Standard and Poor's Corporate Descriptions   New York: Standard and Poor's Compustat Services, Inc.

More than 9,000 publicly held U.S. corporations are included in this database, which is available on CD-ROM. Descriptions include corporate background, income account and balance sheet figures, and stock and bond data.

Dictionaries

Dictionary of Health Services Management, 2d ed.   Thomas C. Timmerick, Editor, Owings Mills, Maryland: National Health Publishing, 1987.

Health services administration, organization, and management terms are defined in this book. Special treatment is given to hospital information.

Encyclopedia and Dictionary of Medicine, Nursing, and Allied Health, 2d ed.   By Benjamin F. Miller and Claire B. Keane, Philadelphia: Saunders Publishing, 1978.

This dictionary can be used by the layperson as well as the professional. The appendix lists sources for educational materials and contains a list of agencies concerned with health.

The New American Medical Dictionary and Health Manual, 5th ed.   By Robert E. Rothenberg, New York: New American Library, 1988.

This all-in-one handbook, dictionary, and manual provides information on health in general and special sections on relevant topics such as the elderly and their special needs.

Directories

American Hospital Association Guide to the Health Care Field   Chicago: American Hospital Association (annually).

This guide is a central reference for information on health care institutions, on the AHA, on organizations and agencies in the health care field, and on national hospital statistical data. The information is divided into sections with each section providing definitions and explanatory information.

Medical and Health Information Directory, 2d ed.   Detroit: Gale Research Company, 1980.

Provides locator information on agencies, institutions, associations, and companies concerned with health care at the state and national level. The directory is a useful resource for locating organizations concerned with different aspects of health care.

Financial Information

Almanac of Business and Industrial Financial Ratios   By Leo Troy, Englewood Cliffs, New Jersey: Prentice-Hall (annually).

This source provides selected financial ratios for key U.S. industries including a variety of health care organizations.

Annual Reports   Washington, D.C.: RC Publications, Inc. (biennially).

Most libraries maintain a file of annual reports for the companies listed in *Fortune 500* as well as other public firms.

Directory of Corporate Affiliation   Skokie, Illinois: National Register Publishing Co. (annually with bimonthly supplements).

> The directory lists 3,500 U.S. parent companies with their domestic and foreign divisions, subsidiaries, and affiliates, as well as 35,000 "corporate children" and their parent companies. Five bimonthly publications update personnel changes, acquisitions, address changes, and so on.

Financial Analyst's Handbook   By Sumner Levine, Homewood, Illinois: Dow Jones-Irwin, 1975.

> The handbook is in two volumes. Volume 1 contains methods, theory, and portfolio management. Volume 2 contains discussions by specialists for a variety of industries. The orientation is toward economic, social, marketing, regulatory, taxation, accountancy, and other topics considered to be of significance to the industries included.

Financial Research Associates' Financial Studies of Small Business   Arlington, Virginia: Financial Research Associates (annually).

> Most industry data is provided for larger business operations. FRA publishes ratios and norms for small businesses with total capitalization that is less than $1 million.

Industry Norms and Key Business Ratios   New York: Dun and Bradstreet Credit Services (annually).

> Over 800 different types of business operations are included. Key industry ratios (including the common ROA, ROI, ROE, current ratio, quick ratio, and so on plus some less common ratios, such as current liabilities to net worth, total liabilities to net worth) and industry norms are presented.

Q-File   St. Petersburg, Florida: Q-Data Corp., 1982.

> An extensive microfiche file, this source contains corporate annual reports and 10-K reports for firms listed on the New York Stock Exchange (NYSE) or the American Stock Exchange (AMEX), and for public firms traded over the counter (OTC). The master index and updates are usually available in printed form in a loose-leaf binder as well as on microfiche.

Robert Morris Associates' Annual Statement Studies   Philadelphia: Robert   Morris Associates (annually).

> Robert Morris is an association of bank lenders that publishes composite financial data (activity, profitability, liquidity, market price ratios, and so on) for nearly 300 lines of business representing manufacturers, wholesalers, retailers, providers of services (including health care), and contractors. Financial ratios are computed for each industry included.

Handbooks and Guides

Administrator's Handbook for Community Health and Home Care Services, 3d ed. By Anne S. Smith, New York: National League of Nurses, 1988.

> This specialized book would be useful to nurses as well as other health administrators. The publication includes discussions of strategic planning, marketing, management, and evaluation of community and home health care services.

A Guide to Health Data Resources   By Ira D. Singer, Millwood, Virginia: Center for Health Affairs Project HOPE, 1985.

> This guide offers descriptions of resource documents on health care that have been published by public- and private-sector organizations in the United States. Complete

bibliographic information is given for each item. An added feature is a general description as well as an abridged table of contents when applicable.

Handbook of Health Care Management   By W. Jack Duncan, Peter M. Ginter, and Linda E. Swayne, Malden, Massachusetts: Blackwell Publishers, 1997.

The handbook contains fifteen relevant topics for practicing health care managers as well as students of health administration.

The Health Care Supervisor's Handbook, 2d ed.   By Norman Metzger, Rockville, Maryland: Aspen Systems Corporation, 1982.

The handbook addresses the complex and varied responsibilities of today's health care supervisor. Features include sample supervisor evaluations, a leadership questionnaire, and a description of the leadership selection process.

Health Services Administration: Education and Practice   By Karen M. Lorentz, St. Louis: W. H. Green, 1988.

This basic guide and text would be beneficial to any new professional to the health care field. Recent developments in the education of health administrators are the primary focus of this guide.

Health Statistics: A Guide to Information Sources   By Freida Weise, Detroit: Gale Research Company, 1980.

This inclusive resource annotates and evaluates the references cited in the following areas: birth and mortality, marriage and divorce, morbidity, health care facilities, health personnel, use of health services, health care costs and expenditures, health professions, education, and population characteristics.

Hospital Health Promotion   By Neil Sol, Champaign, Illinois: Human Kinetics Books, 1989.

This book represents a strategic approach to hospital health promotion and is designed to make health care administrators aware of the current and future importance of marketing. Divided into six parts, Part 3 offers a "how-to" strategy for program development, management, marketing, selling, and delivery.

Human Resource Management in the Health Care Sector: A Guide for Administrators and Professionals   By Amarjit S. Sethi, New York: Quorum Books, 1989.

Health facilities, personnel management in the health services field, and hospital administration are all topics in this important addition to the health administration literature. This guide would be very useful to the practicing administrator.

The White Labyrinth: A Guide to the Health Care System   By David B. Smith, Ann Arbor, Michigan: Health Administration Press, 1986.

This detailed analysis of the health care delivery system includes external environmental issues shaping financial and regulatory providers, an in-depth account of the structural shifts in health care delivery, and a presentation of the health care system's operational issues. It is organized into sections that include figures and tables as part of the text.

Indexes

Business Index   Forest City, California: Information Access Company (monthly).

This source is available on 16-mm computer-output microfilm for viewing on a microfilm reader, which provides more rapid availability and more complete accumulation of information. Over 375 business periodicals are indexed, as well as acquisitions, mergers, and corporate promotions from the *New York Times* and the *Wall Street Journal.*

Business Periodicals Index   New York: H. W. Wilson Co. (monthly).

BPI is a cumulative index to English-language periodicals pertaining to business. Approximately 300 periodicals are indexed primarily by subject. Articles about a company are indexed under the name of the company. Volumes are issued monthly, with a cumulative quarterly update and a cumulative annual update published.

Cumulative Index to Nursing and Allied Health Literature   Glendale, California: Seventh Day Adventist Hospital Association (five per year with annual accumulations).

This index is not limited to nursing journals. Health care delivery and other special topics are also included.

Funk and Scott (F & S) Index of Corporations and Industries   Cleveland: Predicasts, Inc. (annually).

F & S is an excellent source to locate information concerning specific industries and companies. It indexes business-related journals, some newspapers, trade publications, newsletters, and loose-leaf services. This index is divided into two sections: industry and company. The industry section is arranged by SIC number; the company section is arranged alphabetically by company name. To identify the SIC code for an industry, check the *Standard Industrial Classification Manual* usually kept at the reference desk at most libraries.

Hospital Literature Index   Chicago: American Hospital Association (quarterly, with annual and quinquennial accumulations).

This is a major index service providing information about hundreds of health journals. It is arranged by author and subject. Cumulative indexes are published periodically.

New York Times Index   New York: The New York Times Company (semimonthly).

Published semimonthly with quarterly updates and a yearly cumulative issue, the *NY Times Index* abstracts news and editorial matter classified by appropriate subject, geographic, organization, and personal name headings. Entries are by subject whenever possible and are alphabetized.

Wall Street Journal Index   New York: Dow Jones and Company.

This index covers articles published in the *Wall Street Journal.* There are two sections: general news, where articles concerning various subjects are arranged alphabetically, and corporate news, where articles about companies are arranged by company name.

Health Care and Management Journals

Allied Health Care

Education and the Health Professions   Beverly Hills, California: Sage Publications (quarterly).

Health Care Supervisor   Frederick, Maryland: Aspen Publishers, Inc. (quarterly).

Journal of Allied Health   Chicago: College of Associated Health Professions, University of Illinois (quarterly).

Nursing Administration Quarterly   Rockville, Maryland: Aspen Systems (quarterly).

Business (General)

Administrative Science Quarterly   Ithaca, New York: Cornell Graduate School of Business (quarterly).

Business Horizons   Bloomington, Indiana: Indiana University School of Business (bimonthly).

California Management Review   Berkeley: University of California at Berkeley, School of Business (quarterly).

Harvard Business Review   Boston: Harvard University, Graduate School of Business Administration (bimonthly).

Journal of General Management   Sussex, England: Braybrooke Press, Ltd. (quarterly).

Finance and Economics

Health Care Financing Review   Baltimore: U.S. Department of Health and Human Services, Health Care Financing Administration (quarterly).

Healthcare Financial Management   Westchester, Illinois: Healthcare Financial Management Association (monthly).

Hospital Capital Finance   Chicago: American Hospital Association (monthly).

Journal of Finance   New York: American Finance Association, Stern School of Business, New York University (monthly).

Journal of Health Care Finance   Gaithersburg, Maryland: Aspen Publishers, Inc. (quarterly).

Journal of Health Economics   Amsterdam, Netherlands: North Holland (quarterly).

Topics in Health Care Financing   Frederick, Maryland: Aspen Publishers, Inc. (quarterly).

Health Administration Management (General)

Frontiers of Health Services Management   Ann Arbor, Michigan: Health Administration Press (quarterly).

Health Care Executive   Chicago: American College of Healthcare Executives (six issues per year).

Health Care Management Review   Frederick, Maryland: Aspen Publishers, Inc. (quarterly).

Health Services Management Research   Harlow, England: Longman Group, UK (three issues per year).

HMQ (Hospital Management Quarterly)   Evanston, Illinois: American Hospital Supply Corporation (quarterly).

Hospital and Health Services Administration   Chicago: Foundation of the American College of Healthcare Executives (quarterly).

Journal of Health Administration Education   Arlington, Virginia: Association of University Programs in Health Administration (quarterly).

Health Care (General)

American Journal of Public Health   Washington, D.C.: American Public Health Association (monthly).

Annual Review of Public Health   Palo Alto, California: Annual Reviews, Inc. (annually).

Hastings Center Report   Briarcliff Manor, New York: Hastings Center Studies (bimonthly).

Health Affairs   Chevy Chase, Maryland: People-to-People Health Foundation, Inc. (quarterly).

Healthcare Forum Journal   San Francisco: Healthcare Forum (bimonthly).

Health Policy   Amsterdam, Netherlands: Elsevier Science Publishers (nine issues per year).

Health Progress   St. Louis: Catholic Health Association of the United States (ten issues per year).

Health Services Research   Ann Arbor, Michigan: Health Care Administration Press (bimonthly).

Inquiry   Chicago: Blue Cross/Blue Shield (quarterly).

Journal of American Health Policy   Washington, D.C.: Faulkner and Gray (bimonthly).

Journal of Community Health   New York: Human Sciences Press, Inc. (bimonthly).

Journal of Health and Human Services Administration   Montgomery, Alabama: Southern Public Administration Education Foundation (quarterly).

Journal of Health and Social Behavior   Washington, D.C.: American Sociological Association (quarterly).

Journal of Public Health Policy   Burlington, Vermont: Journal of Public Health Policy (quarterly).

Milbank Quarterly   New York: Blackwell Publishers (quarterly).

Mobius   Berkeley: University of California Press (quarterly).

Modern Health Care   Chicago: Crain Communications, Inc. (weekly).

Public Health Reports   Rockville, Maryland: U.S. Public Health Service (bimonthly).

U.S. Healthcare   Lakewood, Colorado: Health Data Analysis, Inc. (monthly).

Human Resources

Journal of Health and Human Resources Administration   Montgomery, Alabama: Southern Public Administration Education Foundation (quarterly).

Information Systems

Computers in Health Care   Englewood, Colorado: Cardiff (monthly).

Datamation   Newton, Massachusetts: Cahners Publishing Company (twenty-four issues per year)

Health Care Informatics   Lakewood, Colorado: Health Data Analysis (monthly).

Healthcare Computing and Communications   Littleton, Colorado: Health Data Analysis (monthly).

Health Management Technology   Atlanta, Georgia: Argus, Inc. (monthly).

Journal of AHIMA   Chicago: American Health Information Management Association (twelve times per year).

International Health

International Journal of Health Planning and Management   Essex, England: John Wiley and Sons (quarterly).

International Journal of Health Services   Amityville, New York: Baywood Publishing Company (quarterly).

International Journal of Mental Health   Armonk, New York: M. E. Sharpe, Inc. (quarterly).

Social Science and Medicine   Tarrytown, New York: Pergamon Press, Inc. (bimonthly).

World Health   Geneva, Switzerland: World Health Organization (bimonthly).

World Hospitals and Health Services   London, England: International Hospital Federation (three issues per year)

Legal and Ethical

Health Law Bulletin   Chapel Hill, North Carolina: Institute of Government (irregular).

Health Law Digest   Washington, D.C.: National Health Lawyers Association (monthly).

Journal of Health Politics, Policy and Law   Durham, North Carolina: Duke University (quarterly).

Journal of Law, Medicine, and Ethics   Boston: American Society of Law, Medicine, and Ethics (quarterly).

Law, Medicine and Health Care   Boston: American Society of Law and Medicine (bimonthly).

Management (General)

Academy of Management Executive   Ada, Ohio: Academy of Management (quarterly).

Academy of Management Journal   Ada, Ohio: Academy of Management (six issues per year).

Academy of Management Proceedings   Ada, Ohio: Academy of Management (annually).

Academy of Management Review   Ada, Ohio: Academy of Management (six issues per year).

Journal of Business Strategy   New York: Warren, Gorham, and Lamont (six issues per year).

Journal of Management   Bloomington, Indiana: Indiana University School of Business (quarterly).

Journal of Management Studies   Oxford, England: Basil Blackwell, Ltd. (annually).

Long Range Planning   Tarrytown, New York: Pergamon Press, Inc. (six issues per year).

Organizational Dynamics   New York: American Management Association (quarterly)

Medicine (General)

Academic Medicine   Washington, D.C.: Association of American Medical Colleges (monthly).

Journal of the American Medical Association   Chicago: American Medical Association (weekly).

Journal of Medical Systems   New York: Plenum Press (quarterly).

Medical Care   Philadelphia: J. B. Lippincott Co. (monthly).

Medical Care Research and Review   Chicago: American College of Healthcare Executives (quarterly).

Medical Care Review   Ann Arbor, Michigan: Health Administration Press (quarterly).

Medical Economics   Montvale, New Jersey: Medical Economics Publishing Company (every two weeks).

New England Journal of Medicine   Waltham, Massachusetts: Massachusetts Medical Society (weekly).

Provider Type

American Journal of Hospital Pharmacy   Philadelphia: Philadelphia College of Pharmacy and Science (monthly).

Emergency Health Services Review   Binghamton, New York: Haworth Press (quarterly).

Home Health Care Services Quarterly Binghamton, New York: Haworth Press, Inc. (quarterly).

Hospice Journal Binghamton, New York: Haworth Press, Inc. (quarterly).

Hospital Forum San Francisco: Association of Western Hospitals (bimonthly).

Hospital Topics Sarasota, Florida: Hospital Topics (bimonthly).

Hospital Trustee Ottawa, Canada: Canadian Hospital Association (bimonthly).

Hospitals and Health Networks Chicago: American Hospital Publishing, Inc. (quarterly).

Journal of Ambulatory Care Management Frederick, Maryland: Aspen Publishers, Inc. (quarterly).

Journal of Ambulatory Health Management Netherlands: Swet and Zeithinger BV (quarterly).

Journal of Ambulatory Health Marketing Binghamton, New York: Haworth Press, Inc. (quarterly).

Journal of Emergency Medical Services Solana Beach, California: JEMS Publishing (monthly).

Journal of Long Term Care Administration Alexandria, Virginia: American College of Health Care Administrators (quarterly).

Journal of Medical Practice Management Baltimore, Maryland: Williams and Wilkins (quarterly).

Journal of Mental Health Administration Washington, D.C.: Association of Mental Health Administrators (semiannually).

Journal of Nursing Administration Philadelphia: J. B. Lippincott, Co. (monthly).

Journal of Rural Health Kansas City, Missouri: National Rural Health Association (semiannually).

Medical Group Management Denver, Colorado: Medical Group Management Association (bimonthly).

Trustee Chicago: American Hospital Association (monthly).

Strategic Management and Marketing

Health Care Strategic Management Ann Arbor, Michigan: Chi Systems (monthly).

Health Marketing Quarterly Binghamton, New York: Hawthorne Press, Inc. (quarterly).

Journal of Health Care Marketing Chicago: American Marketing Association (quarterly).

Planning Review Oxford, Ohio: International Society for Strategic Management and Planning (bimonthly).

Strategic Management Journal Sussex, England: John Wiley and Sons, Ltd. (eight issues per year).

Loose-Leaf Services

Health Administration: Laws, Regulations and Guidelines Towson, Maryland: National Health Publishing Limited Partnership.

Direct federal regulation of the health care industry is covered in this service, which provides current updates of federal regulation of the health care industry.

Hospital Law Manual   Germantown, Maryland: Aspen Systems.

This unique set of books has separate volumes for use by health administrators as well as attorneys. Topics are conveniently organized according to subject. All sections are periodically updated with recent developments in health care law.

Industry Information

Economic Census   Washington, D.C.: U.S. Government Printing Office.

The U.S. Bureau of the Census publishes an economic census every five years for years that end in 2 or 7. This government document includes manufacturers, retail, wholesale, service, construction, transportation, and mineral industries. The data include number of establishments, value of shipments or sales, cost of materials, employment, and payroll, arranged by line of business.

Forbes Magazine   New York: Forbes, Inc. (monthly).

Annually *Forbes* publishes a special issue (in January) that reviews the performance of major American industries and ranks the identified firms by profitability and growth.

Fortune Magazine   New York: Time-Warner, Inc. (biweekly).

Annually the *Fortune 500* is published in May, reviewing the performance of the 500 largest industrials in the United States; the *Services 500* is published in June; and the *International 500* is published in August.

Statistical Abstract of the United States   Washington, D.C.: U.S. Government Printing Office (annually).

A standard summary of statistics on the social, political, and economic organizations in the United States, this source includes data from many statistical publications, both government and private. Emphasis is on national data, but regional, state, and metropolitan data is also included.

Survey of Current Business   Washington, D.C.: U.S. Government Printing Office.

This publication provides up-to-date leading economic indicators, as well as general business indicators, and analyses for selected industries.

U.S. Industrial Outlook   Washington, D.C.: U.S. Government Printing Office (annually).

Industries are profiled along with forecasts for industry activity for the next decade.

Sources of Financial Information

Moody's Manuals   New York: Moody's Investors' Service, Inc. (annually).

A subsidiary of Dun and Bradstreet, Moody's publishes manuals annually in five areas: industrial, bank and finance, public utility, transportation, and OTC (over-the-counter) industrial. Detailed financial information is provided for companies that represent investment opportunities. The information for the industries includes location and history of the firm, type of business, property, reserves, subsidiaries, officers, directors, annual meetings, balance sheets and income statements for several years, earnings, dividends, loans, debts, securities issued, market prices of securities, and related data. Similar information, tailored to other types of organizations, is provided in the different manuals. Each manual is updated by the loose-leaf *News Reports.*

Standard and Poor's Corporation Services   New York: Standard and Poor's Corporation.

Standard and Poor's lists corporations and other organizations offering investment opportunities. Information is arranged alphabetically by company and includes capitalization, corporate background, financial statements, properties, officers, stock data, numbers of stockholders, price range of securities, dividends, and other data.

Value Line Investment Survey   New York: A. Bernard (weekly).

Although this source is designed to guide private investors, professional analysts, corporate executives, purchasing agents, and sales managers, it does provide timely information on corporate developments and analysis of financial position as well as a brief industry overview. More than 1,500 companies in a variety of industries are covered in the weekly publication. Data include a ten-year statistical history of the firms in the survey, estimates of the next three-to-five-years' sales, estimates of quarterly sales, earnings, and dividends.

On-Line Search Engines

The world wide web (WWW) offers a wealth of information from your computer. Many hospitals have developed web pages as have most pharmaceutical companies, health insurance companies, medical equipment companies, and so on. Some companies encourage you to purchase their products from their web page (direct marketing), whereas others use their web page to provide information about the organization itself or about various diseases, treatments, tips to maintain health, and so on. "Chat pages" have been established as support groups for a variety of health problems. Accessing the specific information that you want on the web is sometimes a daunting task, but it can be simplified by use of search engines that allow use of normal language to search for the topic of interest. If one of the following moves too slowly, try a different one. (See Perspective 9–5 for the ten best health care web sites).

Search Engine	Address
Altavista	http://altavista.digital.com
Infoseek	http://www2.infoseek.com
LYCOS	http://www.lycos.com
Webcrawler	http://www.webcrawler.com
Yahoo	http://www.yahoo.com.search/html

Statistical Sources

Facts at Your Fingertips: A Guide to Sources of Statistical Information on Major Health Topics, 6th ed.   Hyattsville, Maryland: U.S. Department of Health and Human Services, National Center for Health Statistics, 1982.

Many sources of statistical information on major health topics are listed in this publication. It provides citations for individual sources and also includes information on persons to contact with phone numbers and addresses.

Hospital Statistics   Chicago: American Hospital Association (annual).

This detailed statistical compendium presents current and trend data about hospitals in the United States. The tables are compiled from a survey response. Data are arranged according to geographic area, type of organization reporting, and services provided. It also offers comprehensive statistics on the number of hospitals, beds, and patients.

Standard Medical Almanac, 2d ed.   Chicago: Marquis Academic Media, 1979.

A periodically updated publication with an overall focus on health personnel and health services statistics. Divided into six parts, this publication covers human resources, budgeting, licensing, facilities management, general health care, and federal information. There are also three separate indexes: subject, organization, and geographic.

Bibliography for Health Care Researchers and Strategists

Appendix E

Aaker, D. A. *Developing Business Strategies,* 4th ed. New York: John Wiley & Sons, Inc., 1995.

Abrahams, J. *The Mission Statement Book: 301 Mission Statements from America's Top Companies.* New York: Ten Speed Press, 1995.

Ackerman, F. K., III. "The Movement Toward Vertically Integrated Regional Health Systems." *Health Care Management Review* 17, no. 3 (Summer 1992), pp. 81–88.

Agho, A. O., and S. T. Cyphert. "Problem Areas Faced by Hospital Administrators." *Hospital and Health Services Administration* 37, no. 1 (Spring 1992), pp. 131–135.

Akin, B. V., L. Rucker, F. A. Hubbell, R. W. Cygan, and H. Waitzkin. "Access to Medical Care in a Medically Indigent Population." *Journal of General Internal Medicine* 4 (May/June 1989), pp. 216–220.

Alexander, J. A. "Adaptive Change in Corporate Control Practices." *Academy of Management Journal* 34, no. 1 (March 1991), pp. 162–193.

Alexander, J. A., and L. L. Morlock. "CEO-Board Relationships Under Hospital Corporate Restructuring." *Hospital and Health Services Administration* 33, no. 4 (Winter 1988), pp. 435–448.

Alexander, J. A., and M. A. Morrisey. "Hospital-Physician Integration and Hospital Costs." *Inquiry* 25, no. 3 (Fall 1988), pp. 388–401.

Alexander, J. A., and M. A. Morrisey. "Hospital Selection into Multihospital Systems." *Medical Care* 26, no. 2 (February 1988), pp. 159–176.

Alexander, J. A., and T. G. Rundall. "Public Hospitals Under Contract Management." *Medical Care* 23, no. 3 (March 1985), pp. 209–219.

Alexander, J. A., and T. L. Amburgey. "The Dynamics of Change in the American Hospital Industry: Transformation or Selection?" *Medical Care Review* 44, no. 2 (Fall 1987), pp. 279–321.

Alexander, J. A., B. L. Lewis, and M. A. Morrisey. "Acquisition Strategies of Multihospital Systems." *Health Affairs* 4, no. 3 (Fall 1985), pp. 49–66.

Alexander, J. A., L. L. Morlock, and B. D. Gifford. "The Effects of Corporate Restructuring on Hospital Policymaking." *Health Services Research* 23, no. 2 (June 1988), pp. 311–338.

Alexander, J. A., M. A. Morrisey, and S. M. Shortell. "Effects of Competition, Regulation, and Corporatization on Hospital-Physician Relationships." *Journal of Health and Social Behavior* 27 (1986), pp. 220–235.

Alter, C. "An Exploratory Study of Conflict and Coordination in Interorganizational Service Delivery Systems." *Academy of Management Journal* 33, no. 3 (1990), pp. 478–502.

Amara, R., J. I. Morrison, and G. Schnid. *Looking Ahead at American Health Care.* Washington, D.C.: McGraw-Hill Book Company, Health Information Center, 1988.

American Hospital Association. *Vision, Environmental Values, Viability Assessment 1989–1990.* Chicago: American Hospital Association, 1988.

Amit, R., and P. J. H. Schoemaker. "Strategic Assets and Organizational Rent." *Strategic Management Journal* 14 (1993), pp. 33–46.

Andersen, R. M., T. H. Rice, and G. F. Kominski, eds. *Changing the U.S. Health Care System: Key Issues in Health Services, Policy, and Management.* San Francisco: Jossey-Bass Publishers, 1996.

Ansoff, H. I., and E. J. McDonnell. *Implementing Strategic Management,* 2d ed. Englewood Cliffs, New Jersey: Prentice-Hall, 1990.

Arndt, M., and B. Bigelow. "Vertical Integration in Hospitals: A Framework for Analysis." *Medical Care Review* 49, no. 1 (1993), pp. 93–115.

Arnold, R. J., and L. M. DeBrock. "Competition and Market Failure in the Hospital Industry: A Review of the Evidence." *Medical Care Review* 43, no. 2 (Fall 1986), pp. 253–292.

Atchison, T. A. *Turning Health Care Leadership Around: Cultivating Inspired, Empowered, and Loyal Followers.* San Francisco: Jossey-Bass, 1990.

Austin, C. J. *Information Systems for Health Services Administration,* 4th ed. Ann Arbor, Michigan: AUPHA Press, 1992.

Autrey, P., and D. Thomas. "Competitive Strategy in the Hospital Industry." *Health Care Management Review* 11, no. 1 (Winter 1986), pp. 7–14.

Azzibem, G., and U. Bertele. "Measuring Resources for Supporting Resource-Based Competencies," *Management Decision* 33, no. 9 (1995), pp. 57–58.

Barker, J. A. *Future Edge: Discovering the New Paradigms of Success.* New York: William Morrow and Company, 1992.

Barney, J. B. "Firm Resources and Sustained Competitive Advantage." *Journal of Management* 17, no. 1 (1991), pp. 99–120.

Barney, J. B. "Looking Inside for Competitive Advantage." *Academy of Management Executive* 9, no. 4 (1995), pp. 49–61.

Barney, J. B., and M. H. Hansen. "Trustworthiness as a Source of Competitive Advantage." *Strategic Management Journal* 15, no. 3 (1994), pp. 175–190.

Barsky, A. "A Radical Prescription for Hospitals." *Harvard Business Review* 66, no. 3 (May/June 1988), pp. 100–104.

Bates, D. L., and J. E. Dillard, Jr. "Wanted: A Strategic Planner for the 1990s." *Journal of General Management* 18, no. 1 (1992), pp. 51–62.

Baum, J. A. C., and H. J. Korn. "Competitive Dynamics of Interfirm Rivalry." *Academy of Management Journal* 39, no. 2 (1996), pp. 255–291.

Baysinger, B., and R. E. Hoskisson. "The Composition of Boards of Directors and Strategic Control: Effects on Corporate Strategy." *Academy of Management Review* 15, no. 1 (January 1990), pp. 72–87.

Beam, H. H. "Strategic Discontinuities: When Being Good May Not Be Enough." *Business Horizons* 33, no. 4 (July/August 1990), pp. 10–14.

Beckham, D. "Making Speed a Priority." *Marketing to Doctors* 5, no. 11 (November 1992), pp. 1–3.

Beckham, J. D. "The Longest Wave." *Healthcare Forum Journal* 36, no. 6 (November/December 1993), pp. 78, 80–82.

Bell, R. "Laying the Groundwork for a Smooth Transition to TQM." *Hospital Topics* 71, no. 1 (1993), pp. 23–26.

Bennis, W., and R. Townsend. *Reinventing Leadership: Strategies to Empower the Organization.* New York: William Morrow and Company, Inc., 1995.

Berkowitz, D. A., and M. M. Swan. "Technology Decision Making." *Health Progress* 74, no. 1 (January/February 1993), p. 42–47.

Berry, L. L. "Five Imperatives for Improving Service Quality." *Sloan Management Review* 31, no. 4 (Summer 1991), pp. 29–38.

Berry, L. L. "Services Marketing Is Different." *Business* (May/June 1980), pp. 24–30.

Berwick, D. M. "Health Services Research and Quality of Care: Assignments for the 1990s." *Medical Care* 27, no. 8 (August 1989), pp. 763–771.

Berwick, D. M., A. B. Godfrey, and J. Roessner. *Curing Health Care: New Strategies for Quality Improvement.* San Francisco: Jossey-Bass, 1990.

Bezold, C. "Five Futures." *Healthcare Forum Journal* 35, no. 3 (1992), p. 29.

Bezold, C. "The Future of Health Care: Implications for the Allied Health Professions." *Journal of Allied Health* 18, no. 5 (Fall 1989), pp. 435–458.

Biehl, B. *Stop Setting Goals If You Would Rather Solve Problems.* Nashville: Moorings, 1995.

Biendon, R. J. "The Public's View of the Future of Health Care." *Journal of the American Medical Association* 259, no. 24 (1985), pp. 3587–3593.

Bigelow, B., and J. F. Mahon. "Strategic Behavior of Hospitals: A Framework for Analysis." *Medical Care Review* 46, no. 3 (Fall 1989), pp. 295–311.

Bigelow, B., and M. Arndt. "Ambulatory Care Centers: Are They a Competitive Advantage?" *Hospital and Health Services Administration* 36, no. 3 (Fall 1991), pp. 351–363.

Blair, J. D., and C. J. Whitehead. "Too Many on the Seesaw: Stakeholder Diagnosis and Management for Hospitals." *Hospital and Health Services Administration* 33, no. 2 (Summer 1988), pp. 153–166.

Blair, J. D., and M. D. Fottler. *Challenges in Health Care Management: Strategic Perspectives for Managing Key Stakeholders.* San Francisco: Jossey-Bass, 1990.

Blair, J. D., C. R. Slaton, and G. T. Savage. "Hospital-Physician Joint Ventures: A Strategic Approach for Both Dimensions of Success." *Hospital and Health Services Administration* 35, no. 1 (Spring 1990), pp. 3–26.

Blair, J. D., G. T. Savage, and C. J. Whitehead. "A Strategic Approach for Negotiating with Hospital Stakeholders." *Health Care Management Review* 14, no. 1 (Winter 1989), pp. 13–23.

Blumenthal, D., and B. R. Berenson. "Health Care Issues in Presidential Campaigns." *New England Journal of Medicine* 321, no. 13 (September 28, 1989), pp. 908–912.

Bodenheimer, T. "The Fruits of Empire Rot on the Vine: U.S. Health Policy in the Austerity Era." *Sociology, Science and Medicine* 28, no. 6 (1989), pp. 531–538.

Boeker, W. "Strategic Change: The Effects of Founding and History." *Academy of Management Journal* 32, no. 3 (September 1989), pp. 489–515.

Boles, K. E., and J. K. Glenn. "What Accounting Leaves out of Hospital Financial Management." *Hospital and Health Services Administration* 31, no. 2 (Summer 1986), pp. 8–27.

Borys, B., and D. B. Jemison. "Hybrid Arrangements as Strategic Alliances: Theoretical Issues in Organizational Combinations." *Academy of Management Review* 14, no. 2 (April 1989), pp. 234–249.

Boscarino, J. A. "Hospital Wellness Centers: Strategic Implementation, Marketing, and Management." *Health Care Management Review* 14, no. 2 (Spring 1989), pp. 25–29.

Bowman, E. H., and D. Hurry. "Strategy Through the Option Lens: An Integrated View of Resource Investments and the Incremental-Choice Process." *Academy of Management Review* 18, no. 4 (October 1993), pp. 760–782.

Bracken, J., J. Calkin, J. Sanders, and A. Thesen. "A Strategy for Adaptive Staffing of Hospitals Under Varying Environmental Conditions." *Health Care Management Review* 10, no. 4 (Fall 1985), pp. 43–53.

Breindel, C. L. "Nongrowth Strategies and Options in Health Care." *Hospital and Health Services Administration* 33, no. 1 (Spring 1988), pp. 37–45.

Bridgers, W. F. *Health Care Reform: The Dilemma and a Pathway for the Health Care System.* St. Louis: G. W. Manning, 1992.

Brown, M. "The 1990s: Just Around the Corner." *Health Care Management Review* 13, no. 2 (Spring 1988), pp. 81–86.

Brown, M. *Health Care Marketing Management.* Gaithersburg, Maryland: Aspen Publishers, 1992.

Brown, M., and B. P. McCool. "High-Performing Managers: Leadership Attributes for the 1990s." *Health Care Management Review* 12, no. 2 (Spring 1987), pp. 69–75.

Brown, M., and B. P. McCool. "Vertical Integration: Exploration of a Popular Strategic Concept." *Health Care Management Review* 11, no. 4 (Fall 1986), pp. 17–19.

Broyles, R. W., and B. J. Reilly. "Physicians, Patients, and Administrators: A Realignment of Relationships." *Hospital and Health Services Administration* 33, no. 1 (Spring 1988), pp. 5–14.

Brumagim, A. L. "A Hierarchy of Corporate Resources." In *Advances in Strategic Management: Resource-Based View of the Firm,* edited by Paul Shrivastava, Anne S. Huff, and Jane E. Dutton, pp. 81–112. Greenwich, Connecticut: JAI Press, 1994.

Buller, P. F., and L. Timpson. "The Strategic Management of Hospitals: Toward an Integrative Approach." *Health Care Management Review* 11, no. 1 (Spring 1986), pp. 7–13.

Burns, L. R. "Matrix Management in Hospitals: Testing Theories of Matrix Structure and Development." *Administrative Science Quarterly* 34, no. 2 (June 1989), pp. 349–368.

Burns, L. R., and D. P. Thorpe. "Trends and Models in Physician-Hospital Organization." *Health Care Management Review* 18, no. 4 (Fall 1993), pp. 7–20.

Burns, L. R., R. M. Andersen, and S. M. Shortell. "The Impact of Corporate Structures on Physicians Inclusion and Participation." *Medical Care* 27, no. 10 (October 1989), pp. 967–982.

Butcher, A. H. "Supervisors Matter More Than You Think: Components of a Mission-Centered Organizational Climate." *Hospital and Health Services Administration* 39, no. 4 (1994), pp. 505–520.

Byars, L. L., and T. C. Neil. "Organizational Philosophy and Mission Statements." *Planning Review* 15, no. 4 (July/August 1987), pp. 32–35.

Camillus, J. C. "Reinventing Strategic Planning." *Strategy & Leadership* 24, no. 3 (1996), pp. 6–12.

Cantrell, L. E., Jr., and J. A. Flick. "Physician Efficiency and Reimbursement: A Case Study." *Hospital and Health Services Administration* 31, no. 4 (Winter 1986), pp. 43–50.

Carpman, J. R., and M. A. Grant. *Design That Cares: Planning Health Facilities for Patients and Visitors,*

2d ed. Chicago: American Hospital Publishing, 1993.

Carroll, A. B. "The Pyramid of Corporate Social Responsibility: Towards a Moral Management of Organizational Stakeholders." *Business Horizons* 34, no. 4 (July–August 1991), pp. 39–48.

Carroll, G. R. "A Sociological View on Why Firms Differ." *Strategic Management Journal* 14, no. 4 (1993), pp. 237–249.

Carroll, P. E., C. W. Daly, and J. C. Kowalski. "Materials Management." In *Effective Health Care Facilities Management,* edited by V. James McLarney. Chicago: American Hospital Publishing, 1991.

Carson, K. D., P. P. Carson, C. W. Roe, J. P. Authement, and R. Yallapragada. "Increasing the Effectiveness of Healthcare Managers." *Hospital Topics* 71, no. 3 (Summer 1993), pp. 16–19.

Cartwright, S., and C. L. Cooper. "The Role of Culture Compatibility in Successful Organizational Marriage." *Academy of Management Executive* 7, no. 2 (May 1993), pp. 57–70.

Casalou, R. F. "Total Quality Management in Health Care." *Hospital and Health Services Administration* 36, no. 1 (Spring 1991), pp. 134–146.

Chaffee, E. E. "Three Models of Strategy." *Academy of Management Review* 10, no. 1 (January 1985), pp. 89–98.

Champy, J. *Reengineering Management: The Mandate for Leadership.* New York: HarperBusiness, 1996.

Champy, J., and N. Nohria. *Fast Forward: The Best Ideas on Managing Business Change.* Boston: Harvard Business Review Press, 1996.

Chang, Y., and H. Thomas. "The Impact of Diversification Strategy on Risk-Return Performance." *Strategic Management Journal* 10, no. 3 (May/June 1989), pp. 271–284.

Chen, M. "Competitor Analysis and Interfirm Rivalry: Toward a Theoretical Integration." *Academy of Management Review* 21, no. 1 (1996), pp. 100–134.

Chilingerian, J. A. "New Directions for Hospital Strategic Management: The Market for Efficient Care." *Health Care Management Review* 17, no. 4 (Fall 1992), pp. 73–80.

Choi, T., R. F. Allison, and F. Munson. "Impact of Environment on State University Hospital Performance." *Medical Care* 23, no. 7 (July 1985), pp. 855–871.

Chow, C. W., K. M. Haddad, and K. Wong-Boren. "Improving Subjective Decision Making in Health Care Administration." *Hospital and Health Services Administration* 36, no. 2 (Summer 1991), pp. 191–210.

Christianson, J. B., M. Shadle, M. M. Hunter, S. Hartwell, and J. McGee. "The New Environment for Rural HMOs." *Health Affairs* 5, no. 1 (Spring 1986), pp. 105–121.

Christianson, J. B., S. M. Sanchez, D. R. Wholey, and M. Shadle. "The HMO Industry: Evolution in Population Demographics and Market Structures." *Medical Care Review* 48, no. 1 (Spring 1991), pp. 3–46.

Clement, J. P. "Corporate Diversification: Expectations and Outcomes." *Health Care Management Review* 13, no. 2 (Spring 1988), pp. 7–13.

Clement, J. P. "Does Hospital Diversification Improve Financial Outcomes?" *Medical Care* 25, no. 10 (October 1987), pp. 988–1001.

Clement, J. P. "Vertical Integration and Diversification of Acute Care Hospitals: Conceptual Definitions." *Hospital and Health Services Administration* 33, no. 1 (Spring 1988), pp. 99–110.

Clement, J. P., T. D'Aunno, and B. L. M. Poyzer. "The Financial Performance of Diversified Hospital Subsidiaries." *Health Services Research* 27, no. 6 (February 1993), pp. 741–763.

Cleverley, W. O. "Financial Policy Formation: Principles for Hospitals." *Hospital and Health Services Administration* 30, no. 1 (Spring 1985), pp. 29–42.

Cleverley, W. O. "How Boards Can Use Comparative Data in Strategic Planning." *Healthcare Executive* 4, no. 3 (May 6, 1989), pp. 32–33.

Cleverley, W. O. "Is a Leveraged ESOP a Possibility for the Voluntary Hospital?" *Hospital and Health Services Administration* 33, no. 3 (Fall 1988), pp. 385–405.

Cleverley, W. O. "Promotion and Pricing in Competitive Markets." *Hospital and Health Services Administration* 32, no. 3 (Fall 1987), pp. 329–341.

Cleverley, W. O. "Strategic Financial Planning: A Balance Sheet Perspective." *Hospital and Health Services Administration* 32, no. 3 (Fall 1987), pp. 1–20.

Cleverley, W. O. "Three Ways to Measure A Strategic Plan's Viability." *Healthcare Financial Management* 31, no. 1 (January 1989), pp. 63–69.

Cleverley, W. O., and R. K. Harvey. "Competitive Strategy for Successful Hospital Management." *Hospital and Health Services Administration* 37, no. 1 (Spring 1992), pp. 53–69.

Cleverley, W. O., and R. K. Harvey. "Critical Strategies for Successful Rural Hospitals." *Health Care Management Review* 17, no. 1 (Winter 1992), pp. 27–33.

Coddington, D. C., and K. D. Moore. *Market-Driven Strategies in Health Care.* San Francisco: Jossey-Bass, 1987.

Coddington, D. C., D. J. Keen, K. D. Moore, and R. L. Clark. *The Crisis in Health Care: Costs, Choices, and Strategies.* San Francisco: Jossey-Bass, 1990.

Coddington, D. C., L. E. Palmquist, and W. V. Trollinger. "Strategies for Survival in the Hospital Industry." *Harvard Business Review* 63, no. 3 (May/June 1985), pp. 129–138.

Coile, R. C., Jr. "Re-Visioning Health Care." *Health Management Quarterly* 11, no. 4 (1990), pp. 2–3.

Collins, J. C., and J. I. Porras. "Organizational Vision and Visionary Organizations." *California Management Review* 34, no. 1 (1991), pp. 30–52.

Collis, D. J., and C. A. Montgomery. "Competing on Resources: Strategy in the 1990s." *Harvard Business Review* 73, no. 4 (July/August, 1995), pp. 118–128.

Collis, D. J. "Research Note: How Valuable Are Organizational Capabilities?" *Strategic Management Journal* 15, no. 2 (1994), pp. 143–152.

Conger, J. A. "Inspiring Others: The Language of Leadership." *Academy of Management Executive* 5, no. 1 (February 1991), pp. 31–45.

Conrad, D. A., S. S. Mick, C. W. Madden, and G. Hoare. "Vertical Structures and Control in Health Care Markets: A Conceptual Framework and Empirical Review." *Medical Care Review* 45, no. 1 (Spring 1988), pp. 49–100.

Cook, D. "Strategic Plan Creates a Blueprint for Budgeting." *Healthcare Financial Management* 44, no. 5 (May 1990), pp. 21–25.

Cool, K., and I. Dierickx. "Rivalry, Strategic Groups and Firm Profitability." *Strategic Management Journal* 14, no. 1 (1993), pp. 47–59.

Coombs, T. W., and S. J. Holladay. "Speaking of Visions and Visions Being Spoken." *Management Communication Quarterly* 8, no. 2 (1994), pp. 165–189.

Costello, M. M. "Caution: Business Opportunity Ahead." *Hospital and Health Services Administration* 31, no. 4 (Winter 1986), pp. 19–31.

Coulson-Thomas, C. "Strategic Vision or Strategic Con: Rhetoric or Reality?" *Long Range Planning* 25, no. 1 (1992), pp. 81–89.

Counte, M. A., G. L. Glandon, D. M. Oleske, and J. P. Hill. "Total Quality Management in a Health Care Organization: How Are Employees Affected?" *Hospital and Health Services Administration* 37, no. 4 (Winter 1992), pp. 503–518.

Coyne, J. S. "A Comparative Financial Analysis of Multi-Institutional Organizations by Ownership Type." *Hospital and Health Services Administration* 30, no. 4 (Winter 1985), pp. 48–63.

Coyne, J. S. "A Financial Model for Assessing Hospital Performance: An Application to Multi-Institutional Organizations." *Hospital and Health Services Administration* 31, no. 2 (Summer 1986), pp. 28–40.

Crawford-Mason, C., and L. Dobyns. *Quality or Else.* Boston: Houghton Mifflin Company, 1991.

Culhane, D. P., and T. R. Hadley. "The Discriminating Characteristics of For-Profit versus Not-For-Profit Freestanding Psychiatric Inpatient Facilities." *Health Services Research* 27, no. 2 (June 1992), pp. 177–194.

Cyphert, S., and J. Rohrer. "A National Medical Care Program: Review and Synthesis of Past Proposals." *Journal of Public Health Policy* (Winter 1988), pp. 456–471.

Daniel, D. J., and W. D. Reitsperger. "Linking Quality Strategy with Management Control Systems: Empirical Evidence from Japanese Industry." *Accounting, Organizations, and Society* 16 (1991), pp. 601–618.

Darr, K. *Ethics in Health Services Management,* 2d ed. Baltimore: Health Professions Press, 1991.

D'Aunno, T. A., and H. S. Zuckerman. "A Life-Cycle Model of Organizational Federations: The Case of Hospitals." *Academy of Management Review* 12, no. 3 (July 1987), pp. 534–545.

D'Aunno, T. A., and H. S. Zuckerman. "The Emergence of Hospital Federations: An Integration of Perspectives from Organizational Theory." *Medical Care Review* 44, no. 2 (Fall 1987), pp. 323–343.

D'Aunno, T. A., R. Hooijbert, and F. C. Munson. "Decision Making, Goal Consensus, and Effectiveness in University Hospitals." *Hospital and Health Services Administration* 36, no. 4 (Winter 1991), pp. 505–523.

D'Aveni, R. A. "Coping with Hypercompetition: Utilizing the New 7S's Framework." *The Academy of Management Executive* 9, no. 3 (1995), pp. 45–60.

D'Aveni, R. A. "The Aftermath of Organizational Decline: A Longitudinal Study of the Strategic and Managerial Characteristics of Declining Firms." *Academy of Management Journal* 32, no. 3 (September 1989), pp. 577–605.

Davenport, T. H. "Need Radical Innovation and Continuous Improvement? Integrate Process Reengineering and TQM." *Planning Review* 22, no. 3 (May/June 1993), pp. 6–12.

Davis, T. R. V., and M. S. Patrick. "Benchmarking at the SunHealth Alliance." *Planning Review* 21, no. 1 (January/February 1993), pp. 28–31ff.

Day, G. S. *Market Driven Strategy: Processes for Creating Value.* New York: Free Press, 1990.

De Bono, E. *Serious Creativity: Using the Power of Lateral Thinking to Create New Ideas.* New York: HarperBusiness, 1992.

Delbecq, A. L., and S. L. Gill. "Developing Strategic Direction for Governing Boards." *Hospital and Health Services Administration* 33, no. 1 (Spring 1988), pp. 25–35.

DeMuro, P. R. *The Financial Manager's Guide to Managed Care and Integrated Delivery Systems.* Burr Ridge, Illinois: Irwin Professional Publishing, 1996.

Depree, M. *Leadership Is an Art.* New York: Doubleday, 1989.

Desai, H. B., and C. R. Margenthaler. "A Framework for Developing Hospital Strategies." *Hospital and Health Services Administration* 32, no. 2 (Summer 1987), pp. 235–248.

DeSimone, L. D. "How Can Big Companies Keep the Entrepreneurial Spirit Alive?" *Harvard Business Review* 73, no. 5 (1995), pp. 183–186.

Dixit, A. K., and B. J. Nalebuff. *Thinking Strategically: The Competitive Edge in Business, Politics, and Everyday Life.* New York: W. W. Norton & Company, 1991.

Drucker, P. F. *Managing in Turbulent Times.* New York: HarperBusiness, 1980.

Drucker, P. F. *Managing the Nonprofit Organization.* New York: HarperCollins Publishers, 1990.

Duncan, W. J. "When Necessity Becomes a Virtue: Do Not Get Too Cynical About Strategy." *Journal of General Management* 13, no. 2 (Winter 1987), pp. 29–43.

Duncan, W. J., P. M. Ginter, and L. E. Swayne, eds. *Handbook of Health Care Management.* Malden, Massachusetts: Blackwell Publishers, 1997.

Duncan, W. J., P. M. Ginter, and S. A. Capper. "Identifying Opportunities and Threats in Public Health." *European Journal of Public Health* 3 (1993), pp. 54–59.

Duncan, W. J., P. M. Ginter, and W. K. Kreidel. "A Sense of Direction in Public Organizations: An Analysis of Mission Statements in State Health Departments." *Administration and Society* 28, no. 1 (May 1994), pp. 11–24.

Dutton, J. E., and E. Ottensmeyer. "Strategic Issue Management Systems: Forms, Functions, and Contexts." *Academy of Management Review* 12, no. 2 (April 1987), pp. 355–365.

Dutton, J. E., and R. B. Duncan. "The Creation of Momentum for Change Through the Process of Strategic Issue Diagnosis." *Strategic Management Journal* 8, no. 3 (May/June 1987), pp. 279–295.

Dutton, J. E., and R. B. Duncan. "The Influence of the Strategic Planning Process on Strategic Change." *Strategic Management Journal* 8, no. 2 (March/April 1987), pp. 103–116.

Dutton, J. E., and S. E. Jackson. "Categorizing Strategic Issues: Links to Organizational Action." *Academy of Management Review* 12, no. 1 (January 1987), pp. 76–90.

Dutton, J. E., and S. J. Ashford. "Selling Issues to Top Management." *The Academy of Management Review* 18, no. 3 (July 1993), pp. 397–428.

Dwore, R. B., and B. P. Murray. "Hospital Administrators in a Market Environment: The Case of Utah." *Hospital and Health Services Administration* 32, no. 4 (Winter 1987), pp. 493–508.

Dychtwald, K., and M. Zitter. "Developing a Strategic Marketing Plan for Hospitals." *Healthcare Financial Management* 42, no. 9 (September 1988), pp. 42–46.

Eastaugh, S. R. "Hospital Specialization and Cost Efficiency: Benefits of Trimming Product Lines." *Hospital and Health Services Administration* 37, no. 2 (Summer 1992), pp. 223–235.

Eastaugh, S. R. "Hospital Strategy and Financial Performance." *Health Care Management Review* 17, no. 3 (Summer 1992), pp. 19–31.

Eastaugh, S. R., and J. A. Eastaugh. "Prospective Payment System: Steps to Enhance Quality, Efficiency, and Regionalization." *Health Care Management Review* 11, no. 4 (Fall 1986), pp. 37–52.

Ehreth, J. "Hospital Survival in a Competitive Environment: The Competitive Constituency Model." *Hospital and Health Services Administration* 38, no. 1 (Spring 1993), pp. 23–44.

Enthoven, A. "The History and Principles of Managed Competition." *Health Affairs,* Supplement (1993), pp. 24–48.

Enthoven, A., and R. Kronick. "A Consumer-Choice Health Plan for the 1990s." *New England Journal of Medicine* 320, no. 1 (January 5, 1989), pp. 29–37.

Enthoven, A., and R. Kronick. "A Consumer-Choice Health Plan for the 1990s." *New England Journal of Medicine* 320, no. 2 (January 12, 1989), pp. 94–101.

Erickson, G. M., and S. A. Finkler. "Determinants of Market Share for a Hospital's Services." *Medical Care* 23, no. 8 (August 1985), pp. 1003–1018.

Estes, R. *Tyranny of the Bottom Line.* San Francisco: Berrett-Koehler Publishers, 1996.

Fahey, L., and V. K. Narayanan. *Macroenvironmental Analysis for Strategic Management,* 2d ed. St. Paul: West Publishing Company, 1986.

Falbe, C., M. Kriger, L. Larwood, and P. Miesing. "Structure and Meaning of Organizational Vision." *Academy of Management Journal* 38, no. 3 (1995), pp. 740–767.

Fallon, R. P. "Profitability Planning in Not-for-Profit Organizations." *Health Care Management Review* 16, no. 3 (Summer 1991), pp. 47–61.

Farson, R. *Management of the Absurd.* New York: Simon & Schuster, 1996.

Fennell, M. L., and J. A. Alexander. "Governing Boards and Profound Organizational Change in Hospitals." *Medical Care Review* 46, no. 2 (Summer 1989), pp. 157–187.

Fennell, M. L., and J. A. Alexander. "Organizational Boundary Spanning in Institutionalized Environments." *Academy of Management Journal* 30, no. 3 (September 1987), pp. 456–476.

Ferrand, J. D., M. Chokron, and C. M. Lay. "An Integrated Analytic Framework for Evaluation of Hospital Information Systems Planning." *Medical Care Review* 50, no. 3 (Fall 1993), pp. 327–366.

Fetter, R. B., and J. L. Freeman. "Diagnosis Related Groups: Product Line Management Within Hospitals." *Academy of Management Review* 11, no. 1 (January 1986), pp. 41–54.

Files, L. A. "Strategy Formulation in Hospitals." *Health Care Management Review* 13, no. 1 (Winter 1988), pp. 9–16.

Findelstein, S. "Power in Top Management Teams: Dimensions, Measurement, and Validation." *Academy of Management Journal* 35 (1992), pp. 505–538.

Flannery, T. P., D. A. Hofrichter, and P. Platten. *People, Performance, and Pay.* New York: Free Press, 1996.

Floyd, S. W., and B. Wooldridge. "Managing Strategic Consensus: The Foundation of Effective Implementation." *Academy of Management Executive* 6 (November 1992), pp. 27–35.

Folger, J. C. "Integration of Strategic, Financial Plans Vital to Success." *Healthcare Financial Management* 43, no. 1 (January 1989), pp. 22–32.

Folger, J. C. "Strategic Plans Provide Lasting Solutions to Rural Crisis." *Healthcare Financial Management* 44, no. 4 (April 1990), pp. 25–30.

Fontaine, S. J. "Evaluating the Use of Environmental Analysis in Health Care." *Health Care Strategic Management* 5, no. 12 (December 1987), pp. 15–18.

Foster, J. T. "Hospitals in the Year 2000: A Scenario." *Frontiers of Health Services Management* 6, no. 2 (Winter 1989), pp. 3–29.

Fottler, M. D., and L. J. Repasky. "Attitudes of Hospital Executives Toward Product Line Management: A Pilot Survey." *Health Care Management Review* 13, no. 3 (Summer 1988), pp. 15–22.

Fottler, M. D., H. L. Smith, and H. J. Muller. "Retrenchment in Health Care Organizations: Theory and Practice." *Hospital and Health Services Administration* 31, no. 3 (Fall 1986), pp. 29–43.

Fottler, M. D., J. D. Blair, C. J. Whitehead, M. D. Lau, and G. T. Savage. "Assessing Key Stakeholders: Who Matters to Hospitals and Why?" *Hospital and Health Services Administration* 34, no. 4 (Winter 1989), pp. 525–546.

Fottler, M. D., R. L. Phillips, J. D. Blair, and C. A. Duran. "Achieving Competitive Advantage Through Strategic Human Resources Management." *Hospital and Health Services Administration* 35, no. 3 (Fall 1990), pp. 341–364.

Fox, I., and A. Marcus. "The Causes and Consequences of Leveraged Management Buyouts." *Academy of Management Review* 17, no. 1 (January 1992), pp. 62–85.

Fox, W. L. "Vertical Integration Strategies: More Promising than Diversification." *Health Care Management Review* 14, no. 3 (Summer 1989), pp. 49–56.

France, K. R., and R. Grover. "What Is the Health Care Product?" *Journal of Health Care Marketing* 12, no. 2 (June 1992), pp. 32–45.

Fredrickson, J. W. "Effects of Decision Motive and Organizational Performance Level on Strategic Decision Processes." *Academy of Management Journal* 28, no. 4 (December 1985), pp. 821–843.

Fredrickson, J. W., and T. R. Mitchell. "Strategic Decision Processes: Comprehensiveness and Performance in an Industry with an Unstable Environment." *Academy of Management Journal* 27, no. 2 (June 1984), pp. 399–423.

Fredrickson, J. W., ed. *Perspectives on Strategic Management.* New York: HarperBusiness, 1990.

Frenzel, C. W. *Management of Information Technology.* Boston: boyd & fraser, 1992.

Friedman, B., and S. M. Shortell. "The Financial Performance of Selected Investor-Owned and Not-for-Profit System Hospitals Before and After Medicare Prospective Payment." *Health Services Research* 23, no. 2 (June 1988), pp. 237–267.

Friedman, E. *Choices and Conflict: Explorations in Health Care Ethics.* Chicago: American Hospital Publishing, 1992.

Frize, M., and M. Shaffer. "Clinical Engineering in Today's Hospital." *Hospital and Health Services Administration* 36, no. 2 (Summer 1991), pp. 288–299.

Frost, P. J., L. F. Moore, M. L. Louis, C. C. Lundberg, and J. Martin, eds. *Reframing Organizational Culture.* Newbury Park, California: Sage Publications, 1991.

Gabler, J. M. "Information Systems: A Competitive Advantage for Managing Healthcare." In *Healthcare Information Management Systems,* edited by Marion J. Ball, Judith V. Douglas, Robert I. O'Desky, and James W. Albright. New York: Springer-Verlag, 1991.

Gabrieli, E. R. "Aspects of a Computer-Based Patient Record." *Journal of AHIMA* 64, no. 7 (July 1993), pp. 70–82.

Gallon, M. R., H. M. Stillman, and D. Coates. "Putting Core Competency Thinking into Practice." *Research Technology Management* 38, no. 3 (1995), pp. 37–39.

Gallupe, R. B., A. R. Dennis, W. H. Cooper, J. S. Valacich, L. M. Bastianutti, and J. F. Nunamaker, Jr. "Electronic Brainstorming and Group Size." *Academy of Management* 35, no. 2 (June 1992), pp. 350–369.

Gapenski, L. C. "Capital Investment Analysis: Three Methods." *Healthcare Financial Management* 47, no. 8 (August 1993), pp. 60–66.

Gapenski, L. C., W. B. Vogel, and B. Langland-Orban. "The Determinants of Hospital Profitability." *Hospital and Health Services Administration* 38, no. 1 (Spring 1993), pp. 63–80.

Garnick, D. W., H. S. Luft, J. C. Robinson, and J. Tetreault. "Appropriate Measures of Hospital Market Areas." *Health Services Research* 22, no. 1 (April 1987), pp. 69–89.

Garrett, T. M., R. J. Klonoski, and H. W. Baillie. "American Business Ethics and Healthcare Costs." *Health-care Management Review* 18, no. 4 (1993), pp. 44–50.

Gay, E. G., J. J. Kronenfeld, S. L. Baker, and R. L. Amidon. "An Appraisal of Organizational Response to Fiscally Constraining Regulation: The Case of Hospitals and DRGs." *Journal of Health and Social Behavior* 30, no. 1 (1989), pp. 41–55.

Gehani, R. R. "Quality Value-Chain: A Meta-Synthesis of Frontiers of the Quality Movement." *Academy of Management Executive* 7, no. 2 (1993), pp. 29–42.

Gehrt, K. C., and M. B. Pinto. "Assessing the Viability of Situationally Driven Segmentation Opportunities in the Health Care Market." *Hospital and Health Services Administration* 38, no. 2 (Summer 1993), pp. 243–265.

Gersick, C. J. G. "Revolutionary Change Theories: A Multilevel Exploration of the Punctuated Equilibrium Paradigm." *Academy of Management Review* 16, no. 1 (January 1991), pp. 10–36.

Ghoshal, S., and D. E. Westney. "Organizing Competitor Analysis Systems." *Strategic Management Journal* 12, no. 1 (1991), pp. 17–31.

Ghoshal, S., and C. A. Bartlett. *The Individualized Corporation.* New York: HarperBusiness, 1996.

Giardina, C. W., M. D. Fottler, R. M. Schewchuk, and D. B. Hill. "The Case for Hospital Diversification into Long-Term Care." *Health Care Management Review* 15, no. 1 (Winter 1990), pp. 71–82.

Gibson, C. K., D. J. Newton, and D. S. Cochran. "An Empirical Investigation of the Nature of Hospital Mission Statements." *Health Care Management Review* 15, no. 3 (Summer 1990), pp. 35–46.

Gift, R. G., and C. F. Kinney, eds. *Today's Management Methods: A Guide for the Health Care Executive.* Chicago: American Hospital Publishing, 1996.

Gill, S. L., and S. S. Meighan. "Five Roadblocks to Effective Partnerships in a Competitive Health Care Environment." *Hospital and Health Services Administration* 33, no. 4 (Winter 1988), pp. 505–520.

Gillock, R. E., H. L. Smith, and N. F. Piland. "For-Profit and Nonprofit Mergers: Concerns and Outcomes." *Hospital and Health Services Administration* 31, no. 4 (Winter 1986), pp. 74–84.

Ginn, G. O., and G. J. Young. "Organizational and Environmental Determinants of Hospital Strategy." *Hospital and Health Services Administration* 37, no. 3 (Fall 1992), pp. 291–302.

Ginsberg, A. "Measuring and Modeling Changes in Strategy: Theoretical Foundations and Empirical

Directions." *Strategic Management Journal* 9, no. 6 (November/December 1987), pp. 559–575.

Ginsberg, A., and A. Buchholtz. "Converting to For-Profit Status: Corporate Responsiveness to Radical Change." *Academy of Management Journal* 33, no. 3 (September 1990), pp. 445–477.

Ginsberg, A., and E. Abrahamson. "Champions of Change and Strategic Shifts: The Role of Internal and External Change Advocates." *Journal of Management Studies* 28 (March 1991), pp. 173–190.

Ginter, P. M., W. J. Duncan, and S. A. Capper. "Keeping Strategic Thinking in Strategic Planning: Macro-Environmental Analysis in a State Department of Public Health." *Public Health* 106 (1992), pp. 253–269.

Ginter, P. M., A. C. Rucks, and W. J. Duncan. "Characteristics of Strategic Planning in Selected Service Industries and Planner Satisfaction with the Process." *Management International Review* 29, no. 2 (1989), pp. 66–74.

Ginter, P. M., A. C. Rucks, and W. J. Duncan. "Planners' Perceptions of the Strategic Management Process." *Journal of Management Studies* 22, no. 6 (1985), pp. 581–596.

Ginter, P. M., W. J. Duncan, S. A. Capper, and M. G. Rowe. "Evaluating Public Health Programs Using Portfolio Analysis." *Proceeding of the Southern Management Association.* Atlanta, November 1993, pp. 492–496.

Ginter, P. M., W. J. Duncan, W. D. Richardson, and L. E. Swayne. "Analyzing the Health Care Environment: 'You Can't Hit What You Can't See.'" *Health Care Management Review* 16, no. 4 (Fall 1991), pp. 35–48.

Ginzberg, E. "Health Personnel: The Challenges Ahead." *Frontiers of Health Services Management* 7, no. 2 (Winter 1990), pp. 3–20.

Ginzberg, E. "Medical Care for the Poor: No Magic Bullets." *Journal of the American Medical Association* 259, no. 22 (1988), pp. 3309–3311.

Giola, D. A., and K. Chittipeddi. "Sensemaking and Sensegiving in Strategic Change Initiation." *Strategic Management Journal* 12, no. 6 (September 1991), pp. 433–448.

Glenesk, A. E. "Six Myths That Can Cloud Strategic Vision." *Healthcare Financial Management* 44, no. 5 (May 1990), pp. 38–43.

Godfrey, P. C., and C. W. L. Hill. "The Problem of Unobservables in Strategic Management Research."

Strategic Management Journal 16, no. 7 (1995), pp. 519–534.

Goldberg, J., and H. J. Martin. "Control and Support: What Physicians Want from Hospitals." *Hospital and Health Services Administration* 35, no. 1 (Spring 1990), pp. 27–37.

Goldman, R. L. "Practical Applications of Health Care Marketing Ethics." *Healthcare Financial Management* 47, no. 3 (March 1993), pp. 47–54.

Goldsmith, J. "A Radical Prescription for Hospitals." *Harvard Business Review* 67, no. 3 (May/June 1989), pp. 104–111.

Gomes, H. *Quality Quotes.* Milwaukee, Wisconsin: Quality Press, 1996.

Goodstein, J., and W. Boeker. "Turbulence at the Top: A New Perspective on Governance Structure Changes and Strategic Change." *Academy of Management Journal* 34, no. 2 (June 1991), pp. 306–330.

Goody, B. "Defining Rural Hospital Markets." *Health Services Research* 28, no. 2 (June 1993), pp. 183–200.

Goold, M., and J. J. Quinn. "The Paradox of Strategic Controls." *Strategic Management Journal* 11, no. 1 (January 1990), pp. 40–50.

Goold, M., and K. Luchs. "Why Diversify? Four Decades of Management Thinking." *Academy of Management Executive* 7, no. 3 (August 1993), pp. 7–25.

Gould, S. J. "Macrodynamic Trends in Health Care: A Distribution and Retailing Perspective." *Health Care Management Review* 13, no. 2 (Spring 1988), pp. 15–22.

Gourley, D. R., and M. E. Moore. "Marketing and Planning in Multihospital Systems." *Hospital and Health Services Administration* 33, no. 3 (Fall 1988), pp. 331–344.

Govindarajan, V. "Implementing Competitive Strategies at the Business Unit Level: Implications of Matching Managers to Strategies." *Strategic Management Journal* 10, no. 3 (March/April 1989), pp. 251–269.

Graham, J. W., and W. C. Havlick. *Mission Statements: A Guide to the Corporate and Nonprofit Sectors.* New York: Garland Publishing, 1994.

Grant, R. M. *Contemporary Strategic Analysis: Concepts, Techniques, Applications.* Cambridge, Massachusetts: Blackwell Business, 1995.

Gray, B. H. "Why Nonprofits? Hospitals and the Future of American Health Care." *Frontiers of Health Services Management* 8, no. 4 (Summer 1992), pp. 3–32.

Greaf, W. D. "Public Hospital Strategic Planning: Does it Differ From Voluntary, Not-for-Profit Hospital

Strategic Planning?" *Health Care Management Review* 13, no. 3 (Summer 1988), pp. 7–14.

Greer, C. R., and T. C. Ireland. "Organizational and Financial Correlates of a Contrarian Human Resource Investment Strategy." *Academy of Management Journal* 35 (1992), pp. 956–984.

Gregory, D. "Strategic Alliances between Physicians and Hospitals in Multihospital Systems." *Hospital and Health Services Administration* 37, no. 2 (Summer 1992), pp. 247–258.

Greifinger, R. B., and M. S. Bluestone. "Building Physician Alliances for Cost Containment." *Health Care Management Review* 11, no. 4 (Fall 1986), pp. 63–72.

Griffith, J. R. "Voluntary Hospitals: Are Trustees the Solution?" *Hospital and Health Services Administration* 33, no. 3 (Fall 1988), pp. 295–309.

Grim, S. A. "Win/Win: Urban and Rural Hospitals Network for Survival." *Hospital and Health Services Administration* 31, no. 1 (Spring 1986), pp. 34–46.

Gupta, A. K. "SBU Strategies, Corporate-SBU Relations, and SBU Effectiveness in Strategy Implementation." *Academy of Management Journal* 30, no. 3 (September 1987), pp. 477–500.

Gutknecht, J. E., and J. B. Keys. "Mergers, Acquisitions, and Takeovers: Maintaining Morale of Survivors and Protecting Employees." *Academy of Management Executive* 7, no. 3 (August 1993), pp. 26–36.

Halal, W. E. *The New Management: Democracy and Enterprise Are Transforming Organizations.* San Francisco: Berrett-Koehler Publishers, Inc., 1996.

Halberstam, D. *The Reckoning.* New York: William Morrow, 1986.

Halé, J. *From Concepts to Capabilities.* New York: John Wiley and Sons, 1996.

Hall, R. "A Framework Linking Intangible Resources and Capabilities to Sustainable Competitive Advantage." *Strategic Management Journal* 14, no. 8 (November 1993), pp. 607–618.

Halseth, M. J., and J. R. Paul. "The Coming Revolution in Information Systems." *Computers in Healthcare* 13, no. 11 (November 1992), pp. 43–44.

Hambrick, D. C. "Some Tests of the Effectiveness and Functional Attitudes of Miles and Snow's Strategic Types." *Academy of Management Journal* 26, no. 1 (March 1983), pp. 263–279.

Hambrick, D. C., I. C. MacMillan, and D. L. Day. "Strategic Attributes and Performance in the BCG Matrix: A PIMS-Based Analysis of Industrial-Product Business." *Academy of Management Journal* 25, no. 3 (September 1982), pp. 510–531.

Hamel, G., and C. K. Prahalad. "Competing in the New Economy: Managing out of Bounds." *Strategic Management Journal* 17, no. 1 (1996), 237–242.

Hamel, G., and C. K. Prahalad. "Strategy As Stretch and Leverage," *Harvard Business Review* 71, no. 3 (March/April, 1993), pp. 75–84.

Hamel, G., and C. K. Prahalad. *Competing for the Future.* Boston: Harvard Business School Press, 1994.

Hammer, M. "Reengineering Work: Don't Automate, Obliterate." *Harvard Business Review* 68, no 4 (July/August 1990), pp. 104–112.

Hammer, M., and J. Champy. *Reengineering the Corporation: A Manifesto for Business Revolution.* New York: HarperBusiness, 1993.

Harper, S. C. "The Challenges Facing CEOs: Past, Present, and Future." *Academy of Management Executive* 6, no. 3 (August 1992), pp. 7–25.

Harrell, G. D., and M. F. Fors. "Planning Evolution in Hospital Management." *Health Care Management Review* 12, no. 1 (Winter 1987), pp. 9–22.

Harrington, C., R. J. Newcomer, and T. G. Moore. "Factors That Contribute to Medicare HMO Risk Contract Success." *Inquiry* 25, no. 2 (Summer 1988), pp. 251–262.

Harris, C., L. L. Hicks, and B. J. Kelly, "Physician-Hospital Networking: Avoiding a Shotgun Wedding." *Health Care Management Review* 17, no. 4 (Fall 1992), pp. 17–28.

Harris, S., K. W. Mossholder, and S. Oswald. "Vision Salience and Strategic Involvement: Implications for Psychological Attachment to Organization and Job." *Strategic Management Journal* 15, no. 3 (1994), pp. 477–489.

Hart, S. L. "A Natural-Resource-Based View of the Firm." *Academy of Management Review* 20, no. 4 (1995), pp. 986–1014.

Hart, S. L. "An Integrative Framework for Strategy-Making Processes." *Academy of Management Review* 17, no. 2 (April 1992), pp. 327–351.

Hatten, K. J., and M. L. Hatten. "Strategic Groups, Asymmetrical Mobility Barriers and Contestability." *Strategic Management Journal* 8, no. 4 (1987), pp. 329–342.

Hax, A. C. "Redefining the Concept of Strategy and the Strategy Formation Process." *Planning Review* 18, no. 3 (May/June 1990), pp. 34–40.

Hayes, R. H., G. P. Pisano, and D. M. Upton. *Strategic Operations.* New York: Free Press, 1996.

Henderson, J. C., and J. B. Thomas. "Aligning Business and Information Technology Domains: Strategic Planning in Hospitals." *Hospital and Health Ser-*

vices Administration 37, no. 1 (Spring 1992), pp. 71–87.

Henderson, R., and I. Cockburn. "Measuring Competence? Exploring Firm Effects in Pharmaceutical Research." *Strategic Management Journal* 15, no. 1 (1994), pp. 63–84.

Herbert, T. T., and H. Deresky. "Generic Strategies: An Empirical Investigation of Typology Validity and Strategy Content." *Strategic Management Journal* 9, no. 2 (February 1987), pp. 135–147.

Herzlinger, R. E. "The Failed Revolution in Health Care—The Role of Management." *Harvard Business Review* 67, no. 3 (May/June 1989), pp. 95–103.

Heshmat, S. "The Role of Cost in Hospital Pricing Decisions." *Journal of Hospital Marketing* 6, no. 1 (1991), pp. 155–161.

Heskett, J. L., W. E. Sasser, Jr., and C. W. L. Hart. *Service Breakthroughs—Changing the Rules of the Game.* New York: Free Press, 1990.

Hickman, C. R. *Mind of a Manager, Soul of a Leader.* New York: John Wiley & Sons, Inc., 1992.

Higgins, C. W., and E. D. Meyers. "Managed Care and Vertical Integration: Implications for the Hospital Industry." *Hospital and Health Services Administration* 32, no. 3 (Fall 1987), pp. 319–327.

Hiller, M. D. *Ethics and Health Administration: Ethical Decision Making in Health Management.* Arlington, Virginia: Association of University Programs in Health Administration, 1986.

Hillestad, S. G., and E. N. Berkowitz. *Health Care Marketing Plans: From Strategy to Action,* 2d ed. Gaithersburg, Maryland: Aspen Publishers, 1991.

Hilmer, F. G., and L. Donaldson. *Management Redeemed.* New York: Free Press, 1996.

Hinterhuber, H. H., and W. Popp. "Are You a Strategist or Just a Manager?" *Harvard Business Review* 70 (January/February 1992), pp. 105–113.

Hitt, M. A., R. E. Hoskisson, and J. S. Harrison. "Strategic Competitiveness in the 1990s: Challenges and Opportunities for U.S. Executives." *Academy of Management Executive* 5, no. 2 (May 1991), pp. 23–33.

Hitt, M. A., R. E. Hoskisson, and R. Nixon. "A Mid-Range Theory of Interfunctional Integration, Its Antecedents and Outcomes." *Journal of Engineering and Technology Management* 10, no. 1 (1993), pp. 26–40.

Hood, John M. *The Heroic Enterprise.* New York: Free Press, 1996.

Hoskisson, R. E., and R. A. Johnson. "Corporate Restructuring and Strategic Change: Effect on Diversification Strategy and R&D Intensity." *Strategic Management Journal* 13, no. 8 (1992), pp. 625–634.

Hosmer, L. T. "Strategic Planning As If Ethics Mattered." *Strategic Management Journal* 15, no. 1 Special Issue (1994), pp. 17–34.

Huff, A. S., and R. K. Reger. "A Review of Strategic Process Research." *Journal of Management* 13, no. 2 (Summer 1987), pp. 211–236.

Hughes, W. L., and S. Y. Soliman. "Short-Term Case Mix Management with Linear Programming." *Hospital and Health Services Administration* 30, no. 1 (Spring 1985), pp. 61–71.

Hunter, S. S. "Marketing and Strategic Management: Integrating Skills for a Better Hospital." *Hospital and Health Services Administration* 32, no. 2 (Summer 1987), pp. 205–217.

Hurley, R. E. "The Purchaser-Driven Reformation in Health Care: Alternative Approaches to Leveling Our Cathedrals." *Frontiers of Health Services Management* 9, no. 4 (1993), pp. 5–35.

Hurst, D. K. *Crisis and Renewal: Meeting the Challenge of Organizational Change.* Boston: Harvard Business School Press, 1995.

Hutchinson, R. A., K. E. White, and D. P. Vogel. "Development and Implementation of a Strategic-Planning Process at a University Hospital." *American Journal of Hospital Pharmacy* 46 (May 1989), pp. 952–957.

Ireland, R. D., and M. A. Hitt. "Mission Statements: Importance, Challenge, and Recommendations for Development." *Business Horizons* 35 no. 3 (1992), pp. 34–42.

Ireland, R. D., M. A. Hitt, R. A. Bettis, and D. A. DePorras. "Strategy Formulation Processes: Differences in Perceptions of Strengths and Weaknesses Indicators and Environmental Uncertainty by Managerial Level." *Strategic Management Journal* 8, no. 4 (July/August 1987), pp. 469–485.

Jackson, S. E., and J. E. Dutton. "Discerning Threats and Opportunities." *Administrative Science Quarterly* 33, no. 3 (September 1988), pp. 370–387.

Jacobson, C. K. "A Conceptual Framework for Evaluating Joint Venture Opportunities Between Hospitals and Physicians." *Health Services Management Research* 2, no. 3 (Summer 1989), pp. 204–212.

Jacobson, R. "The 'Austrian' School of Strategy." *Academy of Management Review* 17, no. 4 (October 1992), pp. 782–807.

Jaeger, B. J., A. D. Kaluzny, and K. Magruder-Habib. "A New Perspective on Multiinstitutional Systems

Management." *Health Care Management Review* 12, no. 4 (Fall 1987), pp. 9–19.

James, K. "Process and Culture Impediments to Health Care Innovation." *Hospital and Health Services Administration* 35, no. 3 (Fall 1990), pp. 395–407.

Javalgi, R. G., T. W. Whipple, M. K. McManamon, and V. L. Edick. "Hospital Image: A Correspondence Analysis Approach." *Journal of Health Care Marketing* 12, no. 4 (December 1992), pp. 34–39.

Jerrell, S. L. "Strategic Adaptation by Community Mental Health Centers." *Academy of Management Proceedings,* August 1986, pp. 87–90.

John, J., and A. R. Miller. "Strategic Planning for Nursing Homes: A Market Opportunity Analysis Perspective." *Health Care Management Review* 14, no. 4 (Fall 1989), pp. 11–19.

Johnson, D. E. L. "Health-Care Futurists Face New Scenarios in Planning." *Health Care Strategic Management* 6, no. 6 (June 1988), pp. 2–3.

Johnson, E. A. "Ethical Considerations for Business Relationships of Hospitals and Physicians." *Health Care Management Review* 16, no. 3 (Summer 1991), pp. 7–13.

Johnson, E. A. "The Competitive Market: Changing Medical Staff Accountability." *Hospital and Health Services Administration* 33, no. 2 (Summer 1988), pp. 179–187.

Johnson, G. "Managing Strategic Change—Strategy, Culture, and Action." *Long Range Planning* 25, no. 1 (1992), pp. 28–36.

Johnson, R. A., R. E. Hoskisson, and M. A. Hitt. "Board of Director Involvement in Restructuring: The Effects of Board Versus Managerial Controls and Characteristics." *Strategic Management Journal* 14, Special Issue (1993), pp. 33–50.

Jones, K. R., and S. G. Sloate. "Academic Health Center Hospitals: Alternative Responses to Financial Stress." *Health Care Management Review* 12, no. 3 (Summer 1987), pp. 83–89.

Jones, P., and L. Kahaner. *Say It and Live It: The 50 Corporate Mission Statements That Hit the Mark.* New York: Doubleday, 1995.

Jones, S. B., M. K. DuVal, and M. Lesparre. "Competition or Conscience? Mixed-Mission Dilemmas of the Voluntary Hospital." *Inquiry* 24, no. 2 (Summer 1987), pp. 110–118.

Jones, W. "Letting Technology Dictate Design." *Health Care Strategic Management* 6, no. 11 (November 1988), pp. 10–12.

Judge, W. Q., and C. P. Zeithaml. "An Empirical Comparison Between the Board's Strategic Role in Non-

profit Hospitals and in For-Profit Industrial Firms." *Health Services Research* 27, no. 1 (April 1992), pp. 47–64.

Kaluzny, A. D., L. M. Lacey, R. Warnecke, D. M. Hynes, J. Morrisey, L. Ford, and E. Sondik. "Predicting the Performance of a Strategic Alliance: An Analysis of the Community Clinical Oncology Program." *Health Services Research* 28, no. 2 (June 1993), pp. 159–182.

Kaluzny, A. D. "Revitalizing Decision Making at the Middle Management Level." *Hospital and Health Services Administration* 34, no. 1 (Spring 1989), pp. 39–51.

Kaluzny, A. D., and H. S. Zuckerman. "Strategic Alliances: Two Perspectives for Understanding Their Effects on Health Services." *Hospital and Health Services Administration* 37, no. 4 (Winter 1992), pp. 477–490.

Kaluzny, A. D., C. P. McLaughlin, and C. P. Simpson. "Applying Total Quality Management Concepts to Public Health Organizations." *Public Health Reports* 107, no. 3 (1992), pp. 257–264.

Kaluzny, A., and H. S. Zuckerman. "Strategic Alliances Ensure TQM's Full Potential." *Healthcare Executive* 8, no. 3 (May/June 1993), p. 33.

Kamath, R. R., and J. Elmer. "Capital Investment Decisions in Hospitals: Survey Results." *Health Care Management Review* 14, no. 2 (Spring 1989), pp. 45–56.

Kaplan, R. S., and D. P. Norton. *The Balanced Scorecard: Translating Strategy into Action.* Boston: Harvard Business School Press, 1996.

Keen, P. G. W. *Shaping the Future: Business Design Through Information Technology.* Boston: Harvard Business School Press, 1991.

Kellinghusen, G., and K. Wubbenhorst. "Strategic Control for Improved Performance." *Long Range Planning* 23, no. 3 (1990), pp. 30–40.

Kennedy, M., J. A. Prevost, M. P. Carr, and J. W. Dilley. "A Roundtable Discussion: Hospital Leaders Discuss Quality Improvement Implementation Issues." *Journal of Quality Improvement* 18 (March 3, 1992), pp. 78–97.

Kets de Vries, M. F. R. "The Leadership Mystique." *Academy of Management Executive* 8, no. 3 (1994), pp. 73–83.

Kiernan, M. J. "The New Strategic Architecture: Learning to Compete in the Twenty-First Century." *Academy of Management Executive* 7, no. 1 (February 1993), pp. 7–21.

Kimberly, J. R., and E. J. Zajac. "Strategic Adaptation in Health Care Organizations: Implications for Theory and Research." *Medical Care Review* 42, no. 2 (Fall 1985), pp. 267–302.

Klein, H. E., and R. E. Linneman. "Environmental Assessment: An International Study of Corporate Practices." *Journal of Business Strategy* 5 (1984), pp. 69–77.

Kolb, D. S., and J. Ryan. *Assessing Organizational Readiness for Capitation.* Chicago: American Hospital Publishing, 1996.

Kotabe, M., and E. P. Cox III. "Assessment of Global Competitiveness: Patent Applications and Grants in Four Major Trading Countries." *Business Horizons* 36, no. 1 (1993), pp. 57–64.

Kotler, P., and R. N. Clarke. *Marketing for Health Care Organizations.* Englewood Cliffs, New Jersey: Prentice-Hall, 1987.

Kotler, P., and S. J. Levy. "Broadening the Concept of Marketing." *Journal of Marketing* 33, no. 1 (January 1969), pp. 10–15.

Kotter, J. P. *The New Rules: How to Succeed in Today's Post-Corporate World.* New York: Free Press, 1995.

Kotter, J. P., and J. L. Heskett. *Corporate Culture and Performance.* New York: Free Press, 1992.

Kouzes, J. M., and B. Z. Posner. "Envisioning Your Future: Imagining Ideal Scenarios." *The Futurist* 30, no. 3 (1996), pp. 14–19.

Kouzes, J. M., and B. Z. Posner. *The Leadership Challenge: How to Keep Getting Extraordinary Things Done in Organizations.* San Francisco: Jossey-Bass, 1995.

Kovner, A. R., and M. J. Chin. "Physician Leadership in Hospital Strategic Decision Making." *Hospital and Health Services Administration* 30, no. 4 (Winter 1985), pp. 64–79.

Kralewski, J. E., R. Feldman, B. Dowd, and J. Shapiro. "Strategies Employed by HMOs to Achieve Hospital Discounts." *Health Care Management Review* 16, no. 1 (Winter 1991), pp. 9–16.

Kralewski, J.E., G. Gifford, and J. Porter. "Profit Versus Public Welfare Goals in Investor-Owned and Not-for-Profit Hospitals." *Hospital and Health Services Administration* 33, no. 3 (Fall 1988), pp. 311–329.

Kropf, R., and A. J. Szafran. "Developing a Competitive Advantage in the Market for Radiology Services." *Hospital and Health Services Administration* 33, no. 2 (Summer 1988), pp. 213–220.

Ledford, G. E., J. T. Strahley, and J. R. Wendenhof. "Realizing A Corporate Philosophy." *Organizational Dynamics* 23, no. 3 (1995), pp. 4–19.

Leebov, W., and G. Scott. *Health Care Managers in Transition.* San Francisco: Jossey-Bass, 1990.

Lemieux-Charles, L. "Ethical Issues Faced by Clinicians/Managers in Resource-Allocation Decisions." *Hospital and Health Services Administration* 38, no. 2 (Summer 1993), pp. 267–286.

Lengnick-Hall, C. A. "Innovation and Competitive Advantage." *Journal of Management* 18, no. 2 (1992), pp. 399–429.

Lengnick-Hall, C. A. "Customer Contribution to Quality: A Different View of the Customer-Oriented Firm," *Academy of Management Review* 21, no. 3 (1996), pp. 791–824.

Levitz, G. S., and P. P. Brooke. "Independent Versus System-Affiliated Hospitals: A Comparative Analysis of Financial Performance, Cost, and Productivity." *Health Services Research* 20, no. 3 (August 1985), pp. 315–339.

Liedtka, J. M. "Formulating Hospital Strategy: Moving Beyond a Market Mentality." *Health Care Management Review* 17, no. 1 (Winter 1992), pp. 21–26.

Linder, J. C. "Outcomes Measurement in Hospitals: Can the System Change the Organization?" *Hospital and Health Services Administration* 37, no. 2 (Summer 1992), pp. 143–166.

Linder, J. C. "Outcomes Measurement: Compliance Tool or Strategic Initiative?" *Health Care Management Review* 16, no. 4 (Fall 1991), pp. 21–33.

Long, C., and M. Vickers-Koch. "Using Core Capabilities to Create Competitive Advantage." *Organizational Dynamics* 24, no. 1 (Summer, 1995), pp. 7–22.

Longest, B. B., Jr. "Interorganizational Linkages in the Health Sector." *Health Care Management Review* 15, no. 1 (Winter 1990), pp. 17–28.

Longest, B. B., Jr., K. Darr, and J. S. Rakich. "Organizational Leadership in Hospitals." *Hospital Topics* 71, no. 3 (Summer 1993), pp. 11–15.

Lubatkin, M., and R. C. Rogers. "Diversification, Systematic Risk, and Shareholder Return." *Academy of Management Journal* 32, no. 2 (June 1989), pp. 454–465.

Luft, H. S., J. C. Robinson, D. W. Garnick, R. Hughes, S. J. McPhee, S. Hunt, and J. Showstack. "Hospital Behavior in a Local Market Context." *Medical Care Review* 43, no. 2 (Fall 1986), pp. 217–251.

Luke, R. D. "Local Hospital Systems: Forerunners of Regional Systems?" *Frontiers of Health Services Management* 9, no. 2 (1992), pp. 3–51.

Luke, R. D. "Spatial Competition and Cooperation in Local Hospital Markets." *Medical Care Review* 48, no. 2 (Summer 1991), pp. 207–237.

Luke, R. D., and J. W. Begun. "Strategic Orientations of Small Multihospital Systems." *Health Services Research* 23, no. 5 (December 1988), pp. 597–618.

Luke, R. D., and J. W. Begun. "The Management of Strategy." In S. M. Shortell and A. D. Kaluzny, eds., *Health Care Management.* New York: John Wiley & Sons, 1988.

Luke, R. D., J. W. Begun, and D. D. Pointer. "Quasi Firms: Strategic Interorganizational Forms in the Health Care Industry." *Academy of Management Review* 14, no. 1 (Winter 1989), pp. 9–19.

Lumsdon, K. "The 1990s: A Time for Developing Creative Financial Vision." *Healthcare Financial Management* 43, no. 10 (October 1989), pp. 19–30.

Lynn, M. L., and D. P. Osborn. "Deming's Quality Principles: A Health Care Application." *Hospital and Health Services Administration* 36, no. 1 (Spring 1991), pp. 111–120.

MacStravic, R. S. "A Customer Relations Strategy for Health Care Employee Relations." *Hospital and Health Services Administration* 34, no. 3 (Fall 1989), pp. 397–411.

MacStravic, R. S. "Market and Market Segment Portfolio Assessment for Hospitals." *Health Care Management Review* 14, no. 3 (Summer 1989), pp. 25–32.

MacStravic, R. S. "Product-Line Administration in Hospitals." *Health Care Management Review* 11, no. 1 (Winter 1989), pp. 35–43.

MacStravic, R. S. "The Patient As Partner: A Competitive Strategy in Health Care Marketing." *Hospital and Health Services Administration* 33, no. 1 (Spring 1988), pp. 15–24.

Manheim, L. M., S. M. Shortell, and S. McFall. "The Effect of Investor-Owned Chain Acquisitions on Hospital Expenses and Staffing." *Health Services Research* 24, no. 4 (October 1989), pp. 461–484.

Manton, K. G., M. A. Woodbury, J. C. Vertrees, and E. Stallard. "Use of Medicare Services Before and After Introduction of the Prospective Payment System." *Health Services Research* 28, no. 3 (August 1993), pp. 269–292.

March, B., P. Schavoir, J. Y. Gueguen, G. Shaw, and P. Cholmondeley. "How to Identify and Enhance Core Competencies." *Planning Review* 22, no. 6 (1994), pp. 24–26.

Markides, C. C., and P. J. Williamson. "Related Diversification, Core Competencies, and Corporate Performance." *Strategic Management Journal* 15, no. 3 (1994), pp. 149–165.

Marszalek-Gaucher, E., and R. J. Coffey. *Transforming Healthcare Organizations.* San Francisco: Jossey-Bass, 1990.

McCain, G. "Black Holes, Cash Pigs, and Other Hospital Portfolio Analysis Problems." *Journal of Health Care Management* 7, no. 2 (June 1987), pp. 56–64.

McCue, M. J. "A Profile of Preacquisition Proprietary Hospitals." *Health Care Management Review* 13, no. 4 (Fall 1988), pp. 15–24.

McCue, M. J., and R. W. Furst. "Financial Characteristics of Hospitals Purchased by Investor-Owned Chains." *Health Services Research* 21, no. 4 (October 1986), pp. 515–527.

McCue, M. J., and Y. A. Ozcan. "Determinants of Capital Structure." *Hospital and Health Services Administration* 37, no. 3 (Fall 1992), pp. 333–346.

McCue, M. J., T. McCue, and J. R. C. Wheeler. "An Assessment of Hospital Acquisition Prices." *Inquiry* 25, no. 2 (Summer 1988), pp. 290–296.

McDermott, D. R., F. J. Franzak, and M. W. Little. "Does Marketing Relate to Hospital Profitability?" *Journal of Health Care Marketing* 13, no. 2 (Summer 1993), pp. 18–25.

McDermott, S. "The New Hospital Challenge: Organizing and Managing Physician Organizations." *Health Care Management Review* 13, no. 1 (Winter 1988), pp. 57–61.

McDevitt, P. "Learning by Doing: Strategic Marketing Management in Hospitals." *Health Care Management Review* 12, no. 1 (Winter 1987), pp. 23–30.

McFall, S. L., S. M. Shortell, and L. M. Manheim. "HCA's Acquisition Process: The Physician's Role and Perspective." *Health Care Management Review* 13, no. 1 (Winter 1988), pp. 23–34.

McGill, S. G., Jr. "Security." In V. James McLarney, ed., *Effective Health Care Facilities Management.* Chicago: American Hospital Publishing, 1991.

McKinney, M. A., A. D. Kaluzny, and H. S. Zuckerman. "Innovation Diffusion Networks in Multihospital Systems and Alliances." *Health Care Management Review* 16, no. 1 (Winter 1991), pp. 17–23.

McLafferty, S. "The Geographical Restructuring of Urban Hospitals: Spatial Dimensions of Corporate Strategy." *Social Science and Medicine* 23, no. 10 (1986), pp. 1079–1086.

McLarney, V. J., ed. *Effective Health Care Facilities Management.* Chicago: American Hospital Publishing, 1991.

McLean, R. A. "Outside Directors: Stakeholder Representation in Investor-Owned Health Care Organizations." *Hospital and Health Services Administration* 34, no. 1 (Spring 1989), pp. 255–268.

McLean, R. A. *Financial Management of Health Care Organizations.* Albany, New York: Delmar Publishing, 1997.

McMahon, L. F., R. B. Fetter, J. L. Freeman, and J. D. Thompson. "Hospital Matrix Management and DRG-Based Prospective Payment." *Hospital and Health Services Administration* 31, no. 1 (Spring 1986), pp. 62–74.

McRath, R. G., I. C. MacMillian, S. Venktaraman. "Defining and Developing Competence: A Strategic Process Paradigm." *Strategic Management Journal* 16, no. 3 (1995), pp. 251–275.

Mechanic, D. "America's Health Care System and Its Future: The View of a Despairing Optimist." *Medical Care Review* 50, no. 1 (Spring 1993), pp. 7–47.

Mechanic, D. "Changing Our Health Care System." *Medical Care Review* 48, no. 3 (Fall 1991), pp. 247–260.

Medley, G. J. "WWF UK Creates a New Mission." *Long Range Planning* 25, no. 2 (1992), pp. 63–68.

Mercer, D., ed. *Managing the External Environment.* London: Sage Publications, 1992.

Meyer, R. H., M. N. Mannix, and T. F. Costello. "Nursing Recruitment: Do Health Care Managers Gear Strategies to the Appropriate Audience?" *Hospital and Health Services Administration* 36, no. 3 (Fall 1991), pp. 447–453.

Michael, J. G., and D. C. Hambrick. "Diversification Posture and Top Management Team Characteristics." *Academy of Management Journal* 35 (1992), pp. 9–37.

Mick, S. S., and Associates. *Innovations in Health Care Delivery.* San Francisco: Jossey-Bass, 1990.

Mick, S. S., and D. A. Conrad. "The Decision to Integrate Vertically in Health Care Organizations." *Hospital and Health Services Administration* 33, no. 3 (Fall 1988), pp. 345–360.

Milakovich, M. E. "Creating a Total Quality Health Care Environment." *Health Care Management Review* 16, no. 2 (Spring 1991), pp. 9–20.

Miller, D. "Preserving the Privacy of Computerized Patient Records." *Healthcare Informatics* 10, no. 10 (October 1993), p. 72.

Miller, D. "Relating Porter's Business Strategies to Environment and Structure: Analysis and Performance Implications." *Academy of Management Journal* 31, no. 2 (June 1988), pp. 280–308.

Miller, R. H., and H. S. Luft. "Managed Care: Past Evidence and Potential Trends." *Frontiers of Health Services Management* 9, no. 3 (1993), pp. 3–37.

Miner, J. B. "The Validity and Usefulness of Theories in an Emerging Organizational Science." *Academy of Management Review* 9, no. 2 (April 1984), pp. 296–306.

Mintzberg, H. "The Design School: Reconsidering the Basic Premises of Strategic Management." *Strategic Management Journal* 11, no. 3 (March/April 1990), pp. 171–195.

Mintzberg, H. "The Fall and Rise of Strategic Planning." *Harvard Business Review* 72, no. 1 (January/February 1994), pp. 107–114.

Mintzberg, H. *The Rise and Fall of Strategic Planning.* New York: Free Press, 1994.

Mohr, R. A. "An Institutional Perspective on Rational Myths and Organizational Change in Health Care." *Medical Care Review* 49, no. 2 (Summer 1992), pp. 233–255.

Molinari, C., L. L. Morlock, J. A. Alexander, and C. A. Lyles. "Hospital Board Effectiveness: Relationships Between Governing Board Composition and Hospital Financial Viability." *Health Services Research* 28, no. 3 (August 1993), pp. 357–377.

Montgomery, C. A., and M. E. Porter, eds. *Strategy: Seeking and Securing Competitive Advantage.* Boston: Harvard Business School Publishing, 1991.

Montgomery, C. A., B. Wernerfelt, and S. Balakrishnan. "Strategy Content and the Research Process: A Critique and Commentary." *Strategic Management Journal* 10, no. 2 (March/April 1989), pp. 189–197.

Morefield, F. L. "Combining EDI and the Electronic Patient Record: The Information Infrastructure That Is Needed for Healthcare." *Journal of AHIMA* 64, no. 11 (November 1993), pp. 56–61.

Morgan, M. J. "How Corporate Culture Drives Strategy." *Long Range Planning* 26, no. 2 (1993), pp. 110–118.

Moriarty, D. D. "Strategic Information Systems Planning for Health Service Providers." *Health Care Management Review* 17, no. 1 (Winter 1992), pp. 85–90.

Morlock, L. L., and J. A. Alexander. "Models of Governance in Multihospital Systems." *Medical Care* 24, no. 12 (December 1986), pp. 1118–1135.

Morlock, L. L., J. A. Alexander, and H. M. Hunter. "Formal Relationships Among Governing Boards, CEOs and Medical Staffs in Independent and System

Hospitals." *Medical Care* 23, no. 12 (December 1985), pp. 1193–1213.

Morrisey, M. A., and J. A. Alexander. "Hospital Acquisition or Management Contract: A Theory of Strategic Choice." *Health Care Management Review* 12, no. 4 (Fall 1987), pp. 21–30.

Moynihan, J. J., and K. Norman. "Networking Providers—Data Highways of the '90s." *Journal of AHIMA* 64, no. 11 (November 1993), p. 42.

Mullaney, A. D. "Downsizing: How One Hospital Responded to Decreasing Demand." *Health Care Management Review* 14, no. 3 (Summer 1989), pp. 41–48.

Muller, H. J., and H. L. Smith. "Retrenchment Strategies and Tactics for Healthcare Executives." *Hospital and Health Services Administration* 30, no. 3 (Fall 1985), pp. 31–43.

Mullner, R. M., R. J. Rydman, D. G. Whites, and R. F. Rich. "Rural Community Hospitals and Factors Correlated with Their Risk of Closing." *Public Health Reports* 104, no. 4 (July/August 1989), pp. 315–325.

Murphy, R. F. "Venture Profile Analysis." *Hospital and Health Services Administration* 30, no. 4 (Winter 1985), pp. 80–95.

Murray, V. V., and T. D. Jick. "Taking Stock of Organizational Decline Management: Some Issues and Illustrations From an Empirical Study." *Journal of Management* 11, no. 3 (September 1985), pp. 111–123.

Nackel, J. G., and I. W. Kues. "Product-Line Management: Systems and Strategies." *Hospital and Health Services Administration* 31, no. 2 (Summer 1986), pp. 109–123.

Naidu, G. M., and C. L. Narayana. "How Marketing Oriented Are Hospitals in a Declining Market?" *Journal of Health Care Marketing* 2, no. 1 (1991), pp. 30–42.

El-Namaki, M. S. S. "Creating a Corporate Vision." *Long Range Planning* 25, no. 6 (1992), pp. 25–29.

Nanis, B. *Visionary Leadership.* San Francisco: Jossey-Bass, 1992.

Nash, H. O., Jr., J. R. Barrick, E. S. Lipsey, Jr., and B. B. Blount. "Engineering and Maintenance." In V. J. McLarney, ed., *Effective Health Care Facilities Management.* Chicago: American Hospital Publishing, 1991.

Navarro, V. "The Arguments of a National Health Program: Science or Ideology." *International Journal of Health Services* 18, no. 2 (1988), pp. 179–188.

Navarro, V. "Why Some Countries Have National Health Insurance, Others Have National Health Services, and the U.S. Has Neither." *Social Science and Medicine* 18, no. 9 (1989), pp. 887–898.

Nayyar, P. R. "Performance Effects of Information Asymmetry and Economies of Scope in Diversified Service Firms." *Academy of Management Journal* 36, no. 1 (February 1993), pp. 28–57.

Nelson, R. F. W. "Four-Quadrant Leadership." *Planning Review* 24, no. 1 (1996), pp. 20–25, 37.

Newman, G. "Worried About Vision? See an Optometrist." *Across the Board* 19 (October 1992), pp. 7–8.

Norman, R., and R. Ramirez. "From Value Chain to Value Constellation: Designing Interactive Systems." *Harvard Business Review* 71, no. 4 (1993), pp. 65–77.

Nutt, P. C. "How Top Managers in Health Organizations Set Directions That Guide Decision Making." *Hospital and Health Services Administration* 36, no. 1 (Spring 1991), pp. 57–75.

Nutt, P. C. "Identifying and Appraising How Managers Install Strategy." *Strategic Management Journal* 8, no. 6 (January/February 1987), pp. 1–14.

Nutt, P. C. "Tactics of Implementation." *Academy of Management Journal* 29, no. 2 (June 1986), pp. 230–261.

Nutt, P. C., and R. W. Backoff. "Transforming Public Organizations with Strategic Management and Strategic Leadership." *Journal of Management* 19 (Summer 1993), pp. 299–347.

Nutt, P. C., and R. W. Backoff. *Strategic Management of Public and Third Sector Organizations: A Handbook for Leaders.* San Francisco: Jossey-Bass, 1992.

Nystrom, P. C. "Organizational Cultures, Strategies, and Commitments in Health Care Organizations." *Health Care Management Review* 18, no. 1 (Winter 1993), pp. 43–49.

O'Leary, M. "Reinventing the Heal." *CIO Magazine* 6, no. 7 (February 1993), pp. 1–5.

Oliver, C. "Determinants of Interorganizational Relationships: Integration and Future Directions." *Academy of Management Review* 15, no. 2 (April 1990), pp. 241–265.

Oliver, C. "Strategic Responses to Institutional Processes." *Academy of Management Review* 16, no. 1 (January 1991), pp. 145–179.

Oster, S. M. *Modern Competitive Analysis,* 2d ed. New York: Oxford University Press, 1994.

Ozcan, Y. A., and R. D. Luke. "A National Study of the Efficiency of Hospitals in Urban Markets." *Health*

Services Research 27, no. 6 (February 1993), pp. 719–739.

Parkhe, A. "Strategic Alliance Structuring: A Game Theoretic and Transaction Cost Examination of Interfirm Cooperation." *Academy of Management Journal* 36, no. 4 (August 1993), pp. 794–829.

Parry, M., and A. E. Parry. "Strategy and Marketing Tactics in Nonprofit Hospitals." *Health Care Management Review* 17, no. 1 (Winter 1992), pp. 51–61.

Pearce, J. A., II, and F. David. "Corporate Mission Statements and the Bottom Line." *Academy of Management Executive* 1, no. 2 (May 1987), pp. 109–116.

Pearson, E. "Marketing Audit Reveals Holes and Opportunities." *Health Care Strategic Management* 8, no. 7 (July 1990), pp. 17–18.

Pegels, C., and K. A. Rogers. *Strategic Management of Hospitals and Health Care Facilities.* Rockville, Maryland: Aspen Publishers, 1988.

Pelfrey, S., and B. A. Theisen. "Joint Ventures in Health Care." *Journal of Nursing Administration* 19, no. 4 (April 1989), pp. 39–42.

Penrod, J. I. "Methods and Models for Planning Strategically." In M. J. Ball, J. V. Douglas, R. I. O'Desky, and J. W. Albright, eds., *Healthcare Information Management Systems.* New York: Springer-Verlag, 1991.

Perry, D. L. "Keys to Creating an Effective Ethics Program." *Healthcare Executive* 8, no. 2 (March/April 1993), p. 26.

Petchers, M. K., S. Swanker, and M. K. Singer. "The Hospital Merger: Its Effect on Employees." *Health Care Management Review* 13, no. 4 (Fall 1988), pp. 9–14.

Peteraf, M. A. "The Cornerstones of Competitive Advantage: A Resource-Based View." *Strategic Management Journal* 14, no. 3 (March 1993), pp. 179–191.

Peters, J. P. *A Strategic Planning Process for Hospitals.* Chicago: American Hospital Publishing, 1985.

Peters, T. *Liberation Management: Necessary Disorganization for the Nanosecond Nineties.* New York: Alfred A. Knopf, 1992.

Pettigrew, A. M. *The Management of Strategic Change.* Oxford: Basil Blackwell, 1987.

Pettigrew, A. M., E. Ferlie, and L. McKee. *Shaping Strategic Change.* London: Sage Publications, 1992.

Pickett, G. "Local Public Health and the State." *American Journal of Public Health* 79, no. 8 (August 1989), pp. 967–968.

Pickett, G. "The Future of Health Departments: The Governmental Presence." *Annual Review of Public Health* 9, no. 1 (1988), pp. 298–322.

Pitts, T. "The Illusion of Control and the Importance of Community in Health Care Organization." *Hospital and Health Services Administration* 38, no. 1 (Spring 1993), pp. 101–109.

Pogue, J. F. "Capitation Strategies." *Integrated Healthcare Report* (December 1994), pp. 1–10.

Pointer, D. D. "Offering-Level Strategy Formulation in Health Services Organizations." *Health Care Management Review* 15, no. 3 (1990), pp. 15–23.

Pointer, D. D., and J. Zwanziger. "Pricing Strategy and Tactics in the New Hospital Marketplace." *Hospital and Health Services Administration* 31, no. 4 (Winter 1986), pp. 5–18.

Pointer, D. D., J. W. Begun, and R. D. Luke. "Managing Interorganizational Dependencies in the New Health Care Marketplace." *Hospital and Health Services Administration* 33, no. 2 (Summer 1988), pp. 167–177.

Pol, L. G., and R. K. Thomas. *The Demography of Health and Health Care.* New York: Plenum Press, 1992.

Porter, M. E. *Competitive Strategy: Techniques for Analyzing Industries and Competitors.* New York: Free Press, 1980.

Powell, T. C. "Total Quality Management As Competitive Advantage." *Strategic Management Journal* 16, no. 1 (1995), pp. 15–37.

Prahalad, C. K., and G. Hamel. "The Core Competence of the Corporation." *Harvard Business Review* 68, no. 3 (May/June 1990), pp. 79–91.

Prescott, J. E., and D. C. Smith. "The Largest Survey of 'Leading-Edge' Competitor Intelligence Managers." *Planning Review* 17, no. 3 (1989), pp. 6–13.

Priem, R. L. "Top Management Team Group Factors, Consensus, and Firm Performance." *Strategic Management Journal* 11, no. 6 (1990), pp. 469–478.

Provan, K. G. "Environmental and Organizational Predictors of Adoption of Cost Containment Policies in Hospitals." *Academy of Management Journal* 30, no. 2 (1987), pp. 219–239.

Provan, K. G. "Organizational and Decision Unit Characteristics and Board Influence in Independent Versus Multihospital System-Affiliated Hospitals." *Journal of Health and Social Behavior* 29, no. 3 (September 1988), pp. 239–252.

Pyenson, B. S., ed. *Calculated Risk: A Provider's Guide to Assessing and Controlling the Financial Risk of*

Management Care. Chicago: American Hospital Publishing, 1995.

Rakich, J. S. "The Canadian and U.S. Health Care Systems: Profiles and Policies." *Hospital and Health Services Administration* 36, no. 1 (Spring 1991), pp. 25–42.

Rakich, J. S., and K. Darr. "Outcomes of Hospital Strategic Planning." *Hospital Topics* 66, no. 3 (1988), pp. 23–27.

Ramajujam, V., and P. Varadarajan. "Research on Diversification: A Synthesis." *Strategic Management Journal* 10, no. 6 (November/December 1989), pp. 523–551.

Rayport, J. F., and J. J. Sviokla. "Exploiting the Virtual Value Chain." *Harvard Business Review* 73, no. 6 (1995), pp. 75–85.

Reed, R., and M. Reed. "CEO Experience and Diversification Strategy." *Journal of Management Studies* 26 (June 1989), pp. 251–270.

Reed, R., D. J. Lemak, and J. C. Montgomery. "Beyond Process: TQM Content and Firm Performance." *Academy of Management Journal* 21, no. 1 (1996), pp. 173–202.

Reeves, P. N. "Issues Management: The Other Side of Strategic Planning." *Hospital and Health Services Administration* 38, no. 2 (Summer 1993), pp. 229–241.

Reger, R. K., and A. S. Huff. "Strategic Groups: A Cognitive Perspective." *Strategic Management Journal* 14, no. 2 (1993), pp. 103–123.

Reisler, M. "Business in Richmond Attacks Health Care Costs." *Harvard Business Review* 63, no. 1 (January/February 1985), pp. 145–155.

Reynolds, J. X. "Using DRGs for Competitive Positioning and Practical Business Planning." *Health Care Management Review* 11, no. 3 (Summer 1986), pp. 37–55.

Rhyme, L. C. "The Relationship of Strategic Planning to Financial Performance." *Strategic Management Journal* 7, no. 5 (September/October 1986), pp. 423–436.

Ries, A., and J. Trout. *Positioning: The Battle for Your Mind.* New York: McGraw-Hill, 1981.

Roberts, C. C. "Getting to Hospitals of the Year 2000: Evolution or Revolution?" *Frontiers of Health Services Management* 6, no. 2 (Winter 1989), pp. 35–40.

Robertson, P. J., D. R. Roberts, and J. I. Porras. "Dynamics of Planned Organizational Change." *Academy of Management Journal* 36, no. 3 (June 1993), pp. 619–634.

Robinson, R. K., G. Franklin, and R. L. Fink. "Sexual Harassment at Work: Issues and Answers for Health Care Administrators." *Hospital and Health Services Administration* 38, no. 2 (Summer 1993), pp. 181–195.

Rogers, M. M., and K. Rothe. "Integrating Capital Budgeting Techniques." *Health Care Strategic Management* 11, no. 2 (February 1993), pp. 7–10.

Rood, D. L. "Beyond Synoptics and Incrementalism: Interpretivism and the Social Construction of Reality." In D. F. Ray, ed., *Southern Management Proceedings,* November 1988, pp. 377–379.

Rosen, E. D. *Improving Public Sector Productivity: Concepts and Practice.* Newbury Park, California: Sage Publications, 1993.

Rosenberger, H. R., and K. M. Kaiser. "Strategic Planning for Health Care Management Information Systems." *Health Care Management Review* 10, no. 1 (Winter 1985), pp. 7–17.

Rosenstein, A. H. "Hospital Closure or Survival: Formula for Success." *Health Care Management Review* 11, no. 3 (Summer 1986), pp. 29–35.

Ross, J. W., J. W. Glaser, D. Rasinski-Gregory, J. M. Gibson, and C. Bayley. *Health Care Ethics Committees.* Chicago: American Hospital Publishing, 1993.

Rothschild, W. E. "A Portfolio of Strategic Leaders." *Planning Review* 24, no. 1 (1996), pp.16–19.

Rouse, W. B. *Start Where You Are: Matching Your Strategy to Your Marketplace.* San Francisco: Jossey-Bass, 1996.

Sahney, V. K., and G. L. Warden. "The Quest for Quality and Productivity in Health Services." *Frontiers of Health Services Management* 7, no. 4 (Summer 1991), pp. 2–40.

Saint-Onge, H. "Tacit Knowledge: The Key to the Strategic Alignment of Intellectual Capital." *Strategy and Leadership* 24, no. 2 (1996), pp.10–14.

Sapienza, A. M. "Imagery and Strategy." *Journal of Management* 13, no. 3 (Fall 1987), pp. 543–555.

Saunders, R., J. J. Mayerhofer, and W. J. Jones. "Strategic Capital Planning Scenarios for the Future." *Healthcare Financial Management* 48, no. 4 (April 1993), pp. 50–55.

Savage, C. M. *Fifth Generation Management: Co-creating Through Virtual Enterprising, Dynamic Teaming, and Knowledge Networking.* Boston: Butterworth-Heinemann, 1996.

Savage, G. T., J. D. Blair, M. J. Benson, and B. Hale. "Urban-Rural Hospital Affiliations." *Health Care*

Management Review 17, no. 1 (Winter 1992), pp. 35–49.

Savage, G. T., T. W. Nix, C. J. Whitehead, and J. D. Blair. "Strategies for Assessing and Managing Organizational Stakeholders." *Academy of Management Executive* 5, no. 2 (May 1991), pp. 61–75.

El Sawy, O. A., and T. C. Pauchant. "Triggers, Templates and Twitches in the Tracking of Emerging Strategic Issues." *Strategic Management Journal* 9, no. 5 (September/October 1988), pp. 455–474.

Scardina, A. "Environmental Services." In V. James McLarney, ed., *Effective Health Care Management Facilities.* Chicago: American Hospital Publishing, 1991.

Schauffler, H. H., and T. Rodriguez. "Managed Care for Preventive Services: A Review of Policy Options." *Medical Care Review* 50, no. 2 (Summer 1993), pp. 153–198.

Schendel, D. "Introduction to Competitive Organizational Behavior: Toward an Organizationally Based Theory of Competitive Advantage." *Strategic Management Journal* 15, no. 1 (1994), pp. 1–4.

Schmeling, W. *Facing Change in Health Care: Learning Faster in Tough Times.* Chicago: American Hospital Association Press, 1995.

Schmitz, H. H. "Decision Support: A Strategic Weapon." In M. J. Ball, J. V. Douglas, R. I. O'Desky, and J. W. Albright, eds., *Healthcare Information Management Systems.* New York: Springer-Verlag, 1991.

Schoemaker, P. J. H. "How to Link Strategic Vision to Core Capabilities." *Sloan Management Review* 34, no. 1 (1992), pp. 67–81.

Schoemaker, P. J. H. "Multiple Scenario Development: Its Conceptual and Behavioral Foundation." *Strategic Management Journal* 14, no. 3 (March 1993), pp. 193–213.

Scholz, C. "Corporate Culture and Strategy—The Problem with Strategic Fit." *Long Range Planning* 20, no. 8 (August 1987), pp. 80–90.

Schonberger, R. J. "Is Strategy Strategic? Impact of Total Quality Management on Strategy." *Academy of Management Executive* 6, no. 3 (August 1992), pp. 80–87.

Schriefer, A. "Getting the Most Out of Scenarios: Advice from the Experts." *Planning Review* 23, no. 5, (1995), pp. 33–35.

Schwartz, G. F., and C. T. Stone. "Strategic Acquisitions by Academic Medical Centers." *Health Care Management* 16, no. 2 (Spring 1991), pp. 39–47.

Schwartz, H. *Century's End: An Orientation Manual Toward the Year 2000.* New York: Doubleday, 1996.

Schwenk, C. "A Meta-Analysis of the Comparative Effectiveness of Devil's Advocacy and Dialectical Inquiry." *Strategic Management Journal* 10, no. 3 (May/June 1989), pp. 303–306.

Scott, W. R. "The Organization of Medical Care Services: Toward an Integrated Theoretical Model." *Medical Care Review* 50, no. 3 (Fall 1993), pp. 271–302.

Selbst, P. L. "A More Total Approach to Productivity Improvement." *Hospital and Health Services Administration* 30, no. 3 (Fall 1985), pp. 85–96.

Senge, P. M. "The Leader's New Work: Building Learning Organizations." *Sloan Management Review* 32 (Fall 1992), pp. 7–22.

Sharon, R., and R. Gority. "Bridging the Visions of Competing Catholic Health Care Systems." *Health Care Strategic Management* 11, no. 7 (1993), pp. 16–19.

Shelton, N. "Competitive Contingencies in Selective Contracting for Hospital Services." *Medical Care Review* 46, no. 3 (Fall 1989), pp. 271–293.

Sheridan, J. E. "Organizational Culture and Employee Retention." *Academy of Management Journal* 35, no. 6 (December 1992), pp. 1036–1056.

Shortell, S. M. "New Directions in Hospital Governance." *Hospital and Health Services Administration* 34, no. 1 (Spring 1989), pp. 7–23.

Shortell, S. M. "Revisiting the Garden: Medicine and Management in the 1990s." *Frontiers of Health Services Management* 7, no. 1 (Fall 1990), pp. 3–32.

Shortell, S. M. "The Evolution of Hospital Systems: Unfulfilled Promises and Self-Fulfilling Prophesies." *Medical Care Review* 45, no. 2 (Fall 1988), pp. 177–214.

Shortell, S. M., and E. J. Zajac. "Internal Corporate Joint Ventures: Development Processes and Performance Outcomes." *Strategic Management Journal* 9, no. 6 (November/December 1988), pp. 527–542.

Shortell, S. M., E. M. Morrison, and B. Friedman. *Strategic Choices Facing American Hospitals: Managing Change in Turbulent Times.* San Francisco: Jossey-Bass, 1990.

Shortell, S. M., E. M. Morrison, and S. Hughes. "The Keys to Successful Diversification: Lessons from Leading Hospital Systems." *Hospital and Health Services Administration* 34, no. 4 (Winter 1989), pp. 471–492.

Shortell, S. M., E. M. Morrison, and S. Robbins. "Strategy Making in Health Care Organizations: A Framework and Agenda for Research." *Medical Care Review* 42, no. 2 (Fall 1985), pp. 219–266.

Shortell, S. M., E. M. Morrison, S. L. Hughes, B. Friedman, J. Coverdill, and L. Berg. "The Effects of Hospital Ownership on Nontraditional Services." *Health Affairs* 5, no. 4 (Winter 1986), pp. 97–111.

Shortell, S. M., M. A. Morrisey, and D. A. Conrad. "Economic Regulation and Hospital Behavior: The Effects on Medical Staff Organization and Hospital-Physician Relationships." *Health Services Research* 20, no. 5 (December 1985), pp. 597–628.

Shortell, S. M., R. R. Gillies, D. A. Anderson, K. M. Erickson, and J. B. Mitchell. *Remaking Health Care in America.* San Francisco: Jossey-Bass, 1996.

Shrivastava, P. "Rigor and Practical Usefulness of Research in Strategic Management." *Strategic Management Journal* 8, no. 1 (January/February 1987), pp. 77–92.

Sieveking, N., and D. Wood. "Hospital CEOs View Their Careers: Implications for Selection, Training, and Placement." *Hospital and Health Services Administration* 37, no. 2 (Summer 1992), pp. 167–279.

Simmons, J. "Integrating Federal Health Care Resources at the Local Level." *Hospital and Health Services Administration* 34, no. 1 (Spring 1989), pp. 113–122.

Simon, J. K., and B. A. Cohen. "Reorganization/Diversification: Six Years Later." *Health Care Management Review* 14, no. 4 (Fall 1989), pp. 77–84.

Singer, A. E. "Strategy As Moral Philosophy." *Strategic Management Journal* 15, no. 3 (1994), pp. 191–213.

Siu, A. L., E. A. McGlynn, H. Morgenstern, M. H. Beers, D. M. Carlisle, E. B. Keeler, J. Beloff, K. Curtin, J. Leaning, B. C. Perry, H. P. Selker, W. Weiswasser, A. Wisenthal, and R. H. Brook. "Choosing Quality of Care Measures Based on the Expected Impact of Improved Care on Health." *Health Services Research* 27, no. 5 (December 1992), pp. 619–650.

Size, T. "Managing Partnerships: The Perspective of a Rural Hospital Cooperative." *Health Care Management Review* 18, no. 1 (1993), pp. 31–41.

Slack, G. D. "Clinical Engineering." In V. James McLarney, ed., *Effective Health Care Facilities Management.* Chicago: American Hospital Publishing, 1991.

Smith, C. T. "Hospital Management Strategies for Fixed-Price Payment." *Health Care Management Review* 11, no. 1 (Winter 1986), pp. 21–26.

Smith, C. T. "Strategic Planning and Entrepreneurism in Academic Health Centers." *Hospital and Health Services Administration* 33, no. 2 (Summer 1988), pp. 143–152.

Smith, D. B. "One More Time: What Do We Mean by Strategic Management?" *Hospital and Health Services Administration* 32, no. 2 (Summer 1987), pp. 219–233.

Smith, D. B., and J. L. Larson. "The Impact of Learning on Cost: The Case of Heart Transplantation." *Hospital and Health Services Administration* 34, no. 1 (Spring 1989), pp. 85–97.

Smith, D. G., and J. R. C. Wheeler. "Strategies and Structures for Hospital Risk Management Programs." *Health Care Management Review* 17, no. 3 (Summer 1992), pp. 9–17.

Smith, H. L., and N. F. Piland. "Does Planning Pay Off? A Look at the Experience of New Mexico's Rural Hospitals." *Hospital Topics* 71, no. 1 (1993), pp. 27–35.

Smith, H. L., N. F. Piland, and M. J. Funk. "Strategic Planning in Rural Health Care Organizations." *Health Care Management Review* 17, no. 3 (Summer 1992), pp. 63–80.

Snell, S. A. "Control Theory in Strategic Human Resource Management: The Mediating Effect of Administrative Information." *Academy of Management Journal* 35, no. 2 (June 1992), pp. 292–327.

Snell, S. A., and M. A. Youndt. "Human Resource Management and Firm Performance: Testing a Contingency Model of Executive Controls." *Journal of Management* 21, no. 4 (1995), pp. 711–731.

Sobczak, P. M., M. D. Fottler, and D. Chastagner. "Managing Retrenchment in French Public Hospitals: Philosophical and Regulatory Constraints." *International Journal of Health Planning and Management* 3, no. 1 (January 1988), pp. 19–34.

Sofaer, S., and R. C. Myrtle. "Interorganizational Theory and Research: Implications for Health Care Management, Policy, and Research." *Medical Care Review* 48, no. 4 (Winter 1991), pp. 371–409.

Solovy, A. "Health Care in 1990s: Forecasts by Top Analysts." *Hospitals* 63 (July 20, 1989), pp. 34–46.

Spiegel, A. D., and H. H. Hyman. *Strategic Health Planning: Methods and Techniques Applied to Marketing and Management.* Norwood, New Jersey: Ablex Publishing, 1991.

Sprague, R. H., Jr., and B. C. McNurlin. *Information Systems in Practice,* 3d ed. Englewood Cliffs, New Jersey: Prentice-Hall, 1993.

Stacey, R. "Strategy as Order Emerging from Chaos." *Long Range Planning* 26, no. 1 (1993), pp. 10–17.

Stacey, R. *Complexity and Creativity in Organizations.* San Francisco: Berrett-Koehler Publishers, 1996.

Starkweather, D. B., and J. M. Carman. "The Limits of Power in Hospital Markets." *Medical Care Review* 45, no. 1 (Spring 1988), pp. 5–48.

Stein, H. "Organizational Psychohistory." *The Journal of Psychohistory* 21 (Summer 1993), pp. 97–114.

Steiner, G. A., J. B. Miner, and E. R. Gray. *Management Policy and Strategy,* 2d ed. New York: Macmillan, 1992.

Stevens, R. A. "The Hospital as a Social Institution, New-Fashioned for the 1990s." *Hospital and Health Services Administration* 36, no. 2 (Summer 1991), pp. 163–173.

Stier, R. D., and C. L. Pugh. "The Strategic Linkage of Marketing and Finance." *Healthcare Forum Journal* (March/April 1989), p. 37.

Stone, R. A. "Mission Statements Revisited." *SAM Advanced Management Journal* 61, no. 1 (Winter 1996), pp. 31–43.

Strasser, S., L. Aharony, and D. Greenberger. "The Patient Satisfaction Process: Moving Toward a Comprehensive Model." *Medical Care Review* 50, no. 2 (1993), pp. 219–248.

Sullivan, J. M. "Health Care Reform: Toward a Healthier Society." *Hospital and Health Services Administration* 37, no. 4 (Winter 1992), pp. 519–532.

Sussman, G. E. "CEO Perspectives on Mission, Healthcare Systems, and the Environment." *Hospital and Health Services Administration* 30, no. 2 (Summer 1985), pp. 21–34.

Sutton, R. I. "The Process of Organizational Death: Disbanding and Reconnecting." *Administrative Science Quarterly* 32, no. 4 (December 1987), pp. 542–569.

Swett, J. N. "Reconstitution of the Not-for-Profit Hospital: New Ethics, New Equity." *Hospital and Health Services Administration* 30, no. 3 (Fall 1985), pp. 20–30.

Sykes, C. S., Jr. "The Role of Equity Financing in Today's Health Care Environment." *Topics in Health Care Financing* 12, no. 3 (1986), pp. 1–3.

Thakur, M., W. English, and W. Hoffman. "Cost Containment in Small Hospitals: Targeting Strategies Beyond This Decade." *Hospital and Health Services Administration* 31, no. 3 (Fall 1986), pp. 34–44.

Thomas, A. S., R. J. Litschert, and K. Ramaswamy. "The Performance Impact of Strategy-Manager Coalignment: An Empirical Examination." *Strategic Management Journal* 12 (1991), pp. 509–522.

Thomas, J. B., and R. R. McDaniel, Jr. "Interpreting Strategic Issues: Effects of Strategy and the Information-Processing Structure of Top Management Teams." *Academy of Management Journal* 33, no. 2 (June 1990), p. 288.

Thomas, J. B., D. J. Ketchen, Jr., L. K. Trevino, and R. R. McDaniel, Jr. "Developing Interorganizational Relationships in the Health Sector." *Health Care Management Review* 17, no. 2 (Spring 1992), pp. 7–19.

Topping, S., and M. D. Fottler. "Improved Stakeholder Management: The Key to Revitalizing the HMO Movement?" *Medical Care Review* 47, no. 3 (Fall 1990), pp. 365–393.

Topping, S., and S. R. Hernandez. "Health Care Strategy Research, 1985–1990: A Critical Review." *Medical Care Review* 48, no. 1 (Spring 1991), pp. 47–89.

Trautwein, F. "Merger Motives and Merger Prescriptions." *Strategic Management Journal* 11, no. 4 (1990), pp. 283–295.

Traxler, H., and T. Dunaye. "Emerging Patterns in Transitional Care." *Health Affairs* 6, no. 2 (Summer 1987), pp. 57–68.

Trotter, J. P. *The Quest for Cost-Effectiveness in Health Care: Achieving Clinical Excellence While Controlling Costs.* Chicago: American Hospital Publishing, 1996.

Tucker, L. R., and R. A. Zaremba. "Organizational Control and Marketing in Multihospital Systems." *Health Care Management Review* 16, no. 1 (Winter 1991), pp. 41–56.

Turner, B. R. "Future Role of Academic Medical Centers." *Health Care Management Review* 14, no. 2 (Spring 1987), pp. 73–77.

Tushman, M. L., W. H. Newman, and E. Romanelli. "Convergence and Upheaval: Managing the Unsteady Pace of Organizational Evolution." *California Management Review* 29, no. 1 (Winter 1986), pp. 29–44.

Tuttle, W. C., N. F. Piland, and H. L. Smith. "The Evolving Role of Health Care Organizations in Research." *Hospital and Health Services Administration* 33, no. 1 (Spring 1988), pp. 47–56.

Ulrich, D. *Human Resource Champions: The Next Agenda for Adding Value and Delivering Results.* Boston: Harvard Business School Press, 1996.

Ulrich, R. S. "Effects of Interior Design on Wellness: Theory and Recent Scientific Research." *Health Care Interior Design* 3 (1991), pp. 97–109.

Van Wart, M. "The First Step in the Reinvention Process: Assessment." *Public Administration Review* 55, no. 5 (1995), pp. 429–438.

Vance, M. and D. Deacon. *Think out of the Box.* Franklin Lakes, New Jersey: Career Press, 1995.

Venable, J. M., Q. Li, P. M. Ginter, and W. J. Duncan. "The Use of Scenario Analysis in Local Public Health Departments: Alternative Futures of Strategic Planning." *Public Health Reports* 108, no. 6 (1994), pp. 701–710.

Vessey, J. T. "The New Competitors: They Think in Terms of 'Speed to Market.' " *Academy of Management Executive* 5, no. 2 (May 1991), pp. 23–33.

Vladeck, B. C. "Health Care Leadership in the Public Interest." *Frontiers of Health Services Management* 8, no. 3 (Spring 1992), pp. 3–26.

Vogel, W. B., B. Langland-Orban, and L. C. Gapenski. "Factors Influencing High and Low Profitability Among Hospitals." *Health Care Management Review* 18, no. 2 (Spring 1993), pp. 15–26.

Vraciu, R. A. "Hospital Strategies for the Eighties: A Mid-Decade Look." *Health Care Management Review* 10, no. 4 (Fall 1985), pp. 9–19.

Vraciu, R. A., and J. Harkey. "Strategies for Small Community Hospitals Operating in the Shadow of a Medical Center." *Health Care Management Review* 17, no. 4 (Fall 1992), pp. 65–72.

Walker, L. R., and M. D. Rosko. "Evaluation of Health Care Service Diversification Options in Health Care Institutions and Programs by Portfolio Analysis: A Marketing Approach." *Journal of Health Care Management* 8, no. 1 (March 1988), pp. 48–59.

Walsh, J. P., and R. D. Kosnik. "Corporate Raiders and Their Disciplinary Role in the Market for Corporate Control." *Academy of Management Journal* 36, no. 4 (August 1993), pp. 671–700.

Watson, D., and L. Strasen. "The Integration of Respiratory Therapy into Nursing: Reorganization for Improved Productivity." *Hospital and Health Services Administration* 32, no. 3 (Fall 1987), pp. 369–398.

Webster, J. L., W. E. Reif, and J. S. Bracker. "The Manager's Guide to Strategic Planning Tools and Techniques." *Planning Review* 17, no. 6 (1989), pp. 4–13.

Weiner, A. J., and J. A. Alexander. "Hospital Governance and Quality of Care: A Critical Review of Transitional Roles." *Medical Care Review* 50, no. 4 (Winter 1993), pp. 375–409.

Weinstein, B. M. "Situation Analysis and Strategic Development in a Public Hospital." *Hospital and Health Services Administration* 31, no. 4 (Winter 1986), pp. 62–73.

Weiss, A. *Our Emperors Have No Clothes: Incredibly Stupid Things Corporate Executives Have Done While Reengineering, Restructuring, Downsizing, TQM'ing, Team-Building, and Empowering . . . in Order to Cover Their Ifs, and "Buts."* Franklin Lakes, New Jersey: Career Press, 1995.

Welge, W. L. "Managed Care Is Limited by the Information System." *Topics in Health Care Financing* 19, no. 2 (Winter 1992), pp. 23–32.

Westley, F. R. "Middle Managers and Strategy: Microdynamics of Inclusion." *Strategic Management Journal* 11, no. 5 (1990), pp. 337–352.

Wheeler, J. R. C., T. M. Wickizer, and S. M. Shortell. "Hospital-Physician Vertical Integration." *Hospital and Health Services Administration* 31, no. 2 (Summer 1986), pp. 67–80.

Wheeler, K. E., and T. Porter-O'Grady. "Barrell Technology: A Strategic Factor in Hospital Planning." *Health Care Management Review* 10, no. 2 (March/April 1985), pp. 55–63.

White, S. L., and T. N. Chirikos. "Measuring Hospital Competition." *Medical Care* 26, no. 3 (March 1988), pp. 256–262.

Whitehead, C. J., J. D. Blair, R. R. Smith, T. W. Nix, and G. T. Savage. "Stakeholder Supportiveness and Strategic Vulnerability: Implications for Competitive Strategy in the HMO Industry." *Health Care Management Review* 14, no. 3 (Summer 1989), pp. 65–76.

Widra, L. S., and M. D. Fottler. "Determinants of HMO Success: The Case of Complete Health." *Health Care Management Review* 17, no. 2 (Spring 1992), pp. 33–44.

Widra, L. S., and M. D. Fottler. "Survival of the Hospital Emergency Department: Strategic Alternatives for the Future." *Health Care Management Review* 13, no. 3 (Summer 1988), pp. 73–83.

Wiersema, M. F., and K. A. Bantel. "Top Management Team Demography and Corporate Strategic Change." *Academy of Management Journal* 35, no. 11 (March 1992), pp. 91–121.

Wilke, C. L. F., and T. Choi. "Changing Criteria for Hospital Acquisitions." *Health Care Management Review* 13, no. 3 (Summer 1988), pp. 23–34.

Williams, J. R. "How Sustainable Is Your Competitive Advantage?" *California Management Review* (Spring 1992), pp. 29–51.

Williams, J. R., B. L. Paez, and L. Sanders. "Conglomeration Revisited." *Strategic Management Journal* 9, no. 5 (September/October 1988), pp. 403–414.

Wilson, I. H. "Realizing the Power of Strategic Vision." *Long Range Planning* 25, no. 5 (1992), pp. 18–28.

Wilson, I. H. "The Five Compasses of Strategic Leadership." *Strategy and Leadership* 24, no. 4 (1996), pp. 26–31.

Wodinsky, H. B., D. Egan, and F. Markel. "Product Line Management in Oncology: A Canadian Experience." *Hospital and Health Services Administration* 33, no. 2 (Summer 1988), pp. 221–236.

Wood, D. J. "Corporate Social Performance Revisited." *The Academy of Management Review* 16, no. 4 (October 1991), pp. 691–718.

Wernerfelt, B. "The Resource-Based View of the Firm: Ten Years After." *Strategic Management Journal* 16, no. 3 (1995), p. 173–177.

Yip, G. S. "Who Needs Strategic Planning?" *Journal of Business Strategy* 6, no. 2 (Fall 1985), pp. 30–42.

Young, G., R. I. Beekun, and G. O. Ginn. "Governing Board Structure, Business Strategy, and Performance of Acute Care Hospitals: A Contingency Perspective." *Health Services Research* 27, no. 4 (October 1992), pp. 543–564.

Young, J. P. "Pawns or Potentates: The Reality of America's Corporate Boards—An Interview with Jay W. Lorsch." *Academy of Management Executive* 4, no. 4 (1990), pp. 85–87.

Yuan, G. *Lure the Tiger out of the Mountains: The 36 Stratagems of Ancient China.* New York: Simon & Schuster, 1991.

Zahra, S. A., and S. S. Chaples. "Blind Spots in Competitive Analysis." *Academy of Management Executive* 7, no. 2 (1993), pp. 7–28.

Zajac, E. J., and M. H. Bazerman. "Blind Spots in Industry and Competitor Analysis: Implications of Interfirm (Mis)perceptions for Strategic Decisions." *Academy of Management Review* 16, no. 1 (January 1991), pp. 37–56.

Zeithaml, V. A., A. Parasuraman, and L. L. Berry. *Delivering Quality Service.* New York: Free Press, 1990.

Zelman, W. A. *The Changing Health Care Marketplace: Private Ventures, Public Interests, Uneasy Partnerships among Doctors, Hospitals, and Health Plans.* San Francisco: Jossey-Bass, 1996.

Zelman, W. N., and D. L. Parham. "Strategic, Operational, and Marketing Concerns of Product Line Management." *Health Care Management Review* 15, no. 1 (1990), pp. 29–35.

Zentner, R. D., and B. D. Gelb. "Scenarios: A Planning Tool for Health Care Organizations." *Hospital and Health Services Administration* 36, no. 2 (Summer 1991), pp. 211–222.

Zuckerman, H. S. "Redefining the Role of the CEO: Challenges and Conflicts." *Hospital and Health Services Administration* 34, no. 1 (Spring 1989), pp. 25–38.

Zuckerman, H. S. "The Strategies and Autonomy of University Hospitals in Competitive Environments." *Hospital and Health Services Administration* 35, no. 1 (Spring 1990), pp. 103–120.

Zuckerman, H. S., and A. D. Kaluzny. "Strategic Alliances in Health Care: The Challenges of Cooperation." *Frontiers of Health Services Management* 7, no. 3 (Spring 1991), pp. 3–23.

Zuckerman, H. S., and T. A. D'Aunno. "Hospital Alliances: Cooperative Strategy in a Competitive Environment." *Health Care Management Review* 15, no. 2 (Spring 1990), pp. 21–30.

PART 6

Cases in the
Health Care Sector

Allina Medical Group: A Division of Allina Health System

Introduction

In July 1994, Allina Health System was formed through the merger of HealthSpan Health Systems Corporation and Medica, making it the largest health care organization in the twin cities of Minneapolis and St. Paul. With that merger, Allina announced the formation of a multidisciplinary medical group practice organization to be derived from HealthSpan's Group Practice Organization. The Allina division, which eventually adopted the name Allina Medical Group (AMG), was formed to manage Allina's network of about 400 owned and contracted physicians and fifty clinics spread over a 10,000-square-mile area in Minnesota and western Wisconsin. As the major owned portion of Allina's provider network, the AMG was an important part of Allina's vision of creating "an integrated health care system to affordably enhance the health status of people living and working in communities we serve."

This case was written by J. Stuart Bunderson, Shawn M. Lofstrom, and Andrew H. Van de Ven of the Strategic Management Research Center at the University of Minnesota in collaboration with managers and clinicians of the Allina Medical Group. The case was prepared to promote class discussion and learning. It was not designed to illustrate either effective or ineffective management. The case includes information that no longer reflects accurately the Allina Organization, its strategies or structures as they exist today. To protect confidentiality, fictitious names of Allina individuals are used in the case.

Hal Patrick, M.D., a private practice physician trained in internal medicine, was appointed as the first president of the new organization. Patrick's vision was to create a group practice organization with the personalized feel of a private practice but the efficiency and market power of a large organization. In order to accomplish this objective, Patrick and the AMG needed to meet a number of significant challenges. These challenges included the integration of the AMG's three regions, fifty clinics, and seventy-five providers into a system with a common strategy and structure, the management of the numerous clinic acquisitions that were constantly being added to the AMG, and the negotiation of the AMG's role within the larger hospital- and health plan–oriented Allina organization.

Allina Health System

Allina Health System was a not-for-profit, integrated health care system serving the needs of health care consumers in Minnesota and western Wisconsin. Allina offered a broad range of health care services including hospitals, nursing homes, transportation services, home care, primary care, and a variety of health plan products. Allina employed 19,376 people (making it the third-largest employer in the state of Minnesota) and provided coverage for 960,634 lives. Allina operated twelve owned hospitals (1,720 staffed beds), six managed hospitals (224 staffed beds), a medical group with fifty clinics and 423 employee providers, and it maintained relationships with 8,700 providers in its network (5,700 physicians). In 1994, revenues from all operations totaled $1.8 billion and were expected to reach $2 billion in 1995.

History and Background

Allina Health System was formed by the July 27, 1994 merger of HealthSpan Health Systems Corporation and Medica. HealthSpan Health Systems contributed hospitals, clinics, nursing homes, ambulance services, a preferred provider network, and other diversified businesses, while Medica contributed managed-care products and preferred provider networks. At the time of the merger, HealthSpan had $1.05 billion in assets and revenues of $970 million (40 percent from HMOs/PPOs) and Medica reported revenues of around $890 million.

The merger between HealthSpan and Medica was precipitated in part by anticipation of health care reform, which was the subject of debate and legislation at state and national levels in 1992, followed in 1993 by enactment of the "MinnesotaCare" legislation. A secondary environmental event that prompted thinking about the merger was a 1992 RFP (request for proposal) issued by the Business Health Care Action Group (an organization of twenty leading employers in the Twin Cities area) that called for an integrated system of health care delivery with the discipline, quality, and cost-effectiveness to meet the needs of multiple purchasers. HealthSpan was interested in meeting this challenge and saw three options that it could pursue: (1) contract with an existing health plan or health plans, (2) develop a health plan, or (3) partner with an existing health plan. The first option was rejected because it would leave HealthSpan with limited control over its future. The second option required expertise that most providers, including HealthSpan, did not possess and did not have the time to develop. This left the third option as the most viable alternative.

The next question concerned whether partnering with an existing health plan should take the form of a joint venture or a merger. A full merger was eventually chosen over a joint venture because both Medica and HealthSpan believed it was the only way to achieve a truly integrated system. It was argued that a full merger allowed for the alignment of incentives, the ability to bear large-scale risk, accountability for population health, a seamless system, single signature authority, and wholesale organizational change. Consequently, in September 1993, HealthSpan began discussions with Medica and other parties regarding the formation of an integrated service network (ISN). On December 7, 1993, Medica and HealthSpan signed a letter of intent to merge and after seven months of antitrust scrutiny, the merger was approved and became effective on July 27, 1994.

The merger that created Allina in 1994 was the latest in a series of mergers and acquisitions that had occurred throughout the history of the organization. Exhibit 1–1 presents the "heritage" of Allina Health System, beginning with the creation of the Christ Church Orphan Home in 1857 and ending with the creation of Allina in 1994. This heritage highlighted the fact that Allina, as the product of at least eleven distinct mergers/acquisitions (not including the acquisitions of individual group practices), was truly a melting pot of organizational backgrounds.

The Twin Cities Health Care Market

The very competitive health care marketplace in the Twin Cities metropolitan area, as in many other markets, was changing significantly in response to increased emphasis on cost containment by health care purchasers and more state and federal legislative initiatives. All health care service providers, including physicians and hospitals, felt these pressures. There was wide acceptance of managed care by consumers in the Twin Cities market with 70 percent of the population covered by a managed-care plan—22 percent in HMOs, 40 percent in PPOs, and 5 percent in government HMOs. The growth in managed-care enrollment in the Twin Cities over the past ten years had been rapid, moving from 500,000 enrollees in 1984 to almost 3 million in 1994.[1] As an increasing number of health care services in the Twin Cities were offered via managed-care programs, hospitals felt pressure to consolidate into integrated systems in order to remain competitive and efficient. As a result of these dynamics, health care costs in the Twin Cities were on average 18 percent to 22 percent lower than in other parts of the country.

One of the factors influencing the competitive nature of the Twin Cities market was the influence of powerful purchaser groups. For example, the Business Health Care Action Group joined together in

Exhibit 1–1 • The Heritage of Allina to 1995

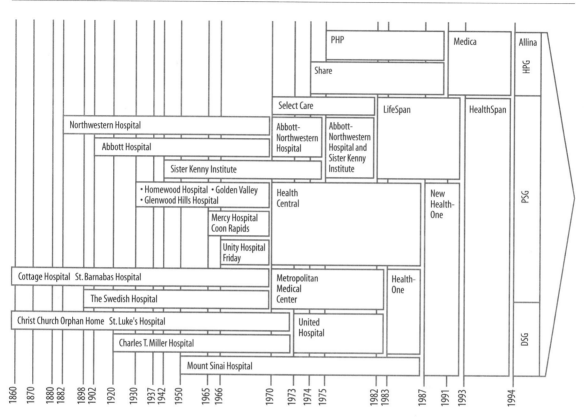

Source: Michael Howe Presentation, AHA Learning Lab, November 10, 1995.

1992 to negotiate health benefit contracts for their employees. Similarly, the Employers Association, Inc. was established to represent over 300 small and medium-sized employers (over 100,000 people) in contracting with service providers. These purchaser groups exerted a significant influence over the organization of health care delivery in the Twin Cities market.

The public debate over health care reform in Minnesota and the legislation that emerged had a dramatic effect on the organization of health care in the Twin Cities as well. Most concrete was the 1993 passage of the "MinnesotaCare" legislation that encouraged providers to develop integrated service networks to provide consumers with the most cost-efficient full range of services at reasonable prices.

Although the outcome of federal legislation was uncertain, there was a willingness on the part of many providers to anticipate future federal regulations by organizing in ways favored by possible health care reform.

In recent years, a few major systems emerged as market leaders in the Twin Cities marketplace. These included Allina, HealthEast, Fairview, and Health Partners. HealthEast operated four hospitals, Fairview operated three large hospitals and some smaller community hospitals, and Health Partners operated one hospital and a number of clinics. These four major systems, as well as third-party payors such as Blue Cross, were actively involved in building integrated service networks involving hospitals, physicians, and clinics.

Exhibit 1–2 presents comparative information on the major health care systems in the Twin Cities, including Allina, as of year-end 1994. As illustrated in Exhibit 1–2, Allina was the largest of the Twin Cities health care systems. Exhibit 1–3 summarizes 1995 market share information for the hospital and health plans of Allina's operations. Allina had 23 percent of the health plans market (second only to Blue Cross/Blue Shield), 28 percent of the hospital market (first in the market), and 20 percent of the primary-care market (second in the market).[2]

Structure and Organization

When Allina was formed in 1994, it divided its operations into three business groups: the Delivery Services Group, the Professional Services Group, and the Health Plans Group. The Delivery Services Group included Allina's hospitals, nursing homes, medical transportation services, home health care, and medical equipment business. The Professional Services Group included the AMG, a medical policy group, and some physician support services. The AMG made up 95 percent of the Professional Services Group in terms of employees and 99 percent in terms of revenue. The Health Plans Group included Allina's health plans and managed-care products: four fully funded commercial products, four self-funded products, six Medicare products, one Medicaid product, and one dental care product. Each of these three groups—Delivery Services, Professional Services, and Health Plans—was led by a vice president who reported directly to the executive officer.

In addition to these three operating groups, Allina employed a corporate staff in each of the following areas: human resources, communications, marketing/planning, legal services, finance/administration, quality, public affairs, and information systems. Representatives from each of these areas were "deployed" to those operating groups where they were needed although they still maintained accountability to the functional vice presidents. This matrix structure encouraged cross-fertilization through staff involvement in different parts of the organization. A 1995 organization chart depicting the three operating groups and the eight support functions is shown in Exhibit 1–4.

Allina adopted a dual physician-management leadership structure in its executive office as well as at other levels of the organization. Gordon Sprenger, Allina's executive officer, received his training in health care management whereas Allina's president, James Ehlen, M.D., was a trained physician. This dual management approach was designed to ensure that both physician and management interests were represented in decision making.

Exhibit 1–2 • Comparing Allina with Its Major Twin Cities Competitors

	Allina[*]	Fairview[†]	HealthEast	Health Systems[‡]	Health Partners[§]	Blue Cross
Employees	19,376	8,700	3,000	4,700	≈5,000	n/a
Enrollees	960,634	400,000	–	–	580,000	1,200,000
Contracted Providers	8,688	3,200	–	–	≈3,200	10,000
Employed Providers	423	100	50	365	350	85
Owned Hospitals	12	5	4	1	1	–
Staffed Beds	1,720	1,276	740	301	≈200	–
1994 Net Revenue ($ millions)	1,800	500	250	320	≈900	1,100

[*] 1995 numbers for Allina only
[†] Includes Preferred One PPO, 60% owned by Fairview.
[‡] Park Nicollet/Methodist Hospital.
[§] Includes Ramsey Hospital Clinic.
Source: D. Grazman and A. Van de Ven, "Building Allina's Group Practice Organization for the Future," Strategic Management Research Center Case, University of Minnesota, 1994.

Exhibit 1–3 · 1995 Market Share Information for Allina Hospitals and Health Plans

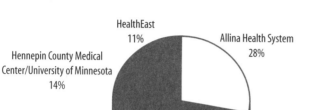

1995 Market Share for Twin Cities Hospitals

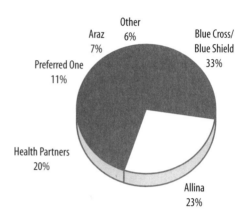

1995 Market Share for Minnesota Health Plans

Source: Sprenger and Ehlen, 1995.

Balanced representation was an important part of Allina's board configuration. The Allina board was made up of 50 percent doctors and 50 percent community members. Furthermore, given IRS guidelines for not-for-profits (that limit doctor membership on hospital boards), physicians with a direct interest in the community constituted only 33 percent of the board membership. The rest of the physician contingent on the Allina board was made up of "disinterested" physicians (doctors who work outside of Minnesota).

Strategy and Vision

Allina's vision was to "offer an integrated healthcare system to affordably enhance the health of people living and working in communities we serve." There were two aspects of this vision that had particular significance: (1) the commitment to an integrated system and (2) the goal of community health. Allina believed that real improvements in community health, improvements that addressed fundamental causes rather than consequences, could only be realized through "the integration of all components of healthcare delivery management and financing." Gordon Sprenger, Allina's chief executive officer, cap-

tured the reasoning behind this vision: "Economic integration will allow all parts of the system to be rewarded for their contributions to efficient, high-quality outcomes that enhance health, whereas in the past, each part has had to compete for its share of the health care pie. . . . New integrated delivery systems like Allina, with all parts allocating the scarce resources, are the only way to make the shift to healthy communities."

Allina's vision of integration was well captured in its name and logo. The name "Allina" was chosen to emphasize the idea that hospitals, clinics, and health plans were "aligned" under one corporate umbrella. The logo showed a letter "A" against a dark elliptical background (see Exhibit 1–5). The three sides of the triangle created by the letter "A" represented the three groups within Allina. The ellipse symbolized that despite very diverse activities, there was one common vision of community health driving all Allina activities.

Sprenger and other Allina leaders not only believed that integrated health care was more effective but that purchasers of health care actually preferred a "single point of accountability" from a health care system rather than the multiple points existing

Exhibit 1–4   •   Allina Organization Chart as of December 1995

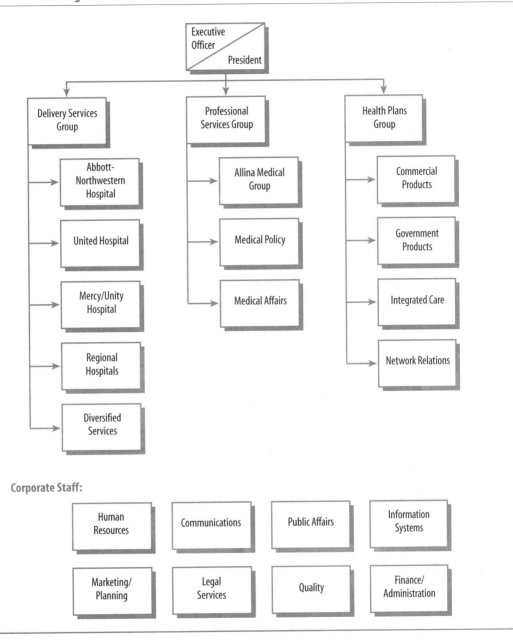

under the traditional market model. Allina therefore emphasized a single point of access into an integrated system in their marketing efforts. In August 1995, Allina launched its first large-scale advertising campaign to "enter the market with clear messages about who we are and the value we bring to the communities we serve." Television, print, and outdoor advertisements emphasized that Allina's system of

Exhibit 1–5 • **Allina Logo**

doctors, hospitals, and health plans was uniquely qualified to address all of an individual's health care needs throughout a lifetime. Advertisements were designed to present Allina as straightforward and plain-talking, clearly understanding fears and concerns about health care, and caring enough to provide consumers with health care choices.

Role of the Allina Medical Group

Allina's provider network was an important part of its strategy to achieve an integrated health care delivery system. In 1995, the 423 physicians and 100 other providers of the Allina Medical Group, spread across fifty clinic sites, represented the major owned or employed portion of Allina's provider network to complement Allina's 8,700 contracted providers. As the owned portion of the Allina provider network, the AMG ideally exemplified the benefits to be gained through system integration. The AMG was one of the largest primary-care group practice organizations in the Twin Cities, with 20 percent of the primary-care market, challenged only by Health Partners and Health Systems Minnesota in terms of employed providers (refer to Exhibit 1–2).

The impact of the AMG on other groups within the Allina system was measured in two ways: (1) in terms of the referrals sent to Allina hospitals by AMG clinics and (2) in terms of the number of enrollees in Allina health plans that utilized AMG clinics. AMG referrals accounted for between 15 percent and 60 percent of inpatient business at Allina's metro hospitals. It was estimated that each AMG physician directed a significant dollar value of care annually to

other parts of the Allina system. This was in addition to the care delivered directly by each physician. In terms of the AMG's contribution to Allina's health plan business, 20 percent of AMG patients were Medica enrollees and contracts while AMG providers made up about 17 percent of the Health Plans Group's business.

The Allina Medical Group

About half of the AMG's fifty clinics were in the Twin Cities metro area. Of the 423 providers that staffed these clinic sites, 75 percent of them were primary care providers (25 percent were specialists) and 75 percent were physicians (25 percent were nonphysician clinicians). Fifteen hundred other employees supported the activities of this provider group, making the AMG the second-largest nonacademic medical group in Minnesota and the fifteenth largest in the United States. The AMG had about 2.0 million patient visits each year and maintained 850,000 active charts.

History and Background

Although the history of the Allina Medical Group as an organized, self-directed entity began in 1994, the historical roots of the AMG can be traced back much further. Because the AMG was originally created out of the various primary-care clinics owned by Health-Span hospitals, the historical origins of the AMG were tied to the history of clinic ownership and management among the different hospitals that eventually combined to form the HealthSpan system. This history could be simplified into three general periods that represented different ways of thinking about clinic ownership and management among the various HealthSpan hospitals.

First Period: Ensuring Primary-Care Services and Maintaining Referrals

Before the mid-1980s, clinic acquisitions by what would eventually become Allina hospitals (Abbott-Northwestern, Unity, Mercy, United) were largely driven by three motives. First, hospitals often acquired clinics in their referral base that were not doing well financially either as a result of poor management or because the clinic was simply unable to keep up with the rising cost of medical technology. Second, a hospital might agree to help fund a doctor who was interested in establishing a new practice in the community. Third, retiring doctors were often unwilling to invest the money required to update their practices and keep them viable; therefore a hospital might intervene to help in that transition. In all three cases, the general motives were a desire to ensure the availability of primary-care services, thereby maintaining or strengthening patient referral patterns in a hospital's service area.

Hospitals typically adopted a laissez-faire style of management with regard to these acquired practices, allowing them almost complete autonomy in the management of their operations. When acquired clinics had financial difficulties, the hospital would often step in to help the practice meet its financial obligations. Nevertheless, there was little or no attempt to manage clinics to any specified standards during this period. Furthermore, clinic acquisition was typically not a stated objective in a hospital's strategic plan.

Second Period: Active Acquisition

In the mid- to late 1980s, more and more primary-care practices began to sell out to large hospital systems or HMOs in response to pressures from payors, the rising costs of medical technology, changing Medicare and Medicaid legislation, and a growing sentiment among many practitioners that managed care was an inevitable trend. As a result, many hospitals began to view clinic acquisitions as a strategic imperative to ensure a steady stream of referrals and to preempt competitor acquisition activity. Clinic acquisitions during this second period were more strategic and proactive than they had been in the first period.

Nevertheless, the management of clinics during this period continued to be based on what one Allina manager called an "oversight" philosophy. Clinics maintained almost complete autonomy in the management of their operations and hospital management did little to influence the behavior of clinicians.

Third Period: Integration

When HealthOne and LifeSpan merged to form HealthSpan in 1992, there were about forty primary-care clinics that had been acquired by the various HealthSpan hospitals over the years. Prior to the merger, discussions occurred in both organizations about the need to be more strategic in the management of these various clinics. With the merger of the two organizations, a vision of a truly regional delivery system with hospitals, clinics, and other elements such as transportation and home care emerged. The idea of a group practice organization that would be responsible for managing the primary-care element of that delivery system was a central part of this emerging vision.

Therefore, in 1992 a search was begun for someone who could take the lead in creating this new group practice. It was decided that the person chosen should be a physician, someone who could manage the group practice from a physician's perspective. In July 1994, at the time of the merger of HealthSpan and Medica to form Allina, Hal Patrick, M.D., was appointed president of what was then called the Allina Group Practice Organization. In July 1995, the name of the yearling group practice was officially changed to Allina Medical Group.

Structure and Organization

AMG operations were divided into three regions, east, north, and west, with regional dividing lines roughly following hospital referral patterns (United Hospital in the east, Mercy/Unity Hospital in the north, and Abbott-Northwestern Hospital in the west). The East Region was made up of eighteen clinic sites spread throughout St. Paul and the eastern suburbs with some presence in southeastern Minnesota (Hastings, Farmington, Northfield). The North Region consisted of fifteen clinic sites located in the northern suburbs and in the non-metro areas north of the Twin Cities (Braham, Cambridge). The West Region had seventeen sites, eleven of which were in the Minneapolis area and western suburbs and six of which were in non-metro areas west of the Twin Cities (Litchfield, Cokato, Annandale).

The three AMG regions varied considerably in terms of their managed-care experience, the degree of market power they exercised, and the contribution they made to Allina hospitals. The East and North Regions were considered to be the most established, aided considerably by the contribution of two major groups—the former River Valley Clinic in the east and the former Comprehensive Medical Clinic in the north—each of which had a long history of managed-care experience and market dominance. In contrast, the West Region consisted primarily of small, independently minded clinics, not one of which represented a formidable market presence.

Three regional vice presidents directed operations in the three AMG regions. With the addition of Hal Patrick, M.D., and two other operations personnel, this group comprised the executive team of the AMG. With three physicians and three professional managers, the AMG executive team maintained the same balanced representation that was evident at other levels of the Allina organization. The executive team was supported by Allina-deployed administrative personnel in each of the following areas: communications, strategic planning/marketing, finance, payor relations and contracting, and human resources. These support personnel joined the executive team to make up the senior management team of the AMG.

The three AMG regions were further divided into geographically organized districts. Each district was assigned a district director (typically a professional manager) who was responsible for supervising clinic administration for the sites in his or her district. Exhibit 1–6 presents an organization chart of the AMG.

At the clinic level, management and administration was carried out through a dual physician-manager leadership structure. Each clinic site was managed by both a clinic manager (typically a professional management person) and a lead physician—a physician who worked directly with the clinic manager in the direction of "all activities that contribute to the operational and business functions of the practice." Although these two individuals had similar job descriptions, they might have different reporting relationships. Whereas the clinic manager reported to the district director, the lead physician often reported directly to the regional vice president.

Management of clinical practice issues at the AMG was accomplished using a second leadership structure. Each region was assigned a regional medical director who was responsible for coordinating clinical integration and clinical practice issues for his or her region. This person worked directly with site medical directors—physicians at each clinic who were responsible for clinical care issues at their respective sites. The responsibilities of medical directors included the development and implementation of clinical guidelines, service and clinical quality initiatives, and educational or teaching programs within the site or region.

The management of the AMG was overseen by an AMG board of directors consisting of Hal Patrick, M.D., one other member of the senior management team, and several physicians from across the AMG. A new board was in the process of being chosen to conform with 501(c)(3) stipulations that there be no more than 20 percent interested parties in the governing group.[3] This new board would likely include Hal Patrick, M.D., as the AMG-interested party, as well as individuals with experience on the boards of other Allina divisions (hospitals, health plans). In addition, a new management advisory group would be formed to provide a mechanism for ongoing physician involvement in major strategic and operational decisions. Similar groups might be formed at the regional or district level.

Financial Performance

Exhibit 1–7 presents the 1994 and estimated 1995 financials for the AMG. The AMG operated at a loss since its creation in 1994. Although there were several explanations for the financial performance of the AMG, three issues were especially salient. First, the clinic acquisitions that had been made throughout the history of the AMG were not always profitable. Many of the clinics that the AMG inherited from Allina hospitals were initially purchased because they were losing money, not because they were prof-

Exhibit 1–6 • AMG Organization Chart as of December 1995

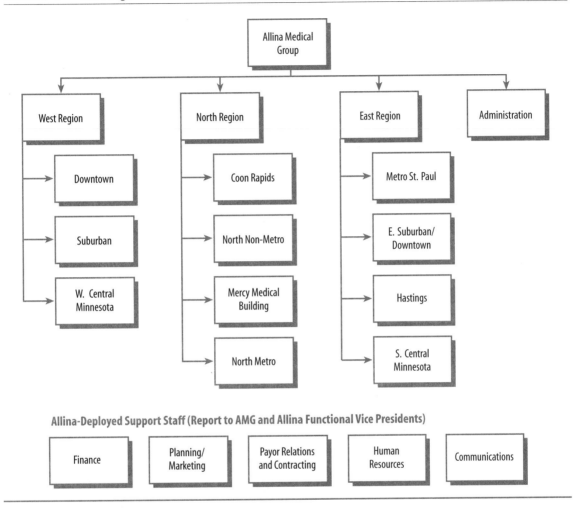

itable investments. Hospitals bought these clinics and kept them alive through cash infusions in order to maintain the availability of primary-care services within the hospital's service area, thereby protecting the hospital's referral base. Consequently, some of the clinics remaining in the AMG system were simply not competitive in their respective markets because of poor market position or other factors. In other clinic acquisition agreements, salaries, the purchase of accounts receivable, and so on were written so as to persuade strategically important clinics to join the Allina system. Even though these might be strong clinics, the AMG could still be losing money on them because of financial obligations that would not be justified based only on the particular clinic's financial contribution.

A second explanation for the AMG's current financial performance was the removal of incentives for productivity at the provider level. Some argued that providers who were employed by a large, managed-care system were less motivated to work long hours and were less conscientious with regard to cost control than were their colleagues in private practice. If these dynamics were present at the

Exhibit 1–7 · 1994 and Estimated 1995 Financials for Allina Medical Group

	1994	1995 (est.)	Percent Change
Revenue			
(dollars in thousands)			
Gross Charges	119,380	160,311	34%
Discounts	24,393	39,260	61%
Other Income	4,277	5,199	22%
Net Revenue	99,264	126,250	27%
Expenses			
Provider Compensation	43,210	60,950	41%
Support Staff	37,681	43,451	85%
Other Operating Expenses	41,794	48,597	16%
Total Expenses	122,685	152,998	25%
Other			
(actual numbers)			
Visits	1,149,096	1,703,300	48%
Charges per Visit	103.89	94.12	−9%
Discount Rate	20.43%	24.49%	20%
Net Revenue per Visit	86.88	74.12	−15%
Provider FTEs	313	426	36%
Support FTEs	1,107	1,452	31%

AMG, even clinics that were profitable before acquisition might not remain profitable once direct market incentives for increased productivity were removed through acquisition. In order to avoid these problems, AMG management spent considerable time and effort developing provider compensation systems that rewarded providers for productivity and quality.

A third explanation for the AMG's financial performance was that payors were simply not reimbursing the AMG enough for services provided. When the AMG entered into a contract with a payor, it often agreed to a fee schedule that reflected substantial discounts from actual AMG charges. Some argued that the AMG had too many payor contracts with unfavorable discount rates and was therefore being forced to operate with slim or nonexistent margins. This issue was aggravated by the fact that different payors agreed to very different discount rates, ranging from the AMG's lowest commercial payor (Medica, Allina's own health plan) at a 29 per-

cent discount rate to the AMG's highest commercial payor at a 17 percent discount rate.

Strategy and Vision

Hal Patrick and his management team believed that their organization was moving into an important transition period. In the past, the key strategy for the AMG was one of clinic acquisition. Between 1993 and 1995 alone, the AMG provider base grew over 100 percent from 231 providers to 423 providers as a result of aggressive acquisition. Nevertheless, Patrick and his team felt that the current strategy for the AMG must move from clinic acquisition to clinic management and ultimately to care management.

In order to move from clinic acquisition to clinic management, the AMG was attempting to implement systemwide approaches to management in areas such as human resources (compensation, staffing, promotions), finance (billing, reporting, budgeting), communications (advertising, signage), and information systems (patient medical records). The goal of these efforts was to increase management efficiency and reduce costs through integrating and streamlining clinic and system operations.

The move from clinic management to care management, on the other hand, involved efforts to implement practices such as clinical quality initiatives, service quality programs, and superior, system-wide approaches to dealing with specific clinical issues (e.g., pregnancy care, care of the elderly). The goal of this transition was to enhance the AMG's ability to achieve its mission of "improving the experience and results of care."

AMG management believed that their organization had two key competitive advantages in the Twin Cities health care market: (1) a private practice mentality with a primary-care, service focus and (2) membership in a large, integrated health care system. The management team recognized that these two advantages stood in opposition to one another—it was difficult to maintain a private practice mentality and at the same time achieve the benefits of integration into a larger system. Nevertheless, the mission, vision, goals, and organizing principles that the AMG developed and continued to develop represented their struggle to maintain this difficult balance.

According to the AMG's mission statement, the purpose of the Allina Medical Group was "to improve the experience and results of care." This basic mission was supported by the following values statements of how AMG members would treat one another in their efforts to achieve their mission:

- Customer needs and values drive everything we do.
- We support and encourage each other.
- We recognize and reward team, as well as individual, contributions.
- We welcome and leverage diversity.
- Our work environment is free of harassment and prejudice.
- We are interdependent with the rest of Allina.
- We emphasize collaboration rather than competition.
- Employees are recognized and developed as our greatest asset.

The AMG further identified a list of "organizing principles," statements that attempted to paint "a future picture of what we're creating." These principles maintained that the organization would:

- be focused on local health needs;
- provide continuous clinical and service innovation;
- provide leadership in care redesign;
- be accountable for managing clinical quality, service quality, and cost;
- be multidisciplinary;
- provide a superior work environment;
- have high expectations for participation in AMG goals;
- provide sharing experiences and learning across the AMG;
- be collaboratively managed by a core physician and administrative team;
- provide input from practitioners regarding strategies, priorities, decisions, and care redesign;
- be supported by common administrative systems and processes; and
- be geographically focused in central Minnesota and west central Wisconsin.

As mentioned previously, the name Allina Medical Group had only been used since July 1994. Before that time, the AMG went by the name Allina Group Practice Organization (and previously Health-Span Group Practice Organization). The name change signaled an important opportunity for the AMG to establish its identity in the market as a single, unified organization rather than a collection of independent and loosely affiliated clinics. For example, clinics began to use the name Allina Medical Group as a tag line (below the clinic site name) and started to use the Allina Medical Group name on clinic materials and in advertising (e.g., in the Yellow Pages). This usage was standardized in 1996.

An important strategic issue that the AMG management team continued to address involved the role that owned, primary-care clinics (i.e., the AMG) played within the larger Allina system. In the past, ownership of primary-care clinics was viewed primarily as a strategy for securing a referral base for Allina hospitals. Nevertheless, Patrick and his management team had a much broader vision of how the AMG could contribute to the Allina system. They pointed out that AMG physicians not only directed a significant dollar value of care to other parts of Allina, they formed an important deterrent to the growth of any competing health plans in the Twin Cities—no competing plan could grow without using AMG clinics. Furthermore, Allina's vision of improving community health required an investment in health improvement at the level of the primary-care physician because he or she was in the best position to deal with the origins of health problems. Hal and his team felt that one of their major objectives was to communicate this vision to other parts of the Allina system to ensure continued support of the AMG.

Challenges of Change at the AMG

As Hal Patrick, his management team, and Allina management looked forward to 1996, they identified a number of issues that would continue to affect their ability to operationalize the corporation's vision of a fully integrated health care delivery system.

Challenges of Creating a Large Group Practice

Group practice organizations became commonplace throughout the United States to deal with the increasing complexity of health care delivery. Nationwide, approximately two-thirds of all physicians practiced in small group practices, usually numbering from three to nine physicians.[4] Nevertheless, group practice organizations the size of the AMG were still a very new and relatively rare phenomenon. Consequently, the AMG was working to create a new type of organization without the benefit of an established precedent and with few counselors who had gone through the process.

One consequence of this pioneer status was that the AMG's senior management team was developing the expertise they needed as they progressed. Although all of the six individuals in the AMG operating group had experience managing a group practice, none had managed anything as large or as complex as the AMG. In the words of one manager, "There are not very many people in this country with the skills to manage this practice because

there's nothing like it. So do you go out and buy it and then wait for them to figure out the marketplace or do you take the people you've got and try to make them better?"

In the process of developing this expertise, the management team often found itself in disagreement about the best decision to be made given a certain set of circumstances. These differences were at least partially because of the different backgrounds and management experiences that team members had. As one manager stated, "How does this AMG management team of people that were independent administrative types come together? We have diverse backgrounds and diverse visions of where to go. . . . I think it would be really helpful if we could figure out what dynamics create those differences and how to work through them."

Different views regarding the strategy and organization of the AMG were often based on fundamental differences in the assumptions that individuals held about the appropriate drivers for organization and management in health care. Some individuals favor a *physician-driven* model wherein physician self-control and autonomy were viewed as central and physicians were seen as the key organizational decision makers. The following comment illustrated the physician-driven logic: "In health care, people at the top aren't that much smarter—they're actually less smart—than the guys down here. That's why it won't work until we figure out that the real wisdom in this company is right down on the front line."

Others subscribed to a *market-driven* model, suggesting that profit maximization and market position should be the principal criteria driving decisions about organization and management. The following quote was an example of a market-driven approach to decision making: "So the motive for integrating as a group provider organization (GPO) was purely market-leverage in the marketplace. We wanted leverage." And in another quote: "This company is about money. . . . They're about making money. The biggest success for this company is the financials."

A third group adopted a *system-driven* perspective, arguing that decisions about organization and management should be driven by the demands of efficiency and focused on goal attainment. The following quote captured the logic behind a system-driven model of decision making: "So what we're trying to do is to challenge our physicians to look at ways to get higher quality and more efficiency. And if we can have standardization of some things but still the flexibility to individualize when necessary for a specific patient problem, we'll be more successful."

Finally, a fourth group favored a *community-driven* model wherein the health of the community and the welfare of society were the principal criteria by which decisions were made. The following quote exemplified community-driven thinking: "If you really want to improve the health status of a community, who's your enemy? The enemy is the disease." Exhibit 1–8 summarizes some of the differences between these four models of organizing.

Another challenge for the AMG was to decide how it would address the competing requirements called for by these four different models. In the words of one manager, it required a "ying and yang"

kind of thinking where old ways of framing the business were revised and "you create an overall value out of balancing tensions by aligning the interests of all parties." Although a key objective, balancing the four different models within one organization represented a significant challenge. One manager commented on this challenge as follows, "If you look out there, most everyone is struggling to implement one or two of these models, but no one else is trying to integrate all four models simultaneously."

Challenges of Provider Integration

Another important issue that the AMG had been dealing with and would continue to deal with was the integration of physicians and other providers into the AMG organization. Before becoming members of Allina, most AMG providers were either in private practice or in smaller group practices. The move to a larger organization therefore represented a significant

Exhibit 1–8 · Alternative Models of Organization Present within AMG

	System Driven	Market Driven	Physician Driven	Community Driven
Central Characteristics	Rational Administrative Bureaucracy	Utilitarian Capitalistic Entrepreneurial	Professional "Occupational community"	Altruistic Humanitarian Socialist
Organizational Purpose	Efficient attainment of system goals	Profit maximization	Self-control of profession's work and membership	Address a social need, benevolence
Organization Design Principles	Division of labor Specialized Competency Impersonal Procedures Hierarchical authority Standardized rules	Strategic advantage Marketing Proprietary Technology Customer authority Economic Competition	Self-defined membership Professional identity Peer reference group Expert authority Work ideology/culture	Needs assessment Social mission/cause Community Organizing Indigenous Leadership Compete against nature
The Role of the Individual	Organizational position	Entrepreneur	Occupational identity	Servant, civic activist
View of Work	Work for a living	Make a living	Work is living	Work for greater good
Career Development	Hierarchical advancement	Economic growth and ownership	Work achievement Profession centrality	Inclusion and status in social community
Incentives	Inducements and contributions	Wealth accumulation	Peer recognition and social relations	Intrinsic task/need accomplishments
Failure	Bureaupathologies Demotions	Loss of profit and assets	Loss of self-control of occupational matters	Loss of commitment to cause

change in work roles and relationships for many providers. Some still struggled with the requirements and expectations of these changing roles.

For example, in smaller practices, physicians had much greater involvement in decisions regarding all aspects of the practice. In a larger system such as the AMG, many of the administrative roles that physicians used to fill were being filled by professional management and full-time staff. Although this allowed the physicians to avoid many of the "headaches" associated with running a practice (e.g., payor relations, finances, payroll), it also made for a more rigid and bureaucratic work environment where policies and procedures took the place of informal interaction and spot decision making. One manager explained it as follows: "In the past, if a physician wanted a new EKG machine, they went out to buy one; but now they have to fit it into projected budgets."

Additionally, the incentive structure for providers changed with membership in an organization such as the AMG. In private practices, providers usually shared the formal ownership of the clinic, bearing the risks and potentially high returns associated with entrepreneurship. Ownership acted as a powerful incentive encouraging individual contributions to clinic productivity. In an organization like the AMG, these incentives were restructured as providers traded the risks of ownership for the security of a salary. This could have an important effect on provider motivations and behaviors. One manager explained it this way, "Something changes in terms of the mind set when it's my money versus your money. Do we need a full-time nurse or a half-time nurse? Those issues are raised when you're on your own but not when you are part of somebody else's deal."

The meaning of provider leadership and management changed as providers moved from small practices to a large organization. In small practices, provider leadership entailed informal interactions, personal relationships, and spot decision making with the interests of the clinic as the principal criterion in decisions. In a large organization such as the AMG, provider leadership involved the ability to coordinate clinic activities within an organizational context, draw on organizational resources as needed for clinic operations, and focus on system as well as clinic effectiveness. This was a very different set of leadership requirements—a set that was critical for the growth of the AMG but that took time to develop. In the words of one manager, "We need to develop physician leadership. Physician leadership has been developed out of medical societies and hospital staffs and that's different than organizational leadership. These are fundamental issues about what it means to be a physician. If we can't do that, I have some fundamental concerns about whether we're going to be able to do this."

Still other changes in provider work practices were actually required by the legal implications of membership in an organization such as the AMG. For example, one provider told of his clinic's long-standing practice of providing charity care to local seminary students. When his clinic became a member of the AMG, he was told that he could no longer perform this service because it created legal problems for the AMG. In order for the AMG to maintain its status as a not-for-profit, it could not provide free or discounted care except on the basis of need.

In sum, the move from a small practice to a larger organization represented a significant change in roles and role relationships for many providers. The ability of the AMG to develop systems, structures, and practices that facilitated this transition would be key to the AMG's future performance.

Apart from the change in organizational milieu, there were many who would argue that professionals (i.e., physicians) simply did not function well in organizational contexts. Professionals required autonomy and the freedom to direct their own work activities. In contrast, organizations required control through standardization and the reduction of variance. As a result, professionals made poor organizational citizens. The AMG's ability to resolve this tension between professional autonomy and organizational citizenship would be another important part of its future success.

One area in which this tension was apparent was in the implementation of clinical practice guidelines. Many people within Allina, as well as in other health care organizations, believed that standard guidelines for clinical care would help to improve the consistent quality of care that a patient received. In the Twin Cities, organizations such as the Institute for Clinical Systems Integration were dedicated to developing these guidelines in the hope that they would become adopted industry-wide. For some providers, however, the implementation of clinical guidelines was viewed as a threat to autonomy and to a provider's ability to exercise professional discretion in the treatment of patients. One manager described it this way: "We will, over time, get to the place where physician performance will be evaluated by the degree to which they practice within those decision support guidelines. That doesn't mean that they follow blindly but that they can't be constant outliers." Indeed, during a February 1996 AMG workshop on clinical improvement, workshop facilitator Brent James, M.D., of InterMountain Health Care emphasized that "some variation in practice is necessary to achieve appropriate care for each patient. Quality improvement seeks to eliminate variation that does not add value." The issue will be whether physicians view clinical practice guidelines as supporting effectiveness in the practice of medicine or as interference in their professional autonomy.

One additional issue regarding the integration of AMG providers was the stereotypes that people held about one another. People often stereotyped physicians as "very concrete," "always looking for data," and "quick to make a judgment about what's going on and what needs to be done." Professional managers, on the other hand, were often viewed as numbers-driven, insensitive to the "loftier" goals of medicine, and concerned only with "making money." Although these stereotypes described some individuals, they were clearly impoverished ways of thinking about and interacting with an entire group of people. Furthermore, if interactions between physicians and managers at the AMG became driven by stereotypes rather than an open exploration of differences, real progress toward integration would become extremely difficult.

Challenges of Corporate Membership

Another set of challenges faced by the AMG derived from the fact that the AMG was one group within a larger, integrated health care system. As a member of Allina, the AMG was expected to integrate its activities with other parts of the system (hospitals, health plans, affiliated providers) to contribute to Allina's goal of providing seamless delivery of care. At the same time, the AMG was expected to operate as profitably and efficiently as possible. These two objectives often proved to be at odds with one another as the interests of different Allina groups came into conflict. As a result, the AMG (and the larger Allina system) was forced to develop ways of dealing with situations wherein the best decision for one Allina division might not be the best decision for another.

An example of this divergence of interests was found in the AMG's efforts to renegotiate with payors. In order to increase revenue and take advantage of its market leverage, the AMG attempted to negotiate higher rates with some of its key payors. In some of these negotiations, the AMG suggested that if a payor did not raise its rates, the AMG would no longer be able to provide services to the patients of that payor. If the AMG were a stand-alone operation, payors might have a difficult time responding to this threat but because the AMG was a part of Allina, payors had some strong reactions. One payor responded by pointing out that the rates of Allina's own health plan (Medica) were the lowest on the market and that if the AMG needed money, they should ask their own health plan to raise its rates. Another payor responded by accusing Allina of unfair market practices, suggesting that Allina was using the AMG to eliminate health plan competition. As a result of these payor concerns, the AMG had a very difficult time making progress in payor renegotiations.

Further, conflicts of interest occurred between the AMG and Allina's affiliated provider network. In the Twin Cities metro area, all physicians on staff at Allina's metro hospitals (including AMG physicians) were organized into physician-hospital organizations (PHOs). These PHOs provided an opportunity for physicians to gain leverage in negotiations with payors. There were three PHOs in the metro area, corresponding to Mercy/Unity Hospital in the north, United Hospital in the east, and Abbott-Northwestern Hospital in the west. The AMG made up roughly 50 percent of the PHO at Mercy/Unity, 90 percent at United, and 30 percent at Abbott-Northwestern. Because the AMG negotiated with payors apart from the PHO, the two groups were often competing for particular payor contracts. Consequently, non-AMG physicians often complained to Allina that the AMG was stealing their business. In such cases, Allina often sided with the PHO to avoid losing precious provider relationships.

Another area where the interests of different Allina groups diverged was in the way that the AMG's value was represented in company financials. As previously mentioned, the AMG expected to report a sizable loss in 1995. This loss was in stark contrast to the performance of Allina hospitals and health plans, which reported significant gains for 1995. Although some members of Allina concluded from these data that the AMG did not add value to the company, Patrick and others responded that the problem was in the way that value was represented. They pointed out that although each AMG physician directed a significant dollar value of care to other parts of Allina, these contributions were not represented in AMG financials. Consequently, either the AMG should not be expected to operate profitably, or money should be transferred from the hospitals and health plans to the AMG to more accurately reflect the AMG's contribution. As might be expected, hospitals and health plans expressed considerable resistance to the second alternative.

The existence of conflicting interests within Allina led some to question whether Allina's current divisional structure with hospitals, clinics, and health plans operating as separate groups was really the best structure to facilitate integration. Some argued that although the current division was necessary to enable the AMG to differentiate itself from the hospitals and establish its own identity, it was now a hindrance to achieving integration. In the words of one manager, "We initially thought this was a good idea because the hospitals were dominating us too much and we have to have some independence and control in decision making. But if we are truly going to integrate, having separate companies may cause problems."

Challenges of Defining a Role within Allina

A final set of challenges that the AMG faced as it looked to the future was really a set of challenges that the AMG shared with all of Allina. Allina was in the process of creating something relatively novel in the health care industry—the integration of formerly independent hospitals, clinics, and health plans into one integrated system. Although the three different pieces of this strategy were in place, Allina was still working to understand how these pieces could best be combined to realize its vision of seamless care and community health. The decisions that were made and the understandings that emerged would have important implications for the future role of the AMG within Allina.

For example, the AMG's poor financial performance led some to question whether clinic ownership was really a strategy that Allina should pursue. These people suggested that Allina did not need to own providers in order to obtain the referred care that providers brought. Instead, provider cooperation could be achieved through creative contracting that would allow Allina to enjoy the benefits of provider cooperation without assuming all of the risk. Proponents of clinic ownership responded that contracting was an uncertain strategy, that ownership was sometimes the only option (e.g., when a clinic was about to go under or would sell to a competitor if not purchased), and that a contracting strategy did not allow for the creation of an efficient group practice organization with a powerful presence in the market. The outcome of this debate would clearly have important implications for the future of the AMG within Allina.

Another debate within Allina, as well as within the larger Twin Cities market, centered around whether the market really wanted the kind of integrated system that Allina offered. The merger that created Allina was originally motivated by government legislation (MinnesotaCare) and purchaser requests (Business Health Care Action Group) calling for the creation of integrated service networks. These activities were developed in anticipation of health care reforms at the national level that did not materialize. As a result, some have questioned whether Allina's integrated delivery system was designed to meet a need that no longer existed. Given that other powerful organizations in the Twin Cities market proposed a very different model based on open access and broad choice, this was a strategic question that had important implications for the future of Allina (and the AMG).

The Future

The Allina Medical Group faced an exciting future as it moved ahead in an environment of change—changes in health care, the Twin Cities market, Allina, and in the AMG itself. The way in which the AMG met the challenges created by this changing context would help to determine the success of Allina as well as the structure of health care in the Twin Cities. These challenges included creating a large group practice, integrating providers, becoming corporate citizens, and establishing a role within Allina. The process of meeting these challenges would almost certainly be indeterminate, incremental, and difficult to plan. It would also be fascinating to watch.

Notes

1. G. M. Sprenger and K. J. Ehlen, "Going Vertical in a Horizontal World," *Hospitals and Health Networks: Pacesetters* Action Learning Lab Series (Chicago: American Hospital Association, 1995).
2. *1995 Minnesota Managed Care Review.*
3. The AMG achieved 501(c)(3) status in early 1994.
4. D. Grazman and A. Van de Ven, "Building Allina's Group Practice Organization for the Future," Strategic Management Research Center Case, University of Minnesota, 1994.

Life Images:
3-D Ultrasound

In April 1994, Tony Dagnone, CEO of University Hospital, London, Ontario, had to decide how to commercially launch the revolutionary 3-D ultrasound invented in the lab. Should he license the technology, form a strategic alliance with a medical technology company, or create a for-profit subsidiary with venture capital to develop, produce, and market the device?

Background

University Hospital was a 390-bed not-for-profit regional medical center and research institute that served as the major teaching hospital for Western Ontario University's College of Medicine. The hospital had 2,500 employees. Although admissions were increasing, the hospital's provincially supported budget had remained flat. Rising health care costs, combined with an economic recession, had placed downward pressure on the provincial government's support for hospital care. Revenues were not keeping up with patient care demands. Research dollars from both government and foundations were slowing as well. Faced with similar circumstances, the J. P. Robarts Institute, a research affiliate of the hospital, was itself considering the option of placing a hiring

moratorium and a wage freeze on administrative salaries in order to compensate for the reduction in grant support.

As stated in its annual report, the mission of the hospital was to "provide exemplary care; to protect the dignity and rights of patients, their families, and our staff; to expand knowledge through innovative research; to provide health care professionals with high quality clinical education; and to maintain our role as a world-class leader in health care teaching and research."

The 3-D Ultrasound Project

On the morning of April 19, 1994, Tony Dagnone, University Hospital's CEO, and Greg Weiler, the director of planning and finance, met with the director of the imaging lab, Dr. Aaron Fenster. At the meeting, Fenster announced that the prototype three-dimensional (3-D) ultrasound computer enhancement device, which had been developed in the hospital's research laboratory, was ready for commercial development. Weiler had prepared a study that assessed the potential North American market demand. Weiler distributed the report to the group. Three basic opinions were outlined in the report: license the technology; joint venture with a leading medical technology firm; and create a for-profit subsidiary with the aid of venture capital to develop and market the system.

The market study was designed to help inform their thinking. The hospital's board of trustees had requested a recommendation at its next meeting.

Dr. Fenster's invention was state of the art and all copyright protections had been secured. However, in an age of rapid technological change and competition, speed to market was critical to the success of any of the options before them.

The Product

The product, consisting of proprietary software and image-acquisition hardware, was configured to use an Apple Macintosh computer to enhance conventional two-dimensional ultrasound images. It had several competitive advantages over current products. The system used a unique approach to create a three-dimensional image of the targeted anatomy. The 3-D system was a specially designed computer-controlled rotation device that was added to a conventional ultrasound machine. Conventional ultrasound machines collect two-dimensional images across the target. The 3-D device was a complex computer software program that mathematically generated a three-dimensional ultrasound image.

The imaging system was an improvement over existing diagnostic techniques in several ways. It recorded one hundred images in fifteen seconds and reconstructed a 3-D image in any rotation to reveal the desired anatomy. This approach benefited the patient by reducing the duration of an uncomfortable examination from ten to twenty minutes to two minutes. The internal architecture of the anatomy in question could be better appreciated in a 3-D image. At an estimated purchase price of US$30,000 per unit, it was relatively inexpensive when compared to magnetic resonance imaging (MRI) priced at US$6 million and computerized tomography (CT) scanning priced at US$1 million. The fact that existing two-dimensional ultrasound machines could be adapted to use the new 3-D computer-imaging software meant that hospitals and physicians did not have to scrap existing expensive equipment.

Clinical Applications and Market Opportunities

Applications had been developed for the imaging of prostate cancers and eye abnormalities. In addition,

work was under way to develop prototype systems to image human breast cancer and heart disease. Each application required a new software program. Updates would be an expected by-product of experience. Volunteers had been scanned for each of these applications. The results had been promising.

Prostate Cancer Market

Prostate cancer was and continued to be the most common human cancer and was found at autopsy in 30 percent of men at the age of fifty and almost 90 percent of men at the age of ninety. It was the leading cause of death due to cancer in men worldwide and the third leading cause of death in Canada. Patients with prostate cancer often did not exhibit symptoms until tumor growth was quite extensive. Only 65 percent of men were diagnosed while the disease was locally confined. When prostate cancer was diagnosed at an early stage, it was highly curable. Even at later stages, treatment was effective, but treatment options varied. Prognosis worsened when diagnosis occurred at advanced stages. Clearly, early diagnosis and ability to assess the severity of the cancer (staging the disease) were important in the management of prostate cancer. The American Cancer Society estimated that, in the United States alone, mass screening using current modalities, treatments, and complications from treatments cost about $28 billion annually. Prostate cancer was most frequently diagnosed with a digital rectal examination, commonly known as the "finger test." This type of examination was easily administered, but missed 40 to 50 percent of tumors that were beyond the reach of the finger or were too small to be detected by touch. Prostate-specific antigen blood tests correctly detected cancer in only about 40 percent of the cases, and so it had limited reliability and predictive value.

Breast Imaging

Breast cancer killed 45,000 women a year in the United States. Approximately 15 million women would undergo mammography to screen for this disease annually. X-ray mammography was the most common form of screening for breast tumors. Although mammography was sensitive to detecting breast tissue abnormalities, it frequently failed to provide enough diagnostic information to determine if the abnormality was cancerous or benign. Of the estimated half-million women referred to surgical biopsy procedures, 70 percent would be found to have nonmalignant lesions.

MRI was an ideal technology to determine whether an abnormality was cancerous or benign. Its biggest drawback was the high cost of acquiring and installing the equipment. Therefore, the research team was excited about the potential use of 3-D ultrasound in the detection and management of breast cancer.

Cardiology Market

Approximately one in four individuals in North America suffered from some form of heart or blood vessel disease or stroke. These diseases affected both middle-aged and elderly people. Forty-three percent of all hospital discharges for patients with heart disease or stroke occurred among people aged forty-five to sixty-five. Clearly, ways to prevent cardiovascular disease would be a huge benefit to society. Work was under way to use the 3-D technology as an easy, non-invasive method to both calculate blood flow using ejection fractions and imaging of the left ventricle muscle mass from the chest surface.

Diagnostic Image Market Trends

Between 75,000 and 100,000 ultrasound units were estimated to have been installed worldwide. An estimated 5,200 U.S. hospitals had purchased and installed over 14,500 ultrasound systems. The annual replacement rate was projected at 3,300 units.

An industry report prepared by the Canadian Industrial Innovation Center estimated that annual world sales of three-dimensional imaging systems (MRIs, CT scans) would triple from $429 million in 1993 to $1.5 billion in 1998. Worldwide ultrasound sales could see annual increases of at least 5 to 10 percent due to the technology's relatively low cost, expanding clinical capabilities, and ongoing replacement or upgrading of older machines. The report concluded that ultrasound would remain a major contributor to the revenue of both hospitals and physician office practices. Weiler estimated that the 3-D ultrasound market could grow from 9 percent of the total three-dimensional imaging market in 1995 to 28 percent in 1998.

The U.S. customer base for medical diagnostic equipment was made up of hospitals, outpatient clinics, and physician offices. One-third of all imaging procedures were performed in nonhospital settings. Seventy-five percent of the 5,200 hospitals in the United States were privately owned. Major chains of hospitals such as Columbia/HCA, Galen, NME, and alliances such as Voluntary Hospitals of America engaged in centralized purchasing. Government hospitals represented 10 percent of all U.S. hospitals. University teaching hospitals accounted for 7 percent of the total.

Teaching hospitals were an excellent arena for introducing new technologies and brand names to medical students, thus building future customer loyalty. Cost containment continued to be a driving force in both the Canadian and U.S. markets. In both markets, outpatient care increased and pre-admission testing was used to reduce the length of hospital stays. The growth of managed care in the United States forced many physicians and hospitals to balance the quality and cost of patient care and to pay attention to prevention and early detection.

The Business Opportunity

The new technology provided better information to the physician than the conventional two-dimensional ultrasound image. This, the developers believed, would lead to earlier diagnosis, better treatments, reduced overall health care costs, and possibly fewer deaths. Over $2 million had been invested in developing this product.

University Hospital had been assigned all intellectual property rights to the technology including patents, copyrights, and trademarks ("Life Images"). The strength of the patents remained to be determined. Three-dimensional images were used in other modalities such as MRI and CT scanning. Three-D was being explored by several ultrasound manufacturers using different approaches. Even with a patent, there were no guarantees that it would preclude the marketing of 3-D systems by competitors who used different approaches.

Regulatory Barriers

Canadian regulatory approval would be straightforward since 3-D ultrasound technology did not include an implantable device or use radiation. Federal Drug Administration (FDA) approval would have to be obtained before the technology could be sold in the United States. Expedited 510(K) approval would be sought on the basis that the 3-D technology used and enhanced the diagnostic capabilities of existing two-dimensional ultrasound probes and equipment. This process could take as little as three months or as long as two years. To be eligible for FDA 510(K) approval, the efficacy and safety of the product must be demonstrated through clinical trials. Normal industry practice was to sell the product to the institutions participating in clinical trials. To do so, an FDA investigational device exemption (IDE) was required.

Should the FDA dispute the 510(K) application, a full premarket approval (PMA) was required. PMA was required if the device was novel and no similar device had received approval. The PMA process could take from two to seven years to complete.

Alternative Business Development Options

The components of the proprietary 3-D ultrasound software and hardware, along with proprietary knowledge, could be licensed to a major ultrasound equipment manufacturer for integration into their new generations of equipment on an OEM (original equipment manufacturer) basis. Given the high concentration of market share among a few major manufacturers (e.g., ALT, Acuson, Hewlett-Packard, or Toshiba), significant worldwide market penetration could potentially be achieved only with a strategic alliance with one of these firms. Preliminary discussions with these manufacturers to form a strategic alliance had revealed their negotiating positions. The manufacturers demanded the right of exclusivity in the development of all current and potential clinical applications in exchange for their role in putting up the required capital for continuous product development, production, and marketing. Manufacturers typically proposed licensing agreements with a 4 to 5 percent royalty on the purchase price of each unit sold. None, however, would outline and guarantee the aggressiveness of their market strategy.

Although the medical technology industry was highly competitive, it would be a significant challenge to develop the market for the 3-D technology. Weiler's report indicated that he believed that the hospital was capable, with appropriate funding and governance structure, of creating a for-profit spin-off to develop and to market the technology. He also noted that venture capital could be secured, given the tax incentives and credits offered to investors willing to support investments in projects designed to reverse the trend of U.S. companies exploiting Canadian discoveries. Several inquiries from venture capitalists had already been received.

Weiler's report assumed that each option could access a minimum of 10 percent of the installed and replacement ultrasound units annually within five years. The report outlined the cost of developing the unit as an independent company. Administrative and marketing costs were estimated at 5 percent and 15 percent of sales. An estimated $6.8 million would be needed for additional product development, regulatory approvals, and clinical evaluations during the first three years. Given the nature of the software, production costs would be minimal. The unit price was set at $30,000. The report established a minimum after-tax profit goal of 10 percent of sales and identified the option of going public after five years. When projected revenues were accounted for, $4.5 million would be needed to finance the start-up of the new company.

As Dagnone examined each of the alternatives, he contemplated the validity of the assumptions. Did the potential benefits outweigh the risks? What should he recommend to the board?

The Visiting Nurses Association of the Greater Ledgerton Area: Working through the Tightening Web of Health Care Regulation

Case 3

When Randy Everitt, the Visiting Nurses Association (VNA) board president, prepared for the January 1996 board of directors' meeting, he reviewed the report from the December 1995 board and finance committee meetings. Costs had increased, revenues decreased, and things did not look very positive for the financial health of the VNA. It was obvious that the board needed to consider changes in the current organizational strategy.

Three years ago Randy had been pleased to be nominated for membership on the board of directors for the VNA in Ledgerton, Ohio. Upon acceptance as a member, he was immediately recruited to serve a two-year term as vice president, then succeeded to the presidency a year ago. However, turbulence in the health care industry resulted in this position having a much greater responsibility for decision making than expected. Much of the board's time during monthly meeting deliberations was spent evaluating strategic decisions that would ensure survival of the organization.

For Randy, the VNA was the epitome of what a provider organization should be. It had a distinguished history of health care support that extended to a broad spectrum of society, and he was proud to be involved with an organization that had such an illustrious background.

Background

VNAs were freestanding, not-for-profit organizations governed by voluntary boards of directors and usually financed by tax-deductible contributions as well as by earnings. Their mission was to provide innovative, cost-effective, comprehensive, compassionate, high-quality home and community care to all people in their communities, regardless of their ability to pay.

History of the Visiting Nurses Associations of America

"Visiting Nurses" originated from a concept developed in England by Florence Nightingale and William Rathbone. In 1880, Albany, New York, became the first VNA site established in the United States. As early as 1885, the Visiting Nurses Associations recognized that providing both health care and assistance with daily activities in the home helped people to get well. Early VNA responsiveness meant establishing milk banks and cleaning homes to ensure infant survival, combating infectious diseases in mining camps, and providing care for the poor during massive flu epidemics. Today's VNAs evolved from those original organizations that provided this basic health and hygiene care for a relatively small, indigent, and immigrant population.

Description of the Home Health Care Industry

VNAs comprised about 8 percent of all home health agencies and about 48 percent of all not-for-profit home health agencies. Other types of organizations that provided home health care included public health agencies, proprietary for-profit agencies, private not-for-profit agencies, and hospital-based agencies. Compared to most other home health agencies, VNAs offered a wider variety of services. Medical services included skilled nursing, personal care and support, medical services, pharmaceuticals, antibiotics, rehabilitation, parenteral and enteral nutrition, renal dialysis, home infusion therapy, chemotherapy, telemetry and respiratory care.[1] (See Appendix A of this case for an explanation of home-care insurance reimbursement.)

Local Organization

The VNA of the Greater Ledgerton Area was organized in 1904. Its original board of trustees had established four committees: nursing, finance, supply, and executive. The current board offered services that had expanded over the years. Its organizational chart included a trustee board that was required to have no more than twenty-five, but no fewer than fifteen, elected members. The officers (president, vice president, secretary, treasurer, and assistant treasurer, along with the immediate past

president) formed the membership of the executive committee. These individuals supervised the actions of the executive director and seven board committees: advisory, child health, finance, medical advisory (which monitored clinical record review activities), nominating, personnel, and publicity/public relations (see Exhibit 3–1).

The executive director presided over the staff positions of office manager, risk manager, bookkeeper/personnel records manager, a receptionist, a file clerk, and additional support personnel who covered duties associated with data entry, billing, and scheduling.

A director of nursing, who reported directly to the executive director, supervised the activities of four team coordinators, each of whom represented one of four geographic areas and additionally was responsible for one of four different segments of home health care. These four team coordinators were identified as home health aide case coordinator, mental health team coordinator, high-technology team coordinator (e.g., for services to patients who required intravenous [IV] monitoring), and a rehabilitation team coordinator. The nursing director also supervised two intake coordinators and a case worker who organized funded programs (see Exhibits 3–2 and 3–3).

Increasingly restrictive funding on the part of both private and government health care insurance

Exhibit 3–1 • Visiting Nurses Association Board of Trustees Organizational Chart

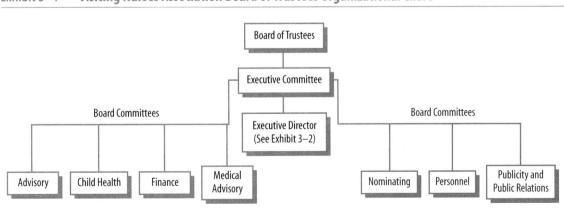

Exhibit 3–2 • Visiting Nurses Association Organizational Chart

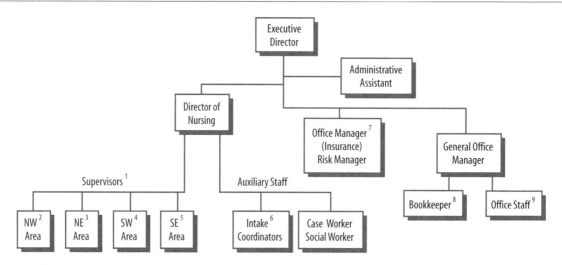

[1] Supervisors (team coordinators) are physically located in four separate geographic areas.
  • Although each is in a different location, the specialty service is made available throughout the region.
  • Each geographic location has a representative on the wound care team and the high-tech team.
[2] Home health aide case coordinator—maximizes utilization of home health aides for scheduling of case load.
[3] Mental health team coordinator—This team includes a psychologist and social worker.
[4] High-tech team coordinator (e.g., intravenous cases).
[5] Rehabilitation team coordinator.
[6] Two RNs who interview and register new case referrals. They function as liaisons between the referral source and the VNA.
[7] These jobs overlap. They include workers' compensation cases and the identification of risk to clients and employees.
[8] Includes accounts payable, payroll, and personnel records.
[9] Personnel who deal with data entry, billings, scheduling, filing, and the receptionist.

providers, along with the VNA's continued adherence to the philosophy of providing services regardless of a client's ability to pay resulted in a deteriorating "bottom line" on financial statements. Some problems were immediately apparent. For example, the total number of billable visits was increasing, whereas income received from insurance and other outside funding sources was decreasing (see Exhibit 3–4).

In addition to fees paid for services, as indicated in Exhibit 3–4, the United Way contributed some annual funding. Other support was provided through income from foundations, a revocable trust, and miscellaneous grants.

As Randy thought more about the events that had occurred in the past two years, he decided to review his files of board and finance committee reports. Bits of information, like pieces of a puzzle,

started to emerge, forming a kind of "big picture." For example, the actual budget deficit as shown in the balance sheet of July 31, 1994 was over $42,000 and continued to increase throughout 1994 and 1995. However, it was hoped that a Medicaid reimbursement reconciliation process currently under way by the State would reduce much of the shortfall.

During the September 1995 meeting, the VNA executive director, Susan Schelly, had suggested using capital fund-raising as a possible way to fill in a financial shortfall. Subsequently, the board set up a development committee to investigate the idea, a development consultant was contacted, and the project was initiated. Within a month, the consultant developed a statement of need and objectives (see Exhibit 3–5), and suggested a timetable for its implementation.

Exhibit 3–3 • Programs Offered by the Ledgerton VNA

Home Care (Homemaker)

This program provided housekeeping services, including housecleaning, laundry, essential shopping, errands, and meal preparation to patients receiving home health aide services. Emphasis was on frail, homebound, over 75 years of age, low-income, minority elderly.

Funding: Eighty-five percent of the cost of this program was underwritten by Title III-B of the federal government through the Area Agency on Aging, plus United Way matching funds.

Geriatric Counseling

1. Geriatric nurse counseling services were available to residents of six high-rise apartments for the elderly and two locations of the Ledgerton County nutrition program for the elderly. The VNA nurse provided both health assessment and counseling to the clinic patients, health teaching, and referrals to available community resources as appropriate.

2. The VNA nurse made visits to designated homebound patients for the purpose of preventive health and early detection of disease. Health assessment, patient teaching, and counseling were done during these visits.

Funding: Federal Grant Title III, with United Way matching funds.

Operation Search and Help

This program provided medicine for disabled children (e.g., asthmatics and diabetics). It was grant funded through the Hale Foundation, which also gave financial assistance under certain conditions.

Funding: Private foundation.

Home Care (Home Care)

The VNA provided in-home, high-quality nursing, home health aide, physical therapy, occupational therapy, and speech therapy to individuals of all ages and income levels in the Greater Ledgerton area.

Funding: Medicaid program fees (which covered approximately 60 percent of service costs) with some United Way backup.

Geriatric Nutrition and Health Assessment

1. This program provided a platform used to evaluate the nutritional status of clients of the senior citizen nutrition program, as well as to those who receive meals-on-wheels.

2. Counseled clients whose responses indicate a moderate or greater health risk. Referrals were made to private physicians or appropriate social service agencies for patients identified as high risk . The nurse assessed home safety while in the home.

3. Advised clients of potential medication problems such as adverse side effects and drug interactions.

Funding: Federal Grant Title III with United Way matching funds.

Randy remembered that Susan was happy the board considered outside fund-raising. At that time, recent changes in insurance reimbursement formulas were putting a stranglehold on the VNA's budget, and it was apparent that new methods for acquiring additional monies for operations were needed.

Since the mid-1980s, VNA income had come solely from fee sources, trust and foundation funding, and the United Way (for operating expenses), with no other community support or additional fund-raising. Part of the reason for this became apparent upon reviewing the membership of the VNA board. Most of these individuals were either professional retirees or in staff or middle management positions, and they had no ties to the financial community (board members of most human services agencies in the area usually had such affiliations). They were not prone to thinking about fund-raising. In fact, potential members were recruited to the board by portraying the VNA as one of the few not-for-profit agencies *not* participating in fund-raising.

Emerging Competition

In 1986, a single VNA competitor, Care Providers, entered the community. It was bought out in 1989

Exhibit 3–4 • Comparison of 1993–1995 Billable* Revenue Sources

Origin	Number of 1993 Visits	Percent of Total	Number of 1994 Visits	Percent of Total	Number of 1995 Visits	Percent of Total
Medicare	32,874	76.5	40,548	79.5	43,427	79.3
Medicaid	6,393	14.9	5,945	11.7	4,542	8.3
Major Medical	1,515	3.5	1,681	3.3	2,095	3.8
Part./Private Pay	1,546	3.6	720	1.4	769	1.4
VA/WC[†]	642	1.5	283	0.5	74	0.1
PSSPRT/Privam[‡]			955	1.9	3,130	5.7
Title XX[§]			897	1.8	752	1.4
Total Visits	42,970		51,029		54,789	

* Causes for *non-billable* visits include:
  • If a fee source only pays for a visit by an aide, a nurse or supervisor of that aide must check the client periodically. This visit by the nurse or supervisor was a *non-billable* visit.
  • A need to return to VNA for supplies.
  • Patient "not home, not found."

[†] VA/WC = Veteran's Administration or Workers' Compensation.

[‡] PSSPRT = A Medicaid waver program.

[§] TITLE XX = Federal funds are a fee source used to provide personal care for those seniors who do not qualify for Medicare services.

Source: VNA Records

Exhibit 3–5 • VNA Statement of Need

The need to create programs, services, and philanthropic opportunities designed to further ensure the financial stability of the Visiting Nurses Association of the Greater Ledgerton Area is greater than ever. The realization of the need to develop a sound approach to sustained financial resource development must come from those who are willing to project their minds into the future and make decisions *now* that will have bearing upon the capability of the Visiting Nurses Association to fund itself as it serves future constituencies and continues to adapt to changing economic times.

by the North State Care System, a multiple-hospital corporation in the area. Physicians with privileges at North State Care System were requested to refer clients to Care Providers when they were in need of home care. This left the VNA to rely primarily on St. Steven's Hospital, a large, 500-bed local hospital, for most of its referrals. Even though this represented a reduction in referral sources, the growth in home-care demand in the late 1980s was so great that the VNA realized a decrease in home visits for only the first full year of this competition. By 1990, the number of VNA home visits was again increasing. In that year, St. Steven's extended an offer to the VNA for purchase or joint venture, but it was refused. In 1992, St. Steven's began a restructuring plan to dra-

matically downsize staff, and it announced that it planned to open its own home-care agency.

Susan Schelly had been only partially aware of this whole sequence of events. She was a relative newcomer to the human services segment of the health care industry. Hired as executive director of the VNA in March 1992, she came with a background of twenty years' experience in middle management at St. Steven's. Susan was one of the few *non*-nurses to head an area home health care organization. Moreover, she had no experience in home care. This precipitated a certain amount of distrust by many of the staff who assumed her role was one of financial management and cost containment, not commitment to quality of care or concerns for staff.

For approximately nine months prior to Susan's assuming the director's position, a VNA nurse supervisor had been covering as acting director. This individual had no business training, and she was not prepared to handle the changing demands for services. As a result, referrals were refused when staff was not readily available to handle additional cases. It was in this time period that St. Steven's announced plans to open its own home-care agency.

The first change Susan instituted was that no case was to be refused due to lack of staff. Evening visits were arranged, and overtime hours were increased. This move precipitated different problems because although VNA nurses were unionized, their wage scale in 1992 was not competitive. Therefore, nurse turnover was significant because hospitals paid higher wages, as did competing, for-profit home-care agencies. Because of this combination of circumstances, Susan decided to open the union contract to increase nursing wages; she felt that this cost increase (approximately 15 percent) could be borne by the Medicare cost reimbursement system, since at that point in time the VNA's costs were significantly below the Medicare cap for services reimbursement. A three-year contract negotiated in 1994 raised wages even higher, with a 3 percent annual step increase for each of the first ten years of employment and an agencywide 3 percent cost-of-living adjustment. Thus the VNA was to see almost a 6 percent increase in wage costs within two years.

In 1992, St. Steven's provided approximately 75 percent of VNA referrals; physician referrals comprised most of the remaining 25 percent. In 1993, St. Steven's home-care agency opened, which eliminated a major referral source to the VNA. Susan therefore initiated steps to hire an intake coordinator. The person she subsequently employed was a nurse with excellent phone and people skills. This individual was well qualified to take referrals in addition to making personal contact with physicians to maintain and improve working relationships with them. This was especially important because physicians were often responsible for guiding patients' decisions about which home health care provider was chosen. By the end of 1994, St. Steven's accounted for 25 percent of referrals and physicians accounted for 75 percent, but the VNA caseload based on number of visits continued to increase by at least 10 percent each year.

In 1994, the Ledgerton VNA depended on profits from its major medical (private insurance) caseload (3.3 percent of total cases) to support the losses from its Medicaid caseload (11.6 percent of total). Medicaid reimbursed the VNA at barely 60 percent of its costs. At the same time, private insurance companies were also negotiating for lower rates with the VNA. Therefore, the Medicaid caseload had to be reduced and the private insurance caseload increased. For the first time in its history, the VNA informed referral sources that it would only take a percentage of Medicaid cases in proportion to the number of private insurance cases referred for its services.

January Blues

Several disturbing pieces of information emerged during the January 1995 board meeting. Although the objective set for number of billable visits in 1994 was 52,560, the actual number was found to be closer to 50,000. Growth slowed noticeably toward the end of that year and was projected to continue into 1995. The problem was attributed to aggressiveness of the local home-care competition, most significantly, the agency owned by St. Steven's. At the meeting, Susan announced her intention to discuss the matter with the CEO of that facility, because some VNA clients were not being referred back to the VNA after their hospital stays.

There were reports concerning additional indications of the aggressive strength exhibited by other home health care organizations. For example, after twenty years of holding the senior nutrition services contract to provide in-home delivery of prepared meals, a well-known not-for-profit organization lost that funding support to a recent newcomer (for-profit) in the home-care field. To top it off, more for-profit and not-for-profit competition was emerging along with a shift to managed care. Managed care was an approach to health care that included both the *procedure* used to determine what individual or agency will provide care as well as the amount of *reimbursement* that will be paid for services. It included the concept of individual freedom to choose one primary-care physician who contracted to an insuring agency to provide all regular health care needs for an individual who subscribed through a particular insurer. The physician agreed to provide all regular health care needs of an individual for a contracted monthly fee. Referrals to a specialist or a specific agency for that individual could only be acquired through his or her designated primary-care physician.

Under a managed-care program, the VNA was considered to be a provider of special services; therefore, a client's primary-care physician must refer any home-care needs specifically to the VNA so the insurer will reimburse for the services provided. Recent proliferation of home health care competition in the Ledgerton area occurred because several hospitals developed their own home health care organizations using the strategy of related horizontal integration. Therefore, they had a built-in market share acquired through the physicians on staff.

1995 Summary of Information and Events

The January VNA program activities summary presented to the board included a report about the new rehabilitation program that was recently added. Information was included about a social services program that was needed. This particular service was predicted to expand the psychiatric program into a full-service mental health program and entice major medical insurance companies to use VNA services.

Susan reported that the United Way had changed its philosophy about fund-raising and asked agencies to try to raise funds for themselves to supplement United Way support. In 1994, the United Way allocated $63,000.

Good News/Bad News

At the February 1995 meeting, Susan relayed information about a new organization being formed in the area that might offer some benefits of membership. It was as yet unnamed, however in concept it would be devised as a network of Northern Ohio Visiting Nurses Associations. Some potential benefits included sharing ideas about goals, marketing strategies, nursing staff, and other types of resources. In addition, the network might negotiate managed-care contracts as a unit.

Information was presented that indicated how tough the government Medicare program could make things for health service organizations that did not follow the rules. The chairperson of the advisory committee recounted a health care administration service report about a national for-profit business that was found guilty of Medicare fraud and lost its license to practice for seven years.

At the end of the February meeting, Randy stayed behind to talk with Susan. During their conversation she told him she would be traveling to Columbus in March to testify in a class action Medicaid suit against the state. A final decision could hold positive financial benefits for the VNA. An audit of Medicaid reimbursements for 1991 to 1994 indicated that nearly 50 percent of visits paid for may not have met the criteria for Medicaid necessity. Therefore, the government might have a valid legal case to demand these monies be returned, and the amount could be as much as $400,000.

There was, however, a lawsuit pending in the state of Ohio based on a Medicaid legislated regulation that the state must have developed a method to determine the reimbursable rate. The suit was based on the fact that the state developed no formalized method and that the VNA was reimbursed at an inappropriate rate. Such suits have been filed in at least four other states and all have won. Therefore, the Ledgerton VNA had reason to believe that it might recoup up to $200,000 when the case was finally decided.

Susan also indicated that a search had been initiated to recruit a social worker. This person was needed to provide additional VNA counseling services. Locating someone qualified was no easy task. In a meeting with Family Services held to discuss the possibility of sharing staff resources, it was revealed that they had been recruiting for some time, but had not yet found a social worker for their staff.

At the March meeting there was some evidence of a productive outcome from additional networking activities. The VNA had formed subcontracts with a durable medical equipment supplier and with a pharmaceutical drug supplier. In addition, Susan asked for, and received, finance committee approval to pursue a joint venture with a local pharmacist to purchase IV supplies. These business relationships were sought more for their future strategic value than for current income.

The board approved a purchase of scheduling software. Using this package, one clerical person could do the work of two registered nurses, who were inputting the scheduling data at that time. This left the nurses free to do more specialized work.

A recap of staffing activities revealed that staff supervised by the director of nursing had recently been increased by two people, an additional intake coordinator and a staff development position. This brought the number of staff directly and indirectly supervised by the nursing director (which also included registered nurses, licensed practical nurses, home health aides, and therapy staff) to ninety-two, a 15 percent increase over the past two years.

New, specialized programs were developed, and some existing programs were strengthened:

1. A rehabilitative team was developed to coordinate physical, occupational, and speech therapy with restorative nursing.
2. A wound care team was developed and a comprehensive wound care program was implemented.
3. A registered nurse with an M.S. degree in nursing was hired to participate in the psychiatric nursing program.
4. Home health aide services were expanded by implementing "flex hours" to meet the after-hours and weekend needs of VNA clients.
5. The flu shot program was reported to have expanded significantly. Approximately 1,700 flu shots were given in 1994 compared to the 200 given in 1993.

Spring; a Long, Hot Summer; and Then There Was Fall

A record number (4,807) of billed visits was reported to the board in May (the agency budgeted for 4,500 visits per month), but the accrual report indicated a $30,123 year-to-date deficit. Along with that dismal report came the news that proposed cuts for Medicare and Medicaid included the possibility of a co-pay for both. The effect on home-care agencies would be additional paperwork and cash flow problems.

Additional Information Reported at the May Meeting

- A survey of the Ledgerton VNA by the Department of Health for compliance with home-care regulations revealed deficiencies in the area of charting visit frequency.
- Board members registered some surprise at hearing the results of a study that analyzed a survey of residents' perceptions of services offered by local home-care agencies. Apparently the VNA services were not well recognized by many professionals, certain age groups, and in some geographic sectors of the area (see Exhibit 3–6).
- The 1996 proposed United Way budget was presented at the September board meeting. Increased funding needs were reflected in retirement (due to funding necessities of the retirement plan) and employee health, due to a significant increase in 1995 and the proposed 1996 Blue Cross/Blue Shield health insurance premiums.

Other Items of Note Found in the Board's "September Song"

1. A projected net gain from the flu vaccine campaign fell in the range of $15,000 to $20,000.
2. It was suggested that a development campaign be instituted to raise funds for capital expenditures.
3. Due to a training program initiated in June, the deficiencies in charting frequency were corrected and the VNA was in compliance with the Department of Health Home Care regulations.
4. Two more new positions were scheduled for implementation:
   A. A risk manager, needed because of the increasing number of worker's compensation clients and their accompanying Joint Commission on Accreditation of Healthcare Organizations (JCAHO) claims. The risk manager would need documentation requirements for the skills assessment of those clients.
   B. An additional clerical person was needed to run the software scheduling program. This

Exhibit 3-6 • VNA Market Survey

Problem Statement

The VNA was experiencing competition from an increasing number of organizations in the home health care field. The percent of increase in market share for the 1994–1995 period was significantly lower compared to the 1993–1994 period. Therefore, although the service was experiencing an increase in number of home visits, there was *not* an increase in market share as evidenced by the number of patients served.

Based on this information, it was determined that a market study could be helpful in determining how the VNA was perceived by the general population and the level of awareness for the services they provided. This information was needed to identify possible ways to gain greater recognition by the general public. There was an additional need to develop a description of the target market—segmented by age groups and profiles of decision makers who were responsible for determining which home health care agency would be chosen should the need arise.

Results

Of the eight largest home health care agencies listed on the survey, the VNA was the most often chosen to be contacted if the need for such care arose. Forty percent of the respondents were aware that the VNA existed.

In a cross listing of awareness of VNA services, the following data were reported:

- The forty-six to fifty-five age group was the largest group not aware that the VNA does skilled-nursing assessments.
- That same group was the largest group unaware of the availability of home health aide services.
- The thirty-six to forty-five age group was unaware that VNA provided the following services:

  Rehabilitation services

  Intravenous therapy services

  Psychiatric nursing services

  Geriatric clinic services

- The forty-six to fifty-five age group was unaware that the VNA provided pediatric assessment services.

---

individual was needed to increase efficiency by monitoring the overlap of visits by a supervisor and an aide. (Each individual visit was billed separately, and increasing instances were found when both were scheduled for the same day. When that occurred, the bill for a supervisor visit was denied.)

5. Two offers from outside concerns were received. Both wished to purchase the VNA. These were two out of a number that had come in during previous months. They represented attempts by national corporations to gather larger shares of the home-care market.

6. In late summer, the VNA participated in a fundraiser, "Charity Night with JC Penney." The project netted about $250, which did not seem to be worth the time and effort expended to develop it.

7. Preparation began for a JCAHO survey in early 1996. The JCAHO was a peer review group that was given status by the Health Care Financing Administration (HCFA)—the overseer of Medi-

care. JCAHO accreditation was often required by managed-care organizations.

8. A strategic planning committee composed of board and staff members was formed to immediately begin sessions designed to revise the VNA mission and develop a new strategic plan along with goals and objectives. The committee was charged with the development of a planning draft for the VNA of the Greater Ledgerton Area, which included:

   A. assessment and revision of the current mission statement;

   B. analysis of macroenvironmental changes in the past five years;

   C. perceptions of current and future target markets; and

   D. identification of critical issues facing the VNA.

Leafing Through October . . .

1. September's deficit balance ($45,204) was a big concern. It appeared that the revenue decrease

corresponded directly to the 10 percent decrease in home visits.

2. The strategic planning committee proposed four areas for strategic development.
   A. Image and marketing (the VNA is more technologically advanced than ever before);
   B. Funding;
   C. Expansion of services; and
   D. Collaboration with other organizations.

December 1995: It's a Jolly Holiday!

1. The board held its annual luncheon meeting.
2. New members and next year's slate of officers were installed.
3. The new president noted three challenges:
   A. Negative income,
   B. Negotiations with VNA staff, and
   C. Strategic planning—the goal program (VNA needs to set goals for the next five years).

Future Concerns

Although a change was possible, up to January 1996, nonreimbursable cost centers (nonhome health care programs) had to write off the same percentage of indirect costs even if the program could be more efficient. For example, with the Hale Foundation–funded services, there was really no need to hire a case worker *and* a billing clerk. However, regulation required that the Hale program write off the same percentage of indirect costs as the Medicare program; it had to share the cost of the billing clerk services. Because of this situation, many home-care agencies developed two companies, one Medicare certified and one non-Medicare certified. The nonreimbursable cost centers were placed in the non-Medicare–certified company, and those services were free of the Medicare regulatory impact.

If the VNA were to start a second, non-Medicare-certified company, a number of pertinent issues should be considered:

1. The federal government may adopt a DRG-type prospective payment system although no one was sure when—it had been under consideration for a number of months. In that case reimbursement would be determined on a per-case basis.

2. On July 1, 1996, health management organizations were scheduled to become available to Medicaid patients on an elective basis. Predictions were that an initial 40 percent of Medicaid-eligible individuals would enroll with an HMO. The reimbursement for each patient under any such plan was 60 percent of the billable fee. In addition, Medicare HMOs were under development, to become available in Ohio on July 1, 1997.

Appendix A: Historical Development of Insurance Reimbursement for Home Care

Until the advent of Medicare and Medicaid in 1966, the VNA was the only provider of home health care in the Ledgerton area. Its delivery of services was almost 100 percent dependent upon donations from the community. The type of care was centered around what was then called "community health" and consisted primarily of well-baby care and treatment of communicable diseases. Until then, individuals who needed extensive treatment or monitoring of their disease processes were treated in the hospital, and their fees were paid out-of-pocket or by health insurance. Because senior citizens, who comprised over 50 percent of the hospitalized population, frequently had no income, they were treated as "charity" patients and placed in hospital wards in charity or teaching institutions.

When Medicare and Medicaid entered the American health system as fee sources, they also required nondiscrimination of health care. Seniors and the poor could no longer be placed in wards; their treatment and housing was mandated to be the same as individuals who paid for their stay. To assure this nondiscrimination, Medicare reimbursed hospitals for all costs, including capital expenditures.

Cost-based reimbursement, as defined by Medicare, recognized all reasonable costs for a program and reimbursed the provider the percentage of these costs based on the percentage utilization by Medicare patients. This method of payment was known as type A and applied to both hospital and home health care. Medicare B, as with all of Medicaid, utilized a fixed-fee payment form and was applicable to physicians' fees, drugs, and medical equipment.

Because Medicare and Medicaid each had provisions of payment for home health care, the VNA's need for financial support from the community diminished. Some operations, such as well-baby care, were maintained, and a significant portion of the population still had no fee source (i.e., did not qualify for Medicare, Medicaid, or had no health insurance).

The next major change that affected home health care and the VNAs was the institution of diagnosis related groups (DRGs) reimbursement by Medicare for hospitals. This form of Medicare reimbursement gave hospitals a set fee according to the patient's discharge diagnosis. If a hospital were cost effective, it realized an excess of revenue over expenses, or profit. Many hospitals could not keep their costs at or below the reimbursement rate and closed. An effective way for hospitals to cut costs was found to be to discharge patients to home care as early as possible.

Thus, home care experienced rapid growth in the 1980s. Many hospitals opened their own home health care agencies if there was an insufficient supply to meet their needs. Insurance companies, such as Blue Cross, and private insurers, such as Metropolitan, followed Medicare's lead to cut costs by lowering the number of days they would reimburse hospitals for care.

Proprietary (for-profit) agencies sprouted up to meet this excess demand. Medicare's cost-based method recognized a 2 percent return on equity for the for-profit agencies as a reasonable expense. But more important, the private insurance companies (that were charged above cost rates) offered a possible profit to home health care agencies. The private payors often negotiated rates similar to Medicare reimbursement.

Proprietary home health care agencies often accepted only insurance or private pay cases. Thus, they cut costs by ignoring Medicare's burdensome conditions of participation. Many not-for-profit or voluntary home health agencies opened second companies based on this principle.

Notes

1. *Basic Statistics on Home Care, 1994,* National Association for Home Care; Statistics on not-for-profit and Visiting Nurses Association Agencies, *Managed Care Digest,* Long-Term Care Ed., 1994, Marion, Merrill, & Dow.

HEALTHSOUTH Corporation: Becoming the Dominant Player in the Market

Richard M. Scrushy, chairman and CEO of HEALTH-SOUTH Corporation, was not surprised by many things when it came to his business. The April 22, 1996, issue of *Forbes* magazine, however, surprised even him. *Forbes* listed HEALTHSOUTH as the nation's fourth-largest company in market value growth in 1995. HEALTHSOUTH grew by 298 percent in market value, only surpassed by Ascend Communications, U.S. Robotics, and FORE Systems. Scrushy commented, "I was just surprised because I would have thought there would be more than three companies that outgrew us in market value growth." He was elated that the company he founded only thirteen years ago "was now on lists with big conglomerates we've known about our entire life."

HEALTHSOUTH Corporation was the nation's largest provider of outpatient and rehabilitative health care services, as well as the largest ambulatory surgery center provider. In 1996, the company changed its name from HEALTHSOUTH Rehabilitation Corporation to HEALTHSOUTH Corporation to clearly indicate that it was not just a rehabilitation company anymore but retained its symbol on the

New York Stock Exchange as HRC. At the close of 1995, HEALTHSOUTH operated over 700 locations throughout the United States and Canada. Its goal was clear: "To be the dominant outpatient health care provider in the nation's top 300 cities with 100,000 or more population" through the placement of all components of the integrated service model in these markets.

HEALTHSOUTH Corporation was one of the most successful business ventures in modern health care. The corporation's growth could only be described as "explosive" since its acquisition of National Medical Enterprise's rehabilitation business in December 1993. Yet, growth involved its own challenge, and explosive growth involved even greater challenges. As Scrushy reviewed selected operating results at the end of 1995 and reflected on the company's position as it neared the end of its first decade of growth, he wondered about HEALTHSOUTH's future (see Exhibits 4–1, 4–2, and 4–3).

The ultimate direction of health care reform remained uncertain. "Would there be significantly more competition in the rehabilitation market?" Scrushy realized that, to sustain growth, continued hard work was even more necessary than during the start-up period. Additionally, he realized that some key strategic decisions would have to be made: "What was the optimum mix of businesses for HEALTHSOUTH Corporation? How far should HEALTHSOUTH go with its integrated 'virtual hospital' model? What pitfalls were ahead? Could success continue?"

This case was prepared by W. Jack Duncan and Peter M. Ginter of the University of Alabama at Birmingham, Michael D. Martin and Kellie Flanagan McIntyre of HEALTHSOUTH Corporation. It is intended as a basis for classroom discussion rather than to illustrate effective or ineffective handling of an administrative situation. Used with permission from Richard Scrushy.

635

Exhibit 4–1 • HEALTHSOUTH Corporation and Subsidiaries: Consolidated Balance Sheets

Assets:	December 31, 1994 (000)	December 31, 1995 (000)
Current Assets:		
Cash and Cash Equivalents	$ 73,438	$ 104,896
Other Marketable Securities	16,628	4,077
Accounts Receivable, Net of Allowances for Doubtful Accounts and Contractual Adjustments of $147,435,000 in 1994 and $212,972,000 in 1995	246,983	336,818
Inventories	27,398	33,504
Prepaid Expenses and Other Current Assets	69,092	70,888
Deferred Income Taxes	3,073	13,257
Total Current Assets	436,612	563,440
Other Assets:		
Loans to Officers	1,240	1,525
Other	41,834	60,437
Property, Plant, and Equipment—Net	872,795	1,100,212
Intangible Assets—Net	426,458	734,515
Total Assets	$1,778,939	$2,460,129
Liabilities and Stockholders' Equity		
Current Liabilities:		
Accounts Payable	$ 88,413	$ 90,427
Salaries and Wages Payable	34,848	59,540
Accrued Interest Payable and Other Liabilities	57,351	58,086
Current Portion of Long-Term Debt	19,123	27,913
Total Current Liabilities	199,735	235,966
Long-Term Debt	1,032,941	1,253,374
Deferred Income Taxes	9,104	15,436
Other Long-Term Liabilities	9,451	5,375
Deferred Revenue	7,526	1,525
Minority Interests-Limited Partnerships	15,959	20,743
Commitments and Contingent Liabilities		
Stockholders' Equity:		
Preferred Stock, $.01 Par Value–1,500,000 Shares Authorized; Issued and Outstanding–None		
Common Stock, $.01 Par Value–150,000,000 Shares Authorized; Issued 78,858,000 in 1994 and 97,359,000 in 1995	789	974
Additional Paid-In Capital	388,269	740,763
Retained Earnings	138,205	208,653
Treasury Stock, at Cost (91,000 Shares)	(323)	(323)
Receivable from Employee Stock Ownership Plan	(17,477)	(15,886)
Notes Receivable from Stockholders	(5,240)	(6,471)
Total Stockholders' Equity	504,223	927,710
Total Liabilities and Stockholders' Equity	$ 1,778,939	$ 2,460,129

Exhibit 4–2 • **HEALTHSOUTH Corporation and Subsidiaries: Consolidated Statements of Income (in thousands except per share amounts)**

	December 31, 1994	December 31, 1995
Revenues	$ 1,274,365	$ 1,556,687
Operating Expenses:	930,845	1,087,554
Operating Units Corporate General and Administrative	48,606	42,514
Provision for Doubtful Accounts	27,646	31,637
Depreciation and Amortization	89,305	121,195
Interest Expense	66,874	91,693
Interest Income	(4,566)	(5,879)
Merger and Acquisition Related Expenses	6,520	34,159
Loss on Impairment of Assets	10,500	11,192
Loss on Abandonment of Computer Project	4,500	0
	1,180,230	1,414,065
Income Before Income Taxes and Minority Interests	94,135	142,622
Provision for Income Taxes	34,788	48,091
	59,347	94,531
Minority Interests	8,864	15,582
Net Income	$50,483	$78,949
Weighted Average Common and Common Equivalent Share	86,461	94,246
Net Income per Common and Common Equivalent Share	$ 0.58	$ 0.84
Net Income per Common Share Assuming Full Dilution	$ 0.58	$ 0.82

The Beginning of Success

HEALTHSOUTH was organized in 1983 as AMCARE, Inc., but in 1985 it changed its name to HEALTH-SOUTH Rehabilitation Corporation. The company was founded by a group of health care professionals, led by Scrushy, who were formerly with LifeMark Corporation, a large publicly held health care services chain that was acquired by American Medical International (AMI) in 1984.

In 1982, Richard Scrushy reflected on how he first recognized the potential for rehabilitation services:

I saw the TEFRA (Tax Equity and Fiscal Responsibility Act) guidelines and the upcoming implementation of Medicare's prospective payment system (PPS) as creating a need for outpatient rehabilitation ser-

vices. It was rather clear that lengths of stay in general hospitals would decrease and that patients would be discharged more quickly than in the past. It became obvious to me that these changes would create a need for a transition between the hospital and the patient's home.

Medicare provided financial incentives for outpatient rehabilitation services by giving comprehensive outpatient rehabilitation facilities an exemption from prospective payment and allowed the services of these facilities to continue to be reimbursed on a retrospective, cost-based basis.

Scrushy recalled:

I also saw that LifeMark, my current employer, would suffer significant reductions in profitability as the use of the then

Exhibit 4–3 · HEALTHSOUTH Corporation and Subsidiaries: Consolidated Statements of Stockholders' Equity

	Common Shares	Common Stock	Additional Paid-In Capital	Retained Earnings	Treasury Stock	Receivable ESOP	Notes Receivable from Stockholders	Total Stockholders' Equity
Balance—December 31, 1994	$78,767	788.6	$388,269	$138,205	(323)	(17,477)	(5,240)	$504,223
Adjustment for ReLife Merger	2,732	27.3	7,114	(3,734)	0	0	0	3,407
Proceeds from Issuance of Common Shares	14,950	149.5	330,229	0	0	0	0	330,379
Proceeds from Exercise of Options	819	8.2	8,499	0	0	0	0	8,507
Income Tax Benefits Related to Incentive Stock Options	0	0	6,653	0	0	0	0	6,653
Reduction in Receivable from Employee Stock Ownership Plan	0	0	0	0	0	1,591	0	1,591
Increase in Stockholders' Notes Receivable	0	0	0	0	0	0	(1,231)	(1,231)
Purchase of Limited Partnership Units	0	0	0	(4,767)	0	0	0	(4,767)
Net Income	0	0	0	78,949	0	0	0	78,949
Balance—December 31, 1995	$97,268	$973.6	$740,764	$208,653	$(323)	$(15,886)	$(6,471)	$927,711

lucrative ancillary inpatient services was discouraged under the new reimbursement guidelines. I discussed my concerns about the upcoming changes in Medicare with LifeMark management and proposed that we develop a chain of outpatient rehabilitation centers. I saw that the centers I proposed were LifeMark's chance to preserve its profitability under PPS, and when they rejected my proposal, I saw cutbacks and a low rate of advancement in the future.

I repeated my proposal for AMI's management when it acquired LifeMark, but AMI could not implement the program immediately after such a major acquisition. So, I resigned and founded HEALTH-SOUTH Rehabilitation Corporation in conjunction with three of my colleagues from LifeMark.

Early Development

HEALTHSOUTH Corporation's initial focus was on the establishment of a national network of outpatient rehabilitation facilities supported by a rehabilitation equipment business. In September 1984, HEALTH-SOUTH opened its first outpatient rehabilitation facility in Little Rock, Arkansas, followed by another one in Birmingham, Alabama. Within five years, the company was operating twenty-nine outpatient facilities located in seventeen states throughout the Southeastern United States. By the end of 1995, HEALTHSOUTH operated in more than 700 locations—from California to New Hampshire, from Florida to Wisconsin and into Canada. Business was booming. HRC started providing inpatient rehabilitation services in June 1985 with the acquisition of an eighty-eight-bed facility in Florence, South Carolina. Between 1985 and 1990, the company established eleven more inpatient facilities in nine states.

South Highlands Hospital

A key development in HEALTHSOUTH's strategy was the December 1989 acquisition of the 219-bed South Highlands Hospital in Birmingham, Alabama. Although South Highlands had been marginally profitable, its inability to obtain financing meant that it was unable to meet the needs of its physicians, particularly James Andrews and William Clancy, both world-renowned orthopedic surgeons. As Scrushy noted:

> My immediate concern was to maintain the referral base that Drs. Andrews and Clancy provided. HRC had benefited from the rehabilitation referrals stemming from the extensive orthopedic surgery the doctors performed at South Highlands. The surgeons needed a major expansion at South Highlands to practice at maximum effectiveness and Drs. Andrews and Clancy would seek the facilities they needed elsewhere if something wasn't done. On the surface, our acquisition of South Highlands was defensive.

However, purchase of South Highlands Hospital for approximately $27 million was far more than a defensive move. Renamed HEALTHSOUTH Medical Center (HMC), the hospital was developed into a flagship facility. HRC immediately began construction of a $30 million addition to the hospital. Even during construction, referrals continued to flow from HMC to other HRC facilities. The construction created interest in the medical community, which in turn, created business. The emergency facility at HMC eliminated the necessity of delaying evaluation and treatment of athletic injuries that could be quickly transferred to the facility through HRC's extensive linkages with almost 400 high school and college athletic programs.

The acquisition of additional medical centers was an outgrowth of HEALTHSOUTH's rehabilitative services. The medical centers provided general and specialty health care services emphasizing orthopedics, sports medicine, and rehabilitation. In each market where a medical center had been acquired, HEALTHSOUTH enjoyed well-established relationships with the medical communities serving the facility. Following each acquisition, it was HEALTHSOUTH's goal to provide resources for improving the physical plant and expanding services through the introduction of new technology. All HEALTHSOUTH medical centers were JCAHO accredited and participated in the Medicare prospective payment system.

Inpatient Services

In December 1995, HRC operated seventy-seven inpatient rehabilitation facilities with 4,618 beds. This represented the largest group of affiliated proprietary inpatient rehabilitation facilities in the United States. Inpatient rehabilitation patients were typically those who experienced significant physical disabilities because of various conditions. Inpatient facilities provided the medical, nursing, therapy, and ancillary services required to comply with local, state, and federal regulations as well as accreditation standards of JCAHO and the Commission on Accreditation of Rehabilitation Facilities. All inpatient rehabilitation facilities used an interdisciplinary team approach and involved the patient, the patient's family, and the payor in the determination of the goals for each patient. At the end of 1995, the company's inpatient facilities achieved an overall bed utilization rate of just over 70 percent.

Surgery Centers

During 1995, HEALTHSOUTH finalized pooling-of-interest mergers with Surgical Health Corporation (thirty-seven outpatient surgery centers in eleven states) and Sutter Surgery Centers, Inc. (twelve outpatient surgery centers in three states), as well as stock purchase acquisitions of the rehabilitation hospitals division of NovaCare, Inc. (eleven inpatient rehabilitation facilities, twelve other health care facilities, and two certificates of need [CONs] in eight states), and Caremark Orthopedic Services, Inc. (120 outpatient rehabilitation facilities in thirteen states). In addition, the company entered into agreements to acquire Surgical Care Affiliates, Inc. (sixty-seven outpatient surgery centers in twenty-four states) and became the largest operator of outpatient surgery centers in the United States. At the end of 1995, HRC operated over one hundred freestanding surgery centers with others under development. Most of

Exhibit 4–4 · Integrated Service Model

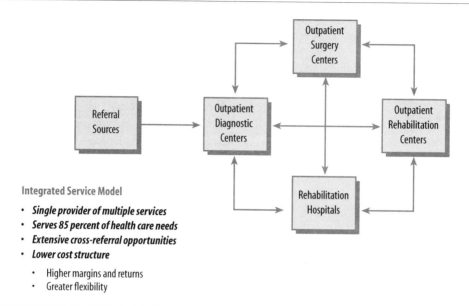

Integrated Service Model

- *Single provider of multiple services*
- *Serves 85 percent of health care needs*
- *Extensive cross-referral opportunities*
- *Lower cost structure*
  - Higher margins and returns
  - Greater flexibility

the surgi-centers were located in markets served by the company's outpatient and rehabilitative service facilities, creating the potential of significant synergies through cross-referrals between surgery and rehabilitative facilities as well as centralization of administration.

The entry of the outpatient surgery market provided an important ingredient in the realization of HEALTHSOUTH's integrated service model (illustrated in Exhibit 4–4). In light of developments in managed care, this integrated service model offered payors convenience and cost-effectiveness because they dealt with a single provider for a variety of services (one-stop shopping). With this model, Scrushy noted:

> We are laying the foundation for HEALTH-SOUTH to be the health care company of the twenty-first century. We are establishing the platform on which we will build. Health care in the next century will not be based on the traditional hospital model. Rather, the emphasis will be less intrusive surgical interventions, more efficient diagnostic procedures, and less restrictive environments. . . .

Health care in the future will develop around the virtual hospital—an integrated service delivery model that replaces many of the functions of the acute-care hospital with lower-cost outpatient facilities.

HRC estimated that full implementation of the integrated service model in the 300 target markets represented a market potential of $20 to $30 billion.

Industry Overview

Every year more than four million people needed rehabilitative health care services as the result of automobile and industrial accidents, sports and recreational injuries, crime and violence, or cardiac, stroke, and cancer episodes. It was estimated that at any particular time, 13 percent of the U.S. population and almost one-half of Americans over seventy-five years of age required some form of rehabilitative health services. The aging population suggested even higher demand for rehabilitative health services in the future.

Medical rehabilitation involved the treatment of physical limitations through which therapists attempted to improve their patients' functional independence, relieve pain, and ameliorate any permanent disabilities. Patients using medical rehabilitation services included the handicapped and those recovering from accidents, strokes, surgery, and fractures; disabilities associated with diseases; and conditions such as multiple sclerosis, cerebral palsy, arthritis, and heart disease. Over 80 percent of those people receiving rehabilitative health care services returned to their homes, work, schools, or active retirement.

Rehabilitation Services

Medical rehabilitation services included inpatient rehabilitation in dedicated freestanding hospitals and distinct units of acute-care hospitals; comprehensive outpatient rehabilitation facilities; specialty rehabilitation programs (such as traumatic brain injury and spinal cord injury); pediatric rehabilitation; and occupational and industrial rehabilitation.

The availability of comprehensive rehabilitation services was limited in the United States. Provision of rehabilitation services by outpatient departments of acute-care hospitals was fragmented because services were provided through several departments, and private practice therapists rarely provided a full-range of comprehensive rehabilitation services. Often, patients requiring multidisciplinary services would be treated by different therapists in different locations, which could result in uncoordinated care.

Comprehensive inpatient rehabilitation services were provided by freestanding rehabilitation hospitals, distinct units in acute-care hospitals, and skilled nursing facilities. Analysts with Solomon Brothers estimated that the rehabilitation services segment of the health care industry in the United States would grow at a rate of 13 to 15 percent in 1996 and that HEALTHSOUTH Corporation should increase its earnings per share by 20 to 22 percent over the next three years. They predicted HRC would significantly outperform the rehabilitation market in general. However, a number of factors would drive industry growth and ultimately affect HRC's performance.

The incidence of major disability increased with age. Improvements in medical care have enabled more people with severe disabilities to live longer. Data compiled by the National Center for Health Statistics showed that in 1995, 35 million people in the United States (one out of every seven people) had some form of disability. The National Association of Insurance Commissioners pointed out that seven out of ten workers would suffer a long-term disability between the ages of thirty-five and sixty-five. Increases in leisure time among the middle-aged population resulted in more physical activity and thus more sports injuries, a major portion of HEALTH-SOUTH's business. At the same time, the greater proportion of the population in the over sixty-five age group increased the demand for rehabilitation services associated with the elderly, such as treatments for strokes and amputations. As a direct result of improved technology, three million people a year survived automobile crashes, sports injuries, strokes, and heart attacks and required rehabilitation services to restore normal functions.

Purchasers and providers of health care services, such as insurance companies, health maintenance organizations, businesses, and industry were seeking economical, high-quality alternatives to traditional health care services. Rehabilitation services, whether outpatient or inpatient, represented such an alternative. Often early participation in a disabled person's rehabilitation prevented a short-term problem from becoming a long-term disability. Moreover, by returning the individual to the workforce, the number of disability benefit payments was reduced, thus decreasing long-term disability costs. Independent studies by insurance companies have shown that of every dollar spent on rehabilitation, a savings of $30 occurred in disability payments. Insurance companies generally agreed that every rehabilitation dollar spent on patients with serious functional impairments saved from $10 to $30 in long-term health care costs such as nursing care.

As noted previously, inpatient rehabilitation services, organized as either dedicated rehabilitation hospitals or distinct units, were eligible for exemptions from Medicare's prospective payment system. Outpatient rehabilitation services, organized as comprehensive outpatient rehabilitation facilities or rehabilitation agencies, were eligible to participate in the Medicare program under cost-based reimbursement. Inpatient and outpatient rehabilitation services were typically covered for payment by the major medical portion of commercial health insurance policies.

Moreover, Medicare reimbursement and the policies of private insurance companies encouraged early discharge from acute-care hospitals thereby providing opportunities for outpatient rehabilitation, home health, and long-term-care facilities.

Advances in medical science and trauma care made it possible to save the lives of increasing numbers of victims of accidents, violence, and serious sports injuries. These victims were provided with therapeutic options that offered opportunities for inpatient and outpatient rehabilitation facilities. Although HEALTHSOUTH was no longer simply a rehabilitation company, rehabilitative services remained the core of its integrated services model. Expansion into medical centers and outpatient surgery augmented and capitalized on the company's reputation and relationships in the markets it served.

Rehabilitation and Outpatient Surgery

At the close of 1992, HEALTHSOUTH's primary inpatient rehabilitation services competitors were National Medical Enterprises, Inc., Continental Medical Systems, ReLife, NovaCare, and Advantage-HEALTH. By the beginning of 1996, HEALTHSOUTH had acquired all the relevant operations of these competitors except Continental Medical Systems. It was estimated that HEALTHSOUTH presently controlled about 15 percent of the inpatient rehabilitation beds and approximately 6 percent of the outpatient rehabilitation beds.

Within one year of entry into the market, HEALTHSOUTH became the industry leader in ambulatory surgical centers. According to Alex. Brown & Sons, of the roughly 2,100 freestanding ambulatory surgery centers, approximately 75 percent were single-site and physician owned. This market, in other words, was highly fragmented and represented a major opportunity for HEALTHSOUTH. The company owned slightly less than 10 percent of the freestanding surgical centers.

HRC's operating units were located in forty-two states, the District of Columbia, and Canada (see Exhibit 4–5). The company owned 5 medical centers, 15 diagnostic centers, 497 outpatient clinics, and 112 outpatient surgery centers. The competition faced in each of these markets was similar although unique aspects existed, arising primarily from the number of health care providers in specific metropolitan areas. The primary competitive factors in the rehabilitation services business were quality of services; projected patient outcomes; responsiveness to the needs of the patients, community, and physicians; ability to tailor programs and services to meet specific needs; and the charges for services.

HEALTHSOUTH's rehabilitative facilities competed on a regional and national basis with other providers of specialized services such as sports medicine, head injury rehabilitation, and orthopedic surgery. Competitors and potential competitors included hospitals, private practice therapists, rehabilitation agencies, and so on. Some of the competitors had significant patient referral support systems as well as financial and human resources. HEALTHSOUTH medical centers competed directly with local hospitals and various nationally recognized centers of excellence in orthopedics, sports medicine, and other specialties.

HEALTHSOUTH's surgery centers competed primarily with hospitals and other operators of freestanding surgery centers in attracting patients and physicians, in developing new centers, and in acquiring existing centers. The primary competitive factors in the outpatient surgery business were convenience, cost, quality of service, physician loyalty, and reputation. Hospitals had a number of competitive advantages in attracting physicians and patients.

The market for outpatient rehabilitation services was estimated to be approximately $7.9 billion. Inpatient rehabilitation services were estimated to be another $7.7 billion, and the market for outpatient surgery centers was estimated to be approximately $6 billion. HEALTHSOUTH's estimated market share in each of these markets is shown in Exhibit 4–6.

Reimbursement

Aggressive acquisition and managed-care marketing efforts had radically altered the payor mix of HEALTHSOUTH over the past five years. Reimbursement for services provided by HRC were divided into four distinct categories: commercial or private pay, workers' compensation, Medicare, and "other," which included a relatively small amount of Medicaid and HMOs and PPOs. The percentage of each

Exhibit 4–5　•　Location of HEALTHSOUTH Facilities as of January 1, 1996

Location	Outpatient Centers	Inpatient Centers	Medical Centers	Surgery Centers	Diagnostic Centers	Location	Outpatient Centers	Inpatient Centers	Medical Centers	Surgery Centers	Diagnostic Centers
Alabama	19	9	1	5	4	Mississippi	3	0	0	0	0
Alaska	0	0	0	1	0	Missouri	30	4	0	6	0
Arizona	17	3	0	2	0	Nebraska	2	0	0	0	0
Arkansas	2	1	0	2	0	Nevada	2	0	0	0	0
California	46	1	0	18	0	New Hampshire	7	1	0	0	0
Colorado	21	0	0	4	0	New Jersey	18	2	0	2	0
Connecticut	1	0	0	0	0	New Mexico	3	1	0	1	0
Washington, DC	1	0	0	0	1	New York	12	0	0	0	0
Delaware	4	0	0	0	0	North Carolina	13	1	0	3	0
Florida	47	8	2	20	1	Ohio	24	0	0	1	0
Georgia	8	3	0	4	1	Oklahoma	9	1	0	1	0
Hawaii	3	0	0	0	0	Ontario, Canada	1	0	0	0	0
Idaho	0	0	0	1	0	Pennsylvania	19	8	0	0	0
Illinois	46	0	0	2	0	South Carolina	6	5	0	0	0
Indiana	13	1	0	2	0	Tennessee	13	6	0	6	1
Iowa	3	0	0	0	0	Texas	42	13	1	14	3
Kansas	3	0	0	0	0	Utah	1	1	0	1	0
Kentucky	2	1	0	2	0	Virginia	10	3	1	1	1
Louisiana	2	1	0	1	0	Washington	23	0	0	1	0
Maine	2	0	0	0	0	West Virginia	1	4	0	0	0
Maryland	15	1	0	5	3	Wisconsin	1	0	0	4	0
Massachusetts	1	0	0	1	0						
Michigan	1	0	0	1	0	Total	497	79	5	112	15

varied by business segment and facility. As illustrated in Exhibit 4–7, commercial or private payment represented about 34 percent of total company receipts, Medicare accounted for 41 percent of overall HRC revenues, workers' compensation comprised 11 percent of overall revenues, and all "other" sources accounted for 14 percent.

Commercial or Private Payment　Approximately 80 percent of the population under age sixty-five had medical insurance coverage. The extent of the coverage varied by location. Generally, charges for inpatient rehabilitation were completely (100 percent) reimbursed under general hospitalization benefits, and outpatient rehabilitation was reimbursed similar to other outpatient services. Studies conducted by the Life Insurance Marketing and Research Association found that more than 70 percent of the employers in their sample provided some financial assistance for employees who participated in company-approved rehabilitation programs. Northwestern National Life Insurance Company reported that complete rehabilitation was possible in 66 percent of the light-industry injuries and in 62 percent of heavy-industry injuries. Of particular significance was the fact that HEALTHSOUTH's size and leadership made possible an aggressive managed-care contracting strategy. In 1993, for example, HRC had 265 managed-care contracts. In 1995, the number increased to 1,200. Almost two-thirds of all HRC's commercial revenues were under managed-care contracts (compared to only one-third in 1993).

Exhibit 4–6 • **HEALTHSOUTH** Corporation Market Share

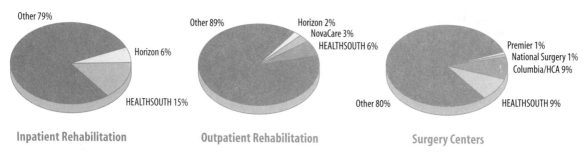

Inpatient Rehabilitation   **Outpatient Rehabilitation**   **Surgery Centers**

Inpatient rehabilitation services acquisitions include NME, ReLife, NovaCare, and AdvantageHEALTH.
Outpatient rehabilitation services include Caremark and AdvantageHEALTH acquisitions.
Surgery centers include Surgical Care Affiliates, Sutter, and Surgical Health acquisitions.

Exhibit 4–7 • **HEALTHSOUTH** Corporation Revenue Sources

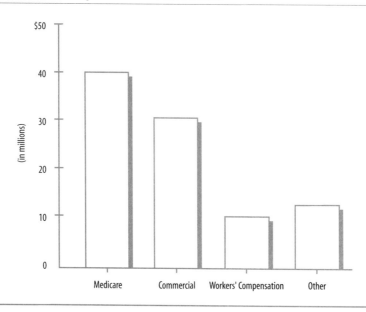

Medicare Although the rehabilitation services market had grown significantly, it continued to represent a relatively small portion of Medicare expenditures. As a result of the Social Security Act Amendments of 1983, Congress adopted a prospective payment system to cover the routine and ancillary operating costs of most Medicare inpatient hospital services. Although PPS applied to most acute-care inpatient services, as of 1995, Medicare continued to pay cer-

tain freestanding rehabilitation facilities and certified outpatient units on the basis of "reasonable costs" incurred during a base year (the year prior to being excluded from Medicare's prospective payment system or the first year of operation), adjusted by a market basket index. As a result, PPS was an advantage for the rehabilitation segment of the health care industry because the economic pressure on acute-care hospitals to discharge patients as soon as possible resulted in increased demand for outpatient rehabilitation services that were currently exempt from PPS. Even inpatient rehabilitation units in acute-care facilities could obtain exemption from PPS upon satisfaction of certain federal criteria.

Workers' Compensation Increasingly, managed care attempted to include workers' compensation into seamless products. About 40 percent of the costs associated with workers' compensation claims were medical costs, and many of these could be reduced through discount purchasing, utilization management, and outcomes-based treatment programs. Much of HEALTHSOUTH's expansion over the past several years was motivated by the need to pursue managed care as an opportunity rather than retreat from it as a threat. By becoming the largest rehabilitation services provider and building a network of inpatient and outpatient facilities nationwide, HRC was able to sign national contracts with payors and directly with large, self-insured employers, gain market share, and offset any erosion in margin. Workers' compensation was estimated to be about 15 percent of HRC's total rehabilitation business and accounted for almost 40 percent of outpatient revenues.

Regulation

The health care industry was subject to regulation by federal, state, and local governments. The various levels of regulatory activity affected organizations by controlling growth, requiring licensure or certification of facilities, regulating the use of properties, and controlling the reimbursement for services provided. In some states, regulations controlled the growth of health care facilities through CON programs.

The company faced competition every time it initiated a CON project or sought to acquire an existing facility. The competition would arise from national or regional companies or from local hospitals that filed competing applications or that opposed the proposed CON project. Although the number of states requiring CON or similar approval was decreasing, HRC continued to face this requirement in several states. Organizations planning to open new facilities or purchase expensive and specialized equipment must convince a regulatory or planning agency that such facilities or equipment were needed

to satisfy unmet demand and would not merely move patients from one provider to another. They served as an important barrier to entry and potentially limited competition by creating a franchise to provide services in a given area.

Licensure and certification were separate but related regulatory activities. The former was usually a state or local requirement, and the latter was a federal requirement. In almost all instances, licensure and certification would follow specific standards and requirements set forth in readily available public documents. Compliance with the requirements was monitored by periodic on-site inspections by representatives of various government agencies.

To receive Medicare reimbursement, a facility had to meet the applicable conditions of participation set forth by the U.S. Department of Health and Human Services relating to the type of facility, equipment, personnel, and standards of medical care, as well as compliance with all state and local laws and regulations. In addition, Medicare regulations generally required entry into such facilities through physician referral.

HEALTHSOUTH's Goal

HEALTHSOUTH's primary objective was to be the provider of choice for patients, physicians, and payors for outpatient and rehabilitative health care services throughout the United States. Its growth strategy was based on four interrelated elements: (1) implementation of the company's *integrated service model* in appropriate markets; (2) successful marketing to managed-care organizations and other payors; (3) provision of high-quality, cost-effective health care services; and (4) expansion of its national network.

- *Integrated Service Model.* HEALTHSOUTH attempted to offer an integrated system of health care services including outpatient rehabilitative services, inpatient rehabilitative services, ambulatory surgery services, and outpatient diagnostic services as illustrated previously in Exhibit 4–4. The company believed that such an integrated model offered patients and payors convenience and offered substantial referral opportunities. HEALTHSOUTH estimated, for example, that one-third of its outpatient rehabilitative patients had outpatient surgery; virtually all inpatient and outpatient rehabilitation patients required some form of outpatient rehabilitation; and almost all inpatient and outpatient rehabilitation patients had some type of diagnostic procedure. In 1995, the integrated service model was fully implemented in 30 of the 300 target markets. In two-thirds of these markets, at least one component of the model operated. Actions were under way to "backfill" the missing component or components in these markets.

- *Marketing to Managed-Care Organizations and Other Payors.* Since its inception, HEALTHSOUTH had focused on the development of contractual relationships with managed-care organizations, major insurance companies, large regional and national employers, and provider alliances and networks. The company's documented outcomes with thousands of patients and its reputation for quality provided competitive advantage over smaller organizations.

- *Cost-Effective Services.* An important corporate goal was to provide high-quality, cost-effective health care services. The company had developed standardized clinical protocols that resulted in the application of "best practices" techniques throughout all HEALTHSOUTH facilities. The company's reputation for its clinical programs was enhanced by its relationship with major universities and its support of clinical research facilities. The company believed that outpatient and rehabilitative services were inherently less expensive than comparable services delivered in an inpatient environment. To this end, HEALTHSOUTH was committed to the "virtual hospital" or "hospital without walls" concept whereby services are delivered more cost effectively by avoiding the heavy overhead burden of the acute-care hospital.

- *Expansion of the National Network.* As the largest provider of outpatient and rehabilitative health care services in the United States, HEALTHSOUTH was able to realize economies of scale and competed successfully for national

contracts with national payors and employers while retaining the ability to respond to the unique needs of local markets. The national network offered payors the convenience of dealing with a single provider, greater buying power through centralized purchasing, more efficient costs of capital and labor, and greater efficiency in recruiting and retaining physicians.

Functional Considerations

HRC's management was a group of young energetic professionals. In 1995, HEALTHSOUTH was formally organized around four operating divisions, each with its own president who reported to the corporate president and chief operating officer. The corporate president and chief operating officer reported to Scrushy, who remained as chairman of the board and chief executive officer. The operating divisions were HEALTHSOUTH Inpatient Operations (included medical centers), HEALTHSOUTH Outpatient Centers, HEALTHSOUTH Surgery Centers, and HEALTHSOUTH Imaging Centers (see Exhibit 4–8). The average age of the executive officers was forty-three years with a range from thirty-six to fifty-five. Despite the relative youth of the executive officers, the team as a whole had an average tenure with the company of slightly over eight years. The range was one year to twelve years. Four of the twelve executive officers had been with HEALTHSOUTH from its inception.

The corporate climate was characterized by a sense of urgency that was instilled in all of HEALTHSOUTH's employees directly by the chairman and CEO. Scrushy founded HEALTHSOUTH at the age of 32. As with many entrepreneurs, he was a visionary, but had the ability to make things happen. He worked virtually 365 days a year, sixteen to twenty hours a day for the first five years, waiting until 1989 before taking his first vacation. His pace remained furious, working many hours per week.

As a result of Scrushy's "hands-on" style, HRC was run; it did not drift. One of the company's most effective tools was a weekly statistical report, compiled every Thursday and distributed on Friday. The report included weekly statistics and trends such as payor mix, census, and revenue. It was reviewed

Exhibit 4–8 • HEALTHSOUTH Corporation Market Share

Outpatient Rehabilitation	Medical Centers*	Surgery Centers	Inpatient Rehabilitation	Diagnostic Centers
Services Include:	**Services Include:**	**Services Include:**	**Services Include:**	**Services Include:**
• Aquatic therapy	• Cardiology	• Ear, nose, and throat	• Aquatic therapy	• Computed tomography
• Audiological screenings	• Day surgery	• Gastroenterology	• Amputee	• Electromyography
• Biofeedback	• Diagnostic imaging	• General surgery	• Arthritis	• Magnetic resonance imaging
• Driving assessments	• Dial-a-nurse	• Gynecology	• Brain injury	• Mammography
• Family education	• Emergency room	• Lithotripsy	• Burns	• Nerve conduction velocity
• Foot and ankle	• Foot and ankle	• Ophthalmology	• Cardiac	• Nuclear medicine
• Functional capacity evaluations	• Gastroenterology	• Oral surgery	• Cerebral palsy	• Radiographic fluoroscopy
• General orthopedics	• General surgery	• Orthopedics	• Community reentry	• Ultrasound
• Hand therapy	• Hand surgery	• Pain management	• General rehabilitation	
• Headache	• Joint replacement	• Plastic surgery	• Joint replacement	
• Injury prevention	• Lithotripsy	• Podiatry	• Multiple sclerosis	
• Neurology	• Neurological sciences	• Urology	• Neurobehavioral	
• Neuropsychology	• Occupational health		• Orthopedics	
• Occupational therapy	• Oncology		• Orthotics and prosthetics	
• Pain	• Orthopedics		• Pain management	
• Physical therapy	• Pain management		• Pediatrics	
• Speech therapy	• Plastic surgery		• Pulmonary	
• Spine rehabilitation	• Spine		• Renal dialysis	
• Sports therapy	• Sports medicine		• Spinal injury	
• Urinary therapy	• Urology			
• Vision therapy				
• Work hardening				
• WCA/FCA				

* *(Not an Operating Division)*

over the weekend; and, if there was a negative trend, it was corrected. Thus, any problem was short lived. In this manner the management team was focused on real and developing problems.

Another tool was effective communications. Every Monday morning at 7:00 A.M. there was a meeting of the company's officers that included personnel from operations, development, finance, and administration. In this meeting, each employee made a presentation, detailing what he or she accomplished in the previous week and what was planned for the current week. Questions were answered and problems were resolved. One additional benefit was that each employee was held accountable for his or her actions. Although this could be perceived to be overkill, it was believed to be necessary and helpful to the participants. At one time the meetings were stopped for about six weeks. After the company

experienced a slight dip in performance and coordination, the meetings were reinstated.

Staffing and Compensation

Unlike many other health care companies, HEALTHSOUTH had not experienced staffing shortages. Clinicians were in short supply, but HRC was able to recruit and maintain excellent personnel. The ability to offer a challenging environment was a key factor. A HEALTHSOUTH inpatient facility in a metropolitan location typically competed favorably against other hospitals and nursing homes for the skills of new therapists. HEALTHSOUTH's outpatient facilities offered an attractive alternative to the clinician by offering eight-hour workdays with weekends and holidays off.

All of the company's employees were competitively compensated. One compensation tool used was employee incentive stock options, granted to key corporate and clinical personnel. The options required a vesting period of five years with 20 percent of the amount being vested annually. If the employee left for another job, the options were lost. With the tremendous success of the company, the stock options had created "golden handcuffs." Additionally, in 1991 the company created an employee stock ownership plan (ESOP) for the purpose of providing substantially all employees with the opportunity to save for retirement and acquire a proprietary interest in the company.

Marketing

The company's marketing efforts were similar for each business segment. Demand was controlled by physicians, workers' compensation managers, insurance companies, and other intermediaries. HRC administrators and clinicians were all involved in the marketing effort. The company hired a number of individuals who were formerly case managers with local intermediaries, such as insurance companies and HMOs, to assist in the marketing efforts. Every outpatient clinic had its own marketing director.

HRC entered into contracts to be the exclusive provider for rehabilitation services directly to industry. Firms such as Ford Motor Company were excellent targets because they had many employees in various markets that HEALTHSOUTH served. In such cases, significant new business could be generated, and in return HEALTHSOUTH could afford to discount its charges. HRC expanded its marketing efforts to include a focus on national contracts with large payors and self-insured employers.

HEALTHSOUTH established a national marketing effort with training programs, national account managers, case managers, and a carefully developed marketing plan for each facility based on a number of factors, including population demographics, physician characteristics, and localized disability statistics. The objective was to put into place a consistent sales methodology throughout HEALTHSOUTH and take advantage of its national system of rehabilitation facilities. This national coverage enabled HEALTHSOUTH to provide services for national as well as regional companies.

Marketing programs were directed toward the development of long-term relationships with local schools, businesses and industries, physicians, health maintenance organizations, and preferred provider organizations. In addition, HRC attempted to develop and enhance its image with the public at large. One example was the company's joint promotional arrangement with the Ladies Professional Golf Association, whereby HRC provided and staffed a rehabilitation van for the players while they were on tour.

HEALTHSOUTH's pricing was usually lower than that of competition. However, this was not used as a major selling point, but rather a bonus. HEALTHSOUTH focused mainly on quality of services and outcomes as the best marketing tool.

Financial Structure

HEALTHSOUTH's growth was funded through a mix of equity and debt. The company raised $13 million in venture capital before going public in 1986. Because of the company's start-up nature, commercial banks were reluctant to lend significant funds for development in its early years. After the company's initial public offering, commercial bankers were more responsive to financing growth plans. HRC continued to use a conservative mix of equity and debt and believed its cost of capital was the lowest in the health care industry. A decision to give up ownership was an easy one. The founders understood that a smaller percentage ownership of a larger company would be worth more and would not carry as much risk.

Earnings increases were significant, with compounded earnings growth of 416 percent from 1986 to 1990. During the 1990 to 1993 period, growth rates declined as expected, but remained impressive by industry standards. Operating revenues for 1995 increased about 22 percent over 1994. Revenues were estimated to grow between 10 to 15 percent from 1996 to 1999. The large ($7.9 billion) outpatient rehabilitation market was fragmented, and HRC was one of the few providers that had the ability to develop a powerful network. In 1995 it was estimated that HRC's outpatient revenue grew about 32 percent (34 percent in visits and 2 percent in pricing). Surgery center growth was expected to be about 15 to 20 percent, which should result from a combination of continued acquisitions and same-store volume and price increases. Inpatient services would continue to be the cash cow for HRC. Inpatient rehabilitation and specialty medical centers accounted for about 46 and 11 percent of 1995 revenues respectively. The outlook for these businesses remained encouraging.

Where Does HEALTHSOUTH Go from Here?

Richard Scrushy returned to reviewing company projections. He could not help but wonder if it were possible for HRC to continue such rapid growth. All the questions raised earlier were in his thoughts. "What will I need to do to make it happen? Are there things we should be doing differently? How can I ensure that HEALTHSOUTH does not outgrow its resources (capital and management)? Does the market provide ample opportunity to grow at 20 to 30 percent per year? What external factors do we face? What should we do to ensure that medical rehabilitation continues to be favorably reimbursed? What is the real number of facilities needed, and how many acquisition targets are there? Are our current strategies what they should be?"

Scrushy focused on answering the questions. He knew that he could formulate a plan to ensure HEALTHSOUTH's success. The key for future success, he believed, was in the company's ability to successfully implement the integrated service model in the 300 key health care markets throughout the nation. The work would be hard; but the rewards, professionally and financially, would be great.

References

Sources used for quotes and information to supplement public documents of HEALTHSOUTH include the following:

Alex. Brown & Sons, Inc. Research Report, Health Care Group, December 28, 1995.

Alex. Brown & Sons, Inc. Research Report, Health Care Group, February 16, 1996.

Jeffrey Hansen, "HEALTHSOUTH Finishes Deal Doubling Size," Birmingham News (January 6, 1994), pp. 6D and 10D.

"HEALTHSOUTH Wins Notice of Forbes, Wall Street." Birmingham News (April 19, 1996), pp. 1E–4E.

W. G. Hicks, M. Willard, K. Miner, and M. Sullivan, "Consolidation Steamroller Continues to Move Ahead," Gowen Perspectives (February 28, 1996), p. 7.

HEALTHSOUTH Corporation, Form 10-K. (For year ended December 31, 1995) and Annual Report (1995).

United States Equity Research, Health Services, Soloman Brothers (March 13, 1996).

U.S. Investment Research, "Trailblazing into the Northeast," HealtHRCare Services, Morgan Stanley (January 2, 1996).

Marvin Wilder, "The Powerhouse Behind HEALTHSOUTH," Rehabilitation Today (May 1991), pp. 22–31.

The University of Texas Health Center at Tyler

The health care industry in the United States was in transition, and as a result, so was the University of Texas Health Center at Tyler (UTHCT). Evidence of this transition could be seen in the unwillingness of both public and private payors of health care costs to accept rising prices. This focus on cost led to rural hospital closings, rapid growth in health maintenance organizations (HMOs), strategic alliances and realignments of medical institutions, government reimbursement reductions, and rising levels of indigent care. Compounding the complexity of the change were such forces as rapidly advancing and costly technology and the increasing competition among health care providers. Ironically, in an era of cost-consciousness, the rapid advancement of costly technology dictated investments in gigantic infrastructures at both local and regional levels.

Against this backdrop, the University of Texas Health Center at Tyler attempted to fulfill its three-part mission of providing patient care, conducting research, and educating M.D.s and the public concerning cardiopulmonary diseases as well as training physicians for a career in family practice. Because the Health Center received a percentage of its operating resources from the State of Texas, it was

This case was prepared by Mark J. Kroll, the University of Texas at Tyler, and Godwin Osuagwu, Texas College. It is intended to be used as a basis for classroom discussion rather than to illustrate effective or ineffective handling of an administrative situation. Used with permission from Mark Kroll.

required to provide certain levels of indigent health care to the poor in its region. In addition, it was required to provide care to indigents with tuberculosis from anywhere in the state. Nevertheless, the center had never refused services to any Texas indigent regardless of the nature of their illness. As health insurance premiums rose, more and more people lost their coverage. As a result, private hospitals frequently refused treatment and referred patients to state-supported institutions. This trend, in conjunction with the closings of many of the region's rural hospitals, as well as federal reimbursement reductions, compelled many individuals to seek care at the Health Center under indigency or charity status. In fact, most indigent patients erroneously believed that UTHCT was a "free" hospital.

Unfortunately, state funding levels for this type of care had not kept pace with demand, seriously undermining the financial base of the institution. Moreover, the Health Center had to provide competitive wages in order to attract nursing and selected allied health care personnel who were in short supply. Although other private health care organizations could provide minimum staffing, UTHCT was required to meet state standards for staffing-to-patient ratios. Additionally, the Health Center operated in a competitive local hospital market for paying patients as well as using costly technology and instrumentation. Most of the major strategic issues confronting the Health Center were ultimately related to the dilemmas faced by the entire health care industry. Compounding the Health Center's problems, however, were reductions in state general revenue appropriations as a percentage of the total operating budget for research, operations, and maintenance.

The Health Center was, as were most health care providers, undergoing a transition from providing most of its services on an inpatient basis to providing more outpatient care. Local competition for specific patient groups had also increased, as health care organizations formed HMOs. As a typical example, the Health Center's major competitors launched a major push into geriatric ambulatory care for senior citizens in order to strategically position themselves for Medicare HMOs.

In addition to the issues mentioned, there was the unique issue of the hospital's research mandate. The Health Center was successfully increasing its levels of grant-funded research, but in more recent years its grant-funded research revenues had flattened out.

History

The Health Center was established in 1947 as a state tuberculosis sanitarium. It operated under the State Board of Control by act of the 50th Texas Legislature. Over the years, the institution changed in a number of ways. Its role and scope were expanded to adapt to new medical technology and to the changing health care needs of the state and region.

The institution was established at the site of a deactivated World War II army infantry training base, Camp Fannin, located eight miles northeast of Tyler, Texas. The state acquired 614 acres and the existing facilities of the base hospital from the federal government. Most of the base's 1,000 beds were in rows of wooden barracks, with each barrack accommodating 25 beds in an open ward. The first patients were accepted in 1949.

Supervision of the East Texas Tuberculosis Sanitarium was later transferred to a newly formed Board of Texas State Hospitals and Special Schools. In 1951, the Texas Legislature changed the hospital's name to the East Texas Tuberculosis Hospital. Its role and scope were changed from simple custodial care to treatment using newly developed drugs.

Although there were several legislative bills enacted during the 1940s and 1950s changing the

institution's governing authority, it was not until 1969 that its scope was expanded beyond the care and treatment of tuberculosis patients. In that year the legislature authorized the institution to develop pilot programs aimed at treating other respiratory diseases such as asthma, lung cancer, chronic bronchitis, emphysema, and occupational diseases related to asbestos. In 1971, the Texas Legislature approved a broader mission for the institution to include education and research as well as patient care. The name was changed to the East Texas Chest Hospital to be operated under the Texas Board of Health. This program expansion into education and research reflected the increasing stature of the facility and its scientific capabilities.

In 1977, Texas State Senator Peyton McKnight of Tyler introduced legislation transferring control of the hospital to the Board of Regents of the University of Texas (UT) System. This legislation authorized the regents to use the institution as a teaching hospital and to change its name to the University of Texas Health Center at Tyler. The UT System controlled six medical schools and research/teaching hospitals around the state. In addition, it reaffirmed the institution's role and scope as a primary state referral center for patient care, education, and research in diseases of the chest.

The physical face of the institution had changed dramatically over the years. In 1957, the state completed a 320-bed, six-story brick and masonry structure that allowed for removal of most of the wooden barracks. A few of these structures still remained and had over the years been renovated for use as research laboratories. Other major building programs were initiated in the late 1960s and early 1970s. An outpatient clinic was added to the hospital in 1970. In 1976, the state appropriated $17 million for construction of a completely modern hospital facility. A six-story, 320-bed hospital was built adjacent to the original structure, doubling the size of the complex. At the same time, the lower three floors of the old hospital building were renovated for support services. In 1984, the top three floors of the old hospital were renovated to house additional offices and allow for expansion of programs in cardiac and pulmonary rehabilitation and cancer treatment.

The Watson W. Wise Medical Research Library was dedicated in 1984, supporting an expanded research faculty and the addition of new departments such as biochemistry, microbiology, and physiology. In 1987, the Health Center's Biomedical Research Building was completed. Construction was completed on an $11 million expansion of UTHCT's ambulatory-care facilities that housed the outpatient clinic, clinical laboratory, radiology, and surgical facilities. The addition facilitated delivery and handling of ambulatory patient services. In addition, the facility provided space for the family practice residency program and other clinics, as well as space for clinical research. Many of these activities had been carried out in converted hospital inpatient space as the center reduced its bed count and increased its ambulatory-care volume.

In terms of medical staff, the Health Center had sixty primary-care and specialty physicians. Ninety-five percent of UTHCT's physicians were board-certified, and many were certified in two or three areas.

In carrying out the mission and purpose of the institution, UTHCT changed from custodial care only to a three-fold purpose of patient care, education, and research. Open-heart surgery became available in 1983, and the Health Center's Pediatric Pulmonary Service was designated as one of the state's regional cystic fibrosis centers. In 1985, the Health Center was designated as a national cystic fibrosis satellite center. The first postgraduate medical education program in East Texas, residency training in family practice, was launched in 1985 in cooperation with two Tyler hospitals. In 1995, the Health Center had eighteen residents in the three-year family practice program and was graduating six each year. Additionally, the Health Center was performing a host of surgical procedures (see Exhibit 5–1). In 1995, the Health Center was given a $1 million grant by the Texas Legislature to establish a center for pulmonary infectious disease control.

Grant research funding increased rapidly in the 1980s, but growth tapered off in recent years. In 1983, research funding was $78,347; and by 1985, funding reached $808,836. Completion of the biomedical research building in 1987 and recruitment of research scientists resulted in more external funding. In 1988, $2,896,061 in external research grant dollars were received. For the past three years, the number and amounts of grants remained about the same (see Exhibit 5–2 for details). External research funding came from sources such as the National Institutes of Health, the Texas Affiliate of the American Heart Association, the American Lung Association of Texas, the Muscular Dystrophy Foundation, private medical-research foundations, and several industrial and pharmaceutical firms. The Health Center was awarded its first two biomedical research patents in 1992, and in the following year it was awarded two more biomedical research patents. In addition to external grant funds, as noted in Exhibit 5–2, the state maintained its support for research at about $4 million annually.

The Competition

Although UTHCT had historically been a specialized, state-supported center for the treatment of cardiopulmonary diseases, more recently the center had entered the fray for paying customers in response to rising costs, lower state appropriations, and increased indigent care demands. However, its two major competitors—Trinity-Mother Frances Health System and East Texas Medical Center—were very formidable and highly competitive.

The Trinity-Mother Frances Health System, founded in 1937 by the Sisters of the Holy Family of Nazareth, was started as a sixty-bed facility with a handful of attending physicians. It had become a 350-bed hospital at the hub of a medical complex with over 350 affiliated physicians, ten satellite rural health clinics, a huge outpatient clinic on the hospital's campus, a large OB/GYN unit, a home health care center, a 13,000-square-foot wellness center, an emergency medical services system authorized to provide level II trauma care, an acclaimed heart and lung institute, a spine and joint institute, a cancer care institute, and an eye institute. The merger of Mother Frances and Trinity Clinic, the region's largest group practice, integrated over seventy-five specialists into the hospital's network. This made Trinity-Mother Frances a formidable regional competitor, capable of offering a comprehensive list of medical services.

Exhibit 5–1 • The University of Texas Health Center at Tyler, Operative Procedures

	Fiscal Year 1993	Fiscal Year 1994	Fiscal Year 1995
Coronary Bypass	77	64	92
Angioplasty	48	60	58
Thoracic	135	133	115
Vascular	126	204	354
Abdominal Procedures	175	283	274
All Other Procedures*	1,134	1,009	1,347*
Total Procedures Performed	1,695	1,753	2,240
Inpatient	894	810	909
Outpatient	368	457	589
Total Patients	1,262	1,267	1,498

*The following is a list of "all other procedures" performed in the operating room.			
Amputation			33
Bone Marrow Biopsy			74
Breast			112
Bronchoscopy			218
Hernia			110
Mediastinoscopy			13
Pacemaker/Defibrillator			19
Rectal			44
Thyroid/Parathyroid			19
Tracheostomy			9
Vital Port			83
Lesion			105
Cyst			35
Temporal Artery			11
Carpal Tunnel			16
Gynecological			110
Orthopedic			18
Podiatry			29
Ear, Nose, and Throat			82
Miscellaneous			207
Total			1,347

Trinity-Mother Frances aggressively moved to strengthen its position in other ways. It negotiated HMO and preferred provider organization (PPO) agreements with several of the area's largest employers. Developing HMO and PPO relationships with employers was facilitated by the affiliation of Mother Frances with Trinity Clinic, as the combined organization provided virtually any inpatient or outpatient service needed. Additionally, Trinity-Mother Frances negotiated referral relationships with smaller, less-comprehensive hospitals in the region (that were not part of the East Texas Medical Center organization).

Exhibit 5–2 • **Extramural and State Research Grant Support**

	Fiscal Year 1993	Fiscal Year 1994	Fiscal Year 1995
Federal	$1,335,711	$1,295,579	$1,245,144
Private	384,774	173,391	496,712
Other	665,786	602,745	374,927
Total	$2,386,271	$2,071,715	$2,116,783
Number of Grants	22	16	21
Extramural Funds/Investigator	$82,285	$64,741	$72, 992
State Funding	$3,522,051	$4,151,697	$4,271,067

These referral relationships fed patients into the various specialized care units, such as the heart and lung institute that had performed over 30,000 heart procedures in the past twelve years.

The largest health care organization in the East Texas region was East Texas Medical Center (ETMC). In 1996, ETMC was the primary referral facility for a network of five rural community hospitals, three affiliated rural hospitals, fourteen rural clinics, and fourteen home health care locations. ETMC's emergency medical services unit was responsible for providing emergency medical services for Smith County (where Tyler is located) and ten surrounding counties. This network had a radius of over 100 miles from Tyler and essentially overlapped the service region of UTHCT. The parent organization of ETMC was East Texas Medical Center Regional Health Care System, a not-for-profit corporation founded in 1949.

ETMC had undergone a number of expansions since it was first opened, including the addition of numerous specialized service units. In addition to the primary 410-bed hospital, ETMC operated a level II trauma center that treated over 36,000 patients a year. It housed a recognized cancer institute and cardiac-care center that were equipped with state-of-the-art technology. The ETMC was home to the East Texas Neurological Institute as well as the Behavioral Health Center, which provided comprehensive mental health services. The emergency medical services unit operated the largest not-for-profit ambulance program in Texas. ETMC was supported by over 300 staff physicians.

Funding and the Quest for Paying Patients

UTHCT's operating budget was comprised of general revenue appropriations from the State of Texas, research grant funding, and locally generated revenues from services rendered to patients who were able to pay. Over the years, the composition percentage of the operating budget coming from appropriated versus locally generated funds changed significantly. General revenue appropriations decreased from 66 percent of the operating budget for fiscal year 1982 to 36 percent of the operating budget for fiscal year 1995. Consequently, the Health Center had been forced, as had its competitors, to generate local funds through the paying patient base (see Exhibit 5–3).

Complicating matters was the fact that the Health Center's operating budget was required to support educational programs as well as some of the research activities. State appropriations for indigent patient care, in actual dollars, remained relatively constant over the past ten years. However, the indigent care provided had dramatically increased over the same period. In 1983, indigent care and bad debt write-offs were about $12 million. In 1988 that amount was about $16 million. The most recent analysis of state funding and medical care losses was for fiscal year 1993 (see Exhibit 5–4).

As a result of the growing gap between funds received from the state to provide indigent care and the amount actually provided by the Health Center, the institution was competing for paying patients with other local hospitals. Because the Health Center,

Exhibit 5-3 • The University of Texas Health Center at Tyler, Financial Statements

	Fiscal Year 1993	Fiscal Year 1994	Fiscal Year 1995
Current Revenues			
State Appropriations	$19,057,480	$27,211,218	26,163,857
Federal Grants and Contracts	1,543,153	1,379,879	1,238,273
State Grants and Contracts	609,322	672,446	756,335
Private Gifts, Grants, and Contracts	1,287,677	1,433,463	2,282,365
Endowment Income	17,869	19,566	30,029
Sales and Services of Hospitals	35,051,548	27,675,077	28,285,473
Sales and Services of Auxiliary Enterprises	179,180	184,764	188,289
Professional Fees	7,200,056	7,279,864	7,580,420
Other Interest Income	331,054	205,189	237,167
Other Sources	539,412	670,741	705,497
Medicare Cost Recovery	2,957,397	3,478,158	5,016,828
Gains/Losses on Investments		(23,914)	(9,723)
Total Current Revenues	**$68,774,148**	**$70,186,451**	**$72,474,810**
Current Expenditures			
Education and General Instruction	$2,646,937	$2,937,540	$3,206,049
Research	$5,500,613	$5,974,905	$6,142,470
Hospital	$43,229,374	$46,978,306	$48,992,977
Institutional Support	$8,919,614	$10,709,241	$11,104,922
Operation and Maintenance of Plant	$3,843,867	$4,381,307	$3,729,309
Total Educational and General Expenditures	**64,140,405**	**70,981,299**	**73,175,727**
Auxiliary Enterprises	**$149,706**	**$171,112**	**$174,330**
Total Current Expenditures	**$64,290,111**	**$71,152,411**	**$73,350,057**
Excess of Revenues over Expenditures	**$4,484,037**	**($965,960)**	**($875,247)**

Trinity-Mother Frances Hospital, and ETMC offered similar health care services such as cardiology and cardiovascular surgery, competition for market share was intense. Both ETMC and Trinity-Mother Frances aggressively advertised and promoted their institutional images, services, and facilities.

Although the Health Center did not advertise in a competitive or comparative manner with the local hospitals, it did begin to use some print and television advertisements to build customer awareness and institutional image. Its advertising stressed that it was both a health care provider and a research facility, and therefore provided state-of-the-art medicine. It used the tag line, "UTHCT—bringing you tomorrow's medicine today." Unfortunately, the Health Center had a somewhat higher ratio of risk as

its patients were disproportionately older or had advanced tuberculosis or other serious pulmonary diseases. High-risk status generally accompanied indigency status because patients did not receive basic health care and waited longer before seeking medical attention, at which point, the disease process was advanced. The higher risk ratio put the Health Center at somewhat of a competitive disadvantage because such patients required longer hospital stays and were more costly to treat.

Given the Health Center's mission of patient care, education, and research, the focus of the institution was not on direct competition with local hospitals. Although the Health Center was a hospital in the traditional sense, it was much more. In order to achieve all three dimensions of its mission, the hospi-

Exhibit 5–4 • Sources and Uses of State Funds and Indigent Care and Bad Debt Losses

State Funds Received	*$17,019,533*
Use of State Funds:	
Instruction:	$2,740,452
Library	
Primary-Care Residency	
Continuing Education	
Other	
Research (total general revenue cost)	$4,116,158
Indigent Care (hospital and physician pure charity)[*]	$12,254,665
Actual Indigent Care Delivered	$14,346,407
Deficit of State Funds to Cover Above Costs:	*($2,091,742)*

[*]In addition to the pure charity cost which was classified as indigent care,
the Health Center had the following adjustments to hospital and physician revenue:

Contractual Allowances and Other Adjustments	$14,093,409
Bad Debt Write-Off	3,535,805
Subtotal	$17,629,214
Indigent Care (total from above)	$14,346,407
Total Write-Off	*$31,975,621*

tal's financial and managerial resources had to be divided, as it was the combination of the three elements that composed the Health Center's "product." For example, in the treatment of asbestos-related diseases, the patient benefited significantly through specialized treatment that was unavailable at the local hospitals. Grant-funded research provided the combined efforts of a clinical researcher, who worked at the molecular level of the disease, with an experienced pulmonary disease physician specialist. The patient could participate in clinical trials, such as a new drug therapy, that would most likely lead to improvements in treatment of the disease. Further, the Health Center's advanced technology instrumentation base (including three electron microscopes) improved diagnostic capabilities. These microscopes provided ultrahigh magnification for enhanced research studies and patient care.

Customers (Market)

The Health Center was located in the middle of Smith County, Texas, in an area known as East Texas. The hospital's primary patient base was derived from the surrounding population of its twenty-five county service area. It based its forecasts for future patient loads and program implementation on the demographics of this region. East Texas, similar to the rest of the state, was increasing in population. The Health Center service area had a population of approximately 1,108,900. Analysts projected a 1.4 percent to 2.1 percent annual population increase through the year 2000. Age was another important factor in the analysis of the Health Center service area demographics. Percentages of the state's population by age group is included as Exhibit 5–5.

For the years 1980 through 2030, the birth to seventeen-year-old age group of the Texas population was expected to decline from 28.6 percent of the population to 22.7 percent, whereas the forty-five to sixty-four group was expected to increase from 17.1 percent to 23.6 percent of the population. The sixty-five and older group of the Texas population was expected to increase from 10.1 percent to 17 percent. The population in Texas was both aging and growing. These trends would obviously have an impact on the direction of patient care for the elderly at the Health Center as well as for Texas and the nation.

Exhibit 5–5 • Texas Population by Age, 1990 and 2030

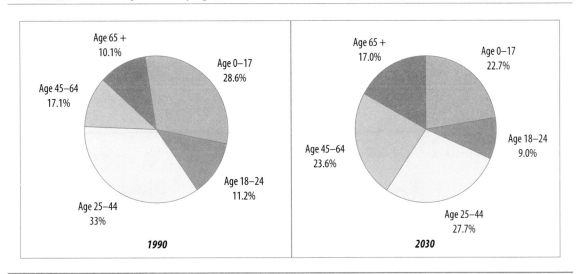

1990 *2030*

Many hospitals and physicians statewide referred patients to the Health Center for diagnosis and treatment, especially when pulmonary problems were suspected. However, the bulk of patients came from the surrounding twenty-five-county East Texas service area (see Exhibits 5–6 and 5–7).

Patient referrals were from group practices, physicians, hospitals, governmental agencies, and self-referrals. Most patients admitted for diagnosis and treatment were referred because their clinical problems required specialized diagnosis and treatment provided by the Health Center. Many times, referrals were made for acutely ill pulmonary patients requiring longer-than-average intensive care. This was especially true for advanced tuberculosis and asbestosis cases.

Exhibit 5–6 • The University of Texas Health Center at Tyler, Population of Service Area by County

	1994	2030		1994	2030
Anderson	50,029	56,620	Kaufman	57,692	133,968
Angelina	73,701	99,762	Marion	10,069	11,506
Bowie	83,435	85,547	Morris	13,215	13,256
Camp	10,566	11,117	Panola	22,543	25,089
Cass	30,574	36,129	Rains	7,198	9,982
Cherokee	42,457	56,459	Rusk	44,496	56,260
Franklin	8,178	10,545	Shelby	22,538	26,131
Gregg	109,502	127,451	Smith	159,434	204,633
Harrison	59,348	85,475	Titus	25,495	36,386
Henderson	62,288	88,240	Upshur	33,280	44,814
Hopkins	30,636	39,036	Van Zandt	40,062	52,337
Houston	21,722	22,450	Wood	31,544	55,522
Hunt	67,114	83,131	*Total*	1,117,116	1,471,846

Exhibit 5–7 • The University of Texas Health Center at Tyler, Service Area by County

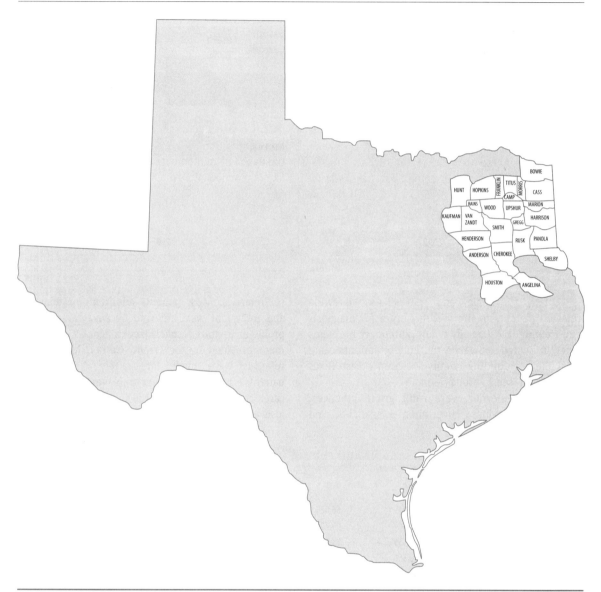

It was important to recognize that the Health Center had an unusual patient population because of its specialties in pulmonary care (that attracted older patients), commitment to indigent care, and aging population. These factors, especially its pulmonary referral status, resulted in greater demands being placed on the center for medical services. A great deal of indigent care had been provided not only to people in counties within the service area, but also to a large number of Texans outside the hospital's service area. Tuberculosis tended to be concentrated in indigent populations. Approximately 28 percent of the indigent care the Health Center provided was to patients residing outside the immediate East Texas service area. This accounted for about 30 percent of the total cost of indigent care services. In one attempt to rein in indigent care costs, the Health Center started limiting the prescription drugs it would provide free of charge and placed limits on the amount of indigent care provided by the general medicine clinic and the family practice clinic.

To capture more of the insured patient market, UTHCT attempted to establish itself as an HMO service provider for some of the region's larger employers (see Exhibit 5–8 for a listing). After negotiating with several providers, the Health Center signed a contract with one of the area's largest employers. On January 1, 1993, UTHCT became the primary-care provider for the company's 2,000 employees. The Health Center provided contracted medical care to Smith County's jail inmates beginning in October 1994. In September 1995, the center adopted an HMO plan for its own 1,100 employees and those of the University of Texas at Tyler, an academic unit of the UT System also located in Tyler. In addition, the Health Center negotiated preferred provider contracts with a number of large insurance companies. The Health Center aggressively marketed its occupational health services that were primarily targeted to help employers reduce the risks of their workers suffering work-related injury or illness, thus reducing medical and disability costs.

As was true for many health care organizations, UTHCT had seen a major shift in its patient volume away from inpatient toward outpatient services. As Exhibits 5–9, 5–10, and 5–11 indicate, the Health Center reduced its number of beds and converted the space to outpatient services. Although the number of beds declined, the occupancy remained relatively flat. In contrast, the number of outpatient or ambulatory visits increased about 25 percent in the past two years. It was in anticipation of a continuation of this trend that the Health Center completed the new $11 million outpatient treatment center and family practice clinic in October 1996.

Regulation and Economics

In the health care field, regulations were an integral part of the economics that drove the industry. Regulations were promulgated by numerous government and industry agencies. Operational regulations for the Health Center were imposed by the State of Texas and the University of Texas System. Although these entities prescribed the operational parameters, the prospective payment system for Medicare and Medicaid reimbursement had the most significant impact on the health care industry and the Health Center. Enacted in October 1984, the system established diagnosis-related groups (DRGs), whereby Medicare or Medicaid reimbursement payments to health care providers were based entirely on the

Exhibit 5–8 • Major Private Employers in the Region

Employer	Product/Service	Number of Employees
Brookshire Grocery Company	Grocery Retailing	2,000
Trane Company	Heating/Cooling Equipment	1,992
Tyler Pipe Corporation	Cast Iron Pipe	1,548
Kelly-Springfield	Auto and Truck Tires	1,521
Carrier Air Conditioning	Heating/Cooling Equipment	1,200
Loggins Meat Company	Meat Packing	425
Howe-Baker Engineering	Petrochemical Process Equipment	350
LaGloria Refining Company	Petroleum Refining	250
Celebrity, Inc.	Silk Flower Imports	250
Black Sheep, Inc.	Life Jackets and Gun Cases	245

Exhibit 5–9 · **The University of Texas Health Center at Tyler, Hospital Financial Analysis, Fiscal Years 1993, 1994, and 1995**

Financial	Fiscal Year 1993	Fiscal Year 1994	Fiscal Year 1995
Inpatient	$36,293,171	$32,637,506	$33,389,305
Outpatient	13,524,552	13,892,494	14,786,423
Gross Revenue	$49,817,723	$46,530,000	$48,175,728
Inpatient	$18,906,664	$18,403,385	$17,285,969
Outpatient	9,469,428	9,903,129	10,572,309
Cash Collections	$28,376,092	$28,306,514	$27,858,278
Miscellaneous Patient Care Revenue	$323,103	$345,484	$289,292
Revenue/Bed	$218,634	$225,086	$271,458
Collections/Bed	$113,896	$126,920	$140,536
Days in Accounts Receivable	72.18	72.11	66.58

Exhibit 5–10 · **The University of Texas Health Center at Tyler, Hospital Statistical Analysis, Fiscal Years 1993, 1994, and 1995**

Statistical	Fiscal Year 1993	Fiscal Year 1994	Fiscal Year 1995
Operating—Staff Beds	166	145	123
Revenue/Bed	$218,634	$225,086	$271,458
Collections/Bed	$113,896	$126,920	$140,536
Staff/Bed Ratio (Adjusted)	3.69	4.07	4.80
Cost/Bed Ratio	$994	$1,090	$1,140
Admissions	3,520	3,134	3,280
Inpatient Days	36,530	29,937	29,292
Average Daily Census	100.1	82.0	80.3
Average LOS—TB/ATB[*]	61.7	42.6	40.9
Average LOS without TB	7.5	7.1	6.6
Total Average LOS	10.7	9.1	9.3
Occupancy Rate	62.3%	56.6%	65.4%
Observation Occupancy	3.3%	2.8%	3.5%
Total Occupancy Rate	65.6%	59.4%	68.9%

[*] LOS: Length of Stay
TB: Tuberculosis Cases
ATB: Atypical Tuberculosis Cases

Exhibit 5–11 · **The University of Texas Health Center at Tyler, Annual Clinic (Ambulatory) Summary, Fiscal Years 1993, 1994, and 1995**

Statistical	Fiscal Year 1993	Fiscal Year 1994	Fiscal Year 1995
Total Visits	80,178	91,097	100,245
Visits/Day	265.5	293.8	326.3
Visits/PCP* (Non-FP)†	2,482.4	2,982.4	2,607.9
Visits/FP†	2,151.1	1,999.0	2,275.2
Clinic Rooms	77	97	96
Staff/Rooms	1.2	1.1	1.6
Staff/MD	2.39	2.48	2.61

* Primary-Care Physicians (PCP), Include Internal Medicine, Managed Care, General Pediatrics
† Family Practice Clinic Physicians (FP)

diagnosis of the patient. This system did not reimburse for actual costs incurred for patient care if the required treatment varied from the average costs related to the "normal" treatment routine. It only paid the health care provider the average costs associated with a particular course of treatment. For example, a given rate and length of hospital stay was established for open-heart surgery. If complications arose and the patient care costs exceeded the given rate and length of stay (a common occurrence when dealing with the poor), the provider did not receive federal reimbursement payment for the additional costs over the predetermined rate. In addition, many treatments were only reimbursable as an outpatient charge. A material portion of UTHCT's losses on care provided came from the mismatch between reimbursement rates and actual costs. (The amount is under "Contractual Allowances and Other Adjustments" in Exhibit 5–4.)

The initial intent of PPS was to standardize rates, force efficiency, reduce utilization rates among Medicare and Medicaid patients, and shift some of the health care cost burden from the federal to the state level. Cost control became a real objective for the health care industry. As a result, the Health Center converted inpatient hospital rooms to outpatient clinics and the construction of the ambulatory-care clinic became a priority.

Another reduction in federal reimbursements was expected because of the Federal Budget Agreement of 1990 that targeted Medicare spending. The act specifically identified the reimbursement adjustment factor for indirect medical education, such as the residency program at the Health Center, as a target to reduce. As a teaching facility that received this benefit, the Health Center would obviously be negatively impacted, though the magnitude was not yet clear as the federal government was still studying what percentage reduction should apply to teaching hospitals. The economic implications of all the factors discussed were enormous for the Health Center, as 40 percent of the institution's paying patients were covered by Medicare. This percentage was projected to increase significantly, based on the projection that the Medicare patient base would double by the year 2025.

Governance

The UT System was presided over by a board of regents, made up of members from diverse professions and backgrounds including business people, educators, and physicians. Each was considered to be knowledgeable and successful in a given field. They were external to the University of Texas System, and typically had significant positions of power and influence in their chosen career fields. In addition, the members usually had political and persuasive powers with the Texas Legislature in order to secure funding and associated legislation for the UT System. The board of regents set financial and operating guidelines through operating budgets, capital expenditure approvals, program implementation, and related activities confirmations. The board essentially supported or rejected recommendations from the administrators of the universities and medical centers in the system. The board of regents' decisions were implemented through the chancellor of the University of Texas System.

The management of UTHCT was organized along functional lines according to business, research, and medical classifications. The organizational chart for the Health Center is illustrated in Exhibit 5–12. The clinical division was directed by an Executive Associate Director, who was a physician and held an MBA. He possessed a keen business mind geared toward quality, cost-effectiveness, efficiency, and productivity. He was supported by assistant administrators and physician leaders along functional lines. A search was in progress for the replacement of the deceased Associate Director for Research. The business division was directed by the Executive Associate Director for Administration and Business Affairs, who held a masters degree in health administration. He was supported by assistant administrators along functional lines.

The group of directors, administrators, and assistant administrators comprised the administrative staff. They met weekly to develop policy, implement strategic plans, and perform various administrative functions.

The strategic plans were developed by the directors and distributed to administrators and the next lower management level, the department heads. Based on input from these groups, the plan was revised by a committee that included representation from the medical, research, and education divisions. The strategic plan that emerged forms part of the basis for budget requests for special programs, operating funds, equipment, and personnel.

Strategic decision-making authority was vested in the administrative staff. Both the department heads and administrative staff were responsible for making operational decisions. Most routine opera-

tions were managed by department heads who controlled departmental budgets. Accountability at each management level was maintained through a criteria-based job performance evaluation system.

Standing committees formed another important part of the Health Center's management structure. These committees utilized several techniques to communicate with employees at various levels of the organization. Formal meetings, hearings, interviews, questionnaires, and review of documentation enabled the committees to perform their assigned functions. Most of the committees were required by health care accrediting and governmental agencies as well as the University of Texas System.

The communication network between management levels varied among the divisions. Medical management divisions generally communicated through formal meetings and memos. Weekly medical staff meetings were conducted by the Chief of Staff to discuss medical concerns, distribute policy changes, and solicit feedback from the staff.

Monthly department head meetings provided an avenue for communication among the medical, educational, business, and research groups. This was a critical communication link because of the complex and unique nature of a university health center. In addition, routine informal information exchange occurred at all levels in managing operations. A recently created public affairs department produced three separate Health Center internal newsletters, as well as a number of patient information and education brochures.

Given the Health Center's threefold mission, faculty members were appointed to positions in either research or clinical areas. All new faculty members initially received one-year appointments that were reviewed annually. To be considered for promotion, the clinical faculty member was required to demonstrate competence in four areas: clinical practice, service to the institution, research, and teaching.

Physician faculty were in effect employed by the Health Center full time; therefore, they did not have private medical practices. To fulfill the clinical practice dimension of their positions, physicians were provided with private offices, an outpatient clinic area, laboratory, radiology, and ancillary services. In addition, they were provided nursing, clerical, and

Exhibit 5–12 • Organization Chart: The University of Texas Health Center at Tyler

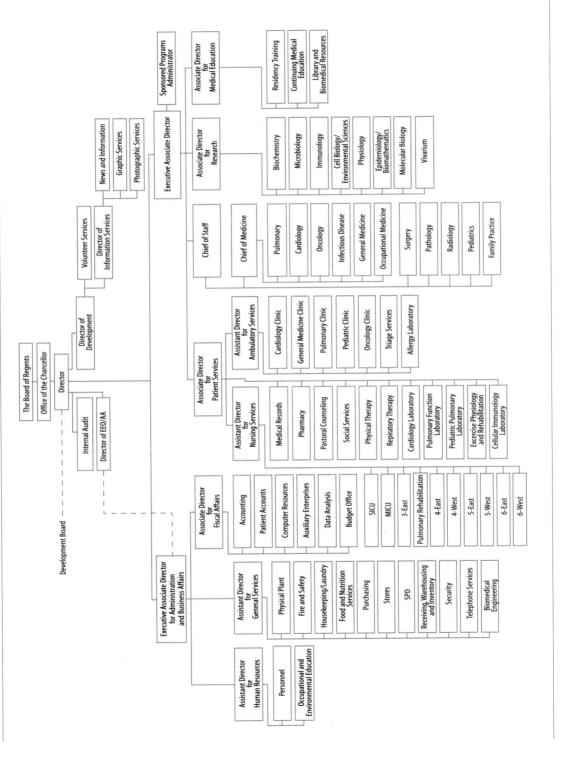

support staff personnel, medical malpractice liability insurance, legal assistance, retirement plans, and other benefits. All physicians were salaried; however, increases in patient visits and resultant income for the Health Center could lead to additions in a physician's base salary.

Looking Ahead

The UT Health Center at Tyler had made significant progress in the implementation of its threefold mission to provide patient care, conduct research, and provide education. Patient volume grew over the years, especially outpatient (ambulatory-care) services. These services were provided by nationally recruited, highly qualified, and published clinical physicians and consulting staff. The Health Center acquired additional medical and surgical intensive-care suites, a heart-catheterization laboratory, and an open-heart operating suite. The Health Center provided a full range of services for cardiovascular diagnosis, treatment, and rehabilitation, including coronary angioplasty and coronary bypass. When the new ambulatory-care center opened, UTHCT had more than adequate space and state-of-the-art facilities. Nationally known for its pulmonary disease capabilities, the Health Center had the most highly developed program for comprehensive evaluation and treatment of occupational lung diseases in Texas. In addition, it was conducting some of the most advanced research in the world in such areas as pneumonia and asbestosis.

In fiscal year 1995, hospital admissions were 3,280 inpatients who spent a total of 29,292 days at the Health Center (see Exhibit 5–10). In 1995, the Health Center saw over 100,000 outpatients, graduated new family practitioners from its family practice residency program, and became a significant player in the region's HMO competition. However, changing economic conditions, reductions in both state and federal funding, and the increasing costs of providing health care programs presented both opportunities and challenges. Being partially state funded required the Health Center to provide indigent health care. In actuality the Health Center had to absorb large losses in indigent care because many private hospitals in the region refused to treat the indigent and referred

them to state institutions. State and federal funding, however, had not kept pace with the increases in recent years, nor did it appear that adequate funding for future indigent care would be forthcoming. Future funding of Medicare and Medicaid appeared suspect. Improving services to paying patients and increasing that portion of the center's business became a clear priority to offset indigent care losses.

In the future, UTHCT planned to continue its tripartite mission of providing health care services to the East Texas region, conducting research primarily on pulmonary diseases, and providing education and training. However, in order to respond to the new realities of the health care environment, the Health Center adopted several key strategies to pursue. First, it wanted to maintain the relationships it had with its two HMO clients. Second, the Health Center would use its occupational medicine program (that grew out of its asbestos treatment work) to market additional health care services to the region's employers and attract more insured, industry-related pulmonary cases from across the state. Third, the Health Center would play a pivotal role in developing a regional Medicaid managed-care network. Fourth, UTHCT would develop and market a Medicare HMO as well as one for its own employees. Fifth, the Health Center wanted to elevate its stature in the region as the premier provider of outpatient services. It wanted to become the region's provider of choice for such services rather than "the state chest hospital." Finally, the Health Center planned to develop relationships with medical care providers (physician groups and clinics) who were not directly employed by the Health Center to become more of a comprehensive marketing conduit for managed-care services.

To build its status as a research institution, the Health Center had to more aggressively pursue external research grants. Given the stagnation in state support for research, attracting alternative funds became more and more critical. Although UTHCT had come a long way from its days as a tuberculosis hospital housed in converted army barracks, the challenges were as great as ever. The Health Center needed to simultaneously become a more aggressive competitor in the health care services marketplace and grow in its role as a center of research and learning.

Calumet Community Hospital

Introduction

"When we hired a consulting firm to develop a long-range plan, we expected to receive a step-by-step plan for staged growth," commented hospital administrator Jon L. Smyth. "However, it seems we may be facing one or two giant steps instead."

Like most not-for-profit hospitals, Calumet Community Hospital operated near the break-even point. Extensive renovation of the hospital building or major new construction would require far greater financial reserves than Calumet had available at the time.

Other issues facing Smyth were increased competition from larger hospitals and other health providers, declining inpatient revenue due in part to a change in Medicare reimbursement, and a shortage of physicians. Smyth and the Calumet Board of Directors faced tough decisions on future directions.

This case was prepared by V. Aline Arnold. It is intended to be used as a basis for class discussion rather than to illustrate effective or ineffective handling of an administrative situation. The names of the organizations, individuals, and locations, as well as statistical information have been disguised to preserve the anonymity of the organization. Presented and accepted by the refereed Midwest Society for Case Research. All rights reserved to the author and the MSCR. Copyright ©1988 by Aline Arnold. Used with permission.

Background

Calumet Community Hospital was a forty-five-bed general acute-care hospital located in a small, rural community in the Southwest. As a hospital, it was one of the more complex organizational types in modern society.

The hospital originally was established in 1935 as the Jones Memorial Hospital. The present building was constructed on twelve acres leased from the nearby Central State University and opened for service on April 1, 1976.

The organization operated forty-five beds for general acute medical and surgical care until 1986. The number of days of care for medical and surgical patients had been slowly declining since 1983 (see Exhibit 6–1). In addition, the advancing age of the two physicians who accounted for over 75 percent of the hospital's revenue and increasing competition forced the hospital to look for new sources of revenue.

Similar to other hospitals, Calumet began searching for ways to reduce the hospital's dependence on inpatients. The home health program was instituted in 1986 and now accounted for an average of seventy-five patients per week (see Exhibit 6–2).

In years past, the hospital did only one-fourth of its own laboratory work and contracted for the remainder. Now, about 99 percent of the lab work was done in-house. In addition, the laboratory was contracting with physicians' offices and the veterinary clinic at the university. The lab procedures

665

Exhibit 6–1 • Inpatient Care Volume and Bed Utilization, Fiscal Years 1983–1987

	Fiscal Year Ending September 30,						Fiscal Year Ending September 30,				
	1983	1984	1985	1986	1987		1983	1984	1985	1986	1987
Patients						***Average Daily Census***					
Medicine/Surgery	1,353	1,298	1,224	1,197	1,138	Medicine/Surgery	15.0	14.1	13.2	12.3	11.3
Obstetrics	239	187	207	279	328	Obstetrics	1.9	1.6	1.4	1.8	2.1
Pediatrics	38	43	69	118	219	Pediatrics	0.3	0.3	0.5	0.8	1.4
Subtotal, General Acute	1,630	1,528	1,500	1,594	1,685	Subtotal, General Acute	17.2	16.0	15.1	14.9	14.8
Substance Abuse	0	0	0	146	299	Substance Abuse	0	0	0	8.6	14.0
Total	1,630	1,528	1,500	1,740	1,984	Total	17.2	16.0	15.1	23.5	28.8
Newborn	192	149	150	194	217	Newborn	1.6	1.2	1.1	1.6	1.8
Days of Care						***Occupancy Percentage***					
Medicine/Surgery	5,465	5,132	4,824	4,487	4,118	General Acute	38.1	35.3	33.6	32.9	32.8
Obstetrics	707	571	571	650	758	Substance Abuse	0	0	0	61.3	99.6
Pediatrics	99	102	184	277	525	Total	38.1	35.3	33.6	47.1	66.2
Subtotal, General Acute	6,271	5,805	5,579	5,414	5,401	Newborn	20.0	15.0	13.8	20.0	22.5
Substance Abuse	0	0	0	3,133	5,092	***Beds***					
Total	6,271	5,805	5,579	8,547	10,493	General Acute	45	45	45	31	31
Newborn	568	454	388	587	669	Substance Abuse	0	0	0	14	14
Average Length of Stay						Total	45	45	45	45	45
Medicine/Surgery	4.0	4.0	3.9	3.7	3.6	Newborn Bassinets	8	8	8	8	8
Obstetrics	3.0	3.1	2.5	3.0	2.9						
Pediatrics	2.6	2.4	2.7	2.3	2.4						
Subtotal, General Acute	3.2	3.2	3.0	3.0	3.0						
Substance Abuse	0	0	0	21.5	17.0						
Total	3.2	3.2	3.0	24.5	20.0						
Newborn	3.0	3.0	2.6	3.0	3.1						

increased dramatically since these actions were taken (see Exhibit 6–2).

In 1986, the hospital administrator decided to convert fourteen beds from medical and surgical care to treatment of substance abuse and alcoholism in a unit called CareUnit. Calumet provided the beds, and Care Corporation, in exchange for a share of the profits, provided the unit's professional counseling staff. This unit was running at 100 percent occupancy most of the time.

The service mix for the forty-five beds was now six obstetric, two pediatric, fourteen alcohol or substance abuse, and twenty-three medical and surgical. Statistical information relating to utilization of these beds since 1983 is shown in Exhibit 6–1.

Hospital Mission

Calumet Community Hospital's mission statement was as follows:

> Calumet Community Hospital's mission is to provide hospital services for Calumet, Randolph County, and the surrounding area by sustaining and strengthening its position in quality and scope of services:
>
> • a general hospital where patients and their families receive personalized, efficient care under high technical standards in a setting that focuses on local needs;

Exhibit 6–2 • **Volume of Selected Diagnostic and Treatment Services, Fiscal Years 1983–1987**

Services	Fiscal Year Ending September 30,				
	1983	1984	1985	1986	1987
Emergency Room Visits	2,789	2,370	3,417	3,342	3,155
Operating Room					
Inpatient	533	487	490	492	474
Outpatient	20	28	18	35	116
Total	553	515	508	527	590
Diagnostic Radiology Procedures					
Inpatient	1,947	2,180	2,097	2,436	2,136
Outpatient	2,744	2,816	3,205	2,436	2,262
Total	4,691	4,996	5,302	4,872	4,398
Laboratory Tests					
Inpatient	9,513	9,734	11,112	61,054	63,592
Outpatient	8,794	8,912	8,797	23,024	23,828
Total	18,307	18,646	19,909	84,078[2]	87,420
Delivery Room Live Births	189	160	150	192	217
Respiratory Therapy Treatment					
Inpatient	1,878	1,641	11,552	11,297	13,448
Outpatient	144	161	438	421	429
Total	2,022	1,802	11,990	11,718	13,877
Physical Therapy Treatments	0	0	0	0	1,925[1]
Speech Therapy Treatments	0	0	0	0	267
Electrocardiograms (Ecg)					
Inpatient	609	440	644	909	1,159
Outpatient	184	219	188	175	226
Total	793	659	832	1,084	1,385
Home Health Visits	0	0	0	2,814	4,066

[1] Ten months of operation.
[2] Change in recording methodology.

- a center for the private solo or group practice of medicine, where physicians can concentrate their practices with maximum support from management and personnel staff, modern facilities, and a productive professional environment for themselves and their patients;

- an economically sound and responsible not-for-profit entity that develops revenues and other resources effectively and achieves maximum volume from the use of these resources;
- a Calumet-centered institution and an active corporate citizen dedicated to serving residents of Calumet and its

trade area and to enhancing the region's status through civic leadership and a wide range of contributions to the local economy; and

- an employer in a setting where talented personnel with a service attitude and initiative can practice and grow in their profession or vocation and receive job satisfaction and appropriate rewards for good performance.

Board of Directors

Calumet Community Hospital had an eleven-member board of directors (see Exhibit 6–3). The board was appointed by the governing authority of Randolph County for a two-year term on a rotating basis.

The board of directors was legally responsible for the operation of the hospital. In addition, the board established goals and objectives for evaluating the hospital's performance relative to those goals. The board recruited, selected, and evaluated the hospital's chief executive officer, called hospital administrator, who represented the board in implementing policies.

Smyth often called on board members for their expertise but at the same time tried to keep them from being involved in day-to-day internal operations.

Management and Organization

Calumet's organizational structure was fairly typical of small hospitals (see Exhibit 6–4). All department heads reported directly to Smyth. Smyth noted, "One of my strengths is my open-door policy and my accessibility when the department heads need me to make a quick decision. I also practice 'management by wandering around' to keep on top of things in the hospital."

Smyth had been with the hospital for the past nine years. Prior to joining Calumet, he was an assistant administrator at Union County Hospital in Eureka. He held a bachelor's degree in psychology from a small church-related university and was a member of the American College of Healthcare Executives. In addition he was an active and participating member of the State Hospital Association.

During Smyth's tenure at Calumet, the hospital had been financially successful and experienced

---

Exhibit 6–3 · Calumet Community Hospital Board of Directors

Kenneth Owens (Board Chairperson)
President
First National Bank

Marjorie Crow
Housewife

Gene Barnett
Editor
Calumet Daily News

Joe Marchman
Retired Schoolteacher

Harold Borman
Office Manager
Calumet Paper Co.

Verna Shepperd
Principal
Armstrong Elementary School

James Stuckey
Owner
Stuckey's Feed and Seed

Andy Arthur
Private Investments

John Stuart
Owner
Stuart Insurance Agency

Eileen Fordham
Owner
Fordham Furniture

Bill Blake
Attorney
Blake, Jones and Associates

Exhibit 6–4 • **Calumet Community Hospital Organization Chart**

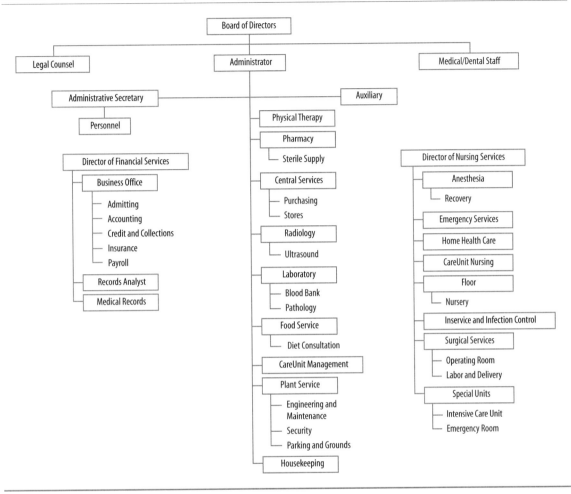

steady growth until 1984. Smyth attributed much of the hospital's past success to his participatory style of management. Twice a month, department heads met to develop ideas and discuss problems. A department head who brought a problem to the meeting was asked to bring at least one solution to the problem. This approach tended to keep the meeting from turning into a "gripe" session. New programs were discussed and old programs were examined to decide whether to retain or discontinue them.

Management by objectives was not practiced at Calumet because of time constraints. According to

Smyth, "In facilities where MBO is used, the people spend all their time writing and hardly any time working. Too much time is spent deciding if goals are met, and assigning rewards and punishments instead of caring for patients." Smyth continued, "This is not to say Calumet is not goal oriented. I spend a great amount of my time helping personnel set goals and work toward those goals. Salary increases are based on employees reaching their goals."

Smyth was very popular with the hospital staff because of his friendly nature and willingness to roll up his sleeves and help out when necessary. It was not unusual to see him answering the telephone while the receptionist took a coffee break or filling the soft drink machine when it was empty.

Smyth maintained control of billing and collections by working with the billing clerk on a regular basis. In addition to billing and collections, he "kept on top" of purchasing. All purchase orders, except for food and pharmaceutical items, required his approval before issuance. Although he often worked late into the evening on his paperwork, he felt this control was important if the hospital was to remain financially sound.

The Medical Staff

As was the practice of most hospitals, physicians applied for admission to the medical staff and were appointed by the hospital's board of directors (see Exhibit 6–4). Upon approval of the board of directors, a physician was granted the privilege of admitting patients to Calumet Community Hospital. The physician might be appointed to "active" medical staff, "courtesy" medical staff, or "consulting" medical staff. The difference between these categories was usually determined by how active a physician wished to be in Calumet Community Hospital. Active status included full rights and voting privileges along with an obligation to attend medical staff meetings and participate in medical staff committees. The active medical staff currently listed twenty-one physicians. However, only twelve physicians routinely admitted patients to Calumet Community Hospital. Eight of the twelve physicians had offices in Calumet, and the other four practiced in Eureka, ten miles away. Of the eight Calumet physicians, two family practitioners generated over 75 percent of the hospital's revenues; one was age sixty-five and the other was age sixty.

The specialties of these twelve physicians were as follows: family/general practitioners (7), otolaryngologist (1), general surgeon (1), obstetrician/gynecologist (1), cardiologist (1), and urologist (1).

The active medical staff membership declined during the past five years. "To make my job even more difficult," noted Smyth, "the medical staff is fragmented and not pulling in the same direction. I end up spending a great deal of time solving problems created by the doctors."

The medical staff was governed by its own bylaws, rules, and regulations and was accountable to the board of directors. It conducted business through the executive committee, credentials committee, medical records committee, and medical audit committee. In addition, there was a joint conference committee consisting of three members each from the medical staff and board of directors. The administrator served as an ex officio member of that committee.

The hospital administrator was the liaison officer between the board of directors and the medical staff. The administrator facilitated the work of the medical staff by providing administrative assistance to the officers and committees on a routine basis. The administrator did not have direct line authority over the medical staff.

Smyth employed a physician search agency to recruit an orthopedic surgeon. An orthopedic surgeon was needed to overcome the community's perception that the hospital's emergency room was only a "first-aid" station. Currently, orthopedic cases that were too complicated for the attending physician were transferred to Eureka.

Physicians were particularly important to Calumet for two main reasons:

1. Only physicians admitted patients and initiated treatment.
2. Physicians specified products and quantities purchased from the hospital (e.g., number of laboratory and X-ray tests, days of care required, and so on).

Thus, physicians often were considered the hospital's most important marketing target. Hospitals had to first market to their medical staff if they were to succeed in marketing their services and attracting patients.[1]

Service Area

The hospital's primary service area, Randolph County, had a population of 16,000. The population of the city of Calumet was approximately 11,000. In addition, 4,200 students attended Central State University; half of these students lived in Calumet during the regular school session.

The university was a liberal arts institution and included a School of Nursing. The hospital benefited from the nursing students who received part of their clinical training at the hospital. In addition, the university conducted a "wellness program" and used the hospital's classroom for lectures from time to time.

A small retirement village located a block from the hospital had approximately eighty-five residents. Residents of the service area, however, were younger than average; only 7 percent were over the age of sixty-five compared to the national average of 11 percent.

Although agriculture was the main industry in the local economy, the university was the largest employer. There were also several small industrial plants in the county, including a printing plant that employed 160 persons.

Competition and the Market Situation

Calumet was a county-owned hospital, so it benefited from the tax support of Randolph County. Between 1986 and 1988, tax revenue totaled $1,119,000. These funds covered the cost of the care of indigent patients and the loss on bad debts. In addition, Calumet was just about able to break even from operations after absorbing the difference between Medicare reimbursement and actual cost of serving Medicare patients.

Although there had been a decline in occupancy rate and Medicare reimbursement, direct charges to patients were generally 10 percent to 20 percent lower than in other area hospitals. According to Smyth, "This gives Calumet a competitive advantage over the other hospitals." In spite of lower rates, Calumet felt the impact of competition from area hospitals and other health providers. Although there were no other hospitals in Randolph County, there were several hospitals in adjacent counties (see Exhibit 6–5).

Eureka, a city of approximately 162,000 population, was ten miles from Calumet. Eureka had three large hospitals: Main General, a 350-bed for-profit hospital; Union County, a 210-bed not-for-profit hospital; and St. Mary's, a 280-bed not-for-profit church-affiliated hospital.

Only two facilities within a fifty-mile radius treated alcohol- or substance-abuse patients. The CareUnit operated by Calumet had fourteen beds. The fifteen-bed Central Alcohol Recovery Center, located in Eureka, was operated by a private not-for-profit corporation.

All three large hospitals in Eureka planned to open adult or adolescent substance-abuse units in the immediate future. Main General planned an adolescent chemical-dependency unit, Union County Hospital planned to open a twenty-one-bed adult substance unit, and St. Mary's planned to open a twenty-bed adolescent unit in six months.

Calumet also competed with alternative health delivery systems including hospice organizations, home health agencies, and medical clinics.

The Consultants' Recommendations

In late 1987, Smyth obtained approval from the board of directors to hire consultants to perform a marketing analysis of the service area and prepare a long-range plan that examined changes within the industry and competition from other health care providers. General Consultants, Inc., a national firm specializing in health facilities, was employed in October 1987. In March 1988, the consultants completed their study and presented Smyth with the hospital's new long-range plan, the first written plan for the hospital.

In the process of the study, the consultants did an analysis of strengths, weaknesses, opportunities, and threats (SWOT). The findings included the following:

Strengths

- Current services are of good quality.
- The medical staff is dedicated and qualified.
- The hospital is well equipped for its size.

Exhibit 6–5 · **Calumet Community Hospital Location Map**

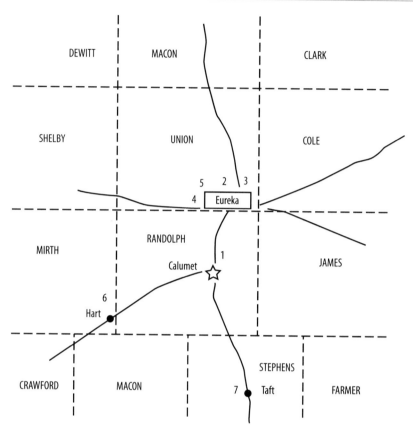

Map Key	Hospital	City	County	Beds	Distance from Calumet (in miles)
1.	Calumet Community Hospital	Calumet	Randolph	45	—
2.	Main General Hospital	Eureka	Union	350	10
3.	Union County Hospital	Eureka	Union	210	10
4.	Doctors' Memorial Hospital	Eureka	Union	40	10
5.	St. Mary's Hospital	Eureka	Union	280	10
6.	Smithville Hospital	Hart	Mirth	65	24
7.	Stillwater Hospital	Taft	Stephens	24	30

- Department heads are dedicated.
- All rooms in the hospital are private.
- This is the only hospital in Calumet.
- The hospital has strong administrative leadership.

Weaknesses and Problems

- There is heavy dependence on two physicians.
- Many active medical staff have left over the past five years.

- There are factions within the medical staff.
- The hospital is small so there are no economies of scale.
- The hospital is reputed to resist change.
- Some citizens lack a positive image of the hospital.
- There are limited public relations and marketing activities.
- The hospital has lost 60 percent of all county patients in its primary service area to other hospitals.
- There are inadequate plans and insufficient resources to meet increased competition.

Opportunities

- Recruit physician specialists in selected fields.
- Establish a physicians' office building to assist in attracting new physicians.
- Create a public relations/marketing program to enhance the hospital's image and attract patients.
- Expand home health services.
- Improve student medical services.
- Improve emergency and outpatient care.

Threats

- There is increased competition from larger hospitals nearby.
- Consumers expect more specialized services than the hospital can afford to offer.
- The government's reimbursement system for Medicare patients is a potential problem.
- There is competition from other substance-abuse units.
- There are limited resources to stay current with the increasing technology in the health field.
- There is a reduction in the county's tax support.

The consultants' final recommendations centered on five construction projects that would provide Calumet Community Hospital with additional space by 1995. The projects were as follows:

1. Construct a medical office building at an estimated cost of $900,000.
2. Expand CareUnit by fourteen beds, for an estimated cost of $238,000.

3. Remodel and expand the dietary area, for an estimated cost of $150,000.
4. Construct a twenty-bed adolescent treatment unit at an estimated cost of $460,000.
5. Construct an addition to the existing building to accommodate a new classroom and additional laboratory space, for an estimated cost of $62,000.

Where Do We Go from Here?

The consultants' report left the administrator and board with some hard decisions about what direction to take. A major problem was that almost no single part of the construction suggested could be undertaken without putting more pressure on available space—what one of the consultants called the "domino effect."

How soon any of the projects could be undertaken and how to pay for them were still under consideration. The board decided to investigate other alternatives before implementing the consultants' recommendations. These alternatives would be to:

- affiliate with one of the larger hospitals;
- convert the hospital to an outpatient and emergency center; and
- convert the hospital to a day-care facility for senior citizens and offer skilled-nursing home services.

A referendum was required to raise funds or "float bonds" to support any remodeling or major capital expenditures. However, what alternatives would the citizens of Randolph County have for primary health care if the mission of Calumet Community Hospital was drastically changed? The decisions would not be easy.

Appendix A: Rural Health Care Industry Note

The health care industry had changed dramatically in recent years. Advanced technology, changing medical practices, increased specialization, intense competition, government regulations, and alternative health delivery systems have forced hospitals to develop new and evolving goals. Systematic, strategic planning was more important now than ever before.

For the past few years, prophets of doom predicted the closing of many small rural hospitals in this country. They questioned whether rural hospitals could remain economically viable in today's competitive environment and predicted the demise of many of them before the year 2000.[2] A 1987 study conducted by a large accounting firm predicted that 700 U.S. hospitals would close by 1995.[3]

DRG Reimbursement

In 1983, the federal government began reimbursing hospitals for services to Medicare and Medicaid patients on a preestablished fee based on treatment appropriate to the individual patient's admitting diagnosis rather than on the actual cost of service. This case-specific method was constructed around diagnostic related groups (DRGs). The concept behind DRGs was that certain categories or groups of medical diagnoses consumed similar types and quantities of hospital resources. The DRG system subdivided inpatient hospital care into 383 separate diagnostic categories. Except for the fees of the attending physician, all other medical expenses were covered. The hospital was reimbursed one flat fee per illness rather than by patient day, service, or procedure rendered. In addition, some procedures and services were covered only on an outpatient basis.

The DRG system was phased in at hospitals over a four-year period. In 1983, 25 percent of total reimbursement to hospitals was under the new system, 50 percent in 1984, 75 percent in 1985, and 100 percent in 1986.

Problems of Rural Hospitals

An almost immediate impact of the DRG system was a dramatic decrease in hospital inpatient admissions. Although all hospitals experienced lower occupancy rates and inadequate payments from the Medicare program, rural hospitals were especially hard hit. For example, DRG reimbursement for a pneumonia patient hospitalized for 4.5 days might be $950 less than reimbursement under the previous actual-cost-of-service method.

Between 1984 and 1986, 163 hospitals closed. Seventy-four were classified as small or rural.[4] When the DRG system was implemented, rural hospitals such as Calumet Community Hospital began receiving reimbursement for care of Medicare and Medicaid patients at a lower fee than that paid to larger city hospitals. For example, rural hospitals received up to 30 percent less than urban hospitals for treating the same diagnosis, even though rural hospital costs were only 10 percent to 15 percent less. In addition, rural hospitals had difficulty attracting physicians and other health professionals and often had to pay premium salaries to attract qualified individuals.

Another concern for rural hospitals was the outmigration of patients to larger medical centers in nearby cities. More than four of ten consumers in rural areas indicated they did not believe specialized medical services were available in their area.[5] As many as 42 percent of rural residents traveled to urban areas to receive medical treatment, usually to gain access to specialists and more sophisticated testing facilities than were available locally.[6]

Approximately 52 percent of rural hospitals were owned or leased by local governments. These organizations often faced complex governmental structures that were unable to react quickly to changes in reimbursement, technology, and competition.

To increase revenues, and in some instances simply to survive, hospitals established satellite emergency centers or outpatient clinics, eliminated unprofitable services, merged with other facilities, added services such as home health and hospice, and diversified into other businesses (medical office buildings, management consulting services, laundry services, food-catering services, and so on).[7] Small rural hospitals had limited options for revenue enhancement, which complicated their planning for survival. However, many did find a specific market niche to fill in their service area.

Historically, small rural hospitals did not feel a need to utilize marketing techniques or develop long-range strategic plans.[8] However, that attitude changed significantly in recent years. A 1987 study of 476 small or rural hospitals, conducted by the American Hospital Association, noted that nearly 60 percent were active in marketing. Because of financial constraints, the administrator often was in charge of marketing and planning activities. Such activities were frequently restricted to public relations and advertising. So, the question remained, how effective were the marketing and planning functions when carried out on a part-time basis by the administrator?

Notes

1. Julian G. Franks, "Zeroing in on the Targets," *L and H Perspective* (Fall/Winter 1980), p. 37.
2. Michael J. Rabinowitz and James J. O. Keefe III, "Rx for Rural Hospitals: Heal Thyself," *L and H Perspective* (Fall/Winter 1980), p. 28.
3. Arvin Rodrigues et al., "Strategic Planning for Rural Hospitals," *Proceedings of the 1989 Conference of the Business and Health Administration Association,* Midwest Business Administration 25th Annual Meeting, Chicago, March 1989, p. 32.
4. Ibid.
5. Joyce Jensen and Ned Miklovic, "Declining Censuses Plague Hospitals: Administrators Expect Further Drops," *Modern Healthcare* (August 16, 1985), pp. 86–87.
6. Ibid.
7. Sarah A. Grim, "Win/Win: Urban and Rural Hospitals Network for Survival," *Hospital and Health Services Administration* 31, no. 1 (Spring 1986), pp. 1–13.
8. Verna Aline Arnold, "The Application of Selected Marketing Concepts in the Hospital Planning Process," doctoral dissertation, North Texas State University, 1978, pp. 158–161.

References

Jonas, Steven. *Health Care Delivery in the United States,* 2d ed. New York: Springer Publishing Company, 1981.

Rakich, Jonathon S., et al. *Managing Health Services Organizations,* 2d ed. Philadelphia: W. B. Saunders Co., 1985.

Roberts, Carolyn, and James G. Schuman. "Planning and Marketing in Small and Rural Hospitals." *Healthcare Planning and Marketing* (January/February 1988), pp. 4–9.

Sherman, James F., and Albert Zezulinski. "A New Procedure for Hospital Survival." *L and H Perspective* 11, no. 2 (1985), pp. 55–58.

Snook, I. Donald. *Hospitals: What They Are and How They Work.* Rockville, Maryland: Aspen Publishers, 1981.

Tye, Larry. "The Ins and Outs of Hospitals." *St. Louis Post-Dispatch* (September 9, 1989), p. 1D.

Sisters of Charity of the Incarnate Word Health Care System: Health Care Mission Plan

Case 7

The Sisters of Charity Health Care System (SCHCS) was a multihospital corporation whose eleven hospitals served three major markets: Southern California, North Central Louisiana, and Southeastern Texas (see Exhibit 7–1). At its meeting the previous night, the SCHCS Board of Trustees had approved the "system goal" as part of the SCHCS mission plan. The "system goal" was designed to clearly and concisely communicate to a variety of constituencies the short-term direction of the SCHCS. It read as follows:

> Emphasizing collaboration with compatible partners, we will be a catalyst and leader in developing integrated community health networks that meet the identified needs and improve the health status of our communities.

The task imperative for SCHCS's management team was simply to translate this vision into reality. "With whom should they collaborate? Should they form alliances with other hospitals, divest poorly performing assets, joint-venture with an existing insurer, or develop their own insurance capability? What was the best way to engage physicians into the integrated community health network strategy? How many and what kind of physicians would they need? How can they reengineer the cost of health care delivery

This case was written by Martin B. Gerowitz of Xavier University. It was prepared as a basis for classroom discussion rather than to illustrate effective or ineffective handling of an administrative situation. Used with permission from Martin Gerowitz.

while maintaining measurable and superior quality of care? Could the system goal be implemented the same way in each of SCHCS's markets?"

History and Context

In 1866, C. M. Dubois, Bishop of Galveston, Texas, traveled to France seeking sisters to take charge of "our hospitals, refuges, and asylums." Three sisters volunteered to form a new congregation dedicated to caring for the mind, body, and spirit of the individual with particular attention to the most vulnerable members of the community. In 1867, they opened St. Mary's Infirmary (later renamed St. Mary's Hospital) in Galveston. From this auspicious beginning, the SCHCS had grown to become a leader in U.S. health care with eleven acute-care hospitals, four long-term-care centers, numerous clinics, and a variety of health-related entities in five states. SCHCS ranked among the top five Catholic health care systems in the nation with assets of $2 billion, including a fund balance of $1 billion.

SCHCS had flourished during the past ten years. SCHCS's management strategy placed initiative with the managers at each hospital. The system was a recognized leader in the continuous quality improvement movement and had diversified into long-term care, home care, and third-party administration. The result was a sizable base of retained earnings. The system reported operating income of $196.3 million and net patient revenues of $1.2 billion in 1993. Yet Stan Urban, president and chief executive officer of the system, was concerned. As he viewed the market

Exhibit 7–1 • Sisters of Charity Health Care System Facilities

California

San Bernardino, California

Acute-Care Hospital
St. Bernadine's Medical Center (449 beds)

Primary-Care Clinic
Inland Healthcare Group (seven locations)

Home-Care Services
St. Bernardine's Home and Health Hospice

Long Beach, California

Acute-Care Hospital
St. Mary's Medical Center

Primary-Care Clinics
Hungtinton Beach Family Practice
Seaview Clinic
Priority One Industrial Medicine Clinic
Ambulatory Medicine Clinic
OB Clinic

Home Health Services
Home Care of St. Mary's Medical Center

Louisiana

Alexandria, Louisiana

Acute-Care Hospital
St. Francis Cabrini Hospital

Home-Care Services
The Cabrini Home Health/Hospice Program

Primary-Care Clinics
The Family Medicine Center
Pediatric Associates
Rainbow Pediatrics
Carlton and Luke Clinic (managed by SCHCS)
Mayaux Family Clinic (managed by SCHCS)
Three Physician Offices (managed by SCHCS)
Garcia Clinic of Internal Medicine (managed by SCHCS)
Quick Care (two locations)
Cabrini Center for Occupational Medicine (two locations)

Shreveport, Louisiana

Acute-Care Hospital
Schumpert Medical Center

Home-Care Services
Schumpert Home Health Services

Primary-Care Clinics
First Care (South and West)
S.I.M.S. (Schumpert Internal Medicine Specialists)
The Diagnostic Clinic Internists
Mansfield Family Medicine
Northwood Family Medicine
Ringold Family Medicine
Michael Hammer, M.D.
Pines Road Family Medicine
Drs. Gayle and Taylor

Community Clinic
Martin Luther King Health Clinic

Lake Charles, Louisiana

Acute-Care Hospital
St. Patrick Hospital

Home-Care Services
Health Care at Home

Texas

Beaumont, Texas

Acute-Care Hospital
St. Elizabeth's Hospital

Home-Care Services
St. Elizabeth's Home Care

Community Clinic
11th Street OB Clinic

Galveston, Texas

Acute-Care Hospital
St. Mary's Hospital

Home-Care Services
St. Mary's Home Health

Community Clinic
Bishop Dubois Clinic

Houston, Texas

Acute-Care Hospital
St. Joseph's Hospital

Primary-Care Clinic
St. Joseph's Primary Care Tingled

Community Clinic
St. Joseph's OB Clinic

Nassau Bay, Texas

Acute-Care Hospital
St. John's Hospital

Primary-Care Clinics
Bay Medical Associates
St. John's Pediatric Group
Pineloch Clinic
South Shore Harbor

Home Health Services
St. John's Home Health

Port Arthur, Texas

Acute-Care Hospitals
St. Mary's Hospital

Primary-Care Clinic
Bishop Byrne Wellness Center

Home-Care Services
St. Mary's Home Health

Texarkana, Texas

Acute-Care Hospital
St. Michael's Healthcare Center

Rehabilitation Hospital
St. Michael's Rehabilitation Hospital

Primary-Care Clinic
St. Michael's Family Clinic

Home-Care Services
St. Michael's Home Health

---

trends in managed-care penetration and its impact upon utilization across the country, he noticed the vast variances in regional experiences. "What," he wondered, "were the implications of these trends for the SCHCS?" High penetration of managed care had challenged the health care providers that operated as autonomous players to integrate the roles of ambulatory, acute-care, and insurer functions through alliances, mergers, and acquisitions to create competing systems that offered continuity of care across the continuum for a set price.

This represented a significant paradigm shift—a shift away from the acute-care production-based incentives that rewarded for admissions and increased length of stay to incentives that rewarded providers based on delivering medically necessary care early in the disease process in the lowest cost setting. Emphasis was on treating the patient outside the hospital walls. Day surgery and home health care were growing rapidly. In 1992, the number of outpatient visits performed by hospitals outpaced the number of inpatient visits for the first time. This trend had already reduced hospital occupancy rates and would be fueled further by increased managed-care penetration.

There was an obvious excess capacity in the acute-care component of the health care system. How many hospitals would survive? Despite the SCHCS success, Stan Urban knew that in a changing market, nothing failed like success. He shared these concerns with the board, and the board had responded by adopting a "systems goal." The future, they had agreed, belonged to those willing to create integrated community health networks—networks of providers who had the capability to offer a full continuum of health services, cover a geographic region, accept fixed payment and risk for defined populations, and improve the health status of defined (enrolled) populations.

SCHCS delegated significant responsibility to its member hospitals. Each had taken the initiative to develop home-care programs and primary-care clinics. SCHCS had pioneered what the popular management literature was now advocating—less hierarchical, less centralized, and less bureaucratic structures. Such structures, management gurus argued, were more flexible and promoted organizational learning. In fact, SCHCS had long ago yielded significant control over their organizational units. Each hospital reported to Urban's COO, Dan Walterman. Yet each hospital CEO was accountable to his or her hospital board and had to deal with the sensitivities of the medical staff.

Urban sensed that these new advances in computer-mediated communication technologies and the accelerating demands for scale economies, measurable quality, and customer responsiveness would require managers to have greater flexibility in developing new options for creating continuous improvement and competitive advantage. The task of selecting partners was a daunting one. Freestanding community hospitals would be difficult to manage efficiently under increased competition and requirements for health systems integration. On the other hand, alliances and mergers in other industries had left a trail of failed efforts. Gayle Capozzalo, senior vice president of organizational development, suggested to the group the following list of criteria:

- Did the candidate provide complementary coverage in terms of geographic and service scope?
- Did the candidate demonstrate clinical quality and a high level of patient satisfaction?
- Did the candidate possess a strong financial position?
- Did the candidate place a premium on physician integration?
- Did the candidate embrace and engage physicians as full decision-making partners in integration?
- Did the candidate express values compatible with those of SCHCS?

SCHCS's California Market

If one wanted to see the future, to witness the stresses of rightsizing, alliance building, the converting of fee-for-service to capitation, and the transforming of the stand-alone hospital and the solo or small-group practice into the integrated delivery system of the twenty-first century, one need only go to California. Southern California was characterized by many small hospitals, many large physician group practices, and a market penetration in managed care that was double the U.S. rate. The smaller physician practice and the solo hospital were in the process of becoming as extinct as the dinosaur. They were being displaced by regional provider-driven managed-care networks striving to provide high-quality health care at affordable prices. In contrast to the rest of the nation, California health care providers were pushing managed competition further into the future. Physician groups were merging to form larger physician groups and networks to gain leverage when negotiating and contracting with insurers and hospitals. Each round of mergers resulted in another round of merger frenzy between physician groups and among hospitals as each created new alliances and expanded delivery networks with each other to balance the imbalances created from the previous round.

The latest round of mergers between physician group practices and health care providers in Southern California had created new alliances and alliances of alliances. Cedars-Sinai Medical Center in Los Angeles and a network of three Adventist Health Systems/West hospitals was announced. Cedars-Sinai Medical Center was a subsidiary of UniHealth America. It planned to purchase the assets of the Medical Group of Beverly Hills, a twenty-seven-physician group that served 16,000 managed-care enrollees. Another provider organization, the Southern California Health Care Network Foundation had acquired the Glendale Multispecialty Medical Group composed of 32 primary-care and 132 multispecialty physicians serving 23,000 managed-care enrollees as well as Family Medical Associates, a practice with 11 primary-care and 32 specialty physicians. Primary-care physicians (e.g., family practitioners, internists, OB/GYNs, and pediatricians) were the "portals" into the system. Over the years, physicians had opted to specialize. As a consequence, fewer primary-care physicians were available than needed. This, combined with the rapid movement toward integration, had placed primary-care physicians at the front of the "food chain."

The San Diego market was also entering a new phase. Established networks such as the Scripps Institute, Sharp Health Care, and Kaiser Permanente had revamped their current structures and strategies to accommodate capitation, new cost controls, and potential new partners. Kaiser had abandoned its tightly controlled system by offering a point-of-service option. This allowed enrollees to go outside the system for care if they were willing to pay higher

deductibles and co-payments. It also had experimented with a new program that blended its traditional medical coverage with workers' compensation coverage. Sharp Health Care consisted of five acute-care hospitals, fifteen clinics, and seven specialty facilities; 2,200 affiliated physicians; and 13,000 covered lives enrolled in a health maintenance plan initiated in January 1993.

In March, the San Francisco–based Catholic Health Care West, Mercy Health Care of San Diego, and La Jolla–based Scripps announced that they would form an exclusive alignment primarily to pursue state and regional managed-care contracts (see Exhibit 7–2). The combination of these three California health care systems would create a provider network consisting of twenty-two hospitals with a total of 5,740 beds and 5,595 physicians in three states (Arizona, California, and Nevada). The Oakland-based Kaiser Permanente operated thirty hospitals with a total of 6,351 beds and 7,676 physicians in three western states and Ohio.

In addition, the four leading hospital-based managed-care delivery systems in California had joined together to form the California Heath Network, a single statewide network to pursue contracts with large employers. The network was a joint venture of California Health Systems, Sharp Health Care, Adventist Heath Systems/West, and Loma Linda University Medical Center.

The SCHCS had several options in Southern California. They could sell the hospitals to a for-profit system, they could create an alliance with another compatible system, or they could compete head on.

St. Bernadine's Medical Center

St. Bernadine's was a 443-bed tertiary referral center located approximately thirty-five miles east of Los Angeles. Given its distance from Los Angeles and the Pacific coast, the region was referred to as the "Inlands." The hospital operated at 50 percent occupancy. Its major clinical services included cardiovascular surgery, neuroscience, NICU/maternity, and orthopedics. Twenty percent of its 175 active physicians were primary care (family/general practice, internal medicine, pediatrics, or OB/GYNs). The

Exhibit 7–2 · The Emerging California Networks

System	Acute-Care Hospitals	Number of Physicians	Licensed Beds	Market Area
Catholic Health Care West San Francisco	16	3,102	4,135	Arizona California Nevada
Mercy Health Care San Diego	1	500	520	San Diego County
Scripps Health La Jolla	5	1,993	1,085	San Diego County

majority of the staff were independent, solo practitioners. The hospital and its physicians were late entrants into a rapidly maturing managed-care market in which more than 30 percent of the payor mix was managed care (see Exhibit 7–3). The Inland market had experienced 460 bed days per 1,000 and the bed days per 1,000 was predicted to reach 260 by 1998. Overall hospital occupancy rates for all hospitals in the Inlands area was 37 percent. The area had experienced an accelerated level of consolidation of managed-care lives between physicians and payor organizations including Kaiser (415,000 lives), Pacific Physician Services (270,000 lives), and PrimeCare/Aetna (Desert Valley Hospital, 200,000 lives). The remaining 300,000 managed-care lives were held by local group/IPAs.

The decline in inpatient utilization had resulted in reduced demand for specialists. The impact on specialists had manifested itself in declining incomes, resistance and denial, fear and anxiety, and resignations. The hospital's ability to respond to market forces was hampered by minimal control and influence over the patient base, primary-care delivery, and health plan contracts. The hospital's ability to promote integrated delivery as a strategy had been impacted by control issues between the hospital and the physicians, a void in physician leadership, and physician indecision regarding how best to respond to marketplace forces.

The key element in the hospital's strategy was the expansion of its Inland Community Health Network (ICHN) through acquisition or affiliation with medical groups and IPAs. The foundation of the ICHN was the Inland Health Group (IHG), which consisted of seventeen employed physicians in six clinic locations with 29,000 managed-care lives. It was in negotiation with several primary-care physicians and physician groups with over 50,000 managed-care lives. Despite the appreciation of the fact that health plans were shifting costs and risks to providers, thus forcing physicians to align with larger organizations that could offer greater leverage and resources to manage risk, physicians were immobilized by the multiple choices for affiliation. The ICHN was offering physicians an ownership position in the ICHN and a role in its governance. The ICHN, however, lacked an established track record and was in stiff competition from several well-established medical groups and physician-driven delivery networks that resonated with physicians who believed that the ICHN was hospital controlled, that physicians should create and control managed-care delivery systems, and that hospitals should only have contractual relationships.

St. Mary's Medical Center

Located in Long Beach, St. Mary's Medical Center (SMMC) had 551 licensed beds with special services in trauma, open-heart surgery, and kidney transplantation. It had an affiliation with the UCLA School of Medicine and carried out several community outreach programs including CARE (Comprehensive AIDS Resources Education), Southeast Asian Health

Exhibit 7–3 • **St. Bernadine's Payor Mix**

Payor	Percent of Market Share
Medicare	34
Managed Care	31
Medi-Cal (California's Medicaid)	24
Commercial	4
Other/Self-Pay	7

Project, OB Clinic, Medicine Clinic, and Geriatric Assessment Center; it was also a member of the Mobile Pediatric Clinic Coalition. In addition, it operated a comprehensive outpatient service, home health care, surgi-center, cancer care/radiation center, older adult services, geropsych, and three satellite clinics.

St. Mary's market share within the primary Long Beach service area was 21 percent and 7 percent for the total service area. Over 40 percent of its payor mix was accounted for by Medi-Cal. Nearly 25 percent of the patients were Medicare recipients. A goal of SMMC had been to maximize the number of covered lives served at the lowest possible cost per life by promoting physician integration, regional integration, and hospital networking. Physicians of Greater Long Beach (PGLB) was the largest IPA in Long Beach and had 20,000 covered lives. SMMC was their only hospital. PGLB was dominated by specialists. In the past year, PGLB's enrollment had been flat.

SCHCS's Louisiana Market

With a population of four million people, the State of Louisiana consisted of two geographic markets—the Greater New Orleans/Baton Rouge market area of southern Louisiana and the northern part of the state. The largest employer was the state government. When state Medicaid beneficiaries were included, the State of Louisiana was the largest single purchaser of health care services.

The state was considering the move toward capitating its Medicaid population as well as the benefit structure for state employees. The ability to put these contracts up for bidding statewide would be cost effective for the state. Issuing and monitoring one contract would be less costly and time consuming than negotiating contracts with different provider groups in each submarket. Hospitals that could set up statewide networks (attractive to managed-care plans) would have a competitive advantage in Louisiana. The state did not have a certificate of need (CON) law. However, the state legislature was considering one as a means of generating revenue from CON application fees to shore up a $600 million shortfall.

SCHCS Hospitals and Services

The SCHCS operated three hospitals and one nursing home in Louisiana. These facilities were located outside the New Orleans/Baton Rouge market. Two of the hospitals, St. Francis Cabrini Hospital (304 beds) in Alexandria and Schumpert Medical Center (625 beds) in Shreveport, were located in the northern end of the state, 200 miles from Baton Rouge. The third, St. Patrick Hospital, was located in Lake Charles, 125 miles west of New Orleans and Baton Rouge. Each hospital had established its own array of diversified services. These included primary-care centers, community clinics, and home-care services.

Potential Partners

General Health Based in Baton Rouge, General Health was the parent corporation of the 396-bed Baton Rouge General Hospital. It was the state's largest provider of managed-care services with 140,000 enrollees. Tom Sawyer, CEO of General Health, had been discussing with state officials the notion of developing a more coordinated system of care that would involve the state public hospital in Baton Rouge and the Earl K. Long Hospital, a 153-bed facility operated by the Louisiana Health Authority. The state was considering a replacement facility for Earl K. Long estimated at $52 million.

Louisiana Health Authority The Health Authority operated Louisiana's nine public health hospitals. Louisiana insurance commissioner, Jim Brown, had proposed privatizing the state Medicaid system in order to make private providers, not the state's public hospital system, the primary purveyor of health care to the poor.

Ochsner Medical Institutions The Ochsner Medical Institutions represented the Ochsner Clinic, the Alton Ochsner Medical Foundation, and the Ochsner Health Plan. The Ochsner Clinic was the largest medical group practice in Louisiana. It had 400 physicians and surgeons who practiced in 64 specialties and subspecialties. Its main clinic was in central New Orleans with ten neighborhood clinic locations throughout the Greater New Orleans metropolitan area. It was one of the largest employers in New Orleans. It also operated the Ochsner Clinic of Baton Rouge along with three neighborhood clinics in that community. The Ochsner Clinic was founded in 1941 as a private partnership. It was named after Dr. Alton Ochsner, a world-renowned surgeon who was the first physician to draw a connection between cigarette smoking and lung cancer.

The Alton Ochsner Medical Foundation operated the not-for-profit, 532-bed Ochsner Foundation Hospital and the Freeman Research Institute. Annually it admitted 18,000 patients and treated about 30,000 patients in its emergency department. It was known for specialty treatment in the areas of cardiovascular care and cancer. Patients came from throughout the United States, particularly the south Gulf. Ochsner Health Plan (OHP), founded in 1984, had grown to be the largest health maintenance plan in Louisiana with more than 80,000 members. Over the past ten years OHP had developed significant competencies in marketing health benefit plans, managing physician group practices, and containing costs while maintaining high member satisfaction.

SCHCS's Texas Health Care Market

The SCHCS presence in Southeast Texas consisted of five hospitals. St. Joseph's Hospital (840 beds), located in downtown Houston, provided specialized services and was a teaching affiliate of the University of Texas–Houston School of Medicine. The four general/community hospitals included St. Mary's Hospital in Port Arthur, Texas (278 beds); St. Mary's Hospital in Galveston, Texas (556 beds); St. John's Hospital in Nassau Bay, Texas (130 beds); and St. Michael's Health Center in Texarkana, Texas (239 beds).

In addition, SCHCS, operating through a for-profit subsidiary unit, managed the largest PPO (preferred provider organization) in Southeast Texas. It managed a capitated contract awarded by the Department of Defense to serve 31,000 retired military personnel and their dependents under CHAMPUS. In addition, SCHCS operated a management service organization in Southeast Texas that had ten physician employees and managed twenty practices.

There were seventy-three hospitals in the Southeast Texas market that surrounded the Greater Houston Metropolitan area. This area encompassed over four million people, the fifth largest urban center in the United States. Nearly 50 percent of these hospitals were consolidated into one of four large systems: Health Trust (twelve hospitals with 2,850 beds); Columbia/HCA (ten hospitals with 2,726 beds); Memorial (seven hospitals with 1,163 beds); and the Sisters of Charity (five hospitals with 2,708 beds). Methodist Hospital, a freestanding hospital system, had 1,527 beds. Health care reform in the form of managed care, however, had hardly scratched the surface. The two largest HMOs in the area—Prudential Health Care Plan and Sanus/New York Life Health Plan—had only enrolled about 373,000 members. This was less than 10 percent of the Houston market.

The Texas Medical Center (Methodist Hospital, St. Luke's Hospital, M. D. Anderson Hospital, and Hermann Hospital)

These five institutions were located in close geographic proximity to each other in central Houston. Though independent institutions, these five hospitals appeared to share a common campuslike setting that reinforced the image of the Texas Medical Center as a regionally recognized center of medical excellence.

Under the leadership of its CEO, Larry Mathis, Methodist Hospital took on a $150 million expansion in the late 1980s. This expansion made Methodist the nation's largest freestanding hospital with 1,527 beds. Mathis was an industry leader. In 1993, Mathis was elected chairperson of the American Hospital Association. Mathis's philosophy had so embodied the spirit of this giant hospital that people sometimes referred to it as "Mathodist." In addition to his building spree, Mathis staunchly refused to take managed-care contracts. The *Wall Street Journal* labeled him a health care "troglodyte" who was out of step with the rest of the industry. Mathis was perhaps best known in Texas for his stance in a lawsuit filed in 1991 by the state attorney general. The suit contended that the not-for-profit hospital was not providing enough charity care to justify its tax-exempt status. The lawsuit was won by Methodist, but the dispute prompted the state legislature to pass a new law requiring not-for-profit hospitals to provide specific levels of charity care. In 1993, Methodist Hospital reported $20 million in net operating income on net patient revenues of $586.6 million. The system reported assets of $1.3 billion.

Located across the street from Methodist Hospital, St. Luke's Episcopal Hospital with 646 beds had been reported to be discussing a merger or affiliation with Methodist, its traditional rival. According to HCIA, a Baltimore health care research firm, St. Luke's had a net income of $10.1 million on net patient revenues of $303.3 million in 1992. A merger of St. Luke's and Methodist would create a system of over 2,000 beds and would align competing and highly respected programs in cardiovascular surgery and orthopedics. A spokesperson for Methodist Hospital, in response to a reporter inquiry noted that "a merger with St. Luke's is only one of many options Methodist is exploring with various providers." This was followed by a jointly issued statement by Methodist and St. Luke's that "speculation on the details of any alignment is premature since we are in the very earliest stages of discussion."[1]

David R. Page was the CEO of Houston's Hermann Hospital. Page had followed an aggressive strategy of physician acquisition. The aggressiveness of this strategy, however, had caught the attention of the Justice Department, which had sued the hospital in federal court.[2] Organizations were eligible for federal tax-exempt status under the Internal Revenue Code in Section 501(c)(3) if they met the following tests: (1) a charitable purpose test; (2) political activities test; (3) private benefit test; and (4) the private inurement test. Hermann's suspected conduct included physician income guarantees, subsidized office personnel, free office space, unpaid loans, subsidized parking, and "purchases and other transactions" that may have benefited former board members and other individuals.[3]

HCA/Columbia

Rick Scott, the forty-one-year-old CEO of Columbia Hospital, led the successful acquisition of HCA in 1993. This acquisition created the largest for-profit hospital management company in the nation with annual revenues exceeding $15 billion. The chain publicly vowed to acquire between 500 and 1,000 additional hospitals over the next several years. Scott did not intend to keep all these facilities open. When interviewed by the *Wall Street Journal* he said, "You could close 30 percent of the hospitals in this country today, and nobody would miss them, as long as people could go to a good hospital nearby." Columbia/HCA had spent $100 million buying facilities that it promptly closed, eliminating competition for other Columbia/HCA facilities. For example, in 1988, Scott, who owned two hospitals in El Paso, proceeded to borrow $11 million dollars to purchase a third hospital nearby that was serving fifty patients per day. He promptly closed this hospital and shifted forty patients (an 80 percent patient retention) to the two remaining facilities. In June 1994, Columbia/HCA announced its intentions to consolidate services in Houston by selling Heights Hospital and merging its operations with nearby facilities. In a related development, Columbia/HCA had met with about 300 physicians to provide information about syndicating the Houston market. Columbia/HCA had syndicated other markets in Texas and Florida. The strategy was to woo doctors' loyalty by offering them the chance to become equity partners in the company's operation in their local markets. Scott gave similar incentives to local management by giving equity opportunities to the CEO, COO, CFO, and nursing executive. Typically they sold a 20 percent interest in the local networks to area physicians and administrators.

Scott focused his strategy in seven states (Texas, Florida, Louisiana, Tennessee, Kentucky, Virginia, and Georgia). These states accounted for 213 of Columbia/HCA's 311 hospitals. Some referred to Columbia/HCA as the Wal-Mart of health care. It used volume buying, strict cost controls, and size to offer a broad range of services at a competitive price. Urban had been approached by Scott in 1993. They discussed industry trends. Scott noted that "the Catholic mission was to take care of charity patients. That mission is past." Mr. Scott also noted that "universal acccess will provide the indigent with care. I have no problem with their [Catholic] canon of ethics." When asked if Columbia could keep growing at its current pace, it was noted that when Columbia went to the banking community in January 1993 to fund a $3 billion line of credit, the banks were eager to take part. Urban, stating SCHCS's interest in seeking partners to meet community needs, promised to keep the dialogue open. Columbia/HCA controlled eight of Houston's twenty-nine acute-care hospitals.

Memorial Health System

The Memorial Health Care System began in 1907 as the dream of a twenty-seven-year-old Baptist minister who recognized Houston's need for high-quality health care. Memorial was chartered that year as the Baptist Sanatorium, the second Baptist Hospital in the nation.

Memorial operated as a community-based multi-hospital system with five community general hospitals, all situated in Houston suburbs. Dan Wilford, Memorial's CEO, unlike Methodist's Mathis, had vigorously sought out managed-care contracts and had succeeded in developing fifty-seven contracts with managed-care plans. Thirty-two percent of Memorial's revenues were derived from managed-care contracts. It operated an HMO in a joint venture with Aetna. In a recent interview, he had acknowledged Memorial's interest in going into the insurance business.

Physicians and Physician Groups

There were over 7,500 patient care physicians in Southeast Texas with over 3,800 primary-care specialists (family practice, general practice, internal medicine, pediatricians, and OB/GYNs). The population-to-physician ratio was 218 to 1. There was a lack of physician organization. With the exception of a few moderately sized medical groups, most of the physicians practiced solo or belonged to two-person practices. According to regional planners, the distribution of primary-care and specialist physicians were in disequilibrium. Although managed care accounted for less than 10 percent of the market share, national carriers (Prudential, CIGNA, and MetLife) were gearing up to enter the Texas market.

Business Coalitions

A business coalition had been organized in the mid-1980s to influence the direction of health care in the region. Recently it formed the Houston Health Care Business Coalition. It consisted of thirty Houston area employers with 250,000 employees. Its goal was to create a collective purchasing alliance and to implement value-based purchasing in the nation's fourth-largest health care market. Organizers of the Houston Coalition said "their approach focused on making long-range changes in health care practices rather than seeking short-term discounts."[4]

The Recommendation

Stan Urban knew that there would have to be long-range changes in health care practices. He was determined to make the best decisions about what those changes should be in order for SCHCS to continue to fulfill its mission. "Which of the possible partners in each of the major market areas would contribute to that mission? Would he recommend pursuing different strategies in each of the three markets? Was Rick Scott right that the Catholic mission to care for charity patients was past?" His preliminary recommendations would have to be made in the morning as the board continued its meeting.

Notes

1. S. Lutz, *Modern Healthcare* (June 14, 1994), p. 16.
2. W. Aseltyne, *Topics in Health Care Financing* 20, no. 3 (Spring 1994), pp. 46–53.
3. B. Broccolo, "Hermann Agreement Updates IRS Guidelines for Incentives," *Healthcare Financial Management* 49, no. 1 (1995), pp. 64–67.
4. D. Wise, "Houston Group Goes Against the Grain," *Business and Health* 12, no. 6 (June 1994), pp. 61–62.

"And learn to play the game fair, no self-deception, no shrinking from the truth; mercy and consideration for the other man, but none for yourself, upon whom you have to keep an incessant watch."

Sir William Osler
Physician and Educator (1849–1919)

Prologue

Mr. Blackwell decided to consult the institutional ethics committee (IEC) of Regional Memorial Hospital. Blackwell was the CEO of this large, public health facility that had over 900 beds and served a countywide population of over one million. His concerns centered around two cases that plagued his administrative staff for months. The questions just did not go away. The free baby formula case and the vendor ethics case were fairly typical, and they raised ethical issues that were troublesome and not easily managed. Actually, the major issue in both cases was conflict of interest.

W. H. Shaw explained the problem clearly when he wrote that "a conflict of interest arises when employees at any level have a private interest in a transaction substantial enough that it does or reasonably might affect their independent judgment."[1]

This case was written by John M. Lincourt, the University of North Carolina at Charlotte. It was prepared as a basis for class discussion rather than to illustrate either effective or ineffective handling of an administrative situation. Used with permission from John M. Lincourt.

Patients and hospitals had the right to expect those who made decisions to be as free as possible from conflicts of interest. Because of perceived conflicts of interest in the cases, Blackwell sought the advice of the hospital's IEC on the fair course of action.

Background

R. E. Cranford and A. E. Doudera's description of hospital ethics committees was useful: "Institutional ethics committees are interdisciplinary groups within health care institutions that advise about pressing ethical problems that arise in clinical care."[2] IECs were founded on the primary assumption that cooperative, reasoned reflection was likely to assist decision makers to reach better conclusions. These committees provided information and education to staff and the surrounding communities about ethical questions, proposed policies related to ethically difficult issues, and reviewed patient care situations (prospectively and retrospectively) in which ethical questions were at stake. Assets provided by IECs were that they (1) served as a locus for discussion, clarification, dialogue, and advice (not decision); (2) supplied protection and support for health care providers making difficult decisions; and (3) increased awareness of and sensitivity to ethical dimensions of clinical cases.

IECs were not without their critics. Some claimed such advisory groups threatened to undermine the traditional doctor-patient relationship and imposed new and untested regulatory burdens on patients, families, physicians, and hospitals. Labeling an issue as "ethical" removed it from the category of those that were strictly medical or managerial and declared that relevant considerations were not just technical in nature. Many health care providers were unaccustomed to working in this area of ethical values, and some insisted their training and experience provided scant preparation for it. Conversely, others claimed that ethics was woven into the very fabric of medical practice and management thereby rendering them eminently capable, if not the most capable, to make such decisions. These individuals tended to view IECs as "God Squads," that is, generally lacking in moral authority and ill-equipped to handle the ethical challenges of vexing and sometimes urgent hospital decisions. Such attitudes still persisted in some quarters.[3]

The operation of IECs was similar to other hospital committees, but there were some important differences. These included the interdisciplinary composition, sliding orientation period, and varied utilization pattern. IECs tended to be large committees having between ten and twenty members. Membership included nurses and physicians (frequently from oncology and pediatrics); administrators, including an outside attorney; members of the clergy and social services; a citizen or two; plus an ethicist (if available). Orientation for a new committee or new members ranged from a week or two up to a full year. Typically, this period was devoted to a careful review of institutional and community standards of care, an introduction to the bioethical literature (that was becoming vast), and most importantly, practice sessions involving ethics cases. Such reviews were usually retrospective in nature and came from that institution, one of similar status, or the literature.

Committee utilization patterns varied as well. The IEC might be convened on a case requiring immediate action, the careful review of past cases that were known to include ethical misjudgments, and cases that after review were not considered to be ethical issues at all but rather some other problem or issue (e.g., legal or procedural). Finally, the Patient Self-Determination Act, passed by Congress as part of the Omnibus Reconciliation Act of 1990 (effective December 1, 1991), helped to legitimize IECs and to socialize them more completely into hospital medical practice.

Increasingly, the arenas of business ethics and biomedical ethics intersected in important ways. No longer was the assertion heard that health care was not a business but rather a profession that somehow stood above the adversarial and competitive features of typical business practices. Hospitals were businesses and health care was an industry. In fact, the business aspects of health care were now the object of much discussion, concern, debate, and study. Such was the case with baby formula.

Free Baby Formula

The business–health care overlap was highlighted in the way three hospitals dealt with the issue of breast-feeding. At question was a curious phenomenon. Health professionals were virtually unanimous in the belief that breast milk was best for infants. Evidence was overwhelming that breast milk reduced a baby's susceptibility to illnesses such as ear infections and stomach flu and played a positive role in many other ways such as mental and hormonal development.

Why then did so many mothers who gave birth in hospitals choose synthetic baby formula? The reasons were many and varied, including opposition from family and friends, lack of good information, unsympathetic work settings, and reasons of custom and fashion. However, many health professionals believed hospitals undermined breast-feeding by the widespread practice of giving new mothers free formula supplied by formula manufacturers. Research indicated the practice did make a difference. One study at Boston City Hospital, cited in the *Wall Street Journal,* found that 343 low-income women, who received free formula from the hospital, breast-fed their infants for a median duration of 42 days, compared with 60 days for those who received no free formula—a difference of 30 percent. The article concluded with the observation that breast-feeding rates were not much higher than they were ten years ago.

At a joint meeting of the IECs of the three local hospitals, this issue of conflict of interest between formula manufacturers who supplied the free formula and the three hospitals was raised. Presently, all three hospitals accepted free baby formula. One breast-feeding proponent candidly described her suspicion of the close ties between hospitals and formula companies hoping to promote their product. Discussion of the issue by IEC members at this joint meeting resulted in four main options for dealing with the issue: (1) accept no free formula at all despite its availability; (2) give no free formula to those who breast-feed; (3) charge patients a nominal fee for the free formula, so families considered the cost of formula when making the breast-feeding decision; and (4) continue to issue free formula but also distribute information about the benefits of breast-feeding. The four options were not prioritized.

At Mr. Blackwell's request, the IEC of Regional Memorial Hospital met to advise him on a morally justifiable course of action relative to the hospital's free baby formula practice.

Vendor Ethics

Hospitals were not self-sustaining, independent entities. They depended on the goods and services provided by others. These ranged from the rare to the commonplace and included such items as radioactive materials, laboratory testing, security apparatus, laundry services, waste removal, and a vast array of drugs, medicines, and surgical instruments. A current label among health care managers to describe this operation was "outsourcing." All of these goods and services were outsourced by hospitals to vendors. Conflicts of interest involving vendors occurred when the self-interest of employees of the hospital led them to carry out their duties in ways that might not be in the best interest of the patients, health care providers, or the hospital itself.

A leading cause of conflicts of interest between hospitals and vendors was the perk. Promotional perks were marketing incentives provided by vendors to influence the decisions of hospital purchasing agents. So overzealous were some of these marketing practices that the distinction between persuasion and bribery was often blurred.

Vendors offered a wide range of incentives. These included dinners and concerts, trips to resorts, tickets to sporting events, frequent flier miles, use of company planes, free drug samples, and other expensive inducements such as computers, fax machines, and cellular phones. Inexpensive gratuities such as pens, doughnuts, and tee-shirts were standard practice. Employees who defended the practice argued that because health care was an industry, it was unrealistic, if not foolish, to think standard business practices would not come into play. They rejected the argument that perks jeopardized their objectivity and independent judgment. They claimed further that if a conflict did arise, it was invariably transparent and easily managed, so as not to compromise the trust the employee held by virtue of his or her office.

Conversely, the practice of offering gratuities to employees who are responsible for vendor access and sales raised important ethical concerns for hospital administrators. They worried about the real or perceived conflict of interest between the employee working for the overall welfare of the institution and the distracting effect gifts from vendors had on such decisions. One caveat deserved mentioning. This was the mutual need to establish reliable and trustworthy relationships between hospitals and vendors. Hospitals needed to believe that goods ordered from vendors would be delivered on time, in the right way, to the appointed location, and at the agreed-upon price. Conversely, vendors needed to believe that unreasonable demands would not be made, invoices would be paid on time, and company representatives would not be abused but treated in a professional and respectful manner.

The specific issue which brought Mr. Blackwell to the IEC was a rumor he heard and later confirmed. It involved a purchasing agent employed by the hospital. She was responsible for overseeing a fairly extensive landscaping project. The work cost over $100,000 and took a full year to complete. One part of the project involved the purchase and installation of twenty-four Japanese cherry trees. These were ornamental hybrids—*Prunus serrulata*—with a minimum height of 20 feet. The going price for the trees was reported by the agent to be $600 per tree.

On visiting the purchasing agent's home, Blackwell saw firsthand three twenty-foot Japanese cherry trees in the front yard. Somewhat embarrassed by the surprise visit, the agent explained to her CEO that when the nursery learned the agent was relandscaping her property they provided the trees. "It was merely a gesture of goodwill. That's all," the agent explained. Asked if she felt the free trees influenced her choice of nursery for the hospital, she replied: "Absolutely not, I would have chosen Green Thumb Nursery even if they had not given me the trees. I decided objectively. Mr. Blackwell, I know my job and I am always impartial."

Mr. Blackwell's first thoughts were "precedent setting." He knew that his decisions regarding such matters would be the subject of much discussion by a variety of people and indeed set precedent. The purchasing agent had been an excellent employee.

He would refer this case to the IEC for a full, open hearing.

Notes

1. W. H. Shaw, *Business Ethics* (Belmont, California: Wadsworth Publishing Co., 1991), p. 258.
2. R. E. Cranford and A. E. Doudera, "The Emergence of Institutional Ethics Committees," *Proceedings of the American Society of Law and Medicine,* April 1983, p. 13.
3. M. Siegler, "Ethics Committees: Decision by Bureaucracy," *Hastings Center Report* 16 (June/July 1986), pp. 3, 22.

Helicopter Emergency Medical Services at the Medical College of Georgia Hospital and Clinics

Case 9

Introduction

The Medical College of Georgia Hospital and Clinics was the health sciences campus of Georgia located in Augusta. The 590-bed hospital and associated clinics functioned as integral parts of the Medical College of Georgia (MCG) teaching and research programs. The hospital was clearly recognized as a high-quality tertiary-care provider. (A tertiary-care provider was a hospital that provided state-of-the-art subspecialty services, such as neonatal intensive care.)

The city of Augusta was the health care center not only for its metropolitan statistical area (MSA) of 450,000 people, but also for the surrounding predominantly rural area within a 100-mile radius. The MCG Hospital and Clinics, as providers of tertiary care, served an even larger rural area.

University Health, Inc. (UH), a recently reorganized, aggressive, state-of-the-art, 840-bed acute-care hospital with a full range of support services, satellite services, and alternative delivery systems, was the largest inpatient facility in the Augusta MSA. UH also provided some tertiary specialties including neonatal care and the area's only heart transplant program. Augusta's emergency care was coordinated by UH, which also operated the area's predominant ambulance service.

Other area hospitals carved out market niches by serving specialized populations. Humana Hospital, Inc. concentrated on burn care and renal dialysis. St. Joseph's Hospital provided home health services and family-oriented inpatient care. Augusta was also the home of a major military installation that included a regional military referral hospital. In addition, three major Veterans Administration facilities were located in Augusta.

Augusta was a city in which health care was a major industry. Health care providers were major employers and health care topics were covered extensively by the news media. The citizens of Augusta and the surrounding rural areas came to expect exceptional health care services; and despite the apparent abundance of such facilities, most area hospitals operated at high occupancy rates (75 percent to 90 percent). These rates were attributed to population growth in the local area, as well as increasing referrals from the surrounding region.

In June 1985, after tiring of attempts to collaborate with other area hospitals, UH unilaterally started a helicopter emergency medical services (HEMS) program, dubbed Carebird. This move was in character with UH's aggressive posture and heavy involvement in emergency care. Unfortunately for UH, however, only a quarter of the patients transported by helicopter were delivered to its hospital. Most patients transported by helicopter were taken to either MCG Hospital, the area's Level I trauma cen-

This case was prepared by Harry R. Kuniansky and Phil Rutsohn. It is intended as a basis for classroom discussion rather than to illustrate either effective or ineffective handling of an administrative situation. Used with permission from Harry Kuniansky and Phil Rutsohn.

ter, or to Humana Hospital for burn care. Some unfortunate incidents, negative publicity, aircraft vendor problems, and sizable revenue losses prompted UH to discontinue Carebird in November 1987.

In January 1988, UH approached area hospitals (MCG Hospital in particular) with a proposal for a HEMS consortium. Based on lessons learned with Carebird, a restructured HEMS program would apportion program costs based on a given hospital's use of the service. MCG Hospital, as the single largest potential user, was considering UH's proposal.

Helicopters in Health Care

Helicopter use in civilian health care grew out of the heavily publicized successful military experience, especially during the Vietnam era. Because of their effectiveness in reducing mortality, medical specialists began to view helicopters as logical extensions of trauma care programs, especially those serving rural areas where a disproportionately high percentage of trauma injuries occurred.

The first civilian programs were started in the mid-1970s; and now an estimated 150 to 200 programs were in operation, most of which had been established outside of certificate-of-need (CON) legislation. (CON legislation required that institutional capital expenditures that exceeded an established threshold be reviewed by a state agency that had the authority to approve or disapprove the expenditure.) Almost every metropolitan area had a helicopter transport program. Some metropolitan areas had competing programs, and some rural communities had overlapping coverage areas of competing helicopter services.

Safety

Unfortunately, the safety record of HEMS programs was poor. HEMS aircraft experienced thirty times the normal helicopter accident rate and one hundred times the scheduled airline accident rate. In 1986, HEMS aircraft were involved in twenty-one accidents, resulting in eleven deaths. This was not an isolated bad year, but part of a continuing trend, which the industry had not been able to reverse.

Safety became a major industry concern. Television programs such as *60 Minutes* and other media attention made it a public concern as well. A few states, not including Georgia, attempted HEMS regulation through legislation, but most HEMS programs operated in an environment that was minimally regulated by the health care industry and the Federal Aviation Administration (FAA). Indeed, pilot rest requirements were due to be relaxed in the near future.

Meetings of the American Society of Hospital Based Emergency Air Medical Systems (ASHBEAMS) have provided a forum for safety discussions. Data presented at those meetings included the following:

- About 70 percent of fatal accidents resulted from flights at night, in marginal weather, or in unfamiliar terrain, and these were attributed to pilot error.
- The remaining 30 percent of fatal accidents were due to helicopter mechanical problems.

The industry appeared to have concluded that multiple engine helicopters with redundant flight systems were an appropriate safety response. "Pilot error," however, was more difficult to address. The industry suggested:

- setting ceiling and visibility minimums, regardless of the nature of the injury reported;
- placing strict limits on pilot duty time, and requiring at least three pilots per helicopter in seven-day, twenty-four hour programs;
- using only instrument-rated pilots; and
- establishing better criteria for the air versus ground transport decision.

HEMS Benefits

On the positive side, major studies had shown reduced mortality with helicopter-transported patients, especially severely injured or critically ill patients in rural service areas. One study of more than 900 helicopter-transported trauma victims indicated that helicopter transport was essential to the victims' well-being in 14 percent of those cases, helpful in another 13 percent, and not a factor in 57 percent of cases. Despite treatment and transport, 16 percent of the victims died as a result of injuries. Another study found a 39 percent mortality in ground-transported trauma patients compared to a 36 percent mortality in helicopter-transported trauma victims.

Patient Profiles

Various other studies yielded the following:

- Of those transported by helicopter, 60 percent to 75 percent were legitimate traumas or critical illnesses.
- Of those qualifying as legitimate, 75 percent were trauma victims and 25 percent were critically ill patients.
- Only 30 percent of helicopter transports came from accident scenes; the remainder were transports from other hospitals.
- Helicopters seemed most effective within an area farther than twenty miles but less than one hundred miles from the receiving hospital.
- A study of nearly 3,600 helicopter-transported patients indicated the following distribution by diagnostic category:

Diagnostic Category	Number of Patients
Trauma	916
Cardiac	723
Neurologic	407
Neonatal	361
General Surgery	226
Burns	156
Toxic Ingestion	107
OB/GYN	96
Other	600
Total	3,592

Costs

Nationwide, first-year costs for HEMS programs were in the $900,000 to $2 million range. Thereafter, continuing annual costs ranged from $700,000 to $1.6 million. Costs usually included operation and maintenance of one helicopter, pilots, flight nurses, dispatchers, administrative personnel, and some flight physician expenses.

Many options existed to configure a one-aircraft operation. The institution could (1) purchase or lease the aircraft, contract for aviation management services, and provide its own medical staff; (2) do the same, except hire the aviation management expertise from another operating system; (3) contract for the aircraft and aviation management services and provide its own medical staff; or (4) contract for a complete turnkey operation, including flight and medical service.

Most not-for-profit institutions opted for an agreement in which the contractor provided the aircraft, pilots, maintenance, and aviation management. Most vendors of this type of contract provided backup aircraft availability as a bonus. These vendors usually did not compete based on price but rather on services offered. Most were regional companies that also provided other commercial helicopter services. Exhibit 9–1 shows national average vendor prices for three basic helicopter types. Other costs for helicopter programs are shown in Exhibit 9–2.

Reimbursement

Medicare and Medicaid currently reimbursed at the ground ambulance rate of $125 for critical-care transports plus a mileage rate of $1.50 per mile to the county line. No major carrier had established a rate for reimbursement for helicopter services. Most commercial third-party payors would reimburse part of the cost of helicopter transport under major medical, if the treating physician stated that the helicopter was medically necessary. These claims were handled on a case-by-case basis and reimbursement was not consistent.

No program currently in operation was breaking even. Revenues generated by patient transport did not cover the fixed and variable operating costs. Programs generally covered only 30 percent to 50 percent of operating costs from individual and third-party payments. Most programs considered the marginal inpatient revenues from new inpatient stays in their cost/benefit assessments because these "new captures" were patients who probably would not have been inpatients at the current institution if not for the helicopter system.

Carebird

In June 1985, UH made the unilateral decision to begin a trial program, which meant accepting all

Exhibit 9–1 • **Typical Helicopter Costs**

	Helicopter Categories		
Options	*Single-Engine Light*	*Twin-Engine Light*	*Twin-Engine Medium*
Purchase	$350,000	$800,000	$1,500,000
Lease Monthly	29,500	37,500	56,000
Lease Hourly (per flight hour)	300	305	415
Fuel (per hour)	40	50	50

Exhibit 9–2 • **Other Associated Program Costs**

Helipad	$10,000
Communications	1,000
Staff*	
5 EFT RN @ .70 Time	93,000
5 EFT EMT @ .70 Time	66,500
1 EFT Secretary	13,500
0.5 EFT Management	12,500
Fringe Benefits	25% of staff costs
Indirect Costs	25% of staff costs
Ground Transport (per trip)	$25

*EFT = Equivalent Full Time; RN = Registered Nurse; EMT = Emergency Medical Technician

risks and potential rewards. Metro Air Ambulance from Atlanta (approximately 150 miles from Augusta) offered UH a ninety-day free trial. Metro provided the helicopter, crew, and flight service, and UH provided medical flight personnel. Dispatching and medical ground control were provided through UH's emergency room.

The ninety-day trial was deemed a success, and Carebird began operations. Through October 1986, 958 missions involving approximately 2,000 flight hours were completed. Pertinent information concerning Carebird missions is shown in Exhibit 9–3. Of those transported, 59 percent went to MCG Hospital, 25 percent to UH, 14 percent to Humana Hospital, and the remaining 2 percent to other area hospitals.

For comparison, experience from other MSAs in the region is shown in Exhibit 9–4. Although a sin-

gle helicopter could approach 700 flights per year, the national average is 1.5 flights per day. One major provider of helicopter services estimated annual usage at thirty flights per 100,000 people within a 100-mile radius. The reimbursement history of the program is shown in Exhibit 9–5.

Carebird was staffed by one full-time pilot twenty-four hours a day. He was occasionally relieved by another pilot from the Metro base. The service utilized a Bell Jet-Ranger helicopter. Medical staffing was provided by the EMT at the scene of the accident or the first available EMT was picked up by the pilot from a ground ambulance.

Several articles were written in the local newspaper concerning the appropriate use of the helicopter for transportation of patients. Some articles were negative, emphasizing safety problems and the fact

Exhibit 9–3 • **Carebird Trips**

Year	No. of Trips	Annualized
1985 (24 weeks)	166	360
1986 (52 weeks)	425	425
1987 (42 weeks)	367	454

Types of patients transported by Carebird were as follows:

Diagnostic Category	Percent of Total Patients
Trauma	40
Cardiovascular	20
Burns	14
Neonates	8
Other	18

Exhibit 9–4 • **Air Ambulance Service Growth Rate**

	Jacksonville	Atlanta	Memphis	Pensacola
First three months' flights	110	39	48	50
First six months' flights	256	107	140	128
First full year's flights	633	304	306	366
Second full year's flights	755	420	450	630
Population within 50 miles	750,000	2,000,000	1,000,000	400,000
Population within 100 miles	1,000,000	3,000,000	1,500,000	750,000

Exhibit 9–5 • **Carebird Financial Review**

	1985	1986	1987
Charges			
Air ambulance charges	$143,143	$331,857	$514,870
Supply charges	7,006	15,454	25,272
Total	$150,149	$347,311	$540,142
Receipts			
Paid by third party	$75,027	$134,971	$84,205
Paid by guarantor	6,899	18,654	7,035
Payment expected from third party or guarantor	0	23,027	328,357
Public relations (nonbillable)	10,282	5,068	947
Total	$92,208	$181,720	$420,544
Bad debt	$57,941	$165,591	$119,598

that ground ambulances were more efficient; and some were positive, pointing out that lives were saved by the rapid transportation provided by the helicopter.

In late 1987, plagued by operational problems, negative publicity, a deteriorating relationship with Metro, and sizable financial losses, the contract with Metro was terminated after proper notice. Since then, the Augusta MSA and surrounding rural areas have been without local medical helicopter services.

Medical College of Georgia

The MCG Hospital was exclusively controlled by MCG and the State University System of Georgia. The MCG Hospital and Clinics mission was to support the MCG mission, which included teaching, research, patient care, and community (state) service.

MCG Clinics accommodated 225,000 visits per year. The MCG Hospital was a modern 590-bed tertiary-care facility with an overall occupancy rate of 84 percent. Of the 590-bed total, 50 beds were configured for intensive or trauma care. Those beds had an occupancy rate of 91 percent. The average length of stay for all MCG patients was 7.8 days. The average length of stay for trauma victims was nearly fourteen days. MCG was a relatively high-cost provider,

with daily inpatient variable costs of $300. Charges per inpatient day were approximately $800. The collection rate for all patients was 66 percent of charges.

The MCG emergency services volume had increased steadily over the past few years. This was attributed to a combination of population growth, increased emphasis on emergency medicine teaching programs, and designation as the area Level I trauma center. Trauma cases currently arrived at MCG via ground transport.

The MCG Hospital and Clinics strategic plan for the next three to five years called for increased emphasis on ambulatory care, emergency care, intensive care, and the care of children. New facilities were now being designed to increase the number of trauma/intensive-care beds and to supplement corresponding ancillary and support services. Expanded teaching programs in emergency medicine were planned to coincide with facility improvements.

MCG was also becoming more concerned with its community image as competition for paying and tertiary-care patients increased. Planners at MCG were examining the UH HEMS proposal. Assuming that dispatching continued from UH, planners estimated HEMS nonflight costs as shown in Exhibit 9–6.

Exhibit 9–6 • HEMS Nonflight Cost Estimates

Helipad	$10,000
Communications	1,000
Staffing*	
3.5 EFT RN (5 @ .70 time)	93,000
3.5 EFT EMT	66,500
1.0 EFT Secretary	13,500
0.5 EFT Management	12,500
	185,500
Fringe Benefits	46,375
Indirect Costs	46,375
Total Annual Hospital Costs	$289,250

* EFT = Equivalent Full Time; RN = Registered Nurse;
EMT = Emergency Medical Technician

Area Outlook

Exhibits 9–7 and 9–8 provide population data and projections for the Augusta MSA. The Augusta health care service area included another twenty-one counties outside the MSA with an additional 500,000 persons, based on 1985 estimates.

The Decision

Barbara Hoskens, vice president for hospital services for MCG, was contemplating a plan submitted by Darren Whitten of UH, which proposed a cost-shar-ing consortium of area hospitals to support restarting helicopter emergency medical services in Augusta. The anticipated service would be similar operationally to Carebird with ground medical control provided by UH's emergency room. Two notable differences from the previous Carebird situation would be the cost sharing among hospitals and the use of a twin-engine helicopter to improve safety and increase range and capacity.

Whitten believed time to be of the essence and requested that MCG Hospital along with the other area hospitals respond to the proposal within sixty days.

Exhibit 9–7 • **Population Data, December 31, 1987**

	Population	Percent of U.S. Pop.	Pop./Sq. Mi. (Density)	Household Total	Percent of U.S. Households
Total	378,700	.1571	193	133,300	.1508
County A	190,700	.0791	585	65,100	.0736
County B	53,100	.0220	183	18,100	.0205
County C	115,000	.0477	105	43,100	.0488
County D	19,900	.0083	78	7,000	.0079

Exhibit 9–8 • **MSA Population Trends/Projections**

Year	Augusta	County A	County B	County C	County D	MSA Total*
1980	47,532	181,629	40,118	105,625	18,546	345,918
1988	49,147	208,390	59,164	118,278	20,621	406,453
1990	—	207,884	62,116	130,000	21,511	421,511
2000	—	237,160	88,153	150,000	24,088	499,401

*1980 Census data with estimates by Augusta Planning Commission.

Merck & Company, Inc., 1994

Major changes occurred at Merck in 1994. Under a new chief executive officer (CEO), Merck attempted to transform itself into a truly globally competitive pharmaceutical company. Although global growth had been one of Merck's goals, it was now becoming the centerpiece of its strategy. In addition, Merck reexamined its business concept and made significant changes in its product mix but retained its strong commitment to innovation. Along with these changes the company embarked on a wide-ranging alignment of its operations, systems, and structure. Merck was intent on thriving, despite its increasingly hostile competitive environment.

Intense competition and unfavorable governmental interventions caused Merck to lose its seven-year standing as "America's Most Admired Corporation." This coveted title signified the U.S. leading executives' admiration of Merck's financial position, commitment to social responsibility, and dedication to innovation. Every year, *Fortune* magazine conducted a survey of the largest 500 U.S. industrial corporations. And, for seven consecutive years, Merck emerged as the leading company of this venerable group of corporations. However, when the 1994 results were announced, Merck was rated eleventh.[1]

This case was developed by Patricia H. Zahra, consultant, and Shaker A. Zahra, Georgia State University. It was prepared as a basis for class discussion rather than to illustrate effective or ineffective handling of an administrative situation. © 1994 Shaker A. Zahra. Used with permission.

The *Fortune* magazine rating of Merck, although still respectable, reflected the tough time the company and its industry were experiencing. The growth of generic-drug makers affected Merck and its operations. Further, similar to other pharmaceutical companies, Merck had come under public attack as a major cause for the high cost of the nation's health care system. Merck responded to the high drug prices by providing discounts and starting voluntary price restraints. Merck was able to provide the public with price reductions while still maintaining the needed revenue for its research and development for new, breakthrough drugs.

In July 1993, Merck's biggest change was the acquisition of Medco Containment Services, Inc., an unregulated, mail-order distributor of discount prescription drugs. This was a totally new direction for Merck. The company's management hoped to coordinate the objectives and expertise of both companies to provide a drug delivery system that would further reduce costs while maintaining patient care and satisfaction.

Merck's leadership was also undergoing significant change. The president and CEO, P. Roy Vagelos, M.D., was about to retire. He had been the key element for the firm in his vision and in his ability to lead Merck's research and development to produce a phenomenal number of innovative drugs in the 1980s and early 1990s. The board's chosen successor was recruited from outside the company. The new president would bring a new perspective.

History[2]

Merck started as a small, family apothecary in Darmstadt, Germany in 1668. After 150 years the Merck family decided to transform the business from a pharmacy to a manufacturer of its own drugs. In 1827, the Merck factory opened its own operations to manufacture its first drug. By 1887, Merck started a small manufacturing branch in New York to begin competing in the U.S. market. Before long, the Merck & Company partnership was formed. Shortly thereafter, in 1903, Merck set up its manufacturing operations of drugs and specialty chemicals in Rahway, New Jersey (the current corporate headquarters). By 1908, Merck & Co. was incorporated in New York, and in 1919 it sold its first public stock.

Although Merck continued to grow in its manufacturing expertise, a competitor close by, Sharp and Dohme, was concentrating on the research for new drugs. Seeing the advantage of putting their expertise together, the two companies merged in 1953. The new company quickly became known for its excellent research and development (R&D) and manufacturing of drugs and specialty chemicals. Merck grew and expanded into new areas and new markets throughout the United States. However, during the past ten years, Merck expanded its operations outside the United States. Merck defined its business as "a worldwide organization engaged primarily in the business of discovering, developing, producing and marketing products and services for the maintenance or restoration of health."[3]

Industry Segments and Products

Merck's business was divided into two industry segments: human and animal health products and services and specialty chemical products. Exhibit 10–1 shows the distribution of sales between the two segments. As Exhibit 10–1 shows, the majority of

Exhibit 10–1 • **Consolidated Sales (dollars in millions)**

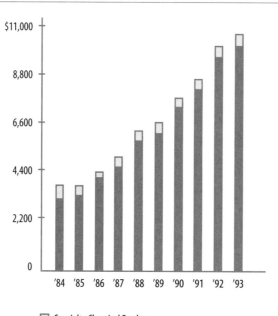

☐ Specialty Chemical Products

■ Human and Animal Health Products and Services

Merck's sales were derived from its human and animal health products and services segment.

Specialty Chemical Products

This area consisted of two divisions—Kelco and Calgon Vestal Laboratories. Kelco was the world's largest manufacturer and marketer of a variety of alginates and biogums. These ingredients had a wide range of applications in health care, food processing, oil exploration, paper, textiles, and personal care. One of Kelco's standard products was a xanthan gum that could be used as a fat-replacing ingredient for the healthy foods market. A new, gellan gum (gelling agent) improved the flavor and texture of a variety of foods. Because of the growing segment of health-conscious individuals, in 1993 Kelco entered the new field of nutraceuticals (nutrition and good health) involving food ingredients that contributed to personal health.

Merck's second division was Calgon Vestal Laboratories, which provided patient skin care products (primarily sold to hospitals and nursing homes) as well as wound management products. Recently, Calgon Vestal introduced new wound management products to existing international markets. Calgon Vestal was also expanding its core alginate products to Europe and Asia. In the 1990s, several new products were introduced to the market. Helistat was an absorbable collagen sponge for use in surgical procedures. Kaltostat was a calcium sodium alginate wound dressing that would be expanded to hospitals and long-term-care facilities. A new technology called Ozone was used to launch a new line of products: Geo-Guard, an environmentally sound water treatment alternative; Algistat, a U.K.-produced alginate for use in surgical procedures; and Vesta-Syde, a decontamination system for instruments used in the operating room.

Distribution of products and services in the specialty chemical products segment was made to industrial users, health care providers, distributors, municipalities, and utilities. The two divisions were successful in their operations. In 1993, Merck made the decision to sell its Calgon Water Management Division in order to concentrate on its core health care businesses.

Human and Animal Health Products

Merck's growth and financial success was due primarily to its human and animal health products. The product portfolio includes sixteen products in nineteen therapeutic categories that exceeded $100 million in annual sales.[4]

Exhibit 10–2 shows the overall distribution of Merck's human and animal health products as a percent of sales.

Merck's most recent product breakthrough came in 1992 with the introduction of Proscar. It

Exhibit 10–2 • **Overall Distribution of Human and Animal Health Products**

Products	Percent of Sales
Cardiovasculars	48.3
Anti-ulcerants	13.2
Antibiotics	8.7
Vaccines/biologicals	5.2
Ophthalmologicals	4.5
Anti-inflammatories/analgesics	3.4
Other human health	4.5
Other Medco sales	3.0
Animal health/crop protection	9.2
	100.0

Source: Annual Report 1993, p. 3.

was the first drug for the treatment of symptomatic benign prostate enlargement—a condition that was prevalent among the aging male population. Proscar was now available in fifty countries with annual sales exceeding $100 million and rising. Proscar was so promising that additional research was under way to determine if it could be used for the prevention of prostate cancer.

Two of Merck's prescription drugs continued to be leading products in their categories. Mevacor was used for the treatment of high cholesterol. There were an estimated 60 million people with high cholesterol who were yet untreated and targeted for Mevacor usage. In 1993, Mevacor experienced slower growth because of competition. However, the annual sales for Mevacor exceeded $1 billion. Mevacor's companion drug was Zocor, the second cholesterol-lowering agent. Zocor's annual sales were between $500 million and $1 billion. Together, these two drugs had a 40 percent share of the worldwide market.

The second leading drug was Vasotec, considered to be the world's leading brand in the cardiovascular market. Vasotec was used in the treatment of high blood pressure and all stages of symptomatic heart failure. Recently, the Food and Drug Administration (FDA) approved Vasotec for expanded use as a preventive measure for decreasing the rate of development of possible heart failure. Vasotec's annual sales were over $1 billion. Merck produced a similar drug, Prinivil, that was also used for reducing high blood pressure.

Two of Merck's health products targeted the gastrointestinal market. Pepcid and Prilosec were widely used to treat ulcers and gastroesophageal reflux disease. Pepcid was licensed to Merck by a Japanese company, and Prilosec was licensed by AB Astra of Sweden. Each product ranged from $500 million to $1 billion in annual sales. A similar formulation of Pepcid was used in one of Merck's newest over-the-counter (OTC) drugs, Pepcid AC. Although a new drug application was filed with the FDA in the United States in 1993 to market this product, Pepcid AC sales were launched in the United Kingdom in February 1994.

Merck's many products remained very strong in their highly competitive markets. Ongoing research and clinical studies promised to produce additional new drugs. In 1993, Merck received U.S. market clearance for Timoptic-XE, a once-a-day treatment for elevated intraocular pressure associated with glaucoma. It had been cleared for use in several countries. Two drugs, Fosamax, for the prevention and treatment of osteoporosis, and Vaqta, a vaccine for the prevention of hepatitis A infection, were being clinically tested for human use. In addition, applications were pending at the FDA for Cozaar, a daily therapy for high blood pressure and heart failure; Trusopt, the first topical treatment for elevated intraocular pressure associated with glaucoma; and Varivax, a vaccine for the prevention of chicken pox.

Merck's quality drugs and innovative products extended to animal health, crop protection, and poultry genetics through Merck AgVet. The introduction of many of Merck AgVet's products into other countries led to their prominence worldwide. For example, Paraban, a new computer modeling program, was introduced in South America in 1992. Paraban assists veterinarians and cattle producers in controlling parasites. Thus, Merck AgVet's sales force was able to tailor the program to fit an individual customer's needs in animal management while controlling for local climate conditions. Since its introduction, Paraban's use was expanded to include the United States, France, Spain, and New Zealand. The product was introduced in Germany and Canada in 1994.

Merck AgVet also included products for domestic animals. For instance, Enacard was a new therapeutic breakthrough for the treatment of heart failure in dogs. It was marketed in the United States, the United Kingdom, Ireland, Australia, Canada, and The Netherlands. The company also had an active crop protection program. It established the resistance management program to help crop growers fight the resistance developed by specific pests over time.

Distribution for Merck's human health products included drug wholesalers and retailers, hospitals, managed-care providers, government agencies, and other health care institutions. The animal health segment distributed its products to veterinarians, feed manufacturers, veterinary suppliers, and laboratories, as well as general wholesalers and retailers.[5]

Management

From the time he became CEO in 1985, P. Roy Vagelos helped to propel Merck to becoming one of the premier pharmaceutical companies. Through his vision as a research scientist, Vagelos made R&D Merck's number one priority. Vagelos continued the philosophy of George W. Merck that "medicine is for the patient . . . . It is not for the profits."[6] During his tenure as CEO, Vagelos increased R&D yearly while decentralizing the R&D management. Researchers were given autonomy to pursue their investigations. Vagelos also organized the different units into project teams that focused around specific disease targets or compounds to better enable researchers to discover new drugs. Vagelos stayed in touch and close to Merck's scientists and researchers. In doing so, he was able to create programs and provide them with incentives to achieve their best performance.

In the early 1990s, Vagelos knew that in addition to the changes in the pharmaceutical industry, the nation's health care system was under scrutiny and future reform was needed. Although maintaining a strong R&D, Vagelos knew that aggressive marketing was necessary. As a result, at the time he announced his retirement plans, Vagelos named his heir-apparent. On December 16, 1992, Richard J. Markham, a marketing executive, was chosen and accepted the CEO position. However, on July 9, 1993, he abruptly resigned, leaving the company in turmoil. For a while, it appeared as though there would be no successor for the person whose vision had made Merck the biggest pharmaceutical company in the world.

About six months later, the group of outside directors on Merck's board took control and set out to find Vagelos's replacement after his retirement in November 1994. Raymond V. Gilmartin was chosen to be the new CEO of Merck—the first outsider to hold this position in 103 years.

Mr. Gilmartin's background was interesting. He was an electrical engineer with an MBA from Harvard. He had no drug industry experience and no scientific credentials. Gilmartin's last position was CEO of Becton Dickinson & Co., a medium-sized manufacturer of medical equipment. Because of pricing pressures and restructuring in the 1980s, Gilmartin was able to turn a struggling Becton Dickinson around to a sound, profitable company. Gilmartin had proven himself to be a strategic thinker and an effective cost-cutter. He was skilled in dealing with people through team building and leading by consensus.[7] Similar to Vagelos, Gilmartin should be able to lead and work with the employees and guide Merck into a new era of the managed-care world.

Other members of Merck's management team made decisions to leave the company. Prior to the appointment of Mr. Gilmartin, John L. Zabriskie, executive vice president of Merck, took another position. Effective January 1994 he was named chairman and CEO of Upjohn Co.[8] In addition, Cecil B. Pickett, former senior vice president of Merck's Canadian research laboratory left the company. He became executive vice president in charge of research at Schering-Plough Corp.[9] Richard J. Markham, Dr. Vagelos's original choice to head Merck, joined Marion Merrell Dow as president and COO.[10]

Research and Development

R&D had been the centerpiece of Merck's strategy. With its aggressive R&D, Merck was able to provide new innovative products for cures and improvements in human and animal health. Merck's research strategy was "characterized by strong investments in programs, people and technology."[11] R&D was so important for Merck that Vagelos himself traveled to the best schools and universities to recruit the best people.

Merck's long-term goal was to perform the highest quality research for every major disease. However, discovering cures for present-day diseases was very difficult, time consuming, and costly. After a potential cure was found, the task was still not complete. To commercialize the drug, especially in the United States, a lengthy process of clinical work was needed to prove that the drug was safe and effective for human use. Once this was accomplished and approval granted by the FDA, then, and only then, could the drug be released to the market. This arduous R&D process required large financial resources.

Merck accomplished this by investing in research and first-rate R&D facilities. In 1993, Merck spent almost $1.2 billion in R&D. The company planned to spend more than $1.3 billion in 1994. As noted in Exhibit 10–3, Merck had a long history of high R&D expenditures, with the goal of making research its principal source of growth.[12]

As noted, Merck invested a large amount of capital in its R&D facilities. In the United States alone, Merck completed a new research building in West Point, Pennsylvania in 1993. There were three more facilities under construction: a small-scale organic pilot plant in Rahway, New Jersey, and two biological support laboratories (one in Pennsylvania and one in New Jersey). There were additional research facilities located around the globe. A major facility was located in Japan with plans for an additional plant. There was a research building in Italy in conjunction with its joint venture. Merck had also expanded its Canadian research laboratory to make it the largest biomedical facility in Canada.

When Merck began its in-depth research for drugs to help prevent and cure major human diseases, it started in the field of chemistry looking for compounds and solutions to defeat the causes of these diseases. As science and technology advanced, it became apparent that the search for new drugs would fall into the area of biomedical/biotechnology research. To remain at the forefront with its research capabilities and to continue to recruit and maintain some of the world's top scientists, Merck had to move into the most modern areas of research. Merck's R&D activities were enhanced to cover all areas of research including biotechnology, molecular biology, high-resolution nuclear magnetic resonance, X-ray crystallography, and molecular modeling.[13]

Merck's R&D achievements were outstanding. For instance, in 1989, Merck was the first to identify the HIV-1 protease enzyme that targeted AIDS; and they solved the structure of the enzyme that produced the virus.[14] Merck entered its protease inhibitor in early clinical trials in 1993. Thus, Merck might be the first to develop a new drug for the treatment of AIDS. Another example of Merck's most recent research developments was its identification of small molecules in the treatment of human growth hormone deficiency. This research might lead to developments in the treatment of growth in children and

Exhibit 10–3 • R&D Expenditures

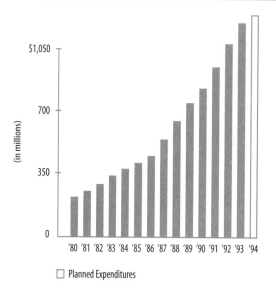

☐ Planned Expenditures

Source: Annual Report 1993.

adults, burn patients, and patients with bone fractures such as the elderly.

Advertising

Recently, Merck altered its advertising techniques. In the past, Merck concentrated most of its efforts on direct, personal contact with the health care physician. With the rise of managed-care organizations, such as health maintenance organizations (HMOs), and the fact that the average person was becoming more health-conscious and taking more responsibility for their own health, Merck had to rethink its strategies. Although FDA regulations for advertisements was very strict and detailed, Merck expanded its coverage to include pharmaceutical ads directed to the individual consumer. Merck's newest drugs, Proscar and Mevacor, were now being advertised in popular magazines to be read directly by the customer.

Also, because of its highly competitive environment and the onslaught of generic drugs, Merck improved its advertising. Not only was their sales force highly trained, each salesperson was given a laptop computer that provided the technical and health information necessary to discuss the company's drugs with the physicians.

Back in 1887, Merck developed *Merck's Bulletin*, the first of many publications throughout the years to provide technical information to its customers. Over the years and many updates later, the company finally put together the *Merck Manual*, which still exists. It provided technical information on Merck's drugs in addition to the signs and symptoms of most diseases. The *Merck Manual* was found in many homes as well as on the physician's bookshelf. It also was available on the Franklin Digital Book System.[15]

International—Foreign Sales

Merck successfully marketed its products around the globe. In addition to the United States, Western European and Japanese markets added substantially to Merck's business. In competing in foreign markets, Merck contended with currency fluctuations and local government regulations that differed greatly from those in the United States. The main strategy for dealing with other governments was to provide assurance that the drug was considered safe and effective for human use. Merck had been successful in dealing with foreign governments in manufacturing and marketing its products.

With the opening of Eastern Europe and the Commonwealth of Independent States, new markets were available. To prepare for these opportunities Merck opened offices in the Czech Republic, Hungary, Poland, Russia, Slovakia, the Ukraine, and Uzbekistan. In addition, Merck expanded in Latin America, the Pacific Rim, and the Middle East. Plans were to open new operations in China, Mexico, Taiwan, and Turkey.[16]

Strategic Alliances

To maintain its position as one of the world's leading pharmaceutical companies, Merck benefited greatly from its strategic alliances. Merck pursued a two-prong worldwide strategy: a strong commitment to internal discovery and development programs and external alliances to expand its research capabilities.

In 1989, Merck and Du Pont joined equally to form the Du Pont Merck Pharmaceutical Company providing research and drugs in several therapeutic classes including heart disease, cancer, and AIDS. Du Pont Merck marketed pharmaceutical and imaging agent products in eighty countries. The company itself continued to grow by having licensing agreements with Merck to have the marketing rights to five products in France, Germany, Italy, Spain, and the United Kingdom. In 1991, Du Pont Merck opened a subsidiary in Italy, and in 1992, it opened another subsidiary in Spain. Then, in 1993, the company received marketing rights to a brain-imaging agent in several European countries and Japan. Du Pont Merck underscored its long-term commitment to R&D by reinvesting 30 percent of its sales back into research. After only three years of operations, Du Pont Merck was listed among the *Fortune 500* companies.

In 1989, Merck formed a new business named Merck Consumer Healthcare Group. This business formed a joint venture with Johnson & Johnson (J&J) to provide OTC drugs in the United States and Europe. Merck provided the prescription drugs, and

J&J provided the sales and marketing expertise. By 1993, the joint venture became the leader in OTC medicines. Mylanta, purchased from ICI Americas Inc., became the leader in the antacid market in the United States. The company became the leader for an ibuprofen brand analgesic in Germany, and it had the second largest market share in Spain of an OTC product for coughs and colds.

Another successful strategic alliance was with AB Astra, a Swedish pharmaceutical company. AB Astra and Merck had worked together since 1982. Merck was marketing three of Astra's products in the United States. According to their agreement, if sales reached a certain level by December 31, 1993, a new, separate entity would be formed in which Merck would have the U.S. rights to the products currently licensed from Astra as well as most research discoveries. The annual sales topped the agreed limit in July 1993. The Astra-related business was expected to be transferred to the United States by 1995 to open a new joint venture. Astra had the right to purchase 50 percent of the venture, if it chose under agreed-upon terms and conditions.

Merck engaged in other strategic alliances. A joint venture was formed with Sigma Tau, the leading Italian pharmaceutical company, to do research on viral diseases. An agreement was reached with a competitor, SmithKline Beecham, to jointly promote Zocor (the cholesterol-lowering drug) in the United States. The new Proscar drug was already licensed to Japanese firms. In January 1994, a joint venture was formed with Tularik Inc. to research a remedy to deter the progress of several sexually transmitted viruses.[17] By October 1994, Merck and Pasteur Merieux Serums et Vaccins received approval from the European Commission to form a joint venture in Europe. This new entity would be working to develop a "super cocktail" of vaccines for children.[18] Merck was already working with Merieux's U.S. affiliate, Connaught, to conduct further R&D on new combinations of pediatric vaccines for marketing in the United States. These and other strategic alliances gave Merck access to new markets and new technologies.

Merck was very successful in developing new and innovative drugs that were extremely costly and took years to develop into a marketable product. However, patents for some of these drugs were due to expire soon, allowing competitors to imitate and market "me too" drugs. In addition, there was an ever-increasing number of companies producing generic drugs that competed directly with existing brand-name drugs. In response, Merck decided to establish a generic arm with the West Point Pharma Division to enter this market segment. In addition, Du Pont Merck recently formed Endo Laboratories to research, manufacture, and distribute generic drugs.

The most surprising step made by Merck over the years was the acquisition of Medco Containment Services, Inc., an unregulated, mail-order distributor of discount prescription drugs. Merck had always been known for its R&D of new, high-margin prescription drugs. Medco was, however, a purely marketing company and one that appealed to the cost conscious. Merck saw this as an opportunity to sell its products directly to major employers in managed-care plans. Medco's database of prescription drugs at the time of the acquisition was 95 million prescription drugs per year (used by 33 million people). This would give Merck the revenue-raising opportunities while maintaining its long-term focus on conducting R&D for new prescription drugs. Because this strategy was such a complete shift from what Merck had done over its long history, there were some difficult issues that needed to be addressed. Could Merck successfully merge two companies with such distinct visions, strategies, and cultures? Prior to the acquisition, Medco was always able to persuade drugmakers to give their lowest possible prices on their drugs so Medco could pass those savings on to their customers. Would this be a conflict of interest in the merger of the two companies?

Organization and Structure

With the company's domestic and international expansion, Merck determined that restructuring was needed. Merck moved from a centralized, bureaucratic organization to a decentralized structure. The major emphasis was on decentralizing R&D management. Therefore, the R&D function was broken into project teams organized around specific disease targets or compounds, gaining more autonomy for the researchers.

Merck combined its chemical manufacturing division and its pharmaceutical manufacturing division (thirty-one plants) into one global organization, known as the Merck Manufacturing Division. Merck consolidated its U.S. and international marketing into the Merck Human Health Division to develop the strongest marketing strategies worldwide. A new Merck Vaccine Division was established to seek growth opportunities through internal R&D for new vaccines.

In addition, as mentioned previously, a new division—West Point Pharma—was created to market generic versions of widely used products. In 1994, Merck decided to increase their sales of low-priced, generic copies of several brand-name drugs from other companies.

Manufacturing and Operations

Merck continued to invest in its manufacturing capabilities. Its facilities were computer-integrated to streamline operations and to become more cost effective. Merck installed automated lines using robotics and intelligent vision systems. The sensors in these systems ensured the reliability of drugs being produced. Merck used an information system that allowed it to employ computer modeling in the development of its drugs.

To maintain its long-term focus on discovering new drugs, Merck invested $1.0 billion in capital expenditures in 1993, compared to $1.1 billion in 1992, and $1.0 billion in 1991. Of these expenditures $759.7 million in 1993 and $784.0 million in 1992 were in the United States. The 1993 capital expenditures were allocated to support the focus on new drugs: $260.1 million for R&D facilities; $218.5 million for production facilities; $136.5 million for safety and environmental projects; and $397.6 million for administrative and general site projects. Capital expenditures of $79.3 million were incurred by Merck's joint ventures that were not included in the above figure.[19]

Employees

Merck continued to recruit the best people believing that they were what made the company maintain its competitive edge and allowed it to compete globally. Merck recruited successfully on college campuses. In 1993, Merck hired more than 400 graduates; 50 percent were women and 26 percent were members of minority groups.[20] Currently, Merck had 48,700 employees (38,400 originally from Merck and 10,300 employees from Medco).

Merck had several programs that helped to attract the most talented employees and provide them with incentives. For example, Merck emphasized pay-for-performance in its compensation programs. In addition, Merck increased the number of employees who were eligible to participate in their compensation programs that provided cash awards and stock options. A World-Shares Stock Option Program, started in 1991, granted employees around the world an option to buy 300 shares of Merck stock.[21] This was part of an ongoing program to increase employee ownership in Merck and to better align employee interests with those of the company's other shareholders.

Merck set up a work-family benefit program that included job sharing. In addition, Merck completed one on-site child-care center for its employees. Merck was well known for providing employment to the disabled. It had a special task force that ensured that the company complied with all aspects of the Americans with Disabilities Act.[22]

Due to restructuring and emphasis on cost containment, Merck offered its employees a voluntary retirement program in the areas of the company where this was necessary. The program made it possible for Merck to achieve its goal without adversely affecting its human resources.

Health Care Reform

With rising costs, limited resources, and the growing number of individuals unable to get needed health care, the federal government and the private sector explored ways to reform the nation's health care system. Merck was actively involved from the outset in deciding what changes would be beneficial for everyone concerned. The rising costs of prescription drugs was a major item to be addressed because it affected the pharmaceutical industry.

As early as 1990, Merck started the Equal Access to Medicines Program in several states. This program helped reduce the cost of drugs by giving the best price discounts to state Medicaid programs in exchange for patient access to all of Merck's products.[23] In addition, Merck proposed a voluntary price restraint program on its products. The company had not increased its product prices on a weighted average basis beyond the Consumer Price Index in the past three years. Even by doing this, Merck was aware that cost constraints enforced by a governmental agency could reduce the company R&D expenditures. In the long term, this would adversely affect the search for medicines and cures of some of the most devastating diseases. Merck, therefore, believed that, "any reform effort must rest on four critical 'cornerstones.' Namely: broadening patient access, protecting America's unmatched capability for medical innovation, rationally managing costs, and maintaining the high quality of medical care."[24]

Merck believed restraining costs through governmental reform would ultimately jeopardize the necessary R&D to develop new drugs. Instead, Merck believed that cost constraints could be managed effectively through the market system. This allowed costs of prescription drugs to remain low and still provided for the needed revenue to undertake quality R&D to discover new drugs.

Merck's managers believed that prescription drugs that either prevented or cured existing diseases ultimately brought down the total cost to the consumer; they either did not get the disease, or did not require as extensive a treatment program because the disease was less severe. Thus, medical science and cost management could coexist. One example was the acquisition of Medco, where Merck integrated all the components of providing optimum health care and meeting cost constraints.

Financial Performances

Merck did well financially in 1993. As Exhibit 10–4 illustrates, total sales increased 9 percent from 1992, which was down by 3 percent from the growth from 1991 to 1992. This reduction in sales growth was affected by the acquisition of Medco Containment Services, Inc. and the divestiture of the Calgon Water Management business.

In human and animal health products and services, sales grew 10 percent. Merck's strongest performing products were Vasotec, Mevacor, Zocor, Pepcid, and other drugs such as vaccines. Merck's newest drug, Proscar, did not do as well as projected. Still, it did well for the first year, and predictions indicated expanded use in the future. Merck's older and more mature drugs continued to generate strong revenues. Their unit volumes declined, primarily because of fierce competition from generic drugs.

The sales in the specialty chemical products segment declined by 14 percent. This was directly due to the sale of the Calgon Water Management business. If this transaction was excluded, sales in this segment showed an increase of 6 percent over 1992.

Overall, Merck's domestic sales grew 17 percent. If the acquisition of Medco was excluded, sales would be up 11 percent. Foreign sales were done pri-

Exhibit 10–4 • **Sales by Industry Segment (dollars in millions)**

	1991	1992	1993
Human and Animal Health	$ 8,019.5	$ 9,067.6	$ 9,987.9
Specialty Chemical	583.2	594.9	510.3
Total	$ 8,602.7	$ 9,662.5	$10,498.2

Source: Annual Report 1993, p. 34.

marily through subsidiaries. Because of the strong U.S. dollar, foreign sales in 1993 were reduced by two percentage points. However, there was a 3 percent growth for the year.

Exhibit 10–5 presents Merck's sales by geographic segment over the past three years. Due to poor economic conditions and difficult governmental policies, Merck had to divest or restructure its facilities in some foreign countries. The company, therefore, pursued its business interests in countries where they earned at least a fair market return.

Exhibit 10–6 shows a good, overall picture of the consolidated sales comparing domestic and foreign sales from the year 1984 through 1993. Overall sales increased substantially over this ten-year period. As displayed, foreign sales remained about 50 percent of the total sales.

The next three Exhibits (10–7, 10–8, and 10–9) display the financial results for Merck. As noted in Exhibit 10–7, the consolidated statement of income, and Exhibit 10–9, the selected financial data, there was a restructuring charge of $775.0 million. This charge encompassed two programs. The first was a short-term program that involved a

permanent reduction of the workforce by approximately 2,100 positions to be achieved primarily through early retirements in the United States. The second was a long-term program that consisted of consolidating the manufacturing and distribution facilities, as well as an additional reduction of the workforce outside the United States. This two-tier restructuring program reduced employment costs and provided savings from fewer facilities. As displayed in the three exhibits, Merck's financial position remained strong.

Industry and Competition

Merck ranked first in profits and third in sales in the pharmaceutical industry (a total of sixteen companies) according to the 1994 *Fortune 500* list of the largest industrial corporations. Johnson & Johnson and Bristol-Myers/Squibb were the only two companies that had greater sales than Merck. Competition in the industry was fierce and continued to intensify. In addition, the industry's overall earnings declined because of price discounts and voluntary price restraints. Because of these two factors, growth in

---

Exhibit 10–5 · **Geographic Segments (dollars in millions)**

	1991	1992	1993
Customer Sales			
Domestic	$ 4,616.4	$ 5,180.1	$ 5,914.3
Foreign: Western Europe, Canada, Australia, New Zealand, and Japan	3,812.1	4,262.4	4,201.1
Other	174.2	220.0	382.8
Affiliate Sales			
Domestic	1,093.9	1,215.9	1,263.6
Foreign: Western Europe, Canada, Australia, New Zealand, and Japan	132.1	117.5	185.7
Other	38.9	68.0	103.6
Eliminations	(1,264.9)	(1,401.4)	(1,522.9)
Total	$ 8,602.7	$ 9,662.5	$10,528.2

Source: Annual Report 1993, p. 50.

Exhibit 10–6 · **Consolidated Sales (dollars in millions)**

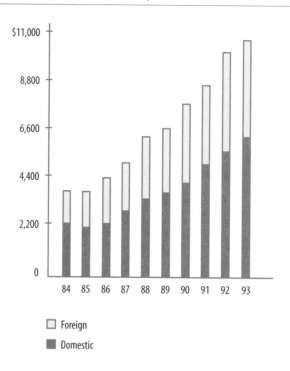

☐ Foreign

■ Domestic

Source: Annual Report 1993.

the industry was expected to slow down. The average earnings growth was expected to drop to a range of 8 to 12 percent in the next several years. This was below the 1992 rate of 15 percent.[25]

Despite a decline in earnings, R&D remained crucial to success in the pharmaceutical industry. R&D investment had doubled every five years since 1970. In 1993, the industry invested $12.6 billion in R&D, a 14.5 percent increase over 1992. This represented 16.7 percent of the total sales, which was more than double the amount of R&D that was invested in any other high-tech industry.[26]

Companies had to have aggressive R&D programs to generate new streams of drugs. Searching for innovative drugs for long-term diseases was especially important. Exhibit 10–10 displays the R&D expenditures of major companies in the industry over a three-year period. As noted, every company had increased the amount spent on R&D each year. Merck planned for another increase in 1994.

Several changes were expected to affect the industry. The first was price discounting of prescription drugs. The rapidly growing managed-care business had a significant effect on drug prices. These providers worked as a collective unit to obtain discounted prices by ordering in large quantities. Moreover, insurance companies became more powerful in making decisions on what drugs were prescribed as well as in negotiating lower prices. This trend was expected to reduce industry prices and, consequently, earnings.

A second change was the weakened economies in some foreign countries where drug companies exported or had subsidiaries. These companies were very sensitive to, and affected by, the variety of the different business conditions and government regulations. In addition, fluctuations in the value of the U.S. dollar could have a major impact on the industry's earnings.

A third trend was the increased number of generic and OTC drugs. Already the generic market

Exhibit 10–7 • **Consolidated Statements of Income and Retained Earnings (in millions except per share data)**

Consolidated Statement of Income

Year Ended December 31	1991	1992	1993
Sales	$ 8,602.7	$ 9,662.5	$ 10,498.2
Costs and expenses			
Materials and production	1,934.9	2,096.1	2,497.6
Marketing and administrative	2,570.3	2,963.3	2,913.9
Research and development	987.8	1,111.6	1,172.8
Restructuring charge	–	–	775.0
Other (income) expense, net	(57.0)	(72.1)	36.2
	5,436.0	6,098.9	7,395.5
Income before taxes and cumulative effect of accounting changes	3,166.7	3,563.6	3,102.7
Taxes on income	1,045.0	1,117.0	936.5
Income before cumulative effect of accounting changes	2,121.7	2,446.6	2,166.2
Cumulative effect of accounting changes			
Postretirement benefits other than pensions	–	(370.2)	–
Income taxes	–	(62.6)	–
Postemployment benefits	–	(29.6)	–
Net income	$ 2,121.7	$ 1,984.2	$ 2,166.2
Earnings per share of common stock			
Before cumulative effect of accounting changes	$1.83	$2.12	$1.87
Cumulative effect of accounting changes			
Postretirement benefits other than pensions	–	(.32)	–
Income taxes	–	(.05)	–
Postemployment benefits	–	(.03)	–
Net income	$1.83	$1.72	$1.87

Consolidated Statement of Retained Earnings

Year Ended December 31	1991	1992	1993
Balance, January 1	$ 6,387.3	$ 7,588.7	$ 8,466.0
Net income	2,121.7	1,984.2	2,166.2
Common stock dividends declared	(920.3)	(1,106.9)	(1,239.0)
Balance, December 31	$ 7,588.7	$ 8,466.0	$ 9,393.2

Source: Annual Report 1993, p. 40.

was having a significant effect on the prescription drug market. In the next few years, more and more patents were to expire leaving room for an influx of generics. Thus, competition was expected to increase. Merck started to counteract this trend by opening its West Point Pharma Division to produce its own generic drugs.

OTC drugs were another major threat. The average individual was becoming more health conscious, educated, and more responsible for his or her own health. People were, therefore, more willing to make decisions concerning their own medications by choosing OTCs. There was a growing trend for the aging population to self-medicate with OTCs. Companies

Exhibit 10–8　·　**Consolidated Balance Sheet (in millions)**

	December 31, 1992	1993		December 31, 1992	1993
Assets			Liabilities and Stockholders' Equity		
Current assets			Current liabilities		
Cash and cash equivalents	$575.1	$829.4	Accounts payable and accrued liabilities	$1,461.9	$2,378.3
Short-term investments	518.4	712.9	Loans payable	825.2	1,736.0
Accounts receivable	1,736.9	2,094.3	Income taxes payable	1,043.8	1,430.4
Inventories	1,182.6	1,641.7	Dividends payable	286.4	351.0
Prepaid expenses and taxes	386.7	456.3	Total current liabilities	3,617.3	5,895.7
Total current assets	4,399.7	5,734.6	Long-term debt	495.7	1,120.8
Investments	1,415.6	1,779.9	Deferred income taxes and noncurrent liabilities	1,343.0	1,744.9
Property, plant, and equipment, at cost			Minority interests	627.1	1,144.4
Land	210.3	212.5	Stockholders' equity		
Buildings	2,122.1	2,386.1	Common stock		
Machinery, equipment, and office furnishings	3,435.0	3,769.0	Authorized—2,700,000,000 shares	204.7	4,576.5
Construction in progress	763.5	805.2	Issued—1,480,611,247 shares—1993		
	6,530.9	7,172.8	—1,366,572,924 shares—1992		
Less allowance for depreciation	2,259.8	2,278.2	Retained earnings	8,466.0	9,393.2
	4,271.1	4,894.6		8,670.7	13,969.7

Goodwill and other intangibles (net of accumulated amortization of $97.2 million in 1993 and $69.0 million in 1992)	153.5	6,645.5	Less treasury stock, at cost
			  226,676,597 shares—1993
			  221,878,127 shares—1992
				3,667.8	3,948.0

Other assets	846.1	872.9	Total stockholders' equity	5,002.9	10,021.7
Total assets	11,086.0	19,927.5	Total liabilities and stockholders' equity	$11,086.0	$19,927.5

Source: Annual Report 1993, p. 41

had the opportunity, however, to protect their markets by converting their patented, prescription drugs to OTCs. There were four advantages for doing this: (1) it was a counterattack on the generic market; (2) if the prescription drug was cleared for OTC sale, the drug received two additional years of patent protection; (3) OTC drugs did not have any price restrictions; and (4) OTCs did not require long, time-consuming paperwork as needed by the FDA with prescription drugs.[27]

A fourth important industry-wide change was the possible increase in governmental controls of prescription drugs. It was believed that the drug industry's profit margins were too high. Because of the high price of drugs, which was passed on to the consumer, the nation's overall health care was too

expensive and therefore not available to all individuals. By making the reform of the health care system a national priority, the government was pressuring the pharmaceutical companies to reduce drug prices. Therefore, some companies, including Merck, established voluntary price restraints on their drug prices. In addition, the prospect of government controls spurred company restructuring as well as mergers with biotechnology firms and companies that could enhance R&D activities. Merck had been active in strategic alliances to gain a competitive edge.

The pharmaceutical industry maintained a positive, international trade balance despite increased competition. Exhibit 10–11 shows the major U.S. drug companies that competed in the foreign market.

Exhibit 10–9 • Selected Financial Data (in millions except per share data)711

	1983	1984	1985	1986	1987	1988	1989	1990	1991	1992[1]	1993[2]
Results for Year											
Sales	$3,246.1	$3,559.7	$3,547.5	$4,128.9	$5,061.3	$5,939.5	$6,550.5	$7,671.5	$8,602.7	$9,662.5	$10,498.2
Materials and production costs	1,263.4	1,424.5	1,272.4	1,338.0	1,444.3	1,526.1	1,550.3	1,778.1	1,934.9	2,096.1	2,497.6
Marketing/administrative expenses	905.1	945.5	1,009.0	1,269.9	1,682.1	1,877.8	2,013.4	2,388.0	2,570.3	2,963.3	2,913.9
Research/development expenses	356.0	393.1	426.3	479.8	565.7	668.8	750.5	854.0	987.8	1,111.6	1,172.8
Restructuring charge	—	—	—	—	—	—	—	—	—	—	775.0
Other (income) expense, net	25.6	9.8	(17.2)	(32.1)	(36.0)	(4.2)	(46.7)	(47.4)	(57.0)	(72.1)	36.2
Income before taxes	696.0	786.8	857.0	1073.3	1,405.2	1,871.0	2,283.0	2,698.8	3,166.7	3,563.6	3,102.7
Taxes on income	245.1	293.8	317.1	397.6	498.8	664.2	787.6	917.6	1,045.0	1,117.0	936.5
Net income	450.9	493.0	539.9	675.7	906.4	1,206.8	1,495.4	1,781.2	2,121.7	2,446.6	2,166.2
Per share of common stock	$.34	$.37	$.42	$.54	$.74	$1.02	$1.26	$1.52	$1.83	$2.12	$1.87
Dividends on common stock											
Declared	210.8	224.0	235.1	278.5	365.2	546.3	681.5	788.1	920.3	1,106.9	1,239.0
Paid per share	$.16	$.17	$.18	$.21	$.27	$.43	$.55	$.64	$.77	$.92	$1.03
Capital expenditures	272.8	274.4	237.6	210.6	253.7	372.7	433.0	670.8	1,041.5	1,066.6	1,012.7
Depreciation	135.2	151.6	163.6	167.2	188.5	189.0	206.4	231.4	242.7	290.3	348.4
Year-End Position											
Working capital	734.9	1,076.5	1,106.6	1,094.3	798.3	1,480.3	1,502.5	939.2	1,496.5	782.4	(161.1)
Property, plant, and equipment (net)	1,715.2	1,912.8	1,882.8	1,906.2	1,948.0	2,070.7	2,292.5	2,721.7	3,504.5	4,271.1	4,894.6
Total assets	4,214.7	4,590.6	4,902.2	5,105.2	5,680.0	6,127.5	6,756.7	8,029.8	9,498.5	11,086.0	19,927.5
Long-term debt	385.5	179.1	170.8	167.5	167.4	142.8	117.8	124.1	493.7	495.7	1,120.8
Stockholders' equity	2,409.9	2,518.6	2,607.7	2,541.2	2,116.7	2,855.8	3,520.6	3,834.4	4,916.2	5,002.9	10,021.7
Financial Ratios											
Net income as a percent of:											
Sales	13.9%	13.8%	15.2%	16.4%	17.9%	20.3%	22.8%	23.2%	24.7%	25.3%	20.6%
Average total assets	11.5%	11.2%	11.4%	13.5%	16.8%	20.4%	23.2%	24.1%	24.2%	24.1%	14.0%
Year-End Statistics											
Average number of shares of common stock outstanding (in millions)	1,331.0	1,322.0	1,282.7	1,253.9	1,221.2	1,186.9	1,188.3	1,172.1	1,159.9	1,153.5	1,156.5
Number of stockholders	51,800	50,200	47,000	48,300	56,900	68,500	75,600	82,300	91,100	161,200	231,300
Number of employees	32,600	34,800	30,900	30,700	31,100	32,000	34,400	36,900	37,700	38,400	47,100[3]

[1] 1992 results of operations exclude the cumulative effect of the accounting charges.
[2] 1993 amounts include Medco Containment Services, Inc. from the date of acquisition (November 18, 1993). Excluding the effect of the acquisition, earnings per share would have been $1.94 and the ratio of net income to average total assets would have been 18.5%. 1993 amounts also include a nonrecurring restructuring charge of $.45 per share.
[3] Includes 10,300 Medco employees.
Source: Annual Report 1993, p. 52.

Exhibit 10–10 • Research and Development Expenditures (dollars in millions)

Company	1990 R & D Expenditures	1990 Percent of Sales	1991 R & D Expenditures	1991 Percent of Sales	1992 R & D Expenditures	1992 Percent of Sales
Abbott	567	9	666	10	772	10
American Home Products	369	5	431	6	552	7
Bristol-Myers/Squibb	873	9	983	9	1,083	10
Johnson & Johnson	834	7	980	8	1,127	8
Eli Lilly	703	14	767	13	925	15
Glaxo	748	13	841	14	1,047	15
Marion Merrell Dow	358	15	393	14	465	14
Merck	*854*	*11*	*988*	*11*	*1,112*	*12*
Pfizer	640	10	757	11	863	12
Schering-Plough	380	11	426	12	522	13
SmithKline Beecham	700	9	756	9	841	9
Syntex	271	18	316	17	374	18
Upjohn	427	14	491	14	549	15
Warner-Lambert	379	8	423	8	473	8
Wellcome	343	16	385	15	455	15

Source: Standard and Poor's Industry Surveys, 1993, p. H21.

Merck was second only to Johnson & Johnson in dollars of foreign sales. Merck received nearly half of its total sales from foreign sales.

Exhibit 10–12 displays the export trade patterns for U.S. pharmaceutical companies.

As the European economic unification unfolded, there were three important issues being negotiated by the European Community (EC) for the future of the industry. First, there was a proposal for centralized product registration that would allow a pharmaceutical company to go through a single approval process applicable to all countries within the EC. Second, there would be free-market pricing. Presently, each country set its own pricing structure according to its own regulations. The new proposal would let the market of the EC as a whole set the prices. Third, there would be universal patent protection. It was suggested that a central agency represent all countries in protecting a company's intellectual rights. If these steps were incorporated into the final agreement of the EC, companies in the industry would be able to export drugs more efficiently and at a much lower cost.[28]

To maintain its positive trade balance and remain highly competitive, the industry must overcome international obstacles. For instance, it must currently compete within the weak world economy. It must also compete in countries where there was no protection for intellectual property (patents and copyrights). Moreover, each country had its own price controls and regulations that must be dealt with on a country-by-country basis. Also, there was a shortage of hard currency in developing countries where some pharmaceutical companies were doing business.

The pharmaceutical industry was doing well in its competitive environment. In 1993, the drug companies exported more than $7.2 billion in products and had a trade surplus of $500 million. Nearly 50 percent of all exports went to the EC, which remained the largest importer of U.S. pharmaceuticals. The projected U.S. overall economic growth outlook for 1994 was 2 percent.[29]

The forecast for the pharmaceutical industry was positive long-term growth. The aging population was one element that helped support this. People

Exhibit 10–11 • Foreign Sales of Major U.S. Drug Companies (dollars in millions)

Company	1990 Foreign Sales	1990 Percent of Total Sales	1991 Foreign Sales	1991 Percent of Total Sales	1992 Foreign Sales	1992 Percent of Total Sales
Abbott	2,245	36	2,501	36	2,934	37
American Home Products	2,168	32	2,202	31	2,487	32
Bristol-Myers/Squibb	3,201	33	3,399	32	3,794	34
Johnson & Johnson	5,810	52	6,199	50	6,850	50
Eli Lilly	2,470	48	2,732	48	2,988	48
Marion Merrell Dow	675	27	850	30	1,102	33
Merck	*3,782*	*49*	*4,157*	*48*	*4,668*	*48*
Pfizer	2,933	46	3,141	45	3,342	46
Schering-Plough	1,433	43	1,498	41	1,892	47
Syntex	475	31	561	31	617	30
Upjohn	1,200	40	1,290	38	1,391	38
Warner-Lambert	2,242	48	2,444	48	2,784	50

Source: Standard and Poor's Industry Surveys, 1993, p. H24.

Exhibit 10–12 • U.S. Export Trade Patterns in 1992

Countries/Regions	Value (dollars in millions)	Share (percent)
Canada and Mexico	986	14.6
European Community	3,260	48.1
Japan	963	14.2
East Asia—Newly Industrial Countries	329	4.9
South America	291	4.3
Other	944	13.9
World Total	6,773	100.0
Top Five Countries		
Japan	963	14.2
Canada	844	12.5
Germany	768	11.3
Italy	561	8.3
France	499	7.4

Source: U.S. Industrial Outlook 1994, p. 43.

over the age of sixty-five consumed three times more drugs than those under that age. In the years ahead, as this aging group increased, a larger market would be available.

As companies continued to innovate and discover new drugs, they would have the assurance that these drugs were shielded through the long years of patent protection.

The Future

Merck's mission was "to provide society with superior products and services—innovations and solutions that satisfy customer needs and improve the quality of life....To better meet the challenge of the dramatic changes in the health care marketing environment...."[30] This mission was tested during a dramatic period of change in the pharmaceutical industry and a changing societal view of the existing health care system. The national debate on health care reform pressured Merck to lower drug prices and made these drugs more accessible to more people.

Merck was able to reduce its prices while still generating the necessary revenue for extensive R&D of new therapeutic drugs. The company planned to shortly introduce Varivax, the first chicken pox vaccine, and a new drug for treating asthma. This was to be followed by the next generation of Merck's leading drug, Vasotec, that reduced high blood pressure. Merck's commitment to R&D was never stronger. However, new marketing, distribution, and manufacturing skills were needed to succeed in tomorrow's fiercely competitive markets. The company's executives believed that for "those who master change, redefine themselves, and respond to society's needs... there will be enormous opportunities for growth and success."[31] Would Merck reclaim its position as "America's Most Admired Corporation"? Would it succeed in its global expansion? What additional strategic changes were needed to succeed in tomorrow's pharmaceutical industry? Could the new CEO maintain Merck's organizational culture? Would he retain the company's lead in R&D? These and similar questions were no doubt being asked today. If the past was any indication, Merck was on the verge of transforming itself into a truly global competitor.

Notes

1. All information in this case was collected from secondary references.
2. Lloyd Byars, "Merck & Co., Inc." in *Strategic Management: Formulation and Implementation, Concepts and Cases*, 3d ed. (New York: HarperCollins Publishers Inc., 1991), pp. 373–376.
3. *Annual Report 1993*, p. 32.
4. *Ibid.*, p. 3
5. Form 10-K, March 25, 1993, p. 3.
6. Lloyd Byars, "Merck & Co., Inc." p. 375.
7. J. Weber, J. Byrne, M. McNamee, and G. McWilliams, "Merck Finally Gets Its Man," *Business Week* (June 27, 1994), p. 24.
8. D. Lavin and E. Tanouye, "Merck's Zabriskie Is Named Chairman, Chief of Upjohn; Vagelos Heir Unclear," *Wall Street Journal* (December 8, 1993), p. 7.
9. D. Lavin and E. Tanouye, "Schering-Plough Taps Merck's Cecil Pickett for Research Position," *Wall Street Journal* (August 11, 1993), p. 8.
10. J. P. Miller, "Marion Merrell gives Markham Two Top Posts," *Wall Street Journal* (September 22, 1993), p. 3
11. *Annual Report 1991*, p. 8.
12. *Annual Report 1993*, p. 11.
13. *Ibid.*, p. 10.
14. *Ibid.*
15. T. Friend, "A Digital Doctor of Your Own," *USA Today* (May 26, 1994), p. 1.
16. *Annual Report 1992*, p. 14.
17. "Tularik Inc.," *Wall Street Journal* (January 7, 1994), p. 3.
18. "Joint Venture for Vaccines," *New York Times* (October 8, 1994), p. 21
19. *Annual Report 1993*, p. 38.
20. *Ibid.*, p. 30.
21. *Ibid.*
22. *Annual Report 1992*, p. 27.
23. Martha Galser, "Majority of States Give Nod to Merck Discount Plan," *Drug Topics* (August 20, 1990), pp. 63–64.
24. *Annual Report 1992*, p. 5.
25. "Rx Needed for Ailing Pharmaceutical Industry," *Standard and Poor's Industry Surveys* (September 9, 1993), p. H18.
26. *U.S. Industrial Outlook 1994* (U.S. Department of Commerce, January 1994), p. 43.
27. "Rx-to-OTC Conversions to Boost Market," *Standard and Poor's Industry Surveys* (September 9, 1993), p. H31.
28. "Rx Needed for Ailing Pharmaceutical Industry," *Standard and Poor's*, p. H24.
29. *U.S. Industrial Outlook 1994* (U.S. Department of Commerce, January 1994), p. 6, 20.
30. *Annual Report 1993*, inside front cover.
31. *Ibid.*, p. 2.

HMA and Its Riverview Regional Medical Center Facility

As Jon Vollmer scanned another résumé for the executive director's position at Riverview Regional Medical Center (RRMC) located in Gadsden, Alabama, he knew that whoever was selected would need to maintain the overall growth of the facility and entice area employers to the facility to be successful. Mr. Vollmer considered the progress of RRMC since being acquired five years earlier by Health Management Associates, Inc. (HMA) to be excellent! He himself had served as RRMC's executive director from the time of HMA's acquisition until January 1995 when he was promoted to corporate vice president for operations. In June 1996, RRMC's executive director of sixteen months resigned, and Vollmer resumed the position of executive director in addition to his vice presidential duties. Although Vollmer operated out of RRMC, he was responsible for seven hospitals located in Alabama, Arkansas, Kentucky, Mississippi, and West Virginia. His vice presidential duties along with his increased travel schedule left him scant time to properly manage RRMC. He knew that filling the executive director's position was an important move for keeping RRMC on track and for building on the foundation he had established.

This case was prepared by Beth Woodard, Donna J. Slovensky, and Woodrow D. Richardson, all of the University of Alabama at Birmingham. It is intended as a basis for class discussion rather than to illustrate effective or ineffective handling of an administrative situation. Used with permission from Woody Richardson.

Health Care Providers

In 1993, Merrill Lynch predicted, "In the larger urban areas, HMOs would . . . continue to be the coordinator and provider of health care services. However, in non-urban markets, . . . the hospital would be the cornerstone and coordinator of health care services for the health alliance purchasing cooperatives which would be formed under managed competition proposals."[1]

At the individual provider level, some experts insisted that the financial power base was moving away from solo practices and independent small groups toward integrated, cost-competitive, comprehensive systems that produced a single patient bill including the charges of the physicians, the hospital, and the outpatient services. Integrated systems required a corporate structure to facilitate shared capitated risk. Over the past decade, mergers and other types of strategic alliances between physicians' practices, and hospitals and physicians' practices, had increased as providers struggled to reduce costs and become price competitive. Small group practices often lacked the administrative and management expertise as well as the material resources necessary to improve efficiency. They were advised to look for such capabilities when they sought potential partners.

Many physicians remained skeptical that mergers, partnerships, and alliances offered any competitive advantage. That skepticism occurred most often in areas where managed care was absent or limited.

Exhibit 11–1 shows the penetration of managed care in selected southern states.

Rural and Non-Urban Health Care Market

Forty-nine percent of the U.S. population resided in counties classified as rural or non-urban. Non-urban areas had 44 percent fewer doctors per 100,000 residents than urban areas. Since 1981, more than 200 non-urban hospitals had closed. Many hospitals continued to underperform and were failing due to ineffective operations.[2]

Rural and non-urban hospitals had become hot acquisition targets for investor-owned health care companies. For the nation's 2,400 rural hospitals—acute-care facilities located outside of a metropolitan statistical area—the status quo was not acceptable.[3] Hospitals that chose to stand alone faced an uncertain market where 60 percent to 75 percent of revenues were attributed to Medicare. Threatened by the prospect of declining federal reimbursement, coupled with the lack of resources to invest in costly information systems, many local governments that owned rural and non-urban hospitals were looking for a way out.[4]

According to company chief executive officer and chairman of the board, William Schoen, when it came to the "field of dreams" logic that small hospitals used in the past, they would not succeed. "Whereas other hospitals think, 'We are here and you will come,' we're in the customer service business," said Schoen. No other firm had been as suc-cessful as Health Management Associates, Inc. in the non-urban markets.

Health Management Associates

Health Management Associates was ahead of the growing throng of firms targeting rural and non-urban markets where the presence of managed care was less intense and good opportunities were perceived by physicians. Schoen understood that his customers were not only patients, but physicians as well. When HMA acquired a facility, it was with the premise that the facility's expansion would be financed and assistance would be available to recruit personnel; however the facility was responsible for its own community service activities.

Founded in 1977, HMA acquired, improved, and operated hospitals in high-growth, non-urban areas in the Southeast and Southwest, where the growing population created a need for comprehensive health care services. This focus was changing. In addition to 200 "acquisition opportunities" in those regions, the company had identified another 175 to 200 facilities in other areas of the country, primarily in the Midwest and mid-Atlantic states. The hospitals that HMA chose to acquire:

- had a clear demographic need;
- demonstrated high potential for growth;
- were located in communities with populations of 40,000 to 300,000;
- were preferably located in states with certificate of need (CON) regulations;

Exhibit 11–1 · Managed-Care Penetration in Selected States

State	Percentage
Texas	10
Florida	18
Georgia	7
Alabama	under 7
California (reference point)	40 or more

Source: http://www.hoovers.com/ICF/16060icf.html; Physician Corporation of America, 1997.

- possessed an established physician base; and
- were available at a reasonable price.

HMA was using a strategy of acquiring rural facilities in communities where they had the opportunity to "be the dominant provider." Its management strategy incorporated a decentralized decision-making approach with centralized operating systems. HMA consistently turned hospitals into efficient, state-of-the-art medical facilities that provided high-quality care. HMA owned twenty-five hospitals in eleven states and had quite successfully operated them in the black despite intense cost pressure.

In 1995, HMA had net income of $63.3 million on net patient service revenues of $531.1 million. In 1995, HMA watched its average Medicare patient length of stay (LOS) drop to 6.2 days from 6.8 days in 1994. However, this LOS compared favorably to the national average of 8.0 days, as reported by the Department of Health and Human Services' (DHHS) Health Care Financing Administration.[5]

There had been few changes at HMA in recent years. The corporation maintained small corporate overhead. Most of the forty-four employees in the Naples, Florida, corporate office were secretarial staff. In fact, the 50,000-square-foot HMA building had less than 15,000 square feet actually allocated for the health care company. The remaining space was leased to other businesses. HMA credited the stability of its top management as a key selling point to communities. The company's four-person top executive team had been intact for fourteen years. Exhibit 11–2 provides information on the corporate officers.

Corporate Philosophy and Mission

In 1992, HMA published "A Statement of Corporate Philosophy" that defined its goals and principles as a health care provider, employer, and publicly traded company. The corporate officers believed that success in the health care industry was determined by the ability of providers to deliver services in the most cost-effective and efficient manner possible. HMA's guiding objectives were stated as follows:

- Providing the highest quality service to our patients, physicians, and the communities we serve.

- Providing an attractive return on investment to those who are investors in our company.
- Providing employees with a satisfying and rewarding work environment.
- Functioning as a good corporate citizen in the communities we serve.
- Managing HMA in a manner that maintains uniform strength and identity while allowing individual hospitals the degree of independence necessary to maximize innovation and efficiency and meet the individual needs of the communities we serve.

Furthermore, they believed that the experience of contracting directly with employers to provide health care services would be very important in the future. For that reason, HMA had established its own PPO in some of the markets with low managed-care penetration.

Corporate Strategy

When originally established in 1977, HMA intended to compete as a national firm by owning, leasing, and managing hospitals throughout the United States. In 1983 HMA redirected its focus to a niche strategy—ownership of hospitals located in non-urban communities in the Southeast and Southwest with 40,000 to 300,000 in population. The officers believed the very nature and size of the facilities (generally 200 beds or fewer) located in non-urban communities precluded the individual, non-system-affiliated hospitals from attracting experienced and professional medical practitioners in each area of specialty. On the other hand, they believed that through system-affiliation with HMA and its concomitant infusion of capital and management expertise, the same financially troubled hospitals could become profitable.

In other words, in order to optimally penetrate the niche markets, HMA executives believed it was necessary to provide the management expertise and medical technology in specific areas to reduce costs, attract physicians, increase the scope and quality of service within a profitable framework, and halt the outmigration of patients to larger metropolitan areas for as many surgical procedures as possible. They believed that achieving these objectives allowed the communities they served to forge the viable and

Exhibit 11–2 • HMA Corporate Officers

Name	Age	Position	Year Elected
William J. Schoen	59	Chairman, Board of Directors, President and CEO	1983
Kent P. Dauten	39	Director	1981
Robert A. Knox	42	Director	1985
Charles R. Lees	73	Director	1988
Kenneth D. Lewis	47	Director	1991
Earl P. Holland	49	Executive Vice President	1982
Robb L. Smith	50	Senior Vice President	1982
Stephen M. Ray	46	Senior Vice President	1983

William J. Schoen joined the company's board of directors in February 1983 and in December 1983 became its president and chief operating officer. He became co-chief executive officer in December 1985 and chairman of the board of directors and chief executive officer in April 1986. From 1982 to 1987, Mr. Schoen was chairman of Commerce National Bank, Naples, Florida, and from 1973 to 1981 he was president, chief operating officer, and chief executive officer of the F & M Schafer Corporation, a consumer products company. From 1971 to 1983, Mr. Schoen was president of the Pierce Glass subsidiary of Indian Head, Inc., a diversified company. In addition to serving on the company's board, Mr. Schoen also serves on the board of directors of First Union National Bank of Florida.

Kent P. Dauten served as a director of the company from March 1981 through May 1983, and again from June 1985 through September 1988. He was again elected a director in November 1988. Mr. Dauten is a senior vice president of Madison Dearborn Partners, Inc., which is the management company both for Madison Dearborn Capital Partners, L.P., a private equity investment fund, and for Madison Dearborn Advisors, L.P., which provides venture capital investment advisory services to First Chicago Corporation. Mr. Dauten was formerly a senior vice president of First Chicago Investment Corporation and First Capital Corporation of Chicago, the venture capital subsidiaries of First Chicago Corporation, where he had been employed in various investment management positions since 1979. He is a general partner of Madison Dearborn Partners, IV, a venture capital investment partnership. In addition, he serves on the board of directors of Genesis Health Ventures, Inc.

Robert A. Knox has been a director of the company since June 1985. Mr. Knox has been employed by the Prudential Insurance Company of America since 1975, and since 1984 he has been president of Prudential Equity Investors, Inc., a venture capital firm. He also serves on the board of directors of Lechters, Inc.

Charles R. Lees served as director of the company from April 1988 through September 1988. He was again elected a director in February 1989. Mr. Lees has been in the private practice of law, concentrating in tax matters, since May 1985. He was a project director for the Governor's Tax Reform Advisory Commission in California from August 1984 to September 1985. From 1979 to 1983 he was a visiting professor at the School of Accounting, University of Southern California. For more than twenty years prior to his retirement in 1979, Mr. Lees was a partner of the accounting firm of Peat, Marwick, Mitchell and Co., specializing in tax matters.

Kenneth D. Lewis was elected to the company's board of directors in May 1991. He is president of NationsBank Corporation, a position that he has held since December 1991. Prior to that, Mr. Lewis was employed by NCNB Corporation in various capacities since 1969, including president of NCNB—Texas from 1988 to 1990, and president of NCNB National Bank of Florida from 1986 to 1988.

Earl P. Holland joined the company in 1981 as senior vice president of operations. He became senior vice president of marketing and development in 1984 and executive vice president of operations and development in 1989. For more than five years prior to 1981, he was employed by Humana, Inc., where he served as assistant regional vice president and as the executive director of two hospitals.

Robb L. Smith joined the company as vice president and general counsel in 1981 after eleven years of private law practice in Louisville, Kentucky. His private practice included representing the company as outside counsel. Mr. Smith was appointed secretary in 1986, and senior vice president and general counsel in 1988.

Stephen M. Ray, a certified public accountant, joined the company in 1981 as controller and became a vice president in 1983. In 1992, Mr. Ray was promoted to senior vice president of administrative services. He served as treasurer from 1987 to 1988. He is currently responsible for the company's systemwide supply procurement and contract negotiations. From 1979 until 1981, Mr. Ray was employed by Hospital Affiliates International, Inc., a hospital management company, where he was responsible for reporting compliance and corporate technical accounting.

Sources: Merrill Lynch et al. *Prospectus,* February 2, 1993; Health Management Associates, Inc., *Annual Report 1995.*

effective health care delivery facilities that they desperately needed.

Facilities

In 1995, HMA operated twenty-two facilities. Eighteen were general acute-care hospitals (totaling 2,440 beds) that offered a broad range of inpatient and outpatient health services with an emphasis on primary care. Inpatient programs at all facilities included a broad range of medical and surgical services, diagnostic services, intensive and cardiac care, plus emergency services that were staffed by physicians at all times. At various facilities, other specialty services such as full-service obstetrics, oncology, and industrial medicine were available. In addition, HMA operated four freestanding psychiatric hospitals. Exhibit 11–3 presents information with respect to the corporation's facilities as of August 1996.

Selected Financial Data and Operating Statistics

Approximately 63 percent, 65 percent, and 67 percent of gross patient service revenue, for fiscal years 1993, 1994, and 1995, respectively, related to services rendered to patients covered by Medicare and Medicaid programs. Exhibit 11–4 shows the financial performance of the corporation for fiscal years 1993 through 1995, along with selected operating statistics.

HMA had a number of hospital renovations/expansion projects under way as fiscal year 1995 ended. In addition, the company planned to replace four of its existing hospitals over the next five years, subject to approval by the appropriate regulatory agencies. There were hospital renovation and expansion commitments of approximately $7.7 million outstanding, of which $1,336,000 was paid September 30, 1995.

Riverview Regional Medical Center

The 281-bed acute-care facility was originally chartered in the 1940s as The Holy Name of Jesus Hospital—the first hospital built in Etowah County. Owned and operated by an order of Catholic nuns, it remained under their ownership and control until financial considerations persuaded them to sell the hospital to HMA in August 1991. At that time the name was changed to Riverview Regional Medical Center. RRMC's mission statement was written at that time:

> Riverview Regional Medical Center will provide quality personalized health care in a courteous, quantifiable, and cost efficient manner, responding to the needs of our patients, their families, physicians, employees, and the community.

Local Demographics

RRMC was located in the city of Gadsden, Etowah County, in northeastern Alabama. Etowah County was the ninth-largest county in the state of Alabama. Exhibit 11–5 shows population growth in Alabama by county. Etowah County was comprised of twelve incorporated cities with a total population of 99,832 people in 1995. Gadsden was the largest city in Etowah County as well as the county seat. Exhibit 11–6 shows the relationship and proximity of the cities in Etowah County to one another.

Gadsden was a growing transportation hub connecting many of the major metropolitan areas in the southeastern region of the country. It was located at the southern foothills of the Appalachian Mountains in an area sixty miles northeast of Birmingham, 70 miles southeast of Huntsville, 110 miles west of Atlanta, and 95 miles southwest of Chattanooga. Situated astride Lookout Mountain and the Coosa River, the city had grown from sparsely populated Indian country in the early 1800s to a city with a population that peaked at more than 58,000 residents in the early 1960s. The population had since declined to slightly more than 43,000 residents. Exhibits 11–7, 11–8, and 11–9 show the population trends for Etowah County and Gadsden between 1940 and 1990, and populations of surrounding counties. Exhibit 11–10 shows the major manufacturers in the region.

Health Care Competition

As mentioned previously, unlike many of the other facilities operated by HMA, RRMC was neither the sole community provider, nor even the dominant provider of health care in its service area. Gadsden Regional Medical Center (GRMC) had approximately

Exhibit 11–3 · HMA Facilities in 1996

Location	Hospital	Facility Type	Licensed Beds
Alabama			
Anniston	Stringfellow Memorial Hospital	General Medical/Surgical	175
Gadsden	Riverview Regional Medical Center	General Medical/Surgical	281
Arkansas			
Van Buren	Crawford Memorial	General Medical/Surgical	103
Florida			
Haines City	Heart of Florida	General Medical/Surgical	51
Lakeland	Palmview Hospital	Psychiatric	66
Marathon	Fishermen's Memorial Hospital	General Medical/Surgical	55
Orlando	University Behavioral Center	Psychiatric	100
Punta Gorda	Charlotte Regional Medical Center	General Medical/Surgical	208
Sebastian	Sebastian River Medical Center	General Medical/Surgical	133
Sebring	Highlands Regional Medical Center	General Medical/Surgical	126
Tequesta	Sandy Pines	Psychiatric	60
Georgia			
Statesboro	Bullock Memorial Hospital	General Medical/Surgical	158
Kansas			
Topeka	Parkview Hospital	Psychiatric	101
Kentucky			
Paintsville	Paul B. Hall Regional Medical Center	General Medical/Surgical	72
Mississippi			
Biloxi	Biloxi Regional Medical Center	General Medical/Surgical	153
Clarksdale	Northwest Mississippi Regional Medical Center	General Medical/Surgical	175
Natchez	Natchez Community Hospital	General Medical/Surgical	100
North Carolina			
Hamlet	Hamlet Hospital	General Medical/Surgical	64
Louisburg	Franklin Regional Medical Center	General Medical/Surgical	85
Mooresville	Lake Normal Regional Medical Center	General Medical/Surgical	121
Oklahoma			
Durant	Medical Center of Southeastern Oklahoma	General Medical/Surgical	102
Midwest City	Midwest City Regional Medical Center	General Medical/Surgical	208
South Carolina			
Gaffney	Upstate Carolina Medical Center	General Medical/Surgical	125
Hartsville	Byerly Hospital	General Medical/Surgical	100
West Virginia			
Williamson	Williamson Memorial Hospital	General Medical/Surgical	76

Source: *1996 The Hospital Phone Book*. Published by the U.S. Directory Service. Copyright © Reed Elsevier, Inc. (1996).

Exhibit 11–4 · HMA Summary of Financial Statements (in thousands, except per share data)

	Year Ended September 30		
	1993	1994	1995
Income Statement			
Net operating revenue	$346,767	$438,366	$531,094
Total costs and expenses	290,328	356,636	426,845
Income before taxes and cumulative effect of accounting change	56,439	81,730	104,249
Cumulative effect of change in accounting for income taxes	-----	(2,550)	-----
Net income	32,245	46,536	63,331
Earnings per share			
Before accounting change	.48	.69	.88
Accounting change	---	(.04)	---
Net income per share	.48	.65	.88
Weighted average number of common and common equivalent shares outstanding	66,738	71,069	72,056

	Year Ended September 30	
	1994	1995
Balance Sheet		
Total current assets	$177,564	$173,378
Net property, plant, and equipment	214,255	283,279
Funds held by trustee	343	72
Deferred charges and other assets	6,651	10,269
	$398,813	$466,998
Total current liabilities	$39,563	$50,631
Deferred income taxes	19,299	18,399
Other long-term liabilities	11,254	12,297
Long-term debt	75,769	67,721
Total stockholders' equity	252,928	317,950
	$398,813	$466,998

the same number of beds as RRMC. Both acute-care hospitals located in Gadsden were among the nine largest employers in the county. Unlike the key GRMC medical staff members who were housed in a hospital-owned professional office building, RRMC's key medical staff members and group practices maintained separate offices throughout the city. For the most part, the two hospitals had a common medical staff membership, with the exception of the Emergency Department physicians. Exhibit 11–11 shows a comparison of the services offered by RRMC and GRMC.

Primary Market Area Although not owned by the Goodyear Tire and Rubber Company (Etowah County's largest employer and fourth-largest taxpayer), GRMC was located on property adjacent to the Goodyear plant. The hospital, formerly known as Baptist Memorial Hospital, was sold to Quorum Health Group/Quorum Health Resources and renamed GRMC in 1994.

According to *Modern Healthcare*'s 1996 multi-provider survey, Quorum was the largest provider of hospital contract management by bed size and number

Exhibit 11–5 • Population Growth of Counties in Alabama

How counties compared to state average

☐ Declining population

▨ Lower than average growth

▮ Above average growth

Source: Gadsden Times, Etowah County Fact Book—1993.

of facilities. Quorum owned sixteen hospitals, managed sixteen others, and operated in forty-three states plus the District of Columbia. Since Quorum took over, the entire GRMC administration, with the exception of nursing administration, had changed.

On June 21, 1996, GRMC's top two administrators resigned by mutual agreement. At the same time, RRMC's executive director resigned.

Both RRMC and GRMC were accredited by the Joint Commission on Accreditation of Healthcare

Exhibit 11–6 • Relationship and Proximity of Cities in Etowah County

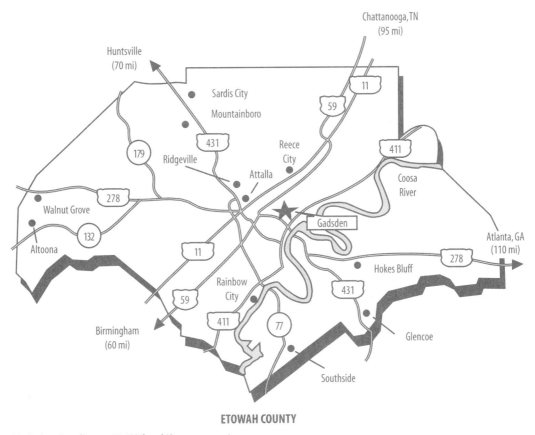

ETOWAH COUNTY

Source: Birmingham News (January 25, 1991), p. A12.

Organizations, certified for participation in the Health Insurance for the Aged (Medicare) Program by the DHHS, and contracted or participated in Blue Cross Plans as reported by the Blue Cross Association. However, only GRMC had a cancer program approved by the American College of Surgeons. Both RRMC and GRMC were controlled by investor-owned (for-profit) corporations. Exhibit 11–12 shows a comparison of the two facilities.

The only other competitor for inpatient services in Gadsden was Mountain View Hospital, a psychiatric and chemical dependency hospital for children, adolescents, and adults. Although Mountain View Hospital was not a direct competitor of RRMC by vir-

tue of its target population, it nonetheless influenced local market forces with respect to certain health care services.

Mountain View Hospital implemented professional and educational programs by recruiting national specialists in the field of mental health. Through a relationship with Northeast Alabama Psychiatric Services, neuropsychiatry was available as well as extensive outpatient services. In addition, the hospital specialized in the treatment of attention deficit hyperactivity disorders in children and adolescents. In June 1991, an adult psychiatric unit was opened to treat depression, stress, anxiety, and panic disorders. An intensive-care center for psychiatric care

Exhibit 11-7 · Population Trends, Etowah County/Gadsden 1960-1990

	Year			
	1960	1970	1980	1990
Etowah County	92,980	96,980	103,057	99,840
Altoona	744	781	928	960
Attalla	8,257	7,510	7,737	6,859
Gadsden	58,088	53,928	47,565	42,523
Glencoe	2,592	2,901	4,648	4,670
Walnut Grove	237	224	510	717
Hokes Bluff	1,619	2,133	3,216	3,739
Rainbow City	1,626	3,107	6,792	7,673
Reece City	470	496	718	657
Southside	436	983	5,139	5,580
Mountainboro	—	311	266	261
Sardis City	—	368	883	1,301
Ridgeville	—	—	182	178

Exhibit 11-8 · Population Demographics

Population within 30-mile radius of Gadsden	342,000
Gadsden population	42,523
Metro population	71,044
County population	99,840
Male	47.3%
Female	52.7%
White	85.4%
Black	13.8%
Under 18	24.6%
18 to 39	31.3%
40 to 64	28.2%
65 or over	15.9%

Source: Gadsden Area Chamber of Commerce

was opened in January 1993. Other services provided by Mountain View Hospital included substance-abuse treatment, a year-round academic program, a state-licensed private school, partial hospitalization, community education, and free twenty-four-hour crisis evaluation. Physicians were being recruited from various nationally respected hospitals throughout the country with specialized areas of expertise in the field of mental health.

RRMC increased its presence in nearby Anniston. In fact, there was a cardiologist that had his primary practice in Anniston, but he sent his angioplasty patients to RRMC. With the Military Base Realignment and Closure of Fort McClellan's Noble

Exhibit 11–9 · Population of Surrounding Counties

County	Area	Population	County Seat	Workforce
Blount	643 sq. miles	40,306	Oneonta	
Calhoun	611 sq. miles	116,404	Anniston	48,204
Cherokee	553 sq. miles	19,860	Centre	8,880
De Kalb	778 sq. miles	55,909	Fort Payne	16,750
Etowah	542 sq. miles	99,832	Gadsden	43,280
Marshall	567 sq. miles	73,524	Guntersville	34,140
Jefferson	1,119 sq. miles	657,674	Birmingham	300,450
St. Clair	646 sq. miles	53,290	Ashville	23,630

Source: http://isl-garnet.uah.eduAlabama_kCounty/

Exhibit 11–10 · Selected Manufacturers of Etowah County

Name of Company	Number Employed	Year Est.	Location	Products
AAA Plumbing Pottery	151–200	1949	Gadsden	Vitreous china, plumbing fixtures
AMC Pattern and Tooling	1–5	1991	Rainbow City	Patterns
Accucare Health Technologies	6–10	1991	Gadsden	Pharmaceutical-intravenous solutions
Airco Industrial Gas	1–5	1983	Gadsden	Oxygen, nitrogen, acetylene/ welding supply distribution
Arkridge's Cabinet Shop, Inc.	1–5	1965	Gadsden	Custom cabinets
Alabama Contractors and Equipment	41–50	1957	Gadsden	Rent contract equipment and industrial supplies
Alabama Earth Products	1–5	1992	Gadsden	Sludge de-watering, animal feed ingredients, composting material
Alabama Easel Company	6–10	1970	Gadsden	Floral easels
Alabama Gas Corporation	51–75	1978	Gadsden	Public utility
Alabama Outdoor Advertising	11–15	1950	Gadsden	Advertising displays, outdoor advertising
Alabama Power Company	201–250	1907	Gadsden	Public utility
Alabama Structural Beams	11–15	1949	Gadsden	Steel H-beams for mobile homes
Associated Tool	21–30	1980	Gadsden	Dies, parts
Attalla Cabinet Works	1–5	1971	Attalla	Custom kitchen cabinets
AVCO Meat Company	41–50	1976	Gadsden	Pork processing
BACCA Sportswear	16–20	1992	Sardis	Cut and sew blue jeans
Barricks Manufacturing Co.	21–30	1982	Gadsden	Institutional furniture
Bearings and Hydraulic Co.	1–5	1990	Gadsden	Hydraulic hose assembly, band saw blades, electric motors
Beaver Cleaning Systems	1–5	1983	Gadsden	Detergent chemicals
Betty Lane Bow Co.	76–100	1989	Gadsden	Hair bows and accessories
Bigelow Septic Tank Products Co., Inc.	6–10	1950	Attalla	Concrete septic tanks
Bin-Bak, Inc.	16–20	1984	Gadsden	Steel containers, container repairs
Birch Andersen and Company, Inc.	1–5	1915	Gadsden	Commercial printing

continued

Exhibit 11–10 · Continued

Name of Company	Number Employed	Year Est.	Location	Products
Boaz Lowbed International	31–40	1991	Gadsden	Semitrailers
Bolin Cabinet Shop	6–10	1949	Attalla	Kitchen cabinets for mobile homes
Bragg's Factory Outlet	6–10	1977	Glencoe	Storm windows, wood doors
Buffalo Rock Company, Inc.	101–150	1977	Gadsden	Bottling
Burns Fabricating Co.	1–5	1957	Gadsden	Step rails, fences, staircases, burglar bars
C & H Manufacturing	6–10	1992	Hokes Bluff	Truck parts, truck rebuilding
C F & G Inc.	1–5	1983	Gadsden	Truck parts, truck rebuilding
Calhoun Asphalt Company, Inc.		1948	Gadsden	Paving mix
Center Star Manufacturing	76–100	1991	Gadsden	T-shirts, sweatshirts, jogging pants
Choice Fabricators, Inc.	76–100	1979	Attalla	Sheet metal fabrication, stamping, precision machining
Cleaners Hangers Company, Inc.	41–50	1939	Gadsden	Wire garment hangers
Cloud Pulpwood Company	1–5	1940	Attalla	Logging, pulpwood
Cofield Quick Printing	1–5	1980	Rainbow City	Offset printing, quick signs, banners
Coil Clip, Inc.	11–15	1990	Gadsden	Metal cutting
Commercial Printing Co., Inc.	1–5	1945	Gadsden	Printing
Connie Signs	1–5	1940	Gadsden	Signs and advertising displays
Conservation Management, Inc.	6–10	1991	Gadsden	Nonhazardous wastewater treatment plant
Coosa Millwork and Components, Inc.	21–30	1971	Glencoe	Wood windows, door, custom cabinets
Coosa Valley Steel, Inc.	21–30	1977	Attalla	Steel fabrication
Craft Plating and Finishing Co.	11–15	1955	Attalla	Electroplating metals
Custom Creations	6–10	1988	Attalla	Athletic sportswear and uniforms
Data Preparation, Inc.	101–150	1971	Gadsden	Data processing
Dean Sausage Co., Inc.	51–75	1955	Attalla	Sausage processing and packing
Dixie-Pacific Mfg. Co., Inc.	151–200	1967	Gadsden	Colonial wood columns, turnposts
EMCO , Inc.	650–750	1978	Gadsden	Military ordnance
ESI Metals Corporation	51–75	1948	Gadsden	Sheet metal fabrication
East Gadsden Manufacturing	21–30	1991	Gadsden	Ladies' sportswear
Equity Group Alabama, Keystone	301–350	1988	Gadsden	Further processed poultry
Etowah Asphalt Company, Inc.	6–10	1977	Attalla	Paving mix
Flowers Distributing Company	31–40	1989	Gadsden	Bakery product distribution
Gadsden Printing Company, Inc.	1–5	1930	Gadsden	Commercial printing
Gadsden Times	101–150	1861	Gadsden	Newspaper publishing, printing
Gadsden Tool Inc.	41–50	1985	Rainbow City	Tools
Goodyear Distribution Center	101–150	1952	Gadsden	Tire warehousing / distribution
Goodyear Tire and Rubber Co., Inc.	2,001–2,500	1929	Gadsden	Automobile, truck, and tractor tires, tubes, tread rubber
Gulf States Steel, Inc.	2,001–2,500	1986	Gadsden	Carbon steel plates, hot-, cold-rolled steels
Haney Company	51–75	1952	Glencoe	Custom machines, machine parts
Hanna Steel Corporation	41–50	1953	Gadsden	Steel processing (service center)
Holiday Lamp and Lighting, Inc.	21–30	1982	Glencoe	Lamps, lighting fixtures
International Jets, Inc.	6–10	1989	Gadsden	Aircraft purchase and reassembly
Jeffrey's Steel Co., Inc.	21–30	1989	Attalla	Steel fabrication

Exhibit 11–10 · **Continued**

Name of Company	Number Employed	Year Est.	Location	Products
Jones Sawmill Inc.	21–30	1925	Gadsden	Lumber, sawed and planed
KANS, Inc.	41–50	1985	Rainbow City	Refuse containers
Kentucky Farm Kitchens	21–30	1992	Attalla	Precooked sausage products
L B Chemical Company, Inc.	6–10	1950	Gadsden	Commercial chemicals, soaps, detergents
L & M Matkin Machine Shop	6–10	1991	Sardis	Screw machine products
Lemanco	51–75	1958	Gadsden	Storage bins, containers, silos
Liberty Trouser Company	76–100	1988	Altoona	Men's, boys', and children's trousers
Liberty Trouser Company	101–150	1991	Sardis	Men's, boys', and children's trousers
M & M Chemical Co., Inc.	41–50	1976	Attalla	Solvent distillation, fuel from ignitable liquid waste
Martin's Grill Meats	21–30	1939	Gadsden	Beef processing and packaging
Max Packaging Co.	51–75	1990	Attalla	Plastic tableware
Meadow Gold Dairies, Inc.	151–200	1956	Gadsden	Dairy products, juices
Mid-South Electrics, Inc.	451–550	1977	Gadsden	Appliances, computer assemblies, electric assemblies
Mindis Recycling Inc.	101–150	1947	Attalla	Metal processing
Miss Martha Originals, Inc.	76–100	1980	Glencoe	Doll figurines
Osborn Brothers, Inc.	76–100	1947	Gadsden	Commercial food distribution
Post Welding Supply Company	10–15	1943	Rainbow City	Welding supplies
Praxair (formerly Union Carbide)	41–50	1961	Gadsden	Oxygen, nitrogen, argon
Rainbow Mattress Co., Inc.	11–15	1920	Gadsden	Mattresses, box springs
Sherman Ready-Mix Co.	31–40	1921	Glencoe	Ready-mix concrete, concrete block
South Central Bell	151–200	1883	Gadsden	Telephone communications
Stamped Products	31–40	1983	Glencoe	Metal stamping
Stephenson Diversified Electronics, Inc.	75–100	1988	Gadsden	Electronic circuit boards
Trambeam Corp.	41–50	1983	Attalla	Overhead cranes, monorails, miscellaneous fabricated products
Tyson Feed Mill	31–40	1987	Attalla	Feed grains
Tyson Foods, Inc.	1,001–1,500	1970	Gadsden	Poultry processing
Vulcan Materials Co., Inc.	11–15	1930	Glencoe	Crushed stone

Army Base Hospital, RRMC was successful in obtaining the government contract for Tri-Care, thus bringing the area's military retirees to RRMC for service. In addition, HMA was present in Anniston in that it was in the second year of a three-year management agreement that would result in the acquisition of Stringfellow Memorial Hospital.

As for the services RRMC provided, they were again renovating their obstetric services (this was the first area concentrated on during the recent renovation project). RRMC was looking into rehabilitation. The competitor—GRMC—submitted a forty-bed CON for rehabilitation beds at the same time that HMA submitted a twenty-bed CON for RRMC and a twenty-bed CON for Stringfellow. Outcomes of the CONs were pending.

Outmigration to Birmingham None of the hospitals in Gadsden could ignore the opportunity for residents to travel outside the local area for nonemergency care. As shown earlier in Exhibit 11–6, Gadsden's proximity to the interstate network facilitated outmigration to urban areas boasting larger medical facilities. Although exact figures were

Exhibit 11–11 • Major Services Offered by RRMC and GRMC

Service Available and Reported by the Institution	RRMC	GRMC	Service Available and Reported by the Institution	RRMC	GRMC
Angioplasty	√	√	Medical/surgical intensive-care unit	√	√
Birthing room—LDR room LDR/P room	√	√	Nutrition programs	√	√
Breast cancer screening/mammogram	√	√	Obstetrics unit	√	√
Cardiac catheterization laboratory	√	√	Occupational health services	√	√
Cardiac intensive-care unit	√	√	Oncology services	√	√
Case management	√	√	Open-heart surgery	√	√
Community health status-based service planning	✘	√	Outpatient surgery	√	√
Community outreach	√	√	Patient education center	√	√
CT scanner	√	√	Patient representative services	√	√
Diagnostic radioisotope facility	√	√	Physical rehabilitation outpatient services	√	√
Emergency department	√	√	Psychiatric acute inpatient unit	✘	√
Extracorporeal shock wave lithotripter (ESWL)	✘	√	Psychiatric emergency services	✘	√
Geriatric services	√	✘	Radiation therapy	√	√
Health fair	√	√	Single photon emission computerized tomography (SPECT)	√	√
Health information center	√	✘	Social work services	√	√
Health screenings	√	√	Sports medicine	√	✘
Home health services	√	√	Support groups	✘	√
Hospice	✘	√	Trauma center (certified)	√	✘
Hospital-based outpatient care center—services	√	√	Ultrasound	√	√
Magnetic resonance imaging (MRI)	√	√	Volunteer services department	√	√
Meals on wheels	√	✘	Women's health center/services	√	√

√ = Yes   ✘ = No

Source: AHA Guide to the Health Care Field 1995–96 Edition. Published by the American Hospital Association; Chicago, 1995.

unknown, the volume was estimated to be in excess of 25 percent.

The Birmingham metropolitan area included approximately twenty hospitals, many of which offered specialty programs attractive to individuals who were predisposed to self-select health care services. Among those hospitals were HEALTHSOUTH (an internationally acclaimed sports medicine and rehabilitation facility), Baptist Medical Centers and St. Vincent's Hospital (religious, not-for-profits that were negotiating an alliance to strengthen their ability to provide specialty services), Brookwood Medical Center (a Tenet Healthcare Corporation facility), the Veterans' Administration Medical Center, and the University of Alabama at Birmingham (UAB) Medical Center.

The UAB Medical Center campus was located approximately one hour's drive from Gadsden via Interstate 59. It was a world-renowned patient care, education, and research complex, comprised of the Schools of Medicine, Dentistry, Nursing, Optometry, Health Related Professions, and Public Health, the University of Alabama Hospital, Children's Hospital of Alabama, and the Eye Foundation Hospital.

The Medical Center was dominated by the University of Alabama Hospital, a 903-bed teaching facility with more than fifty clinical services. University Hospital encompassed the Alabama Heart Hospital, the Lurleen Wallace Complex for comprehensive cancer treatment, Spain Rehabilitation Center, and the Diabetes Hospital. More than twenty-five educational, instructional, and patient care "centers of excellence" and approximately twenty specialty units providing treatment, screening, and laboratory services were sponsored by the hospital. The UAB Hospital was

Exhibit 11–12 · **Facility Comparison**

Category	RRMC	GRMC
Number of Beds	281	287
Number of Admissions	6,416	12,234
Census	117	193
Outpatient Visits	44,037	139,127
Births	260	1,385
Expense (in thousands of dollars)	*	78,535
Payroll (in thousands of dollars)	*	31,278
Personnel	720	1,154

* Data not reported.

Source: AHA Guide to the Health Care Field 1995–96 Edition. Published by the American Hospital Association; Chicago, 1995.

listed as one of America's best hospitals in a report published in the August 12, 1996, issue of *U.S. News and World Report*.[6] The report looked at 1,961 major medical centers, most of them teaching hospitals. Out of sixteen specialties, UAB ranked eighth in rheumatology, eighteenth in cardiology, twenty-sixth in geriatrics, and thirty-first in gastroenterology.

The medical staff (faculty for the UAB School of Medicine) practiced privately in the Kirklin Clinic, an ultramodern, high-technology facility that opened in 1992. The multispecialty Kirklin Clinic marketed aggressively throughout and beyond the Birmingham market area.

RRMC Operations

At the time Mr. Vollmer was named executive director of RRMC, he had more than ten years of experience in hospital administration and held an MBA from Cornell University. Early in his administration at RRMC substantial tangible and intangible changes were introduced into the organization. The members of the administrative team changed to some degree, as a new financial officer was brought on board in the reorganization and the information services manager chose to make a lateral move within the hospital when HMA's proprietary cost-management and information systems were implemented. A downsizing was initiated through consolidation of jobs, elimination of some positions, and attrition. In all, staffing decreased by about sixty full-time-equivalent posi-

tions. These changes occurred without reducing the services offered by RRMC.

Policies at RRMC were revised to decentralize decision making and give the department heads more operational control. The organizational culture began evolving from the previous one of strict conformity (under the administration of the Catholic order), which discouraged risk taking and participation in problem solving, to a culture in which the administrator was much more visible throughout the hospital and encouraged and reinforced employees' and management's input.

All of these changes were in keeping with the objectives of a well-orchestrated plan that included improving bottom-line accountability by spending the capital necessary to bring the facility up to date, increase efficiency, and improve accounts receivables. In addition, RRMC's objective was to expand and improve the services offered based on the geographic, demographic, and economic characteristics of the community.

Although the overall turnaround strategy was formulated at the corporate level, the details for implementation were developed and refined at the hospital level through the work of the administrative team and the managers, with particular support from the board of trustees and the marketing department.

RRMC's strategy was to provide excellent patient care in a cost-efficient manner. To achieve this, they worked closely with employees to provide quality care to their patients. RRMC utilized a series of surveys: ongoing patient surveys, annual physician surveys, and annual or biannual employee surveys. The results of each were widely dispersed. The physicians were brought together to discuss the outcomes, and employees were able to pick up the results in the Human Resources office.

Physical Plant Changes at RRMC

Physical changes in the plant were begun in 1991 on a large scale, and by 1996, the facility was in the final stages of a five-year, $20 million renovation project that began with the hospital's entrance and the emergency department (ED). The completely remodeled ED paralleled a level of medical sophistication usually observed only in larger urban hospitals. The ED was expanded to eighteen patient treatment rooms with monitoring capabilities that included hardwired and telemetry electrocardiograms, noninvasive blood pressure measurement, noninvasive arterial blood gases, respiratory rate, and temperature. The ED was supported by a full-service, fully equipped twenty-four-hour lab, and state-of-the-art CT and ultrasound imaging units.

In 1994, HMA purchased the Medical Arts Building a few blocks from the hospital. Several of the older physician practices were located in this building, and they were reluctant to make technological and appearance upgrades. Thus, as tenants moved out, new tenants were hard to attract.

RRMC's ED benefited from renovations that created separate entrances for outpatients and ED patients. Annual patient visits to the ED had increased from 23,000 to 26,000 since the renovation, and excess capacity still existed. Six months into 1996, ED utilization was projected to be 25,000 visits. It was found that patients were having higher acuity levels.

Since the 1991 acquisitions, new capital purchases increased the hospital's technological capabilities, and new services and programs were added in areas such as women's health, where the previous administration had not kept pace with the community's needs. Not only were clinical services changing, but innovative programs such as "Nurse First," "One Call Scheduling," and "MedKey," aimed at

marketing the hospital's new efficient and upscale image, were also implemented.

Innovative Programs

Targeted at potential patients, the Nurse First program emphasized RRMC's commitment to patient care. The first person a patient saw in the ED was a nurse, not someone from the registration department. The ED utilized a computerized protocol system approved by an emergency department physician that aided in the triage of patients. Eventually the patient was registered. The computer system then kept track of admitting physician problems (i.e., clinically inappropriate care). Vollmer emphasized, "The Emergency Department is an important front door."

Targeted at potential physicians, the One Call Scheduling program attempted to simplify the admission process for physicians. The admitting physician called a dedicated number at RRMC. The operator set up a conference call with all concerned departments at RRMC (preadmission testing, anesthesia, surgery scheduling, etc.). The key to the success of this program was "knowing your customers and tailoring your programs to meet their needs," according to Vollmer.

Aimed at individuals and potential employers, the MedKey system employed computer technology to streamline patient registration and admission procedures through the use of a plastic "smart card" with a magnetic strip on which pertinent patient information was encoded and updated quickly and easily, as necessary. MedKey translated into increased operational efficiency and better service for patients by substantially decreasing the amount of time required to process an admission and verify insurance coverage. All of the above programs portrayed a patient- and physician-oriented rather than a profit-oriented image.

Marketing

Subsequently, the MedKey system was utilized as a focused marketing strategy that used the patient database to promote RRMC facility utilization through membership incentives and rewards via discounts and extra services for MedKey "members." Marketing efforts were directed at recruiting potential individual members as well as employer-group memberships. As a marketing vehicle, MedKey was viewed by Mr. Vollmer as more effective and cost efficient than mass advertising. Begun in 1991 with approximately 4,000 members, membership swelled to approximately 34,000 in 1996.

An in-house newsletter, featuring new and existing programs and services as well as new benefits for MedKey members was developed and mailed on a regular basis. Promotional flyers were developed and mailed to inform members of upcoming events and activities.

The MedKey program created a win/win/win situation for area businesses, RRMC, and MedKey members. The hospital would win by improving its membership incentives through the discounts provided by the cosponsoring enterprises. The companies would win by reaching a larger market through the hospital's direct-mailings to the ever-growing list of MedKey members to promote upcoming events, new services, and membership discounts. The members would win by receiving savings on services at RRMC as well as savings on the products and services of co-sponsoring enterprises.

Operational

The hospital employed approximately 700 employees including nurses and housekeeping staff. The dietary department was contracted out, and the laundry service was provided by a local rather than a national vendor. This decision allowed for a perceived luxurious amenity in that the hospital had monogrammed towels as opposed to those with a stamped-on hospital logo available from national vendors.

RRMC attempted to attract top-notch physicians. They were able to attract a neurosurgeon from Loma Linda, California. The neurosurgeon rented his office space from RRMC and performed 95 percent of his procedures at RRMC. RRMC had recently recruited a neurologist to work with him.

In an effort to achieve a quality-driven level of patient-focused care, the patients had direct access to a number of service departments. Patient telephones provided direct access to the nurse manager, housekeeping, and food service (in the event of an error in dietary-restricted meals). This direct contact with the service provider resolved issues quickly rather than waiting for information to pass through a chain of command.

In 1994, RRMC was doing approximately 220 open-heart cases per year; in 1996 it had increased to approximately 300. The hospital operated two open-heart surgery programs.

Length of stay had decreased due to the employment of physician assistants (PAs). The hospital employed the PAs to make sure the required tests had been performed and the proper paperwork assembled for the attending physician when he or she arrived at the hospital to see the patient.

Operational efficiencies and the quality of the physical plant had improved markedly. RRMC had an average daily census of 130. In 1996, RRMC had an 8 percent increase in inpatient visits per year and a 20 percent increase in outpatient visits.

Future Challenges for RRMC

Vollmer was concerned about the tightening of health care dollars, especially the further cutbacks in Medicare. It was clear that facilities unable to profit from Medicare and Medicaid in 1996 would have greater financial difficulty in the future.

Vollmer identified two major issues that needed further consideration: first, how to maintain rapid growth, and second, how to entice more area employers (such as Goodyear) to utilize RRMC services and thus slow the outmigration to Birmingham facilities. In an effort to compete for patients in an area with low managed-care penetration, RRMC planned to approach the local Goodyear plant (that employed approximately 2,200 employees) to explain that its rates were $200 per day lower than GRMC's and $400 per day lower than facilities in Birmingham.

Vollmer felt that managed care had not really had an impact on how RRMC delivered services. However, there was a primary-care physician independent practice association (IPA) associated with RRMC and a specialist IPA associated with GRMC.

The doctors in the Gadsden area were fiercely independent. GRMC had chosen to align themselves with older area physicians with lower market presence.

Mr. Vollmer knew that modifications to HMA's efficiency-focused "success formula" would need to be made in the near future, and he was contemplating what crucial information was necessary to support any proposals he would make. Although the trend toward managed care presented an opportunity for RRMC, the medical staff as a group opposed the PPO concept and the majority of large businesses in the area were insured by Blue Cross. In order for the plan to have optimum strategic value, Mr. Vollmer recognized that proposals for future activity and growth must seriously consider the increasing political movement toward simpler and more comprehensive service arrangements.

Notes

1. Merrill Lynch, Health Management Associates, Inc. *New Buy Recommendation* (June 23, 1993).
2. Ernst & Young, Health Management Associates, Inc. *1995 Annual Report* (January 1996).
3. B. Japsen, "Investor-Owned Chains Seek Rich Rural Harvest," *Modern Healthcare* 26, no. 27 (July 1, 1996), pp. 32–37.
4. Ibid.
5. Ernst & Young, Health Management Associates, Inc. *1995 Annual Report* (January 1996).
6. "America's Best Hospitals," *U.S. News and World Report* 121, no. 6 (August 12, 1996), pp. 52–87.

Dr. Louis Mickael: The Physician as Strategic Manager

Industry Background

In the early 1900s, hospitals were perceived by the majority of the population in this country as places where very sick people went to die. However, in the past five decades, rapid progress in medical technology, knowledge base, and expertise enhanced professional capability, and the public now demanded high levels of health care services.

In fifty years, many demographic changes occurred. The population, longevity, and standard of living continued to increase. To address the needs of this changing population, government health care insurance programs for the older and needy segments of society were instituted. Private insurance companies proliferated, and although workers had begun to expect employers to share with them the financial responsibility for their health service needs, employers were searching for less expensive ways to provide such care. The government was also attempt-ing to reduce costs associated with the insurance programs it sponsored.

By the early 1980s, costs to provide these health care services reached epic proportions; and the financial ability of employers to cover these costs was being stretched to the breaking point. In addition, new government health care regulations had been enacted that have had far-reaching effects on this U.S. industry.

The most dramatic change came with the inauguration of a prospective payment system. By 1984, reimbursement shifted to a prospective system under which health care providers were paid preset fees for services rendered to patients. The current procedural terminology codes that were initiated at that time designated the maximum number of billed minutes allowable for the type of procedure (service) rendered for each diagnosis. A diagnosis was now identi-fied by the *International Classification of Diseases, Ninth Revision, Clinical Modification,* otherwise known as *ICD-9-CM.* The two types of codes, proce-dural and diagnosis, must logically correlate or reim-bursement was rejected.

Put simply, regardless of which third-party payor insured a patient for health care, the bill for an office visit was determined by the number of min-utes that the regulation allowed for the visit. This was dictated by the diagnosis of the primary problem that brought the patient into the office and the justifi-able procedures used to treat it.

These cost-cutting measures initiated through the government-mandated prospective payment regulation

This case was prepared by C. Louise Sellaro of Youngstown State University. It is intended as a basis for class discussion rather than to illustrate effective or ineffective handling of an administrative situation. The names of the firms, indi-viduals, locations, and financial information have been dis-guised to preserve the organization's desire for anonymity. Presented and accepted by the Referred Society for Case Research. All rights reserved to the author and S.C.R. Copyright © 1992 by C. Louise Sellaro. Used with permis-sion from Louise Sellaro.

added to physicians' overhead costs because more paperwork was needed to submit claims and collect fees. In addition, the length of time increased between billing and actual reimbursement, causing cash flow problems for medical practices unable to make the procedural changes needed to adjust. This new system had the effect of reducing income for most physicians, because the fees set by the regulation were usually lower than those physicians had previously charged.

Almost all other operating costs of office practice increased. These included utilities, maintenance, and insurance premiums for office liability coverage, workers' compensation, and malpractice coverage (for which costs tripled in the past few years). This changed the method by which government insurance reimbursement was provided for health care disbursed to individuals covered under the Medicare and Medicaid programs. Private insurers quickly adopted the system, and health care as an industry moved into a more competitive mode of doing business.

The industry profile of today differed markedly from that of only a decade ago. Hospitals became complex blends of for-profit and not-for-profit divisions, joint ventures, and partnerships. In addition, health care provided by individual physician practitioners had undergone change. These professionals were forced to take a new look at just who their patients were and what was the most feasible, competitively justifiable, and ethical mode of providing and dispensing care to them.

For the first time in his life, Dr. Lou read about physicians who were bankrupt. In actuality, Dr. Charles, who shared office space with him, was having a financial struggle and was close to declaring bankruptcy.

January 6, 1994

The last patient had just left, and Dr. Lou Mickael ("Dr. Lou") sat in his office thinking about the day's events. He had been delayed getting into work because a patient telephoned him at home to talk about a problem with his son. When he arrived at the office and before there was time to see any of the patients waiting for him, the hospital called to tell him that an elderly patient, Mr. Spence, admitted through the emergency room last night had taken a turn for the worse.

"My days in the office usually start with some sort of crisis," he thought. "In addition to that, the national regulations for physician and hospital care reimbursement are forcing me to spend more and more time dealing with regulatory issues. The result of all this is that I'm not spending enough time *with* my patients. Although I could retire tomorrow and not have to worry financially, that's not an alternative for me right now. Is it possible to change the way this practice is organized, or should I change the type of practice I'm in?"

Practice Background

When Dr. Lou began medical practice over thirty-five years ago, the northeastern city's population was approximately 130,000 people, most of whom were blue-collar workers with diverse ethnic backgrounds. By 1994, suburban development surrounded the city, more than doubling the population base. A large representation of service industries were added, along with an extensive number of upper and middle managers and administrators typically employed by such industries.

Location

Dr. Lou kept the same office over the years. It was less than one-half mile from the main thoroughfare and located in a neighborhood of single-family dwellings. The building, constructed specifically for the purpose of providing space for physicians' offices, was situated across the street from City General, the hospital where Dr. Lou continued to maintain staff privileges. Three physicians (including Dr. Lou) formed a corporation to purchase the building, and each doctor paid that corporation a monthly rental fee, which was based primarily on square footage occupied, with an adjustment for shared facilities such as a waiting room and rest rooms.

Office Layout

One of the physicians, Dr. Salis, was an orthopedic surgeon who occupied the entire top floor of the building. Dr. Mickael and the other physician, Dr.

Charles, were housed on the first floor. Total office space for each (a small reception area, two examining rooms, and private office) encompassed a 15' × 75' area (see Exhibit 12–1). The basement was reserved for storage and maintenance equipment.

The reception area and each of the other rooms that made up the office space opened onto a hallway that Dr. Lou shared with Dr. Charles. The two physicians and their respective staff members had a good rapport; and because the reception desks opened across from each other, each staff was able to provide support for the other by answering the phone or giving general information to patients when the need arose.

The large, common waiting room was used by both physicians. After reporting to their own doctor's reception area, patients were seated in this room, then paged for their appointment via loudspeaker.

Dr. Charles was in his mid-forties and in general practice as well. His patients ranged in age from eighteen to their mid-eighties, and his office was open from 10:00 A.M. until 7:30 P.M. on Mondays and Thursdays, and from 9:30 A.M. until 4:30 P.M. on Tuesdays and Fridays; no office hours were scheduled on Wednesday. He and Dr. Lou were familiar with each other's patient base, and each covered the other's practice when necessary.

Staff and Organizational Structure

Dr. Lou's staff included one part-time bookkeeper (who doubled as office manager) and two part-time assistants. The assistants' and bookkeeper's time during office hours was organized in such a way that one individual was always at the reception desk and another was "floating," taking care of records, helping as needed in the examining rooms, and providing office support functions. There were never more than two staff people on duty at one time, and the assistants' job descriptions overlapped considerably (see Exhibit 12–2 for job descriptions). Each staff member could handle phone calls, schedule appointments, and usher patients in the examining rooms for their appointments.

Although Dr. Lou was "only a phone call away" from patients on a twenty-four-hour basis, patient visits were scheduled only four days a week. On two of these days (Monday and Thursday) hours were from 9:00 A.M. to 5:00 P.M. The other two were "long days" (Tuesday and Friday), when office hours officially were extended to 7:00 P.M. in the evening, but often ran much later.

The fifth weekday (Wednesday) was reserved for meetings, which were an important part of Dr.

Exhibit 12–1 • Shared Office Space of Dr. Mickael and Dr. Charles

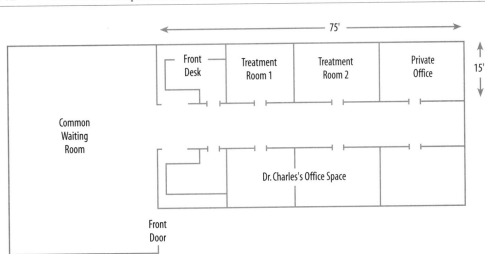

Exhibit 12–2 · Job Descriptions for Dr. Mickael's Office Staff

Job Description: Bookkeeper/Office Manager

In addition to responsibility for bookkeeping functions, ordering supplies, and reconciling the orders with supplies received, this person knows how to run the reception area, pull the file charts, and usher patients to treatment rooms. In addition, she can handle phone calls, schedule appointments, and enter office charges into patient accounts using the computer.

Job Description: Assistant 1

The main responsibility of this position is insurance billing. Additional duties include running the reception area, pulling and filing charts, ushering patients to treatment rooms, answering the phone, scheduling appointments, entering office charges into patient accounts, and placing supplies received into appropriate storage areas.

Job Description: Assistant 2

This is primarily a receptionist position. The duties include running the reception area, pulling and filing charts, ushering patients to treatment rooms, answering the phone, scheduling appointments, entering office charges into patient accounts, and placing supplies received into appropriate storage areas.

Lou's professional responsibilities because he was a member of several hospital committees. He was one of two physicians residing on the ten-member board of the hospital, and this, along with other committee responsibilities, often demanded attendance at a variety of scheduled sessions from 7:00 A.M. until late afternoon on "meetings" day. Wednesday was used by the staff to process patient insurance forms, enter patient data into their charts and accounts receivables, and prepare bills for processing.

When paperwork began to build after the PPS regulations came into effect in the 1980s, patients had many problems dealing with the forms that were required for reimbursement of services received in a physician's office. It was the option of physicians whether to "accept assignment" (the standard fee designated by an insurance payor for a particular health care service provided in a medical office). A physician who chose to *not* accept assignment must bill patients for health care services according to a fee schedule ("a usual charge" industry profile) that was preset by Medicare for Medicare patients. Most other insurances followed the same profile. Dr. Lou agreed to accept the standard fee, but the patient had to pay 20 percent of that fee, so the billing process became quite complicated.

In 1988, Dr. Lou decided that he needed to computerize his patient information base to provide support for the billing function. He investigated the possibility of using an off-site billing service, but it lacked the flexibility needed to deal with regulatory changes in patient insurance reporting that occurred with greater and greater frequency. Dr. Charles was asked if he wished to share expenses and develop a networked computer system. But the offer was declined; he preferred to take care of his own billing manually.

An information systems consultant was hired to investigate the computer hardware and software systems available at that time, make recommendations for programs specifically developed for a practice of this type, and oversee installation of the final choice. After initial setup and staff training, the consultant came to the office only on an "as needed" basis, mostly to update the diagnostic and procedure codes for insurance billing.

Computerization was an important addition to the record-keeping process, and the system helped increase the account collection rate. However, at times problems would arise when the regulations changed and third-party payors (insurance companies) consequently adjusted procedure or diagnosis codes. For example, there was often some lag time between such decisions and receipt of the information needed to update the computer program. Fortunately, the software chosen remained technologically sound, codes were easily adjusted, and vendor support was very good.

Although the new system helped to adjust the account collection rate, fitting this equipment into the cramped quarters of current office space was a problem. To keep the computer paper and other supplies out of the way, Dr. Lou and his staff had to constantly move the heavy boxes containing this stock to and from the basement storage area.

January 8, 1994 (Morning)

On Dr. Lou's way in that day, the bookkeeper told him that something needed to be done about accounts receivable. Lag time between billing and reimbursement was again getting out of hand, and cash flow was becoming a problem (see Exhibits 12–3

Exhibit 12–3 • Trial Balance at December 31

	1991	1992	1993
Debits			
Cash	$15,994	$9,564	$8,666
Petty cash	50	100	100
Accounts receivable	19,081	25,054	28,509
Medical equipment	11,722	11,722	11,722
Furniture and fixtures	3,925	3,925	3,361
Salaries	117,455	124,608	132,325
Professional dues and licenses	1,925	1,873	1,816
Miscellaneous professional expenses	1,228	2,246	3,232
Drugs and medical supplies	2,550	1,631	2,176
Laboratory fees	2,629	524	1,801
Meetings and seminars	2,543	838	3,880
Legal and professional fees	5,525	2,057	5,400
Rent	16,026	16,151	18,932
Office supplies	4,475	3,262	4,989
Publications	1,390	406	401
Telephone	1,531	1,451	2,400
Insurance	8,876	9,629	11,760
Repairs and maintenance	3,547	4,240	5,352
Auto expense	1,009	1,487	3,932
Payroll taxes	3,107	2,998	3,780
Computer expenses	846	938	1,905
Bank charges	438	455	479
	$225,872	$225,159	$256,918
Credits			
Professional fees	$172,281	$172,472	$204,700
Interest income	992	456	210
Capital	46,122	43,137	40,117
Accumulated depreciation (furniture and fixtures)	1,692	2,151	2,796
Accumulated depreciation (medical equipment)	4,785	6,943	9,095
	$225,872	$225,159	$256,918

through 12–6 for financial information concerning the practice).

Cash flow had not been a problem prior to PPS, when billing for the health care provided by Dr. Lou was simpler, and payment was usually retrospectively reimbursed through third-party payors. However, as the regulatory agencies continued to refine the codes for reporting procedures, more and more

Exhibit 12–4 • Gross Revenue and Accounts Receivable

| | December 31 | |
	1979	1986
Gross revenue	$116,951	$137,126
Accounts receivable	15,684	32,137

Exhibit 12–5 • Statements of Income for the Years Ended December 31

	1991	1992	1993
Operating Revenues			
Professional fees	$172,281	$172,472	$204,700
Interest income	992	456	210
Total revenues	173,273	172,928	204,910
Operating Expenses			
Salaries (Dr. Mickael, Staff)	117,455	124,608	132,325
Professional dues and licenses	1,925	1,873	1,816
Miscellaneous professional expenses	1,228	2,246	3,232
Drugs and medical supplies	2,550	1,631	2,176
Laboratory fees	2,629	524	1,801
Meetings and seminars	2,543	838	3,880
Legal and professional fees	5,525	2,057	5,400
Rent	16,026	16,151	18,932
Office supplies	4,475	3,262	4,989
Publications	1,390	406	401
Telephone	1,531	1,451	2,400
Insurance	8,876	9,629	11,760
Repairs and maintenance	3,547	4,240	5,352
Auto expense	1,009	1,487	3,932
Payroll taxes	3,107	2,998	3,780
Computer expenses	846	938	1,905
Bank charges	438	455	479
Total operating expenses	175,100	174,794	204,560
Net Income (Loss)	($1,827)	($1,866)	$350

Exhibit 12–6 • **Balance Sheets at December 31**

	1991	1992	1993
Assets			
Capital equipment			
Medical equipment	$11,722	$11,722	$11,722
Furniture and fixtures	3,925	3,925	3,361
Less-accumulated depreciation	(6,477)	(9,094)	(11,891)
Total capital equipment	9,170	6,553	3,192
Current assets			
Cash	15,994	9,564	8,668
Petty cash	50	100	100
Accounts receivable	19,081	25,054	28,509
Total current assets	35,125	34,718	37,275
Total assets	$44,295	$41,271	$40,469
Liabilities			
Current liabilities			
Income taxes payable	($639)	($653)	$123
Dividends payable	1,158	1,154	1,154
Total current liabilities	519	501	1,277
New income	(1,188)	(1,213)	229
Less dividends	1,158	1,154	1,154
Retained earnings	(2,346)	(2,367)	(925)
Capital	46,122	43,137	40,117
Total owner's equity	46,122	40,770	39,192
Total liabilities and owner's equity	$44,295	$41,271	$40,469

pressure was being placed on physicians to use additional or extended codes in reporting the condition of a patient. Speed of reimbursement was a function of the accuracy with which codes were recorded and subsequently reported to Medicare and other insurance companies. In part, that was determined by a physician's ability to keep current with code changes required to report illness diagnoses and office procedures.

Cathy, the receptionist, had a list of patients who wanted Dr. Lou to call as soon as he came in. She also wanted to know if he could squeeze in time around lunch hour to look at her husband's arm; she believed he had a serious infection resulting from a work-related accident. The wound looked pretty nasty this morning, and Cathy thought maybe it should not wait until the first available appointment at 7:00 P.M.

"I'm just starting to see my patients, and I've already done a half-day's work," Dr. Lou thought when he buzzed his assistant to bring in the first patient. He was forty-five minutes late.

Patient Profile

When Dr. Lou walked into Treatment Room 1 to see the first patient of the day, Doris Cantell, he was thinking about how his practice had grown over the years. His practice maintained between 800 and 900 patients in active files. In comparison to other solo practitioners in the area, this would be considered a fairly large patient base.

"Well, how are you feeling today?" he asked the matronly woman. Doris and her husband, like many of his patients, were personal friends.

In the beginning years of practice, Dr. Lou's patients had been primarily younger people with an average age in the mid-thirties; their average income was approximately $15,000. Their families and careers were just beginning, and it was not unusual to spend all night with a new mother waiting to deliver a baby. Although often dead tired, he enjoyed the closeness of the professional relationships he had with his patients. He believed that much of his success as a physician came from "going that extra mile" with them.

Many things had changed. Today all pregnancies were referred to specialists in the obstetrics field. His patients ranged in age from three to ninety-seven, with an average of fifty-eight years; their median income was $25,000. Most were blue-collar workers or recently retired, and their health care needs were quite diverse.

Approximately 60 percent of Dr. Lou's patients were subsidized by Medicare insurance, and most of the retired patients carried supplemental insurance with other third-party payors. Three types of third-party payors were involved in Dr. Lou's practice: (1) private insurance companies, such as Blue Cross and Blue Shield; (2) government insurance (Medicare and Medicaid); and (3) preferred provider organizations.

Preferred provider organizations and health maintenance organizations were forms of group insurance that emerged in response to the need to cut the costs of providing health care to patients, which resulted in the prospective payment system. Both types of organizations developed a list of physicians who would accept their policies and fee schedules; using the list, subscribers chose the doctor from whom they preferred to obtain health care services.

Contrary to reimbursement policies of most other major medical third-party payors, PPOs and HMOs covered the cost of office visits, and the patient might not be responsible for any percentage of that cost. Although the physician must accept a fee

schedule determined by the outside organization, there was an advantage to working with these agencies. A physician might be on the list of more than one organization, and a practice could maintain or expand its patient base through the exposure gained from being listed as a health service provider for such organizations.

Those patients who were working usually had coverage through work benefits. Some were now members of a PPO. Dr. Lou was on the provider list of the Northeast Health Care PPO; only a few of his patients were enrolled in the government welfare program.

"How's your daughter doing in college?" Dr. Lou asked. He had a strong rapport with the majority of his patients, many of whom continued to travel to his office for medical needs even after they moved out of the immediate area. "Are you heading south again this winter, and are you maintaining your 'snowbird' relationship with Dr. Jackson?"

It was not unusual for patients to call from as far away as Florida and Arizona during the winter months to request his opinion about a medical problem, and Doris had called last year to ask him to recommend a physician near their winter home in the South. Because of this personal attention, once patients initiated health care with him, they tended to continue. Dr. Lou lost very few patients to other physicians in the area since he began to practice medicine. The satisfaction experienced by his patients provided the only marketing function carried out for the practice. Any new patients (other than professional referrals) were drawn to the office through word-of-mouth advertising.

Dr. Lou: Profile of the Physician

Dr. Lou had grown older with many of his patients. His practice spanned more than three generations; a lot of families had been with him since he opened his doors in 1961. Caring for these people, many of whom had become personal friends, was very important to him. However, as the character of the health care industry was changing, Dr. Lou was beginning to feel that he now spent entirely too much time dealing with the "system" rather than taking care of patients.

Eighty-year-old Mr. Spence was a good example. Three weeks ago he was discharged from the hospital after having a pacemaker implanted. He had been living at home with his wife, and although she was wheelchair bound, they managed to maintain some semblance of independence with the assistance of part-time care. Lately, however, the man had become more and more confused. The other night he wandered into the yard, fell, and broke his hip. His reentry to the hospital so soon meant that a great deal of paperwork would be needed to justify this second hospital admission. In addition, Dr. Lou expected to receive calls from their children asking for information to help them determine the best alternatives for the care of both parents from now on. He had never charged a fee for such consultation, considering this to be an extension of the care he normally provided.

"Things are really different now," he thought. "Under this new system I don't have the flexibility I need to determine how much time I should spend with a patient. The regulations are forcing me to deal with business issues for which I have no background, and these concerns for costs and time efficiency are very frustrating. Medical school trained me in the art and science of treating patients, and in that respect I really feel I do a good job, but no training was provided to prepare me to deal with the business part of a health care practice. I wonder if it's possible to maintain *my* standards for quality care and still keep on practicing medicine."

Local Environment

The actual number of city residents had not changed appreciably since the early 1960s, although suburban areas had grown considerably. In the mid-1970s, a four-lane expressway, originally targeted for construction only one mile from the center of the downtown area, was put in place about eight miles farther away. Within five years, most of the stores followed the direction of that main highway artery and moved to a large mall situated about five miles from the original center of the city. Many of the former downtown shops then stood empty. Now, government offices, banking and investment firms, insurance and real estate offices, and a university occupied some of this vacated space; and it was used for quite different (primarily service-oriented) business activities.

A number of residential apartments devoted to housing for the elderly and low-income families were built near the original, downtown shopping area. Several large office buildings (where much space was available for rent) and offices for a number of human services agencies relocated nearby.

As he headed across the street to lunch in the hospital dining room, Dr. Lou was again thinking about how things had changed. At first, he had been one of a few physicians in this area. Within the past ten years, however, many new physicians moved in.

Competition

Two large (500-bed) hospitals within easy access of the downtown area had been in operation for over forty years. One was located immediately within the city limits on the north side of the city; the other was also just inside city limits on the opposite (south) side. They were approximately three miles apart and competed for a market share with City General, a 100-bed facility. This smaller hospital was only two blocks from the old business district; it was the only area hospital where Dr. Lou maintained staff privileges. Exhibit 12–7 contains a map showing the location of the hospitals and Dr. Lou's office.

The two large hospitals had begun to actively compete for staff physicians (physicians in private practice who paid fees to a hospital for the privilege of bringing their patients there for treatment). In addition, these two health care institutions offered start-up help for newly certified physicians by providing low-cost office space and ensuring financial support for a certain period of time while they worked through the first months of practice.

City General recently began subsidizing physicians coming into the area by providing them with offices inside the hospital. Most of these physicians worked in specialty fields that had a strong market demand, and the hospital gave them a salary and special considerations, such as low rent for the first months of practice, to entice them to stay in the area.

Exhibit 12–7 • Map of the Hospitals and Dr. Mickael's Medical Office

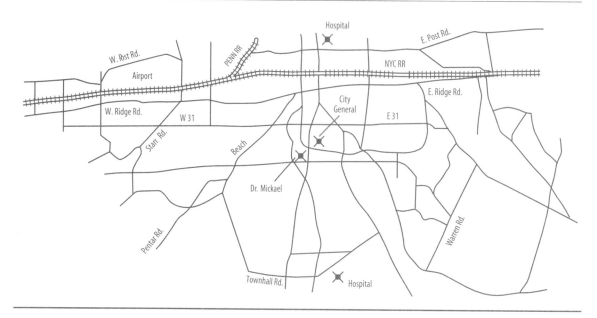

These doctors served as consultants to hospital patients admitted by other staff physicians and could influence the length of time a patient remained in the hospital. This was an extremely important issue for the hospital, because under the new regulations a long length of stay could be costly to the facility. All third-party insurers reimbursed only a fixed amount to the hospital for patient care; the payment received was based on the diagnosis under which a patient was admitted. Should a patient develop complications, a specialist could validate the extension of reimbursable time to be added to the length of stay for that patient.

In the past few years, many services to patients provided by all these hospitals changed to care provided on an outpatient basis. Advancements in technology made it possible to complete in one day a number of services, including tests and some surgical procedures, which formerly required admission into the hospital and an overnight stay. Many such procedures could also be done by physicians in their offices, but insurance reimbursement was faster and easier if a patient had them done in a hospital. As an example of the degree of change involved, in the mid-1980s, outpatient gross revenue was only 18 percent of total gross revenue for City General. In 1992, this figure was projected to be approximately 30 percent.

January 8, 1994 (Lunchtime)

"May I join you?"

Dr. Lou looked up from his lunch to see Jane Duncan, City General's hospital administrator standing across the table. "I'd like to talk with you about something."

Dr. Lou thought he knew what this was about. The hospital had been recruiting additional staff physicians, doctors who owned private practices in and around the city. A number of these individuals held family practice certification, a prerequisite for staff privileges in many hospitals. The recruitment program offered financial assistance to physicians who were family practice specialists wishing to move into the area, and also subsidized placement of younger physicians who had recently completed their residencies. In contrast to physicians designated as gen-

Exhibit 12–8 • Industrial Medicine as a New Career for Dr. Mickael

"Industrial Medicine" is an emerging physician specialty. Training in this new field entails postgraduate work and board certification.

As yet, only a few schools provide such training. One is located in Cincinnati, Ohio, which is geographically close enough to be feasible for Dr. Mickael. The time spent in actual attendance amounts to one two-week training period beginning in June of the year in which a physician is accepted for the training. Two additional training periods are each one week in duration: these take place in the following months of October and March. After this, the physician is expected to individually study for and take the board certification exams, which are given only once per year; the exams are comprehensive and extend over a two-day period.

Training Program Costs: Industrial Medicine

University Residency:	
Three, on-site class sessions	$4,000.00
Per night cost for room	47.87
Books and supplies (total)	580.53
Transportation, Air:	
Three, round-trip fares	$1,650.00
Transportation, Ground:	
Car rental, per week with unlimited mileage	$125.45

eral practitioners, who had not received training beyond that received through medical school and a residency, "family practitioners" received additional training and passed state board exams written to specifically certify a physician in that field.

Last week after a hospital staff meeting, Duncan had caught him in the hall and wanted to know if Dr. Lou had thought about his retirement plans. "It's really not too soon," she had said. Dr. Lou knew that one of the methods used to bring in "new blood" was to provide financial backing to a physician wishing to ease out of practice, helping pay the salary of a partner (usually one with family practice certification) until the older physician retired.

"She wants to talk to me again about retirement and taking on a partner," he thought. "But I'm only in my late fifties. And I'm not ready to go to pasture yet! Besides, there was really no room to install a partner in my office."

January 8, 1994 (Afternoon)

After lunch Dr. Lou ran back to the office to take a look at Cathy's husband's arm before regular office hours started. This was a work-related case. As he

treated the patient, he began thinking about industrial medicine as an alternative to full-time office practice. Right then the prospect seemed quite appealing. He had investigated the idea enough to know that there were only a few schools that provided this kind of training but one was within driving distance (Exhibit 12–8 contains information on industrial medicine).

As health costs rose over the past decade, manufacturing organizations began to feel the cost pinch of providing health care insurance to employees. Some larger companies in the area began to recognize the cost benefit of maintaining a private physician on staff who was trained in the treatment of health care needs for industrial workers. Dr. Lou had been considering going back for postgraduate training in industrial medicine, and while wrapping the man's arm, he began to think about working for a large corporation.

"Work like that could have a lot of benefits; it would give me a chance to do something a little different, at least part time for now," he thought. "The income was almost comparable to what I net for the same time in the office, and some days I might even get home before 9:00 P.M.!"

End of the Day

As he was putting on his coat and getting ready to leave, Dr. Charles, the physician from across the hall, phoned to ask if Dr. Lou might be interested in buying him out. "I think you could use the space," he said, "and my practice is going down the tubes. I can't seem to get an upper hand with the finances. I've had to borrow every month to maintain the cash flow needed to pay *my* bills because patients can't keep up with theirs. City General has offered me a staff position, and I'm seriously considering it. I thought I'd give you first chance." After some minutes of other "office talk," Dr. Charles said good night.

"If I wanted to take on a new partner, that could work out well," thought Dr. Lou. "It might be interesting to check into this. I wonder what his asking price would be? It could not be too much more than the value of my practice; although his patients are a bit younger and some of his equipment is a little newer. The initial hospital proposal to buy me out indicated that my practice was worth about $175,000. So that means I should be able to negotiate with Dr. Charles for a little less than $200,000."

It was 9:30 P.M. when Dr. Lou finally left the office, and he still had hospital rounds to make. "This is another situation caused by these insurance regulations," he thought. "I feel as though I'm continuously updating patients' hospital records throughout the day, and more of my patients require hospitalization more often than they did when they were younger. All things being equal, I'm earning considerably less for doing the same things I did a decade ago, and in addition the paperwork has increased exponentially. There has to be a better way for me to deal with this business of practicing medicine."

Louisiana Office of Public Health: Challenges to the Strategic Planning Process

Getting Started

The Louisiana Office of Public Health (OPH) was directed by an assistant secretary, Eric Baumgartner, who was appointed to the post by Governor Edwin Edwards in 1993. In recent years, Dr. Baumgartner, Liz Sumrall, and Joe Kimbrell had participated in various public health strategic planning and leadership forums that impressed them with the importance of public health's need to organize and reengineer in the context of the relevant changes afoot in this country. In 1994, the OPH management team was convinced that immediate action was needed to involve the agency staff in strategic planning, but they recognized that guidance and assistance was necessary to achieve the excellent results they desired. That meant seeking outside consultation to direct an agencywide strategic planning process, in concert with existing planning and executive management staff. A strong mission and strategic plan could be his legacy as health officer.

The money to hire consultants had to be found and approved by the Department of Health and Hospitals (DHH) before developing a request for proposals. Eric hoped the entire process could be completed before the next gubernatorial election because most

This case was prepared by Woodrow D. Richardson, Peter M. Ginter, W. Jack Duncan, Linda E. Swayne, Eric Baumgartner, and Jimmy Guidry. It is intended as a basis for class discussion rather than to illustrate effective or ineffective handling of an administrative situation. Used with permission from Woody Richardson.

health officers did not survive the political process in Louisiana. However, initiating the process took much longer than he anticipated.

The Design of the Planning Process

For the strategic planning process to be successful, the Office of Public Health would need to develop the capacity to do its own planning. Organizations learn by doing strategic planning. Externally generated plans often have little "buy-in" from the rank and file. Therefore, wide participation in the strategic planning process was essential. Employees from all levels and all functions within OPH were asked to participate. Over one hundred volunteered to serve on one or more of the task forces; additional employees became involved through subcommittees and networking.

Exhibit 13–1 shows the organization of the strategic planning process. The internal, external, and mission/vision task forces were responsible for performing situational analysis that would become input to the steering committee charged with strategic decision making and direction setting. The implementation task force was charged with developing operational plans in support of the decisions made by the steering committee.

Kick-off meetings were held in New Orleans, Alexandria, and Lafayette to solicit participation from OPH employees. Rather than concluding the twelve-month process by election time, the kick-off meetings were held just prior to the November 1995 elections. Exhibit 13–2 depicts the milestone chart for the entire year-long strategic planning process.

Exhibit 13–1 · OPH Strategic Management Task Force Structure

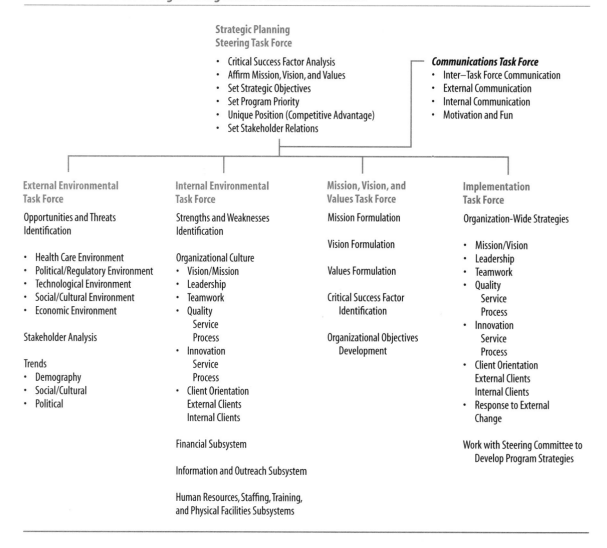

The State of Louisiana

History

In 1682, Robert Cavelier, Sieur de la Salle, named the land at the mouth of the Mississippi "Louisiana" in honor of King Louis XIV. The French ceded Louisiana to the Spanish in 1762. The colony grew as Americans, Spaniards, and Acadian refugees from Nova Scotia settled in Louisiana. In 1800, Napoleon forced the Spanish government to return Louisiana to French rule only to sell it to the United States to keep it from falling into British hands. In 1803, President Thomas Jefferson made the "Louisiana Purchase" for $15 million.

During the early to mid-1800s, Louisiana enjoyed great prosperity. The state produced sugar and cotton on the delta lands and hogs and cattle on the hills of the north and southwest. At the time of the Civil War, nearly half of Louisiana's population were slaves. Thousands of Louisiana residents (black and white) died in this conflict. Large landowners, bankers, businessmen, and politicians dominated

Exhibit 13–2 • OPH Strategic Management Milestone Chart

Months	October	November	December	January	February	March	April	May	June	July	August	September
Weeks	1 2 3 4	1 2 3 4	1 2 3 4	1 2 3 4	1 2 3 4	1 2 3 4	1 2 3 4	1 2 3 4	1 2 3 4	1 2 3 4	1 2 3 4	1 2 3 4

TASKS

- Organization of the Process
  - Create Task Forces
  - Set Up Communications
  - Strategic Planning Retreat
- External Environmental Assessment
  - Opportunities and Threats Identification
  - Stakeholder Analysis
  - Futures Scenario Development
  - Louisiana Trends Identification
- Internal Environmental Assessment
  - Strengths and Weaknesses Identification
  - Financial Subsystem
  - Information and Outreach
  - Human Resources, Staffing, and Physical Facilities
  - Assess Organizational Culture
- Mission, Vision, and Values
  - Mission Formulation
  - Vision Formulation
  - Values Formulation
  - Critical Success Factor Identification
  - Development of Objectives
- Steering Committee
  - Strategic Planning Retreat
  - Critical Success Factor Analysis
  - Affirm Mission and Vision
  - Affirm Values
  - Set Strategic Objectives
  - Program Evaluation
  - Set Program Strategies
  - Set Organization-Wide Strategies
- Operational Plans
  - Set Program Objectives
  - Set Organization-Wide Objectives
  - Develop Program Strategies
  - Develop Organization-Wide Strategies
  - Coordinate All Strategies
- Debrief and Set Up Next Year's Strategic Planning Process

Weeks	1 2 3 4	1 2 3 4	1 2 3 4	1 2 3 4	1 2 3 4	1 2 3 4	1 2 3 4	1 2 3 4	1 2 3 4	1 2 3 4	1 2 3 4	1 2 3 4
Months	October	November	December	January	February	March	April	May	June	July	August	September

state government after the Civil War. The populist movement and the social reforms associated with it were held in check until the election of Huey P. Long as governor in 1928. From 1928 to 1960 the Long family dominated state politics (Huey 1928–1935, his brother Earl, three-time governor, and Huey's son Russell, as U.S. senator). During the Long Era, Louisiana developed into a major petrochemical-manufacturing center. Oil and gas tax revenues fueled unprecedented spending on welfare, highways, and education.

Geography

Louisiana was approximately 237 miles across (east to west) and roughly the same distance from north to south. It was the thirty-first largest state in the United States. The highest elevation in Louisiana was 535 feet above sea level whereas the lowest was 5 feet below sea level. Louisiana had almost 11,000 square miles of wetlands, the most of any state. Exhibit 13–3 presents a map of Louisiana.

Population

In 1994, the population of Louisiana was approximately 4.3 million. Twenty-first in population, the state was projected to grow less than 1 percent by the year 2000. Louisiana's sixty-five and older population was expected to grow from 526,000 in 1990 to 604,000 by the year 2010. Approximately 44 percent of the population resided in rural parishes. The percentage of African Americans in Louisiana was more than twice the national average: 30.8 percent in Louisiana compared to 12 percent nationally. Individual parishes ranged from less than 10 percent to more than 80 percent African American.

Education

Despite having twenty-four colleges and universities, just 10 percent of the population had earned at least a bachelor's degree. Approximately 22 percent of Louisiana's population had not completed high school; the dropout rate was the highest in the United States— 13.7 percent compared to 9.3 percent nationally.

Economy

Louisiana produced about 30 percent of the nation's natural gas valued at $3.4 billion. It produced oil that was valued at $2.4 billion. Job growth for the remainder of this century was predicted to come from services.

Culture

Louisiana's diverse roots produced several distinct cultural variations within the state. The largest metropolitan area was New Orleans with over 1.25 million residents, most of whom were of the Catholic faith. Tourism and shipping gave New Orleans a cosmopolitan feel not found elsewhere in the state. Most of the state north of Baton Rouge was Protestant, rural, and very similar to the surrounding states of Arkansas and Mississippi. South of Baton Rouge the Cajun culture dominated.

Politics

Through the years Louisiana politics could be described as "colorful." Governor Huey P. Long's administrations produced stories of legendary proportions. In more recent years, a governor was convicted of fraud and a sheriff was elected while serving a jail term. The 1995 gubernatorial election culminated in Republican businessman Mike Foster, who promised less government and greater efficiency, winning the office. Foster appointed Bobby Jindal as secretary of the Department of Health and Hospitals (DHH). He asked Eric Baumgartner to stay on as head of OPH.

The Office of Public Health

The Office of Public Health was a program office under the DHH. DHH was responsible for assuring all public health services for the State of Louisiana through four program offices. DHH operated on an annual budget in excess of $3 billion and had more than 13,000 employees statewide. DHH was administered by a secretary, who reported to the governor, and each program office, including the Office of Public Health, was headed by an assistant secretary.

OPH provided a wide range of community services, offering public health related community leadership at the state, regional, and local levels; sponsoring health education programs; and developing public health policies. OPH enforced the State Sani-

Exhibit 13–3 • **Map of Louisiana**

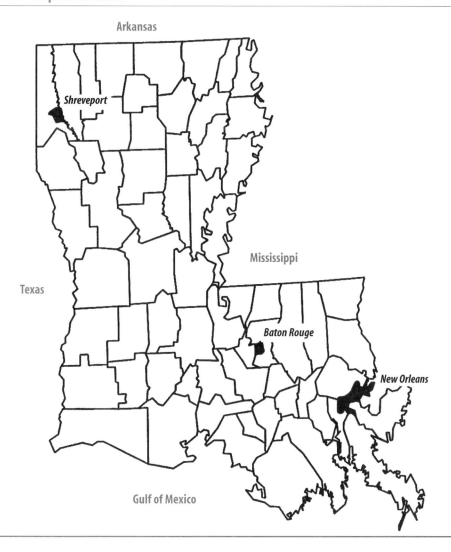

tary Code; tested food products; monitored, tested, and reported on drinking and shellfish harvesting waters; conducted environmental health programs in food, seafood, water, and sewage safety; coordinated emergency medical services; provided preventive and primary health care in more than one hundred public health facilities in sixty-three parishes throughout the state (all except Plaquemines Parish); and administered various health-related programs. Orleans Parish administered its own health department supplemented by services provided by OPH.

OPH had its official central administrative office in Baton Rouge, however its main body resided in New Orleans, seventy-five miles to the southeast of Baton Rouge. The Louisiana parishes were divided into nine regions that were managed through regional offices, each headed by a regional

Exhibit 13–4 • OPH Organization Chart

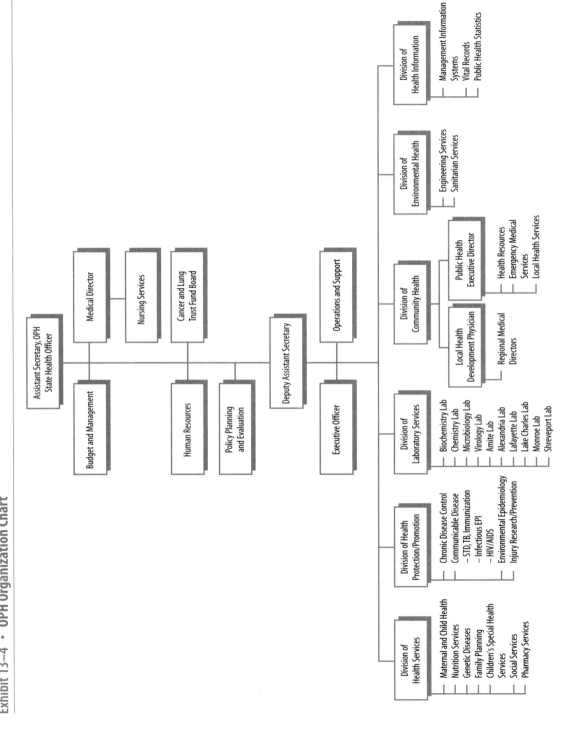

administrator. Exhibit 13–4 depicts the organization structure and programs for OPH. OPH operated on a budget of over $202 million and employed over 2,400 statewide.

OPH Top Management

Eric Baumgartner, M.D., M.P.H., became the director of Local Health Development in the Louisiana Office of Public Health in 1989. In 1993, he was appointed assistant secretary of the Office of Public Health. Prior to working in Louisiana, Baumgartner worked in public health in Hawaii and Mississippi.

He graduated from Louisiana State University School of Medicine in 1981 and served his general pediatric residency at Children's Hospital in Little Rock, Arkansas, from 1981 to 1984. He completed his residency in general preventive medicine while concurrently pursuing and earning the master of public health at Tulane University's School of Public Health and Tropical Medicine. Baumgartner served as an adjunct faculty at the school from 1985 to 1992 and as a clinical instructor in pediatrics at Tulane's School of Medicine beginning in 1985. Dr. Baumgartner was a fellow of both the American Academy of Pediatrics and the American College of Preventive Medicine.

Joe Kimbrell was appointed deputy assistant secretary of OPH in 1985. Mr. Kimbrell was the deputy assistant secretary for the Office of Health Services and Environmental Quality from 1979 to 1985. He had worked as a coordinator of federal programs and a program administrator at local health departments within Louisiana.

Kimbrell earned a bachelor and masters degree from Notre Dame Seminary and a master of social work degree from Tulane University. He was a board certified social worker and a member of the National Association of Social Workers

Liz Sumrall was director of Policy Planning and Evaluation at OPH. She was responsible for directing and overseeing strategic planning, policy development, legislative monitoring, and grants development. Previously, she worked as parent involvement coordinator and evaluation specialist for the Mental Health Association in Louisiana where she was the recipient of the "Supporting Families" Award. She

earned a B.A. in sociology from the University of Southwestern Louisiana and a master of public administration from Louisiana State University.

Growing Uncertainty at OPH

Governor Foster was elected on a platform promising less government. The OPH budget figures for fiscal year 1996–1997 certainly reflected that promise. Although the budget had not been finalized, the impact on OPH was significant. Dr. Baumgartner had trimmed 95 positions through attrition; the proposed budget called for at least 169 additional position cuts—or over 10 percent of OPH employees. The last layoff had occurred in 1987.

Strategic Planning Retreat

Eric Baumgartner warmly greeted the OPH employees from around the state as they filed into the balloon-decorated ballroom of the Hotel Bentley. All of this was in preparation for hearing the culmination and summary messages from the committees that had worked so diligently in the past months to fulfill OPH's vision for strategic planning. "Welcome to everyone and thank you for participating in this very important strategic planning process." He continued, "And a special thanks to the Communications Committee for the festive atmosphere."

Then a voice came over the public address system. "Ladies and gentlemen, please give a warm OPH welcome to Errricky and the Sparkettes!" The music to "FIRE" by The Ohio Players came blaring over the loudspeakers and Dr. Baumgartner and eight members of the Communications Committee came onto the stage. As Dr. Baumgartner painfully struggled with the lead vocals, the Sparkettes danced and provided back-up vocal accompaniment. The words to the song were created by the Communications Committee especially for the strategic planning retreat being held to disseminate the results of the situation analysis phase and to bolster morale and support for OPH's strategic planning efforts. The assemblage of OPH employees applauded and cheered as their chief health officer paraded back and forth across the stage.

FIRE!

We're on FIRE
OPH will aspire
We'll meet the goals we desire
And set our sights even higher

Oh! Yes indeed . . . we'll heed . . . Public
Health-care need . . .
We will be there, now . . . (yes, we will)
Because from birth, our worth is the best health
deal on earth . . .
Gotta lot to share now . . . uh-huh

With SHOTS for TOTS . . . Well-Baby, WIC and
lots
Of health-care know-how . . . uh-huh

We'll check kids' eyes and ears . . . Make sure
they see and hear . . .
And . . . yeah, yeah, yeah, yeah, yeah, yeah . . .
Help them grow now . . .

Fire . . . OPH is on FIRE
Gotta keep, gotta keep, gotta keep on burnin'
Gotta keep, gotta keep, gotta keep on learnin'
How to keep, how to keep the folks returning

TB . . . STD . . . BP . . . and pregnancy . . . We
test and treat now . . . uh-huh

And we can cure your sewer . . . make sure
your water's pure . . .
We can't be beat, now . . . uh-huh . . .

We've been around . . . we're sound . . . Got
both feet on the ground . . .
And we're still in the game . . .

We'll make our mark in the dark . . . we'll turn
our golden spark . . .
Into a brilliant flame . . . In Louisiana . . .

DO YOUR PART . . . PASS THE SPARK . . . WIN
THE GAME . . .
SHARE THE FLAME . . . GET ON FIRE . . .
REACH UP HIGHER

Gotta keep, gotta keep, gotta keep on burnin'
Gotta keep, gotta keep, gotta keep on learnin'
How to keep, how to keep the folks returning . . .
(Repeat chorus × 2)

As he left the stage exhausted and exhilarated he thought, "If the other committees are as committed as the Communications Committee, then the retreat will be a great success."

The enthusiasm in the ballroom was infectious—a sharp contrast to the mood of the employees for the past couple of weeks. The budget figures being bandied about during this legislative session were alarming. Furthermore the governor had proposed completely privatizing public health in the Baton Rouge region as an experiment. The details of this proposal had not been fleshed out, but because of the seniority system in the state, it would mean that several hundred OPH workers in the Baton Rouge region would be given one chance to "bump" their more junior counterparts in other regions, thereby creating turmoil throughout the organization. The privatization experiment proposal and the outcome of this legislative session cast a cloud over today's retreat. Eric wished once more that this initial attempt at strategic planning had been completed before this legislative session had begun. "The whole process has been plagued by 'Murphy's Law.' What could go wrong did," he thought. "Oh well, at least the retreat got off to a good, if slightly 'off-key' start."

As Eric Baumgartner listened to the results of the situation analysis phase of the strategic planning process, he was amazed at the enthusiasm pulsing through the room. The information being shared at the strategic planning rally was the culmination of four months' work by over one hundred people.

Report of Values, Vision, and Mission Task Force

The group was quite satisfied with its efforts to develop a mission, vision, and values statement for OPH (see Exhibits 13–5, 13–6, and 13–7).

Report of the External Analysis Task Force

The external environmental task force organized itself into social/cultural, health care, economic, political/regulatory, and stakeholder subcommittees (See Exhibit 13–8). Each of the subcommittees developed sources of information within and outside OPH to gather primary and secondary information

Exhibit 13–5 · OPH Mission Statement

The mission of the Office of Public Health is:

- To provide leadership in the prevention and control of disease, injury, and disability in the State of Louisiana.
- To enforce regulations to protect the environment and investigate health hazards in the community.
- To promote health through education and the importance of individual responsibility on matters relating to health and wellness.
- To assure universal access to essential health services.
- To collect and distribute information that can be used for decision making on matters relating to the health and environment of Louisiana.
- To assure the quality of health services provided in the state.
- To create a work environment where employees value teamwork, work to the best of their abilities, are empowered by their skills, and make independent decisions.

Our commitment is to enhance the quality of life in Louisiana by providing the information necessary for individuals to assume responsibility for their own health and ensuring the availability of basic health care services for those in need. Accomplishment of our mission relies on our ability to capitalize on the diversity of our population and our employees so as to develop healthy and happy communities.

Exhibit 13–6 · OPH Statement of Values

The Office of Public Health aspires to promote health for the people of Louisiana by providing leadership, being innovative, and focusing on prevention.

- We honor diversity and respect all people as individuals.
- We are dedicated to serving people and communities in a caring, compassionate manner.
- We are committed to excellence and continuous improvement.
- We seek through education, teamwork, and collaboration to empower each other, our communities, and the people we serve.
- We insist on high ethical standards and integrity in all we do. We pledge to be good stewards of the resources entrusted to us.

Exhibit 13–7 · OPH Statement of Vision

We see a future where all the people of Louisiana are born healthy and have the opportunity to grow, develop, and live in an environment that is nurturing, supportive, safe, and promotes the physical, mental, and social health of individuals, families, communities, and the state.

We see a future where the Office of Public Health is a key leader and influential partner in creating and sustaining a healthy and prosperous Louisiana.

on OPH's external environment. The data collection resulted in numerous issues for each subcommittee. The identified issues and stakeholders were then analyzed for duplication and convergence. After eliminating duplication, a list of thirty-four issues and a stakeholder list emerged (see Exhibit 13–9).

The task force was confident of the relevance of the issues identified, but wanted confirmation from additional OPH personnel and external stakeholders. A questionnaire was developed and analyzed to further check on the relevance of the issues (see Exhibits 13–10 and 13–11). Twelve stakeholders

Exhibit 13–8 · **External Environmental Task Force Approach**

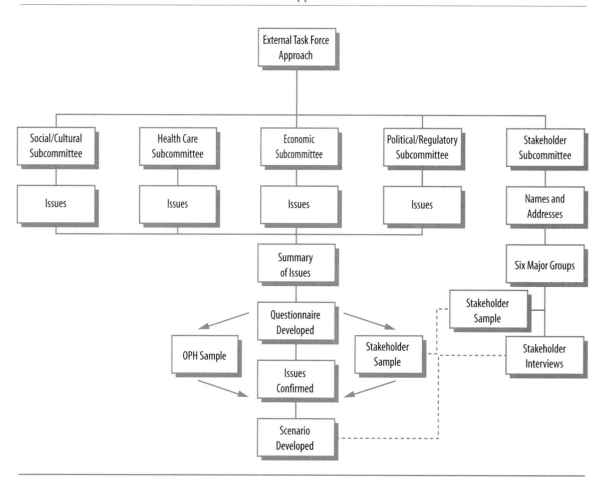

were interviewed either in person or by telephone concerning the issues facing the stakeholder's organization. See Exhibit 13–12 for the interview protocol and the common responses for each question.

The surveys and interviews resulted in confirmation of the issues identified by the various subcommittees. The task force then articulated the implications of the top ten issues identified by the survey results (see Exhibit 13–13). Finally, all the issues were used to develop a scenario of the most likely future facing OPH in the year 2000 (see Exhibit 13–14).

Report of the Internal Analysis Task Force

The internal task force was charged with identifying OPH's strategic capabilities in the form of its strengths and weaknesses. The task force divided itself into five subcommittees: organizational culture; operations and support/facilities; financial; information; and human resources.

Cultural Assessment Subcommittee An initial Organizational Excellence Questionnaire was developed by the subcommittee. It was sent to all 2,427 employ-

Exhibit 13–9 • Summary of Identified Issues/Trends by the External Analysis Task Force

Social/Cultural	Code	Health Care	Code	Economic	Code	Political/Regulatory	Code
Increasing number of homeless	S-1	Limited access to health care by adolescents, rural residents, and the uninsured	HC-1	Increasing number of uninsureds due to health insurance premiums and low-wage jobs	E-1	Increasing regulation of health care	P-1
Rise in teenage pregnancy	S-2	Movement away from fee-for-service to managed care	HC-2	No real growth in state revenues	E-2	Further reductions in Medicaid funding	P-2
Rising number of single-parent households	S-3	Increase in health problems due to lifestyle choices	HC-3	Rising unemployment and low-paying service sector jobs	E-3	Block grants that may result in reductions in OPH funding	P-3
Lack of community involvement in health care	S-4	Increased incidence of infectious diseases	HC-4	Continuing low rates of educational achievement	E-4	Increasing political and market pressure for OPH to assume a role in managed care	P-4
The state lacks adequate transportation services	S-5	Continued privatization of state-supported health systems	HC-5	Difficulty in attracting new business to the state	E-5	Increasing pressure to estimate costs and justify fees or fee changes for services	P-5
Increasing number of migrant and immigrant workers in the state	S-6	Increased number of technological advances in communication, disease detection, and telemedicine	HC-6	Rising levels of violence	E-6		
Many health care decisions made in the political arena	S-7	Increasing attention to environmental factors	HC-7	Increasing the health care millage at the parish level	E-7		
Publicity of negative health care outcomes	S-8	Increasing demand for universal health care coverage	HC-8	Market value fees for recipients of OPH services who can afford to pay	E-8		
Increasing proportion of elderly population	S-9	Greater need for continuing education of health professionals	HC-9	Increasing levels of poverty	E-9		
Communities lack awareness of public health activities	S-10						
The location and poor condition of many public health units	S-11						

ees of the Office of Public Health. A total of 1,116 usable questionnaires were returned for a response rate of 45.6 percent.

Examples of assessment results indicated several areas of general agreement: the Office was responsive to its clients/customers; the most important element of jobs within the Office was serving clients/customers; and employees generally understood how their work related to the work of other members of the group.

Respondents did not agree with the following statements: Office employees have a clear understanding of where the Office needs to be in the next five years; leadership is more concerned with employees than administrative rules and procedures; the leadership is concerned with the welfare and

Exhibit 13–10 • Key Trends and Issues Survey, OPH and Stakeholder Mean Scores

Trends/Issues	Code	OPH Mean	OPH Percent Not Sure	Stakeholder Mean	Stakeholder Percent Not Sure
1. Increasing regulations of health care, particularly with regard to quality assurance, outcomes, and worker safety.	P-1	3.29	4.3	2.90	4.7
2. Further reductions in Medicaid funding.	P-2	3.65	3.3	3.21	9.4
3. Block grants that may result in reductions in OPH funding.	P-3	3.63	4.3	3.40	7.0
4. Increasing political and market pressure for OPH to assume a role in a managed-care system of health care delivery.	P-4	3.36	3.3	2.95	7.0
5. Increasing pressure to estimate costs and justify fees or fee changes for public health services.	P-5	3.32	4.3	3.02	2.3
6. Increasing number of uninsureds due to increases in health insurance premiums and low-wage jobs within the state.	E-1	3.44	4.3	3.29	4.7
7. No real growth in state revenues.	E-2	3.41	6.4	3.27	4.7
8. Rising unemployment and low-paying service sector jobs.	E-3	3.11	4.3	3.10	2.3
9. Continuing low rates of educational achievement.	E-4	3.26	4.3	3.31	2.3
10. Difficulty in attracting new business to the state.	E-5	3.02	2.2	2.85	4.7
11. Rising levels of violence.	E-6	3.42	1.1	3.41	4.7
12. Increasing the health care millage at the parish level.	E-7	3.02	4.3	3.06	18.7
13. Market value fees for recipients of OPH services who can afford to pay.	E-8	3.13	3.3	3.30	7.0
14. Increasing levels of poverty.	E-9	3.23	1.1	3.14	2.3
15. Increasing number of homeless.	S-1	2.95	3.3	3.19	0
16. Rise in teenage pregnancy.	S-2	3.64	2.2	3.50	2.3
17. Rising number of single-parent households.	S-3	3.29	2.2	3.10	4.7
18. Lack of community involvement in health care.	S-4	3.33	1.1	3.42	11.6
19. The state lacks adequate transportation services.	S-5	2.81	1.1	2.45	7.0
20. Increasing number of migrant and immigrant workers within the state.	S-6	2.43	11.7	2.58	11.6
21. Many health care decisions are made in the political arena.	S-7	3.39	5.4	3.33	2.3
22. Publicity of negative health care outcomes.	S-8	3.07	4.3	2.95	14.0
23. Increasing proportion of elderly population.	S-9	3.18	1.1	3.07	4.7
24. Communities lack awareness of public health activities.	S-10	3.36	2.2	3.29	4.7
25. The location and poor condition of many public health units.	S-11	3.29	1.1	3.00	7.0
26. Continued limited access to health care by adolescents, rural residents, and the uninsured.	HC-1	3.22	2.2	3.39	11.7
27. Continued movement away from fee-for-service system of health care delivery to managed-care systems.	HC-2	3.25	3.3	2.97	9.3
28. Increase in health problems due to lifestyle choices (e.g., smoking, diet, exercise, and safety restraints).	HC-3	3.27	1.1	3.23	9.3
29. Increased incidence of infectious diseases (tuberculosis, STDs, hepatitis A, and HIV/AIDS).	HC-4	3.61	1.1	3.60	2.3
30. Continued privatization of traditionally state-supported health care systems.	HC-5	3.13	9.6	2.85	7.0

(1 = Very Important, 4 = Not Important)
(137/237 = 58% Response Rate)

Exhibit 13–10 • **Continued**

Trends/Issues	Code	OPH Mean	OPH Percent Not Sure	Stakeholder Mean	Stakeholder Percent Not Sure
31. Increasing number of technological advances in communication, disease detection and tracking, and telemedicine, which have the potential to improve health care delivery and environmental services.	HC-6	3.14	2.2	3.32	4.6
32. Increasing attention to environmental factors (e.g., indoor/outdoor air quality, water contamination, toxicity, etc.) related to the health of individuals.	HC-7	3.43	2.2	3.21	0
33. Increasing demand for universal health care coverage for all citizens.	HC-8	3.06	4.3	3.05	4.6
34. Greater need for continuing education of health care professionals.	HC-9	3.09	1.1	3.32	4.6

Exhibit 13–11 • **Comparison of OPH and Stakeholder Issues/Trends Ranked by Mean Score**

OPH Rankings	Trends/Issues	External Stakeholders Rankings	OPH Rankings	Trends/Issues	External Stakeholders Rankings
1	Medicaid funding	17	18	Educational achievement	10
2	Teen pregnancy	2	19	Movement to managed care	27
3	Block grants	5	20	Poverty	19
4	Infectious diseases	1	21	Access to health care	6
5	Number of uninsured	12	22	Aging population	22
6	Environmental factors	16	23	Technological advances	8
7	Violence	4	24	Market value fees	11
8	No growth in revenues	14	25	Privatization of health care	32
9	Politics of health care	7	26	Unemployment	21
10	OPH involvement in managed care	28	27	Continuing education	9
11	Community awareness of OPH	13	28	Publicity of negative health care outcomes	29
12	Community involvement in health care	3	29	Universal health care	24
13	Pressure to justify fees	25	30	Parish health care millage	23
14	Single-parent households	20	31	Attracting new business	31
15	Location and condition of health units	26	32	Homelessness	18
16	Regulation of health care	30	33	Inadequate transportation services	34
17	Lifestyle health problems	15	34	Migrant and immigrant workers	33

happiness of those who work in the Office; and the Office periodically assesses employee satisfaction.

Operations and Support/Facilities Subcommittee

A total of one hundred personal interviews were conducted by subcommittee members with a mixture of regional, parish, and central office interviewees. At the parish and regional levels, interviewees were from four areas: facilities, property control, purchasing, and telecommunications. The interview results were summarized and discussed by subcommittee members and staff. From the discussion, a draft list of

Exhibit 13–12 • External Environmental Stakeholder Interview Protocol and Summary of Results

Purpose: The Office of Public Health is engaged in an organization-wide strategic planning effort. As a part of that effort we are interviewing important stakeholders of OPH. Could you spend a few minutes to assist us in these efforts, or could we schedule a more convenient time to call or visit with you?

1. Could you describe the nature of your (or your organization's) relationship with OPH.

Relationships described as: *sporadic*   *ongoing*
                               ad hoc   *contractual*
                               issue oriented

2. What is the best thing about your relationship with OPH?

                               Talented staff   *Enabling*
                               Committed staff   *Information repository*

3. What is the worst thing about your relationship with OPH?

                               Communication   *Bureaucracy*
                               - Inefficient listening to stakeholder needs   *- Too many layers*
                               - Difficult to access OPH information   *- Too much central staff*
                               - Internal communications are inadequate   *- Too removed from action in Baton Rouge*

4. How could OPH improve its relationship with you or your organization?
                               Communicate the scope of OPH responsibilities   *Reduce bureaucracy*
                               Streamline access to OPH information   *Move central office to Baton Rouge*
                               Create newsletter to inform stakeholders of
                               *   ongoing OPH activities*

5. What are the major issues facing your organization that OPH could assist you with?
                               Many different and organization-specific issues were mentioned.

strengths and weaknesses was developed, circulated, and critiqued. A final list of strengths and weaknesses was determined by the subcommittee (see Exhibit 13–15).

Financial Systems Subcommittee A total of 200 questionnaires were mailed to a mixture of regional, parish, and central office personnel including senior administration, all regional administrators, and a nonrandom sample of other personnel. Results were tabulated and summarized by the subcommittee chair and discussed by subcommittee members and staff. After a draft list of strengths and weaknesses was developed, circulated, and critiqued, the subcommittee determined a final list of strengths and weaknesses (see Exhibit 13–16).

Information Systems Subcommittee A total of seventy face-to-face and telephone interviews were conducted throughout OPH by subcommittee members. The interview results were categorized, tabulated, summarized, and discussed by subcommittee members and staff. As with other subcommittees, a draft list of strengths and weaknesses was developed, circulated, and critiqued before a final list was determined (see Exhibit 13–17).

Human Resources Subcommittee A total of fifty personal interviews were conducted by subcommittee members with a mixture of regional, parish, and central office personnel. A format similar to other subcommittees was followed to develop a list of strengths and weaknesses (see Exhibit 13–18).

Exhibit 13–13 • Strategic Implications of Key Issues/Trends

1. *Further reductions in Medicaid funding.* Reductions in Medicaid could transform the role of the Parish Health Unit from providers of services to coordination and monitoring of services. Without the phase-in of state matching funds, Secretary Jindal has stated that the Medicaid program would be one-third smaller than current levels.

   The federal budget impasse notwithstanding, there will be reduced Medicaid funding for the year. If the "entitlement" status is removed (via MediGrants), there will be increased competition for funds at the state level. Adequate health services for those traditionally guaranteed services (i.e., pregnant women and children) could be jeopardized. Without the protective net of entitlement status, public health could see an increase in the number of persons needing services. However, this possibility must be viewed in light of the direction being set by the new state administration—away from the state providing direct services.

2. *Rise in teenage pregnancies.* The number of births to unmarried teens per 1,000 females ages fifteen to nineteen increased from 29.5 in 1985 to 42.5 in 1992. The children of teenage mothers are at a higher risk for low birth weight, accidents, congenital defects, sexually transmitted diseases, and child abuse and neglect.

   In Louisiana, 18.7 percent of all births were to women under 19 years of age. Of these teen pregnancies, 22.2 percent had no health insurance. Teenage childbearing is particularly problematic because it diminishes the opportunities of both the child and the mother. Children born to unmarried teenage mothers have a relatively low probability of obtaining the emotional and financial resources they need to develop into independent, productive, well-adjusted adults. Research shows that children born to single parents are more likely to drop out of school, to give birth out of wedlock, to divorce or separate, and to be dependent on welfare. Teen mothers will require programs that focus on preconceptual care, well-baby health care, and family life education.

3. *Block grants may result in reductions in OPH funding.* Much of the previous discussion of Medicaid funding applies to this issue. Reductions in funding would fuel a reduced role in providing direct services and a greater role in coordination and monitoring of services.

4. *Increased incidence of infectious diseases.* Each year new HIV infections account for $150 million in future Louisiana medical costs. Louisiana ranks eleventh in the United States in AIDS cases per 100,000 residents.

   The private sector relies on public health to be the "experts" on control of communicable diseases. However, collaboration between public health and private providers will increase involvement in achieving the Healthy People 2000 objectives. The use of midlevel practitioners can increase the access to care. Full-service clinics and labs, along with monitoring and evaluation programs, follow-up, and intervention services, can be used to further reduce the spread of infectious diseases.

5. *Increasing number of uninsureds due to increases in health insurance premiums and low-wage jobs within the state.* In Louisiana, 1.1 million residents or 25 percent of the population have no health insurance. Approximately 988,700 residents are covered by Medicaid, 555,000 by Medicare, and approximately 40 percent are privately insured.

   As the number of uninsureds grows, the demand for state services increases. New or redesigned programs must be developed to cover the growing number of Louisiana residents with no health insurance. OPH, through its monitoring and evaluation capabilities, will be in a unique position to delineate areas and populations with need for services.

6. *Increasing attention to environmental factors related to the health of individuals.* EPA statistics show that two in five Americans live in areas where air is dangerous to breathe and 40 percent of the country's rivers and lakes are not suitable for drinking, fishing, or swimming. Louisiana, which produces one-fourth of the nation's bulk commodity chemicals, ranked first in the nation on the EPA's Toxic Release Inventories for three consecutive years (1991–1993).

   Contamination of fish and drinking water were also ranked as health risks. Louisiana private water wells that provide a significant percentage of the population's drinking water, are not routinely tested to determine if they are safe. In addition, over 8,000 pesticides are registered for use statewide with about 1,000 for agricultural purposes. The increased issuance of health/fish consumption advisories in Louisiana, especially for mercury contamination, is directly related to the increased number of areas sampled.

   There is a continued need for environmental health programs that serve and educate populations about the issues surrounding health and the environment. Public and professional preventive health educational programs would have the greatest impact on preventing exposure to environmental pollutants. Informed and involved citizens and communities are the most potent weapon against morbidity and mortality associated with environmental contamination.

7. *Rising levels of violence.* The monetary cost of all crime in Louisiana is estimated to be over $1 billion. The medical costs resulting from violent crime in Louisiana was $114 million in 1993. Violence is linked to many other issues: teen pregnancy, poverty, homelessness, drug use, and others.

   The costs to police, bring to trial, and incarcerate criminals place great demands on state and federal resources. The judicial system tends to compete with public health for shrinking dollars.

continued

Exhibit 13–13 · **Continued**

8. *No real growth in state revenues.* No real economic growth is expected for the near future. Low educational achievement will make it difficult to attract new industry to the state. Growth in gaming seems uncertain and would generate low-wage jobs (many with no health insurance). The unemployment rate for Louisiana increased from 7.4 percent in 1993 to 8.0 percent in 1994—the fourth highest in the nation. Approximately 27 percent of Louisiana workers are employed in the service sector, 60 percent of whom receive no health insurance.

   The lack of real growth in state revenues will impact all state agencies' ability to maintain current funding and procure new funding. Public health must do a better job of competing for new sources of funding. This may require more coordination or reorganization to identify, disseminate, and apply for funding opportunities.

9. *Many health care decisions are made in the political arena.* There is a growing trend to cut the state and federal funding to public health programs. The multitude of service demands in the face of shrinking state and federal resources necessitates tough choices. Many times the decisions emerging from the political processes in Washington and Baton Rouge do little to improve the health status of vulnerable segments of the population.

   Public health clients tend not to be mainstream members of their community and often are not vocal in their support of public health programs. Public health clients tend to be silent users of the public health system. The location of the central office in New Orleans may silence OPH's voice in the legislature (located in Baton Rouge).

   Public health systems cannot expect the users of their services to be strong proponents of the system to nonusers or political leaders. Active communication with community groups is necessary for public health to build a more vocal constituency. Strong, visible community relations will be advocates for the continued funding of essential services to public health's silent clients.

   Legislation has been proposed, which would privatize OPH services in the Baton Rouge region. The privatization would result in management of all DHH direct services (including those provided by OPH) currently being provided in that region. OPH must proactively secure its role in one of the proposed systems for revamping health care delivery.

10. *Increasing political and market pressure for OPH to assume a role in a managed-care system of health care delivery.* U.S. managed-care enrollment grew from 6 million persons in 1976 to over 51 million in 1994. Medicaid managed-care enrollment grew from 800,000 in 1983 to 7,800,000 in 1994. There are eighteen licensed HMOs in Louisiana and nineteen parishes have primary-case management for Medicaid patients. A Medicaid waiver has been applied for to develop fully capitated managed care for Louisiana Medicaid recipients.

    Governor Foster and Secretary Jindal have stated that the state should reduce its role as providers of direct services. The administration believes that the state should "shift its focus from being a health care provider to a wise purchaser of services." As direct service is diverted from OPH to managed-care organizations (MCOs), opportunities exist to engage in core public health areas such as health education, health promotion, quality assurance, and systems development.

    Collaborations between OPH and MCOs will need to address issues such as communicable diseases and environmental health, which do not recognize boundaries of health plans or insured or uninsured. Public and private purchasers of health care, particularly large employers, HCFA, and state Medicaid agencies have a direct interest in promoting quality health care and could be natural partners with OPH in improving health outcomes.

    OPH could bring valuable skills and experiences to partnerships. Experience with surveillance and prevention strategies, epidemiological and laboratory skills, case management, and accessing vulnerable populations could prove useful to many managed-care organizations.

The Challenges Continue

The internal task force was winding down its presentation when Dr. Baumgartner felt the all-too-familiar buzz on his hip. He glanced at his beeper to confirm what he already knew—the governor's office was calling. He was required to appear before the legislature to respond to the budget.

On his way to build his case with the legislature, he thought about what he had heard that morning at the OPH retreat. He still wondered if the employees fully grasped the changing nature of public health in Louisiana and the nation. From his discussions with other state health officers and the mood in Baton Rouge and Washington, it seemed certain that OPH would move away from personal health services. He recognized that many representatives in the legislature did not fully comprehend what this change would mean. After all, personal health services were fairly quantifiable (number of immunizations, office visits, and so on) and could be related to how much money was allocated to OPH.

Exhibit 13-14 • External Environment Scenario (Year 2000)

"Clinton listed successes of the past four years despite a Republican Congress. Government was downsized—two cabinet positions eliminated; federal employees were cut by 10 percent; Medicaid spending was cut by reform and entitlements were removed; block grants to states saved federal dollars by capping expenditures and at the same time gave the states more autonomy; and welfare reform led to a 25 percent decrease in welfare rolls."

The Republican Congress killed health care reform; efforts of the early 1990s were dead in the water. Managed care became the predominant delivery system for health services in the United States. Eighty percent of Americans with third-party payment were enrolled in managed care. Companies faced soaring health care costs by moving to managed care and decreasing workers' health care benefits. The uninsured in America reached an all time high. Costs of health insurance were still out of reach for many working Americans. Welfare and Medicaid reform led to fewer people being eligible for Medicaid. Studies showed that lifestyle choices—smoking, alcohol, and others—were associated with the major causes of death in America. Violence and AIDS were markedly increased.

Federal reforms affected state services for the indigent. The new health and social service block grants let Louisiana decide how to spend the money. There was a 20 percent decrease in providers, and consumer advocacy groups vied for the shrinking federal dollars.

Medicaid recovered from the budget problems of the mid-1990s through establishment of Medicaid managed care and deep cuts in ancillary program services. Most hard hit by federal reforms were pregnant women and children when Medicaid entitlement requirements were removed. Strict requirements for social service programs such as Aid to Families with Dependent Children and time limits for benefits were impacted by decreasing the numbers of beneficiaries eligible for Medicaid.

In a related story, managed-care organizations (MCOs) reported a remarkable growth in the past few years. The number of MCOs in the state have doubled. Linked to the increase in MCOs was increasing private sector utilization as well as the enrollment in managed care of all Medicaid patients. Seventy percent of Louisiana's population was covered by managed care.

Louisiana income did not keep up with inflation. Unemployment was low but opportunities were primarily in service and trade industries. Many small businesses were unable to provide comprehensive health insurance benefits due to escalating costs. The numbers of uninsured in the state grew from the 1.1 million in 1996 to 1.5 million today (2000).

Mounting costs of care for citizens with communicable disease have placed new burdens on the state. This was best seen in the care of people with HIV/AIDS—each year new HIV infections obligated Louisiana to $150 million in future medical costs. Syphilis and gonorrhea cases have declined but TB cases continued to increase although at a slowed rate. Increased attention to prevention was mandatory.

State budget cuts in the mid-1990s and downsizing of state agencies resulted in a reorganization of the state health services. State-supported hospitals and clinics were brought together into a Louisiana Health Alliance System to serve all state citizens. The system served increasing numbers as the uninsured in the state rose.

Public health environmental programs continued to benefit the public. Clean air and water programs as well as inspection and monitoring services survived state budget cuts of the 1990s with outstanding successes. Cooperative efforts of citizens, government agencies, and industry led by the Office of Public Health were cited as the reasons for success. Public water supplies were safe, and air and land pollution was eliminated with the cooperation of the Department of Environmental Quality; food was free from pesticides in cooperation with the Department of Agriculture; and sources of pollution of fish have been eliminated in cooperation with the Departments of Health, Environmental Quality, Agriculture, and Wildlife and Fisheries.

Violence continued to be a major killer of youth in Louisiana and an increasing drain on state resources. The severity of the injuries increased along with the number of crimes committed. Beyond the human factors, costs of violence included the loss of potential earnings as well as the actual health care costs. Costs for violence-related injuries were rising to all time levels especially among the young.

The Story We Would Like to See (The date is unknown but is sometime in our future.)

Louisiana now ranks in the top ten healthiest states —teen pregnancy rates have fallen; new cases of STDs and HIV/AIDS are on the decline; cases of TB have decreased; infant mortality is below the national average; immunization rates for children have reached 100 percent; no foodborne illnesses occur; all homes are connected to a community sewage system; life expectancy for Louisianans rises above the national norms; and all citizens have access to quality health care.

The Office of Public Health has led the way. Success has come through:

1. Development of integrated delivery systems through coordination and consolidation of services among all health care providers.

2. Development and enforcement of standards for health services.

3. Monitoring programs for health status and outcomes.

4. Public education programs on matters related to health including effects of lifestyle on health as well as prevention of disease.

5. Innovative programs bringing in community, private, and other public organizations as partners to meet the Office of Public Health's mission to "protect and enhance the health of Louisiana citizens by helping to create conditions under which all residents can enjoy the best of health."

All of this is a result of the Office of Public Health's 1996 strategic planning effort.

Exhibit 13–15 • Operations and Support/Facilities Strengths and Weaknesses

Strengths

- There is an ongoing effort by many local parish governments to upgrade public health facilities.
- Professional architectural and design support for public health facilities are consistent and of high quality.
- The Office of Telecommunications Management provides good support for equipment specification and equipment-use training.

Weaknesses

- Public health facility quality is highly variable throughout the state with security concerns at some locations.
- Response time from Operations and Support Services to telecommunications repair is often inadequate.
- There is no user-friendly computer network for E-mail and sharing of information statewide.
- Existing policies and methods for tagging, accounting for, and disposition of equipment do not function well as a centralized management process.
- Responsiveness and accuracy of central pharmacy is inadequate.
- ISIS System for supplies is not user friendly.

Exhibit 13–16 • Financial System Strengths and Weaknesses

Strengths

- Financial reports that are currently produced are accurate, complete, and received on a timely basis.
- Fiscal office staff are knowledgeable and respond to questions in a timely manner.

Weaknesses

- There is insufficient financial data to develop budgets, and program managers have expressed concerns about management of budgets due primarily to an inability to control expenditures.
- Problems with the purchasing process have resulted in some vendors and contractors not being paid on a timely basis, and this has inhibited operations.
- Training is insufficient to properly use the financial information that is supplied.
- Insufficient financial resources continue to weaken public health work.

Exhibit 13–17 • Information Systems Strengths and Weaknesses

Strength

- Staff throughout OPH are eager to become more knowledgeable in the use of MIS.

Weaknesses

- MIS lacks visibility or an "organizational presence," and hence employees feel they do not know what MIS does or what services to expect from it.
- MIS is perceived to be more responsive to central office needs and less so to the regional and parish level needs.
- There is no clear plan for information systems development.

Exhibit 13–18 · **Human Resources Strengths and Weaknesses**

Strength

- Human Resources staff respond to requests for assistance in a cooperative and collegial manner.

Weaknesses

- There does not appear to be a rational and objective process for allocating the number and types of positions to various units within OPH.
- Interpretation of personnel policies for employees is inconsistent and at times inaccurate.
- Human Resources does not appear knowledgeable about public health work, specifically relative to the functions and responsibilities of professional personnel.
- At the regional level, DHH Human Resources and OPH Human Resources are not well coordinated.
- Human Resources is too slow and at times nonresponsive to requests for hiring, promotion, or disciplinary actions.
- Employees do not feel that reward and recognition is related to important job skills and/or productivity.
- There is lack of consistent written guidelines for personnel actions.
- Training policies and opportunities are inadequate and inappropriate.

OPH needed to expand its core public health areas and build internal public and political enlightenment of its importance. The building of core functions was not without its critics within OPH. Central office personnel were largely involved in core public health whereas the parishes provided personal health services. Further attempts to strengthen the core functions would be seen as siphoning resources from the parish level, especially in light of the shrinking budgets.

Eric knew that "reinventing" public health would be a tough sell both within and outside of OPH. He felt that strategic planning was one way to help redefine and communicate the changes in public health. Because of all the turbulence and uncertainty facing OPH, he was now more convinced than ever that persevering through the strategic planning process was the correct course of action. The steering committee had a formidable task in front of them. Digesting the work of the other task forces and developing program priorities from that information would take much hard work. The resulting direction and the supporting logic was just what he needed to show the governor and the legislature.

The Veterans Administration Medical Care System

As he climbed the steps of the Veterans Administration (VA) building in Washington, D.C., on the way to his office, Chief Medical Director John Gronvall's glance came to rest on the immortal words of Abraham Lincoln etched across the entrance: "Care for him who shall have borne the battle and for his widow, and his orphan."

"How ironic those words seem," Gronvall thought, "given the current situation: a medical system $221 million short of needed cash with 13,000 beds out of service and 7,000 medical jobs vacant." With a budget proposal for the next fiscal year already $604 million short, they could not even begin to treat all the patients they had treated last year, much less fulfill Lincoln's lofty goal. Somehow, the VA Medical Care System had to provide quality medical treatment to this country's veterans amid budget constraints and demands to decrease public spending. "What was the answer? Would the current strategy work? Should he seek a more radical alternative?"

History and Background

The origin of the VA can be traced to the time immediately after the Civil War when the National Asylum for Disabled Volunteer Soldiers was founded. Union veterans who had suffered economic distress from disabilities incurred during the war were eligible. Concurrently, a number of states established homes for the domiciliation of disabled soldiers and sailors. Operated initially at state expense, in 1888 the homes started receiving federal aid for the care of certain disabled soldiers and sailors at the annual rate of $100 for each veteran domiciled in a state home. At that time, medical care was only ancillary to residency at the federal and state homes.

Growth in Programs and Facilities

Significant changes in benefits to veterans occurred after World War I, including medical and hospital care for those suffering from wounds or diseases incurred while in service. Due to the lack of facilities, medical care had to be provided by the Public Health Service or through contracts with civilian hospitals as well as Army and Navy hospitals. Eventually, a number of the Public Health Service hospitals were transferred to the Veterans Bureau. In 1930, the Veterans Bureau, Pension Bureau, and the National Home for Disabled Veterans were consolidated into a new agency, the Veterans Administration. At that time, it had a budget of $100 million for the operation of forty-seven hospitals (22,732 beds), ten branches of the National Home, and a sanitarium.

World War II caused further expansion in benefits and medical care for veterans. Seventy-two new hospitals were authorized. In 1946, the Department of Medicine and Surgery was established to be headed by a chief medical director who reported directly to the administrator of veteran affairs. Under this department, a three-point program—medical

This case was prepared by Sharon Topping and Peter M. Ginter. It is intended as a basis for class discussion rather than to illustrate effective or ineffective handling of an administrative situation. Used with permission from Sharon Topping.

care, research, and education—was initiated to improve the quality of care to veterans.

At that time, affiliations with medical schools began. In a little over three decades, this program grew to 107 medical school and 58 dental school affiliations. Today, the VA provides residency training for one-third of all U.S. physicians. Numerous affiliations also exist with schools of pharmacy, nursing, psychology, social work, and other allied health disciplines. The research program began with a budget of $1 million; today, its budget is well over $150 million. Moreover, two VA researchers, Rosalyn Yalow and Andrew Schally, were awarded the Nobel Prize.

Over the years, the VA has become one of the largest federal agencies, with approximately 250,000 employees and a budget of over $28 billion. Recently, Congress voted to make it the fourteenth cabinet department, thereby giving veterans a voice in policy making at the White House. A major part of the VA budget is related to the provision of medical services. In 1988, the Department of Medicine and Surgery spent over $10 billion on VA medical programs. The medical system has over 350 facilities that include over 28,000 medical beds, 16,000 surgical beds, 23,000 psychiatric beds, and 10,000 nursing home beds. From a budget of $100 million and sixty facilities, the VA medical system has become the single-largest centrally directed health care system in the country.

The Eligibility Criteria

Initially established to provide medical care for the veteran with service-connected disabilities, VA eligibility criteria changed many times throughout the years. In 1920, the lack of community facilities encouraged Congress to permit the VA to provide care for needy veterans with nonservice-related problems. Through the years, Congress gradually returned to the idea of entitlements in terms of disabilities. A veteran with service-related disabilities was given care on an inpatient and outpatient basis; a veteran with a nonservice-connected condition was treated on an inpatient basis only. This meant that the latter had to have a serious ailment that required hospital care but had no legal right to care before or after hospitalization.

In the 1960s, changes again were made in the criteria. Care was authorized before and after hospitalization, nursing home care was authorized within the VA (or by contract with community nursing homes), and comprehensive care for veterans totally disabled from service was granted. The requirement that veterans aged sixty-five or more had to certify their inability to defray the cost of hospital care for nonrelated conditions was removed. As would be expected, these changes led to a sharp drop in the average length of stay in the hospitals.

Currently, all veterans with an honorable discharge were technically eligible for VA services. Whether this request was granted was determined by a three-tiered system of priorities that was established in 1986 along with a "means test" where appropriate. This system is described in Exhibit 14–1. At the same time, Congress removed the automatic age eligibility of those sixty-five or over. Now, a co-payment indexed to the Medicare deductible was required.

Exhibit 14–1 • Three-Tiered System of Eligibility Priorities

First Priority:	Veterans requesting treatment for service-connected illness or injury.
Second Priority:	Veterans with service-connected injuries or illnesses, whose current injury or illness is not service related.
Space-Available Priority:	Veterans without service-related injuries or illnesses who sign an affidavit stating that they are unable to pay for medical care elsewhere.
"Means" Test Thresholds:	Income that falls at or below $15,000 for single veterans and $18,000 for veterans who have one dependent (with this increasing $1,000 for each dependent).
Special Groups:	Prisoners of war (POW), World War I veterans, and VA pension recipients receive medical care from the VA.

Source: D. Koloski, C. Austin, and E. Borgatta, "Determinants of VA Utilization," *Medical Care* 25 (1987), pp. 830–846.

The income levels were adjusted annually and based on the increment associated with increases in VA pensions. Taken as a whole, the new eligibility criteria changed the focus of VA medical services to place emphasis on veterans with disabilities related to military service and with low incomes. Veterans who did not have service-connected conditions and who had higher incomes could use the health care system only on a space-available basis.

The overriding goal of the VA medical care program was to provide timely high-quality care within government laws and regulations to eligible veterans now and in the future (see Exhibit 14–2).

As ways to decrease the deficit continued to be sought, the question of eligibility received more and more attention. The question always came back to whether the American taxpayer should pay for veterans' care regardless of income or the existence of a service-related disability. It was estimated that without eligibility constraints the cost of VA medical care would exceed $30 billion by the year 2000. In addition, there were problems with the definition of *service-related disability,* for it included a wide range of conditions that might be incurred or aggravated during military service. For example, a knee problem for which an inductee was not exempted but that became worse before discharge was presumed to be service related and treatable by the VA. There were also fifty-seven chronic illnesses and tropical diseases that, if discovered within one to seven years of discharge, qualified the veteran for VA medical benefits.

Environmental Demands: The Aging Population

The issue of eligibility involved not only budget reduction but also demographics. In 1900, individuals age sixty-five and over were 4 percent of the population; by 1987, they were 14.6 percent. By 2020, one in every five persons was expected to be over sixty-five. However, the veteran population was aging at an even faster rate because the population served by the VA was about ten years older than the general population. The aging peak that would occur in the general population in 2020 would hit the VA in 2010. Furthermore, an increasing proportion of elderly men would be veterans. In 1987, over 30 percent of all American men over sixty-five were veterans. By the year 2000, this proportion was expected to be 63 percent (two out of every three).

The Veteran Population

Veterans tended to cluster in age groups that related to service in major conflicts or wars. Although there was a steady influx of veterans during peacetime, these numbers were small compared to the number of those who entered the military after a major mobilization. Therefore, there were large peaks in the veteran population that represented the last three conflicts: World War II, the Korean War, and the war in Vietnam. The veterans from the first two currently were entering into the age group that sought the most medical care. Although woman veterans tended to cluster in similar age groups, it should be noted

---

Exhibit 14–2 • **Veterans Administration Mission and Goals**

The Veterans Administration will serve America's veterans and their families with dignity and compassion and will be their principal advocate in ensuring that they receive the care, support, and recognition earned in service to this nation.

Medical: To ensure quality medical care is provided on a timely basis to eligible veterans.

Benefits: To ensure benefits and services are provided to eligible veterans and their families in an efficient, timely, and compassionate manner.

Memorial Affairs: To ensure the memorial affairs of eligible veterans and dependents are conducted with dignity and compassion.

Leadership: To serve as the leader and advocate within the federal government on all matters directly affecting veterans and their families.

People: To ensure the people of the Veterans Administration receive quality leadership, adequate compensation, decent working conditions, necessary training and education, equal opportunity, and earned recognition.

Management: To integrate technological advances and innovative management techniques into an efficient system for providing quality care and benefits.

that they constituted less than 3 percent of the total veteran population.

The total veteran population increased steadily during the 1970s because of the war in Vietnam (see Exhibit 14–3). It had been declining since 1980 and was estimated to decrease by 13.5 percent by the year 2000. According to VA Chief Medical Director Gronvall, the only age group that would increase between 1986 and 2000 was the group aged sixty-five and older. In 1980, 10 percent of veterans were sixty-five or older. This should increase to 37 percent by 2000 and peak at approximately 47 percent by 2020. Currently, VA facilities served 10 percent to 12 percent of all veterans each year. The larger elderly veteran population was expected to place new stresses on the VA, for this was the age when they were more likely to seek care. People who were sixty-five or older tended to have diseases that were generally chronic and required more long-term care.

Persons in that age group also tended to affect hospital utilization rates because they required more care. In 1980, the average hospital stay of patients age sixty-five or older was 28.9 days. No other group had an average stay of longer than 22.5 days. Because of a growing population of veterans in this age group, long-term-care beds should be in demand. It was estimated by some that in 1990 the system would be providing nursing home care to 90 percent more veterans than received care in 1980. This was especially true in states such as Florida with growing elderly populations. In that state, new facilities would be added to the five already in existence, and contracts with community hospitals would be used to meet the demands.

In addition, of the population of male veterans aged twenty-five and older, the elderly were the poorest (see Exhibit 14–4). Over 50 percent of those veterans sixty-five years or older had annual incomes below $20,000. In a recent survey conducted by Louis Harris and Associates for the VA, which was restricted to veterans over the age of fifty-five, information was obtained on the sources of medical care that age group would select if they needed it. Of those below the $10,000 income level, 42 percent would use VA hospitals and 13 percent would use VA outpatient clinics. As income increased, the number who would use the VA facilities declined rapidly. Furthermore, for veterans with good insurance coverage, their choices of medical care providers were private physicians followed by non-VA hospitals. For those who lacked insurance, VA hospitals replaced all sources of care most likely to be used.

The Veteran Patient

A number of recent studies found that those who use the VA system were somewhat different from the rest of the population. On the average, VA patients were more likely to have lower educational attainment, to have less annual income, to be retired due to health reasons, to be out of the labor force and live alone, to be unable to perform usual activity due to limitations of chronic conditions, and to rate health status as poor.

Exhibit 14–3 • Veteran Population by Age, 1970–2000 (in thousands)

Age	1970	1980	1986	1990*	2000*
Total	27,976	28,640	27,682	26,914	23,951
Under 45	13,652	11,189	9,538	8,349	4,940
45–64	11,111	14,283	12,637	11,515	10,140
65–74	1,292	2,308	4,395	5,586	5,063
75 and over	921	860	1,112	1,464	3,808

*Projected

Source: J. A. Gronvall, "Medical Care of Low-Income Veterans in the VA Health Care System," Health Affairs (Spring 1987), pp. 167–175.

Exhibit 14–4 • Veterans' Total Family Income in 1986 by Age

Age	$1–$9,999	$10,000–$19,999	$20,000–$39,999	$40,000 or More	None or Not Available
Under 25	106,800	91,000	48,100	3,400	13,900
25–44	557,600	1,113,700	2,868,600	2,745,000	568,500
45–64	1,003,700	1,649,600	3,677,400	4,319,900	1,500,700
65 or over	1,204,300	1,794,100	1,376,700	776,900	741,500

Source: Veterans Administration, 1987 Survey of Veterans, U.S. Bureau of the Census, Washington, DC, 1989, p. 103.

From these characteristics, certain outcomes have been inferred. For instance, research findings have shown that there are higher death rates in the lower-income classes. Persons of lower income, regardless of race, stayed in the hospital an average of two days longer than those in other income levels. They had more trouble securing medical care, which in turn led to more incidence of delayed care and more serious ailments when access to the system was finally obtained. The health problems of the poor tended to be more numerous and more complex than those in middle- and upper-income levels. Between the ages of forty-five and sixty-four, chronic conditions such as arthritis, diabetes, hearing and visual impairments, heart condition, and hypertension were two to three times higher for those with low incomes.

According to certain authorities, these characteristics affected the need for care in varying ways:

> Patients with multiple diagnoses, chronic conditions, and lower health status required more intensive medical and nursing care and closer observation and assessment when they were hospitalized. They required additional services such as discharge planning, nutritional counseling, and other patient education programs on a more frequent basis. The lower health status and presence of complicating chronic conditions extended the required length-of-stay per admission. In addition, more

intensive resource utilization per admission would occur.[1]

Past VA hospital usage tended to support many of these conclusions. For instance, VA studies have shown that the hospital discharge rates in the system decreased when income levels increased. Those in the lowest income groups were hospitalized almost twice as much as those with incomes over $10,000. In addition to income, the availability of insurance played a large role in determining the users of VA health care. According to a 1987 Bureau of the Census report, 46.8 percent of the veterans using a VA hospital were not covered by health insurance. Of those covered, there was a reliance on nonprivate types of insurance such as Medicare, Medicaid, and military programs.

Other Problems in the VA's Future

The VA was not only struggling to keep pace with a growing number of elderly veterans but also was facing a growing AIDS problem, the threat of more debilitating diseases among the aging veterans, and significant staffing shortages.

AIDS among Veterans

The VA estimated that it would spend $40 million annually to provide treatment to veterans with AIDS. In January 1987, the VA was treating 1,600 AIDS patients. Of the VA's 172 medical centers, 112 were actively treating AIDS, but 77 percent of the cases were concentrated in 24 facilities. Manhattan Veterans Medical Center treated more cases than any other in the country. Twenty-three of its 120 acute-care beds were occupied by AIDS patients. Presently, the VA was establishing separate, specialized treatment units for veterans with AIDS.

According to the eligibility requirements, veterans unable to pay for care were entitled to free care. AIDS patients usually fell in this category. According to VA statistics, the length of stay for an AIDS patient was twenty-four to twenty-five days at an estimated cost of $50,000 per admission; some AIDS patients were admitted four or five times a year. The Centers for Disease Control in Atlanta estimated that the average general hospital care for each AIDS patient could range as high as $147,000 annually.

Debilitating Diseases

The VA was becoming increasingly strained by the long-term-care needs of those with Alzheimer's disease and other forms of dementia. An increase in these types of diseases was expected. By the year 2000, the VA predicted the number of veterans with dementia to reach 550,000, up from 200,000 in 1983. To prepare for the influx of veterans with Alzheimer's disease, the VA had community-based test projects that provided respite care for family members who cared for veterans with dementia at home. Currently, only one existed, in Bedford, Massachusetts.

Staff Retention and Recruitment

A 1986 survey found the average turnover rate at the VA was 16.1 percent among registered nurses, 22.6 percent for pharmacists, 23.4 percent for occupational therapists, and 25.5 percent for physical therapists. The most severe shortages were in the major metropolitan areas, the northeast, and California. The VA was attempting to enhance its image as an employer by increasing its tuition reimbursement and scholarship programs. It spent approximately $2.5 million on tuition reimbursement in 1990 with funds directed at areas with the largest shortages. The VA planned to broaden its scholarship program, which had traditionally been for nurses only. Under this plan, the program would be increased for nurses

and would add physical therapists. This could lower turnover as 73 percent of the full-time nurses who received scholarships remained at the VA after completing their programs, while 100 percent of the part-time nurses who received scholarships stayed.

Another way that the VA was approaching the turnover problem was through supplemental pay. Because the pay scale in some areas was not competitive, the VA allocated about $36 million for special pay rates in fiscal year 1987 with the expectation that the amount would increase to $50 million in 1988. About 9,700 employees were paid based on a special rate scale. For registered nurses, pharmacists, and physical therapists, salaries were provided that were 4 percent to 21 percent higher than the normal pay scale. In 1987, an entry-level registered nurse earned an average salary of $20,340. At the VA, the same nurse would earn $16,500 on regular pay with an additional 19 percent supplement for a total of $19,700. Nurses were offered the supplemental rate in ninety markets. A task force had been appointed to deal with recruitment and retention problems. Among the many options they considered were provision of child care services, recruitment bonuses, and improved working conditions.

The Political Situation

The VA was scrutinized by congressional committees, veterans' service organizations, and the President's Office of Management and Budget (OMB). The House and Senate Veterans Affairs Committees had legislative authority over the VA; and they were highly protective of this interest, as were the House and Senate Appropriations subcommittees that approved the VA annual budget. In addition, both the House and Senate Committees on Aging, although they had no authority to legislate, exerted pressure on the VA through public hearings and published works. These groups became particularly active if the department was trying to close or relocate a facility. In addition, an individual legislator became a factor in these situations, usually when the questionable facility was in his or her district.

Congress powerfully influenced priorities in the VA medical construction program. For instance, the

House and Senate Appropriations Committees tried to mandate the location of outpatient ambulatory clinics, although the construction program was an area on which the legislators did not always agree. The House Veterans Affairs Committee tended to favor continued construction, whereas its Senate counterpart tended toward promoting alternatives to outpatient care. Congress had been known to become involved at times in some of the smallest details concerning the VA. On different occasions, for example, they directed the VA to hire an assistant medical director for geriatrics and service chiefs for podiatry and optometry at its central office.

The "Iron Triangle"

Actually, the VA and its advocates represented an "iron triangle" of interests in Washington policy making. The triangle was made up of the department itself, congressional committees that oversaw and promoted its interests, and veterans' service organizations. Members of this triangle never missed an opportunity to support the cause of the VA. Never had the influence of this lobby been felt more than by the Reagan administration.

The Reagan administration experienced the power of the VA's vast lobby in its first assault on the budget deficit, the Omnibus Budget Reconciliation Act of 1981. Packaged in this act was a scheme to decrease VA spending by $863 million, nearly two-thirds of which was to come from reductions in medical care and construction programs. To get approval in a Democratic Congress, Reagan needed more than the Republican vote, so the administration tried to put together a block of votes from conservative Democrats. One of these was the chairman of the Veterans Affairs Committee. He, of course, objected to the reductions in VA medical care and would support other cuts only if VA medical care was maintained. Furthermore, for his vote, he elicited an informal agreement from the administration that they would not seek any sizable VA budget reductions in the future.

Commitment by Congress to the VA was steadfast over the years, but would be tested in the future in light of the department's need to shift resources, convert hospital beds into long-term care, and prepare for the care of the elderly veteran. Republican leaders in the Senate were more willing to trim VA spending in the early 1990s. One outgrowth was the decision by Congress to focus the VA's limited dollars on veterans with service-connected injuries in an attempt to improve services and decrease the budget. Federal legislators were encouraging resource-sharing agreements between community hospitals and the VA as an alternative to building or replacing VA hospitals. For instance, one proposed bill would allow for contracting private health care whenever VA medical services were geographically inaccessible.

Political Opponents

A powerful lobby that was opposed to the VA from its inception was the American Medical Association (AMA), which represented private medicine. At the end of World War II, the AMA mounted a major but unsuccessful offensive. Recently, a report by the National Academy of Sciences recommended the integration of VA health facilities with those of the community, with the ultimate goal of relegating the department's functions to the private sector. This was supported but not pursued by the Reagan administration.

Although the budget-reduction efforts failed, the Reagan administration did not give up its attack on the VA. For instance, the General Accounting Office (GAO) released a report in August 1985 that said:

> GAO performed two different reviews of patients at VA hospitals. In one review of seven hospitals, GAO's consultant team of physicians and nurses from the Washington State Professional Standards Review Organization reviewed 350 randomly selected medical files of patients who had been discharged from these hospitals during fiscal year 1982. Based on the consultants' review, GAO estimated that nearly 43 percent of the total days spent by medical and surgical patients at these seven hospitals were medically avoidable. About 20 percent of the total days were attributable to the absence of efficient manage-

ment practices at the hospitals, while 23 percent were attributable to the unavailability of less costly levels of care. The VA service chiefs in the hospitals agreed with 86 percent of the avoidable days identified by the consultant.[2]

The second review during fiscal year 1984 found similar results; however, in both instances, the GAO pointed out that less-costly levels of care for patients were often not available.

The VA Budget

Total spending for veterans (including income security, medical care, education, training, and rehabilitation) peaked in 1976 in inflation-adjusted terms. A decline in spending would continue if the projections for 1990 were sustained. Spending for the medical care program in 1975 was $3.5 billion; this had grown marginally in inflation-adjusted terms from $5.7 billion in 1981 to $6.6 billion in 1982, $7.4 billion in 1983, $7.8 billion in 1984, and $8.9 billion in 1985. The 1989 fiscal year budget proposal was for approximately $11 billion.

In the past, VA medical centers received a finite amount of funding each year. Called a *target allowance,* it represented the historical share of what the VA received from Congress. Using this method, the reward for efficiency and cost containment for each center was survival, and it was effective to a degree in containing cost. In 1981, private hospital cost per patient rose 15.9 percent. According to VA sources, the system's cost rose 8 percent.

Currently, with the prospective payment system using diagnostic-related groups, the budget was distributed differently. The distribution was determined by the efficiency of each hospital within the overall system. This motivated many of the systems to attempt improvements. West Side Medical Center in Chicago, for instance, implemented a venture capital program in which a pool of capital within the budget was set aside for trial implementation of ideas that would decrease costs or increase revenues. They saved $40,000 a year by hiring a wheelchair mechanic instead of contracting out the repair.

The Organization of the VA

To decentralize the provision of medical care, the VA was organized into seven major geographic groupings within the United States: Northeastern, Mid-Atlantic, Southeastern, Great Lakes, Midwestern, Western, and Southwestern (see Exhibit 14–5). The regions were divided into twenty-eight districts that contained several hospitals and medical centers.

Administratively, the VA was divided into three major divisions: Department of Medicine and Surgery, Department of Benefits, and Department of Memorial Affairs. The Department of Medicine and Surgery was headed by the chief medical director. The organization of the department is shown in Exhibit 14–6. The administrator of each hospital in a particular district reported directly to the regional director.

The VA Strategy

The VA had been involved in a "grassroots" planning process involving the administrators of each medical center who studied the demographic changes in the VA's twenty-eight districts. Given the assumption that there would *not* be another war, all districts identified the aging veteran's medical needs as a prime concern. Therefore, the critical issue was how to meet the needs of aging veterans between now and at least the year 2010. A new comprehensive plan would remove VA hospitals from the center of medical services and strengthen ambulatory care and alternative services such as adult day care and hospital-based home care. Exhibit 14–7 describes some of these services. If the aging plan was successful, the hospital would function only as the support system; the focal point would be outpatient and noninstitutional care.

The 1988 fiscal budget of $28 billion contained no allocation for construction of new nursing homes. Rather, the budget called for conversion of 282 hospital beds to long-term-care beds and a $26.9 million increase in expenditures for state and community nursing homes. Usually, the VA was criticized for spending too much on capital expansion and not enough on alternatives to construction. According to

Exhibit 14–5 • Veterans Administration Department of Medicine and Surgery (DM & S)

DM & S Regions

1) **Northeastern**
2) **Mid-Atlantic**
3) **Southeastern**
4) **Great Lakes**
5) **Midwestern**
6) **Western**
7) **Southwestern**

Source: VA documents.

the Office of the VA Chief Medical Director, the strategy was to rely increasingly on state and community homes. Community hospitals and nursing homes would be called to help especially during peak years—the year 2000 for VA hospitals and the year 2010 for long-term-care services.

Other Strategic Alternatives

The VA faced an uncertain future especially in light of so many opposing factors: the humanitarian instincts of society, the political emphasis on decreased public spending, a population of veterans that was rapidly aging, and a private health sector

that might have more hospital beds and physicians than needed. As a result, various groups developed their own proposals as to what the VA's future strategy should be.

Mainstreaming Services

This proposal called for phasing out the VA's direct involvement in the provision of medical care. It was believed that the VA should finance rather than provide services through some form of insurance or voucher system that would allow veterans to purchase health care. Often, partial "mainstreaming" was advocated where either outpatient or hospital care for acute illness would be phased out. Proponents

Exhibit 14–6 • Organizational Chart, Department of Medicine and Surgery, Veterans Administration

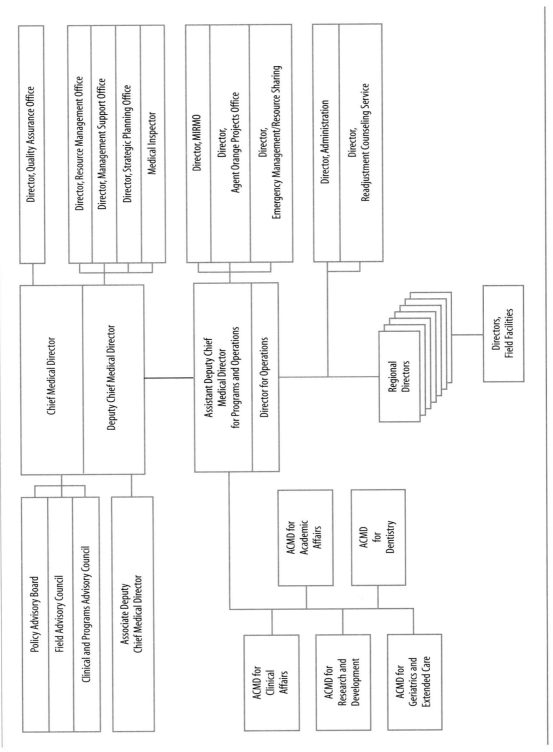

Exhibit 14–7 · Geriatric and Extended-Care Programs

VA Nursing Home Care: One hundred fifteen nursing homes located in VA medical centers.

Community Nursing Home Care: Contract program for veterans who required skilled- or intermediate-nursing care to assist in transition from a hospital to the community.

VA Domiciliary Care: Located in fifteen medical centers and one independent facility for eligible ambulatory vets who were disabled by age, disease, or injury and were in need of care but not hospitalization or skilled services.

Hospital-Based Home Care: Forty-nine medical centers provided chronically ill veterans with services in their own homes. In 1985, there were 219,000 home visits to 11,353 patients.

Community Residential Care Programs: One hundred twenty-five medical centers provided residential care in privately operated facilities to veterans who did not require hospitalization or nursing home care, but who could not resume independent living due to health conditions.

Adult Day Health Care: Provided health maintenance and therapeutic activities in eight VA centers for veterans who otherwise would require institutionalization.

Geriatric Evaluation Units: Fifty units provide assessment of older patients' medical, functional, psychological, and social-economic status in order to improve diagnosis, treatment, and placement.

State Veterans Home Program: Per diem program to aid states in providing direct hospital, nursing home, and domiciliary care to eligible veterans.

Source: J. H. Mather and R. W. Abel, "Medical Care of Veterans," *Journal of the American Geriatrics Society* 34 (1986), pp. 757–760.

---

believed that full or partial mainstreaming would ensure quality control because quality of services was monitored directly by the customer. Proponents of this proposal often based their rationale on the assumption that a national health care system was inevitable.

On the other hand, opponents of this proposal often cited the Medicaid program as evidence against it. They believed that poor patients were shifted to the community unsuccessfully in Medicaid. Furthermore, many believed that if the VA did not meet the burden of the aging veteran, it would be shifted onto state and local governments. Regardless, the needs would have to be met by one social agency or another, and the VA at least knew the veteran population.

Integration into the Private Health Care System

In this proposal, VA health services would be integrated into the larger system of health and social services for older Americans. This would allow both systems to achieve economies of scale and it would eliminate the problem of the VA constructing facilities where underutilized ones already existed in the community. Proponents believed that in attempting to solve the problem of the aging veteran, the political atmosphere must be considered. They thought that this plan was the only politically realistic one

that simultaneously provided a basis for good health care for the elderly.

Conversely, others believed that this plan, like the mainstreaming alternative, would shift the burden of aging veterans onto state and local governments or onto what they perceived as an already failing Medicaid program. As Representative G. V. (Sonny) Montgomery, a Mississippi Democrat and chairman of the House Veterans' Affairs Committee, asked, "Why dump all of those people on a system that does not work very well—Medicare and Medicaid?"[3]

Specialization in Long-Term Care

Many believed that the VA should narrow its focus and specialize in the provision of long-term care. The VA developed a reputation for providing better long-term care than was available in the general health care system. By focusing on this area, it could take advantage of its distinctive competency. Others believed that this area was less well covered by public and private insurance; therefore, as veterans age, more would turn to the VA for nursing home care. The advantages from specialization should lower costs and increase the quality of care. On the other hand, opponents of this alternative regarded the eligible VA population as an attractive market whose needs would be best served by the private sector. Amid problems of federal budget constraints, they asserted that the VA could not obtain the budgetary increases required to build and support the facilities necessary to meet this growing demand.

Construction of Long-Term-Care Facilities

The Veterans Affairs Committees in Congress were supporting the addition of major long-term-care construction projects. This alternative was also supported by the Paralyzed Veterans of America, who feared that there was not enough planning for the long-term needs of the elderly. They believed that most public facilities were running near or at full capacity and could not accommodate the growing elderly population as called for by the VA plan. With this proposal, veterans' medical services would remain with the VA; there would be no change except for the emphasis on construction of long-term-care facilities. This alternative was opposed not only by those who maintained that the quality of care provided by the VA was suspect but also by those who believed that the VA would not be able to meet the future demands of the aging veterans.

Integration with the Military

This proposal called for the gradual integration of the VA with the armed forces. Many believed that this solution would maintain the organizational integrity of the VA and help solve the military problem of physician shortages. However, the opposite view was that neither the VA nor the armed forces could provide adequate care; therefore, the merging of the two would resolve no problems while creating worse obstacles to veteran care.

Operational Efficiency Focus

One alternative proposed to change the focus of the VA strategy to increasing operational efficiency. GAO reported that nearly 43 percent of the VA medical and surgical days reviewed were medically avoidable. Some were the result of poor management practices; others were attributable to the unavailability of less-costly levels of care. From this, the proponents believed that the reimbursement mechanism provided incentives to keep the beds filled; therefore, to focus on operational efficiency, incentives would be

changed. The opponents did not believe that a new focus would change any of the existing problems such as the long-term needs of an aging veteran population or the perceived lack of quality care.

Expansion of the Array of Services

This proposal was based on the fact that 30 percent of VA nursing home care was provided by community facilities. It was believed that this should be eliminated so that the veteran could obtain all services from the VA. This would allow substitution of one more-costly service by another of lesser cost. It was believed that when acute care was delivered in one service system while long-term care was delivered elsewhere, providers had little incentive to substitute one for the other to reduce costs. Moreover, the movement of patients between the two disrupted the continuity and quality of care. Inherent in this proposal was the need to broaden the patient base to include all veterans regardless of eligibility. Others, such as spouses of veterans, could even be included. This alternative, however, was considered politically impracticable by many. Among other things, there was the concern of Congress to reduce costs coupled with the perceived reluctance of the taxpayer to support all veterans' medical expenses regardless of service-related disability.

The Future Direction of the VA Health Care System

With Lincoln's quote still in mind, Dr. Gronvall reflected on the many changes facing the VA medical care program in the future. Knowing that the agency was moving into a period fraught with more uncertainty than ever before in its history, he could not help but question the appropriateness of the current strategy. "Would the conversion of existing VA beds and reliance on state and community facilities meet the long-term-care needs of the aging veterans both now and in the year 2010? Would the VA be able to successfully refocus from hospital-based care to outpatient and alternative means of care? Or, given the future environment, would a more radical strategy be feasible, such as mainstreaming services, specializing in long-term care, or even integrating with the armed forces medical organization?"

Notes

1. M. Randall, K. E. Kilpatrick, J. F. Pendergast, K. R. Jones, and W. B. Vogel, "Differences in Patient Characteristics Between Veterans Administration and Community Hospitals," *Medical Care* 25, no. 11 (1987), p. 1104.
2. J. K. Iglehart, "The Veterans Administration Medical Care System Faces an Uncertain Future," *The New England Journal of Medicine* 313, no. 18 (1985), p. 1172.
3. J. Davidson, "Veterans Are Angry over Proposals to Trim Health-System Budget," *Wall Street Journal* (April 22, 1985), p. 19.

References

Alexander, C. F. "Fifty Years of VA Health Care." *Urban Health* (July–August 1980), p. 10.

Andries, G. H., Jr. "Venture Capitalism at the Veterans Administration." *Hospital and Health Services Administration* 31, no. 4 (Winter 1986), pp. 25–31.

Davidson, J. "Veterans Are Angry over Proposals to Trim Health-System Budget." *Wall Street Journal* (April 22, 1985), pp. 1, 19.

Farber, S. J. "The Future Role of the VA Hospital System: A National Health-Policy Dilemma." *New England Journal of Medicine* 298, no. 11 (1978), pp. 625–628.

Firshein, J. "AIDS Stretching VA's Ability to Treat Veterans." *Hospitals* (February 20, 1986), pp. 33–34.

Franklin, B. A. "Congress Approves Making VA a Cabinet Department." *New York Times* (October 19, 1988), p. 8.

Gronvall, J. A. "Medical Care of Low-Income Veterans in the VA Health Care System." *Health Affairs* (Spring 1987), pp. 167–175.

Horgan, C., A. Taylor, and G. Wilensky. "Aging Veterans: Will They Overwhelm the VA Medical System?" *Health Affairs* 2, no. 3 (1983), pp. 77–86.

Iglehart, J. K. "The Veterans Administration Medical Care System Faces an Uncertain Future." *New England Journal of Medicine* 313, no. 18 (1985), pp. 1168–1172.

Kosloski, D., C. Austin, and E. Borgatta. "Determinants of VA Utilization." *Medical Care* 25, no. 9 (1987), pp. 830–846.

Maino, J. H., T. I. Messer, and D. H. Messer. "Veterans Administration Residency Programs: An Overview." *Journal of the American Optometric Association* 58, no. 5 (1987), pp. 378–379.

Mather, J. H., and R. W. Abel. "Medical Care of Veterans." *Journal of the American Geriatric Society* 34, no. 10 (1986), pp. 757–760.

Randall, M., K. E. Kilpatrick, J. F. Pendergast, K. R. Jones, and W. B. Vogel. "Differences in Patient Characteristics Between Veterans Administration and Community Hospitals." *Medical Care* 25, no. 11 (1987), pp. 1099–1104.

Romeis, J. C., K. N. Gillespie, and R. M. Coe. "Older Veterans' Future Use of VA Health Care Services." *Medical Care* 26, no. 9 (1988), pp. 854–866.

Schlesinger, M., and T. Wetle. "Care of the Elder Veteran: New Directions for Change." *Health Affairs* (Summer 1986), pp. 59–71.

Special Medical Advisory Group of the Veterans Administration. "Helping to Meet the Health Care Needs of the Nation." *Journal of the American Medical Association* 220, no. 10 (1972), pp. 1334–1337.

Thomas, J. W., S. E. Berki, L. Wyszewianski, and M. L. E. Ashcraft. "Classification of Hospitals Based on Measured Output: The VA System." *Medical Care* 21, no. 7 (1983), pp. 715–723.

Veterans Administration. *1987 Survey of Veterans* (Washington, D.C.: U.S. Bureau of the Census, 1989).

Wagner, L. "VA Hospitals Struggling to Keep Pace with Patient Demands, Staff Shortages." *Modern Healthcare* (June 5, 1987), pp. 162–164.

Wallace, C. "VA's New Aging Plan Downplays Hospitals, Stresses Alternatives." *Modern Healthcare* (May 15, 1984), pp. 172–174.

Wolinsky, F. D., R. M. Coe, and R. R. Mosely. "Length of Stay in the VA." *Medical Care* 25, no. 3 (1987), pp. 250–253.

Wolinsky, F. D., R. M. Coe, R. R. Mosely, and S. M. Homan. "Some Clarification About Health Planning in the VA." *Medical Care* 25, no. 11 (1987), pp. 1105–1110.

Wolinsky, F. D., R. M. Coe, R. R. Mosely, and S. M. Homan. "Veterans' and Nonveterans' Use of Health Services." *Medical Care* 23, no. 12 (1985), pp. 1358–1371.

Wills Eye Hospital: A Specialty Hospital Survivor

Introduction

D. McWilliams Kessler, chief executive officer and executive director of Wills Eye Hospital in Philadelphia, was deep in thought as he prepared to present his 1996 annual report to the Board of Directors of City Trusts. The past year had been a successful one for Wills by hospital industry standards, and Wills enjoyed an international reputation for quality in the care and treatment of the eye. Indeed, Wills had been listed consistently among the top hospitals in the nation by *U.S. News and World Report* in its "Annual Guide to America's Best Hospitals." In 1996 Wills was ranked third best in the United States.[1]

Kessler knew better than most, however, that the health care industry was in the midst of a radical transformation, one that would become more turbulent as political and market reforms continued. Not all hospitals would survive the shakeout. Research by the American Hospital Association revealed two ominous trends—hospital closings and mergers—were both on the rise.[2]

As Kessler reflected on the past year's experience, he was both pleased and concerned. Wills's

This case was prepared by Elizabeth B. Davis and Stephen J. Porth of St. Joseph's University and Linda E. Swayne of the University of North Carolina at Charlotte. It is intended as a basis of class discussion rather than to illustrate effective or ineffective handling of an administrative situation. Used with permission from Linda Swayne.

reputation and recent financial performance were sources of pride. At the same time, the momentum for health care reform and the costs of keeping pace with medical technologies threatened the very existence of small, highly specialized hospitals such as Wills. As the area's least efficient hospital (as measured by capacity utilization), Wills was beginning to feel the squeeze.

In consultation with his executive team, Kessler had formulated a set of options to be examined over the upcoming planning period. Although maintaining the independence of the institution continued to be a primary goal, industry pressures and uncertainty forced the team to consider all options, including strategic alliances, mergers, and acquisitions.

Hospital Industry Trends

The health care industry from 1970 throughout the 1990s had continually demonstrated not only its complexity but its volatility as well. The industry comprised a myriad of products and services and a corresponding variety of organizational types. The health care industry was defined as those companies and institutions that directly provide care for patients and those that supply medical products or services to the primary providers.[3] Organizational types included hospitals, clinics, HMOs, nursing homes, medical and dental practices, manufacturers of medical products and technologies, and pharmaceutical companies. These organizations fell into the categories of both not-for-profit and for-profit institutions.

Slowing the growth rate of national health care expenditures had been the subject of great debate beginning in the 1980s and continuing in the 1990s. Health care spending exploded from $25.4 billion in 1960 to over $730 billion in 1991, a compound annual growth rate of 11.8 percent. By comparison, the GNP expanded at an annual rate of 8.5 percent over the same period. Between 1984 and 1994 health care expenditures grew at an average of 9.1 percent annually compared to a 6 percent growth in GDP. Health care costs in 1995 were approximately 14 percent of GNP or $1.0 trillion (a 7 percent increase) compared to $950 billion in 1994 (a 7.5 percent increase). It appeared that market forces were having some impact on slowing health care cost increases; however there was considerable debate concerning whether it could continue. A common question was "What do you cut when there's no fat left in the system?" There was no guarantee that growth in health care expenditures would remain moderate.[4]

Government Health Care Programs

In the 1960s the government enacted the Medicare and Medicaid programs. Jointly funded by state and federal governments, Medicaid was a program that provided medical aid for people who were unable to finance their own medical expenses. Medicare was a program under the Social Security Administration that provided medical care for the aged. These programs experienced tremendous growth over the years, with the Medicare program representing close to 40 percent of hospital revenues, on average.

In 1984, the government enacted a new prospective payment system (PPS), in which reimbursement moved from a cost-based approach to a fixed-fee reimbursement system. That is, health care providers were paid based not on the costs of services rendered but on a predetermined schedule established for various medical conditions known as diagnosis-related groups (DRGs).

The enactment of PPS along with the growth of the Medicare and Medicaid programs resulted in fundamental changes in the delivery of health care services. The changes led to declining trends in hospital admissions, reductions in the average lengths of stay and other utilization measures, and a corresponding increase in services provided in less expensive settings, such as outpatient clinics and home health care. The proliferation of government policy and regulation aimed at solving the rising health care cost problem produced uncertainty and instability, and contributed to the high-risk, high-cost environment of the hospital industry.

Demographic Shifts

The "graying of America" (i.e., the aging U.S. population) created a natural increase in demand for medical services and contributed to rising national health care expenditures. As the elderly segment of the population grew, there was a corresponding increase in medical services designed to serve this population's needs. This increased demand produced a deficit-ridden Medicare program, with predictions of bankruptcy in the early years of the twenty-first century.

Medical Technology

The rapid increase and development of new medical technologies created a fast-paced health care system in which organizations fought to maintain and provide the best quality services through capital equipment acquisitions. These expensive technologies contributed to higher operating costs and, in many cases, shifted medical procedures from inpatient to outpatient services or from hospital to off-site delivery.

Third-Party Payor Systems

Most consumers of health care services had been insulated from rising health care costs through the evolution of the third-party payor system. The majority of U.S. medical expenditures was made by third-party payors such as large corporate employers, the government, and insurance companies. When corporate medical expenses increased 20.4 percent in 1990, companies began in earnest to make changes. In addition, the caps placed on reimbursement under the Medicare and Medicaid programs caused hospitals to increasingly incur uncompensated costs. Hospitals shifted the burden of these uncompensated costs to the private insurers. The corporate response was the creation of managed-care organizations and capitated contracts to control utilization of medical services, thereby controlling corporate expenses.

Although individuals were relieved of a good portion of their health care costs under the fee-for-service system, it provided incentives for hospitals to expand medical-related diagnostic testing and the provision of services. Managed care and capitation provided incentives for hospitals to reduce testing and provision of some services. More patients were treated as outpatients and others left the hospital "quicker and sicker" to be cared for in nursing homes, subacute facilities, or home care.

Delaware Valley Health Care Industry

The Philadelphia metropolitan area was well known for its heavy concentration of health care institutions. Nationally, the Philadelphia area ranked second in the number of teaching hospitals and medical schools behind the New York/northern New Jersey area.[5] The region had six medical schools, twenty-four teaching hospitals, and annually prepared over 4,000 students for medicine.[6] In addition, approximately 63 hospitals were considered part of the Philadelphia metropolitan region,[7] along with over 125 pharmaceutical, biotechnology and research institutions employing over 14,000 people.[8] Total health care employment in the area was about 73,000 people in 1996, a decline from 1992 when over 75,000 people were employed in health care.[9] Exhibit 15-1 provides data on the Philadelphia metropolitan hospital industry, comparing the years 1987, 1992, and 1995.

The Delaware Valley Hospital Council reported that two out of every three hospitals in the city of Philadelphia and one out of every three in the surrounding suburbs ended fiscal year 1990 with operating losses. Average operating margins were between 0 and 1 percent, far below the 4 percent margin that most health care experts say is needed to maintain the physical property. Philadelphia hospitals operated at a profit margin of 0.6 percent in 1995, a better rate than 1994 when the margin was a negative 0.3 percent.[10] Exhibit 15-2 provides operating margins for general and specialty acute-care hospitals in the area.

The overall weak financial performance of Delaware Valley hospitals set the tone for a highly competitive hospital arena. The focus of Delaware Valley hospitals in the years to come would be survival. Both failing and profitable institutions were searching for strategies that would guarantee their viability in the twenty-first century. Wills Eye Hospital was hardly immune to the pressure being exerted by its external environment. Potential alliance partners for Wills were dictated in part by physical proximity of general acute-care hospitals (i.e., urban environment) and medical staff teaching, research, and practice affiliations as well as the emerging systems.

Emerging Competitive Systems

The Philadelphia market was dominated by not-for-profit hospitals. Only one for-profit health care provider, Primary Health System, was involved with negotiating to buy a hospital in the area—Roxborough Memorial Hospital. However, Columbia/HCA had announced it would open an office in June 1997.

Philadelphia was not a mature managed-care market. Most of the hospitals had remained independent longer than many areas in the northeast;

Exhibit 15-1 • Philadelphia Metropolitan Hospitals

	1987	1992	1995
Outpatient visits	4.4 million	6 million	7.4 million
Inpatient days	4.9 million	4.6 million	4.2 million
Beds	18,158	16,862	15,723
Average stay	7.9 days	7.5 days	6.9 days
Occupancy	73.3%	74.9%	73.1%

Source: American Hospital Association Statistical Yearbook, 1996–1997

Exhibit 15–2 • **Operating Margins for Selected Philadelphia-Area Hospitals**

Hospital	Operating Margin 1994	Operating Margin 1995
Albert Einstein Medical Center	3.0%	4.1%
Chestnut Hill Hospital	1.2	2.3
Children's Hospital of Philadelphia	12.3	8.9
Episcopal Hospital	1.3	0.6
Frankford Hospital of the City of Philadelphia	4.7	7.4
Germantown Hospital and Medical Center	−5.5	−3.4
Girard Medical Center	n/a	−0.8
Graduate Health System—City Avenue	−6.0	−3.0
Parkview Hospital	−8.1	−6.8
Graduate Hospital	1.3	−2.2
Hahnemann University Hospital	−14.6	3.0
Hospital of the University of Pennsylvania	17.6	13.6
Jeanes Hospital	1.8	0.7
John F. Kennedy Memorial Hospital	−1.4	1.0
Kensington Hospital	−33.7	−23.1
Medical College Hospitals	2.9	3.1
Mercy Catholic Medical Center	−4.8	0.7
Methodist Hospital	−1.5	−1.8
Mount Sinai Hospital	2.0	−0.6
Nazareth Hospital	−4.3	−1.0
Neumann Medical Center	0.3	6.9
Northeastern Hospital	−11.0	−10.9
Pennsylvania Hospital	−0.7	0.2
Presbyterian Medical Center of Philadelphia	0.5	−0.6
Roxborough Memorial Hospital	−3.8	−3.9
Saint Agnes Medical Center	−0.3	0.6
Saint Christopher's Hospital for Children	3.4	7.6
Saint Joseph's Hospital	n/a	−0.8
Temple University Hospital	13.1	6.4
Thomas Jefferson University Hospital	4.8	4.0
—Ford Road	−28.2	−61.4
Wills Eye Hospital	4.0	2.4

Source: Philadelphia Online "Hospital Financial Reports for Pennsylvania, 1994–1995: http://www.phillynews.com/packages/hospitals/.

however pressures from employers for coverage of their employees spread over the Delaware Valley area was causing change. In 1992 there were nearly 125 hospitals in the Delaware Valley. In early 1996 that number had decreased to sixty-three and four major systems were beginning to emerge (see Exhibit 15–3).

Competitive strategies of nearby hospitals in recent years ranged from the Graduate Hospital's ongoing practice of acquiring failing hospitals and executing turnarounds to Pennsylvania Hospital's conservative search for alliances with premier revenue-generating programs and services. Both hospitals and their corporate offices were within a twelve-block

Exhibit 15–3 • Emerging Systems in the Philadelphia Area

Allegheny Health, Education, and Research Foundation
Allegheny University Hospitals
    Bucks County (Warminster General Hospital)
    Elkins Park (Rolling Hill Hospital)
    Medical College of Pennsylvania
Saint Christopher's Hospital for Children
Lawndale Community Hospital (closed)
Hahnemann University Hospital
Currently negotiating to join Allegheny:
    Graduate Health System including:
    Graduate Hospital
    City Avenue Hospital
    Parkview Hospital
    Mount Sinai Hospital
    Rancocas Hospital

Jefferson Health System
Thomas Jefferson University Hospital
Methodist Division, Thomas Jefferson University Hospital
Main Line Health System
    Lankenau Hospital
    Bryn Mawr Hospital
    Bryn Mawr Rehabilitation Hospital
    Paoli Memorial Hospital
In negotiations with Jefferson:
    Albert Einstein Medical Center

Moss Rehabilitation Hospital
Belmont Center for Comprehensive Treatment

University of Pennsylvania Health System
Hospital of University of Pennsylvania
Taylor Hospital
Germantown Hospital and Medical Center
Presbyterian Medical Center
Holy Redeemer Hospital and Medical Center
Pennsylvania Hospital
Phoenixville Hospital

Temple University Health System
Temple University Hospital
Northeastern Hospital
Neumann Medical Center
Jeanes Hospital

Catholic Health Initiatives
Nazareth Hospital
St. Agnes Medical Center
St. Mary Medical Center

Mercy Health System
Mercy Fitzgerald Hospital
Mercy Community Hospital
Mercy Hospital of Philadelphia (formerly Misericordia)

---

radius of Wills. The Graduate Health System was in the process of negotiating to join Allegheny Health System. The University of Pennsylvania Health System had merged Presbyterian into its system. The Presbyterian Hospital, located on the fringe of center city Philadelphia in the area known as University City, was still relatively close to Wills, Jefferson, and Graduate Hospitals. Presbyterian had strong teaching and practice affiliation with the Hospital of the University of Pennsylvania and maintained a robust activity in ophthalmology through the Scheie Eye Institute.

Thomas Jefferson Hospital had been affiliated with Wills Eye Hospital for many years. Occupying a side-by-side physical arrangement with Wills, it maintained a formal arrangement in which the ophthalmologist in chief of Wills had an appointment in

the Jefferson system as chair of the Ophthalmology Department. Thomas Jefferson had merged with Main Line Health System.

As a multi-institutional system, Main Line Health had succeeded in recent years in building a corporate suburban structure that included not just Lankenau but the Bryn Mawr Hospital, Paoli Memorial Hospital, Bryn Mawr Rehabilitation Hospital, and Community Health Affiliates. This made Main Line Health one of the more powerful players in the Delaware Valley region. The system tended to serve the more affluent communities of Philadelphia; and as a consequence, its financial performance was better than some of its center city Philadelphia counterparts.

In August 1996, the Allegheny System included 4,000 beds, 25,768 employees, and 450 primary-care physicians. A Pittsburgh-based company, it purchased Warminster General Hospital and renamed it Bucks County Campus of the Allegheny Health Education and Research Foundation. Rolling Hill Hospital's name was changed to Elkins Park Campus. Additional hospitals included in the system were: Medical College of Pennsylvania, United Hospitals, Inc., St. Christopher's Hospital for Children, Lawndale Community Hospital (closed after it was purchased), and Hahnemann University Hospital. In addition, extended negotiations were occurring with the Graduate Health System (five hospitals—Graduate Hospital, City Avenue Hospital, Parkview Hospital, Mt. Sinai Hospital, Rancocas Hospital) and Zurbrugg Memorial Health Center.

The fourth major system was developed by Temple University. It included the Temple University Hospital, Neumann Medical Center, Port Richmond Hospital, Jeanes Hospital, and Northeastern Hospital. Temple took over the troubled Northeastern Hospital, which lost $5.4 million in 1995 (following a $6.2 million loss in 1994).

Cost Pressures Affecting the Delaware Valley

In October 1994, the state of Pennsylvania enrolled 650 Medicaid recipients from Philadelphia and its four surrounding counties into a managed-care plan called "Health Choice." Health Choice was operated by a variety of private contractors who wanted to deal with providers that could serve many Medicaid recipients in a cost-effective way.

Philadelphia is over-bedded by most any standards. Many experts in health care delivery believe that closings in the market are inevitable. Consolidation led to some closings or at least affected how some facilities were used. Estimates were that the 29,000 licensed beds in the city was about 10,000 too many; or if managed-care were to become the norm in the region, the beds could be cut to 13,000. According to a study by the Sachs Group, 30 midsize hospitals in the Delaware Valley could close and the remaining hospitals would still have empty beds.

Until 1993, hospital jobs were growing in the Philadelphia area. Health services jobs accounted for 13 percent of the total employment. Up to 40,000 jobs might be eliminated (mostly from hospitals), and

only one-half of those employees would be able to find another job in health care. Many of those would be in lower-paying nonhospital jobs.

Philadelphia had a longer length of stay (LOS) than most parts of the country. The U.S. average LOS declined from 5.5 days in 1992 to 5.0 days in 1994. Philadelphia's comparable figures were 6.6 days in 1992 to 5.8 days in 1994.

In 1995, eight of twenty-six general, acute-care hospitals lost money, based on a report by the Pennsylvania Health Care Cost Containment Council. Germantown, Graduate Health System/City Avenue, Graduate Health System/Parkview, Kensington, Methodist, Northeastern, Nazareth, and Roxborough lost money. Four others took in less revenue than their costs, but donations and income from investments kept them in the black: Graduate Hospital, North Philadelphia Health System components of Girard, St. Joseph's, and Presbyterian Medical Center.

Alan Hillman, a health economist at the University of Pennsylvania pointed out that hospitals were not always going to be able to cut the fat out of the system. At some point they would run out of fat and cut into the bone. Hospitals in the area operated with a "thin" profit margin of 0.06 percent in 1995, but the four suburban counties—Bucks, Montgomery, Chester, and Delaware—were better off with a 3.8 percent profit margin.

History and Background of Wills Eye Hospital

Wills Eye Hospital was founded in 1832 through a bequest of James Wills, Jr., a Quaker merchant. At the time of his death in 1825, James Wills left the city of Philadelphia $108,000 to build an institution for the relief of the indigent blind and lame. The first Wills Hospital was a three-story, seventy-bed institution.

Before Wills's founding, general surgeons treated ophthalmic patients. Specialized training was rare. Wills played a vital role in establishing ophthalmology (the medical field encompassing treatment of the eye) as a separate branch of medicine in the United States. The first cataract operation was performed at Wills in 1834, by a Wills physician, Dr. Isaac Parish. In 1839, just seven years after the hospital's founding, Wills further helped the growth of ophthalmology by establishing the first ophthalmology residency with the enrollment of Dr. John Neill.

In the 1960s, Wills remained at the forefront of ophthalmic care and began to develop subspecialty services in addition to its General Ophthalmology Service (now the Cataract and Primary Eye Care Service). During the 1980s, Wills treated approximately 1 million patients, including over 107,000 operating room cases, 46,000 day surgery cases, 180,000 emergency room cases, 570,000 outpatient visits, and 78,000 inpatient admissions. In 1996, Wills employed over 600 people and occupied a six-floor building with 115 inpatient beds in center city Philadelphia.

The mission of Wills was as follows:

Wills Eye Hospital, through its dedication to the preservation of vision, serves as a comprehensive center for ophthalmology and other specialized services. Wills is committed to excellence in the provision of patient care to all those in need, to support of its medical staff, to education of healthcare professionals, and to participation in medical research.

Its vision:

Wills seeks to remain the preeminent center for excellence for ophthalmology by creating a continuum of care accessible and responsive to the needs of the community. Additionally, Wills seeks to expand its services and become known as a center of excellence in other select medical and surgical programs.

Wills was structured in a unique way. Overseeing the institution was the Board of Directors of City Trusts. The board was a group of political appointees, made up primarily of local business people and politicians, who oversaw Wills as well as 120 other organizations. The primary function of the board was to review and decide the fate of new strategic initiatives developed by Wills's executive staff. The board had the authority to make policy and develop strategies for Wills, but it had not assumed this role. Since 1985, the executive staff of Wills had, without

exception, obtained the approval of the board for each of its strategic initiatives. The board included a five-member subcommittee on hospital and research whose primary function was to advise the CEO of Wills on administrative issues.

Reporting directly to the board was not only the executive director/CEO (D. McWilliams Kessler), but also the ophthalmologist in chief (William Tasman, M.D.). Exhibit 15–4 details this arrangement. As executive director and CEO, Kessler was responsible for management and administration of the business side of Wills. This included, for example, strategic and financial planning, operations, purchasing, budgeting, human resources, accounting, and MIS. Exhibit 15–5 is an organizational chart of the business side of the hospital.

Also reporting directly to the board was the ophthalmologist in chief (OIC), Dr. Tasman. The OIC was responsible for the medical staff at Wills, which consisted of approximately 200 private practice physicians and 9 service chief physicians. The service chiefs were appointed by the OIC and acted as department heads, responsible for medical care within their respective departments. Wills physicians rented office space and equipment from the hospital and practiced in the fee-for-service, private practice mode (and therefore were not salaried employees of the hospital). Exhibit 15–6 provides information on the background and expertise of the key decision makers at Wills.

The structural arrangement shown in Exhibit 15–4 created special challenges for strategic planning at Wills. Specifically, it meant that both the business side and the medical side of the institution needed to agree on strategy. Because the business executives and physicians often saw things from different points of view and had different sets of priorities for the institution, achieving this agreement was a formidable task.

The case of cataract operations illustrates the difference in perspectives of the medical and executive staffs. Cataract operations, one of the most common procedures performed at Wills, had shifted from inpatient to almost exclusively outpatient delivery. This shift had little impact on physicians: they continued to be paid the predetermined fee for the procedure.

Exhibit 15–4 · Relationship of Wills Eye Hospital with Board of Directors of City Trusts

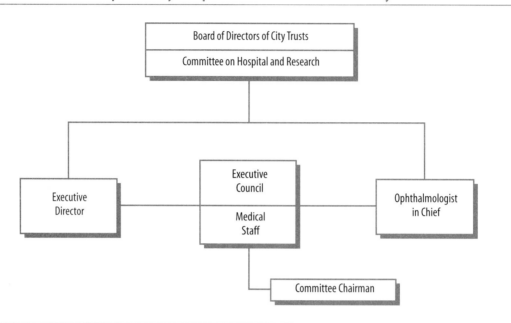

This was not so for the hospital, however, which was squeezed by a reimbursement system that was not cost based (and typically did not cover all costs). The burden to cover overhead expenses (e.g., operating room, emergency room, educational programs) fell primarily on inpatient services at the same time that Wills was performing a steadily decreasing proportion of these services. "We are moving our patients out . . . and now we have all those empty beds and high costs," said Kessler. "The trend creates a problem because it leaves an almost empty hospital with only the most expensive cases to treat. Add the costs of training doctors and performing research and Wills doesn't appear very attractive to HMOs and other insurers scrambling to cut deals with low-cost providers. We're too expensive. And these networks aren't necessarily interested in subsidizing these other things that make Wills's Eye what it is.

"Take the case of cataract surgery—one of the most common and until recently the most lucrative procedures performed at Wills—local HMOs are will-

ing to pay between $800 and $1,200 per operation. At Wills, we're talking about double that amount.

"Finding ways to subsidize under-reimbursed outpatient services, educational programs, and medical research is one key for the future of Wills," according to Kessler. "Another is to utilize our slack resources to produce new income."

Despite a distressed industry, Wills had succeeded in posting an operating margin that was consistent with national standards. Wills had increased its charges in 1992, and the new Geriatric Psychiatry Service was increasing the overall length of stay for the hospital. Occupancy from 1991 to 1992 had increased from 31.9 to 39.1 percent, but it had decreased to 36.5 by the end of 1995. Financial statements are provided in Exhibit 15–7, a "Statement of Revenues and Expenses," and Exhibit 15–8, "Operating Funds Balance Sheet." It is important to note that board-designated assets (i.e., funds held by trustee- and board-designated investments) were not restricted funds.

Exhibit 15–5 • Wills Eye Hospital Organization Chart (Non-Medical)

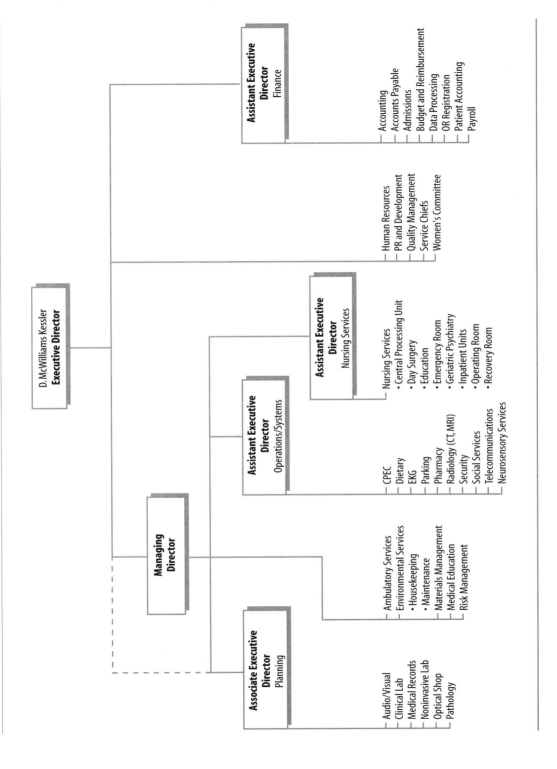

Exhibit 15–6 • Wills Eye Hospital Executives

D. McWilliams Kessler, Executive Director and CEO

Sixteen years' experience in management, finance, planning, education, research, marketing, and development in general and specialty acute-care teaching hospitals. Appointed CEO in 1985, after serving as the associate executive director and COO for the previous four years. Special expertise in financial turnarounds, strategic planning, product development, marketing, physician recruitment, and service diversification.

Kessler was regarded by his executive team as a creative, strategic thinker with vision. Although his relationships with the physicians on staff at the hospital had been stormy at times, he repeatedly demonstrated his finesse and skills at negotiation. This combined with his participatory approach toward his management team had fostered great loyalty and commitment on the part of his staff.

James Mulvihill, Managing Director

Twenty years' experience in hospital management with special expertise in physician recruitment, purchasing, and operations management. Appointed COO in 1985, after serving as assistant executive director since 1979. Mulvihill had been asked to speak about current health care issues at various national meetings and was instrumental in organizing a national buying group to purchase hospital surgical supplies and pharmaceuticals at volume discount prices.

His career was in the operational aspects of the institution with a particular focus on cultivating physician relations. His title was changed to managing director in 1995.

William Tasman, M.D., Ophthalmologist in Chief (OIC)

Tasman, a retina specialist, came to Wills as a resident in 1959. After several hospital appointments as attending surgeon and consulting surgeon, in 1985 he was named the chairman of the Department of Ophthalmology for Thomas Jefferson University Hospital, located next to Wills. Later that same year he was appointed OIC of Wills Eye Hospital.

Tasman had long been a figure in the international medical ophthalmic arena and was a well-known lecturer in his field. His many years of experience in the medical care system made him decisive in his actions and unpredictable in his approach toward management. Senior to most of the young management team at Wills, he was an independent thinker.

These monies were not donor-endowment assets with restrictions as to eventual use or generated yearly income suffering a restriction.

Strategic Options

Wills Eye Hospital had gone through a decade of major strategic changes in the midst of the government regulations and demographic shifts described earlier. One change was in the hospital's mix of inpatient versus outpatient services. Before 1982, all of Wills's services were inpatient. By 1992, fully half of Wills's services were outpatient.

One physician on staff at Wills described the magnitude of this change when he remarked, "When I was considering whether to join the staff at Wills in 1985, I was advised by more than one colleague to stay away. Wills had just finished building a new six-floor, 115-bed hospital. At the same time government regulations were making it increasingly difficult to fill the beds by putting pressure on hospitals

to serve more patients in an outpatient mode. Some people at the hospital were afraid the new building was a white elephant that would intensify the financial burdens on Wills."

As feared, filling beds was a challenge at Wills where occupancy rates lagged behind other area hospitals (see Exhibit 15–9). Further, Wills served a disproportionately high percentage of Medicare patients and was forced to absorb costs not covered because of Medicare reimbursement caps.

In the early 1980s, top management recognized the need to expand the hospital's range of services to fill more beds and attract a greater proportion of non-Medicare patients. As a result, new specialty programs and services, such as the hand center unit (performing hand operations such as carpal tunnel surgery) and the geriatric psychiatry unit, were established. These changes produced a modest level of diversification for Wills but occupancy rates continued to lag behind other area hospitals. The changes created internal controversy at Wills as some of the

Exhibit 15–7 · Statement of Revenues and Expenses

	Year ended June 30			
	1992	1993	1994	1995
Operating revenue				
Net patient service revenue	50,586,601	46,875,521	47,188,341	55,261,920
Other operating revenue	3,524,522	3,218,543	3,190,196	3,689,649
Total operating revenue	54,111,123	50,094,064	50,378,537	58,951,569
Operating expenses				
Salaries, wages, and fees	18,070,941	19,051,555	19,148,621	22,123,725
Supplies and other expenses	21,098,548	21,692,075	22,153,653	27,685,695
Interest expense	1,051,327	1,023,740	930,024	678,110
Depreciation and amortization	2,387,888	2,520,516	2,589,188	3,052,020
Provision for bad debts	3,562,232	3,430,931	3,551,890	4,015,654
Total operating expenses	46,170,936	47,718,817	48,373,376	57,555,204
Excess of revenues over expenses from operations	7,940,187	2,375,247	2,005,161	1,396,365
Nonoperating revenue				
Investment income				
Endowment funds	116,029	108,897	122,927	106,229
Unrestricted	2,183,383	3,381,547	3,127,003	4,089,233
Assets whose use is limited				
Board-designated funds	820,592	797,136	970,102	1,059,869
Trustee-held funds	885,069	627,851	454,651	29,981
Unrealized gain (loss) on marketable securities			(1,197,023)	1,197,023
Unrestricted gifts	362,709	1,718,976	505,958	760,006
Total nonoperating revenue	4,367,782	6,634,407	3,983,618	7,242,341
Extraordinary loss			(247,328)	
Excess of revenues over expenses	$12,307,969	$9,009,654	$5,741,451	$8,638,706

medical staff, who were used to thinking of Wills as a renowned eye hospital, resisted any attempt by management to expand outside of eye care. Exhibit 15–10 provides some insight into Wills's changing mix of services and revenue sources from 1987 to 1992.

As CEO of Wills, Kessler was concerned. Few local competitors could compare to the preeminent medical expertise located at Wills or offer the full range of ophthalmologic services that were housed there. For the time being, however, even these competitive advantages would not suffice. The strategic challenge was survival in the uncontrollable and unpredictable climate of health care reform and technology revolution.

Wills had not yet run at a deficit; however revenues were declining. "I thought our S&P [Standard and Poor's] rating might decline because of our lower profitability, but it actually went up. They tell me the increase was based on our liquidity and our management's strategy for the future," said Mick Kessler. He continued, "That strategy—approved by the City Trusts Board—was internal development of two areas with an emphasis on utilizing hospital beds.

"Our view of the future is that primary care and urgent care will continue to increase and inpatient hospital care will continue to decline. We expect quaternary care to increase. By quaternary care we

Exhibit 15–8 · Operating Funds Balance Sheet

Assets	June 30,			
	1992	1993	1994	1995
General Funds				
Current				
Cash and cash equivalents	25,212,650	20,953,474	23,287,345	15,664,824
Marketable securities	25,837,008	35,897,958	38,737,386	42,367,958
Accounts receivable, net for allowances	371,959	116,020	118,252	777,649
Inventories	566,797	564,382	547,597	737,813
Due from restricted funds	394,496	0	0	0
Other current assets	960,120	1,424,277	1,258,078	1,125,280
Total current assets	53,343,030	58,956,111	63,948,658	60,673,524
Assets whose use is limited				
By board for future expansion	3,991,752	4,180,359	18,361,925	11,687,265
By board for research	1,646,346	1,685,958	1,613,949	1,690,601
By board—other	7,230,696	7,450,757	7,533,905	8,425,064
Under bond indenture agreement held by trustee	18,033,179	20,401,022	0	33,959
Assets whose use is limited	30,901,973	33,718,096	27,509,779	21,836,889
Other investments	0	0	0	4,686,032
Property, plant, and equipment, net	18,887,145	19,405,679	23,585,123	32,827,651
Deferred financing costs, net of amortization	330,296	300,396	456,036	405,508
	103,462,444	112,380,282	115,499,596	120,429,604
Restricted Funds				
Specific purpose funds				
Cash and cash equivalents	3,742,124	2,786,749	2,918,685	3,042,909
Investments	1,001,520	1,855,617	1,747,357	1,877,693
Grants receivable	130,349	14,962	26,790	52,972
Due from general fund	0	97,928	67,350	147,030
	4,873,993	4,755,256	4,760,182	5,120,604
Plant replacement and expansion funds				
Cash and cash equivalents	234,792	241,671	250,737	264,944
Accrued interest	47	448	0	0
Due from general fund	38,493	38,493	38,493	38,493
	273,332	280,612	289,230	303,437
Endowment funds				
Cash and cash equivalents	673,739	610,955	1,346,620	1,090,128
Investments	4,768,730	4,889,893	5,532,618	6,445,665
Due from general fund	89,627	91,966	73,647	107,064
	5,532,096	5,592,814	6,952,885	7,642,857

mean beyond tertiary care. This is high-end surgery that will utilize hospital beds. It's too sophisticated to be done on an outpatient basis.

"We have a two-pronged strategy. First, we have built two outpatient surgery centers—one in Cherry-hill, New Jersey, and one in Bucks County, Pennsyl-

Exhibit 15–8 · **Continued**

Liabilities and Fund Balances	June 30 1992	1993	1994	1995
General Funds				
Current				
Current portion long-term debt	470,000	500,000	830,000	830,000
Accounts payable	3,213,699	2,846,702	3,572,759	3,688,616
Accrued salaries and expenses	2,498,806	2,699,836	2,706,466	1,900,069
Due to restricted funds	128,120	228,387	179,490	292,587
Payable to third parties	5,686,600	5,839,475	4,599,079	1,194,760
Total current liabilities	11,997,225	12,114,400	11,887,794	7,906,032
Long-term debt less current portion	14,915,000	14,415,000	12,450,000	11,620,000
Fund balance				
Board designated	12,868,794	13,317,074	27,509,779	21,802,930
General fund	63,681,425	72,533,808	63,652,023	79,100,642
Total fund balance	76,550,219	85,850,882	91,161,802	100,903,572
	103,462,444	112,380,282	115,499,596	120,429,604
Restricted Funds				
Specific purpose funds				
Due to general fund	394,496	0	0	0
Fund balance	4,479,497	4,755,256	4,760,182	5,120,604
	4,873,993	4,755,256	4,760,182	5,120,604
Plant replacement and expansion				
Fund balance	273,332	280,612	289,230	303,437
	273,332	280,612	289,230	303,437
Endowment funds				
Fund balance	5,532,096	5,592,514	5,592,895	7,642,857
	5,532,096	5,592,514	5,592,895	7,642,857

vania. These are general outpatient surgery centers. They'll do eye, orthopedic, ENT [ear, nose, and throat], and some gynecology surgeries. We plan to build six more in the Delaware Valley area around Philadelphia. We think this network of outpatient surgery centers will make us unique. No other hospital in the area has it.

"These low-cost surgical centers—initially—will allow us to perform lower cost cataract surgery, which should help attract managed-care contracts. This will develop a revenue stream to help subsidize the hospital, which will continue to handle the more complicated cases. If we get these surgery centers up

and running, we would be the major player in ambulatory surgical centers in the Delaware Valley.

"Our second strategic thrust was to begin doing brain surgery. Some people find this unusual but our physicians are already doing complicated surgeries involving nerves. We hired the best brain surgeons, bought all the 'toys' they could want, and we're doing the second-highest number of brain surgeries in the area. As there are sixty-five hospitals and five medical centers in the area you can see that we've really made a commitment to doing quaternary care.

"One of these strategies has to work for Wills or I'll not be here. We're working diligently to make

Exhibit 15–9 · Philadelphia-Area Hospitals, Inpatient Data—1996

Hospital	Code	Service	Beds	Admissions	Occupancy
Allegeny	UM	10	582	27,786	85.7%
Graduate	UM	10	222	11,210	79.7%
University of Pennsylvania	U	10	471	22,179	84.0%
Presbyterian*	U	10	325	12,611	84.0%
Temple	UM	10	450	19,433	78.6%
Thomas Jefferson	U	10	607	26,312	80.6%
Wills Eye	U	20	115	4,413	36.5%

Legend:
U = Urban
S = Suburban
M = Multi-institutional System
10 = General Medicine/Surgery
20 = Specialty Medicine

*Includes Scheie Eye Institute.
Source: AHA Guide to the Health Care Field, 1996–1997

Exhibit 15–10 · Wills Eye Hospital, Activity and Revenue, 1987/1992

Hospital Activity/Service	Activity		Revenue Percent	
	1987	1992	1987	1992
Ophthalmology/inpatient surgery cases	5,695	5,293	45.6	41.8
Ophthalmology/outpatient surgery cases	5,740	6,714	32.5	33.7
Other services/clinic visits, ER, ancillary	85,262	68,872	19.9	18.5
Hand surgery cases	336	296	2.0	1.5
Geriatric psychiatry cases	0	167	0	4.5

them both successful, but one of them has got to work. We're fortunate at Wills that over time we have built a lot of working capital. We're using some of that now to implement these two strategies internally.

"The traditional Wills physicians are not thrilled with this strategy. . . . We have to educate them that under global payments [capitation], they are better off with a well-managed, cost-efficient hospital. By that I mean the physicians are more likely to maintain their share of the revenue pie if the hospital operates efficiently. The amount of money to be paid for health care will be determined at the capitated amount. If the hospital is inefficient, its share of the revenue pie will be larger, leaving a smaller share for the physician. We can generate more revenue through increased inpatient days doing brain surgery and more outpatient visits to our less expensive top operating surgery centers.

"The Philadelphia hospitals are beginning to affiliate and merge. I expect there will be four or maybe five large systems in the end. We have to look at what is right for Wills. We have cash, an international reputation for high quality-care, and hopefully a network of outpatient surgery centers to offer."

Exhibit 15–11 · Strategic Alliance Options, Hospital Inpatient Data, 1996

Hospital	Expense (thousands)	Payroll (thousands)	Personnel	Total Revenue (millions)
Allegheny	$396,888	$158,815	4,552	n/a
Graduate	175,648	60,263	1,564	n/a
University of Pennsylvania	444,076	167,574	5,408	$397.3
Presbyterian	149,292	64,242	1,644	n/a
Temple	256,433	120,959	2,580	n/a
Thomas Jefferson	357,283	161,162	4,121	639.8
Wills Eye	53,540	22,124	596	58.5

n/a = Data not available.
Sources: Annual reports of the respective organizations, 1992; *AHA Guide to the Health Care Field,* 1996.

Exhibit 15–12 · Hospital Statistics

Hospital	Admissions 1989	1992	1995	Occupancy Percent 1989	1992	1995	Total Expenses (Thousands) 1989	1992	1995
Allegeny*			27,786			85.7			396,888
Graduate	11,619	11,601	11,210	82.8	73.4	79.7	n/a	158,167	175,648
University of Pennsylvania	17,569	22,179	n/a	77.6	76.9	n/a	152,391	238,218	444,076
Presbyterian	9,888	11,589	12,611	73.9	85.3	84.0	92,216	127,122	149,292
Temple		17,147	19,433		85.4	78.6		197,478	256,433
Thomas Jefferson	24,629	26,312	n/a	86.0	80.6	n/a	273,476	357,283	n/a
Wills Eye	5,782	5,481	4,413	35.0	39.1	36.5	35,210	42,609	53,540

* Allegheny was new to the Philadelphia area.
n/a = Data not available.
Source: AHA Guide to the Health Care Field, 1990, 1993, 1996.

Kessler considered his strategic options. Given the number of hospitals in the region, Kessler had ample opportunity to consider potential strategic alliances, joint ventures, or integration with a wide variety of partners. Exhibits 15–9, 15–11, and 15–12 provide data on potential strategic partners for Wills Eye Hospital.

Kessler's task as CEO of Wills was to work with his executive staff, the medical staff, and the board, to chart a course for the twenty-first century. The upcoming board meeting appeared to pose no immediate threat for Kessler, however, the future was anything but certain. His frustration was evident when Kessler remarked, "I wish I would only have to be as accountable for my predictions as are economists and meteorologists."

Notes

1. "1996 Annual Guide, America's Best Hospitals," *U.S. News and World Report* (August 12, 1996), p. 87.
2. Jay Greene, "Hospitals Now Merge Rather Than Close," *Modern Healthcare* (July 6, 1992), pp. 20–21.

3. *Standard and Poor's Industry Surveys, Health Care Products and Services* (September 7, 1995), pp. H-15–17.

4. Ibid.

5. "Delaware Valley Hospital Council Facts and Data Sheet on Hospitals," *Directory of American Medical Education,* Association of American Medical Colleges, 1996.

6. Center for Greater Philadelphia Economic Development Coalition, 1992.

7. American Hospital Association, *Hospital Statistics 1996–1997,* p. 132.

8. *Philadelphia Economic Monitoring Project R & D Survey,* 1990.

9. *American Hospital Association Statistical Yearbook, 1996–1997.*

10. Mariam Uhlman, "Philadelphia Hospitals Report Slim Earnings and Restructuring" *Philadelphia Inquirer* (November 26, 1995), pp. 1A, 29.

C. W. Williams Health Center: A Community Asset

The Metrolina Health Center was started by Dr. Charles Warren "C. W." Williams and several medical colleagues with a $25,000 grant from the Department of Health and Human Services. Concerned about the health needs of the poor and wanting to make the world a better place for those less fortunate, Dr. Williams, Charlotte's first African American to serve on the surgical staff of Charlotte Memorial Hospital (Charlotte's largest hospital), enlisted the aid of Dr. John Murphy, a local dentist; Peggy Beckwith, director of the Sickle Cell Association; and health planner Bob Ellis to create a health facility for the unserved and underserved population of Mecklenburg County, North Carolina. The health facility received its corporate status in 1980. Dr. Williams died in 1982 when the health facility was still in its infancy. Thereafter, the Metrolina Comprehensive Health Center was renamed the C. W. Williams Health Center.

"We're celebrating our fifteenth year of operation at C. W. Williams, and I'm celebrating my first full year as CEO," commented Michelle Marrs. "I'm feeling really good about a lot of things—we are fully staffed for the first time in two years, and we are a significant player in a pilot program by North Carolina to manage the health care of Medicaid patients in Mecklenburg County (Charlotte area) through pri-

vate HMOs. We're the only organization that's approved to serve Medicaid recipients that's not an HMO. We have a contract for primary-care case management. We're used to providing care for the Medicaid population and we're used to providing health education. It's part of our original mission (see Exhibit 16–1) and has been since the beginning of C. W. Williams."

Michelle continued, "I've been in health care for quite awhile but things are really changing rapidly now. The center might be forced to align with one of the two hospitals because of managed-care changes. Although we don't want to take away the patient's choice, it might happen. In order for me to do all that I should be doing externally, I need more help internally. I believe we should have a director of finance. We have a great opportunity to buy another location so that we can serve more patients, but this is a relatively unstable time in health care. Buying another facility would be a stretch financially, but the location would be perfect. The asking price does seem high, though. . . ." (Exhibit 16–2 contains a biographical sketch of Ms. Marrs.)

Community Health Centers[1]

When the nation's resources were mobilized during the early 1960s to fight the War on Poverty, it was discovered that poor health and lack of basic medical care were major obstacles to the educational and job training progress of the poor. A system of preventive and comprehensive medical care was necessary to

This case was prepared by Linda E. Swayne and Peter M. Ginter. It is intended as a basis for class discussion rather than to illustrate effective or ineffective handling of an administrative situation. Used with permission from Linda Swayne.

Exhibit 16–1 • C. W. Williams Health Center Mission, Vision, and Values Statements

Mission

To promote a healthier future for our community by consistently providing excellent, accessible health care with pride, compassion, and respect.

Values

- Respect each individual, patient, and staff as well as our community as a valued entity that must be treasured.
- Consistently provide the highest quality patient care with pride and compassion.
- Partner with other organizations to respond to the social, health, and economic development needs of our community.
- Operate in an efficient, well-staffed, comfortable environment as an autonomous and financially sound organization.

Vision

Committed to the pioneering vision of Dr. Charles Warren Williams, Charlotte's first Black surgeon, we will move into the twenty-first century promoting a healthier and brighter future for our community. This means:

- C. W. Williams Health Center will offer personal, high-quality, affordable, comprehensive health services that improve the quality of life for all.
- C. W. Williams Health Center, while partnering with other health care organizations, will expand its high-quality health services into areas of need. No longer will patients be required to travel long distances to receive the medical care they deserve. C.W. Williams Health Center will come to them!
- C. W. Williams Health Center will be well managed using state-of-the-art technology, accelerating into the twenty-first century as a leading provider of comprehensive community-based health services.
- C. W. Williams Health Center will be viewed as Mecklenburg County's premier community health agency, providing care with RESPECT:

    Reliable health care
    Efficient operations
    Supportive staff
    Personal care
    Effective systems
    Clean environments
    Timely services

Exhibit 16–2 • Michelle Marrs, Chief Executive Officer of C. W. Williams Health Center

Michelle Marrs has over twenty years' experience working in a variety of health care settings and delivery systems. On earning her B.S. degree, she began her career as a community health educator working in the prevention of alcoholism and substance abuse among youth and women. In 1976, she pursued graduate education at the Harvard School of Public Health and the Graduate School of Education, earning a masters of education with a concentration in administration, planning, and social policy. She worked for the U.S. Public Health Service, Division of Health Services Delivery; the University of Massachusetts Medical Center as director of the Patient Care Studies Department and administrator of the Radiation Oncology Department; the Mattapan Community Health Center (a comprehensive community-based primary-care health facility in Boston) as director; and as medical office administrator for Kaiser Permanente. Marrs was appointed chief executive officer of the C.W. Williams Health Center in November 1994.

battle poverty. A new health care model for poor communities was started in 1963 through the vision and efforts of two New England physicians—Count Geiger and Jack Gibson of the Tufts Medical School—to open the first two neighborhood health centers in Mound Bayou, in rural Mississippi and in a Boston housing project.

In 1966, an amendment to the Economic Opportunity Act formally established the Comprehensive Health Center Program. By 1971, a total of 150 health centers had been established. By 1990, more than 540 community and migrant health centers at 1,400 service sites had received federal grants totaling $547 million to supplement their budgets of

$1.3 billion. By 1996, the numbers had increased to 700 centers at 2,400 delivery sites providing service to over 9 million people.

Community health centers had a public health perspective; however they were similar to private practices staffed by physicians, nurses, and allied health professionals. They differed from the typical medical office in that they offered a broader range of services, such as social services and health education. Health centers removed the financial and nonfinancial barriers to health care. In addition, health centers were owned by the community and operated by a local volunteer governing board. Federally funded health centers were required to have patients as a majority of the governing board. The use of patients to govern was a major factor in keeping the centers responsive to patients and generating acceptance by them. Because of the increasing complexity of health care delivery, many board members were taking advantage of training opportunities through their state and national associations to better manage the facility.

Community Health Centers Provide Care for the Medically Underserved

Federally subsidized health centers must, by law, serve populations that are identified by the Public Health Service as medically underserved. Half of the medically underserved population lived in rural areas where there were few medical resources. The other half were located in economically depressed inner-city communities where individuals lived in poverty, lacked health insurance, or had special needs such as homelessness, AIDS, or substance abuse. Approximately 60 percent of health center patients were minorities in urban areas whereas 50 percent were white/non-Hispanics in rural areas (see Exhibit 16–3).

Typically, 50 percent of health center patients did not have private health insurance nor did they qualify for public health insurance (Medicaid or Medicare). That compared to 13.4 percent of the U.S. population that was uninsured (see Exhibit 16–4). Over 80 percent of health center patients had incomes below the federal poverty level ($28,700 for a family of four in 1994). Most of the remaining 20 percent were between 100 percent and 200 percent of the federal poverty level.

Community Health Centers Are Cost Effective

Numerous national studies have indicated that the kind of ongoing primary-care management provided by community health centers resulted in significantly lowered costs for inpatient hospital care and specialty care. Because illnesses were diagnosed and treated at an earlier stage, more expensive care interventions were often not needed. Hospital admission rates were 22 to 67 percent lower for health center patients than for community residents. A study of six New York city and state health centers found that Medicaid beneficiaries were 22 to 30 percent less costly to treat than those not served by health centers.[2] A Washington state study found that the average cost to Medicaid per hospital bill was $49 for health center patients versus $74 for commercial

Exhibit 16–3 • Ethnicity of Urban and Rural Health Center Patients

Urban Health Center Patients		Rural Health Center Patients	
African American/Black	37.0%	African American/Black	19.6%
White/Non-Hispanic	29.9%	White/Non-Hispanic	49.3%
Native American	0.8%	Native American	1.1%
Asian/Pacific Islander	3.2%	Asian/Pacific Islander	2.9%
Hispanic/Latino	27.2%	Hispanic/Latino	26.5%
Other	1.9%	Other	0.6%

Exhibit 16–4 · Insurance Status of U.S. Health Center Patients, C. W. Williams Health Center Patients, the U.S. Population, and North Carolina Population

	Health Center Patients	U.S. Population	North Carolina Population	C. W. Williams Health Center Patients
Uninsured	42.7%	13.4%	14%	**21%**
Private Insurance	13.9%	63.2%	64%	**10%**
Public Insurance	42.9%	23.4%	22%	**69%**

sector patients.[3] Health center indigent patients were less likely to make emergency room visits—a reduction of 13 percent overall and 38 percent for pediatric care. In addition, defensive medicine (the practice of ordering every and all diagnostic tests to avoid malpractice claims) was less frequently used. Community health center physicians had some of the lowest medical malpractice loss ratios in the nation.

Not only were community health centers cost efficient, patients were highly satisfied with the care received. A total of 96 percent were satisfied or very satisfied with the care they received, and 97 percent indicated they would recommend the health center to their friends and families.[4] Only 4 percent were not so satisfied, and only 3 percent would not recommend their health center to others.

Movement to Managed Care

In 1990, a little over 2 million Medicaid beneficiaries were enrolled in managed-care plans; in 1993, the number had increased to 8 million; and in 1995, over 11 million Medicaid beneficiaries were enrolled. Medicaid beneficiaries and other low-income Americans had higher rates of illness and disability than others, and thus accumulated significantly higher costs of medical care.[5]

C. W. Williams Health Center

C. W. Williams was beginning to recognize the impact of managed care. Like much of the South, the Carolinas had been slow to accept managed care. The major reasons seemed to be the rural nature of many Southern states, markets that were not as attractive to major managed-care organizations, dominant insurers that continued to provide fee for service ensuring choice of physicians and hospitals, and medical inflation that accelerated more slowly than in other areas. Major changes began to occur, however, beginning in 1993. By 1996 managed care was being implemented in many areas at an accelerated pace.

Challenges for C. W. Williams

Michelle reported, "One of my greatest challenges has been how to handle the changes imposed by the shift from a primarily fee-for-service to a managed-care environment. Local physicians who in the past had the flexibility, loyalty, and availability to assist C. W. Williams by providing part-time assistance or volunteer efforts during the physician shortage are now employed by managed-care organizations or involved in contractual relationships that prohibit them from working with us. The few remaining primary-care solo or small group practices are struggling for survival themselves and seldom are available to provide patient sessions or assist with our hospital call-rotation schedule. The rigorous call-rotation schedule of a small primary-care facility like C. W. Williams is frequently unattractive to available physicians seeking opportunities, even when a market competitive compensation package is offered. Many of these physician recruitment and retention issues are being driven by the rapid changes brought on by the impact of managed care in the local community. It is a real challenge to recruit physicians to provide the necessary access to medical care for our patients."

She continued, "My next greatest challenge is investment in technology to facilitate this transition to managed care. Technology is expensive, yet I know it is crucial to our survival and success. We also need more space, but I don't know if this is a good time for expansion."

She concluded, "One of the pressing and perhaps most difficult efforts has been the careful and strategic consideration of the need to affiliate to some degree with one of the two area hospitals in order to more fully integrate and broaden the range of services to patients of our center. Although a decision has not been made at this juncture, the organization has made significant strides to comprehend the needs of this community, consider the pros and cons of either choice, and continue providing the best care possible under some very difficult circumstances."

Hospital Affiliation

Traditionally, the patients of C. W. Williams Health Center that needed hospitalization were admitted to Charlotte Memorial Hospital, a large regional hospital that was designated at the Trauma I level—one of five designated by the state of North Carolina to handle major trauma cases twenty-four hours a day, seven-days per week (full staffing) as well as perform research in the area of trauma. Uncompensated inpatient care was financed by the county. Charlotte Memorial became Carolinas Medical Center (CMC) in 1984 when it began a program to develop a totally integrated system. In 1995, C. W. Williams provided Carolinas Medical Center with more than 3,000 patient bed days; however the patients were usually seen by their regular C. W. Williams physicians. As Carolinas Medical Center purchased physician practices (over 300 doctors were employed by the system) and purchased or managed many of the surrounding community hospitals, some C. W. Williams patients became concerned that CMC would take over C. W. Williams and that their community health center would no longer exist.

"My preference is that our patients have a choice of where they would prefer to go for hospitalization. Our older patients expect to go to Carolinas Medical, but many of our middle-aged patients have

expressed a preference for Presbyterian. Both hospitals have indicated an interest in our patients," according to Michelle. She continued, "We may not really have a choice, however. We recently were sent information that reported the twelve largest hospitals in the state, including the teaching hospitals—Duke, University of North Carolina at Chapel Hill, Carolinas Medical Center, and East Carolina—have formed a consortium and will contract with the state to pay for Medicaid patients. At the same time all twenty of the health centers in the state—including us at C. W. Williams—are cooperating to develop a health maintenance organization. We expect to gain approval for the HMO by July 1997. Since 60 percent of our patients are Medicaid, if the state contracts with the new consortium, then we will be required to send our patients to Carolinas Medical Center."

Services

C. W. Williams Health Center provides primary and preventive health services including medical, radiology, laboratory, pharmacy, subspecialty, and inpatient managed care; health education/promotion; community outreach; and transportation to care (Exhibit 16–5 lists all services). The center was strongly linked to the Charlotte community, and it worked with other public and private health services to coordinate resources for effective patient care. No one was denied care because of an inability to pay. A little over 20 percent of the patients at C. W. Williams were uninsured.

The full-time staff included five physicians, two physician assistants (PAs), two nurses, one X-ray technician, one pharmacist, and a staff of twenty-eight. Of the five physicians, one was an internist, two were in family practice, and two were pediatricians. The PAs "floated" to work wherever help was most needed. With the help of one assistant, the pharmacist filled more than 20,000 prescriptions annually.

Patients at C. W. Williams

All first-time patients at C. W. Williams were asked what type of insurance they had. If they had some type of insurance—private, Medicare, Medicaid—an appointment was immediately scheduled. If the new patient had no insurance, he or she was asked if they

Exhibit 16–5 · C. W. Williams Health Center Services

Primary-Care and Preventive Services

Diagnostic Laboratory

Diagnostic X-ray (basic)

Pharmacy

EMS (crash cart and CPR-trained staff)

Family Planning

Immunizations (M.D.-directed as well as open clinic—no relationship required)

Prenatal Care and Gynecology

Health Education

Parenting Education

Translation Services

Substance Abuse and Counseling

Nutrition Counseling

Diagnostic Testing

   HIV

   Mammogram

   Pap Smears

   TB Testing

   Vision/Hearing Testing

   Lead Testing

   Pregnancy Test

   Drug Screening

would be interested in applying for the C. W. Williams discount program (the discount could amount to as much as 100 percent, but every person was asked to pay something). The discount was based on income and the number of people in the household. If the response was "no," the caller was informed that payment was expected at the time services were rendered. Visa, Mastercard, cash, and personal check (with two forms of identification) were accepted. At C. W. Williams, all health care was made affordable.

C. W. Williams made reminder calls to the patient's home (or neighbor's or relative's telephone) several days prior to the appointment. When patients arrived at the center, they provided their name to the nurse at the front reception desk and then took a seat in a large waiting room. The pharmacy window was near the front door for the convenience of patients who were simply picking up a prescription. The reception desk, pharmacy, and waiting room occupied the first floor.

When the patient's name was called, he or she was taken by elevator to the second floor where there were ten examination rooms. After seeing the physician, physician assistant, or nurse, the patient was escorted back down the elevator to the pharmacy if a prescription was needed and then to the reception desk to pay. Pharmaceuticals were discounted and a special program by Pfizer Pharmaceuticals provided over $60,000 worth of drugs in 1995 for medically indigent patients.

The center's patient population was 64 percent female between the ages of fifteen and forty-four (see Exhibit 16–6). Nearly 80 percent of patients were African Americans, 18 percent were white, and 2 percent were other minorities. Patients were quite satisfied with the services provided as indicated in

Exhibit 16–6 · C. W. Williams Health Center Patients by Age and Sex

Females	1991	1992	1993	1994	1995
<1	343	408	263	198	101
1–4	434	552	692	647	417
5–11	322	572	494	641	658
12–14	376	197	150	148	124
15–17	361	168	146	121	92
18–19	264	152	85	82	67
20–34	749	1,250	967	964	712
35–44	869	617	479	532	467
45–64	583	567	617	658	658
65+	400	488	531	527	524
	4,701	4,971	4,424	4,518	3,820
Males					
<1	367	471	328	199	119
1–4	439	516	707	625	410
5–11	440	644	598	846	738
12–14	171	175	128	120	104
15–17	180	133	79	76	155
18–19	126	67	28	23	69
20–34	296	389	219	187	126
35–44	313	296	182	205	132
45–64	229	316	273	294	235
65+	151	248	190	190	181
	2,712	3,255	2,732	2,765	2,269
Total	7,413	8,226	7,156	7,283	6,089

patient surveys conducted by the center. Paralleling national studies, 97 percent of C. W. Williams patients would recommend the center to family or friends. Selected service indicators by rank from the patient satisfaction study are included as Exhibit 16–7.

C. W. Williams Organization

The center was managed by a board of directors, responsible for developing policy and hiring the CEO.

Board of Directors   The federal government required that all community health centers have a board of directors that was made up of at least 51 percent patients or citizens who lived in the community. The board chairman of C. W. Williams, Mr. Daniel Dooley, was a center patient. C. W. Williams had a board of fifteen, all of whom were African Americans and four of whom were patients and out of the workforce. Two members of the board were managers/directors from the Public Health Department (which was under the management of CMC). There were two other health professionals—a nurse and a physician. Other board members included a CPA, a financial planner, an insurance agent, a vice president for human resources, an executive in a search firm, and a former professor of economics. A majority of the board had not had a great deal of exposure to the changes occurring in the health care industry (aside

Exhibit 16–7 · **Patient Satisfaction Study**

Rank	Selected Service Indicators	Mean Score
1	Helpfulness/attitudes of medical staff	3.82
2	Clean/comfortable/convenient facility	3.65
3	Relationship with physician/nurse	3.58
4	Quality of health services	3.28
5	Ability to satisfy all medical needs	3.20
6	Helpfulness/attitudes of nonmedical staff	2.72

from their own personal situations) nor were they trained in strategic management.

The Staff The center was operated by Michelle Marrs as CEO, who had an operations officer and medical director reporting to her (see Exhibit 16–8 for an organization chart).

Recently the director of finance, who had worked at the center for over ten years, resigned. "She was offered another position within C. W. Williams," said Michelle, "but she declined to take it. Frankly, I have to have someone with greater expertise in finance. With capitation on the horizon, we need to do some very critical planning to better manage our finances and make sure we are receiving as much reimbursement from Washington as we are entitled."

There were some disagreements between the board and Ms. Marrs over responsibilities. Employees frequently appealed to the chairman and other members of the board when they felt that they had not been treated fairly. Ms. Marrs would prefer the board to be more involved in setting strategic direction for C. W. Williams. "A two-year strategic plan was developed late in 1995 that has not been moved along, embraced, and further developed. Committees have not met on a regular basis to actualize stated objectives."

C. W. Williams Is Financially Strong

The center received an increasing amount of federal grant money for the first ten years of its operation as the number of patients grew, but has leveled off as

most government allocations have been reduced (see Exhibit 16–9). Although the amount collected from Medicare was increasing, the amount collected compared to the full charge was decreasing (see Exhibit 16–10). Exhibits 16–11 to 16–14 provide details of the financial situation.

Carolina ACCESS—A Pilot Program

In fiscal year 1994 (July 1, 1994 to June 30, 1995), North Carolina served more than 950,000 Medicaid recipients at a cost of over $3.5 billion. The aged, blind, and disabled accounted for 26 percent of the eligibles and 65 percent of the expenditures. Families and children accounted for 74 percent of the eligibles and 35 percent of the expenditures. Services were heavily concentrated in two areas: inpatient hospital—accounting for 20 percent of expenses—and nursing-facility/intermediate-care/mentally retarded services—accounting for 34 percent of expenses. Mecklenburg County had the highest number of eligibles within the state at 50,849 people, representing 7 percent of the Medicaid population.

What started out in 1986 as a contract with Kaiser Permanente to provide medical services for recipients of Aid to Families with Dependent Children in four counties became a complex mixture of three models of managed care. Carolina ACCESS was North Carolina Medicaid's primary-care case management model of managed care. It began a pilot program named "Health Care Connections" in Mecklenburg County on June 1, 1996.

Exhibit 16–8 • Metrolina Comprehensive Health Center, Inc. dba C. W. Williams Health Center

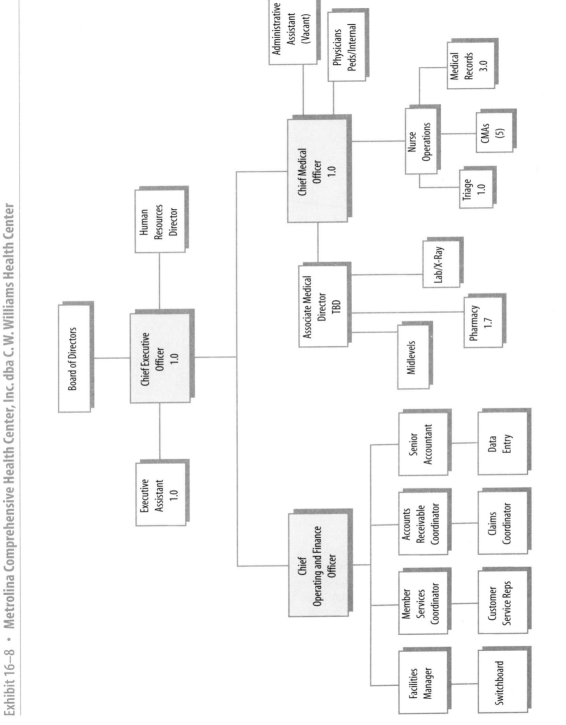

Exhibit 16–9 • **C. W. Williams Funding Sources**

Funding Source	1991	1992	1993	1994	1995
Grant (Federal)	740,000	666,524	689,361	720,584	720,584
Medicare	152,042	157,891	258,104	260,389	301,444
Medicaid	381,109	453,712	641,069	562,380	456,043
Third-Party Pay	25,673	14,128	84,347	90,253	51,799
Uninsured Self-Pay	300,748	441,508	174,992	262,817	338,272
Grant (Miscellaneous)	0	0	0	11,500	48,000
Total	1,599,572	1,733,763	1,847,873	1,907,923	1,916,142

Exhibit 16–10 • **Funding Accounts Receivable**

	1994		1995	
	Full Charge	Amount Collected	Full Charge	Amount Collected
Medicare	436,853	260,389	369,306	301,444
Medicaid	914,212	562,380	725,175	456,043
Insured	99,202	90,253	61,021	51,799
Patient Fees	899,055	262,817	754,864	338,272

Health Care Connections

The state of North Carolina wanted to move 42,000 Mecklenburg County Medicaid recipients into managed care. The state contracted with six health plans and C. W. Williams, as a federally qualified health center, to serve the Mecklenburg County Medicaid population. Because one organization was dropped from the program, Medicaid recipients were to choose one of the following to provide their health care:

Plan Name	Type	Hospital Affiliation
Atlantic Health Plans	HMO	Carolinas Medical Center, University Hospital, Mercy Hospital, Mercy South, Union Regional Medical, Kings Mountain Hospital
Kaiser Permanente	HMO	Presbyterian Hospital, Presbyterian Hospital—Matthews, Presbyterian Orthopedic, Presbyterian Specialty Hospital
Maxicare North Carolina, Inc.	HMO	Presbyterian Hospital,

Plan Name	Type	Hospital Affiliation
		Presbyterian Hospital—Matthews, Presbyterian Orthopedic, Presbyterian Specialty Hospital
Optimum Choice/ Mid-Atlantic Medical	HMO	Presbyterian Hospital, Presbyterian Hospital—Matthews, Presbyterian Orthopedic, Presbyterian Specialty Hospital
The Wellness Plan of NC, Inc.	HMO	Carolinas Medical Center, University Hospital, Mercy Hospital, Mercy South, Union Regional Medical, Kings Mountain Hospital
C. W. Williams Health Center	Partially federally funded, community health center	Carolinas Medical Center, University Hospital, Mercy Hospital, Mercy South, Union Regional Medical, Kings Mountain Hospital or Presbyterian Hospital, Presbyterian Hospital—Matthews, Presbyterian Orthopedic, Presbyterian Specialty Hospital

An integral part of the selection process was the use of a health benefits advisor to assist families in choosing the appropriate plan. By law, none of the organizations was permitted to promote its plan to Medicaid recipients. Rather, the Public Consulting Group of Charlotte was awarded the contract to be an independent enrollment counselor to assist Medicaid recipients in their choices of health care options.

"More than 33,000 of the Medicaid recipients were women and children. Sixty percent of the group had no medical relationship. Slightly over 50 percent of C. W. Williams patients are Medicaid recipients," said Michelle Marrs. See Exhibit 16–15 for C. W. Williams users by pay source.

"We have about 8,000 patients coming to us for about 30,000 visits," according to Michelle (see Exhibit 16–16). "So there are approximately 4,000 people who currently come to us for health care that are now required to choose a health plan. The state decided that an independent agency had to sign people up so that there would be no 'bounty' hunting for enrollees. In the first month, about 2,300 Medicaid recipients enrolled in the pilot program. Almost half of the people who signed up chose Kaiser Foundation Health Plan. It has a history of serving Medicaid patients. We received the next highest number of enrollees, because we too have a history of serving this market. We had 402 enrollees during that first month. Of those, only 38 were previous patients. What we don't know yet is whether we have lost any patients to other programs. The lack of up-to-date information is frustrating. We need a better information system."

Michelle continued, "We decided that we could provide care for up to 8,000 Medicaid patients at C. W. Williams. I embrace managed care for a number of reasons: patients must choose a primary-care provider, patients will be encouraged to take an active role in their health care, and there will be less duplication of medical services and costs. In the past, some doctors have shied away from Medicaid patients

Exhibit 16–11 · C. W. Williams Health Center Balance Sheets

	1992–1993	1993–1994	1994–1995	1995–1996
Assets				
Current Assets				
Cash	280,550	335,258	339,459	132,925
Certificates of Deposit	23,413	24,496	25,446	529,826
Accounts Receivable (net)	213,815	285,934	202,865	160,230
Accounts Receivable (other)	5,661	4,721	2,936	10,069
Security Deposits	1,847	97	-0-	-0-
Notes Receivable	-0-	-0-	29,825	10,403
Inventory	26,191	23,777	30,217	26,844
Prepaid Loans	12,087	21,605	9,722	11,159
Investments	269	269	269	51,628
Total Current Assets	563,833	696,157	640,739	933,084
Property and Equipment				
Land	10,000	10,000	10,000	10,000
Building	311,039	311,039	311,039	311,039
Building Renovations	904,434	904,434	909,754	915,949
Equipment	282,333	312,892	328,063	387,178
Less Depreciation	(393,392)	(452,432)	(523,384)	(597,275)
Total Property and Equipment	1,114,414	1,085,933	1,035,472	1,026,891
Total Assets	1,678,247	1,782,090	1,676,211	1,959,975
Liabilities and Net Assets				
Liabilities				
Accounts Payable	11,066	31,582	13,136	34,039
Vacation Expense Accounts	36,694	42,857	19,457	28,144
Deferred Revenue	42,641	37,910	43,400	59,433
Total Liabilities	90,401	112,349	75,993	121,616
Net Assets				
Unrestricted				1,838,350
Temporary Restricted	-0-	-0-	-0-	-0-
Total Net Assets	1,587,846	1,669,741	1,600,218	1,838,350
Total Liabilities and Net Assets	1,678,247	1,782,090	1,676,211	1,959,976

because they didn't want to be bothered with the paperwork, the medical services weren't fully compensated, and Medicaid patients tended to have numerous health problems.

"There are seven different companies that applied and were given authority to provide health care for Medicaid recipients in Mecklenburg County. Although I understand one had to withdraw, we are the only one that is not a health maintenance organization—an HMO. Although we don't provide hospitalization, we do provide for patients' care whether they need an office visit or to be hospitalized. Our physicians provide care while the patient is in the hospital."

She continued, "Medicaid beneficiaries have to be recertified every six months. We are three months into the sign-up process or approximately

Exhibit 16–12 • Statement of Support, Revenue, Expenses, and Change in Fund Balances

	1992–1993	1993–1994	1994–1995	1995–1996
Contributed Support and Revenue				
Contributed	720,712	720,584	732,584	768,584
Earned Revenue				
Patient Fees	1,213,919	1,186,497	1,183,904	1,129,030
Medicare				465,248
Contributions				5,676
Interest Income	7,228	9,666	12,567	14,115
Dividend Income				2,387
Rental Income				1,980
Miscellaneous Income	5,962	5,941	4,772	11,055
Total Earned	1,227,109	1,202,104	1,201,243	1,629,491
Total Contributed Support and Revenue	1,947,821	1,922,688	1,933,827	2,398,075
Expenses				
Program	1,782,312	1,840,447	2,002,633	2,157,768
Other	442	349	217	2,166
Total Expenses	1,782,754	1,840,796	2,002,850	2,159,934
Increase (decrease) in Net Assets	165,062	81,892	(69,523)	238,141
Net Assets (beginning of year)	1,310,155	1,587,849	1,669,741	1,600,218
Adjustment	112,629[*]	-0-	-0-	-0-
Net Assets (end of year)	1,587,846	1,669,741	1,600,218	1,838,359

[*] Federal grant funds earned but not drawn down in prior years were not recognized as revenue. The error had no effect on net income for fiscal year ended March 31, 1992.

halfway. Kaiser has enrolled the highest number, about one-third of the beneficiaries (see Exhibit 16–17). We have enrolled over 12 percent. The independent enrollment counselor is responsible for helping Medicaid recipients enroll during the initial twelve months. I expect the numbers to dwindle for the last six months of that time period. Changes will primarily come from new patients to the area and patients who are unhappy with their initial choice."

Medicaid patients were going to be a challenge for managed care. Because many of them were used to going to the emergency room for care, they were not in the habit of making or keeping appointments. Some facilities overbooked appointments to try to utilize medical staff efficiently; however, the practice caused very long waits at times. Other complicating factors included lack of telephones for contacting patients for reminder calls or physician follow-ups, lack of transportation, the number of high-risk patients as a result of poverty or lifestyle factors, and patients that did not follow doctors' orders.

Health Connection Enrollment

Medicaid recipients were required to be recertified every six months in the state of North Carolina. During this process, a time was allocated for the Public Consulting Group of Charlotte to make a presentation about the managed-care choices available. The presentation included:

- a discussion of managed care and HMOs and how they were different and the same from previous Medicaid practices;

Exhibit 16–13 · Statement of Functional Expenditures, Fiscal Year Ended March 31

	1992–1993	1993–1994	1994–1995	1995–1996
Personnel				
Salaries	937,119	1,016,194	1,102,373	1,181,639
Benefits	190,300	210,228	210,674	211,705
Total	1,127,419	1,226,422	1,313,047	1,393,344
Other				
Accounting	5,250	5,985	6,397	7,200
Bank Charges	840	300	213	1,001
Building Maintenance	38,842	54,132	49,586	53,828
Consultants	26,674	2,733	39,565	44,923[a]
Contract M.D.s	-0-	-0-	-0-	87,159
Dues/Publications/Conferences	17,371	21,655	22,066	24,258
Equipment Maintenance	28,732	27,365	30,402	27,352
Insurance	15,182	3,146	3,215	3,292
Legal Fees	688	2,774	3,652	3,582
Marketing	6,358	1,958	5,734	15,730
Patient Services	28,959	28,222	35,397	43,815
Pharmacy	271,542	237,761	225,762	188,061
Physician Recruiting	14,171	32,929	56,173	21,395
Postage	8,435	11,622	10,019	14,182
Printing	729	963	2,405	9,696
Supplies	73,020	62,828	72,977	84,064
Telephone	16,755	17,967	20,914	25,002
Travel—Board	2,713	1,202	4,977	3,476
Travel—Staff	13,889	14,576	12,631	15,978
Utilities	15,782	18,305	16,548	16,536
Total Other	585,932	546,423	618,633	690,530
Total Personnel and Other	1,713,351	1,772,845	1,931,680	2,083,874
Depreciation	(68,966)	(67,604)	(70,952)	(73,891)
Total Expenses	1,782,317	1,840,449	2,002,632	2,157,765

[a] Includes contracted medical director.

- benefits of Health Care Connections such as having a medical home, a twenty-four-hour, seven-day-a-week hotline to ask questions about medical care, physician choice, and plan choice; and
- methods to choose a plan based on wanting to use a doctor that the patient has used before, hospital choice (some plans were associated with a specific hospital), and location (for easy access).

If Medicaid recipients did not choose a plan that day, they had ten working days to call in on the hotline to choose a plan. If they had not done so by that deadline, they were randomly assigned to a plan. Public Consulting Group's health benefits advisors (HBAs) made the presentations and then assisted each individual in determining what choice he or she would like to make and filling out the paperwork. More than 80 percent of the Medicaid recipients

Exhibit 16–14 • C. W. Williams Health Center Statement of Cash Flows, Fiscal Year Ended March 31

Net Cash Flow from Operations	1992–1993	1993–1994	1994–1995	1995–1996
Increase in Net Assets	165,062	81,892	(69,523)	238,141
Noncash Income Expense Depreciation	68,966	67,604	70,952	73,891
Increase in Deposits	(1,750)	1,750	-0-	-0-
Decrease in Receivables	(86,620)	(71,179)	55,028	65,328
(Increase) in Prepaid Expenses	(2,277)	(9,518)	11,980	(1,437)
(Increase) Decrease in Inventory	(4,105)	2,414	(6,440)	3,373
Increase in Payables	14,094	20,516	(18,445)	20,903
Increase (Decrease) in Vacation Expense Accrual	(8,583)	6,163	(23,400)	8,688
(Increase) in Notes Receivable	-0-	-0-	-0-	(10,403)
Increase in Deferred Revenue	(2,992)	(4,731)	5,490	16,032
Net Cash Flow from Operations	141,795	94,911	25,642	414,516
Cash Flow from Investing Purchase Fixed Assets	(52,547)	(39,120)	(20,491)	(65,311)
Purchase Marketable Securities	-0-	-0-	-0-	(51,359)
Net Cash Used by Investments	(52,547)	(39,120)	(20,491)	(116,670)
Net Cash from Financing Activities	112,629	-0-	-0-	-0-
Increase in Cash	201,877	55,791	5,151	297,846
Cash + Cash Equivalents				
Beginning of Year April 1	130,274	332,151	387,942	393,093
End of Year March 31	332,151	387,942	393,093	690,939

who went through the recertification process and heard the presentation decided on site. Most others called back on the hotline after more carefully studying the information. About 3 percent were randomly assigned because they did not select a plan.

New Medicaid recipients were provided individualized presentations because they tended to be new to the community, recently developed a health problem, or were pregnant. Because they might have less information than those who had been "in the system" for some time, it took a more detailed explanation from the HBA.

HBAs presented the information in a fair, factual, and useful manner for session attendees. For the first several months they attempted to thoroughly explain the difference between an HMO and a "partially federally funded community health center," but the HBAs decided it was too confusing to the audi-

ence and did not really make a difference in their health care. For the past month they explained "managed care" more carefully and touched lightly on HMOs. C. W. Williams was presented as one of the choices, although some of the HBAs mentioned that it was the only choice that had evening and weekend hours for appointments.

Strategic Plan for C. W. Williams

With the help of Michelle Marrs, the C. W. Williams Board of Directors was beginning to develop a strategic plan. Exhibit 16–18 provides the SWOT analysis that was developed. "Part of our strategic plan was to go to the people—make it easier for our patients to visit C. W. Williams by establishing satellite clinics. We recently became aware of a building that is for sale that would meet our needs. The owner would

Exhibit 16–15 • Users by Pay Source

Source	Percent of Users	Number of Users	Income to C. W. Williams	Number of Encounters
1994–1995				
Medicare	13%	791	301,444	2,392
Medicaid	56%	3,410	456,043	10,305
Full Pay	10%	609	318,424	1,840
Uninsured	21%	1,279	42,421	3,865
		6,089	1,118,332	18,402
1993–1994				
Medicare	12%	1,037	195,352	2,880
Medicaid	53%	4,579	585,446	12,720
Full Pay	11%	950	178,525	2,640
Uninsured	24%	2,074	101,569	5,760
		8,640	1,060,892	24,000
1992–1993				
Medicare	10%	853	189,927	2,304
Medicaid	36%	3,072	401,355	8,294
Full Pay	10%	853	158,473	2,304
Uninsured	44%	3,755	186,708	10,138
		8,533	936,463	23,040
1991–1992				
Medicare	20%	1,614	162,980	4,032
Medicaid	30%	2,419	312,680	6,048
Full Pay	10%	806	157,101	2,016
Uninsured	40%	3,225	159,855	8,064
		8,064	792,616	20,160

like to sell to us. He's older and likes the idea that the building will 'do some good for people,' but he's asking $479,000. The location is near a large number of Medicaid beneficiaries plus a middle-class area of minority patients that could add to our insured population. I just don't know if we should take the risk to buy the building. We own our current building and have no debt. We are running out of space at C. W. Williams. We have two examination rooms for each physician and all patients have to wait on the first floor and then be called to the second floor when a room becomes free. I know that ideally for the greatest efficiency we should have three exam rooms for each doctor.

"We have had an architect look at the proposed facility. He estimated that it would take about $500,000 for remodeling. According to the tax records, the building and land are worth about $250,000. Since we don't yet know how many patients we will actually receive from Health Care Connection or how many of our patients will choose an HMO, it's hard to decide if we should take the risk."

Exhibit 16–16 • C. W. Williams Health Center Patient Visits

Primary-Care Visits	
Internal Medicine	8,248
Family Practice	4,573
Pediatrics	2,643
Gynecology	236
Midlevel Practitioners	3,609
Total	19,309
Subspecialty/Ancillary Service Visits	
Podiatry	82
Mammography	101
Immunizations	1,766
Perinatal	429
X-ray	1,152
Dental	17
Pharmacy Prescriptions	20,868
Hospital	1,762
Laboratory	13,103
Health Education	412
Other Medical Specialists	1,032
Total	40,724

Exhibit 16–17 • ACCESS Enrollment Data for the Week Ended September 6, 1996

	Atlantic	Kaiser Permanente	Maxi-care	Optimum Choice	Wellness Plan	C. W. Williams	Total
Week Totals	229	347	66	114	189	**124**	1,069
Month-to-date	229	347	66	114	189	**124**	1,069
Year-to-date	3,708	5,384	1,164	1,507	2,238	**2,016**	16,017
Project-to-date	3,708	5,384	1,164	1,507	2,238	**2,016**	16,017

What To Do

"At the end of the week I sometimes wonder what I've accomplished," Michelle stated. "I seem to spend a lot of time putting out fires when I should be concentrating on developing a strategic plan and writing more grants."

Notes

1. This section is adapted from Mickey Goodson, "A Quick History," National Association of Community Health Centers Publication, undated.

Exhibit 16–18 • C. W. Williams Health Center SWOT Analysis

Strengths	Weaknesses
Community-based business	Need for deputy director
Primary-care provider with walk-in component	Lack of RN/triage director
Large patient base	Staffing and staffing pattern
Fast, discounted pharmacy	Managed-care readiness
Cash reserve	Number of providers
Laboratory/X-ray	Recruitment and retention
Clean facility in good location	Limited referrals
Satellites	Limited services
Good reputation with community and funders	No social worker/nutritionist/health educator
Resources for disabled patients	No on-site Medicaid eligibility
Strong leadership/management	Weak relationship with community M.D.s
Growth potential	Limited hours of operation
Property owned with good parking	Transportation
Excellent quality of care	Organizational structure
Culturally sensitive staff	Management information systems
Nice environment	Market share at risk of erosion
Dedicated board and staff	Staff orientation to managed care

Opportunities	Threats
Many in the community are uninsured and have multiple medical care needs	Uncertain financial future of health care in general
A number of universities are located in the Charlotte area	Health care reform
Health care reform	Competition from other health care providers for the medically underserved
Oversupply of physicians means that many will not set up private practices or be able to join just any practice	Loss of patients as they choose HMOs rather than C.W. Williams
Managed care	Managed care
Charlotte market	Reimbursement restructuring
	Shortage of health care professionals

2. *Utilization and Costs to Medicaid of AFDC Recipients in New York Served and Not Served by Community Health Centers*, Center for Health Policy Studies, Columbia, MD, June 1994.

3. *Using Medicaid Fee-for-Service Data to Develop Community Health Center Policy*, Washington Association of Community Health Centers and Group Health Cooperative of Puget Sound, Seattle, 1994.

4. *Key Points: A National Survey of Patient Experiences in Community and Migrant Health Centers*, Commonwealth Fund, New York, 1994.

5. *Health Insurance of Minorities in the U.S.*, Report by the Agency for Health Care Policy and Research, U.S. Department of Health and Human Services, 1992, and *Green Book, Overview of Entitlement Programs Under the Jurisdiction of the Ways and Means Committee*, U.S. House of Representatives, 1994.

Columbia/HCA Health Care Corporation: A Growth and Acquisition Strategy

To Tommy Frist, Chairman of the Board of Columbia/HCA Healthcare Corporation, it seemed like only yesterday that his company, Hospital Corporation of America (HCA), had merged with Columbia. The newspapers hailed the merger as the "mega-marriage" of hospital firms, praising the perfect fit that would position the $10 billion hospital chain to dominate American health care. Since the merger, Columbia/HCA had successfully pursued its strategy; the latest announcements were the acquisition of HealthTrust, Inc., the joint venture with Blue Cross and Blue Shield of Ohio, and the dramatic increase in 1995 stock prices. Already, the company had expanded to 338 hospitals, while becoming the largest provider of outpatient services in the country. However, with the uncertain future in the health care industry, Frist could not help but worry. Had he made the right decision to merge HCA? Was Columbia/HCA pursuing the right strategy? Managed care was moving into Columbia/HCA's strongholds, such as Texas and Tennessee, and it would be forced to compete head-on. At the same time, Columbia/HCA was beginning to acquire hospitals in managed-care-dominated states. How would Columbia/HCA meet the challenge?

This case was prepared by Sharon Topping and Peter M. Ginter. It is intended as a basis for class discussion rather than to illustrate effective or ineffective handling of an administrative situation. Used with permission from Sharon Topping.

Hospital Corporation of America Before the Merger

The original Hospital Corporation of America was founded in 1968 by father and son physicians, Thomas F. Frist Sr. and Jr., and several Nashville businessmen. At the founding, the company owned only one hospital, Park View Medical Center, in Nashville, Tennessee. By the end of 1970, the company owned twenty-nine hospitals, most of which were located in the southeast and southwest. A decade later, HCA was considered to be the world's largest hospital management company with a network of hospitals in numerous states and foreign countries. Although a large number of the hospitals were owned by the company, over 30 percent were under management contract. Refer to Exhibit 17–1 for a history of HCA's hospital expansion strategy from 1970 through 1993, when the Columbia/HCA merger took place.

The Years of Growth and Diversification

The 1980s marked a decade of increased government regulation, including the change to prospective payment for medical/surgical hospitals with Medicare patients. Instead of reimbursing hospitals for costs, they were paid predetermined, average rates for specific diagnoses, thereby rewarding those operating efficiently.[1] It was during this time that a noteworthy shift occurred in HCA's expansion strategy. Early in 1980, HCA owned three psychiatric hospitals. By 1981, they owned twenty-four. A major part of this expansion occurred when HCA acquired Hospital Affiliates International, increasing operations by

Exhibit 17–1 · HCA Hospitals, 1970–1993

	General Hospitals—U.S.		General Hospitals—International		Psychiatric Hospitals—U.S.		Total Hospitals
	Owned	*Managed*	*Owned*	*Managed*	*Owned*	*Managed*	
1970	28	0	0	0	1	0	29
1971	37	2	0	0	1	0	40
1972	45	2	0	0	1	0	48
1973	52	4	0	0	2	0	58
1974	54	6	0	0	2	0	62
1975	58	10	0	2	2	0	72
1976	63	17	0	2	3	0	85
1977	70	19	0	2	3	0	94
1978	82	28	4	2	3	0	119
1979	85	46	12	2	3	0	148
1980	111	56	15	3	3	0	188
1981	164	145	13	2	24	1	349
1982	162	143	20	2	24	0	351
1983	169	171	24	2	25	0	391
1984	163	187	25	3	36	0	414
1985	190	196	27	5	40	0	458
1986	185	202	28	7	41	0	463
1987	82	199	27	6	50	0	364
1988	79	191	25	2	52	0	349
1989	78	0	0	0	53	0	131
1990	75	0	0	0	53	0	128
1991	74	0	0	0	54	0	128
1992	73	0	0	0	26	0	99
1993	73	0	0	0	23	0	96

fifty-seven hospitals. Approximately half of these hospitals were psychiatric, making HCA the leader in psychiatric hospitals almost overnight.

Over the next four years, HCA started acquiring insurance and health services companies in order to offer a comprehensive program of health care benefit plans to employers. President Frist described the action as critical to HCA's goal of becoming the world's premier integrated health care company:

> By using our own provider hospitals, we can manage health care expenses and prevent excesses. HCA has demonstrated that we can reduce our own health insurance costs. Now we want to use that expertise

to provide high-quality health care to other companies at a reasonable cost.

In 1986, a joint venture with Equitable Life Assurance Society was announced that combined HCA Health Plans and the Equitable Group Health Insurance Company to create Equicor, a group health plans company. This was viewed as a quick way for HCA to build a national organization to market its hospitals.

Other diversification activity increased throughout the 1980s including the acquisition of Johnson & Johnson's home health care subsidiary; Hill Richards & Co. and Co-Ordinated Benefits Plans, Inc., two claims-processing businesses; HPI Health Services, a

Exhibit 17–2   •   Key Dates in the History of HCA

1968—HCA founded

1970—Listed on the New York Stock Exchange

1972—Formed X-ray, laboratory, and retail pharmacy subsidiary

1973—International expansion of hospitals

    First hospital management contract

    First cash dividend

1977—Formed Parthenon Insurance Company

1979—Acquired HMO in Brazil (with hospitals)

1980—Acquired General Health Services (acute-care hospitals)

1981—Acquired 18 percent of Beverly Enterprises

    Acquired Hospital Affiliates International

    Acquired Health Care Corporation

1982—Opened extended-hour family practice clinics

1983—Introduced PriMed, employee health benefit plan

1984—Acquired American Medical Centers (acute-care and psychiatric hospitals)

    Acquired Hill Richards & Co.

    Acquired Johnson & Johnson's home health care subsidiary

    Acquired HPI Health Services

1985—Acquired New Century Life Insurance Co. (licensing in thirty-five states and D.C.)

    Acquired acute-care division of Forum Group, Inc.

    Acquired Co-Ordinated Benefits Plans, Inc.

    Acquired Healthgroup International, Health Care Plus, and United Medical Plan (HMOs)

    Acquired CyCare Systems

1986—Formed joint venture with Equitable Life Assurance Society (Equicor)

    Joined with Caremark to provide home health care

    Joint venture with the Institute of Clinical Pharmacology

1987—Takeover bid for HCA

    Divested 104 hospitals to HealthTrust (ESOP)

1988—Repurchase of 12 million HCA shares ($51/share)

1989—LBO of HCA ($6 billion restructuring)

    Divested Allied Clinical Laboratories subsidiary

    Divested HCA Management Co. to Quorum Group (ESOP)

    Divested international operations

1990—Divested share of Equicor

1991—Received cash ($600 million) from HealthTrust when it went public

1992—Goes public with sale of stock

    Sold entire interest in HealthTrust, Inc. for $160 million

1993—Restructuring of its debts

1993—Announced merger with Columbia (September)

pharmacy management service; and CyCare Systems, a provider of computerized information services, among others. Key dates in HCA history, including all acquisition activity, are shown in Exhibit 17–2.

The Good Times End

Although revenues and profits grew continuously throughout the early history of the company, growth started to decline in the mid-1980s. This was attributed to two reasons: (1) the failure of government reimbursement for Medicare patients to keep up with hospital costs, and (2) the excess capacity in the industry of approximately 25 percent. In 1986, HCA reported a 48 percent drop in profits. One year later, the company reported a loss. The occupancy rate for its acute and psychiatric hospitals dropped to 48.5 percent, a twenty-point drop from 1980; the average length of stay of a patient had been declining since 1984.

Adding to the tumult, two former Hospital Affiliates International executives, Charles R. Miller and Richard E. Ragsdale, and a Dallas lawyer, Richard L. Scott, offered in April 1987 to buy HCA for $5 billion or $47 a share. The offer was met with considerable skepticism on Wall Street since the three men, virtually unknown in the health care industry, failed to reveal their source of financing. Even if they secured the $5 billion, many analysts believed that, "they would have to sell off large portions of the company in order to pay for a deal of this magnitude."[2] Less than two weeks after the offer, HCA's Board of Directors met and rejected the bid as "not in the best interest of the HCA's stockholders." Because the offer hinged on the takeover being friendly, the bidding group withdrew it immediately.

In response to falling profits and the takeover scare, HCA implemented a restructuring plan that included the divestiture of its less-profitable hospitals. Under the proposal, HCA sold 104 of its small, mostly rural or suburban hospitals to an employee stock ownership plan (ESOP), HealthTrust.[3] The result was a new HCA, slimmed downed to seventy-eight large metropolitan hospitals and fifty psychiatric facilities, all primarily in the south. Their average size was 236 beds, a substantial change from the 160-bed average in 1975.

The Leveraged Buyout and Going Public

One year after the HealthTrust spin-off, HCA again surprised the hospital industry as well as the financial world by announcing a buyout proposal that would take the company private. Chairman Frist explained:

> In today's health care and financial environment, there is no benefit for HCA to remain a public company. HCA has sound properties and assets. With our strong internal cash flow, we do not need access to the public equity market to keep our facilities modern and up-to-date.

Completed in 1989, the leveraged buyout (LBO), led by Frist, Jr., along with other members of senior management, was for approximately $3.6 billion or $51 per share. Financing of the deal involved $4 billion in bank debt and $300 million in equity. Although the reactions of the financial community were mixed, many of the financial analysts believed that it gave "Frist's management team the freedom to make long-term decisions rather than respond to short-term demands by investors."[4]

According to Victor Campbell, vice president of investor relations, "HCA's three goals as it entered the LBO were to sell assets, repay debt, and improve cash flow."[5] As a result, the company sold off most of its nonhospital assets. The emergency medical department, the ambulatory surgery centers, the clinical laboratories, and the international hospitals division were divested. In addition, the hospital contract management division was sold to senior managers and an investment firm for $43 million, and its 50 percent stake in Equicor was sold to Cigna Corporation.[6] This allowed HCA to trim to its core business of operating hospitals. Chairman Frist explained, "Streamlining has eliminated more than $50 million in operating expenses for the company."[7] HCA tried to sell the psychiatric company to a subsidiary of senior management and employees, but failed because of financing problems.

Post-Buyout: HCA Goes Public Again

Two-and-a-half years after going private, HCA filed documents with the Securities and Exchange Commission in Washington, D.C., outlining its plans to go public for the second time. By February 26, 1992, the company had completed its initial public offering and was trading on the New York Stock Exchange the next day. Netting about $800 million from the offering, the company had no trouble selling its stock. One health care analyst remarked that "the company's ability to reduce its debt through asset sales and improvements in financial performance greatly enhanced the value of the company."[8] Since going private, HCA took on $6 billion in debt that it was able to decrease to $4.2 billion, making it one of the most successful LBOs during the 1980s.

The New Strategy

Going public gave HCA access to capital, allowing it not only to reduce debt and interest expense but also to become more flexible in financing expansion and development of hospitals. As a result, debt as a percent of total capital was reduced from 86 percent at the end of 1991 to 63 percent by the end of 1992. Furthermore, HCA's overall strategy involved the operation of a select number of well-positioned, high-quality, technologically sophisticated urban hospitals in the United States. According to Frist, the focus was on "reinvesting cash flow into existing facilities, like outpatient and ambulatory care tied to our medical centers. . . ."[9] This strategy positioned HCA as an efficient provider of high-quality health care services, strengthened the market positions of its facilities,

and enabled the hospitals to expand their contracts with managed-care providers.

After the restructuring, HCA was no longer a health care conglomerate but a very pure hospital company that owned the hospitals it managed. By the end of the third quarter 1993, the company owned seventy-four medical/surgical hospitals (refer to Exhibit 17–3 for locations), and sold, consolidated, or closed over half of its psychiatric hospitals, leaving only twenty-three.[10] The vice president for corporate and investor relations explained, "When the company went public in February, it planned to hang on to all of its psychiatric hospitals. But in the second quarter, we saw greater declines." He attributed the problems to shorter lengths of stay, increased competition, and pressures from insurance companies and

Exhibit 17–3 • Geographic Distribution of HCA Hospitals, 1993

State	Number of General Hospitals (total number of beds)	Number of Psychiatric Hospitals (total number of beds)
Arkansas	1 (304)	0
California	1 (187)	1 (146)
Colorado	0	1 (80)
Delaware	0	1 (68)
Florida	18 (4,128)	1 (60)
Georgia	8 (1,544)	1 (92)
Illinois	0	3 (412)
Kansas	1 (578)	0
Kentucky	2 (364)	0
Louisiana	3 (434)	2 (142)
Missouri	0	1 (100)
New Hampshire	2 (191)	0
New Mexico	2 (370)	1 (92)
North Carolina	2 (287)	1 (88)
Oklahoma	2 (528)	0
South Carolina	3 (626)	1 (47)
Tennessee	8 (1,861)	3 (249)
Texas	13 (2,345)	1 (120)
Utah	1 (233)	0
Virginia	5 (1,568)	4 (469)
West Virginia	2 (332)	1 (110)
Total	74 (15,880)	23 (2,275)

Source: *The AHA Guide to the Health Care Field,* American Hospital Association, 1993.

employers seeking to trim health care costs. In addition, operations had been hurt by negative publicity about competitors. For instance, ten insurance companies filed suit in 1992 accusing National Medical Enterprises Inc. of charging for services that either were not needed or not provided. Although most of the industry applauded HCA's move, there were some who questioned whether the company had gone far enough. Given the problems in the psychiatric hospital industry, one analyst wondered, "Why are they keeping the remaining ones?"[11]

The Financial Picture Before the Merger

For the nine months ended September 30, 1993, HCA earned $270 million on $3.8 billion in operating

revenues; at the end of 1992, it earned $28.2 million on $5.1 billion in operating revenues.[12] The latter included $394 million in charges related to the restructuring of the psychiatric division, including the loss due to the sale of the hospitals. About one-third of the net operating revenues of HCA hospitals was normally from Medicare recipients, and the majority of the remainder of the net operating revenues was from privately insured patients. See Exhibits 17–4 and 17–5 for operating statistics between 1988 and 1993.

Approximately 88 percent of HCA's net operating revenues for the year 1992 came from its medical/surgical hospitals and roughly 8 percent came from the psychiatric hospitals (includes revenues from hospitals sold or closed).[13] Net operating reve-

Exhibit 17–4 · Operating Statistics, HCA Medical/Surgical Hospitals, 1988–1993

Years	1988	1989	1990	1991	1992	1993
Number of Hospitals	79	78	75	74	73	73
Number of Licensed Beds	18,399	18,434	17,712	17,480	17,324	17,653
Average Bed Capacity	18,255	17,965	17,650	17,176	16,977	17,116
Average Daily Census	9,571	9,393	9,194	8,941	8,616	8,399
Occupancy Rate	52%	52%	52%	52%	51%	49%
Admissions	574,600	560,600	554,700	544,900	541,500	399,500
Average Length of Stay	6.1	6.1	6.0	6.0	5.8	7.7

Source: Columbia Healthcare Corporation and HCA-Hospital Corporation of America Joint Proxy Statement and Prospectus, December 14, 1993, p. 9.

Exhibit 17–5 · Operating Statistics, HCA Psychiatric Hospitals, 1988–1993

Years	1988	1989	1990	1991	1992	1993
Number of Hospitals	52	53	53	54	26	23
Number of Licensed Beds	5,450	5,745	5,684	5,759	2,999	2,844
Average Bed Capacity	5,078	5,199	5,377	5,129	2,612	2,407
Average Daily Census	3,105	3,043	3,012	2,812	1,360	1,201
Occupancy Rate	61%	59%	56%	55%	52%	50%
Admissions	46,400	48,900	53,800	57,000	33,100	23,800
Average Length of Stay	24.5	22.7	20.4	18.0	15.0	13.7

Source: Columbia Healthcare Corporation and HCA-Hospital Corporation of America Joint Proxy Statement and Prospectus, December 14, 1993, p. 9.

nues from the psychiatric hospitals decreased approximately 9 percent in 1992 (excluding hospitals sold). For the psychiatric hospitals, the inpatient days were broken down as follows: (1) adult programs—58 percent; (2) adolescent and child programs—31 percent; and (3) substance abuse programs—11 percent. Approximately 77 percent of patient revenues was generated by room, board, and nursing services. This was typical of psychiatric hospitals because ancillary services were limited to pharmacy charges and some miscellaneous medical services. Although there were few outpatient charges for the HCA hospitals, the industry trends pointed to a rise in demand for this type of service.

Columbia Healthcare Corporation—Before the Merger

Columbia Healthcare Corporation, founded in 1987 by Dallas health care attorney, Richard Scott, and Texas financier, Richard Rainwater, began as a small regional hospital company.[14] Through a series of acquisitions aimed at building strong networks in targeted markets, it became a major player at the national level (see Exhibit 17–6).

Columbia's Network Strategy

Columbia's overall strategy—the development of integrated health care networks in targeted metropolitan markets—was accomplished by acquiring a substantial market share in each market through acquisitions and subsequent consolidations and by attracting local physicians as investors. Thus, Columbia positioned itself to offer one-stop shopping—facilities, services, and physicians—to managed-care organizations and large employers in each of its markets. Health care analysts believed this strategy was perfectly suited to the "managed competition" era of health care.[15]

The development of the El Paso market was illustrative of Columbia's strategy. In 1988, Columbia was successful in putting together a diversified health care system in El Paso consisting of acute-care hospitals, a psychiatric hospital, physical therapy centers, skilled nursing services, cardiac rehabilitation services, home health care infusion-therapy providers, and outpatient diagnostic centers. Columbia entered the El Paso market by purchasing two troubled acute-care hospitals (Sun Towers and Vista Hills) and two diagnostic centers. Sun Towers Hospital, a 252-bed former nursing home, was located within blocks of two more prominent competitors, both with excellent reputations and extensive marketing experience. The other acquisition, Vista Hills Medical Center, with 201 beds, had an occupancy rate below 50 percent and was avoided by most patients whenever possible.

Acquiring both properties at reasonable prices, Columbia executives concentrated first on winning back the business of referring physicians. This was achieved by promising close consultation with them on capital expenditures and facility operations and by inviting them to acquire an ownership stake in the local facilities. Obstetrician Jose Hernandez says, "They came in with the proper mental attitude."[16] He recalled how he had complained to the previous Vista Hills administration about a shortage of fetal monitors but had been ignored. However, when he brought this up with a Columbia executive, the needed machines were leased immediately.

Exhibit 17–6 • Columbia's Growth, 1990–1993 (dollars in millions)

Year	1991	1992	1993
Number of Hospitals	12	24	95
Revenues	$499.4	$819.3	$5,124.0
Assets	$485.3	$1,072.0	$4,483.0
EBITDA	$80.8	$136.7	$1,934.1

Source: Modern Healthcare, February 14, 1994, p. 28.

Besides improving facilities by increased capital spending, Columbia invited local physicians to acquire an ownership stake in the local facilities. This resulted in a limited partnership in which physicians made between a $15,000 and $20,000 investment in the company. In El Paso, the direct stake held by physicians was about 20 percent, roughly the percentage maintained in other Columbia networks. This included about 135 of the city's 500 physicians and accounted for 40 percent of Columbia's local business. Critics contended that such business relationships lead to unnecessary treatments, but the company believed that physician ownership was necessary to keep costs down. One of the largest managed-care networks in El Paso said that it had not detected any suspicious billing patterns among Columbia's physician-investors. "I think they know they are under the microscope," said the president.[17]

In addition, Columbia gained business from local physicians by limiting the health care choices in the city through consolidation of other facilities. For instance, two other hospitals in El Paso that were acquired by Columbia were closed and most patients and equipment were transferred to either Sun Towers or Vista Hills. The closure reduced the number of licensed hospital beds in the market by 15 percent. Additionally, Columbia opened one psychiatric hospital and acquired another. It closed the latter and consolidated into the surviving hospital, thereby becoming El Paso's dominant provider of inpatient psychiatric services. Later, Columbia acquired and closed its three primary competitors in the diagnostic-imaging business, acquired two physical therapy centers, and opened a cancer treatment center.

This same aggressive strategy was implemented successfully in other markets, including Miami/Fort Lauderdale, Houston, Corpus Christi, and Southwest Florida. By merging with Galen Health Care, Inc. in late 1993, Columbia was able to begin implementing its strategy in fifteen new markets (see Exhibit 17–7 for geographic locations of the hospitals). However, when looking at the company's ability to lower cost, there were questions about whether the Columbia strategy over time reduced or increased costs to patients and third-party payors. In El Paso, Columbia was in the middle range in terms of its charges when compared to others in the area. According to the American Hospital Association, from 1988 to 1991, expenses per inpatient hospital day in the El Paso market increased by 40 percent to $803. On a nationwide basis, the increase was 28 percent or $745.[18]

Exhibit 17–7 • Geographic Distribution of Columbia Hospitals, Including Galen, 1993

State	Number of Hospitals (total number of beds)	State	Number of Hospitals (total number of beds)
Alabama	7 (1,219)	Kentucky	8 (1,905)
Alaska	1 (238)	Louisiana	7 (647)
Arizona	2 (413)	Mississippi	1 (101)
California	4 (748)	Nevada	1 (688)
Colorado	2 (380)	Tennessee	2 (250)
Florida	26 (6,146)	Texas	20 (4,129)
Georgia	5 (675)	Utah	1 (120)
Illinois	2 (837)	Virginia	1 (200)
Indiana	1 (144)	West Virginia	2 (201)
Kansas	2 (465)	Total	95 (19,506)

Source: The AHA Guide to the Health Care Field, American Hospital Association, 1993.

Columbia's Financial Position
Before the Merger

In 1992, Columbia's revenues totaled $819.3 million, an increase of 65 percent from 1991; and its pretax net income was $42.7 million, an increase of 71.0 percent.[19] Including Galen Health Care System, revenues for the nine months ending September 30, 1993 were $3.8 billion, an increase of 7 percent; and pretax income was $193 million, a 9 percent decrease. Outpatient revenue increased from 21 percent in 1989 to 28 percent in 1992. Medicare as a percentage of revenue increased and was expected to continue because of the aging population and Columbia's market in Florida. For instance, Medicare was 51 percent of revenue at the Fort Myers, Florida, facilities. Additionally, the Florida market was subject to seasonal residency of aged persons; and during the winter months, these hospitals reported higher utilization than the rest of the year. Columbia was the only hospital chain that issued its own commercial paper, gaining a significant competitive advantage with the low interest rates of 3.3 percent.

The Merger: Columbia/HCA

The merger of Columbia Healthcare and HCA created the nation's largest for-profit hospital company with 187 hospitals, over 72,000 beds, and more than 125,000 employees in twenty-six states and two foreign countries. This was nearly one-third of all the for-profit hospitals in the country, although it was only about 3 percent of all U.S. hospitals.

Columbia/HCA was better positioned to compete successfully in a managed-care environment, because its large size gave it the clout needed to bargain with the big buyers of health care services. Furthermore, the economies of scale in such a system provided Columbia/HCA with the ability to reduce costs to the patients and third-party payors. According to Frist, "We feel that this clearly will enable us to be the low-cost quality provider in the vast majority of our markets."[20] Columbia/HCA spent $2 billion a year on medical supplies. If it guaranteed regular suppliers a specific volume of business then it could obtain lower prices. This method was estimated to cut $80 million to $100 million in costs in the next year. The chief financial officer thought he could double that savings in two years.

The merged company continued to use limited partnerships with physicians and hospital administrators. Columbia/HCA maintained about 80 percent ownership of properties.

Most experts agreed that the market was definitely moving in the direction of managed health care. The national market was made up of hundreds of thousands of health purchasers who eventually might consolidate into several hundred large buyers. If this happened, the more than 6,000 hospitals and 550,000 physicians in the United States would consolidate as well in order to compete on the basis of cost and quality of services. Columbia/HCA's strategy was designed to succeed in such an environment. The company would be able to position itself in each of the markets as a significant provider with a reputation for quality health care services as well as simultaneously being one of the lowest-cost providers.

Although the merger was viewed as a positive move by most in the health care industry, not everyone agreed. Joe Millsap, a health care analyst for Morgan Keegan remarked:

> Health care's going to be a very tough business in the '90s, and I think HCA was a perfectly positioned delivery system going into the teeth of reform. I believe they sought to realize a short-term gain for shareholders, but I don't think it's a good long-term decision. The deal might create an unwieldy company that could lose sight of the fact that health care is a "regional, micro-market business." HCA's carefully selected medical/surgical facilities were market-share leaders.
>
> They were also quasi-teaching universities in terms of their quality of care and services offered to the community. I believe that reform would have allowed those facilities to gain market share. Bigger is not necessarily better—certainly not in the acute-care hospital market.[21]

Others had mixed reviews. "HCA's hospitals have better operating profit margins and closer relationships with their physicians. Columbia has been building a network that emphasizes the relationship between the physician and the hospital," stated one analyst in the *Tennessean*.[22] However, he was quick to point out that more than seventy of Columbia's hospitals were former Humana hospitals where the relationship between the hospital and insurance company was more important.

The Team: Frist and Scott

After the merger, Tommy Frist, at fifty-six, became the chairman of the board and Rick Scott became president and CEO.

A former Air Force physician, Tommy Frist was executive vice president during HCA's first ten years. He was named president and chief operating officer in 1977, president and chief executive officer in 1982, and chairman of the board in 1985. At HCA, he was known for his ability to learn from more experienced others. This was reflected in the composition of HCA boards that included members of the financial community, the medical community, and a number of current and former chairmen of some of the largest and most successful corporations in the nation. He was known on Wall Street as someone who "listens well and learns well."[23]

In addition, Tommy Frist was characterized as someone who possessed the ability to get others to stretch their own limits, a quality necessary in successful organizations. A comment made by a close personal friend and running buddy illustrated this characteristic: "He came up to us one day and said that we were going to run a marathon and he was going to train us. I never thought I could do it and if it hadn't been for Tommy, I never would have."[24] However, Frist always challenged himself as well. After knee trouble stopped his marathon running, he took up bicycling, soloing from Aspen to Denver across the Great Divide.

Richard Scott, as President and CEO of Columbia/HCA, was a very powerful man who was almost completely unknown in the health care industry. At forty-one years of age, he put together one of the largest health care companies in the nation and became recognized as an industry spokesman. How-

ever, as a young boy going to school in North Kansas City, Missouri, he was so shy that he often sat in the back row of the classroom to avoid being noticed. Still, upon first meeting him, he came across as just a nice guy who made it big; however, many in the industry described him as aggressive and opinionated. This was especially true when he campaigned against the Clinton health care plan in 1994. He claimed that it would "ruin the Cadillac industry we have today."[25]

Scott's management team was composed of people similar to himself—young and aggressive. The top individuals were David Vandewater (43), chief operating officer and David Colby (40), chief financial officer. Along with Scott, they had a reputation for putting in long days and nights.

The Strategy: Acquisitions and Growth

At the time of the merger, Scott predicted, "Columbia/HCA will acquire between thirty and forty hospitals a year for the next few years as well as add services it lacks in its markets."[26] These acquisitions involved the buying of individual facilities, allowing Columbia/HCA to continue its strategy of increasing market share in targeted locations. Included in this growth strategy was the formation of regional networks through limited partnerships with not-for-profit hospitals. Columbia/HCA acquired a percentage ownership in the hospital, thereby becoming the managing general partner. In this way, not-for-profits that wanted to sell but also wanted to retain oversight were acquired. For example, in 1995, Columbia/HCA completed the nation's first ownership deal between a for-profit and a Catholic hospital system, the Cleveland-based Sisters of St. Augustine. The partnership strategy extended to teaching hospitals and university medical schools as well. Columbia/HCA undertook joint ventures with the University of Louisville, University of Miami, Tulane University, and the Medical University of South Carolina.

In addition to individual facilities, the company made two other major acquisitions since the Columbia/HCA merger (see Exhibit 17–8). To extend its

Exhibit 17–8 · Major Acquisitions by Columbia

Companies	Galen	HCA	Medical Care America	HealthTrust
Facilities	73 hospitals	96 hospitals	96 surgi-centers	116 hospitals
Beds	16,500	21,000	n/a	16,000
Price (in stock)	$2.8 billion	$5.9 billion	$742.6 million	$3.45 billion

Source: Wall Street Journal, October 6, 1994, p. A-3.

range of services, coming closer to its vision of being a one-stop shopping center for medical services, Columbia/HCA acquired Medical Care America, Inc., the nation's largest provider of outpatient surgery and home infusion care. In late 1994, National Medical Enterprises began negotiating a two-way acquisition of HealthTrust, Inc. and American Medical Holdings, which, if successful, would have created the second-largest hospital chain behind Columbia/HCA. To block this deal, Columbia/HCA made its second major move, the acquisition of HealthTrust for $3.45 billion in stock while assuming $1.8 billion in HealthTrust debt. According to the *Wall Street Journal,* this "outcome signals that the ambitions of Columbia/HCA extend far beyond its urban and suburban base and into the nation's hinterlands, where most of HealthTrust facilities are located."[27] The acquisitions by Columbia/HCA expanded its operations in major states such as Florida and Texas, as well as gaining hospitals in smaller towns such as Pulaski, Virginia, and Vicksburg, Mississippi. Refer to Exhibit 17–9 for the geographic locations of the hospitals.

The smaller-market acquisitions from Health-Trust were a way of enhancing Columbia/HCA's ability to secure managed-care contracts with large statewide and regional employers. Furthermore, the hospitals in rural areas would act as feeders to its larger urban ones, attracting more patients and bringing down unit prices. In addition, the acquisition of HealthTrust added home health agencies, and skilled nursing units gave Columbia/HCA the size and breadth of operations to make it a formidable negotiator in an environment of managed care.

Despite this leverage, the company extended its strategy by entering the HMO business as well. A joint venture with Blue Cross and Blue Shield of Ohio gave Columbia/HCA control over the managed-care operations. Since Humana's 1980s debacle in the insurance business, most hospital companies stayed away from managed care ownership so as not to alienate other insurance companies and HMOs that referred patients. Columbia/HCA's move into managed care was considered a serious risk by some in the industry. The head of marketing at a large HMO commented, "We do business with Columbia all over the country. Let's just say we are watching them very closely. If they do move into our territory, it will be easy to shift our business."[28]

Columbia/HCA's growth and acquisition strategy was fueled by its strong financial position. In 1995, earnings per share increased 21 percent, net revenues rose 22 percent, and net income increased 26 percent (see Exhibit 17–10 for selected financial data). This successful performance resulted in a 39 percent increase in stock price. Much of this success was due to Columbia/HCA's ability to cut costs throughout its operation. Its cost-cutting effort involved consolidation of services in each market, using less-skilled, lower-paid workers where possible, and centralized purchasing. In addition, the company used equity investment incentives for physicians to encourage them to take a more active role in improving operations. Although few questioned Columbia/HCA's ability to extract efficiencies from the industry, the still uncertain future for health care in this country leaves some in doubt about the long-term viability of the overall strategy. As one Salomon

Exhibit 17–9 · Geographic Distribution of Columbia/HCA Hospitals, 1995

State	Number of Hospitals (total number of beds)	State	Number of Hospitals (total number of beds)
Alabama	8 (1,218)	Nevada	1 (688)
Alaska	1 (238)	New Hampshire	3 (295)
Arizona	5 (777)	New Mexico	2 (381)
Arkansas	3 (554)	North Carolina	7 (980)
California	13 (1,755)	Ohio	3 (1,168)
Colorado	10 (2,324)	Oklahoma	7 (1,131)
Delaware	1 (74)	Oregon	2 (198)
Florida	55 (13,378)	South Carolina	5 (903)
Georgia	19 (3,207)	Tennessee	28 (4,372)
Idaho	2 (436)	Texas	69 (13,318)
Illinois	9 (2,964)	Utah	10 (1,277)
Indiana	2 (466)	Virginia	15 (3,155)
Kansas	3 (1,260)	Washington	1 (110)
Kentucky	14 (2,946)	West Virginia	6 (909)
Louisiana	22 (3,413)	Wyoming	1 (70)
Mississippi	2 (264)	International	6 (787)
Missouri	3 (786)	Total	338 (65,802)

Note: The international hospitals include: one in Switzerland (185 beds) and five in the United Kingdom (602 beds).
Source: Moody's Industrial Manual, Moody's Investors Service, Inc., 1996, p. 2964.

Brothers' analyst succinctly put it, "The jury is still out on whether huge hospital networks will be able to compete more effectively than one hospital alone."[29]

Notes

1. The prospective payment system (PPS) legislation set pre-determined, fixed rates by diagnostic related groups (known as DRGs) for reimbursement of hospitals treating Medicare patients. This resulted in declining occupancy rates and average length of stay for hospitals and increased the number of outpatient visits. Psychiatric, rehabilitation, and children's hospitals were exempt from PPS.

2. C. Schulze, "Offer Withdrawn After HCA Spurns Trio's Takeover Bid," *Nashville Banner,* April 22, 1987, p. C-8.

3. As part of the proposal, HCA made a financial commitment to HealthTrust by agreeing to an investment of $460 million aggregate principal amount in preferred stock. In addition, it received warrants to purchase up to 34 percent of the fully diluted common stock of HealthTrust and agreed to buy an additional $40 million in preferred stock in the event HealthTrust failed to meet its cash flow projections.

4. E. Gregory, "Frist Action Keeps HCA in Town, Intact," *The Tennessean,* November 17, 1988, pp. D-1, D-5.

5. T. Tanton, "No Plans for HCA to Go Public," *Nashville Banner,* November 29, 1990, p. B-3.

6. Under terms set by CIGNA, HCA agreed not to compete until April 1, 1995, in the ownership or operation of HMOs or PPOs selling health insurance or managed-care products to employers or consumers.

7. T. Tanton, "Streamlined HCA Charts New Course," *Nashville Banner,* November 6, 1989, pp. B-9, B-12.

8. E. Gregory and D. Fox, "HCA Back to Regain Reputation," *The Tennessean,* December 20, 1991, p. A-12.

9. "Hospital Corporation of America," *The Tennessean,* February 7, 1993, p. B-1.

Exhibit 17–10 • Columbia/HCA Healthcare Corporation, Selected Financial Data (dollars in millions except per share amounts)

	For the Years Ended December 31,				
	1991	1992	1993	1994	1995
Summary of Operations:					
Revenues	$ 11,722	$ 12,226	$ 12,678	$ 14,543	$ 17,695
Salaries and benefits	4,924	5,062	5,202	5,963	7,101
Supplies	1,774	1,948	2,015	2,144	2,558
Other operating expenses	2,153	2,292	2,351	2,722	3,418
Provision for doubtful accounts	638	652	699	853	998
Depreciation and amortization	647	670	689	804	981
Interest expense	748	506	415	387	460
Investment income	(83)	(88)	(74)	(69)	(100)
Merger, facility consolidation, and other costs	521	532	151	159	387
	11,322	11,574	11,448	12,963	15,803
Income from continuing operations before minority interest and income taxes	400	652	1,230	1,580	1,892
Minority interest in earnings of consolidated entities	24	25	18	40	113
Income from continuing operations before income taxes	376	627	1,212	1,540	1,779
Provision for income taxes	158	334	492	611	715
Income from continuing operations before extraordinary item and cumulative effect of a change in accounting principle	218	293	720	929	1,064
Discontinued operations:					
Income (loss) from operations of discontinued health plan segment	16	(108)	16	–	–
Costs associated with discontinuance of health plan segment	–	(17)	–	–	–
Extraordinary charges on extinguishment of debt	(114)	(23)	(97)	(115)	(103)
Cumulative effect on prior years of change in accounting for income taxes	–	51	–	–	–
Net income	$120	$196	$639	$814	$ 961
Earnings (loss) per common and common equivalent share:					
Income from continuing operations	$ .59	$ .75	$ 1.75	$ 2.16	$ 2.37
Discontinued operations:					
Income (loss) from operations of discontinued health plan segment	(.05)	(.27)	.04	–	–
Costs associated with discontinuance of health plan segment	–	(.05)	–	–	–
Extraordinary charges on extinguishment of debt	(.34)	(.06)	(.20)	(.27)	(.23)
Cumulative effect of a change in accounting for income taxes	–	.13	–	–	–
Net income	$ .30	$ .50	$ 1.55	$ 1.89	$ 2.14
Shares used in earnings per common share computations (in thousands)	334,676	394,378	413,036	429,295	448,714
Net cash provided by continuing operations	$1,607	$1,776	$1,585	$1,747	$2,254

continued

Exhibit 17–10 · **Continued**

	For the Years Ended December 31,				
	1991	**1992**	**1993**	**1994**	**1995**
Financial Position:					
Assets	$ 13,081	$ 12,773	$ 12,685	$ 16,278	$19,892
Working capital	917	899	835	1,092	1,462
Net assets of discontinued operations	411	376	–	–	–
Long-term debt, including amounts within one year	6,380	4,735	4,682	5,672	7,380
Minority interest in equity consolidated entities	44	51	67	278	722
Stockholder's equity	3,219	4,241	4,158	6,090	7,129
Operating Data:					
Number of hospitals	301	281	274	311	319
Number of licensed beds	54,616	53,457	53,245	59,595	61,347
Weighted average licensed beds	54,072	51,955	53,247	57,517	61,617
Average daily census	25,819	23,569	22,973	23,841	25,917
Occupancy rate	48%	45%	43%	41%	42%
Admissions (in millions)	1,486.2	1,448.0	1,451.0	1,565.5	1,774.8
Average length of stay (days)	6.3	6.0	5.8	5.0	5.3

10. For the six-month period ending June 30, 1992, the psychiatric hospitals that HCA sold, consolidated, or closed had a decline in operating profits of nearly 75 percent from the same period a year earlier. The hospitals kept by HCA had an increase of 23 percent for the same period.

11. H. Cooper, "HCA Hospital Plans to Sell 22 Facilities," *Wall Street Journal,* September 21, 1992, p. A-4.

12. The sources of revenues were (a) the federal government and state governments under Medicare, Medicaid, CHAMPUS (the Civilian Health and Medical Program of the Uniformed Services), and other programs; (b) Blue Cross and other private indemnity insurance carriers, HMOs, PPOs, and other managed-care programs; (c) self-insured employers; and (d) patients directly.

13. A breakdown of operating revenues between medical/surgical and psychiatric hospitals was not available for 1993.

14. The company was founded as Columbia Hospital Corporation, but the name was changed to Columbia Healthcare when it acquired Galen.

15. R. Tomsho, "Columbia Hospital Corporation Scores Success with a 'One-Stop' Health-Care Strategy," *Wall Street Journal,* June 25, 1993, p. B-1.

16. Ibid.

17. Ibid.

18. Ibid.

19. This does not include the Galen figures. If the Galen system were included, the revenues were $4.8 billion, an increase of 4 percent, while pretax net income was 329 million, a decrease of 41.0 percent. The 1993 figures in Exhibit 17–7 include Galen.

20. T. Tanton and P. Newman, "Health Care Reform Drives HCA, Columbia Merger," *Nashville Banner,* October 4, 1993, p. A-2.

21. P. Newman, "Hospital Firms' Mega-Marriage Draws Praise, Too," *Nashville Banner,* October 6, 1993, pp. D-1, D-4.

22. E. Gregory, "HCA Merging, May Move," *The Tennessean,* October 3, 1993, pp. A-1, A-2.

23. E. Gregory, "HCA Chief Says Firm's Buyout 'A Rebirth'," *The Tennessean,* March 19, 1989, p. D-1.

24. Ibid.

25. S. Lutz, "Scott Still Speaks Quietly, But Learns to Wield Power," *Modern Healthcare,* February 14, 1994, p. 28.

26. Ibid.

27. R. Tomsho, E. de Lisser, and R. L. Rundle, "Columbia's HealthTrust Deal Ended Merger Contest Among Four Hospital Firms," *Wall Street Journal,* October 6, 1994, p. A-3.

28. P. Berman and B. Condon, "Columbia Healthcare Versus Managed Care," *Forbes,* June 3, 1996, p. 52.

29. R. Rundle, "Hospital Pact Would Cut Costs—and Choices," *Wall Street Journal,* September 21, 1994, p. B-11.

The *Premier* Health Care Alliance Emerges

"Significant changes have been occurring for health care alliances," said Ben Latimer, president and CEO of SunHealth Alliance until November 1995. "Consolidation, integration, and growth and acquisitions by investor-owned health care organizations are all impacting alliances. Take for example, what happened in St. Louis. Barnes Hospital, Jewish Hospital, and Christian Health Services merged to form BJC Health System. Each one of them belonged to a different health care alliance—Barnes was associated with Voluntary Hospitals of America [VHA], Jewish was allied with Premier, and Christian was a member of American Healthcare Systems. After the merger BJC extensively studied the three different alliances and chose one—VHA."

In 1995, there were over 700 hospitals involved with mergers or acquisitions and 1996 would probably have more, based on the number that occurred in the first half of the year. Ben continued, "Although consolidation has occurred somewhat more slowly in the South, we are observing more and more of it. SunHealth had the largest market share in our fifteen-state area, but we had little room to grow. Consolidation meant that SunHealth was going to gain some partners and lose some oth-

ers. It was a real challenge to grow in that kind of environment.

"In addition, investor-owned health care organizations were acquiring hospitals. Many of those that they purchased were for-profits, but increasingly they were not-for-profits in need of cash. The Columbia/HCAs and Tenets were ready to buy these hospitals and in some instances, after purchasing them, closed them.

"The investor-owned organizations tout their ability to buy at lower prices. They promote this idea to combat the profit-making image and to induce communities to sell the local hospital to them. Because they own the hospital, they can mandate compliance. They also require that all their units buy from a single source in order to obtain those lower prices.

"Integrated networks or health care systems have been formed in many areas of the country. This organizational alternative, if it is of sufficient size, was able to compete with SunHealth if we didn't continue to grow. We wanted to grow, but not at the cost of sacrificing quality.

"One way we could get larger was to require our partners to belong only to SunHealth Alliance and set a specific amount of purchasing that was required. But then we would have to decide if we would require partners to disassociate if they didn't meet these requirements and whether we would pay them a 'market value' for their shares and how we would determine that market value.

"Another way to grow would have been to acquire another regional alliance in New England or

This case was prepared by Linda E. Swayne and Peter M. Ginter. It is intended as a basis for class discussion rather than to illustrate effective or ineffective handling of an administrative situation. Used with permission.

the West, but our partners' goal was to be a 'premier' alliance. They wanted to be part of a strong alliance with a great deal of market power as well as prestige. So we began thinking about becoming much larger and the way to do that was through a merger.

"We began talking with VHA in February 1995 about a possible merger. I signed a nondisclosure and confidentiality agreement but it was not limiting—meaning that I was not prohibited from talking with others. Consultants were hired to determine the interest and compatibility of the two organizations. The consultants and lawyers had been talking for nine months when Robert O'Leary of AmHS contacted me at the American Hospital Association annual meeting with a proposal that SunHealth merge with the very new AmHS/Premier. Those two alliances had merged in August. I owed it to the Sun-Health partners to talk with O'Leary.

"We quickly realized that AmHS/Premier had a good geographic fit with SunHealth and there was a good fit with services. We had some overlap with VHA. In addition, there was a difference in the organization of SunHealth and VHA. VHA was organized by regions. SunHealth and AmHS/Premier had similar organizations.

"One month after the contact with O'Leary, our Board approved a merger of equals with AmHS/Premier. We think it was the right choice for us. Sun-Health partners liked Rob O'Leary's vision and the 'fit' between the organizations. In the final analysis, the 'fit' was the most important variable."

History of SunHealth Alliance

In 1969, SunHealth was founded as Carolinas Hospital and Health Services, Inc. (CHHS), by the state hospital associations of North Carolina and South Carolina as a freestanding, not-for-profit, shared services corporation. The South Carolina Hospital Association (SCHA) had contacted the Duke Endowment, a major foundation, to determine whether it had any interest in helping SCHA set up something similar to a California program—the Commission for Administrative Services to Hospitals (CASH). In the mid-1960s, hospitals cooperated more than they competed, and CASH and other similar organizations were emerging to assist with planning and applying

industrial and management engineering techniques to hospitals for increased efficiencies.

Although receptive, the Duke Endowment leadership was concerned that the twenty or so hospitals in South Carolina were too few to be able to develop such a program. In addition, they knew that a similar group was under way in North Carolina. The Duke Endowment proposed one organization with a board of directors comprising hospital CEOs from both states. The two Carolinas had many commonalities, including culture, social structure, and economy. The hospital communities were similar in philosophy and maintained close ties. In addition, the Duke Endowment was chartered to improve higher education and health care in both North Carolina and South Carolina and saw an opportunity to leverage its grants to benefit more hospitals in the two states.

The two state hospital association CEOs developed the plan and bylaws for the organization. Dr. John Canada, a professor at North Carolina State University, put together a proposal for introducing management engineering and management education for the hospitals. Canada took the responsibility for finding the first staff. According to Ben Latimer, "He considered a number of folks, I understand, but he had some contact with Dr. Harold Smalley at Georgia Tech who suggested that I be considered. I met with the eight-member board and was fortunate to be selected by that group."

Ben Latimer Assumes Leadership of CHHS

Ben W. Latimer earned a BME degree from Georgia Tech University in 1962 and then worked for somewhat over a year at Procter & Gamble in the Department of Industrial Engineering as a management trainee. He returned to Georgia Tech and studied under Dr. Harold Smalley, one of the pioneers in applying industrial engineering and quantitative analysis techniques to health care. (The term *management engineering* was more acceptable to hospital administrators and physicians and thus was used in health care.) Just before he completed the master of science degree in industrial engineering, Latimer was recommended by Smalley for a position with Methodist Hospital in Memphis, Tennessee. There he worked on improving staffing and scheduling, particularly in the area of nursing. He realized early on that management techniques would be interwoven with the newly developing computer technology and management information systems. Although satisfied with the progress he was making in introducing management engineering at Methodist Hospital, he was intrigued by the opportunity at CHHS.

"Though independent of direct hospital association control or ownership, CHHS did serve *in effect* as the associations' operational arm for some services developed or wanted by them for hospital members," wrote Ben Latimer and Pat Poston in a 1976 *Topics in Health Care Financing* article. As an example, they cited group purchasing that was researched and developed by the South Carolina Hospital Association but operationalized by CHHS. Ben stated, "However, CHHS was never limited to implementing only those activities assigned it by the associations. In fact, CHHS operated as an expansion-minded company and would assess user needs and organize services to meet those needs.

"This organizational model was especially applicable to states in which size, density, and health care patterns precluded the existence of enough mid-sized hospitals to support shared services economically," commented Ben. "In addition, the separate but 'associated' corporation provided additional benefits—services could cross state lines, we had to be cost effective in order to survive, we had greater flexibility to recruit and pay employees differently than the associations, we could provide some services that associations were not able to provide, and members did not pay 'dues' but rather membership fees plus fees for the services that they selected. . . .

"The first service provided was management engineering known originally as the Carolinas Hospital Improvement Program or CHIP. It was designed to move hospital administration toward developing strategies for quality improvement and cost containment. It included such things as work and cleaning schedules and management education because most hospital administrators were educated in various health professions and had to learn management skills 'on the job.' For the CHIP program, all the development support came from the Duke Endowment. But as that was followed by other programs in the biomedical engineering and clinical engineering areas, the W. K. Kellogg Foundation supported our efforts as did the Kate B. Reynolds Health Care Trust.

"We used foundation support for development funds to establish new programs; however, each service we added was designed to be self-supporting. If the service was not good enough that the member hospitals weren't willing to pay for it, then it was not continued."

The Growing Alliance Expanded Beyond the Carolinas

When CHHS was originally developed, the support from the Duke Endowment and the composition of the governing board dictated that it was a service organization for the two Carolinas. "It never crossed our mind to serve anyone other than North and South Carolina," Ben said. "In the mid-1970s the question was first raised about offering services beyond our two states. The board decided that it would not harm the current partners and would allow for a larger staff that would have the opportunity to gain more from a broader representation of health organizations, and there would be broader forums for development and expansion.

"Up until the mid-1970s, CHHS served all sizes of hospitals in the Carolinas. Because of our location and the mix of hospitals in the area, most people probably thought we only served small and medium-sized hospitals. Some of the large hospitals—those with 400-plus beds—thought they had more in common with other large-sized hospitals across a broader region. So we formed the Sun Alliance, which corresponded loosely with the geographic area of the Southeastern Hospital Conference. We [CHHS] provided services for Sun Alliance."

CHHS Becomes SunHealth Alliance

"Eventually we determined that having two separate organizations was not beneficial. On the advice of Dr. Howard Zuckerman, a consultant from the University of Michigan, we merged the two organizations into SunHealth Corporation in 1985," Ben stated. The planning consultants laid out the concept of a regional health services network and encouraged the development of a network organization that in effect mirrored the composition of the hospital industry in the region—small community hospitals, large hospital systems, university hospitals, public hospitals, and so on. Given that the purpose of SunHealth was to provide health services to a large share of the population in the region, the consultants encouraged alignment of hospitals corresponding to actual patient flow patterns among facilities and physicians.

The board and management of SunHealth did not want the organization to be thought of as an "investment vehicle designed to return earnings," but rather as a service organization to help partners fulfill their missions. *Partner* was consciously selected to be used when referring to shareholder hospitals to constantly remind all involved parties that SunHealth was a shared alliance where partners worked together to share risk and improve health care.

Requirements for SunHealth Membership

SunHealth Alliance offered membership to hospitals that met the following criteria:

1. A candidate must be a tax-exempt organization engaged principally in the operation, directly or through an affiliated entity, of a not-for-profit hospital with total assets of $5 million or more.
2. It must not be contract managed by an entity other than one that is controlled by or under common control with the member.
3. It must have approval in accordance with board policies and procedures.

In terms of recruiting for new partners in the Alliance, priority was given to (1) hospital organizations in population areas not served by existing partners, (2) those readily able to hold equity interest, and (3) those demonstrating interest in existing alliance activities, and (4) commitment to improve region-wide health care delivery.

A new partner was evaluated on the basis of the characteristics it conveyed in its management team, relationships with other providers (competing and cooperative), recommendations from existing members, and the candidate's objectives in seeking network membership. SunHealth used the term *multihospital system* to refer to partners who operated multiple hospital facilities in different service areas. The term *emerging integrated health care system* was used to refer to those partners that operated

acute-care hospitals but had related (diversified and nondiversified) hospital services.

Because of its regional orientation, the SunHealth Alliance (more so than other major alliances in the country) was composed of diverse segments of membership, including public, general, denominational, rural, community, not-for-profit, and regional referral hospitals plus academic medical centers that served patients from throughout the world. Some of the implications of this diversity among members was reflected in the establishment of membership criteria and requirements. Although members shared some objectives in networking, their local strategies were typically diverse. Some members, constrained by law, organizational relationships, or philosophy, could not make certain types of institutional commitments. For example, public general hospitals and tax-district hospitals were subject to public bidding. Denominational, university, and foundation-operated hospitals were subject to systems or organizational investment requirements for purchasing.

A partner's rights might be terminated if that shareholder failed to continue to meet the technical eligibility requirements, such as loss of its tax exemption, being no longer engaged in the operation of a not-for-profit hospital, being acquired or contract managed by a nonrelated organization, or failure to pay its approved assessment.

SunHealth's Goals and Benefits for Partners

SunHealth's overarching goal was supporting partners to achieve their goals. "I think that our support is one of the things that distinguishes SunHealth from other multihospital organizations and arrangements," said Latimer. "We are so committed to helping our partners reach their goals. We do that through a variety of means:

- collecting and sharing information and experience;
- creating new and better ways through research, development, and testing; and
- supporting the installation and implementation of new and better ways at alliance hospitals."

Services Provided for Partner Hospitals

The impact of the prospective payment system (implemented in 1983) on hospitals caused considerably more concern with improving efficiency. Because hospitals were reimbursed at a predetermined level for each diagnosis related group, those hospitals that could provide the service at a cost below the reimbursement rate had greater revenues over costs and thus greater flexibility. The hospital could choose to spend the money on expansion, development of new services, new technology, and so on. Therefore, CHHS served the hospital members by helping them to increase efficiency.

After CHIP, Carolinas Hospital Engineering Support Services (CHESS) was established to assess and provide feedback on the rapidly emerging new health care technologies. CHIP and CHESS were followed shortly by group purchasing developed in the mid-1970s to offset inflation, the money crunch, and cost-justification requirements. SunHealth did not actually purchase or warehouse items that partners needed. Rather it negotiated terms and conditions to ensure the quality of goods and services plus sought value-added arrangements.

To provide the best in quality and price, SunHealth developed "corporate partnerships" in the mid-1980s with a small number of selected companies. SunHealth Alliance partners purchased approximately $2 billion annually, encouraging vendors to provide an array of value-added offerings as well as an excellent price. Purchasing included medical and surgical supplies, dietary products, pharmaceuticals, medical imaging products, capital equipment, and laboratory supplies. According to Latimer, "We go beyond trading volume for price. With our corporate partners we want to work closely together for our mutual benefit. Some of our corporate partners are Johnson & Johnson, Abbott Labs, duPont, Juran, and General Medical."

Consulting and Other Services

SunHealth's consulting unit had been in operation for more than twenty years. A variety of consulting services allowed hospitals to increase their efficiency in both administrative and clinical areas. Consulting expertise included nursing management, financial management, cost management, decision support, quality management, telecommunications, materials management, facilities management, human resources management, productivity management, health care planning (both strategic and operational), managed-care issues, information systems, and medical staff services.

"Each consulting service provided partners with new techniques or new services not previously employed to maximum benefit in typical hospitals in the region," Ben said. As SunHealth was better able than individual hospitals to locate, recruit, and compensate scarce technical and professional personnel, these programs made staff expertise available economically on a shared basis.

Partner hospitals were able to obtain support services that assisted in the planning, development, operation, and management of integrated managed-care programs, including contract evaluation and negotiation. The SunHealth staff provided assistance to hospitals in strategic consulting and health care planning services designed to strengthen alliance members as market leaders and improve interactions among hospitals, physicians, patients, and payors.

SunHealth joined with a variety of outside organizations to assist in the planning, development, and management of more specialized areas such as malpractice, general liability and workers' compensation insurance services, mental health, addictive disease and rehabilitation service, financial management consulting, human resources consulting, executive and physician search, medical claims collection, housekeeping, dietary plan operations and laundry management, electronic claims processing, employee health benefits, and utilization review services.

"Our services offered to partners must be of sufficient value to be used by the hospitals without resorting to mandates or dues. In essence, we had to be self-sufficient, including generating some surplus so that we could develop new programs or improve existing programs that were of benefit for our partners."

Partners were charged for the consulting and clinical technology services they used in three different ways. One was the per diem rate or a fixed amount per "expert day." Another was a per project charge: "We quote a charge to carry out the project and if the quote is off we have to absorb the loss, or if it comes in under the quote, it is to our advantage," Latimer explained. The third way was a continuing service arrangement. "We place a full-time industrial engineer in the hospital to manage a department. The hospital reimburses us for the compensation of the individual.

"We use incentives to encourage purchasing from SunHealth vendors," Ben stated. "Financial incentives are offered in those situations that are likely to produce financial results. For example, volume purchasing achieves greater savings for the alliance; the savings are returned to partners through rebating of the service fees. Other services, such as consulting, are offered purely on a fee basis as volume usage does not generate discounts."

SunHealth in 1995

Approximately 650 employees at SunHealth provided services to its 151 partners. The partners provided nearly $25 billion worth of health services annually through 350 hospitals that accounted for over 72,000 licensed beds. Located primarily in fifteen southeastern and south central states, hospital bed-size of partners varied as illustrated in Exhibit 18–1. SunHealth had clearly stated its mission and vision (see Exhibit 18–2).

SunHealth was extremely successful in serving its partners' needs and remaining financially strong, as evidenced by its key indicators and comparisons of its hospitals with other hospitals nationally and regionally (see Exhibit 18–3). Purchasing volume was $1.5 billion for fiscal year 1992 or $28,253 per adjusted occupied bed.[1] Purchasing incentives of $1.9 billion plus $16.6 million in vendor dividends were credited to partner organizations in fiscal year 1992.

Exhibit 18–1 • SunHealth's Partners by Bed Size

Number of Adjusted Occupied Beds	Percent of Partners
1–199	34.2
200–299	32.2
300–399	10.7
400–499	12.2
Over 500	10.7

Exhibit 18–2 • SunHealth Mission and Vision

Vision

Together, we improve the health status of people in our communities.

Purpose and Mission

The SunHealth Alliance is a working partnership committed to improving the health status of people in our communities. The alliance exists to help partners and their allies succeed in carrying out this commitment by:

* Providing sustained leadership for the positive transformation of health services organization and delivery;
* Transferring knowledge and experience relating to health services delivery, and developing new methods and knowledge;
* Supporting the linkage of efforts and integration of services in networks, so as to serve communities better; and
* Providing cost-effective resources for the improvement of health status.

Exhibit 18–3 · SunHealth Key Financial Indicators

Key Indicator	FY1991	FY1992	FY1993	FY1994
Current ratio	2.4	2.2	1.9	1.6
Total assets	$14.2 million	$16.2 million	$18.3 million	$20.8 million
Total shareholder equity	$8.8 million	$9.5 million	$9.8 million	$10.0 million
Book value per share	$123.98	$130.68	$131.00	$132.00
Enrollment of alliance	141	145	149	155

Comparisons of SunHealth Hospitals with Other Health Care Institutions

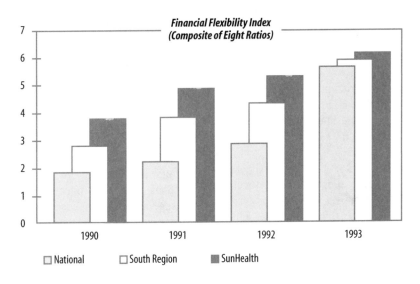

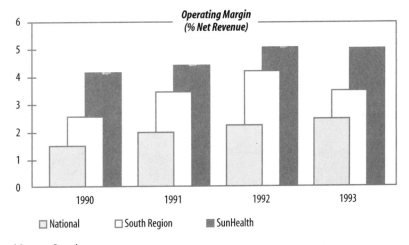

Source: HFMA Reports and Company Records.

History of AmHS[2]

American Healthcare Systems (AmHS), located in San Diego, California, restricted its membership to hospital systems. AmHS was founded in 1984 by merging two previous alliances, Associated Health Systems headquartered in Phoenix, Arizona, representing eleven systems, and United Health Care Systems, located in Kansas City, Missouri, with fourteen systems. By 1995, its board was comprised of forty CEOs of the shareholder systems that owned, leased, or operated 397 hospitals and had affiliation agreements with 528 other hospitals. AmHS shareholders and affiliates were located in forty-six states and the District of Columbia.

Since its founding in 1984 the organization had three different leaders. First was Charles Ewell who left in 1986 to become president of the Governance Institute in La Jolla, California. From 1986 to 1995, Monroe Trout, M.D., was president, chief executive officer, and chairman. Robert O'Leary assumed the position in 1995.

In January 1987, AmHS adopted a strategic plan that called for eliminating programs that directly involved the alliance in health care delivery and expanded services that could best be offered on a national scale.[3] The plan had the following objectives:

- AmHS will develop profit-making ventures that offer high-quality products and services to AmHS shareholders and other health care providers. These ventures will complement rather than compete with AmHS shareholders.
- AmHS will broaden its shareholder base to achieve maximum geographic coverage. This will permit AmHS to take full advantage of economies of scale and mass purchasing, as well as to provide a wide base for distribution of its products.
- AmHS will remain financially self-sufficient by sustaining a variety of revenue sources.
- AmHS will strengthen its key core services, including marketing and the AmHS Institute's representational and educational endeavors.

AmHS developed a number of ventures to benefit shareholders. AmHS Insurance Management Services (IMS) was designed to improve AmHS shareholders' access to cost-effective liability insurance coverage. It created two insurance companies (AEP and ADRL) to share risk, exerting a measure of stability and control over the market in areas such as excess liability insurance. IMS group purchased insurance from major insurers at substantial discounts, often with profit-sharing provisions.

AmHS Capital Corporation was a financial services company that provided customized programs such as a taxable medium-term rate program (when tax-exempt financing was an issue), a consolidated credit card program to serve hospitals and nonacute-care sites such as doctors' offices, and a capital asset protection program to better manage and control capital equipment servicing expenses.

The AmHS Business Group focused on initiating new programs. As an extension of the strategic partnering concept, AmHS Business Group attempted to add value for shareholders by reducing operating costs while maintaining or improving medical efficacy. It purchased equity positions in various manufacturers in exchange for achieving market-share objectives, assessed products and services of health care suppliers (such as those that provided high technology equipment for potential investment by AmHS), and coordinated two venture capital funds in which AmHS was a special limited partner. By 1995, more than $45 million had been invested in emerging medical companies.

The AmHS Institute, located in Washington, D.C., was the organization's public policy center. The Institute served three functions: advocacy, education, and communication. New initiatives were in the areas of managed care, physician integration, information systems, and alternative care purchasing for nonacute-care facilities.

These ventures, and AmHS's corporate partnerships in the purchasing area, were structured to generate capital for the corporation and the systems. AmHS prided itself on its small, highly professional management staff. With a total roster of less than one hundred employees, fewer than any other similar-sized alliance, AmHS made the best possible use of shareholders' assets—maximizing benefits while minimizing overhead expenses. AmHS was able to maintain this staffing level by relying on the talents of its multihospital system shareholders.

In the summer of 1989, AmHS initiated a program to improve member compliance in some group purchasing programs.[4] The compliance improvement program encouraged members to participate at specified levels. Shareholders were rewarded for total compliance in the program with up to 10 percent of annual dividends. Shareholders falling below specified levels were penalized. The eventual goal was 100 percent compliance, which would result in higher returns on investments for members. In 1995, AmHS had accomplished better than 90 percent compliance. If a purchasing group cannot guarantee commitment from its members, it had no bargaining leverage. It was not only the number but the commitment that vendors desired.

AmHS was a shareholder-driven national alliance of forty distinguished multihospital systems working together to improve their competitive positions, realize the economic advantages of size, and create innovative solutions addressing common needs. Its statement of mission is included as Exhibit 18–4.

To be considered as a shareholder in AmHS, an applicant should:

- be a not-for-profit health care corporation;
- be a high-quality prestigious health care organization;
- have a mission consistent with that of AmHS;
- complement the operations of existing shareholders;
- have a sizable market share within its major markets;
- have a strong financial position and be large enough to participate fully;
- have a well-respected management team;

- be able to fulfill certain AmHS program commitments, such as a requirement to participate in the AmHS purchasing program; and
- not participate in any other national alliance.

In July 1995, Quorum Health Group became a corporate affiliate of AmHS. Quorum was a for-profit corporation but its 105 affiliated hospitals were not-for-profit organizations.

History of Premier Health Alliance[5]

Westchester, Illinois-based Premier Health Alliance began in 1983 as a consortium of sixteen Jewish hospitals that agreed to develop a formal arrangement to handle common concerns. Originally the organization limited its membership to community teaching hospitals. The leadership did not plan for growth because of its focus on community teaching hospitals.

Alan Weinstein became the first president. Two years later the organization changed its name to Premier Hospitals Alliance to reflect the admission of non-Jewish members. It changed names again in 1993 to Premier Health Alliance as many of its members became health care systems rather than single hospitals.

Premier offered a wider range of services to its members than other broader-based alliances. This was because its member hospitals had similar needs and wants and the group was small enough so that the staff maintained personal contact with each hospital. Premier services fell into three areas: services that saved hospitals money directly, such as group purchasing and investment programs; services that enhanced the member's market share, such as home care, imaging, and physician bonding; and information sharing services.[6] Premier had seventy programs that were evaluated continuously. A program that did

---

Exhibit 18–4 • AmHS Mission

AmHS mission is to ensure the availability of high-quality health care services to patients at a reasonable and affordable cost. AmHS supports this mission by linking outstanding multihospital systems that share this goal and recognize the benefit of leveraging their resources through collaboration. It is through the strengthening of its shareholders that the success of AmHS can be measured.

not meet its expectations was marked and studied to see if it should be dropped. Between seven and twelve programs were dropped in a year, but at least that many were added. Premier was expanding its managed-care consulting and management services for its members.[7]

In 1995, fifty-five hospitals and health systems owned Premier, representing 280 hospitals. Together the hospitals accounted for nearly $2 billion in purchasing. Premier developed a committed buying program that was designed to reward the hospitals that bought more of their products and services from vendors that Premier had under contract. Hospitals that agreed to buy 80 percent of applicable products under five national contracts earned 12 percent lower prices, on average, than other Premier contracts.

According to Alan Weinstein, president of Premier Health Alliance, "Our commitment to being a member-driven organization is the cornerstone to our success. No alliance offers more to its members in program depth and breadth, quality, or service. We have high expectations of those we work with and serve. Premier boasts a proud heritage that will carry us well into the future, side by side with our membership." Premier's mission statement is included as Exhibit 18–5.

Premier's operating philosophy incorporated the following:

- Premier provides programs and services that support members as they pursue cost savings, management efficiencies, medical excellence, and the integration of health services in their communities.

- Premier delivers meaningful, strategic solutions to the management, clinical, and operating issues facing members during an era of unprecedented health reform.

- Premier programs are tailored to serve members in their individual environments and foster collaboration with other local health organizations. Programs must provide immediate financial value, long-term strategic value, or both.

- Premier is governed by its owners, yet is responsive to the needs of its member organizations.

- While voluntary in nature, Premier strives to build compliance in and, thereby, increase the success of its programs.

- Premier members' staffs participate in Premier projects at every step lending their expertise and ensuring relevance and appropriateness. Premier's own employees are an equally valuable asset, and the alliance is committed to their ongoing training, development, and recognition.

- All Premier relationships—with owners, members, business partners, and employees—are characterized by personal service, mutual respect, integrity, and the highest ethical standards.

AmHS and Premier Merge

In July 1995, AmHS and Premier agreed to merge. In August the organization formally became AmHS/Premier—the largest hospital alliance representing over one quarter of all community hospitals in the United States and $8 billion in purchasing. Robert O'Leary,

---

Exhibit 18–5 • Premier Health Alliance Mission

Premier Health Alliance is a national alliance owned by preeminent hospitals, systems, and provider networks that are responsible for improving the health of the people who live in their communities.

Premier provides hospitals, systems, and provider networks strategic advantages to improve health—through collaborating with other organizations, sharing meaningful information, pursuing economies of scale, and preserving community resources. Premier provides member hospitals, systems and provider networks the strategies and services they need to sustain a leadership role in healthcare excellence, community service, education, and research.

CEO of AmHS became CEO of the new organization, and Alan Weinstein, president of Premier, became president and chief operating officer. AmHS brought shareholders experience in systems and competing in managed-care environments. Premier had developed expertise in technology assessment, information systems, and quality measurement.

AmHS/Premier had ninety-five shareholders operating 400 facilities representing 1,400 hospitals with 240,000 licensed beds in forty-nine states. They operated in most major metropolitan areas providing the potential for the development of regional networks. The new company was less well represented in the Southeast and the Rocky Mountain areas. It represented $45 billion in revenues making it three times larger than Columbia/HCA and 30 percent larger than the next largest alliance, VHA.

A thirteen-member board was to govern the organization—four members from AmHS, four from Premier, three outside members, and O'Leary and Weinstein. Joint committees were expected to draft new policies for the merged organization; a high level of compliance was a priority. AmHS required that 90 percent of eligible goods be bought under its corporate contracts, and Premier guaranteed 80 percent compliance under selected contracts.

AmHS/Premier and SunHealth Agree to Merge

Four months later in November 1995, the recently merged AmHS/Premier formally merged with SunHealth. The new alliance had 240 shareholders with 650 facilities and 1,700 hospitals in fifty states. It represented over 30 percent of the community hospitals in the United States and was five times larger than Columbia/HCA in terms of members and purchasing volume. Annual purchases would be $10 billion, making it a formidable customer and competitor. SunHealth provided geographic coverage in the Southeast, added buying clout, and enhanced services including technology assessment, benchmarking, and physician integration. Exhibit 18–6 provides a map of the location of the new organization's hospitals.

"There was a time in the mid-1980s that we actually became a shareholder in AmHS." Ben explained, "VHA and Aetna were having conversations about joining together to create a national HMO brand name. AmHS wanted to counterbalance that strong association with one of its own. AmHS offered SunHealth Alliance, Yankee Alliance, Adventists System, and several others an opportunity to develop a national brand name approach to the market through Provident Insurance Company. They only required that SunHealth buy one share of AmHS stock to be a part of the enterprise. We purchased a share as it seemed to be a low-risk opportunity. However, we decided fairly quickly it was not for us. Subsequently, AmHS decided that members of its alliance should be required to do all their purchasing through AmHS and the deal with Provident fell through. We withdrew, as did the Adventists who decided to join with us."

Characteristics of the Three New Partners

Each of the new partners had similarities and differences. Exhibit 18–7 summarizes the general characteristics of the organizations before the mergers.

The new leadership team became Robert O'Leary as chairman of the board and chief executive officer, Ben Latimer as vice chairman of the board, and Alan Weinstein as president and chief operating officer. The first board of directors meeting was held in February 1996. Each of the organizations provided five members to the board that also included O'Leary, Latimer, and Weinstein for a total of eighteen members. The organization used AmHS/Premier/SunHealth until March 1996 when the name Premier and the corporate logo were adopted.

Competition

Alliances were created to offer independent members the same buying clout and economies of scale enjoyed by national investor-owned systems plus the opportunity to contract with employers as part of a national health care delivery network.[8] For a variety of reasons many independent hospitals belonged to more than one alliance or purchasing group. Nationally hospitals belonged to an average of 2.8 purchasing groups,

Exhibit 18–6 • Geographic Location of AmHS/Premier/SunHealth Hospitals

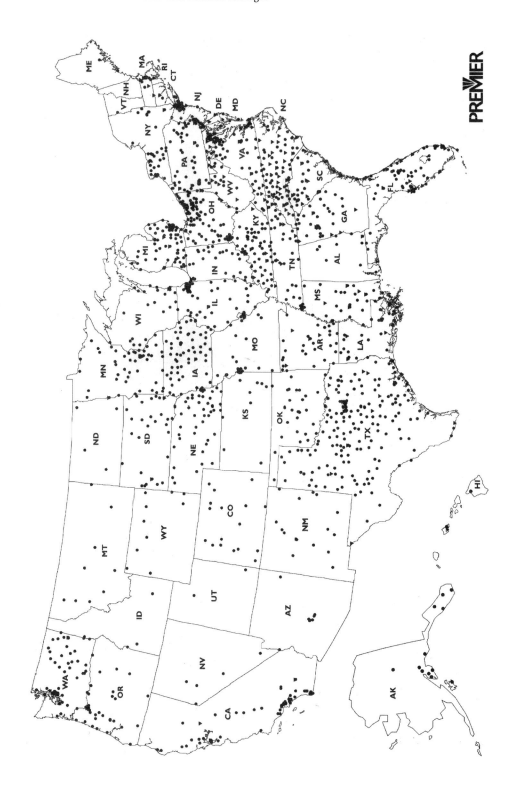

Exhibit 18–7 · Comparison of AmHS, Premier, and SunHealth

	AmHS	PHA	SunHealth
Founded	**1984**	**1983**	**1969**
Leadership	1984–1986, Charles Ewell 1986–1995, M. Trout, M.D. 1995–, Robert O'Leary	1983–, Alan Weinstein	1969–, Ben Latimer
Stakeholder Terminology	Shareholder	Owner	Partner
Geographic Strength	Northeast, Midwest, Northwest	Major metropolitan markets	Southeast
Number of Stakeholders	40 Shareholders	55 Owners	152 Partners
Number of Owner and Affiliate Hospital Units	925	280	355
Orientation Toward Fee-for-Service	Low	Medium	High
Number of Employees	100	130	650
Purchasing Compliance	100% required, but dual source	Moving toward 80% required	Sole source with incentives
Corporate Structure	Parent corporation and LLP	Cooperative corporation C(6)	Cooperative corporation C(6)
Revenues of Stakeholders	$36 billion	n/a	$24.8 billion
Collected Revenues of Division	$78.6 million	$28 million	$61.5 million

although in New York and Pennsylvania, they belonged to four buying organizations.[9]

Industry Competitors

Within the industry there were over 200 purchasing groups. The undercutting of prices led some industry analysts to comment that group purchasing was turning into a commodity industry.[10] However, a purchasing group differed from an alliance in that there was usually no financial or leadership commitment to the purchasing group. An alliance expected member organizations to participate in its governance, sharing of information, and assisting other members as well as paying membership fees.

Many hospital systems and networks were large enough to obtain their own volume buying discounts. Some questioned whether there was still a need for alliances.

There were five major alliances in the United States: AmHS, Premier, SunHealth, University Hospital Consortium (UHC), and VHA. After the merger, Premier became the largest, followed by VHA. UHC was the smallest. Exhibit 18–8 provides a comparison of Premier with its two major competitors.

University Hospital Consortium

University Hospital Consortium, located in Oakbrook, Illinois, was started in 1980 by several CEOs of university hospitals. UHC targeted a specific group of hospitals, those owned by universities and whose staffs were controlled by medical schools. It began a group purchasing program in 1984 to provide university institutions with increased clout in purchasing pharmaceuticals, insurance, supplies, and services. In 1993, UHC surpassed $1 billion in group purchases on behalf of its members. Sixty-five university hospitals in the United States were members of UHC.[11] According to Samuel Schultz II, Ph.D., vice president for information services at UHC, the organization had grown so much because its member hospitals were "in dire straits."[12] General university funding was severely restricted across the United States during this period of a weakened economy. University hospitals, as part of the university, were affected as well.

University hospitals tended to see their mission to be on the cutting edge of health care as they saw patients, gathered data, and performed research. Thus, they had specific needs for the very newest technology

Exhibit 18–8 · **Competitive Organizational Comparison**

	Premier	Columbia/HCA	VHA
Total number of acute-care hospitals	1,757	307	1,136
Total membership	1,757	363	1,332
Shareholders	131	n/a	97
States	50	36	47
Beds	276,000	61,400	253,000
Admissions	9.3 million	1.9 million	7.8 million
Surgical operations	6.8 million	0.6 million	5.7 million
Emergency visits	26.8 million	0.5 million	21.8 million
Percentage of community hospital beds	30.5%	6.8%	28.0%
Estimated purchasing volume 1996	$6–10 billion	$2.5 billion	$7 billion

Source: "The New Premier: One Year After the Merger," *IN VIVO The Business and Medicine Report,* July/August 1996, p. 25.

and in fact were often involved with developing that technology. Many academic health centers faced the dilemma of being the site not only where new drugs and technologies were first used but also where the cost ramifications first emerged. Therefore UHC was very involved in cost and reimbursement assessments. UHC did not offer consulting services for investments in technology or services designed to acquire patients. Services included group purchasing, materials management, a national traveling nurse placement service, a nurse recruiting service, risk-management insurance services, advice on winning contracts for clinical research with pharmaceutical companies, managed-care planning, and information-sharing services.[13]

Strategic goals recently formulated for UHC included an aggressive quality agenda with a dozen programs in management reengineering and quality of care plus development of tools for members to perform market assessments.[14] A major growth area was development of information services for clinical and technology assessment. UHC served as a clearinghouse for information on new technology and was setting up information-sharing systems that would assist member hospitals in clinical research by sharing outcomes information. UHC was developing a clinical information network—a vehicle for collecting members' clinical, financial, and administrative data to investigate quality of care and resource management issues.[15] The ability to share data among academic centers, whose information system architecture varied from archaic paper systems to PC LANs to minis to mainframes to client-server setups, was a challenging task but one that was being tackled at UHC.

Voluntary Hospitals of America

Voluntary Hospitals of America, located in Irving, Texas, was the nation's largest hospital alliance in number of beds prior to the Premier merger. It was founded by thirty hospitals in 1977 and grew to include ninety-seven shareholders and more than 1,300 members at the end of 1995.[16] In 1989, VHA Enterprises divested a variety of business activities that were considered strategically less valuable: VHA Physician Services that offered physician bonding products; VHA Capital; VHA Consulting Services, sold to Arthur Andersen and Co., Chicago; VHA Long-Term Care and VHA Physician Placement Services to their respective managements; and VHA Diagnostic Services to a group of outside investors.[17]

At that time, VHA renewed its emphasis on managed care. "We're probably the only alliance that is appropriately in the managed-care business on a national level, because we have the broadest national presence," according to Bruce Brennen, VHA's vice president for communication.[18] VHA retained 50 percent stake in Partners National Health Plans, a joint venture with Aetna Life Insurance Company of Hartford, Connecticut. With substantially over 2 million members enrolled in thirty-three states, Partners was the third-largest managed-care program in the United States (Kaiser Permanente was the largest). Brennen said that VHA was keeping its managed-care operations because it helped hospitals in local markets and would be strategically important in the future. About 90 percent of VHA members were involved with Partners, which operated a number of PPOs and HMOs.[19] However, by the end of 1993, VHA sold its 50 percent share to Aetna.[20]

New initiatives for VHA included an in-house educational program on implementing best practices, a separate satellite network program for educating top executives, a program to help its members choose and implement information technologies, and a joint program with the Catholic Health Association to market a software program that measured the benefits that hospitals provided for their communities.

VHA was not pleased with SunHealth's decision to merge with Premier. It released a statement that read, "Over the past year, VHA initiated a relationship with SunHealth by participating in task forces and jointly developing a community-ownership advocacy initiative. These joint activities led to further discussions of how a merger might bring value to our members. VHA did not view a potential merger as crucial to its long-term success and acknowledged that several local market conflicts presented potential roadblocks. Despite these challenges, our conversations with SunHealth focused on the potential benefits of bringing our organizations together. During our discussions, SunHealth, without prior notification, began exclusive negotiations with AmHS/Premier that resulted in their recent decision to merge."

The Future of Alliances

Not all hospital CEOs are satisfied with alliances. The primary disadvantage reported is that programs did not meet the needs of individual hospitals.[21] The larger the alliance, which was good for purchasing volume, the more challenging it became to tailor services that met the needs of individual partners.

For alliances to survive, they had to think strategically for their members, be financially sound, and provide the desired services. Specific factors that appeared to be important for alliances to survive included:

- the ability to drive compliance;
- the ability to provide successful, comprehensive services beyond purchasing;
- the willingness to take risks and be creative in finding solutions for their members;
- homogeneity in alliance members;
- the ability to provide value-added services to both members and vendors;
- the ability to focus on the "top-down sell" (meaning hospital CEO involvement); and
- the ability to implement at the local level.[22]

Because of the complexity of current agreements, it was becoming increasingly difficult for hospitals to determine the real value of individual contracts. Hospitals more often were finding that their best strategy was to make a commitment to the group that they believed could best meet their needs on an overall basis—price was not the only criterion. Hospitals might not be able to assess the actual value of group purchasing contracts because they had to weigh the value of available services such as inventory management, electronic data interchange, in-service programs, and remote order entry.

Manufacturers' attitudes toward groups were changing, as well.[23] Vendors were becoming more selective in their dealings. They were targeting groups that could best deliver compliance and market share. This selectivity prompted some manufacturers to refuse to sign contracts with certain groups if they could not deliver the business in return for price concessions. As a result, some groups might close. This made it even more important for hospitals to develop an understanding of which groups could best serve their needs. The consequence of not understanding a group's direction was that a hospital paid higher prices for the products and services it purchased, which could mean clinical and competitive obsolescence.[24]

Sandwiched between trade associations and multihospital systems, facing aggressive competition from the proliferation of shared service and group purchasing, not-for-profit alliances were searching for unique identities and strategies that provided a sustainable competitive advantage for their members. The diversity of needs and interests among members of an alliance made consensus building, setting priorities, and strategic planning efforts very difficult. The alliances that survived would be those that achieved value for member organizations.

Gerald McManis believed that successful alliances would:

- develop and communicate a concise vision for the future and clearly state long-term strategy and objectives;
- establish a member network that shared the vision and had a good structural fit with the alliance's strategy;
- implement programs and services that capitalized on the unique competence of the organization and its membership;
- operate a lean, professionally managed organization, concentrating on adding real value for members, not simply its own growth and self-perpetuation; and
- build long-term relationships with members based on trust, commitment, and value.[25]

Network growth might eliminate the need for purchasing alliances. Some networks grew large enough to buy on their own or at least became a different type customer. Alliances might need to add alternative-site members to grow—clinics, long-term-care facilities, and so on. Among purchasing groups, alternative-site members increased 27.5 percent, but hospital membership only grew 1.2 percent.[26]

Looking Toward the Future of the Premier Alliance

At the first major meeting of the newly merged organization, Rob O'Leary "vowed the giant group would produce the best prices and the most innovative programs. Our role and our responsibility now is to help reshape the American delivery system."[27] He predicted that Premier would launch a physician equity company—Premier Practice Management—that would go public, a similar company that would be an alternative to selling to a for-profit chain, and use the organization's tremendous leverage to reduce prices to member organizations. In addition, Premier offered a full complement of services for its shareholders and affiliates (see Exhibit 18–9).

The first renegotiated contracts were signed in June 1996. DuPont offered a 30 percent lower price to be the sole supplier of film. Glaxo Wellcome agreed to use the same pricing for acute-care drugs and outpatient-care drugs, something the pharmaceutical industry had been resisting. This was an important breakthrough for those organizations that managed care.

In October 1996, Premier announced agreements with Alliant Foodservice, Inc. and Cerner Corporation. Alliant won the sole-source contract valued at approximately $1 billion. Premier agreed to exclusively endorse Cerner as the preferred supplier of clinical data repository systems. Cerner provided Premier members a package named "Premier Foundations," an open clinical data foundation that supported a desktop management information system for clinicians as well as support applications. The use of this architecture by over 30 percent of U.S. hospitals had far-reaching implications.

Things were happening rapidly within Premier, but the melding of the organizations would take some time. As a first step in integrating the three different organizations, each one appointed committee members to tackle important issues in merging the organizations. One of the first outcomes was a statement of values developed by the employees of the new Premier and adopted by the board in April 1996 (see Exhibit 18–10).

Each of the former CEOs knew that merging the three separate organizations to accomplish the synergy they wanted was going to be a real challenge. Using Jim Collins and Jerry Porras's "core ideology" and "envisioned future" framework, Premier was developing a draft of its foundation statements.[28] The organizational leadership had a draft of core values,

Exhibit 18–9 • Premier's Products and Services

Cost Reduction Tools

Purchasing program

- Supplies group purchasing for medical/surgical, laboratory, operating room, food service, cardiology, and support services
- Materials management consulting
- Support services including contract management consulting and operations improvement consulting
- Pharmacy group purchasing
- Pharmacy benefit management services
- Pharmaceutical biotechnology information program
- Drug Intelligence Center
- Regional clinical pharmacy coordinators

Clinical and operational design

- Benchmarking (clinical and operational)
- Process design and reengineering consulting
- Clinical operations consulting
- Premier CareLinks (clinical resource management)
- On-site management engineering and consulting (community-based performance services)
- Emergency room design using simulation software
- Care management/clinical pathways programs
- Collaborative groups consulting

Insurance management services

Risk bearing

- Excess liability
- Directors and officers liability
- Excess workers' compensation

Group sponsored

- Property
- Managed-care liability
- Employee medical benefit stop loss
- Long-term disability
- Group life and accidental death and dismemberment insurance
- Payroll deduction universal life insurance
- Group self-insured workers' compensation
- Universal life insurance program

Financial resources

- Business office management services
- Consulting and analysis for ambulatory patient groupings classification
- GE medical tax-exempt financing

System Development and Integration Strategies

Strategic planning, managed-care, and operations services

- Strategy and business planning
- Managed-care consulting
- Integrated delivery system development
- Government contracting
- Managed-care organization development
- Implementation management
- Medical management
- Physician practice management
- Integrated HealthCare Report

Technology Management Resources

Clinical equipment management

- Biomedical equipment repair
- Imaging equipment repair
- Technology assessment
- Technology life cycle management
- Buying, selling, upgrading, de-installation, and disposal of preowned equipment
- Network Technologies biomedical and imaging equipment accessories and parts dealership
- Clinical engineering department support and management
- Capital Asset Protection Program for lower capital equipment maintenance costs
- Capital equipment purchase negotiations and group buys

Clinical research

Facilities management

- Facilities consulting
- Cable Healthcare
- Energy monitoring and conservation

Information technology resources and management

- Support materials—A health information network white paper, readiness assessment tool kit, planning and deployment methodology, and a managed-care information technology white paper
- An alliance information technology directory and vendor catalog
- Information-system strategic planning
- Information technology network consulting
- Vendor selection and contract negotiation assistance
- Information technology system integration and implementation
- Operations redesign following systems implementation
- Telecommunications consulting

continued

Exhibit 18–9 • **Continued**

Networking and Knowledge Transfer Opportunities

Advocacy

- Grassroots program initiation
- Policy development
- Advocacy publications

Education and experience sharing

- Continuing medical education
- Customized workshops, seminars, and retreats
- Managed-care and IDS education
- Nurse leadership courses
- Physician education
- Physician practice manager training
- Technology Futures Panel conference
- Research and library services
- Peer group networking meetings

Human resources management

- Custom local and regional wage and salary surveys
- Human resources reference desk
- Annual wage and salary surveys
- Physician incentive program design

Legal, regulatory, and JCAHO compliance

- JCAHO/NCQA accreditation preparation services are available and JCAHO decision grid score reports are prepared and compared with those of other organizations. Mock surveys and staff training also can be arranged.
- Employment, labor law, and other specialized services can be accessed through discounted arrangements negotiated by Premier staff.

Market and customer research

- A comprehensive, modular health assessment involving quantitative and qualitative evaluation of health needs, risks, behaviors, and existing community resources.
- Research services focusing on customer perceptions including community psychographics, focus group facilitation, moderator training, and patient, physician, and employer survey tools.

Measuring and comparing performance

- Comparing clinical and financial data with that of other health care facilities
- Critical care decision support (APACHE)
- Decision support and cost accounting system assistance
- A functional assessment tool to measure a patient's physical and mental well-being
- A quality indicator comparative database
- A service quality satisfaction survey

Organizational effectiveness

- Organizational effectiveness training
- Change management consultation
- Self-managed team development
- Organizational diagnosis
- Mission, vision, and values development
- Executive team building
- Health care organizational performance self-assessment
- Strategic visioning conferences

---

core purpose, and core roles (see Exhibit 18–11). Using these as a point of departure, they were working on refining and gaining consensus on the core ideology and the development of Premier's "envisioned future."

"For us to focus on survival of the acute-care hospital is wrong," Ben Latimer emphatically stated. "Success will be increasing the health status of our partners' communities without acute care. It is our task to help our partners achieve this paradigm shift and deliver care—wellness promotion as well as illness care—in new ways that lead to improved health status."

Notes

1. Adjusted occupied bed (AOB) is computed by multiplying total annual patient care revenues by the average twelve-month census and dividing by total annual inpatient revenues:
   AOB = total annual patient care revenues × average 12-month census ÷ total annual inpatient revenues.
2. Much of the information for this section was taken from *Building Value for Our Systems,* an American Healthcare Systems brochure.

Exhibit 18–10 · Premier Values Statement

Premier consists of leading systems and networks of healthcare organizations that have created this enterprise to further their responsibility for improving the health of communities. *Premier exists to bring value to its owners and affiliates.* We provide value through quantifiable economic advantage and meaningful strategic solutions to the management and clinical issues facing our constituency. Premier's strength comes from its ability to provide leveraged solutions while recognizing the need for market flexibility.

Values

We believe our success is dependent on creating partnerships that bring value. We think of every encounter as an opportunity for a partner relationship. This includes encounters with our owners, affiliates, business partners, and employees. We are a responsible and accountable organization within the healthcare industry and the larger society. We work together to achieve our mission through the following core values:

We act ethically

- We are honest and fair
- We treat individuals with equality and respect
- We are accountable, both individually and corporately, for our actions
- We use our influence responsibly
- We actively embrace our fiduciary responsibility

We deliver exemplary and customized service

- We ask and listen to our partners
- We provide meaningful and timely products and services to meet our partners' needs
- We work as a team to provide coordinated services
- We openly communicate meaningful and timely information
- We empower employees to make decisions

We enhance value

- We optimize revenue growth and owner return on investment
- We deliver cost-effective performance improvement in our operations and our business solutions
- We are committed to maximizing profitability
- We develop strategic solutions through knowledge transfer

We lead and embrace change

- We are visionary, yet respectful of our heritage
- We deliver innovative solutions
- We reward creative thinking and responsible risk taking
- We actively challenge our assumptions and the way we conduct business
- We work beyond traditional norms and practices
- We commit to personal and organizational development, recognizing individual accountability for our own growth
- We commit to transforming the industry to benefit the broader society

We Commit to be The Best

- We attract and retain the best partners
- We deliver the best products and services
- We create the best work environment and support the balance between work and personal life
- We continually raise our standards as we try for new levels of excellence
- We invest in developing leadership expertise throughout the organization

We celebrate our accomplishments and have fun in what we do while serving our communities and patients.

April 4, 1996

Exhibit 18–11 · Premier Core Ideology (Draft)

Foundation Statements

Core Ideology

Core Values

- Integrity that shines in the individual and the enterprise
- Enduring respect for others' worth and for the principles that uphold our communities
- A passion for performance and a bias for action: creating real value, engaging change, leading the pace

Core Purpose

- To improve the health of communities

Core Roles of the Enterprise

- Producing cost savings and quality improvements
- Providing alternative revenue sources
- Providing strategic vehicles
- Facilitating the rapid transfer of knowledge and experience

---

3. Howard Larkin, "Alliances: Changing Focus for Changing Times," *Hospitals* 63 (December 20, 1989), pp. 34–35.
4. Howard Larkin, "Alliances Argue Merits of Compliance Incentives," *Hospitals* 63 (December 20, 1989), p. 37.
5. Much of the information for this section was taken from a Premier Health Alliance brochure.
6. Larkin, "Alliances: Changing Focus for Changing Times," pp. 34–35.
7. "Collaborative Efforts Enhance Program Development," *Health Care Strategic Management* 11, no. 2 (February 1993), p. 23.
8. Gerald L. McManis, "Not-for-Profit Alliances Need to Focus on Value," *Modern Healthcare* (October 15, 1989), p. 20; and Larkin, "Alliances: Changing Focus for Changing Times," pp. 34–38.
9. Lisa Scott, "Group Purchasing Evolution," *Modern Healthcare* (September 27, 1993), p. 52.
10. Jim Montague, "Can Purchasing Alliances Adapt?" *Hospitals and Health Networks* 69, no. 16 (August 20, 1995), pp. 30–34.
11. Membership information was provided by University Hospital Consortium corporate offices in a telephone interview.
12. Carolyn Dunbar, "A New Era Dawns for the University Hospital Consortium," *Computers in Healthcare* 13, no. 13 (December 1992), p. 32.

13. Ibid., p. 34.
14. Ibid.
15. Ibid.
16. Current membership information was supplied by VHA corporate offices in a telephone interview.
17. Larkin, "Alliances: Changing Focus for Changing Times," p. 35.
18. Ibid.
19. Ibid.
20. Information supplied in a telephone interview.
21. Larkin, "Alliances: Changing Focus for Changing Times," p. 35.
22. John A. Henderson, "Hospitals Should Reassess Group Purchasing," *Modern Healthcare* (March 10, 1989), p. 80.
23. Ibid.
24. Ibid.
25. McManis, "Not-for-Profit Alliances," p. 20.
26. Scott, "Group Purchasing Evolution," p. 58.
27. Lisa Scott, "Giant Alliance Shares New Name, Bold Plans with Hospital Members," *Modern Healthcare,* March 18, 1996, p. 5.
28. For a complete discussion see James C. Collins and Jerry I. Porras, "Building Your Company's Vision," *Harvard Business Review* 88, no. 5 (September/October 1996), pp. 65–77.

Index